The
International Critical Commentary

on the Holy Scriptures of the Old and

New Testaments.

UNDER THE EDITORSHIP OF

THE REV. SAMUEL ROLLES DRIVER, D.D., D.LITT.,
Regius Professor of Hebrew, Oxford;

THE REV. ALFRED PLUMMER, M.A., D.D.,
Master of University College, Durham;

AND

THE REV. CHARLES AUGUSTUS BRIGGS, D.D., D.LITT.,
Professor of Theological Encyclopædia and Symbolics,
Union Theological Seminary, New York.

A

CRITICAL AND EXEGETICAL COMMENTARY

ON

THE BOOK OF PSALMS

BY

CHARLES AUGUSTUS BRIGGS, D.D., D.Litt.

GRADUATE PROFESSOR OF THEOLOGICAL ENCYCLOPÆDIA AND
SYMBOLICS, UNION THEOLOGICAL SEMINARY, NEW YORK

AND

EMILIE GRACE BRIGGS, B.D.

(In Two Volumes)

VOL. II

EDINBURGH:

T. & T. CLARK, 59 GEORGE STREET

PRINTED IN GREAT BRITAIN BY PAGE BROS (NORWICH) LTD.,
BOUND BY HUNTER & FOULIS LTD., EDINBURGH.

FOR

T. & T. CLARK LTD., EDINBURGH

0 567 05012 2

LATEST IMPRESSION 1986

CONTENTS

v

xxxi, l. 19. *Protestantische* for *Protestanische*.

xli, l. 30. Sidney for Sydney.

cv, l. 1. Del. Asterius († 410) already given ciii, l. 36.

cv, l. 12. Rhabanus for Rhabamus.

cviii, l. 31. Add after 1889⁵ Minocchi 1905.

cix, l. 1. Davison for Davidson.

cix, l. 2. Add after 1904 Davies 1906.

27, l. 10. 12⁶ for 18⁸.

34, l. 12 sq. α β γ δ ε for *a b c d h*.

41, l. 26. Hithp. for Hiph.

45, l. 22. 18⁴⁷ for 1¹.

49, l. 26. 90¹³ for 90³.

50, l. 26. § 35 for § 39.

l. 39. עָרֵשׁ for עֶרֶשׂ.

58, l. 21. Before **8** insert — צִוִּיתָ] Pi. pf. rel. clause √‡ [צוה], not used in Qal, but Pi.: (1) *give charge to*, c. לֹ pers. 105⁸ Ex. 1²² (E) Is. 13³; c. acc. pers. לֹ concerning whom, Ps. 91¹¹ Nu. 32²⁸ (P); (2) *charge, command*, c. acc. *pers. et rei*, Pss. 78⁵ 119⁴·¹³⁸ ברית 111⁹; (3) *commission*, c. acc. חָסָד 42⁹ ברכה 133³; (4) *appoint, ordain*, in creation 33⁹ 148⁵ Is. 45¹², providence Ps. 78²³ Am. 6¹¹ 9⁹; redemption Pss. 7⁷ 44⁵ 68²⁰ 71³.

60, l. 34. קְוָקֹד for קְוְקֹד.

82, l. 25. After **6** insert — גָּעַרְתָּ] Qal pf. 2 sg. † גָּעַר vb. Qal *rebuke* in ψ alw. of God: 9⁶ 68³¹ 106⁹ 119²¹ Is. 17¹³ 54⁹ Na. 1⁴ Zc. 3²·² Mal. 2³ 3¹¹, of man Gn. 37¹⁰ (E) Ru. 2¹⁶ Je. 29²⁷.

85, l. 17. Before **20** insert — **19**. ‡ תִּקְוָה n.f. (1) *hope* 62⁶; (2) ground of *hope* 71⁵ Jb. 4⁶; (3) things *hoped for*, here as Ez. 19⁵ 37¹¹ and WL.

104, l. 8. Maskilim for Maskelim.

122, l. 26. *qametz* for *quametz*.

PAGE

134, l. 26. *10²* for *10⁴*.

151, l. 6. **2** for **1**.

152, l. 5. § 1 for § 35.

173, l. 18. Add cf. 25^{10} 78^{56} 93^{5} 99^{7} 132^{12}. These with pl. forms in 119 usually derived from [עָרָה] ; but Mas. pointing is artificial ; *v.* BD*B*.

174, l. 16. Before **11** insert : Elsw. ψ [צדק] Qal *be justified* by acquittal 143^{2} Is. 43^{26} ; *be just*, of God 51^{6}, Hiph., *do justice* 82^{3}.

228, l. 37. פנה for פנה.

276, l. 23. Maskilim for Maskelim.

333, l. 38. טבה for טבח.

373, l. 5. שָׁחָה for שָׁחָה.

A COMMENTARY ON THE BOOK OF PSALMS.

A COMMENTARY ON THE BOOK OF PSALMS.

PSALM LI., 4 STR. 10³.

Ps. 51 is a penitential prayer of the congregation in the time of Nehemiah : (1) Petition that Yahweh in His kindness will cleanse His people from sin (v.³⁻⁴), who confess it in vindication of His just judgment (v.⁵⁻⁶). (2) The sin goes back to the origin of the nation, in antithesis with the faithfulness in which Yahweh delights (v.⁷⁻⁸) ; cleansing alone will give joy (v.⁹⁻¹¹). (3) Petition for renewal of heart, the continued presence of the Holy Spirit, and the joy of salvation (v.¹²⁻¹⁴) ; with a vow to teach the divine ways and praise His righteousness (v.¹⁵⁻¹⁶). (4) The sacrifices of Yahweh are the praises of a contrite spirit (v.¹⁷⁻¹⁹). The final petition is that He will rebuild the walls of Jerusalem and accept the sacrifices there (v.²⁰⁻²¹).

BE gracious to me (Yahweh), according to Thy kindness;
    According to Thy compassion blot out my transgressions.
    Wash me thoroughly from mine iniquity,
    And purify me from my sin.
    For my transgressions I am knowing,
    And my sin is before me continually.
    Against Thee, Thee only, have I sinned,
    And the evil in Thine eyes have I done;
    That Thou mightest be just in Thy (words),
    (That) Thou mightest be clear when Thou judgest.
BEHOLD in iniquity I was brought forth,
    And in sin did my mother conceive me.
    Behold in faithfulness Thou dost delight;
    The confidence of wisdom Thou makest me know.
    Cleanse me from sin with hyssop, and I shall be pure;
    Wash me, and I shall be whiter than snow.
    Let me hear joy and gladness,
    The bones which Thou hast crushed will exult.
    Hide Thy face from my sins,
    And all mine iniquities blot out.

3

THE heart into a pure one transform for me,
  The spirit into a steadfast one renew.
  Cast me not away from Thy presence,
  And Thy holy Spirit take not away.
  Restore the joy of Thy salvation,
  And with the princely Spirit uphold me.
  I will teach transgressors Thy ways,
  And sinners unto Thee will return.
  Deliver me from bloodshed (Yahweh).
  My tongue will ring out Thy righteousness.
O LORD, my lips mayest Thou open;
  And my mouth will declare Thy praise;
  For Thou delightest not in peace-offering,
  In whole burnt-offering Thou takest no pleasure:
  Sacrifices of a broken spirit,
  A heart crushed, Thou wilt not despise.
  O do good in Thy good pleasure unto Zion;
  Mayest Thou rebuild the walls of Jerusalem:
  Then wilt Thou delight in peace-offering and whole burnt-offering;
  Then will they offer bullocks on Thine altar.

Ps. 51 was in 𝔇 and 𝔐, then in 𝔈 and 𝔇𝔎 (*v.* Intr. §§ 27, 32, 33). The historical allusion was already attached to the Ps. in 𝔇 as a conjectural illustrative situation, but without historical value. It is impossible to adjust the Ps. to the situation. The language is related chiefly to Literature of the Exile or early Restoration. (1) Is.¹·² seem to have been chiefly in mind: (*a*) in the conception of the purification of the nation's sins v.³·⁴·⁹; cf. Is.1¹⁸, the use of מחה Is. 43²⁵ 44²², כבס for the person Je. 2²² 4¹⁴, טהר Je. 33⁸ Ez. 36³³ 37²³ Mal. 3³. The vb. חטא for purification from sin is elsw. only in P when applied to the person, but is in Ez. when applied to the altar. It does not therefore necessarily imply P. אזוב is used in J as well as P, and was doubtless ancient. (*b*) For the personal experience of v.⁵, cf. Is. 59¹². (*c*) ששון ושמחה v.¹⁰, cf. Is. 22¹³ 35¹⁰ 51³·¹¹. (*d*) רוח קדש v.¹³, elsw. only Is. 63¹⁰·¹¹. (*e*) For the bruised spirit v.¹⁹, cf. Is. 66². (*f*) For the son of the mother v.⁷, cf. the sin of the first father Is. 43²⁷ and of Zion the mother 54¹⁻⁸. (2) Other linguistic traces are: כליל v.²¹, an early syn. of עולה, cf. Dt. 33¹⁰ 1 S. 7⁹; יחם v.⁷, for conception, cf. Gn. 30⁴¹ 31¹⁰ (E). (3) Evidences of later date are: רוח נדיבה v.¹⁴, cf. Ex. 35⁵·²² (P); but see Ps. 110³, also רוח נכון v.¹² 57⁸·⁸ 108²; v.⁶ is prob. earlier than 19¹⁰, which agrees with it in use of Qal of צדק. (4) The only substantial evidences of very late date are: בטחות v.⁸, cf. Jb. 38³⁶, but prob. txt. err., explained by סתם, prob. gl. The Ps. in its theology depends on the postexilic sections of Is.², and in its deep penitence represents the spirit of the people of the Restoration in the time of Nehemiah. The prayer for rebuilding the walls of Jerusalem was probably real and not ideal, and indicates that the author was one of the companions of Nehemiah in the great effort to give the city walls.

Str. I. has a syn. tetrastich and a hexastich composed of three syn. couplets. — **3-4.** *Be gracious to me*], show favour, usually in the bestowal of redemption from enemies, evils, and sins, a characteristic term of 𝕯 ; with the two syn. nouns : *kindness*, the loving disposition to do acts of kindness (*4⁴*), and *compassion* (*25⁶*), the affectionate sympathy, especially of parent to a child, cf. 103¹³. — *Yahweh*], here and throughout the group, Ps. 51–72, for which 𝕰 substituted *Elohim*. — *My transgressions*], sins, conceived as rebellion, transgression of the Law, or will of God, with the two chief syns., *iniquity*, sin as a distortion or perversion of right, and *sin* as a failure from the norm or aim of life. These three terms for sin are antithetical to the three terms for the divine kindness, and have three mediating terms for its exercise in cleansing the nation. The transgressions stain the people, blackening their reputation and character, therefore *blot out*, wipe out, obliterate them, so that they no longer can be seen, cf. 109¹⁴. The iniquity soils them as a filthy garment, therefore *wash me*, cleanse all this filth away, so that I may be clean ; do it so thoroughly that not the least trace may remain, cf. v.⁹. The sins produce religious pollution, unfitting for the worship of God ; therefore *purify me*, apply the appointed means of purification, that I may enjoy communion again, cf. v.⁹. The poet doubtless had in mind Is. 1¹⁶⁻¹⁸, thinking of sin in its subjective effects on the person, rather than of its objective effects upon the places of divine presence. It is therefore the ritual of purification that he has in mind, rather than the ritual of sacrifice. He feels that the nation needs something more than the ritual ; they need the personal favour of Yahweh Himself ; His interposition as the administrator of this national cleansing. — **5.** *I am knowing*], present, active, personal, experimental knowledge of sin, as thus staining, soiling, polluting, the nation. — *before me continually*]. I cannot escape from seeing it and contemplating it in all its odiousness, cf. Is. 59¹². — **6.** *Against Thee*], emphatic in position, to indicate that the sin was especially against Yahweh, intensified by, *Thee only*]. The national sin was against their God, " not against the Babylonians," as Theodore of Mopsuestia, Theodoret, cited by Bä. with approval ; or indeed against the Persians, or the minor nations who so cruelly used them, opposing every effort of Israel to reëstablish himself in Jerusalem. — *in Thine eyes*], before the face of God, in His very presence ; and so high-handed, without excuse, which exposed to just retribution, relief from which could come only from His kindness. — *That Thou mightest be just ‖ be clear*], final clauses, not dependent on the act of sin as if the commission of sin was in order to justify God in dealing with it ; but on the confession of sin against God only. This public confession made it evident that God's dealings with His people during their long exile and in the long-continued afflictions of the people, in their efforts to restore the national life and worship in Jerusalem, were in accordance with His law, and so just. — *Thy words*], referring to the Ten Words of the primitive Law by which the nation is judged here, as in 50[16-20], so 𝔊, 𝔙, 𝔍, Rom. 3[4], and not " when Thou speakest," 𝔥, EV[s]., which gives a form *a.λ.*, assimilated by copyist's error to — *when Thou judgest*] that is, according to these Words ; as 𝔥, 𝔍, AV., RV., 50[4], which is to be preferred to 𝔊, 𝔙, Rom. 3[4], PBV., " when Thou art judged," as if the poet thought of a higher judgment seat before which God Himself could be tried, a conceit which, however suited to Greek and modern ideas, was not suited to the religion of the Old Testament.

Str. II. is an antistr., beginning with confession in a tetrastich of two syn. couplets, and concluding with a hexastich of petition of three syn. couplets. — **7.** *Behold*], calling emphatic attention to the antithesis between Yahweh's requirements and the actual historic condition of His people, the latter coming first. — *I was brought forth*], not referring to the iniquity of the parent, or to an iniquitous condition of the infant when brought forth ; implying the doctrine of original sin, transmitted from Adam and Eve in accordance with Traducianism, or imputed to the child as created as part of a sinful race, according to Creationism. I myself hold to the speculative dogma of Traducianism ; but I must say that neither of these doctrines has any support whatever in the OT. The poet here alludes to the historic origin of the nation in their patriarchal ancestors, as in Is. 43[27]. Their first father committed sin, and all his posterity since his day have followed him in transgression. — *did my mother conceive me*]. This is certainly not the mother of David, as if she were especially a sinner at the time of her conception, or as if sin were attached to the unborn fœtus which she conceived ; but the mother here is Mother Israel, in accordance with the conception of Is.², especially Is. 54¹⁻⁸. — **8**. *in faithfulness*], fidelity to Yahweh and His words ‖ *the confidence of wisdom*, the confidence in Yahweh which true wisdom imparts. This, by the misunderstanding of an early copyist, has been interpreted as a word, elsewhere only Jb. 38³⁶, and variously explained by 𝔥 and Vrss. as referring to the reins or inward parts of the man. It was defined by the addition of a late Hebrew word meaning " closed," or secret place of the breast, making the line too long, and compelling an explanation of the line, as referring to the future and so as out of parallelism with its mate in the couplet. In fact, both lines set forth the divine requirements, over against the sin of the past history of the nation in the father Jacob and the mother Zion ; and so the verbs are presents. — *Thou dost delight*], that is, the confidence is acceptable as satisfying the divine requirements, giving gratification and delight to Yahweh. — *Thou makest me know*], by the teaching of the Words of the Law, carrying on the idea of v.⁶ᶜ. These words impart true wisdom, and so confidence in Yahweh the great Teacher. — **9**. *Cleanse me from sin*], a term of the ritual Ez. P. — *with hyssop*], a bunch of small branches of the caper plant, used in the ritual, to gather up the water or blood, and scatter it upon the person or thing to be cleansed. This is a renewal and intensification of v.⁴ — *and I shall be pure*], in the religious sense, as thus cleansed in accordance with the ritual ; which is intensified in *I shall be whiter than snow*. The poet is evidently, in the use of the terms of Is. 1¹⁸, thinking of the sins of the nation as scarlet and crimson in their colour, of bloodguiltiness ; for they had committed a high-handed, death-deserving sin, cf. v.¹⁶. — **10**. *joy and gladness*], phr. of Is. 22¹³ 35¹⁰ 51³·¹¹, which they at the same time *hear* and also utter. Even *the bones* exult in sympathy with the exhilaration of the soul. This was expressed by voice, and probably also by dancing, though the bones had been *crushed* by Yahweh Himself in the afflictions He brought upon the nation. The bones are personified as those of an individual, severally suffering. The bones ache with the anxiety of the soul, cf. 22¹⁵ 32³. — **11**. *Hide Thy face from my sins*], do not look upon them, overlook them (*10¹¹*), take no account of them, cf. 32² ; another conception of Yahweh's gracious attitude

toward sin. This is in some respects the reverse of the conception of the syn. line, which is a simple renewal of v.3⁵, although
the word for sin varies.

Str. III. has a hexastich of three syn. couplets of petition, followed by two syn. couplets, the latter the climax of the Str. —
12. *Transform ‖ renew*]. These verbs do not imply creation out
of nothing, which indeed the Hebrew בָּרָא never means (*v.* BD*B.*) ;
or creation of a new heart out of other material in place of the
old heart, views which depend on a misunderstanding of the terms
in Vrss.; but the transformation of the former heart, or mind, of
the nation into a heart of an entirely different character, the making of the spirit, or disposition of the nation, over new into an
entirely different spirit. According to the previous context they
had been stained, soiled, and polluted ; they were to be made *pure*
and *steadfast*, the former in accord with v.⁹, the latter in accord
with the faithfulness and confidence of v.⁸. —*for me*], as 𝔍,
not " in me," of 𝔊, 𝔙, and most Vrss., which is an inexactness
of translation, not implying a different text. — **13.** *Cast me not
away from Thy presence*], banish from the sacred places of
worship in Jerusalem, cf. 42³. — *Thy holy Spirit take not away*].
The divine Spirit was holy, as it was the presence of the holy
God, requiring His people to be holy, not in the sense of ethical
perfection, but in the sense of consecration, a keeping apart from
all that was impure or defiling, in accordance with the conception
of holiness in H and Ez. The phr. is used elsewhere only Is. 63¹⁰· ¹¹,
where the divine Spirit is identified with the theophanic angel of
the Presence who led Israel up out of Egypt into the Holy Land.
The people had then grieved Him. The poet conceives that the
same Holy Spirit now dwells in Israel of the Restoration, just as
Hg. 2⁵ Zc. 4⁶ conceives of the divine Spirit as standing in their
midst and about to fulfil all divine promises. The poet fears lest
owing to the guilt of the people the Holy Spirit may depart from
their midst, leaving them desolate — **14.** *Restore the joy of Thy
salvation*], the joy that salvation will produce, cf. v.¹⁰. — *And with
the princely Spirit uphold me*], so 𝔊, 𝔙, 𝔍, in accord with previous
verse, thinking of the divine Spirit, with the attribute noble, princely,
on account of its being the leader and guide of the nation, the
princely representative of the King Yahweh Himself; cf. PBV.,

AV., " Thy free Spirit." This best suits the verb, always used of God's sustaining His people (3^6). RV. and most moderns think of the spirit of man or the nation, the steadfast spirit of v.[12] becoming the free, voluntary spirit, or disposition to serve God, especially in songs of praise. — **15.** *I will teach transgressors Thy ways*]. This line doubtless refers to the transgressors in Israel, who might still remain after the nation itself had been purified as a whole. The nation, cordially accepting the divine words and ways, will become a great teaching body. This is in the spirit of the times of Nehemiah, cf. 32^9. — *And sinners will return*], in repentance from sin, unto their God Yahweh, cf. Is. 42^{24}. — **16.** *Deliver me from bloodshed*], in accordance with usage (cf. 16^4), the shedding of blood in death, the affliction of the nation by banishment from Yahweh and withdrawal of the Holy Spirit, reaching its climax in death, so Ols., Hi., Bä. ; but EV[s]. and most moderns think of " bloodguiltiness " in accord with v.[9], a meaning possible to the Hebrew word, but not sustained by usage. — *Yahweh*], the original divine name for " Elohim," which was intensified by an ancient glossator by adding " God of my salvation," making the line just these two words too long.

Str. IV. has a hexastich of three syn. couplets and a tetrastich of two syn. couplets. — **17.** *My lips* ‖ *my mouth*], the organs of speech, thus far used in confession of sin and humble pleading for purification, anxious now to *declare* the *praise* in public worship of Yahweh, if only He will enable them so to do by granting their prayers, cf. v.[10. 14. 16], and thus *open* their lips to this glad service. — **18.** *For Thou delightest not* ‖ *takest no pleasure*], syn. terms for acceptance of the ritual worship as expressed in the *peace-offering*, characteristic of festivals, and *whole burnt-offering*, characteristic of the ordered worship at all sacred times. Such sacrifices were easily made, and habitually offered, even while the nation was most stained with sin, cf. Is. 1^{12-20} Ps. 50^{7-15}. — **19–21.** The sacrifices that really were acceptable to Yahweh and which He did not *despise*, as He did the merely external sacrifices, were " sacrifices of God " = " sacrifices of righteousness," v.[21]. These qualifications of the sacrifices were both explanatory glosses, in accordance with Dt. 33^{19} Ps. 4^6. They are not to be regarded as in antithesis to the ritual sacrifices, as if the sacrifices of God,

those which He required, were altogether internal states of soul,
without external expression in ritual. Those sacrifices were also
peace-offerings and whole burnt-offerings, consisting especially of
the most costly animals, *bullocks*, offered on the divine *altar* in
Jerusalem ; only the external sacrifices were to be offered by a
nation purified from sin, and living righteously in accordance with
the words and ways of Yahweh ; and indeed by a nation truly
penitent for all past and present sins and transgressions.   They
are *sacrifices of a broken spirit*, made by a broken spirit ; *a heart
crushed*, by divine discipline, v.¹⁰, cf. Is. 57¹⁵ 66² Pss. 34¹⁹ 147³. —
O do good unto Zion], bestow good things upon her, treat her well.
This is especially defined as *rebuild the walls of Jerusalem*, which
the people needed for safety from their enemies, and for the
honour of Yahweh Himself in His royal city. — *in Thy good
pleasure*], accepting her repentance and purifying her ; taking delight in her sacrifice, offered now with a contrite, pure, righteous,
steadfast disposition. He might justly deal kindly with her. This
verse is not a late addition to the Ps., as many have thought,
because of a mistaken reference of it to the experience of David,
or to a misinterpretation of the previous context, as if there were
an unreconcilable antithesis between the Ps. and this conclusion ;
rather it is essential to the completeness of the Str., and expresses
the historical situation of the poet.

3-4. חָנֵּנִי] Qal imv. חנן (*4²*), characteristic of 𝔇, but not of 𝕴 or 𝕬, || חֶסֶד
kindness (*4⁴*) and רחמים pl. abstr. *compassion* (*25⁶*). — אלהיב] for an original
יהוה, as throughout 𝔇, used by 𝕰. — כְּרֹב] though in 𝕲, 𝕵, is intensification,
making l. too long. 𝕲, 𝕵, also intensify in previous l., 𝕲 κατὰ τὸ μέγα ἔλεός
σου, 𝕵 *secundum magnam misericordiam tuam*. — מָחֵה] Qal imv. (*9⁶*) *blot out*,
as v.¹¹; with sins elsw. in Qal Is. 43²⁵ 44²², Niph. Ps. 109¹⁴ Ne. 3³⁷, syn. כִּבְּסֵנִי
Pi. imv. ‡ כבס vb. Pi. *wash*, person elsw. only v.⁹ Je. 2²² 4¹⁴; || טַהֲרֵנִי vb. Pi.
imv. ‡ טהר, a technical term for ceremonial purification, so v.⁹ (Qal) by the
use of hyssop ; common in P, but also Je. 33⁸ Ez. 36³³ 37²³ Mal. 3³ +. —
הרבה] Kt. הֶרֶב Hiph. inf. abs. רבה as adv. 130⁷, so 𝕲 ἐπὶ πλεῖον, 𝕵 *multum*,
Ges.⁷⁵ ᶠᶠ· to be preferred to Qr. הֶרֶב abr. Hiph. imv., Ges.⁷⁵ ᵍᵍ·. — וּמֵחַטָּאתִי] has
two tones. — **5.** אֲנִי] makes l. too long, unnecessary gl. — אֵדָע] Qal impf. i.p.
present experience, || וְנֶגְדִּי רְמִיד, cf. *16⁸* Is. 59¹². — **6.** לְךָ לְבַדְּךָ] emphatic ‡ בַּר
n.m. *separation ;* with לְ, in a state of separation, *alone*, by oneself ; always
of God in ψ, elsw. 71¹⁶ 72¹⁸ 83¹⁹ 86¹⁰ 136⁴ 148¹³. — וְהָרַע בְּעֵינֶיךָ עָשִׂיתִי] adj. רע
with article, emphatic ; phr. of 𝔇, Dt. 4²⁵ 9¹⁸ 17² 31²⁹ + 57 t. — לְמַעַן] conj.
final clause with impf. as 9¹⁵ 30¹³ 48¹⁴. — תִּצְדַּק] Qal impf. 2 m. *be just*, as

19[10]. — [בְּרַבְּרֶךָ] form a.λ. Qal inf. cstr. attracted to form of בשפטך; but 𝔊, 𝔍,
Rom. 3[4] pl. דְּבָרֶיךָ, referring to words of *Law*, then resembling still more Ps. 19.
— [תִּזְכֶּה] Qal impf. † [זכר] vb. Qal (1) *be clean, pure*, of man in the sight of
God Jb. 15[14] 25[4]; (2) *be clear*, in justice, of God Ps. *51*[6] Mi. 6[11]. Pi. *make
or keep pure*, the (ב) זכ Ps. 73[13] Pr. 20[9], ארח Ps. 119[9]. Hithp. *make oneself
clean* Is. 1[16]. 𝔊 νικήσης, cf. Rom. 3[4]; so Σ, Θ, 𝔙, 𝔍, after Aram. usage.
𝔊 also prefixes καί, which may be for an original כי needed for measure,
omitted in 𝔐 because of previous בְּ_. 𝔊 Rom. 3[4], 𝔙, PBV., also interpret
בשפטך as passive, which is improbable. — **7.** [הֵן ‡] interj. *lo! behold!* used in
early prose but chiefly in poetry, so v.[8] 68[34] 78[20] 139[4], for the more frequent
הנה. — [חֵטְא ‡] n.m. (1) *sin* v.[11] Is. 31[7] Ho. 12[9] Dt. 19[15]; (2) *guilt* of sin v.[7]
103[10] Is. 1[18] Dt. 15[9] 21[22] 23[22. 23] 24[15]. — [יֶחֱמַתְנִי] Pi. pf. † [יחם] Pi. elsw. only
of conception of cattle Gn. 30[41. 41] 31[10] (E). This form is for the normal
יֶחֱמַרְנִי, cf. Ju. 5[28] Ges.[64 h]. — **8.** † [טֻחוֹת] n.fpl. in Jb. 38[36], acc. to 𝔗 and Rabb.
reins, but impossible there, as refer. is to dark cloud layers ; *inward parts*,
*B*DB., as covered over, concealed, 𝔊 τὰ ἄδηλα, 𝔙 *incerta*, 𝔍 *absconditum ;*
𝔊, 𝔙, 𝔍, all attaching to next l. — [יִסְתֹם] is doubtless a gl. explanatory of
בטחות Qal ptc. pass. ‡ סתם *stop up*, in Qal and Pi. of stopping wells ; in a higher
sense Dn. 8[26] 12[4. 9] (Qal) of shutting up prophetic words, here of the closed
chamber of the breast, therefore *late*. All this is improbable ; it gives no
suitable parall. Rd. with Hi. בטחות abstract pl. בטחה *confidence, security*, cf.
Is. 30[15] Jb. 12[6]; cstr. before הכמה (*37*[30]), the confidence or security that Wisdom affords. — **9.** [תְּחַטְּאֵנִי] Pi. juss. *purify from sin ;* elsw. in this sense, of
person, only P; Nu. 19[19] (Pi.) Nu. 8[21] + 7 t. (Hithp.); of place (altar, house)
Ez. 43[20] + 4 t. Ez. Lv. 8[15] + 2 t., all P (Pi.). — [אֵזוֹב] n.m. the *hyssop*, prob.
caper, described by Tristram. "The stem has short, recurved spines below
the junction of each leaf. The leaves are oval, of a glossy green, and in
warmer situations evergreen." The plant is mentioned 1 K. 5[13]; elsw. in
ritual use for sprinkling blood at Passover Ex. 12[22] (J), for cleansing of leper
Lv. 14[4. 6. 49. 51. 52] (P), for cleansing from contact with the dead Nu. 19[6. 18] (P),
of cleansing from sin here only. — [וְאֶטְהָר] ו subord., the final ה omitted in late
style ; so also with אֶלְבִּין Hiph. impf. † לבן vb. denom. Hiph. (1) *make white*
= purify (ethical) Dn. 11[35]; (2) *shew whiteness, become white*, of tree Jo. 1[7],
of moral purity cf. שלג Is. 1[18] and here; Hithp. *be purified* Dn. 12[10]. —
10. [שָׂשׂוֹן וְשִׂמְחָה] phr. Is. 22[13] 35[10] 51[3. 11]. — [דִּכִּיתָ] Pi. pf. rel. clause ; cf. v.[19]
10[10]. — **12.** [בְּרָא] Qal imv. ברא *create* in the sense of *transform*, as Is. 41[20]
65[17. 18]. — [אֱלֹהִים] is gl. making l. too long. — [רוּחַ נָכוֹן] נכון Niph. ptc. כון,
firmly established in the religious and moral sense, cf. נכ ן לב 57[8. 8] 108[2], also
78[37] 112[7]. — [חַדֵּשׁ] Pi. imv. † חדשׁ Pi. (1) *renew*, only here in religious sense,
of face of ground 104[3], kingdom 1 S. 11[14], years I.a. 5[21], witnesses Jb. 10[17];
(2) *repair*, cities Is. 61[4], temple 2 Ch. 24[4. 12], altar 2 Ch. 15[8]. Hithp. *renew*,
youth Ps. 103[5]. — [בְּקִרְבִּי] is a gl., making l. too long. — **13.** [אַל־תַּשְׁלִיכֵנִי] is
neg. juss. Hiph. with two accents. — [תִּקַּח] expl. gl. — **14.** [הָשִׁיבָה] Hiph. imv.
cohort. לי is expl. gl. — [שָׂשׂוֹן יִשְׁעֶךָ] phr. a.λ. *v. 12*[6]. — [רוּחַ נְדִיבָה] phr. a.λ.,
but נְדָבָה רוּחוֹ Ex. 35[21] (P), cf. נדיב לב Ex. 35[5. 22] (P) 2 Ch. 29[31], willing, **freely**

offering oneself; 𝕲 ἡγεμονικῷ, 𝖁 *principali*, 𝕵 *potenti* in the other mng. *noble, princely*, so Street. — **15.** אֲלַמְּדָה] Pi. cohort. — **16.** דָמִים] abst. pl. *bloodshed*, Ols., Hi., Bä.; most think of blood-guiltiness. — אלהים אלהי תשועתי] amplification, only one name needed for measure; rd. יהוה, for which אלהים was substituted by 𝕰. — תְּרַנֵּן] Pi. juss., apod. of imv. (5[12]). — **18.** לֹא] neg., so 𝕵, but 𝕲 לֻא conditional particle due to וְאֶתֵּנָה Qal cohort. נתן, apod., which certainly implies a previous conditional clause. But this vb. makes l. too long and is doubtless an expl. gl. — **19.** אלהים] is gl. in both ll.; it puts God in 2d and 3d pers. in same v. זִבְחֵי is then cstr. before רוח. It is prob. that נשבר after לב is an expl. gl. inserted before the unusual נִדְכֶּה. — **20.** הֵיטִיבָה] Hiph. imv. cohort. יטב (33[3]). 𝕲, 𝕵, insert אדני, but at expense of measure. — **21.** עוֹלָה] is expl. gl. for the unusual ‡ כָּלִיל n.m. *whole, entire offering*, as Dt. 33[10] 1 S. 7[9]; for other mng. *v.* 50[2].

PSALM LII., 2 STR. 6^5.

Ps. 52 is a didactic poem of the time of Jeremiah: (1) denouncing a crafty noble who worked mischief with his lying tongue (v.[3-6]); predicting his speedy downfall (v.[7]); (2) triumphing in the antithesis between the noble's vain trust in his wealth, and the sure trust of the righteous in Yahweh (v.[8-11a]). The Ps. concludes with a liturgical gloss (v.[11b]).

WHY boastest thou of evil, thou mighty man, all day long?
Engulfing ruin thou devisest, thy tongue is as a whetted razor;
Thou dost love evil rather than good, lying rather than right;
Thou dost love all devouring words, the deceitful tongue.
'El also will pull thee down, forever He will snatch thee away;
He will pluck thee up out of thy tent, and so root thee out of the land of the living.

THEN the righteous will see and revere, and will laugh at him:
"Behold (the mighty man) that used not to make (Yahweh) his refuge,
But used to trust in the abundance of his riches, used to be strong in his (wealth).
As for me, I am in the house of (Yahweh) as a luxuriant olive tree;
I trust in the kindness of (Yahweh) forever and ever.
I will laud Thee that Thou hast done it, and I will wait on Thy name."

Ps. 52 was a מַשְׂכִּיל at first in 𝕯, and subsequently in 𝕰 and 𝕯𝕽 (*v.* Intr. §§ 26, 27, 32, 33). In 𝕯 it had the following historical reference: בְּבוֹא דוֹאֵג הָאֲדֹמִי וַיַּגֵּד לְשָׁאוּל וַיֹּאמֶר לוֹ בָּא־דָוִד אֶל־בֵּית אֲחִימֶלֶךְ = "When Doeg the Edomite came and told Saul, and said unto him, David is come to the house of Abimelech." This is based on 1 S. 22[9-10], but makes a clumsy use of the narrative. This reference was made not with the view that the Ps. was actually composed at that time; but that it might be conceived as expressing the emotions of David under those circumstances. In fact the Ps. in some respects would suit the situation; but in others not. Both the internal and the external evidence make such a time of composition impossible. The גבור v.[3. 9] refers to a warrior, and evidently, in the context, to a false and wicked one such as Doeg certainly was. But it is easy to think also of Shebna (Is. 22[15 sq.]), Pashhur (Je. 20[1 sq.]), Hananiah (Je. 28[1 sq.]), or Sanballat (Ne. 6). But these were doubtless only representatives of a class constantly appearing in Jewish history and denounced by the prophets. The זיח רענן v.[1)] = Je. 11[16] does not involve dependence on Je., for the simile is an easy one and the use of it is not the same. The reference to the house of Yahweh, however, implies either preëxilic or postexilic times, when the temple was the established place of worship. The crafty and lying use of the tongue denounced in the Ps. is especially prominent in the denunciations of the pre-exilic prophets, cf. Je. 9[3 sq.] Mi. 6[12]. The same is true of the early Restoration. But subsequently falsehood, under Persian influence, assumes a more ethical character, and is denounced not only for its injurious effects, but for its own immoral nature. The language and style favour a preëxilic date. The Ps. is best explained from the time of Jeremiah.

Str. I. has a tetrastich of three syn. lines explaining the first, and an antith. syn. couplet. — **3.** *Why boastest thou, . . . thou mighty man ?*] Some noble, a rich and powerful warrior, is referred to, such as Shebna (Is. 22[15 sq.]), Pashhur (Je. 20[1 sq.]), Hananiah (Je. 28[1 sq.]), or Sanballat (Ne. 6), who was indulging in self-confident boasting of his success and impunity in *evil*. This was all the more irritating that it was continuous, *all day long*. An ancient glossator impatient for the antithesis v.[10], attached to the margin the "kindness," making that "all day long." This subsequently came into the text at the expense of the measure, and the simplicity of the movement of thought in its parallelism. The Vrss. greatly differ here. — **4.** *Engulfing ruin*]. The evil is explained as a ruin in which one falls and is engulfed or swallowed up, a term of ₪, 5[10] 38[13] 55[12] 57[2]. Such overwhelming ruin he *deviseth* against the righteous. He has a definite plan and purpose to ruin them, and it is expressed in crafty words of false witness. — *thy tongue is as a whetted razor*], phr. a.λ., cf. Ps. 7[13] Je. 36[23]. The tongue has a deadly purpose, and so it is compared to a razor which has been whetted in order to make it as sharp as possible. The glossator added "working deception," as 101[7], making the line too long whether referring to the tongue or the man, whether in apposition or vocative. The Vrss. differ. —

5-6. *Thou dost love*], emphatic present, repeated in syn. line for greater emphasis.   The evil tongue represents an evil nature, whose affection is set on *evil rather than good*, defined more precisely as the evil of *lying rather than* the good of speaking that which is just and *right*.   The climax is reached in *all-devouring words*, whose purpose is to swallow up and devour, cf. v.⁴, — *the deceitful tongue*], as 120²·³ in apposition ⅁, ⅍, ⅄, to be preferred to the vocative: "O thou deceitful tongue" of EVˢ. and most moderns. — **7.** *'El also*] on His part, as an additional actor, appears unexpectedly to the wicked noble.   This divine name was left in the Ps. by 𝔈.   Vbs. are heaped up, two in each line, to indicate the great variety of motions by which God overthrows this vainglorious noble. — *will pull thee down*] from a firm position ; — *snatch thee away*] elsewhere of snatching up coals from a hearth with tongs or shovel ; — *pluck thee up out of thy tent*], out of and away from the inmost dwelling, the very home ; — *and so root thee out of the land of the living*].   It is extermination, leaving neither root nor branch behind in the land where only the living dwell, v. 27¹³.

Str. II. has a line introducing the words of the triumphant *righteous* which declare in an antith. couplet the trust of the wicked noble, and, in a syn. triplet, the trust of the righteous. — **8.** *See and revere*], see the fall of the wicked noble, and revere, in reverential fear of Yahweh who overthrew him, cf. 40⁴. — *and will laugh at him*], the triumphant laugh of scorn and derision.   This is just as appropriate for the people of Yahweh when Yahweh triumphs over His enemies and theirs, as it is for Yahweh Himself, Ps. 2⁴. — **9.** *Behold the mighty man*], the same person as in v.³ ; but 𝔐 and Vrss. by a different pointing of the same consonant letters, interpret the term as the more general and comprehensive "man." — *used not to make Yahweh his refuge*], frequentative, of habitual action ; so probably the following vbs. also.   EVˢ., after 𝕵, render "strength" or "stronghold," but improperly, *v.* 27¹. — *in the abundance of his riches*].   This noble had great riches as well as great power, and in these he used to trust, instead of in his God, as every true Jew should have done. — *used to be strong in his (wealth)*] so ⅍, 𝕿, and most moderns, as best suited to context.   𝔐 gives the same form as v.⁴, which is variously explained by Vrss. and interpreters. But, if correct, it must be interpreted as their "engulfing ruin," and we must think of his strengthening himself in the ruin he has brought on others, building himself up on their ruins. — **10**. *As for me*], emphatic antithesis. — *as a luxuriant olive tree*], fresh, green, fat, and flourishing in the richest soil; not that the olive tree was *in the house of Yahweh* and therefore especially luxuriant, but that the righteous man was a guest there and on that account was to be compared to such a tree. His trust was in the kindness of Yahweh, in antithesis with the trust of the wicked noble in his riches; and therefore he would continue to flourish after the wicked noble had been overthrown with his wealth. — **11**. *I will laud Thee*], the vow of public worship in the temple in thanksgiving, as usual at the conclusion of Pss. — *that Thou hast done it*]. The special theme of the praise was that which Yahweh had done to the proud oppressor of the righteous. — *and I will wait on Thy name*]. Although this phr. is α.λ., yet the name of Yahweh frequently takes the place of Yahweh Himself in other phrases, and there is no good reason why it should not do so here. The remainder of the v. is too much for the measure and Str. — *for it is good in the sight of Thy pious ones*]. This is doubtless a gloss. The name is good, benign. The pious so regard it as they contemplate it. The name of Yahweh in late usage is for Yahweh Himself.

3. [הִתְהַלֵּל] Hithp. impf. *make one's boast*, as 49⁷. — [הַגִּבּוֹר] vocative, as usual with article. — [חֶסֶד אֵל] is a gl., originally in margin simply as חסד, from v.¹⁰, referring to the kindness of Yahweh, antith. to the wickedness of this boaster. But 𝕲 ἀνομίαν, Aq., Quinta, ὄνειδος = חסד as Aram. *shame*, *reproach*, elsw. Pr. 14³⁴ Lv. 20¹⁷. אֵל was a later insertion in 𝔐, 𝔍, to define חסד as God's. But it is interpr. by 𝕾, Houb., Oort, We., Du., as inexactness for עֵל חסיר. Hi., Dy., rd. עֵל חֶסֶר adv. inf. But all are improbable and unsatisfactory. The two words in fact destroy the measure. — **4**. [הַוּוֹת] emph. *engulfing ruin*, v. 5¹⁰. — [כְּתַעַר מְלֻטָּשׁ] phr. α.λ. ‡ תַּעַר n.m., *razor*, as Is. 7²⁰ Ez. 5¹. לטש, v. 7¹³, of sword. — [עשה רמיה] is explan. gl. — **5**. [מְדַבֵּר צֶדֶק] phr. elsw. Ps. 58². צדק of rightness of speech, elsw. Pr. 8⁸ 12¹⁷ 16¹³, cf. צדקה Is. 45²³ 48¹ 63¹ Je. 4² Zc. 8⁸. The vb. is a gl. making the l. too long, so Bä. — **6**. [דִּבְרֵי־בָלַע] phr. α.λ. † בֶּלַע n.[m.] *devouring*, elsw. Je. 51⁴⁴, v. Ps. 55¹⁰, also vb. 21¹⁰. It is tempting with Be., Che., to rd. בְּלִיַּעַל. — [לְשׁוֹן מִרְמָה] phr. α.λ. in apposition, not vocative; usual phr. שֶׁקֶר ל 109² Pr. 6¹⁷ 12¹⁹ 21⁶ 26²⁸, רמיה ל Ps. 120². ³ Mi. 6¹². — **7**. [נֶס־אֵל]. Two tones are needed. Therefore rd. וְנֵס אֵל as usual in such cases. — [יִתָּצְךָ] Qal future ‡ נתץ vb. Qal (1) *pull down*, a structure

Ex. 34[13] (J) Dt. 7[5] + ; (2) a nation Je. 1[10] 18[7], an individual Jb. 19[10], so here ; the jaw teeth of lions Ps. 58[7]. — יְהָתֵּף] Qal impf. † חתה vb. *snatch up*, coals from hearth Is. 30[14], cf. Pr. 6[27] 25[22]; here fig. involved. — וַיִּחְתָּה] i coörd. Qal impf. † נסח vb. Qal *tear away*, as Pr. 2[22] 15[25]; Niph. Dt. 28[63]. — וְשָׁרְשֶׁךָ] i consec. after the impf. expressing result ; † שרשׁ vb. demon. Pi. *roct ou*, elsw. Jb. 31[12]; Pu. Jb. 31[8]; Poel Is. 40[24]; Poal Je. 12[2]; Hiph. also *strike root* Ps. 80[10] Is. 27[6] Jb. 5[3]. — **8.** 𝕲 attaches καὶ ἐροῦσιν, which is implied indeed, but not usually expressed in poetry. — **9.** הַגֶּבֶר] so 𝔐 and all Vrss.; but certainly a mispointing for גְּבוּר, v.[3]. — לֹא־יְשִׂים] neg. rel. clause, vb. frequent. — אלהים] for original יהוה as throughout 𝐄. — וַיִּבְכָּח] i consec. after impf., emph. change of tense ; improb. It should be i coörd. and vb. frequent. — בְּרֹב עָשְׁרוֹ] original of 49[7]. — יָעֹז] Qal freq. *be strong*, 9[20]. — בְּהַוָּתוֹ] as v.[4], but dub. rd. with 𝔖, 𝕿, Lag., Gr., Bi., Bä., Oort, Du., Dr., *BDB.*, בְּהוֹנוֹ *in his wealth*, v. 44[13]. — **11.** לְעֵילָם] is gl., making l. too long. — אֲהַוֶּה שִׁמְךָ] phr. a.λ., but קוה with acc. י frequent. The substitution of *name* for *Yahweh* is common with other vbs., why not with this? It is however not suited to כִּי־טוֹב נֶגֶד הַסִּידֶיךָ, and therefore Dy., Hi., Gr., *BDB.*, rd. אֲהַוֶּה, Hu., Oort, אקרא. But in fact this last heterogeneous clause makes an additional l. to the Str. however we may divide the ll. It is indeed a double gl.: כי טוב (v. 25[8]); נגד חסידיך still later, cf. 79[2] 89[20] 132[9] (= 2 Ch. 6[41]) 145[10].

PSALM LIII.

Ps. 53 is an Elohistic edition of Ps. 14, with variations of text and editorial changes, all of which are discussed under Ps. 14.

PSALM LIV., 2 STR. 6[3].

Ps. 54 is a prayer for national victory in the early days of Josiah. (1) Petition to Yahweh to save the nation from its terrible foreign foes (v.[3-5b]), (2) that the enemy may be exterminated, and the people gaze in triumph upon them (v.[6-7. 9]). Glosses assert that the enemy ignores God (v.[5c]), and vow praise and sacrifice in the temple (v.[8]).

> YAHWEH, by Thy name save *me*,
> And by Thy might execute judgment for *me.*
> Yahweh, hear *my* prayer ;
> Give ear to the words of *my* mouth :
> For (proud ones) have risen up against *me*,
> And terrible ones have sought *my* life.

L O, Yahweh, Helper to *me!*
   Yahweh, Upholder of *my* life!
   Let evil return to *my* watchful foe;
   In Thy faithfulness exterminate (*mine* enemy);
   From all trouble deliver *me*,
   And on mine enemy let *mine* eye look.

Ps. 54 was a *Maskil* in 𝔈. It was then taken up into 𝕯𝕽, and received the assignment בְּנִינֹת. It was also taken up into 𝕰. The historical reference בְּבֹא הַזִּיפִים וַיֹּאמְרוּ לְשָׁאוּל הֲלֹא דָוִד מִסְתַּתֵּר עִמָּנוּ, refers to the incident mentioned 1 S. 23¹⁹ ˢq·, cf. 26¹ ˢq· (*v.* Intr. §§ 26, 27, 32, 33, 34). This Ps. could not have been composed by David at this time, but the circumstances there referred to might illustrate some of the features of the Ps. It is a prayer for national deliverance in peril from enemies; and indeed זָרִים, powerful, cruel, and terrible ones, v.⁵, such as the Babylonians, cf. 37³⁵ 86¹¹ Is. 13¹¹ 29⁵. The language and style are of the earlier Pss. of 𝕯. The reference to temple worship and sacrifice, v.⁸, is a gloss. The prayer that they might look in triumph on their enemies, v.⁹, implies a preëx. situation, in which the armies of Judah were still in the field and might hope to overcome their enemies in battle. The early years of Josiah best suit this situation.

Str. I. has three syn. couplets, the last giving the reason of the prayer. — **3.** *By Thy name*]. The name of Yahweh, as known to His people and made known to their enemies, is a saving name, giving confidence to His people, and invoking fear in their enemies, owing to the renown of His previous historical achievements, *v.* 20⁶· ⁸ 33²¹ 44⁶ 89¹³· ¹⁷· ²⁵ 105³ 118¹⁰· ¹¹· ¹² 124⁸. — *Thy might*], as exhibited in the putting forth of warlike power, *v.* 20⁷ 21¹⁴ 80³ 89¹⁴. — *save me*], as the context shows, by deliverance from enemies in war, implying victory over them ‖ *execute judgment for me*], vindicate my cause in battle, *v.* 110⁶. — **4.** The petition of the previous couplet is indeed *prayer*, as expressed in *words of my mouth*, oral prayer, which *Yahweh* is urged to *hear* ‖ *give ear to*, usual terms in such circumstances, *v.* 4⁴ 5². — **5.** The reason for this petition is given in this couplet, *proud ones*], the probable original, as 𝔗 and many codd. 𝕳, rather than "foreigners," foreign enemies, of most codd. 𝕳 and other Vrss. These are defined as *terrible ones*, such as the Assyrians, Is. 29⁵, and Babylonians, Is. 13¹¹ Ez. 28⁷. — *have risen up against me*], in war ‖ *have sought my life*], to destroy the nation so that it could no longer have national independence or existence. A glossator, without regard to the structure of the Ps. as composed of couplets, added

c

a line to give another characteristic of these enemies, " they do not set God before their eyes," cf. 10^4 $14^1 = 53^2$, probably influenced by the latter passage.

Str. II. has also three syn. couplets. — **6.** *Lo*], calling emphatic attention to the wish expressed in v.[7], introduced by the vocatives in v.[6]. — *Helper to me*], not predicate of *Yahweh*, as Vrss.; but in apposition to Yahweh, as His characteristic. — *Upholder of my life*] the One who had been throughout history the sustainer of His people, maintaining their national existence in every peril and against all enemies. — **7.** *Let evil return*], so Kt., in requital, cf. 7^{17} 94^{15}, to be preferred to Qr., 𝕲, 𝔍, " He will return," " requite," as $18^{21.\ 25}$ 28^4 79^{12}, which requires the interpretation of Yahweh as subj. in the 3d pers. against the uniform usage of this Ps., which is a prayer to Him, in the 2d pers. Such an interpretation is indeed forbidden by the syn. imv. *exterminate*, otherwise the transition from the one person to the other in a syn. couplet would be exceedingly abrupt and uncalled for. — *In Thy faithfulness*]. The usual meaning of the Hebrew word is alone appropriate here ; namely, the faithfulness of Yahweh to His people, as helper and sustainer. The EV[s]. give the unusual meaning " truth," which has no propriety in this context. These enemies of v.[5] are here described as *my watchful foes*], who lie in wait, a term of 𝔻, *v. 5^9;* also in general as *mine enemy*, an insertion which the uniform assonance of this Ps. in *ı* requires, as well as the measure, in place of the suffix " them," of 𝖍, Vrss. — **8.** This vow disturbs the order of the prayer and the structure of the Str. ; but was needed to make the Ps. appropriate for public worship in later times. — *In voluntariness will I sacrifice to Thee*], so Vrss., AV., cf. PBV., expressing the glad, voluntary participation in public sacrifice, cf. 51^{14}. RV. " freewill offering," while a possible rendering of the Hebrew word, is a specific kind of sacrifice which was only appropriate on special occasions, and not at all characteristic of public sacrifice in the temple, or indeed appropriate to it. — *I will laud Thy name, Yahweh, (saying) for He is good*], the oral choral praise, with the Rf. of the Hallels, *v.* 135^3, and Intr. § 35. — **9.** *From all trouble deliver me*], continuation of the prayer, the verb being interpreted as imv. MT., 𝔍, 𝕿, pf. 3 sg., 𝕲, 𝕾, pf. 2 sg., are due to the insertion of the gloss v.[8], separating v.[9] from its

connection with the imv. v.[7b]. — *Let mine eye look*]. The context
of the original Ps. requires the jussive here, as against pf. of 狺
and Vrss., due to the gloss. The eye of Israel hopes to gaze in
triumph upon the enemy, defeated and exterminated, cf. 112[8]
118[7].

3. אלהים] for an original יהוה; also v.[4. 6.] — וכנבירכך] has two tones, as usual
in long words, with ו conj. — יביט] Qal juss. after imv. (7[9]). — **4.** [לאמרי־פי
two tones, the first thrown back from ultima to penult of אמרי as usual; *v.* 2[12],
phr. Pss 19[15] 78[1] 138[1] Dt. 32[1] +. — **5.** [ירים] marked as dub. by Paseq, was
prob. originally ידיב, as 𝕿 and many codd. MT.; so Oort, Gr., Bä., Du. —
עירי] the usual prep. with קום, but the pl. sf. impairs the assonance in ־ָי.
Rd. therefore בי as 27[12]. — [ריציב] pl. adj., as 37[35] 86[14], both 𝔐; cf. Is. 13[11]
29[5]. — [ין יצו ארהים רנורב] is an extra l. to the Str., lacks the characteristic
rhyme, and is doubtless a gl. — **6.** [ער לי] phr. 30[11] (𝔐). — [אדני] prob. for
original יהוה. — [ןס בי] 𝕲 ἀντιλήμπτωρ, 𝕵 *sustentans*, imply sg. without ־ָ; the
latter is due to the interpretation of form as pl., and is prob. not original,
v. 3[6]. — **7.** [ישוב] Kt.; ישיב Qr., so 𝕲, 𝕵; the former is more suited to the
context if יהוה is vocative in foregoing, the latter if it is subject of clauses;
the former more probable, only it should be juss. — [ישרבי] pl. is against
assonance; rd. sg. *v. 5[9].* — [רצייר]. The suffix is contrary to the assonance
in ־ָי characteristic of Ps. A word is also missing for the measure: rd. איבי. —
8. ‡ [ורבה] n.f. (1) *voluntariness* of love Ho. 14[5], of volunteering for military service Ps. 110[3], of copious rain 68[10], of voluntary offering of sacrifice
54[8], adv. acc. Dt. 23[24]; elsw. always *freewill offering*, in ψ only 119[108] unless
this mng. be found here also — [אינבה] Qal cohort. I sg. expressing resolution;
the accent is retracted before לי whether Makkeph is used or not; cf. v.[4]. —
[איבה שבך] Hiph. impf. cohort. יד, *v.* Intr. § 35, cf. 44[9], 99[3], 138[2] 142[8]. —
יהוה] suspicious in 𝔈. The rhyme does not appear in this v. It is a gl.
— [יריטוב] *v.* 52[11]. — **9.** ה is a gl. of interp. — [רצייני] Hiph. pf. 3 sg. changes
from 2d to 3d pers. without sufficient reason: 𝕲, 𝕾, 2d pers., so Horsley, Gr.,
Che.; rd. imv. יצילני as Street — [ריבר] Qal pf. 3 f. is not suited to context,
even if explained as future pf. or pf. of sure future. The original Ps. required,
as Street, ראה juss. The text has been changed from imv. and juss. because
of intervening gl. — [בי] should be sg. sf. as above.

PSALM LV.

**Ps. 55 is composite. (A) A prayer for deliverance, with the
longing to flee away from the terrible anxiety to a sure refuge
(v.[2-3. 5-9a]). (B) Imprecations upon treacherous foes within the
holy city (v.[9b-12]), and upon a treacherous friend (v.[13-16a 21-22. 24ab]).**

Glosses express confidence in Yahweh (v.[23.24c]), make vows of public prayer (v.[17-18]) and urgent petition (v.[-6a]), refer to deliverances from battle (v.[19]), and enlarge upon various features of the original (v.[4.16b.20b]).

$$A. \quad v.^{2-3.5-9a}, \; 3 \; STR. \; 4^3.$$

O GIVE ear, (Yahweh), to *my* prayer;
    And hide not Thyself from *my* supplication.
    O attend to me, and answer *me*.
    I am depressed, and I moan in *my* complaint.
M Y heart writhes within *me*,
    And terrors have fallen upon *me*.
    Fear comes upon *me*,
    And trembling and shuddering cover *me*.
PINIONS O that *I* had!
    As a dove *I* would fly away and settle down,
    So I would make afar off *my* flight.
    I would haste away to *my* place of escape.

$$B. \quad v.^{9b-10a.21-22.24ab}, \; 3 \; STR. \; 5^5.$$

W ITH a tempestuous wind, O Lord, divide their tongues.
    For I see violence and strife in the city;
    Day and night they go round about upon the walls thereof.
    Trouble and mischief are in the midst of it, engulfing ruin in its (square);
    And oppression and deceit depart not from its square.
F OR it is not an enemy who reproaches me, I could get away (from him).
    It is not he that hateth me that magnifieth himself against me, I could have hidden from him.
    But thou, a man mine equal, mine associate and my familiar acquaintance!
    Together we used to hold sweet counsel, we used to walk in concord.
    Let death come treacherously upon them, let them descend alive to Sheol.
H E put forth his hands against his confederate: he profaned his covenant;
    His face was smoother than curds; but war was in his mind.
    His words were softer than oil, but they were drawn swords.
    But, O Thou, (Yahweh), bring them down to the Pit of Sheol.
    Let not men of blood and deceit live out half their days.

Ps. 55 was in 𝔇, of the class מַשְׂכִּיל, which is justified by the original Ps.A, not by the present Ps. It was taken up into 𝔈, when the divine name was changed as elsw. It was also in 𝔇𝕽, where it was assigned בנגינת (*v*. Intr. §§ 26, 27, 32, 33, 34). The Ps. has an unusual number of glosses. (1) V.[17] has יהוה. This could not have been in 𝔈, or in 𝔇𝕽, which follows its sources in its use of divine names. The three hours of prayer, v.[18], appear elsw. Dn. 6[11] as a late usage. V.[19] belongs with v.[18]. It implies deliverance from a recent battle. These verses all come from a Maccabean editor adapting the Ps. to the circumstances of his times. V.[20b] belongs also to the same hand,

and it is probable that he changed v.[20a], which was an earlier marginal gl. with ענה in the sense of *answer*, to ענה in the sense of *humiliation* of the enemies. V.[4] is a couplet of similar tone, and probably came from him also. (2) V.[23] has יהוה also, and must have been a gl. later than 𝕯𝕽. It expresses, however, a calm confidence in Yahweh which was more characteristic of the Greek period before the Maccabean trials. V.[23] is based on 22⁹ 66⁹. The Aramaic יהב is also an evidence of late date. V.[24c] is also a trimeter gl., concluding the Ps. with an expression of trust in Yahweh. After the glosses have been removed, the Ps. is composite of an early Maskil, v.[2-3. 5-9a] and a later impr. catory Ps., v.[9b-10a. 21-22. 24ab]. The former was a little prayer, which originally was apart by itself, resembling Ps. 54. It was doubtless in 𝕰, because the original יהוה has been changed to אלהים. The combination with the prayer may have been made by 𝕰. The imprecatory Ps. is based in v.[10a] upon the story of the dispersion from Babel Gn. 11[1-9] (J); in v.[16] on the story of Korah and his company Nu. 16[33] (P). The traditional ascription of the Ps. to David in the time of the treachery of Ahithophel, 2 S. 15, has no other propriety than that Ahithophel was just such a person as is described in v.[13-15. 21-22]; but he could hardly have been regarded as the equal of the king. The reference to Pashhur, Jer. 20, would be more probable, if we could suppose that the Ps. was composed by Jeremiah ; but this is improbable, and there is no evidence that Pashhur was such an intimate friend as is here described. The reference to the walls of the city and its public squares, v.[11-12], prevents us from thinking of the times of the restoration previous to Nehemiah. It is therefore probably a Ps. of the time of Nehemiah, when there was no special peril from foreign enemies, but great corruption, violence, and strife in the city itself.

PSALM LV. *A.*

Str. I. 2–3 is a prayer in a syn. tristich with a synth. line giving reason. — **2-3**. *O give ear* ‖ *O attend to me*, and the climax, *answer me*, are usual terms of petition. — *and hide not Thyself*]. Yahweh seems to hide His face from His people if He gives no response to their prayers when they are in trouble; cf. 10¹. — *I am depressed*], lit. brought down in humiliation, as 𝕵, favoured also by paraphrase of 𝕲, PBV., AV., to be preferred to 𝕳, RV., and most moderns, from a different Hebrew stem, " I am restless." — *I moan*], as v.[18], 𝕲, 𝕵, RV., to be preferred to 𝕳, " am distracted." — *in my complaint*], plaintive expostulation with Yahweh for leaving him in this condition.

Str. II. is a syn. tetrastich, continuing the description of suffering. — **5**. *My heart writhes*], in the pain and anguish of the situation. — *And terrors*] of the consequences which will result if

Yahweh does not save him. The specification "of death" was
due to dittography, and was not original, as indeed it makes the
line too long for the measure. — **4** is a pentameter gloss, assigning
a reason for the anxiety. The *enemy* and *wicked* are a plurality
of foreign enemies, as v.[17-20]. These *dislodge trouble*], a metaphor
of rolling stones down from heights upon enemies in the valley
beneath, or in a siege from walls upon those assailing them. —
cherish animosity]. They habitually and with set purpose, due
to *anger*, take every opportunity of hostile action. — **6.** *shuddering*] is an intensification of *fear* and *trembling*. These have not
only *come upon* him, as a dark and gloomy cloud, but *cover* over,
enveloping and shutting him in from any relief except from his God.

Str. III. is a tetrastich of stairlike advance. — **7-9** a. *O that
I had*], the usual formula of the wish. — *pinions*]. He is unable
to escape in any other way than by the wings of a bird. — *As a
dove*]. This belongs to the second line. The poet is thinking
not simply of flying, but that he himself is like a dove, too weak
to resist the enemy, whose only hope is in flight. — *I would fly
away*], seeking refuge in clefts of the rocks, Ct. 3[14]. — *and settle
down*], in safety. — *afar off*], away from the danger of the city. —
I would lodge in the wilderness], abandoning the metaphor of the
bird for that of the traveller, as Je. 9[1]. This is not suited to the
context, it destroys the measure of the line, and is doubtless a gloss
from Je. — *hasten*], syn. with previous lines and so intransitive.

PSALM LV. *B.*

Str. I. is a pentastich, giving an introductory line of imprecation and the reason for it in a syn. tetrastich. — **9** *b.* *with a tempestuous wind*]. There is here a conflation, due to textual error,
of "stormy wind" and "devouring tempest." All of these words
except "devouring" are attached to previous lines by 𝔊 and
Vrss. at the expense of measures and right connection of the two
Pss. As so connected it represents a wayfarer flying for refuge
from an impending storm, but really it belongs with the next v.
as the instrument used by Yahweh for the purpose of division. —
10-12. *O Lord, divide their tongues*], imprecation upon persons
not mentioned as yet, a divine visitation such as that upon the
builders of Babel, Gn. 11[1-9], and indeed in the same way by a

theophanic storm. — *For I see*]. The reason for the previous wish is now given, and the peril is explained as something that was distinctly seen. The places are *in the city*], Jerusalem ; *upon the walls thereof*], the place of watchful defence ; *in the midst of it*], in its public square, a place of public concourse. This is as much as to say, in its enclosing walls and in its public places, within the city in its entirety. — *violence and strife*], these as personified are guilty of preying on the city instead of defending it, ‖ *trouble and mischief, engulfing ruin, oppression and deceit*], heaping up epithets, to describe the utter corruption that prevailed in the city, especially among its rulers and soldiers, who ought rather to have defended the city from all such things.

Str. II. is a pentastich, with four lines syn. and the fifth synth. thereto as an imprecation, thus in the reverse order of Str. I. on the principle of inclusion. — **13–15.** *For it is not an enemy*], neither foreign, as v.[4][16,19], nor even domestic, *he that hateth me*], a personal enemy ; but the very reverse, — *Thou, a man mine equal*], of like estimation, of the same rank and public esteem as himself. — *mine associate*], in close social relations. — *my familiar acquaintance*], well known by friendly personal intercourse. — *Together used to hold sweet counsel*], accustomed to meet together in the intimacy of a confidential circle and take counsel together, and this was made sweet by mutual words and acts of friendliness. — *we used to walk in concord*], ⅊, 𝔙, " as friends " PBV., which is greatly to be preferred to RV. " with the throng," thinking of the procession in the temple as 42[5], which latter meaning has no appropriateness if " the house of God " is regarded as a gloss, making, as it does, the line too long. Indeed, there is no good reason for limiting the walking in concord to the walk in temple processions, which would not be suggested by anything else in this Ps. Such was the man who was at the bottom of all this trouble, and such were the circumstances under which he had acted. — *who reproaches me*]. The man who was not an enemy acts as an enemy, and makes false representations and bitter taunts. He who did not hate now acts as if he hated, by making unworthy comparisons with his equal, by magnifying himself in hostility to his friend. This inconsistency between their present and former relations made it extremely difficult to act wisely. — He *could get away from* an open enemy ; he *could have hidden from* a man that was pronounced in his hatred ; but what could he do in this strange situation in which his best friend had become his worst enemy ? — **16.** *Let death come treacherously upon them*]. These are the enemies led by the treacherous friend ; cf. the personified attributes of wickedness v.[10b-12]. This is an imprecation upon them. The wish is that death may beguile them, coming upon them when they least expect it, taking them unprepared. — *Let them descend alive to Sheol*]. The author is thinking of Korah and his company, Nu. 16[33] (P), who by divine visitation were swallowed up by an earthquake, and, without the experience of death, descended living into the gulf and went down to the cavern of Sheol. A glossator thought it needful to append a reason for the imprecation : —*for evils are in their dwellings*], the place where the enemies dwell, their houses, the enemies being resident in the same city as the author.

Str. III. is a further description of the false friend. The pentastich has an introductory line and two syn. couplets. — **21–22.** *He put forth his hands*]. His reproaches had advanced to personal violence, cf. v.[10], and that *against his confederate*, the one who was in a covenant of peace and friendship with him, sealed as it was in the times of the Psalmist by the communion meal and the joint application of the blood of the victim ; and so he *profaned his covenant*], defiled it, as a sacred thing in which God, by the sacrifice, was also involved, and so was guilty of impiety toward the God of the covenant. The false friend is now described in the inconsistency between his words and deeds, his profession and practice. — *His face*], so 𝔊, required by pl. vb. ; better than " his mouth," 𝔐, which has been assimilated to *his words*. The antith. between face and mind is more natural. The face *was smoother than curds*]. With a round, smiling, beaming face, he addressed his friend ; but in his mind, hidden away in secret, was *war*, which he was only waiting for a convenient opportunity to wage. — *softer than oil*], were his words ; they were smooth, oily, flattering in appearance, but in reality they were drawn swords, sharp, taunting, piercing reproaches. This Str. is interrupted by a gloss which inserts a comforting exhortation to the afflicted before the imprecation :

> Cast upon Yahweh thy lot and He will sustain thee,
> He will not forever suffer the righteous to be moved.

23. *Cast upon Yahweh thy lot*], cf. 22^9 37^5; an exhortation to take up the burden of trouble and cast it upon Yahweh, that He might bear it for them. This is the lot, portion, or way, assigned one in this life, however difficult it may be. — *He will sustain thee*], give personal support in the trouble, enabling to endure it. This is enforced by an antithetical couplet, gnomic in character: *He will not suffer the righteous to be moved*]. They will be enabled to bear their burdens, endure the lot given them to endure, and will stand firm under it, not tottering from their position. — *forever*]. The sustaining will go on and the restraint from trouble without ceasing.

24. *But, O Thou, Yahweh*], strong antith. — *bring them down to the Pit of Sheol*]. The final imprecation wishes them to descend by a violent deed of God into the Pit, the place of punishment in Sheol. — *Men of blood and deceit*], such as the false friend described above and the treacherous enemies in the city. — *Let them not live out half their days*]. This in the original was doubtless jussive as the context requires, and not indicative, " will not live," as 𝔐, Vrss., because of the gl. — **24** *c. But as for me, I trust in Thee*], certainly a more appropriate conclusion for a Ps. used in public worship.

A series of glosses was inserted v.[17-20] :

> But as for me, unto God will I call, and Yahweh will save me.
> Evening and morning and at noon I will make complaint and moan;
> And He heard my voice, He ransomed me in peace,
> From the battle that I had : for with many were they against me.
> May 'El hear and answer them, even He that is enthroned of old !
> There are no changes for them that fear not God.

17–18. *But as for me*]. The Jewish nation speaks here a vow of worship. — *unto God will I call*], in supplicatory prayer, and this in the syn. line at the three hours of daily prayer of later Judaism, *evening and morning and at noon.* — *I will make complaint and moan*]. The prayer is a complaint for the evils experienced from enemies, and moaning in the pain involved in them. The prayer is not doubtful of its result, — *Yahweh will save me*], that is, by giving victory over these enemies. — *And he heard my* *voice*]. This begins a new line, and should not be attached to previous line, as a consequence of its petition, against the measure. It refers to a deliverance already experienced as a basis for a plea for another act of deliverance. — **19.** *ransomed me in peace*]. The peace is peace from war, the ransom is from enemies ; and so it is defined, *from the battle that I had*], doubtless in the Maccabean wars in which the Jews had won the victory, and that notwithstanding the fact that : *with many were they against me*]. Their enemies had been very numerous. This is therefore a later gl., with no original connection with its context. — **20.** '*El*], the ancient divine name, ‖ *He that is enthroned of old*], the King of Israel, enthroned on His heavenly throne, reigning as their king from the most ancient times. These are poetic expressions which do not suit the method of the Maccabean editor. They, with the imvs. *hear* ‖ *answer*, were probably a gloss, which the Maccabean editor found and adapted to his purpose by interpreting the latter vb. as from another stem meaning " humble," or "afflict," thinking of the enemy thus as humbled by defeat and slaughter. The Vrss. and interpreters find great difficulty with this v. — *There are no changes for them*]. The enemies have no changes of fortune to expect ; they will meet the same defeat in the future as in the past, because they *fear not God*]. Only the God-fearing people may expect salvation and victory.

LV. *A.*

2. האזינה] Hiph. imv. cohort., *v. 5*². — אלהים] for original יהוה, as usual in 𝔈. — תתעלם] Hithp. juss.; Ges.⁵⁴· ⁽³⁾ ᵏ. — [תחניתי] *v. 6*¹⁰ 119¹⁷⁰. — **3.** [אריד Hiph. impf. † רוד vb., cf. Arab. stem, *go to and fro;* Qal Ho. 12¹ (𝕲 otherwise) Je. 2³¹ (txt. err., prob. וירד); Hiph. Gn. 27⁴⁰ *show restlessness* (dub. *B*DB.). There is no certain use of the form in Heb. Here 𝕲 has ἐλυπήθην, 𝔙 *contristatus sum*, and 𝔍 *humiliatus sum*, which favour an original אריד, as Is. 15³. — [אשיח 1 sg. sf. ‡ שיח n.m. (1) *plaint, complaint*, so 64² 102¹ 142², elsw. Pr. 23²⁹ Jb. (5 t.) ; other mngs. dub. in ψ only, (2) *muse* 104³⁴, as 1 K. 18²⁷ (E). The word should be at the end of l. for rhyme in ֽ. — אהימה] dub. *B*DB., as most, Hiph. cohort. † [הים or הום] *show disquietude*, elsw. Mi. 2¹² (of fold and pasture) ; but Hi., De., Now., Qal *be driven about, distracted;* elsw. Dt. 7²³ *discomfit* by defeat ; Lag., Gr., Bu., אהמה, as v.¹⁸; Du. Niph. אהימה, as 1 S. 4⁵ Ru. 1¹⁹ 1 K. 1⁴⁵ *be in a stir*. In all these cases the form is cohort. and must be given a modal force not easy in the context. Ols., Che., Bä., rd. אהמיה, as 77⁴, √המה; Lag., Gr., Bu., Dr., אהמה √המה,

which is favoured by 𝕲 ἐταράχθην, 𝖩 *conturbatus*, v.¹³ and Ps. 39⁷. 𝕳 makes
the sentence close here, but 𝕲, 𝖩, make the subsequent context depend on
this vb. — **4.** קתַ:] cstr. קֵהָ n.f. *a.λ. pressure*, √קוץ; Aram. *press a.λ.* Am. 2¹³
(txt. err. for פוק). The only other form from this stem in Heb. מוּיָקָה n.f. *a.λ.*
Aramaism Ps. 66¹¹, 𝕲 θλίψεις, 𝖸 *tribulationes*. Here 𝕲 θλίψεως, 𝖩 *perse-
quentis*, interpret קתְ/ as מוּעָקָה, and that is best suited to context. עֲקַת, suggested by Ol., Dy., Now., is syn. with ?ו ; but the sense *cry of distress* suits
not the wicked adversary, but rather the singer of the Ps. It is easier to think
of a defectively written אֲקַת cstr. † צוּקָה n.f. *distress* Is. 8²² 30⁵ Pr. 1²⁷; the
substitution of Aram. for Heb. form easy for a later scribe. — יִשְׂטְמוּני] Qal
impf. † [שֲׂטַם] vb. Qal *cherish animosity against*, c. acc. pers., as Gn. 27⁴¹ (J)
49²³ (Poem) 50¹⁵ (E) Jb. 16⁹ 30²¹. This v. is of different measure from its
context and is an explanatory gl. — **5.** לִבִּי] emph. in position. — יָחִיל] Qal
impf. descriptive, *writhe in pain*, √חור, as 77¹⁷ 97⁴. — [אֵימוֹת] pl. ‡ אֵימָה n.f.
terror, poetic word, elsw. ψ, 88¹⁶; cf. Ex. 15¹⁰ Dt. 32²⁵. — יָּוֶת] dittog. of
previous word, as Che. — **6.** Not in 𝕲ᴮ. † רַעַד n.m. elsw. Ex. 15¹⁵. It belongs in the next l. for measure. — וַיְכַסֵּני] ו consec. impf. after impf., improb.
here ; rd. ו coörd. It was interp. as result of previous movement. — † פַּלָּצוּת]
n.f. *shuddering*, as Is. 21⁴ Ez. 7¹⁸ Jb. 21⁶; but 𝕲 ᶜ·ᴿ·ᵀ·ᴬ σκότος, צלמות, so 𝖩
caligo, 𝖸 *tenebrae*, so 𝖲, Gr., Che., but Σ φρίκη. — **7.** [וָאֹמַר] prosaic gl., as
often ; not usual in poetry. — מִי־יִתֶּן־לִי] *wish*, as 14⁷ = 53⁷, should close the
l. for rhyme. — † אֵבֶר] n.m. *pinions* of dove, elsw. eagle Is. 40³¹ Ez. 17³. —
‡ יוֹנָה] n.f. *dove*, elsw. 56¹ 68¹⁴. A new l., as Che., and not as MT. at close
of l. — וְאֶשְׁכֹּנָה] ו coörd. Qal cohort. שכן for an original וישכנתי, required for
rhyme. — **8.** אַרְחִיק] Hiph. impf. רחק (22¹²), although not cohort. in form
must, between cohortatives of v.⁷·⁹, be cohort. in mng. Prob. the cohort.
ending has been omitted by an early copyist. — נָדֹד] Qal inf. cstr. obj. previous vb., which has force of auxiliary or adverb It should have sf. for
rhyme in י_. — **9.** אָחִישָׁה] Hiph. cohort. חוש (22²⁰) *hasten ;* so Aq., Θ, Σ, 𝖩,
but 𝕲 προσεδεχόμην, 𝖸 *expectabam* = אוֹחִילָה Hiph. יהל (31²⁵), so 𝖲. — [מִפְלָט]
a.λ. n.m. acc. obj. *escape*, Hu., Bä., or acc. direction, taking previous vb. as
intrans. *haste ; place of escape*, We., Du ; but 𝕲 τὸν σώζοντά με, so 𝖲, 𝖸,
imply לִי מְפַלֵּט Pi. ptc. (17¹³), cf. 144². 𝕳 is most prob.

LV. B.

סֹיָה] *a.λ.* ptc. סיה *rushing*, as in cognate Syr. and Arab. stems, ᴮDB., but
dub.; 𝕲 ὀλιγοψυχίας, 𝖸 *pusillanimitate spiritus* = סַעַר, as Is. 51¹⁴, but this
is improb.; 𝖩 *spiritu tempestatis ;* Aq., O, λαιλαπώδους. Gr., Hu., Dy., rd.
‡ סוּפָה n.f. *storm wind* 83¹⁶ Am. 1¹⁴ Na. 1³. It is prob. txt. err., variation of
† סַעַר n.m. *tempest*, elsw. 83¹⁵ Am. 1¹⁴ Jon. 1⁴·¹² Je. 23¹⁹ 25³² 30²³. — **10.** [בַּלַּע]
Pi. imv. (21¹⁰) attached to this l. as בְּרַע (48¹⁴), although pointing of latter
attracted to former, Ges.⁵²⁽²⁾ⁿ; but rd. prob. בְּלִי, as 52⁶, because it is dependent on סַעַר. It is prob. that we have conflation here. סער נרי is expl. of
רוח סיה. The original was מרוח סער. The מן is then instrumental, qualifying

the following vb. — [אדני פלג לשונם] refer to Gn. 10²⁵. — **11.** [און ועמל] phr., cf. [עמל ואון] 10⁷ 90¹⁰. — **12.** [חוית] *v. 5¹⁰*, rightly attached to previous l. by ⅏; necessary to complete its measure. — [נתרבה] improb. repetition, not in ⅏. A word is, however, needed for measure. It was prob. הרהבה. The copyist was confused between the two words, and attaching one to this l. he naturally used קרבה; whereas if one were attached to the previous l. he would have used רחבה. — [תשיש] Hiph. impf. freq. ‡ שוש Qal *depart*, not in ψ. Hiph. trans. *remove*, not in ψ; but intrans. here, as Ex. 13²² 33¹¹ Na. 3¹ +. — [תוך ומרמה] cf. *10⁷*. — **13.** [לא־אויב] emph. in position. ⅏ takes it as לא conditional; but context favours 𝔈, 𝔍. — [יחרפני] Pi. impf. freq., prob. relative clause. — [ואשא] the apod. as ⅏, only of an implicit, not explicit, prot. as Dr., and not ו subord. as 𝔍 *ut sustineam*, so Bä. The l. is defective, needing חמני as truly as syn. l. נשא here in the sense of *lift up* the foot in going away, *betake oneself away*, *get away*, so 139⁹, as Gn. 29¹; not *bear*, *endure*, which is against the syn. vb. — [צלי הגדיל] as 35²⁶ 38¹⁷. Σ adds ירב, as 41¹¹, but it makes l. too long and indeed is out of place there. — **14.** [ואנוש] emph. antith. — ‡ [ערך] n.m. (1) *order*, *row*, not in ψ, but (2) *estimate*, *valuation*, of like estimation with myself, only here. — † [אלוף] adj. (1) *tame*, of animals; *docile*, of lamb Je. 11¹⁹, of cows Ps. 144¹⁴ (usually as אלף *thousand*); (2) of friends, intimates, here as Mi. 7⁵ Je. 3⁴ 13²¹ Pr. 2¹⁷ 16²⁸ 17⁹, but ⅏ ἡγεμών μου, 𝔙 *dux meus* = אלופי, as Ex. 15¹⁵. — [מידעי] as 31¹² 88⁹. ¹⁹. — **15.** [אשר] is prosaic gl. — [נמתיק] Hiph. impf. 1 pl. freq. † [מתק] denom. *be* or *become sweet;* Qal Ex. 15²⁵ Pr. 9¹⁷ Jb. 21³³, suck Jb. 24²⁰ (?); Hiph. Jb. 20¹², with סור only here. ⅏ ἐδέσματα = either ציד or סעד n. α.λ. from סעד vb. as 𝔖. — [בבית אלהים] is a gl. of definition. — [ברגש] α.λ. *company*, *companionship*, or *concord*, ⅏ ἐν ὁμονοίᾳ, *v.* רגשה 64³, רגשו 2¹. — **16.** [ישימות] Kt. α.λ. pl. [ישימה] n.f. *desolation* √ישם improb., Qr. ישי מות, as ⅏, 𝔙, 𝔍; ישי Hiph. impf. defective for ישיא √† נשא *beguile*, Ges.⁷⁴ ⁽³⁾ ᵏ; Niph. *be beguiled* Is. 19¹³; Hiph. *beguile*, c. acc. pers. Gn. 3¹³ (J) Je. 37⁹ 49¹⁶ Ob.³. ⁷ 2 K. 19¹⁰ = Is. 37¹⁰ 2 Ch. 32¹⁵; sq. ל 2 K. 18²⁹ = Is. 36¹⁴ Je. 4¹⁰ 29⁸; c. על only here, pregnant, implying descent, Ges.¹¹⁹ ⁽⁴⁾. ⅏, 𝔙, 𝔍, give the vb. the mng. *come upon*, which is prob. paraphrase. — [עלימו] archaic poetic sf. There is a reference to Nu. 16¹³. It is possible therefore that with Brüll we should rd. יבלעמו. — [יירב] n. sf. 3 pl. † [יור] n.[m.] *sojourning* place, elsw. pl. Jb. 18¹⁹, ארץ מ׳ Gn. 17⁸ 28¹ 36⁷ 37¹ Ex. 6⁴ (P) Ez. 20³⁸, שני מ׳ Gn. 47⁹, ימי מ׳ Gn. 47⁹, בית מ׳ Ps. 119⁵⁴. But ⅏, 𝔖, have pl., and it seems prob. that the form has been attracted to בקרבם. There are in this v. three trimeters, and the clause with כי is doubtless a gl. — **17.** The use of יהוה in 𝔈 is improb. It is in ⅏, 𝔍, and is doubtless original, though 𝔖 has אלהים only. It indicates that the entire v. is a gl. — **18.** [אציתה] Qal cohort. שיח (6⁷). — [ואהמה] ו coörd. Qal impf. also cohort. המה (39⁷), *v.* v.³. — [וישמע] ו consec. result of prayer; goes with פדה of next v. ⅏ makes both impfs. and interprets ו as conjunctive; so Gr., Du., We. These vbs. are usually regarded as pfs. of certainty. — **19.** [קרב] n.m. *battle*, *war*, as v.²² 68³¹ 78⁹ 144¹ Zc. 14³ Jb. 38²³ Ec. 9¹⁸, so Ra., Ki., EV⁸., Now., Du.; but Vrss. Qal inf. cstr. קרב *draw nigh*, Hi., De., Bä. But the former is favoured, if the l. begins here. — [ברבים]

The בְּ is taken as כ *essentiae* by Bä., Dr., after Σ, 𝕵; but 𝕲 ἐν πολλοῖς, so Du., Now. — שְׁעָרַי‎] *against me*, as Σ πρὸς ἐμέ, 𝕵 *adversum me*, cf. בְּ 94[16]. — **20.** תַּעֲנֶם‎] ۱ conj. Qal impf. sf. 3 pl. בַּ‎; *answer*, as usual after שׁוּב‎. But 𝕲 καὶ ταπεινώσει αὐτούς, 𝕵 *humiliabit eos*, so 𝕾. יְעַנֵּה‎ Pi. ענה‎. The sf. is often an interp. and is prob. incorrect. It really refers to the psalmist. The original was without sf. — חֲלִיפוֹת‎] pl. ‡ [חֲלִיפָה‎] n.f. *change* (1) of garment Gn. 45[22. 22] Ju. 14[19]; (2) relays 1 K. 5[28] Jb. 10[17], or relief from service Jb. 14[14]. We may think of changes of character here in accord with (1) Now., or of changes of fortune, vicissitudes, in accord with (2) Calv., Dr., Kirk., al. — **21.** שָׁרַי‎] for אישׁ שׁרּחַבמי‎ 41[10], cf. יעורמי‎ 7[5], possibly here שָׁרַי‎; 𝕲 ἐν τῷ ἀποδιδόναι, 𝕵 *in retribuendo*, interp. as Pi. inf. cstr. שׁלם‎ *recompense* (22[26]), but 𝕵 *pacifica sua*. — חֲרֵל בְּרִיחוֹ‎] as 89[5] Mal. 2[10]. — **22.** חָלְקוּ‎] Qal *be smooth*, a.λ. (Ho. 10[2] from other stem, so 𝕲 here); Hiph. *v.* 5[10]. — **22.** יְתָחָאֵה‎] a.λ. pl. cstr. *butter-words* for usual חֶמְאָה‎ n.f. *curd, curdled milk*, not in ψ; but dub., as Vrss. take מ as prep. ‖ יָשְׁעֵי‎, which is most prob.; point therefore מֵחֲמַאת‎. 𝕲 ἀπὸ ὀργῆς τοῦ προσώπου αὐτοῦ rd. מֵחֲרַ ת פניו‎ from חֵמָה‎ n.f. *burning anger*, so 𝕾, 𝕵, but other Vrss. as 𝕳; פניו‎ is prob. correct, as vb. is pl. — רַכּוּ‎] Qal pf. 3 pl. † [רכך‎] vb. *be tender, soft:* (1) of heart, *fearful* Is. 7[4] Je. 51[46] Dt. 20[3]; *softened, penitent,* 2 K. 22[19] = Ch. 34[27]; (2) of treacherous words, only here. Pu. *be softened* with oil Is. 1[6]; Hiph. caus. of Qal (1), Jb. 23[16]. — [פְּחוֹת‎ a.λ.; pl. [פְּתָחָה‎] n [f.] *drawn* sword; why not Qal ptc. pl. פֹּחוֹת‎, as Qal for drawing swords 37[14]. — **23.** הַשְׁלֵךְ‎] Hiph. imv. שׁרּךְ‎, cf. 22[9] 37[5], all עַל יהוה‎. יהוה‎ in 𝕳 evidence that not only this word, but entire v. is a gl. — יְהָבְךָ‎] a.λ. n.m. sf. 2 m. *lot,* Aramaism, *BDB.;* 𝕲 τὴν μέριμνάν σου, dub.; יְהַבְךָ‎ Qal impf. יחב‎, as Aq., Σ, Quinta, Sexta, ἀγαπήσει σε, 𝕵 *caritatem tuam.* But this vb. also Aramaism; in OT. only Dt. 33[3]. In any case the word is late and another evidence of glossator. — הוא‎] emph. demonst. — וְלְהָבְךָ‎] Pilp. impf. fut. ‡ כּוּל‎ vb. Pilp. *sustain, support;* elsw. acc. pers. Gn. 45[11] 50[21] (E) Zc. 11[16] +, acc. rei Ps. 112[5]. — ‡ מוֹט‎] n.m. *shaking,* obj. נֶר‎, as 66[9], cf. 121[3]; cf. vb. (*10⁶*). — **24.** וְאַָרָה‎] emphatic change of pers. — ‡ בְּאֵר‎] n.f. *pit,* specif. here and 69[16], the Pit of Sheol = בּוּר‎ (7[16]), which Bä., Du., rd. — שַׁחַת‎ *v.* 7[16]. — אנשׁי דמים‎] = 26[9] 59[3] 139[19] Pr. 29[10]. — יֶחֱצוּ‎] Qal impf. ‡ חצה‎ vb. denom. חֵצִי‎ *half,* so *halve, divide in half;* cf. Is. 30[28]. — וְאֲנִי אבטח בך‎ 𝕲 had יהוה‎ also, but improb. in 𝕳, and even then l. is too short. Du. adds also אלהי‎, necessary if l. be original; but it is doubtless a gl.

PSALM LVI., 4 STR. 6³, RF. 3³.

Ps. 56 is a national prayer for deliverance from enemies: (**1**) petition that Yahweh will be gracious because of the enemy who is fighting them and treading them down (v[2-4]) ; (**2**) that He will weigh out retribution to them for their crafty lying in wait for Israel's life (v.[6-8]) ; (**3**) assurance that the enemy will be defeated

because of Yahweh's attention to His people's troubles (v.$^{9-11a}$) ; (4) **promise of votive and thank-offerings for the accomplished deliverance** (v.$^{13-14}$). **Rf. is a resolution of boastful song of praise and fearless trust in Yahweh** (v.$^{5.\ 11b-12}$).

BE gracious unto me, for man doth tread me down;
All day long the fighter presseth me;
All day long my watchful foes do tread me down;
For many are fighting against me.
O Most High, in the day I fear,
Unto Thee I trust.
Of Yahweh I boast with a word of song.
In Yahweh do I put my trust without fear.
What can flesh do unto me?

ALL day long with words they vex me.
Against me are all their plans.
For evil they gather themselves together; they lurk;
They watch my footprints,
Even as they wait for my life.
Because of trouble, weigh out to them.
Of Yahweh I boast with a word of song.
In Yahweh do I put my trust without fear.
What can flesh do unto me?

(I MAKE known, I recount them, Yahweh;)
My tears are put (before Thee).
Mine enemies will turn backward.
In the day I call, I know it.
For Yahweh is for me,
Of Yahweh I boast with a word of song.
Of Yahweh I boast with a word of song.
In Yahweh do I put my trust without fear.
What can flesh do unto me?

UPON me is (the obligation of) Thy votive offerings,
I will pay Thee thank-offerings;
For Thou hast delivered my life from death,
And my feet from being pushed down,
That I may walk before Yahweh
In the light (of the land) of the living.
Of Yahweh I boast with a word of song.
In Yahweh do I put my trust without fear.
What can flesh do unto me?

Ps. 56 was in the earlier collection of מכתמים, then taken up into 𝔇 and 𝔈 (*v.* Intr. §§ 25, 27, 32). The reference באחז אותו פלשתים בגת, cf. 1 S. 27, was in 𝔇. Like all such historical references, it was not designed to indicate the circumstances of composition, but circumstances illustrating certain features of the Ps. In 𝔇ℜ it received the assignment על־יונת אלם רחקים (*v.* Intr. §§ 33, 34). The Ps. is ornate, having 4 Str. 6^3 with Rf. 3^3, which is retained after

Strs. 1 and 3, but omitted after Strs. 2 and 4. The Ps. is a national prayer for deliverance from numerous and powerful enemies. The language and style are ancient. Words are often repeated: יְבָאַף v.²·³, רחם v.²·³, כָל חיום v.²·⁸·⁶, אירא v.⁴·⁵·¹², בטח v.⁴·⁵·¹². There are rare words: רחם v.²·³, elsw. 35¹·¹; שאף v.²·³, as 57⁴ Am. 8⁴ Ez. 36³; יגורו v.⁷ as 59⁴ 140³ Is. 54¹⁵; נֹרִי v.⁹ a.λ. dub., prob. txt. err.; סְפָרָה v.⁹ a.λ. also prob. txt. err.; יהֹ v.¹⁴ = 116⁹. There are also rare uses of words: מרום v.³, as 92⁹; יְקְבִי יִשְׁמֹרוּ, phr. a.λ. v.⁷; חֶרֶשׁ v.⁸; as 32⁷, but more prob. פרס, as 58³; אור החיים v.¹⁴, phr. elsw. Jb. 33³⁰. V.¹⁴ is cited 116⁸⁻⁹, and is therefore much earlier. The temple worship is in existence, with words of song, votive offerings, and thank-offerings, v.¹¹·¹³. The people have been delivered from their enemies, though they are still in peril. The Ps. dates therefore from the Babylonian period before the exile.

Str. I. has a syn. tetrastich and an antith. couplet. — **2-3.** *Be gracious unto me*], usual petition in peril, *v.* 4². — *for man*], collective for the enemy of the nation, 9²⁰⁻²¹ 10¹⁸ 66¹², — *fighter*], engaged in *fighting*, v.³ᵇ ‖ *watchful foes, v.* 5⁹. — *doth tread me down*], repeated in v.³ᵃ; of the trampling under foot by the victorious enemy, so 𝕲, 𝔍, and other Vrss., as 57⁴, greatly to be preferred to " swallow me up," EVˢ., which is based on a Hebrew word of similar form. — *presseth me*], the pressure of conflict on the battle-field ; for the context shows that the fighting was still in progress. The enemy is powerful and numerous, and the danger is great. — *O Most High*], as 𝔍, PBV., AV., is better suited to the context than adv. " proudly," RV., which, though favoured by many moderns, is not so well sustained by Hebrew usage, and is not in accord with the position of the word, which the measure requires should be in l. 5 and not in l. 4. — **4.** *in the day I fear*], the time of extreme peril in battle, when there was every reason to fear, I yet will *trust* in Yahweh. This leads to the Rf., which is a syn. couplet with a synth. line of challenge. — **5.** *Of Yahweh I boast with a word of song*]. Usage requires that we should render " boast," and not " praise," as 𝕲, 𝔍, EVˢ., due to interpreting " word " as word of promise. While this is possible, it is not suggested by the context. " His word " of 𝔚 is not sustained by " my words " of 𝕲 ; but the simple " word " of 𝔍 is sustained by v.¹¹, 𝔚, Vrss. This is most naturally explained as the word of song, as Dt. 32⁴⁴ Pss. 18¹ 45² 137³, cf. Ju. 5¹² Jos. 10¹². The people boast in song of the victory they are assured that Yahweh will eventually give them. — *trust without fear*]. The trust in divine help is so firm and sure that the fear natural under the circumstances passed away and no longer existed. — *What can flesh do unto me ?*] Sure of speedy victory over foes, the poet challenges their power to do any permanent or real harm. They are but *flesh*, and therefore impotent to resist God. In v.[12] "flesh" is changed to "man." This may have been an intentional variation of Rf., but in view of the author's style of frequent repetition, it is more probable that the variation is due to the taste of an editor.

Str. II. has a syn. pentastich and a synth. line of imprecation. — **6-7.** *with words they vex me*], as 𝔍. The words are those of the enemy, as the plans are *their plans*. "My words" of 𝔐, 𝔊, EV[s]., interpret the words as those of the author, which might suit a reference of the Ps. to an individual, or a group of individuals ; but hardly to the nation. The words are threatening words, which pass over into plans and finally into deeds of violence. — *For evil*]. The measure requires that this should go with l. 3 and be connected with : *they gather themselves together*, as the purpose of the gathering. Their activity in carrying out their evil purpose is graphically described. They *lurk*, hiding in ambush to spy upon the people and take them unawares ; *they watch my footprints*, every movement that is made, following at my heels and tracing out my path. — *wait for my life*], in the climax. Their hope is, that they may take the life of the people of God, destroy the nation altogether. Therefore the final petition. — **8.** *Because of trouble weigh out to them*]. The enemies have made great trouble for the people of God. As deliverance had been implored in the previous Str., so here retribution upon the enemies. It is hoped that this may be weighed out in the exactness of justice. The Vrss. differ from 𝔐 in this line, and it is difficult to explain any of them. The difficulty originated from a copyist's mistake of a single letter, by which he gave a word meaning "escape," instead of the word meaning "weigh out." The only way to explain 𝔐 is as interrogatory, "shall they escape?" EV[s]., which probably occasioned the insertion of an additional line, making the Str. too long : "In anger cast down the peoples."

Str. III. has a tristich composed of syn. couplet, a synth. line, and a synth. tristich. — **9.** *I make known*]. This emendation seems to explain, in a measure at least, the many different terms of 𝕳 and Vrss. This is emphasized by the cognate verb, *I recount them*], namely, the tears of the next line. The 1 sg. of 𝕲, 𝕾, is to be preferred to 2 sg. of 𝕳, "Thou tellest," EV[s]., "hast counted," Dr., Kirk. — *My tears are put before Thee*]. So 𝕲, which is to be preferred to 𝕳, "in Thy flask," as better suited to the context and simpler. 𝕳 gives a figure of speech, which is indeed striking and touching, especially if in parall. with the next clause of 𝕳, "are they not in Thy book." This is as much as to say that Yahweh not only records in His book of record the sufferings of His people; but every tear that these sufferings produce is treasured up in the flask, rather the skin bottle of the Orient, which He uses for the purpose. But this last clause is an explanatory gloss, destroying the measure, and the reference to flask, standing alone, is less probable. — **10**. *Mine enemies will turn backward*]. The attention of Yahweh to the sufferings of His people makes it certain that their enemies will be overcome, and that they will be compelled to a disastrous retreat, cf. 9[4] 44[11]. — *In the day I call, I know it*]. As in v.[4], the time of extreme peril, the time of fear, was also the time of trust, so here the time when they call upon Yahweh for help is the very time in which they know that Yahweh is able to give them the deliverance they implore. This is emphasized in 𝕳 by the insertion of "lo," both unnecessary and at the expense of the measure. — *For Yahweh is for me*], as PBV., AV., is to be preferred to RV., "that Yahweh is for me," connecting it with "know" in the same line as its obj., which is against the measure.

Str. IV. has two syn. couplets and a synth. couplet. — **13**. *Upon me*], incumbent as a duty, or an assumed obligation, because of the deliverance granted. — *Thy votive offerings*], sacrifices vowed and offered up in accordance with such vows, cf. 22[25] ‖ *thank-offerings*, sacrifices expressing gratitude for blessings received, cf. 50[14. 23]; first distinguished in code of D. — **14**. *And my feet from being pushed down*]. The phr. cited 116[8] is dub. But the use of the verb makes it evident that the peril was from thrusts or pushes of the enemy, which would result in his stumbling and falling prostrate in death, unless delivered. — *that I may walk before Yahweh*], in the presence of Yahweh, resident in His temple in

D

Jerusalem ; the city of Jerusalem being conceived as the royal
city, and the land as His land. — *in the light of the land of the
living*]. The Holy Land is a land rejoicing in the light shining
forth from Yahweh's presence in the temple, and so it is the land
of the living, in which those living by the favour of Yahweh truly
live. An ancient copyist reduced the line to " light of the living,"
a phr. elsw. Jb. 33[30], but it was cited before that mistake was made
in 116[9] as " lands of the living," cf. 27[13] 52[7] 142[6]. The measure
requires both words.

2. אלהים] ⅏ κύριε. The divine name is a gl., making l. too long. — יְ] gl.
of interpretation. — שְׁאָפַנִי] Qal pf. שאף *pant after*, as 119[131] Je. 2[24] 14[6], so
Du., Dr.; but ⅏ κατεπάτησέν με, 𝔍 *conculcavit me* † שׁאף II. v.[3] 57[4] Am. 2[7] (?) 8[4]
Ez. 36[3], so Bä. — אֱנוֹשׁ] coll. antith. God 8[5] 9[20. 21], cf. בשׂר v.[5], ארם v.[12]. —
כל היום thrice repeated, v.[2. 3. 6]. It should begin the l. [3] as in other cases.
— יִלְחָצֵנִי] Qal impf. ‡ לחץ vb. Qal *squeeze, oppress*, as 106[42] Ex. 22[20] 23[9] (E)
Ju. 2[18] Am. 6[14]. — **3.** מָרוֹם] ⅏[B] inserts מרום before כי רבים, so Aug.,
Cassiodorus, by txt. err., rendering ἀπὸ ὕψους ἡμέρας = ממרום or מָרוֹם, which
meaning is unknown to Heb. usage. ⅏[ᶜ. ᵃ. ᶜ. ᵀ. λ] attach it as 𝔥. ⅏[A], Eusebius
rd. מרום, but divide as 𝔥, so Houb., מרום, should, however, go with יום as
the measure requires. מרום usually is the height of heaven, 7[8] 10[5] 18[17], but
92[9] *Most High*, ⅏ ὕψιστος, so here 𝔍 *altissime*, Aq., 𝕿, Quinta, Ki., Calv., AV.
It is also used of heavenly beings Is. 24[4]. Bu. gives it adverbial force, *with
pride, proudly*, as Σ, Luther, Geier, Moll., RV., Now., Kirk., *with high looks*,
Dr., but this is the only example proposed and is dub. The measure requires
מרום in v.[4], and *Most High* gives best sense and is better sustained. — **4.** יום]
with impf. as v.[10], cf. with inf. 20[10], time when, graphically conceived as a day.
— אירא] Qal impf. of state; but ⅏ φοβηθήσονται makes it prob. that we should
rd. inf. ירא, capable of both interpretations. — אני] emph. — **5.** = v.[11b. 12],
a Rf. to be inserted also after v.[8ᵃ 14]. — אֲהַלֵּל] Pi. impf. *v.* 56[6]; c. ב, as in 44[9],
boast of; c. acc. *laud, praise.* ⅏ inserts כל היום from 44[9] and interprets vb. as
ἐπαινέσω, so 𝔍 *laudavi.* — דבר] ⅏ רברי, both interp. of דבר, 𝔍 as v.[11]; 2d acc.
after הלל *with a word*, cf. קול 3[5], etc. — בבשׂר] *flesh, v.* 16[9]; for man antith.
God, cf. 78[39] Gn. 6[3] (J) Je. 17[5] and the phr. כל בשׂר Pss. 65[3] 145[21] ‖ ארם v.[12], which
latter is prob. editorial substitution. — יְ] should precede בשׂר for better measure. — **6.** דְּבָרָי] if obj. must be taken in the sense of *affairs*, Bä., Du.; but 𝔍
has *sermonibus* דברי, which is most prob. — יְעַצֵּבוּ] Pi. impf. 3 pl. i.p. ‡ [עצב]
vb. *hurt, pain, grieve;* Pi. *vex*, as Is. 63[10]; Hiph. idem Ps. 78[40]. ⅏ has
ἐβδελύσσοντο which translates יתעבו 5[7] 106[40] 107[18] 119[163], but improb. — עלי]
emph. — כל־מחשׁבתם] has two beats 33[10] Je. 6[19] 18[12] 29[11] +. — לרע] makes
l. too long; should go with next in emph. position, which indeed needs it. —
7. יָגוּרוּ] Qal impf. גור ⅏ παροικήσουσιν, usual mng. *sojourn, v.* 5[5]; but 𝔍
congregabuntur, so Σ, 𝕿, EVˢ., from another stem † גור mng. *gather together*,

as Ki., Ges., De., Now., elsw. 59⁴ 140³ Is. 54¹⁵. But *B*DB. after Hi., Ew.,
Di., Bä., makes stem = גרה with mng. *stir up strife, quarrel*, in all these passages. Gr., Du., after AE rd. here and in 59⁴ יגורו Qal impf. גור *troop together*,
as 94²¹, where, however, Ols. rds. יגורו. — יצפינו] Kt. Hiph. impf. 3 pl., so
Jb. 14³ Ex. 2³, but Qr. Qal; in either case *hide, lurk, spy*, as Ps. 10⁸. — [הֵמָּה]
emph. referring to same persons. MT. attached to previous vb., but 𝕲 more
properly to following in accord with measure. — [עֲקֵבַי יִשְׁמֹרוּ] phr. α.λ. but
idea 89⁵². — [כַּאֲשֶׁר] *according as*. La., Bi., rd. כארי *as a lion*, but ארי not in
ψ (22¹⁷ txt. err.), and the change unnecessary and improb. — **8.** [עַל־אָוֶן פַּלֶּט־לָמֵוֹ]
is difficult in this context. Most who retain the text interpret as a question;
but it is certainly abrupt and improb. 𝔍 has *quia nullus est salvus in eis* =
עַל אין פלט למו, taking עַל = אשר עַל, cf. 119¹³⁶, and אין negative; but this does not
suit the context. 𝕲 has ὑπὲρ τοῦ μηθενὸς σώσεις αὐτούς, taking אֶוֶן as noun,
nothing and vb. as imv. ‖ הורד. This gives good parall., but a lame idea.
The text is certainly corrupt. Bach., Bä., propose אוֶן אין, 𝔚, Aq., Σ, 𝕿,
retaining one, 𝕲, 𝔍, Quinta, 𝕾, 𝔙, the other. This would be easier were
it not for the subsequent l. with its imv. But that is an interp. gl. making the
Str. too long. Ew., Ols., Hu., Dy., Now., Du., change פלט to † פלס vb. denom.
Pi. (1) *weigh out*, as 58⁶; (2) *level*, a path, 78⁵⁰, as Pr. 4²⁶ 5⁶·²¹ Is. 26⁷. The
Rf. which should follow favours imv., and פלס gives a most suitable sense.
— **9.** [נֹדִי] α.λ. נוד n. [m.] sf. 1 sg. *wandering B*DB., or possibly agitation, √נוד
vb. *move to and fro, v. 11¹*. But 𝕲 τὴν ζωήν μου, 𝔙 *vitam meam*, 𝔍 *secretiora
mea*, 𝕾 *my confession*, Σ τὰ ἔνδον μου, are difficult to explain on the basis of
𝔚. Some simple word with sf. 1 pl. or coll. sg. is needed ‖ דמעתי having a
mng. suited to the vb. ספר. Bä., Ecker, think that there is word-play with
נאדך, and that 𝔚 is thereby verified; but this is dub. Che. suggests אנחתי,
which is certainly an appropriate word, but the derivation of all the texts and
translations therefrom is difficult. It is easier to start from 𝕾. This might be
הדהי, Hiph. inf. cstr. ידה, cf. הודי, the same from נגר. If we suppose that נדי
and ספרתה have been transposed, the final ה of the vb. which is unknown to
𝕲, 𝕾, would belong to the noun. This would give us הנדי, an easy error for
הגר. In this case the ζωήν of 𝕲 and *secretiora* of 𝔍 are what is made known;
and 𝕾 interprets it of confession. This would give us a still better word-play,
especially if with 𝕲, 𝔍, 𝕾, we read נגרך for נאדך. — [סָפְרָה] Qal pf. 2 m. fully
written, but 𝕲, 𝕾, סָפְרִי makes it evident that אֶרְה was not in original text. It
is dittog. The l. as in 𝕲 has אלהים at the beginning, making measure complete. — [שִׂימָה] MT. Qal imv. cohort. improb., שִׂימֶךְ ptc. pass. f. is to be preferred, cf. ἔθου, 𝕲, 𝕾, so Ew., Hu., Bö., Hi., De. — [נֹאדֶךָ] *thy skin bottle*, cf.
33⁷ 119⁸³; but 𝕲, 𝔍, 𝕾, נגדר, as Street most prob. — [הֲלֹא בְּסִפְרָתֶךָ] is tautological, a defective l., making the Str. just this l. too long. It is doubtless a
gl. or txt. err. by dittog. of ספרתה above, or conflation, as Street. הלא is not in
𝕲, which has ὡς καὶ, or in 𝔍, which has *sed non*, all interpretative. † [סִפְרָה]
n.f. α.λ. possibly *book;* but 𝕲 ἐν τῇ ἐπαγγελίᾳ σου, 𝔍 *in narratione tua*. —
10. אָז] 𝔚, 𝔍, but not in 𝕲; a gl. making l. too long. — [זֶה] 𝔚, 𝔍, emph., pointing to the following; but 𝕲 ἰδού; both interpretative gl. — [כִּי אלהים לי] 𝕲 ὅτι

θεός μου εἶ σύ, so 𝔍 *quia deus meus es.* This is correct if אלהים be original ; but if אלהים stands for original יהוה, לי is *for me, on my side, espousing my cause,* which is better suited to context. — **11.** כאלהים אהלל דבר] bis in 𝔐, 𝔊, 𝔍, all Vrss. It is tempting to think of dittog., as the only difference is that in v.¹¹ᵇ. 𝔐 has יהוה ; but 𝔊, 𝔍, have אלהום in both lines, so that the variation is dub. The first clause is needed to complete the Str., the second is the first l. of Rf. — **13.** עָלַי] emph., *incumbent on me* as an obligation, as 7¹¹ 10¹⁴ 16² 22¹¹ 37⁵ 40⁸ 55²³ 62⁸ 71⁶. — **14.** This v. is also in 116⁸⁻⁹, derived from this Ps. The variations are : (1) חלצת 116⁸ for הצלת 56¹⁴; (2) the insertion in 116⁸ of עיני מן דמעה, ,עי־, which is a gl. even there, and is not in 56¹⁴; (3) את־רגלי 116⁸ is doubtless original for רגלי הלא of 56¹⁴. רלא is interpretative gl. and abrupt, only ו of 𝔊 should be prefixed. † [דְּחִי] n. [m.] *stumbling,* α.λ. these two passages. (4) את־הלך 116⁹ for inf. לְהִתְהַלֵּךְ 56¹⁴ is an intentional variation. (5) לפני יהוה 116⁹ = לפני אלהים 56¹⁴; יהוה is certainly original. Ps. 116 was composed before 56 went into 𝔈. (6) ארצות החיים 116⁹, cf. אור ההיים 56¹⁴. The original was אור ארץ החיים, as measure requires.

PSALM LVII.

Ps. 57 is composite : **(A)** a prayer of the community of the Restoration for deliverance from enemies : (1) seeking refuge in Yahweh (v.²) ; (2) crying for interposition from heaven (v.³⁻⁴) ; (3) describing the serious situation (v.⁵). **(B)** a national hymn in a later peaceful time : (1) praising Yahweh in the morning in the temple with mind and music (v.⁸⁻⁹) ; (2) exalting Him to all peoples because of the manifestations of His kindness and faithfulness (v.¹⁰⁻¹¹). **The Rf. exalts Him above heaven and earth (v.⁶· ¹²). A gloss represents the enemies as fallen into their own pit (v.⁷).**

A. v.²⁻⁵, 3 STR. 4³.

B̲E gracious to me, Yahweh, be gracious :
    For in Thee I take refuge ;
    Yea, in the shadow of Thy wings I seek refuge,
    Till the engulfing ruin be overpast.
I̲ CRY to 'El, 'Elyon,
    To 'El who dealeth bountifully with me.
    May He send from heaven to save me,
    May He send His kindness and His faithfulness.
I̲ AM in the midst of lions ;
    I must lie down among those who consume the sons of mankind,
    Whose teeth are spears and arrows,
    Whose tongue is a sharp sword.

B. v.^{6. 8-12}, 2 STR. 4³ RF. 2³ = PS. 108²⁻⁶.

O be exalted above the heavens, Yahweh ;
And above all the earth be Thy glory.

MY mind is fixed, Yahweh ;
  With my mind let me sing and let me make melo·'y.
  My glory, O wake with the harp,
  With the lyre let me waken the dawn.
LET me praise Thee among the peoples, Adonay.
  Let me make melody to Thee among the nation.,
  For above the heavens is Thy kindness,
  And unto the skies Thy faithfulness.
    O be exalted above the heavens, Yahweh ;
    And above all the earth be Thy glory.

Ps. 57 was in 𝔇 from the collection of מכתמים. It was taken up into 𝔈. The reference בברחו מפני־ישאול במערה was in 𝔇 (*v*. Intr. §§ 25, 27, 32). As in similar cases, it did not imply that such was the circumstance of its origin ; but that some features of the Ps. might be illustrated. It is doubtful which cave is referred to, whether Adullam 1 S. 22, or that in the wilderness of Engedi 1 S. 24. The Ps. was also taken up into 𝔇𝕂, when it received the musical assignment אל־תשחת (*v*. Intr. §§ 33, 34). The Ps. is really composite : *A* = v.²⁻⁵ a prayer for deliverance, 3 Str. 4³, which alone was in 𝔇 with the title מכתם ; *B* = v.⁶. ⁸⁻¹², 2 Str. 4³ with an introductory and concluding Rf. 2⁸. V.⁷, a pentameter couplet, is a late gl. The second Ps. except v.⁶ is also contained in the composite Ps. 108²⁻⁶. The use of אלהים in v.⁶. ⁸. ¹² makes it probable that this Ps. was also in 𝔈, and that the combination of the two Pss. was made in 𝔈, or they may have been separate and adjoining Pss. in 𝔈. Ps. 108 however uses יהוה v.⁴ for אדני 57¹⁰, but אלהים v.². ⁶. Inasmuch as it uses אלהים in its second part, also a Ps. of 𝔈, אדני was prob. original and יהוה due to a late copyist. In Ps. 57 the language is that of 𝔇. The unusual forms are glosses or errors of copyists. V.³ נמֵר for נמֵר 𝔊, v.⁴ חרֶף gloss, v.⁵ לבאים mispointing for לביאים, לְהָטִים mispointing for (:)לְהַטִּים; ה־ה as Is. 49² Ez. 5¹. The situation seems to be the perilous one of the feeble community of the Restoration before Nehemiah. The enemies are the lesser nations who took advantage of the unwalled city to keep the people in constant peril and alarm. Ps. 57*b* is a morning hymn to be sung, שיר־מזמר, in the temple with the use of נבל and כנור v.⁹. The poet has a wide outlook over all nations and all the earth. This Ps. cannot be earlier than the Persian period subsequent to Nehemiah, when the people were in a peaceful and happy condition. The structure of the Ps. with opening and closing Rf., as well as its tone, resembles Ps. 8.

PSALM LVII. *A.*

Str. I. has a syn. and a synth. couplet. — **2.** *Be gracious*] repeated for emphasis, cf. 56². — *I take refuge*], a usual term of 𝔇 ; first in pf. emphatic present, laying stress upon the act as a fact, then in impf. representing the action as a continuous activity in the present. נַפְשִׁי is, as usual in Hebrew poetry, for the personal pronoun "I," and should not be translated, "my soul," EV⁸., as if there were any stress upon the activity of the soul as distinguished from the body. — *In the shadow of Thy wings*], a graphic metaphor for *in Thee*, of syn. line, as 17^8 36^8 63^8, referring to the cherubic wings guarding the divine presence. — *till the engulfing ruin be overpast*]. The people were in great danger of being engulfed by the peril in which they were situated; but they were assured it could be only temporary; it would eventually pass over. In the meanwhile they need relief, which can only come from Yahweh. In His presence they are in a place of refuge and safety, while their enemies rage in vain.

Str. II. has a synth. and a syn. couplet. — **3.** *'El, 'Elyon*], the "most High," and the primitive *'El;* divine names are heaped up as usual in urgent pleading. — *who dealeth bountifully with me*]. That is the characteristic of "'El," as expressed by the Hebrew ptc.; so 𝔊, 𝕵, cf. 13^6 116^7 119^{17} greatly to be preferred to 𝔐, Aq., and most, which render a slightly varying verb in an Aramaic sense possible elsewhere only 138^8 "completeth for me," inexactly given in EV⁸. "performeth for me"; only to be explained by the insertion of "all things," and then not at all easy to understand, especially in this context. — **4.** *May He send from heaven*]. The people invoke divine interposition, and that from heaven itself; not here as often theophanic in character, but as defined in syn. line, by sending *His kindness and His faithfulness*]. These are personified and conceived as angelic messengers coming forth from Yahweh in heaven, as 43^3 85^{11-14}, *to save* His people. This strophe does not state the peril or the enemies. An ancient scribe inserted, probably in the margin, a reference to them: "Those that trample upon me taunt." This subsequently crept into the text at the expense of the measure, making the construction of v.⁴ difficult. These two words and their combination are variously explained by Vrss. and commentators, but with no satisfactory result in this context. This scribe was thinking of such taunts as 42^4, which the enemies were constantly making because of the apparent failure of prayers for divine interposition. The enemies are described by the term used in the previous Ps. $56^{2\ 3}$.

Str. III. has two syn. couplets. — **5.** *I am in the midst of* ‖ *I must lie down with*]. The people are surrounded by enemies. They are not besieged by a powerful enemy, but rather the city is beset by treacherous foes who keep the people in constant peril. This was just the situation of the people of unwalled Jerusalem prior to Nehemiah. These enemies are described as *lions*, because of their strength and ferocity. The figure is then left for the warriors themselves : their *teeth are spears and arrows* and their *tongue is a sharp sword,* in syn. couplet. It is most natural therefore in the previous difficult line to think of their breath as compared with flames *that consume the sons of mankind.* The Vrss. ancient and modern differ greatly in their interpretation of this line. EV⁸. following 𝕳 make the ptc. Qal " that are set on fire," and then take the " children of men " as in apposition with it, making an awkward construction difficult to explain. Moreover, the term " sons of mankind " is commonly employed in Hebrew for those who are afflicted and not for warlike enemies.

PSALM LVII. *B.*

Rf. 6 = 12, a syn. couplet at the beginning and close of the hymn, as Ps. 8. — *O be exalted, Yahweh*], as the subsequent context indicates as an object of praise and adoration, as 113⁴. If it were connected with the previous context it would be in victory over enemies, as 18⁴⁷ 21¹⁴ 46¹¹ 138⁶.

7 is a syn. pent. couplet, representing the enemies as hunters, cf. 7¹⁶ 9¹⁶ ˢᑫ·. It is a gloss, due to a misinterpretation of the previous couplet of Rf.

> Snares they prepared for my steps that I might bow down ;
> They dug before me a pit, they fell into its midst.

— *Snares they prepared* ‖ *They dug a pit*]. The first line states their purpose : *that I might bow down.* The Heb. נַפְשִׁי is for the personal pronoun as usual, and it is the person who bows down with his feet caught in the snares. Various other explanations are given, the usual one, " my soul is bowed down," AV., RV., refers it to internal humiliation, which is unsuited to the context. The second line states the antith. result : *they fell into its midst*]. The enemies had dug the pit for the people of Yahweh, but into it they plunged themselves.

Str. I. is a syn. tetrastich. **8.** *My mind is fixed*], repeated in 57 but not in 108 聀. It is amplification at the cost of the measure. The mind is firmly set and resolved to public praise. — *With my mind*] belongs to the second line and not to the previous one. — *let me sing and let me make melody*] with vocal and instrumental music in the temple; the mind expresses its religious emotion in worship. — **9.** *My glory*], poetic for the soul, the seat of honour in man, his noblest part, as 7^6 16^9 30^{13} 108^2. — *O wake with the harp*], rouse thyself to the service of public praise ‖ *With the lyre let me waken the dawn*]. The dawning sun preceded by the music of temple praise, is said to be aroused by that music. When the sun appears, it seems as if it had been summoned by the morning worship.

Str. II. has two syn. couplets. **10.** *Let me praise Thee among the peoples*]. The public praise is to be not only in temple worship, but world-wide, wherever the people of Yahweh are assembled in their synagogues throughout the Dispersion. — **11.** *For above the heavens is Thy kindness*]. Above the heavens is the seat of Yahweh's throne; there is the source of His kindness, cf. 36^6. It comes from thence to mankind, and therefore extends over all beneath the heavens. This corresponds with the world-wide praise, as giving the reason for it. — *And unto the skies Thy faithfulness*], as 36^6. This divine attribute extends in its vastness of reach up into the heights of the skies, cf. also 85^{11-14}.

LVII. *A.*

2. הְכָּיָה] Qal pf. 3 f. הסה *v.* 2^{12} for הְסָתָה Ges.[75. u] Kö. I. 547. The original radical is preserved in the form in order to retract accent to antepenult. — עַד יַעֲבֹר הַוּית] neglect of agreement, sg. vb. with abstr. pl. Ges. [145 (7)]; but Bi., Du., rd. הַעֲבֹרֵנָה; change unnecessary. ־ דּוֹ in ψ only pl., *v.* 5^{10}; Du. compares Is. 26^{20} עַד יַעֲבֹר זַעַם for the original idea. It is a similar thought, but in different relations, and there is no sufficient reason for dependence. — **3.** אלהים עליון] originally עֶלְיוֹן יְ־ל. — מֵר] Qal ptc.; so 聀, Aq.; but ⅏ τὸν εὐεργετήσαντά με, Street, Luzzato, Gr., Bi., Che., Du., ־. : *deal bountifully with*, is best suited to context and date of Ps. ℑ *ultorem* is from same stem in bad sense. Σ ἐπιτιμήσαντα = יְ־ר. — **4.** יִשְׁיְעֵנִי] Hiph. impf. ישע, *v.* 3^8, with subordinate expressing purpose, and not with coörd. — חֵרֵף שֹׁאֲפִי] is dub. and difficult. חֵרֵף Pi. pf. always man subj. שֹׁאֲפִי is variously explained here as $56^{2, 3}$. If subj., the clause must be rel. and most likely of time when, as Bä., Dr.; but l. is incomplete and awkward, especially as closing l. of Str.

𝕲 ἔδωκεν εἰς ὄνειδος, so essentially 𝔈, 𝔍, 𝔖, 𝔗, give a mng. to הרף appropriate enough in itself, but without usage to justify it. In that case it is better to rd. יהרף, the initial י having fallen out by haplog. But still the l. is defective. It is best to regard it as a gl. influenced by 56². ³. — **5.** לְרָאֵם] mispointing for לְבִיאִים pl. לָבִיא *lion* Gn. 49⁹ Dt. 33²⁾ Ho. 13⁸ +. 𝕲 καὶ ἐρύσατο τὴν ψυχήν μου ἐκ μέσου σκύμνων; so essentially 𝔖, supply vb. from previous v. — לֹהֲטִים] ptc. pl. √ ‡ להט † Qal *blaze up, flame*, elsw. איש להט *flaming fire* 104⁴, both dub. prob. Pi. *burn, burn up*, Dt. 32²² Pss. 83¹⁵ 97³ 106¹⁸; so prob. here, Pi. ptc. with בני אדם as obj., all the more that בני אדם is used of the humble and rather בני איש of strong enemies. 𝔍 makes the ptc. adj. of lions, *leonum ferocientium*, but against mng.; 𝕲 τεταραγμένος, 𝔈 *conturbatus*, ptc. as sg. qualifying vb., usual rendering for בהל or רגז. — ‡ חָרָה] adj. *sharp*, only f. sg.; elsw. Is. 49² Pr. 5⁴ Ez. 5¹.

LVII. B. = 108²⁻⁶.

6 = v.¹². Rf. at beginning and end, but it goes with v.⁸⁻¹², not with v.²⁻⁵. **7.** הֵכִינוּ רֶשֶׁת] phr. α.λ. less graphic and later than the usual שית רשת 9¹⁶ 31⁵ 35⁷. ⁸, cf. 140⁶. — לִפְעָמַי] as 58¹¹ 74³ 140⁵, for idea, cf. Je. 18²². — כָּפַף] Qal pf. † כפף vb. Qal *bend low down*, inf. Is. 58⁵ of head. Ptc. pass. כפופים *those bowed down in distress* Pss. 145¹⁴ 146⁸, Niph. *bow oneself* Mi. 6⁶. The pf. 3 ms. here difficult, for נפש is f. and the enemies pl. and the Qal is elsw. intrans. 𝕲 κατέκαμψαν τὴν ψυχήν μου makes it trans. and pl., which may however be interpretation and not imply a different text. 𝔍 *ad incurvandam* implies inf. as Is. 58⁵, and that would explain 𝕲 also; so Street. — שִׁיחָה‏] כָרוּ phr. elsw. 119⁸⁵ Je. 18²² (Kt.); שׁוּחה c. כרה Je. 18²⁰, c. בור Ps. 7¹⁶. The v. is a pentameter couplet based on Je. 18²⁾. ²², and is a gl. — **8.** לִבִּי‏ נָכוֹן] bis. 108². ‏𝔊‎ omits second נכון, but it is given in 𝕲. It is doubtless amplification. It impairs measure, as Street, Che. For phr. cf. 51¹² 78³⁷ 112⁷. — אָשִׁירָה] Qal impf. cohort. ‖ אזמרה. MT. closes v. here, but 108² with אף כבודי, omitting first עורה of 57⁹. In 108² 𝕲 has ἐν τῇ δόξῃ μου, 𝔍 *sed et gloria mea*. אף and first עורה are both gls. of amplification. — **9.** עוּרָה‏] Qal imv. cohort. עור v. 7⁷, invocation to כְּבוֹדִי for נפש, as 16⁹ 30¹³ 108². — ‡ שָׁחַר] i.p. *the dawn*, elsw. 22¹ 108³ 139⁹; here personified as Ra., Ew., Ols., Hu., Bä, Dr., Du., not acc. of time *at dawn*. — **10.** אוּרֶךָ] Hiph. cohort., the sf. prevents the cohort. form from appearing, but context requires it. — אֲדֹנָי‏] = יהוה 108⁴. ארני is more likely to be original. — אֲזַמֶּרְךָ] with sf. 30¹³ 138¹, all ‖ אורך, cf. 47⁷; usually with ל, doubtless here אזמרה לך as measure requires, cf. 101¹ 105². — **11** is essentially the same as 36⁶. 108⁵ has מְּ שָׁמַיִם for עד ש of 57¹¹; in other respects it is the same. But 36⁶ has בעצמיך, and אמונה־ך for אמתך, this latter a variation in form from same stem, and it omits גדל which is certainly a gl., making l. too long and interpretative. מעל is doubtless original. עד is assimilation to l. 2.

PSALM LVIII., 2 STR. 8⁴, RF. 2⁴.

Ps. 58 was written in the early Hebrew monarchy : (1) complaining of unjust rulers for their violence, venomous lying, and
deafness to the pleas of the people (v.²⁻⁶) ; (2) describing the
punitive judgment of Yahweh upon them in several similes, concluding with a firm confidence in Yahweh as judge (v.⁷⁻¹⁰ ¹²). A
gloss expresses the joy of a Maccabean editor in bloody vengeance
(v.¹¹).

> *But do ye indeed speak justice ?*
> *In equity judge the sons of mankind ?*

N AY, in the mind ye do iniquity ;
>> In the land ye weigh violence with your hands.
>> The wicked become estranged from the womb,
>> Those who speak lies go estray from the belly.
>> They have poison like a serpent,
>> They are like a cobra, deaf and stopping his ear,
>> Which hearkeneth not to the voice of the charmers,
>> The binder of spells, the exceedingly skilful.

Y AHWEH doth break down their teeth in their mouth,
>> Yahweh doth tear down the jaw-teeth of the young lions.
>> They melt away as water, they flow of themselves.
>> Are they luxuriant as green grass, so they wither away.
>> As a snail, that melts away, they go.
>> Hath fire fallen, they do not behold the sun ;
>> Before they perceive it, they become like brambles ;
>> As still living, in hot anger, He sweeps them away in a storm.

>> *Ye sons of mankind, surely there is fruit for the righteous ;*
>> *Surely Yahweh is judging in the land.*

Ps. 58 was originally in the group of מזמרים, then in �, subsequently in 𝐄
and also in 𝐃𝐑, where it received the musical direction אל תשחת (*v.* Intr.
§§ 25, 27, 32, 33, 34). It has 2 Str. of 8 tetrameters each, with introductory
and concluding couplets, which, while varying in detail, are yet of the nature
of Rfs., cf. Pss. 8, 57. The language and style are primitive and difficult. It
is rich in antique similes and expressions. The Ps. complains of unjust rulers
in the style of the preëxilic prophets, and expresses confidence in the
retributive judgment of Yahweh. The Ps. is doubtless one of the oldest in
the Psalter.

Str. I. has an introductory syn. couplet in form of a question,
which receives a negative answer in four syn. couplets. This is of
the nature of a Rf., beginning the Ps. as a corresponding Rf.

closes it. — **2**. *Do ye indeed speak justice ?*]. The question is addressed, as the context shows, to the rulers of the people, || *in equity judge ?* The couplet is not easy to render. Text and Vrss. differ. In the first line the same Hebrew consonants with varying vowels give four different interpretations. That which is here preferred is the interpretation of 𝕲, 𝕵, taking the word אֶלֶם as adv. emphasizing more strongly the initial " indeed " ; so JPSV, " Do ye in very deed." But 𝕳, followed by most moderns, interprets the form as an unusual word, " in silence," RV., in accordance with the thought of v.⁶. Ki. interprets as Aram. word " band," so Calv., PBV., AV., " congregation." Many moderns interpret as still another word, " gods," for rulers, as 82¹· ⁶. — *sons of mankind*]. Those judged, as most moderns, referring, according to usage of the term, to the common people. But 𝕲, 𝕵, EVˢ., interpret as the rulers, as if it were the antithetical term, " sons of men." — **3**. *Nay*]. A strong asseveration in negative reply to the question. These rulers were the very reverse of what they ought to be. — *in the mind*], mentally, their secret resolution in antith. to the execution of their purpose. — *in the land,* and also *with your hands*]. The hands are graphically conceived as using scales and balances, and thus as weighing out what they are to deliver to others. This should have been in accordance with the conception of justice : just, equal, right measure, which could not be questioned. In fact, it was the reverse : *weigh violence.* — **4**. *Become estranged* || *go estray*], that is, from the principles of justice, the practice of equity. — *from the womb* || *from the belly*], so soon as they are born, they at once begin to stray from right to wrong. This does not refer, as older interpreters thought, to the impulses of original sin or innate depravity ; but specifically to the *wicked* in antith. to the " righteous," v.¹². They begin the practice of their wickedness in their earliest youth. The wicked are here especially judges : *Those who speak lies*] ; not lies in general, in the later and higher ethical sense that the lie as such is wicked ; but in the early sense, lies as injurious, such as accompany acts of violence, false witness before the judges, or false and lying decisions by the judges themselves against the common people, and in favour of the oppressors. — **5–6**. *They have poison*]. They are venomous in their violence and lies, and so they are *like a serpent* || *a* *cobra*], an especially venomous kind of serpent, which adds to its venom another dangerous characteristic, that it cannot be charmed by *the charmers*. *The binder of spells*, accustomed to charm all other serpents, can do nothing with this one. Though *exceedingly skilful*, expert in all the arts of the charmer, he utterly fails. This cobra is *deaf, stopping his ear*. So these wicked judges are so intent upon violence to the people and injurious lies, that no pleading, no arguments, however just and right, no influence whatever, can prevent them from executing their wicked will.

Str. II. is an antistr., having a syn. couplet, then six syn. similes describing the divine judgment coming upon the wicked judges. — **7.** *Yahweh doth break down their teeth ‖ tear down the jaw teeth*], so 𝕲 interpreting the vbs. as pfs., and the subsequent vbs. as impfs., describing the judgment itself; which is to be preferred to taking the vbs. as imvs., and the subsequent vbs. as jussives, imprecating the divine judgment, as MT. and most Vrss. and interpreters. — The wicked rulers are first compared to *young lions*. Their teeth are all broken down to make them harmless. — **8.** *They melt away as water*]. Water is a frequent simile of instability and weakness. So here the first simile compares the judges to water melting away. So weak are they and unstable that they need no one to make them unstable ; *they flow of themselves*, of their own inherent weakness and instability. — *Are they luxuriant as green grass*]. The second simile compares them to green grass, which is the common symbol of rapid growth and speedy withering away, cf. 37^2 90^5. But 𝔅, by the wrong attachment of a single letter to the previous instead of the following word, changed the former to the vb. "tread," and the latter to the word "his arrow," and so got a phrase for the usual "tread the bow," which cannot be explained satisfactorily in this context. An archer, aiming his arrows, even if their points are broken, is not a good simile of weakness from the point of view of the context. The grass is luxuriant enough in its growth, but it has a short duration ; so these judges *wither away*. The rendering "cut off" is a possible translation of a Hebrew word cognate to that rendered above in the usual meaning "wither" ; but no other example of such a meaning can be found. Some refer the cutting off to the arrows, as AV., RV., others to the wicked judges, as

PBV. — **9.** *As a snail*], so most moderns after 𝔗 ; but 𝕲, 𝔖, 𝖸,
Arab. " wax," and other Vrss. various other renderings, making
the meaning exceedingly dubious.   But whatever the thing may
be, as it *melts away*, so the wicked rulers *go*.   If it be the snail,
the reference is to the slimy track it leaves behind it as it moves
along. — *Hath fire fallen, they do not behold the sun*], so 𝕲, 𝔖, 𝖸,
the fire of the divine anger ; the lightning suddenly descends
from heaven upon these wicked judges, they are instantaneously
consumed, never more will they see the sunlight.   This is in
accord with the subsequent context, and the common reference to
such visitations in the OT. and the Koran.   But MT., 𝔍, influenced probably by Jb. 3^{16} Ec. 6^3, by different vowel points with
the same Hebrew text, get " an untimely birth of a woman " ; but
find difficulty in the tense and number of the vb., as is evident
from the various renderings of Vrss. and commentators.   The
propriety of comparing such strong vigorous enemies with a premature birth of a child already dead, and never really alive, may be
questioned. — **10.** *Before they perceive it, they become like thorns*].
This continues the thought of the suddenness of the divine visitation.   The wicked are taken unawares ; before they perceive it,
the fire comes upon them, and they are consumed by it like dry
thorns.   The text has been made difficult by an early copyist,
before 𝕲, making a misconnection of two letters, attaching them
to the previous word as the suffix " your," when they belong to the
following word as prep. " like."   A variant gloss to thorns also
made it possible to think of a kindred word " pots," and so the
interpretation arose — " before your pots perceived the thorns,"
which conceives of pots containing flesh placed above thorns
kindled to make a fire with which to cook a meal.   Before these
pots are at all heated, the judgment comes upon them.   With this
interpretation the subsequent line, which contains the principal
clause, must be made to correspond, and here still greater difficulty arises.   Several words must be given meanings, possible in
themselves, but not justified by Hebrew usage.   The simple meaning, giving every word its well-attested usage, is in accord with
the previous context ; *as still living*, while in the full vigour of
life, so 𝕲, 𝔍, 𝔖, as Nu. 16^{30} ; *in hot anger*, the heat of the divine
anger, syn. with the " fire " above ; *He sweeps them away in a*

storm], the storm of wind and rain or hail accompanying the fire of lightning, as usual in such divine visitations. — **11**. *The righteous will be glad when he beholdeth vengeance*]. This gratification of the righteous in looking upon their enemies suffering under divine vengeance, is especially characteristic of the Maccabean age, when this v. was inserted as a gloss. It makes the Str. just these lines too long. — *His feet he will wash in the blood of the wicked*] is an expression of vengeful feelings against foreign enemies in war, and so contrary to the theme of the Ps., which has to do with wicked rulers in Israel. The attitude of mind is distinctly Maccabean. — **12.** This is the closing Rf. *Ye sons of mankind*], vocative, as in accordance with v.²ᵇ. It has been misinterpreted in 𝕳 and Vrss. as subj. of the verb " shall say," at first understood as usual in poetry, afterwards introduced into the text, and so destroying the similarity of the two Rfs. — *surely*], emphatic expression of assurance and certainty of the divine interposition in behalf of the *righteous*, the people. — They have *fruit;* that is their righteousness will not in the end be unprofitable, but successful. — *Yahweh is judging the land*]. Though the wicked rulers do not judge in equity, but oppress the people of the land, Yahweh Himself interposes, and undertakes Himself their vindication and the punishment of their enemies.

2. הַאֻמְנָם] interrog. ה with † אָמְנָם adv. (√אמן) always interrog. *verily, truly, indeed*, so Nu. 22³⁷ (E) 1 K. 8²⁷ = 2 Ch. 6¹⁸; without ה Gn. 18¹³ (J). — † אֵלֶם] n.[m.] *silence* 56¹ (title) and here. Dr. "in dumbness," after Aq., Ges.; but 𝕲 ἄρα, as v.¹²; 𝔙, 𝔍, *utique* = אֵלָךְ = אוּלָם = *but, indeed*, strong adv., not elsw. ψ, but Gn. 28¹⁹ 48¹⁹ Ex. 9¹⁶ +. This gives good sense. אלהים Houb.; אֵלֶם Lowth., Dathe, Street, Ol., De., Ew., Dy., Gr., Bä., 𝐵DB., as 82¹· ⁶, is not suited to the context. אלם = *band;* Ki., Calv., Ains., Ham., AV., PBV., *congregation* √אלב *bind*, not elsw. Bibl. Heb. — תְּדַבֵּרוּן] Pi. impf. 3 pl. archaic ending ; so we should have תשפטון in assonance at close of l., as תפלסון, תפעלוּן, v.³. — בְּנֵי אָדָם] *v. 8⁵, sons of mankind*, the judges over against God, so 𝕲, 𝔍, Luther, PBV.; but 𝕿, Pe., Bä., Dr., Du., most moderns, *mankind* as obj. of vb. If judges were referred to, בני איש would be more suitable. — **3.** אַף] emph. answer to question, cf. 44¹⁰. — בְּלֵב] *in mind, in themselves, to themselves*, their secret resolution and purpose, antith. to בארץ *in the land.* 𝕲 takes both עולה and הבם as acc. after vb., so Dr., Bä., Du. Many think בלב not appropriate to context. The use of בלב by itself in this sense is not usual, but אמר בלב is common. Bä. suggests כֻּלְּכֶם *all of you*, after 𝕾. Du. בְּלָט *in secret* is better antith. to בארץ. But 𝕳, 𝕲, 𝔍, 𝕿, all have same text. —

חֲמֵס ידיכם] *violence of your hands*, so Aq., Σ, Ϫ. But 𝔊, 𝔖, Θ, Quinta, 𝕿, all make חָמֵס abs. It is not necessary, however, to suppose with Bä. that they took ידיכם as subj. of vb. and that they rd. תְּפַלֵּסוּן, for they would render תפלסון חמס in the same way if they regarded ידיכם as 2d subj., as קוֹר 3⁵; cf. דבר 56⁶, *with your hands*. This is the best interp. — בארץ] emph. in position, *in the land*, in their administration of justice ; not *on the earth* or *on earth*. It is attached to the first l. in 𝕳, 𝔊, to second in Ϫ. — תְּפַלֵּסוּן] Pi. impf. 3 m. archaic ending, *v. 56⁸*. — **4.** זֹרוּ] only here for זָרוּ Qal pf. 3 m. זוּר, as באו Je. 27¹⁸ for בָּאוּ, Kö.[I. 445], *become estranged*. Cf. בנים זרים Ho. 5⁷ ‖ יִתְּעוּ, both aorists. — מֵרָ֫חֶם] i.p. with prep. מִן. Another beat is needed, rd. יֵ֫לֵ֫כוּ. — דֹּבְרֵי כָזָב] subj. of vb., and not qualifying it. 𝔊, however, rd. pf. ἐλάλησαν, but Ϫ *loquentes*. — **5.** חֲמַת־לָ֫מוֹ] *heat of poison*, as Dt. 32²⁴·³³, cf. Ps. 140⁴ Jb. 6⁴. לָ֫מוֹ archaic sf. with ־ of possession. חֲמַת before נחש is gl.; not in 𝔊. — ‡ דְּמוּת] n.f. *likeness, similitude*, used here adverbially, as Is. 13⁴ Ez. 23¹⁵. — כְּמוֹ] archaic stronger form of prep. כְּ, so v.⁸·⁹·¹⁰. — † פֶּ֫תֶן] *venomous serpent*, perhaps *cobra*, *BDB.*, Tristram[N.H. 271 f.]; elsw. 91¹³ Dt. 32³³ Is. 11⁸ Jb. 20¹⁴·¹⁶. — חֵרֵשׁ] adj. *deaf*, a.λ. in connection with serpent; form elsw. 38¹⁴. Cf. vb. חרש 28¹. — יַאְטֵם] a.λ. Hiph. juss., cf. Dr.[173. obs.], the juss. force being lost; rel. clause Dr. "that stoppeth his ear." 𝔊 has καὶ βνούσης τὰ ὦτα αὐτῆς = וְאָטְמָה. This is more natural, esp. as † אטם vb. elsw. always ptc. Qal either active Is. 33¹⁵ Pr. 17²⁸ 21¹³, or pass. Ez. 40¹⁶ 41¹⁶·²⁶ 1 K. 6⁴. — **6.** אֲשֶׁר] rel. referring to the פֶּתֶן and explaining חרש ואטם. — מְלַחֲשִׁים] Pi. ptc. pl. a.λ. *whisperers, charmers*, לחשׁ, *v. 41⁸*; cf. לַחַשׁ *serpent charming* Is. 3³ Ec. 10¹¹. — חוֹבֵר חֲבָרִים] *tie magic knots* (*v.* RS.[JPh. XIV. 1885, p. 123]), vb. only used with cognate acc. Dt. 18¹¹ in this sense. ‡ חבר vb. elsw. Pu. *be allied* Ps. 94²⁰⁾, *joined together* 122³. † חֶבֶר n.[m.] (1) *company, association*, Ho. 6⁹ Pr. 21⁹ 25²⁴; (2) *spell*, elsw. Dt. 18¹¹ cf. Is. 47⁹·¹² of Babylonian magic. — מְחֻכָּם] Pu. ptc. only here and Pr. 30²⁴ *learned, skilled* (*v. 19⁸*). The l. is defective. We may add the kindred ‡ חָכָם adj. *skilful man*, one of the class of magicians Gn. 41⁸ (E) Ex. 7¹¹ (P) Is. 44²⁵ Je. 50³⁵ 51⁵⁷; elsw. in ψ *wise* (ethical and religious sense) 49¹¹ 107⁴³. — **7.** אלהים] for original יהוה, as usual in 𝔈. — הֲרָס־] Qal imv. הרס vb. (*v. 11³*). — וְרֹעַ] (*v. 52⁷*) *break down*, here only of teeth. 𝔊 gives both vbs. as Pfs. and this is better suited to v.⁸ᵇ. — יְמוֹ] archaic poetic sf. for rhythm, in both nouns for usual מ־. Characteristic of the Ps. is the use of מוֹ. — מַלְתְּעוֹת] a.λ. for מְתַלְּעוֹת Jo. 1⁶ Pr. 30¹⁴ Jb. 29¹⁷. — יהוה] is suspicious in 𝔈, though in 𝔊. A divine name is needed for measure. Doubtless it was originally יהוה, changed to אלהים in 𝔈, and then subsequently back to יהוה. — **8.** יִמָּאֲסוּ] Niph. impf. either juss. or indicative † מָאַס vb. Niph. *flow, run*, elsw. Jb. 7⁵ regarded as variation of מסס vb. *melt, dissolve* (*22¹⁵*), probably both fully written forms from מסה *melt* (6⁷). — יִתְהַלְּכוּ] in apposition with previous vb. and not rel. clause. — לָמוֹ] ethical dative with vb. of motion Ges.[119. s] *of themselves*. — יִדְרֹךְ חִצּוֹ] phr. elsw. only 64⁴. הִצּוֹ Kt., חִצָּיו Qr. *arrows* for τόξον 𝔊, *arcum* Ϫ, קשׁת דרך 7¹³ 11² 37¹⁴; an abrupt transition; not suited to context. Rd. with Bi., Che., We., הַצִּיר, which is favoured by vb. יִתְמֹלָ֫לוּ, cf. יְחֶרָצִיר יְכַלֶּה 37², also 90⁵. The כ of ידרך prob. goes with הציר and we should rd. ידרו Qal impf. דָּרָה vb. α.λ. Heb.; but the same stem in Ar. is used of herbage, *be abundant, luxuriant;* then כמו = *so,* and יִתְמֹלָלוּ is Hithp. of מלל vb. *wither, fade,* as 37², favoured by 𝔊 ἀσθενήσουσιν; and not of † [צָלַל] vb. Qal *circumcise* Jos. 5² Niph. Gn. 17¹¹ and Hithp. only here *cut off.* 𝔊 ἕως οὗ, 𝔍 *donec,* interpret the vb. as final clause, disregarding כמו. — **9.** [שַׁבְּלוּל] α.λ. traditional rendering *snail* as 𝔗; but 𝔊 κηρὸς, 𝔖, 𝔘, Arab. *beeswax,* Aq. γῆς ἔντερον *earthworm,* 𝔍 *vermis,* Σ χόριον, AE. שָׁבֹּלֶת *flood.* — [חֶמֶס] α.λ. n. (√ חסם) *melting away,* dub.; 39¹² we have the form וַתֶּמֶס כָּעָשׁ Hiph. impf. 2 m. מסה, *cause to flow, dissolve.* — [יַהֲרֹךְ] Qal impf. fuller form for usual יֵלֵךְ, as 91⁶ Je. 9³ Jb. 14²⁰ 16⁶ 20²⁵ (6 t. in all), cf. ההלך Ps. 73⁹ Ex. 9²³, אהלך Jb. 16²² 23⁸. יהלך here as יַהֲלֹךְ v.⁸. 𝔊 and 𝔍 take it as pl. — [נֵפֶל אֵשֶׁת] so 𝔍 *quasi abortivum mulieris* and Aq., Σ, Θ, 𝔗. † נֵפֶל n.m. *untimely birth,* as Jb. 3¹⁶ Ec. 6³, but dub. on acc. of late date of these two uses. 𝔊 has ἐπέπεσε πῦρ = אֵשׁ יָפֵל, so 𝔖, 𝔘. אֵשֶׁת is usually taken as variant form of אִשָּׁה as Dt. 21¹¹ 1 S. 28⁷. — [חָזוּ־דָר] Qal pl. 3 m., most naturally as in other vbs. refers to the wicked; so 𝔊, 𝔖, 𝔘, Aq., Σ, PBV., the pf. for the impf. But 𝔍, RV., and prob. MT. interpret it as rel. clause with the previous נפל coll., influenced prob. by Jb. 3¹⁶ Ec. 6³. The context on the whole favours 𝔊. — **10.** [סִירֹתֵיכֶם] is difficult, both in the form itself and in the sf. 2 pl. It is against the context which gives always 3 pers. However the sf. 2 pl. is in 𝔊, 𝔍; and 𝔊 even makes sf. with vb. ישׁערו 2 pl. against 𝔐 and other Vrss. Most moderns think of ‡ סִיר I. n.m. *pot,* (1) used for boiling, Ex. 16³ (P) Je. 1¹³ Ez. 11⁸ +; (2) for washing, Ps. 60¹⁰ = 108¹⁰; (3) in sanctuary Je. 52¹⁹ Zc. 14²⁰ +. But 𝔊, 𝔘, 𝔍, 𝔗, Σ, all follow † סִיר II., (1) *thorn,* pl. סירים, Is. 34¹³ Ho. 2⁸ Ec. 7⁶ Na. 1 ¹⁰(?); (2) *hook,* pl. סירות, Am. 4². The objection that *thorn* elsw. has pl. סירים is not valid; for there is no sound reason why it should not also have pl. f. in (1) as well as in (2), or indeed סיר sg. in the one word as well as in the other. We should prob. rd. סירה כמו, and prob. סירה was originally only a marginal variation of † אָטָד n.m. *bramble, buckthorn,* as Gn. 50¹⁰. ¹¹ Ju. 9¹⁴. ¹⁵. ¹⁵. The vb. יבינו is never used for perception through touching inanimate things, and this weighs strongly against the usual modern interp., "*before your pots can feel the thorns,*" AV., RV. 𝔍 *crescant,* Σ αὐξηθῶσιν, so 𝔗 rd. יכון. — [כְּמוֹ חַי]. חי is taken by those who think of the *pot* hanging over burning brambles, as *living, fresh* brambles, so Ges., Ew., Hu., Ol., Pe.; but there is no other example of such a use. So חרו is taken in antith. for *burning* brambles, but this has no justification in usage. Others, De., Ri., Che., Bä., Now., refer חי to the *raw flesh* in the pot, as 1 S. 2¹⁵ Lv. 13¹⁰. ¹⁴. ¹⁵. ¹⁶ (P). But it is most natural to interpret כמו חי as *living,* so 𝔊, 𝔘, 𝔍, ἔτι ζῶντα Σ, cf. Nu. 16³⁰, where the rebellious go down alive into the pit of Sheol. — [כמו־חרון] 𝔊 has ὡσεὶ ἐν ὀργῇ, 𝔍 *quasi in ira.* Both had חרי, but interpreted חרון as instrumental acc. This suggests however, as Bä., that original reading may have been במו. — [וִישְׂעָרֶנּוּ] Qal. impf. strong sf. שׂער Qal, *storm away,* only here in ψ, but Niph. *v.* 50³. — **11.** ‡ יֶחֱזֶה α.λ. ψ, but Ez. 24⁸+; the vengeance taken by Yahweh upon His wicked enemies. 𝔊 adds ἀσεβῶν which is interpretative, not in 𝔍. — [פעמיו] *his feet* or *footsteps,* so Σ, 𝔍, 𝔗, cf. 57⁷. 𝔊 has

χεῖρας, so 𝔙, 𝔖. — 12. וַיֹּאמֶר אָדָם [ו coörd. Qal impf., cf. בני אדם v.², which we
would expect here. 𝔊, 𝔍, had אדם *mankind* in general. But ויאמר is prosaic
and suspicious; we would expect vocative as v.². It is prob. gl. and בני אדם
the original. — אלהים] 𝔊 ὁ θεὸς, 𝔍 *Deus;* if so, not predicate, but for an
original יהוי. Bä. interprets as pl. *gods.* If אֱלִים is to be read in v.², it would
be probable here. It is indeed favoured by שפטים, although אלהים in 𝔈 of
Hex. is sometimes used with pl., cf. 2 S. 7²³. But 𝔊 κρίνων αὐτοὺς = שֹׁפְטָם.
The sf. may be interpretative as often, and misunderstood in MT.

PSALM LIX., 2 STR. 12³, RF. 4³.

Ps. 59 was a national prayer in the early Restoration : (1) for
deliverance from bloodthirsty enemies, who without justification
have broken their treaties and are prepared to attack Israel, concluding with an invocation to Yahweh to awake and visit them (v.²⁻⁶).
(2) Petition for kindness to the people and the unpitying defeat
and destruction of their enemies, because of their cursing, falsehood, and pride ; concluding with the wish for the extension of
Yahweh's rule to the ends of the earth (v.¹¹⁻¹⁴). Rf. describes the
enemies as greedy dogs, running about the environs of the city in
snarling packs (v.⁷˙ ¹⁵), concluding with a vow of public praise of
Yahweh, the High Tower (v.¹⁰˙ ¹⁸). Glosses emphasize the falseness
of the enemy (v.⁸), their greed (v.¹⁶), Yahweh's derision of them
(v.⁹), and the thanksgiving of the people (v.¹⁷).

FROM mine enemies, O *my* God, deliver *me ;*
   From them that rise up against me, set *me* on high;
   From the workers of trouble, deliver *me ;*
   And from men of blood, save *me.*
   For lo, they lurk for *my* life ;
   Strong ones gather together, without transgression of *mine ;*
   They run up, without sin of *mine ;*
   They station themselves, without iniquity of *mine.*
   O awake to meet me and see,
   Thou, Yahweh, Sabaoth !
   O arise to visit the nations ;
   Be not gracious to all the treacherous troublers.
      They snarl again and again like a dog.
      They go round about the city in the evening.
      My Strength, unto Thee I will make melody ;
      For Thou, Yahweh, art my High Tower.
MAY my God come to meet me with His kindness !
   May Yahweh let me look upon my watchful foes !

E

Do not (have compassion), lest they forget.
Make them wander up and down by Thine army, my sovereign Lord.
Bring them down, O my shield!
Bring them to punishment for the sin of their mouth,
The iniquity of the word of their lips,
And let them be taken in their pride.
Because of the cursing, and because of the lying which they speak,
Consume (in Thy wrath) that they be no more.
And it shall be known that it is the God of Jacob,
Ruler to the ends of the earth.
They snarl again and again like a dog.
They go round about the city in the evening.
My Strength, unto Thee I will make melody;
For Thou, Yahweh, art my High Tower.

Ps. 59 was one of the מכתמים, then in 𝔇, afterward in 𝔈. The reference to the situation in the life of David, בשלח שאול וישמרו את־הבית להמיתו, was in 𝔇. When it was taken up into 𝔇ℜ it was assigned for rendering אל־תשחת, as 57, 58 (*v.* Intr. §§ 25, 27, 32, 33, 34). The reference to the story of David's escape by night from the messengers of Saul, 1 S. $19^{8\,sq.}$, only illustrates in small part the situation in the Ps. The editor had no thought of assigning its composition to the time of David. In fact, the Ps. does not reflect any situation in the life of David. It is a national Ps. of a much later date. The Ps., like all the מכתמים, is ornate in style, having 2 Str. 12^3, with Rf. 4^3. It is also antique in language and style, and exceedingly difficult. Glosses v.$^{8.\,9.\,16.\,17}$ adapt it for later liturgical use. V.^{2} מתקוממי as 17^7; v.^{4} יגורו as 56^7; עזים, cf. 18^{18}; v.^{5} יכוננו as Nu. 21^{27} Is. 54^{14}; v.^{6} יהוה צבאות as 24^{10}, cf. $80^{5.\,20}$ 84^9; בגדי און phr. α.λ., but separate words ancient, implying violation of covenant relations; v.^{12} הניעמו, cf. Nu. 32^{13} (J) 2 S. 15^{20}; God as shield, as 3^4 7^{11} +; v.^{13} ואון in sense of pride, as Is. 16^6 Je. 48^{29} Zp. 2^{10}+; אלה as 10^7; v.^{14} אלהי יעקב as 20^2. The language throughout is early. So also the frequent use of archaic sf. ־מו. In the glosses v.^{6} אלהי ישראל phr. of 𝔈 of Hex., cf. 69^7; v.^{9} as a citation from 2^4 gives evidence of date of gloss, but not of original Ps. It is possible that v.^{12} contains a reference to the story of Cain in Gn. 4^{12} (J), but it is by no means certain. The Ps. is evidently a national one. The enemies are not wicked individuals; but nations, who have treacherously violated treaties, v.^{6}, therefore not the great world powers, but the neighbouring nations, kindred with Israel. They are described in Rf. as cruel, greedy dogs, who wander about, not in the city but outside the city, round about it, making it perilous to go forth, v.$^{7.\,15}$. They are not besieging it with armies, but besetting it with marauding bands, who lurk with bloodthirsty intent, v.^{3}. The situation is indeed similar to that of Ps. 9-10, the situation of the inhabitants of Jerusalem beset by unfriendly neighbours just before Nehemiah.

Str. I. has three tetrastichs, the first syn.; the second of two syn. couplets, the second synth. to the first; the third in which

lines 1, 3, 4, are syn., but 2 synth. to 1. — **2–3**. *Deliver me*],
repeated for emphasis in v.²; syn. with *set me on high*], literally in
an inaccessible place, but probably without that specific meaning
here ; and *save me*], the more general and comprehensive term.
The peril is from *enemies*, which are described as *them that rise
up against me*], in war, as 17⁷ ; *workers of trouble*], the mischiefs
and sorrows of petty warfare (cf. 5⁶ 6⁹ 14⁴ +) ; *and men of blood*],
bloodthirsty men, bent on bloodshed, cf. 26⁹ 55²⁴ + . They are
still further described v.⁴ as *strong ones*], cf. 18¹⁸, too strong for
the people to resist successfully without divine help ; and finally,
v.⁶ : *treacherous troublers*], those who in their working of trouble
have treacherously violated their covenant, or treaty with the
people ; their natural neighbours and allies ; and yet like the old
Moabites and Ammonites, really their worst foes.   They are
indeed *nations*, not the great nations, the world powers, Assyria,
Babylonia, or Egypt, who could not be thus described ; but the
lesser nations, the treacherous neighbours of Israel, in the early
Restoration, when the feeble community of Jerusalem had to get
on as best they could in an unwalled and unprotected city. —
4–5. The activity of the enemies is vividly described : *they lurk
for my life*], as wild beasts, hiding in ambush, waiting for an
opportunity to strike a deadly blow, cf. 10⁹. — *gather together*],
assemble in bands for a predatory excursion, cf. 56⁷. — *They run
up*], for an attack, as 18³⁰. — *They station themselves*] take a
stand and prepare for the final assault, cf. 3⁷. — *without transgression of mine*]. The enemies had no just cause for their
hostility. This is emphasized by the use of three terms for sin :
transgression, sin, and iniquity, in order to make the affirmation
of innocence as comprehensive and strong as possible.   The
people had in fact been faithful to all their covenant relations
with their neighbours. These neighbours had the sole guilt in
the matter. — **6**. *O awake*], earnest plea for divine interposition,
cf. 7⁷. — *O arise*], from apparent sleep or indifference, 35²³ 44²⁴.
The need for help is imperative. The purpose is : *to meet me*], for
help, as 25¹⁸, — *and see*], the serious situation ; *to visit*, with punishment, as 89³³ ; with the climax : *be not gracious*], implying the
reverse. The divine name is appropriate in this appeal for warlike interference : *Yahweh Sabaoth*, the title of Yahweh as the

God of the battle array of Israel, the God of the Davidic
dynasty, cf. 24¹⁰. A later editor has intensified it at the expense of the measure by adding "God of Israel," cf. 41¹⁴ 68⁹ 69⁷
72¹⁸ 106⁴⁸.

Rfr. The first couplet is synth. — **7 = 15.** *They snarl again and
again like a dog*]. The enemies are compared to the half wild
dogs of the Orient, which are the scavengers of the cities of the
East, prowling about the environs by day and in the streets by
night, and which do not hesitate to prey upon the feeble and
helpless, cf. 22¹⁷ 1 K. 14¹¹ 2 K. 9³⁶. They snarl because they are
angry and ready to snap at their prey. They do it again and
again, as *they go round about the city*], the environs of the city ;
not in the streets of the city, as some render, thinking of evil-doers
in the city itself in hostility to the righteous, which is against the
context and entire conception of the Ps. — *In the evening*], that
is, every evening. As the shades of night begin to fall, these dogs
appear with the shadows and begin their prowling expeditions.
The word properly belongs with the second line, as the measure
and parall. require. A prosaic editor made the couplet into a
prose sentence and put the words in the order of prose, as not
infrequently elsewhere in the Psalter.

8. The two couplets of the Rf. are interrupted by glosses enlarging on the situation. — *Lo, they pour forth with their mouth*].
The simile of the dog is abandoned, and the enemies are described
as to their wicked speech. — *swords are in their lips*]. The words
which are on their lips are compared to swords which cut and
pierce, cf. 57⁵. These are enemies of another kind than those of
the original Ps. — *For who is hearing ?*]. They think that they
can so speak with impunity, for they conceive that the God of
Israel is not hearing or caring. It is only another form of the
scornful challenge of 10⁴ ˢᵠ· 42⁴. It is usual to prefix the word
" say." This or some syn. word must be understood, but here, as
often in poetry, it is not expressed. — **9.** *Verily Thou, Yahweh,
laughest at them*]. The scorn of the people of Yahweh by their
enemies has as its antith. Yahweh's scorn of them. This, indeed,
as well as the subsequent line, is a citation from 2⁴, except that
mockest at all the nations is an adaption to this Ps. to correspond
with v.⁶.

10 = 18 is the second couplet of Rf., separated from the first couplet by the glosses. — *My Strength*]. Yahweh is the strength of His people for defence against their enemies, and so virtually a stronghold, cf. 28[7] 46[2] 84[6] 118[14] 140[8]. — *my High Tower*], the place whither Yahweh lifts His people up on high, as v.[2], cf 9[10] 18[3] 46[8, 12] 48[4] 62[3, 7] 94[22] 144[2]. In this last clause *Yahweh* is not subj. of copula, 3d. pers., as EV[s].; but as 𝔍 here and 𝔊 v.[18], syn. with second pers., as the previous syn. line requires. — *I will make melody*]. The usual vow of public worship, as 9[12] 27[6] 30[5] 47[7] 66[4] +. So v.[18] and 𝔖 here also. 𝔐, 𝔊, 𝔍, give here the variant, "unto thee will I watch," or "keep guard." But the variation is due to a copyist's mistake of a single letter similar in sound, and this one mistake caused all the variations and difficulties in 𝔐 and Vrss.

Str. II. has three synth. tetrastichs. — **11.** *May my God come to meet me with His kindness*]. 𝔐 and Vrss. greatly differ as between "God" and "my God," and "God of my kindness" and "of His kindness," but the translation given above is best sustained. RV., as usual, adheres too slavishly to 𝔐. The invocation resumes that which closed the previous Str. v.[6]. — *Let me look upon*], in triumph, seeing them prostrate in defeat and overthrow, cf. 54[9] 112[8] 118[7]. — **12.** *Do not have compassion on them*]. This emendation, proposed by G. Baur and adopted by several scholars, is in accord with v.[6] and most suitable to the context. An ancient copyist, by misreading ח for ג, gave the antithetical meaning, "slay them not." This is contrary to the subsequent context and has occasioned endless difficulties, which 𝔐 and Vrss. sought to remove by various insertions and explanations, none of which yield good sense. — *lest they forget*], most naturally refers to these nations, which, if Yahweh spared them in compassion, would speedily forget it and renew their depredations. But owing to the mistake above referred to, it became necessary to think of "my people" as the subj. of "forget," and this was indeed inserted in 𝔐; whereas 𝔊, answering the question as to what they were in danger of forgetting, inserted "Thy law." The line is complete without either of them. — *Make them wander up and down*], in confusion after defeat, and possibly with the sense of staggering from severe blows. — *by thine army*]. Most think of an army of angels, cf. $35^{5.6}$, but it is quite possible to think of the army of Israel as the army of Yahweh, as 110^3, cf. Jo. 2^{25}, in accordance with the original meaning of *Sabaoth*, 1 S. 17^{45} Ps. 24^{10}. — *Bring them down*], by a humiliating overthrow, a defeat that will prostrate them. — *my Shield*], so 𝕲, in accordance with context and usage of Ps.; changed by inexactness into "our shield," in 𝔥, 𝔍, cf. 3^4 18^3 $28^7 +$. — *my sovereign Lord*]. The term here retains its original meaning, and really belongs to previous line to complete its measure. — **13**. *for the sin of their mouth* ‖ *The iniquity of the word of their lips*]. Sin has as its usual parallel iniquity, the omission of which, by an early copyist, has made difficulty to Vrss. and interpreters, who differ greatly in their translations. The sin of the mouth is that which the mouth commits in speech. The iniquity of the word is the iniquity which the word of false witness conveys when it issues from the lips. This is defined as *cursing*, and *lying which they speak*, and as connected with *pride* or haughtiness. A verb is missing in the first line, which was probably the verb cognate to the noun " sin," so similar in form that the copyist inadvertently omitted it, namely : *bring them to punishment*]. This then has its counterpart in the closing line : *let them be taken*], probably in the sense of entrapped in the snare of their own words, cf. 9^{16} ; rather than taken captive in war, a usage common in other Heb. Lit., but not found in ψ. — **14**. *Consume*], repeated for emphasis by glossator, making line too long — *in Thy wrath*], the heat of the divine anger excited against them because of their evil conduct above described. — *that they be no more*], cease to exist, utterly perish, as a result of this divine interposition. — *And it shall be known*], indef. subj. rendered best in English by passive ; in accordance with the extent of this knowledge, to : *the ends of the earth*. That which is thus made known is, in accordance with the order of 𝕲, which is doubtless more original than the prosaic order of 𝔥 : *that it is the God of Jacob*, cf. 20^2 $46^{8.12}$; who has wrought this judgment. — *Ruler*]. As sovereign lord of Jacob He also has universal rule, cf. 22^{29} 66^7 89^{10} 103^{19}.

Glosses again interpose between the couplets of the Rf. — **16**. *They wander up and down to devour*]. This is an enlargement of the simile of the dogs, giving the purpose of their prowling. — *If they are not satisfied*], a condition involving a negative answer. — *they growl*], so 𝔊, 𝔘, 𝔍, Aq., cf. " grudge," PBV., AV., in accordance with context and the nature of the dogs. MT., followed slavishly by RV., " tarry all night," from a similar Hebrew word, differing only in vowel points, is unsuited to context. The usual justification of the latter from the antithesis with " morning " of v.[17] is shattered on the fact that both are glosses from different hands. — **17.** This verse is an amplification of v.[18], a tetrastich of two syn. couplets : *I will sing* ‖ *I will ring out*], in public worship in the morning, the time of morning worship in the temple ; not in antithesis with a night of peril, as many. Yahweh is a *High Tower*, as v.[18], and place of refuge to which one flees, as 142[5], — *in the day I have trouble*], as 102[3]. The situation of this glossator is more general and less perilous than that of the author of the Ps.

2-3. הַצִּילֵנִי] Hiph. imv. נצל (7[2]), also v.[3] 𝔊, 𝔍, have different words : v.[2] ἐξελοῦ, *erue ;* v.[3] ῥῦσαί, *libera.* This favours a copyist's assimilation. But 𝔊 renders the same Heb. words elsw. by both Greek words, and the variation may therefore be simply for better style. — אֱלֹהַי] sf. 1 sg. i.p., so 𝔍 ; but 𝔊 ὁ Θεός, which may stand for an original יהוה. — מִמִּתְקוֹמְמַי] Hithp. ptc. pl. sf. 1 sg. קוּם, so 17[7], *those rising up against me.* 𝔊, 𝔍, insert conj.; prob. interp. and not original. The word has two beats for measure. The four verbs v.[2-3] are in assonance in נִי and it is prob. that originally they were all at end of l. — **4.** יָגוּרוּ] *v. 56[7] ;* AE, Dr., Kau., rd. יָרוּ *attack* גרה, 𝔊 ἐπέθεντο, but 𝔍, 𝔗, Ges., De., JPSV., *congregantur,* best suited to context. " Attack " is too strong for the subsequent vbs. עַזִּים] pl. adj. *Mighty ones,* as 18[18] אֹיְבַי עַז, so 𝔊 κραταιοί, 𝔍 *fortissimi,* Dr., Bä., others, עָזִים *with strength,* cf. v.[10] עֻזּוֹ. — יִרְאֶ־חֲטָאִי] shortened for בלא פשעי. This belongs in previous l. for syn. parali. A copyist reduced the two lines to prose. — יהוה] is suspicious, as in all Pss. of 𝔈 ; doubtless gl., as Bä. It makes l. too long. — **5.** בְּלִי־עָוֹן] varia- tion of לֹא ; thus three great terms for sin are used. Rd. prob. עֲוֹנִי, the י absorbed in י of next word. It goes to end of l. for rhyme, with two tones. — יְרֻצוּן] Qal impf. 3 pl. archaic ending, *run* of armed men *18[30] ;* followed by י coörd. with יְכוֹנָנוּ for וְנוּ, cf. Pr. 24[3], Hithp. √כון (7[10]), cf. תְּכוֹנֵן Nu. 21[27], Is. 54[14]. 𝔊 κατεύθυνα (α err. for αν), *station oneself, take a stand,* 𝔍 *prae- parantur.* The first of these vbs. belongs in previous l. for parall. and assonance — קְרָאתִי] inf. cstr. ראה *v. 25[18].* — **6.** יהוה אלהים צבאות] an impos- sible combination. יהוה is doubtless a gl. of variation of reading, and אלהים stands for an original י דר ; so that the text once stood יהוה צבאות, as Kirk. — אֱלֹהֵי יִשְׂרָאֵל] phr. of 𝔈, elsw. in ψ 68[9] 69[7], doxologies 41[14] 72[18] 106[48]; is here a gl. of intensification. The original l. was אֵרֶה יהוה צבאיר. — כָּל־הַגּוֹיִם] so 𝔊, 𝔍, is striking here : prob. כי was introduced from later point of view as suited to next l. — יְלַיֲלָה־עֹיְבֵי אָוֶן] phr. α.λ., 𝔊, 𝔍, פעלי און as v.[3]. 𝔐 can only be understood as pregnant for און בגדי פעלי כל, cf. 25³. It implies treachery in covenants. 獨 as the more difficult is to be preferred. — **7 = 15** Rf. יָשׁוּבוּ] Qal impf. 3 pl. *they return* if we give this vb. its normal force, implying that they have been there before. But there is nothing of this in context, and it does not suit the idea of the Rf. The vb. has auxiliary force, *again*, and, as impf. freq., *again and again*. — יֶהֱמוּ] Qal. impf. after ישבו·. The conj. of 𝕲, 𝔍, misses the construction, as do, after them, most moderns. המה vb., *v. 39*⁷; *growl B*DB., *snarl* Dr., cf. Is. 59¹¹ of bears, Ez. 7¹⁶ of doves. — וִיסֹבְבוּ] goes with the previous vb., therefore ו before סבבו· is incorrect interpretation, although in 𝕲, 𝔍. The first l. is too long and the second too short. יָעִיר has been removed by prosaic copyist from the second l. to the first. It separates the principal vb. from its auxiliary. — **8.** יַבִּיעוּן] Hiph. impf. 3 pl. archaic form נבע (19³) *pour forth*. This vb. is not suited to the previous context. It describes another kind of enemy and is a gl. It has nothing to correspond with it in the second Rf. — בְּפִיהֶם־וַחֲרָבֹות] has two poetic accents. — **9.** Gl. from 2⁴. — ואתה] was taken from v.⁶. — יהוה] not suited to 𝔈. — תִּשְׂחַק־לָמֹו] as (למו) ישחק 2⁴. — תלעג] as ילעג 2⁴, but for למו of 2⁴ לכל־גוים is given as an interp. of it. — **10 = 18** Rf. עֻזֹּי] has no good sense. Rd. with 𝕲, 𝔍, 𝕿, Dr., Kirk., and some codd. MT. עֻזִּי *my strength* (83³) ‖ מִשְׂגַּבִּי (910¹⁰) so Rf. v.¹⁸. — אֶשְׁמֹרָה] Qal impf. cohort. i.p. = אֲשַׁמֵּרָה v.¹⁸; though 𝕲, 𝔍, have the same text here as 獨, yet 𝕾 has the same vb. in both passages, so Houb., Kenn., Street, Ols., Bi., Gr., Bä., Dr. It is improbable that the Rf. would differ. Furthermore, אל is not suited to שמר (12⁸), and although אל is with זמר (7¹⁸) elsw. only v.¹⁸, it is just as suitable here as there, and is a frequent variant with ל after other vbs. — אלהים] for original יהוה. 𝕲 agrees with 獨 here, but not in v.¹⁸, where it has ὁ Θεός μου. 𝔍 has *tu deus* here, but 3d pers. v.¹⁸. The context demands 2d pers. — **11.** אֱלֹהֵי חַסְדִּי] Kt. אלהי חסדי Qr., 𝕲, ὁ Θεός μου τὸ ἔλεος αὐτοῦ, but v.¹⁸ ὁ Θεός μου τὸ ἔλεός μου; 𝔍 v.¹¹ *dei mei misericordia*, v.¹⁸ *deus misericordia mea*. These do not sustain אֱלֹהֵי as cstr., which gives a phr. a.λ. improb. in itself. הַסְדִּי is sustained by v.¹⁸ (MT., 𝕲, 𝔍), and is indeed required by the context. But v.¹¹ is entirely different; a subj. is needed for יקרמני. In v.¹⁸ the phr. is at the close of Ps. after Rf.; in v.¹¹ it begins the second part of the Ps. The Rf. is sufficiently long without it. It is therefore a txt. err. in v.¹⁸ from v.¹¹. If so, the copyist found אלהי חסדי, unless we may suppose that הסי· is a later change to assimilate the word to its context. On the whole 𝕲 is the best guide, and we should rd. אלהי חסדי, as Dr. — **12.** אַל־תַּהַרְגֵם] Qal juss. with sf. 3 pl. is inconsistent with v.¹⁴. Gr. would change this latter. No satisfactory explanation has been given of the text, though it is sustained by Vrss. G. Baur., Now., propose הֲרָחֵמֵם, which is in accord with חֵן· צָל־· v.⁶, and most satisfactory except that sf. is unnecessary. — פֶּן־יִשְׁכְּחוּ עַמִּי] 𝔍 *ne forte obliviscantur populi mei*, 𝕲 μή ποτε ἐπιλάθωνται τοῦ νόμου σου, Jerome Epist. 33 " In Graeco scriptum est: *legis tuae;* sed in LXX. et in Hebraeo non habet *populi tui* sed *populi mei.*" It is probable that עמי of 獨, 𝔍, and חור־ך of 𝕲 are both interpretations of the vb. without subj. and obj. The subj. of ישכחו is the enemies as 9¹⁸, and the whole is a single l., אל־תהרג פן ישכחו. — הֲנִיעֵמֹו] Hiph.

imv. נוע (22⁸) with archaic sf., enemies ; *cause to stagger*, or *wander*, cf. Nu. 32¹³ (J) 2 S. 15²⁰. — וְהוֹרִידֵמוֹ] Hiph. imv. with ו coörd., sf. 3 pl. archaic, with two accents. Lag. הֲנִידֵמוֹ after 𝕊 ; so Du. with reference to Gn. 4¹², נע ונד, tempting but not probable. The longer word is needed for measure, and ארני goes with preceding l., which needs it for completeness. Moreover, this l. begins a new tetrastich, and is not strictly parall. with previous l. — מָגִנֵּנוּ] (3⁴). But 1 pl. is against usage of Ps. ; therefore מָגֵנִי as 𝕲 ὁ ὑπερασπιστής μου. — **13.** הֲרָאת פִּימוֹ] as antith. v.⁴. 𝕲 ἁμαρτίαν στόματος αὐτῶν, 𝔍 *in peccato oris sui.* — דְּבַר־שְׂפָתֵימוֹ] in apposition with previous clause, as 𝔍, 𝕲, acc. and not predicate as many moderns. Two lines are needed for measure. They have been compressed into one by ancient copyist. In the second עין ‖ חמא is needed ; in the first a vb. הֵרָא *bring into punishment*, as Is. 29²¹ Dt. 24⁴. — וְיִלָּכְדוּ] ו seems to imply something to which it is in coördination ; prob. the vb. suggested. Niph. *be caught*, so 9¹⁶, as in snare or trap. — בְגָאוֹנָם ‡ נְאוֹן elsw. ψ 47⁴; here in bad sense *pride*, as Is. 16⁶ Je. 48²⁹ Zp. 2¹⁰ Ez. 7²⁰ 16⁴⁹. A word is missing. 𝔍 has not conj. with אָר.., therefore מָאלה־מו is doubtless correct for ס ומי in accord with usage of Ps. So we should have the fully written במו and read the line וַיִּלְכְרוּ בְמוֹ גְאוֹנָמוֹ. — אָלָה] prep. מִן *because of* and ‡ אָלָה n.f. *cursing,* cf. 10⁷. This begins new quartette. — ‡ כַּחַשׁ] n.m. (1) *lying*, as Ho. 7³ 10¹³ 12¹ Na. 3¹; (2) *leanness* Ps. 109²⁴ (?) Jb. 16⁸. — **14.** יְסַפֵּר] Piel. imv. (18³⁸) bis ; only one is needed for measure, the other is a gl. of intensification. — וְכַחֵשׁ] is attached to the previous כלה by 𝔍, to following by 𝕲. — אלהי יעקב 𝔍, 𝕲 had אלהים מי על ביעקב [אלהים מי על ביעקב rds. *deus dominatur Jacob.* בְּ before יַעֲקֹב is doubtless explanatory gl. 𝕲 is most likely correct. It gives the only good measure. — **16.** This v. is a gl., breaking between couplets of Rf. — וְינוּעוּן] Kt. Qal impf. 3 pl. archaic, יְנִיעוּן Qr. Hiph. impf., cf. v.¹²; 𝕲 διασκορπισθήσονται, 𝔍 *vagabuntur.* — אִם־לֹא] but 𝕲 ἐὰν δὲ, making negative dub. — וְיָלִינוּ] ו consec. after impf., aorist of result, which is not suited to the idea of lodging all night. Σ, 𝕮, 𝕊, have same vb. as 𝔚, but ו coörd. 𝕲, Aq., γογγύσουσιν ; 𝔍 *murmurabunt;* PBV. וְיָרִינוּ Hiph., or וְיֵלִינוּ Niph.; so Du., Bä., Bu., BDB. ‡ לון vb. Niph. *murmur*, cf. Ex. 15²⁴ (JE) Nu. 14² 16¹¹ 17⁶ (P) +, Hiph. same, Ex. 17³ (E) 16⁸ (P) +. — **17** is also a gl., amplification of Rf. v.¹⁸. — וַאֲנִי] emph. antith. to enemies. — אָשִׁיר עֻזְּךָ = עֵי אֹזְרָה v.¹⁸. [משגב לי = עֻזִּי v.¹⁸. — מָנוֹס ‡ם] n.m. (1) *a place of flight, of escape*, elsw. 142⁵ Am. 2¹⁴ Je. 25³⁵ Jb. 11²¹ 2 S. 22³ (?) Je. 16¹⁹ (?) ; (2) *flight* Je. 46⁵. — ביום צר־לי] so 102³ (v. 4²).

PSALM LX.

Ps. 60 is composite. (A) A Ps. of the time of David, citing an ancient oracle, giving Israel possession of the land and supremacy over his neighbours (v.⁸⁻¹²ᵃ). (B) A prayer for deliverance in time of defeat and great humiliation, probably of the reign of Jehoiachin (v.³⁻⁷· ¹²ᵇ⁻¹⁴).

A. v.$^{8-12a}$, 4 STR. 3^3.

YAHWEH spake in His sanctuary :
    " I will exult, I will divide Shechem ;
    " And the Valley of Succoth will I mete out.
" GILEAD is Mine, and Mine is Manasseh ;
    " Ephraim also is the defence of My head ;
    " Judah is My commander's staff.
" MOAB is My washpot ;
    " Unto Edom will I cast My sandal ;
    " Over Philistia will I shout in victory."
O THAT one would conduct me to the entrenched city?
    O that one would lead me unto Edom?
    Wilt not Thou (Yahweh)?

B. v.$^{3-7.\ 12b-14}$, 4 STR. 4^3.

YAHWEH, Thou hast rejected us, hast broken *us* down ;
    Thou wast angry and didst turn *us* backward ;
    Thou didst shake the land, didst cleave it :
    Its breach doth sink down, it doth totter.
THOU hast let Thy people see hard things :
    Thou hast made us drink wine of staggering.
    A sign to them that fear Thee Thou hast given,
    That they might betake themselves to flight (because of (Thy) faithfulness).
THAT Thy beloved people may be delivered,
    O give victory with Thy right hand and answer us ;
    Thou Yahweh, who didst reject us (and put us to shame),
    And wentest not forth with our hosts.
O GIVE us help because of straits,
    For vain is the victory of man.
    Through Yahweh let us do valiantly,
    And He will tread down our adversaries.

Ps. 60 is composite. (*B*) v.$^{3-6}$, 2 Str. 4^3, continued in v.$^{7.\ 12b-14}$, 2 Str. 4^3. This has taken up into its midst an older Ps. (*A*), v.$^{8-12a}$, 4 Str. 3^3. V.$^{7-14}$ is also contained in the composite Ps. 108, which begins with 57^{8-12}. As 108 uses the composite Ps. 60, it was composed subsequent to that composition. Ps. 108 cited 57, 60, from 𝔈, and not from the original group of מכתמים, for the divine name is אלהים throughout. It is therefore unlikely that 108 was in 𝔇. The לדוד of the title is due to the recognition of the fact that the two original Pss. out of which it was constructed were in 𝔇. Ps. 108 was not in 𝔇ℜ, but 60 was, and probably already as composite when it received the musical assignment על־שושן עדות (*v.* Intr. §§ 27, 32, 33, 34). The original מכתם (*v.* Intr. § 25) was only (*A*), which is antique in its language and style. The term לְלַמֵּד is prob. original. It reminds one of the dirge 2 S. $1^{17\ sq.}$ and possibly was also in the Book of Yashar. To it alone the historical reference can apply : בהצותו את ארם נהרים ואת־ארם צובה וישב יואב ויך את־אדום בגיא־מלח

י\שנים עשר אל\ף: When he strove with Aram Naharaim and with Aram Zoba, when Joab returned and smote of Edom in the valley of salt twelve thousand. Cf. 2 S. 8¹³ sq. 10¹⁶ sq. 1 C. 18¹² sq. 19⁶ sq.. The variation in number is prob. due to a corruption of text. But while this Ps. is undoubtedly ancient and might go back to the time of David, yet it is too general to refer to this defeat of Edom (or rather ארם as 2 S. 10), and is an oracle as to the triumph over the lesser neighbours, Aram not being mentioned. (B) was a Ps. of different structure and date. It was a petition for divine interposition after humiliating defeat of the armies of Israel. V.⁶ resembles Je. 4⁶, v.⁵ Is. 51¹⁷·²². It probably refers to the defeat of the armies of Judah by the Babylonians, reducing them to a desperate situation. It reminds us of parts of Pss. 44 and 89, and may express the feelings of the companions of Jehoiachin.

PSALM LX. A.

Str. I. a tristich having a syn. couplet synth. to the first line.— 8. *Yahweh spake in His sanctuary*], so 𝕲, 𝕵, referring to the sacred place of the divine presence, where the oracle of Yahweh was given ; and not, " in " or " by His holiness," of EVˢ. suggesting a divine oath, as Am. 4² Ps. 89³⁶. This oracle goes back to the original conquest of the land. — *I will exult*], in triumph over the inhabitants of the land. Yahweh speaks as the supreme commander of His people, cf. Ps. 24⁷⁻¹⁰ Is. 63¹⁻⁶. — *I will divide*], the conquered land among the tribes, ‖ *will I mete out*, the measurement in connection with the division. — *Shechem*, at the foot of Mt. Gerizim, the chief gathering place in the time of Joshua, stands for the country west of the Jordan, cf. Josh. 24¹. The *Valley of Succoth*], in the valley of the Jordan on the eastern side, near the Jabbok (S. Merrill, *East of Jordan*, 385 sq.), stands for the country east of the Jordan ; possibly with a reminiscence of the two chief places mentioned in the story of the return of Jacob from Haran to Canaan, Gen. 33¹⁷⁻²⁰.

Str. II. is a syn. tristich. — 9. *Gilead*, as distinguished from *Manasseh*, must indicate with it the two chief divisions east of the Jordan, as *Ephraim* and *Judah*, the two chief divisions on the west. Accordingly Gilead, here, is for the southern portion assigned to Reuben and Gad, Nu. 32¹⁻²⁹, and Manasseh, the northern portion, or the land of Bashan. These, says Yahweh, are *Mine*], that is, my possession, my land. Ephraim is *the defence of My head*], the helmet defending the head from the blows of an enemy, in per-

sonal combat in battle. Judah is *My commander's staff*], as
Gn. 49[10]; not the " sceptre," RV., which implies royalty, nor the
"lawgiver," PBV., AV., which implies government; but the baton,
the symbol of military authority, with which the commander directs
the movements of his army and points them to victory.

Str. III. is also a syn. tristich, referring to the three hostile
neighbours who are conceived as subjugated. — **10.** *Moab is My
washpot*]. Moab was the troublesome neighbor of Israel, occu-
pying the region east of the Dead Sea. He is to be so reduced
that he becomes the wash basin which is carried by a slave to pour
water over his master's hands or feet. — *Unto Edom will I cast
My sandal*]. Edom, the troublesome neighbour of Judah, on the
southeast, was also so reduced as to become another slave to
whom the master kicks off the sandals when he would have them
removed to wash his feet. This is better than EV[s]. " over " or
"upon Edom," as though it were a symbol of the taking possession of the land by conquest. — *Over Philistia will I shout in
victory*]. The relations between the Philistines and Israel were
those of mutually respecting warlike neighbours. There is nothing ignominious therefore in the reference to them. They are
defeated, and there is rejoicing in the victory. MT. and Vrss., by
a mistake of a vowel point here, but not in 108[10], compel various
other renderings, none of which suit the context or give a satisfactory meaning.

Str. IV. has a syn. couplet with a synth. line in climax. —
11. *O that one would*], expression of a wish to enjoy the triumph
promised in the oracle cited above, and not a simple question,
" who will " of EV[s]. — *conduct me ‖ lead me*], that is, in victorious entry into *the entrenched city*, the chief fortification and
defence, which being captured, *Edom* itself would come into possession of the conquerors. — **12**a. *Wilt not Thou Yahweh?* This
question implies an affirmative answer in accordance with the
promise of the oracle, and therefore an appropriate climax and
conclusion of this ancient Ps.

PSALM LX. *B.*

Str. I. has a syn. tetrastich. — **3.** *Thou hast rejected us*], cf.
43[2] 44[24]; refused to go with us, or be with us, or help us in war.

‖ *Thou wast angry*], the reason of the rejection. As a result of this : *Thou hast broken us down*]. The army, which should have stood like a wall in defence of the nation, has been broken down, so that it can no longer resist the onset of the enemy. — *didst turn us backward*] in defeat, compelling a disastrous retreat. This meaning is most suited to the context, cf. 44[11]. The Hebrew text is capable of various other renderings which are followed in Vrss. and interpreters, the most probable of which is, " O restore us again." Such a petition, however, comes in too abruptly into the text, and does not suit the context, which continues the description of the divine discipline of the people. It is quite possible, however, that this meaning was designed by the final editor of ψ for liturgical reasons. — **4**. *Thou didst shake the land*]. The national disaster is compared to an earthquake, cf. 46[3. 6] Is. 24[18 sq.]. — *Thou didst cleave it*]. The metaphor is continued. As the earthquake cleaves the land by making rents and cracks in the solid ground, so the nation is all broken up in disorder and confusion. — *Its breach doth sink down*]. The walls of defence have been breached, and the breach sinks down, — *it doth totter*], and is about to fall down in a mass of ruins. The poet is here describing a great national disaster within his own experience.

Str. II. has a syn. couplet and a synth. couplet. — **5**. The *hard things*], the people of Yahweh are seeing are the sad experiences of defeat, disaster, death in battle, captivity, humiliation, and shame. — *wine of staggering*]. They are so overwhelmed with dismay and panic by this unexpected situation that they are dazed, they stagger as if intoxicated, cf. Is. 51[17. 22]. At the same time they know that Yahweh has made them see these things, and He has given them this cup to drink, cf. 80[6]. — **6**. *A sign to them that fear Thee Thou hast given*]. Yahweh distinguishes the God-fearing in the midst of this disaster, and gives them a sign or signal, which enables them to escape in time. — *that they might betake themselves to flight*]. This rendering, sustained by 𝕲, 𝔍, is suited to the context and greatly to be preferred to that of AV., RV., based on Aq., 𝕿 : " that it (the banner) may be displayed," which gives a victory to the God-fearing that does not at all suit the context. It is quite possible, however, that for liturgical reasons the clause was given this turn in the traditions of synagogue use. —

Because of Thy faithfulness]. This is a conjectural emendation of the text, in accordance with the context. It is at the basis of the rendering of Aq., 𝕿, EVˢ., " because of the truth." But 𝕲, 𝔍, 𝖁, RV.ᵐ, " before the bow " is preferred by most.

Str. III. v.⁷·¹²ᵇ has a synth. and a syn. couplet separated by the insertion of v.⁸⁻¹²ᵃ. — **7.** *That Thy beloved people may be delivered*]. The purpose is placed before the imv. for emphasis. The people of Yahweh are named beloved, because they are the special objects of His love, notwithstanding the disasters He has brought upon them. His people cannot think that these can be more than temporary and disciplinary, and that in the end they will be delivered. — *O give victory with Thy right hand*]. The right hand of Yahweh stretched out in behalf of His people is the great instrument of deliverance and victory, cf. 20⁷ 21⁹ 44⁴ 48¹¹+ Ex. 15⁶. The Hebrew word, which means sometimes " give victory," sometimes " save," should not be generalised here. — **12*b*.** *Thou Yahweh, who didst reject us*], resuming the thought of v.³; the very One who rejected His people, is the only One who can give them the victory. When the two Pss. were pieced together, this line had to be adapted to its context, and was condensed with v.¹²ᵃ so as to give " hast Thou not rejected us." For the same reason the closing vb., *and put us to shame*, was omitted. It is given, however, in the citation Ps. 44¹⁰, and should be restored in Ps. 60 for the sake of the measure and strophical organisation. — *And wentest not forth with our hosts*]. A continuation of the statement of the previous line and explanatory of it. Yahweh was not with the armies of His people; they went into battle without Him. His right hand was not stretched out on their behalf. He was indeed angry with them. That was the reason for their defeat. The prayer for victory implies that Yahweh might go forth with the armies of His people and as their chieftain again stretch forth His hand against their enemies.

Str. IV. has two syn. couplets. — **13.** *O give us help*], a renewal of the prayer for victory of the previous Str. — *because of straits*]. This interpretation of 𝕲, 𝔍, PBV., AV., is most probable, as it corresponds with the thought of the previous Str.; although the rendering of RV. " against the adversary," favoured by many moderns, is possible. — *For vain is the victory of man*]. Victory to be won by man in war against the enemy amounts to nothing; it is a vain hope. Victory cannot be brought about by man, but by Yahweh only. — **14.** *Through Yahweh*]. His right hand stretched out in battle. — *let us do valiantly*]. Assured of divine help, the people resolve on their part to fight with all their might. — *and He will tread down our adversaries*]. Yahweh will trample them under foot in His victorious advance.

LX. *B.*

3. אלהים] for original יהוה, so v.⁸· ¹²· ¹⁴. — פְּרַצְתָּנוּ] Qal pf. 2 m., sf. 1 pl. ‡ פרץ Qal (1) *break down* a wall, 80¹³ 89⁴¹ Is. 5⁵ Ec. 10⁸, here of nation, cf. v.⁴ (2) *break in* Ps. 106²⁹. — שׁיבֵב] Polel impf. שׁוב, *restore*, as 23³ Is. 58¹² acc. to Bu., Dr., Du., then juss. *restore us;* 𝕿 *return to us* as petition. 𝕲, 𝔙, Aq., Σ, Quinta, take it as pf. καὶ ᾤκτείρησας ἡμᾶς. This mng. does not suit context. Bä. rds. ותשובב, ו consec. impf., as Je. 50⁶, cf. Ps. 44¹¹, תשיבנו אחור מני צר. The difficulty then is with ל. This is prob. not original but interpretation. The initial ת is dittog. for an original ה. Rd. השׁיבֵנו with two tones, *turn back in retreat*, which alone suits the context and rhyme. — **4.** הִרְעַשְׁתָּה] Hiph. pf. 2 m. fully written, רעשׁ, *v. 18⁸*. But it is prob. that final ה belongs to אֶרֶץ. — פְּצַמְתָּהּ] *a.λ.* Qal pf. 2 m., sf. 3 f. prob. *split open,* dub.; 𝕲 καὶ συνετάραξας αὐτήν, 𝔍 *et disrupisti eam.* — רְפָה] Qal imv. רפה = רפא *heal, v. 6³,* so 𝕲 ἴασαι, 𝔍 *sana;* but רָפָה Qal pf. cf. *37⁸,* *sink, relax,* is more suited to context, with שְׁבָרֶיךָ as subj. The phr. *a.λ.* שֶׁבֶר n.m. *breach* in a wall Is. 30¹³· ¹⁴, ruin of state La. 2¹¹ 3⁴⁷ Am. 6⁶ Na. 3¹⁹. The פֶּרֶץ נֹפֵל Is. 30¹³ *breach ready to fall* is similar idea, and possibly in mind of poet. — כִי־מָטָה] Qal 3 f. sg. מוט (*10⁶*). כי is prob. interpretative gl. because of interp. of רפה as imv. — **5.** ‡ קָשָׁה] adj. f. קָשֶׁה *what is hard* (to bear), in war as 2 S. 2¹⁷; *a.λ. ψ,* common in Lit. — תַּרְעֵלָה] n.f. *reeling, staggering,* elsw. Is. 51¹⁷· ²². — **6.** נֵס] Qal pf. 2 m. fully written, נסס. — ‡ נֵס] n.m. *standard,* as Is. 62¹⁰, so Dr. *B*DB., or *signal,* as Je. 4⁶ (to direct refugees to Zion), so here to direct flight from enemy, 𝕲 σημείωσιν, 𝔍 *signum.* — לְהִתְנוֹסֵס] Hithpolel inf. ‡ נוס Qal. *flee,* of armies 68², of sea 114³· ⁵, cf. 104⁷; Hithp. *take flight,* so 𝕲, 𝔙, 𝔍, Σ, Dr., Du., Bä., Hu., Now., Che., RV.ᵐ. But De. after Aq., 𝕿, Luther, AV., RV., takes it as denom. of נֵס, *that it may be displayed.* The former alone suits the context. — מִפְּנֵי קֹשֶׁט] 𝕲 ἀπὸ προσώπου τόξου, 𝔍 *a facie arcus.* קֹשֶׁט is *bow* in Aram. but not in Heb., which has קֶשֶׁת. קֹשֶׁט is *truth,* Pr. 22²¹ (but Aram gl. acc. to Toy); so here acc. to those who take vb. as denom. of נֵס. The Aram. word has been substituted for Heb. word אֱמוּנָה, which accords with rhyme, by a late copyist. — **7** = 108⁷. למען] למען (for אשר) *emph.* at beginning of sentence, elsw. *ψ* 122⁸· ⁹. יֵחָלְצוּן Niph. impf. 3 pl. archaic form Niph. elsw. 108⁷ Pr. 11⁸· ⁹; but Piel, *v. 6⁵.* — יְדִידֶיךָ] pl. sf. 2 m. † יָדִיד adj. *beloved,* elsw. 108⁷ 84² 127², cf. 45¹; also Dt. 33¹² Is. 5¹· ¹ Je. 11¹⁵. — עֲנֵנוּ] Kt. *answer us,* connects with previous context; עֲנֵנִי Qr. 𝕲, 𝔍, connects

with following context. The reading נִי 108[6] is because of its previous context, which requires 1st pers. Du. rightly connects with previous part of Ps.
and adds v.[12b-14].

LX. A.

8. V[8-12a] = 108[8-14]. The only variations are: v.[9] מִי לִי 108, for וּלִי מִ here,
the latter more correct; v.[10] עָלַי for עֲלֵי, the former doubtless correct;
אתרועע for התרועעי, the former better; v.[11] מִבְצָר for מָצוֹר, the former correct;
v.[12] הֲלֹא אלהים for הֲלֹא אתה אלהים, the latter correct.— בְּקָדְשׁוֹ], cf. 2[6], ᴳ ἐν τῷ
ἁγίῳ αὑτοῦ, Ᵽ in sanctuario suo; so Ew., Du., Bä., in his holy place. But
Now., Dr., Kirk., in or by his holiness, EV[s]., his majestic sacredness, cf. 89[36]
Am. 4[2] c. נִשְׁבַּע.— אֶעְלֹזָה] impf. cohort. v. 28[7], so אֲחַלְּקָה; so prob. in ancient
text אֲמַדֵּד was cohort. also; Piel ‡ מדד vb. Qal measure, † Pi. measure off,
elsw. 108[8] 2 S. 8[2. 2].— סֻכּוֹת] on East Jordan, for Eastern Palestine. Cf.
Gn. 33[17. 18], where same places are mentioned. ᴳ has τῶν σκηνῶν.— **9.** לִי]
should be connected with גלעד by makkeph, but וְלִי is separate word. The
omission of ו in 108[9] impairs the euphony of l.— מָעוֹז] place of refuge, v. 27[1],
but here prob. in the sense of protection, RV. defence; i.e. helmet, Bä. thinks
of horns. ᴳ κραταίωσις, Ᵽ fortitudo, PBV., AV., strength = עֹז.— מְחֹקְקִי] Po.
ptc. ‡ [חקק] vb., measure requires לִי מְחֹקֵק, cf. Gn. 49[10] Nu. 21[18]. ᴳ βασιλεύς
μου, Ᵽ rex meus, improb.— **10.** קִיר רָחְצִי] phr. α.λ. סִיר (v. 58[10]), † רַחַץ n.m.
washing α.λ. Why not inf. cstr. רחץ? (2[6]).— עָלַי פְּלֶשֶׁת הִתְרוֹעָעִי] ᴳ ἐμοὶ ἀλλό-
φυλοι ὑπετάγησαν, so in 108; Ᵽ mihi Palaestina foederata est, but in 108 cum
Philisthim foederabor. Ᵽ takes vb. as Hithp. רעה II., as Pr. 22[24], ᴳ as Hithp.,
רעע II., as Is. 24[19] Pr. 18[24]. Ps. 108 has better אֶתְרוֹעָע עֲלֵי פּ׳. Most moderns,
Du., Bä., Bu., BDB., make vb. Hithp. רוע, v. 41[12], shout in triumph over.—
11. מִי] is not simply interrog. as EV[s]., but expresses a wish, as DeW., Ols.—
מָצוֹר] intrenched (as 31[22]) = 108[11]. ‡ מִבְצָר n.m. elsw. 89[41] Nu. 32[17. 36] Jos. 10[20]
19[29. 35] Je. 4[5] 5[17] 8[14] + fortified place, stronghold. Ᵽ and ᴳ are the same in
both passages. It is prob. that 108[11] is correct. מצור has been written by
copyist under influence of 31[22].— מִי נָחַנִי] Qal pf. sf. 1 sg. נחה, v. 5[9]. ᴳ, Ᵽ,
have impf., which is doubtless correct, the initial י having been omitted by
error after י of מִי.— **12.** הֲלֹא אַתָּה] 108 omits אתה, but it is needed for
measure.

LX. B. (continued).

12[b]–14 belongs with v.[3-7], and not with v.[8-12a]. V.[12b. c] is cited 44[10], where
we are to seek the original of the first l., which is here condensed, זְנַחְתָּנוּ
remaining for אַף זָנַחְתָּ וְהַכְלִימֵנוּ. The אַף was needed for Ps. 44[10], but was not
original. The original contained יהוה for which E אלהים.— **13.** רְבָה-לָּנוּ]
cohort. imv. יהב, v. 29[1], poetic Aram. vb.— עֶזְרָת] Ges.[§80g] for עֶזְרָה, v. 22[20],
cf. עֶזְרָתָה 63[8], help, succour.— מִצָּר] ᴳ ἐκ θλίψεως, Ᵽ in tribulatione, v. 4[2].
But Dr., Bä., Du., against the adversary, v. 3[2] ‖ צרינו v.[14].— הָשִׁיעַת אָדָם] phr.
α.λ. but cf. 146[3], v. 33[17], victory from man, gained by man.— **14.** וְנַעֲשֶׂה-חָיִל]
do valiantly, † phr. 118[15. 16] Nu. 24[18] (JE.) 1 S. 14[48], prob. cohort. of resolution.— יהוא] referring to God, antith. to we.— יָבוּס] Qal impf. trample under
feet, as 44[6].

PSALM LXI., 3 STR. 4⁴.

Ps. 61 is a national prayer of the early monarchy: (1) for deliverance in time of war (v.$^{2. 3b-4}$); (2) with the assurance that the vows for the king have been answered (v.$^{6-7}$); and (3) that he will reign forever, protected by the kindness and faithfulness of Yahweh; for which public praise will be given (v.$^{8-9}$). Glosses give the urgent prayer of an exile (v.^{3a}), and the comfortable assurance of the guests of Yahweh in His temple (v.^{5}).

O HEAR my yell! O hearken to my prayer!
  In that my heart fainteth, on the rock mayest Thou lift me up.
  Mayest Thou lead me, for Thou art a refuge for me,
  A tower of strength from before mine enemy.
THOU, Yahweh, hast heard my vows.
  Thou hast granted the request of them that fear Thy name.
  Days unto the days of the king Thou wilt add.
  His years, as his days, shall be for generation after generation.
HE will sit enthroned before Yahweh forever.
  Kindness and faithfulness (on the right hand) will preserve him.
  So will I make melody to Thy name forever;
  While I pay my vows day by day.

Ps. 61 was originally in 𝔇, then taken up into 𝔈 and 𝔇𝔈, in the latter receiving the musical assignment על נגינת (v. Intr. §§ 27, 32, 33, 34). It is composed of three tetrameter tetrastichs, the first an urgent petition, the last two expressing assurance that the prayer has been answered, reminding of Pss. 20, 21. It is a royal Ps. of the time of the Heb. monarchy; a time of peril, it is true, and yet a time of victory, when the future seemed serene and the perpetuity of the monarchy certain. V.^{6b}, cf. 21^{3}; v.^{7}, cf. 21^{5}; v.^{8}, cf. 21$^{7. 8}$. The Ps. is cited v.^{8b} in Pr. 20^{28}. Glosses indicate a later time: v.^{3} מקצה הארץ implies an exilic glossator; v.^{5} implies a postexilic glossator of the Greek period.

Str. I. has a synth. and a syn. couplet. — **2.** *O hear my yell* ‖ *O hearken to my prayer*], urgent entreaty that Yahweh will attend to His people in their straits. An exilic glossator adds: *from the bounds of the earth*], far distant from the Holy land. — *unto Thee I call*], making the prayer suited to the exilic situation, or that of the Diaspora. — **3.** *In that my heart fainteth*]. A causal clause, giving the reason for the urgency of prayer. The situation is so serious that the heart loses its courage, and is in dismay and despair. — *on the rock mayest Thou lift me up*], so 𝕲, 𝕴, 𝕾; the rock fastness is the usual refuge in early Pss., unto which one is lifted up to safety; cf. 27^5 31^3 62^8. 𝕳, 𝕾, 𝕵, 𝕿, EVs., by a different connection of Hebrew letters give " on the rock that is higher than I," too high for me to climb myself, which, however pleasing a conception, in form makes the line too long, and in meaning is not so easy and natural, and is without analogy. — **4.** *For Thou art a refuge for me*], a place or a person affording refuge, ‖ *a tower of strength*], a tower so strong that it cannot be captured by the enemy, cf. 18^{51} 48^{13}. — **5.** A glossator, of the Greek period, enlarges upon this idea, only he turns from the rock refuge to the temple : *I will be a guest in Thy tent*], have the privilege of a guest, a familiar visitor to the sacred tent, cf. 5^5 15^1 Is. 33^{14}. — *for ages*], a late conception of time conceived as a number of ages, these extended into indefinite periods of time or aeons. — *under the cover of Thy wings*]. The cherubic wings, guarding the Holy of Holies of the divine presence, made all the precincts of the temple a place of refuge, *v.* 27^5 31^{21} 36^8 57^2.

Str. II. has two syn. couplets. — **6.** *Hast heard my vows*]. The prayers, referred to in Str. I., had accompanied votive offerings. These had been accepted by Yahweh, and the accompanying petitions heard. Accordingly the syn. : *Thou hast granted the request*], so most recent scholars, in place of 𝕳 and Vrss. " the heritage," which is due to the mistake of a single letter of the word by an early copyist, giving a meaning not in accordance with the context and difficult to explain. The various efforts that have been made to solve the problem require still more serious modification of the text than that proposed, whether by the addition of sfs., by ungrammatical explanations, or by insertions in thought. There could be no question, in the situation of this Psalmist, of the people having their inheritance given them, or taking that of the enemy. Moreover, the situation is so like that of Ps. 21 that we should expect the use of the same words. — **7.** *The days of the king*], the days of his lifetime, the king being conceived as representing his dynasty. That Yahweh will add days implies a long continuance of his reign. This is intensified in 𝕳 ; *His years, as his days, shall be for generation after generation*]. 𝕳 and Vrss. differ here, 𝕲 giving " days," where 𝕳, 𝕵,

give only the prep., differently interpreted however. The variations do not effect the general sense that the dynasty of the king
is to be perpetual, cf. 21⁵. This doubtless gained a Messianic
significance in later times.

Str. III. has a synth. and a syn. couplet. — **8.** *He will sit
enthroned before Yahweh forever*], cf. Ps. 2⁶; as the anointed
of Yahweh, installed by Him on his throne. His reign will be
perpetual, cf. 89²⁰⁻³⁸. — *Kindness and faithfulness will preserve
him*]. These divine attributes here, as 85¹¹, cf. 43³, are personified and given charge over the king to keep him in safety. 㷌 and
Vrss. differ greatly as to one word of this line, which is needed
for the measure. 㷌, followed by AV., RV., and most moderns,
rd. imv. "O appoint," namely these attributes of God; but this is
not favoured by other Vrss. The analogy of Pss. 45¹⁰ 109³¹ 110¹·⁵+
suggests *on the right hand*, a word so near the Hebrew word that
the mistake could easily have been made. This gives the place
where these guardian angels stand to protect the dynasty. — **9.** *So
will I make melody*], in public worship in the temple, ‖ *pay my
vows*, make frequent votive offerings at the times of daily sacrifice.

2. אלהים] not in 𝕲; gl. — 3. מִקְצֵה הָאָרֶץ]. This and two words that follow, a gl. to adapt Ps. to later situation of the Diaspora. — בַּעֲטֹף] Qal inf. cstr.
with בְּ of reason ‡ עטף vb. Qal *be faint, feeble*, 102¹ (title); רוּחַ Is. 57¹⁶, as לֵב
here. † Hithp. *faint away* La. 2¹², רוח Pss. 77⁴ 142⁴ 143⁴, נפש 107⁵ Jon. 2⁸. —
בְּצוּר־יָרוּם] so Σ, 𝔍, 𝔗; but 𝕲, 𝔖, 𝔘, תְּרוֹמְמֵנִי is better suited to context
and measure, so Street. — 5. עוֹלָמִים] pl. עולם always late, so 77⁶·⁸ 145¹³
1 K. 8¹³ = 2 Ch. 6² Is. 26⁴ 45¹⁷·¹⁷ 51⁹ Dn. 9²⁴ Ec. 1¹⁰. — אֶחֱסֶה בְסֵתֶר כְּנָפֶיךָ]
phr. a.λ., but 𝕲 has σκέπῃ as בצל כנפיך 17⁸ 36⁸ 57² 63⁸, cf. 91⁴ Ru. 2¹², also
Pss. 27⁵ 31²¹ 91¹. — 6. נְדָרָי] i.p., but 𝕲, 𝔘, 𝔍, תפלתי as v.²; not so prob. —
יְרֻשַּׁת] cstr. sg. † יְרֻשָּׁה n.f. *possession, inheritance*, Dt. 2⁵·⁹·⁹·¹²·¹⁹·¹⁹ 3²⁰ Jos. 1¹⁵
12⁶·⁷ Ju. 21¹⁷ Je. 32⁸ 2 Ch. 20¹¹ of holy land; not elsw. in ψ. It does not suit
context. Hu., Kroch., Bi., Du., rd. אֲרֶשֶׁת as 21³, which is to be preferred. —
7. יָמִים תּוֹסִיף] phr. a.λ., but cf. האריך ימים Jos. 24³¹ (D), אֶרֶךְ יָמִים Pr. 3²·¹⁶. —
כְּמוֹ] prep., 𝔍 *donec*, 𝕲 ἕως ἡμέρας. The measure favours כִּימֵיו. — 8. מַן] Pi.
imv. for מֵנָה, ‡ מָנָה Qal *count, number*, 90¹² 147⁴, † Pi. *appoint, ordain*, elsw.
Jon. 2¹ 4⁰·⁷·⁸ Dn. 1⁵·¹⁰·¹¹ Jb. 7³; but 𝕲 τίς, Aram. מַן, or Heb. מִי; omitted
Aq., Σ, 𝔍, and in citation Pr. 20²⁸ הסר ואמת יצרו מלך. Houb., Lowth., suggest
מִי(הוה), but improb. Rd. יָמִין *on the right hand* for protection, cf. 45¹⁰ 109³¹
110¹·⁵. — יִנְצְרֻהוּ] Qal impf. sf. 3 m. for יִצְרוּ, נ is retained of original stronger
form for euphony. The clause is final if מַן is imv., but otherwise and most
prob. ‖ יֵשֵׁב.

PSALM LXII., 2 STR. 2⁶., RF. 2⁶.

Ps. 62 is an expression of confidence in Yahweh only, by a man of position, in the time of Jeremiah (v.²⁻³·⁶⁻⁷). His false foes are only a wall about to fall; they are only taking counsel against him (v.⁴ᵇ⁻⁵ᵃ); they are only breath without real weight (v.¹⁰). Gnomic glosses exhort not to have confidence in extortion and wealth (v.¹¹), and remind that strength and kindness belong to God (v.¹²⁻¹³ᵃ). Other glosses emphasize the several conceptions of the Ps. and adapt them to later circumstances (v.⁴ᵃ·⁵ᵇ·⁸⁻⁹·¹³ᵇ).

Only to (Yahweh) be still, my soul! from Him is my hope.
Only He is my rock and my salvation, my high tower; I shall not be moved.
(Only) a leaning wall, a bulging fence are all of (them).
Only consult do they to thrust (me) out from (my) dignity: they take pleasure in falsehood.

Only to (Yahweh) be still, my soul! from Him is my hope.
Only He is my rock and my salvation, my high tower; I shall not be moved.
Only a breath are the sons of mankind, a falsehood the sons of men.
(Only) to go up in the balances are they, made of breath altogether.

Ps. 62 was originally in 𝔇, then in 𝔐 and 𝔈, and subsequently in 𝔇𝔈, where it received the assignment עַל־יְדוּתוּן (v. Intr. §§ 27, 31, 32, 33, 34). The original Ps. was composed of two hexameter couplets, v.⁴ᵇ⁻⁵ᵃ·¹⁰, with Rf. v.²⁻³·⁶⁻⁷. These use terms of 𝔇 and give evidence of a preëxilic date, being characterised by calm confidence in Yahweh. The Ps. was originally personal, and the author's perils were from crafty personal foes, who strove to thrust him out of a position of dignity. There are two glosses from different hands, of the type of WL., both trimeter tetrastichs, v.¹¹·¹²⁻¹³ᵃ. Other glosses are: a remonstrance addressed to enemies in 2d pl., v.⁴ᵃ; a description of the enemies as false friends, v.⁵ᵇ; a reiteration of the thought of refuge in God, v.⁸; an exhortation to the whole congregation to trust in Him, a trimeter tristich not earlier than the Greek period, v.⁹; and a final statement of God's equitable requital of men, v.¹³ᵇ. These glosses were added from time to time, in the various editings of the Ps.

The original Ps. was composed of two Strs., each of two couplets; the first couplet in both Strs. is an identical synth. Rf. of confidence in Yahweh, and the final couplets are syn. with each other but synth. in themselves, expressing contempt of the feeble, false foes.

Str. I. 2. *Only*], characteristic of the Ps. at the beginning of each of its lines; cf. Ps. 39; an emphatic restriction of the confidence to Yahweh alone, and antith. to the ability of his enemies to do him harm. The EV*. as well as the ancient Vrss. differ greatly in rendering this particle in the several lines, sometimes using the asseverative "surely"; but a uniform rendering alone brings out the real power of the Ps. — *be still*]. The text of 𝕳 has the noun "silence," "resignation," here, and the imv. vb. v.[6]. Such a variation in Rf. is improbable. The imv. is better sustained. The soul in calm expectation waits for the divine interposition, cf. 37[7]. — *from Him is my hope*], so v.[6]; but here "salvation" in texts, assimilated to v.[3]. The use of "hope" in the original is more probable: "hope" for its object, the thing hoped for, deliverance from enemies. — **3.** *He is my rock and my salvation; my high tower*], terms familiar in ψ, cf. 18[3], all emphasizing Yahweh as a refuge. — *I shall not be moved*], also a familiar phr. for the firm, stable position of the one relying upon God, cf. 10[6] 15[5] 16[8] 21[8] 30[7] +. A later editor inserted an enigmatical word, whether as a later form of the adv. *greatly*, to limit the statement, or as a liturgical exclamation, JPSV. — **4.** *How long will you threaten a man?*]. Remonstrance with enemies, address in 2 pl. inconsistent with objective 3 pl. of original Ps.; a late gloss. The vb. is a.λ. and dubious, and is variously rendered in Vrss. — *to commit murder*], so Ben Naphtali, 𝕲, 𝕵, RV., which is to be preferred to "ye shall be slain," MT., AV., PBV., which depends upon close connection with the subsequent context. — *all of them*], the enemies of v.[5]; changed into "all of you" in 𝕳 by assimilation to previous context. *Only* has fallen out by mistake. — *a leaning wall, a bulging fence*]. The enemies are compared to a wall that leans over from its upright position, and therefore is in peril of falling down; and to a fence which has been pushed in, and so bulges and is unsafe. They are only such an unstable wall in antithesis to the psalmist's stability in confidence in his God. — **5.** *From my dignity*], so 𝕲, which is to be preferred to 3 sg. of MT.; both doubtless interpretations of a noun without sf. — *Only consult do they*]. Their enmity amounts to nothing more than consulting together, making plans *to thrust me out*. It does not become effective in action, and therefore is not really disturbing. — *they take pleasure in falsehood*]. They delight in craft; they would be false to the psalmist, but really

they deceive themselves. A glossator explains this by inserting
with their mouth they bless, but inwardly they curse.

Str. II. 6–7. The same Rf. as v.[2-3]. — **8.** A gl. explaining
further the Rf. — *Upon God depends my salvation and my glory*].
The glory of the psalmist is the honour and dignity of his position, cf. v.[5]. — *the rock of my strength*], from which strength comes
to help. — *my refuge is in God*], or as Hi., De., Kirk., interpret
as ‫ ב‬ *essentiae*, "is God." — **9** is also a gloss of exhortation to the
late Jewish congregation, a trimeter tristich. — *Trust in Him, O
whole congregation of the people*], so 𝕲, which is more probable
than ‫יוב‬, "at every time, ye people." — *pour out before Him your
heart*] in public worship, cf. 42[5] 102[1] 142[3]. — **10.** *Only a breath*],
nothing more substantial, *are the sons of mankind,* the common
people of the enemies, as distinguished from *the sons of men,*
their leaders, cf. 49[2], which latter are *a falsehood* to their followers, deceiving them and misleading them to no purpose. So
unsubstantial are they that when weighed *in the balances* they are
without weight and have *only to go up* in the weightless scale.
— *made of breath altogether*], the emphatic conclusion. They
amount in the aggregate to nothing more than this. Thus the
original Ps. reached its striking end. But later editors wished to
give it another conclusion, and so in the times of Hebrew Wisdom
they added two gnomes. — **11.** A trimeter tetrastich, *Trust not
in oppression*], antith. the exhortation to trust in God, cf. v.[9]. —
and of robbery be not vain], become filled with unsubstantial,
delusive hopes, be possessed of unsubstantial self-confidence, cf.
Je. 23[16]. — *Wealth, when it beareth fruit*], in ill-gotten gains, —
do not set the mind on it], as if it were of great value and to be
depended upon for salvation. — **12–13 a.** Another trimeter tetrastich. — *One thing God spake*]. These gnomes were regarded as
divine in their origin, just as prophetic words and priestly laws. —
Two things are there which I have heard], implying that God
had indeed spoken the two things that follow. This method of
numerical intensification is familiar in WL., *v.* Pr. 6[16 sq.] 30[15 sq.]. —
that strength belongeth unto God], that is the first thing, and —
that to Adonay belongeth kindness], that is the second thing. It
is improbable that in the original there was a change of subject
to the 2d pers. The change was due probably to assimilation to

next clause, **13** *b*, which is a still later addition to the Ps. from the point of view of the Levitical Law (*v.* Rom. 2⁶ˢᑫ·).

2. אַךְ] cf. v.³· ⁵· ⁶· ⁷· ¹⁰; asseverative, *surely*, De W., Hu., Bä.; always same, prob. *only*, Ki., Che., Dr., Kirk., Ges., Ew., Hi. The Vrss. vary in verses. — אֶל אלהים = לאלהים v.⁶; latter required by measure in both. אלהים for original יהוה. — דּוּמִיָּה] n.f. *silence, resignation*, dub. *v. 22³*, דֹּמִי v.⁶, so here Bi., Gr., Che., Du., We., BDB.: דֹּמִי Qal imv. 2 f. דמם, *v. 4⁵*. The variation is prob. due to an original דמי הנפש, the sf. afterwards taking place of article. — כי v.⁶, lacking here, is prob. gl. — וִישׁוּעָתִי = תקותי v.⁶, prob. originally the same, the former an assimilation to v.³. — **3.** רַבָּה] used as adv. for רַבַּת 65¹⁰ (?) 120⁶ 123⁴ 129¹· ²; not in v.⁷, dub. and late usage not suited to early Ps.; prob. gl. Phr. so common without it (*v. 10⁶*) that change improb. — **4.** תְּהוֹתֲתוּ] Polel impf. 2 pl. הות *shout at, threaten*, BDB. *si vera*, so De., Du., Bä. Wetzstein, cf. Damascene Arab. הות *rush upon one* with cries and raised fist, so MV. SS.; Ges. התת *attack*. Form is unknown elsw. Hu. תהוללו *be frantic against*, cf. 102⁹; but 𝔊 ἐπιτίθεσθε, Aq. ἐπιβουλεύετε, 𝔍 *insidiamini*, Σ ματαιοπονήσετε. — תְּרָצְּחוּ] Pu. impf. 2 pl. רצח *murder*, Ben Napht. תְּרָצְּחוּ Pi., so 𝔊, 𝔍, Street, De., Bä., al. The absence of obj. is to be noticed. This whole clause is a gl.; change of subj. to 2d pers. from 3d pers. of Ps. — כֻּלְּכֶם] כל with sf. 2 m. pl., 𝔊 πάντες, but prob. כלם in original. This begins third l. of Str. and should have אַךְ, which has fallen out by haplog. — ‡ קִיר] n.m. *wall*, as Nu. 22²⁵ (J) 35⁴ (P) +. — ‡ גָּדֵר] n.m. *wall, fence*, as 80¹³; but more prob. ‡ גְּדֵרָה n.f., as 89⁴¹. — הַדְּחוּיָה] ptc. pass. f. דחה, *pushed in*. The article improb. after articleless n. The ה goes with previous word, as Ols., De., BDB. — **5.** מִשְּׂאֵתוֹ] emph. in position, ‡ שְׂאֵת n.f. *exaltation, dignity*, elsw. Gn. 49³ (poem) Hb. 1⁷; other mngs. not in ψ. 𝔊 has τὴν τιμήν μου, which is doubtless correct, the original here as elsw. being without sf. — לְהַדִּיחַ] Hiph. inf. cstr. נדח *thrust out*, cf. 5¹¹ and דחה v.⁴. — יִרְצוּ] Qal impf. רצה 40¹⁴, so 𝔍. But 𝔊 ἔδραμον ἐν δίψει, יָרֻצוּ, so 𝔖. — בְּפִיו] with pl. vb., err. for פימו as 𝔊, 𝔖, 𝔗. — **8.** יִשְׁעִי] *v. 12⁶* for וִישׁוּעָתִי of original Ps. — צוּר־עֻזִּי] phr. α.λ., cf. מחסי עז 71⁷, עֻז 61⁴. This v. is mere repetition of v.⁷ by another hand: a tetrameter couplet. — **9.** בְּכָל עֵת עָם] so 𝔍; but 𝔊 כל עדת עם is more prob., as Bä. עֵדָה, v. 1⁵. — שִׁפְכוּ לְבַבְכֶם] cf. similar phr. 42⁵ 102¹ 142⁸. This v. is an exhortation in 2 pl. in a trimeter tristich; another late hand. — **10.** ‡ מֹאזֲנַיִם n.[m.] only dual, *scales, balances*, Is. 40¹² Jb. 31⁶ Ez. 45¹⁰ +. This n. emph. It was originally preceded by אך, as other ll. The measure requires this. — מֵהֶבֶל] 𝔊 ἐκ ματαιότητος; מ of what they are composed. — **11.** תֶּהְבָּלוּ] Qal impf. 2 pl. † הבל vb. denom. הֶבֶל v.¹⁰. Qal *become vain, possessed of worthless self-confidence*, cf. Jb. 27¹² Je. 2⁵ = 2 K. 17¹⁵; Hiph. Je. 23¹⁶. — יָנוּב] Qal impf. † נוב *bear fruit*, fig., so of tree 92¹⁵, fig. Pr. 10³¹; Po. *make flourish* Zc. 9¹⁷. — This v. is a trimeter tetrastich, a מישל of type of WL. — **12–13a.** Another trimeter tetrastich, a מישל. — זוּ] relative, as 9¹⁶; וּלְךָ is improb. The original was doubtless וכי לאדני. The change was due either to assimilation to next clause, or to transposition of כ and ל by error.

PSALM LXIII., 3 STR. 4^3.

Ps. 63 is the longing of an exile for Yahweh (v.^{2}), remembering the glory of God in temple worship (v.^{3}), and meditating upon Him in the night (v.^{7}), with vows of perpetual worship (v.^{5}), and adherence to His support (v.^{9}). To this was appended a fragment of a royal Ps., expressing confidence in the overthrow of the enemies (v.$^{10-11}$), and the rejoicing of king and people (v.$^{12a. b}$). Several glosses emphasize various parts of the original (v.$^{4. 6. 8. 12c}$).

(YAHWEH), my God, earnestly I seek *Thee*.
My soul doth thirst for *Thee*.
My flesh doth long for *Thee*;
As a dry land it faints for *Thee*.
AS in the sanctuary I beheld *Thee*,
Seeing Thy strength and *Thy* glory,
So in my life will I bless *Thee*;
I will lift up my palms in *Thy* name.
WHEN on my couch I remembered *Thee*,
In the night watches was musing on *Thee*,
My soul did cleave after *Thee*;
On me did take hold *Thy* right hand.

Ps. 63 was in 𝔇, then in 𝔐 and 𝔈. It had the reference to David's life בהיותו במדבר יהודה in 𝔇. It was not in 𝔇ℜ (*v.* Intr. §§ 27, 31, 32). The original was composed of three trimeter tetrastichs, v.^{2} v.$^{3. 5}$ v.$^{7. 9}$, all in assonance, in ךָ—. The author seems to be in exile, away from the sanctuary, where he used to behold the glory of Yahweh. Now he can only remember his former privileges and persist in prayer and longing for a return. The situation is similar to that of Ps. 42–43. The Ps. probably comes from the early exile. The statement in the title is probably due to the use of בארץ ציה by txt. err. for כארץ ציה, a simile, and not indicating the locality of the author. To this Ps. was attached in 𝔈 a fragment of a royal Ps. v.$^{10-12b}$, a trimeter hexastich which, on account of המלך, was preëxilic, and, on account of תחתיות הארץ, was not earlier than the reign of Josiah. Possibly both Pss. were from a common author, a companion of Jehoiachin. To these Pss. several glosses were added: v.$^{4. 6. 8}$, all later than 𝔈 and all emphasizing temple worship, and therefore making the Ps. more suitable to public use. V.^{12c} is a vindictive conclusion suited to the Maccabean period.

Str. I. A syn. tetrastich. — **2.** *Yahweh, my God*], emphasizing the personal relation to Yahweh as his own God. The archaic *'El* is for the *'Elohim* usual in such combinations. It is improbable, however, that it was to emphasize the original meaning, " strong one," as 𝔍, or that it was predicate as EVˢ. after 𝔚, 𝔍; for the personal pronoun " Thou " was an interpretative insertion, making the line too long. — *earnestly I seek thee*], as one rising with the dawn, cf. Ps. 78³⁴; ‖ *thirst for Thee*], cf. 42² ‖ *long for Thee* ‖ *faints for Thee;* with the simile of *a dry land*], greatly in need of rain, cf. Je. 4³¹ Ps. 143⁶. This is explained by a gloss, " where no water is," interpreting the previous adj. as an additional attribute of land, so Vrss., " dry and weary land without water." — *my soul . . . my flesh*], the whole man.

Str. II. Two antith. syn. couplets. — **3, 5.** *As in the sanctuary*], in the worship of the temple at Jerusalem in my past experience. — *so in my life*], in my future experience. — *I beheld Thee*], explained as *seeing Thy strength and Thy glory*], in the contemplation of public worship, cf. 29¹ 59¹⁷ 68³⁵ 96⁷. In the future life *will I bless Thee*], in perpetual worship : ‖ *I will lift up my palms in Thy name*], a gesture especially of invocatory prayer, cf. 28² 141². This Str. has been enlarged by two glosses. — **4.** *For better than life is Thy kindness*]. Not only did they behold the strength and glory of Yahweh in public worship, but also His kindness ; and it was not only earnestly sought and thirsted after, it was better than life itself. This beholding of Yahweh in His temple was in oral worship : *my lips laud Thee.* As the former public worship was thus emphasized, so the future worship. — **6.** *As with marrow and fatness my soul will be satisfied*]. Doubtless the poet is thinking of the sacrificial feasts which characterised seasons of rejoicing before God in the worship of the temple, cf. 22²⁷ 23⁵ 36⁹. It is true that the fat pieces of animals always went to the altar. The poet is not thinking of them, but of the flesh of the fat young animals which alone were suitable for sacrifice, where the fat meat was eaten by the offerers and their friends, together with bread and wine. But these provisions for the flesh had as their accompaniment provisions for the soul also ; so that soul and flesh were alike and together satisfied. The glossator is evidently thinking more of the satisfaction of soul, for he adds : *and with lips of jubilation will my mouth praise*]. This tautology of 𝔚 is dubious, especially as it is not in 𝔊, which omits " my mouth," and adds to the verb " Thy name." It is probable that both are explanatory additions, and that the original was, "and my lips will praise with jubilation."

Str. III. Two synth. syn. couplets. — *When on my couch ǁ in the night watches*]. Awake during the night in the excitement due to the thirst of soul and flesh, he counted the three watches as they passed, cf. La. 2¹⁹. — *I remembered Thee ǁ was musing on Thee*], recalling the joyous experiences of public worship in the temple described in the previous Str., and doubtless also the experiences of the strength and glory of God in private and public life. — **8.** A glossator inserts a syn. couplet, *For Thou art a help to me; I rejoice in the shadow of Thy wings*], a statement only suitable to one enjoying the privilege of worship in the temple, cf. 17⁸ 36⁸ 57². — **9.** *My soul did cleave after Thee*], in close adherence, not willing to be apart from God; a phr. usual in connection with following the divine word or commands, cf. Dt. 10²⁰, also Ho. 6³; but here in the more personal relation, seeking comfort and strength. Yahweh also adheres closely to His servant. — *on me did take hold Thy right hand*]. The right hand of God is usually stretched forth with power against enemies, here with tenderness to sustain His servant, cf. 3⁶.

The editor of 𝔈 added a fragment of a royal Psalm.

> As for them that seek (his) life,
> They shall go down into the nether parts of the earth;
> They shall be delivered over unto the power of the sword;
> A portion for jackals shall they become;
> But the king will rejoice in God;
> Every one that sweareth by Him will glory.

This little piece has a syn. tetrastich and an antith. syn. couplet. — **10.** *As for them that seek his life*], to take the life of the king. The attachment of this part of the royal Ps. to the Ps. of personal experience led to the variation "my soul," as referring to the poet. This line is intensified by a gloss: that he may go down into Sheol, the place of *desolation, ǁ nether parts of the earth*, a phr. used in Ez. 26²⁰ 32¹⁸·²⁴, and subsequently Is. 44²³ Ps. 139¹⁵, for the deeper regions of Sheol. The enemies sought to send the king of Israel thither, but *they shall go down* thither themselves. Their descent, however, will not be that of ordinary death. They will be slain in battle. — **11.** *They shall be delivered over unto the* *power of the sword*]. It will be not in victory, but in defeat; for their bodies will be abandoned on the battle-field, *a portion for jackals*, which will devour them. EV⁸., "foxes," is erroneous. " It is the jackal rather than the fox which preys on dead bodies, and which assembles in troops on battle-fields to feed on the slain " (Tristram, *Nat. Hist. Bible*, p. 110). — **12**. On the other hand, the victorious *king will rejoice in God,* who gave him the victory ; and the people, *every one that sweareth by Him,* loyal servants, united in the oath of the covenant to God, *will glory*. A Maccabean editor appends to the Ps. a thought appropriate to the affliction of his time : *The mouth of them that speak lies shall be stopped.*

2. אֵלִי] divine name as ⅏, and not *fortitudo mea* of 𝔍. — אַתָּה] 𝔊, 𝔍, not in ⅏, is a gl., making l. too long. — אֲשַׁחֲרֶךָּ] Pi. impf. 1 sg., strong sf. 2 m. ‡ (שחר) vb. denom. שָׁחַר *dawn* (57⁹), Pi. *to seek with the dawn,* early, earnestly 78³⁴ Ho. 5¹⁵ Is. 26⁹ Pr. 8¹⁷. — כָּמַהּ] vb. a.λ., cf. Ar. stem, *be pale of face, weak-eyed, be blind,* so *BDB. faint,* Σ ἱμείρεταί σου, 𝔍 *desideravit,* so 𝔖, 𝔗. Ki. compares כאב, Ra. אוה. ⅏ ποσαπλῶς σοι, 𝔘 *quam multipliciter,* Θ ποσαχῶς = כַּמֶּה, *how often, how long,* not suited to context and improbable. — אֶרֶץ־צִיָּה] phr. 107³⁵ Ho. 2⁵ Je. 2⁶ 50¹² 51⁴³ Is. 41¹⁸ 53² Ez. 19¹³ Jb. 2²⁰; † צִיָּה n.f. with the same mng. *desert land* Is. 35¹ Zp. 2¹³ Jb. 30³ Ps. 78¹⁷ 105⁴¹ (as only pl. dub.) ; *drought* Jb. 24¹⁹. — וְעָיֵף בְּלִי־מָיִם] phr. dub., makes l. too long, and assonance in ךְ missing. בלי־מים is expl. gl., so Bä. ‡ עָיֵף adj. *faint, weary,* as 143⁶, עֲיֵפָה נפש Je. 31²⁵ Pr. 25²⁵, so prob. Je. 4³¹ (for עֲיֵפָה). The simile כארץ עיפה 143⁶ dependent on בארץ ציה ועיף, therefore rd. here כארץ ציה ועיפה. Neglect of agreement of עָיֵף with its noun ארץ, though justified by some, cf. Kö. *Syn.* § 334 f., is improbable. The original of all is doubtless Je. 4³¹ c. לְ. Ps. 143⁶ has לְ also, and לְךָ is demanded here for assonance. The ו is an error of interpretation. The adj. agrees with בשר, and is therefore masc. So לְךָ in two previous lines should be at the end of l. — **3.** כֵּן] has as its complement כֵּן v.⁵. These two couplets belong together in the tetrastich ; and v.⁴ is a gl. — **4.** יְשַׁבְּחוּנְךָ] Pi. impf. full form with sf. 2 sg. † (שבח) vb. Aramaism, Pi. (1) *laud, praise,* elsw. 117¹ 145⁴ 147¹²; (2) *congratulate* Ec. 4² 8¹⁵. Hithp. *boast of* Ps. 106⁴⁷ = 1 Ch. 16³⁵. — **5.** אֲבָרְכֶךָ] Pi. impf. 1 sg., sf. 2 sg., should be at the close of the l. for assonance ; so בשמך. The copyists did not regard the original order. — **6.** רְנָנוֹת] pl. † רְנָנָה n f. *jubilation,* clsw. 100⁹ Jb. 3⁷ 20⁶, late form for רִנָּה (*v. 17¹*). — וְהַלֵּל־פִּי] so 𝔍, but ⅏ αἰνέσει τὸ ὄνομά σου. It is prob. that פי is late gl. of 𝔐 to give vb. subj., and that τὸ ὄνομά σου is gl. of ⅏ to give vb. obj.; neither original. But the vb. 3 sg. is difficult in context of fem. nouns. The phr. שִׂפְתֵי רננות is a.λ., and the syntax is difficult. We should prob. rd. שְׂפָתַי as v.⁴. נפשי is explan. gl. But even as emended this v. is a gl. to the original. — **7.** אִם־זְכַרְתִּיךָ]. This is prosaic order, and assonance

requires הָ at end of l. Better euphony is also given by אִם־יָעַר. אם *when*, as 78³⁴.
— יְצוּעָי sf. 1 sg. i.p. † [יָצוּעַ] n.[m.] *spread, couch*, as 132³ Gn. 49⁴ (J) 1 Ch. 5¹
Jb. 17¹³. — אַשְׁמֻרֹת] pl. † אַשְׁמוּרָה n.f. a *watch* of night, elsw. 90⁴ 119¹⁴⁸ La. 2¹⁹.
— אֶהְגֶּה] impf. frequentative. — **8.** עֶזְרָתָה] archaic f. form ; for better euphony
with לִי, cf. 3⁴ 60¹³. — **10.** וְהֵמָּה] emph. antith. — לִשׁוֹאָה] is dub. שׁוֹאָה n.f.
desolation, v. 35⁸ ‖ with בתחתיות הארץ. ‡ תַּחְתִּי adj. *lower ;* f. תחתית with ארץ
Ez. 31¹⁴· ¹⁶· ¹⁸, שאול Dt. 32²²; תחתיה with שאול Ps. 86¹³; pl. תחתיות with בור 88⁷
= La. 3⁵⁵; with ארץ elsw. Ps. 139¹⁵ Is. 44²³ Ez. 26²⁾ 32¹⁸· ²⁴, all referring to the
deeper, gloomier regions of Sheol. So 𝔗 לקבורתא. For רִשׁוֹאָה, 𝔍 *interficere*.
𝔊 εἰς μάτην, 𝔙 *in vanum*, לשוא (*12³*) is improbable. The form is, as Bä.,
an expl. gl. It makes l. too long. נפשׁ is error of interp. for הנפשׁ referring
to the king v.¹¹. — **11.** יַגִּירֻהוּ] Hiph. impf. 3 pl., sf. 3 sg. † [נגר] vb. Aramaism. Niph. (1) *be poured, spilt*, as water 2 S. 14¹⁴, of the eye with tears
La. 3⁴⁹, fig. *vanish* Jb. 20²⁸; (2) *be extended*, of the hand Ps. 77³. Hiph.
(1) *throw down* stones Mi. 1⁶, (2) *extend* the wine cup to one Ps. 75⁹; phr.
עַל יְדֵי חֶרֶב elsw. Je. 18²¹ Ez. 35⁵; 𝔊 παραδοθήσονται εἰς χεῖρας ῥομφαίας, *BDB*
deliver over to. Hoph. ptc. Mi. 1⁴ of mts. melting in theophany. The vb. is
pl. of indef. subj. The sf. הוּ, sg. for pl., is of dub. originality. It was not
needed and was not in 𝔊. — שְׁלֵּים] pl. † שׁוּעָל. n.m. *jackal* elsw. Ne. 3⁵⁵ Ju. 15⁴
La. 5¹⁸ Ez. 13⁴ Ct. 2¹⁵· ¹⁵. — **12.** יִסָּכֵר] Niph. impf. † [סכר] vb. Aramaism for
סגר Niph., *be stopped*, here of mouth, Gn. 8² (P) of springs. Pi. *shut up*,
deliver up into the hands of, Is. 19⁴. The last half of v. is a pentameter l. if
not prose, and is a gl.

PSALM LXIV., 3 STR. 5⁴.

Ps. 64 is a plaintive cry of Israel to Yahweh for preservation
from enemies who slander and plot against him (v.²· ⁴⁻⁷ᵃ), with the
assurance that the plot will fail, because Yahweh will overcome
them by their own tongues and make them a lesson to all men
(v.⁷ᵇ⁻¹⁰). Glosses pray for hiding from evil companionship (v.³),
and express the assurance of the eventual joy and glory of the
righteous (v.¹¹).

> HEAR, Yahweh, my voice in my plaint;
>> From dread of the enemy mayest Thou preserve my life,
>> Who do whet as a sword their tongue,
>> Do aim their arrow, a bitter speech,
>> To shoot in secret places at the perfect.
> SUDDENLY they shoot at him without fear;
>> They strengthen for themselves an evil speech;
>> They talk to themselves of hiding snares;
>> They say to themselves: Who can see?
>> They search out injustice; they have hidden a plot.

IT is plotted, and each one draws nigh with a deep mind.
Then Yahweh doth shoot at them: sudden is their wound;
And He causeth them to stumble by their own tongue;
And all that look on them wag the head,
And declare His doing and His work consider.

Ps. 64 was in 𝔇, then in 𝔐, 𝔈, and 𝔇ℜ (*v.* Intr. §§ 27, 31, 32, 33). The Ps. has three tetrameter pentastichs. It is a complaint of the community of the early Restoration, encompassed by petty enemies who slander them at the court of Persia. It has two glosses: (1) V.[3], which is not in 𝔊[B], and was probably inserted subsequent to the text on which 𝔊 was based; (2) V.[11] uses יהוה, and was therefore subsequent to 𝔈 and probably also 𝔇ℜ.

Str. I. A synth. couplet and a triplet of two syn. lines and a third synth. thereto. — **2.** *in my plaint*]. Yahweh is called upon in prayer to hear the voice of His people in their perils, going up to Him in plaintive cry. — *mayest Thou preserve my life*]. The life of the nation is in peril from enemies, who make themselves to be dreaded because of their craft and cruelty. — **3.** A glossator enlarges upon these enemies as a *council of evil doers*] gathered in secret to plot their evil scheme; ‖ *companionship of workers of trouble*]; cf. 2^1 55^{15}, which is to be preferred to the "insurrection" of PBV., AV., or the "tumult" of RV., JPSV., neither of which mngs. can be established, or suits the context. From these the Psalmist prays to be hidden. — **4.** *Who do whet as a sword their tongue*, ‖ *Do aim their arrow*]. Speech of a hostile character is compared to weapons of war, the sword and the arrow; so 55^{22} 57^5 59^8. — *a bitter speech*], that which they make in slanderous hostility at the court of Persia against the feeble community of the Restoration, cf. v.[6]. — *in secret places*]. They are like enemies shooting from ambush, cf. 10^8 17^{12}. — *at the perfect*]. Israel as a people, in the unity of his organisation, is a man of integrity. His conduct has been unexceptionable towards the government of Persia and also towards these crafty foes.

Str. II is stairlike in its advance, the first line resuming the thought of the last line of previous Str. and then explaining it in syn. parallelism. — **5.** *Suddenly they shoot at him*], taking him by surprise from ambush, and accordingly *without fear*], because they have taken him altogether unprepared and unable to defend himself. This shooting is now explained as — **6.** *an evil speech*] resuming the " bitter speech " of v.[4], which *they strengthen for themselves*], giving one another mutual support, and fortifying their word by the number of false witnesses. — *They talk to themselves* ‖ *say to themselves*], in their consultation, — *of hiding snares*] that is, from the context, ensnaring words, of treacherous character. — *Who can see ?*] They persuade themselves that even the God of Israel will not see, cf. 10[4. 11. 13]. — **7a.** *They search out injustice*], diligently seek for something that they may wrest to their evil purpose, however unjust that would be. — *They have hidden a plot*]. This is the most probable rendering, and gives an appropriate climax, though sustained by but few Hebrew codd. The ordinary reading is a difficult one, which may be explained either as " accomplished " AV., RV., or as " we are innocent " JPSV.; but neither of these translations suits the context.

Str. III. is also stairlike to Str. II. It is composed of an introductory line, resuming the last line of v.[7a], and then of the antithetical couplet of divine retribution and a closing couplet showing its effect upon all observers. — **7b.** *Each one draws nigh with a deep mind*], so 𝔊, 𝔍, taking the Hebrew form as vb. MT., followed by modern Vrss., takes it as noun : " inward thought of every one " ‖ " mind," of which " deep " is the common predicate. But the connection is difficult, and the thought abrupt. The Psalmist now would say that the enemies have undertaken to carry out their treacherous plans. They draw nigh the Persian court, each and all of them, with their plan deep in their mind. But though it was hidden from Israel, it was not hidden from Yahweh, and He visits them with swift and just retribution before their plans become effective, cf. Is. 29[15]. — **8.** *Then Yahweh doth shoot at them*], in antithesis with the shooting of the enemy at Israel ; and this shooting is not only *sudden* as theirs, but it is effective, because it accomplishes *their wound.* " With an arrow " is an unnecessary explanatory addition at the expense of the measure. — **9.** The divine shooting was also in the use of words. — *He causeth them to stumble by their own tongue*]. Their own words are turned against them to their own hurt : so I venture to amend the text. The text of 𝔐 and the ancient Vrss. is corrupt and dubious as is generally agreed. All efforts to make good sense out of the text have failed. The humiliation is indeed in public in antithesis with the deeply hidden craft. — *All that look on them wag the head*], in scorn and derision, as RV., cf. 22[8] Je. 48[27], which is to be preferred to another reading: "flee away" in horror, of AV., although modern scholars are very much divided in their preferences between the two. — **10**. A glossator explains by the insertion of "and all men shall fear," at the expense of the measure. — *And declare His doing*], that is, Yahweh's, recognising the retribution as His. This is made more definite in the text by the insertion of the divine name for the suffix, making the line just this word too long. — *His work consider*], observe, contemplate, ponder it, reflect upon it and the lesson it conveys of warning and rebuke, cf. Dt. 32[29] Ps. 106[7]. — **11**. This Ps. ends like the previous one, with a similar Maccabean gloss, expressing the confidence that *the righteous* ‖ *all the upright of mind, who seek refuge* in Yahweh in their distress, will ultimately *rejoice* and *glory*, cf. 34[3] 63[12].

2. חַיָּי] but 𝕲 נַפְשִׁי more prob. The former unconscious substitution by a late copyist, owing to his interpretation of נפש as *life*. — **3**. This v. is not in 𝕲[B]; it is of different measure from Ps. and is doubtless a late gl. — רִגְשַׁת] cstr. רְגְשָׁה n.f. a.λ. 𝕲[ᴬᴿᵀ] ἀπὸ πλήθους, 𝔙 *a multitudine*, 𝔍 *a tumultu;* but acc. to context, ‖ סוד prob. *companionship*. Cf. 2[1]. — **4**. דָּבָר מָר] phr. a.λ.; should have retracted accent with דבר for euphony; so v.[6a]. ‡ מַר adj. *bitter, harsh, severe.* Cf. Ju. 18[25] Hb. 1[6]. — **5**. לִירֹת] Qal inf. cstr. ירה (*11*[2]) with לְ purpose; but Hiph. impf. with sf. 3 m. יֹרֻהוּ v.[5b], and וַיֹּרֵם Hiph. impf. sf. 3 pl. with ו consec. v.[8a]. The use of Qal in same Ps. as two Hiphs. with same mng. improb.; rd. לְהֹרֹת. — ‡ פִּתְאֹם] as v.[8] פִּתְאוֹם adv. *suddenly.* Cf. Is. 47[11] 48[3] Je. 4[20] 6[26] +. — ולא יִירָאוּ] Qal impf. i.p. ירא with neg. having force of *without*, in a circumstantial clause, Ges.[156. 3b]. 𝔖, Lowth., Street, Gr., יֵרָאוּ Niph. impf. ראה gives certainly a better parallelism, and is favoured by v.[6b]. — **6**. לָמוֹ] archaic sf. with לְ, reflexive. It is also required for measure and good sense after יספרו, used in the weakened sense of *speak*, as 59[13] 73[15]. But לָמוֹ as obj. of יִרְאֶה is unexampled and improb. It should go with אמרו. It has been misplaced. — **7**. יַחְפְּשׂוּ] Qal impf. 3 pl. ‡ חפשׂ] vb. † Qal *search out, think out*, elsw. *search for* Pr. 2[4], *search, test* La. 3[40] Pr. 20[27]. Pi. *search*, Ps. 77[7]. † Pu. *be searched*, v.[7b] as Pr. 28[12]. † חפשׂ n. [m.] *a λ. device, plot ᴮ*DBB. 𝕲 in second clause ἐξεραυνῶντες ἐξεραυνήσει = חָפַשׂ חִפֻּשִׂים, 𝔙, 𝔍, *scrutantes scrutinio* rd. חפשׂים חפשׂ, as Gr. But the l. is too long. The former goes with previous l. to complete it; the latter as Qal pf. with subsequent l. — תַּמְנוּ] is taken by Bä., Dr., al. as Qal pf. 1 pl. of תמם for תַּמֹּנוּ. But the sudden change of pers. is improb. De., Now., after 𝕲, 𝔙, 𝔍, 𝔖, take it as 3 pl. תמנו for תַּמּוּ Ges. [20. 0]. Du. follows several codd. Kenn., De Rossi, and rds. טמנו, which is favoured

by v.⁶. — וַחֲרֵב] as 5^{10} inward part of man, 𝔍 cogitationibus. But 𝔊 προσε-
λεύσεται, 𝔙 accedet = קָרֵב draw near, as 27^2. — וְלֵב] ו of accompaniment. —
‡עָמֹק] adj. deep, inscrutable, cf. Jb. 12^{22} Ec. 7^{24}. — 8. וַיֹּרֵם] ו consec. dependent on previous pfs. and thus sustaining them, unless we suppose a new
clause begins here with different tense. 𝔊 καὶ ὑψωθήσεται = יָרֻם is improbable. — פִּהְאוֹם] 𝔐 as v.⁵ᵇ, so 𝔍 ; but 𝔊 νηπίων = פְּהָאִים (19^8) the simple, so 𝔙
parvulorum. It is however improbable. — מַכַּתָם] pl. c. sf. 3 pl. ‡מַכָּה n.f.
wound, blow 1 K. 22^{35} Ze. 13^6 Is. 1^6 Je. 10^{19}+. The v. is too long for one l.,
two short for two. הֵן is unnecessary gl. ; not with vb. v⁵; so also הָיוּ. —
9. וַיַּכְשִׁילֻהוּ] Hiph. impf. 3 pl. ו consec. It is improb. that 3 sg. and 3 pl. in
same v. should refer to enemies. 𝔍 et corruent in semetipsos linguis suis, 𝔙
et infirmatae sunt contra eos linguae eorum, seem to have had no sf. but עָלֵימוֹ.
𝔊 καὶ ἐξουθένησαν αὐτὸν αἱ γλῶσσαι αὐτῶν had the sf., but not עָלֵימוֹ; prob.
𝔐 is conflation of the two. עָלֵימוֹ Dy., Hi., Now., as 90^8 is improb. The
prop. reading is with Marti, Du., וּכְשִׁלְמוֹ עָלֵי לְשׁוֹנָם. — יִתְנוֹדְדוּ] Hithp. impf.
3 pl. dub. 𝔍 fugient, Ges., Ew., Hi., BDB, נוד flee away in horror, Bä., Now.,
Du., Dr., Kirk., נוד wag the head, cf. Je. 48^{27}. ו consec. should be prefixed
as in previous and subsequent vbs. — 10. וַיִּרְאוּ כָל־אָדָם] is a gl., making the
specific reference of v.⁹ too universal. — פָּעַל אֱלֹהִים] for an original פָּעֳלוֹ : divine
name makes l. too long. — 11. יהוה] evidence of gl. of l., certainly not in 𝔐.

PSALM LXV., 2 STR. 4⁵.

Ps. 65 is an ancient song of praise in the temple at the time of
votive offering (v.²· ³ᵃ), rejoicing in the privilege of worship there
(v.⁵), and admiring the wonders of Yahweh in nature (v.⁶ᵃ· ⁷· ⁸ᵃ· ⁹ᵇ).
A gloss makes this worship a universal privilege (v.³ᵇ) and these
wonders a ground of universal confidence (v.⁶ᵇ). Another makes
them an object of fear (v.⁹ᵃ). Another thinks of the covering over
of transgression (v.⁴). Later editors add fragments of two harvest
songs in different measures : the former (v.¹⁰⁻¹¹) with reference to
the grain harvest, the latter (v.¹²⁻¹⁴) with reference to the richness
of flocks.

TO Thee a song of praise is recited, Yahweh, in Zion ;
  And to Thee a votive offering is being paid, O Hearer of prayer, in Jerusalem.
  Happy the one whom Thou choosest and bringest near to dwell in Thy courts!
  We shall be satisfied with the goodness of Thy house, the holy place of Thy
   temple.
WITH awful things in righteousness Thou answerest us, O God of our salvation,
  Who establishest the mountains by power, being girded with might;
  Who stillest the roaring of the seas, the roaring of their waves ;
  With Thy wonders the outgoings of the morning and evening Thou makest to
   jubilate.

Ps. 65 was in 𝔇 and then in 𝔐. But previously it was a שׁיר, cf. תהלה v.². It was then in 𝔈 and 𝔇ℜ (v. Intr. §§ 24, 27, 31, 32, 33). The original Ps. was v.²⁻³ᵃ· ⁵· ⁶ᵃ· ⁷· ⁸ᵃ· ⁹ᵇ, two pentameter tetrastichs, a hymn of praise to Yahweh in Zion, in peaceful times of the Restoration. Many codd. 𝔊 (HP), Comp., Ald., have ᾠδὴ Ἰερεμίου καὶ Ἰεζεκιὴλ καὶ τοῦ λαοῦ τῆς παροικίας ὅτε ἔμελλον ἐκπορεύεσθαι; so 𝕴, 𝔙. But this is an impossible assignment. It was written for use in public worship in Palestine. The universalism of v.³ᵇ⁻⁴· ⁶ᵇ· ⁸ᵇ⁻⁹ᵃ is due to a later editor. Two fragments of harvest songs were added, possibly in 𝔈. The first, of five tetrameter lines, v.¹⁰⁻¹¹; the second, of seven trimeter lines, v.¹²⁻¹⁴.

Str. I. has a syn. and a synth. couplet. — **2.** *To Thee*], emphatic in position and repeated at the beginning of the next line. — *a song of praise*], a hymn, as 𝔊, 𝔙, accompanying a *votive offering*, both specific and not general, " praise " and " vow," as EVˢ. — *is recited*], the most probable reading ‖ *is being paid*, to be preferred to " silence," " resignation," 𝔐, 𝔍, 𝔗, or " is becoming," " beseemeth," 𝔊, 𝔖, 𝔙, which seems to be inappropriate paraphrase. The paraphrase of AV., RV., " waiteth," is still less justifiable. — **3.** A later glossator, influenced by Is. 56⁷ 66²³, gives this worship a universal reference by insertion of : *unto Thee all flesh come.* — **4.** A still later glossator makes the Ps. more suitable to ordinary worship by inserting a reference to the covering over of sins. — *matters of iniquities*], interpreted in the ‖ as *our transgressions.* — *have (they) prevailed over (us)*], so 𝔊 ; been too strong for us and so overcome us, involving us in transgression. 𝔐, 𝔍, have " over me," changing the person to pl. in the second clause. If the original was singular, it is still the congregation that is speaking. But the plural is more suitable to the later period of the glossator. This clause is the protasis of the apodosis : *Thou coverest them over*]. This was in the later ritual accomplished by the sin offering ; but more frequently in ψ by the sovereign grace of God without sacrifice, cf. 32¹ 78³⁸ 79⁹. — **5.** *Happy the one*] ; cf. 1¹. — *whom Thou choosest and bringest near to dwell in Thy courts*], not referring especially to the Levitical privileges in the temple, but more generally to all worshippers who have this right of daily worship as members of the sacred community, cf. 15¹ 23⁶ 24³ 27⁴ 84⁵. — *We shall be satisfied with the goodness of Thy house*], the bountiful provisions made there for the body and soul of the worshipper, cf. 36⁹ 63⁶. — *the holy*

G

place of Thy temple], not technically, the holy place as distinguished from the most holy, the palatial reception room, to which
only priests were admitted ; but, as usual in ψ, the holy place as
identical with the temple in its more general sense as embracing
the entire sacred enclosure, cf. 48^{10} 79^1 138^2.

   Str. II.   A tetrastich of introverted parallelism. — **6–9.** *With
awful things*], things or deeds of Yahweh inspiring awe, and so
|| *with Thy wonders*], v.[9]; not miracles in the technical sense,
although this word is often used for them ; but, as the context
shows, the tokens or signs of the divine power in the control
of the great forces of nature. — *in righteousness*], not judicial,
forensic, or legal ; but, as usual in ψ, vindicatory and saving,
and accordingly emphasized in *O God of our salvation.* — *Thou
answerest us*], responding to the prayers and worship of His
people. — *the outgoings of the morning and evening Thou makest
to jubilate*].   It is probable that this does not refer to sunrise and
sunset, the East and West as the extreme limits of the earth, with
universal significance; but rather to sunrise and sunset as the
limits of the day, and so the goings out of morning and evening
worship in the temple.   These jubilate in the assurance that
Yahweh has answered the prayers of His people with salvation.
It is evident, however, that a later editor gave the former interpretation, for he inserts in v.[6b] *the confidence of the extremities of
the earth*, and supplements by *the isles afar off*, which by copyist's
error appears in the text as " the sea of them that are afar off,"
certainly an awkward expression. — *Who establishest the mountains by power*].   The mountains are conceived in ψ as the strong,
stable, and permanent parts of the earth, the most appropriate
representatives of divine power, cf. 36^7 90^2 Pr. 8^{25}. — *being girded
with might*], passive or possibly reflexive, " girding Thyself with
might," cf. 93^1; that is, for so great a task. — *Who stillest the
roaring of the seas*], the other great representatives of power in
nature, cf. 36^7 89^{10} 93^4; defined more closely as *the roaring
of their waves.*   There should be little doubt that the origi-
nal Ps. referred to the real seas || with the real mountains.   But
a later editor, wishing to give it figurative sense, interprets it
as *the tumult of the peoples*, cf. 46^7, but at the expense of
the measure. — Another glossator adds, *and so the dwellers*

in the extremities (of the earth) *fear.* The power of God as put forth upon the sea causes universal fear. But this conception is not homogeneous to its context, or to the thought of the Ps.

A fragment of a hymn for the grain harvest is now appended consisting of five tetrameters.

> Thou dost visit the earth, and water it, to enrich it.
> The brook of God is full of water.
> Thou preparest their grain, yea, thus Thou preparest it,
> Its furrows saturating, settling its ridges;
> Thou meltest it with showers, its growth blessest.

— **10.** *Thou dost visit the earth*]. The poet conceives of God as coming Himself in the storm, and as really present and sending rain upon the earth, cf. Ps. 29 Jb. 38^{25-27}. — *and water it*], the most probable reading. By dittography of a single letter the text gives "makest it overflow," thinking of a drenching, flooding rain. — *to enrich it*]. The impf. subj. expressing purpose. This has been intensified by a later scribe, at the expense of the measure, by the insertion of the adv. "greatly." — *The brook of God is full of water*]. The sources of rain are here conceived in a superterrestrial brook or river, cf. Gn. 1^7 Jb. 38^{25}, and being entirely at the disposal of God, it is especially His river; and as the source of all rain it is always full and never becomes dry. — *Thou preparest their grain*]. The grain harvest is prepared by God Himself; the sending of the rain upon the land is one of the most important parts of that preparation. — *yea, thus Thou preparest it*]. The particle has the intensive rather than the causal meaning. — **11.** *Its furrows saturating, settling its ridges*], that is, the ploughed field after planting. — *Thou meltest it with showers*]. The land, which otherwise would become hardened and compacted by the baking heat of the sun, is kept in a soft condition by a succession of showers during the season of the early germination of the grain. — *its growth blessest*]. This is the result of the whole process. The grain is blessed in its growth, and eventually comes to maturity in the harvest.

The harvest song of the flocks is now appended in a trimeter heptastich.

> Thou dost crown the year of Thy goodness;
> And Thy tracks drip with fatness,
> The pastures of the wilderness drip;
> And the hills gird themselves with rejoicing;
> The (mountains) clothe themselves with flocks;
> And the valleys cover themselves with lambs;
> They shout for joy; yea, they sing.

— **12**. *Thou dost crown the year of Thy goodness*]. The year is
a year characterised by the goodness, the beneficent care of God
over the flocks of His people. Goodness is not that with which
the year is crowned, or brought to its conclusion, as EV⁵.; but
the entire year has been a good year, and it is crowned by the
rich and abundant flocks of the subsequent context. — *And Thy
tracks drip with fatness*]. The tracks or footsteps of God, as He
visits the land to bless it, drip with fatness, or rather with those
refreshing, invigorating, and enriching showers which produce fat
pastures and fat flocks. — **13**. *The pastures of the wilderness drip*].
The wilderness in Palestine is the ordinary place for the pasturing
of flocks. These are so rich that they themselves drip with fatness. — *And the hills gird themselves with rejoicing*]. The hills
of the wilderness are so rich in pasture that they rejoice in their
richness, cf. 96¹¹⁻¹². — **14**. *The mountains*]. This is the most
probable reading, to be preferred to "pastures," 𝕳, AV., RV.,
which is an awkward repetition, or "lambs," ancient Vrss., which
gives a dubious sense. — *clothe themselves with flocks*]. Personified, they put on as clothing flocks of sheep and goats so numerous as to cover them from top to bottom. — *And the valleys
cover themselves over with lambs*]. The ‖ suggests this rendering,
although 𝕳 and Vrss. all give "grain." — *They shout for joy*],
resuming l. 4, and in climax — *yea, they sing*.

2. דְּמִיָּה] n.f. *silence, resignation* (22³). But Vrss. except 𝕿 either ptc. as
Aq. σιωπῶσα, 𝕵 *silens*, or pf. 𝕲 πρέπει = נאוה 𝕾, 𝔙, as 147¹, which latter is
prob. paraphrase, although regarded as the meaning of Qal ptc. דְּמִיָּה √דמה
(17⁴) by Ew., Bä., Du. This mng. has not, however, been sustained, although
the syn. שׁוה has it in late Heb. It is better in this early Ps. to cf. Ho. 12¹¹
דְּמָה *recite a poem*, and point here דְּמֶה Pu. 3 m. 113 codd. HP, 𝕲ᴺ·ᴿ·ᵀ, Compl.,
Ald., 𝔙, add בירושלם; so Hare, Che., PBV., justified by parall. — **3**. שֹׁמֵעַ] Qal
ptc. ‖ אלהיכ, for original יהוה. 𝕲, 𝔙, 𝕵, imv., not so prob. It is the necessary complement of the previous l. and does not go with the following clause,

as 𝔎, Vrss. This clause, a trimeter, is a gl. with a later universalistic reference. — **4.** דִּבְרֵי עֲוֹנֹת] phr. a.λ. *matters* or *affairs of iniquities*, 𝔊 λόγοι ἀνόμων,
𝔍 *verba iniquitatum.* — מֶנִּי] so 𝔍, sf. I sg. not suited to context. 𝔊 has
ἡμᾶς, מִמֶּנּוּ, so Gr., Du. But the whole v. is a gl., and it may be that the two
parts of it had a different origin. The conception of forgiveness of sins was
suitable for liturgical use of Ps. but is not in accord with the context of this
hymn of praise. — **5.** אַשְׁרֵי] pl. cstr. before relative clause, Ges.[155. 2] (*v. 1¹*).
— יִשְׁכֹּן] Qal impf. final clause, Ges.[120. 1b. 2]. — הֲצֵרֶיךָ] pl. sf. 2 m. ‡ חָצֵר n.m.
enclosure, court, ψ always of temple ; elsw. 84[3. 11] 92[14] 96[8] 100[4] 116[19] 135[2]. —
קֹדֹשׁ הֵיכָלֶךָ] phr. a.λ. קָדוֹשׁ *holy place* of the temple, cf. הֵיכַל קָדְשֶׁךָ 5[8] +. While
a transposition is possible, cf. Aq. ναοῦ ἁγίού σου, yet most Vrss. have the
order of 𝔎, as 𝔊 ἄγιος ὁ ναός σου. But 𝔍 *sanctificatione templi tui*, as if
קֹדֶשׁ. This is to be preferred with Bä., as best suited to previous clause and
the vb. — **6.** תַּעֲנֵנוּ] Qal impf. 2 m., present, not juss. as 𝔊, 𝔍, or future EV[s].
— רַחֹקֵי־אֶרֶץ] phr. elsw. 48[11] Is. 26[15]. — וְיָם רְחֹקִים] is not in 𝔊[B], but in 𝔊[א. c. a. R. T],
𝔍 *maris longinqui.* יָם is suspicious with following pl. Accordingly Gr., We.,
Du., rd. אִיִּים, as Is. 66[19]. If the l. were original, the second half would be
needed for measure. The omission of the second half in 𝔊[B] makes it suspicious. This opinion is fortified by its universalism, which is in accord with
v.[8b] but not with this temple Ps. as a whole. — **7.** בְּכֹחוֹ] but 𝔊, 𝔍, כחך, both
sfs. interpretations, rd. כֹּחַ ‖ גבורה. It is tempting to rd. with Gr. נאזרי בכה, as
Ex. 15[6]. — **8.** וַהֲמוֹן] is attached by 𝔎, 𝔍, to previous clause as noun (*37¹⁶*) ;
by 𝔊 to subsequent clause, taking it as vb. ταραχθήσονται, 𝔙 *turbabunter* =
יֶהֱמוּ Qal pf. הָמָה (*39⁷*). If original, the latter is to be preferred, as it makes
a complete and harmonious l.; but it looks like an explanatory gl. — **9.** וַיִּירְאוּ]
ו consec. is not suited to context, unless with Dr. it is interpreted as result,
Ges.[111. 3b]. — קְצָוֹת] a.λ. ψ, pl. קְצָה improb., esp. in view of v.[6] ; prob. קָצֶה, cf.
19[7]. But it is strange that we have not קְצָוֵי ארץ as v.[6]. The whole of this
clause is prob. gl. by same hand as v.[3b], v.[6]. — מֵאוֹתֹתֶיךָ]. מִן gives the ground
and reason, not of the fear, but of the rejoicing. It goes with the subsequent
context to complete the measure and is ‖ נֹרָאוֹת, which begins the Str. ‡ אוֹת
n.m. (1) *sign, token*, 86[17] ; (2) *sign, wondrous deed, miracle*, 74[9] 78[43] 105[27]
135[9], so here ; (3) *standard* 74[4. 4]. Other mngs. not in ψ. — מוֹצָאֵי] as 19[7],
cf. 75[7] ; refers to the dawning sun, but cannot refer to the evening, which is
a place of entrance, not of outgoing. — **10.** וַתִּשְׁקְקֶהָ ו consec. Po. impf. † שׁוּק
Hiph. *overrun, overstream*, Jo. 2[24] 4[13]. Polel causative, *cause to overflow*, a.λ.
here ; but Vrss. all take it as if וַתַּשְׁקֶהָ, and prob. this is the correct reading,
the double ק being dittog. It is possible, however, that they interpreted שֹׁקֵק
= שׁקה, *v.* 36[9]. — רַבַּת] adv. as 120[6] 123[1] 129[1. 2], but 𝔊 ἐπλήθυνας רָבִיתָ followed by impf. of purpose. This certainly best explains the impf., תַּעְשְׁרֶיהָ
Hiph. of עשׁר (cf. 49[17]) with strong sf. 3 f. The l. is, however, pentameter,
like the previous context, when it really goes with the subsequent context,
which is tetrameter. רבת is therefore to be regarded as a gl. of adverbial
intensification. The assonance in ה‑ָ begins with this l. and continues through
v.[11]. — תְּכֹנְנֶהָ] sf. interp., not in Σ ; so Lowth., Street. — **11.** תְּלָמֶיהָ] pf. sf. 3 sg.

† חֶלֶם n.m. *furrow*, elsw. Jb. 31³⁸ 39¹⁰ Ho. 10⁴ 12¹². — רָוָה] Pi. inf. abs. רוה/√
(36⁹), so נחת/√ נַחַת (18³⁵). — גְּרוּדֶךָ] defectively written pl., sf. 3 f. † גְּרוּד *fur-row, ridge, cutting*, elsw. Je. 48³⁷ cuttings upon hands. — † רְבִיבָם] def. written pl., *copious showers*, elsw. 72⁶ Dt. 32² Mi. 5⁶ Je. 3³ 14²². — תְּמֹגְגֶנָה] Po. impf. 2 m., strong sf. 3 f. מוג. — צִמְחָהּ] sf. 3 f. † צֶמַח n.m. *sprouting, growth*, as Je. 23⁵ = 33¹⁵ Zc. 3⁸ 6¹². It should close the l. for assonance. V.¹⁰⁻¹¹ give five tetrameters, a fragment of another Ps. added to the previous one. — **12.** שְׁנַת] cstr. sg. שָׁנָה, so 𝕲; but 𝕵 and EVˢ. take it as abs., which is inadmissible. — יִרְעֲפוּן] full form 3 pl. Qal impf., *v.* v.¹³. † רָעַף] vb. *trickle*, elsw. *drop*, of clouds Jb. 36²⁸, dew Pr. 3²⁰. Hiph. *trickle* Is. 45⁸. — **14.** כָּרִים] pl. כַּר n.m. dub., cf. 37²⁰; usually *pastures*, but 𝕵 *agnis greges*, 𝕲 οἱ κριοὶ τῶν προβάτων. But context suggests הָרִים, as Hare, Street, Houb. — יַעְטְפוּ] Aramaism † עָטַף, elsw. 73⁶ *put on, cover oneself with*, ‖ לבש; 𝕲 πληθυνοῦσιν, 𝔙 *abundabunt*, 𝕵 *plenae erunt.* — בַּר †] n.m. grain, as 72¹⁶ Am. 5¹¹ 8⁵·⁶ Gn. 41³⁵·⁴⁹ 42³·²⁵ 45²³ (E) Je. 23²⁸ Ju. 2²⁴ Pr. 11²⁶. But although sustained by ancient Vrss., it is difficult to see a sufficient reason for passing over from flocks to grain. The most natural word in ‖ is כרים *lambs*, which by copyist's error went into previous l., so making a double difficulty. — יִתְרוֹעָעוּ] Hithp. impf. 3 pl. רוע, *v. 41¹².*

PSALM LXVI.

Ps. 66 is composite: (*A*) **A song of praise to Yahweh** (v.¹⁻². ⁸) for His ancient deliverance of Israel at the Red Sea (v.⁶), His watch over the nations (v.⁷ᵃ· ᵇ), and His present protection of His people (v.⁹); with glosses emphasizing this praise (v.⁴), representing how awe-inspiring His deeds are to enemies in particular (v.³) and to mankind in general (v.⁵): and warning the refractory (v.⁷ᶜ). The editor of 𝔈 adds a reflection upon severe trials through which the nation has passed before Yahweh brought them forth into safety (v.¹⁰⁻¹²). (*B*) **A prayer connected with rich and abundant sacrifices in the temple in fulfilment of vows made in time of distress** (v.¹³⁻¹⁵), a grateful public acknowledgment of the deliverance God had wrought in answer to prayer (v.¹⁶⁻¹⁷· ¹⁹⁻²⁰), with a gloss intimating that the Lord would not have heard, if the people had contemplated wickedness (v.¹⁸).

A. v.¹ᵇ⁻². ⁶⁻⁷ᵇ. ⁸⁻⁹, 3 STR. 2³, RF. 2³.

*S*HOUT *to* (*Yahweh*) *all the earth;*
  Make melody unto His name in a song of praise to Him,
 Who turned the sea into dry land,
 That they might pass through the flood on foot.

(LET all the earth worship Yahweh.)
 Let us rejoice (in His name with a song of praise to Him),
Who ruleth by His might forever:
His eyes over the nations keep watch.
 BLESS (Yahweh), ye peoples;
 And let your voice be heard in a song of praise to Him,
Who setteth us in life,
And doth not suffer our foot to be moved.

B. v.¹³⁻²⁰, 2 STR. 7³.

I WILL come into Thy house with whole burnt offering:
 I will pay my votive offerings to Thee,
 Wherewith my lips opened,
 And which my mouth spake, when I was in distress.
 Fat ones will I cause to ascend to Thee,
 Together with the incense of rams,
 Bullocks together with he-goats.
COME, hearken; and I will tell
 What He hath done for me.
 Unto Him did I call with my mouth,
 And high praise was under my tongue.
 Verily (Yahweh) heard;
 He attended to the voice of my prayer.
 He did not turn away His kindness from me.

Ps. 66 is a Ps. of 𝕳, 𝕰, and 𝕯𝕽 (*v.* Intr. §§ 31, 32, 33). It was originally a שיר, and also a תהלה v.² ⁸, a תפלה v.¹⁹· ²⁰ (*v.* §§ 1, 24). In 𝕲 ἀναστάσεως, so 𝖞, because of liturgical use as a Ps. of the Resurrection; certainly not original. It is one of the two Pss. of 𝕯𝕽, 66–67, which were not in 𝔹, 𝕶, 𝕬. It is indeed a composite Ps., *A* v.²⁻⁹, *B* v.¹³⁻²⁰, with many glosses. The original שיר, תהלה, was probably only *A*, and was composed of three trimeter tetrastichs. It resembles the royal group 96–100 in tone and style, though simpler and earlier. It is doubtless postexilic, and belongs to peaceable times because of its optimistic universalism. V.¹⁰⁻¹² is a beautiful trimeter heptastich, seeming to be a complete strophe of a longer Ps. describing severe national afflictions and deliverance from them. It is in the style of Is. 2 and was earlier than v.²⁻⁹. It was probably added to the previous Ps. in 𝕳. V.¹³⁻²⁰ is a temple Ps. of two trimeter heptastichs, certainly composed in Palestine in connection with sacrificial worship. It was doubtless later than the other two pieces, and may have been added to them by 𝕯𝕽. The glosses are of various kinds. V.³ is a pentameter couplet, implying a divine judgment upon enemies; of uncertain date, but cf. 81¹⁶ for similar use of vb. כחש. V.⁴ is a confused line, modified to suit its present context; but originally the introductory couplet of the 2d Str. of the Ps. V.⁵ is a tetrameter couplet, the first line of which was taken from 46⁹. It was certainly inserted subsequent to v.⁴, separating it from its original connection with v.⁶ᶜ. V.⁷ᶜ has a word used elsw., Ps. 68[7. 19] cf. 78[8], and probably was inserted under its influence. V.[18] is a late qualifying insertion, expressing a legal attitude. V.[20a] is a liturgical ejaculation, adapted to its context. Probably none of these glosses were in 𝔈 or 𝔇ℜ.

PSALM LXVI. *A.*

The three Strs. have each a syn. couplet of the nature of a Rf., a summons to praise ; and a synth. couplet giving the reason. **1–2.** *Shout to Yahweh* ‖ *make melody unto His name*] evidently from the context in public worship in the temple. The call appears as a couplet at the beginning of each strophe in variant terms. *Bless Yahweh* ‖ *let your voice be heard* v.[8]. The second Str. has lost its introductory couplet through the insertion of the glosses v.[3-5]; but probably it was transposed and transformed, and should be *worship Yahweh* v.[4a] ‖ *let us rejoice in His name* v.[6c]. This call is emphasized by a glossator in v.[2] by attaching (in 𝔋, not in 𝔊) *glory* to " His name," and by inserting (in both 𝔋 and 𝔊) *make glorious*; both at the expense of the measure. Moreover, the transposition of the Rf. of Str. II. into connection with v.[3] made it necessary to change the 3d pers. into the 2d pers. — *in a song of praise to Him*], a temple hymn ; repeated in v.[8] and probably also in the missing Rf. — *all the earth*], v.[4a], probably in missing Rf. ‖ *peoples*, v.[8]. The author conceives of Yahweh as the God of the whole world and of all peoples ; and of the religion of Israel as a universal religion in which all men share. The reason for this universal praise is given in the second couplet of the Strophes. — **6.** *Who turned the sea into dry land*], referring to the passage of the Red Sea by Israel when he went up out of Egypt, cf. 74[13] 78[13], based on the narrative Ex. 14[21 sq.] 15[19]. — *That they might pass through the flood on foot*], probably referring to the same event, because of the subord. impf., and not to the subsequent passage of the river Jordan. The attachment of v.[6c] to the foregoing, occasioned the textual error which compels the rendering *There let us rejoice in Him*]. This is usually explained out of the consciousness of the unbroken continuity of national life. But throughout this Ps. the author is addressing the nations, and not the Israelites either of the present or of the past, or in the unity of their national life. — **7.** *Who ruleth by His might forever*], the universal Ruler whose dominion extends also through

all time. It is tempting to think with ℨ, ℭ, Calv., Hi., of עוֹלָם
in the sense of "age of the world," but this meaning is much later
than this Ps. and the vb. requires the prep. and not the acc. —
His eyes over the nations keep watch]. As Kirk., "He is the
world's watchman, sleeplessly on the watch lest any foe should
injure Israel;" but also, as the context implies, in watchful care
of the nations themselves, who are summoned to praise on that
account. — **9**. *Who setteth us in life*], not referring to the birth
of the nation or the individual; but to the preservation of the life
of the nation and deliverance out of peril to life. — *And doth not
suffer our foot to be moved*], of the firm establishment of the
nation, cf. 55²³. A later editor, in an entirely different spirit from
that of the author of the original Ps., who evidently lived in peaceful times of friendliness to the nations, expresses his own unfriend-
liness to them by inserting a warning at the close of v.⁷ — *as for
the refractory*], cf. 68⁷·¹⁹, also 78⁸; those obstinately resisting the
divine rule and refusing to take part in the worship of the universal ruler. — *let them not exalt themselves*], "their head" or
"their horn," cf. 3⁴ 75⁵. — Probably the same hand inserted
3. *Say to God: How awe-inspiring are Thy works!*] cf. 64¹⁰. —
*Because of the greatness of Thy strength Thine enemies come cring-
ing unto Thee*], cf. 18⁴⁵ 81¹⁶. — Another and a later hand inserted
5 a similar thought from 46⁹ᵃ, *Come and see the deeds of God;*
and a variation of 46⁹ᵇ, *Awe-inspiring in doing unto the children
of mankind*.

V.¹⁰⁻¹² is probably a Str. taken from a larger Ps. and added by
the editor of 𝔈.

> Though Thou hast tried us (Yahweh),
> Refined us as silver is refined;
> Didst bring us into a net,
> Didst lay constraint on our loins;
> Didst let men ride over our head;
> We went through fire and water:
> Thou didst yet bring us out into a spacious place.

This heptastich has six syn. lines in protasis, preparatory to a
single line in apodosis. — **10**. *Thou hast tried us*], explained in ‖
as silver is refined. This simile of the testing of affliction is
common in OT., cf. Is. 1²⁵ 48¹⁰ Je. 9⁷ Ze. 13⁹ Mal. 3²·³. — **11**. *bring
us into a net*] Jb. 19⁶, cf. Ez. 12¹³ 17²⁰, favours the more general

reference rather than the specific reference to a net spread by
enemies, Ps. 9^{16}. — *Didst lay constraint on our loins*]. The loins
are the seat of pain, Is. 21^3 Na. 2^{10}, and weakness, Ps. 69^{24}. —
12. *Didst let men ride over our head*]. They were thrown down
in the highway, so that chariots were driven over them, cf. Is. 51^{23}.
We went through fire and water] as the climax, summary statement of trial, cf. Is. 43^2. — *Thou didst yet bring us out*] from all
these afflictions, *into a spacious place*], as ancient Vrss.; a place
where, free from all restraint, they had breathing space, ample
room, and liberty of movement, cf. Ps. 18^{20}. EV^s. "wealthy
place," based upon text of 𝔐, is not so well suited to context, and
improbable.

PSALM LXVI. *B.*

Str. I. Five syn. lines enclosing, after the first two, a synth.
couplet. — **13–15**. *I will come into Thy house*], for public worship
in the temple. The nation is speaking in its unity, and not a
priest or king as an individual. — *with whole burnt offering*], the
usual sacrifice to express public worship. The whole burnt offering consisted of *votive offerings*. This is more suited to ∥ than
"vows" of EV^s; for the entire Str. has to do with whole burnt
offerings, which are then described as *fat ones*, the choicest, fattest
animals, *rams, bullocks, he-goats*, representing the best of the
herds and the flocks, in great numbers such as were appropriate
only for a national sacrifice. These the nation says *I will pay*],
that which was vowed. — *Wherewith my lips opened* ∥ *which my
mouth spake, when I was in distress*] in a time of national trial
from which they had just been delivered. — *will I cause to ascend
to Thee*] in the flames of the altar; as is evident a *whole burnt
offering*, but a glossator inserts this at the expense of the measure;
so also in the next line *I will offer*, which was sufficiently evident
from *the incense of rams*], the sweet odour of the burning flesh, as
1 S. 2^{28} Ps. 141^2 Is. 1^{13}, and not the incense of fine spices burnt at
the altar of incense.

Str. II. is composed of a synth. couplet, a syn. couplet, and a
syn. triplet. — **16**. *Come, hearken; and I will tell*]. The usual
vow to tell of the divine deliverance, publish it, make it known to
the public, to all the world, cf. $22^{23. \, 26. \, 32}$ 32^8 $40^{10. \, 11}$. A later glos-

sator limits the general reference to a particular class : *all ye that fear God;* but the measure does not allow it. — *What He hath done for me*] in delivering me out of the distress of v.¹⁴. The נפשׁי is as usual a poetic expression for the person, and does not refer to the soul as distinguished from the body. — **17**. *Unto Him did I call with my mouth*] in time of distress ; not merely a plaintive prayer for help, but with an assurance of speedy deliverance. —*high praise*], expressed in a hymn of praise, anticipating the deliverance. — *was under my tongue*], ready to burst forth in speech. —**19**–**20**. *Verily Yahweh heard*], emphasizing the fact which is expressed in syn. clauses as *He attended to the voice of my prayer,* and *He did not turn away His kindness from me*]. The latter is explained by a glossator by the unnecessary insertion of *prayer,* and the former is emphasized by the exclamation *Blessed be God!* The Vrss. render the adverb, " but " instead of " verily " ; because of the insertion by a glossator of the qualification : **18**. *If I contemplated wickedness in my mind, the Lord would not hear*]. This is from a more legal point of view than that of the author of the Ps.

LXVI. A.

2. כָּבוֹד שְׁמוֹ]. ﹾ has only שׁמו. The phr. is suspicious. It looks like a variation of שׁימו כבוד which in archaic Heb. would differ only in order of words. The text is a conflation of two variants. The original was זמרו שׁמו תהללתו. So v.⁸ has two ll., not three. — **3** has two pentameters and 2d sg., and is therefore a gl. — **4**. וְיִזַמְרוּ לָךְ] is a duplicate of יזמרו שמך. There is no good measure or propriety in this duplication. The latter prob. goes with v.⁶ᶜ. — **5**. לכו וראו מפעלות אלהים] This l. is tetrameter, a citation from 46⁹ᵃ except וראו for חזו and אלהים for יהוה. The second l. is also tetrameter, and a variation of 46⁹ᵇ. This v. is a late gl. — **6** returns to 3d pers. and continues v.² giving the theme of the hymn of praise. — הָפַךְ] But ﹾ, 𝕾, ptc. as v.⁷· ⁹ more correct. — יַעֲבְרוּ] Qal. impf. is subjunctive after הפך, expressing purpose. — שָׁם נִשְׂמְחָה בּוֹ] is an abrupt change in tone improb. in the original between v.⁶ᵃ· ᵇ and v.⁷. As the previous and subsequent Strs. begin with a couplet of universal praise, we would expect one here. It is prob. that this couplet is only obscured in v.⁴ and v.⁶ᶜ, verses which originally were together before the insertion of v.⁵. The couplet was prob. therefore

השתחוו ליהוה כל הארץ
בשמו נשמחה תהללתו

נשמחה is cohort. 1 pl., and can hardly be used with reference to the past. — **7**. הַסּוֹרְרִים] Qal ptc. pl. ‡ סרר vb. *be stubborn, rebellious,* elsw. pl. 68⁷· ¹⁹, sg.

78[8]. — אַל־יִרִימוּ לָמוֹ] Kt. Hiph. juss. with ראש or קרן to be supplied in thought, and לָמוֹ *dativus commodi ;* Qr. Qal יָרוּמוּ. — 8. אֱלֹהֵינוּ] for אלהים original יהוה as v.[1]. — 9. נַפְשֵׁנוּ] so 𝔍, but 𝔊, 𝔙, נפשי; the same difference in רגלנו, רגלי; both variations of interpretation of an original רגל, נפשׁ. — 10. The 2d pers. begins here and continues through v.[12] in trimeter ll. It is a fragment of an independent Ps. — 11. † מְצוּדָה] n.f. *net* spread by hunter as Ez. 12[13] 17[20], so here 𝔊, 𝔖, 𝔗, 𝔙; fig. *prey* Ez. 13[21]. Aq. Σ, 𝔗, Quinta, *prison,* cf. Ez. 19[9], so Luther, Bä.; but this latter in ψ always of God as refuge, v. 18[3]. מוּצָקָה] n.f. *a.λ. compression, distress, B*DB., 𝔊 θλίψεις, 𝔙 *tribulationes,* 𝔍 *stridorem,* Σ κύκλωσιν. The form is prob. error for מְצוּקָה 25[17]. — † מָתְנַיִם] n.m. dual *loins* as seat of strength and weakness, as 69[24]. — 12. לְרְוָיָה] *to satiety,* as 23[5]; but rd. prob. לְרְוָחָה as 𝔊 εἰς ἀναψυχήν, 𝔙, 𝔍 *refrigerium,* also 𝔗 לִרְוַחְתָּא, 𝔖 רוחתו Σ εὐρυχωρίαν, Gr., Houb., Horsley, Bä., Che., al.

LXVI. B.

13. A change to 1st pers. introduces still another Ps. which continues to v.[20]. — 15. מֵיחִים] fully written for מֵחִים as Is. 5[17] *fat ones.* עֹלוֹת is prob. a gl. of explan. making l. too long. — ‡ קְטֹרֶת] n.f. usually *incense ;* but here, as in Is. 1[13] 1 S. 2[28], the earlier mng. of *odour of sacrifice,* cf. Ps. 141[2]. אֵילִים] pl. ‡ אַיִל n.m. *ram,* the animal as skipping, 114[4. 6]; as a victim offered in sacrifice here as commonly in OT. — ‡ בָּקָר] n.m. usually generic *cattle,* here as often specific *oxen,* sg. coll. — 16. לְכוּ שִׁמְעוּ] two Qal imvs. without conj., emph., with apod. וַאֲסַפְּרָה Pi. cohort. 1 p. — אלהים] But 𝔊 κύριος implies אדני, as v.[18], is most prob. original, and favours the opinion that both clauses are glosses. — 17. פִּי] second subj., cf. 3[5]. — רוֹמַם] Polal רום *he was extolled.* But Ges., Hu., Now., Che., Bä., Bu., BD*B.,* † רוֹמֵם n.[m.] *extolling, high praise, song of praise,* as pl. רוֹמֵמוֹת אֵל 149[6]. Gr. rds. here רוֹמַמְתִּי, the final ת having been omitted by txt. err. because of initial ת of next word. This is most prob., only rd. רוֹמֵמוֹת, the sf. being unnecessary. — 18. אָוֶן] emph. in position ; but whole v. a qualifying gl. as אדני makes most prob. — 20. בָּרוּךְ אלהים אשר] is doubtless a liturgical gl. It destroys the measure. תְּפִלָּתִי is also a gl.

PSALM LXVII., 3 str. 5[3].

Ps. 67 is a summons to all nations to give thanks to Yahweh (v.[4-5a. 6]) and do reverence (v.[8b]), because His salvation is made known to all through the divine benediction of Israel (v.[2-3]) ; He governs all nations in equity (v.[5b. c]), and He blesseth Israel with a fertile land (v.[7]).

> YAHWEH, be gracious to us, and bless us,
>   Make His face shine toward us,
>   (And give peace to us) ;
>   That Thy way may be known in the earth,
>   Thy salvation among all nations.

L ET the peoples give Thee thanks, Yahweh!
   Let the peoples, all of them, give Thee thanks!
   Let the nations be glad, let them jubilate;
   For Thou governest the peoples with equity,
   And leadest the nations in the earth.
L ET the peoples give Thee thanks, Yahweh!
   Let the peoples, all of them, give Thee thanks!
   The earth hath yielded her increase.
   Yahweh our God blesseth us;
   Therefore let all the ends of the earth do reverence.

Ps. 67 was first in 𝕳, then taken up into 𝕰 and 𝔇𝖱 ; but it was composed at an earlier date as a שיר, which expresses its character (*v.* Intr. §§ 24, 31, 32, 33). In 𝔇𝖱 it was assigned to be sung בנגינת (*v.* Intr. § 34). It presupposes the blessing of the high priest, Nu. 6²⁴⁻²⁶, which it paraphrases in v.²; but not necessarily the document P in which that is contained, for the priest's blessing is much more ancient than P, and was one actually used by priests before the Exile. 𝕲 has τῷ Δαυείδ after מזמור, omitting שיר, but that is improbable. בנגינת is also incorrectly rendered ἐν ὕμνοις in 𝕲. The universalism of the Ps. resembles that of 66¹⁻⁹, and presupposes Is.² and a time of peace and friendliness with the nations subsequent to Nehemiah.

Str. I. A synth. triplet and a syn. couplet.—**2.** The priestly benediction Nu. 6²⁴⁻²⁶ is turned into a petition of the nation for itself, and therefore in varied terms, cf. 4⁷ 29¹¹ 31¹⁷ 80⁴· ⁸· ²⁰. It is therefore improbable that the third clause was omitted in the original ; all the more that it is needed to complete the Str. We must add the line omitted, probably for abbreviation in writing, *And give peace to us.* — **3.** *That Thy way*], defined as *Thy salvation*, in the more general sense of blessing as in previous and subsequent context, and not in the more specific sense of salvation from evils. — *may be known*], that is, mediately, through the blessing of Israel. — *in the earth* ‖ *among all nations*.

Str. II. A syn. triplet and a syn. couplet. **Str. III.** A syn. triplet enclosing a syn. couplet.—**4.** *Let the peoples give Thee thanks*], repeated for greater emphasis ; so also at the beginning of the next Str., v.⁶, the first line giving the person to be thanked, *Yahweh*, the second emphasizing the peoples by *all of them*. This thanksgiving is still further emphasized in Str. II., v.⁵ᵃ, by *let the nations be glad and let them jubilate*], and in the last Str., at the close of the Ps., v.⁸ᵇ, by *Therefore let all the ends of the earth do reverence*]. — The reason for this thanksgiving in Str. II. is v.⁵ᵇ·ᶜ·, *Thou governest the peoples with equity ‖ leadest the nations in the earth*], in providential government of the world. The reason in Str. III., v.⁷, is as in Str. I., v.², the divine blessing of Israel, especially in a fruitful harvest: *The earth hath yielded her increase.*

4. ‏יְבָרֵךְ‎] bis, also v.⁶ bis. Hiph. impf. 3 pl. ירה (*v.* Intr. § 39) with sf. 2 m. in 𝔐, 𝔍, but 𝔊 has sfs. only v.⁶, and not v.⁴ It is prob. that they were not in the original, but are in all cases interpretative. — **5.** ‏הַנְחֵם‎] Hiph. impf. 2 m. sf. 3 pl. נחה (5⁹). — **7.** ‏יְבוּלָהּ‎] sf. f. ‡ ‏יְבוּל‎ n.m. *produce* of soil, as 78⁴⁶ 85¹³ Dt. 32²² Ju. 6⁴ Hg. 1¹⁰. — ‏אלהים אלהינו‎]. The original was certainly ‏יהוה אלהינו‎. This makes it evident that the Ps. was older than 𝔈. — **8.** ‏וִיבָרְכֵנוּ אלהים‎] is dittog., later than 𝔈. — ‏אותו‎] makes the l. too long ; is interpretation of a late scribe at the expense of the measure.

PSALM LXVIII., 8 STR. 6⁴.

Ps. 68 is an ode, not based upon any particular historical victory, but upon the victories of Yahweh in the long history of Israel. (1) A reference to Yahweh's rising up in theophany, causing His enemies to perish, to the great joy of the righteous (v.²⁻⁴). (2) A summons to praise Him who interposes in theophany on behalf of orphans, widows, and prisoners (v.⁵⁻⁷). (3) A reference to the theophanic march through the wilderness, with the divine provision for His afflicted people (v.⁸⁻¹¹). (4) A reference to the theophanic interposition at the Kishon, with the great slaughter of the enemies and the rich booty for His people (v.¹²⁻¹⁵). (5) The selection of Zion for the divine abode, and the theophanic entrance into the sanctuary (v.¹⁶⁻¹⁹). (6) The crushing of the enemies in the subsequent wars, probably of the reign of David (v.²²⁻²⁴). (7) The triumphal processions into the sanctuary (v.²⁵⁻²⁶·²⁸). (8) Final petition for deliverance from the world powers and their dependent peoples (v.²⁹·³¹). Many minor glosses emphasize various features of the ode, insert ascriptions of blessedness to Yahweh (v.²⁰⁻²¹·²⁷·³⁶ᶜ), and predictions of the homage of kings to Yahweh in Jerusalem (v.³⁰). A late editor adapts the Ps. to liturgical use by adding Messianic prediction (v.³²), invocation to public praise (v.³³⁻³⁵), and finally adoration of the God of Israel in His sanctuary (v.³⁶ᵃ·ᵇ).

WHEN Yahweh arises, His enemies are scattered;
  And them that hate (Yahweh) flee from His presence.
  As smoke is driven away when (the wind) driveth,
  As wax is melted from the presence of fire,
  The wicked perish from the presence of Yahweh;
  But the righteous are glad, exult with gladness.
SING to Yahweh, make melody to His name.
  Lift up (a song) to the One riding on the clouds of His heaven.
  Exult before Him, the Father of orphans,
  And Judge of widows in His holy habitation,
  Yahweh, who bringeth home the solitary ones,
  Who bringeth forth prisoners into prosperity.
YAHWEH, when Thou wentest forth before Thy people,
  When Thou didst march in the desert, the earth trembled.
  Yea, the heavens dripped at the presence of Yahweh
  A copious rain upon Thine inheritance.
  If it were weary, Thou didst establish it, Yahweh.
  For Thy living creatures Thou providest, for the afflicted, Yahweh.
WORD is given; the women are heralding war.
  The king doth strive; armies flee;
  And the beauty at home divideth the spoil.
  The dove on the wing is covered with silver,
  And her pinions flash with yellow gold.
  But (when the vulture spreadeth her wings), it is like snow on Zalmon.
O MOUNT of Yahweh, fertile mountain!
  O Mount of summits, fertile mountain!
  Mount Yahweh desired for His throne!
  Yahweh, Thou didst ride in Thy chariot from Sinai into the sanctuary.
  Thou didst ascend up on high.   Thou didst lead captives captive.
  Thou didst accept gifts, to dwell among mankind.
YAHWEH will crush the head of His enemies,
  The hairy scalp of the one going on in his faults.
  Yahweh said: " I will recompense them in Bashan.
  I will recompense them in the gulf of the sea, even I;
  That the foot may be bathed in blood;
  And the tongue of dogs may have its portion of the same."
THEY see Thy processions, Yahweh, into the sanctuary.
  The singers go before; behind the musicians;
  In the midst damsels playing on timbrels.
  There is little Benjamin, the conqueror;
  (There) princes of Judah, a heap of them;
  Princes of Zebulon, princes of Naphtali.
YAHWEH, command Thy strength for us,
  Strengthen what Thou hast done for us.
  Rebuke the wild beast of the reeds, Yahweh;
  The assembly of bulls with the calves of peoples;
  Trampling in the mire the favoured ones, refined as silver.
  Disperse the people that delight in war.

Ps. 68 was originally a שׁיר, an ode, when it was taken up into 𝔇. It was then in 𝔐, and subsequently was used in 𝔈 and 𝔇ℜ (*v.* Intr. §§ 24, 27, 31, 32, 33). It has many glosses from different editors. It is based on several older poems. (1) Ju. 5, the song of Deborah : v.$^{8-9}$, the theophanic march Ju. 5^{4-5}; v.^{13}, cf. Ju. 5^{30}; v.^{14}, cf. Ju. 5^{16}; v.^{19}, cf. Ju. 5^{12}; v.^{22}, cf. Ju. 5^{26}; v.^{28}, cf. Ju. 5^{18}. (2) Dt. 33, the Blessing of Moses: v.$^{34.\,35}$, cf. Dt. $33^{26.\,28}$, also Ps. 18^{11}; v.^{18}, cf. Dt. 33^{2}. (3) Nu. 10^{35}, the Song of the Ark, cf. v.^{2}. (4) The *holy habitation* of v.^{6} depends on Dt. 26^{15} Je. 25^{30}. (5) The representation that Yahweh is the *Father of orphans* and *Judge of widows* is Deuteronomic. (6) The triumphal procession into Zion is a later development of Ps. 24. The reference to *prisoners* and *solitary ones* v.$^{7.\,19}$ implies the prison of exile. *The wild beast of the reeds* Egypt v.^{31}, *assembly of bulls* used of Assyria and Edom, probably refer to the Eastern world powers. *The calves of peoples* probably refer to the lesser nations coöperating with them. All this implies a peril of the Jews between the East and the West, which was no less than their being *trampled in the mire.* Egypt, however, seems to be the chief enemy, as in Ps. 80. The peril was not from minor nations alone, as in the early Restoration, but from great ones as well. The reference to the Sanctuary v.$^{18.\,25}$, and the mountain of the throne of Yahweh v.^{17}, as well as to the temple procession with songs and stringed instruments, implies thoroughly organised temple worship, and therefore a date later than the erection of the second temple. The combination of these situations favours the late Persian period, when Persia and Egypt were at war, about 360–350 B.C.

The tributary gifts of kings v.^{30}, and the restoration to Yahweh of Egypt and Cush v.^{32}, are glosses of a prophetic character based on Is. 18^{7} 19^{16-25} 23^{18} 44^{5} 60, $66^{20.\,21}$. All the uses of יה v.$^{5.\,19}$ and ארני v.$^{12.\,18.\,20.\,21.\,23.\,27.\,33}$ are redactional; also the call ברוך v.$^{20.\,27.\,36}$, and many Aramaisms and late uses : סוררים v.$^{7.\,19}$, רצד v.^{17}, גבננים v.^{17}, אלפי שנאן v.^{18}, מושעות v.^{21}, תוצאות v.^{21}, מקהלות v.^{27}. The following α.λ. and strange forms are all errors of copyists: v.^{7} כושרות α.λ. for מושרות; v.^{14} שפתים α.λ. for משפתים; v.^{15} פרש שדי α.λ. for פרש דיה; v.^{16} הר בשן for הר דשן 𝔊; v.^{31} בזר for פזר; v.^{32} חשמנים α.λ. for חשם מני. Apart from these glosses and errors there is no reason for dating the Ps. later than the closing years of the Persian domination.

Str. I. Two syn. and an antith. couplet.—**2.** *When Yahweh arises*], a use of the marching song of the ark Nu. 10^{35}; and so the ode begins with the march from Horeb. Yahweh was conceived as present in theophany with the sacred Ark. He arose in the pillar of cloud as a signal for the march; and when enemies obstructed the way, they were overcome by His divine presence. EV^{s}. follow MT in the translation "let arise," as if the verbs were jussive, making the Ps. begin with a prayer, when really it is in the form of an ode, and the impfs. are graphic description of the

march from Horeb. — *His enemies ‖ them that hate Yahweh ‖ the
wicked*, v.³], usual terms to indicate those who were both the enemies of His people and the enemies of their God. — *are scattered ‖
flee from His presence ‖ perish from the presence of Yahweh*, v.³],
in disastrous, overwhelming defeat and slaughter. This is illustrated by two intervening similes. — **3.** *As smoke is driven away*],
cf. 37²⁰ Ho. 13³, but especially Ps. 1⁴, which suggests the original
reading, — *when the wind driveth*]. By the omission of the noun
by an early copyist at the expense of the measure, an anomalous
Hebrew form has come into the text, which probably rests upon
ancient variations of reading, one of which is followed by EVˢ. in
the imv. "drive them away," making a premature departure from
the simile. — *As wax is melted from the presence of fire*], cf. 97⁵
Mi. 1⁴. These similes suggest that the theophanic presence of
God is that of a thunder storm with a strong blast of wind and the
fire of lightnings, cf. Ps. 18⁹⁻¹⁶. — **4.** *But the righteous*], the people
of Yahweh in antith. with their wicked enemies, — *are glad ‖ exult
with gladness*], in the victories of Yahweh. A glossator emphasizes
this at the expense of the measure by inserting : *exult before God.*

Str. II. Three syn. couplets. — **5.** *Sing to Yahweh, make melody to His name*], a summons to public praise ‖ *lift up a song* to
Him, so 𝔖, 𝔗 ; PBV. "magnify" ; AV., JPSV. "extol," which the
parallelism demands, though it is a rare poetic meaning of the
verb. The more usual meaning is given by 𝔊, 𝔍, RV., "cast up a
highway," which does not suit the context. — *The One riding on
the clouds of His heavens*], the most probable original of a difficult
verse in accordance with the conception of the theophanic
chariot 18¹¹ Dt. 33²⁶. An early copyist mistook the Hebrew word
"clouds" for another meaning "steppe, deserts," which nowhere
else is used with the theophanic chariot ; and that made it necessary to interpret the word rendered "His heavens" as if it were
the same as the word at the close of the previous line, "His
name," and this occasioned the insertion of the divine name
"Yah." — **6.** *The Father of orphans*]. Yahweh is the father of
the fatherless ‖ *and Judge of widows*], their vindicator against
injustice ; both Deuteronomic conceptions, cf. 10¹⁴ 146⁹ Jb. 31¹⁶⁻¹⁸
(*v.* Br.*ᴴ.ᶜ.ᴴ.³ ⁸⁵*). — *In His holy habitation*], the heavenly temple,
as Dt. 26¹⁵ Je. 25³⁰. — **7.** *Who bringeth home ‖ who bringeth forth*].

H

These are different phases of the same action ; for *the solitary ones* are those shut up alone in prison ‖ *prisoners*, and they are brought out of prison to their *home*, their own houses ‖ *into prosperity*], the reënjoyment of the privileges of home in their native land.   It is quite possible that the poet is thinking of the deliverance from Egyptian bondage ; but he uses terms which are more suitable to the time of the captivity in Babylon.   It is probable that the two historic events were mingled in his mind.   A glossator added the line : *Verily the stubborn abide*], remain, abandoned by God, who had released the faithful prisoners, either *in a parched land*, as EV⁸. and most interpreters, referring then to the wilderness of the wanderings ; or possibly, by another explanation " in a dungeon," referring to the prisons of the Exile or of Maccabean times.

Str. III. Syn. couplets. — **8**. *When Thou wentest forth before Thy people ‖ didst march*], the theophanic march of Ju. 5^{4-5}. — *in the desert*], from Sinai to Palestine. — **9**. *the earth trembled*], in earthquake, as usual in theophanies Ex. $19^{16\,sq.}$ Ps. $18^{7\,sq.}$ Hb. $3^{3\,sq.}$. — *Yea, the heavens dripped*], in the theophanic storm, — *at the presence of Yahweh*], His theophanic presence in the storm clouds.   A glossator inserts from Ju. 5^5 : *Yon Sinai at the presence of God, the God of Israel.*   But this gloss separates the verb of the previous line from its object in this line, and so makes the connection of thought obscure. — **10**. *A copious rain upon Thine inheritance*], a theophanic storm with thunder and lightning and heavy rain, usually mingled with hail, cf. 18^{12-16}.   A glossator, misunderstanding the line as an independent sentence, and taking the preposition for a divine name, inserted a verb at the expense of the measure, which is rendered in EV⁸. " send," without sufficient justification.   JPSV. " pour down," *B*DB. " shed abroad," are better suited to the context, but are speculative meanings, without authority in usage. — *If it were weary*], emphatic in position, referring to the inheritance. — *Thou didst establish it*], strengthen it ; remove its weariness and make it vigorous.— **11**. *For Thy living creatures*], as Vrss., including man and animals of the inheritance, connected with the verb, *Thou providest*, and ‖ *for the afflicted*], these living creatures when afflicted with need.   But the insertion, at the expense of the measure, of the gloss, probably a relative clause, "that dwell in it," has been the occasion of another interpretation in modern times, taking the initial noun in an ancient meaning, "community," sustained only by a single passage, and the inserted clause as a principal clause, and so getting the rendering, "Thy community dwelt therein." This is certainly a very weak outcome of a passage of a Ps. which elsewhere is strong and vigorous. The glossator also inserted " in Thy goodness," certainly an unnecessary explanation.

Str. IV. A synth. triplet, and one composed of a syn. couplet with an antithetical line. — **12.** *Word is given*], indef. subj. equivalent to the English passive ; but a glossator prefixed *Adonay ;* as if God were the subject and He gave the message or command, which does not at all suit the context. — *the women are heralding war*]. Women fleeing before the advancing armies herald their approach for battle. A misunderstanding of the proper place of division of the lines put the measures in confusion, and occasioned the rendering "great host," as if there were an army of women with these tidings, which is unexampled in usage and impossible in reality. — **13.** *The king doth strive*]. The reference is certainly based on Ju. 5 and the battle of the Kishon. The king is doubtless the king of Canaan. He is graphically described as striving in battle with Israel. By mistaking the verb for an adjective and attaching it to the previous line the noun was left without a verb and it was necessary to attach it to the following noun, which then, as the two are followed by a plural verb, had to be given as a plural ; and so 墨 gives us, " kings of armies flee." But in fact, as the subsequent context shows, it is the *armies* which *flee*. The repetition of the verb in emphasis is against the measure and improbable. — *And the beauty at home divideth the spoil*]. So 𝕲, 𝖄, 𝕴. This is evidently based on Ju. 5[30], where the reference is to the mother of Sisera, here to the fair wives and daughters of the victors of Israel. It is a mistaken interpretation of the initial word to render it, as EV[s]., " she that tarrieth at home." — **14.** A glossator inserts, probably at first on the margin, from Ju. 5[16] the reproof of the Reubenites for their neglect to take part in the holy war : " Will ye lie down among the sheepfolds ? " This has made the passage difficult, and indeed a crux of interpretation ; and there is no agreement among commentators. De. thinks of Israel as

God's turtle dove basking in the sunlight of prosperity ; but this is certainly against the context. It would be more suited to the citation from Ju. 5[16] to think of a reproof of those Israelites who preferred to live the peaceful life of the dove in her cotes to the perils of war ; but why then the emphasis upon silver and gold? Before I saw that v.[14a] was a gloss, it seemed best, Br.[MP.434], to think of these words as carrying on the words of the messengers summoning the people to arms : " the winged dove is covered with silver " ; that is, if you would share in the spoil, you must not remain in the dovecotes, but take flight to the battle-field. But the removal of the gloss removes the difficulty of interpretation, and makes evident the reference to the fleeing enemy. — *The dove on the wing*]. The fleeing armies are compared to a dove fleeing from its enemies — *is covered with silver* ‖ *her pinions flash with yellow gold*], the brilliant colours of the dove in the sunlight as she wings her flight from her enemies, a metaphor of the spoil of gold and silver abandoned by the fleeing armies in their tracks. — **15.** *But when the vulture spreadeth her wings*]. The victorious Israelites, pursuing the defeated and helpless fugitives, are compared to a vulture flying after a dove. An early copyist, by dittography of **ש**, substituted for the Hebrew word " vulture " the divine name "Almighty," which made it necessary to give the verb the meaning " scatter " without justification in usage, and to supply the object " kings," and the place " in it " all at the expense of the measure and to the confusion of the sense. — *it is like snow on Zalmon*]. The silver and gold colours of the dove in flight have as their antithesis the snow-white colour of the bones of the slaughtered army, as they have been picked clean by the vultures. Zalmon is the still unidentified place where the bones of those slain in battle were so thickly spread that they seemed like snow covering the ground. Those who retain the present text think, some of a theophanic snow storm, others of a comparison with snow of glistening armour dropped in flight (cf. Hom. *Il.* XIX. 357–361), or of bleached bones on the battle-field (cf. Vir. *Aen.* V. 865, XII. 36), and still others of " snow-flakes swept along by a hurricane," Kirk.

Str. V. A tristich of two syn. and one synth. line, and a tristich with a single line whose first part has its syn. in the second line, its second in the third line. — **16–17.** *Mount of Yahweh*], described as *fertile mountain* and as *Mount of summits*, of many rounded peaks, and still further as *Mount Yahweh desired for His throne*, can be no other than Mount Zion. But the change in 𝔐 of " Yahweh " to " Elohim " made it possible to think of " mountain of God " as a gigantic mountain, cf. 36⁷, and then more naturally of the giant peaks of Palestine; and so by an easy copyist's mistake in late texts of 𝔐 " Mount Bashan " takes the place of " fertile mountain " of the ancient Vrss. The many peaks were then conceived to be those of Bashan instead of the several hills of Jerusalem; and it became necessary to explain the antith. between the gigantic Bashan and the mount of the divine residence by the gloss: " Why hop ye " PBV., " leap ye " AV., better "look askance," RV., JPSV., " ye mountain of summits? " A glossator also emphasized the perpetuity of the divine residence by inserting the clause: " Yea, Yahweh dwelleth for ever." — **18.** *Yahweh, Thou didst ride in Thy chariot from Sinai into the sanctuary*]. This seems to be the original of a line which has been so expanded by glosses that there are no measures left and the meaning is most difficult. This Str. represents that Yahweh took possession of His permanent residence in the sanctuary of Zion by a theophanic ride from His earlier residence in Sinai. The errors and insertions of copyists made the present text, the best translation of which is that of Dr.: " The chariots of God are twenty thousand, even thousands redoubled; the Lord is come from Sinai into the sanctuary." This lays the stress upon the angelic army of God. But a more strict adherence to MT. gives in the last clause, " Sinai in sanctity "; that is, making the new residence in Zion as sacred as ancient Sinai. — **19.** *Thou didst ascend up on high; Thou didst lead captives captive*], based on Ju. 5¹². This is the victorious ride of Yahweh on the heights of battle-fields, rescuing captive Israelites from their enemies and leading them in triumphal procession to the sanctuary. It is a general reference to all the triumphs of Yahweh from Sinai until the erection of the temple by Solomon and the taking up the divine residence there after its consecration. — *Thou didst accept gifts*], gifts of tribute from enemies, especially of offerings from His people made at the sacred place. — *to dwell among mankind*], in order to dwell in His temple among mankind, in antith. with His heavenly abode. A glossator inserted " even the stubborn " to emphasize the fact that the divine residence in Israel was notwithstanding the stubbornness of the people in their historic relation to Him ; and this made it necessary to insert the divine name "Yah" and its Qr. " 'Elohim." An editor, thinking of a liturgical use of the Ps., inserted at this point an ascription of blessedness to Yahweh : **20–21.** *Blessed be Adonay day by day, who beareth burdens for us, the God of our salvation. God is unto us a God to save. To Yahweh Adonay belong escapes from death*]. The reasons for the praise of God here given are general, and not in accord with the context of this warlike Ps. They are : (1) that Yahweh bears the burdens, cares, anxieties of His people ; (2) gives them salvation from enemies and troubles ; (3) is their hope for escape from death.

Str. VI. has three syn. couplets. — **22.** *Yahweh will crush the head* ‖ *the hairy scalp*], cf. Ju. 5²⁶ Hb. 3¹³. Yahweh will trample under foot and stamp upon the heads of the prostrate foes, putting them to the most extreme humiliation. — *His enemies* ‖ *the one going on in his faults*], persisting in offences against Him and His people, until they have heaped up a vast store for retribution. — **23.** *Yahweh said :*], in resolute determination, — *I will recompense*], repeated for emphasis. This meaning is required by previous and subsequent context ; although it is possible to render with PBV., AV., after 𝕮, " I will bring again (my people)," or with RV., JPSV., leave the object indefinite and think with many moderns of a pursuit of the enemy in order to bring them back to the sacred place for punishment. But the thought of the restoration of Israel here, though favoured by the preposition " from," is an intrusion, however suitable it might have been for public worship ; and the preposition was doubtless an error of interpretation. The thought of bringing the enemies back from their places of refuge to a place of judgment in Jerusalem is not sustained by Am. 9²⁻³, which is a pursuit in order to slay them wherever found. — *Bashan* ‖ *gulf of the sea*] are accusatives of place, and, as suggested by Am. 9²⁻³, indicate in antith. the lofty peaks of the mountains and the depths of the sea as places where the enemies have fled for refuge ; but in vain, for the divine retribution overtakes them even there. — **24**. *That the foot may be bathed in blood*], the blood of the slain enemies flowing like a stream. — *and the tongue of dogs may have its portion of the same*], lapping up the blood as predatory dogs do in Palestine. The explanatory gloss " of enemies " impairs the simplicity of the thought as well as the measure.

Str. **VII**. Synth. hexastich.— **25**. *They see*], people generally; indef. subj. equal to passive " are seen." — *Thy processions, Yahweh*], the triumphal processions of the victorious Yahweh. — *unto the sanctuary*], entering the holy city, ascending the holy hill, and entering into the courts of the temple. This has been intensified by a glossator at the expense of the measure by the repetition : *processions of my God, my King.* — **26**. *The singers go before, behind the musicians, in the midst damsels playing on timbrels*]. The procession is preceded by the temple choirs, the singers and the players on stringed instruments being separated by the damsels playing on the timbrels. These latter from the earliest times took part in triumphal processions, Ex. 15^{20}. This was not strictly a temple service. MT. should be rendered " in the midst of the damsels," as RV., the damsels marching on both sides of the singers and musicians, so Kirk., but we cannot rely on the pointing of MT., and such an order of procession is improbable. The editor here introduces another ascription to God. — **27**. *In assemblies*], possibly choirs, 26^{12}. — *bless ye Yahweh Adonay, the fountain of Israel*], cf. Je. 2^{13} 17^{13} Ps. 36^{10}. By dittography of an ancient scribe the text arose, " from the fountain of Israel," which must then be interpreted as RV. : " ye that are of the fountain of Israel," genuine sons of Jacob, cf. Is. 48^1 $51^{1.2}$ Dt. 33^{28} — **28**. *There*], graphic, an onlooker pointing to the place, — *is little Benjamin, the conqueror*], doubtless referring to Saul of Benjamin, the first king of Israel, — *princes of Judah, a heap of them*], the numerous princes of the line of David, — *princes of Zebulon, princes of Naphtali*], representative of the northern tribes. The omission of Ephraim and the trans-Jordanic tribes is a sufficient evidence that the onlooker is only mentioning a few of the tribes, and that he does not attempt to describe the entire procession.

Str. **VIII**. A syn. couplet and a syn. tetrastich. — **29**. *Yahweh, command Thy strength ‖ O strengthen*]. Imperatives, as 𝔊, 𝔖, 𝔙, 𝔖, 𝔗, 𝔍, and not pf., as 𝔐, followed by EV⁸., " hath commanded," which is inharmonious with the imperative that follows. The final Str. is a supplication, based on the ode, for divine victories in the time of the Psalmist also. 𝔥 interprets incorrectly by adding the sf. " Thy " to " God," and compels the interpretation of " Thy strength," as referring to the strength of Israel, which is contrary to the parallelism. — *what Thou hast done for us*], in the history of Israel as set forth in the previous context of the ode. An editor introduces here a prediction with Messianic significance : **30.** *Because of Thy temple at Jerusalem to Thee kings will bring presents*], based on Is. 60[7 sq.] 66[20], cf. Hg. 2[7] Zc. 2[11 sq.] 6[15] 8[21 sq.]. — **31.** *Rebuke the wild beast of the reeds*], the hippopotamus, Egypt ; cf. Ps. 80[14] Jb. 40[21] ; " company of spearmen," PBV., AV., has no justification whatever. — *the assembly of bulls*], the eastern nations under the dominion of Persia, — *with the calves of peoples*], the lesser tributary nations, cf. Je. 46[20, 21]. — *Trampling in the mire*], under foot in arrogant, overwhelming force. Israel was ruthlessly trampled under foot in the mire by these nations traversing her territory to war upon one another. — *the favoured ones*], the people having the divine favour, though they are *refined as silver*, cast as it were into the furnace of affliction, to come out as pure silver with all the dross removed. This indicates very severe affliction of Israel by Egypt and her allies. Glossators, misunderstanding this difficult clause, after the omission of an important word, left it in such a state that it has always been a crux of interpreters and Versions. PBV., " so that they humbly bring pieces of silver," AV., " (till every one) submit himself with pieces of silver," RV., " trampling under foot the pieces of silver," JPSV., " him that submitteth himself offering bars of silver," are only specimens of well-nigh universal disagreement, making it evident that the fault is with the text. — *Disperse the peoples that delight in war*], all these warlike nations, Egypt, Persia, and the nations under her dominion. The imperative of 𝔊, 𝔖, 𝔘, 𝔍, followed by AV., is demanded by the context rather than the pf. of MT., followed by PBV., RV., JPSV., whether interpreted as referring to the past or as a prophetic perfect. These Vrss. are all the more to be followed if the Ps. originally ended here.

A later editor made the Ps., as he thought, more appropriate for common use by adding v.[32-36]. These verses have varied contents. — **32.** *Swift messengers will come out of Egypt*], the most probable rendering of a difficult passage after ancient Vrss. "Princes" of EV[s]. cannot be sustained even by the erroneous form of שׂר due to dittography. JPSV., "Hashmanim" leaves the word untranslated and without meaning. — *As for Cush*], Biblical name of Ethiopia, — *his hands will run out to God*, in the gesture of supplication. This is a prediction of the conversion of Egypt and Ethiopia in accordance with Is. 19[19 sq.] 43[3] 45[14] 60[5 sq.] Zp. 3[10]. — **33–36.** A universal summons to praise. — **33.** *Ye kingdoms of earth*], all of them, — *sing to God*], take part in the public worship in the temple in Jerusalem, cf. 96[7 sq.] 97[1] 98[4] 99[1 sq.]. — **34.** *Lift up to Him that rideth upon the ancient heavens*], based on v.[5] and Dt. 33[26]. A later glossator prefixes as an interpretation: *make melody to Adonay;* and still later the original verb is interpreted as Selah. A glossator emphasizes the theophanic ride of Yahweh in the heavens by the usual reference to the thunder storm: *Lo! He uttereth with His voice*]. — **35.** The summons to praise continues: *with a strong voice ascribe strength to God*], with loud praise of vocal and instrumental music; and probably also thinking of the blowing of horns, with blasts of the sacred trumpets — *Whose majesty is over Israel, and whose strength is in the skies*]. God in His theophanic ride is conceived as majestic and strong in the skies; but as Dt. 33[26] it is all for Israel, in Israel's behalf, that the theophanic ride has been made. — **36.** *Awe-inspiring in His sanctuary*], as ancient Vrss. The change to the second person in שׂר, followed by EV[s]., is improbable. The earthly sanctuary is here in antith. with the heavenly. — *the God of Israel*], emphasis upon the peculiar relation between God and His people, — *Giver of strength and great might to the people*]. The strength that He exhibits in His theophanic ride in the heaven is bestowed upon His people on earth. The Ps. concludes in its present form with the liturgical phrase: *Blessed be God*, cf. v.[20. 27].

---

2. יָקוּם] Qal impf. indicative, not juss. יקם of Vrss.; so יָפוּצוּ (*18[15]*), יָנוּסוּ (*60[6]*), not future, but temporal clause and apod. without conj., as frequent in poetry. The v. is adapted from Nu. 10[35], the marching song of the ark, where קוּמָה Qal imv. cohort. is used with 2 pers. sfs. and ו with the shortened forms יָנֻסוּ, יָפֻצוּ; and יהוה, which here, as throughout this Ps., was the original of אלהים of 𝔈. In other respects the sentence is the same. The measure requires יהוה מפני for מפניו, as v.³ᶜ. — **3.** כְּהִנְדֹּף] MT. is an anomalous form, prob. an ancient variation of reading between תִּנְדֹּף and הִנָּדֵף, the latter favoured by ‖ כְּהֵמֵס (22¹⁵) and the masc. עָשָׁן. תִּנְדֹּף cannot, from context, be 2 m., but 3 f., implying רוּחַ, Bö. as ¹⁴, which indeed is required for measure. The clause is then a temporal clause. — **4.** וְיַעַלְצוּ לִפְנֵי אֱלֹהִים] makes difficult measure. It is essentially the same as וְעָלְזוּ לְפָנָיו v.⁵ᶜ, except that עָלַץ for עָלַז is an improbable variation in the same Ps. Besides, לִפְנֵי אלהים is tautological immediately after מִפְנֵי אלהים. It is therefore prob. txt. err. or gl. of amplification. — **5.** סֹלּוּ] Qal imv. ‡ [סלל vb. Qal *cast up* a highway Je. 18¹⁵ Is. 57¹⁴ 62¹⁰, so 𝔊, 𝔍, and most here; but ‖ justifies *lift up* (*a song*), so 𝔖, 𝔗, Street, Gr., cf. Pilp. *exalt* Pr. 4⁸ and Hithp. *exalt oneself* Ex. 9¹⁷ (J) BS. 39²⁴ 40²⁸; cf. also סֶלָה (*v.* Intr. § 41). — רֹכֵב] Qal ptc. רכב, as *18¹¹*, cf. v.³⁴, all theophanic. — עֲרָבוֹת] so 𝔊, 𝔍, pl. ‡ עֲרָבָה n.f. *steppe*, not elsw. ψ, but Je. 2⁶ 17⁶ 50¹² Is. 33⁹ +; not suited to theophanic chariot ride, therefore with Gr. rd. עָבוֹת, as Is. 19¹ Ps. 104³; cf. v.³⁴ *18¹²* Dt. 33²⁶. — בְּיָהּ שְׁמוֹ] is dub.; usually explained as ב *essentiae*, Ges.¹⁵⁴·³, with יָהּ abbreviated יהוה, cf. יָהּ v.¹⁹ (*v.* Intr. § 32). Hare, Dy., Oort, Du., rd. שמחו, which is better suited to context; Gr. ברכו שמו is improb., the vb. does not in any way correspond with letters of text, which is sustained by all Vrss. These words, according to the measure, go with the previous l., which needs another word. V.³⁴ suggests שמיו, as Dt. 33²⁸, which interpreted as שמו would lead to the insertion of בְּיָהּ. — עָלְזוּ לְפָנָיו] so 𝔍; but 𝔊 has ἀγαλλιᾶσθε ἐνώπιον αὐτοῦ· ταραχθήσονται ἀπὸ προσώπου αὐτοῦ, which is evidently a conflation of עלזו and ירגזו. But the latter is an error not suited to the context. — **6.** ‡ דַּיָּן] n.m. *judge*, as 1 S. 24¹⁶. — אלהים־] makes this l. too long. It has come up from v.⁷ᵃ, where it is needed. — מְעוֹן קָדְשׁוֹ] as Dt. 26¹⁵ Je. 25³⁰ Zc. 2¹⁷ 2 Ch. 30²⁷, cf. *268*. — **7.** מוֹשִׁיב] Hiph. ptc. ישב, so 𝔊, 𝔍. But Lag., Bä., Du., משיב Hiph. ptc. שוב ‖ מוֹצִיא is more probable. Then יחידים (22²¹) are *solitary ones* ‖ אֲסִירִים pl. † אָסִיר n.m. *prisoner*, elsw. 69³⁴ 79¹¹ 102²¹ 107¹⁰ Gn. 39²⁰·²² (Qr. J) Is. 14¹⁷ Zc. 9¹¹·¹² La. 3³⁴ Jb. 3¹⁸, cf. Ju. 16²¹·²⁵ (Kt.). — כּוֹשָׁרוֹת] a.λ. pl. [כּוֹשָׁרָה] n.f. *prosperity*, BDB. But √כשר Aram. and the form improb. 𝔊 ἐν ἀνδρείᾳ, 𝔙 𝔍, *in fortitudine*, Σ εἰς ἀπόλυσιν, Θ εἰς εὐθύτησιν, all lead to an original מִישָׁרוֹת pl. abstr. of מִישׁוֹר = מֵישָׁר 26¹², *level place, condition of prosperity*, as 26¹². Rd. also במו. — אַךְ־סוֹרְרִים] Qal ptc. pl. as v.¹⁹ 66⁷. But 𝔊 ὁμοίως τοὺς παραπικραίνοντας, 𝔙 *similiter eos qui exasperant* = מררים, cf. Ex. 1¹⁴; *v.* v.¹⁹, where the phr. is in 𝔊 καὶ γὰρ ἀπειθοῦντες. 𝔍 has *increduli autem* v.⁷, *insuper et non credentes* v.¹⁹. — צְחִיחָה] a.λ. BD*B*. n.f. *parched land*, 𝔊 ἐν τάφοις, 𝔙 *in sepulcris*, prob. † צְרִיחַ n.[m.] *underground chamber* Ju. 9⁴⁶·⁴⁹·⁴⁹ 1 S. 13⁶; or possibly † שְׁחִית *pit*, as La. 4²⁰ Ps. 107²⁰ = שחת, 𝔍 *in siccitatibus*, cf. אֶרֶץ צִיָּה 63². — This l. is prob. a late gl., qualifying the previous context. — **8–9** is a condensation of Ju. 5⁴⁻⁵. — לִפְנֵי יֶמֶךָ] takes the place of מִשֵּׂעִיר, generalising the first l. — בְּצֵעַדְךָ] Qal inf. sf. 2 m. with ב temporal, of the march of Yahweh, as Ju. 5⁴; cf. Hb. 3¹². — בִּישִׁימוֹן] takes the place of מִשְּׂדֵה אֱדוֹם ‡ יְשִׁימוֹן n.m. *waste, wilderness*, as Dt. 32¹⁰ Pss. 78⁴⁰ 106¹⁴ 107⁴ Is. 43¹⁹·²⁰. — אַף] in place of גם of original. The subsequent lines were condensed by the omission of

מפני יהוה, which were re- שמים נטפו between גם עבים נטפו מים נטפו הרים נזלו
tained, only יהוה was subsequently changed in 𝔈 to אלהים as elsw. † נטף vb.
Qal *drop, drip*, here as Ju. 5⁴ Jo. 4¹⁸ Ct. 4¹¹ 5⁵· ¹³ Pr. 5³, intrans. Jb. 29²².
Hiph. idem Am. 9¹³, of speech c. עַל Am. 7¹⁶, אֶל Ez. 21²· ⁷, לְ Mi. 2⁶· ¹¹. —
זֶה סִינַי] introduces a l. too long for the measure, making the Str. too long.
It is a gl. from Ju. 5⁵. The lines of Ju. are thus reduced to three in Ps. —
10. ‡ גֶּשֶׁם] n.m. *rain, shower*, 105³² Gn. 7¹² 8² (J) +. — נְדָבוֹת] *v. 54⁸*, 𝔊 ἑκού-
σιον. — תָּנִיף] Hiph. impf. 2 m. ‡ נוף † Qal *besprinkle* Pr. 7¹⁷ (couch with myrrh),
Hiph. *swing to and fro, wave*, in the ritual for the presentation of the priest's
share to God, often in P. 𝔊 ἀφοριεῖς, Aq., Θ ; 𝔍 *elevasti* for the syn. הרים, so
𝔗 ארימת. But *BDB.* gives with hesitation a mng. corresponding with Qal,
shed abroad, here only. Lag., Gr., Now., Du., rd. תַּטִּיף Hiph. נטף *drip*. The
vb., however, requires אל or עַל for the second obj., and if this is supplied it
makes the l. too long; for נחלתך belongs with this l. as 𝔊, and the ו with נלאה
in 𝔐, 𝔊 (not 𝔍), attaches it most naturally to the next l. The divine name
אלהים makes the first l. too long, and is needed in the second. A copyist
probably mistook אֶל for אֵל and wrote it אלהים, and then omitted the אלהים
of the second l. The force of the vb. נטפו was then carried over from the
previous l. to this. — וְנִלְאָה] Niph. pf. 3 f. sg. ‡ לאה Qal, Niph. prot. of temporal
clause, *be weary* Is. 1¹⁴ Je. 9⁴ 20⁹ +, 𝔊 καὶ ἠσθένησεν. 𝔍 interprets as ptc.
laborantem, which would strictly require article. Ols., Now., would prefix it.
— **11.** חַיָּתְךָ] dub., 𝔊 τὰ ζῶά σου, so 𝔖, 𝔙, 𝔍, *animalia tua*, cf. v.³¹; so Hu.,
De., Pe., with various explanations. But most moderns think of † חַיָּה n.f.
community, as 2 S. 23¹³; so essentially Ges., EVˢ., Hi., Ri., Ols., Du., Bä.,
Dr., Kirk., Now., but not sufficiently sustained by a single passage. — יֵשְׁבוּ־בָהּ]
seems to be an expl. gl., m. pl. vb. when subj. is f. sg. בְּטוֹבָתְךָ is also a gl. of
amplification. With these removed, the difficulty of explaining חַיָּתְךָ in its
ordinary sense disappears. It is the acc. of vb. הכין with לְ pers. נלאה ‖ לְעָנִי,
and then refers to the animals, not with Hu. the quails as complementary
to the manna of previous clause ; but as the rain suggests grain, so the living creatures, cattle large and small, are provided for. — **12.** אֲדֹנָי] is dub.,
makes l. too long ; prob. gl. of interp., cf. v.¹⁸· ²⁰· ²¹· ²³· ²⁷· ³³. — יִתֶּן־אֹמֶר] *v. 5²* ;
without אדני indef. subj., as Hb. 3⁹, the thunder of a theophany acc. Now., who
cf. נתן קול Ps. 18¹⁴ Am. 1² Jo. 2¹¹ 4¹⁶. But such usage unexampled. אֹמֶר is
somewhat different from קוֹל. — הַמְבַשְּׂרוֹת] Pi. ptc. pl. f. women heralding glad
tidings (*40¹⁰*), elsw. ψ and Is. 40⁹· ⁹ 41²⁷ 52⁷· ⁷ of victory and salvation ; so
most here. But it may also mean simply *bringing tidings*, as 1 S. 4¹⁷
2 S. 18¹⁹· ²⁰· ²⁶ 1 K. 1⁴²; that depends upon our interp. of the context. 𝔊, 𝔍,
𝔙, all make this ptc. second acc. to יתן. It is prob. that ה does not belong
to the ptc. making it a relative clause, but with the previous noun, which
should be read אִמְרָה (*12⁷*). Then the ptc. is in an independent verbal clause.
— צָבָא רָב] in 𝔊 δυνάμει πολλῇ, 𝔙 *virtute multa*, 𝔍 *fortitudinis plurimae*.
This is more prob. than EVˢ. *great company* or *host*, which is unexampled in
such a fig. sense, of women or messengers. It must mean either a real *army*
or *war*. If רב belongs to it, it is *great army* as obj. of ptc. If, as is prob.,

רב belongs to subsequent l., it is *war* that is heralded. רב is then Qal pf. ריב
strive in battle (*v. 35¹*) with מֶלֶךְ sg. as in 𝔊 and as subj.. — מלכי צבאות] phr.
α.λ. and improb. צבאות is subj. of next vb. — **13.** יִדֹּדוּן] twice Qal impf. נדד
most prob.; but 𝔍 *foederabuntur* √ידד vb. not used in Heb. 𝔊 τοῦ ἀγαπη-
τοῦ = יְדִיד adj. (*60⁷*). The repetition is, however, prob. a gl. of intensification, certainly not in original if רב belongs to this l. — נְוַת־בַּיִת] phr. α.λ. *she
that is abiding at home*, BDB. [נָוֶה] adj. f., cf. [נָוֶה] *pasture, meadow, 23²*.
But 𝔊 ὡραιότητι, 𝔍 *pulchritudo*, = נָוֶה = יָאֶה, as Je. 6², *the comely, beautiful one*,
v. 33¹. — [הִחֵלֶק שָׁלָל] Pi. impf. 3 f., phr. dependent on Ju. 5³⁰. — **14.** אִם־תִּשְׁכְּבוּן
[בֵּין שְׁפַתַּיִם] is derived from Ju. 5¹⁶ לָמָּה יָשַׁבְתָּ בֵּין הַמִּשְׁפְּתַיִם, cf. Gn. 49¹⁴ רֹבֵץ בֵּין
הַמִּשְׁפְּתָיִם. שְׁפַתַּיִם α.λ. prob. error for †מִשְׁפְּתַיִם. Cf. other passages: Gn. 49¹⁴
stalls, Ju. 5¹⁶ *sheepfolds*, here from context *dovecotes*. The clause is prob. a
gl., not suited to context and misleading for subsequent lines; so We., Du.
— כַּנְפֵי יוֹנָה] with נחפה Niph. pt. f. sg. Ges.¹⁴⁵. k, agreeing with principal noun
rather than construct, as if "winged dove." † [חָפָה] vb. Qal, *cover*, as
2 S. 15³⁰· ³⁰ Je. 14³· ⁴ Est. 6¹² 7⁸. Niph. *be covered*, here only. Pi. *overlay*
2 Ch. 3⁵· ⁵· ⁷· ⁸· ⁹. — [אֶבְרוֹתֶיהָ] pl. f. sf. 3 f. †אֶבְרָה n.f. *pinion*, elsw. Dt. 32¹¹
Ps. 91⁴ of eagle, Jb. 39¹³ ostrich; cf. אֵבֶר 55⁷ of dove. — [בִּירַקְרַק] n. with בּ,
†יְרַקְרַק adj. (1) *pale green* of plague spots Lv. 13⁴⁹ 14³⁷; (2) *BDB. n. green-
shimmering* only here. This improb. Another word is needed for measure;
rd. ברקה בירק. ברק vb. *flash* of lightning *18¹⁵;* cf. n. used also of arrow
Jb. 20²⁵, sword Dt. 32⁴¹, spear Na. 3³ Hb. 3¹¹, cf. *glitter* of weapon Ez. 21¹⁵· ²⁰· ³³;
so here the golden coloured pinions in the sunlight. יֶרֶק (*37²*) *greenness*
of grass, cf. As. *arḳu, yellow*, Sab. ורק *gold*, so Eth. †חָרוּץ n.m. *gold*, as Pr. 3¹⁴
8¹⁰· ¹⁹ 16¹⁶. — **15.** [בְּפָרֵשׂ] Pi. inf. cstr. פרשׂ *spread out*, always in Pi. unless here
and Zc. 2¹⁰, where some render *scatter;* but in both cases without sufficient
reason. 𝔊 ἐν τῷ διαστέλλειν, 𝔍 *cum divideret* = פרם *break in two, divide*,
used in Qal of breaking up bones in kettle Mi. 3³; so possibly interp. of 𝔐
here. Indeed, מלכים and רָב demand some such sense. But l. is just these
words too long, and they are prob. interp. glosses. If so, we may interpret פרשׂ of the spreading of wings of a bird, with wings omitted as 1 Ch.
28¹⁸. — ‡שַׁדַּי] pointed as divine name, MT. as 91¹, so Nu. 24⁴· ¹⁶ (Poems
Balaam) Ru. 1²⁰· ²¹ Is. 13⁶; Gn. 49²⁵ Jo. 1¹⁵ Ez. 1²⁴ dub.; but Jb. 31 times.
אל שדי characteristic of P as speculative conception of God of patriarchs;
Ez. 10⁵ dub. The use of שַׁדַּי dub. here. It has given the chief difficulty in
dealing with previous vb. Du. suggests שָׂדַי *field*, of battle-field, as local acc.
But it is more prob. that שׂ is dittog. and that we should rd. †דַּיָּה n.f. *bird of
prey* Is. 34¹⁵ Dt. 14¹³ דָּאָה Lv. 11¹⁴, cf. דאה vb. *fly swiftly* of eagle Je. 48⁴⁰
49²², in both cases ‖ פרשׂ כנפיו, *v. 18¹¹*. This gives us the bird of prey pursuing the dove of the previous context, which is indeed implied in the previous metaphor as most agree. — תַּשְׁלֵג] Hiph. juss., vb. α.λ., juss. sense
improb. in context. The vb. itself is suspicious; rd. prob. שֶׁלֶג n. as 51⁹, with
כ as Bi., Du., cf. Jb. 9³⁰. Lag. בהר השלג for בה תשלג does not give good sense.
— †צַלְמוֹן] n. pr. loci, Ju. 9⁴⁸ wooded mountain near Shechem, not yet identified; prob. here the same, as Bä., Du. If the reference is to the battle of

the Kishon, Ju. 5, we must think of some ridge of or near Carmel, famed for
its forests. Rob. BR.[III. 116 sq.] mentions *El Mutesellim*, of which he says:
"As we stood upon the noble Tell with the wide plain and Taanach there
before us, we could not but feel that here had been the scene of the great
battle of Deborah and Barak." This tell would satisfy all the conditions
of both passages. If the snow is a simile of bones which have been
stripped by birds of prey, there is no need of thinking of a snow mountain.
— **16.** הר־אלהים] either as הררי אל 36[7], cf. 80[1] if referring to gigantic mountains, as Bashan or Hermon; or for an original הר יהוה, if referring to Zion.
— הר־בָּשָׁן] 𝔐, Mt. E. Jordan and Gennesaret from the Jabbok to Syrian
Hauran, Wettstein, Golan, Now., Bu., Hermon Bä. But 𝔊 πῖον, 𝔍 *pinguis*,
so Σ, 𝔈, 𝔖, all favour דשן, as 36[9] בית דשן the fat things, rich blessings of the
temple on Zion, cf. Is. 5[1]. This is most prob. — הר־גַּבְנֻנִּים † [וַיִּבֶז] n.[m.]
peak or *rounded summit; many peaked* as adj., or in apposition *peaks*,
the latter favoured by הרים גבנים v.[17]. 𝔊 τετυρωμένα, 𝔈 *coagulatos*, as גְּבִינָה *milk*,
curds, Jb. 10[10]. 𝔍 *excelsus excelsi*, as if נבהים. — **17.** הֵרְצְדוּן] Pi. impf. archaic
3 pl. רצד a.λ. 𝔐 *look askance*, 𝔊 ὑπολαμβάνετε, 𝔍 *contenditis*, Aq. ἐρίζετε
dub. The l. is a late gl. — לְשִׁבְתּוֹ] Qal inf. cstr. sf. preg. sense, for His sitting
enthroned. — אף־יהוה] improb. in 𝔈; the whole l. doubtless a gl. — **18.** רֶכֶב]
coll. of heavenly army, cf. 2 K. 2[11] 6[17]. — רִבֹּתַיִם] a.λ. dual רִבּוֹ, Aramaism,
myriad dub., whether two myriads or myriadfold, v. Ges.[97. h]. 𝔊 μυριοπλά-
σιον, 𝔍 *innumerabiles*. — שִׁנְאָן] a.λ. *repetition*, *B*DB., "in a multiplicative
sense," Ges.[97. h], for שְׁנָן Kö.[II. 1. 99. b] √שנה, Aram. הנא *repeat*, so 𝔍 *millia
abundantium*, Aq., Σ, Bä., שאון, cf. Je. 48[45], but not suited to the context.
Lag., Bi., al., ישראל favoured by Nu. 10[36] רבכות אלפי ישראל, but it is difficult
to explain how the easy reading could give place to so difficult a one, especially as ישראל and שנאן are not easy to interchange. 𝔐, 𝔍, most prob., but
evidently a late phr. and **a** prosaic gl., doublet of רבתים, so Kau. — כָּם סִינַי]
though sustained by 𝔊 ἐν αὐτοῖς ἐν Σινὰ, 𝔍 *in eis, in Sina*, is difficult. Köster,
Ols., Now., Dr., Kau., rd. בא מסיני as Dt. 33[2]. — בַּקֹּדֶשׁ] either the holy place
of Zion as the goal of the march, as Now., Dr., or in majestic holiness, as
Ex. 15[11] Ps. 77[14], Ew., Bä. The l. is dub. and prosaic. The 3d pers. with
אדני is improb. for the 2d pers. characteristic of Ps. A single l. of four words
underlies this conglomerate. We first throw out שנאן אלפי as doublet and gl.
אדני is also improb., if there was originally only one l. כָּם is also explanatory
of the clause סיני בקרש. That leaves רכב יהוה רבתים סיני בקרש. רבתים סיני
is txt. err. for an original רבכת מסיני. רֶכֶב was prefixed to explain רבתים. The
original was therefore the theophanic ride of Yahweh from Sinai to the sanctuary in Zion שביתָ שֶּׁבִי בקרש — **19.** יהוה רכבת מסיני בקרש. שָׁבָה vb.
leud captives 106[46] 137[3] with שֶׁבִי n.m. collective *captives, captivity*, elsw.
Dt. 21[10] Ju. 5[12] 2 Ch. 28[17]; with מן Nu. 21[1], cf. 2 Ch. 28[5. 11]. שְׁבִי elsw. ψ
alone 78[61]. — מַתָּנוֹת] pl. מַתָּנָה n.f. *gift*, esp. of offerings. — בָּאָדָם does not
qualify the previous word, but לשכן. It is defined by סוררים ואף. See v.[7].
This phr. is prob. a gl., as it makes l. too long. — לִשְׁכֹּן] Qal inf. cstr. as לשבתו
v.[17]. — יָהּ] v. v.[5], is gl. — The various expl. of this difficult l. are due to a

failure to recognise the proper measures and the glosses, and therefore need not detain us. — **20.** וַיְעַמֵּס לָנוּ] Qal juss. ‡ עמס vb. Qal *load upon* Gn. 44¹³ (E) Ne. 13¹⁵, *carry as a load* here, as Zc. 12³ Is. 46¹· ³; 𝕲 κατευοδώσει paraphrase. 𝕴 *portabit*, as Aq., Σ βαστάσει. — רָאֵל יְשׁוּעָתֵנוּ]. The article improb. אֵל has been assimilated to האל v.²¹. It is doubtless cstr. as 𝕲, 𝕴. — **21.** מוֹשָׁעוֹת] α.λ.; prob. Aram. inf. ישׁע, 𝕲 τοῦ σῴζειν, 𝕴 *deus salutis*, as above. — לֵיהוה] in 𝕰, also evidence of gl. — תֵּצְאוֹת] pl. ‡ תּוֹצָאָה] n.f. only pl., (1) *outgoings, extremities of territory*, J, E, P, *outskirts* of city, Ez. 48³⁰ 1 Ch. 5¹⁶; (2) ת׳ חיים Pr. 4²³ (?) as מוצא (3); (3) *escapes*, *BDB.*, here only; cf. הוֹצִיא (2) v.⁷. — **22.** וַיִּמְחַץ רֹאשׁ] as 110⁶ Hb. 3¹³, cf. Ju. 5²⁰. — קָדְקֹד שֵׂעָר] *hairy scalp*, phr. α.λ.; for use of קדקד, cf. 7¹⁷. — בַּאֲשָׁמָיו] ‡ אָשָׁם] n.m. *offence*, *fault* (*v. 5¹¹*), 𝕲 πλημμελίαις, 𝕴 *delictis*. — **23.** אָמַר אֲדֹנָי] introduces an oracle. — אָשִׁיב] bis, Hiph. impf. 1 sg. in the sense of *bring back*, either the enemies in defeat, 𝕲, 𝕰, or dispersed Israel in restoration, 𝕴, 𝕮, the former an incongruous idea, the latter not suited to the context. It is better to interp. vb. as *requite, recompense* (*18²¹*) the enemy, which admirably suits the context. מִן with בשן and מצלות is improb., due to misinterp. It is really in both cases sf. with vb. אשיבכם. 𝕲 indeed has ἐν βυθοῖς though ἐκ βασὰν. A word is missing from second l., prob. אֲנִי. — **24.** לְמַעַן] final clause with תִּמְחַץ Qal impf. assimilated to v.²², unsuited to context. Rd. with 𝕲, 𝕾, 𝕮, תרחץ, so Hare, Kenn., Bö., Ols., We., al. — רַגְלְךָ] with sf. 2 sg., so כְּלָבֶיךָ is against the usage of Ps. It is due to the oracle which is cited here as in v.²³, referring to Israel. — מִנֵּהוּ] so 𝕲 παρ᾽ αὐτοῦ, 𝕰 *ab ipso*, 𝕴 *a temetipso*, Σ ἀπὸ ἑκάστου. A vb. or noun is missing which is needed to give sense. It is not necessary with Ols., Dy., Hu., Bi., Dr., We., Du., Kirk., to read מְנָתוֹ (*11⁶*) for מנהו. It is better to regard both as original, the former omitted by txt. err.; then מאויבים is an interpretative gl. — **25.** רָאוּ] Qal pf. 3 pl. indef. subj. to be rendered by passive. — הֲלִיכוֹתֶיךָ] pl. † הֲלִיכָה] n.f. (1) *travelling company, caravan*, Jb. 6¹⁹; (2) *going*, Na. 2⁶ Pr. 31²⁷ (Qr.); *procession*, here bis of God; so Hb. 3⁶. — הֲלִיכוֹת אֵלִי מַלְכִּי] a gl. of amplification, improb. here in original. — בַּקֹּדֶשׁ] *into the sanctuary*, Street, Horsley, Dr., Hu., Pe., Bä., Du.; *in holiness*, Ew., Hi., De. But 𝕲 τοῦ βασιλέως τοῦ ἐν τῷ ἁγίῳ; Ols., Gr., suggest קָדֵשׁ, *Kadesh*. — **26.** אַחַר] prep. *after*, but 𝕲 ἐχόμενοι, cf. 45¹⁵ 49¹⁴ 94¹⁵; prob. paraphrase Hu., Now., adv. — שָׁרִים] Qal ptc. שִׁיר as 87⁷, so Σ, 𝕴, 𝕮; 𝕲 ἄρχοντες, 𝕰 *principes*, so 𝕾; שׂרים not so well suited to context. — נֹגְנִים] Qal ptc. pl. נגן (*v. Intr. § 34*) improb.; rd. Pi. ptc. מנגנים as elsw. — בְּתוֹךְ] as prep. *in the midst of*, so Vrss. It is possible that תּוֹךְ should be rd. — עֲלָמוֹת] pl. עַלְמָה n.f. *young woman* (*v. Intr. § 34*). — תּוֹפֵפִיה] α.λ. Qal ptc. pl. f. תפף denom. תֹּף n.m. *timbrel* Ex. 15²⁰ Je. 31⁴ +, usually played by dancing women in the Orient, cf. Na. 2⁸. Polel ptc. מתפפות (dub. 𝕲 מצפצפות). Prob. the word has two tones, and we should rd. Pi. ptc. — **27.** מַקְהֵלוֹת] *assembly, choir*, as 26¹². — מְקוֹר] if correct, rel. clause; but phr. α.λ. and improb. Elsw. ψ מקור (*36¹⁰*), the source of life in Yahweh, as Je. 2¹³17 ¹⁸, so prob. here. מ prep. is dittog. The whole verse is a gl. — **28.** ‡ צָעִיר] adj. *little*, with the idea of insignificance, as 119¹⁴¹ Mi. 5¹ Je. 49²⁰ 50⁴⁵ Is. 60²², mng. *young* not in ψ. — רֹדֵם] Qal ptc. רדה (*49¹⁵*) with sf. 3 pl., for רְדָם or רְדִיהֶם, as 𝕿 refer. to Saul, 𝕵 *continens eos*, Aq. ἐπικρατῶν αὐτῶν, Θ παιδευτὴς αὐτῶν. But 𝕲 νεώτερος ἐν ἐκστάσει interprets רֹדֵם as ptc. † [רדם] vb. *be in ecstasy*, cf. 76⁷. Both the vb. and noun are used not for ecstatic song and dancing, but only for deep and profound sleep, cf. תַּרְדֵּמָה n.f. *deep, ecstatic sleep*, Gn. 2²¹; similarly 𝔖, 𝔙. Grill., Now., Du., would rd. רֹדֵם as above, v.²⁶. But the easiest explanation lies in antith. of the insignificant number of rulers of Benjamin with the heap of princes of Judah. — רִגְמָתָם] a.λ. [רִגְמָה] n.f. *heap* of stones, and so of people, Now. The phr. *heap of people*, common in South of the United States and suitable in antith. with the few princes of Benjamin. Hu., Bä., Pe., Bi., Dr., *BDB*., רִגְשָׁתָם as 64³, cf. 55¹⁵. But the mng. given by them to רגשׁ is improb. (*v.* 2¹), and therefore it gives no help here. 𝕲 ἡγεμόνες αὐτῶν, so 𝔖; 𝕵 *in purpura sua*, אַרְגָּמָן n.(m.) *purple* garments, as Nu. 4¹³ Ju. 8²⁶ Je. 10⁹. שֹׁם is needed to complete the measure of l. — **29.** צַוֵּה] Pi. pf. with אלהיך as subj. is not suited to context. 𝕲 ἔντειλαι θεὸς implies אלהים צַוֵּה, so 𝔖, 𝔙, Σ, 𝕵, 𝕿, Ew., Hu., Pe., Bä., Du. The sf. of 𝕳 is interpretation. — עֻזָּה] Qal imv. cohort. עזז, *be strong, prevail*, given by 𝕲, 𝕵, as transitive, but against usage. — זוּ] relative (9¹⁶) — לנו is needed for measure at close of first l., and אלהים is not needed in the second. — **30.** מֵהֵיכָלֶךָ is dub. (5⁸), 𝕲 ἀπὸ τοῦ ναοῦ σου, 𝕵 *de templo tuo*, so Du. ; but Σ διὰ τὸν ναόν, so Ew., Bä., Dr., most prob. — [יוֹבִילוּ שַׁי] Hiph. impf. יבל phr. 76¹² Is. 18⁷. † שַׁי n.m. *gift*, only in this phr. The v. is prosaic, not suited to context ; goes with v.³² rather, and is a gl. — **31.** חַיַּת קָנֶה] phr. a.λ. *wild beast of reeds*. ‡ קָנֶה n.m. *reed*, the water reeds of the Nile, cf. 1 K. 14¹⁵ Is. 19⁶ 35⁷. The hippopotamus, symbol of Egypt, cf. Ps. 80¹⁴. The l. prob. closes here, and the divine name is needed for measure. — עֲדַת אַבִּירִים]. For עֵדָה *v.* 1⁵, cf. espec. עדת לאמים 7⁸, ע׳ עריצים 86¹⁴. אַבִּירִים of strong enemies 22¹³, king of Assyria Is. 10¹³, Edomites Is. 34⁷, here confederate princes. — עֶגְלֵי עַמִּים]. These are not the people as calves following the bulls as their chiefs, but the subject peoples, the lesser nations. — מִתְרַפֵּס] Hithp. ptc. † רפס, variation of רפשׁ vb. *stamp, tread;* Qal c. acc. water Ez. 32² 34¹⁸. Niph. a fountain befouled Pr. 25²⁶. Hithp. *humble oneself* Pr. 6³ (RV.ᵐ Toy *bestir oneself*) ptc. only here *stamping, trampling* (?) *BDB*. ; cf. † [מִרְפָּשׂ] (water) *befouled* (by the feet) Ez. 34¹⁹; † רֶפֶשׂ n.[m.] *mire* Is. 57²⁰. 𝕲ᴮ τοῦ μὴ ἀποκλεισθῆναι τοὺς δεδοκιμασμένους τῷ ἀργυρίῳ makes מִן of neg. consequence as 39² 69²⁴ 102⁵ 106²³, *v.* *BDB*. ת must then be err. for ה of Niph. inf. Bä. suggests הִסָּכֵר. But 𝕲 uses ἀποκλείω for סגר. 𝕲ᴺ·ᶜ·ᵃ·ᴿ·ᵃ, omit μὴ, so 𝔙 *ut excludant eos qui probati sunt argento*, Hilary, Cassiod., *ut non excludantur*, Aug. Psalter Rom. *ut excludantur*. The negative seems to reverse the idea which the context demands. Ptc. is sustained by other Vrss. The vb. best suits the hippopotamus, with the meaning *trampling in the mire*. Then those trampled must be Israel. — [בְּרַצֵּי] 𝕲, Σ, give no evidence of ב, which is prob. interp. For רצי, 𝕲 צֹרְפֵי Qal ptc. pl. cstr. צרף *refine* (12⁷), which is well suited to כֶּסֶף; representing therefore Israel as refined as silver and yet trodden in the mire by the hippopotamus Egypt. Σ τοὺς εὐδοκήτους ὡς δοκιμὴν ἀργυρίου rd. כסף צרף רצוי. רָצוּי ptc. pass. רצה *favoured one* (40¹⁴), and also צָרֵף *refined*. ὡς is prob. explanatory. This gives the best explanation, and indeed the missing word of the line. 𝕲 took one of the two similar words, 𝕳, Aq., 𝔍, the other. Aq., 𝔍, interpret רצי as noun, pl. *runners, wheels*, from רוץ vb. *run*, thinking of silver wheels ; but such a noun, though possible, is not known in Heb. Lit. — בַּזַּר] Pi. pf. error for imv. בַּזֵּר as context demands ; so 𝕲, 𝔍. † בזר vb. *scatter*, Qal Dn. 11²⁴, Pi. only here. Prob. this is late copyist's error for פזר.— הְרָבוּת] pl. הְרָב *battle, war* (55¹⁹) rel. clause. — **32.** יֶאֱתָיוּ] Qal impf. 3 pl. ‡ אתה *come* Dt. 33². ²¹ Is. 41²⁵ 56¹²; here the form is Aramaism, Ges.⁷⁵· Anm. ⁴. — הַשְׁמַנִּים] α.λ. dub. ; 𝕲, 𝔖, 𝓤, πρέσβεις, *legati, ambassadors, nobles,* Σ ἐκφανέντες, Aq. ἐσπευσμένως, 𝔍 *velociter*, so Hilg., Pont., Che., חשם ptc. pass. חוש. Then נים would be dittog. from חֵמִי, archaic strong form of מן for tone measure. It is possible that 𝕲 also had חשׁב, thinking of swift messengers. — ‡ מִצְרָיִם] n. pr. *Egypt*, elsw. 78¹²· ⁴³· ⁵¹ 80⁹ 81⁶· ¹¹ 105²³· ³⁸ 106⁷· ²¹ 114¹ 135⁸· ⁹ 136¹⁰.— ‡ כּוּשׁ n. pr. *Ethiopia*, elsw. 7¹ 87⁴.— תָּרִיץ יָדָיו] phr. α.λ. Hiph. 3 f. רוץ with subj. land sg. f. Ges. L· ¹¹⁶· ², but 3 pl. m. sf. with יד makes it improb. It is better to regard ידיו as the subj. with Bö., Ols., Grill., Hu., Now., Ges.¹⁴⁶· ³. This couplet is a gl. based on Is. 45¹⁴. — **33.** זַמְּרוּ אֲדֹנָי]. The vb. is repeated in 𝕲 with לְרֹכֵב v.³⁴, cf. v.⁵ סֹלּוּ לָרֹכֵב. אדני is, as usual in this Ps., a gl. A vb. is needed with לרכב. It is not certain whether it was זמרו as 𝕲, or סלו as v.⁵, for which סלה, a misinterp. ; prob. the latter. — **34.** שָׁמֵי] has been repeated by dittog. שְׁמֵי קֶדֶם, cf. 44². — הֵן יִתֵּן בְּקוֹלוֹ] cf. 18¹⁴ 46⁷; the thunder accompanying the theophany. Here it is a gl., separating the clauses that belong together. — קוֹל־עֹז prob. goes with next clause to make a complete tetrameter. — **35.** וְאוֹתוֹ וְעֻזּוֹ בַשְּׁחָקִים] is derived from Dt. 33²⁶.— **36.** נוֹרָא] Niph. ptc. ירא.—אֱלֹהִים] is gl. making l. too long.— מִמְּקְדָּשֶׁיךָ]. But 𝕲 במקרשיו ἐν τοῖς ὁσίοις αὐτοῦ, 𝓤 *in sanctis suis*, 𝔍 *in sanctuario suo ;* so Σ, 𝔖, 𝕿, and 24 codd. Kenn., 30 De Rossi, have sg. Sf. in all cases and pl. are interpretations of an original מקדש, which is best interpreted as sg. referring to the sanctuary, as 74⁷ 78⁶⁹ 96⁶, cf. 73¹⁷. — אֶל ישראל] cf. אל יעקב 146⁵. — הוּא] is gl. of interp., though in 𝕲. — ‡ תַּעֲצֻמוֹת α.λ. pl. n.f. *might,* √עצם *be mighty* 38²⁰ — בָּרוּךְ אֱלֹהִים] liturg. addition as v.²⁷.

PSALM LXIX.

Ps. 69 is composite : (A) a prəyer (1) petition for salvation from deadly peril, represented under the figure of drowning in the rapids of a stream with miry bottom (v.²⁻³) ; explained as deadly enemies, numerous and false, who require retribution for offences wrongly charged (v.⁵) ; (2) a plea for the faithful, that they be not put to shame through the sufferer (v.⁷), and that in kindness and faithfulness he may be delivered from the overwhelming flood and the covered Pit (v.¹⁴ᵇ⁻¹⁶) ; (3) renewed plea for an answer in haste (v.¹⁷⁻¹⁸), for ransom from enemies (v.¹⁹), and exaltation from affliction (v.^{30}); with the concluding vow of public praise, which the author conceived to be more acceptable to God than sacrifices of animals (v.$^{31-32}$). Glosses intensify the suffering (v.^{4}), represent it as due to the folly and fault of the people (v.^{6}), and that the prayer is offered in a time of acceptance (v.^{14a}). (*B*) The lamentation of a sufferer who has been persecuted for his fidelity to God and zeal for the temple (v.$^{8-10}$). His fasting made him the derision of the idle and the drunkards (v.$^{11-13}$). His heart was broken because of the pitiless conduct of his adversaries, who gave him gall and vinegar instead of food and drink (v.$^{20b-22}$). He imprecates that their table may become a snare, their eyes and loins enfeebled, and that they may be overtaken by the divine anger (v.$^{23-25}$); that their dwellings may be without inhabitants, their guilt so great that they may have no salvation, and that their names may not be recorded with the righteous in the book of life (v.$^{26\ 28-29}$). This sufferer is doubtless the ideal community of Ps. 22, Is. 53. Glosses attribute the suffering to the divine visitation (v.^{27}); represent that God knows the reproach borne (v.^{20a}); that his salvation will give joy to all the afflicted (v.^{33}), and honour Yahweh as the deliverer of poor prisoners (v.^{34}). All nature is summoned to praise the Saviour of Zion and rebuilder of the cities of Judah for the abode of His servants and their seed (v.$^{35-37}$).

A.   v.$^{2-3.\ 5.\ 7.\ 14b-19.\ 30-32}$,   3 STR. 6^5.

SAVE me, Yahweh; for waters are come unto my life.
  I am plunged into the mire of the abyss, where there is no standing.
  I am come into depths of water, and a flood doth overwhelm me.
  Those hating me without cause are more than the hairs of my head.
  My false enemies are stronger in number (than my bones).
  What I have not spoiled, that I must repay.
LET not those that wait on Thee be ashamed through me, Yahweh Sabaoth.
  Let not those that seek Thee be upbraided through me, God of Israel.
  In the abundance of Thy kindness answer me, in the faithfulness of Thy
    salvation.
  Deliver me, and let me not be overwhelmed in the depths of water.
  Let not the flood overwhelm me, and let me not be swallowed up;
  And let not the Pit keep guard over me with its mouth.
ANSWER me according to the goodness of Thy kindness, according to the
    abundance of Thy compassion.
  And hide not Thy face; in my straits O make haste!
  Draw near unto me; O ransom, on account of mine enemies.

I

Afflicted and sorrowful, let Thy salvation, Yahweh, lift me on high.
I will praise Thy name with a song, and I will magnify it with thanksgiving:
And it will please better than an ox, a bullock horned and hoofed.

B. v.$^{8-13.\ 20b-26.\ 28-29}$, 5 STR. 6^3.

FOR Thy sake I have borne reproach;
Upbraiding hath covered my face.
I am become a stranger to my brethren,
A foreigner to the sons of my mother.
Zeal for Thine house consumed me;
And Thy reproaches have fallen on me.
WHEN I afflicted my soul with fasting,
It became a reproach unto me.
When I made my garments sackcloth,
I became a taunt song to them.
Those sitting in the gate composed (a song) against me.
Winebibbers made me a theme for their lyres.
BEFORE Thee are all mine adversaries.
Reproach hath broken my heart.
When I hoped for some one to pity, there was none;
For some to have compassion: I found them not.
And they gave me gall in my eating,
And in my thirst vinegar they gave me to drink.
LET their table become a snare,
Their peace-offerings before them a trap.
Let their eyes be darkened that they cannot see,
And their loins be continually tottering.
Pour upon them Thine indignation,
And let the heat of Thine anger overtake them.
LET their habitation become desolate,
And in their tents let there be no inhabitant.
Add iniquity to their iniquity,
And let them not come into Thy righteousness.
Let them be blotted out of the book of the living,
And with the righteous let them not be inscribed.

Ps. 69 was originally in 𝔇 (*v.* Intr. § 27); that is, its earliest part which we shall designate as *A*. This Ps. had three pentameter hexastichs, v.$^{2-3.\ 5.\ 7.\ 15-19.\ 30-32}$. It resembles other Pss. of 𝔇: עצם v.^{5}, as 38^{20} $40^{6.\ 13}$; איבי שקר, שנאי חנם v.^{5} = 35^{19}; באר v.^{16} for Pit of Sheol, as 55^{24}; צר לי v.^{18}, as 18^7, cf. 66^{14}; למען איבי v.^{19}, cf. 5^9 27^{11}. The conception of inward worship as more acceptable to Yahweh than animal sacrifices v.^{32} is as Pss. 40, 51; the figurative representation of trouble as peril of drowning, is as Ps. 18^{17}, cf. 42^8. Several other words and phrases are to be noted: יהוה צבאות v.^{7}, אלהי ישראל v.^{7}, שבלת v.$^{3.\ 16}$, as Ju. 12^6 Is. 27^{12}; מעמד α.λ. v.^{3} and עני וכואב α.λ. v.^{30}. The peril is the overwhelming trouble of the Exile, and the situation is that of Pss. 40, 51. This Ps. was taken up into 𝔈, and then subsequently into 𝔇ℜ, where it received the direction אל שושנים (*v.* Intr. §§ 32, 33, 34). It is however quite possible that 𝕯𝕽 had not *A*, but only *B* ; and that the combination of *A* and *B* came later ; for the שושנים Ps. 80 is a trimeter. *B* is a trimeter poem of five hexastichs : v.[3-13. 20b-26. 28-29]. This Ps. has its special features : v.[8], cf. Ps. 44[16. 23] Je. 15[15] Zp. 3[18]; v.[9], cf. Jb. 19[15]; v.[10] zeal for the temple, cf. Nu. 25[11] (P) for God ; v. 11 בצום as Ps. 35[13]; v. 12 לבושי שק as 35[13]; משל as 44[15]; v.[18] שותי שכר a.λ.; v.[21] שברה as 34[19] 51[19], ואנושה as Je. 15[18] Mi. 1[9]; v.[22] ברותי a.λ., but cf. בָּרוּת La. 4[10]; v.[28] מוקש cf. Ps. 18[6] 64[6]; פח 91[3] 141[9]; שלום as Mi. 7[3] Ho. 9[7] Is. 34[8]; v.[24] המער as Ez. 29[7]; v.[25] חרון אף phr. of J, cf. Ps. 78[49] 85[4]; v.[26] טירה as Gn. 25[16] (P) Nu. 31[10] (P) Ez. 25[4]; v.[29] ספר חיים, a.λ. cf. Ex. 32[32. 33] (E), ארץ (ה)חיים Pss. 27[13] 52[7] 142[6]. The terms are not later than Nehemiah. The imprecations imply a severe strain from unscrupulous foes of the time when Nehemiah began his reforms. The zeal for the temple is characteristic of the same situation. *C*. There are several glosses to this Ps. : (1) v.[14a] עת רצון = Is. 49[8], cf. also Is. 58[5] 61[2]. This l. is a seam uniting *A* and *B*. It seems to have an original יהוה and is therefore later than 𝕰. If 𝕯𝕽 combined the two, it was composed by him; if later, whoever combined them is responsible for it. (2) V.[4] כלו עיני as La. 2[11] 4[17], יגע as Ps. 6[7]. This tetrameter couplet is not late in style, but it introduces a different conception of suffering in the midst of a simile. It was prob. originally a marginal note which subsequently crept into the text. (3) V.[27] חלליך as Je. 51[52] La. 2[12] Ez. 26[15] 30[24]. This v. is not late in style ; but it breaks up a str. of the trimeter poem, which 𝕯𝕽 would not do. It must be later than 𝕯𝕽. (4) V.[6] אולת as 38[6], elsw. Pr. 23 t. אשמה usage of P, Chr. לְ acc. late Aramaism. This v. disturbs the pentameter poem. אלהים is prob. original. This gl. belongs to the Greek period. (5) V.[20a] the use of ידע, as in v.[6] indicates prob. the same hand. (6) V.[33-34. 36-37] are based on Ps. 22[24. 25. 27] a gl. from the Maccabean period. (7) V.[35] is a later insertion in the above gl.

PSALM LXIX. *A*.

Str. I. has a syn. tristich, a syn. couplet, and a concluding line. **2.** *Save me, Yahweh*], as the context indicates from deadly peril ; an individual servant of Yahweh, a prophet like Jeremiah. —*for waters are come unto my life*]. He is drowning in waters which have so risen up about him, that he is in peril of death. — **3.** *I am come into depths of water*]. He is beyond his depth in the stream. — *and a flood doth overwhelm me*]. He is in the rapids of the Jordan ; and the waters, swiftly descending, come upon him like a flood. This is doubtless figurative, as 18[17] 42[8], and not real. — A glossator inserts another description of the sufferings : **4.** *I am weary with my calling : my throat is hot : Mine eyes do fail in waiting for my God*]. He has so long called for divine help that his throat has become heated and feverish. His eyes fail because of weeping hot tears. This is not altogether suited to the context, and it makes the Str. too long even if the measure of this v. were the same as that of this Ps. — **5.** *Those hating me without cause* ‖ *my false enemies*]. The figure of drowning in the rapids of a river passes over into its explanation as perils from enemies. — Their causeless hatred is explained in the last clause : *what I have not spoiled*]. He is falsely accused of having taken spoil from his enemies or their friends by violence or injustice, and this they insist upon. — *I must repay*] make retribution for it ; not simply make restoration, for their purpose is a deadly one : they *would destroy my life*]. These enemies are not only false, without justification and deadly ; but they are very numerous : — *more than the hairs of my head* ‖ *strong in number*]. — A glossator explains the suffering as due to the folly and fault of the sufferer, in a line of different measure from the context : **6.** *Thou knowest* ‖ *from Thee are not hid*] positively and negatively : all is known to God. — *my folly* ‖ *my faults*], both terms of late usage in the time when the legal type of righteousness was mingled with the more ethical type of Hebrew Wisdom.

Str. II. has a syn. couplet, and a tetrastich whose second and third lines are syn., the first and fourth introductory and concluding. — **7.** *Let not those that wait on Thee* ‖ *that seek Thee*], the real worshippers. — *Yahweh Sabaoth* ‖ *God of Israel*], divine names which in themselves are pleas for help in the mouth of an Israelite. — *be ashamed* ‖ *be upbraided*], suffer disgrace and humiliation. — *through me*], as an example of a worshipper of Yahweh delivered over into the hands of enemies. — A later editor now inserts a portion of another Ps., v.[8-13], which in trimeter measure describes the sufferings of a persecuted prophet. Then **14 a** was inserted as a seam. — *But as for me*], antith. enemies. — *my prayer is to Thee, Yahweh, at the time of acceptance, O God*]. This expresses an assurance and certainty of redemption, which is not in harmony with the context. "The time of acceptance," phr. elsw. Is. 49[8], is the time when the prayer will be favoured by God with an answer of salvation. **14 b–16.** *In the abundance of Thy kindness*, intensified by *in the faithfulness of Thy salvation*]. The attributes of kindness and faithfulness are those upon which salvation is usually based. When these are intensified by abundance, superabounding every need, they constitute an invincible plea. On them are heaped up a number of verbal pleas, at first more general : *answer me* || *deliver me*, then more specifically, referring to the figure of v.[3] : *Let me not be overwhelmed in the depths of water* || *Let not the flood overwhelm me, and let me not be swallowed up*], concluding with deliverance from the Pit of Sheol : *Let not the Pit keep guard over me with its mouth*]. Let me not go down into the Pit of Sheol, and be shut up there, kept in ward by a safely fastened door at its mouth. Those who think of the dungeon in which Jeremiah was confined, Je. 38[6], fail to see the incongruity between the figure of the rapids of a river and that of a damp, miry dungeon.

Str. III. has two synth. tristichs. — **17.** *Answer me*], a renewal of the petition, v.[14b], with slightly varying terms : *according to the goodness of Thy kindness, according to the abundance of Thy compassion*]. This was enlarged by an ancient copyist, making the v. into two tetrameters : " answer me, Yahweh ; for Thy kindness is good ; according to the abundance of Thy compassion turn unto me." This reading, although sustained by 𝕲 and other Vrss. and followed by EV[s]., cannot be justified save at the expense of the measure and strophical organisation of the Ps. and at the cost of the correspondence of the v. with v.[14b]. — **18.** *And hide not Thy face*], so as not to see, cf. 10[1]. A glossator adds *from Thy servant — in my straits*], as elsw. ; but a glossator enlarges it with " for I am in straits." — *O make haste*]. The need is imperative, and unless speedy help is given it will be too late. This also was enlarged by a glossator's appending " answer me." All these additions were probably made to assimilate these pentameter lines to the trimeters of the poem, whose second part begins, v.[20b], and continues through v.[29]. — **19.** *Draw near unto me, O ransom, on account of mine enemies*], referring back to v.[5]. The glossator appends " redeem me " to make this line also into two trimeters, as v.[20-29]. — **30.** *Afflicted and sorrowful*], emphatic description of the condition of the pleading sufferer. — *let Thy salvation*], cf. v.[14b]. — *lift me on high*] in safety from the enemies, where they cannot reach me. — **31.** *I will praise Thy name* || *magnify it*], a vow of public praise in the temple. — *with a song* || *thanksgiving*], a song of thanksgiving with vocal music. — **32.** *And it will* *please*], give gratification to God and find acceptance with Him. — *better than an ox, a bullock horned and hoofed*], the choicest animal slaughtered in the thank-offering.

PSALM LXIX. *B.*

Str. I. has three syn. couplets. — **8.** *For Thy sake*], emph. in position to show that the servant of Yahweh suffered for the cause of Yahweh, and for that cause alone, cf. Je. 15^{15} Ps. 44^{23}. — *I have borne reproach ‖ upbraiding hath covered my face*], cf. 44^{16}. Reproaches are heaped upon the servant for his fidelity to Yahweh, in such quantity and intensity that they are hard to bear, and his face is covered over with the shame of them. — **9.** *I am become a stranger ‖ a foreigner*], instead of an acquaintance and native born. — even *to my brethren*], the sons of the same father ‖ *the sons of my mother*], in a polygamous state of society nearer still than sons of a common father. — **10.** *Zeal for Thine house*]. This can hardly be for the erection of the temple in the time of Zerubbabel, or for the purification of the temple in the time of the Maccabees; but rather for the honour of the temple and the worship of God therein, as in the time of Nehemiah, against those unfaithful Jews who were treacherous to their own people and syncretistic in their tendencies. The servant, *consumed* by this zeal as by a fire in his bones, became offensive to those who were annoyed by it. — *And Thy reproaches*], reproaches against God, resuming the thought of v.^{8}. — *have fallen on me*], as espousing the cause of God and interposing on His behalf.

Str. II. has two synth. and a syn. couplet. — **11–12.** *When I afflicted my soul with fasting*], in humiliation and penitence for the neglect of the religion of Yahweh and the dishonour done to their God by compatriots. — *When I made my garments sackcloth*], put on the outward badge of sorrow and fasting, cf. Ne. 9$^{1-2}$. —*it became a reproach unto me*], the impenitent and ungodly reproached him for it ‖ *I became a taunt song to them*], cf. 44^{15}. — They *composed* (*a song*) *against me*], they taunted him in a song, which they composed to hold him up to ridicule and scorn ‖ **13.** *made me a theme for their lyres*]. The taunt song was accompanied with the music of the common sort of stringed instruments used by such people in such places. — *Those sitting*

in the gate], the public place inside the gate where idlers gathered
for gossip, and partisans gathered together in groups ‖ *winebibbers*], as usual in such cases indulging freely in wine, which made
them hilarious and abusive of their opponents. Doubtless the
poet is contrasting in his mind the worship of God with song and
music in the temple with this abuse of song and music by the
ungodly in the public squares.

Str. III. has a synth. and two syn. couplets. — **20 *b. Before Thee*],**
emphatic in position ; in Thy presence, in Thy sight. — *are all
mine adversaries*]. They have done nothing ; they cannot do
anything without the divine knowledge. — **21.** *Reproach*], resuming the term of v.[8. 10-11]. — *hath broken my heart*], cf. Je. 23[9]
Ps. 22[15]. He is heartbroken with sorrow, and the sense of injustice and wrong. — *When I hoped for some one to pity ‖ some to
have compassion*]. In his heartbroken condition he looked about
for sympathy and pity for his sufferings. — *there was none ‖
I found them not*]. He was left alone in his agony like the sufferer of 22[7-8]. — **22.** *And they gave me gall* instead of bread, *in
my eating ‖ vinegar* instead of wine, *gave me to drink, in my thirst*],
to aggravate his hunger and thirst instead of satisfying them ; to
mock him in his misery.

Str. IV. is an imprecation in three syn. couplets. — **23.** *Let their
table*], upon which their food and drink are spread, antith. v.[22] and
therefore ‖ *their peace-offerings*], the flesh of the festal offerings
on the table ; which is certainly to be preferred to AV. " that
which should have been for their welfare," which is without justification ; or RV. " when they are in peace," JPSV. " unto their
friends," which are not well sustained ; or 𝕲, 𝔙, 𝔍, Aq., Rom. 11[9],
" for retribution," which is sustained by good usage, but does not
suit the context. — *become a snare ‖ before them a trap*]. The
context does not indicate in what sense this is meant ; whether
the rich food was to be poisoned by treacherous enemies, or
whether they would be surprised by enemies while indulging at
the table. The author leaves it indefinite purposely, with suggestion of many possible explanations. — **24.** *Let their eyes be darkened that they cannot see*]. Let them be blinded by some sudden
calamity. — *And let their loins be continually tottering*], from some
sudden shock, filling them with terror and despair. — **25.** *Pour*

upon them ‖ *let overtake them*], as a downfall of rain, a deluge, a storm. — *Thine indignation* ‖ *the heat of Thine anger*].

Str. V. has three syn. couplets. — **26.** *Let their habitation* ‖ *in their tents*], the dwellings of the families of these enemies of Yahweh and His servant. — *become desolate* ‖ *let there be no inhabitant*]. Let their wives and children, and all their adherents and posterity perish. — A glossator inserts a reason : **27.** *For whom Thou hast smitten they do pursue, and of the pain of those whom Thou hast pierced they tell*]. This glossator states that the sufferings of the servant of Yahweh are due to the divine visitation, which is contrary to the entire tone of the Ps. : but he thinks at the same time that this aggravates the guilt of the persecutors. — **28.** *Add iniquity to their iniquity*]. Increase this guilt, make them more and more guilty. — *Let them not come into Thy righteousness*], share in the saving righteousness bestowed by God on His faithful servants. — **29.** *Let them be blotted out* ‖ *let them not be inscribed*], registered, *with the righteous*], their names among them, cf. Je. 22³⁰ Ez. 13⁹ Ps. 87⁶. — *the book of the living*], the book recording the names of those who share in everlasting life, cf. Ex. 32³², ³³ Dn. 12¹ also Hb. 2⁴. This brings this simple and impressive Ps. to a conclusion.

A late editor of the Maccabean period, thinking to give the composite Ps. a more appropriate conclusion, added v.³³⁻³⁴, ³⁶⁻³⁷ after the analogy of 22²⁴, ²⁵, ²⁷. **33.** *Have the afflicted seen, they will be glad*]. When the delivered praise God in the temple, they will be seen by others, afflicted as they have been, who will be glad with them. — *Those seeking God*]. His worshippers — *will say: Let your heart live*], as 22²⁷. — **34.** *For Yahweh heareth the poor, and His prisoners He doth not despise*], as 22²⁵. The poor and the prisoners are doubtless those of the Maccabean afflictions. A still later editor inserts here an invocation to universal praise : **35.** *Let heaven and earth praise Him, the seas and all that glideth therein.* — **36.** *For God will save Zion, and rebuild the cities of Judah*]. Zion was still in danger, and the cities of Judah were in ruins owing to the Syrian wars. — *and they will dwell therein, and have it in possession* ‖ **37.** *The seed also of His servants will inherit it, and they that love His name will dwell in it*]. The author looks forward to a long and peaceful residence of the faithful under the protection of God in Zion and in the rebuilt cities of Judah.

LXIX. *A* (*a*).

2. אלהים] for יהוה of 𝔐: wherever יהוה appears in present Ps. of 𝔈 it is either verbal gl. or part of a longer gl. or txt. err., as v.⁷. — מים] עד־נפש phr. cited Jon. 2⁶. — **3.** בִּיָוֵן] elsw. *40³* טיט הַיָוֵן, cf. Je. 38⁶ (בַּטִּיט).— † מָעֳמָד] n.(m.) a.λ. *standing ground, foothold.* — מַעֲמַקֵּי־מַיִם] = v.¹⁵ † מַעֲמַקִּים n.m. pl. (√עמק) 130¹, מַעֲמַקִּי ים Is. 51¹⁰, so here 𝔊; מ׳ מים elsw. Ez. 27³⁴. — ‡ שִׁבֹּלֶת] n.f. † (1) *stream, flood,* elsw. v.¹⁶ Ju. 12⁶ (the Jordan), Is. 27¹² (the Euphrates). (2) *ears of grain* Gn. 41⁵⁻²⁷ Ru. 2² Is. 17⁵. — שְׁטָפַתְנִי] Qal pf. 3 f.s., sf. 1 sg. ‡ שטף vb. *overflow, wash away,* v.¹⁶, cf. Is. 8⁸ 28² 30²⁸ 43² 66¹² Je. 47² Pss. 78²⁰ 124⁴ : for the idea in different terminology, cf. 18⁵ 42⁸. — **4.** יגעתי בקראי], cf. 6⁷ יגעתי באנחתי. 𝔊 κράζων, 𝔍 *clamans* without sf. which is a gl. in 𝔐. — נִחַר] Niph. pf. † חרר vb. Qal *be hot,* Ez. 24¹¹, *burn* Is. 24⁶, of bones in fever Jb. 30³⁰, Niph. (1) *be scorched* Je. 6²⁹ Ez. 15⁴·⁵ 24¹⁹ ; (2) *burn,* of bones in fever Ps. 102⁴ ; *be parched,* of throat here only. Pilp. *kindle* (strife) Pr. 26²¹. — כָּלוּ עֵינַי] *fail,* exhausted by weeping, phr. La. 2¹¹, cf. 4¹⁷ Ps. 119⁸²·¹²³ ; for vb. cf. *18³³* 71⁹ 73²⁶ 84³ 119⁸¹ 143⁷.— מְיַחֵל] Pi. ptc. יהל *31²⁵*, so 𝔍, 𝔊 ἀπὸ τοῦ ἐγγίζειν ἐπὶ τὸν θεόν μου, מְיַחֵל prep. and inf., so Du.; most prob., easiest syntax. — This v. has two tetrameters ; is gl. — **5.** מִשַּׂעֲרוֹת רֹאשִׁי], phr. elsw. 40¹³. — שֹׂנְאַי חִנָּם] phr. elsw. *35¹⁹* = איבי חנם La. 3⁵²: ‖ אֹיְבַי שֶׁקֶר = *35¹⁹*, cf. שנאי שקר *38²⁰*. — עָצְמוּ] *be vast, numerous* ‖ רבו; *38²⁰* 40⁶·¹³ 139¹⁷ Is. 31¹ Je. 5⁶ 30¹⁴·¹⁵. — מַצְמִיתִי] Hiph. ptc. sf. 1 sg. √צמת (*18⁴¹*) *my exterminators,* but improb. The parall. suggests a comparison. Hare, Lowth., Street, Ew., Gr., מִצַּמְרִי *than my locks,* but this mng. dub.; 𝔖 מֵעַצְמוֹתַי *than my bones,* so Ols., Hu., Dy., Kau., Bä., cf. Jb. 4¹⁴, is to be preferred, and this gives us two beats for the measure. A word is missing with reading of 𝔐. It is favoured also by the word play of vb. and noun. — אז] 𝔊 and 𝔍 is difficult unless אשר be regarded as relative of time. If not, we must interpret of logical sequence, as 40⁸ 119⁶·⁹². But we would expect rather a demonstrative זֶה or זֹאת. אז is regarded as a corruption of אני by Lag., Du.; but unnecessary. — **6.** לְאִוַּלְתִּי] ל of acc. of late style, 𝔊 τὴν ἀφροσύνην μου, 𝔍 *stultitiam meam,* אִוֶּלֶת n.f. *38⁶* and here, elsw. Pr. 23 t. ‖ אַשְׁמוֹתַי pl. ‡ אַשְׁמָה n.f. *wrong doing, guiltiness, trespass* a.λ. in ψ, but Lv. 5²⁶ and Chr. 10 t. (action); Lv. 4³ Am. 8¹⁴(?) Chr. 3 t. (guilt); Lv. 5²⁴ 22¹⁶ of bringing trespass offering ; implies late date subsequent to P. — This v. is doubtless a late gl. — **7.** אֲדֹנָי יהוה צבאות] 𝔊 has only κύριε τῶν δυνάμεων, but 𝔍 *domine deus exercituum*: יהוה in 𝔈 cannot be original. 𝔍 is doubtless correct as a conflation of אדני (for יהוה) and אלהים of 𝔈.

LXIX. *B* (*a*).

Another Ps. begins here with trimeter measure. — **8.** כִּי־עָלֶיךָ] cf. 44²³. — נָשָׂאתִי חֶרְפָּה] phr. elsw. Je. 15¹⁵ Zp. 3¹⁸ חֶרְפָּה (*15³*). — כִּסְּתָה כְלִמָּה פָנָי], cf. 44¹⁶ בשת פני כִּסְּנִי. The order here is suspicious. It was at an earlier stage כסתני כלמה מני. For כְּלִמָּה *v. 4³*. — **9.** מוּזָר] Hoph. ptc. זור *estranged* a.λ.; Niph. same sense Is. 1⁴ Ez. 14⁵.— וְנָכְרִי] adj. *foreign, alien,* cf. Jb. 19¹⁵ נכרי בעיניהם. — **10.** קִנְאַת בֵּיתְךָ] phr. a.λ. *zeal for thy house.* ‡ קִנְאָה n.f. *ardour*

(1) of jealousy not in ψ; (2) of zeal for God 2 K. 10¹⁶ Nu. 25¹¹ (P), so here; (3) of anger Ps. 119¹³⁹ Jb. 5² (men); † אש קנאה Ps. 79⁵ Is. 26¹¹ Ez. 36⁵ Zp. 1¹⁸ 3⁸. — [חרפית חורפיך] prob. dittog., makes too long a l. The original was prob. חרפותיך *reproaches against Thee.* It is possible that הרפות came in by error from next v., and that made it necessary to interpret the other form as ptc. — **11.** [וָאֶבְכֶּה] ו consec. prot. temporal clause with Qal impf. 1 sg. ‡ בכה vb. *weep* elsw. in ψ 78⁶⁴ 126⁶ 137¹. This form is dub. with בַצּוֹם נַפְשִׁי *with fasting,* as 35¹³. MT. seems to make נפשי a second subj. of vb, so Ew., Hi., De., Bä., Ges.¹⁴⁴⁽⁴⁾. 𝕵 makes it acc. after vb., so Aq., Σ, interp. Pi., as Ez. 8¹⁴, properly *bewailing oneself, for oneself,* cf. Je. 31¹⁵. This is most prob. with text, as it is suited to the context. But 𝕲ᴮ συνέκαμψα, so 𝕾. מככת suggests either as Houb., Lowth., Lag., Now., אָמֶה Aramaism, cf. Ps. 106⁴³, 𝕲 of 88¹⁶ Jb. 24²⁴ Ec. 10¹⁸, or אֶעֱנֶה assimilated to 35¹³, where alone the same phr. is found with this vb., so Dy., Ols., Hu., Gr., Du. 𝕲ᴺ·ᶜ·ᵃ·ᴿ· συνεκάλυψα, 𝕻 *operui* would represent an original וְאֶכֶּה which is improbable. — **12.** [וָאֶתְּנָה] ו consec. prot. temporal clause, Qal impf. coh. 1 sg. — [וְאֶהִי] *v. 35¹³.* — [לְבוּשִׁי שָׂק] Qal impf. 1 sg. coh. 1 consec. apod., Qal impf. 3 sg. juss. היה. But rhyme requires that it should be at close of l. — [לְמָשָׁל] *for a by-word* or *taunt song,* as 44¹⁵. — **13.** [יָשִׂיחוּ] Qal impf. שׂיח, not (1) *complain,* as 55¹⁸, nor (2) *muse,* so Dr., as 77⁷·¹³; but *compose* (a song), as 105² Ju. 5¹⁰. — [כִּי] makes l. too long unless attached by Makkeph to vb. It also come at close of l. with retracted accent, יָשִׂיחוּ־בִי. — [ישבי שער] *sit in the gate,* as Dr., not *dwell in gate,* cf. Gn. 19¹ c. ב, those who sit in judgment there, rulers, but here, idlers. — [נְגִינוֹת] of stringed instruments (see Intr. § 34), cf. 77⁷(?) Jb. 30⁹ La. 3¹⁴; 𝕲 καὶ εἰς ἐμὲ ἔψαλλον, 𝕻 *in me psallebant,* and 𝕵 *et cantabant,* rd. vb. and sf. Rd. נְגִּנּוּנִי Houb., and put at end of l. — [שֹׁתֵי שֵׁכָר] *drinkers of strong drink,* Qal. ptc. fully written, pl. cstr. ‡ שֵׁכָר n. a.λ. in ψ. Cf. Is. 5¹¹·²² Mi. 2¹¹ +. — **14.** [ואני] emph. antith. to mocking enemies; not original; this v. is a gl., measure is complete without it. — [הִפְּלְתִי־לְךְ] so c. ל 42⁹, cf. 35¹³ (עַל חִיקִי תָשׁוּב). — [יהוה] mark of gl. as in v.⁷. — [עֵת־רָצוֹן] phr. elsw. Is. 49⁸, cf. ר־ יום Is. 58⁵, שנת ר־ Is. 61². — [אלהים] as in 𝕲 goes with first part of v. for an original יהוה.

LXIX. *A (b).*

The pentameter poem is resumed here with v.¹⁴ᵇ. — **15.** [מִמָּטִיט] gl. *(18⁴³).* — [וְאַל־אֶטְבָּעָה] Qal cohort. with ו coörd. See v.³. 𝕲 ἵνα μὴ, so 𝕵 requires ולא; possibly assimilated to other ll., which have אל, possibly phr. is gl. after v.3ᵃ. — [אִנָּצְלָה] Niph. cohort. נצל (7²): doublet of הצילני, improb. The l. is too long. משנאי must go out as gl., so Bä., or the following words as repetition from v.³. But other terms are repeated from v.³ We would expect this phr. also, whereas משנאי is explanatory of trouble and disturbs the metaphor. Rd. ב for מ before מעמקי. — **16.** [אל־תִּשְׁטְפֵנִי] Qal juss., cf. v.³ attached to same noun, only here שבלת מים for שבלת there; prob. מים a later addition, as unnecessary; makes l. too long. — [מְצוּלָה] unnecessary, gl. to give second vb. a subj. — [תֶּאְטַר] vb. a.λ. 𝕲 has συνσχέτω usually for עצר, 𝕵 *coronet* = עטר. Gr. suggests אטם which is not so easy. Better תפער as Is. 5¹⁴ of Sheol, cf. Jb. 16¹⁰. —

בְּאֵר] *pit* of Sheol here as *55²⁴*. — **17.** יהוה] gl. as v.¹⁴. — כִּי טוב] although sustained by Vrss. is not according to ‖ ערב, therefore rd. כטוב with Street, Gr., We., Che., Bä., Du. It has been assimilated to 63⁴ 109²¹. — פנה אלי] does not belong to the l.; it is prob. gl. — **18.** מֵעַבְדְּךָ] (cf. *19¹²*) prob. gl. as Du. — כִּי־צַר־לִי] as 31¹⁰ elsw. always with ב ; בצר ל 18⁷ 66¹⁴ 106⁴⁴ 107⁶· ¹³· ¹⁹· ²⁸ ; cf. צר לי ביום 59¹⁷ 102³ ; so prob. here also. — מַהֵר עֲנֵנִי] two imvs., the first auxiliary, same phr., 102³ 143⁷, cf. 79⁸ (*v. 164*). But ענני is here prob. gl., dittog. of beginning of previous v. — **19.** אֶל־נַפְשִׁי] *unto myself*, cf. v.² — לְמַעַן אֹיְבִי cf. למען שוררים 5⁹ 27¹¹, למען צוררים 8³, in all these cases concluding a clause ; therefore prob. פדני a gl. ‖ גאלה. There has been an effort to change these pentameters into trimeters because of subsequent trimeters. — **20.** אַתָּה] emph., but without apparent reason. L. a gl. — בָּשְׁתִּי (*35²⁶*) ‖ כלמתי, cf. v.⁸ ; חרפתי, cf. v.⁸· ¹⁰· ¹¹· ²¹.

LXIX. B (b).

The trimeter Ps. is here resumed with 20ᵇ. — נֶגְדְּךָ] emph. — **21.** שָׁבְרָה לִבִּי] *v.* 34¹⁹ 51¹⁹ 147³; ℨ *contritum.* 𝕲 has προσεδόκησεν with ἡ ψυχή μου = נפשי as subj. = שִׁבְרָה Pi. *hope, v. 104²⁷* 119¹⁶⁶ 145¹⁵, in accord with subsequent context. לבי of 𝕴 and נפש of 𝕲 both interp. glosses. — וָאֲנוּשָׁה] consec. with Qal cohort. נוּש vb. a.λ. *be sick*, improb. ; is attached to previous context by MT. and Vrss. 𝕲 ταλαιπωρίαν f. ptc. Qal אנוש *to be weak, sick*, as Je. 15¹⁸ Mi. 1⁹, ℨ *disperatus sum*, so 𝕿, Bi., Che. Unpointed 𝕴 would yield ptc. also. — וָאֲקַוֶּה] consec. Pi. impf. I sg. (*25³*) ; prob. this consec. reacted upon previous . — לָנוּד] inf. c. נוד (*11¹*) ; so Jb. 2¹¹ ‖ לְנַחֲמוֹ; cf. Jb. 42¹¹ וַיָּנֻדוּ ‖ וַיְנַחֲמוּ, *condole with, shew sympathy*, only in these passages in this sense. But 𝕲 συλλυπούμενον = ptc. נָד required also by ‖ מנחמים Pi. ptc. pl. (*23⁴*), so Bä., Du. ℨ renders both by rel. clause, and prob. rd. ptc. also. — **22.** בְּבָרוּתִי] *as my food*, ברות a.λ. (√ברה *eat*). 𝕲 εἰς τὸ βρῶμά μου, ℨ *in esca mea* ; cf. inf. Pi. לְבָרוֹת La. 4¹⁰; prob. inf. here with ב of time בְּבָרוּתִי *when I ate.* — † ראשׁ] n.m. (1) *poisonous herb*, elsw. La. 3⁵· ¹⁹ Dt. 29¹⁷ 32³² Am. 6¹² Ho. 10⁴ Je. 8¹⁴ 9¹⁴ 23¹⁵; (2) *venom* Dt. 32³³ Jb. 20¹⁶. — **23.** וְלִשְׁלוֹמִים] MT. pl. of שָׁלֵו, as Ra., *those in security, careless*, cf. 4⁹ 37³⁷; but pl. of שלום always txt. err. (*v.* BDB.). 𝕿 rd. שְׁלָמֶם *their peace-offering*, ל prep. being assimilation in connection with misinterpretation of text, so Houb., Gr., Du. But all other Vrss. are different. 𝕲 has καὶ εἰς ἀνταπόδοσιν καὶ, 𝕱, ℨ, *et in retributiones ad*, Aq. εἰς ἀποδόσεις, Σ εἰς τιμωρίαν, Θ εἰς ἀνταποδόσεις, rd. שְׁלוּמִים pl. שִׁלוּם n.m. *recompense, retribution*, elsw. Mi. 7³ Ho. 9⁷ Is. 34⁸, so Street. The three nouns with ל prob. parallel, and the measure so requires. If the present order of 𝕴 be correct, we must interpret the word after 𝕲 ; but the v. seems to have lost its parall. If לפניהם is transposed to the second l. and לפח to the first, then we get better ‖ by thinking of שלמים as the festal meal. — **24.** תֶּחְשַׁכְנָה] Qal impf. 2 pl. f. ‡ חשׁך vb. Qal *grow dim*, fig. as La. 5¹⁷ Ec. 12³. Hiph. *cause darkness* Ps. 105²⁸, sq. מן 139¹². — הַמְעַד] for הַמְעֵד Hiph. imv., so 𝕲, ℨ, מעד (*18³⁷*), *cause to totter*, cf. Ez. 29⁷, where rd. המעדת with מתנים כל after Sm., Co., Da., Berth. (instead of MT. העמדת). Gr. suggests מעור המעד here, but the change is unnecessary. —

25. חֲרוֹן אַפְּךָ] so 78⁴⁹ 85⁴, early usage J, not E, D², H, P. — **26.** טִירֹתָם] pl.
sf. † טִירָה] n.f. (1) *encampment;* so here ‖ אהליהם, cf. Gn. 25¹⁶ (P) Nu. 31¹⁰
(P) Ez. 25⁴ 1 Ch. 6³⁹; (2) *battlement,* Ct. 8⁹; (3) *row* of stones Ez. 46²³ (?).
— **27.** כִּי אַתָּה] emph., as v.²⁰. But it is singular before אשר; Perles, Du., Che.,
therefore rd. אֶת־אֲשֶׁר. It is a misplaced gl. — הֲלָלֶיךָ] pl. sf. 2 m. ‡ חָלָל n.m.
(1) *pierced, fatally wounded,* here, as Je. 51⁵² La. 2¹² Ez. 26¹⁵ 30²⁴; (2) *slain*
Ps. 88⁶ 89¹¹ Nu. 19¹⁸ +. — יְסַפֵּרוּ] Pi. impf. 3 pl. ספר *tell of,* so ℑ, but it does
not suit the context. 𝕲 has προσέθηκαν, 𝔙 *addiderunt,* 𝕾 אוספו, so Hare, Houb.,
Lowth., Street; Ew., Ol., Gr., Bi., Che., Bä., Du., Dr., יֹסִפוּ Hiph. יסף, *add.*
This v. disturbs the imprecation, and is a late gl. — **29.** יִמָּחוּ] Niph. juss. 3 pl.
מחה (𝕲⁶). — סֵפֶר חַיִּים] phr. α.λ. *book of the living,* cf. Ex. 32³²·³³ (E) Dn. 12¹,
cf. אוֹר הח׳ Ps. 56¹⁴, ארצות הח׳ 116⁹, (ה)חיים ארץ 27¹³ 52⁷ 142⁶.

LXIX. A (c).

The pentameter is here resumed. — **30.** ואני] emph. as above v.¹⁴, but owing
to gl. and not original. — עָנִי וְכוֹאֵב] phr. α.λ. ‡ כּוֹאֵב Qal ptc. *be sorrowful,* cf.
מכאוב v.²⁷. — **32.** ליהוה] is gl. as in 𝔈 always. — מַקְרִן] Hiph. ptc. † קרן denom.
חֶרֶן, *having horns, horned, putting forth horns,* elsw. only Qal, of rays Ex.
34²⁹·³⁰·³⁵ (P). — מַפְרִיס] Hiph. ‡ פרס denom. פַּרְסָה n.f. *hoof,* and so *hoofed;*
only here ψ, but Hiph. elsw., *dividing the hoof* Dt. 14⁶⁻⁸ Lv. 11³⁻⁷·²⁶. —
33. רָאוּ] Qal pf.; Du. makes it imv. — דִּרְשֵׁי אלהים ויחי לבבכם]. 𝕲 has for
this καὶ ζήσεσθε, which paraphrases it, cf. 22²⁷, which is the original passage.
אלהים is gl., ו of ויחי goes with ptc., rd. דרשיו יחי לבבכם. — **34.** יהוה] is gl. —
לֹא בזה], cf. the original 22²⁵. — **35.** רֹמֵשׂ] Qal ptc. ‡ רמש vb. Qal (1) *creep* of
reptiles Lv. 20²⁵ (H) Gn. 9² (P); (2) *glide about* of water animals, here as Lv.
11⁴⁶ (H), Gn. 1²¹ (P); (3) *move about* of wild beasts Ps. 104²⁰ Gn. 1²⁸ (P).

PSALM LXX., 2 STR. 4⁵.

Ps. 70 is a prayer used Ps. 40¹⁴⁻¹⁸, where it has been considered.

PSALM LXXI., 4 STR. 7³.

Ps. 71 is a prayer of the congregation to Yahweh for deliverance
from enemies. He has been the hope of the nation from its infancy,
indeed from birth; and has continually been praised (v.⁴⁻⁶). His
people have become a portent to the nations on that account, and
the praise of Yahweh has ever sounded forth in His temple; therefore the plea not to cast them off when old and feeble (v.⁷⁻⁹). They
continue their hope and their praise of His righteous might and
salvation (v.¹⁴⁻¹⁶). He has taught them from earliest youth;
therefore the renewed plea not to forsake them in old age, but to

let them continue to praise His wondrous deeds to succeeding generations ; concluding with the exclamation that their God is incomparable in His great deeds of salvation (v.$^{17-19}$). There are numerous glosses of enlargement and emphasis (v.$^{1-3.\ 10-13.\ 20-24}$).

MY God, deliver me from the hand of the wicked,
 From the palm of the wrong doer and the violent:
 For Thou art my hope, Adonay,
 My trust from my youth, Yahweh.
 Upon Thee have I stayed myself from the womb;
 From the bowels of my mother Thou drewest me forth.
 Of Thee is my praise continually.
AS a wonder I am become to many,
 Since Thou art my refuge (and) my strength.
 My mouth is full of Thy praise,
 [That I may sing of Thy glory],
 All the day of Thy beauty.
 Cast me not away in the time of old age:
 When my power faileth forsake me not.
I ON my part continually hope,
 And add unto all Thy praise.
 My mouth tells of Thy righteousness,
 All the day of Thy salvation;
 Though I know not how to tell it.
 I will bring Thy might, Adonay.
 I will make mention of Thy righteousness, Yahweh.
THOU hast taught me from youth even until now,
 Even to old age and hoar hairs do not forsake me;
 Until I declare Thy wondrous deeds to a seed,
 To a generation to come Thy might,
 And Thy righteousness, O God (extendeth) to the height,
 The great deeds that Thou hast done.
 O God, who is like Thee!

Ps. 71 is without title in 𝔥. The title of 𝔊, τῷ Δαυείδ, υἱῶν Ἰωναδὰβ καὶ τῶν πρώτων αἰχμαλωτισθέντων, is a late conjecture, due probably to the fact that the Rechabites of Je. 35 were faithful to their father's commands, just as this poet claims Israel to be to those of Yahweh his God. The Ps. was originally composed of four trimeter heptastichs, v.$^{4-9.\ 14-19}$; but glosses of different measure appear in v.$^{10-13.\ 20-24}$, and an introductory trimeter gloss from 31$^{2-4}$. The original Ps. has reminiscences of: 22$^{10-11}$ in v.$^{5-6}$, 22$^{31-32}$ in v.^{18}, 36^6 in v.^{19}, Is. 63^{14} in v.^{8}, Is. 46^4 in v.$^{9.\ 18}$, Dt. 28^{46} in v.^{7}. It is evident that the author must have composed it some time after these writings, and therefore not earlier than the Greek period, and probably late in that period, too late for his Ps. to have been taken up into any of the minor Psalters. The glosses are still more dependent on other Literature: v.^{10}, cf. 56^7; v.^{12a}, cf. 22^{12a} = 35^{22b} = 38^{22b}; v.^{12b}, cf. 40^{14b} = 70^{2b} = 38^{23a}; v.^{13}, cf. 35$^{4.\ 26}$ = 40^{15} =

70³; שׁוֹט, cf. 38²¹; עֹשֶׂה, cf. 109¹⁹· ²⁹; v.²⁰, cf. 63¹⁰ Is. 44²³, also Ez. 26²⁰ 32¹⁸· ²⁴; v.²⁴ᵃ, cf. 35²⁸; v.²⁴ᵇ, cf. 35⁴· ²⁶ 70³ 40¹⁵.   These glosses doubtless come from the Maccabean period.   It is probable that the gloss v.¹⁻³ was prefixed before these, as it has been assimilated to the structure of the Strs. of the original.

This Ps. is introduced by an editor with a Str. taken with slight variations from 31²⁻⁴ : —

> In Thee, Yahweh, have I taken refuge.
> Let me not be shamed forever.
> In Thy righteousness rescue me, and deliver me.
> Incline unto me Thine ear.
> Become to me the rock of my stronghold,
> The house of my fortress to save me ;
> For Thou art my crag and my fortress.

The variations from the original are discussed in the critical notes 31²⁻⁴. The editor adapted it to the strophical organisation of this Ps.

Str. I. Three syn. couplets and a synth. line. — **4.** *My God*] emphatic in position because of the urgent plea : *deliver me — from the hand of the wicked ‖ the palm of the wrong doer and the violent*].   These are national enemies, and not personal ones. — **5–6.** *For Thou art my hope ‖ my trust*], upon whom the people have been relying, — *from my youth*] that of the nation ; the time of the Exodus, cf. Ho. 11. — *Adonay ‖ Yahweh*], the two divine names in syn. lines ; so v.¹⁶.   V.⁶ᵃ· ᵇ is a citation from 22¹¹ ; there used of the ideal sufferer, here of the nation. — *Of Thee*], emphatic in position, — *is my praise*], based on the hope and trust, — *continually*], from the youth of the nation until the present, and ever will be in the worship of the temple.

Str. II. A synth. couplet, a syn. triplet, and a syn. couplet. — **7.** *As a wonder*], emphatic in position ; not on account of the unexampled sufferings, due to abandonment of their God, which, though sustained by Dt. 28⁴⁶, does not suit the context, but rather on account of the wondrous deliverances which they had experienced in their history. — *I am become to many*], the many nations with which they were brought in contact from the Exodus onward. — *since Thou art my refuge*], a circumstantial clause. — *and my strength*], as 46² 62⁸ ; reduced by copyist's error against the measure to the phrase, α.λ. and ungrammatical : " my refuge of strength."

—**8**. *My mouth is full of Thy praise*], resuming v.^{6c} ‖ *that I may sing of Thy glory*], a line preserved by 𝕲, 𝔙, and PBV., and necessary to the completeness of the Str., though omitted by copyist's mistake in 𝕳, followed by AV., RV. ‖ *all the day of Thy beauty*], the manifestation of the divine glory in the beautiful ornaments of the temple worship. — **9**. *Cast me not away* ‖ *forsake me not*], based on v.$^{6a.\ b}$, — *in the time of old age* ‖ *when my power faileth*], in the decline of the nation in power due to its age, over against the support given from youth of v.^{5}.

A late editor inserted several lines v.$^{10-13}$, enlarging upon the peril and making the petition for deliverance more urgent. — **10**. *For mine enemies* ‖ *they that watch for my life*], deadly enemies, — *say of me* ‖ *consult together saying*]. They express their deadly hatred in talk, consulting together to accomplish their wicked desires. — **11**. *God hath forsaken him : pursue and seize him, for there is none to deliver*]. They presume that what the people pray may not take place, has already taken place ; and that their God has already abandoned them as a helpless prey. — **12**. *O God, be not far from me*], urgent entreaty, based on 22^{12} 38^{22}, — *my God, O haste to my help*], based on 38^{23a}. — **13**. *Let them be ashamed and confounded together that are the adversaries of my life* ‖ *Let them put on reproach and confusion that seek my hurt*], pentameter couplet of imprecation based on 70^{3}, cf. 35$^{4.\ 26}$ 40^{15}.

Str. III. A synth. couplet, a syn. triplet, and a syn. couplet. — **14**. *I on my part*], emph. in position, cf. v.$^{5a.\ 7b}$. — *continually hope*], as v.^{5}, — *and add unto all Thy praise*], continually praise God, as v.$^{6c.\ 8}$; and so constantly add to His praise, increasing its amount and volume. — **15**. *My mouth*], as v.^{8a}, — *all the day*], as v.^{8b}, — *tells of Thy righteousness*], vindicatory righteousness, which delivers His people from their enemies, and so ‖ *of Thy salvation.* — *Though I know not how to tell it*], so great is it, so vastly exceeding understanding and narration. — **16**. *I will bring*], the story of the salvation and the praise ‖ *I will make mention of*] — *Thy might*], as chief Vrss. ; to be preferred to " mighty acts " of 𝕳, followed by EV^{s}, because of v.^{18} and the ‖ *Thy righteousness.*

Str. IV. A synth. couplet, two. syn. couplets, and a concluding line. — **17**. *Thou hast taught me from youth even until now*], resuming v.[5], only changing the relation of trust into one of instruction and guidance. — **18**. *Even to old age and hoar hairs do not forsake me*], resuming v.[9] with slight variation. — *Until I declare Thy wondrous deeds to a seed*], the most probable original of a difficult passage, due in part to the mistake of transposing a clause, and in part to the mispointing a word. The line is based on 22^{31}; ‖ *To a generation to come*], as 22^{32}. — *Thy might*], as v.[16a].—**19**. *And Thy righteousness, O God*], resuming v.[15. 16], — *extendeth to the height*], the height of heaven in its reach, cf. 36^6 57^{11}; and so beyond the reach of praise however great, cf. v.[15c]. — *The great deeds that Thou hast done*], in the historic deliverance of Israel. — *O God, who is like Thee!*], concluding with the praise of their God as the incomparable one, in accordance with the ancient song of praise Ex. 15^{11}, cf. Pss. 35^{10} 86^8 $89^{7. 9}$ Mi. 7^{18}.

A later editor, probably the same who inserted v.[10-13], appends v.[20-24]. — **20**. *Who hast caused me to see many troubles and straits*]. This editor lived in more troublous times than the author of the Ps., and not only looks back upon many past troubles in the history of the nation, but seems to speak from his own experience. — *Quicken me again, and from the lowest parts of the earth bring me up again*]. The nation has fallen so low that it has, as it were, died and gone down into the depths of Sheol; and the restoration of the nation is the bringing of the dead to life, cf. Ho. 6^{1-2} Ez. $37^{12 \text{ sq.}}$. — **21**. *Mayest Thou multiply greatness*], doubtless the greatness of God, as 𝕲, 𝔍; " my greatness " of 𝔥, followed by EV[s]., is a misinterpretation of the original. — *and again comfort me*], so most Vrss. By error of a single letter 𝔥, followed by EV[s]., uses a cognate vb. " mayest Thou encompass me," which in PBV. and AV. is rendered " on every side." — **22**. *even me*], needed to complete the previous line v.[21]. It makes the next line too long, and would unduly emphasize the subject of the vb. — *I will give thanks to Thee ‖ make melody to Thee*], in public worship, — *with the harp ‖ with the lyre*], instrumental music. — *Thy faithfulness, my God*], second object of vb. ‖ *Holy One of Israel*], divine name of Is.[1. 2], as Pss. 78^{41} 89^{19}. — **23**–**24**. *My lips will jubilate ‖ my tongue will muse*], oral, vocal celebration. A copyist's mistake inserted against the measure, " Yea, I will make melody," probably dittog. of v.[22b]. The first line has as its complement, *even the person Thou hast ransomed*]. The second line gives the theme, — *Thy righteousness*], as manifested in the ransom, — also the vow of its long-continued celebration, — *all the day*]. It is based on 35²⁸. — *For they are shamed; for they are abashed that seek my hurt*], an expression of certitude of the retribution upon the enemies, substituted for the imprecation of 35²⁶.

1–3 = 31²⁻⁴ᵃ with slight variations. — **4.** עֲוָּל] Pi. ptc. a.λ. † [עול] denom. עָוַל, *act wrongfully*, elsw. Pi. impf. Is. 26¹⁰; a late word. ⅁ has παρανομοῦν-τος, 𝔍 *iniqui*. — חוֹמֵץ] Qal ptc. † [חמץ] vb. a.λ. ⅁ ἀδικοῦντος, 𝔍 *nocentis*, BDB. *ruthless*, dub. Cf. חָמוּץ n.[m.] a.λ. Is. 1¹⁷ also dub. ⅀ הַטוֹף. Cf. חִמֵּם for which it may be txt. err., as Che. — **5–6** cited from 22¹⁰⁻¹¹. — **5.** אֲדנִי יהוה] so 𝔍; ⅁ divides them properly between two lines, so Bä. — וְנִסְמַכְתִּי] Niph. pf. 1 m. סמך (36), *support oneself*, as Ju. 16²⁹ Is. 36⁶. This softens the original השלכתי. — גוזִי] Qal ptc. † גזה vb. a.λ. BDB. *cut off, sever*. ⅁ σκεπαστής for ἐκσπάσας 22¹⁰ prob. originally as De ἐκσπαστής, ⅁ having same form in both passages; 𝔈, 𝔍, *protector*; Ges., Ew., Hu., Pe., *benefactor*; cf. Talm. גוי, but dub.: prob. err. for גחי. — **6.** תְּהִלָּתִי] ⅁ ὕμνησις, 𝔍 *laus*, cf. 22⁴; but Σ חַלָּתִי as 39⁸, so We., Du., which better suits context. In this case תהלתי has arisen from assimilation to v.⁸. — **7.** † מוֹפֵת] n.m. *wonder*, of divine power, as 78⁴³ 105⁵·²⁷ 135⁹, based on Dt. 28⁴⁶. — מַחֲסִי־עֹז] phr. a.λ., both words common apart: מהסה ועז 46², חסִי יְוֵי 62⁸, so prob. here as measure requires. — **8.** ⅁ inserts after תהלתך, ὅπως ὑμνήσω τὴν δόξαν σου, so 𝔈; but it is not in 𝔖, 𝔍, ⅀. It is, however, doubtless original, as the measure requires it; so Du. — תפארתך sf. 2 m. † תִּפְאָרָה n.f. *beauty, glory* of Yahweh, as 78⁶¹ 89¹⁸ 96⁶ Is. 60⁷·¹⁹ 63¹²·¹⁴·¹⁵ 64¹⁰. — **9.** לְעֵת זִקְנָה] for idea Is. 46⁴ as applied to Israel. † זִקְנָה n.f. *old age*, cf. v.¹⁸; elsw. Gn. 24³⁶ (J) 1 K. 11⁴ 15²³. — כְּלוֹת כֹּחִי] Qal inf. cstr. כלה (18³⁸) *finished, spent, exhausted*, cf. 31¹¹ 69⁴ 73²⁶ 102⁴ 143⁷. — **10.** לִי] *of me*, not *to me*. — שֹׁמְרֵי נַפְשִׁי] usually in good sense, but here in bad sense, *watch for my life*, cf. 56⁷. — יַחְדָּו] (4⁹) though in ⅁ is prob. gl., as Bä., Du.; in this phr. elsw. Ne. 6⁷ Is. 45²¹, cf. Ps. 83⁶. — **11.** לֵאמֹר] is prosaic gl., as Bä. — הַפְשּׂוּהוּ] Qal imv. 3 pl. sf. 3 m. תפש *grasp, seize, take prisoner*, only here in ψ in Qal, but Niph. 10²; common elsw., as Je. 34³ Ez. 12¹³ +. — כִּי־אֵין מַצִּיל as 7³ 50²². — **12.** אַל־תִּרְחַק מִמֶּנִּי] = 22¹²ᵃ = 35²²ᵇ = 38²²ᵇ, the latter only with אלהי. — לְעֶזְרָתִי הוּשָׁה] = 40¹⁴ᵇ = 70²ᵇ = 38²³ᵃ, the latter with ארני, the two former with יהוה. חישה Kt. is evidently txt. err. The second of these clauses is not in ⅁ᴮ, but is in ⅁ᴺ·ᴿ. The two, however, belong together. — **13.** יֵבֹשׁוּ יִכְלוּ שֹׂטְנֵי נַפְשִׁי יַעֲטוּ חֶרְפָּה וּכְלִמָּה מְבַקְשֵׁי רָעָתִי]. We should insert יחדו here as in 35⁴ 70³ in accord. with 35²⁶ 40¹⁵, and then we would have two pentameters. These four passages vary in terms slightly, but they all go back to the same original. — יִכְלוּ] Qal impf. 3 pl. כלה is error for יִכָּלְמוּ 35⁴ 40¹⁵; so 𝔖, Hare, Lowth., Ols., Dy., Hu., Oort, Che. — שֹׂטְנֵי נַפְשִׁי] is a variation of מבקשי נפשי 35⁴ 40¹⁵ 70³; שֹׂטְנֵי Qal ptc. pl. cstr. שטן as 38²¹. — מְבַקְשֵׁי רָעָתִי] is a variation of חשבי רעתי 35⁴, שמחי ר׳ 35²⁶, חפצי ר׳ 40¹⁶ 70³. — יַעֲטוּ] is a poetic

variation of ילבשו 35²⁶. ‡ עטה vb. Qal *wrap oneself, enwrap :* of God with
אור as a garment 104²; of men כבגד 109¹⁹, with shame 109²⁰, reproach, so
here. Hiph. *enwrap*, acc. shame, c. עַל 89⁴⁶, subj. בושׁה and acc. blessings 84⁷.
This v. depends on Pss. 35, 38 jointly. — **14.** ואני] emph. antith. — [הִתְהַלָּךְ so
𝕲; but Aq., Σ, 𝔍, 𝔖, pl. הִתְהַלּוּךְ. — **15.** סְפֹרִית] MT. pl. סְפָרָה n.f. a.λ., BDB.
numbers ; T מנינהון, so Houb.; 𝕲ˣ·ᴮ·ᵃ·ᵇ γραμματίας, 𝔖 ספרוהא, 𝔍 *literaturas*,
סְפָרוֹת pl. סְפָרָה *writings, scriptures ;* so Street, Du.; 𝕲 πραγματίας prob. txt.
err. Σ ἐξαριθμῆσαι vb. inf. סְפֹר is favoured by analogy of 40⁶ 139¹⁷·¹⁸
מְסַפֵּר. אֶסְפְּרֵם, עַצמו מספֵּר, so Bä. We might read סְפָרָה and take כי as conces-
sive, as Gr. suggests. — **16.** אָבוֹא בְ] Qal impf., בוא with בְּ *come with, bring*,
as 40⁸ 66¹³. — [גְּבֻרוֹת pl. of mighty deeds of Yahweh ; but 𝕲, 𝔖, 𝔍, Σ, 𝕿, rd.
sg. גְּבֻרַת *might* as v.¹⁸, so Bä. — [אֲדֹנָי יהוה so 𝔍 ; but 𝕲 correctly divides between the two lines. — **17.** [וְעַד־הֵנָּה *and until now*, phr. of time, as 1 Ch. 9¹⁸
12⁹. It goes most naturally with previous context, and then אלהים is gl. —
[אַגִּיד נפלאותיך Hiph. impf. נגד is unsuited to עַד־הֵנָּה. It has come up by
txt. err. from v.¹⁸. It disturbs the couplet made by the previous and following ll. — **18.** [וְגַם עַד־זִקְנָה cf. v.⁹. וגם is gl. of intensification, and אלהים makes
l. overfull. — ‡ [שֵׂיבָה n.m. *old age ;* elsw. in ψ, 92¹⁵, but cf. Is. 46⁴, on which
v. is based, also Ho. 7⁹ Dt. 32²⁵ +. — [זְרוֹעֲךָ עַד־אַגִּיד־זְרוֹעֲ of arm of Yahweh,
symbol of strength and salvation, as Is. 33² 40¹⁰ 51⁵ +, but nowhere else for
that which it accomplishes and improb. here. Rd. יָרֵעַ as in 22²¹ upon which
this v. depends. The sf. is interpretation. The obj. of vb. is then נפלאותיך,
which has gone up with אגיד into previous v. — [לְדוֹר לְכָל 𝕲 πάσῃ τῇ γενεᾷ.
The כל is prob. gl. of intensification, and לדור is followed by יבוא in rel. clause
as in 22³². 𝔖 omits כל, so Oort, Bä., Beer, al.; but other Vrss. give it. —
19. [עַד־מָרוֹם] as the extent of the declaration of divine righteousness ; not
of the righteousness itself, as Bä., who cfs. 36⁶ 57¹¹ 108⁵ where, however,
faithfulness is used. — [אֲשֶׁר עָשִׂיתָ] rel. of obj. as כי עשה 22³², defined by גְּדֹלוֹת.
— **20.** [הִרְאִיתַנִי Kt., Aq., -נִ_ Qr., 𝕲, Σ, Θ, 𝔍, 𝔖, 𝕿. The same difference
in התַחַיֵּנוּ. The first pers. sg. is best suited to the context, but both are interpretations. — [הָשׁוּב Qal impf. 2 m. bis followed by impfs. is auxil. *again ;*
should be juss. הָשֵׁב. [תְּהֹמוֹת הָאָרֶץ] elsw. always of depths of sea ; so Ols.,
We., Du. Rd. תַּחתִּיוֹת הָאָרֶץ 63¹⁰ Is. 44²³; so ארץ התחתית Ez. 26²⁰ 32¹⁸·²⁴. 𝕲
ἀβύσσων τῆς γῆς, repeated 𝕲, in v.²¹ at close. The peril is of death for the
nation, as in other passages. — **21.** [תֶּרֶב Hiph. juss. 2 m. רָבָה *multiply* =
𝕲 πλεονάσας. — [וּדְלִי 𝕲 δικαιοσύνην σου. 𝔍 follows MT. A great number
of codd. H and P τὴν μεγαλωσύνην σου. Both sfs. interpretations. — [וְתִסֹּב
Qal impf. 2 m. סבב (17¹¹) for which 𝕲, 𝔍, 𝔖, תשׁב, which is favoured by ‖ v.²⁰;
so Houb., Lowth., Horsley, Oort, Bä. The l. lacks a word. Gr. attaches
וגם אני. — **22.** [אוֹדְךָ Hiph. impf. 1 sg., sf. 2 m., but better parall. with לְךָ as
usual. — [בִּכְלִי־נֶבֶל cf. בכלי נבלים 1 Ch. 16⁵. 𝕲ᴸ, 103 codd. HP, Compl., Ald.,
𝕷, after אודך rd. ἐν λαοῖς κύριε, as בגוים יהוה, as 18⁵⁰. So Oort, Bä., Beer, Che.,
We., but without sufficient reason. — [הָרוֹיֵב יִשְׂרָאֵל as 78⁴¹ 89¹⁹, characteristic
of Is.¹ (11 t.) Is.² (13 t.). — **23.** [הְרַנֵּנָה so BD., Ginsberg, al.; *v.* Ges.⁴⁴·°.
— [כִּי אֲזַמְּרָה לָךְ temporal clause, but difficult with cohort. Pi. Prob. txt. err.

from previous l. — **24.** נס־לישוני תהוה צדק־ךּ = 35²⁸ ולישוני תהגה צדקך כל־היום תהוה צדק־ךּ
כל־היום התהלך: the only variations נס for ן, צדקה for צדק, and the omission of
יבישו ויהפרו יהדו [כי־בשו כי־חפרו מבקשי רעתי — .התהלך is also variation of 35²⁶
שמחי רעתי. The only differences are in tense of vb., repetition of כי for ן,
substitution of מבקשי as v.¹⁸ for שמחי, and omission of יהרו.

PSALM LXXII., 2 STR. 7⁶.

Ps. 72 was originally a petition for a king on his ascending the
throne : (1) that Yahweh would endow him with justice, that he
might rule righteously, and especially save the afflicted from the
injustice suffered during the previous reign (v.¹⁻⁷) ; (2) that the
king might have pity on the poor and so enjoy their prayers and
blessings, that abundance of grain and cattle might be in the land,
and that he might live and be honoured forever (v.¹³⁻¹⁷ᵃ). An editor
adapted the Ps. for congregational use by giving it Messianic significance, applying to the king from other scriptures the world-
wide reign (v.⁸), the subjugation of enemies (v.⁹⁻¹¹), the deliverance
of the afflicted (v.¹²), and the blessing of the seed of Abraham
(v.¹⁷ᵇ).

YAHWEH, Thy *justice* give to a king, and Thy *righteousness* to a king's son ;
  May he rule Thy *people* in *righteousness*, and *Thine afflicted ones* with *justice*
    (*govern*) ;
  May mountains bear peace to (Thy) *people*, and hills *righteousness ;*
  May he *govern* the *afflicted of* (*Thy*) *people*, save the sons of the *poor*.
  May he (prolong days) with the sun, and before the moon for generations of
    generations ;
  May he descend as rain upon the mowing grass, as showers (besprinkling)
    the earth ;
  May *righteousness* flourish in his days, and *peace* till there be no moon.
MAY he have pity on the weak and *poor*, and the *persons* of the *poor* save ;
  From injury may he redeem their *person*, and precious may their blood be in
    his eyes ;
  May (the king) live, and may there be given to him of the gold of Sheba ;
  And may prayer be made for him continually, all day long may blessing be
    invoked on him ;
  May there be (an aftergrowth) in the land ; on the top of the mountains (sheep),
  (Kine) on Lebanon ; and may flowers blossom (out of the forests) as herbs
    of the field ;
  May his name be forever, and before the sun may he be established.

Ps. 72 has in the title לישלמה, which is neither an ascription of authorship,
nor a reference to the theme of the Ps., but a pseudonym (*v*. Intr., § 30).

After the Benediction, v.¹⁸⁻¹⁹, we have the subscription כלו חפלות דוד בן־יישי.
The prayers (the written prayers) of David the son of Jesse (those contained
in the prayer-book of David) are completed: this is the last of those prayers
(*v.* Intr., §§ 1, 27). This implies that this petition for a king was the last
prayer of this ancient prayer-book. This statement is impossible for the Ps.
in its present form, unless 𝔻 be very late; for: (1) we have a citation from
Zec. 9¹⁰, giving the king a world-wide dominion v.⁸, which could not be
earlier than the Assyrian rule (*v.* Ps. 2). (2) V.⁹⁻¹¹ uses Is. 43, 49, 60, where
the nations pay tribute to Zion and do homage to her, and adapts the language and conceptions to the Messianic King. (3) V.¹⁷ᵇ cites from the
blessing of Abraham Gn. 12³ 18¹⁸ 22¹⁸, especially, in its latest redactional
form, terms which originally applied to the seed of Abraham, and adapts it to
the king. These adaptions could hardly have been made until late in the
Persian period. (4) V.¹² is a citation from Jb. 29¹², which could hardly have
been made prior to the Greek period. Furthermore, these adaptations imply
a time when a Messianic king again absorbed in himself the redemptive ideals
of the nation, a time illustrated also by the additions to Ps. 89. There is such
a contrast between the use of other writings in these lines, v.⁸⁻¹². ¹⁷ᵇ, and the
remaining lines of the Ps. that we are justified in regarding the former
verses as glosses of the Greek or Maccabean times, and in finding an original Ps. in v.¹⁻⁷. ¹³⁻¹⁷ᵃ, and also in thinking that only this original Ps. was
in 𝔻. This is fortified by the fact that these verses, separated by the glosses,
constitute in themselves two complete Strs. of seven hexameter lines each,
and that they are harmonious throughout. The Ps., in this original form, was,
throughout, a prayer for a king on his accession, and therefore most appropriate as the closing prayer of 𝔻. A hint as to the time of composition is
given in the petition that the king may be endowed with justice: there were
poor, weak, and afflicted ones who had suffered from injustice in the previous
reign. The prophets rebuke just such injustice of kings and princes both in
Israel and Judah before the exile. Je. 22¹³⁻¹⁹ uses similar terms for the reign
of Jehoiachim the son of Josiah. But there was no period when there was
so much of it as the reigns of Manasseh and Amon 2 K. 21, and the accession
of Josiah to the throne might or would have encouraged just the petitions
used in this Ps. It is probable, therefore, that this prayer was composed for
that occasion. This Ps. was not in 𝔻𝕽; but it was in 𝔼, for the original
יהוה was changed to אלהים in v.¹ (*v.* Intr., § 32). The Ps. is assigned in the
Roman use for Epiphany, in the Sarum and Roman use for Trinity Sunday,
and in the Gregorian use for the Nativity of Christ.

Str. I. has seven hexameters, a stair-like tetrastich, and an emblematic tristich, all petitions of the people to Yahweh for their new
king. — **1**. *Yahweh, give Thy justice*], so 𝔊 and 𝔍, in accordance
with ‖ *Thy righteousness*, cf. v.²; interpreted as pl. "judgments,"
acts of judgment" in H. — *to a king ‖ to a king's son*]. This

monarch is king by inheritance, and not by appointment or usurpation. Justice and righteousness are conceived as the essential endowments of a king, just as they are the foundation of Yahweh's throne, 89[15]. They are gifts of Yahweh to the king. — **2.** *May he rule Thy people in righteousness*], syn. with second half of previous line. Only the king is now subject instead of Yahweh, and continues so to be throughout the Str. Those whom he rules are the people of Yahweh. — *and Thine afflicted ones with justice*]. This is syn. with first half of previous line. The traditional text has omitted the vb. which the measure requires. It was probably *govern*, as v.[4a]. The people have been afflicted, as the petition suggests, by a previous king whose rule was in the reverse of justice and righteousness ; by such a king as Manasseh and his son Amon 2 K. 21, so that Josiah would suit well the king prayed for at the installation. — **3.** A metaphor appears in the third syn. line. — *mountains and hills*], instead of the king, — may they *bear peace to Thy people*], peace taking the place of justice ‖ *righteousness*. This is not the bearing them, producing them as fruit, cf. Jb. 40[20] Ez. 17[23] 36[8], but the bearing, carrying, bringing as a blessing, cf. Ps. 24[6]. The mountains are personified for the messengers who come over them, proclaiming from all parts the prevalence of peace and righteousness. Cf. the messengers of peace on the mountains Is. 52[7]. The peace here, as substitute for justice and ‖ righteousness, is not peace from war, for no hostile nations are in the mind of the poet, but internal peace as established by the administration of justice ; so that the afflicted ones are no more afflicted, v.[2. 4], and the poor v.[4. 13-14] no more suffer poverty, cf. v.[7]. — **4.** *May he govern the afflicted of Thy people, save the sons of the poor*] ‖ v.[2] ; do them justice against those that afflict them. The afflicted are also poor ; they are sons of the poor, not as children of poor men, but as afflicted with poverty, belonging to the class of the poor ; and, as the context suggests, those reduced to poverty by injustice and unrighteousness. Cf. Je. 22[13-17] for an identical situation in the reign of Jehoiachim, Josiah's son, described in terms similar to those of our Ps. — **5.** *May he prolong days*], have a long reign, so 𝕲, 𝖁, cf. Is. 53[10] Ec. 7[15] ; which is suited to the ‖ *for generations of generations*, and the petition v.[15] ; but 𝕳 and other Vrss. read : " May they fear thee," which changes subj. of vb. to the people contrary to the usage of the Str. — *With the sun*], companion in duration with the sun, — *before the moon*], in the presence of the moon, in duration, cf. 89[37-38]. — **6.** *May he descend as rain*], simile of refreshment, cf. Dt. 32[2] Jb. 29[23] 2 S. 23[4]: may his justice descend, in his administration of it, — *as showers*], cf. Ps. 65[11] Mi. 5[6], — *besprinkling*], interp. as participle, by an easy change of a corrupt text, instead of as noun " dripping," — *upon the mowing grass*], the grass ready for mowing ‖ *the earth.* As rain and especially showers descend upon the grass ready for mowing and refresh it, and make the earth fertile; so the administration of justice by the king refreshes, strengthens, and enriches his people. — **7.** The climax sums up in terms from v.[1, 3, 5] the entire preceding context, changing the subject to the attributes which rule the Str. — *May righteousness flourish*], as 𝔊, 𝕴, 𝕾, 𝖁, cf. v.[1, 2, 3], and not " the righteous," as H, Aq., 𝚺, 𝕮, which introduces a term foreign to the entire Ps. — *and peace*], internal peace, as v.[3]. "Abundance of" is probably a gloss. It suggests prosperity, which may have been in the mind of the glossator. — *in his days*], syn. *till there be no moon*, cf. v.[5]. The psalmist is thinking not only of the king just beginning his reign, but merges him in a dynasty which he prays may administer justice perpetually.

8–12. An editor inserted a series of glosses, to give the Ps. a Messianic meaning and so adapt it for public worship. These glosses are citations or adaptations from several earlier writings. — **8** is cited from Zec. 9[10]. — *And may he rule*], in accordance with the previous context, or "and he will rule," cf. 110[2] 144[2], in accordance with " his rule shall be " of Zc. 9[10]; — *from sea to sea*], from the Mediterranean to the Indian Ocean, *and from the river unto the extremities of earth*], from the Euphrates unto the extreme west coast of the Mediterranean Sea. Cf. Ps. 2[8], where the extremities of the earth are the inheritance of the Messiah. There can be no doubt that this verse sets forth a universal reign of the Messianic king. — **9.** *Before him let adversaries bow*], down to the ground in defeat because overthrown, cf. 18[40]; so by an easy change of text to suit context for " desert dwellers," 𝕳, a term used elsewhere of animals but nowhere else of men. — *his enemies lick the dust*], in the humiliation of defeat, prostrated on the ground, cf. Mi. 7[17] Is. 49[23]. — **10**. *Let kings of Tarshish and the coasts*]. Tarshish is the Phœnician colony of Tartessus, Spain, cf. Ps. 48[8] Is. 60[9] 66[19]. The coasts, including islands, is a favourite term of Is.[2] (12 t.). — *return presents*], cf. 2 K. 17[3], or tribute, cf. Is. 60[9] Ps. 45[13]. — *Let kings of Sheba and Seba*]. Sheba is Arabia Felix, the Sabian empire, cf. Is. 60[6] Je. 6[20] Ez. 27[22] 38[13]. Seba has not been identified, but was most probably on the west coast of the Red Sea, in the Adulic Gulf (*B*DB.), or the region about Massowah in Abyssinia (Dr.), cf. Is. 43[3]. — *bring gifts*], cf. Ez. 27[15]. In these two syn. lines, which are pentameters, the kings in the extreme West are contrasted with those in the extreme Southeast. — **11**. *And let all kings do homage to him*], cf. 1 K. 1[53]. Ps. 45[12] Is. 49[23]; universal homage of kings between the extremities of the earth, of v.[10]. — *all nations serve him*]. He is to have a world-wide empire over all nations, cf. Ps. 2[10-11]. These verses (v.[9-11]) are dependent in phrase and conception on the later Is.[2. 3], especially chapters 43, 49, 60, 66. But the homage there is to Zion, the restored and glorified nation, here to the Messianic king. The glossator adapts the language and conception of these passages to the king. — **12** is a citation from Jb. 29[12], with slight changes. — *For he will redeem the poor, when he crieth for help, and the afflicted and him that hath no helper*]. This is only a variation of v.[4]

This entire section, v.[8-12], is thus a series of glosses, especially citations of a Messianic character, which the editor does not trouble to adapt to the measures of the Ps.

Str. II. is also composed of seven hexameters : three distichs and a line of climax. It continues the petition for the new king of the first Str. without regard to the intervening glosses. — **13**. *May he have pity on the weak and poor*], may his justice take the form of pity. The "weak" are added to the "poor," and take the place of the "afflicted," v.[2. 4]. — *and the persons of the poor save*], cf. v.[4b]. — **14**. *From injury may he redeem their person*]. The injustice had been so great that their life was still in danger. The Hebrew word for "injury" was a rare one, and so a glossator adds in explanation a common one, "and violence," which makes a conflate text and impairs the measure. — *and precious may their blood be in his eyes*]. The shedding of the blood of the poor was characteristic of the unjust princes and kings of the preëxilic times in Israel and Judah. — **15**. A couplet now implores long life and blessing for the king himself, renewing v.[5]. — *May the king live*]. The word "king" of the usual formula, wishing long life to the king (1 S. 10[24] 2 S. 16[16] 1 K. 1[25], cf. Ps. 22[27] 69[33]) was omitted by scribal contraction, but the omission spoils the measure and the meaning. — *and may there be given to him of the gold of Sheba*], not tributary gold from Sheba, as the gloss v.[10] ; but gold from Sheba given him by his own grateful subjects as in the syn. line. — *And may prayer be made for him continually*], to Yahweh on his behalf, in accordance with this entire Ps., which is such a prayer. — *All day long may blessing be invoked on him*], syn. with the giving him of gold, as the prayer for him is syn. with the wishing him long life. A couplet, petitioning for prosperity in vegetation and cattle under his reign, now follows, but the text of 𝕳 is obscure and the Vrss. dubious. It is necessary to make conjectural restorations. — **16**. *May there be an aftergrowth in the land*], that is, after the crops have been gathered in, may there be a second growth, which the land will produce of itself, and which will be exceedingly great. 𝕳 gives a phr. found only here, and which can only be explained by conjectures, none of which explain the Vrss. — *on the top of the mountains sheep*] ; so by an easy change of text. We would expect cattle to be associated with vegetation in the prosperity of the land. — *Kine on Lebanon*] ‖ *sheep* on the mountain tops. 𝕳, "May the fruit thereof shake like Lebanon," gives no good sense. The fruit of corn is in the ear : the standing corn may move to and fro, rustle in the wind, but if the fruit is ripe and shaken, it is beaten to the ground and destroyed. The vb. rendered "shake" elsewhere is always used of earthquake ; but an earthquake shaking the corn is hardly conceivable with the thought of fertility and a rich harvest. 𝕲, 𝕵, imply a different text from 𝕳. — *And may flowers blossom out of the forests as herbs of the field*] ‖ *aftergrowth in the land.* The forest land is naturally associated with Lebanon. Flowers are associated with forest land, especially with Carmel and Lebanon Is. 35[1-3]. 𝕳, " out of the city," implies the subj. " men," which is altogether incongruous with the context. — **17a**. The Str., in conclusion, petitions long life and honour to the king, a most appropriate climax. — *May his name be forever, and before the sun may he be established*], cf. v.$^{5.\ 15}$. The vb. " established " is favoured by 𝔊, 𝔍. 𝔥 is uncertain. The vb. may mean " have issue," RV.^{m}, so Aq., Σ, " sprout forth." *Yinnon* is a name of the Messiah in Talm. *Synh.* 98^{b} based on this passage. — *His name*] is repeated in a second clause by copyist's error.

17*b*. *And all the clans of the earth will bless themselves in him, all nations will pronounce him happy*]. This is also a gloss based on Gn. 12^{3} 18^{18} 22^{18}, the Abrahamic covenant, representing the seed of Abraham as the medium of blessing to all nations. 𝔥 omits by copyist's error, *all the clans of the earth*, which is, however, sustained by 𝔊, and required by first vb. as subject, and also by the measure. The Psalmist here applies to the Messianic king that which, in the covenant of Abraham, was ascribed to the seed of Abraham; just as above v.$^{9-11}$ he applied to the king that which Is.^{2} ascribed to the people of Zion.

1. אלהים] by 𝔈 for an original יהוה of 𝔇. — מִשְׁפָּטֶיךָ] pl., משפט (1^{5}), *acts* or *deeds of judgment*. This is a misinterpretation of later times. 𝔊 τὸ κρίμα σου and 𝔍 *iudicium tuum*, sg. משפטך, which is required by ‖ צדקתך; cf. במשפט v.^{2}. — **2.** יָדִין] Qal impf. דין (7^{9}). 𝔊 has κρίνειν, either reading לדין or more prob. interpreting as subjunctive. — בְּצֶדֶק] between צדקה v.^{1} and v.^{3} is improb.; rd. צדקה. It is prob. that vb. ישפט has fallen off by haplog. after במשפט. It is used v.^{4}. Then the l. would be divided in middle by caesura, as most frequently in hexameters. — **3.** ישאו הרים שלום] phr. α.λ., usually explained after Jb. 40^{20} בול הרים ישאו לו, and so of tree bearing fruit Hg. 2^{19} Jo. 2^{22}, fig. Ez. 17^{23} 36^{8}; but mountains and hills bearing as their produce peace and righteousness is hardly the idea of the poet. Better explain the vb. as *bear, carry*, so a blessing from Yahweh 24^{6}, provision from one person to another. The mountains and hills are personified for the messengers coming over them, and they bear to the people messages of peace and salvation; cf. Is. 52^{7}. — גְּבָעוֹת] in ψ always pl. ‡ גִּבְעָה n.f. *hill*, elsw. 65^{13} $114^{4.\ 6}$ 148^{9}; cf. Dt. 33^{15}. — לָעָם] 𝔊 τῷ λαῷ σου; sf. is interpretation. — בצדקה] as instrument by which the mountains and hills produce peace. But this is later interp. 𝔊 attaches this word to next v. because of the ב, and so destroys the measure of both lines; ב is an interpretative gl. — **4.** לבני אביון] phr. α.λ., ל acc. Aramaism, prob. not original. אביון (9^{19}) coll. v.$^{12.\ 13}$, נפשות אביונים v.^{13}. בני א׳ used for measure, just as עניי עם for עניים. — וִידַכֵּא עוֹשֵׁק] ו conj. Pi. impf. ‡ דכא vb. Qal *crush;* elsw. ψ, 89^{11} 94^{5} 143^{3}. עוֹשֵׁק Qal ptc. ‡ עשק vb. Qal (1) *oppress, wrong* by extortion, elsw. 103^{6} 146^{7} Je. 21^{12} Ec. 4^{1} +; (2) *oppress* a nation Pss. 105^{14} (= 1 Ch. 16^{21}) $119^{121.\ 122}$ +. This clause is a gl., as Bä., appropriate in thought but not suited to context, which does not depart from relation of the king to the poor and afflicted people, and it makes l. just these words too long. Here the context favours individuals, but the glossator probably thought of the nation.— **5.** וְיִירָאוּךָ] Qal impf. 3 pl. ירא with sf. 2 sg. ; but 𝕲 συμπαραμενεῖ = יַאֲרִיךָ, cf. Is. 53¹⁰, יאריך ימים Ec. 7¹⁵ which is more in accord. with דור דורים, so Houb., Lag., Now., Oort, Bä. Change of subj. is striking. In previous and subsequent context the king is subj. of vbs. and also in v.¹⁷. The context favours יאריך, but Σ, 𝔖, 𝔍, 𝕿, agree with 𝔥.— **6.** † גֵז] n.[m.] (1) *shearing*, for wool shorn Dt. 18⁴ Jb. 31²⁰, *fleece*, so here 𝕲, Σ, 𝔖, 𝔍, Houb. ; (2) *mowing* Am. 7¹, and here most prob. *land to be mown* Street, *BDB*.— זַרְזִיף] α.λ. n.[m.] *dripping*, dub. ; cf. זְרִיף *flow together*, NH. זַרְזִיפֵי דמיא *drops of water;* Hu., Bi., *BDB*., impf. Hiph. יַזְרִיף *cause to drip, irrigate.* Krochmal and Gr. rd. ירעיפו. But the Vrss. presuppose a ptc. pl., 𝕲 στάζουσαι = *drops dropping upon,* 𝔍 *inrorantes, bedewing.* Rd. ptc. pl., זרופי ; the י in זרופי has been transposed.— **7.** יִפְרַח] Qal impf. ‡ פרח vb. *flourish, sprout, bloom* of plant or tree, in ψ only fig. of flourishing condition of a man or people, elsw. 92⁸·¹³, as Is. 27⁶ 35² 66¹⁴ Ho. 14⁶·⁸ Pr. 11²⁸; so in Hiph. Ps. 92¹⁴ Jb. 14⁹ Pr. 14¹¹; suited to the simile of the king as rain.— צַדִּיק] so Aq., Σ, 𝕿; but 𝕲, 𝔙, 𝔖, 𝔍, צֶדֶק or צְדָקָה, so Hare, Street, Lag., Oort. שלום in parall. suggests צדקה as above.— רֹב] before שלום is prob. gl., implying interpret. *prosperity*, but צדקה and v.³ suggest *peace.*— Thus far we have had seven hexameter ll., and a complete Str. is before us. V.⁸ begins a change in the thought and construction.— **8.** וְיֵרְדְּ מים ער־ים ומנהר ער־אפסי־ארץ] cf. Zc. 9¹⁰ וּמָשְׁלוֹ מים עד ים ומנהר עד אפסי ארץ; the only difference is the substitution of וְיֵרְדְּ for וּמָשְׁלוֹ, in order to adapt the v. to the context of the Ps. It is evident that the Ps. quotes from the prophet. וְיֵרְדְּ] conj. Qal impf. רדה vb. (49¹⁵); the juss. form here is late style.— **9.** צִיִּים] pl. † צִי] n.m. an animal of the dry desert, 74¹⁴ Is. 13²¹ 23¹⁸ 34¹⁴ Je. 50³⁹. This sense is inappropriate here, and so the צי is thought to be an inhabitant of the thirsty lands ; but there is no authority for this. 𝕲, Aq., Σ, Αἰθίοπες, 𝔙, 𝔍, *Aethiopes* = כוש, 𝕿 אפרפיא, prob. an interpretation due to Is. 43³. 𝔖 rds. איים, which is assimilation to v.¹⁰; Ols., Dy., Oort, Gr., SS., Bu., Du., rd. צרים ‖ איבים, which is appropriate to כרע.— אִיֹּבָיו יְלַחֵכוּ] *lick the dust* in humiliation of defeat, phr. elsw. Mi. 7¹⁷ Is. 49²³. This last passage is so similar that probably it was in the mind of the writer of this l. Vb. Pi. impf. † לְחַךְ] elsw. Qal Nu. 22⁴ of ox, Pi. Nu. 22⁴ (E) 1 K. 18³⁸.— **10.** ‡ תַרְשִׁישׁ] *Tarshish*, the Phoenician colony in Tartessus, Spain ; elsw. ψ only 48⁸ אניות תי *ships of Tarshish*, cf. Is. 60⁹ 66¹⁹.— אִיִּים] pl. ‡ אִי n.m. *coast land*, including islands, fuller form איי הים Is. 11¹¹ 24¹⁵ Est. 10¹; abr. איים Is. 41¹·⁵ 42⁴·¹⁰ Ps. 97¹ Dn. 11¹⁸, so here ; א וישביהם Is. 42¹² 49¹ 51⁵ 59¹⁸ 60⁹ 66¹⁹, *islands* Is. 40¹⁵ ‖ נהרות Is. 42¹⁵.— מִנְחָה יָשִׁיבוּ] phr. elsw. 2 K. 17³; מנחה as *tribute* Ju. 3¹⁵ 2 S. 8² 1 K. 5¹ Ho. 10⁶ +. For the idea in another form cf. Is. 60⁹ Ps. 45¹³.— ‡ שְׁבָא] n. pr. m. *Arabia Felix, Sabian empire,* Is. 60⁶ Je. 6²⁰ Ez. 27²² 38¹³, only here and v.¹⁵ ψ.— † סְבָא] n. pr. m. name of first son of Cush Gn. 10⁷ (P) = 1 Ch. 1⁹, of nation or territory here as Is. 43³; not identified, most prob. on west coast of Red

Sea in Adulic gulf (*B*DB.). — † אֶשְׁכָּר] n.m. elsw. Ez. 27¹⁵ *gift, tribute*. —
12. כִּי אֲמַלֵּט עָנִי מְשַׁוֵּעַ וְיָתוֹם וְלֹא עֹזֵר לוֹ = [כִּי יַצִּיל אֶבְיוֹן מְשַׁוֵּעַ וְעָנִי וְאֵין עֹזֵר לוֹ Jb. 29¹².
the only differences are (1) change to 3d pers. as above, v.⁸, in citation from
Zc.; (2) יתום *orphan*, appropriate to Jb. but not to Ps., and so אביון is taken
as a syn. of עני; (3) ואין is smoother style than ירא; (4) the more common
vb. נצל for syn. מלט. — **13.** יָחֹם] Qal juss. ‡ חוס Qal *pity, spare;* חָיוּם Je. 21⁷;
cf. הָחֹם Dt. 7¹⁶ + 9 t., but הָחֹם Gn. 45²⁰ Ez. 9⁶, (*a*) of God c. עַל Je. 13¹⁴ Ez.
24¹⁴ +, (*b*) of man c. עַל Je. 21⁷ Jon. 4¹⁰ and here. — **14.** וְיֶחֱסַם] is a familiar
word, inserted as gl. explanatory of less familiar הוֹן *violence*. The l. is just
this word too long. — וְיִיקַר דָּמָם] Qal juss., ו coörd. √יקר *be precious;* ⑮, Θ,
τὸ ὄνομα αὐτῶν שמם, so 𝔊, as 1 S. 18³⁰, but Aq., Σ, 𝔖, 𝔗, 𝔍, as 𝔐. — **15.** וִיחִי
וְיִתֶּן־לוֹ מִזְּהַב שְׁבָא]. This is a defective line. The first vb. stands alone without subj. ו coörd. Qal juss. חיה *live*. This suggests same subj. as יִתֶּן, which
is impossible. The missing word is doubtless הַמֶּלֶךְ with לְעוֹלָם. It is prob.
that an ancient copyist used ויחי for the longer formula, and that a later scribe
misunderstood his abbreviation. יחי המלך 1 S. 10²⁴ 2 S. 16¹⁶˙¹⁶ 1 K. 1²⁵˙³¹˙³⁴˙³⁹
2 K. 11¹² 2 Ch. 23¹¹; cf. המלך לעולם יחיה Ne. 2³. — מַזְהָב שְׁבָא] phr. α.λ.; cf.
v.¹⁰. This may have suggested the interpolation of v.⁹⁻¹¹. Gold is usually
associated with Ophir 1 K. 9²⁸ 10¹¹ 22⁴⁹ 1 Ch. 29⁴ 2 Ch. 8¹⁸ 9¹⁰. — וִיבָרֲכֶנְהוּ] Pi.
juss. ברך (5¹³) with strong sf. נְהוּ for הוּ, continues indef. subj., to be rendered by passive. — **16.** פִּסַּת] α.λ. NH. פִּסָּה = extremity of the hand or foot.
כֹּס *piece*, כְּכֹס *thresh grain*, Aram. *piece of bread* = Hebr. פַּת. ⑮ στήριγμα,
𝔍 *firmamentum, foundation, support*, did not read בר, which must therefore
be either a gl. of explanation or part of another word. It is prob. the former,
for ⑮ renders הַסְּעֵד 1 S. 26¹⁹ ἐστηρίσθαι, so prob. here στήριγμα for פסה.
But † סָפִיחַ n.[m.] *aftergrowth* of vegetation, that which grows of itself,
Lv. 25⁵˙¹¹ Is. 37³⁰ = 2 K. 19²⁹, would admirably suit the context, to which
בר might be a more exact definition. 𝔍 *memorabile triticum* is based on
מוֹפֵת הבר, which is an easy error for מִפְתַח בר *one plowing the field*, cf. Is. 28²⁴.
פסה and מפ־ה are easy mistakes for an original ספיח. שפעת Jb. 22¹¹ *overflow,
abundance*, suggested by Lag., Gr., We., SS., gives good sense, but cannot
explain the Vrss. except 𝔖 סוגאא. — בראש הרים] closes the l. according to
MT., but that makes five words for this l. and seven for the next, which is
impossible. — יִרְעַשׁ] Qal impf. רעש (18⁸); elsw. always of earthquake. It is
usually interpreted here of the rustling of the standing grain. But the shaking caused by earthquake and the movement of grain caused by wind are
difficult to reconcile. ⑮ ὑπεραρθήσεται ὑπὲρ τὸν Λίβανον ὁ καρπὸς αὐτοῦ,
𝔍 *elevabitur sicut Libani fructus eius*, imply another word. Ew. suggests
denom. ראש *come to a head, attain the summit;* but no such usage is known
and, if possible, it would not give a poetic conception. Evidently these Vrss.
had not ירעש in their text. It prob. represents יֵרְעַ־שֶׂה *may sheep pasture.*
ירע would then be a gl. to explain an original שֶׂה. This would explain ⑮ and
𝔍, which rd. שׂאת. — כַּלְּבָנוֹן] so 𝔍. But ⑮ ὑπὲρ = כ, which is more prob.,
unless both prep. interpretative. — פִּרְיוֹ] פְּרִי n.m. with sf. 3 sg., referred by
De. to בר, by Hi. to ארץ, by Ri. to ראש; all alike improb. Bä. would rd.

יפרו vb. Qal impf. פרה and connect it closely with following. He suggests it might be a gl. for יציץ, for it is tautological. If שׂה was original in previous l. we would expect פרים here, pl. פַר n.m. *bull*, ו often error for בׇ. — בׇ צ ו] ו coörd. Qal juss. 3 pl. ‡ צוץ vb. *bloom*, of grass or flowers 90⁶ 103¹⁵, so prob. here ; fig. of wicked 92⁸, Israel Is. 27⁶; *shine, gleam*, of royal ornament 132¹⁸. — מֵעִיר] prep. with עִיר; but this, though sustained by Vrss., gives no good sense ; rd. מַיַּעַר *from the forest* (29⁹) ‖ לבנון.—**17.** יְהִי שְׁמוֹ לעולם] so 𝔍 ; but 𝕲 has ἔστω τὸ ὄνομα αὐτοῦ εὐλογημένον εἰς τοὺς αἰῶνας; εὐλογημένον is an interpretative gl. The second שׁמו is prob. a gl. — יִנִּין] Kt. Hiph. impf. ; ינין Qr. Niph. impf., in either case a.λ. ; 𝕲 διαμενεῖ, 𝔍 *perseverabit*, 𝕿 יְזֵמֵי, favour יפון Niph. כון *be established*; Bä., SS., *BDB.*, Aq., Σ, γεννηθήσεται, favour נין vb. denom. נִין n.[m.] *offspring, posterity.* —יתברכו בו כל־גוים יאשרהו]. This is based on Gn. 12³ (J), ונברכו בך כל משפחת האדמה, Gn. 18¹⁸ ונברכו בו כל גויי הארץ, Gn. 22¹⁸ והתברכו בזרעך כל גויי הארץ. It is a paraphrase based on the redactional passage. That which referred to the seed of Abraham is here applied to the dynasty of David. 𝕲 inserts after ויתברכו בו πᾶσαι αἱ φυλαὶ τῆς γῆς from Gn. 12³.— **18–19** = doxology of the second book of ψ. 𝕲 omits אלהים after יהוה. It is conflation of Elohistic and Yahwistic editors. 𝕲 adds after לעולם καὶ εἰς τὸν αἰῶνα τοῦ αἰῶνος, a fuller doxology (*v.* Intr. § 40). — **20** = editorial statement to the effect that this Ps. closed the Prayer-book of David (*v.* Intr. § 1).

PSALM LXXIII., 2 PTS., 5 STR. 4³.

Ps. 73 has two Parts. The first states how near apostasy the psalmist had been because of the prosperity of the wicked (v.²⁻³), who are described as without trouble as other men (v.⁴⁻⁵), proud and violent in their iniquity (v.⁶⁻⁷), mocking and blaspheming (v.⁸⁻⁹), and, while increasing their wealth, denying God's practical knowledge of their doings (v.¹¹⁻¹²). In the Second Part he laments that all his efforts for purity have only resulted in suffering (v.¹³⁻¹⁴), then remonstrates with himself for such a thought as treacherous to God, when the suffering should urge rather to know better (v.¹⁵⁻¹⁶), and as having a mind embittered and being a stupid beast (v.²¹⁻²²), when really God had kept firm hold of him and guided him in this life, and would eventually take him to glory (v.²³⁻²⁴). In this consolation he exclaims that God is his only delight in heaven and on earth, for whom he pines body and soul (v.²⁵⁻²⁶). Besides minor glosses (v.¹· ¹⁰) there are two larger ones : (1) giving a solution of the problem of the Ps. by reflection in the temple upon the calamitous latter end of the prosperous wicked

$(v.^{17-20})$; (2) contrasting the ultimate ruin of apostates with the goodness of God to those drawing nigh to Him $(v.^{27-28})$.

I.

MY feet were almost gone;
  My steps had well nigh slipped:
  For I was envious of the boasters,
  While the prosperity of the wicked I was seeing.
FOR they have no (decisions) ;
  Sound and fat is their (strength).
  In the trouble of (ordinary) men they have no portion,
  Together with (other) men they are not accustomed to be stricken.
THEREFORE pride serves them as their necklace.
  They clothe themselves with violence.
  Their (iniquity) doth come forth from fatness.
  Conceits of the mind overflow.
THEY scoff and speak of evil,
  Of oppression loftily they speak.
  They have set against the heavens their mouth,
  While their tongue goes about in the earth.
AND they do say : " How doth 'El know ?
  And is there knowledge with 'Elyon ? "
  Behold, such as these are the wicked :
  And, being always at ease, they do increase riches.

II.

SURELY in vain have I cleansed my mind,
  And washed in innocency my palms,
  And become one smitten all day long,
  And had chastening every morning.
HAD I said : " I will tell it thus ";
  I would have been treacherous to the generation of Thy sons.
  And so I thought how I might know this.
  A trouble was it in mine eyes.
FOR my mind was embittered,
  And in my reins was I pricked.
  I was brutish, without knowledge ;
  A stupid beast was I with Thee.
YET am I continually with Thee,
  Thou dost hold me by my right hand.
  (Now) with Thy counsel Thou guidest me,
  And afterwards unto glory (Thou) wilt take me.
WHOM have I in heaven?
  And having Thee on earth I delight in nought else.
  My flesh doth pine and my soul,
  My Rock and my Portion forever.

Ps. 73 was originally in 𝕬 as 50; 74–83. It was then in 𝕸. It was subsequently taken up into 𝕰 (v. Intr. §§ 29, 31, 32). The Ps. has two

parts, each of five trimeter tetrastichs: (1) v.[2-9. 11-12], (2) v.[13-16. 21-26]. The
other verses are glosses, v.[1. 10. 17-20. 27-28]. The original Ps. resembles others
of 𝔄: (1) in the use of אל v.[11] as 50[1] 74[8] 77[10. 14. 15] 78[7. 8. 18. 19. 34. 35. 41] 80[11] 82[1]
83[2] (gl.v.[17]); (2) of עליון v.[11] as 50[14] 77[11] 78[17. 35. 56] 82[6] 83[19]; (3) of לֵבָב v.[7. 13]
(gl. v.[1. 21. 26]), as in 77[7] 78[18. 72] (gl.), characteristic of time of Chronicler.
The Ps. has good syntax (1) cohortative v.[15. 16] (gl. v.[17]), (2) ו consec. impf.
v.[13. 14]. There are several interesting words: v.[4] חרצבות, elsw. Is. 58[6], prob.
txt. err. for חרצוה; אולם a.λ., אול, txt. err. for חילם; v.[6] ענקתמו elsw. Dt. 15[14];
יעטף Aramaism, elsw. Ps. 65[14]; שית as Pr. 7[10], interp. gl.; v.[7] משכיות Aramaism;
v.[8] ימיקו, Aramaism, a.λ.; v.[9] תהלך strong form; v.[12] השגו Aramaism Ps. 92[13]
Jb. 8[7]. Phrases to be considered are: v.[5] עמל אנוש a.λ., but both words apart
common; v.[9] ולשונם תהלך בארץ a.λ., cf. Je. 49[31]; v.[12] שלוי עולם a.λ., cf. Je. 49[31];
v.[15] דור בניך a.λ., but words apart common; v.[22] בער as 49[11] 92[7]. V.[13b] is a
citation from 26[6]. V.[24] implies the story of Enoch in its phrasing, and so the
use of Gn. 5[24]. V.[26] in its use of כלה resembles Jb. 19[27]. The Ps. gives the
experience of an individual who contrasts his own experience of sorrow and
trouble with the prosperity of the boastful wicked. He finds his consolation
in the divine guidance in life and a hope of glory after death, indicating a
highly developed eschatology. The wicked are boasters, v.[8], and scornful.
The Ps. came from a commercial period, the beginning of the Greek period.
V.[1] is an introductory liturgical gl., which generalises the Ps. and makes it
applicable to Israel as a people. V.[10] is a gloss, looking to the restoration
of God's people to their own land and a long life for them therein, probably
from Maccabean times. V.[17-20] is a reflection upon the final doom of the
wicked, made in the sanctuary. V.[19] בלהות, cf. Jb. 18[11] +. V.[18] משואות prob.
Aramaism, inf. cstr. נשא, cf. Ps. 74[3] v.[20] ארני. V.[27-29] gives an antithesis between
the final ruin of apostates and the benefits of those who draw near to God in
worship. Both of these glosses are Maccabean. 𝔊 adds a gl. v.[28d], "in the
gates of the daughter of Zion," to accord with v.[17a]. V.[28] קרבת elsw. Is. 58[2]
probably inf. cstr. קרב.

Pt. I. Str. I. has two syn. couplets. A later glossator prefixes a
hexameter which is a sort of summary of the conclusion of the Ps.
— **1.** *Surely*], notwithstanding all appearances and everything that
might be said to the contrary, — *God is good to Israel*], not simply
as a nation, but distributively, distinguishing between the righteous
and the wicked, and so only *to the pure-minded.* — **2.** *My feet ∥ my
steps*], as often for the course of life, emphasized by a glossator
by the prefixing of *As for me.* — *were almost gone ∥ had well nigh
slipped*], in the peril of falling away from God in apostasy. The
reason for this is given in general, — **3.** *For I was envious of the
boasters*], those who were boasting of their success and prosperity,
and so were arrogant toward those less successful than themselves.

— *While the prosperity of the wicked I was seeing*], a circumstantial clause implying an habitual observation of this strange circumstance, so contrary to Deuteronomic principles, which promised prosperity to the righteous and threatened adversity to the wicked. This inconsistency is what troubles this poet, as it did the authors of Pss. 37 (𝔇) and 49 (𝔎), and more especially those of the book of Job. The remainder of Pt. I. is an enlargement upon this couplet.

Str. II. Two syn. couplets. — **4.** *For they have no decisions*]. This is the most probable explanation of a difficult text, where 𝔥, Vrss., and commentators greatly differ. The word rendered "bands," AV., RV., is used elsewhere only Is. 58[6] in the sense of "bonds." This gives a good sense here only by the paraphrase "restraints," JPSV., which, however, is not justified by other usage. The paraphrase "peril," PBV., "torments," Hu., Dr., Ki., has still less justification. Most ancient Vrss. had another reading, which may be conjectured and given as above. The text "in their death," though given by 𝔥 and Vrss., is abandoned by JPSV. and most moderns, for it is against the measure and the context, which is very far from suggesting their death. — *Sound and fat is their strength*], the most probable rendering of a difficult clause, adding to the freedom of the mind from anxiety the full strength of the body. — **5.** *In the trouble of ordinary men*], that which men ordinarily experience, — *they have no portion*], they alone are exempt from trouble, ‖ *together with*, in common with *other men they are not accustomed to be stricken*]. The blows of affliction never strike them as they do repeatedly all others.

Str. III. Two synth. couplets. — **6.** *Therefore pride*], appropriate to the boasters of v.[3], — *serves them as their necklace*], an ornament worn about the neck of men as well as women in those times, cf. Gn. 41[42] Dn. 5[7], and conspicuous as an evidence of wealth and power. — *They clothe themselves with violence*]. Their pride of wealth and power naturally and inevitably leads to violence toward others, and such conduct becomes habitual, a characteristic which they present to others as the dress by which they are recognised. A glossator makes this more definite by inserting the word "clothing." — **7.** *Their iniquity*], so 𝕲, 𝕾, 𝕴, and many moderns ; more appropriate to the context than "their eyes" of 𝔥, 𝕵,

followed by EV⁸. — *doth come forth from fatness*], their fat, gross
mind and body breed iniquity, cf. Dt. 32¹⁵ Ps. 17¹⁰. — *Conceits of
the mind overflow*], their minds are full to overflowing with evil
imaginations and conceits, which flow forth in word and deed,
cf. Hb. 1¹¹. The rendering of AV., RV., "they have more than
heart could wish," is a paraphrase which cannot be justified.

Str. IV. A syn. couplet and an antith. couplet. — **8**. *They
scoff*], so 𝔍, RV., JPSV., and most moderns; the rendering "they
corrupt other" of PBV., "they are corrupt" of AV., cannot be
sustained. — *and speak of evil*], talk with one another about doing
evil, as a suitable and habitual theme ‖ *of oppression they speak*],
cf. v.⁶ᵇ; they propose to oppress the weak. — *loftily*], as if from
on high, far above others in the exaltation of pride and arrogance.
— **9**. *They have set against the heavens their mouth*], as AV.;
blaspheming against God and divine things in accordance with
v.⁸ᵃ ¹¹, which is to be preferred to "in the heavens," of RV.;
explained by Kirk. in accordance with v.⁸ᵇ: "they make an
impious claim of divine authority, and dictate to men as though
the earth belonged to them." — **10**. This verse is difficult. Kt.
can only be explained as a divine promise to afflicted Israel to
restore them to their land and give them abundant prosperity.
This was probably originally a marginal note of consolation, which
subsequently crept into the text. — *Therefore will He bring back
the people thither, and waters of fulness will be drained out to
them*]. The Qr. and ancient Vrss. probably had essentially the
same meaning: "His people will return." This is so against the
context that various explanations have been sought. JPSV. makes
these the words of the prosperous. "Well, then, let His people
turn hither, and water shall be found for them in abundance."
— A promise of prosperity to all people who will come to the
prosperous for prosperity.

Str. V. syn. and synth. couplets. — **11**. *And they do say: "How
doth 'El know? ‖ And is there knowledge with 'Elyon?"*], not
denying the omniscience of God, but the divine practical knowledge
or interest in human affairs, cf. 10⁴· ¹¹· ¹³, and therefore the impunity
of their evil conduct. — **12**. *Behold such as these are the wicked*].
The description of them has now reached its end. It is all summed
up in the final statement: *and being always at ease*]; having ever

an easy and prosperous life, without fear of God and without anxiety because of men, in the full enjoyment of health of body and content of mind. — *they do increase riches*], become ever richer and richer ; since they are unscrupulous as to means, shrink not from evil deeds, and indulge in violence and oppression.

Pt. II. Str. I. has two syn. couplets. — **13.** *Surely in vain*]. It is certain that it has been to no purpose, has not been successful ; emphatic in position. — *have I cleansed my mind*], made and kept it clean from sin ; completed by keeping also the body clean, — *and washed in innocency my palms*], cf. 26[6] ; the conception based on Levitical purifications for public worship ; but here evidently referring to the keeping the palms clean from bribery, robbery, and just those forms of violence (v.[6b]) and oppression (v.[8b]) by which the wicked had to a great extent gained their wealth and prosperity. — **14.** *And become one smitten all day long* || *and had chastening every morning*], in antithesis with the wicked, who had been ever exempt from such blows, v.[5]. This serious inconsistency with the promises and threatenings of the Deuteronomic Law tempted him here to the assertion of the failure of innocence and virtue, as in the previous part to apostasy, v.[2].

Str. II. The statement of the previous Str. was only made to be renounced in two synth. couplets. — **15.** *Had I said : I will tell it thus*]. He had not said it ; but only entertained in his mind the thought of saying it. — *I would have been treacherous to the generation of Thy sons*]. Israel in his national unity is in a relation of sonship to God, Ex. 4[22] Dt. 14[1], in which all the faithful share. Unfaithfulness to this relation of sonship, as well as to the similar relation of marriage, is regarded as treachery, cf. Pss. 25[3] 59[6] Je. 3[20]. Nothing could be more treacherous to the family of God than to assert that His service in innocence and purity of life was all in vain and of no use. — **16.** *And so I thought*], as a result of this experience, — *how I might know this*], gain a practical knowledge and understanding of this difficult problem, this inconsistency between theory and fact. — *A trouble was it in mine eyes*]. It involved toil in anxiety and perplexity of mind, and sorrow in the distressing experiences involved in such a struggle to resist temptation and gain the true solution of the problem. A later editor, not altogether content with the solution given below, v.[21-26], here

1

inserts another one, v.[17-20]. — **17**. *Until I entered into the great
sanctuary of 'El*], the temple at Jerusalem, named the great
sanctuary by the use of the Heb. pl. of intensity.   There, in the
place of public worship, where God was accustomed to manifest
Himself, the perplexed might look for a solution. — *considered
their latter end*], not merely their past and present prosperity, but
what the ultimate result, the final end of it all would be.   This
editor finds the solution of the problem in the final punishment
of the wicked, which would be in dreadful antithesis with their
long-continued prosperity, cf. 37[1 sq.] Ec. 8[11-13].   The description
of this punishment now follows. — **18**. *Surely in slippery places
Thou settest them*], cf. 35[6] Je. 23[12]. — *Thou causest them to fall into
utter ruin*], ere long they slip and fall, and from the fall they rise
no more ; they remain like a fallen wall in utter ruin, cf. 74[3]. —
19. *How have they become a desolation in a moment !*], when the
time of their ruin is come, it is sudden, unexpected, and all accomplished in a moment. — *They have come to an end*, intensified
by *they are finished*], the two vbs. more emphatic than the rendering of AV., RV., "utterly consumed" — *by terrors*], a term of
Job, 18[11] +. — **20**. *as a dream after awakening*], unsubstantial,
in recollection only as a mere phantasm, an image of the imagination ‖ *phantom.* — *Adonay*], divine name of the time of the glossator, — *when Thou rousest Thyself*], in active intervention, in
judicial activity, cf. 7[7] 35[23]. — *Thou despisest*], so trivial, unsubstantial, despicable, the life of these rich, prosperous boasters has
really been in the sight of God.

Str. III. Two syn. couplets. — **21**. *For my mind was embittered*], or soured by the inconsistency of innocence and affliction, cf. v.[13].   This verse is altogether unconscious of v.[17-20], and
depends at once upon v.[13-16]. — *And in my reins was I pricked*].
The reins, the seat of the feelings, were pained as if pricked by a
sword or lance. — **22**. *I was brutish*], cf. 49[11] 92[7] 94[8], — *without
knowledge*], not able to know what it all meant, cf. v.[16], — *a stupid
beast*], the intensive pl. ; "a mere beast," Kirk., "a very beast,"
Dr., — *was I with Thee*], in relation to, and in association and
communion with God.

Str. IV. Syn. and synth. couplets. — **23**. *Yet am I continually
with Thee*], though in knowledge and action stupid as a beast, yet

he knew that he was in communion with God. — *Thou dost hold me by my right hand*], to give support, help, and consolation in time of perplexity and peril, cf. 63⁹. — **24.** *Now*], probably to be inserted to complete the line in antithesis with, *and afterwards — with Thy counsel Thou guidest me*], habitual action, giving constant advice and counsel, as well as support and help. — *Unto glory Thou wilt take me*], in the future, interpreted by some as the latter end of the life of the righteous; by others, AV., RV., JPSV., Pe., De., Bä., more properly as in the life after death, especially as the story of the translation of Enoch, Gn. 5²⁴, cf. Ps. 49¹⁶, seems to be implied in the terms that are used. With the former interpretation Dr., Kirk., after 𝔊, 𝔘, 𝔍, PBV., prefer to interpret כבוד as adv. acc., "with glory" or "honour." The psalmist finds the solution of the inconsistencies of this life in the final reward to the righteous after death, cf. Jb. 19²⁶⁻²⁷, also Ps. 16¹¹.

Str. V. Synth. couplets. — **25.** *Whom have I in Heaven?*], implying the answer that he has no one but God. — *And having Thee*], as v.²³ᵃ, — *on earth I delight in nought else*]. God is the one only and exclusive object of his delight, his only good, cf. 16². — **26.** *My flesh doth pine*], for the realisation of this joyous anticipation, cf. Jb. 19²⁷ Ps. 84³. — *my Rock*], 18³, to which a glossator added the interpretation *of my soul*. — *and my Portion forever*], cf. 16⁵. To this the glossator adds the interpreting "God," which is sufficiently evident from the context. Both of these glosses impair the measure.

The Ps. has now reached the grandest climax; but a later editor added an emphatic antithesis between the fortunes of the righteous and the wicked. — **27.** *For behold those departing from Thee*], those who had acted as this psalmist had been sorely tempted to act, v.², — *will go to ruin*], cf. 1⁶. — *Thou dost exterminate every one that goes whoring from Thee*]. Yahweh was the husband of His people, Ho. 2² Is. 54⁵·⁶ +; apostasy from Him was a rupture of the marriage relation, and so spiritual whoredom. — **28.** *As for me*], in antithesis with such, — *drawing nigh to God is good for me ‖ my making Yahweh my refuge*]. The same glossator as that of v.²⁰ inserts "in Adonay." — *telling of all Thy occupations*], in general care over the righteous; cf. Gn. 2²·³ (P), for creative, Je. 50²⁵ for judicial works of God, where alone elsewhere this word is used of divine work.

1. אַךְ] particle of asseveration, as 23⁶; 𝔊 ὡς, 𝔍 *attamen.* — בְּרִי לֵבָב] cf. בַּר לֵבָב 24⁴; רבב characteristic of this Ps., v.⁷·¹³·²¹·²⁶; so 77⁷. — **2.** וַאֲנִי] makes l. too long; is explan. gl. — וְנָטוּי] Kt. Qal ptc. pass., subj. the man himself, explained by אני, to which רגלי n.f. is secondary subj.; but Qr. נָטָיוּ Qal pf. 3 pl. רגלי subj. — שֻׁפְּכָה] Kt. Pu. pf. 3 f. sg. neglect of agreement; but Qr. שֻׁפְּכוּ 3 pl., subj. אֲשֻׁרָי (4⁵). It is most prob. that MT. has interp. the sg. רגלי, אֲשֻׁרָי as pl. Kt. would then in both cases be correct and the agreement complete. 𝔊, 𝔍, agree with Qr. — **3.** הוֹלְלִים] Qal ptc. *boasters,* as 5⁶ 75⁵, not ἀνόμοις 𝔊, *iniquos* 𝔍. — **4.** חַרְצֻבּוֹת] pl. † [הַרְצֻבָּה] n.[f.], elsw. Is. 58⁶ *bonds;* 𝔊 ἀνάνευσις, 𝔙 *respectus,* 𝔍 *recogitaverint,* Aq. δυσπάθειαι, Σ ἐνεθυμοῦντο, 𝔖 סבא, 𝔗 תּוּהִין. These all may be explained as different interpretations of חרצות, properly *decisions.* — לְמוֹתָם] ל prep., מָוֶת n.m. *death* (6⁶) sf. 3 pl. m.; so Vrss.; but most moderns after Moerlius (scholia 1737), Ew., Hi., Bö., Ols., Oort, לָמוֹ, prep. ל of possession with sf. 3 pl., תָּם adj. *sound, wholesome* (37³⁷). The measure also requires the two words. — בְּרִיא] adj. of cattle, *fat,* Gn. 41²·⁴·⁵·⁷·¹⁸·²⁰ (E) I K. 5³ Ez. 34³·²⁰ Ze. 11¹⁶; of food, Hb. 1¹⁶; of man, Ju. 3¹⁷ Dn. 1¹⁵; here only of אול. — אוּלָם] dub.; *BDB.* [אוּל] n.[m.] α.λ. *body, belly* (in contempt); so, with hesitation, Bä., but improb. 𝔊 ἐν τῇ μάστιγι αὐτῶν, 𝔙 *in plaga* = חֳלָיָם, Σ πρόπυλα, 𝔍 *vestibula* = אוּלָם (אוּלָךְ n.m. *porch*). Rd. חֵילָם *their strength.* — **5.** אֵינֵמוֹ] fully written for אֵינְמוֹ] אֵין with sf. 3 pl. (3³). — **6.** יַעֲנָקְתֵמוֹ] Qal pf. 3 f. sg., archaic sf. 3 pl. † [עֲנַק] vb. denom. *serve as a necklace,* elsw. Hiph. Dt. 15¹⁴·¹⁴. — יַעֲטָף] Qal impf. Aramaism, elsw. 65¹⁴. 𝔊, 𝔍, 3 pl., prob. correct. — † שִׁית] n.[m.] *clothing;* but 𝔊 ἀδικίαν καὶ ἀσέβειαν is prob. interp. gl. — **7.** עֵינֵמוֹ] archaic sf. with עַיִן, so 𝔍; but 𝔊 ἡ ἀδικία αὐτῶν, so 𝔖, 𝔙, Street, Hi., Ew., Ols., De., Oort, Bä., *BDB.,* עֲוֹנֵמוֹ. — מַשְׂכִּיּוֹת] pl. † מַשְׂכִּית n.f. (1) *show-piece, figure,* Nu. 33⁵² Lv. 26¹ (P) Ez. 8¹² (?) Pr. 25¹¹; (2) *imagination, conceit,* Aramaism Pr. 18¹¹ and here; so 𝔍 *cogitationes;* but 𝔊 εἰς διάθεσιν, 𝔙 *in affectum.* — **8.** יָמִיקוּ] vb. Qal or Hiph. מוק or מיק α.λ. *mock, deride,* Aramaism, 𝔊 διενοήθησαν, 𝔍 *iniriserunt.* — מֵרוֹם] so 𝔍; but 𝔊 εἰς τὸ ὕψος, prob. both prep. interp. glosses; subsequent context favours 𝔚. — **9.** הִתְהַלֵּךְ] Qal impf. strong form, Ew.§¹³⁸·ᵇ Ges.⁶⁹·ˣ Kö.ⁱ·⁴¹⁵, for usual יֵלֵךְ. But Lag., Now., Du., מִתְהַלֵּךְ. — **10.** יָשִׁיב] Kt. Hiph. impf. שׁוּב; Qr. יָשׁוּב Qal impf.; so 𝔊, 𝔍. — ‡ הֲלֹם] adv. *hither.* — יְמָמוֹ] so 𝔍; but 𝔊, 𝔖, יְמֵי; both sfs. interpretative. Houb., Lag., Oort, Now., *BDB.,* rd. ייבעמו לחם *satisfy them with bread.* But the v. is prob. gl., and the Hiph. of Kt. should be followed, which gives us the restoration of God's people from exile. — וּמֵי מָלֵא יִמָּצוּ] vb. Niph. impf. 3 pl. מָצָא 𝔊, 𝔙, 𝔖, 𝔍, Σ, cf. מְצָרֵי Nu. 11¹¹; 𝔍 *quis plenus invenietur in eis,* מִי מָלֵא; 𝔊, 𝔙, יְמֵי. Σ διδαχὴ is interp. of 𝔚. מֵי leads most moderns to think of מִצָּה, v. 75⁹; but improb. — **11.** וְאָמְרוּ] ו coörd. connecting with v.⁹, possibly gl. — אֵל] divine name, frequent in 𝔄, v.¹⁷ 50¹ 74⁸ 77¹⁰·¹⁴·¹⁵ 78⁷·⁸·¹⁸·¹⁹·³⁴·³⁵·⁴¹ +. — † דֵּעָה] n.f. *knowledge,* elsw. 1 S. 2³ Is. 11⁹ 28⁹ Je. 3¹⁵ Jb. 36⁴, poetic for usual דַּעַת (19³). — עֶלְיוֹן] divine name, common in 𝔄, 50¹⁴ 77¹¹ 78¹⁷·³⁵·⁵⁶ 82⁶ 83¹⁹, seldom early ψ, v. Intr. § 32. — **12.** שַׁלְוֵי עוֹלָם] phr. α.λ., † שָׁלֵו adj. *at ease, quiet,* Zc. 7⁷ 1 Ch. 4⁴⁰; of quiet, easy life Je. 49²¹ Jb. 16¹² 21²³; abst. Jb. 20²⁰ Ez. 23⁴², both txt. err. — הִשְׂגּוּ] Hiph. pf. † [שָׂגָה] vb. Aram., Qal *grow great,*

as cedar 92¹⁸, cf. Jb. 8⁷· ¹¹, Hiph. *increase riches*, a.λ. here. — **13.** אַךְ] as v.¹.
𝔊 prefixes καὶ εἶπα as v.¹¹, but this evidently a gl. — וָאֶרְחַץ] ו consec. impf.
unusual in late Pss. The phr. apart from ו consec. is cited from Ps. 26⁶. —
14. לִבְחָרִים] as 101⁸; without ר, cf. 5⁴ 55¹⁸. — **15.** אִם־אָמַרְתִּי] conditional
clause with pf. כְּדָרְתִּי (25³) in apod. — אֲסַפֵּרָה] Pi. cohort. expressing resolution, cf. 2⁷. 𝔍 attaches the condition to אספרה. It is possible that אם is
interp. gl. as Bä. — כְּמוֹ] adv. *so*. 𝔊 οὕτως, 𝔍 *sic*. Ew., Dr., add הִנֵּה Bö., Gr.,
rd. כמוהם, Bä. כָּמוֹהָ, which is more prob. because of following ה. The adv.
alone is unexampled. — **16.** היא] Kt. agrees with זאת. הוא Qr. without dis-
crimination, as usual in OT. — **18.** הַפִּלְתָּם מַשּׁוּאוֹת † מישואה] n.f. *place of deception*,
elsw. 74³; √שָׁאָ *beguile* (55¹⁶); but improb. Σ εἰς ἀφανισμούς, 𝔍 *ad interitum* =
מְשׁוּאוֹת pl. מְשׁוּאָה √שׁוּא *ruin*, as Zp. 1¹⁵ Jb. 30³, so Klos., Now., Bä., 𝐵DB.
𝔊ᴮ has not this clause, but 𝔊ᴺ· ᴿ· ᵀ κατέβαλες αὐτοὺς ἐν τῷ ἐπαρθῆναι, 𝔙 *dum
allevarentur*, Aug. *dum extollerentur*, so Horsley, "in their elevation," Aram.
inf. cstr. למשּׂאות as Ez. 17⁹ √נשא *lift up*. — **19.** קָמוּ] Qal pf. 3 m. pl. † סוּף] vb.
Qal *come to an end*, elsw. Am. 3¹⁵ Is. 66¹⁷ Est. 9²⁸. Hiph. *make an end of*
Zp. 1²· ³· ³ Je. 8¹³ (all dub.). — תַמּוּ] Qal pf. 3 m. pl. הַמֵּם emph. coördination.
— בַּלָּהוֹת] pl. † בַּלָּהָה n.f. (1) *terrors* (only pl.) Jb. 18¹¹ 27²⁰ 30¹⁵, spec. of death
Jb. 18¹⁴ 24¹⁷; (2) *calamity* sg. Is. 17¹⁴, elsw. pl. Ez. 26²¹ 27³⁶ 28¹⁹. 𝐵DB.
classes our Ps. with (2), Dr. with (1); more prob. esp. if it be a late gl. 𝔊
διὰ τὴν ἀνομίαν and 𝔙 is interpretative; so also 𝔍 *quasi non sint*. This v. is
a tetrameter gl. — **20.** ‡ חֲלוֹם] n.m. *dream*, only here ψ, but frequent in early
Lit., cf. vb. 126¹. — מֵהָקִיץ] Hiph. inf. קִיץ (3⁶) with מִן temporal, *after*, Ges.¹⁶⁴· ᵍ.
𝔊 ἐξεγειρομένου = מֵקִיץ מֵהָקִיץ, so Σ, 𝔍, 𝔖, 𝔙. — אֲדֹנָי] as 𝔊, 𝔍, MT., belongs
with second clause, making v. hexameter with caesura after the second beat.
— בָעִיר] contr. בְּהָעִיר Hiph. inf. עוּר (7⁷) with ב temporal as 𝕿, Ges.⁵³· ᑫ; so
Oort, Bä., al., and most moderns. 𝔊 ἐν τῇ πόλει σου, sustained by 𝔙, 𝔍, 𝔖, is
an erroneous interpretation, which does not suit the context. — **21.** יִתְחַמֵּץ]
Hithp. impf. 3 sg. † חמץ vb. Qal *be soured, leavened*, Ex. 12³⁴· ³⁹ (E), cf. Ho. 7⁴.
Hithp. *be soured, embittered*, a.λ. ‖ אֶשְׁתּוֹנָן Hithp. impf. 1 sg. שׁנן. — **22.** וְלֹא אֵדָע]
circumstantial, *without knowing:* cf. 14⁴ *unintelligent*, בְּהֵמָה pl. בְּהֵמוֹת (8⁸);
pl. not of number but of intensity ; *stupid* or *great beast*, "a very beast," Dr.;
not the hippopotamus, as De., Hi., Now. — **24.** וְאַחַר כָּבוֹד] adv. term with conj.
and afterwards, as 𝔍, Σ, so most moderns. 𝔊 μετὰ δόξης, 𝔙 *cum gloria*, take
it as prep. But אחר as prep. nowhere has this sense. The vb. לקה does not
admit of the use of אחר in the sense of following after, though Ew., Hi., suggest it as the goal of the taking. The mng. is evident enough, and is open to
no other objection than dogmatic presupposition. The text is only made more
difficult by the emendation of Gr., וְאַחֲרֵיךְ כִּי, though adopted by We., Now.
כָבוֹד is acc. of direction, the place of honour, in the immediate presence of
God, as 16¹¹; cf. 112⁹. — **26.** שְׁאֵרִי] sf. 1 sg. ‡ שְׁאֵר n.m. *flesh*, elsw. 78²⁰· ²⁷ Mi.
3²· ³ Je. 51³⁵+. — צוּר לְבָבִי] phr. a.λ. improb. לבבי is dittog. אלהים is also gl.,
though both in 𝔊. The l. is complete without either. We should rd. צוּרִי (18³)
as חֶלְקִי (16⁵). — **27.** רְחֵקֶיךָ] sf. 2 sg. with pl. adj. רָחֵק a.λ. *departing*, 𝐵DB.
𝔊 οἱ μακρύνοντες ἑαυτοὺς ἀπὸ σοῦ, 𝔍 *qui elongant se a te*. It is more prob.

ptc. ‖ זוֹנֶה. Rd. therefore מְרַחֲקֶיךָ with Gr. — [הִצְמָתָּה] Hiph. pf. 2 m., fully written צמת (*1841*). — [זוֹנֶה] Qal ptc. ‡ זָנָה vb. *commit fornication*, usually in physical sense ; but in religious sense, by forsaking Yahweh for another God, only here c. מִן alone, elsw. c. אחרי, usually Ex. 34¹⁵· ¹⁶ +, מֵעַל Ho. 9¹, מִתַּחַת Ho. 4¹², abs. Ho. 2⁷ 4¹⁵ Is. 57³ Ps. 106³⁹. — **28.** [הָרְבַּת] cstr. † [הָרְבָּה] *B*DB. *approach*, elsw. Is. 58² in same phr.; but 𝕲, 𝕵, interp. as vb. inf., which is more prob., rd. הָרְבָה אל אלהים. — [שִׁבְתִּי] Qal inf. cstr. with sf. 1 sg. שִׁבְתִּ, cf. 49¹⁵, but שִׁיתָ v.¹⁸ makes it improb. that we should have שבת here. There is prob. error of pointing in MT. — [אֲרֹנִי יהוה] is conflation. 𝕲 κύριος for אֲרֹנִי. יהוה in 𝕰 either gl. or evidence that context also is gl. — [בְּיָדֶיךָ] sf. 2 m. pl. ‡ מְלָאכָה n.f. *work*, † of God, elsw. creation Gn. 2²· ²· ³ (P), judgment Je. 50²⁵; of men, 107²³.

PSALM LXXIV., 3 PTS. OF 3 STR. 3⁴.

Ps. 74 is a prayer of the exilic community : I. An expostulation with God for continuous anger against His ancient people and Zion (v.¹· ²ᵃᶜ). The enemies have destroyed the temple (v.³ᵇ· ⁴ᵃ· ⁷) ; they planned the exile of the people and the destruction of their religion (v.⁸⁻⁹). II. The enemies reproach God and He still withholds His hand from them (v.¹⁰⁻¹¹) ; and yet He has wrought wonders in the past (v.¹³· ¹⁵) and He is sovereign of nature (v.¹⁶⁻¹⁷). III. A plea to remember the reproaches of the enemy, and not abandon His people to them (v.¹⁸⁻¹⁹), to look upon the violence and not let the afflicted be confounded (v.²⁰⁻²¹), to rise up for His own cause against His adversaries (v.²²⁻²³). Glosses of various kinds were inserted (v.²ᵇ· ³ᵃ· ⁴ᵇ⁻⁶· ¹²⁻¹⁴).

I.

WHY, O God, dost Thou cast us off forever;
    Smokes Thine anger against the flock of Thy pasture ?
    Remember Thy congregation, which Thou didst get of old ;
    Mount Zion, wherein Thou hast dwelt.
ALL hath the enemy marred in the sanctuary.
    Thine adversaries roared in the midst of Thy meeting place.
    They set on fire Thy sanctuary, (O God).
    To the ground they profaned the dwelling place of Thy name.
THEY said in their mind : " Let their offspring become solitary."
    They made the festivals of God in the land to cease.
    Our signs we do not see :
    And there is not with us one who knows.

II.

HOW long, O God, shall the adversary reproach ;
    The enemy ever contemn Thy name ?

Why drawest Thou back Thy hand, (O God) ;
And Thy right hand in the midst of Thy bosom (retainest) ?
THOU didst divide by Thy strength the sea.
Thou didst break the heads of the dragon by the waters.
Thou didst cleave out springs and brooks.
Thou didst dry up everflowing rivers.
THINE is the day : Thine also the night.
Thou didst prepare luminary and sun.
Thou didst fix all the boundaries of earth.
Summer and harvest Thou didst form.

III.

REMEMBER this : the enemy doth reproach ;
An impudent people do contemn Thy name.
Give not to wild beasts (the person that praiseth Thee).
The life of Thine afflicted forget not forever.
LOOK to (the fat ones) ; for they are full.
The dark places of the earth are dwellings of violence.
Let not the crushed turn away confounded.
Let the afflicted and poor praise Thy name.
ARISE, O God ! O plead Thine own cause.
Remember the reproach of Thee by the impudent.
Forget not the voice of Thine adversaries,
The roar of those who rise up against Thee, going up continually.

Ps. 74 was in $\mathfrak{A}$, of the class משכיל as 78, and subsequently in $\mathfrak{E}$; $v.$ Intr. §§ 29, 32. It has three parts : (1) v.[1. 2ac. 3b. 4a. 7-9], (2) v.[10-11. 13. 15-17], (3) v.[18-23]. Each part has three tetrameter tetrastichs. The glosses are all added to (1) and (2), not to (3). These are : (1) v.[2b], from Je. 10[16]; (2) v.[3a], a petition in time of depression ; (3) v.[4b-6], a Maccabean gl. ; (4) v.[12], a general reference to God as king ; (5) v.[14], a haggadistic gl., the first l. of which is absent from $\mathfrak{G}$. Apart from glosses the Ps. shows no evidence of very late date. The reference to the capture of the temple, the setting it on fire and profaning it to the ground, v.[3. 7], best suits the destruction of the temple by the Babylonians. The reference to the mind of the enemy to make the posterity of Israel solitary and to cause the festivals to cease from the land, v.[8], suits best the Exile. The expostulation which is the ground tone of the Ps. looks back upon these things as so long past that the people of God are justified in remonstrating with Yahweh for their continuance. The reference to the absence of miracle and prophecy, v.[9], usually regarded as evidence of Maccabean times, is a gl. The linguistic and stylistic resemblances are the following : v.[1] יעשן אפך phr. elsw. Dt. 29[19], cf. Ps. 80[5] ($\mathfrak{A}$) ; צאן מרעיתך phr. elsw. Pss. 79[13] ($\mathfrak{A}$) 100[3] Je. 23[1] Ez. 34[31]; v.[2] קנה of getting of Israel by redemption Ps. 78[54] ($\mathfrak{A}$) Ex. 15[16] Is. 11[11]; v.[7] לארץ חלל phr. of 89[40], cf. La. 2[2]; v.[8] ויִּים prob. יין, elsw. Gn. 21[23] Is. 14[22] Jb. 18[19]; מיֹעֲדי אל phr. a.λ., but מועדים common in the sense of *feasts ;* so here as $\mathfrak{G}$. The reference to synagogues has no justification in Hebr. language, and therefore cannot give evidence

of a date of composition after synagogues were established in the land. V.[15]
בקע as Ps. 78[13. 15] (𝕬), נהרות איתן phr. α.λ., cf. נחל א׳ Dt. 21[4] Am. 5[24]; v.[18. 22]
נב׳ as 14[1] Dt. 32[21], referring to national enemy ; v.[20] מחשך as Is. 29[15]. There
are several passages which remind of Ps. 9–10: v.[10], cf. 10[3. 13]; v.[19], cf. 9[13];
v.[20], cf. 10[7]; v.[21], as 9[10] 10[18]. The הנינים v.[13] refers prob. to Egypt of the
Exodus, cf. Ez. 29[3] 32[2]. V.[15] refers to the crossing of the Jordan. On the
whole, the Ps. may be best explained as written with reference to the destruction of Jerusalem by the Babylonians, and to the Exile, by a poet subsequent
to Ez. and prior to Is.[2]. The glosses are partly from the editor of 𝕰, chiefly
from a Maccabean editor who wishes to refer to the desecration of the temple
in the time of Antiochus. To this event the erection of the signs therein and
the ruthless destruction of the ornaments of the temple naturally refer. Such
desecration is not altogether homogeneous with the destruction of the temple
as described in the original Ps. The glosses have also evidence of late style :
v.[3] הרים פעם משאות α.λ. ; v.[6] כשיל, כולפות v.[14] לויתן and לעם לציים.

Pt. I., Str. I. Two syn. couplets. — **1.** *Why, O God, dost Thou
cast us off forever ?*], expostulation with God for the long-continued abandonment of His people during their exile from their
native land. It seems as if it were to last forever, cf. 44[24] 77[8] 79[5]
La. 3[31]. — *Smokes Thine anger*], cf. 18[9] 80[5]. — *against the flock of
Thy pasture*], phr. elsw. Pss. 79[13] 100[3] Je. 23[1] Ez. 34[31]. Israel is
conceived as the flock of God, their Shepherd, who leads them to
pasture ; cf. Pss. 23[1-2] 77[21] 78[52] 80[2]. — **2.** *Remember*], so v.[18. 22]. Recall to mind the facts of the past ; two are mentioned : (*a*) *Thy
congregation which Thou didst get of old*], referring to the Exodus
from Egypt and entrance into the Holy Land, cf. Ex. 15[16] Dt. 32[6-7].
A glossator emphasizes this by inserting from Je. 10[16], *Thou didst
redeem the tribe of Thine inheritance.* — (*b*) *Mount Zion, wherein
Thou hast dwelt*], referring to the selection of Mount Zion as
the permanent place of the divine temple 2 S. 7[12-13] 1 K. 6[11-13]
Ps. 132[13-14], in which the God of Israel had resided from the time
of Solomon until the Exile. — **3** a. A glossator adds for emphatic
enlargement, *which Thy footsteps exalted to everlasting dignity*].
The usual explanation is " continual desolations," such as have so
long continued that they seem to be forever, and so God is urged
to interpose by stepping up to them and inspecting them Himself.
But this is abrupt and awkward in the context, and is not sustained
by ancient Vrss. The translation given above requires no change
in the unpointed text.

Str. II. Synth. tetrastich. — **3 b.** *All*] or "everything," emphatic in position — *hath the enemy marred in the sanctuary*] ; they have left nothing intact : everything has been destroyed. — **4 a.** *Roared*], the uproar of a crowd of *adversaries*, who have captured the temple after a prolonged conflict, and make its ancient walls ring with their shouts of triumph. They have penetrated even into *the midst of Thy meeting place*], the transfer to the temple of the idea of the ancient tent of meeting, where Yahweh met His people. There is no justification for the rendering "Thy congregation" of AV. — **7.** *They set on fire Thy sanctuary*]. After rioting in it, spoiling it of its treasures, and destroying everything that they could not take away with them, they finally set the temple on fire. This probably refers to the destruction of the temple by the army of Nebuchadnezzar 2 K. 25⁹⁻¹⁷. — *They profaned the dwelling place of Thy name*]. The sacred places were reserved for Israelites, who must be consecrated in order to have access to them. These had been profaned by the presence of the heathen soldiery, unconsecrated and defiled with blood. — *to the ground*], utterly, cf. Ps. 89⁴⁰. — A Maccabean editor enlarges upon this description of the destruction of the temple to make it more appropriate to the desecration by Antiochus. — **4 b.** *They have set up their own signs as signs*], probably referring not to the standards of the army in token of victory, but to the religious symbols of the Greeks as a supplanting of the Jewish religion. — **5.** *It was perceived*], lit. "made known " or "became known," namely, that which was done by the enemies in the temple ; so this difficult form should most probably be rendered. Vrss. and interpreters differ greatly in their views of this passage. — *as one who wieldeth upwards axes in a thicket of trees*], simile of a woodman lifting up his ax in a forest to cut down trees, cf. Je. 46²². ²³. **6.** *So now its doors together with hatchets and axes they strike down*], breaking open all the doors of the temple, a graphic description of the desecration of the temple by Antiochus ; cf. 1 Macc. 1. The reference to "doors" of 𝔊, 𝔘, is more probable than that to "carved work " of 𝔐, 𝔍, and modern Vrss.

Str. III. Syn. couplets. — **8.** *They said in their mind*], to themselves, their plan and purpose. — *Let their offspring become solitary*] ; the words of the Babylonian enemy, determining upon the transportation of the people into exile, so that their offspring might be brought up apart from their native land, apart by themselves in a foreign land. The word "offspring" of 𝕲, 𝔍, is better sustained than the vb. of MT. followed by PBV., RV. "let us make havock of them altogether," or "let us destroy them," AV., JPSV. — *They made to cease*], 𝕲; to be preferred to "burnt up" of 𝔥, though sustained by most Vrss., because of the tautology with v.[7a]. — *the festivals of 'El*], so 𝕲, intensified by the later insertion of "all": the abolition of all the sacred feasts prescribed in the laws of Israel from the most ancient times. There is no authority in ancient usage for thinking of the synagogues of Maccabean times, although this is adopted by EV[s]. and most moderns. — **9.** *Our signs we do not see*], the symbols of the religion of Yahweh, such as the Sabbath Ez. 20[12. 20] Ex. 31[13. 17], in appropriate parall. with festivals of previous line, and therefore more probable than "miracles" or "ensigns." It is, however, possible that the glossator who inserted "there is no more a prophet," interpreted them as miracles, thinking of his own time as characterised by the absence alike of miracle and prophecy, cf. 1 Macc. 4[46] 9[27] 14[41]. — *And there is not with us one who knows*]. No one understands what it all means. It is not probable that the author was thinking of a prophet, or that he was thinking of the length of time the exile would last, as the erroneous dittog. of "how long" requires; he was rather thinking that the whole situation was unintelligible, inexplicable, in view of the relation of Israel to God.

Pt. II., Str. I. Syn. couplets. — **10.** *How long*], expostulation as to the length of time, cf. 79[5] 89[47], ‖ *ever.* — *shall the adversary reproach* ‖ *contemn Thy name*], by their maltreatment of the temple which bears the divine name, and in which God dwelt and the people worshipped who were called by His name, cf. v.[18] 10[3. 13] 79[12]. — **11.** *Why drawest Thou back Thy hand?*], to which, for the sake of the measure, *O God* should be added, which has fallen out by mistake. One would expect the very reverse, that God would draw it forth to vindicate Himself. — *And Thy right hand* in ‖, in connection with *in the midst of Thy bosom*, suggests the vb. *retainest*, which was probably in the original Ps., but which was changed by the Maccabean editor to a similar vb. imv. "consume them," implying a vb. "take it forth," or "pluck it forth,"

RV. The hand of God, and especially His right hand, is that which He lifts up (10^{12}), or stretches out (Ex. 15^{12}), in vindicating Himself and His people against their enemies, cf. 44^4 89^{14}. Israel cannot understand why he does not do this now ; why He stands aside, as it were, with His right hand in the bosom of His garment. — **12**. A glossator inserts, as an additional reason for the expostulation, the couplet : *And God is my king of old*]. From the most ancient times He has been king of Israel, cf. 9^8 10^{16} 44^5. — *Worker of victories*], ptc. expressing the characteristic action of the king, who as commander of armies gives victory to His people, cf. 1 S. 14^{45} Is. 26^{18} Pss. 20^6 $21^{2.6}$ 44^5 68^{20} + ; not to be generalised into " salvation " of EV⁵. — *in the midst of the earth*]. His victories were not confined to the Holy Land, but were wrought in other parts of the earth ; interpreting the subsequent context.

Str. II. Synth. couplets. — **13**. *Thou didst divide by Thy strength the sea*], referring to the crossing of the Red Sea by Israel at the Exodus, Ex. $14^{21\ sq.}$. — *Thou didst break the heads of the dragon by the waters*], the military chiefs of Egypt compared to a dragon, Is. 27^1 51^9 Ez. 29^3 32^2. — **14**. A doublet of the previous v. — *Thou didst crush the heads of Leviathan*], probably here the crocodile, another term for Egypt, cf. Is. 27^1. — *that Thou mightest give them for food to the folk of jackals*]. Their dead bodies cast up upon the shore became the prey of the jackals, cf. 63^{11}. The reference of 𝕲, 𝕵, 𝖁, to the Ethiopians has no historical or linguistic propriety. The reference of EV⁵. " to the people inhabiting the wilderness," while possible, has no historical support and is improbable. Aq., ϴ, 𝕮, Quinta, give it a mythological reference to the flesh of Leviathan (cf. Jb. 3^8), which it was supposed would be given as a festal meal to Israel in the latter days. This is more probable in so late a gloss. — **15**. *Thou didst cleave out springs and brooks*], cf. 78^{15} 105^{41} Is. 48^{21}, referring to the miracle of bringing water from the rocks Ex. 17^0 Nu. 20^8. — *Thou didst dry up everflowing rivers*], referring to the crossing of the Jordan Jos. 3.

Str. III. Synth. couplets, passing from the divine power in history to the divine power over nature, both in creation and providence. — **16**. *Thine is the day*] ; it belongs to Thee as its owner. — *Thine also the night*], therefore both day and night, comprehending all time. The reason for this ownership is *Thou didst prepare*, create, *luminary*, that is, the moon, as 𝕲, giving light by night, *and sun*, giving light by day; cf. Gn. 1¹⁴⁻¹⁹ Ps. 104¹⁹⁻²³. — **17**. *Thou didst fix all the boundaries of earth*], which might be interpreted in general of the separation of land and sea Gn. 1⁹ Jb. 38⁸ ˢᵠ· Pr. 8²⁹, or of the boundaries of the nations Dt. 32⁸; but more probably, owing to the qualifying line, refers to the divisions of the seasons Gn. 1¹⁴; for the reason is given : *Summer and harvest Thou didst form*] at the creation, making this the chief boundary in the year.

Pt. III., Str. I. Syn. couplets. — **18**. *Remember this*], renewing the plea of v.², only calling attention now to the enemy instead of to the people of God. The demonstrative, thrown before for emphasis, is defined in the subsequent clauses. — "The enemy" of v.³ is resumed and described as *an impudent people*], so v.²² 14¹. — *doth reproach ‖ contemn Thy name*], resuming v.¹⁰. — **19**. *Give not to wild beasts*], or "wild beast," as RV. after 𝕲, 𝕵, 𝕿, much more probable than "unto the multitude," that is, of the enemies or wicked, of PBV., AV., which depends upon another interpretation of the Hebr. word. — *the person that praiseth Thee*], so 𝕲, 𝖁, favoured by interpretations of other ancient Vrss.; to be preferred to 𝕳, followed by EVˢ., "Thy turtle dove," a pet name for Israel which has no other Biblical authority, and is elsewhere only an image of timidity. — *The life of Thine afflicted*]. The people suffering affliction from their enemies were in mortal peril. — *forget not forever*], cf. 10¹¹⁻¹² 13². God's withholding interposition so long (v.¹⁰) seems like forgetfulness; the reverse of the plea to remember.

Str. II. Synth. couplets. — **20**. *Look to the fat ones*], the sleek enemies made fat by victory and booty, cf. 73⁴, as suggested by Du.; to be preferred to 𝕳, "Look to the covenant," though sustained by ancient and modern Vrss. and most interpreters; because it interrupts the thought by the suggestion of God's neglect of the ancient covenant with Israel, Ex. 24⁸, when the whole context is a plea to consider the attitude of the enemy. The variation in the text as between the two readings is only one of pointing. — *for they are full*], that is, with the booty, which makes them fat.

The measure requires that this vb. should go with the previous clause and not with the following, as EV⁵. — *The dark places of the earth*], referring not to the hiding-places of the persecuted of the Maccabean period 1 Macc. 1⁵³ 2²⁷ ˢᑫ·, to which they were pursued by their enemies and cruelly cut down, and thus justifying the supplementary statement *dwellings of violence*, but to the lands of exile where Israel was, as it were, in the Sheol of national death, away from the light of the divine countenance, and exposed in their weakness to the cruelty of their enemies. — **21.** *Let not the crushed ‖ afflicted and poor*]. The nation had been crushed by the destruction of Jerusalem and the misery of the Exile. In their affliction and poverty they resort to their God for deliverance; they plead that they may not *turn away confounded*], as if unrecognised, unanswered, or refused. On the contrary, let them *praise Thy name*], in antithesis with the enemies who contemn it v.¹⁸.

Str. III. Syn. couplets. — **22–23.** *O arise, O God!*], a still more importunate plea for immediate interposition, cf. 9²⁰ 10¹². — *O plead Thine own cause*], the cause of His people was identical with His own, cf. 43¹. — *Remember* (cf. v.¹⁸) and its antithesis *forget not* (v.¹⁹) are resumed in the climax. — *the reproach of Thee*], cf. v.¹⁸, as expressed in *the voice*, aloud in boldness and defiance, and indeed as *the roar, going up continually*], of a tumultuous assembly of angry and vindictive as well as *impudent* ones ‖ *Thine adversaries* ‖ *those who rise up against Thee*. The psalmist, in his emphatic assertion that they were God's enemies, has lost sight for the moment that they were also enemies of the people of God.

1. לְךָ] expostulation (*2¹*). — אֱלֹהִים] so v.¹⁰· ¹²· ²², prob. original. — בְּ עֶשַׁן אַפְּךָ] phr. elsw. Dt. 29¹⁹. † יֶעְשַׁן vb. denom. Qal *smoke*, elsw. of mountain Ex. 19¹⁸ Pss. 104³² 144⁵; cf. Ps. 80⁵ (without אַף). — צֹאן מַרְעִיתֶךָ] *flock of Thy shepherding;* phr. elsw. Pss. 79¹³ 100³ Je. 23¹ Ez. 34³¹, cf. Ps. 95⁷. † [מַרְעִית] n.f. elsw. *pasturage* Ho. 13⁶ Is. 249⁹ Je. 25³⁶; by meton. *flock* Je. 10²¹. — **2.** זְכֹר] Qal imv. 2 m. (*8⁵*), so v.¹⁸· ²², characteristic of Ps. — קָנִיתָ] Qal pf. 2 m. ‡ קָנָה vb. *get, acquire*, of God (all poetic), (1) by creation or origination 139¹³ Gn. 14¹⁹· ²² Dt. 32⁶ Pr. 8²²; (2) by redemption, here, as Ps. 78⁵⁴ Ex. 15¹⁶ Is. 11¹¹. Other mngs. not in ψ. — וְאָלְךָ שֵׁבֶט וּנְחֲלָ־] gl. from Je. 10¹⁶ = 51¹⁹, cf. Is. 63¹⁷. — זֶה] relative, as 78⁵⁴ 104⁸· ²⁶. — **3.** הָרִימָה פְעָמֶיךָ] phr. a.λ., but cf. vb. with יד Ex. 17¹¹ (E) Nu. 20¹¹ (P) 1 K. 11²⁶· ²⁷, with רגל Gn. 41⁴⁴ (E); vb. is Hiph. imv. cohort. רום. 𝔊 has τὰς χεῖράς σου here, so 𝔙; 𝔖 נְבוּך, 𝔍 sublimitas = הֵרֵמָה, all glosses interp. of the obj. of vb. unexpressed.— ל [לְמַשָּׁאוֹת] prep., pl. [נשׁאׂ], elsw. 73¹⁸ dub. 𝔊 has ἐπὶ τὰς ὑπερηφανίας αὐτῶν = 𝔙 in superbias eorum, as v.²³ (for שְׁאוֹן) both from נשׁא (1), cf. Jb. 13¹¹ 20⁶ 31²³; Σ ἠφανίσθη interprets from נשׁא as Niph. So 𝔖 משׁתקלין; cf. Is. 33¹⁰ Ps. 94². 𝔍 dissipata est interprets from נשׁי beguile, deceive (55¹⁶); cf. Jb. 32²². The l. is a late gl. Ehr. proposes to take הרימה as Hiph. pf. 3 f. in rel. clause with פעמיך as subj.; and so we might render: "which Thy footsteps exalted." This makes better parall. with previous ll. Then it is better to go farther than Ehr. and follow 𝔊 in the interp. of למשׁאות, only giving it a good sense as משׁאת = שׁאו elevation, dignity, and so render the whole as: which Thy footsteps exalted to everlasting dignity. The glossator thus adds to each tetrameter a syn. trimeter in rel. clause. — [כָּל־הֵרֵע] כל is used absolutely, as 8⁷ 145¹⁶, and emph. with vb. in rel. clause, rel. omitted, which then connects it closely with previous l.; but as that is improb. the vb. is rather in a principal clause giving statement of fact. — 4. [מוֹעֲדֶיךָ] sf. 2 m. ‡ מוֹעֵד n.m. (1) appointed time 75³ 102¹⁴ 104¹⁹, so 𝔊 here τῆς ἑορτῆς σου; † (2) appointed place of assembly Zp. 3¹⁸ La. 2⁶. Many codd. MT., so 𝔗, Ki., rd. pl. here as v.⁸ אֵל מוֹעֲדֵי כָל; 𝔍 omnes solemnitates dei; 𝔊 τὰς ἑορτὰς κυρίου without כל. There is no sufficient reason to think of synagogues in v.⁸. — [שָׂמוּ אוֹתֹתָם אֹתוֹת]. This is not in 𝔊ᴮ, but in 𝔊ᴮ·ᵃᵇ·ᵐᵍ·ⁱⁿᶠ·ℵ·ᴿ·ᵀ ἔθεντο τὰ σημεῖα αὐτῶν σημεῖα καὶ οὐκ ἔγνωσαν. אוֹת (65⁹). The mng. standards elsw. only Nu. 2² (P); though after 𝔍, Calv., PBV., JPSV., and many adopt this mng. Most think of religious symbols. This best explains the repetition of the word. But in that case this l. is not suited to the context. — 5. [יִוָּדַע] Niph. impf. ידע; 3 sg. for 3 pl. is noteworthy. It can hardly refer to the enemies of the previous context. This also is not in 𝔊ᴮ. 𝔊ℵ·ᴿ·ᵀ⁺ rd. לֹא יָדָעוּ. 𝔍 manifesta prob. gives the true mng. It is needed for measure. — [כְּמֵבִיא] prep. כ with Hiph. ptc. בוא. 𝔊 has ὡς here as in next clause, but interp. before εἰς τὴν εἴσοδον; 𝔍 in introitu; these rd. מָבִיא. But 𝔊ℵ·ᶜ·ᵃ·ᴿ·ᵃ·ᵀ ἔξοδον; so 𝔙 sicut in exitu. — [לְמָעְלָה] adv. i.p. upward α.λ. ψ, but common elsw. OT.; cf. מַעַל. — [בִּסְבָּךְ] prep. בְ with † [סְבֹךְ] n.[m.] thicket, elsw. Je. 4⁷; cf. סְבָךְ n.[m.] idem Gn. 22¹³, pl. Is. 9¹⁷ 10³⁴. — [הַרְדֻּמוֹת] pl. † [הַרְדֹּם] n.[m.] axe, elsw. Ju. 9⁴⁸ I S. 13²⁰·²¹ Je. 46²². — 6. [וְעַת] Kt.; Qr. וְעַתָּה temporal sequence, so now. 𝔊 ἐξέκοψαν = יָדְעוּ, so 𝔖, 𝔙. Bä. rds. יָרְעַת Pu., as Is. 9⁹. But Σ νῦν δὲ, 𝔍 et nunc. — [פִּתּוּחֶיהָ] pl. sf. 3 f. † פִּתּוּחַ n.m. engraving on metal or stone I K. 6²⁹ Zc. 3⁹ Ex. 28¹¹·²¹·³⁶ 39⁶·¹⁴·³⁰ 2 Ch. 2⁶·¹³; so here, as 𝔍. But 𝔊 τὰς θύρας αὐτῆς = פְּתָחֶיהָ, so 𝔙. — [כַּשִּׁיל] α.λ., Aramaic loan word, BDB. axe. — [וְכֵילַפּׂת] α.λ. n.[f.] axe, Assyrian kalappatu, BDB. — [יַהֲלֹמוּן] Qal impf. 3 pl. fuller form ‡ [הלם] vb. smite with hammer Ju. 5²⁶; fig. Ps. 141⁵; so here with axe. — V.⁵⁻⁶ give two hexameters, a gl. to the tetrameter poem. — 7. [שִׁלְחוּ] Pi. pf. 3 pl. c. בְ instrument and acc. of obj. against which; cf. Ju. 1⁸ 20⁴⁸ 2 K. 8¹². A word seems to be missing. — [מִקְדָּשֶׁךָ] 𝔍 sanctuarium tuum, 𝔊 τὸ ἁγιαστήριόν σου. [דָּאָרֶץ הִלְלוּ] phr. 89⁴⁰, cf. La. 2². — 8. [נִינָם] dub. Qal impf. I pl. with sf. 3 pl. יָנָה oppress 17¹² 123⁴, so 𝔖 נוכר Ki., AE., Hu.³,

De., Bi.; but 𝕲 ἡ συγγενία αὐτῶν, 𝕵 *posteri eorum*, 𝕮 בניהם. †נִין n.m. *offspring*, as Gn. 21²³ Jb. 18¹⁹ Is. 14²²; so Hi., Bä. — יָחַד] i.p. (2²); but rd. יָחִיד *solitary, alone* (in exile) as 25¹⁶ 68⁷ 141¹⁰ (𝕲). — מוֹעֲדֵי אֵל] 𝕲ᴮ κυρίου, but 𝕲ˣ·ᴿ·ᵀ τοῦ θεοῦ more correct; *v.* v.⁴. — שָׂרְפוּ] Qal pf. 3 m., so 𝕵, Σ, Θ, Quinta, 𝕮; but 𝕲 δεῦτε καὶ καταπαύσωμεν, which Jerome supposed to be err. for κατακαύσωμεν (ep. 106 *ad Sun. et Fret.* c. 46), so Sexta. But 𝕾 נובד. It is improbable that burning, which has been mentioned v.⁷, would reappear in v.⁸. The text of 𝕲, 𝕾, was not the same as that of 𝔚 and other Vrss. The use of 2d pers. for God in the Ps. favours 𝕲 that אֵל should be in words of enemy. Ehrt, Moll, suggest עכבו err. for שָׁבַת וכר מוֹעֲדֵי. But ישבתו is itself more prob., cf. La. 5¹⁵ Is. 24⁸. — **9.** אֹתֹתֵינוּ] prep. את with sf. 1 pl., so 𝕵; 𝕲 ἡμᾶς, 𝖅 *et nos*, את def. acc. with sf. But the latter is against the use of 2 pers. for God in the Ps. — נָבִיא] n.m. *prophet*, elsw. ψ only 51² (title) 105¹⁵; gl., so also עד־מה dittog. — **10.** עַד־מָתַי] *until when, how long*, v.⁹; c. impf. elsw. 82² 94³, pf. 80⁵. This expostulation begins Part II. — **11.** יָדְךָ וִימִינְךָ] the second noun an intensification of the first, so 𝕵; but 𝕲 attaches ימינך to next l., which gives better parall. The first l. lacks a word, prob. the divine name. Then ימינך is acc. instrument with כָּלֵה Pi. imv. כרה (18³⁸), cf. 59¹⁴. This was prob. changed by Maccabean editor from an original הכלא, which gives better parall. — הוֹתֵךְ] Kt., err. for הֵיכְךָ Qr. (35¹³). — **12.** The change to 3 pers. between ll. of 2 pers. indicates a gl. — פָּעַל יְשׁוּעוֹת phr. a.λ. *worker of victories for usual* עשׂה יש I S. 14⁴⁵ Is. 26¹⁸. — **13.** פּוֹרַרְתָּ] Poel pf. 2 m. †פָּרַר] BDB. (SS. פור); Qal and Hithp. Is. 24¹⁹; Poel only here, *split, divide*. — תַּנִּין] n.m. (1) *serpent*, 91¹³ Dt. 32³³; רָאשֵׁי תַנִּינִים ‡ (2) *crocodile* or *dragon*, as fig. of Egypt, so here as Is. 27¹ 51⁹, cf. Ez. 29³ 32²; of Babylon Je. 51³⁴; (3) *sea monster*, as whale Gn. 1²¹ Jb. 7¹² Ps. 148⁷. The reference here is to Egypt, and the heads of the monster are the chiefs who were overwhelmed in the Red Sea. — **14.** רִצַּצְתָּ] Pi. pf. 2 m. ‡רצץ] vb. a.λ. ψ *crush in pieces*. — †לִוְיָתָן] n.m. (1) *river monster, crocodile*, Jb. 40²⁵, prob. here fig. of Egypt, cf. Is. 27¹·¹; (2) *sea monster, whale*, Ps. 104²⁶; (3) mythological *dragon* Jb. 3⁸. — This v. is a doublet of previous l. and is doubtless a gl. — תִּתְּנֶנּוּ] Qal impf. 2 m. נתן with sf. 3 m. sg The impf. in the midst of pfs. prob. expresses purpose. — לְ for prep. of late style for genitive, and עַם צִיִּים *yelpers, jackals*, cf. 72⁹. But 𝕲 λαοῖς τοῖς Αἰθίοψιν, 𝕵 *populo Aethiopum*. Aq., Quinta, 𝕮, refer עם to the Jews in accordance with the legend of *Baba bathra* 7⁴, that the pious in the future age would receive the flesh of Leviathan as a festal meal; so Θ λαῷ τῷ ἐσχάτῳ. This l. is also a late gl. — **15.** בָּקַעְתָּ] Qal pf. 2 m. ‡בָקַע vb. Qal *cleave, break open*, צור Is. 48²¹, the sea Ex. 14¹⁶ (P) Ps. 78¹³, so here ארץ, the earth 141⁷. Pi. *cleave* rock Ps. 78¹⁵. — ‡מַעְיָן] n.m. *spring, source*, elsw. ψ, 104¹⁰ 114⁸, but 84⁷ 87⁷ (dub.). — וָנַחַל] i.p. *torrent, brook* (18⁵). — וְהֹרֵיתָ אֵיתָן] phr. a.λ., cf. וַיַּהֲפֹךְ א Am. 5²⁴ Dt. 21⁴. ‡אֵיתָן adj. elsw. as *ever flowing* Ex. 14²⁷ (J) I K. 8²; other sense *permanent, enduring*, not in ψ. — **16.** ‡מָאוֹר] n.m. *luminary*, usually of both sun and moon, here followed by שׁמשׁ. It seems necessary to think of the moon, as 𝕲, although Now. thinks it collective for moon and stars; cf. 90⁸ of God's face as a luminary. — **17.** [חַיָּין וְהֶרֶף] phr. elsw. Gn. 8²² (J) Zc. 14⁸. — † [הֹרֶף] n.m. *harvest time*, elsw. Am. 3¹⁵ Je. 36²² Pr. 20⁴ Jb. 29⁴. — **18.** [זאת] so 𝔍; 𝔊ᴮ has τῆς κτίσεώς σου, but not 𝔊ˣ·ᵀ. — [יהוה] though sustained by 𝔊, 𝔍, must be a gl. in 𝔈. Moreover, it makes l. too long. — [עַם־נָבָל] phr. elsw. Dt. 32⁶ of Israel; but נבל v.²² 14¹ = 53² Dt. 32²¹ (גוי נ) all refer to the heathen as *impudent, shameless.* — **19.** [לְחַיַּת] לְ prep. with חַיַּת repeated in next l. It is impossible to give these words the same mng. in both cases, for *Thierlein*, De., though tempting, has no support in usage. Seventeen codd. de Rossi have לְחָיַת, making it stronger form for חַיָּה. It is prob. that it was so understood by MT., for 𝔗 as well as 𝔊, 𝔍, translate by *wild beast.* But it is easier to point חַיַּת. The other חַיַּת is cstr. חַיָּה in the sense of *life,* as 78⁵⁰ 143³. — [תּוֹרֶךָ] 𝔥, *thy dove,* endearing name for Israel, but there is no Biblical authority for it. It is elsw. only for image of timidity. 𝔊 ἐξομολογουμένην σοι, 𝔙 *confitentes tibi,* so 𝔖, הוֹרֶךָ Hiph. impf. 2 m. ירה (*v.* Intr. § 39) with sf. 2 m. This seems most prob. 𝔍 *eruditam lege tua;* Σ, 𝔗, תּוֹרֶךָ Hiph. impf. 2 m. ירה (*11²*) teach the law. — **20.** [לִבְרִית] (*v. 25¹⁰*) 𝔊 has sf. σοῦ, but it is doubtless interp. This gives no good sense in the context, and to connect it with מלאו and so get good measure is difficult. Rd. with Du. בְּרִיאַת for בְּרִיאֵי *fat persons,* cf. 73⁴. [כִּי־מָלְאוּ] agrees with בריות; cf. 10⁷. — [מַחֲשַׁכֵּי] pl. cstr. † מַחֲשָׁךְ n.m. (1) *dark, secret place,* where the wicked hide and work Is. 29¹⁵; so here; (2) *dark region,* where one loses the way Is. 42¹⁶; (3) *Sheol* Pss. 88⁷· ¹⁹ 143³ La. 3⁶. — **22.** [כִּי־הֵיוֹם] is prob. gl., as it makes l. too long with חֵנִי, which can only be explained as designed for an additional tone before נכל. — **23.** [עֹלֶה] Qal ptc. עֹלָה, relative clause without the usual article agreeing with שאון.

PSALM LXXV., 6 STR. 3³.

Ps. 75 is a song of thanksgiving to God for all His wondrous deeds (v.²), citing an oracle in which God Himself tells of an appointed time of judgment (v.³⁻⁴), warns the boasting wicked (v.⁵⁻⁶) that help cannot come from any quarter (v.⁷⁻⁸), that they must drain to the dregs the cup of judgment (v⁹) ; and declares once for all that the wicked will eventually be hewn off, but the righteous lifted up (v.¹⁰⁻¹¹).

> WE give thanks to Thee, O God,
>> We give thanks and call on Thy name,
>> Tell of (all) Thy wondrous deeds.
> "WHEN I take an appointed time,
>> I in equity judge :
>> The earth and its inhabitants melt away.
> "I SAY to the boasters : 'Boast not';
>> And to the wicked : 'Lift not up the horn.
>> Do not speak arrogantly against the Rock.'

" FOR not from the East or from the West,
  And not from the wilderness or from the mountains.
  Verily, God is about to judge.
" FOR a cup with red wine —
  It is full of mixed wine, and He extends it:
  Yea, its dregs they will drain out.
" VERILY I declare forever,
  That the horns of the wicked I will hew off ;
  But the horns of the righteous shall be lifted up."

Ps. 75 was originally a שׁיר, as indeed is evident from v.² It was taken up into 𝔄, then into 𝔐, 𝔈, and 𝔇ℜ, in which latter it was assigned אל תשׁחת (v. Intr. §§ 24, 29, 31, 32, 33, 34). The Ps., apart from the first Str., is an oracle of God, in five trimeter tristichs. The author was evidently familiar with the song of Hannah 1 S. 2 (v. v.⁵·⁶). The use of the cup of the wine of God's wrath to be drained by His enemies v.⁹ is as Je. 25¹⁵ 49¹² La. 4²¹ Is. 51¹⁷ Ez. 23³³⁻³⁴ Hb. 2¹⁶. The phrs. worthy of note are : v.³, מועד זקח a.λ., cf. 102¹⁴; v.¹¹ גדע קרנים phr. a.λ., but cf. Is. 45² Ps. 107¹⁶. V.⁹ ויגר ו consec. impf. is good old syntax. There are several glosses, chiefly of intensification : v.⁴ᵇ, אנכי for אני v.³·¹⁰; הכנתי late usage of the vb; v.⁶ᵃ, doublet of v.⁵ᵇ; v.⁸ᵇ, enlarged from 1 S. 2⁷; v.⁹ᵈ, amplification; v.¹⁰ᵇ, praise in 1 sg. for 1 pl. of Ps., and interrupting the divine words. The Ps. is ancient, and, apart from the use of אלהים, might be preëxilic. It is written in a calm tone of confidence in God and praise to Him for His wonders. It implies a peaceful condition of the community, probably in Babylonia prior to Nehemiah.

Str. I. Syn. triplet. — **2.** *We give thanks*], repeated for emphasis || *call on Thy name*], so 𝔊, 𝔙, 𝔖, Dr., Kirk., al., well suited to the context. "Thy name is near," of 𝔐, 𝔍, rests upon displacement of a single letter, and is an anomalous phr. difficult to explain, especially in this context, whether we think of "name" as for help or for presence. In the climax, — *Tell of all Thy wondrous deeds*], celebrate them in a song. These are, as the oracle indicates, deeds of impending judgment.

Str. II. Synth triplet. — **3.** *When I take an appointed time*]. God Himself speaks the oracle which takes up the remainder of the Ps. The "appointed time" is the time of judgment, cf. Hb. 2³ ; so RV., JPSV., and most moderns. PBV., AV., "when I receive the congregation," though a possible rendering, is not suited to the context. — *I in equity judge*], as the context indicates, in distributive justice, giving equitable punishment to the wicked and vindication to the righteous, cf. 9⁹ 58² 98⁹. — **4.** *The earth and its inhabitants melt away*], panic-stricken, in terror,

M

cf. Ex. 15^{15} Pss. 46^7 107^{26}. The reference is evidently to them as
wicked, cf. v^{11}, in antithesis with the righteous people of God.
A glossator adds : *It is I that have adjusted its pillars*], cf. 24^2 Jb.
38$^{4 \, sq.}$ 1 S. 2^8. It therefore depends entirely upon God whether
the earth shall remain stable and unshaken, or not.

Str. III. is a syn. triplet. — **5.** *I say to the boasters* ‖ *the
wicked*], a warning to the enemies of His people, — *Boast not*],
as expressed by the external gesture, — *lift not up the horn*], in
self-conscious dignity and supremacy ; cf. 1 S. 2$^{1. \, 10}$ Pss. 89$^{18. \, 25}$ 92^{11}
112^9. — **6.** This is interpreted by a glossator in dittog. by enlarging " horn " to " your horn," and " lift up " to " on high." The
Str. is complete without it. The climax of this boasting and
self-exaltation appears in the warning : *Do not speak arrogantly*].
This, acc. to independent, independent, EV^s., is expressed by the " neck " ; but the
rendering, *against the Rock*], suggested by independent, is followed by most
moderns and is doubtless correct, especially because of the relation
of this Ps. to the Song of Hannah 1 S. 2$^{2-3}$, cf. Dt. 32$^{4. \, 37}$ Hb. 1^{12}.

Str. IV. is a synth. triplet. — **7.** *For not from the East or from
the West*], the two antithetical quarters, complemented by *not
from the wilderness*, the southern quarter, *or from the mountains*,
the northern quarter, thus embracing the four quarters to exclude
them all. The interpretation of AV., RV., JPSV., with many
ancients and moderns, finding in the form the predicate " lifting
up," is improbable ; as is also that of independent, independent, independent, and most moderns,
" mountainous wilderness." Both of these leave the northern
quarter unmentioned. The statement of Kirk., that it is because
of the Assyrian approach from that quarter, is involved in a
mistaken view of the date of the Ps., and is unsatisfactory in any
case. It is usually supposed that these are the words of the
psalmist, excluding help for Israel from every quarter but God.
But this Str. intervening between III. and V. really is in close connection with both, and continues the warning of God to the wicked
enemies that no help can come to them from any quarter : their
judgment is about to begin. — **8.** *Verily God is about to judge*].
A glossator inserts from 1 S. 2^7 a statement of distributive judgment : *the one He putteth down, the other He lifteth up*, a line
making the Str. overfull, and really interrupting the close connection of the previous clause with the following Str.

Str. V. is a stairlike triplet. — **9.** *For a cup with red wine*],
the most probable reading, instead of "that foameth," of MT., a
term used only here of wine and dubious in itself. It was *in the
hand of Yahweh*, without doubt, as is evident from the context;
but it was not necessary to say this. The divine name is not the
one used in this Ps., and the insertion impairs the measure. — *It
is full of mixed wine*], cf. Is. 5²² Pr. 9².⁵ Ps. 102¹⁰. Herbs and
spices of various kinds were used to make it more stimulating and
intoxicating. — *and He extends it*]. God hands it out to the
wicked to drink. This is the most probable explanation of an
Aramaism which is rendered in EVˢ., " He poureth out." " Of it "
is an explanatory addition of a glossator at the expense of the
measure ; enlarged in ⑤, ⑤, ⑤, into " of this . . . of that," thinking
of two different cups. — *Yea, its dregs they will drain out*], interpreted by the gloss, " will drink," and whose subject is also given
without need : " all the wicked of the earth," both at the expense of
the measure. The cup of the wrath of God given to the wicked to
drink is common in OT., cf. 11⁶ 60⁵ Je. 25¹⁵ ˢ𝓺· 49¹² ˢ𝓺· 51⁷ Is. 51¹⁷ ˢ𝓺·.

Str. VI. A single line followed by an antith. couplet. —
10. *Verily I declare forever*], the words of God continued and
brought to their climax in the first person as Str. II., III. The
declaration is an everlasting decree, an unchangeable purpose.
It was, however, interpreted by a glossator as the words of Israel
in public worship, and accordingly a ‖ was inserted : *I will make
melody to the God of Jacob*, cf. 81², which then occasioned in ⑤
the change of the first vb. into " I will rejoice." — **11.** That
which God declares as His eternal purpose is : *That the horns of
the wicked I will hew off*], by a sudden and violent blow against
them, when lifted up by the wicked themselves, v.⁵ᵇ ; and, in
antithesis : *But the horns of the righteous shall be lifted up*], as is
suggested, by God Himself.

2. הֹורִ֫ינוּ] Hiph. pf. 1 pl. bis; when sq. לְ only of ritual worship (*v.* Intr.
§ 39), cf. 79¹⁰. — וְקָרֹ֫וב שְׁמֶ֑ךָ] so 𝔍 ; but phr. α.λ. dub.; ⑤ ἐπικαλεσόμεθα τὸ
ὄνομά σου = קְרוֹ בִישְׁמֶךָ inf. abs. קְרֹא with בְ prep. interp. as 1 pl. pf. — סִפְּרוּ] Pi.
pf. 3 m.; so 𝔍 : but ⑤ has διηγήσομαι, ⑤ *narrabimus*, also interp. inf. abs.
סַפֵּר. ⑤ has 1 pl. in both cases. Street, Du., would rd. 1 pl. Dy., Gr., Oort,
Bä., Kau., We., ptc. קֹרְאֵי. — וּפְלָאיֲךֶ] (9²). ⑤, ⑤, add לֹ, which gives better
measure, so Che. — **3.** כִּי־אֶקַּח מוֹעֵד] phr. α.λ.; כִּי temporal as ⑤, 𝔍 ; cf. 102¹⁴

מֵישָׁרִים אֶשְׁפֹּט] as 58², cf. 98⁹ c. בְ, in uprightness, equity, v. 9⁹. — **4.** נְמֹגִים] Niph. ptc. pl. a.λ. מוג = *melt away*, fig. of terror, *panic-stricken*, cf. Ex. 15¹⁵; in Qal 46⁷, Hithp. 107²⁶. — אָנֹכִי] full form instead of אֲנִי v.³·¹⁰; prob. betrays another hand. — תִּכַּנְתִּי] Pi. pf. † תכן Qal *weigh, prove*, Pr. 16² 21² 24¹². Niph. (1) *be weighed* 1 S. 2³; (2) *be right* of conduct Ez. 18²⁵·²⁹ 33¹⁷·²⁰. Pi. (1) *weigh* Jb. 28²⁵; (2) *measure* Is. 40¹²; (3) prob. late, *set right, adjust*, Is. 40¹³ (?), so here. Pu. *be weighed*, 2 K. 12¹². — עַמּוּדֶיהָ] pl. sf. 3 f. *its pillars*, ‡ עַמּוּד n.m. here of earth, so Jb. 9⁶, of heaven Jb. 26¹¹, of Wisdom's house Pr. 9¹, column of smoke Ps. 99⁷, as Ex. 13²¹·²² (J) + ; usually of pillars supporting house, or of column or pillar standing apart. — **5.** הֵרִימוּ קֶרֶן] so v.⁶·¹¹, cf. 18³ 89¹⁸·²⁵ 92¹¹ 112⁹. The repetition in next l. is doublet and gl. — **6.** הִרְבְּרוּ] without neg. interp. as subordinate if the second הרימו be original, otherwise אל was originally with the vb. — בְּצַוָּאר] so 𝔍, 𝔖; but 𝔊, 𝔙, κατὰ τοῦ θεοῦ = בצור, so Cap., Oort, Bä., Hu.³, Kau., Du., Dr., *B*DB. — עָתָק] *froward, arrogant;* elsw. 1 S. 2³ Pss. *31*¹⁹ 94⁴; nowhere else connected with the *neck*, and improb.; whereas עֹשֶׁק is used in 1 S. 2²⁻³, which was in the mind of this poet. — **7.** ‡ מַעֲרָב n.[m.] *West* Pss. 103¹² 107³ Is. 43⁵ 45⁶ 59¹⁹ +. — מִמִּדְבָּר] so Baer; but 𝔊ⁿ·ᴿ·ᵀ, 𝔙, 𝔍, Ginsburg, and most moderns, מִדְבַּר cstr. with הרים *mountainous wilderness of the South*, but 𝔊ᴮ omits הרים. It is best, after Ew., with We., Du., to rd. either והרים or מֵהָרִים. If author in middle Palestine or Galilee, "the mountains" would be the North ; so also if in Babylonia. The predicate is found by Ki., Hu., Dy., al., in הרים, Hiph. inf. רום *lift up*, so AV. RV., JPSV.; but this is improb. The sentence is aposiopese, and we have to supply in thought יבא עזרנו, cf. 121¹·². — **8.** זֶה־זֶה] *the one ... the other.* This l. is based on 1 S. 2⁷ and is a gl. — **9.** כִּיד יהוה] though in 𝔊, 𝔍, must be gl. in 𝔈. כּוֹס was followed by ו of accompaniment וַיַּיִן. — חָמַר] Qal, rel. clause usually, as *B*DB. = *which foams*, only here of wine and dub., of waters 46⁴; prob. חמר to be rd. † חֶמֶר n.m. *wine* or red wine Dt. 32¹⁴. 𝔊 has here οἴνου ἀκράτου, 𝔙 *vini meri*, Aq. αὐστηροῦ, 𝔍 *vino meraco*. — מָלֵא] Qal pf. 3 m.; but כּוֹס f. Rd. Pi. pf. מִלֵּא God subj. — מֶסֶךְ] n. *mixture* a.λ.; but vb. † מסך *mix* of wine 102¹⁰ Is. 5²² 19¹⁴ Pr. 9²·⁵, so prob. here. — וַיַּגֵּר] Hiph. impf. † נגר vb. Aramaism, *v.* 63¹¹. — מִזֶּה] so 𝔍, referring to the *wine;* but 𝔊 ἐκ τούτου εἰς τοῦτο ; so 𝔖, 𝔙, thinking of two different cups. It is in all cases an interp. gl. — שְׁמָרֶיהָ] pl. sf. 3 f., referring to the cup. † שֶׁמֶר] n.m. *dregs of wine, lees*, as Je. 48¹¹ Zp. 1¹² Is. 25⁶·⁶. — יִמְצוּ] Qal impf. 3 m. modal force. † מָצָה vb. Qal *drain out* dregs, elsw. Ju. 6³⁸ Ez. 23³⁴ Is. 51¹⁷. Niph. Lv. 1¹⁵ 5⁹ Ps. 73¹⁰ (?); 𝔊 here יִמְצְאוּ, as 73¹⁰. — כָּל־רִשְׁעֵי אֶרֶץ] phr. elsw. 101⁸ 119¹¹⁹, prob. also Ez. 7²¹; but here a gl. with the vb. ישתו. — **10.** אַגִּיד] Hiph. impf. נגד, so 𝔍; but 𝔊 (אגילה) is well suited to ‖ אזמרה, though not used elsw. in 𝔄; Hare, Houb., Lowth., Street, Oort, Ehr., al. The 1 sg. here instead of 1 pl. of v.² is striking, but the latter half of v. is not suited to context and is gl.; in original Ps. God speaks as v.³. — אֱלֹהֵי יַעֲקֹב] (20²) 46⁸·¹² (𝔎) 76⁷ 81²·⁵ (𝔄). — **11.** וְכָל־קַרְנֵי]. The וכל is gl., making l. too long. — אֲגַדֵּעַ קֶרֶן] vb. Pi. impf. f. ‡ ורד, phr. a.λ.; but *hew off* bars of iron Is. 45², cf. Ps. 107¹⁶. This can only have God as subj.

PSALM LXXVI., 3 STR. 6³.

Ps. 76 was a song, celebrating an ancient victory of Yahweh over enemies in Jerusalem itself, where He made His greatness known in the destruction of the instruments of war (v.²⁻⁴), became glorious in making the enemies sleep their last sleep (v.⁵⁻⁷), awe-inspiring in judgment upon enemies and in salvation of His people (v.⁸⁻¹⁰). A gloss calls upon all to praise Him in festival even in their wrath, and to bring Him presents (v.¹¹⁻¹³).

GOD made Himself known in Judah;
　　In Israel His name became great:
　　And His covert was in Salem,
　　And His lair was (put) in Zion.
　　He brake the flashings of the bow,
　　Shield and sword and battle.
ILLUSTRIOUS art Thou, (O God),
　　Glorious from the (everlasting) mountains.
　　The stout-hearted slept their (last) sleep,
　　And the men of war did not find (spoil).
　　At Thy rebuke, O God of Jacob,
　　Chariot and horse fell into a deep sleep.
AWE–INSPIRING art Thou, (O God);
　　And who can stand before Thine anger?
　　From heaven Thou didst let Thy sentence be heard.
　　The land feared, and it was quiet,
　　When God arose to judgment,
　　To save all the afflicted of the land.

Ps. 76 was originally a שׁיר. It was taken up into 𝕬 and 𝔐, then into 𝕰 and 𝕯𝕽, in which latter it was given the musical direction בנגינת (v. Intr. §§ 24, 29, 31, 32, 33, 34). It is composed of three trimeter hexastichs and a gloss of much later date, v.¹¹⁻¹³. It resembles Pss. 46, 48, of 𝕶 in commemorating a signal victory of Yahweh over the enemies of His people, probably over Sennacherib. It was probably written in Babylonia in the time of the early Restoration, for the encouragement of the people by reference to their ancient history. שָׁלֵם v.³ as name of Jerusalem, elsw. Gn. 14¹⁰, does not imply dependence, but probably a common traditional explanation of the last part of the compound ירושׁלם. In the original Ps. the terms are those of early poetry: הררי עד v.⁵ = Hb. 3⁶; אבירי לב v.⁶, as Is. 46¹²; אלהי יעקב v.⁷, as 75¹⁰ 81².⁵; כל ענוי ארץ v.¹⁰, as Zp. 2³. The glosses contain evidence of later date: אישׁתוללו v.⁶, Aramaism for השׁתוללו; מֵאָז v.⁸, as Ru. 2⁷, explan. gl.; יביאו שׁי v.¹², as 68³⁰ Is. 18⁷.

Str. I. Three syn. couplets. — **2–3.** *God made Himself known*],
reflexive, as JPSV.; on a historic occasion, probably the defeat
of the army of Sennacherib, cf. 48[4], ‖ *His name became great*],
celebrated, made famous by victory, cf. 48[2] 77[14]. — *in Judah* ‖ *in
Israel*], still more closely defined by *Salem*, poetic term for Jerusalem, cf. Gen. 14[18], ‖ *Zion.* — These were *His covert*] ‖ *His lair;*
probably in the literal sense, conceiving of God as the lion of
Judah, cf. Is. 31[4], although this word is used in Ps. 27[5] for the
temple as a refuge and shelter. — **4.** *was put*], so most probably,
as measure requires, attaching the form to the previous context,
and not "there," as adv. emphatic of MT. and Vrss., making this
line too long. The difference in Hebr. is only one of interpretation of the original unpointed text. — *He brake*], as one overcoming an enemy, taking from him his weapons and breaking them
in pieces, cf. 46[10] Ho. 2[20]. — *the flashings of the bow*], the arrows
in their flight compared with lightning flashes, elsewhere conceived
as the arrows of God, Ps. 18[15]. — To these are added *shield and
sword*, and, in a summary statement, *battle*, by meton. for the
weapons of war used in battle.

Str. II. Syn., antith., and synth. couplets. — **5.** *Illustrious art
Thou*], lighted up, enveloped with glorious light ‖ *glorious* syn.
with v.[2]. — *from the everlasting mountains*], so 𝕲, 𝕵; syn. Zion
v.[3], cf. Dt. 33[15] Hb. 3[6] Pss. 87[1] 110[3]; misinterpreted by 𝕳 and
other Vrss. as "mountains of prey," which then is variously explained as "more than the mountains of prey," AV.; "than the
hills of the robbers," PBV.; or, more properly, "coming down
from mountains of prey," RV., JPSV., as the seat of victory or
booty. This interpretation occasioned the gloss, "are spoiled,"
at the beginning of the next v., which makes the line too long
and is in itself an Aramaism of later use than the date of the Ps.
— **6–7.** *The stout-hearted*], the brave warriors, ‖ *men of war*,
the veterans trained for war, ‖ *chariot and horse*, personified for
the most effective division of an ancient army, in which the greatest warriors always rode. God vanquished and slew them on the
field of battle, and so they *slept their last sleep* ‖ *fell into a deep
sleep*], that of death as distinguished from natural sleep. — The
death of the warriors has as its antithesis they *did not find*], that
is, *spoil*, as Ju. 5[30]. This is all that the measure allows; but a

glossator has otherwise explained it by inserting " all " to emphasize the warriors, and " their hands " either as the obj. of the vb.
to emphasize the paralysis of their strength, AV., RV., or as a
secondary subj. of the vb., " with their hands," cf. PBV. — *at Thy
rebuke*], as expressed not merely in words, but in deeds of divine
judgment, — *O God of Jacob*], the endearing name of God as
the God of the father of the nation, cf. 81$^{2. 5}$.

Str. III. Three synth. couplets. — **8.** *Awe-inspiring art Thou*],
inspiring awe, fear, and even terror in the enemies He has conquered, syn. v.$^{2. 5}$. — *Who can stand before Thine anger ?*], implying a negative answer : none.   This has been enlarged by a
glossator in 𝔥, followed by EV^s., by the insertion of a temporal
particle " when once," which involved the separation of the prep.
from its noun and forced the translation " before Thee when once
Thou art angry? " all of which is at the expense of the measure
and lacks the simplicity and force of the original. — **9-10.** *From
heaven*], emphatic in position.   Though Jerusalem, the capital city,
is the place where God manifests His glory, yet His throne is in
heaven, and from thence He terrifies His adversaries when He
appears in judgment. — *Thou didst let Thy sentence be heard*], of
condemnation, as manifested in the sound of thunder, terrifying
the enemy and overcoming them : ‖ *When God arose to judgment*] to decide between His people and their enemies, to condemn and visit the enemy with the death penalty, and *To save all
the afflicted of the land*], the people of God who had been afflicted
by the enemy. — *The land feared*], that is, Judah and Jerusalem ;
the fear of awe before their God. — *and it was quiet*] had peace
from the disturbances of war after the destruction of the enemy.

The Ps. reached its appropriate conclusion here ; but a later
editor, wishing to give it a more general and practical conclusion,
added v.$^{11-13}$. — **11.** *Let wrath against men ‖ remainder of wrath*],
that still remaining against the enemies after the greater part of it
had been expended in gratification at their destruction.   In this
state of mind let them *praise Thee ‖ keep festival*], in the celebration of victory.   This is the most natural interpretation of a difficult passage, in which 𝔥 and Vrss. greatly differ.   EV^s. follow 𝔥,
which here is not so well grounded as 𝔊.   In the first clause they
all agree essentially in the rendering : " Surely the wrath of man

shall praise Thee," that is, the wrath of the enemies will by their overthrow be turned into praise of God through His glory in victory. The last clause is more difficult, and is variously rendered and explained. PBV. and AV. may be dismissed as unjustified translations of 𝔐 and as altogether mistaken even as paraphrase. RV. " the residue of wrath shalt Thou gird upon Thee," is correct in form, and is followed by Dr., Kirk., al. ; but it is difficult to explain. Is it God's wrath with which He girds Himself in His judgment of enemies? as JPSV. "when Thou girdest a remnant with wrath "? Then " wrath " is used in two different senses in parall., which is improbable. Is it the wrath of the enemies, as in the parall.? Then it is an awkward and unexampled conception, that God should gird Himself with that. Kirk. does not satisfy with his explanation : " God girds on Himself as an ornament the last futile efforts of human wrath, turning them to His own honour ; or girds them on as a sword, making the wrath of His enemies to minister to their final discomfiture." — **12**. *Vow and pay* ‖ *bring presents*], the former, Israel, to *Yahweh your God*, a term for God characteristic of D², but heterogeneous to this Ps. and to all of 𝔄 ; the latter *all that are round about Him*, the neighbouring nations : and therefore to *the Terrible One*], the one who, by His vindication of His people, fills them with fear and terror, as more fully explained in **13**. — *Who taketh away*], so 𝔊, 𝔙, 𝔍, which is more suited to *the spirit*, courage, *of princes* than the stronger word of 𝔐, "cutteth off," or "loppeth short," which is used nowhere else with " spirit," and seems inappropriate to this word. — *is awe-inspiring*], awe, fear, takes the place of courage, — *to the kings of the earth*], the monarchs of all the nations round about Israel.

2–3. וַיְהִי] ו consec. impf. implies previous pf. Therefore נוֹדָע Niph. ptc. ידע should be pf. נוֹדַע reflexive, as 48⁴, aorist referring to a particular event ; so 𝔗, Gr., Che. It has been generalised in 𝔐 and Vrss. — †שָׁלֵם] n. pr. loc., elsw. Gn. 14¹⁸; archaic name for צִיּוֹן in parall. here ; abbrev. from ירושׁלם, the last half of the compound noun being interpreted in this way. It is by no means certain, however, that the Ps. depends on Gn. 14¹⁸. It is quite possible that the reverse is the case. 𝔊 ἐν εἰρήνῃ = בְּשָׁלֵם improb. — סוּכּוֹ] fully written סֻכּוֹ sf. 3 sg. [־וֹ] n.[m.] *thicket, covert, lair*, as 10⁹, implying simile of lion. — מְעוֹנָתוֹ] sf. 3 sg. ‡ מְעוֹנָה n.f. elsw. ψ, 104²² of lair of wild beasts. — **4.** שָׁמָּה] so 𝔐 and Vrss., adv. שָׁם with ה־ local, as 122⁵; but it makes l. too long, and a

word is needed for measure in previous l. Rd. therefore שָׂמָה Qal ptc. pass.
f. שׂים and attach to previous v. —רִשְׁפֵי קָשֶׁת] phr. α.λ. †רֶשֶׁף n.m. *flame* of
fire Ct. 8⁶ Jb. 5⁷, fiery bolts of Yahweh bringing pestilence and death Dt. 32²⁴
Hb. 3⁵ Ps. 78⁴⁸; here of the piercing shafts of arrows. —מִלְחָמָה] summary
statement in climax for כָּל־כְּלֵי מִלחמה; 𝔊ᴮ adds ἐκεῖ συνκλάσει τὰ κέρατα, but
it is not in 𝔊ᴮ· ᵃᵇ· ℵ· ᴿ· ᵀ, and is doubtless a late gl. It makes the Str. too
long. — **5.** נָאוֹר] Niph. α.λ. ptc. prob. should be pf. אור = *become lighted up*,
enveloped with glorious light, Σ ἐπιφανής, 𝔖 נהיר. Aq. φωτισμός, 𝔍 *lumen*, rd.
מָאוֹר; 𝔊 φωτίζεις, 𝔙 *illuminans* = מאיר ‖ אדיר *majestic* (S²) as 93⁴. There is
no sufficient reason to rd. with Oort, Bä., Dr., Che., Ehr., נורא as v.⁸ after Θ
φοβερός. אלהים is required for measure, and אדיר begins the second line of
the couplet. —מֵהַרְרֵי טָרֶף] phr. α.λ.; prep. מִן, long form of הַר (2⁶) for euphony,
cf. 50¹⁰ 87¹ 110³. †טֶרֶף i.p. טָרֶף n. (1) *prey* 104²¹ 124⁶; (2) fig. food provided
by God 111⁵. 𝔊 has here αἰωνίων = עַד (9⁶) as Hb. 3⁶, so Oort, Hi., Bä.,
Ecker. It seems prob. that a copyist substituted טרף for an original עד which
he interpreted in the sense of *prey*, as Gn. 49²⁷ Zp. 3⁸ Is. 33²³. — **6.** This
interpretation occasioned the insertion of the vb. אֶשְׁתּוֹלֲלוּ] Hithpolel pf., Aramaic form אשׁ־ for היׁ־ Heb. Ges.⁵⁴· ᵃ ‡שׁלל vb. Qal *spoil* Hb. 2⁸ Is. 10⁶ Je.
50¹⁰+. Hithp. elsw. Is. 59¹⁵. This Aramaic form is good evidence that the
vb. is a late gl. This is confirmed by 𝔊, which inserts a different vb., ἐτα-
ράχθησαν, another interp. gl. These vbs. destroy the measure. —אַבִּירֵי לֵב]
phr. elsw. Is. 46¹², stout, *valiant mind* (22¹³), 𝔊 οἱ ἀσύνετοι = בַּעֲרֵי. —נָמוּ]
Qal pf. 3 pl. ‡נום vb. Qal only, *be drowsy* Is. 5²⁷ 56¹⁰ Ps. 121³· ⁴ Na. 3¹⁸; of
sleep of death only here. —שְׁנָתָ־ם] pl. sf. ‡שֵׁנָה n.f. *sleep* (1) of sleep at night
Pr. 6⁴ Ec. 8¹⁶+; (2) of sleep of death, here as Ps. 90⁵ Je. 51³⁹. —וְלֹא־מָצְאוּ]
This l. is too long. The כָּל with אַנְשֵׁי חַיִל is gl. of amplification, but this phr.
is certainly original. It is α.λ. ψ, but Ju. 3²⁹ 20⁴⁴· ⁴⁶ Je. 48¹⁵+ for warriors.
This must be taken as subj. of vb. יְדֵיהֶם is then the second subj., defining
the action more closely. Then the vb. is as Ps. 21⁹, of the hand finding out,
reaching the enemy. ידיהם is prob. an interp. gl. — **7.** אֱלֹהֵי יַעֲקֹב] as 75¹⁰
81²· ⁵. —נִרְדָּם] Niph. pf. 3 sg. †רדם] only Niph. *fall into a heavy sleep* Ju. 4²¹
Jon. 1⁵· ⁶ Pr. 10⁵, stunned by dread Dn. 8¹⁸ 10⁹; of death only here. —
וְרֶכֶב וָסוּס]. The double ו = *both* . . . *and;* but the sg. vb. is then improb.,
and we should rather rd. וס׳ נרדמו ר׳, 𝔊 οἱ ἐπιβεβηκότες τοὺς ἵππους rd.
נִרְדְּמוּ רֹכְבֵי סוּס, which is in itself more prob., cf. סוּס וְרֹכְבוֹ Ex. 15¹, רֹכֵב הַסּוּס
Am. 2¹⁵. — **8.** נוֹרָא אַתָּה] אלהים must be added for measure as in v.⁵. —
לְפָנֶיךָ מֵאָז אַפֶּךָ]. This phr. with the vb. makes l. too long. 𝔊ᴮ has ἀντι-
στήσεταί σοι ἀπὸ τῆς ὀργῆς σου, but 𝔊ᴮ· ᵃᵇ· ℵ· ᵀ have τότε also after ἀπό. מֵאָז
may be gl. interpreting מֵאַפֶּךָ as with מִן temporal, as 73²⁾. The sf. with
לפני is also interp. — **9.** וְשָׁרָיּמָה] Qal pf. 3 f. i.p. with ו coördinate. ‡שָׁקְטָה vb.
Qal (1) *be quiet, still*, with none to disturb Ju. 3¹¹ 5³¹ Is. 14⁷ Je. 30¹⁰+, so
prob. here; the ארץ, as in v.¹⁰ᵇ, referring to the holy land itself, as enjoying
quiet and peace after the divine judgment upon enemies. The usual interp.
as stillness of the enemy from *fear* is not justified by usage; (2) *rest*, from
service Is. 62¹ Je. 47⁶, so of God as not helping Ps. 83². Hiph. *give rest* from

evil 94¹³. — **10.** קָל־עַנְוֵי־אָרֶץ] phr. Zp. 2³, without כל Is. 11⁴ Am. 8⁴ Jb. 24⁴ (v. 9¹³). — **11.** חֲמַ־ת אָדָם] is difficult. אדם evidently refers to the enemies of God and His people. Is it the wrath of these enemies, which against their will is turned into praise? So most. But it is better to take it as cstr. of obj. *rage against man*. Is it then the rage of God in judgment? How can God's rage praise God? It is more prob. the rage of the people of God against their enemies, that of the meek of the land of the previous l. Raging against their enemies, they praise God who destroys them. Then חֲמֹת pl. MT. most naturally refers to wrathful deeds of God in accordance with the vb., תחגר of 頂. But 𝕲, 𝕵, take it more prob. as sg. חמה. The final ת is then dittog. of ה of vb. חמה in both cases will have the same mng. Then ἑορτάσει σοι of 𝕲 is most prob. הֶחָגֵּךְ, as Bö., Ew.; תָּהֹגּ רְךָ, Oort, Du., We. (*42⁵*). God's people celebrate the victory by a festival when the residue of their rage still remains. — ‡ שְׁאֵרִית] n. (1) *remnant* of a people Je. 31⁷ Ez. 9⁸+, (2) *posterity* 2 S. 14⁷ Je. 11²³, (3) *remainder* of a thing Je. 6⁹ 39³; so here, what remains of the rage after its first outburst. The vbs. are juss. in accordance with the imvs. of v.¹². — **12.** הוה אלהיכם] sustained by 𝕲, 𝕵, is impossible in 𝕰. Either יהוה is a gl. or the l.; and if the l., the entire final Str. v.¹¹⁻¹³. — בְּיִלוּ שֵׁי] phr. elsw. 68³⁾ Is. 18⁷. — מוֹרָא] of God as object of reverence, as Is. 8¹²·¹³, cf. Ps. 9²¹. 𝕲 interprets same as נורא v.¹·ᵇ, and it was possibly the same word in original text. This l. is tetrameter as it stands. 𝕲 attaches last word to next l. — **13.** יִבְצֹר] Qal impf. of general truth. ‡ [בָּצַר] vb. Qal *cut off*, of grapes Lv. 25⁵+, of fortified places frequent, but not ψ; here only in sense of *take away*, but 𝕲 καὶ ἀφαιρουμένῳ, so 𝕵 *auferenti*, prob. rd. יָבֹךְ. This is the better reading. רוח then has the mng. of *courage*, cf. 77⁴. — [נְגִידִים] pl. ‡ נָגִיד n.m. *prince*, not elsw. ψ, but Pr. 28¹⁶ Jb. 29¹⁰ 31³⁷+.

PSALM LXXVII.

Ps. 77 is composite : (A) a resolution of importunate prayer in distress by one remembering and musing upon God (v.²⁻⁴), all night long musing on divine help in former ages (v.⁵⁻⁷), expostulating with God for ceasing to be favourable and casting off His people (v.⁸⁻¹⁰), taking encouragement from the wondrous deeds of the past (v.¹¹⁻¹³), and in the greatness of God especially as shown in the redemption of His people (v.¹⁴⁻¹⁶) ; (B) a description of a theophany in a storm (v.¹⁷⁻²⁰) ; and a gloss referring to the historic leading of Israel by Moses and Aaron (v.²¹).

A. v.²⁻¹⁶, 5 STR. 6³.

WITH my voice unto 'El I will cry,
 In the day of my distress I do seek (Him),
 My hand is extended without growing numb;

My soul doth refuse to be comforted,
 I will remember God and I will moan,
 I will muse and my spirit will faint.
I DO lay hold of the night watches with mine eyes,
 I am disturbed, and I cannot speak,
 I do consider the days of old,
 The years of former ages will I remember;
 My soliloquising in the night is with my mind,
 I will muse, and with my spirit make diligent search.
" FOR ages will He reject,
 And no more again be favourable?
 Is there a cessation of His kindness forever,
 Has His (faithfulness) come to an end for all generations?
 Has 'El forgotten to be gracious,
 Or shut up in anger His compassion? "
THEN I said: " I have begun with this,
 The years of the right hand of 'Elyon.
 I will commemorate the deeds of Yah,
 Yea, I will remember Thy wonders of old:
 And I will meditate on all Thy work;
 And on Thy doings muse."
O GOD, in sanctity is Thy way.
 Who is a great 'El like Yahweh?
 The 'El who doeth wonders,
 Who made known among the peoples Thy strength?
 Thou didst redeem with Thine arm Thy people,
 The sons of Jacob and Joseph.

B.   v.$^{1f-20}$, 4 STR. 3^3.

THE waters saw Thee, O God.
 The waters saw Thee; they were in pangs:
 Yea, the depths trembled.
THE clouds poured forth water,
 The skies gave their voice;
 Yea, Thine arrows went abroad.
THE sound of Thy thunder was in the whirlwind,
 The lightnings illumined the world,
 The earth trembled and shook.
IN the sea Thou didst tread with Thy horses,
 And Thy paths in the great waters;
 And Thy footprints were not known.

Ps. 77 was a Ps. of 𝕬, taken up into 𝕳 and 𝕰, where יהוה was changed to
אלהים v.[14], and then into 𝕯𝕽, when it received the musical direction עָל ירוּן
(*v.* Intr. §§ 29, 31, 32, 33, 34). It was composed of five trimeter hexastichs,
v.[1-16]. To this Ps. was added at a later date a little poem of four trimeter
tristichs, based on Hb. 3, and also citing (v.[19]) from Ps. 97[4]. This must have
been later than 𝕯𝕽, because 𝕯𝕽 contained Hb. 3, and it is improbable that

a little Ps. based upon that ode or prayer was in the same Psalter. The original
Ps. used the divine names: אל v.[2. 10. 14. 15], עליון v.[11]; and probably יה v.[12], יהוה
v.[14]. אדני v.[3. 8] are glosses. It resembles other Pss. of 𝔄: נגרה v.[3], cf. 75[9];
מאנה v.[3], cf. 78[10]; מעלליס v.[12], cf. 78[7]; פלא v.[12. 15], as 78[12]; עלילות v.[13] as 78[11].
This resemblance to Ps. 78, which is confirmed by its attitude toward ancient
history, suggests the same author. Its style is classic: cohortatives v.[2. 4. 7. 12. 13],
ו consec. v.[11], prob. v.[13a]. The use of לבב v.[7] suggests Deuteronomic influence.
בני יעקב ויוסף v.[16] suggests the usage of other Pss. of 𝔄 and the time of Ob.[18],
when Jacob stood for Judah and Joseph for Ephraim. The situation suggests
the period of the Exile, when the people were still in great distress, and comfort was sought as in Is.[2] from the ancient history of the nation. The little
Ps., v.[17-20], as based on Hb. 3 and Ps. 97, must have been very late, not earlier
than the late Greek period. V.[21] is a couplet in the style of 𝔄, a liturgical
addition, cf. 78[52] 80[2].

PSALM LXXVII. *A*.

Str. I. Two syn. triplets. — **2.** *With my voice unto 'El*], emph.
in position; aloud in prayer; repeated in the next line either by
dittog. or by an editor to get the antithesis between *I will cry* and
" He will give ear unto me "; but the latter is premature and
against the context, and the line makes the Str. just this much too
long. — **3.** *In the day of my distress*], not of an individual but of
the nation, as usual in the ψ, the nation speaking in its unity as an
individual, — *I do seek Him*], that is, God; to find Him and get
a response to prayer. — *My hand*], emphatic in position, *is extended*], the gesture of invocation and importunity; the most
probable meaning of an unusual word, as 𝔍, RV. The rendering
of PBV., AV., " my sore ran," is based upon the usage of " hand "
for "stroke" in Jb. 23[2], which, however, is quite different from
this passage; and upon the interpretation of the vb. as meaning
" flow." Many moderns, as Dr., on the basis of La. 3[49], think that
the original was probably " mine eye poured down "; but these
interpretations are not so simple or natural. " In the night " is
a gloss in antithesis with " the day," making the line too long. —
without growing numb], as the hand would naturally do from long-
continued reaching out after the desired object. — *My soul doth
refuse to be comforted*], by giving up the petition as useless, and
seeking comfort in other ways; but persists in the prayer, seeking
comfort only in God. — **4.** *I will remember God*], a resolution
expressed by the cohortative form, repeated, as characteristic of

the Ps., in v.⁷˙¹². ‖ *I will muse*], that is, upon God ; also characteristic of the Ps. v.⁷ᵇ˙¹³ᵇ. — *and I will moan*], cf. 55¹⁸, in the
anguish of the distress and wrestling with God for help. ‖ *my
spirit will faint*], exhausted from the long-continued pleading, cf.
142⁴ 143⁴ La. 2¹².

   Str. II. Three syn. couplets. — **5.** *I do lay hold of the night
watches with mine eyes*], so 𝔜 and probably 𝔊 ; also Aq., ϴ, interpret this vb. as in subsequent lines as 1 sg. But MT., 𝕿, and most
moderns interpret the vb. as 2 pers. with God as subj., "holdest
eyelids." "Thou heldest (open) the guards of mine eyes ;" Dr.,
thinking of eyelids kept open so that there was no sleep from
anxiety. So JPSV., Kirk., paraphrased by EVˢ. — *I am disturbed*], by long-continued wakefulness and anxiety, and indeed
to such an extent that — *I cannot speak*], either having nothing to
say in explanation of this situation, or speechless in inability to speak
through amazement at the long-continued withholding of help. —
6-7. *I do consider*], emphatic present, in pondering, reflecting,
and so ‖ *I will remember* ‖ *I will muse*, also ‖ *My soliloquising in
the night (is) with my mind*], as 𝔊, 𝔜, cf. 63⁷ 143⁵ ; kept within the
mind and unexpressed, ‖ *and with my spirit make diligent search*],
so essentially 𝚺, ϴ, 𝔖, 𝔍, 𝔜, and probably 𝔊 ; searching out the
whole with the utmost attention and thorough investigation. The
object of it all is *the days of old* ‖ *years of former ages*], during
which God had dealt far otherwise with His people than at present. MT., however, in v.⁷ᵃ has another reading : "my song" (to
the accompaniment of stringed instruments) ; so 𝔍, EVˢ., JPSV.,
which is only possible by attaching the word to the vb. "will
remember." But this destroys the measure of the previous and
subsequent lines, and gives former night-songs as object of remembrance in place of the night of speechless, wakeful anxiety, rather
than the much more sublime "years of former ages." MT. also
by its 3 pers. with 1 consec. makes the action of the vb. a result,
and the "spirit" the subject ; and so whether with AV., RV., we
render, "And my spirit made diligent search," or with JPSV.,
"Then my spirit fainteth," it becomes necessary to connect with
the subsequent context. But this makes the previous Str. just
one line too short and the next Str. just so much too long ;
moreover it disturbs the exquisite harmony of the lines and unity
of the Str.

Str. III. Three syn. couplets. — **8-9.** *For ages*], present and future, in antithesis with " former ages," v.[6b], || *again*], in antithesis with " days of old " v.[6a] || *forever ?* || *for all generations ?* — *Will He reject ?*], cf. 43[2] 44[24] 60[3] 74[1] 88[15] || *no more be favourable*], cf. 44[4] 85[2] 106[4] || *cessation of His kindness*], cf. 42[9] 44[27] 85[8. 11] || *His faithfulness*], as usual || with " kindness "; suggested by Nestle, and certainly more appropriate than " His word " of promise, though sustained by 𝔥 and all Vrss., — *come to an end*] cf. 7[10]. — **10.** *Has 'El forgotten to be gracious ?*], cf. Ex. 34[6 sq.] Ps. 9[13. 16] 10[12] 74[19. 23], — *or shut up His compassion ?*], not permitting it to go forth from hand, cf. Dt. 15[7]; or mouth, cf. Is. 52[15] Ps. 107[42]. — *in anger*], cf. Hb. 3[2]. Anger against His people was the real reason of all this long-continued neglect of them.

Str. IV. One synth. and two syn. couplets. — **11.** *Then I said*], after the complaint of present distress over against past favours. — *I have begun*], that is, to speak ; so 𝔊, 𝔙, which best suits the context. But 𝔥, Σ, Θ, 𝔖, 𝔗, and most, " my piercing wound," probably then best explained as " my suffering and I must bear it," Kirk., cf. Je. 10[19]. Aq., 𝔍, have still another reading, " my weakness," followed by EV[s]., " my infirmity," referring back to the previous complaint as not really justified and only uttered because of his weakness, cf. 73[15 sq.]. But at the beginning of a new Str. these explanations are not so natural as the reading of 𝔊, 𝔙. — *With this*], the object of the vb., belonging to the first line as the measure requires, and not to the second, as 𝔊, 𝔙. It is then defined in the second line as : *The years of the right hand of 'Elyon*], when He stretched forth His right hand in the deliverance of His people, resuming the thought of v.[6]. This is the interpretation of EV[s]., as in v.[6] ; but all ancient Vrss. read instead of " years," inf. abs. of a vb. meaning " change," interpreting in various ways : " that the right Hand of the Most High has changed," or " doth change," or " hath suffered change," or, as in 𝔊, 𝔙, " this is the change of the right hand of the Most High." But such a change is enigmatical here. It is improbable that the poet would have spoken of a change without giving some intimation of what he meant by it. The poet really resumes the thought of v.[6] in order to enlarge upon it. — **12-13.** *I will commemorate*], as Kt., 𝔊, Σ, 𝔍, 𝔖, 𝔗, 𝔙, RV., cf. 71[16] Is. 63[7] ; not only muse upon it in recollection, but make mention of, celebrate. The Qri, followed by PBV., AV., JPSV, " remember " is tautological and improbable, because the ‖ is just this, *I will remember* ‖ *meditate on* ‖ *muse on*, cf. v.[4, 7]. The object here is not God Himself as v.[4], nor the former ages as v.[6]; but what God in these former ages had done for His people : *the deeds of Yah* ‖ *Thy wonders of old* ‖ *all Thy work* ‖ *Thy doings*], in the salvation of Israel and in the judgment upon their enemies, as usual in the use of these terms, and as indeed the context demands.

Str. V. Three synth. couplets. — **14**. *In sanctity is Thy way*], in majestic exaltation, in sacred apartness, so PBV., JPSV., and most moderns, after 𝔖, 𝔖, 𝔗 ; to be preferred to " in the sanctuary," AV., RV., though sustained by 𝔊, 𝔜, 𝔍, and early Jewish authorities. This would be appropriate to the thought of many other Pss., but is not appropriate to the context, which speaks of God's working apart from the temple. ‖ *Who is a great 'El?*], cf. Ex. 15[11], which seems to have been in the mind of the poet. — **15**. *The 'El who doeth wonders*], resuming v.[12]. — *made known Thy strength*], in the doing of these wondrous deeds of judgment and salvation, — *among the peoples*]. God's fame went forth among all the surrounding nations, because of the deliverance He had wrought for His people, cf. Ex. 15[14 sq]. — **16**. *Thou didst redeem with Thine arm*], the outstretched arm of the narrative of the Exodus, cf. v.[11b] Ex. 6[6] Ps. 136[12]. — *Thy people* ‖ *The sons of Jacob and Joseph*], probably using the name " Jacob " for the sons of Israel in general, and the particular name " Joseph " specifically for the Northern kingdom, in accordance with a characteristic preference of 𝔄, cf. 78[67] 80[2] 81[6] Ob.[18].

PSALM LXXVII. *B.*

This Ps. describes the advent of Yahweh in a storm, cf. Pss. 18, 29, 114, Hb. 3. **Str. I.** is a stairlike triplet. — **17**. *The waters saw Thee* ‖ *Yea, the depths*], doubtless referring to the " sea " ‖ " great waters " v.[20], but not specifically to the Red Sea at the time of crossing, as is usually supposed, on the basis of a connection between this Ps. and the references to the song Ex. 15 in v.[14 sq], which is opposed by the independence of the Ps. of its present context and its entire dependence on Hb. 3. — *they were* *in pangs ‖ trembled*], in fear and terror, as elsewhere mountains and earth at the advent of God Hb. 3¹⁰ Pss. 97⁴ 114⁴·⁷.

Str. II. is also a stairlike triplet. — **18**. *The clouds ‖ skies . . . poured forth water*], in downpouring rain. The advent was in a storm, as Ps. 18. — *gave their voice*]. This was a thunder storm with lightning, which is, as usual, conceived as the *arrows* of God. The lightning flashes in their rapidity of movement *went abroad* like arrows, flew hither and hither.

Str. III. A synth. triplet. — **19**. *The sound of Thy thunder*], resuming v.¹⁸ᵇ, — *was in the whirlwind*]. The storm was accompanied by a strong wind. — *The lightnings illumined the world*], cf. 97⁴; resuming v.¹⁸ᶜ in order to the result. — *The earth trembled and shook*], which is a variation of v.¹⁷ᶜ.

Str. IV. has stairlike parall. — **20**. *In the sea Thou didst tread with Thy horses*], so most probably, in accordance with Hb. 3¹⁵; the conception being that God in His cherubic chariot rode in the storm upon the sea. A later glossator, to avoid this apparently mythological conception, reduced it to "Thy way is in the sea" ‖ *Thy paths ‖ Thy footprints . . . were not known*], could not be traced after the storm had subsided.

A later editor added **21**, probably to give the previous Ps. a reference to the crossing of the Red Sea by interpreting it as followed by the leading of the people on to the Holy Land. — *Thou didst lead as a flock*], God being the Shepherd of His people, cf. Ex. 15¹³ Pss. 78⁵² 80², — *by the hand of Moses and Aaron*], the leaders of the people at the Exodus, cf. Is. 63¹¹⁻¹² Mi. 6⁴.

LXXVII. *A.*

2. קוֹלִי] 2d subj. vb., cf. *3⁵;* emph. in position. — וַאֶצְעָקָה] ו with Qal cohort. not capable of good explanation. ו not in 𝔊, 𝔍, is doubtless txt. err. Vb. as v.⁴ implies אמרתי and expresses resolution. — וְהַאֲזִין אֵלַי] Hiph. pf. אזן, with אל pers. elsw. only Is. 51⁴ Dt. 1⁴⁵; in ψ usually c. acc. *5².* This statement of fact is premature. The whole l. with the repeated קוֹלִי אל א´ is a gl., making the Str. too long. — **3.** בְּיוֹם צָרָתִי] as 50¹⁵ (𝔄). — אֲדֹנָי] 𝔊 τὸν θεόν more prob., but both glosses. — [יָדִי] is a gl. in antith. with יום, making l. too long. — וְנִגְּרָה] Niph. pf. 3 f. נגר (*63¹¹*), *be extended*, as 𝔍. 𝔊 ἐναντίον αὐτοῦ = וְנֶגְדָּה is not so prob. There is no need to change the text because of a supposed dependence on La. 3⁴⁹ on the basis of a supposed mng., *flow.* — וְלֹא תָפוּג] Pi. pf. 3 f. ‡ [פּוּג] vb. Pi. *refuse*, elsw. ψ only 78¹⁰, but Gn. 37³⁵ (J) Ex. 22¹⁶ (E) Dt. 25⁷ +. — **4.** וְתִתְעַטֵּף רוּחִי] phr. 142⁴ 143⁴, cf. La. 2¹²; vb. c. נפש Ps. 107⁵ Jon. 2⁸, *v.*

Ps. 61³. — **5.** אָחַזְתָּ שְׁמֻרוֹת עֵינָי] phr. a.λ. *eyelids*, so 𝔗 and most moderns ; 𝔊 προκατελάβοντο φυλακὰς οἱ ἐχθροί μου; 𝔊ᴿ·ᵀ ὀφθαλμοὶ for ἐχθροί, as 𝔙 *anti-cipaverunt vigiliis oculi mei*, with text אחזתי אשמרות, regarding עֵינַי as second subj., and therefore in translating making it the real subj. of the vb. This is most prob. So Aq., Θ, think of the watches of the night. 𝔍 *prohibebam suspectum oculorum meorum*. Σ, 𝔖, had other texts, which are difficult to determine. — נִפְעַמְתִּי] Niph. pf. 1 sg. † [פעם] vb. Qal *thrust, impel*, Ju. 13²⁵. Niph. *be disturbed* here, as Gn. 41⁸ Dn. 2³. Hithp. Dn. 2¹. — **7.** אֶזְכְּרָה], cf. v.⁴; goes with previous l. to complete it, as 𝔊, 𝔖, Σ, 𝔙, Hare, Lowth., Street, and not with the following, as 𝔚, 𝔍. — נְגִינָתִי] sf. 1 sg. with נְגִינָה (v. Intr. § 34) *music of stringed instruments*, or theme for it. 𝔍 *psalmorum meorum* נְגִינֹתַי, but improb. in this context. 𝔊 καὶ ἐμελέτησα, 𝔙 *meditatus sum* = הָגִיתִי as v.¹³, Qal pf. 1 sg. הגה (I²) as 63⁷ 143⁵ *soliloquise*, so Lowth., Street, Ehr., or more prob. inf. cstr. sf. הֲגִיתִי. — לְבָבִי] full form seems to be original, for there is no apparent reason for it rather than לֵב. — וַיְחַפֵּשׂ רוּחִי] phr. a.λ.; vb. Pi. impf. ו consec., so Aq., but improb. after previous impf. Σ, Θ, 𝔖, 𝔍, 𝔙, all rd. 1 sg. יֵאַחְפֵּשׂ. 𝔊ᴮ has 3 sg., but 𝔊ᴮᵃ·ᴺ·*·ᴿᵃ 1 sg. Prob. 1 sg. was original. — **8.** הַלְעוֹלָמִים] has two beats. אֲדֹנָי] is a gl. — **9.** גָּמַר אֹמֶר] phr. a.λ., not in 𝔊, but omission txt. err., because it is needed for measure and is in all other Vrss. So 𝔊ᴺ·ᶜ·ᵃ. אֹמֶר only here in this sense, but not improb. Nestle (*Theol. Stud. aus Würtemberg* 1882 S. 242) suggests אֵמֶר, which is probable because of its constant ‖ חסד, as Che., Ehr. — **10.** חַנּוֹת] Qal inf. cstr. חנן (I²), common in 𝔚, but not elsw. in 𝔄. — † קָפַץ] vb. Qal *shut up*, hand Dt. 15⁷, mouth Is. 52¹⁵ Jb. 5¹⁶ Ps. 107⁴²; here fig. Niph. Jb. 24²¹, Pi. Ct. 2⁸. — **11.** חַלּוֹתִי] Pi. inf. cstr. sf. 1 sg. חלל = *my piercing wound*, so Σ, Θ, Quinta, 𝔖, 𝔗, Ew., Hi., De., Bä., SS., Dr., Kö.ᴵ·³⁴¹; but Aq., 𝔍, *imbecillitas mea* חֲלִיתִי Qal inf. cstr. הרה *be sick*, cf. 35¹³, so Hu., Pe., Bi., but all improb. 𝔊 ἠρξάμην, 𝔙 *coepi* = הַחִלֹּתִי. Hiph. pf. 1 sg. חלל is most prob. — שְׁנוֹת] 𝔊 ἡ ἀλλοίωσις, 𝔍 *commutatio*, and all ancient Vrss. interpret as Qal inf. cstr. שׁנה *change*, cf. 34¹ 89³⁵. It is more prob. that it is the same as שְׁנוֹת v.⁶. — עֶלְיוֹן] divine name (v. Intr. § 32) as 50¹⁴ 73¹¹ 78¹⁷ 83¹⁹; characteristic of 𝔄. — **12.** אַזְכִּיר Kt. Hiph. impf. 1 sg., as 𝔊, Σ, 𝔍, 𝔖, 𝔗, should prob. be cohort. אַזְכִּירָה *commemorate*. — מַעַלְלֵי יָהּ] elsw. מַעַלְלֵי אֵל 78⁷, cf. 28⁴ for מַעַל of wanton deeds of men. — פִלְאֶךָ] v. v.¹⁵ 9²; sf. 2 m., now begins rather abruptly, and continues throughout the Ps. — **13.** וּבַעֲלִילוֹתֶיךָ] has two tones; עֲלִילָה also 78¹¹. — **14.** מִי אֵל גָּדוֹל כֵּאלֹהִים]. 𝔊 has ὁ θεὸς ἡμῶν; אלהים as distinguished from אל must be used as a proper name, prob. as Bä. for an original יהוה. אֵל גָּדוֹל phr. Dt. 7²¹ 10¹⁷ Je. 32¹⁸ Ps. 95³+. — **15.** הָאֵל]. The article to distinguish the God of Israel from the more general use of אֵל in previous v., cf. 18³¹·³³·⁴⁸ 68²⁰·²¹. — **16.** בְּזְרוֹעַ] without sf. is striking, so 𝔍; but 𝔊 appends it, prob. interpretative. The article must either be written or understood, and as such really stands for the possessive. — בְּנֵי יַעֲקֹב וְיוֹסֵף], cf. Ob.¹⁸, where בית יעקב stands for the people of Judah and בית יוסף for Ephraim; cf. Am. 5⁶ and Ze. 10⁶, where בית יוסף ‖ בית יהודה; cf. also Ps. 78⁶⁷ 80² 81⁶.

N

LXXVII. *B.*

17. רָאוּךָ] bis, Qal pf. sf. 2 sg. ראה based on Hb. 3¹⁰. — מַיִם] also bis instead of הָרִים of the original. — יָחִילוּ] as in the original. Qal impf. 3 pl. חור (29⁸) more suited to הרים than מים, but no sufficient reason for substitution, as Gr. מים is sustained by תְּהֹמוֹת (33⁷). The third l. is not in Hb. 3¹⁰. — **18.** זֹרְמוּ] Po. pf. 3 pl. זרם † [זֹרַם] vb. denom. זֶרֶם Qal Ps. 90⁵ *flood away* (?), Po. only here, *pour forth*, *BDB*. The original had זֶרֶם מַיִם עָבוֹת. עָבִית *cloud masses* as *18¹²* might be error for עָבוּ vb. עָבוּ is sustained by Aq., 𝔖, 𝕴, 𝕿; 𝕲 πλῆθος ἤχους ὕδατος, 𝕲ᴺ·ᶜ·ᵃ·ᴿ ὑδάτων. 𝕵 *multitudo sonitus aquarum* = המון מים רב is so different that it implies a variation of text too great to be explained as txt. err. — קוֹל נָתְנוּ] as in Hb. 3¹⁰, only pl. with שחקים for sg. with תהום. The phr. is equivalent to *thunder* 18¹⁴ 29³ˢᑫ·. — הֲצָצֶיךָ יִתְהַלָּכוּ] for original חִצֶּיךָ יְהַלֵּכוּ Hb. 3¹¹; † הָצָץ n.m. *arrow* a.λ. fuller form for חֵץ; elsw. חֵץ is *gravel stone* Pr. 20¹⁷ La. 3¹⁶. The vb. Hithp. for Pi. — **19.** קוֹל רַעַמֶךָ] phr. 104⁷, † רעם n.[m.] *thunder*, elsw. 81⁸ Is. 29⁶ Jb. 26¹⁴ 39²⁵. — ‡ גַּלְגַּל] n.m. *whirlwind* here ; but 83¹⁴ Is. 17¹³ *whirl* of dust or chaff. — רָאִירוּ בְרָקִים הֵבֵל] = 97⁴. — **20.** בַּיָּם דַּרְכֶּךָ] lacks a word to complete measure. The original Hb. 3¹⁵ has דָּרַכְתָּ בַיָּם סוּסֶיךָ. The Vrss. all agree with 𝔚. A word must be supplied ; rd. as Hb. 3¹⁵. — שְׁבִילֶיךָ] Kt. pl. sf. 2 m. † [שְׁבִיל] n.[m.] only pl. *path*, as Je. 18¹⁵ (Qr.). Kt. is sustained by 𝕲, 𝔖, 𝕴. The sg. שְׁבִילְךָ Qr. is sustained only by 𝕿, and was an assimilation to דַרְכֶּךָ. — **21.** כַּצֹּאן] as 78⁵² 80² (𝔄).

PSALM LXXVIII., 4 PTS. OF 5 STR. 4³.

Ps. 78 is a didactic Psalm, using the ancient history of Israel, from the crossing of the Red Sea to the erection of the temple, as a lesson to the people. I. proposes to give in the form of a poetic enigma (v.¹⁻²) the history which has been transmitted from the fathers, and which is to be handed down to the children (v.³· ⁴ᵃ· ⁷ᵇ), that they may not be, as their fathers, rebellious and unreliable (v.⁸⁻⁹). The crossing of the sea is mentioned (v.¹²⁻¹³), the theophanic pillar (v.¹⁴), and the water from the rock (v.¹⁶). II. The people rebelled and tempted their God in asking food (v.¹⁷⁻²⁰), which was given them (v.²³⁻²⁴· ²⁶⁻²⁷), but accompanied by an outbreak of the divine anger (v.³⁰ᵇ⁻³¹). III. The wasting away of the people led them to remember their God (v.³²⁻³⁵), who was compassionate and forgiving (v.³⁸). He considered the weakness of their human nature (v.³⁹), and led them as a flock in the wilderness (v.⁵²). He brought them to the holy land and gave it to them as an inheritance (v.⁵⁴⁻⁵⁵). IV. Yet they rebelled against God and tempted

Him with their infidelity (v.$^{56-57}$). In anger He rejected Shilo (v.^{60}), gave up His ark and His people into captivity (v.^{61}) ; all classes of the people were slain (v.$^{63-64}$). He then selected Judah and Mount Zion (v.$^{67-68}$), and David as the shepherd of His people (v.$^{70-71a.\,b}$). An editor inserted an extract from an ancient poem describing the plagues of Egypt (v.$^{40-48.\,51.\,53}$). Legalistic (v.$^{4b-7a.\,10-11.\,56b}$) and expansive glosses (v.$^{15.\,21-22.\,25.\,28-30a.\,36-37.\,49-50.\,58-59.\,62.\,65-66.\,69.\,71c-72}$) were also added.

I.

O GIVE ear, my people, to my teaching.
　Incline your ears to the words of my mouth.
　I will open my mouth in a poem.
　I will pour forth of ancient times in my enigma.
WHAT we have heard and know,
　What our fathers have told to us,
　We will not hide from their children ;
　That they may not forget the works of God.
THAT they may not be as their fathers,
　A stubborn and rebellious generation.
　Armed with a deceitful bow,
　They turned back in the day of battle.
IN sight of their fathers He did wonders,
　In the land of Egypt, the country of Zoan.
　He clave the sea and made them pass through ;
　And He made the waters stand up as a heap.
AND He led them in the cloud by day,
　And all night long with the light of fire :
　And brought forth streams out of the crag,
　And let waters run down like rivers.

II.

THEN they sinned against Him,
　Rebelled against 'Elyon in the thirsty land ;
　And tempted God in their minds
　By asking food according to their appetite.
THEY said : " Is God able
　To prepare a table in the wilderness?
　Is He also able to give bread,
　Or provide flesh for His people ? "
THEN He commanded the skies above,
　And opened the doors of heaven ;
　And rained down manna upon them.
　And grain of heaven for them.
THEN He led on the east wind,
　And guided by His strength the south wind ;
　And rained down flesh as dust,
　And fowl as the sand of the sea.

THEIR food was yet in their mouths.
  And the anger of God went up;
  And He slew the fattest of them,
  And bowed down the choicest of Israel.

III.

FOR all this they sinned again,
  And believed not in His wonders;
  And He consumed their days as a breath,
  And their years He made to haste away in suddenness.
IF He slew them, they sought Him,
  And again diligently sought 'El;
  And remembered God their Rock,
  And 'El 'Elyon their Redeemer.
BUT He is compassionate (and gracious).
  He covers over and destroys not,
  And many times turns away His anger,
  And stirs not up any of His wrath.
THEN He remembered that they were flesh,
  A breath passing away not to return.
  And He led on His people like sheep,
  And guided them like a flock in the wilderness.
AND He brought them to His sacred border,
  The mountain that His right hand had gotten;
  And drave out nations before them,
  And allotted them the inheritance by measure.

IV.

THEN (again) they tempted God,
  (Again and again) rebelled against 'Elyon;
  And drew back, and dealt treacherously like their fathers,
  And turned aside like a deceitful bow.
THEN He rejected the tabernacle of Shilo,
  The tent He made to dwell among mankind;
  And delivered up His strength to captivity,
  And His ornament into the hand of the adversary.
FIRE devoured their young men,
  And their maidens were not praised in marriage song.
  Their priests fell by the sword,
  And their widows did not sing dirges.
AND He refused the tent of Joseph,
  And chose not the tribe of Ephraim;
  But chose the tribe of Judah,
  Mount Zion which He doth love.
AND He chose David His servant,
  And took him from the sheepfolds;
  From following the ewes that give suck He brought him,
  To be shepherd over Jacob His people.

Ps. 78 was a Ps. of 𝕬 of the class מַשְׂכִּיר. From 𝕬 it was taken up into 𝕰 (v. Intr. §§ 26, 29, 32). It has many glosses. The original Ps. was composed of four parts, each with five trimeter tetrastichs. I. v.[1-2], v.[3. 4a. 7b], v.[8ab. 9bc], v.[12-13], v.[14. 16]; II. v.[17. 18], v.[19bc. 20cd], v.[23-24], v.[26-27], v.[30b-31]; III. v.[32-33], v.[34-35], v.[38], v.[39. 52], v.[54. 55ab]; IV. v.[56a. 57], v.[60-61], v.[63-64], v.[67. 68], v.[70. 71b]. This Ps. is a מָשָׁל and חִידוֹת v.[2], based on the history of God's dealings with Israel from the Exodus to the establishment of the Davidic dynasty. The poem was written under the influence of J, E, D, but not of P, and therefore in the early Persian period. It encloses part of a still older pentameter poem, v.[40-48. 51. 53], giving an account of the plagues of Egypt and the crossing of the Red Sea. This fragment depends on the story of J, E, and knows nothing of any other document of the Hex. It seems therefore to be preëxilic and to precede the reign of Josiah. The glosses are later than 𝕰, and come from the Greek or Maccabean period. The language of the original Ps. shows many features of Pss. of 𝕬, as well as dependence upon other Lit.:
מַעְלְלֵי אל v.[7] = 77[12]; דור סורר ומרה v.[8], cf. Dt. 21[18. 20] Je. 5[23]; אל v.[7. 18. 19. 34. 85] (also in gl. v.[8. 41]); רוֹמֵי קֶשֶׁת v.[9] = Je. 4[29] (rd. prob. קֶשֶׁת רְמִיָּה, as v.[57] Ho. 7[16]); ביום קרב v.[9] = Zc. 14[3]; עָשָׂה פֶלֶא v.[12] = 77[15] 88[11]; שָׁרָה צֹעַן v.[12] = v.[43] (gl.); בִקַע יָם v.[13], cf. Ex. 14[16. 21] (E); יצב כְּמוֹ נֵד v.[13] = Ex. 15[8]; הֶמְרָה v.[17. 40] (gl.) 56, as D, Is. 3[8] Ez. 5[6]; עֶלְיוֹן v.[17. 35. 56], frequent in 𝕬; נסה אל v.[18. 41. 56], as Ex. 17[2. 7] Nu. 14[22] (J); לֵבָב v.[18], characteristic of 𝕬; שְׁאֵר v.[20. 27], as Ex. 21[10]; אַף עָלָה ב v.[31], so v.[21] (gl.), cf. 2 S. 11[20]; דִלְתֵי שָׁמַיִם v.[23], cf. Gn. 7[11] (J); קְנֵה יָמִין v.[54] a.λ.; גְּבוּל קֹדֶשׁ v.[54] a.λ.; דְּגַן שָׁמַיִם v.[24] a.λ.; רוּחַ הוֹלֵךְ וְלֹא יָשׁוּב v.[39] a.λ.; שִׁלּוֹ v.[60], cf. Je. 7[14] 26[9] 41[5]; עֹז for ark v.[61], cf. 132[8]; תִּפְאֶרֶת for ark v.[61] as for temple 96[6] Is. 60[7] 63[15] 64[10]; הוֹלִילוֹ for bridal song v.[63], cf. Ez. 26[17]. The older pentameter poem has the following: הָפַךְ לְדָם v.[44], cf. Ex. 7[17. 20]; יְאוֹרִים v.[44], as Ex. 7[17. 20]; עָרֹב v.[45], as Ex. 8[17]; צְפַרְדֵּעַ v.[45], as Ex.8[2]; בֶּעָרָד v.[48], as Ex. 22[4] Nu. 20[4. 8. 11]; רֵאשִׁית אוֹנִים v.[51], as Gn. 49[8] Dt. 21[17] Ps. 105[36]; כָּסָה הַיָּם v.[53], as Ex. 15[10] Jos. 24[7]. The glosses in some instances have much later language: הֵקִים בְּרִית v.[5], phr. of P; עֵדוּת v.[5], term of P; כֶּסֶל v.[7], 49[14] elsw. WL.; הֵכִין לֵב v.[8], 10[17] Jb. 11[13] 2 Ch. 12[4]; נָכוֹן לֵב v.[37], as 57[8. 8] 112[7]; נָאַמְנָה רוּחַ v.[8], cf. Ne. 9[8] Pr. 11[13]; שָׁמַר בְּרִית v.[10], 1 K. 11[11] Ne. 1[5] 9[32] +; וַיְזְנוּ מִיָּם v.[20], based on Is. 48[21]; הֶעְתִּיר v.[21. 59. 62], elsw. 89[39] Dt. 3[26] Pr. (3 t.); הֶאֱמִין בֵּ(אלהים) v.[22], cf. v.[32], Gn. 15[6] (E) Ex. 14[31] Nu. 14[11] (J); לֶחֶם אַבִּירִים v.[25], phr. a.λ. angels' food, late idea; קְדוֹשׁ יִשְׂרָאֵל v.[41], as Is.[1. 2]; הִתְוָה v.[41], Aramaism a.λ.; מַלְאֲכֵי רָעִים v.[49] a.λ. evil angels, a late idea; יַכְעִיסוּהוּ, יַקְנִיאוּהוּ v.[58], as Dt. 32[16]; מְתֹרֹנָן מִיַּיִן v.[65] a.λ.

Pt. I., Str. I. Two syn. couplets. — **1-2.** *O give ear ‖ incline your ears*], attentively in order to hear — *my teaching ‖ words of my mouth*], instruction to be given by the psalmist, as RV.[m], JPSV., and not " my Law," EV[s]., as if there were a reference to the divine Law. This instruction is to be given in the balanced measure of a *poem* in the emblematic style ‖ *enigma*], setting forth

problems and mysteries difficult to solve and understand, cf. 49⁵.
— *I will open my mouth ‖ I will pour forth*], in the melodies of
sacred song.

Str. II. Two synth. couplets. — **3.** *What we have heard and
know ‖ What our fathers have told us*]. The story has come
down by oral tradition from father to son through many generations. This implies not that there was no written narrative, for
the author gives ample evidence of dependence upon the earlier
prophetic narratives, but that he recognised that the story, though
recorded, was essentially tradition, and not based on original
records. — **4 a.** *We will not hide from their children*]. We will
transmit it in our turn to our successors. — **7b.** *That they may
not forget the works of God*], that the story of the divine works
of redemption and judgment may never be forgotten. A glossator, wishing to emphasize the importance of this oral instruction, added the clause from a legal point of view : *His commands
might keep;* but also inserted a long expansive gloss : **4b–7a,** *telling to a coming generation the praises of Yahweh and His might
and the wondrous deeds that He did*]. This is an expansion of
" the works of God," explaining them as wonders and worthy of
songs of praise. The remainder of the gloss is legalistic : *And He
established a testimony in Jacob ; a Law He appointed in Israel*],
doubtless referring to the legislation of the Pentateuch, using a
term characteristic of P. — *which He commanded our fathers to
make known to their sons ; in order that a coming generation might
know, sons to be born ; that they might rise up and tell them to their
sons*]. A long prosaic sentence enlarging upon the commands, cf.
Ex. 10² 12²⁶⁻²⁷ 13⁸·¹⁴ Dt. 4⁹ 6²⁰⁻²⁵. — *that they might put in God their
hope*], a very late phr. of WL., cf. Ps. 49¹⁴ Pr. 3²⁶ ; an expansive
gloss to v.⁷ᵇ.

Str. III. Two synth. couplets. — **8.** *That they may not be as
their fathers*]. The instruction here takes the form of warning.
— *A stubborn and rebellious generation*], based on Dt. 21¹⁸·²⁰. A
glossator enlarged by adding : *a generation that did not fix its
mind, whose spirit was not faithful with 'El.* — **9.** *Armed with a
deceitful bow*], the most probable original of a difficult passage, cf.
v.⁵⁷ : a bow which in time of use would not bend properly, and so
proved unreliable ; while the bowman, being practically weapon-

less, *turned back in the day of battle*]. A copyist, by error of trans-position, gave the tautological " armed, shooting with the bow " ; and then, as the point of the comparison was lost, the conjecture arose that there must be a reference to some event in which there had been rebellion against God in a cowardly retreat from battle. A glossator could not think this of Israel as a whole ; and so he conjectures that *Ephraim* was at fault, and makes this insertion in the text. The whole context shows that Israel as a whole is in the mind of the poet, and that a specific reference to Ephraim was out of place in the original. A glossator enlarges upon the original : **10**. *They kept not* ‖ *refused to walk in; the covenant of God* ‖ *His Law*]. Their offence from a legalistic point of view was especially violation of Law. — **11**. *And forgat the doings of God; the wondrous deeds*, of judgment and salvation, *that He shewed them ;* as described in the next Str.

Str. IV. A synth. and a syn. couplet. — **12**. *In sight of their fathers*], so that they saw distinctly with their own eyes, — *He did wonders*], the miracles of the plagues, which, however, are not mentioned here in detail ; but cf. v.⁴³⁻⁵¹. — *In the land of Egypt*, especially in *the country of Zoan*] the district of which Zoan, ancient name for *Tanis*, was the capital, situated on the east bank of the Tanitic arm of the Nile. — **13**. *He clave the sea*], phr. of Ex. 14¹⁶ ‖ *made the waters stand up as a heap*], as Ex. 15⁸ (song), fig. of the waters on either side of the shallow bottom which formed the pathway through the sea, — *and made them pass through*], gave them a safe transit through the sea to the other side.

Str. V. Syn. couplets. — **14**. *And led them*], personal leader-ship, in accordance with the ancient narratives, by the theophanic angel, — *in the cloud by day* ‖ *all night long with the light of fire*], as Ex. 13²¹·²² (JE) : the theophanic pillar, changing its appearance as needed for manifestation. — **16**. *And brought forth* ‖ *let run down ; streams out of the crag* ‖ *waters like rivers*], a poetic con-ception of the miracle Ex. 17¹⁻⁷. — A glossator prefixed a doublet in a more prosaic general statement : **15**. *And He clave rocks in the wilderness, and gave them depths to drink of in abundance.*

Pt. II., Str. I. Syn. and synth. couplets. — **17**. *Then they sinned* ‖ *rebelled*]. The instruction was to be for the sake of warning, v.⁸ᵇ ; therefore we are not surprised that the second Pt.

begins with a Str. setting forth the sins of the fathers, — *against Him* ‖ *against 'Elyon*], the ancient poetic name of God, — *again*], in addition to the earlier sin v.[9], — *in the thirsty land*], the wilderness of the wanderings. This sin is more specifically defined **18** as *tempted God in their minds*], put Him to a test, which implied lack of confidence and fidelity ; and still more specifically, — *by asking food according to their appetite*], discontented with what God had given them. A glossator emphasizes the offence at the expense of the measure by adding : **19 a.** *and spake against God.* All this is in accordance with the narrative of JE. in Ex. 16.

Str. **II.** Synth. and syn. couplets. — **19 b–20.** *They said : Is God able ?* repeated for emphasis, — *Is He also able ?*], questioning the power of their God to supply their needs. — *in the wilderness*], the most unlikely place, — *to prepare a table*], laid and furnished for His servants, ‖ *to give bread* ‖ *provide flesh for His people*], bread and flesh, the ordinary and the festal provision of food. A glossator emphasizes this sin by repeating the story of the supply of water to quench their thirst, as making their doubt still more unjustifiable ; but at the expense of the simplicity and harmony of the Str. — *Lo, He smote the rock, and waters gushed out and streams overflowed*], cf. 105[41] Is. 48[21]. Before describing the miracle itself, the glossator asserts with emphasis the anger of God against their unbelief. — **21.** *Therefore Yahweh heard and was wroth ; and fire was kindled against Jacob, and also anger went up against Israel*], cf. Nu. 11[1-3]. The reason is reasserted **22.** *For they did not believe in God, and did not trust in His salvation*]. They had no confidence in the fulfilment of the divine promises made to them, and they had lost their trust in His willingness and ability to save them from peril of starvation in the wilderness.

Str. **III.** Syn. couplets. — **23.** *Then He commanded the skies above*], His authoritative command to them as His servants. — *And opened the doors of Heaven*]. Heaven is here conceived as a granary in which is stored up abundance of grain. The divine proprietor opens the doors in order to distribute the grain. — **24.** *And rained down manna upon them, and grain of heaven for them*]. The manna was conceived as heavenly grain descending from heaven like rain or hail, cf. Ex. 16, Nu. 11[6-9] Dt. 8[3. 16]. A glossator enlarges upon this also. — **25.** *Bread of the mighty*], cf.

103^{20}; probably of the angels, conceived as having their food in this divine ambrosia. — *man did eat*], admitted to the table of angels. — *provision He sent them to satiety*], more than they needed, more than they could eat; which they ate till they were overfull and unable to eat any more, and indeed with a distaste for it. **Str. IV.** Syn. couplets. — **26.** *Then He led on* ‖ *guided by His strength*], the former as dealing with willing servants, the latter as compelling reluctant ones, — *the east wind* ‖ *the south wind*]. The poet conceives that the two winds coöperated, thinking, doubtless, of a southeast wind. — **27.** *And rained down flesh* ‖ *fowl*], the quails of Ex. 16, Nu. 11, in such great quantities that they are compared with *dust* ‖ *the sand of the sea*]. According to Tristram : " The period when they were brought to the camp of Israel was in the spring, when on their northward migration from Africa. According to their well-known instinct, they would follow up the coast of the Red Sea until they came to its bifurcation at the Sinaitic Peninsula, and then would cross at the narrow part " (*Nat. Hist. Bible*, p. 231). A glossator enlarges upon the narrative by **28–30 a.** *And let it fall in the midst of the camp, round about their dwellings*], cf. Ex. 16^{13} Nu. 11^{31}, — *and they ate and were satisfied, and their desire He brought them*]. God gave them their desire to the full. — *and their desire became loathing*]. They ate so much of the flesh and became so satiated with it, that they could not eat any more ; they loathed the sight of it. This is the most probable explanation of a difficult line, which is rendered in EV⁸. after 𝔐, " they were not estranged from their lust," as if ‖ with the line which begins the next Str. ; that is, before they had been surfeited, which is altogether improbable.

Str. V. Synth. and syn. couplets. — **30 b.** *Their food was yet in their mouths*], even while they were still eating. — **31.** *And the anger of God went up*], ascended as smoke from the nostrils. — *And He slew* ‖ *bowed down* in death, *the fattest of them* ‖ *the choicest of Israel*], cf. Nu. 11^{33}. The entire Pt. is given to this rebellion, the two miracles, and the consequences, showing the purpose of the author in warning the men of his generation lest they should repeat the offence.

Pt. III., Str. I. Synth. and syn. couplets. — **32.** *For all this*], notwithstanding the previous historic experience, — *they sinned* *again*], this Pt. beginning as the previous one v.[17]. — *And believed not in His wonders*], in His power and ability to do wonders, cf. v.[19. 20]. — **33**. *And He consumed their days*], used up, exhausted the days of their life, — *as a breath*], as if they were a mere breath, breathed out and gone forever. — ‖ *And their years*, of life, *He made to haste away in suddenness*], the most probable interpretation of a difficult text, correctly given by JPSV. This meaning is alone suited to the context. "In trouble" of PBV., AV., is without justification. The meaning: "in terror," RV.; "sudden terror," Kirk.; "dismay," Dr., is sustained by Lv. 26[16] Is. 65[23], but is not suited to the context.

Str. II. Syn. couplets. — **34**. *If He slew them*], in punishment for their sin, — *they sought Him* ‖ *again diligently sought 'El*], in petition for deliverance. — **35**. *And remembered God their Rock* ‖ *'El 'Elyon their Redeemer*]. It is altogether probable that God was the original object of the remembrance, and that His titles, "their Rock," cf. Dt. 32[4] Ps. 18[3], and "their Redeemer," as well as "'Elyon," are in apposition with "God" ‖ "'El." It is then a mistake to suppose that they are predicates, or that 'El 'Elyon is the compound divine name peculiar to Gn. 14. The insertion of the particle כ in the text was also a mistaken supposition that the clause is an objective one. A glossator now enlarges upon the infidelity of the people: **36–37**. *And they beguiled Him with their mouth*, and *with their tongue lied to Him*], false professions of fidelity and obedience, — *and their mind was not steadfast with Him*], cf. 57[8], — *and they were not faithful in His covenant*], cf. v.[8].

Str. III. Synth. and syn. couplets. — **38**. *But He is compassionate*], citation of Ex. 34[6] (J), cf. Ps. 86[15] 103[8]; add therefore to complete the line: *and gracious*. This is a general statement as to the character of God, in the form of the present, and not of the habitual past. — *He covers over*], as 65[4] 79[9]: the later conception of cancelling, obliteration of sin, for the earlier one of forgiveness of Ex. 34[7]. A glossator adds the object *iniquity*, which was no more needed than the object of the verb *and destroys not*, and so impairs the measure. — *And many times turns away His anger*], so that it will not strike the people, cf. 85[4] 106[23] ‖ *and stirs not up any of His wrath*], maintains a calm, serene attitude, and does not permit any stimulation or excitement of His wrath. These two phrases set forth two sides of the divine self-restraint in His attitude toward His sinning people.

Str. III. Synth. and syn. couplets. — **39.** *Then He remembered that they were flesh*], a return to the historical narration. God remembers on His part, as His people on their part. They recognise Him as their Rock and their Redeemer. He recognises them in antithesis as flesh, frail and perishable; and as a mere *breath passing away not to return*]. Their breath, passing out of the flesh in death, returns no more to the flesh with its impulse of life. The counterpart of v.³⁹ is **52**, though separated by a long insertion. Inasmuch as God remembered that His people were flesh, to pass away in death, He treated them as such, and became to them as the shepherd of a feeble, helpless flock. — *He led on His people ‖ and guided them; like sheep ‖ like a flock,* in their journeys *in the wilderness.*

A late editor, for a reason difficult to determine, inserted between v.³⁹ and v.⁵² a pentameter extract from an older poem, describing the plagues of Egypt in accordance with the narrative of J, which alone this author seems to have known.

How often they rebelled against Him in the wilderness, grieved Him in the desert!
Again and again they tempted 'El, the Holy One of Israel.
They did not remember His hand, the day He redeemed them from the adversary;
When He put His miracles in Egypt, His marvels in the country of Zoan.
When He turned their canals into blood, that they could not drink of their streams;
And sent forth swarms of flies and devoured them; and frogs and destroyed them;
And gave their increase to the caterpillar, and their labour to the locust;
And slew their vines with hail, and their sycamores with frost;
And gave over to the pestilence their cattle, and their herds to the flame of fever;
And He smote all their first-born, the first of their strength.
And He led them in confidence, but their enemies the sea covered.

40-43. Syn. and synth. couplets. — **40-41.** *How often*], exclamation of wonder; in the ‖ positive statement: *again and again*], as JPSV.; a verb with auxiliary force, incorrectly rendered in EVˢ. as " they turned again," away from God. — *they rebelled ‖ grieved*], cf. Is. 63¹⁰ ‖ *tempted*], as v.¹⁸·⁵⁶ 95⁹ 106¹⁴ Ex. 17²·⁷ Nu. 14²² (J) Dt. 6¹⁶, to which a glossator adds in 𝕳, followed by EVˢ., " provoked," in 𝕲, 𝖄, " spurned." — *in the wilderness ‖ in the desert*], the region of the wanderings of Israel, as v.¹⁷·¹⁹. — *the Holy One* *of Israel*], divine name of Is.[1. 2], cf. 71[22] 89[19]. — **42**. *They did not remember*], cf. v.[35], — *His hand*], the lifting it for their redemption, cf. Ex. 3[20], — *the day He redeemed them from the adversary*], probably the day of the crossing of the sea. — **43**. *When He put His miracles ‖ His marvels*], those enumerated in the subsequent context, — *in Egypt ‖ in the country of Zoan*], cf. v.[12].

44–48. A series of six plagues, those of J. — **44**. *When He turned their canals into blood, that they could not drink of their streams*], as Ex. 7[17. 20]. — **45**. *And sent forth swarms of flies and devoured them*], as Ex. 8[17 sq.]; combined in the same line with : *and frogs and destroyed them*], as Ex. 7[27-29] 8[1-9]. — **46**. *And gave their increase to the caterpillar, and their labour to the locust*], plague of Ex. 10[4 sq.]. — **47**. *And slew their vines with hail and their sycamores with frost*], plague of Ex. 9[18 sq.]. — **48**. *And gave over to pestilence their cattle, and their herds to the flame of fever*], the cattle plague of Ex. 9[3 sq.]. 𝔥, sustained by most Vrss., therefore by early txt. err. of a single letter, makes this line to continue the plague of v.[47] in the use of "hail" for "pestilence," and so interprets the following noun as "hot thunderbolts," instead of "the flame of fever"; and omits the cattle plague; all of which is improbable. A late glossator generalises in **49–50**. *He sends forth*], graphic imperfect of the past, ‖ *levels a path for*], to give it direct and swift course, — *the heat of His anger ‖ His anger*]. This is intensified by the heaping up of other terms : *overflowing wrath*, and *indignation and distress*. The divine anger as directed against the enemies of His people is in striking antithesis to the restraint of His anger toward His people, though by a different author, v.[38]. — *a mission of angels of evils*], not evil angels in the ethical sense, as distinguished from good ; but in the physical sense, as executing or bringing evil upon men, angels of punishment. — *and did not spare their life from death*, with the antithesis : *but their life gave over to the pestilence*]. This glossator is thinking of the pestilence of P, which is more extended than the cattle plague of J. — **51**. *and smote*], continuation of the aorists of v.[44-48], — *all of their first-born, the first of their strength*], the final plague of Ex. 11[4 sq.], cf. Ps. 105[36]. To this a glossator adds, at the expense of the measure : *in the tents of Ham*], a phrase α.λ. and late ; cf., however, 105[23. 27] 106[22] for "land of Ham." This extract concludes with **53**, *And led them in confidence*, to which a glossator adds, *without dread*. In antith. with which, — *their enemies the sea covered*.

Str. IV. continues v.[39. 52] in synth. couplets. — **54.** *And He brought them to His sacred border*], the border or boundary of the holy land ; not " the border of His sanctuary " of EV[s], as if it referred to the temple ; so also *mountain* does not refer to Mount Zion, but to the mountainous land, which is characteristic of Palestine, Nu. 13[17. 29] Dt. 1[7], Jos. 11[2]. — *that His right hand had gotten*], by conquest from its original inhabitants through the stretching forth of His right hand as the valiant champion and war-god of His people. — **55.** *And drave out nations before them*], dispossessed them and expelled them from the land to give place to His people, — *and allotted them*], in accordance with the narrative Jos. 23[4], cf. Ps. 105[11], — *the inheritance by measure*], each portion of the people having measured out to them a part of the common inheritance. A glossator adds : *and made the tribes of Israel dwell in their tents.*

Pt. IV., Str. I. Syn. couplets. — **56.** *Then they tempted* ‖ *rebelled against*], as v.[17-18. 40-41] ; but there in two syn. lines, here compressed by a prosaic scribe into a prose sentence, which may be restored to its original form as a couplet by inserting *again* in the first line, and *again and again* in the second line. A glossator adds the legalistic phrase : *and they did not keep His testimonies*], using the legal term of P. — **57.** *And drew back* ‖ *turned aside*], the former explained ethically as *dealt treacherously like their fathers*, cf. 44[19] ; the latter by the simile, — *like a deceitful bow*], which springs the wrong way in time of need ; phrase used elsw. Ho. 7[16], probably also with corrected text v.[9]. To this a glossator adds : **58.** *And provoked Him to anger with their high places, and moved Him to jealousy with their graven images*], the constant Deuteronomic charge against Israel in the redaction of the ancient histories, that they were unfaithful to Yahweh in worship at the ancient high places instead of at the central altar at Jerusalem, and in their use of images in His worship. **59** is also a gloss in the same tone. — *God heard, and was furious ; and refused Israel altogether*]. This last is not harmonious with the subsequent couplet ; and so some have thought that the original was Ephraim instead of Israel.

Str. II. Synth and syn. couplets. — **60**. *Then He rejected the tabernacle of Shilo*], the sacred tabernacle set up at Shilo, north of Bethel, in Ephraim, after the conquest; the chief religious centre of the time of the Judges Jos. 18⁸⁻¹⁰ 21² 1 S. 1–4, Je. 7¹⁴. — *The tent that He made to dwell among mankind*], the sacred tent in which God was supposed to dwell, and whose locality He Himself selected, cf. Jos. 22¹⁹. — **61**. *And delivered up His strength ‖ His ornament*], terms descriptive of the sacred ark, cf. 1 S. 4²¹ ˢᵍ· Ps. 132⁸. — *to captivity ‖ into the hand of the adversary*], the Philistines, in accordance with the narrative 1 S. 4. To this a glossator added : **62**. *And gave up His people to the sword*], duplication of v.⁶⁴ᵃ, — *and became furious against His inheritance*], as v.⁵⁹.

Str. III. Synth. couplets. — **63**. *Fire devoured their young men*], the fire of war; war being conceived as a devouring flame in accordance with the subsequent context. It is improbable that the reference is to the fire of the divine anger. — *And their maidens were not praised in marriage song*]. They must remain unmarried, because of the slaughter of the young men, who might have married them. — **64**. *Their priests fell by the sword*], doubtless referring to the historic event of the slaughter of Hophni and Phinehas, the attendants upon the ark, 1 S. 4¹¹· ¹⁷. — *And their widows did not sing dirges*], the customary funeral solemnities could not be observed on account of the invasion of the land by the enemy and the universal disorder occasioned thereby. A glossator interrupts the narrative by a passionate outburst in accordance with the previous glosses v.⁵⁹· ⁶² : **65**. *Then Adonay awaked*]. He had left His people so long subject to their enemies, that He had seemed *as one asleep*, cf. 7⁷ 10¹ ‖ *like a hero overcome with wine*], as 𝕲, 𝔍, JPSV.: in a heavy, drunken sleep; better sustained by ‖ and usage than EVˢ., "that shouteth by reason of wine," as if, awakening from sleep, He fell upon His enemies with the passionate excitement of one stimulated to frenzy by too much wine. — **66**. *And smote His adversaries backward*], made them retreat in disaster, — *to an everlasting reproach He put them*], phr. of Ez. 22⁴ Jo. 2¹⁹.

Str. IV. Syn. and synth. couplets, antith. to each other. — **67**. *And He refused ‖ chose not*], positive and negative sides of the same idea. — *the tent of Joseph* || *the tribe of Ephraim*]. The rejection of Shilo carried with it the rejection of the tribe of Ephraim, in which it was situated, and the children of Joseph, of whom Ephraim was the leading tribe. — **68**. *But chose*], in place of the rejected : *the tribe of Judah*], and in that tribe, in place of Shilo : *Mount Zion which He doth love*], cf. 47^5 87^2. The love of God for Zion is here stated as a present and abiding fact, and not as the basis of the choice in the past, " He loved," as EV[s]. A glossator interrupts the course of thought by inserting a statement as to the erection of the temple. — **69**. *And built like the heights His sanctuary*], the sanctuary in Jerusalem being modelled after the heavenly abode of God, — *as the earth which He founded forever*], the temple was as firmly founded and as immutable as the earth itself. It is difficult to understand how a late glossator could speak so extravagantly of a temple which had been ruined more than once, and at least once had been destroyed by fire and levelled to the ground ; but doubtless he thought that the foundations were eternal, and that though it were destroyed, it would be rebuilt again in the same place and so abide through all vicissitudes.

Str. V. Syn. couplets. — **70**. *And He chose David His servant*], a usual term for prophets and special ministers of God. David bears this title elsw. 18^1 36^1 $89^{4.21}$ 132^{10} 144^{10} + 28 t. — *And took him from the sheepfolds*]. David's early life was that of a shepherd 1 S. 16^{11} $17^{15.34-37.40}$. — **71**. *From following the ewes that give suck He brought him*]. The shepherd leads his flock in Palestine ; but the ewes that suckle their young need his special attention, and those he follows with his eye and if needful with his steps, to watch over them and protect them from harm, cf. Is. 40^{11}. — *To be shepherd over Jacob His people*]. Israel as the flock of God had the Davidic dynasty as their shepherd, appointed by God as His son and representative in government, cf. Ez. 34^{23}. The Ps. here reaches its proper conclusion ; but a glossator thought it better to emphasize the last clause by the addition of the || *Israel His inheritance*, and to conclude with a laudation of David's reign : **72**. *And he shepherded them* || *used to lead them*], as shepherd king, — *according to the integrity of his mind*]. His rule was one of integrity of purpose. — and *with deeds of understanding of his hands*]. The royal acts of David as wrought with his hands were with intelligence, discernment, and skill. This is an idealisation of the reign of David in the style of the Chronicler and later writings, overlooking and ignoring the blots upon his reign, as recorded in the primitive prophetic histories.

1. אִמְרֵי פִי] phr. 19¹⁵ 54⁴ 138⁴ Dt. 32¹ +. — **2.** חִידוֹת] pl. חִידָה, as *49⁵.* — מֶנִּי] archaic form prep. מִן for euphony. — **3.** וַאֲבִיתֵינוּ סִפְּרוּ לָנוּ] phr. = 44². — **4.** דּוֹר אַחֲרוֹן] phr. elsw. v.⁶ 48¹⁴ 102¹⁹ Dt. 29²¹. — מְסַפְּרִים] Pi. ptc. pl. is difficult. We would expect נְסַפֵּר. But 𝕲, 𝕴, attach the ptc. to subsequent words, which certainly makes better grammar. This ptc. introduces a long prosaic gl. יהוה is used, which was impossible in 𝔈. — † עֱזוּז] n.[m.] *strength,* elsw. 145⁶ Is. 42²⁵ of fierceness of battle. — נִפְלְאֹתָיו אֲשֶׁר עָשָׂה] = 105⁵. — **5.** וַיָּקֶם] ו consec. Hiph. impf. קוּם, in the sense of *appoint,* here only ψ; cf. הֵקִים בְּרִית phr. of P Gn. 6¹⁸ +; ו consec. carries on the previous pf. and then continues gl. Otherwise it is aorist, based on an ideal past. — עֵדוּת] *19⁸* 81⁶ 119⁸⁸ 122⁴; also term of P, ‖ תּוֹרָה. — **6** is prosaic and certainly a gl. — **7.** כֵּסֶל] *confidence,* as 49¹⁴ Pr. 3²⁶ Jb. 8¹⁴ 31²⁴; a late word. — וְלֹא יִשְׁכְּחוּ] introduces the fourth l. of Str. II. after v.⁴ᵃ. — מִצְוֹתָיו יִנְצֹרוּ] cf. 77¹². — מִצְוֹתָיו יִנְצֹרוּ] cf. Dt. 33⁹ Pss. 105⁴⁵ 119² +; as a dimeter is gl. — **8.** דּוֹר סוֹרֵר וּמֹרֶה] phr. α.λ., but cf. Dt. 21¹⁸·²⁰ בֵּן סוֹרֵר וּמוֹרֶה from which it is certainly derived, also Je. 5²³ הֵכִין לִבּוֹ — .לב ס׳ ומ׳] phr. elsw. 10¹⁷ Jb. 11¹³ 2 Ch. 12¹⁴, cf. נכון לב v.³⁷ 57⁸·⁸ (= 108²) 112⁷. — וְאֶת־נֶאֶמְנָה] Niph. pf. 3 f. with רוּחַ, cf. v.³⁷ 89³⁸ 101⁶. — אֶל] as v.⁷·¹⁸·¹⁹·³⁴·³⁵·⁴¹; characteristic of 𝔄, though this part of v. is a gl. — **9.** נֹשְׁקֵי רוֹמֵי קָשֶׁת] phr. dub. and difficult. נשקי קשת 1 Ch. 12² 2 Ch. 17¹⁷ *equipped with the bow,* רוֹמֵי קֶשֶׁת Je. 4²⁹, † רמה vb. *cast* elsw., בַּיָּם Ex. 15¹·²¹. One of these vbs. might be an interp. gl. Hu., Hi., Kau., think of רומי as gl., but נשקי is the later phr. and therefore most prob. the gl., if there be one. It is difficult to see the connection of this v. with context, if בְּנֵי אֶפְרַיִם is original. It indicates a hostile disposition towards the people of the North, not in accordance with 𝔄 elsw. and for which no historic situation can be assigned. The difficulty would be removed, if we could rd. נֹשְׁקֵי קֶשֶׁת רְמִיָּה and suppose that רְמִיָּה had been transposed by txt. err., and that בְּנֵי אֶפְרַיִם had been inserted by late glossator. We would then have the same idea as v.⁵⁷, and this couplet would conclude Str. III. — יוֹם קְרָב] phr. elsw. Zc. 14³, but *v.* Ps. 55¹⁹. — **10.** שָׁמְרוּ בְרִית] phr. elsw. 103¹⁸ 132¹² 1 K. 11¹¹ Ne. 1⁵ 9³² Dn. 9⁴; cf. v.³⁷. — **11.** עֲלִילוֹתָיו] as 77¹³. This v. is a pentameter gl. — **12.** שְׂדֵה־צֹעַן] phr. as v.⁴³. ‡ שָׂדֶה n.m. (1) *field* with flowers 103¹⁵, sown 107³⁷; (2) *country* 132⁶, so here and v.⁴³, † צֹעַן n. pr. loc. *Zanis,* town built seven years after Hebron acc. Nu. 13²², elsw. Is. 19¹¹·¹³ 30⁴ Ez. 30¹⁴, modern Ṣân, in N.W. Delta of Egypt. — **13.** בָּקַע יָם] as Ex. 14¹⁶ Ne. 9¹¹, *v. 74¹⁵;* cf. יַבְקַע צֻרִים v.¹⁵. — וַיַּצֶּב־מַיִם כְּמוֹ־נֵד] cf. כמו נד נֹזְלִים Ex. 15⁸. — **14.** בֶּעָנָן] ‡ עָנָן n.m. (1) *cloud mass* 97²; (2) of the historic, theophanic cloud of the Exodus, here, as 105³⁹ Ex. 34⁵; עמוד ענן Ps. 99⁷, as Ex. 13²¹·²² + 6 t. (JE) Ne. 9¹²·¹⁹. — אוֹר אֵשׁ] phr. α.λ. for עַמוּד (ה)אֵשׁ Ex. 13²¹·²² 14²⁴ (JE) +. — **15.** יְבַקַּע] Pi. impf. for Qal v.¹³ suspi-

cious, also absence of ו consec., which appears again וַיִּשְׁךְ. 𝕲, 𝔍, render it as
v.[18] pf.; prob. the original text was בקע Qal pf. They both rd. צור sg. for
צֻרִים, which is also more prob. 𝕲, 𝔍, take רַבָּה as adj. agreeing with תהמות.
— **16**. [נֹזְלִים] ptc. ‡ [נזל] *flow*, of water 147[18], ptc. *streams, floods*, Ex. 15[8],
so here and v.[44]. — V.[15] and v.[16] are doublets; the latter is more poetic and
more likely original. — **17**. [לַמְרוֹת] for יְהַמְרוּת, Hiph. inf. cstr. מרה; cf. v.[40. 56].
— [עֶלְיוֹן] characteristic of 𝔄, as v.[35. 56] 50[14] 73[11] 77[11] 82[6] 83[19]. — [בַּצִיָּה] for
ארץ ציה 63[2]. — **18**. [וַיְנַסּוּ] ו consec. Pi. impf., cf. v.[41. 56], as Ex. 17[2. 7] Nu.
14[22] (J). — [לִלְבָבָם] fuller form, as 73[1. 7. 13. 21. 26] 77[7]. יְבִי v.[8] is in gl., so לְבָב
v.[37]. — [לְנַפְשָׁם] *according to their appetite*, as 17[9] 63[6] 106[15] 107[5. 9. 18]. —
19. [וַיְדַבְּרוּ בֵאלֹהִים] is doubtless a gl., explan. of אמרו. — **20**. [הֵן הִכָּה צוּר וַיָּזוּבוּ מַיִם]
cf. 105[41], and Is. 48[21] פָּקַח צוּר וַיָּזֻבוּ מָיִם. The earliest of
these is doubtless the last. הכה is used by reference to Ex. 17[6] (E) or
Nu. 20[11] (P). [זוב] a.λ. ψ.—[יִשְׁטְפוּ] Qal impf. 3 pl. (69[3]). This whole
l. is a triplet with v.[14. 15], and is a gl. based on Is. 48[21]. [שְׁאֵר] as v.[27],
v. 73[26]. — **21**. [לָכֵן שָׁמַע יהוה וַיִּתְעַבָּר]. This is prose style. יהוה impossible in
𝔈. [וַיִּתְעַבָּר] ו consec. Hithp. impf. † עבר denom. עֶבְרָה. Hithp. (1) *be furious*,
so v.[59. 62] 89[39], cf. Dt. 3[26] Pr. 26[17]; (2) *be arrogant* Pr. 14[16]; (3) *incite to
fury* Pr. 20[2] (?). — [נִשְּׂקָה] Niph. pf. 3 f. שׂיק BDB. (cf. סלק). Hiph. *kindle*,
set on fire, Is. 44[15] Ez. 39[9] BS. 43[21]. Niph. a.λ. *be kindled*. — **23**. [דַּלְתֵי] pl.
cstr. ‡ דֶּלֶת n.f. *door*, common in OT, but in ψ only here and 107[16], unless דָּל
141[3] is error for דרך, which is prob. For the idea cf. אֲרֻבֹּת הַשָּׁמַיִם Gn. 7[11]. —
24. [וַיַּמְטֵר] cf. v.[27], based on Ex. 16[4] (J). — † [מָן] n.m. *manna*, the divine
provision of bread for Israel in the wilderness Ex. 16[15. 31. 33. 35. 35] Nu. 11[6. 7. 9]
Dt. 8[3. 16] Jos. 5[12. 12] Ne. 9[20]. — [לֶאֱכֹל] Qal inf. cstr. with לְ is a gl., making
l. too long and altogether unnecessary. — [דְּגַן שָׁמַיִם] phr. a.λ.; 𝕲 ἄρτον οὐρανοῦ does not imply different text, but is paraphrase; cf. לחם שמים 105[40]. —
נתן] expansive gl. This v. has been assimilated to v.[25] in measure and so
made tetrameter. — **25**. [לֶחֶם אַבִּירִים] phr. a.λ., prob. referring to angels as
103[20], so 𝕲 ἀγγέλων; a late conception, like the Greek *ambrosia*, the food
of the gods. — † [צֵידָה] n.f. *provision* Gn. 42[25] 45[21] Ex. 12[39] (E) Jos. 1[11] (D)
9[11] (JE) Ju. 7[8] (?) 20[10] 1 S. 22[10] and here. — This v. is a tetrameter couplet
and a late gl. — **26**. [יַסַּע] Hiph. impf. נסע. 𝕲 has καὶ ἐπῆρεν. Indeed ו consec. is necessary to the sense and has been omitted in 𝔐 by err. ‡ נסע vb.
Qal *pull up* (tent) pegs and set out on a journey, common in OT, but not
in ψ. Hiph. † *cause to set out, lead out*, Ex. 15[22] c. acc. pers., Ps. 78[52] people
as flock, 80[9] fig. of vine ; here of wind. — [קָדִים] *East wind*, as Gn. 41[6. 23] (E)
Ho. 12[2] 13[15], elsw. ψ with רוח 48[8]. — ‡ [תֵּימָן] n.f. (1) *the South* Jos. 15[1]
Is. 43[6] +; † (2) poet. *South wind*, here as Ct. 4[16]. The use of the wind is
according to Nu. 11[31]. — **27**. [עֲלֵיהֶם] makes l. too long and is gl. — [שְׁאֵר] as
v.[20]. — [חוֹל יַמִּים] phr. Je. 15[8] Jb. 6[3], ה הַיָּם ח Gn. 32[13] (E) 41[49] Is. 10[22] Ho. 2[1]
Jc. 33[22], cf. Gn. 22[17] (J). ‡ [חוֹל] n.m. *sand*, elsw. ψ 139[18]. — **28**. [מִשְׁכְּנֹתָיו]. The
3 sg. here and in מַחֲנֵהוּ between 3 pl. referring to Israel is striking. 𝕲 has
pl., but 𝔍 agrees with 𝔐. The original Ex. 16[13] Nu. 11[31] מחנה has no sf. at
all, and there is no reference to מִשְׁכָּנוֹת. The sfs. are differences of interp.

o

as usual, and the two nouns are syn. There is no justification for referring משכנות to the *tabernacle*, which is always מִשְׁכָּן. These are the tabernacles of Israel, as 87² Nu. 24⁵. But in fact this v. is an expansive gl. — **29.** [הָאֱוָתָם] emph. in position; sf. 3 pl. הָאֱוָת n.f. (*10¹⁷*) based on Nu. 11⁴· ³⁴, cf. Ps. 106¹⁴ ᵇq·. — [יָבֹא] Hiph. impf. 3 m. is out of harmony with context. It cannot be pf. as ⅏. It does not follow the action of previous vbs.; cf. v.²⁹, which is also a gl. — **30.** [זָרוּ] Qal pf. 3 m. זור *be a stranger to*, but ⅏ ἐστερήθησαν elsw. for מנע, must be interpretation, so 𝔙 *fraudati*, 𝔍 *indiguerunt*. There is an evident reference to זָרָא n.(f.) *loathsome thing*, cf. Nu. 11²⁰ (JE), prob. err. for זרה (Sam.) *B*DB. We should prob. rd. לְזָרָה תַאוָתָם *their lust became loathing*. This accords exactly with the narrative. The usual interp. reverses the narrative and makes the visitation of wrath precede the loathing. — [עֹוד אָכְלָם בְּפִיהֶם] is a variation of הַבָּשָׂר עֹודֶנוּ בֵּין שִׁנֵּיהֶם Nu. 11³³. This l. introduces the next Str. — **31.** [אַף אֱלֹהִים] emph. in position. — [בָּהֶם] is gl., making l. too long. — [בְּמִשְׁמַנֵּיהֶם] has two beats. ב prep. *among*. ‡ מִשְׁמָן n.m. of men *fat, lusty*, of warriors here, as Is. 10¹⁶; so prob. Dn. 11²⁴, as Bevan. — [בַּחוּרֵי] pl. cstr. ‡ בָּחוּר n.m. *young man*, as v.⁶³ 148¹². But ⅏ ἐκλέκτους, 𝔙 *electos*, as בְּחִירֵי, is better suited to parall. — **32.** [בְּכָל־זֹאת] phr. Is. 5²⁵ 9¹¹· ¹⁶· ²⁰ +. — **33.** ‡ [בֶּהָלָה] n.f. *dismay, terror*, elsw. Lv. 26¹⁶ Je. 15⁸ Is. 65²³. ⅏ renders this word μετὰ σπουδῆς, 𝔍 *velociter*. A vb. is needed in last l., prob. בהל *made to haste away, in haste*, best suited to הבל. — **34.** [אִם־הֲרָגָם] temporal force of אִם with pf. in both prot. and apod. The Waws are all coördinate of late style for ו consec. impf., the style of this poem in the original parts. — **35.** [וַיִּזְכְּרוּ] resumes the style of the original. כי before אלהים, though in ⅏, 𝔍, is prob. a gl. to emphasize the fact. — [צוּר] for God, as *18³*. — [אֵל עֶלְיֹון] as 87⁵ (?), cf. אלהים עליון v.⁵⁶ (?) 57³ (?). This gives two names of God, and not, as Gn. 14¹⁸· ¹⁹· ²⁰· ²², a simple compound name. — **36.** ו [וַיְפַתּוּהוּ] consec. Pi. impf. ‡ פתה vb. denom. *be simple*, in ψ only here *deceive*, as 2 S. 3²⁵ Pr. 24²⁸ Je. 20⁷ Ez. 14⁹ +. ⅏ has ἠγάπησαν, 𝔙 *dilexerunt*. — [יְכַזְּבוּ] Pi. impf. ‡ כזב, denom. כָּזָב *tell a lie*, as 89³⁶, elsw. ψ † Qal *to be a liar* 116¹¹. — This v. is tetrameter; it can hardly be original, and is really a later theological interp. of the conduct of the people. It is possible that there was no vb. with כפיהם in the original, and that both יפתוהו and ἠγάπησαν are interpretative, the one for syn. parall., the other for antith. parall. — **37.** though in the same measure as Ps., is yet another dogmatic gl. — [נכון לב] cf. v.⁸, רוח נכון 51¹². — [וְנֶאֶמְנוּ] as v.⁸. — **38.** † [רַחוּם] adj. *compassionate;* Dt. 4³¹, elsw. with חַנּוּן following Pss. 86¹⁵ 103⁸, as Ex. 34⁶ (J), earlier order; preceding Pss. 111⁴ 112⁴ 145⁸ 2 Ch. 30⁹ Ne. 9¹⁷· ³¹ Jo. 2¹³ Jon. 4² later order; more likely the former here. The Pasiq prob. indicates this omission. — [וְיְכַפֵּר עָוֹן] cf. 65⁴ 79⁹, used for נשא of Ex. 34⁶ ᵇq·. This and the following impf. express the present and constant state of character of God. עָוֹן is gl., making l. too long. — [וְהִרְבָּה] ו consec. pf. carrying on habitual action. It has auxil. force with inf., as Is. 55⁷ Ex. 36⁵. — [לְהָשִׁיב אַפּוֹ] cf. vb. with חמה 106²³, חרון אף 85⁴. The space in 𝕳 before v.³⁸, according to *Kiddushin*³⁰ᵃ, indicates the middle of the 5896 στίχοι of ψ. *Maccoth*²²ᵇ states that this v. and Dt. 28⁵⁸· ⁵⁹ 29⁸ were

recited when forty stripes save one were inflicted (v. De. *Com. Ps.*). —
39. [וַיִּזְכֹּר] ו consec. carrying on the thought of v.[35], God's remembrance in
antithesis with Israel's remembrance. — **40.** [בִּישִׁימוֹן] elsw. *68[8]* 106[14] 107[4]
Dt. 32[10]. The vbs. in this v. are so out of harmony with the context that they
must be a reflective gl. Vs.[40-48] are a pentameter extract from an older poem.
— **41.** [וַיָּשׁוּבוּ] ו consec. impf. שוב with auxil. force followed by ' consec. impf.
— [קְרוֹשׁ יִשְׂרָאֵל] divine name of Is. 6[3]; elsw. in ψ, 71[22] 89[19]. — [הִתְווּ] Hiph.
pf. 3 pl. תוה α.λ. Aramaism. 𝕲 παρώξυναν, 𝕵 *concitaverunt*. 𝕲 translates
Is. 5[24] קְרוֹשׁ יִשְׂרָאֵל נִאֵצוּ in the same way, so also נאץ in Ps. 10[3. 13] 74[10. 18] 107[11].
It is possible therefore that נאצו was in 𝕲, and that a later copyist substituted
the Aramaic vb. for it. Part of the l. is original; the vb. makes the l. too
long and must be a later insertion. — **42.** [מִנְּי־צָר] the longer form of prep.
for euphony. צָר n.m. coll. *3[2]*. — **43.** [שָׂם אֹתוֹת וּמוֹפְתִים] phr. elsw. Je. 32[20],
cf. Ps. 105[27]; אוֹת as *miracle* elsw. ψ 65[9] 74[9] ‖ מוֹפְתִים (*v. 71[7]*) 135[9]; c. שִׂים
elsw. Ex. 10[2] (J) Is. 66[19]. — **44.** [וַיַּהֲפֹךְ] ו consec. (*30[12]*), cf. Niph. Ex. 7[17. 20].
— [יְאֹרֵיהֶם] sf. 3 pl. refers to Egyptians of v.[43]. ‡ יְאֹר n.m. *stream of the Nile*
(an Egyptian loan word), derived from Ex. 7[17. 18] + (J). — [בַּל־יִשְׁתָּיוּן] Qal
impf. 3 pl. fuller form with archaic neg. in final clause. — **45.** [יְשַׁלַּח] Pi. impf.
without ו consec. is err., for the context demands ו, unless we rd. pf. — [בָּהֶם]
is prosaic. It makes l. too long. — † [עָרֹב] n.m. *insect swarm*, as Ex. 8[17 + 6 t] (J)
Ps. 105[31]. — † [צְפַרְדֵּעַ] n.f. sg. coll., as Ex. 8[2] (J); pl. Ex. 7[27. 28. 29] 8[1. 3. 4. 5. 7. 8. 9] (J)
Ps. 105[30]. — **46.** † [חָסִיל] n.m. kind of *locust*, elsw. 1 K. 8[37] = 2 Ch. 6[28] Jo. 1[4]
2[25] Is. 33[4]. — ‡ [יְגִיעַ] n.m. (1) *toil*, not in ψ ; (2) *result of toil, produce ;* elsw.
109[11] 128[2] Ho. 12[9] Dt. 28[33]. — ‡ [אַרְבֶּה] n.m. a kind of *locust*, as Ex. 10[4] + 6 t.
(J) Pss. 105[34] 109[23]. — **47.** [יַהֲרֹג] Qal impf. without ו consec. is improb. in
this context. — ‡ [בָּרָד] n.m. *hail*, plague v.[48], Ex. 9[18] + 17 t. (JE) Ps. 105[32];
elsw. ψ of storm 18[13. 14] 148[8]. — ‡ [גֶּפֶן] n.f. *vine*, as 105[33]; in simile of wife
128[3]; allegory of Israel 80[9. 15] Ez. 17[6. 7. 8] Ho. 10[1]. — [שִׁקְמוֹתָם] pl. f., sf. 3 pl.
† [שִׁקְמָה] *sycamore tree*, elsw. שִׁקְמוֹת 1 K. 10[27] 1 Ch. 27[28] 2 Ch. 1[15] 9[27] Is. 9[9]
Am. 7[14]. — [חֲנָמַל] n.[m.] α.λ. prob. *frost*, as 𝕲 ἐν τῇ πάχνῃ, 𝕵 *frigore*. —
48. [לַבָּרָד] so 𝕲, 𝕵, but improb. It has been assimilated to v.[47]; rd. as Ew.,
Dy., Gr., Du., Valeton, after 2 codd., ‡ דֶּבֶר n.m. (1) *pestilence* Ex. 5[3] 9[15] Nu.
14[12] (J) Ps. 91[3. 6]; (2) *cattle plague, murrain*, Ex. 9[3] (J), as here ; cf. v.[50].
— † [בְּעִיר] n.m. *beast*, as Gn. 45[17] Ex. 22[4] Nu. 20[4. 8. 11] (E). — ‡ [מִקְנֶה] n.m.
cattle, as Ex. 9[3] + (J). — [רְשָׁפִים] pl. רֶשֶׁף *fiery shafts* of Yahweh, sending disease and death, as Dt. 32[24] Hb. 3[5]; cf. Ps. 76[4]. — **49.** [יְשַׁלַּח־בָּם] cf. v.[45a]
בָּהֶם.— [חֲרוֹן אַפּוֹ] phr. of J, as 69[25] 85[4]. — [עֶבְרָה וָזַעַם וְצָרָה] a heaping up of syn.
terms. — † [מִשְׁלַחַת] n.f. *sending, mission*, elsw. Ec. 8[8] *dismission ;* cf. שִׁלּוּחַ
mission Est. 9[19. 22]. [מַלְאֲכֵי רָעִים] 𝕲 ἀγγέλων πονηρῶν, 𝕵 *angelorum malo-
rum*, prob. correct. — The v. is a late gl. — **50.** [יְפַלֵּס נָתִיב] phr. α.λ.; פלס vb.
level a path, elsw. Pr. 4[26] 5[6. 21] Is. 26[7]. — † [נָתִיב] n.m. *path* 119[35] Jb. 18[10] 28[7]
41[24] Pr. 12[28], late word ; cf. נְתִיבָה n.f. earlier form 142[4]. — [חַיָּיתָם] syn. with
נַפְשָׁם, has the uncommon mng. *their life*, as 74[19] 143[3]. Possibly MT. so
pointed, supposing that it referred to animals ; as 𝕲 τὰ κτήνη αὐτῶν,
𝕵 *jumenta*, of the more extensive form of the pestilence according to P. —

V.⁴⁹·⁵⁰ are full of late terms and conceptions, and are doubtless glosses. —
51. וַיַּךְ] Hiph. impf. ו consec. נָכָה, carries on v.⁴⁸ from which it has been
separated by gl.—רֵאשִׁית אוֹנִים] phr. elsw. 105³⁶ ראשית לכל אונם, Gn. 49³
ראשית אוני, Dt. 21¹⁷ ראשית אני. These all suggest rather אונִים here, as ﬩.
‡ רֵאשִׁית n.f. *beginning*, elsw. ψ, 111¹⁰ of wisdom. † אוֹן n.m. elsw. *strength*
Jb. 18⁷·¹² 40¹⁶ Ho. 12⁴ Is. 40²⁶·²⁹ Pr. 11⁷; *wealth* Jb. 20¹⁰ Ho. 12⁹, prob. also
Ps. 49⁶. — בְּאָהֳלֵי־חָם] phr. *a.λ.*, not in Ps. 105³⁶; as it makes the l. longer
than the other ll. of the plagues, it is prob. gl. But אֶרֶץ חָם 105²³·²⁷ 106²².
For similar uses of אָהֳלֵי *v.* 83⁷ 120⁵ Hb. 3⁷. Only in these late Pss. is this
usage of ‡ חָם found; elsw. Ham is the name of the son of Noah Gn. 5³² +.
— **52.** ‡ עֵדֶר] n.m. *flock, herd*, only here ψ, but common in OT.; elsw. in simile
Mi. 2¹² Je. 31¹⁰. This v. carries on the thought of v.³⁹. The intervening
material is a long pentameter gl. — **53.** וְלֹא פָחָדוּ] as ﬤ *absque timore*, has
really two tones and is a gl. — פַּחַה הַיָּם] cf. 106¹¹ Ex. 15⁵·¹⁰ (song) 14²⁸ (P)
Jos. 24⁷ (E). This v. concludes the pentameter poem. — **54.** וַיְבִיאֵם] ו consec.
Hiph. בוא resumes the poem, and should follow v.⁵². — גְּבוּל קָדְשׁוֹ] phr. *a.λ.*
‡ גְּבוּל n.m. (1) *border, boundary*, of limit of waters of great deep 104⁹;
(2) *territory* 105³¹·³³ 147¹⁴ and here; cf. ‡ גְּבוּלָה n.f. 74¹⁷. — זֶה] prob. relative, as 74² 104⁸·²⁶, but ﬤ, ﬦ, ﬡ, ﬤ, regard it as demonstrative; if so it must
have the strong force of "yonder," as it is without the article. — **55.** וַיֵּשַׁב]
Hiph. impf. ו consec. This third l. is a gl. — שִׁבְטֵי יִשְׂרָאֵל] שבט for *tribe* in
ψ elsw. only v.⁶⁷·⁶⁸ 74² 105³⁷ 122⁴·⁴. — **56.** וַיְנַסּוּ וַיַּמְרוּ] cf. v.¹⁷·¹⁸·⁴⁰·⁴¹. These
two vbs. seem to be a compression of two ll. — אֶת־אֱלֹהִים] before עֶלְיוֹן makes
one l. too long. If we attach את אלהים to the first vb. and insert עוּר we have
the first l. The second also requires an additional word, prob. יָשׁוּבוּ of v.⁴¹.
— עֵדְוֹתָיו] term of P, c. שמר also 99⁷ 119¹⁴⁶·¹⁶⁷; prob. a gl. — **57.** וַיִּסֹּגוּ] ו consec. Niph. impf. 3 pl. *turn oneself back, prove faithless, v. 14³;* elsw. with
אחור 44¹⁹. — קֶשֶׁת רְמִיָּה] *v.* v.⁹; phr. elsw. Ho. 7¹⁶. — **58.** וַיַּכְעִיסוּהוּ] ו consec.
Hiph. כעם, as 106²⁹; phr. of D, Je. — יַקְנִיאוּהוּ] Hiph. impf. קנא, as Dt. 32¹⁶·²¹.
The force of ו consec. is required, whether we suppose that there has been
a transposition or that the force of the ו with the noun is consec. — בָּמוֹת] for
high places of worship, only here ψ, but common in D, H, and Chr. —
‡ פָּסִיל] n.m. only pl. *idols*, as Ho. 11² Is. 10¹⁰ 21⁹ 30²² Dt. 7⁵·²⁵ 12³ +. This
v. is a tetrameter gl. It could not be the reason for the rejection of Shilo
in so early a writing; cf. Dt. 32¹⁶. — **59.** וַיִּשְׂרָאֵל] here is striking, for the subsequent context suggests Ephraim. But the v. is a late gl. — **60.** שִׁלוֹ] n. pr.
loc., as Ju. 21¹⁹ 1 S. 1²⁴ 3²¹ Je. 7¹⁴ +, usually שִׁלֹה *Shiloh*, a place in Ephraim,
north of Bethel; *Seilûn*, Rob. *Pal.*ᴵᴵᴵ·³⁰³ᶠ — **61.** עֻזּוֹ] is used here, as context
indicates, for עז ארון 132⁸; ‖ תִּפְאַרְתּוֹ (71⁸), attributed to the ark as to the
temple 96⁶ Is. 60⁷ 63¹⁵ 64¹⁰. — **62.** הִתְעַבָּר] is repetition of v.⁵⁹. — **63.** הוּלָּלוּ]
Pu. Pf. הלל, *v.* Intr. § 35, *be praised* in marriage songs; so Aq. ὑμνήθη-
σαν. ﬤ ἐπένθησαν, ﬖ *non sunt lamentatae*, so ﬦ יְלָלוּ √הילילו improbable. —
64. תִבְכֶּינָה] Qal impf. pl. 3 f. בכה (69¹¹), as Σ, ﬡ, must have the specific
sense of weeping or singing dirges. ﬤ, ﬡ, ﬦ, interp. as Niph. passive תִּבָּכֶינָה.
— **65.** וַיִּקַץ] Qal impf. ו consec. † יָקַץ vb. *awake*, as Gn. 41⁴·⁷·²¹ (E) 9²⁴

28¹⁶ (J) Ju. 16¹⁴·²⁰ 1 K. 3¹⁵ 18²⁷ Hb. 2⁷; earlier word than קוּם. — יָשֵׁן] adj. *sleeping*, cf. vb. *3⁶*; also 1 K. 18²⁷ of Baal. — אֲדֹנָי] in this Ps. suspicious. — מִתְרוֹנֵן] a.λ. Hithp. ptc. † [רון] *be overcome* with wine; κεκραιπαληκὼς ἐξ οἴνου 𝕲, *crapulatus* 𝖁, *post crapulam vini* 𝕵; AE., Aug., Ges., De W., Hi., Bä., Du., Kau., Bu., Ehr., most prob.; but AV., RV., De., *B*DB., after Σ, Ki., Flaminius, Hithp. רנן *shout*. — 66. נהז (עוֹלם) [חֶרְפַּת] phr. as Ez. 22⁴ Jo. 2¹⁹. — 69. כְּמוֹ־רָמִים] archaic form prep. with רָמִים Qal ptc. pl. רום; 𝕲 ὡς μονοκερώτων, 𝕵 *monoceroton* רְאֵמִים, so 𝕿 הֵיךְ חַרְנָא וְרִימְנָא. It is better to rd. כַּמְרוֹמִים with Hi.; cf. Ps. 148¹. This v. is a gl. — 71. עָלוֹת] Qal ptc. f. pl. † [עוּל] vb. *give suck*, elsw. Is. 40¹¹ 1 S. 6⁷·¹⁰ Gn. 33¹³ (J). — וּבִישְׂרָאֵל] with subsequent word is a gl. of intensification; so also v.⁷². — 72. הֹם לְבָבוֹ] phr. elsw. 101² Gn. 20⁵·⁶ (E) 1 K. 9⁴. — תְבוּנוֹת כַּפָּיו] phr. a.λ., *v. 49⁴;* pl. *deeas* or *acts of understanding.* — יַנְחֵם] Hiph. impf. נהה with sf. 3 pl. must have sense of pf. and previous ו with noun have force of ו consec., or else it must be in circumstantial clause.

PSALM LXXIX., 2 STR. 6³.

Ps. 79 originally was a lament over the destruction of Jerusa-lem by Nebuchadnezzar, the defiling of the temple and slaughter of the people (v.¹⁻²), with a petition not to remember the iniquities of their ancestors, but speedily to have compassion and save them (v.⁸ᵃᵇ·⁹ᵃᵇ), concluding with a vow of perpetual thanksgiving (v.¹³ᶜᵈ). But many glosses were added by Maccabean editors, making the Ps. appropriate to the desecration of the temple and the cruelty of Antiochus (v.³·⁹ᶜᵈ·¹⁰ᵇᶜ·¹²). Many citations from other scriptures were inserted (v.⁴⁻⁷·⁸ᶜ·¹⁰ᵃ·¹¹·¹³ᵃᵇ), making it more appropriate for religious use; although from a literary point of view it is now a mosaic.

> THE nations are come into Thine inheritance.
> They have defiled Thy holy temple.
> They have laid Jerusalem in ruins.
> They have given the dead bodies of Thy servants
> As food to the birds of heaven,
> Thy pious ones to the wild beasts of the earth.
> REMEMBER not the iniquities of our forefathers.
> Quickly let Thine acts of compassion come to meet us
> Help us, O God of our salvation,
> For the sake of the glory of Thy name.
> We will give thanks unto Thee forever;
> To all generations tell Thy praise.

Ps. 79 was a Ps. of 𝕬, then taken up into 𝕸 and 𝕰, but not into 𝕯𝕽 (*v.* Intr. §§ 29, 31, 32). That applies only to the original Ps. Indeed, the

Ps. in its present form is a mosaic of citations from many different writings.
The original Ps. had only two trimeter hexastichs, v.[1-2] and v.[8ab. 9ab. 13cd]. These
Strs. indicate a date soon after the destruction of the temple by Nebuchadnezzar, to which v.[1-2] clearly refers. The use of שׂמא v.[1] is that of D, H, P,
Ez., cf. Je. 7[30] Ez. 9[7]. שׂם לעיים v.[1] is dependent on Mi. 1[6]; נבלה v.[2] is in its
earlier use for corpse, not the later for carcass of animals. ראשׁנים v.[8] as Dt.
19[14] Lv. 26[45] (H). נקמה v.[10] as Je. 50[28] 51[11]. The glosses are: (a) v.[3] is not
a citation; but is either hexameter or prose. It probably refers to Maccabean
bloodshed; (b) v.[4] is derived from Ps. 44[14], (c) v.[5] from Ps. 89[47], (d) v.[6-7]
from Je. 10[25], (e) v.[8c] from Ps. 142[7]; (f) v.[9cd] is composed of a prosaic gloss
which attributes the suffering to sins; (g) v.[10a] is derived from Ps. 115[2];
(h) v.[11ac] is based on 102[21]; (i) v.[11b] is a citation from Ex. 15[16]; (j) v.[10bc. 12]
are characteristically Maccabean, cf. 89[51. 52]; (k) v.[13ab] is a citation from Ps.
100[3]. These additions to the Ps. were not made in 𝕬, as is evident from the
use of יהוה v.[5] and אדני v.[12]. 𝕭𝕽 did not use it, and therefore that editor
could not have made the addition. The glosses doubtless all came from the
Maccabean editor, adapting the Ps. to his own times. The Ps. is prescribed
in Rabbinical use for the day commemorating the destruction of the temple
(*Sopherim* 18[3]).

Str. I. A synth. tetrastich, concluding with a syn. couplet. —
1. *The nations are come into Thine inheritance*], have invaded
the Holy Land, which God had taken as His own special land
and given as an inheritance to His people, cf. Ex. 15[17] Pss. 74[2]
78[62. 71]. — *They have defiled Thy holy temple*]. Even the entrance
of the uncircumcised and unconsecrated nations into the temple
would have defiled it La. 1[10] Jo. 4[17] Na. 2[1] Is. 35[8] 52[1], and have
made it ceremonially unclean; but it is altogether probable that a
more positive desecration is referred to, such as the desecration
of the sacred vessels and furniture of the sacred places, partly by
putting them to profane use, partly by breaking them up as spoil,
and partly by removing them from the sacred places into distant
lands; all of which was done by the Babylonians 2 K. 25[13-17] La.
2[7]. — *They have laid Jerusalem in ruins*], phr. of Mi. 1[6], cf. Je. 26[18],
also 2 K. 25[9-10]. — **2.** *They have given the dead bodies of Thy
servants ‖ Thy pious ones*], slain in battle about the walls or in
the streets of the captured city, cf. La. 4[13-14] — *as food*], the bodies
left unburied became prey *to the birds of heaven*], the vultures,
and *to the wild beasts of the earth*], especially jackals, cf. 74[14] Je.
34[20]. This simple but graphic description of the ruin wrought by
the Babylonians was enlarged and adapted to later times by later

editors, especially Maccabean. — **3.** *They have poured out their blood like water round about Jerusalem, and there was none to bury them*]. This might be regarded as an enlargement of the previous context, but is more suited to the excessive cruelty of the Maccabean times, cf. 1 Mac. 1³⁷ 7¹⁷. — **4.** *We are become a reproach to our neighbours, a scorn and derision to them that are round about us*]. This is a citation from 44¹⁴. — **5.** *How long, Yahweh? wilt Thou be angry forever? Will Thy jealousy burn like fire?*] This is a citation with slight variation from 89⁴⁷. — **6–7.** *Pour out Thy wrath upon the nations that know Thee not, and upon the kingdoms that do not call on Thy name; for they have devoured Jacob, and his habitation laid waste*]. This is a citation, with few and unimportant changes, from Je. 10²⁵.

Str. II. One antith., one synth., and one syn. couplet. — **8.** *Remember not the iniquities of our forefathers*], according to law Ex. 20⁵, threatening Lv. 26¹⁴ ˢᑫ· Dt. 28¹⁵ ˢᑫ·, prophecy Je. 11¹⁰ ˢᑫ·, and experience La. 5⁷ 2 K. 23²⁶ ˢᑫ· 24³⁻⁴. The posterity in their solidarity of inheritance, both of favour and guilt, must suffer the penalty of their fathers' misdeeds as well as inherit the blessings of their covenant. — *Quickly*], in haste; the need is pressing, — *let Thine acts of compassion*], so most probably, in accordance with usage, as the pl. vb. is used, and not abstr. "compassion" or pl. "compassions," "tender mercies," AV., RV. — *come to meet us*], personified as messengers of God, cf. 21⁴ 43³ 85¹¹⁻¹². A glossator appends as reason a citation from 142⁷: *for we are brought very low.* — **9.** *Help us, O God of our salvation*], carrying on the petition, basing it upon the well-known character of God, cf. 18⁴⁷ 24⁵ 25⁵ 27⁹ 65⁶ 85⁵ Mi. 7⁷ Hb. 3¹⁸ Is. 17¹⁰ 1 Ch. 16³⁵. — *For the sake of the glory of Thy name*], phr. 29² 66² 96⁸, in its conception common and ancient. Such glory was due to His name, and could be given by His people only and not by others, and in the land of the living, not of the dead. The honour of God was involved in the salvation of His people. Several insertions were made here by later editors, — *and deliver us*], specifying the help, — *and cover over our sins for Thy name's sake*]. The editor makes the Ps. more appropriate for use in the synagogue by inserting this petition for the covering over of the sins of the people themselves, as a check upon their inclination, apparently justified by v.⁸, to attribute all their afflictions to the sins of their ancestors, cf. Ez. 18¹⁹ ˢᵠ·. The covering over of sins here is evidently conceived as by the grace of God apart from sacrifices, cf. 65⁴. — **10.** *Wherefore should the nations say: "Where is their God?"*] This is a citation from 115², cf. 42⁴·¹¹. — *Let it be made known among the nations before our eyes, the vengeance for the blood of Thy servants that was poured out*]. This resumes the thought of v.³ with the Maccabean vindictiveness and cry for vengeance ; only the wish is that it may not be deferred, but may be taken in their days and before their very eyes, so that they may have the joy of it ; and also that it may be before all nations, as a public vengeance. — **11.** *Let the groaning of the prisoner come before Thee*], a citation from 102²¹, as also the ‖ *cause to remain alive those condemned to death*], captives in war who yet had incurred the death penalty by violation of some regulation of their conquerors ; especially appropriate to the early Maccabean times, when religious and political rebellion was mingled with acts of unnatural cruelty and barbarism on the part of the Jews, in violation of the rights of war and justly incurring death after capture. The additional clause giving basis for the plea : *according to the greatness of Thine arm*], is a citation from Ex. 15¹⁶. — **12.** *And return to our neighbours sevenfold*], another exhibition of the Maccabean vindictiveness to the neighbouring nations, cf. v.¹⁰ : a demand for vengeance of the most thoroughgoing kind, sevenfold, in the spirit of the ancient Lamech, cf. Gn. 4¹⁵· ²⁴, rather than of the prophets, and indeed *into their bosom*], well-directed, so that it strikes to the very centre, to their very heart. — *the reproach wherewith they reproached Thee, Adonay*]. This is a citation from Ps. 89⁵¹· ⁵². — **13.** *So we, Thy people, and the flock of Thy pasture*]. This is a citation from 100³, to get the antithesis to the evil neighbours, in order to gain a proper subject for the final couplet of the original Ps. — *Will give thanks unto Thee ‖ tell Thy praise*], the usual vow for benefits received, — *forever ‖ to all generations*], doubtless in public song in the temple.

1. אלהים] is a gl. not required for sense or measure. — טִמְאוּ] Pi. pf. ‡ טמא vb. Qal *become unclean*, by sacrificing children 106³⁹. Pi. *defile*, religiously in D, H, P, Je., Ez., as here. — שָׂמוּ לְעִיִּים] phr. as Mi. 1⁶ שֹם לְעִי. † עִי n.[m.] *ruin, heap of ruins*, elsw. עיים תהיה Mi. 3¹² = Je. 26¹⁸. — **2.** ‡ נִבְלָה] n.f.

(1) *corpse*, as Je. 7³³ + 6 t. Je., Jos. 8²⁹ (JE) 1 K. 13²² + 10 t. K, Dt. 21²³ 28²⁶ Is. 5²⁵ 26¹⁹ ; (2) *carcass* of animals in Ez., H, P, Dt. 14²¹. — נבש] makes l. too long. It is a gl. — חיתו־ארץ] phr. Gn. 1²⁴ (P), cf. חיתו שדי Ps. 104¹¹, חיתו יער 50¹⁰ 104²⁰. — 3. A series of glosses begins here, chiefly extracts from older writings. — דמם] phr. v.¹⁰ 106³⁸. — סביבות] pl. f. סביב, either prep. as 18¹² 27⁶ 89⁹, or *parts round about, suburbs*, as v.⁴. — 4 = 44¹⁴, only variation היינו for השימנו ; evidently gl. — 5 = 89⁴⁷; variations: האנף for תערר, and קנאתך (69¹⁰) for תבער ; יהוה was impossible in 𝕰 ; evidently gl. — 6–7 = Je. 10²⁵; variations: אל of late style for על; שמלנות, with wider outlook, for משפחות ; and omission of ואכלהו ויכלהו. — אכל] 𝕸 is evidently err. for pl. of 𝕲, 𝕵, 𝕾, 𝕿, and Je. 10²⁵. — 8. לנו is prosaic ; makes l. too long. — ראשנים] pl. ‡ ראשון adj. elsw. ψ 89⁵⁰ as adj. with הסריב ; here dub., either adj. with עונת as *BDB.*, PBV., AV., 𝕲, 𝕵 ; or as subst. *ancestors*, as Dt. 19¹⁴ Lv. 26⁴⁵ (H), 𝕿, RV., Dr., Bä., Now., Kirk., Ehr. — בער] adv. as 69¹⁸ 102³ 143⁷. — [ני דליינו מאר = 142⁷ only 1 pl. vb. for 1 sg.; a gl. — 9. אלהי ישענו v. 12⁶. — על־דבר as Ps 45⁵ Gn. 20¹¹ (E) Ex. 8² (J). — כבור שמך] phr., v. 29². — ותצילנו] Hiph. imv. נצל with ו separating it from previous context in MT. 𝕵 attaches it to subsequent clause. 𝕲 has κύριε ῥῦσαι ἡμᾶς, making it independent of both clauses. — כפר על] as Je. 18²⁸, c. acc. Pss. 65⁴ 78³⁸. — למען שמך] as 23³ 25¹¹ 31⁴; here gl. — 10. למה ... אלהיהם] = 115²; only variation is omission of particle את. — נקמת דם] cstr. obj. *vengeance for*, phr. α.λ., but cf. ני היכל Je. 50²⁸ 51¹¹. — 11. Based on Ps. 102²¹ in the phrs. אנקת אסיר and בני תמירה ; phrs. and † תמותה n.f. not used elsw. The vbs. are different from those of 102²¹: הותר Hiph. imv. ‡ [יתר] vb. *remain over ;* elsw. ψ Niph. *be left over* 106¹¹. — כגדל זריעך] = Ex. 15¹⁶, only כ for ב and ודל for גדל, a variation not owing to an original difference of text. This v. is therefore a mosaic gl., and is without regard to measure. — 12. שכנים] of reproachful neighbouring nations, elsw. ψ, v.⁴ gl. = 44¹⁴, cf. 31¹² 80⁷ 89⁴². — שבעתים] *sevenfold*, as 12⁷ ; used for vengeance Gn. 4¹⁵⁻²⁴, which were prob. in the mind of the writer. — אל־חיקם] of requital, cf. Is. 65⁶⁻⁷ Je. 32¹⁸. — חרפם אשר חרפוך] is a condensation of 89⁵¹⁻⁵²; and אדני also was derived from that passage. — 13 a = 100³ᵇ, except 2 sg. sf. for 3 sg. with both nouns. — נירה לך] Hiph. impf. 1 pl. ידה ; phr. 6⁶ 75² +. — נספר תהלתך] phr. 9¹⁵ 78⁴ Is 43²¹ cf. Ps. 102²².

PSALM LXXX., 5 str. 6³, rf. 2³.

Ps. 80 is a prayer of Israel for a divine advent for salvation, especially in the Rf. (v.⁴·⁸·¹⁵ᵃ·²⁰) ; that the Shepherd of Israel would shine forth before Northern Israel (v.²⁻³) ; remonstrance against long continued anger, while the people in tears were praying and their neighbours were mocking (v.⁵⁻⁷) ; recalling the earlier, more prosperous history in the allegory of the vine (v.⁹⁻¹¹), and then the subsequent oppression by Egypt and the other world powers (v.¹²⁻¹⁴), with a final petition that Yahweh would visit and save this vine, concluding with a vow of worship (v.[15b. 16. 19]). A Maccabean editor appends an imprecation on the enemies (v.[17]), and a Messianic petition (v.[18]).

SHEPHERD of Israel, O give ear.
    Leader of Joseph as a flock,
    Throned upon the Cherubim, O shine forth.
    Before Ephraim and Manasseh,
    O stir up Thy might,
    And O come for salvation to us.
        Yahweh (Sabaoth) restore us,
        And cause Thy face to shine that we may be saved.

YAHWEH Sabaoth, how long
    Dost Thou smoke during the prayer of Thy people ;
    Dost Thou feed them with the bread of tears ;
    And give them to drink (a measure of wormwood) ;
    Make us a strife to our neighbours,
    That our enemies should mock at us?
        Yahweh Sabaoth restore us,
        And cause Thy face to shine that we may be saved.

A VINE out of Egypt thou removest ;
    Thou dravest out the nations, and didst plant her ;
    Thou didst clear (the way) before her,
    So that she took root and filled the land.
    The mountains were covered with her shadow,
    And with her boughs the cedars of God.
        (*Yahweh Sabaoth restore us,*
        And cause Thy face to shine that we may be saved.)

SHE sends forth her branches unto the Sea,
    And unto the River her shoots.
    Why then hast Thou broken down her walls,
    So that all the passers-by may trample her?
    The boar of (the Nile) tears her down ;
    And the beasts of the field graze upon her.
        Yahweh Sabaoth restore us,
        (*And cause Thy face to shine that we may be saved.*)

LOOK down from heaven, and see,
    And visit the vine (Thou didst get),
    The one Thy right hand did plant,
    The son Thou didst make strong for Thyself.
    And we will not draw back from Thee.
    Quicken us, and on Thy name will we call.
        Yahweh Sabaoth restore us,
        And cause Thy face to shine that we may be saved.

Ps. 80 was in 𝔄, then in 𝔐, subsequently in 𝔈 and in 𝔇𝔕, in which latter it received the direction אל־שׁשׁנים עדות (*v.* Intr. §§ [29. 31. 32. 33. 34]). The Ps.

is composed of five trimeter hexastichs, to which is added identical Rfs. This Rf. is absent in part at close of Str. 4 and altogether at close of Str. 3, owing to copyist's abbreviations. There is but one gloss, v.[17-18], from the Maccabean times. There are many features of 𝕬: Yahweh the Shepherd, Israel the flock v[2], as 74[1] 78[52], cf. 79[13] = 100[3]; the use of Joseph for North Israel v.[2], as 77[16] 78[67] 81[6]; the use of הופיע of theophany v.[2], as 50[2]; of עשן for anger v.[5], as 74[1]; of נסע v.[5], as 78[52]; of הגרש גנים v.[9], as 78[55]; of חזיר מיאר v.[14] referring to Egypt, as 78[44]; of שדי זיז v.[14], as 50[11]. There are several special features, as: שליש v.[6], as Is. 40[12]; מרון v.[7], as Je. 15[10]; ארוו אל v.[11] a.λ., cf. הררי אל 36[7]; פנה v.[10], as Is. 40[3] 57[14] 62[10] Mal. 3[1]. The allegory of the Vine v.[9 sq.] is based on Gn. 49[22], especially the use of בן in v.[16]. The divine name יהוה צבאות was prob. due to the warlike character of the Ps. There are three difficult phrases, which would imply a late date if 𝔐 were correct; but all these are errors: (a) אָרוּהָ v.[13], as Ct. 5[1], both passages incorrect. Rd. here אָרוּהָ. (b) יכרסמנה v.[14a] a.λ., error for יהרסנה. (c) כַּנָּה v.[16], marked by enlarged כ as dubious; rd. קנה, a vb. characteristic of 𝕬. The style of the Ps. is classic in syntax and elegant. The Ps. refers to the ruin wrought by the destruction of Jerusalem. It was written in Babylonia under the influence of D and Is.[2]. The gloss, v.[17-18], contains a Maccabean imprecation, the Aramaism כְּסוּחָה, also a Messianic interp. of איש as איש ימינך, cf. Ps. 110[1], and of בן as בן אדם, cf. 8[5].

Str. I. A hexastich, of which l.[1. 3. 5. 6] are syn., l.[2] emphatically qualifies the subj., l.[4] the obj. of the other lines. — **2-3.** *Shepherd of Israel*], endearing epithet of Yahweh from patriarchal times, cf. Gn. 48[15], a favourite term of 𝕬 74[1] 78[52] ‖ *Leader of Joseph as a flock*]. North Israel seems to be prominent in the mind of the poet, as often in 𝕬 77[16] 78[67] 81[6]; emphasized in *before Ephraim and Manasseh*, the two sons of Joseph, and standing for the chief tribes of the North. To this a glossator has added *Benjamin* at the expense of the measure, without propriety, because this tribe belonged with the South; possibly because it was on the north between Judah and Ephraim, and the glossator thought of help for Judah as coming from the North. — *Enthroned upon the Cherubim*], another ancient epithet of Yahweh 1 S. 4[4] 2 S. 6[2]; originally referring to the divine presence on the cherubic slab above the ark, then in the throne room of the temple, and subsequently to the cherubic chariot in theophany Ez. 1[4 sq.], so doubtless here. The vbs. are all syn.: *O give ear* to the petition ‖ *shine forth* in the brilliant light of theophanic presence, cf. 50[2] 94[1]. ‖ *Stir up Thy might*], rouse to activity the might of the divine arm in interposition, to strike down the enemies and vindicate the people, ‖ *O come for salvation for us*, the people being in need of it.

Rf. 4. *Yahweh Sabaoth restore us, and cause Thy face to shine that we may be saved*]. The Rf. was originally identical at the close of each of the five Strs. But copyists omitted it after Str. III., left off the second line after Str. IV., and thereby occasioned a copyist's error in the last word of the first line ; omitted Sabaoth in the first Rf., and by conflation inserted Yahweh in the last Rf. Doubtless in all cases 𝕷 changed an original "Yahweh" as usual into "'Elohim." The petition in all these cases is that Yahweh Sabaoth, the warlike God of the Davidic dynasty, may interpose in war against the enemies of His people ; let His face shine with the light of favour toward them, cf. Nu. 6^{25} Pss. 4^7 31^{17} 67^2 119^{135} ; that they may be saved from their enemies and restored to their former prosperity.

Str. II. 5–7. *How long ?*], belongs to the first line as an emphatic question of remonstrance, enlarged upon in the five specifications that follow, cf. 6^4 90^{13}. A late copyist by conflation of *Elohim* and *Yahweh* has induced Vrss. and interpreters to attach it to the second line, thereby seeming to limit the question to that line and making the subsequent sentences statements of fact. But the style of the Ps. makes it evident that the question extends over the entire Str. — *Dost Thou smoke*], in anger ; the hard breathing of passion resembling smoke going forth from the nostrils, cf. 74^1 Dt. 29^{19}, — *during the prayer of Thy people*], while the people persist in prayer for deliverance. This seems preferable to AV., RV., "against the prayers," or JPSV., "notwithstanding the prayers," although any of these may be justified by the usage of the Heb. prep. — *Dost Thou feed them ‖ give them to drink*], food and drink making up together the daily nourishment of man ; but instead of the proper nourishment their God gives them *the bread of tears*, cf. 42^4 ‖ *a measure of wormwood*]. This latter is a conjectural reading after Je. 8^{14} 9^{14} 23^5 for the text of 𝕳, which, though sustained by Vrss., does not give a good sense ; whether we render "out of tears," conceived as a cup and defined as a tierce in measure, as is most in accordance with Heb. grammar ; or "with tears tierce-wise," the tierce being a very large measure for a drinking vessel. But the conception and construction are alike awkward, and give nothing more than a tautology, strange for a poet whose style is in other respects so ornate. EV⁵. paraphrase and obscure the meaning of the original. According to the view suggested above the " tierce " is an explanatory gloss defining the " measure " of the original. — *Make us a strife to our neighbours*], an object of contention, as Je. 15¹⁰ ; the lesser neighbouring nations disputing among themselves for the possession of the spoils taken from Israel, whether in land or goods. — *That our enemies should mock at us*], at the weakness of Israel in her inability to protect herself from their incursions.

Str. III. Two synth. couplets and a syn. couplet. — **9–11.** *A vine*], emphatic in position ; an allegory of Israel based on Gn. 49²², cf. Ho. 10¹ Is. 5¹⁻⁷ 27²⁻⁶ Je. 2²¹ 12¹⁰ ˢᵠ· — *Out of Egypt Thou removest*], graphic impf., referring to the Exodus from Egypt, cf. Ex. 15²². — *Thou dravest out the nations*], cf. 78⁵⁵, at the conquest of the Holy Land under Caleb and Joshua, and subsequently ; cf. Ex. 15¹³⁻¹⁷ Ps. 44³. — *and didst plant her*], the final result of the previous divine activities. This vb. is constantly used of the establishment of Israel in the Holy Land, even where the image of a tree or vine is not thought of. — *Thou didst clear the way before her*], resuming the first part of v.⁹ᵇ, and explaining the driving out of the nations in accordance with the allegory as the clearing of the ground of all other plants, the removal of stones and all such other things in the soil as the vine-dresser would remove in making a vineyard. — *So that she took root*], resuming the second part of v.⁹ᵇ, continuing the allegory : the vine striking her roots deep in the fertile soil which had been carefully prepared for her. — *and filled the land*], an advance in the thought ; so greatly did the vine flourish that it filled with its growth the entire vineyard, the entire land of Palestine. — *The mountains were covered with her shadow*], a most stupendous growth, an exaggeration of the allegory, not uncommon in Hebrew poetry. The vine has grown so greatly that it has climbed and covered the mountains, and still more *the cedars of God*]. The gigantic cedars of Lebanon, the loftiest of all trees, were covered *with her boughs*]. The branches of the vine climbed these gigantic trees to the very top and covered their great limbs. Thus had Yahweh prospered Israel in ancient times.

Str. IV. Two syn. couplets and an intervening synth. couplet.
— **12–14.** *She sends forth her branches unto the Sea*]. The
Mediterranean Sea on the west is the limit of the extent of Israel,
and so of the branches of the vine that represent her. — *And unto
the River her shoots*], the river Euphrates, the extreme limit of
Israel on the east according to the tradition of the conquests of
David 2 S. 8³ 1 K. 4²⁴. These extreme limits of conquest bring
Israel into conflict with the great nations. On this account this
couplet begins the Str. to prepare the way for the subsequent
disasters. — *Why then hast Thou broken down her walls ?*], resuming the remonstrance of Str. II. in connection with the allegory. The walls probably refer to the limits of the land guarded
by the armies of Israel. They had been defeated on the frontiers
and driven back, and the land was invaded by the enemy. — *So
that all the passers-by may trample her*]. These are doubtless
the neighbouring nations, who usually took advantage of the invasions of Israel by the world powers to get spoil for themselves by
inroads upon the imperilled borders. They trample the vine of
Israel under foot like wild beasts with no thought of the damage
they are doing. — *The boar of the Nile*], the most probable reading, referring then to Egypt, which by incursion so often laid
waste the land ; but the usual reading, " of the wood," the forest,
gives it a more general reference, possibly to the Syrian neighbours. — *the beasts of the field*], possibly the Philistine neighbours.
— *tears her down*], destroys the branches. — *graze upon her*],
using the vineyard as their pasture, and the tender branches of
the vine with its foliage as their food.

Str. V. A single line advances by stairlike parallelism to the
second line, which begins a syn. triplet, the whole concluding with
a syn. couplet. — **15 b–16.** *Look down from heaven and see ‖ and
visit*], resuming the plea for a divine advent of Str. I. — *the vine
‖ the one ‖ the son*], that is, of the vine, as Gn. 49²². — *Thou didst
get*], take to Thyself as Thine own. This is the most probable
reading ; ‖ *Thy right hand did plant ‖ Thou didst make strong for
Thyself*, all resuming the thought of Str. III. But 𝕳 is doubtful,
and Vrss. disagree whether the form כנה is noun or vb., and none
yield a meaning appropriate to the context, or a text of good
measures ; whether with PBV. we paraphrase by " place of the

vineyard," or with AV. think of "the vineyard" itself, or with
RV. "the stock," JPSV. "the stem," all taking it as noun, or
with 𝕲, 𝔍, we regard it as vb. in the sense of "prepare." —
17. A later editor inserts a couplet, reasserting the damage
wrought by the enemies in another form : *She is burned with fire ;
she is cut off*] ; in order to an imprecation : *At the rebuke of
Thy countenance let them perish.* — **18.** The same, or possibly
another editor, thinking to give the Ps. a Messianic significance,
repeats v.[16] in a form which makes it applicable to his purpose :
Let Thy hand be upon the man of Thy right hand], either thinking of Israel as placed at the right hand of God, or more probably of the Messianic king of 110[1]. — So in the parall. *upon the
Son of Man Thou didst make strong for Thyself*]. This probably
refers to the Son of man of 8[5]. — **19.** The original Ps. is here
resumed, the first line depending on v.[15b-16]. — *And we will not
draw back from Thee*], a vow of fidelity, — and a renewed plea :
Quicken us, and on Thy name will we call.

2. נֹהֵג כַּצֹּאן] Qal ptc., nominal force, as רֹעֶה, יֹשֵׁב. The conception of God
as shepherd and of Israel as flock is characteristic of 𝔄 74[1] 78[52], cf. also 79[13]
= 100[3]. — יוֹסֵף] stands for North Israel, as 77[16] 78[67] 81[6]. — יֹשֵׁב הַכְּרוּבִים] as
99[1] Is. 37[16] 1 S. 4[4] 2 S. 6[2]+ ; originally the cherubim of the ark, later of the
innermost room of the temple, still later of the cherubic theophanic throne, so
probably here, as in Ez. 1[4 sq.], cf. Rev. 4[6 sq.]. — הוֹפִיעָה] Hiph. imv. cohort. יפע,
theophanic shining forth, as 50[2] 94[1]. — **3.** וּבִנְיָמִן] makes l. too long, and is in
itself improb., though in all Vrss.; for why should Benjamin be associated
with North Israel, Manasseh, and Ephraim? Possibly it was inserted because
of an association of איש ימינך of v.[18] with Benjamin. — עוֹרְרָה] Polel imv. cohort.
a.λ. ψ, *rouse, incite to activity;* but Qal 7[7] Hiph. 35[23]. — לִישֻׁעָתָה] poetic
lengthened form for euphony, in order to prevent two accents in immediate
sequence ; for יְשׁוּעָה (3[3]) cf. Ges.[90. 2e]. — **4.** אלהים] requires צְבָאוֹת as its complement for measure, as in other Rfs. v.[8. 15. 20]. In v.[20], as v.[5], it is then preceded by יהוה, which, as in 59[6] 84[9], must be regarded as conflation ; for in all
these cases the measure is impaired, and one of the divine names must be
regarded as a gloss. אלהים in all such cases stands for an original יהוה, otherwise it would be אלהי צבאות. — וְהָאֵר] 1 coörd. Hiph. imv. אור, of divine face,
theophany, 4[7] 31[17] 67[2] 119[135]; cf. Nu. 6[25]. — וְנִוָּשֵׁעָה] 1 subord. purpose, Niph.
impf. cohort. — **5.** עַד־מָתַי] belongs with previous context, as the measure
requires after that יהוה is thrown out. — עָשַׁנְתָּ] Qal pf. עשן denom. עָשָׁן *smoke;*
subj. אף 74[1] Dt. 29[19]; here God Himself. The pf. does not state a fact, but
is dependent on עד מתי, as pfs. in all subsequent ll. of Str. — בְּתִפְלַּת]. The
prep. ב is not ב of hostility, as Gr., Bä., Dr., Che., Kirk., AV., RV.; or *in spite*

of, Hu., Du., so JPSV. *notwithstanding*, cf. 78⁸²; but *in*, *during*, as De W., Ew., Hi., De., Pe., cf. PBV., "with thy people that prayeth"; 𝕲, Σ, have ἐπί, 𝖁 *super*, 𝕵 *ad*, but their interp. improb. — **6.** רָחֵם דִּמְעָה] phr. α.λ., but cf. 42⁴. — [וַתַּשְׁקֵמוֹ] ו consec. Hiph. impf. with archaic sf. 3 pl., c. ב as usual with vbs. of drinking. — [דְּמָעוֹת] pl. is dub., especially after דמעה coll. in previous l. We should prob. rd.: בְּמִדַּת לַעֲנָה, *of a measure of wormwood*, cf. Je. 8¹⁴ 9¹⁴ 23¹⁵, the measure being defined by a glossator as שׁלישׁ, a third measure, a tierce; cf. Jb. 28²⁵ for such a use of מדה for liquids. † שלישׁ elsw. Is. 40¹². 𝕲 ἐν μέτρῳ, 𝕵 *tripliciter*. — **7.** [תְּשִׂימֵנוּ] impf.; change of tense to express the habitual condition of the people. — ‡ מָדוֹן n. (1) *strife, contention*, Hb. 1³, elsw. Pr. 15 t.; (2) object of contention, here as Je. 15¹⁰. — [לָמוֹ] ethical dative, *according to their desire;* but 𝕲, 𝕵, לָנוּ is more prob. — **9.** [גֶּפֶן] emph. in position as theme of the allegory, which is based on Gn. 49²². — [תַּסִּיעַ] Hiph. impf. 2 sg. נסע; elsw. ψ, 78⁵², also of removal of Israel from Egypt (cf. Ex. 15²²) and 78²⁶ of God's leading out the wind. — [תְּגָרֵשׁ גּוֹיִם] elsw. ψ, 78⁵⁵. — [וַתִּטָּעֶהָ] ו consec. after impf., emph. change of tense into aorist. — **10.** [פִּנִּיתָ] Pi. pf. *turn away, clear away;* in this sense usually with דֶרֶךְ Is. 40⁸ 57¹⁴ 62¹⁰ Mal. 3¹, so prob. here. The omission of דֶרֶךְ txt. err. — [וַתַּשְׁרֵשׁ שָׁרָשֶׁיהָ] ו consec. Hiph. שׁרשׁ (52⁷); as Is. 27⁶ Jb. 5³, but these without the cognate acc., which is indeed prob. a gl. to get a subj. for תְּמַלֵּא other than God, the subj. of all previous vbs. But the subj. is really גֶּפֶן. This gives us better measure. 𝕳 gives the v. as three dimeters. — **11.** [כֻּסּוּ] Pu. pf. for usual כָּסוּ, כִסָּה (*32¹*). — [צִלָּהּ] (*17⁸*) acc. remote obj. Ges.²⁷³⁽⁵⁾. — [אַרְזֵי אֵל] gigantic cedars of Lebanon, cf. הררי אל 36⁷. The Rf. should come in here. It has been omitted in writing as elsw. (*v.* Intr. § 12.) — **12.** † [קְצִיר] n.m. coll. *boughs*, elsw. Jb. 14⁹ 18¹⁶ 29¹⁹ Is. 27¹¹; late word, ‖ † [יוֹנֶק] n.f. *shoot*, elsw. Ho. 14⁷ Ez. 17²² Jb. 8¹⁶ 14⁷ 15³⁰. — **13.** [וְאָרוּהָ] ו consec. pf., change of tense to get frequentative. † ארה vb. elsw. Ct. 5¹ *pluck, gather*, 𝔅DB; but as Gr., one does not pluck myrrh, but smell it, and he regards Ct. 5¹ txt. err. for הרחתי √רוח *smell*. Gr. suggests עֵרוּהָ after 𝖘, *trample her*. Che. ערוה, *lay her bare*, is not so good. — **14.** [יְכַרְסְמֶנָּה] Pi. impf. † [כִרְסֵם] α.λ. *tear off*, 𝔅DBᵃ, as NH. It is txt. err. for † יְהַרְסֶיהָ *tear down;* so in Niph. of walls of vineyard Pr. 24³¹. — [חֲזִיר] n.m. *swine, boar*, elsw. Dt. 14⁸ = Lv. 11⁷ Is. 65⁴ 66³· ¹⁷ Pr. 11²². — [וְיָעַר] Qr. *forest* (*29⁹*); suspended ע indicates a change of the original text, prob. to get a reference to Rome. The original was doubtless יאר, referring to Egypt as the river swine, cf. 78⁴⁴. — [וְזִיז שָׂדַי] as 50¹¹ (𝔄), referring to other nations. — **15.** The first l. is a relict of the Rf. which belongs here. 𝕲 had הֲשִׁיבֵנוּ here also, for which 𝕳 שׁוּב וְ אִן is copyist's error. The second l. has been left out. — [הַבֵּט מִשָּׁמַיִם] Hiph. imv. נבט; phr. elsw. 33¹⁸ Is. 63¹⁵ La. 1¹¹· ¹² 2²⁰ 5¹. — **16.** [וְכַנָּה]. The enlarged כ indicates here a doubtful reading. 𝕲 καὶ κατάρ-τισαι αὐτήν = Qal imv. sf. כֻּנָּה from כון acc. Ri., De., but this is improb.; rd. rather Polel כּוֹנְנָה. But 𝕵 *radicem*, so 𝖘, 𝕿, take it as noun. 𝔅DB. כַּנָּה n.f. α.λ. *root, stock;* but this again is improb. Gr., Che., Ehr., would rd. גַּנָּה n.f. *enclosure, garden*. As Du. says, גֶּפֶן זאת is improb. in previous line. It is bad measure and bad syntax. It is prob. err. He suggests זוֹר־הִמְנָה. It is easier,

however, to read תִּהְיֶה in accordance with the preference of 𝔄 for קנה. Then
it is improb. that the next l. began with אישר. It should be איש, as in v.[18a];
איש being used as Gn. 15[10]; syn. with בֵּן, of the vine, Gn. 49[22]. — [עֲלֵי־בֵן] has
been assimilated to v.[18b]; in 𝔊 ארם has also been added. The עֲלֵי is correct
after הָיִי יָדְךָ v.[18a], but not before בֵּן there any more than before אישר. This
insertion made the difficulty with the previous word, urging its interpretation
as vb. sq. עַל. — [אְמַצְתָּה] Pi. pf., fully written 2 m. אמץ, cf. 89[22] Is. 44[14]. —
17. [יְשֹׂרְפָה] Qal ptc., cf. *46[10]*, interrupts the thought, is a Maccabean gloss. —
[כְּסוּחָה] Qal ptc. f. † [כסח] vb. Aramaism *cut off,* or *away;* elsw. Is. 33[12] of
thorns. — [יֹאבֵדוּ] Qal juss.; imprecation upon the enemies. — **18.** doublet of
v.[16], interpreting it in the Messianic sense as referring to the royal Messiah;
based on 8[5] 110[1]. — **19.** [וְלֹא נָסוּג] should be two beats, without Makkeph.
Vb. is Qal impf. סוג ‖ נקרא; cf. 53[4] Zp. 1[6].

PSALM LXXXI.

**Ps. 81 is composite : (A) a call to the celebration of the Pass-
over, based on its divine institution at the Exodus (v.[2-6b]);
(B) a paraphrase of the divine words to Israel at the Exodus, as
to deliverance from Egypt (v.[6c-8a]), the fundamental word as to the
exclusive worship of Yahweh (v.[8b. 9a. 10]), rebuke for disobedience
(v.[12-13]), and exhortation to obedience with promise of victory over
enemies (v.[14-15]). Glosses add varied material (v.[8c. 9b. 11ab. 16-17]).**

A. v.[2-6b], 2 STR. 5[3].

Ring out your joy unto God our strength :
    Shout to the God of Jacob.
    Lift up a melody; sound the timbrel,
    The pleasant lyre with the harp,
    Blow the horn on the new moon.
On the full moon, (is) our feast day :
    For it is a statute to Israel,
    A judgment of the God of Jacob,
    A (festival) that He made in Joseph,
    When he went forth from the land of Egypt.

B. v.[6c-8b. 9a. 10. 12-15], 4 STR. 4[3].

A lip unknown was heard (saying) :
    " I have removed from the burden his shoulder;
    His palms from the basket shall go free.
    In distress thou didst call, and I delivered thee.
" I respond to thee in the secret place of thunder :
    ' Hear, my people Israel !
    There shall not be with thee a strange god;
    And thou shalt not worship a foreign god,'

P

> " BUT my people did not hearken to my voice;
>   And Israel would none of me.
>   And so I let them go in the stubbornness of their mind:
>   And they went on in their own counsels.
> " O THAT my people had hearkened unto me!
>   That Israel would walk in my ways!
>   In a little while their enemies I would subdue,
>   And against their adversaries I would turn my hand."

Ps. 81 was in 𝔄, then in 𝔈 and in 𝔇𝔕, in which last it received the direction עַל הַגִּתִּית (v. Intr. §§ 29, 32, 33, 34). It is a composite Ps.; v.²⁻⁶ᵇ has two trimeter pentastichs, and is a call to the celebration of the feast of Passover, composed not earlier than the late Persian or early Greek period. It was in 𝔈 as is shown by divine names, but probably not in 𝔄. This Ps. was prefixed in 𝔈 to an older Ps. of 𝔄, which in its original form had four trimeter tetrastichs, all the words of God to Israel. It seems incomplete at the beginning. The introductory Str. was probably omitted when v.²⁻⁶ᵇ were prefixed. This Ps. shows dependence on D and Je., and therefore cannot be earlier than the late exile. It is a remonstrance with Israel for not hearkening to the divine words in the matter of the exclusive worship of their God. The command v.¹⁰ᵃ is a הק of the type of D, v.¹⁰ᵇ a דבר of the earlier type (v. Br.ᴴᵉˣ· ²⁴³· ²³⁰); אל זר v.¹⁰ = 44²¹; אל נכר v.¹⁰ = Dt. 32¹² Mal. 2¹¹; לא אבה לי v.¹², cf. Is. 1¹⁹ Dt. 13⁹; v.¹³ is dependent on Je. 7²⁴. There are several glosses: (1) v.⁸ᶜ, a reference to the testing of God at the waters of Meribah, cf. Dt. 33⁸; (2) v.¹¹ᵃ, a reference to the preface of the Ten Words, cf. Dt. 5⁶ 20¹; (3) v.¹¹ᵇ, based on v.¹⁷ from Dt. 32¹³· ¹⁴; (4) v.¹⁶, based on Ps. 18⁴⁵, cf. 66³; עָֽתַם, as 31¹⁶. The Ps. in its present form was assigned to the Feast of Tabernacles, because of the reference in its second part to the giving of the Law.

PSALM LXXXI. *A.*

Str. I. is a syn. pentastich. — **2–4** a. *Ring out your joy ‖ shout*], loud, tumultuous expression of joy, as usual at the pilgrim feasts, cf. 47² 66¹. This was accompanied by the *melody* of song and music of instruments: *timbrel . . . lyre . . . harp* and *horn*, cf. 98⁴⁻⁶. — *unto God our strength*], cf. Ex. 15² = Is. 12² = Ps. 118¹⁴ Mi. 5³ Is. 49⁵. — *the God of Jacob*], also v.⁵, as 75¹⁰ 76⁷ 84⁹. — *on the new moon*]. Each new moon was celebrated as a minor feast from very early times, and in later times the ritual prescribed sacrifices appropriate to the occasion Nu. 28¹¹⁻¹⁵; the new moons of the months of Passover and Tabernacles were especially sacred.

Str. II. has introverted parall.: the first and fourth are syn. lines enclosing the syn. second and third, while the fifth line is synth. to the fourth. — **4** *b*. *On the full moon*]. This might be either Passover or Tabernacles. The Jewish tradition is strongly in favour of the latter, and if the Ps. is taken as a whole in its composite form the stress on the giving of the Law in v.$^{9-11}$ certainly favours that opinion and justifies the use of the Ps. on that occasion. But if v.$^{1-6b}$ was originally a separate Ps., it seems more appropriate to the Passover. — *is our feast day*], specifically, as one of the three great pilgrim feasts. — **5-6** *b*. *For it is a statute*], an earlier form of the ‖ *judgment;* both in their original usage, referring to laws given by courts of law, but here in a later and more general sense for religious laws given by God Himself. — *A festival*], so probably in the original, resuming in the climax the feast day rather than " testimony " of MT. which introduces a late term for Law with two earlier ones, and gives a legal climax instead of the more natural festal climax. — *to Israel* ‖ *in Joseph*], as usual in 𝕬, *v*. 8o^2. — *When he went forth from the land of Egypt*], at the Exodus of Israel, designating the time of the institution of the Passover Ex. 12^{37}–13^{10}. This is according to the text of 𝕲, 𝖁, 𝕵, followed by PBV., and is much more natural than 𝕳, which refers to God as subject, whether we think of His going out *against* the land, with JPSV., Dr., Kirk., and most moderns, or " *through* the land," AV., or " *over* the land," RV. The text of 𝕳 was doubtless due to the interpretation of this line in accordance with the subsequent context, whereas 𝕲, 𝖁, 𝕵 more properly connect it with the previous context.

PSALM LXXXI. *B*.

Str. I has a syn. couplet enclosed in lines introductory thereto. — **6** *c*. *A lip unknown was heard*]. This is the most natural interpretation of this difficult passage. Taking the vbs. as ptcs. best explains the interpretation of 𝕲, 𝖁, 𝕵, PBV., as 3d pers., and of 𝕳 followed by AV., RV., as 1st pers., "where I heard a language that I knew not," or "understood not," made more specific in its reference to Israel by JPSV., "then I heard the speech of Him that I had not known." But the use of the 1st pers. sg. for Israel here immediately before its use for God is improbable. It was the lip of their God speaking that Israel heard. Though He had been the God of their fathers, He had not spoken to Israel in Egypt, and was to them a God of whom they had no practical knowledge. They had been accustomed to the speech of the taskmasters; now they hear the word of a redeemer. — This is, then, introductory to the words of God which follow: **7.** *I have removed from the burden his shoulder ‖ His palms from the basket shall go free*]. Israel in Egypt was in bondage under hard taskmasters, requiring them especially to make bricks and carry them in baskets on their shoulders to the great buildings that were in process of erection; cf. Ex. 1^{11-14} 3^{7-9} 5^{4-19} 6^{6-19}. — **8 a.** *In distress thou didst call*], referring to the bitter cries of Israel for help, finally answered by God in the words given above, which may all be summed up in the sentence: *I delivered thee*].

Str. II. Synth. and syn. couplets. — **8 b.** *I respond to thee in the secret place of thunder*], that is, in the theophany at Mount Horeb, when the Ten Words were spoken aloud in connection with a storm of thunder and lightning, cf. Ex. 19–20 Dt. 5. — The remaining lines of the Str. give this response of Yahweh to the call of the people. A glossator adds another response of Yahweh: *I tried thee at the waters of Meribah* (cf. Nu. 20^{13} (P) Dt. 33^8 Ps. 106^{32}), which has no manner of propriety in this context, and, as usual in such cases, impairs the measure. — **9.** *Hear, my people Israel*], words of essential importance to this Ps., as is evident from their repetition in negative form in v.^{12} and as a wish in v.^{14}. A glossator enlarges them by an addition from Ps. 50^7, *and I will testify against thee,* and a conditional clause, *If thou wilt hearken unto me,* neither of which is suited to the context and both of which are against the measure. — **10.** *There shall not be with thee a strange god ‖ And thou shalt not worship a foreign god*]. These are the first and second of the Ten Words, or the two parts of the First Word, as they are differently counted, cf. Ex. 20^{3-6} Dt. 5^{7-10}, without the reasons or specifications, and in the use of the terms of Dt. 32^{12}, cf. Ps. 44^{21} Mal. 2^{11}, limiting Israel to the worship of their own national God to the exclusion of all foreign deities. This was the fundamental religious law. — **11.** A glossator adds the preface of the Ten Words: *I am Yahweh, thy God, who brought thee up out of the land of Egypt;* and also a conditional promise: *Open wide thy mouth and I will fill it;* their God will give to the full extent of the asking.

Str. III. Two syn. couplets. — **12.** *But my people did not hearken to my voice ‖ Israel would none of me*], referring to the historic disobedience of Israel to the divine Law, and their frequent lapses into idolatry prior to the Exile, cf. Is. 1³. — **13.** *And so I let them go ‖ and they went*], in their course of life, their conduct. — *in the stubbornness of their mind*], a phrase elsewhere peculiar to Je. 3¹⁷ 7²⁴ 9¹³ 11⁸ 13¹⁰ 16¹² 18¹² 23¹⁷, or derived from Je. in Dt. 29¹⁸, ‖ *in their own counsels*], cf. Je. 7²³·²⁴; left entirely to themselves, without the guidance of the divine Law or the divine help, to plan out their own life and live in accordance with their own desires.

Str. IV. Two syn. couplets. — **14.** *O that my people had hearkened unto me!*], probably referring to the past; ‖ *That Israel would walk in my ways*], referring to the present. If this divine wish had been fulfilled by His people, then He on His part, in the apodosis, would have continued to deliver them from all enemies and distresses, as He had delivered them from the Egyptians. — **15.** *In a little while their enemies I would subdue ‖ and against their adversaries I would turn my hand*], the hand of God, as often, being lifted up to smite the enemies of His people; cf. Am. 1⁸ Is. 1²⁵.

A later editor, not content with this simple and strong conclusion of the Ps., makes several additions: **16.** *May the haters of Yahweh come cringing unto Him*], as 66³ 2 S. 22⁴⁵ (= Ps. 18⁴⁵). This is probably to be interpreted as a wish of the congregation, and not as a prediction, or as the continuation of the divine word. — *But let their fortune be forever*], that is, the good time of Israel, as 31¹⁶, antith. with the previous line. The form of the vb. is jussive, and it most probably has full jussive force, and is not to be rendered as simple future or to be given the force of "should" of EVˢ. — **17** is a free citation from Dt. 32¹³⁻¹⁴ and probably in the historical form with historical reference: *And He gave them to eat of the fatness of wheat, and from the rock He satisfied them with honey*]. 𝕲, 𝕵, 𝕾 give 3d pers. in both clauses. 𝔋, followed by EVˢ., uses 3d pers. in the first clause and 1st pers. in the second, which is so incongruous that many moderns change the text of the first clause to the 1st pers. in order to make the entire couplet a continuation of the words of God, and accordingly a promise to Israel.

LXXXI. *A.*

2. עוּזֵּנוּ] for עָזְנוּ; cf. Ex. 15^2 = Is. 12^2 = Ps. 118^{14}, Mi. 5^3 Is. 49^5; ⅏ τῷ βοηθῷ ἡμῶν. — **3.** זִמְרָה] *melody* of Psalm, ⅏ ψαλμὸν, v. Intr. § 1. — ‡ תֹּף] n.m. *timbrel,* as Ex. 15^{20} Pss. 149^8 150^4. — נֵבֶל נָעִים] *sweetly sounding lyre,* ⅏ ψαλτήριον τερπνὸν; cf. 2 S. 23^1 (Dr. in *l.c.*). — **4.** שֹׁדֶשׁ] *in the new moon;* not elsw. ψ, but Am. 8^5 Is. 1^{13} Ho. 2^{13} +. — † כֶּסֶה] *full moon;* elsw. Pr. 7^{20}. יוֹם הַכְּסֵא. — לְיוֹם חַגֵּנוּ] ל is interp.; phr. not in ⅏, Ƴ, which interpret it as in apposition with כסה; it is really predicate, beginning a new Str. — **5.** לֵאלֹהֵי] ל of author, as 𝔍, not τῷ θεῷ ⅏. — **6** *ab.* עֵדוּת] term of P for Law 19^8 78^5 119^{14} + 122^4; improb. here; rd., as climax demands, מוֹעֵד. — יְהוֹסֵף] enlarged form of יוֹסֵף Ges.$^{53.q}$. — בְּצֵאתוֹ עַל] so Aq., Σ; but ⅏ ἐκ, 𝔍 *de;* the original prob. without prep., which in both cases is interpretation.

LXXXI. *B.*

𝕖 c. ידעתי אשמע] but ⅏, Ƴ, 𝔍, 𝔖, 3d pers. in both vbs.; prob. all interp. original ptcs. ידע שמע. — **7.** הַסִירוֹתִי] so 𝔖; but ⅏, 𝔍, have 3d pers. here also, prob. both interps. of an original הסיר. — מִשֶּׁכֶל שְׁכְמוֹ] phr. α.λ., † סֵבֶל n.[m.] *load, burden,* elsw. 1 K. 11^{28} Ne. 4^{11}, usually † סִבְלָה] n.f. Ex. 1^{11} $5^{4.5}$ (J) 2^{11} (E) $6^{6.7}$ (P) ; cf. † סֹבֶל] Is. 9^3 10^{27} 14^{25}. — ‡ דּוּר] n.m. *basket* Je. $24^{2.2}$ 2 K. 10^7; elsw. *pot, kettle,* 1 S. 2^{14} 2 Ch. 35^{13} Jb. 41^{12}, the former alone appropriate here. — **8.** וָאֲחַלְּצֶךָּ] ו consec. impf. with strong sf. apodosis ($⅏^5$). — אֶעֱנְךָ] change to graphic historical impf. — בְּסֵתֶר רַעַם] cf. 18^{12}. — † מֵי מְרִיבָה] as Dt. 33^8 Nu. $20^{13.24}$ (P) Ps. 106^{32}; but מֵי מְרִיבַת קְדֵשׁ Nu. 27^{14} Dt. 32^{51} (P) Ez. 48^{28}; cf. Dt. 33^2 Ez. 47^{19}, also Ex. 17^7 (J) Ps. 95^8. — **9.** יִשְׂמַע עַמִּי] ⅏ adds καὶ λαλήσω σοι, and thus makes the v. as far as בך identical with Ps. 50^7. It is doubtless a gl. — **11.** הַרְחֶב פִּיךָ] phr. elsw. Is. 57^4 Ps. 35^{21}, but in different sense. — **13.** † בִּשְׁרִירוּת לִבָּם] phr. elsw. Je. 3^{17} 7^{24} 9^{13} 11^8 13^{10} 16^{12} 18^{12} 23^{17} Dt. 29^{18}. — בְּמוֹעֲצוֹתֵיהֶם] two accents, as 5^{11}; cf. Je. 7^{24}. — **15.** כִּמְעַט] *quickly,* as 2^{12}; cf. 73^2. — אָכְנִיעַ] Hiph. ‡ כנע Niph. *be humbled* 106^{42}. Hiph. *humble,* 107^{12} Is. 25^5 Jb. 40^{12} 2 Ch. 28^{19}; here *subdue,* as 2 S. 8^1 +. — **16.** יהוה] in a Ps. of 𝔄 is a sure indication of a gl. — יְכַחֲשׁוּ לוֹ] phr. 66^3, cf. 2 S. 22^{45} (= prob. Ps. 18^{46}). — וִיהִי] juss.; not final clause, or result, but expression of wish. — עִתָּם] as 31^{16} *their fortune.* — **17.** וַיַּאֲכִילֵהוּ] so ⅏, 𝔍, and other Vrss.; but ‖ אַשְׂבִּיעֶךָ 𝔐 leads many, as Houb., Kau., Bä., to rd. יַאֲכִילְךָ, ו coörd. with 1st pers. But ⅏, Ƴ, 𝔍, rd. 3d pers. also הִשְׂבִּיעֵהוּ, which is most prob. Both go back upon an inf. abs. הִשְׂבִּיעַ without sf. or indication of pers.

PSALM LXXXII., 3 STR. 4^3.

Ps. 82 is didactic and dramatic, representing God Himself in an assembly of rulers, calling the wicked ones to account for their partiality (v.$^{1-2}$), commanding them to do justice to the poor and weak (v.³⁻⁴), and warning them that, although their position is divine, they are but men (v.⁶⁻⁷). A gloss enlarges upon the evil results of their injustice (v.⁵) ; another makes an urgent appeal to God to rise up to judgment (v.⁸).

> GOD doth stand in the assembly of God :
>   In the midst of gods He judgeth :
>   " How long will ye judge iniquitously,
>   And the persons of the wicked respect?
> " JUDGE the feeble and orphan.
>   To the afflicted and destitute do justice.
>   Deliver the feeble and poor ;
>   From the hand of the wicked rescue them.
> " I SAY : ' Though ye are gods,
>   And sons of 'Elyon, all of you ;
>   (Ye) as mankind shall die,
>   And as one of the princes fall.' "

Ps. 82 was in 𝔄, and then taken up into 𝔐 and 𝔈 (v. Intr. §§ 29, 31, 32). It is similar to Ps. 58. The rulers of the nations, among whom Israel was scattered as a poor, weak, and afflicted people, are gods and sons of the Most High in their capacity as governors. They are rebuked by God for their injustice, and threatened with overthrow. The Ps. is probably exilic. It had three trimeter tetrastichs. V.⁵ is a gloss of further explanation of the serious condition of God's people. V.⁸ is an urgent plea for divine interposition. The Ps. is assigned to the third day of the week in ancient Jewish liturgy.

Str. I. Two syn. couplets. — 1. *God doth stand ‖ He judgeth*]. He hath taken His stand and is in the act of giving sentence. — *in the assembly of God*], summoned by God Himself for a judicial session. — *In the midst of gods*], the session is composed of gods ‖ *sons of 'Elyon, all of you* v.⁶ ; they have been acting as judges, and some of them at least have been guilty of gross injustice. These judges are not evil angels, who in later Judaism were regarded as guardians of nations and responsible to God for the misdeeds of the rulers, so 𝔖, cf. Is. 24²¹⁻²². They are not wicked rulers in Israel, 𝔗, cf. Ex. 21⁶ 22⁸·⁹·²⁸. But they are the wicked governors of the nations holding Israel in subjection, cf. Ez. 28¹¹⁻¹⁹. All of these are called gods, because as rulers and judges they reflect the divine majesty of Law and order in government. — 2. *How long will ye judge iniquitously ?*] These judges had for a long time carried on their injustice in the government of the people

of God. God calls them to account with a question which implies a negative answer, that it cannot go on any longer. This
iniquity was especially manifest by their showing *respect* to *the
persons of the wicked*], an injustice expressly forbidden in the
Law and the Prophets Ex. $23^{2.\ 3.\ 6-8}$ Lv. $19^{15.\ 35}$ Dt. 1^{17} 16^{18-19} Mal. 2^9.

Str. II. Syn. tetrastich. — **3-4.** A command in four imvs. : to
judge ǁ do justice in favour of the *feeble, orphan, afflicted, destitute, poor;* probably not individuals so much as the people of
Israel, helpless in the hands of their foreign governors, and accordingly to *deliver ǁ rescue* them *from the hand of the wicked*,
who were taking advantage of their weakness and inability to
defend themselves. — **5.** A glossator states in strong language the
serious results of this injustice : *They do not know ; they understand not*], syn. statements to emphasize the ignorance and blind-
ness of the judges, according to the usual interpretation. But the
injustice of these judges was not the result of ignorance : they
thoroughly understood what they were doing. That interpretation
is due to the failure to discern that this v. is a gloss. It really sets
forth throughout the serious consequences of the injustice to those
who were oppressed. They could not understand it ; *they walk
about in darkness*], not moral, of ignorance ; but of misfortune, as
Is. 8^{22} 50^{10} Pr. 2^{13}. — *All the foundations of the earth are shaken*].
The whole civil order was disturbed, public confidence destroyed,
and all social and commercial relations were unsettled by the
injustice of these governors, cf. 11^3 75^4.

Str. III. Antith. couplets. — **6-7.** *Ye as mankind shall die*],
not as it were sharing the common lot of mankind in eventual
death ; but as ǁ *as one of the princes fall*, by being cast down,
slain by an adversary ; for the death here is evidently a penalty
impending upon these unjust judges from God Himself. This
penalty they could not escape, though exalted in their position as
gods and sons of 'Elyon. They were not really divine, but human.
They were not exalted to be among the immortals. They were
still mortals, subject to the death penalty. — **8.** A later editor,
wishing to make the Ps. suitable for public worship, adds the
petition appropriate at all times : *O arise, O God! O judge the
earth*], a plea that God would do just what He has been represented as doing in the Ps. ; but probably also in the more compre-

hensive sense of a final advent, as in $94^{1\,sq.}$ $96^{10\,sq.}$ 98^9. — *Since Thou wilt take possession of all nations as an inheritance*]. Israel was the special inheritance of God from the most ancient times. But in the universalism of later times, all nations were conceived as under the divine government, subject to His judgment, and having a share also in redemption, cf. Ps. 87 Is. 19.

1. אֵל] so 𝔍, favoured by measure, which requires one accent for עֲרָת־אֵל; but 𝔊 אֵלֶם, Θεῶν is favoured by ‖ אלהים and by בני עליון v.⁶, so Aq. *ἰσχυρῶν*, 𝔖 *angels.* — **3.** דל ויחום]. 𝔊 transposes nouns. — **5.** An expansive gl. — **6.** אני אמרתי] pronoun emph.; but unnecessary, makes l. too long. — בני עליון] phr. *a.λ.* for rulers; but no sound reason against it, that would not equally apply to בני אל or to בני אלהים. — **7.** אֲכֵן] adv. asseveration, cf. 31^{23} 66^{19}; so 𝔍; but 𝔊 אַתֶּם more probable. — **8.** A gl. of petition.

PSALM LXXXIII., 4 STR. 8^3.

Ps. 83 is an urgent invocation of God in the time of Nehemiah, for deliverance from the conspiracy made against Israel by the neighbouring nations with the purpose of exterminating him (v.²⁻⁵), enumerating them to show the extremity of the peril (v.⁶⁻⁹), then imprecating upon them the destruction that God had sent upon the ancient enemies of His people (v.¹⁰⁻¹³), and that which is wrought by the great forces of nature (v.¹⁴⁻¹⁷ᵃ ¹⁸). Glosses make the Ps. more appropriate for public worship by softening the imprecation, making its final purpose the conversion of the nations and the recognition of the God of Israel as the God of all the earth (v.¹⁷ᵇ· ¹⁹).

O GOD, let there be no quiet to Thee;
And be not still, 'El:
For lo! Thine enemies are in uproar,
And those that hate Thee do lift up the head:
Against Thy people they take crafty counsel,
And they conspire together against Thy treasured ones:
" Come, and let us cut them off from being a nation,
That Israel may be remembered no more."
FOR they have consulted with one mind;
Against Thee they make an alliance.
The tents of Edom, and the Ishmaelites,
The (land) of Moab, and the Hagrites,
(The lords of) Ammon, and Amalek,
The Philistines with the dwellers in Tyre;
(Samaria) also is joined with them,
They have become an arm to the sons of Lot.

DO to them as to Sisera,
As to Jabin at the brook Kishon.
Let them be destroyed (as Midian) at En (Harod).
Let them become dung for the ground,
May their nobles become as Oreb and Zeeb,
As Zebah and Zalmunna their princes.
They said: "Let us take it to ourselves for a possession.
Let us enjoy the dwelling-places of God."
O MY God, make them like whirling dust,
As stubble before the wind,
As fire that burneth up the forest,
As flame that setteth ablaze the mountains;
So mayest Thou pursue them with Thy whirlwind,
And with Thy tempest terrify them.
Fill their faces with ignominy,
And let them be confounded forever, and let them perish.

Ps. 83 was one of the Pss. of 𝔄. It was called a שיר, for what reason it is difficult to determine. The term was possibly attached to the Ps. before it was taken up into 𝔄. The Ps. was subsequently in 𝔐 and 𝔈, but not in 𝔇ℜ (*v.* Intr. §§ 24, 29, 31, 32). It is composed of four trimeter octastichs, the first pair in antithesis with the last. The only glosses are at the close of the Ps., v.$^{17b.19}$, in which the divine name יהוה is prominent. In the original Ps. the following words and phrases are noteworthy: אל דמי לך v.^{2}, cf. Is. $62^{6.7}$; יהמיון v.^{3}, as Ps. 46^{7}; ברית כרת v.^{6}, phr. J, E, D, Is. 61^{8} +; אהלי ארום v.^{7}, cf. Hb. 3^{7}; נלוה עם v.^{9} *α.λ.*, elsw. c. אל Gn. 29^{34} (J) +; c. על Nu. $18^{2.4}$ +; דֹּמֶן v.^{11}, elsw. Je. 4 t. 2 K. 9^{37}; נריבים v.^{12}, as Pss. 47^{10} 107^{40} $113^{8.8}$ 118^{9} 146^{3}; נסיכים v.^{12}, as Jos. 13^{21} Mi. 5^{4} Ez. 32^{30}; נאות v.^{13}, as La. 2^{2} Je. 25^{37}; גלגל v.^{14}, as Is. 17^{13}, cf. Ps. 77^{19}; תלהט הרים v.^{15}, as Dt. 32^{22}. The language and phrases are those of the late exile and early Restoration. There are many *α.λ.*: יערימו סוד v.^{4}, צפוניך v.^{4}, נועצו לב אחד v.^{6}, מלא פנים v.^{17}, all graphic and original, without use of late words. The nations mentioned v.$^{7-9}$ are chiefly the neighbours. The most prominent are the sons of Lot, Ammon and Moab. To these were joined Edom, Philistia, and various Arabian peoples. The Arabian peoples are joined, Ishmael to Edom, Hagrites to Moab, Amalekites to Ammon. The names are old ones and general in character. They do not indicate any specific tribe. This is all the more significant that the Midianites are so prominent in the later imprecations. Attached to the Philistines are inhabitants of Tyre. These are also undoubtedly subordinate. A similar reference to the Tyrians as slave-dealers is in Jo. 4^{4-6}. There is no need to think of them in any other relation. The difficulty with the passage is that *Asshur* is called the arm of the sons of Lot. This was in itself impossible at any period of history. The Assyrian army was never at the disposal of the allies as a weapon against Judah. "Asshur" must be an error. While it is possible to suppose that Asshur might stand as the symbol of a great world power or supreme enemy at any later period, whether we think of Persia, Babylonia, or the Greek Syria, yet none of these could ever have been the arm of the sons of Lot. Geshur, suggested by Gr., was never of sufficient importance to be such an arm. Asshur must therefore be a mistake for some other power of intermediate importance. Leaving this for the moment, three chief theories have been proposed to account for the situation: (1) the earlier view is that of the confederation against Jehoshaphat 2 Ch. 20; so De. But while the Moabites and Ammonites seem to have been at the head of this league v.¹, and Edom seems to have belonged to it v.¹⁰·²², and it is probable that they were accompanied by Arabian allies, yet the Philistines and especially the Tyrians are not mentioned, and there is nothing to correspond with the difficult yet important Asshur. Moreover, it is impossible, for other reasons, that the Ps. could be so early. (2) The most common modern view, going back on Theodore of Mopsuestia, Diodorus, Van Til and Bengel, Hi., Ols., Gr., Bä., assigns the Ps. to the time of 1 Mac. 5. While the neighbouring nations were then hostile, yet there was no actual league, and Edom, not the sons of Lot, was the principal. It is true Tyre and Philistia appear, but Asshur finds no suitable explanation; and in other respects the Ps. betrays no evidence of so late a date. (3) The view of Ew., Di., that it belongs to the time of Nehemiah, is best sustained; for Sanballat, a Horonite of Moab, and Tobiah, the Ammonite, are the two chief conspirators. To these were joined Geshem, the Arabian, and Ashdodites (Philistines) Ne. 2¹⁹ 4⁷ 6¹⁻². The Edomites and Tyrians, it is true, are not mentioned; but it is evident from Ob. that they were most hostile at this time, and from Jo. 4⁴⁻⁶ that the Tyrians were slave-dealers, hostile to Judah and greedy to seize them as slaves. The difficult *Asshur* may best be explained after the ancient Theodoret as referring to the Samaritans. It was indeed upon the army of Samaria that Sanballat chiefly relied as his arm against the Jews Ne. 4². The whole situation suits the time of Nehemiah, when he was building up the wall of Jerusalem. The reference to the stories of Ju. 4–5, 7–8, implies a knowledge of the book in essentially its present form, combining J, E, D ; and all this favours the same period. At the same time, the historical sense of the author is the same as that which appears in 𝕬 generally, as intermediate between D and P.

Str. I. A syn. couplet, followed by three syn. couplets in stairlike advance. — **1.** *O God, let there be no quiet to Thee* ‖ *be not still*], emphasized by a gloss, against the measure, *keep not silence;* an importunate plea that God would no longer refrain from interposition on behalf of His people, but immediately act, without a moment's rest, in their behalf, cf. Is. 62¹·⁶·⁷. — **2.** *For lo, Thine enemies* ‖ *those that hate Thee*]. They are the enemies of God Himself as well as of His people ; they hate Him as bitterly as they hate Israel. — *are in uproar*]. They are gathered in a tumultuous, noisy assembly, giving vent to their anger in loud cries. — *do lift up the head*], in arrogant hostility and readiness for aggressive action. —**4**. *They take crafty counsel* ‖ *they conspire together*]. Their gathering is in secret, and they conspire not for open, honourable warfare, but for crafty, treacherous movements, doubtless referring to their intrigues at the court of Persia as well as with disaffected members of the Jewish community. — *against Thy treasured ones*], a phr. a.λ. ‖ *Thy people*, indicating that God watched over them and guarded them as His treasure, cf. 17^8, and in time of trouble kept them safe from their enemies 27^5 31^{21}. — **5**. *Come and let us cut them off from being a nation*]. The enemies propose nothing less than the extermination of Israel as a nation, an extermination so complete that *Israel may be remembered no more*]. They desire that the history of God's people may pass into everlasting oblivion, cf. 9^{6-7}.

Str. II. A syn. couplet, a syn. tetrastich, and a syn. couplet. — **6**. *For they have consulted with one mind*], the most probable reading, enlarged by conflation of two readings in 獇, literally "together with one mind," paraphrased by EV⁸. as "together with one consent." — *they make an alliance*], a treaty of confederacy in war, cf. Ez. 16^{61} 30^5 Ho. 12^2 Ob.⁷; to be preferred to "covenant" of RV., which does not in ordinary usage convey the correct meaning. The nations that took part in this alliance are enumerated in the remaining lines of the Str. — **7**. *The tents of Edom*], poetic phrase for the nation (cf. 78^{51} 120^5), which was so hostile to Judah in its decline and in the entire period of the Restoration, cf. 137^7. Associated with Edom closely were *the Ishmaelites*, a general term for the Bedouin tribes which harassed Judah from the south. It should be remembered that the murderer of Gedaliah Je. $40^{1\text{ sq.}}$ was an Ishmaelite. — *The land of Moab*]. An early copyist omitted "land," or some other such word, at the cost of the measure. Moab was also intensely hostile to Judah. Sanballat, one of the chief enemies of Nehemiah, was probably a Moabite. Associated with Moab were *the Hagrites*, another general name for Arabian tribes, probably conceived as attacking Israel from the region of the lower Jordan. — **8**. *The lords of Ammon*], the most probable original, for which, by copyist's mistake, an enigmatical "Gebal" appears in 獇, with a variant " Naibal " in ⅏, which is not only difficult to explain, but is a departure from the usage in this passage of giving a principal and a subordinate enemy in each line. Tobiah the Ammonite was one of the chief enemies of Nehemiah. — *Amalek*], the ancient enemy of Israel, is attached to Ammon as helping him. It is probably used as another general term for Bedouin tribes; for ancient Amalek was in the South country, and had long ago been practically exterminated. — *The Philistines*], the ancient enemies on the coast of the Mediterranean. The Philistine Ashdod is mentioned as one of the enemies in the time of Nehemiah Ne. 4⁷. With them are associated *the dwellers in Tyre*], probably as slave-dealers, camp followers, cf. Jo. 4⁴⁻⁶. — **9.** *Samaria*]. This seems to have been the original reading here; for it best explains the situation, and is in accord with the history of the times of Nehemiah. The reading " Assyria " of ⅏ cannot be explained in this context, especially in such a subordinate position as is involved in the phrase : *an arm to the sons of Lot*], Sanballat and Tobiah. The army of Samaria was just that upon which these conspirators relied for an attack upon Jerusalem, Ne. 4².

Str. III. A syn. hexastich and a syn. distich. — **10–12.** *Do to them*], imprecation upon the enemies of divine action intensified in : *Let them be destroyed; let them become dung for the ground*], their dead bodies rotting upon the ground and becoming fertilizers of the soil, cf. 2 K. 9³⁷ Je. 8². The author imprecates the same destruction as that which had come on the ancient enemies of his people. — *as to Sisera*], the commander of the army of *Jabin*, king of Hazor, defeated by divine interposition *at the brook Kishon* in the plain of Esdraelon near Megiddo, Ju. 4–5, 1 S. 12⁹. — *As Midian at En Harod*]. Thus the text should be reconstructed in accordance with Ju. 7. A late copyist by error transposed Midian to the first line in v.⁹, in the couplet with Sisera and Jabin, and changed En Harod into the more familiar En-dor, with the result that the destruction of the Midianites is separated from that of the princes of Midian v.¹². It also destroys the measure of two lines, and the parallelism. Moreover, the assigning of two places to the defeat of Sisera and Jabin is altogether improbable, and the mention of En-dor has no historical or geographical propriety. — *as Oreb and Zeeb*], princes of Midian Ju. 7²⁵ Is. 10²⁶. — *As*

Zebah and Zalmunna], kings of Midian Ju. 8[5-21]. — **13**. *They said :*], interpreted as relative clause by ancient copyist, and so the relative was inserted against the measure. It may be interpreted as relative clause without the relative, which is commonly omitted in poetry; but it is more emphatic as an independent sentence. — *Let us take it to ourselves for a possession ‖ Let us enjoy*]. So probably the prosaic sentence of the text should be reconstructed, with the rare vb. " enjoy " instead of the sign of the def. acc. — *the pastures of God*], the entire land being conceived as the pastures of God, where as a shepherd He pastures His people. The reference here is to the confederates of the previous Str. upon whom the imprecation is made in this Str.

Str. IV. Two syn. couplets, enclosing an emblematic tetrastich, all of imprecation. — **14**. *My God*] emphasizing by sf. the personal relation. — *Make them like whirling dust ‖ as stubble before the wind*], cf. Ps. 1[4] 68[3] Is. 17[13] Je. 13[24]. The "wheel" of PBV., AV., though a possible translation, cannot be justified in this context. — **15**. *As fire ‖ as flame*], in syn. parallelism with wind as a destructive agent, — *burneth up the forest ‖ setteth ablaze the mountains*], the forest-clad mountains. — **16**. *So mayest Thou pursue them ‖ terrify them*]. The point of comparison is not the fire and the burning, but the rapidity of the destruction wrought by a forest fire, and so very properly compared with that wrought by *whirlwind ‖ tempest.* — **17–18**. The similes are now explained in the climax : *Fill their faces with ignominy ‖ And let them be confounded forever, and let them perish*], with the shame of defeat, the flight of a panic-stricken army, and the abandonment of their dead upon the battle-field to vultures and jackals. A glossator enlarges this imprecation v.[18] by the insertion of two vbs. frequently used in such connections, cf. 35[26] 40[15] 70[3] 71[24], *let them be ashamed* and *let them be abashed.* A later editor gives another turn to the thought, to make the Ps. more appropriate for public worship, and with a universalistic spirit v.[17b], — *that they may seek Thy name, Yahweh ‖* **19**. *that they may know that it is Thy name alone, Yahweh,* enlarged in 𝔥 by the marginal doublet, *Thou — 'Elyon above all the earth,* cf. 97[9].

2. דְּמִי [אַל־דֳּמִי־לָךְ] n.[m.] *quiet*, as Is. 62⁶·⁷; but 𝔊 τίς ὁμοιωθήσεταί σοι, **Ψ** *quis similis erit tibi*, מִי יִרְמֶה as 89⁷, so 𝔖. 𝔊 must have read מי אלהים. The second מ dittog. of first, or else original and omitted by haplog. The v. is too long for trimeter measure. אל תחרש is prob. interp. gl. — [אֵל] as often in 𝔄. — **3.** [יֶהֱמָיוּן] poetic fuller form; cf. 46⁷. — **4.** [יַעֲרִימוּ סִיד] phr. *a.λ.*, cf. 55¹⁵ † [ערם] vb. *be shrewd, crafty :* Qal 1 S. 23²², Hiph. elsw. 1 S. 23²² Pr. 15⁵ 19²⁵ (all Qal acc. Ges.§ 63. n., Bu.). — [וַיִּתְיָעֲצוּ] ı coörd. Hithp. *conspire against;* *a.λ.* in this form, but for other forms *v.* 16⁷. — [צְפוּנֶיךָ] Qal ptc. pass. צפן ; usually *treasured ones.* 𝔊 קְדֹשֶׁיךָ, so **Ψ**, interpretation ; but Aq., Σ, sg. ; 𝔍 *arcanum tuum*, referring to temple. — **5.** [אָמְרוּ] gl., making l. too long ; usually omitted in poetry. — [וְנַכְחִידֵם] ı coörd. cohort. כחד (40¹¹), as Ex. 23²³ (E) 1 K. 13³⁴ Zc. 11⁸. — [מִגּוֹי] pregnant, מִהְיוֹת גּוֹי, Σ μὴ ὦσιν ἔθνος, cf. Je. 48² Is. 7⁸ 17¹; *v.* Ges. 1¹¹⁹. ³. d. 1. — [שֵׁם־יִשְׂרָאֵל] שֵׁם is gl. of amplification, makes l. too long. עוֹד also is intensification of glossator. — **6.** [נֽוֹעֲצוּ לֵב יַחְדָּו] phr. *a.λ.*, but without לֵב 71¹⁰ Is. 45²¹ Ne. 6⁷. There seems to be a conflation of two readings : the one the usual one, the other with לֵב אחד, which is approved by most moderns, Ols., Dy., Bi., Bä., Now., Du.; the latter, as the unusual phr., is to be preferred to לֵב יחדו, which is not euphonic. — [בְּרִית כרת] phr. of J, E, D, Pss. 50⁵ 89⁴ Je. 11¹⁰ +. — **7.** [אָהֳלֵי אֱדוֹם] poet. phr. for the nation, cf. 78⁵¹ 120⁵. — ‡ [וְיִשְׁמְעֵאלִים], the *Ishmaelites*, a general name for Arabian tribes, cf. Gn. 37²⁵ Ju. 8²⁴. — [מוֹאָב] as 60¹⁰; needs a complementary word for measure, either אהלי as previous l., or עַרְבוֹת Dt. 34¹·⁸ Jos. 13³² +, or ארץ Dt. 1⁵ Ju. 11¹⁵ Je. 48²⁴ +. — ‡ [הַגְרִים] pl. n. pr. gent., elsw. 1 Ch. 5¹⁰·¹⁹·²⁰, a general name for Arabian tribes, from Hagar, mother of Ishmael. — **8.** [גְּבָל] usually n. pr., *a.λ. Gebal*, Gebalene mountainous region south of Dead Sea. But this is improb. with *Ammon*. Three names improb. in l. syn. with ll. where two are used. One name in each of the other ll. is preceded by a noun in cstr. We might rd. here וּנְבוּלֵי ; or after 𝔊 Ναιβὰλ = בני בל or בני בעל, a conflation of בני and בעלי, the latter prob. correct. — ‡ [עֲמָלֵק] n. pr. m. *Amalek*, ancient enemies of Israel, usually in the Negeb Ex. 17⁸ Ju. 3¹³ 1 S. 14⁴⁸ 30¹⁸; used here as a general name for Arabian invaders. — ‡ [פְּלֶשֶׁת] n. pr. terr. *Philistia*, elsw. ψ, 60¹⁰ = 108¹⁰ 87⁴. — [יֹשְׁבֵי צוֹר] prob. restricts צוֹר to some of its inhabitants, the slave-dealers ; cf. Jo. 4⁴⁻⁶. ‡ צוֹר usually צֹר n. pr. loc. *Tyre*, as 45¹³ 87⁴. — **9.** ‡ [אַשּׁוּר] n. pr. terr. *Assyria ;* not elsw. ψ, improb. here. 𝔗 paraphrases by Sennacherib, king of Asshur. At no period of history could Assyria have been regarded as so dependent upon the Ammonites and Moabites. Lag., Gr., rd. וּשְׁאוֹר, as 2 S. 2⁹ (em. txt.), a small territory on Hermon ; but this was too insignificant a place to be regarded as the *arm* of the children of Lot. Ew. thinks of Persia, and Hi., Ols., Du., think of Syria, as nearest Assyria in later times ; but neither Persia nor Syria could ever have been so dependent on Moab and Ammon. Theodoret suggested Samaria. This is most probable, especially if the Ps. belongs to the time of Nehemiah, for it was just the Samaritan army under Sanballat, Ne. 4¹ sq., which could with propriety be called "the arm of the children of Lot." — נִלְוָה [וְנִלְוָה] Niph. pf. ‡ לוה vb. *be joined*, Qal only Ec. 8¹⁵. Niph. either reflexive or passive: c. עָם only here; elsw. c. אֶל Gn. 29³⁴ (J) Is. 56³ Je. 50⁵ Zc. 2¹⁵; c. עַל Nu. 18². ⁴ Is. 14¹ +. — בְּנֵי־לִיט] phr. elsw. Dt. 2⁹. ¹⁹. — **10.** ‡ מִדְיָן] n. pr. m. the tribe, as Is. 9³ Ju. 6–8. — ‡ סִיסְרָא] the commander of the army of Jabin, Ju. 4–5, 1 S. 12⁹. This is here a doublet of ‡ יָבִין, the Canaanitish king of Hazor, Ju. 4. These three names in close proximity make a prose sentence. One of them belongs with v.¹¹ᵃ. It is probable that *Midian* has been brought forward. — † קִישׁוֹן] always נַחַל קִ Ju. 4⁷. ¹³ 5²¹. ²¹ 1 K. 18⁴⁰, river of plain of Esdraelon, modern *Nahr-el-Mukatta*. — **11.** † עֵין־דֹּאר] n. pr. loc., elsw. Jos. 17¹¹ 1 S. 28⁷, a village on the north side of little Hermon. Gr. would change to עין הרד, the place of Midian's defeat. It does not altogether suit the place of the defeat of Sisera. If we attach *Midian* to this clause, and think of עֵין הרד as the place of defeat, the whole becomes clear. We would expect Midian's defeat to precede v.¹², and not to be separated from it by a reference to the defeat of Sisera, which occurred at quite another time. — † דֹּמֶן] n.m. *dung*, always of corpses lying on the ground as offal 2 K. 9³⁷ Je. 8² 9²¹ 16⁴ 25³³. — **12.** שִׁיתֵמוֹ] imv. poet. sf., obj. defined by וּנְדִיבֵמוֹ; but it makes l. too long. Either noun or vb. must be gl.; prob. the latter from v.¹⁴. — נְסִיכֵמוֹ] all n. pr. m., princes of Midian, cf. Ju. 7–8. — צַלְמֻנָּע, זֶבַח, זְאֵב, עֹרֵב v. 26. — כָּל] gl. of intensification. — **13.** אֲשֶׁר אָמְרוּ] makes a prose sentence. אשר gl. This v. in antith. with v.⁵. — נֵאוֹת אֵת] is prosaic and improb.; cannot have two tones. 𝔊 θυσιαστήριον is interp., does not imply a different text. The error is ancient. Rd. וַאֵת נֵאוֹת; נֵאוֹת Niph. 1 pl. † אות vb. only Niph. *consent, agree*, Gn. 34¹⁵. ²². ²³ 2 K. 12⁹; here as NH. *enjoy*. נֵאוֹת pl. cstr. [וֵיר] v. 23². — **14.** אֱלֹהַי] takes the place of אלהים, doubtless original. — גַּלְגַּל] v. 77¹⁹. — † קַשׁ] n.m. *stubble*, as driven by wind; elsw. Is. 40²⁴ 41² Je. 13²⁴. — הִבְעֵר] relative clause. Qal only here trans. c. acc.: rd. Pi. *BDB*. — **16.** וּתְסוּף־ךְ] has two beats; cf. 55⁹. — **17.** מַלֵּא פְנֵיהֶם] phr. α.λ., but cf. יהוה 44¹⁶ 69⁸. — חָלוֹן] v. 38⁸. — is evidence of gl. for the sentence with which it is connected. — יבקשו שמך] phr. α.λ. for ב׳. כ׳ פני. — **18.** וְיִבָּהֲלוּ] coörd. Niph., as 6³. ⁴. ¹¹ 30⁸ 48⁶; for Pi. v.¹⁶ 2⁵. This vb. unusual in imprecations, and prob. original; so also יחפרו and ויאברו. — יֵבֹשׁוּ עֲדֵי] as 92⁸ 132¹². ¹⁴. — יבשו and ויחפרו] glosses, making the v. pentameter. These are usual vbs. of imprecation, cf. 35²⁶ 40¹⁵ 70³ 71²⁴. — **19.** וְיֵדְעוּ] final clause, usually sq. כִּי, as 4⁴ 20⁷ 41¹² 46¹¹ 56¹⁰ 59¹⁴ +. — אַתָּה] was not in 𝔊. It is prob. a variation of שְׁמָךְ. — יהוה] is additional evidence of gl. — עֶלְיוֹן עַל כָּל־הָאָרֶץ] phr. from 97⁹, where כי אתה יהוה appears also.

PSALM LXXXIV., 3 STR. 6⁵, RF. 1⁵.

Ps. 84 is a pilgrim song, composed just before the Exile: (1) longing for the sacred places where Yahweh's praise is continuous (v.²⁻⁵); (2) though the pilgrim band passes through a vale of weeping, it is transformed into blessings as they advance with prayer to the presence of Yahweh (v.⁶⁻¹⁰) ; (3) one day of prostration at the sacred threshold, in love to Yahweh, the Sun and Shield, is to be preferred to an age in the tents of the wicked (v.¹¹⁻¹³).

HOW beloved are Thy tabernacles, Yahweh Sabaoth!
My soul doth long, yea, doth pine for the courts of Yahweh;
Where my mind and my flesh jubilate 'El, the God of my life.
Yea, the bird doth find a home for herself,
And the swallow a nest for herself, where she may lay her young.
At Thy altars, they praise Thee ever, my King and my God.
Yahweh Sabaoth, happy are they that dwell in Thy house!

THE highways are in the minds of those who pass on in the vale of weeping.
He maketh it a place of springs; yea, the early rain clotheth it with blessings.
They go on from battlement to battlement in order to appear before God,
Yahweh in Zion, Yahweh the God of Hosts;
(Saying) "O hear my prayer; O give ear, God of Jacob!
See our shield, and look on the face of Thine anointed."
Yahweh Sabaoth, happy are they whose stronghold is in Thee.

FOR, one day in Thy courts is better than a thousand.
I choose to be prostrated at the threshold of the house of my God.
Better than an age in the tents of the wicked is to love Yahweh;
For a Sun and Shield is Yahweh my God;
Kindness and faithfulness, grace and glory, He giveth.
Yahweh withholdeth not any good thing from them that walk in integrity.
Yahweh Sabaoth, happy are they that trust in Thee.

Ps. 84 was a pilgrim song, resembling the group of שיר המעלות Ps. 120–134; cf. מסלות 𝔊 ἀναβάσεις v.⁶. It was first in 𝕴, then taken up into 𝕱 and 𝔇𝕽, when it received the direction על הגתית (v. Intr. §§ 28, 31, 33, 34). It was not in 𝕰, the selection from which closes with Ps. 83, although אלהים is used v.⁸ for יהוה by attraction to previous אל v.⁹ by error for אלהי 𝔊 ; and v.¹⁰ as late gloss, for the line is just this word too long; so also v.¹² אלהים is prob. for אלהי, which is characteristic of this Ps., cf. v.^{4. 11}. Ps. 84 resembles 42–43, and prob. had the same author The same devotion to worship in the sacred places is manifest, though the latter Ps. was the lament of an exile, the former the song of one who shared in the pilgrim procession v.⁶, cf. 42⁵, and therefore composed before the destruction of the temple. משכנותיך v.² = 43³, cf. 46⁵; מזבח(י) v.⁴ = 43⁴; אל חי (י) v.³ = 42^{3. 9}, cf. 42¹⁰ 43^{2. 3}; יראה אל v.⁸ = 42³; שמש v.¹², cf. אור 43³ 44⁴. Moreover, these Pss. have the same pentameter measure and the same organisation, in three Strs. with Rfs., although the number of lines is not the same. There are also resemblances with other Pss. of 𝕴: אלהי יעקב v.⁹ = 46^{8. 12}; צבאות(אלהי)יהוה v.^{2. 4. 6. 9. 13} = 46^{8. 12} 48⁹; מֶלֶךְ of Yahweh v.⁴ = 44⁵ 47^{3. 7. 8. 9} 48³. מגן prob. of the king v.¹⁰ ‖ משיחך reminds of 89^{19–21}. The psalmist's prayer for his king as the anointed of Yahweh and shield of the nation implies the monarchy as still in existence; and the temple worship, to

Q

which pilgrim bands ascend, implies either the first or the second temple. The two together imply the first temple. There is no sufficient reason to doubt that the Ps. comes from the time of trouble and anxiety (v.[7]) just before the Exile.

Str. I. has two syn. couplets, enclosed by two syn. lines, followed by Rf. — **2.** *How beloved*], the object of strong affectionate love, lovable, " lovely," RV.[m]. The ancient meaning of " amiable " EV[s]. is now practically obsolete. This is as much as to say that the *tabernacles*, the sacred precincts of the temple of *Yahweh Sabaoth*, the God of the battle array of Israel, the God of the covenant and of the dynasty of David (cf. 24[10]) were beloved with a love that was too great for expression. — **3.** Absence from the sacred precincts was intolerable. — *My soul doth long*], emphatic present, with intense desire, so intense that it *doth pine* and wastes away, is consumed, becomes faint and sick in anxious desire, *for the courts of Yahweh*, to which the festal processions were made. — *Where my heart and my flesh*], emphatic in position, the inner and the outer man, cf. 16[9], the body sympathizing with the soul in this worship. Because of the change of tense from pf. to impf. and the attitude of longing of previous lines, it is necessary to interpret this line as a relative clause with a frequentative verb, — *jubilate*], accustomed to take part in the sacred shouting, the roar of the pilgrim bands, cf. 42[5]. — *'El, the God of my life*], as 42[3. 9]: misread by MT. and Vrss. as " unto the living God," which makes unexampled syntax, and a sentence difficult to explain in accordance with the usage of the verb. — **4-6 a.** *Yea, the bird*],

general term, cf. 8[9], which cannot be rightly rendered by " sparrow," EV[s].; the specific term is the *swallow* — *doth find a home* ‖ *nest*], both followed by *for herself*, as the measure requires. The little birds have the free and habitual access to the sacred precincts that the singer so greatly desires. He envies their privilege, and could almost wish he were a bird. As Tristram says: " Still the swallow seeks the temple enclosure at Jerusalem, and the mosque of Omar, as a secure and safe resting-place " (*Nat. Hist. Bible*, p. 206). — *At Thy altars they praise Thee ever*]. The altars are not to be attached to the previous clause, as EV[s]., with the view that the birds had their nests even there, for altars were places for sacrifices made by fire, and not places to which birds would resort. The meaning is hardly to be weakened into "its neigh-bourhood," Kirk. It begins a new line, as the measure requires. Confusion has been made by an ancient copyist, whose eye has transposed to the next line the two words which originally followed here. This gives a proper parallelism. As the birds are ever in the sacred precincts, the singers who sing in the temple Hallels are ever there in continual service. 𝕲, 𝖁, PBV., rightly interpret this phrase; but 𝕳, 𝕴, by mispointing read "still," which is diffi-cult to understand in this context.— *My King and my God*]. The personal relation is emphasized by the sf. The God of Israel is his king, as usual in 𝕽; the temple is His palace. The Rf., as reconstructed, is thus: *Yahweh Sabaoth, happy are they that dwell in Thy house*], those like the birds having constant access there, and like the birds also singing constantly in the sacred Hallels.

Str. II. has one antith. and two synth. couplets. — **6 *b*–7**. An early scribe removed the Rf. of this Str. from its close v.[10b] to the beginning. The Str. should begin with: *The highways are in the minds of those*]. These are the highways leading up to Jerusalem, on which the pilgrim bands go up to the three great pilgrim feasts, Passover, Pentecost, and Tabernacles. These are in the minds of such pilgrims, in accordance with the longing for the divine Pres-ence in Jerusalem of the previous Str. — *who pass on in the vale of weeping*]. On their way to Jerusalem the pilgrim bands pass through a valley. This is interpreted by many as the vale of Baca, unknown, it is true, and yet one so called from the balsam trees which characterised it: "Some dry, cheerless valley," Dr. But all Vrss. interpret the unusual form as equivalent to a similar word meaning "weeping"; reflecting the experience of sorrow in which the pilgrims approach the sacred places, due probably to the perils which threatened them shortly before the Exile. This tempers the joyous prospect and their intense longing. Cf. the vale of Achor Ho. 2[15], and the valley of dense darkness Ps. 23[4]. — *He maketh it*], so 𝕲, with God as subj., which is best suited to context. MT., 𝕴, EV[s]., give the 3d pl., making the pilgrims the subj. — *a place of springs*], carrying on the figure, the refreshing springwater, for the divine presence and favour, satisfying the thirst after God, as 42[2-3]. — *the early rain*], which in the autumn, in Palestine, refreshes the soil, and thus fitly represents the divine favour descending from heaven, cf. Dt. 32^2 2 S. 23^4 Ho. 10^{12}. — *clotheth it with blessings*], so ⑮, ℭ, RV., as a final interpretation of the figure, antith. to " weeping " ; to be preferred to " pools," PBV., AV. — **8–9**. *They go on from battlement to battlement*], as R. Jehuda, AE., Horsley ; from one walled town to another, on account of the peril of the journey, or, coming to the gates of Jerusalem, they pass from one battlement to another, cf. 48^{14}, on their way to the temple, — *in order to appear before God*], cf. 42^3. This is to be preferred to " from strength to strength," EV[s]. after ancient Vrss., becoming more and more invigorated as they approached Zion. The measure requires that the line should close here, the next emphasizing the goal of the journey, the divine Presence, by heaping up terms : *Yahweh in Zion, Yahweh the God of Hosts*. — *O hear my prayer*], cohort. imv., urgent petition in the prayer, which now begins ‖ *O give ear*, terms constantly used in public worship, cf. 4^4 5^2. — *God of Jacob*], phrase of endearment 20^2 $46^{8.\ 12}$ 75^{10} 76^7 $81^{2.\ 5}$ 94^7 Is. 2^3 = Mi. 4^2. — **10**. *See* ‖ *look on*], pregn. with consideration and favour. — *our shield*], the king, as 89^{19}, cf. 47^{10} ‖ *Thine anointed*, cf. 2^2 18^{51} $89^{39.\ 53}$ 132^{10}, the king of the Davidic dynasty. " Shield " is not to be referred here to God, as EV[s]. after ⑮, 𝔍, 𝔖, Aq., Σ, because of v.^{12}, against the parall. The Rf. v.^{6a} should follow, wrongly removed by ancient copyist to the beginning of Str. : *Yahweh Sabaoth, happy are they whose stronghold is in Thee*], cf. 8^3 46^2. The abstr. " strength " of EV[s]. is not so suited to the context.

Str. III. has three syn. couplets. — **11**. *Yea*], intensive, as beginning Str., is better than causal " for," EV[s]. — *one day*], so ⑮, 𝔖, PBV. ; " one " is needed for measure and antith. with *thousand*, though omitted by 𝔐, AV., RV. — *I choose*], pf. emphatic present, deliberate choice, — *to be prostrated at the threshold*], acc. to ⑮, of the humblest position ; more suited to the context than the paraphrase of this unexampled and difficult form, " doorkeeper," EV[s]. — *Better than an age*], interpreting 𝔐 as a usual form, best suited to the context. — *in the tents of the wicked*], as ⑮, to be preferred to the abstr. " wickedness " of MT., 𝔍, EV[s]. The line is defective. We must supply as subj. of sentence, *to love Yahweh*, which, while given in ⑮, is wrongly attached and explained. Thus we get a beautiful syn. parall. with

the prostration at the threshold, and an idea harmonious with v.².
— **12.** *For a Sun*], only here of God ; but cf. "light," as used of
God's face, especially in theophanic or gracious manifestations in
the temple to worshippers 4^7 27^1 36^{10} 43^3 44^4 89^{16}. — *and Shield
is Yahweh my God*], as the God of Hosts, the warlike God, who
defends His people from their enemies, cf. 3^4 7^{11} $18^{3.31.36}$ 28^7 33^{20}
59^{12} +. — *Kindness and faithfulness*], in $\mathfrak{G}$, although misplaced ;
not in 狽, 𝔍, but needed for measure ‖ *grace and glory*, all objects
of the divine benefaction. — *He giveth* ‖ *withholdeth not*], these
favours. — *them that walk in integrity*], cf. 15^2, those in complete
accord with Yahweh in their course of conduct. — **13.** This third
Rf. emphasizes their trust in Yahweh, as the second that Yahweh
was their stronghold, and the first their dwelling in the temple
precincts.

2. יְדִידוֹת] adj. pl. *beloved*, elsw. of persons Dt. 33^{12} Is. $5^{1.1}$ Je. 11^{15} Pss. 60^7
= 108^7 127^2 and שִׁיר ידות *epithalamium*, cf. 45^1 (*v*. Intr. § 24). — **3.** וְגַם]
makes l. too long. $\mathfrak{G}$, 𝔍, ו only. — כָּֽלְתָה] Qal pf. 3 f. כלה *be spent*, in the
sense of *pine*, also 69^4 $119^{81.82.123}$, pfs. for emphatic present. — יְרַנְּנוּ אֶל] phr.
α.λ. c. acc. theme 51^{16} 59^{17} 145^7; c. ב 20^6 33^1 63^8 89^{13} 92^5; c. ל 95^1. אֶל, $\mathfrak{G}$
ἐπί; but prob. dittog. 𝔍 *laudabunt deum*. The impf. is frequentative, im-
plying relative clause. — אֶל חָי] rd. אֶל חַי as $42^{3.9}$, and then measure is complete without אֶל. — **4.** בַּיִת] in $\mathfrak{G}$, followed by לָהּ, better parall. הֵן לָהּ, and
gives better measure. — אֶת־מִזְבְּחֶךָ]. In any case the two tones make l. too
long. אֶת is an interpretative gl. This word begins a new line. By txt. err.
there has been a transp. of יהוה צבאות with עוֹד יְהַלְלוּךָ, destroying Rf. —
5. עוֹד] so 𝔍 *adhuc;* but $\mathfrak{G}$ עַד εἰς τοὺς αἰῶνας τῶν αἰώνων, which better suits
context, especially if transposed to previous l. as the measure and the Rf.
require. — **6.** אַשְׁרֵי] cf. 1^1. אדם here and v.^{13} prob. gl. of interp.; not needed
and injuring measure. It is the Rf. of Str. II. at the beginning instead of at
the end by copyist's misjudgment. — לוֹ] defines rel., which was omitted as
usual in poetry. — מְסִלּוֹת] **α.λ.** ψ, but common in OT. $\mathfrak{G}$ ἀναβάσεις, 𝔙 *ascensi-
ones* = מְעִלּוֹת, Oort, Bä., Du., is tempting, but $\mathfrak{G}$ may paraphrase. — בִּלְבָבָם]
full form; cf. לְבִי v.^{3}; has no sufficient reason and is improb. The double ב is
dittog. as 28^3. $\mathfrak{G}$ ἐν τῇ καρδίᾳ αὐτοῦ, 𝔙 *in corde suo*, suggests that both sfs.
are interp. and not original ; rd. בלב. — **7.** עֹבְרֵי] Qal ptc. as 𝔍, but $\mathfrak{G}$ διέθετο,
though in Pss. elsw. for כרה, may here possibly represent an original עבר —
בְּעֵמֶק הַבָּכָא]. $\mathfrak{G}$ ἐν τῇ κοιλάδι τοῦ κλαυθμῶνος, $\mathfrak{G}$^{N. c. a. A. T} εἰς τὴν κοιλάδα, 𝔙 *in
valle lacrymarum*, 𝔍 *in valle fletus*, so essentially all Vrss. and Mas. = בְּכִי
weeping. *B*DB. thinks of בכא, *balsam*, cf. בכאים 2 S. 5^{24}, and so desert land.
— מַעְיָן] 𝔍 *fontem*, so Aq., Σ, 𝔗, as 74^{15} 81^7 104^{10}; but $\mathfrak{G}$ τόπον; so 𝔙.
מעון *dwelling place*, so Hu., Bä., We., here and 87^7. — יְשִׁיתֻהוּ] 3 pl., so 𝔍 ; but
$\mathfrak{G}$ sg. ὃν ἔθετο, 𝔙 *quem posuit* more prob. — יוֹרֶה] early rain, as Aq.; but $\mathfrak{G}$

ὁ νομοθετῶν, 𝔍 *doctor*, are sustained by 𝔖, Σ, 𝕿, 𝕱, Quinta, Sexta. — [וַיְעַטֵּה]
Hiph. impf. *v.* 71¹³. 𝕲 δώσει prob. paraphrase. — **8.** [מֵחַיִל] so 𝕲 ἐκ δυνάμεως,
𝔍 *de fortitudine*, *B*DB., Du., Dr.; but R. Jehuda in AE., Horsley, Bä., מֵחֵל
from wall or *rampart*, cf. 48¹⁴. — [יֵרָאֶה] *v.* 42³. — [אֶל אֱלֹהִים] so Σ, 𝔍; but 𝕲
ὁ θεὸς τῶν θεῶν = אל אלהים, so 𝔖, 𝕱, Aq., ἰσχυρὸς θεός. Oort, Bä., Du., rd.
אֵל. This is best sustained. Then l. should close with אל, and אלהים for an
original יהוה should begin the next l. — **9.** [יהוה אלהים צבאות] is improb. 𝕲
אלהי צבאות is most prob. The measure requires the three forms, and they
with יהוה בציון constitute a l. — **11.** [מֵאֶרֶף] should precede בחצריך for better
rhythm. The present order of 𝔚 is prosaic. 𝕲 μία, so 𝔖, rd. אחר after יום,
which is indeed needed for measure. — [הִסְתּוֹפֵף] a.λ., Hithp. ספף denom. סף
stand at threshold as guard, or *in service*; 𝕲 παραριπτεῖσθαι, 𝕱, 𝔍, *abjectus*,
seem to imply הסתפח, Hithp. סכה = סרף *prostrate*, Niph. Je. 46¹⁵. Another
word is needed for measure. The original was prob. סף, הסתחף, compressed
into הסתופף. — [מדור] a.λ. Qal inf. † דור *dwell*, as Aram., cf. Gen. 6³, where some
rd. ידור for ידרון, but both Aramaisms and dub., though sustained here by 𝕲
οἰκεῖν, 𝔍 *habitare*, *B*DB., Du., Bä., al. It is better to rd. דור *generation*, *age*.
— [רֶשַׁע] so 𝔍, more prob. concrete רָשָׁע with 𝕲. — **12.** [כִּי שֶׁמֶשׁ וּמָגֵן יהוה אלהים]
so 𝔍, Σ, Aq., but not 𝕲, which had instead ὅτι ἔλεον καὶ ἀλήθειαν ἀγαπᾷ
κύριος, ὁ θεός, so Θ = כי אהב יהוה אלהים חסר ואמת. The ll. are defective in
measure in either case. Both texts are needed. The omission of the l. of 𝔚
by 𝕲 brought חסר ואמת immediately after אהב יהוה, which latter is really
needed to complete v.¹¹ᶜ and give suitable parallelism. Rd. therefore : —

מדור באהלי רשע אהב יהוה
כי שמש ומגן יהוה אלהי
חסר ואמת חן וכבור יתן

PSALM LXXXV., 4 STR. 6³, RF. 2³.

Ps. 85 is a prayer of the congregation of the Restoration :
(1) rehearsing the favour experienced in the past (v.²⁻⁴) ; (2) petition for salvation from present troubles (v.⁶⁻⁸) ; (3) confidence that
salvation is near (v.⁹⁻¹⁰) ; (4) the divine attributes bring salvation
and peace (v.¹¹⁻¹². ¹⁴). The Rf. is an earnest petition that God will
turn from His vexation and save them (v.⁵). V.¹³ is an expansive
gloss.

THOU didst favour Thy land, Yahweh ;
 Thou didst restore the prosperity of Jacob ;
 Thou didst forgive the iniquity of Thy people ;
 Thou didst cover all their sins ;
 Thou didst gather away all Thy rage ;
 Thou didst turn away the heat of Thine anger.
  Turn to us, God of our salvation,
  And remove Thy vexation towards us.

WILT Thou forever be angry against us,
  Draw out Thine anger to all generations?
  Wilt Thou not again quicken us?
  And shall not Thy people be glad in Thee?
  Shew us, Yahweh, Thy kindness;
  And Thy salvation give to us.
      Turn to us, God of our salvation,
      And remove Thy vexation towards us.
WHAT will God speak?
  Verily He will speak peace,
  Unto His people and unto His favoured ones,
  And unto those that turn their heart to Him.
  Surely His salvation is near to them that fear Him,
  That glory may dwell in our land.
      Turn to us, God of our salvation,
      And remove Thy vexation towards us.
KINDNESS and faithfulness are met together,
  Righteousness and peace kiss each other;
  Faithfulness sprouteth forth from the earth,
  And kindness doth look down from heaven;
  Righteousness goeth before Him,
  And peace doth march in His footsteps.
      Turn to us, God of our salvation,
      And remove Thy vexation towards us.

Ps. 85 was in 𝕳, then in 𝕸, and subsequently in 𝔇𝕽 (*v.* Intr. §§ 28, 31, 33) It looks back upon the restoration from exile as long past, v.²⁻⁴; it prays for deliverance from trouble, probably that of the late Persian period, subsequent to Nehemiah. Ps. 85 resembles 44, but the trouble was not so critical. The personification of divine attributes resembles 43³, only the situation is later and better. The language and style are simple and classic: v.² שבות יעקב = Ez. 39²⁵; v.³ כסה חטאה, cf. Ps. 32⁵; v.⁵ כעס of Yahweh, as Dt. 32¹⁹. ²⁷; v.¹¹ נפגשו, as Pr. 22² 29¹³. The Rf. v.⁵ has been omitted, as often in Pss., from all Strs. but one.

Str. I. has three syn. couplets. — **2.** *Thou didst favour Thy land*], bestow favour upon it, the land for the people. — *Jacob*], the term of endearment for the chosen people of Yahweh. The vb. is an aorist and refers to a definite event in the past, probably the rebuilding of Jerusalem by the returned exiles, and those of the survivors in the land, who united with them. The syn. is: *Thou didst restore the prosperity*], cf. 14¹, and not the specific "turned the captivity," restored from exile, although sustained by 𝕲, 𝕵, and other Vrss. — **3.** *Thou didst forgive*], by taking up the iniquity of the people as a burden, and putting it far away from them and from Himself. — *cover*], in the ritual by the cleansing blood of the sin-offering, applied to the divine altars to obliterate the stain of guilt adhering to them. But here, as 32¹, entirely apart from the ritual, the sins are cancelled by the favour of Yahweh. — **4.** *Thou didst gather away*], taking the anger up as something objective to Himself, withdrawing it from the sinful but penitent people, and removing it with the sins. — *turn away the heat of Thine anger*], give it another direction, so that instead of spending it upon His people it will have an opposite purpose. — **5.** The Rf., omitted by later scribes from other Strs. — *Turn to us*], that is, the divine face in favour, as v.²ᵃ. — *remove Thy vexation*], so ⅏, for 𝕳 "break off," which originated here, as 89³⁴, by mistake of a letter; paraphrased by EVˢ. Vexation with the people carries on the idea of the previous rage and heat of anger in a milder form, as applied to the present situation, which the poet conceives as less guilty than that for which the nation had been visited in the great Exile. — *God of our salvation*], the God who had so often saved His people that He could be regarded as having salvation as His characteristic, cf. 18⁴⁷ 24⁵ 25⁵ 27⁹ 65⁶ 79⁹.

Str. II. has two syn. couplets, enclosing a synth. couplet. — **6.** *Draw out Thine anger*], prolong it so that it will extend to all generations, and so intensify the continuance of the anger forever by His own deliberate purpose and sustained effort. The question implies a negative answer, for such a thing was incredible to the people of Yahweh, in view of the past experience of the nation. — **7-8.** *Wilt Thou not again quicken us ?*], the question implying a positive answer; for the "again" is based on previous experience of quickening, that is, the revival of the nation by the impartation of new life and vigour to them. Such a quickening will make His people *glad;* it will be a letting them see His *kindness* and bestowing upon them salvation.

Str. III. has three syn. couplets. — **9.** *Let me hear*], cohort. impf., is the gloss of an impassioned reader, which has crept into the text and brought with it great difficulty of interpretation. It is improb. that 1 sg. would only here take the place of 1 pl. — *What will God speak ?*]. The question is put in order to the emphatic response, *Verily He will speak peace*], not peaceably, in antithesis with vexation and anger, but peace from trouble, in accordance with the previous prayer and the subsequent confidence, v.[11]. Those to whom He speaks so favourably are emphasized in three descriptive phrases : *unto His people, His favoured ones*, and especially *those that turn their heart to Him*, so properly ⅏, 𝔙 ; but 𝔐 by error of transcription so rearranges the letters as to make an entirely different sentence, which is not only difficult Hebrew syntax, but also interrupts the easy flow of thought characteristic of this Ps. It is then variously rendered, either "let them not turn again to folly," AV., RV., or "unto self-confidence," Dr., Kirk. — **10.** *That glory may dwell in our land*], that the glory of the divine theophanic presence may again come to the land, as in ancient times, and dwell as the Shekinah in the Holy of Holies of the temple, the palace of the king Yahweh.

Str. IV. has three syn. couplets. — **11–12, 14.** The divine attributes *kindness and faithfulness* are constantly associated, 25^{10} $40^{11.\ 12}$ 57^4 61^8 115^1 138^2 ; *righteousness and peace*, only associated here, because of the emphasis upon " peace," v.[9], which takes the place of the term "justice," usually coupled with " righteousness." These four attributes are personified as angel messengers of Yahweh, cf. 43^3 89^{15}. They have been on separate missions in different directions. Returning from these missions they all meet in the Holy Land ; the first pair *are met together*. — *Kindness*, which by a copyist's mistake, at an early date, has been replaced by " righteousness," destroying the parallel, *doth look down from heaven*, cf. 36^6, expecting and waiting to meet *faithfulness*, which *sprouteth forth from the earth*, rising toward heaven to meet her sister, the messenger from heaven and the messenger returning from earth coming together as it were midway above the land. The second pair *kiss each other* in affectionate embrace, when they meet ; the one, *righteousness, goeth before Him*, in His advent to His land and people ; the other, *peace, doth march in His footsteps*, in accordance with the parallel. But an early copyist, by attaching ל to the following instead of to the previous word, made an error, followed by all Vrss., which is variously rendered and explained : PBV. " direct his going in the way," AV. " set us in the way of his steps," RV. " make his footsteps a way to walk in," and the like ; no one of which gives an appropriate meaning, or a suitable close to this beautiful and artistic Ps.

13 is a gloss, interrupting the thought and making the Str. so much too long.

> Yea, Yahweh will give prosperity,
> And our land will yield her increase.

The divine attributes will also bring a blessing to the soil of the land. — *Prosperity* ‖ *increase*]. The *land*, fertilized by the divine presence, will *yield* to its owners.

2. רָצִיתָ] pf. aorist; not emphatic present PBV., proper pf. AV., RV., or pluperf. Bä., Dr.; c. acc., as 44⁴ 147¹¹. — שַׁבְתָּ שְׁבוּת] Kt., שבית Qr., *v. 14⁷*. — **4.** חרון אפך] phr. of J (Ex. 32¹² Nu. 25⁴ +) Pss. 69²⁵ 78⁴⁹, also preëxilic prophets, esp. Je.; uncommon in late writers. — הֲשִׁיבוֹתָ מ׳] s.v. preg., supplying *Thyself*, as Dr.; פנים Du., but improb. The usual construction is with acc., אף 78³⁸, also חמה 106²³, מן pers. מ׳ prob. represents an original מֵהֶם, but that makes the l. too long. It was prob. an interpretative gl. 𝕲, 𝔍, take vb. as Qal. It is difficult to explain Hiph. of 𝕳. — **5.** הָפֵר] Hiph. imv. [פרר] *break, violate*, not suited to the context. 𝕲 ἀπόστεψον, so 𝖄, suggest הָסֵר, which was doubtless original here and 89³⁴; so Bi., Du. — כַּעַס] *vexation*, of Yahweh; not elsw. ψ in this sense, but Dt. 32¹⁹·²⁷ 1 K. 15³⁰ 21²² 2 K. 23²⁶. — **7.** הֲלֹא אַתָּה] so 𝔍, 𝕿; but 𝕲 הָאֵל אתה, so 𝖄, assimilation to v.⁹. אתה is a gl., making l. too long. — הָשׁוּב] has auxil. force followed by subord. impf. — **9.** אֶשְׁמְעָה] cohort. impf. I sg., only example in the midst of I pls., is improb. It is not needed for measure and is a gl. of an impassioned, impatient copyist. — הָאֵל יהוה]. 𝕲 inserts ἐν ἐμοί, 𝖄 *in me*, an interp. gl. followed by PBV., possibly influenced by Hb. 2¹. יהוה is a gl., as it makes l. too long. The less common האל is more prob., especially in 𝕳. — וַיְדַבֵּר שָׁלוֹם] phr. a.λ. of peace with God; but cf. 28³ 35²⁰ Je. 9⁷ Est. 10³, not the same as לישלום Gn. 37⁴ (J). — וְאַל יָשׁוּבוּ]. This negative requires juss. form; but it is inappropriate to the context. Aq., Σ, 𝕾, 𝔍, all make it final clause ולא. — † לְכִסְלָה] n.f. *self-confidence*, elsw. Jb. 4⁶; as כסל 49¹⁴, and not *folly, stultitiam* 𝔍, Aq., Σ, omitted by 𝕾. 𝕲 καὶ τοὺς ἐπιστρέφοντας πρὸς αὐτὸν καρδίαν, 𝖄 *et in eos qui convertuntur ad cor* = וְאֵלָיו שָׁבֵי לְבָם לֹה, so Street, Bä., Now., Du., is doubtless correct. 𝕳 has in time of Egyptian Aramaic script mistaken כס for כם and wrongly arranged the letters of the sentence. — **11.** ‡נפגשׁו] Niph. pf., elsw. Pr. 22² 29¹³; Qal *encounter*, not in ψ. — **13.** גַּם יהוה יִתֵּן]. 𝕲 καὶ γὰρ, 𝔍 *sed et*. This additional ideal interrupts the personification of v.¹¹⁻¹²·¹⁴. The v. is doubtless a gl., as it makes the Str. just these two ll. too long. — **14.** וְיָשֵׂם לְדֶרֶךְ] is improb., as it gives no proper parall. Rd. with Dy., We., Du., שָׁלֹם דָּרַךְ. 𝕳 transposes ל by txt. err.

PSALM LXXXVI., 5 STR. 4^4.

Ps. 86 is a prayer composed for public worship in the synagogue, entreating Yahweh to answer His afflicted servant (v.$^{1-2}$), whose prayer continues all day long (v.$^{3-4}$), pleading His goodness in forgiveness and His incomparable works of deliverance (v.$^{5.\ 8.\ 10a}$), asking for instruction (v.$^{11-12}$), and concluding with thanksgiving for deliverance from Sheol and abundant kindness and faithfulness (v.$^{13.\ 15}$). Glosses were added of entreaty for an answer (v.$^{6.\ 7}$), expressing the assurance that all nations would eventually worship Him (v.^{9}), stating the peril from terrible enemies (v.^{14}), and final importunate pleading (v.$^{16-17}$).

INCLINE Thine ear (unto me), Yahweh,
Answer me; for afflicted and poor am I.
O keep my life; for pious am I.
Save Thy servant, who trusteth in Thee.
(O THOU my God)! be gracious to me, O Lord:
For unto Thee I call all the day.
Make glad the soul of Thy servant, O Lord:
For unto Thee I lift up my soul.
YEA, Thou, O Lord, art good and ready to pardon,
And abundant in kindness to all that call upon Thee.
There is none like Thee, and there are none like Thy doings;
For Thou art great and a doer of wonders.
TEACH me Thy way: I will walk in Thy faithfulness.
Let my heart rejoice in fearing Thy name.
I will thank Thee, O Lord, with all my heart;
And I will glorify Thy name (my God), forever.
FOR Thy kindness is great upon me,
And Thou hast delivered me from the nether Sheol;
For Thou, O Lord, art a God compassionate and gracious,
Slow to anger, and abundant in kindness and faithfulness.

Ps. 86 was a תפלה. It was not in 𝔈 or 𝔇ℜ. It is composed of five tetrameter tetrastichs, and is light and graceful in movement. Its phrases are chiefly those of 𝔇, due probably to familiarity with the Davidic Pss. It implies Ex. 15^{11} in v.^{8}, Dt. 32^{22} in v.^{13b}, Ex. 34^{6} in v.^{15}. It shows dependence on Is.^{2} in its use of עבד for Israel v.$^{2.\ 4}$; and on D in its use of לבב v.$^{11.\ 12}$, and of יראה שם v.^{11}. The author was, however, original, and uses several phrases α.λ.: v.^{2} כי חסיד אני; v.^{5} טוב וסלח; v.^{8} אין כמעשיך; v.$^{8.\ 12}$ כבד שם; v.^{13} חסד גדול על. It was composed for public worship in the synagogue, probably after 𝔇 had been edited. It is probable, therefore, that the Ps. was not in 𝔇, but that לדוד in the title, as in Ps. 108, was due to the resemblance of this Ps. to Pss.

of 𝕭. There are several glosses: v.[6], an intense petition in usual terms; v.[7], a statement of habit of prayer and answer; v.[9], an assurance of the ultimate worship of all nations; v.[14], from 54[5]; v.[16–17], a petition based on 116[16].

Str. I. Syn. couplets. — **1–2.** *Incline Thine ear unto me*], as 31[3] 71[2] 102[3] ‖ *answer me*] as usual in prayers; explained by *O keep my life*], as 25[20] from the peril of death, cf. v.[13]. ‖ *save*]. Here as usual the people pray in the 1st pers. sg. in the consciousness of their unity before God. Israel conceives himself to be the *servant* of Yahweh, as in the exilic Isaiah. As such he is *pious* (*v. 4[b]*), and *trusteth in* Yahweh, cf. 4[6] 31[7]; though *afflicted and poor*, cf. 35[10] 37[14] 40[18].

Str. II. Synth. couplets. — **3–4.** *O Thou my God*], displaced in original text and put into previous Str. It emphasizes the personal relation to God by the sf.; intensified by *O Lord*], a characteristic divine name of this Ps., used also v.[4. 5. 12. 15] besides the glosses v.[8. 9]. — *be gracious to me*], a familiar expression, cf. 4[2]; more specifically, — *Make glad the soul of Thy servant*], give the joy of salvation. The people are now engaged in prayer: *For unto Thee I call* ‖ *lift up my soul*], the soul ascending to God in prayer with the uplifted hands, cf. 25[1], and indeed *all the day*, long, continuous pleading.

Str. III. Syn. couplets. — **5.** *Yea*], emphatic assertion of the fact, to be preferred with JPSV. to "for" of EV[s]., giving an additional reason for the pleading. — *Thou art good and ready to pardon*], phr. α.λ.; "good" in the sense of "being good to" His people, and so ‖ *abundant in kindness*, ready to pardon the sins of the people, cf. v.[15] Ex. 34[6] Ps. 103[3]. — **8.** *There is none like Thee*], comparable with Thee, cf. Ex. 15[11]. There can be no other thought than "among the gods" of other nations; but it was not necessary to express this, and the glossator who added it thereby injured the measure. The second half of the tetrastich defines the first half more closely by *there are none like Thy doings*], a phr. original and peculiar to this Ps., but very proper as an introduction to **10 a.** *For Thou art great and a doer of wonders*], cf. Ex. 15[11]. The Ps. asserts at once the kindness of God in the pardon of sin and His greatness in wonders of deliverance of His people in the past. All this belongs together and is strong in its simplicity and historic reference.

Glossators greatly enlarged this Str., breaking into its several lines and interrupting them. — **6.** is a plea for a hearing, in the usual style : *O give ear, Yahweh, unto my prayer ; and O hearken unto the voice of my supplications*, cf. 28² 130². — **7** is an assertion of general experience : *In the day of my trouble I call on Thee, for Thou answerest me*], cf. 17⁶ 77³. — **9** is a universalistic reference to the eventual conversion of the nations : *All nations whom Thou hast made will come and worship before Thee, O Lord, and glorify Thy name*], cf. 22²⁸. — **10 b.** emphatic repetition of v.¹⁰ᶜ as in 𝕲, *Thou, God, alone art great,* or an assertion of the unity of God as 𝕳, " Thou art God alone," so EVˢ.

Str. IV. Two syn. couplets. — **11–12.** *Teach me Thy way*], cf. 27¹¹ ; petition for divine instruction and guidance in the Law, conceived as a way or course of life.   Then the apodosis of imv. : *I will walk in Thy faithfulness*], cf. 26³ ‖ *Let my heart rejoice*], so 𝕲, 𝕾, 𝕿, cf. v.⁴ ; to be preferred to 𝕳, 𝕵, Aq., 𝚺, 𝕿, followed by EVˢ. : " unite my heart," a phr. α.λ. and difficult to explain in this context, — *in fearing Thy name*], the reverential fear of worship, which is associated with songs of praise and rejoicing ; phr. Dt. 28⁵⁸ Ps. 61⁶ 102¹⁶ +. — *So I will thank Thee ‖ I will glorify Thy name*], doubtless in public worship in the temple.

Str. V. Synth. couplets. — **13.** *For Thy kindness is great upon me*], phr. α.λ., but cf. 103¹⁷.   It is conceived not only as great in intensity, 145⁸ Nu. 14¹⁹ ; and in extent, even to heaven, Ps. 57¹¹ 108⁵ ; but here as extending to *nether Sheol,* cf. Dt. 32²², the world below, the abode of the dead, whither Israel as a nation had gone when exiled from the Holy Land.   Divine kindness descended upon him there in order to bring him up thence, so that he may now say : *Thou hast delivered me from* it.   The original Ps. con-cluded with **15**, an emphatic assertion of the kindness and faith-fulness of God in the citation of the classic passage Ex. 34⁶.

A glossator inserts **14** from Ps. 54⁵, in order to show that Israel had been in mortal peril from terrible foes : *O God, the proud rose up against me, and the congregation of the terrible sought my life, and they did not set Thee before them.*   A later editor for liturgical reasons added **16–17** in different measures : *Turn unto me,* cf. 25¹⁶, *and be gracious to me,* resuming v.³ᵃ, — *O give Thy strength ‖ O give salvation,* resuming v.², *to Thy servant ‖ to the* *son of Thine handmaid*, cf. 116¹⁶. — *Make with me a sign for good*], give some assurance that He was good to His people. It is not necessary to think of a miracle or a theophany, which could hardly have been in the mind of the editor of this late passage; but of some practical exhibition of favour in real life, cf. Ezr. 8²² Ne. 5¹⁹ 13³¹. — *that they that hate me may see with shame*], cf. 6¹¹ 35⁴, — *that*], the fact seen, and not " because " of EVˢ., — *Thou, Yahweh, hast helped me and hast comforted me*], cf. Is. 49⁸· ¹³.

1. הַטֵּה אָזְנֶךָ] elsw. of God, abs. 2 K. 19¹⁶ = Is. 37¹⁷ Dn. 9¹⁸; in ψ either sq. ל 17⁶ 88³ 116², or אֶל 31³ 71² 102³; so here, needed for measure, as Du. — יהוה] is doubtless original. — כִּי עָנִי ואביון] phr. 109²²; without כי 35¹⁰ 37¹⁴ 40¹⁸ (= 70⁶) 109¹⁶, all 𝔅, and 74²¹. — **2.** אהה אלהי] makes l. too long; is needed to complete first l. of v.³. — **3.** אֲדֹנָי] characteristic of this Ps., also in v.⁴· ⁵· (⁸)· (⁹)· ¹²· ¹⁵; possibly in original mng. *my Lord ‖ my God.* — **4.** אליך אִשָּׂא נַפְשִׁי] phr. elsw. 25¹ 143⁸, both 𝔅, and Dt. 24¹⁵ +. — ארני] belongs to first l. to complete the measure. — **5.** טוב וְסַלָּח] phr. α.λ. † סַלָּח α.λ. adj. *ready to pardon;* rd. rather ptc. סֹלֵחַ, as 103³. — רַב חֶסֶד] phr. Nu. 14¹⁸ (J) Ne. 9¹⁷ (Qr.) Jo. 2¹³ Jon. 4² Ps. 103⁸, contr. רב הסד ואמת v.¹⁵ Ex. 34⁶ (J, E). — **6.** הַתְחֲנוּנֹתָי] α.λ. for הַתַחֲנוּנִי 28² +. This v. is a trimeter couplet and a gl. — **7** is a gl. of five words, prosaic in form; cf. 17⁶ 77³. — **8.** באלהים ארני] makes l. too long and is a gl., interp. what is plain enough already. — אֵין כְּמֹעֲשֶׂיךָ] phr. α.λ. intensification of אין כמוך, cf. Ex. 15¹¹; מעשה for *deeds* of Yahweh in deliverance and judgment, cf. 33⁴ +. — **9.** וְיִשְׁתַּחֲווּ]. The ו is either coörd. or introduces a final clause. — וִיכַבְּדוּ לִשְׁמֶךָ] cf. v.¹² without ל; elsw. God Himself 22²⁴ 50¹⁵· ²³. This whole v. is a universalistic gl., not suited to the original prayer. — **10.** The last l. in 𝔐 is defective. 𝔊 supplies גדול, but l. is prob. gl. — **11.** יהוה] makes l. too long and is an insertion from 27¹¹, where same phr. is used. — אֲהַלֵּך] apod. of imv. c. באמת, phr. 26³ 1 K. 2⁴ 3⁶ 2 K. 20³ Is. 38³. — יַחֵד] Pi. impf. ‡ יחד *unite*, as Aq., Σ, 𝔗, 𝔍, Bä., Du.; but 𝔊 εὐφρανθήτω = יַחֵד Qal impf.; so 𝔖, 𝔈, Gr., Bi., חדה *rejoice*, as Ex. 18⁹ Jb. 3⁶, Pi. Ps. 21⁷. — לְלֲבָבִי] full form as v.¹²; both doubtless original, as in Pss. 15, 20, 24, 25, 101, 139 (𝔅). — לְיִרְאָה שְׁמֶךָ] Qal inf. with ל, as Dt. 4¹⁰; phr. Pss. 61⁶ 102¹⁶ Dt. 28⁵⁸ Is. 59¹⁹ Mal. 3²⁰ Ne. 1¹¹. — **12.** ארני אלהי] a prosaic copyist has combined these divine names, but one is needed for each l. — **13.** שְׁאוֹל תַּחְתִּיָּה] = Dt. 32²²; cf. ארץ ה׳ Ez. 31¹⁴· ¹⁶· ¹⁸ +, ארץ(ה) תחתיות Pss. 63¹⁰ 139¹⁵. — **14** is a gl. from 54⁵. The only differences are: זדים for זרים, an error; the insertion of ערת; sf. for אלהים. — **15.** אל רחום וחנון] phr., as Ex. 34⁶ (J) Ps. 103⁸, earlier order; the later חנון ורחום 111⁴ 112⁴ ו45⁸ 2 Ch. 30⁹ +. — **16** has three trimeters, and is doubtless a gl. — בֶּן אֲמָתֶךָ] phr. elsw. 116¹⁶. — **17.** אוֹת לְטוֹבָה] phr. α.λ., cf. Gen. 4¹⁵ Jos. 2¹² (J) Jb. 21²⁹. — וְיִרְאוּ] apod., or final clause, or juss., as it is variously explained. — וְיֵבֹשׁוּ] is subordinate to the previous vb., and qualifies it with adverbial force, so that it does not disturb the force of כי, which is the objective *that*, and not the causal *for*.

PSALM LXXXVII., 3 STR. 3⁵.

Ps. 87 is a hymn in praise of Zion. (1) Zion is beloved of
Yahweh and glorious (v.$^{1-3}$); (2) the greater and minor nations
alike become her citizens, she their mother (v.$^{4-5a}$); (3) Yahweh
establisheth her, and all her inhabitants keep festival (v.$^{5b-7}$).

HIS foundations on the sacred mountains Yahweh loveth;
 The gates of Zion more than all the tabernacles of Jacob.
 Glorious things He is speaking of thee, O city of God.
I MAKE mention of Rahab and Babel: This one belongs to them that know me,
 Lo, of Philistia and Tyre: This one was born there;
 And Zion I will name: Mother. Every one was born in her.
AND He establisheth her, 'El, 'Elyon, Yahweh;
 He counteth in the register of peoples: This one was born there.
 They sing as well as dance, all whose dwelling is in Thee.

Ps. 87 was originally a שׁיר, then in 𝔅 and 𝔐 (*v.* Intr. §§ 24, 28, 31). It
is a song of praise of Zion. The love of Yahweh to Zion v.^{1} shows dependence
on Je., Zph. The use of רהב for Egypt v.^{4} is as Is. 30^{7}. The mention of
Babylon v.^{4} implies the Babylonian period; of Philistia and Tyre v.^{4} implies
these as the most prominent neighbours. The city is a glorious place, the
resort of Egyptians and Babylonians alike, and of Tyrians and Philistines.
This implies a peaceful time, such as the early reign of Josiah. The friendliness to the nations resembles Is. 19. There is no internal evidence of late
date.

Str. I. is a synth. triplet. — **1.** *His foundations*], the sacred
city of Yahweh v.^{3}, founded by Him as His dwelling place and
capitol. — *on the sacred mountains*], probably referring to the
several hills on which Jerusalem, like Rome, Constantinople, and
other great cities, was situated ; especially in view of the great
increase of citizens implied in the subsequent context. These
hills are all regarded as sacred because they are parts of the city
made sacred by the divine residence in the temple on one of them,
cf. Je. 3$^{14-18}$ 31$^{38-40}$ Zph. 3$^{8-20}$ (Br.$^{MP.\ 225\ sq.\ 242\ sq.\ 255\ sq.}$). — **2.** *Yahweh
loveth*], the complement of the previous trimeter, making the
pentameter complete, having its direct object in the previous context, as RV.^{m}, and not in the following, although the latter is sustained by 𝔐 and Vrss. ancient and modern. — *The gates of Zion*],
as the public places of concourse, for the city itself ; and so parall.
" foundations " above, and the second complementary object of

the verb " love." These are compared, as the object of the
divine Love, *with all the tabernacles of Jacob*], cf. 78²⁸ ; a poetic
term for the other cities of the Holy Land, which were indeed
loved by Yahweh, but not so much as His royal seat Zion. —
3. *Glorious things*], emphatic in position, the obj., not the subj.,
of vb. ; referring to the predictions of the prophets, especially
Je., Zp., Is.², upon which the poet depends, summed up by himself v.⁴⁻⁷. — *He is speaking*], the passive with indefinite subj., here,
as often in Heb., to be rendered by active in English, referring to
divine words, as in subsequent context, and not to words of men,
repeating to themselves and others these promises.

Str. II. is a syn. triplet. — **4–5** a. *I make mention of*], Yahweh
Himself speaks, calling the roll of those He has enrolled as citizens
of Zion. These are : (*a*) *them that know me*], in the religious
sense of practical acquaintance in worship, and obedience to the
divine Law, cf. 9¹¹ 36¹¹ 79⁶ 91¹⁴ ; (*b*) *those born in her*], not in the
sense of physical descent, but of moral and religious adoption by
Yahweh, so that they are as truly regarded as citizens as those who
were actually born of citizens. This latter phr. is twice repeated
for emphasis in v.⁵ and again in v.⁶. Other nations are here enrolled with Israel as the people of Yahweh, cf. Is. 19¹⁸⁻²⁵. These
are *Rahab*, an emblematic name of Egypt, as Is. 30⁷, conceived as
a monster on account of her oft-repeated devouring of Israel ; and
Babel, the ancient capital of Babylonia on the Euphrates Ps. 137¹·⁸.
Israel, in the time of Josiah, was indeed a little state, separating
these two great warlike powers, both represented by parties in
Jerusalem, struggling for the mastery. — *Lo, of Philistia and Tyre*],
the chief of the minor nations, on the sea-coast of the Mediterranean, the nearest nations to Israel, and in a like situation with
her in relation to the two great world powers. A glossator inserted,
at the expense of the measure, a reference to Cush, a country south
of Egypt. He was probably influenced by Zp. 3¹⁰, whether he
meant to say, " with Cush," 𝔥, 𝔍, or, " people of Cush," 𝔊. But
this nation would go rather with Egypt than with Philistia and
Tyre, and in any case its introduction here destroys the symmetry
of the pairs of nations. — *And Zion I will name : Mother*], so 𝔊,
giving an appropriate climax to the Str., representing Zion as the
mother of these nations, which are born in her as her children ;

carrying on the idea of Je., Zp., Is.², that Zion is the wife of Yahweh and mother of all her pious inhabitants. 𝔐, followed by other Vrss. : " Of Zion it shall be said," is rather tame, especially for a climax.

Str. III. is a synth. triplet. — **5 b.** *And He*], emphatic demonstrative, referring to Yahweh, defined by a heaping up of divine names for emphasis in the complement of the line : 'El, 'Elyon, *Yahweh;* the force of which is lost in 𝔐 and Vrss. by attaching Yahweh to the next line at the expense of the measure of both lines, and by the omission of 'El. — *establisheth her*], the strengthening and enlarging of the city, as 48⁹, in accordance with its importance as the mother of the nations. — **6.** *He counteth in the register of peoples*], resuming the thought of v.⁴⁻⁵ᵃ. The love of Yahweh for His city is so great that He takes a particular interest in each one of its inhabitants, going over each name enrolled in her register and counting it, making, as it were, a census. — **7.** *They sing as well as dance*], Aq., 𝔍, RV.; keeping festival in sacred dances and processions, cf. 30¹² 149³ 150⁴. This is greatly to be preferred to " trumpeters," PBV., or " players on instruments," AV., explaining Heb. vb. as from a different stem, meaning, " playing on the pipe," or less specifically, " making merry," as 𝔊, 𝔙. — *all whose dwelling is in Thee*], after 𝔊, 𝔙, in accordance with the conception of the new birth, enrolment, and citizenship of the previous context. EVˢ., thinking of another Heb. word, render " all my fountains are in Thee," which then must be regarded as the words of the merry-makers, and interpreted as referring to the fountains of salvation, cf. Is. 12³ Ps. 36⁹.

---

1. יְסוּדָתוֹ] *a.λ.* for usual יסוד Mi. 1⁶ Ps. 137⁷; sg., so 𝔍, but 𝔊 pl. θεμέλιοι αὐτοῦ. — **3.** מְדֻבָּר] Pu. ptc. with indef. subj., for active ; 𝔊 ἐλαλήθη, 𝔍 *dicta sunt;* so 𝔊 περὶ σοῦ, 𝔍 *in te;* prob. בָּךְ was originally at the end of l., as v.⁷. — **4.** אַזְכִּיר] Hiph., so 𝔍 ; but 𝔊 αζκΰρ Qal. — † רַהַב] n.m., mythical sea monster 89¹¹ Is. 51⁹ Jb. 9¹³ 26¹², but emblem Egypt Is. 30⁷; so here. — לְיֹדְעָי] as belonging to the class of, with Qal ptc. pl. sf. 1 sg. i.p. A word is missing from measure; prefix יה, as v.⁴ᵇ·⁶. — עַם־זוּ] so 𝔍, Aq., Σ, but 𝔊 עֵם. The phr. in either case is prob. gl. from Zp. 3¹⁰, as it makes l. too long and destroys the symmetry of the two pairs of nations, major and minor. — **5.** וּלְצִיּוֹן] so 𝔍, Aq., Σ, if ‖ לְיֹדְעַי, לְ belonging to ; but this not suited to vb. 𝔊 μήτηρ Σειών, so 𝔏, Aug., Cassiod. = אֵם צִיּוֹן without לְ, is more prob. as suitable climax. The original was אִם צִיּוֹן אמר, אִם being omitted in 𝔐 by haplog., the

R

prep. and impf. vb. being interpretative. Point אָמַר with the mng. *name,* as Gn. 22². ⁸ (E). יהוה is then subj. with Du., as usual in ψ. Bä., Ecker, after Field, Hexapla, think μήτηρ Σειών txt. err. for μὴ τῇ Σειών, 𝖸 *num quid,* but this is improb. 𝕲 attaches first איש to previous vb., the second to the following. This is due to ו between them. If אם is original, ואיש cannot be. Rd. איש־איש. — **6.** בִּכְתֹּב] Qal inf. cstr. with בְּ, so Aq., 𝕿; but 𝕲 ἐν γραφῇ, so Θ, Quinta, 𝕾; 𝕵 *scribens,* so Σ. — יְסַפֵּר] Qal, so 𝕾, 𝕵; but 𝕲 διηγήσεται, Aq., Pi. — **7.** וְשָׁרִים] ptc. pl. Qal √שׁיר *sing;* but 𝕲 λαῶν καὶ ἀρχόντων τούτων τῶν γεγενημένων ἐν αὐτῇ = מילד בה זה ושרים ועמים takes זה as pl., as it does in v.⁴, and ptc. for pf.; בה is assimilation to v.⁵; שָׂרִים *princes, rulers.* But this does not suit the context, and destroys the measure of the entire Str. — חֹלְלִים] 𝕲 εὐφραινομένων, 𝖸 *laetantium,* ptc. pl. √חלל denom. *play the pipe.* But Aq., 𝕵, *in choris* ptc. Polel, √חול *whirl in the dance* Ju. 21²³; so Pe., De., Bä., Dr., Du. — מַעְיָנַי] *my springs,* words of singers, Aq., Σ, 𝕵, Dr., Du.; but 𝕲 κατοικία, 𝖸 *habitatio* = מָעוֹן *dwelling,* without sf., sf. of 𝕸 being, as often, interpretative; 𝕾 מְעֻנַּי *humbled,* cf. Is. 53⁴, improb. = Pu. ptc. עֻנָּה. Hu. מְעַנַּי, Bö. מַעֲנַי Hiph. ptc. are not justified by usage. כל is before a relative clause, the copula and relative being omitted.

PSALM LXXXVIII., 3 STR. 12³.

Ps. 88 is a national lamentation : (1) crying for help from the Sheol into which the nation has been brought by defeat and captivity (v.²⁻⁶) ; (2) expostulation for leaving them in this state of gloom and misery, where they cannot even laud their God (v.¹⁰ᵇ⁻¹¹. ⁷⁻¹⁰ᵃ) ; (3) cry and expostulation, intensified in the extreme peril into which Yahweh's rejection and wrath have brought them (v.¹⁴⁻¹⁹). Glosses were added (v.¹²⁻¹³).

MY God (I cry for help) by day ;
　I cry in the night in Thy sight :
　Let my prayer come before Thee,
　Incline Thine ear unto my yell.
　My soul is sated with evils,
　And at Sheol my life has arrived ;
　I am counted with them that go down to the Pit ;
　I am become a man without (God).
　Among the dead am I as the slain,
　(Who are cast forth) to lie down in the Grave ;
　Whom Thou rememberest no more,
　Seeing that from Thy hand they are cut off.

I CALL upon Thee, Yahweh, every day ;
　I spread forth my palms unto Thee.
　To the dead wilt Thou do wonders ?
　Will the shades rise up to laud Thee ?

Thou hast put me in the Pit below,
In the dark places, in dense darkness.
Upon me Thy wrath hath laid its hand,
And all Thy breakers Thou hast brought upon me.
Thou hast removed mine acquaintances from me;
Thou hast made me an abomination to them.
I am shut up that I cannot come forth;
Mine eye wasteth away by reason of affliction.

UNTO Thee, Yahweh, I cry for help;
And in the morning my prayer goes to meet Thee.
Why, Yahweh, rejectest Thou me?
Hidest Thy face from me?
Afflicted and ready to expire from my youth,
I endure, I am brought low, I am turned backward;
The outbursts of Thy wrath have gone over me,
Thy terrors exterminate me;
They have encompassed me as it were with waters all day long;
They enclosed me about altogether.
Thou hast removed from me mine acquaintances,
Even lover and friend, in the Place of Darkness.

Ps. 88 has a double title: (1) שיר מזמור לבני קרח is prefixed to למנצח against the usage elsewhere. This is an evidence that the Ps. was not derived from 𝕳 by 𝕯𝕽, but that this title was prefixed to 𝕯𝕽. 𝕯𝕽 did not derive the Ps. from 𝕳, and therefore it was not in 𝕳 as that editor knew it. The statement was prefixed by a later editor after 𝕯𝕽, and therefore it must have come into 𝕳 after 𝕯𝕽 used it, or else be a conjectural mistake (v. Intr. §§ 28, 33). The Ps. differs from the style of 𝕳 so much that internal evidence favours the opinion that the statement is incorrect. The original title ascribes the Ps. to *Heman, the Ezrahite*, להימן האזרחי, with which we may compare לאיתן האזרחי Ps. 89. Both are משכילים. Ps. 88 was taken up into 𝕯𝕽, and the musical direction given על מחלת לענות (v. Intr. §§ 26, 30, 34). Heman is mentioned among the חכמים of Solomon 1 K. 5¹¹ (4³¹), but he is there classed with Calcol and Darda as בני מחול, Ethan alone being האזרחי. 1 Ch. 2⁶, however, gives Zimri, Ethan, Heman, Calcol, and Darda as five בני זרח of the tribe of Judah. But in 1 Ch. 6¹⁸ ˢᑫ˙ ⁽³³ ˢᑫ˙⁾ 15¹⁷˙ ¹⁹ Heman, of the family of Kohath, Asaph, of the family of Gershom, Ethan, of the family of Merari, were all Korahites of the tribe of Levi. According to 1 Ch. 25⁵ Heman was the king's seer. It is evident that the title of this Ps. is independent of the statement of 1 K. 5¹¹, and is in accord with the later Chr. The Ps. could not have been written either by the sage or the singer. The author probably used the name of the ancient worthy as a pseudonym, just as Ethan is used in 89 and Moses in 90. There are so many resemblances with Jb. that De. thought of a common author. But these are more numerous than striking, and due largely to a common theme. V.⁶ חפשׁי, cf. Jb. 3¹⁹, but dubious in Ps. and prob. error for נפשׁי; v.¹⁰ ראב vb., cf. דאבה n. Jb. 41¹⁴ a.λ., but vb. Je. 31¹²˙ ²⁵; v.¹¹ רפאים, Jb. 26⁵, but also Is. 14⁹ Pr. 2¹⁸ +; v.¹² אבדון,

Jb. 26⁸ 28²² 31¹², elsw. Pr., but this v. is a gloss ; v.¹⁶ חֲנֻנֵּר, cf. Jb. 33²⁵ 36¹⁴, elsw. Pr. 29²¹, not necessarily original in Jb., an easy substitute for נעָרים ; v.¹⁶ אֵמֶיךָ, cf. Jb. 20²⁵, but 𝕲 אמץ more probable ; v.¹⁷ בעָת, cf. Jb. 6⁴ 7¹⁴, but also Ps. 18⁵. The evidence for common author or dependence is insufficient. On the other hand, v.⁵ יורד בור is phr. of Ez.; v.⁶, cf. Is. 14¹⁹; נגזרו, cf. Is. 53⁸; v.⁷ בור החתיות = La. 3⁵⁵ ; v.⁷˙ ¹⁹ מחשכ(ים), cf. La. 3⁶; v.¹⁹ אהב ורע = Ps. 38¹². The resemblance is chiefly with exilic Lit. The Ps. is best explained as a national lament during the extreme distress of the Exile, and it resembles 22, 69, of 𝔅 in situation. This is the view of 𝔖, 𝔗, Theodore of Mopsuestia, Ra., Ki., De W., Bä.

Str. I. has three tetrastichs, the first syn., the second introverted, the third syn. pairs. — **2–3.** *My God*], the personal relation to God is the strongest plea, intensified by the gloss " Yahweh," the name of the national God, making the the line too long, — *I cry for help*], so by emendation of a phr. α.λ. in accord with v.¹⁴, and ‖ *I cry*, defined by *my prayer* and intensified in *my yell*, the shrill, piercing cry expressive of intense anxiety and pain, cf. 17¹. This continues *by day* and *in the night*], all the time, continually, without ceasing, cf. 22³. The prayer is made in the sight of Yahweh so far as the people in their exile can come in front of His heavenly throne, seeking by every means to attract His attention ; while they feel that something obstructs the way of their prayer in its ascent *before* God. This they would have removed, so that He will look upon their evil situation, and *incline the ear* to hear them, cf. 17⁶. — **4–5.** *Sated with evils*]. Misfortunes, calamities, have come upon them in such numbers, and to so great an extent, that they have had more than enough, more than they are able to endure. — *I am become a man without God*], in a helpless condition, with no God to help. — *At Sheol*], emphatic in position, the abode of the dead, even of nations, cf. 9¹⁸, — *my life has arrived*], having made the journey toward it and actually arrived there. — *them that go down to the Pit*], descending in death to the abode of the dead, and going still further down into the Pit, in Sheol, the abode of the wretched dead, cf. 28¹ 30⁴ 143⁷. They were already *counted*, or enumerated, among such, as if they were among the dead. — **6.** *I*], " my soul," so Du., Dr., as v.⁴ᵃ. 𝕳, though sustained by 𝕲, 𝕵, " Free among the dead," PBV., AV., does not suit the context ; and the phr., " cast off among the dead," RV., cannot be sustained by the etym. or usage of the Heb. word. The exiles in the Sheol of captivity and national death were in a condition the reverse of free. — *as the slain*], connected with the previous context as the measure requires, and not with the subsequent, as EV⁸. The slain are those slain in the warfare that resulted in the capture of Jerusalem and the slaughter or captivity of its inhabitants. Cf. Ez. 37 for the working out of this symbolism. — *Who are cast forth*], so 𝕲; unfortunately omitted in 𝔐, but needed for the measure : cf. Is. 14¹⁹ Je. 14¹⁶. — *lie down in the grave*], as the climax of the description, cf. Ez. 32²¹⁻²³. In this condition of national death and burial, the most heartrending reflection is : absence from their God. On the one side it seems as if He *remembereth no more*, has utterly forgotten them, cf. v.¹⁵ ; and on the other that His people *are cut off* from Him, so that they can no longer reach Him ; and especially from His *hand*, the putting forth of which has so often given the nation victory and salvation in the past.

Str. II. has also three tetrastichs, the first of which, v.¹⁰ᵇ⁻¹¹, has been transposed after the second and third, v.⁷⁻¹⁰ᵃ, all having two syn. couplets. — **10 b**. *I call upon Thee, Yahweh, every day*], renewing the plea of v.². ‖ *I spread forth my palms*], extend the open hand upward in order to receive, a gesture of prayer especially in the form of invocation, petition, or intercession, cf. La. 3⁴¹ Pss. 44²¹ 63⁵ 119⁴⁸ 141². — **11**. *To the dead*], emphatic in position, ‖ *the shades*, the ghosts of the dead, having a weak existence, a shadowy reflection of their former life, cf. Is. 14⁹ 26¹⁴·¹⁹. — *Wilt Thou do wonders*], not resurrection, as most interpreters, but divine acts of judgment upon enemies and redemption of His people. Such marvels had been wrought often enough in the history of Israel, cf. Ex. 15¹¹ Is. 25¹ Pss. 77¹⁵ 78¹² ; but to a nation having national existence in their own land. But how can such wonders be wrought for a nation already dead and buried? This is what presses upon the poet's mind. He apparently knows not, or has forgotten, Ez. 37, and certainly has never heard of Is. 26¹⁹. On the other hand the disembodied shades cannot *rise up to laud* Yahweh. The conception here is the same as Is. 38¹⁸ Ps. 6⁶, that in Sheol the worship of Yahweh ceases, and so also in the Sheol of national exile. This does not mean that prayer and

praise of a personal kind are impossible ; the Ps. itself is a prayer ;
but that national worship in the ritual of the temple can no longer
be carried on. The dead could not render that worship in Sheol.
How can they rise up in resurrection so that they may do it?
This poet longs for a speedy restoration, because he seems to
imply a negative answer to his question, and to suggest that if the
nation really dies, a national resurrection is not to be thought of.
And yet this was exactly what later poets learned to be the purpose of their God. — **7**. *Thou hast put me*]. Although the calamity had come upon the nation through their enemies, the proud
and all-powerful Babylonians, yet these were but the instruments
for executing the divine Will. — *in the Pit below*], in the extreme
depths of the cavernous underworld, the Pit in Sheol emphasized
as La. 3^{55} Ez. 26^{20} 31^{14} 32^{18}, doubtless at the basis of the bottomless
Pit of Rev. 9^1 11^7 17^8 20^1. — *in dense darkness*]. The original
meaning of a Heb. word, rendered here by 𝕲, 𝕾, 𝖁, "shadow of
death," owing to a misinterpretation of the form (*v.* 23^4). 𝕳, 𝕵,
EV^s., "in the deeps," is based upon another Heb. word, due to a
copyist's transposition of letters, which can only be understood of
subterranean waters ; possibly due to an assimilation to v.^{6b}. —
8. *Upon me Thy wrath hath laid its hand*]. Wrath is personified
here, as the divine attributes elsewhere, cf. 85^{11-14}, and as such lays
its hand upon the nation. The usual interpretation of the vb. as
intransitive "lieth hard upon," EV^s., is not justified by usage. —
And all Thy breakers], fig. of troubles, cf. 42^8. Yahweh's because
these troubles came from Him. — *Thou hast brought*], as 𝕲, 𝕾,
𝖁. 𝕳, 𝕵, Aq., Σ, follow another Heb. word, which is difficult to
explain in the context, AV., RV., "afflicted me with all Thy
waves." — **9**. *Thou hast removed mine acquaintances from me*].
These were the friendly nations, as 31^{12}. The phr. does not imply personal relations between individuals. In exile, Israel was
widely separated from his friendly neighbours as well as from the hostile ones. — *an abomination to them*]. This does not imply, either
in figure or reality, a loathsome disease ; but national calamities
so great that even the friendly nations could only look upon Israel
with abhorrence, dreading and fearing a share in his misfortunes,
cf. 31^{12}. — *I am shut up*], in the dungeon of captivity, as 𝕿, cf.
Je. 32^{2-3}, involving also the figure of Sheol, from which it was im-

possible to *come forth*, to escape, cf. La. 3⁷. — **10** *a*. Because of this terrible situation *Mine eye wasteth away by reason of affliction*], that is, by continual weeping, cf. 6⁷.

A later editor inserted a pentameter and two trimeters to amplify this idea, v.¹²⁻¹³.

> Shall Thy kindness be recounted in the Grave, Thy faithfulness in Abaddon ?
> Shall Thy wonders be known in the Dark Place ;
> Or Thy righteous acts in the Land of Forgetfulness ?

The realm of the dead is described in four syn. terms : (1) *Grave*, as the place of entombment ; (2) *Abaddon*, a term elsewhere WL. as a syn. of " Pit," usually incorrectly rendered in EVˢ. as abstract, " destruction " ; it refers to that part of Sheol in which the wicked go to utter ruin ; (3) *the Dark Place*, as v.⁷, La. 3⁶, referring to the darkness and gloom which characterise this subterranean, cavernous region ; (4) *Land of Forgetfulness*, a poetic term unknown elsewhere, suggesting probably that the dead were forgotten by the dwellers upon earth and also by God, as v.⁶, rather than that they are forgetful of their life in this world, Jb. 14²¹. This editor questions whether the divine attributes *kindness* and *faithfulness*, as expressed in *wonders* and *righteous acts*, shall be made known in this realm of the dead, implying a negative answer.

Str. III. has three tetrastichs, each of two syn. couplets. — **14.** *Unto Thee, Yahweh*], repeating essentially v.². The editor inserted " as for me," making the line too long ; not suitable to the context after v.⁹, but made necessary by its present position after v.¹³. — *my prayer goes to meet Thee*], a stronger and richer expression than v.³, with personification of the prayer, which is represented as going forth on a journey to meet Yahweh, who is conceived as on His way. This is followed by strong expostulation : **15.** *Why rejectest Thou me ?*], cf. 43² 44²⁴ 89³⁹. The nation cannot understand the reason for this continuation of rejection. — *Hidest Thy face*], as 13² 22²⁵ 27⁹ 69¹⁸, so as not to see. — **16.** *Afflicted and ready to expire*]. So severe was the affliction that the nation had been for a long time on the brink of death, and was now virtually already dead, as in the previous context. Only the poet conceives this situation as having a long history back of it. It extended even to the early history of the nation, from its *youth*. The author probably had in mind Dt. 26⁵. In fact, Israel always had been a small and weak nation, in constant peril from the great world powers. But by the wondrous deliverances wrought by Yahweh, it had escaped utter ruin again and again. The climax had now been reached in the Exile. This cannot be explained to suit a reference of the Ps. to an individual sufferer, and so many unsuccessful emendations have been suggested, without help from ancient Vrss. — *I endure, I am brought low, I am turned backward*]; three vbs. in accordance with 𝕲, 𝔙, 𝔖, although they interpret the first as in antithesis with the other two, and translate it " exalted." 𝔐, followed by EVˢ., interprets the second word as a noun, the object of the first vb., " terrors," and the third word as another vb., a.λ., which is rendered " distracted," AV., RV., " benumbed," 𝐵DB., but without sufficient evidence. — **17**. *The outbursts of Thy wrath*], phr. a.λ., but which in accordance with usage of pl. must mean wrath in action in several manifestations or acts, probably renewing the figure of the breakers, v.⁸; cf. v.¹⁸. — *Thy terrors exterminate me*], a phr. a.λ.; but both words, though unusual, sufficiently evident in meaning. The nation is indeed in terror, and on the brink of extermination. — **18**. *They have encompassed ‖ enclosed me*]. These outbursts of wrath are like *waters ‖ terrors*; in time, *all day long*, and in place, *altogether;* so that from every point of view the situation is extremely critical. — **19**. The first line is identical with v.⁹ᵃ in the corrected text. 𝔐 has, by error of transposition, separated *lover* from *friend*, the two belonging together, as 38¹², and emphasizing *acquaintances*. These are all, as v.⁹ᵃ, friendly nations. — *In the Place of darkness*], a local accusative indicating the place of the nation, in exile as v.⁷, and not of the other nations, as AV. Ancient Vrss. give various other explanations, which are, however, unsatisfactory.

2. יהוה] is gl., as 𝕲 v.³. It makes l. too long. — אלהי ישועתי] pl. a.λ. Rd. שִׁוַּעְתִּי, as v.¹⁴ᵃ. The initial י is dittog.; so Hare, Kenn., Gr., Bi., Che., Bä., Ehr. — יום] txt. err. for יומם, 𝕲, Gr., Bi., Che., Bä., Du.; cf. 22⁸ 42⁹ 91⁵ 121⁶, all ‖ לילה. — **5**. אֵיל אֵין] a.λ. † איל n.m. *help*, 𝐵DB. after Lag., loan word Aram. 𝕲 ἀβοήθητος, but 𝔍 *invalidus, without strength*. Ehr. rds. אֵל, which is prob. — כְּגֶבֶר]. The כ prob. gl.; makes it a simile and weakens the thought.

— **6.** ‡ חָפְשִׁי] adj. *free*, as slave from master Ex. 21[2. 5] (E) Jb. 3[19], from captivity Is. 58[6]; so 𝔊, 𝔍, but against context. Rd. נְפָשִׁי, as Dy., Dr. — כמו הללים]
are needed for measure of previous l.; but then rd. כהללים, the poetic form
of prep. in any case impairs the measure. 𝔊[B] ἐρριμμένοι, omitted 𝔊[א. c. a. A. T],
implies מֻשְׁכָּבִים Je. 14[16], which, though not in 𝔐, is needed for measure, and
enables us to arrange ll. in better parall. — נִגְזָרוּ] Niph. pf. ‡ ג.ר. Qal *divide,
cut in two*, 136[13]; Niph. *be cut off from*, here as Is. 53[8]. — **7.** בּוֹר תַּחְתִּיּוֹת] phr.
= La. 3[55], cf. Pss. 63[1) 86[13] Ez. 26[2)] 31[14. 16. 18] 32[18. 24] Is. 44[23]. — מַחֲשַׁכִּים] cf.
La. 3[6] Ps. 143[3]; so prob. v.[19] for מַחְשָׁךְ, and v.[13] for בחשך, *v.* 74[20]. — מְצֹלוֹת]
cf. 69[3. 16] gulf, of deep hole ‖ Pit. But 𝔊, 𝔙, 𝔖, Houb., Kenn., Che., Ehr.,
צלמות more prob. — **8.** עִנִּיתָ] Pi. pf. ענה *afflict*, cf. 90[15]. Aq., Σ, 𝔍, add sf.,
but this is prob. interp. This vb. is not suited to מִשְׁבָּרֶיךָ. 𝔊 ἐπ᾽ ἐμὲ ἐπήγα-
γες, followed by 𝔖, 𝔙, is better. Gr., Bä., Du., rd. אָנִי, as Ex. 21[13] Ps. 91[10].
It is easier to rd. יְהִי. — **9.** תוֹעֵבֹת] pl. seems unnecessary. 𝔊, 𝔍, rd. sg.
The term is used in legal sense in D, Ez., and is ethical in Pr. and subsequently. The conception of Israel as slain suggests the abomination of the
dead body. — לָמוֹ] poetic sf. for euphony. — **10.** דָאֲבָה] pf. Qal 3 f.; vb. † דאב
elsw. Je. 31[12. 25] *become weary, languish;* † רָאֲבָה n. Jb. 41[16]. 𝔊, 𝔙, ἠσθένησαν,
𝔍 *infirmatus*. But Σ, 𝔗, 𝔖, as Aram. דב *flow*. — מִנִּי] archaic prep. for euphony. — עֳנִי] i.p. עֲנִי, *v.* 9[14]. — שִׁטַּחְתִּי בָךְ] phr. a.λ. ‡ שטח. Vb. Qal *spread
out*, in sense of *scatter, disperse*, Je. 8[2] Jb. 12[23] Nu. 11[32. 32] (J) 2 S. 17[19],
here only Pi. of the palms; cf. פרש כף Ps. 44[21]; נשא כף 63[5] 119[48] 141[2]. —
11. † רְפָאִים] n.m. pl. *shades*, the weak ghosts of the dead in Sheol Is. 14[9]
26[14. 19] Pr. 2[18] 9[18] 21[16] Jb. 26[5]. Original mng. dub.; 𝔊 ἰατροί = רֹפְאִים improb.
— **12.** Pentameter gl. We might supply הלל and make it a trimeter couplet.
But this and v.[13] seem rather amplifying glosses, destroying the symmetry of the
Str. — † אֲבַדּוֹן] n.f., the place of ruin in Sheol ‖ בּוֹר and never abstr. Jb. 26[6]
28[22] 31[12] Pr. 15[11] 27[2)] (Qr.). — **13.** † אֶרֶץ נְשִׁיָּה] phr. a.λ. — **14.** וַאֲנִי] a gl.,
making l. too long. — **16.** † נֹעַר] n.m. abstr. *youth* Pr. 29[21] Jb. 33[25] 36[14], for
the usual נערים. — אָפוּנָה] cf. Ps. 55[5]; but 𝔊, 𝔖, 𝔙, אֶמַךְ Niph. † מכך vb. Qal
be low, humiliated, of perverse Israel 106[43]; Niph. *sink in decay*, of timbers
of house Ec. 10[18]; Hoph. *be brought low* Jb. 24[24]. — אָפוּנָה] a.λ. BDB., Qal
impf. cohort. מ פון = פוג as 38[9], so Ols., Hu., Dy., Gr., We., Du.; cf. 77[3]. But
𝔊, 𝔖, 𝔙, 𝔍, אָפְנֶה, Hoph. impf. 1 sg. √פנה, *be turned back* in confusion, cf.
Je. 49[8]. — **17.** בְּעִיתֻנִי] pl. sf. † בעתים] n. pl. *terrors* Jb. 6[4] √בעת vb. *overwhelm* Ps. 18[5], *terrify* Jb. 7[14]. — צִמְּתֻתוּנִי] a.λ. impossible form. Hi., Bä. rd.
צְפַרְתַנִי as 119[139]; but prob. as Ges.§[55. 2], Pi. 3 pl. sf. √צמת (18[41]) *exterminate*.
A word is missing; rd. אתי. 𝔐 is conflation of ני and אתי. — **19.** אהב ורע] =
38[12]. 𝔊[B] omits ירע, but it is needed for measure, and is given by 𝔊[א. c. a A. R. T].
𝔐 transposes מירעי. — מַחְשָׁךְ] prob. *the dark place*, as v.[7], but 𝔊 ἀπὸ ταλαιπω-
ρίας, 𝔙 *a miseria;* so Luther interprets מ as prep. 𝔍 *notos meos abstulisti*,
translates מירעים חשך, vb. חשך *restrain*, as 19[14]; so Bä.

PSALM LXXXIX.

Ps. 89 is composite. (*A*) A Ps. of praise sets forth the faithfulness of Yahweh and His deeds of kindness, especially in the creation and government of the world, as the theme of praise for the people, the holy angels, and the great objects of nature (v.$^{2-3.\ 6-15}$), with a liturgical tetrameter tristich attached (v.$^{16-17}$). (*B*) A lamentation in four parts gives a paraphrase of the Davidic covenant, (*a*) in its institution (v.$^{18-22.\ 4-5}$), (*b*) in its promises (v.$^{23-30}$), (*c*) in the conditions attached and the consequences of their violation (v.$^{31-38}$), and then describes the penalties endured in the humiliation of a king, probably Jehoiachin (v.$^{39-46}$). (*C*) An editor, in troublous times, combined the Pss., and appended an impatient longing for the interposition of Yahweh in behalf of His humiliated people, and for the restoration of the monarchy (v.$^{47-52}$).

A. v.$^{2-3.\ 6-15}$, 6 STR. 4^4.

OF kindness, Yahweh, will I sing forever,
　To all generations will I make known Thy faithfulness;
　By command kindness is built up forever,
　In the heavens where Thou establishest Thy faithfulness.
AND the heavens celebrate Thy wonderfulness, Yahweh,
　Yea, Thy faithfulness in the assembly of holy angels.
　For who in the sky can be compared to Yahweh?
　Be like to Yahweh among the sons of gods?
'EL, awe-inspiring in the circle of holy angels,
　And greatly to be revered above all round about!
　Yahweh, God of Hosts, who is like Thee?
　Thy kindness, Yah, and Thy faithfulness are round about Thee.
THOU art ruler over the swelling of the sea;
　When its waves heave Thou stillest them.
　Thou didst crush Rahab as one deadly wounded;
　With Thy strong arm Thou didst scatter Thine enemies.
THINE are the heavens, yea, Thine is the earth,
　The world in its fulness, Thou didst found them.
　North and South, Thou didst create them.
　Tabor and Hermon in Thy name ring out joy.
THINE is an arm (that is endued) with might.
　Thou strengthenest Thy hand, exaltest Thy right hand,
　Righteousness and justice are the foundation of Thy throne;
　Kindness and faithfulness come to meet Thy face.

B. v.$^{18-22. 4-5. 23-46}$, 4 PTS., 4 STR. 4^3.

I.

THOU art the glory of our strength,
    And by Thy favour Thou exaltest our horn.
    For Yahweh's is our shield,
    And to the Holy One of Israel belongs our king.
THEN Thou didst speak in a vision;
    To Thy son Thou gavest a word,
    (Saying) : I have laid help on a hero;
    I have exalted one chosen from the people.
I FOUND David My servant,
    With My holy oil I anointed him.
    My hand is established with him;
    Yea, Mine arm doth strengthen him.
I MADE a covenant with My chosen,
    I sware to David My servant:
    Forever will I establish thy seed,
    And build thy throne for all generations.

II.

THE enemy shall not come treacherously upon him,
    And the son of wrong shall not any more afflict him.
    But I will beat his adversaries to pieces before him,
    And them that hate him will I smite before him.
BUT My faithfulness and My kindness shall be with him,
    And through My name shall his horn be exalted.
    I will set his hand also on the sea,
    And his right hand (will I put) on the river.
HE will call Me : My Father,
    My God, and the Rock of my salvation.
    Yea, I will make him My first-born,
    Most high above the kings of earth.
FOREVER will I keep My kindness for him,
    And My covenant shall be firm for him;
    And I will set his seed forever,
    And his throne as the days of heaven.

III.

IF his sons forsake My Law,
    And walk not in My judgments;
    If they profane My statutes,
    And keep not My commands;
THEN will I visit their transgressions with a rod,
    And (chastise) their iniquity with stripes:
    But My kindness I will not (remove) from him,
    And I will not belie My faithfulness.

I WILL not profane My covenant,
   And that which has issued from My lips I will not change.
   Once have I sworn by My holiness;
   I will not lie unto David.
H IS seed shall be forever,
   And his throne as the sun before Me.
   As the moon shall it be established forever,
   And (forever as) the sky be firm.

IV.

B UT Thou hast cast off and rejected:
   Thou art become enraged with Thine anointed.
   Thou hast spurned the covenant of Thy servant;
   Thou hast profaned to the ground his crown.
T HOU hast broken down all his fences;
   Thou hast made his fortresses a ruin.
   All the passers-by spoil him:
   He is become a reproach to his neighbours.
T HOU hast exalted the right hand of his adversaries;
   Thou hast gladdened all his enemies.
   Yea, Thou turnest back his sword,
   And hast not made him stand in the battle.
T HOU hast taken away the sceptre of majesty,
   And his throne flung down to the ground.
   Thou hast shortened the days of his youth;
   Thou hast wrapped him up in shame.

C. v.$^{47-52}$, 2 STR. 6^4.

H OW long, Yahweh? wilt Thou hide Thyself forever?
   Shall Thy hot wrath burn like fire?
   Remember, Adonay, what duration is,
   For what nothingness Thou hast created all the sons of men.
   What is man that he should live and not see death?
   Can he deliver his life from the hand of Sheol?
W HERE are Thy former deeds of kindness, Adonay?
   Which Thou didst swear to David in Thy faithfulness?
   Remember, Adonay, the reproach of Thy servants,
   My bearing in my bosom the shame of the peoples,
   With which Thine enemies reproached, Yahweh,
   With which they reproached the footsteps of Thine anointed.

This Ps. is the closing Ps. of the third book of the Psalter, which with the second book embraces 𝔄, 𝔎, and 𝔈, and with the first book the majority of the Pss. of 𝔇, 𝔇𝔎. It was not in any of these, and was probably given its present position by the final editor. It bears in the title משכיל לאיתן האזרחי. It belongs to the משכילים, and the ל is probably ל *auctoris*. The only איתן האזרחי known is the sage of the court of Solomon 1 K. 5^{11} (4^{31}); but it is impossible to regard him as the author, and there is no reason why tradition

should assign this Ps. to him. It is probable, therefore, that the author
selected this ancient worthy as his pseudonym, and there was possibly in his
mind a play upon the word אזרח, which means *native* Israelite Lv. 23⁴²(H)
Nu. 15¹³ (P) +, איתן perennial, permanent, imperishable, cf. Nu. 24²¹ Je. 49¹⁹,
and would hint at the perpetuity of the native kingdom or people of Israel.
Such a pseudonym would be most suitable if, as we shall show, the author
was one of the captives who accompanied King Jehoiachin in his exile. This
title was not attached to the Ps. when finally edited in its present form, but
belonged to the original trimeter poem, v.¹⁸⁻²². ⁴⁻⁵. ²³⁻⁴⁶. This poem, in four
parts of four tetrastichs in each part, gives a paraphrase of the covenant of
David, citing v.⁴⁻⁵. ²⁰⁻³⁸ from the version in 2 S. 7. It uses the divine name
קרוש ישראל v.¹⁹, characteristic of the two Isaiahs. It uses terms for legal
obedience v.³¹. ³² which betray the influence of the code of H, and suggest
a companion of the prophet Ez. It uses other terms characteristic of these
writers, so הלל v.³². ³⁵. ⁴⁰. It limits the extension of the Davidic monarchy to
the region extending from the sea to the river, v.²⁶, and knows nothing of a
world monarchy such as we see in 72⁸ = Zc. 9¹⁰. This primitive conception
is not consistent with a late date. It applies בכור of Ex. 4²²⁻²³ (J) and עליון
of Dt. 26¹⁹ 28¹, both originally used of Israel, to the king v.²⁸. This does not
imply a date much later than D. The fourth part describes the humiliation
of the king in such a realistic and graphic way that it may most naturally be
referred to a real historical experience, such as that of Jehoiachin 2 K. 24¹⁰⁻¹⁶;
and it makes no reference to the calamities attached to the destruction of
Jerusalem. All favour the opinion that the Ps. was written by one of the
exiles who accompanied Jehoiachin in his captivity, prior to the final invasion
of Palestine and the destruction of the Holy City. A later editor attached
this Ps., setting forth the faithfulness and kindness of Yahweh to the Davidic
monarchy, to another much later Ps. praising the faithfulness and deeds of
kindness of Yahweh in general terms in connection with the creation and
government of the world. This poem, without a title, is complete in itself,
composed of six tetrameter tetrastichs v.²⁻³. ⁶⁻¹⁵, with a liturgical addition
v.¹⁶⁻¹⁷. This Ps. throughout indicates composition for public worship. The
assembly or council of holy angels v.⁶. ⁸, in antithesis to an assembly of pious
Israelites ; the use of the term קרשים for angels v.⁶. ⁸, elsw. Zc. 14⁵ Jb. 5¹ 15¹⁵
Dn. 8¹³. ¹⁸; בני אלים v.⁷, only here and 29¹, but cf. Jb. 1⁶ 2¹ 38⁷ Gn. 6². ⁴ (J),
imply a period of fully developed angelology, not earlier than the late Persian
period. The reference to the mythical sea monster *Rahab* v.¹¹, elsw. Jb. 9¹⁸
26¹², probably Is. 51⁹, used as emblematic name of Egypt Ps. 87⁴ Is. 30⁷,
implies influence of Babylonian mythology. The Ps. indicates a period of
peace and quietness in which the public worship of Yahweh in the temple
was enjoyed by Israel, and this not until the troubled times of the Restoration
were over, some time subsequent to Nehemiah, when peace and prosperity
were enjoyed under the Persian rule of Artaxerxes II. (458–404 B.C.). The
later Ps. was prefixed to the earlier one, and that it might not be mere patch-
work v.⁴⁻⁵, the Rf. of the first part of the trimeter poem, which sums up so

well its characteristic features, was removed so as to come immediately after the tetrastich giving the theme of the tetrameter poem. This editor was adapting these Pss. for use in public worship in his own day. It is probably he who added the two concluding tetrameter hexastichs. These reflect times of trouble, a long hiding of Yahweh's presence until His people were in despair and impatiently pled for interposition. He thinks of the reproach of the people more than of the shame of the monarchy, and is overwhelmed with the experience of the vanity of life and the peril of death. He probably wrote at the close of the Greek period, during the troubles brought upon the nation by Antiochus before the heroic outbreak of the Maccabean wars.

PSALM LXXXIX. *A.*

Str. I. The Ps. begins with a syn. tetrastich in praise of the kindness and faithfulness of Yahweh. — **2–3.** *Of kindness*]. This and other like terms for the divine attributes in the singular are abstr., " kindness " v.^{3a} ‖ *faithfulness* v.$^{2b. 3b}$; but in the plural " deeds of kindness," " acts of faithfulness." The pl. of the former is improb. only here in Ps. ; besides, it compels the transl. " of Yahweh's deeds of kindness," whereas *Yahweh* is more prob. vocative 2d pers., as in syn. l. — *will I sing forever*], in public worship, ‖ *To all generations will I make known*], to the congregation of worshippers rather than to the great world. — *By command*], attaching word to the third line and removing the suffix.

𝕳 " with my mouth " makes the second line too long, and is tautological and unpoetical. 𝕳 begins the third line with " for I have said," but 𝕲 and 𝕵 " thou hast said." This was a prosaic addition, based on the interpretation that the words of Yahweh begin here rather than in v.^{4}. — *kindness is built up forever* ‖ *Thou establishest Thy faithfulness*], not a promise for the future, but an existing and long-established experience. — *In the heavens*], the seat and centre of the divine kindness and faithfulness, cf. Pss. 36^6 57^{11}.

4–5. This trimeter tetrastich, separating tetrameter tetrastichs and interrupting the current of their poetic utterance, was placed here by an editor who pieced together an original trimeter poem with this later tetrameter poem. It was necessary to remove this piece containing the theme of the trimeter poem to this place, immediately after the statement of the theme of the tetrameter poem, in order to make the combination effectual. The justification was in the fact that the kindness and the faithfulness of Yahweh were especially exhibited in the covenant with David. The passage may be more appropriately interpreted in its original place after v.[22].

Str. II. has two syn. couplets, the second synth. to the first. This Str. sets forth the praise of Yahweh by angels, as the former by men. — **6**. *The heavens*], taking up the thought of v.[3b], in which the kindness and faithfulness were built up and established. — *celebrate*], sing and make known. — *Thy wonderfulness*], cf. 88[13]; as an attribute of Yahweh taking the place of kindness, cf. "shew extraordinary kindness" 4[4] 17[7] 31[22]. This usage and the context indicate that it is the wonderfulness of kindness that the poet has in mind. — *in the assembly of holy angels*]. The angels are regarded as gathered together in an assembly for the worship of Yahweh, cf. v.[8], just as the pious on earth, cf. 22[23. 26] 35[18] 40[10-11] 107[32] 149[1]. — **7**. *For who in the sky*], what holy or divine being in the heavens, *can be compared to Yahweh*, ‖ *be like to Yahweh*], implying a negative answer. He is incomparably above all other beings, cf. Ex. 15[11]. — *among the sons of gods*], not sons of gods in the sense of polytheism, but in the sense that angels are of the class of divine beings, cf. 8[6] 29[1]; usually, however, sons of God Gn. 6[2. 4] Jb. 1[6] 2[1] 38[7].

Str. III. is syn. with the previous praise of Yahweh in the heavens. It has two couplets, the first syn., the second synth. — **8**. *'El*], taking up the divine name of the previous line; vocative, and so *awe-inspiring*] is in apposition and not predicate, cf. 10[18] ‖ *to be revered*. — *in the circle of holy angels*], the intimate fellowship of the innermost circle, ‖ "assembly of holy angels" v.[6b]. — *Greatly*] is attached by MT. to first l., but it makes l. too long and is needed to complete the measure of second l. — *above all round about*]; the sf. of 𝕳, Vrss., is interp. but improb., as it destroys the force of the vocative in heaping up divine names. — **9**. *Yahweh, God of Hosts*]. The ancient warlike God is now conceived as God of a host of angels. — *who is like Thee*], renewing v.[7]. — The closing line specifies the challenge by recurring to the terms which constitute the main theme of the poem: *Thy kindness* and *Thy faithfulness*. 𝕳 is sustained by 𝕲 and 𝕵, EV[s]., in the use of a word found only here in Heb., "strong," "mighty," or " potent " ; but this is improbable in itself, and the change of a single letter gives us the keyword of the poem, " kindness," which is ‖ with " faithfulness " v.²⁻³. — *Yah*], an abbreviation of Yahweh not uncommon in late Pss. — *are round about Thee*]. The divine attributes are here personified, as often, and are regarded as constantly in His company, attending upon Him and ready to execute His pleasure, cf. 85¹¹⁻¹⁴.

Str. IV. has two syn. couplets. It begins a series describing the power of Yahweh in the creation and government of the world, which were regarded by the poet as expressing His kindness v.²; for His power was always beneficent, and destructive only of the powers of evil. The first couplet asserts his beneficial government of the sea. — **10.** *Thou art ruler over the swelling of the sea*], the lifting up of the sea in its pride and power, — *When its waves heave Thou stillest them*], as an act of kindness putting forth power to stay them and cause them to cease from doing harm. — **11.** *Thou didst crush Rahab*]. The reference to the sea in the previous couplet favours the opinion that Rahab has its usual meaning, the mythical sea monster of Semitic mythology, the " Tiamat " of the Assyrians and Babylonians ; so Jb. 9¹³ 26¹², probably Is. 51⁹. It is an emblematic name for Egypt Ps. 87⁴ Is. 30⁷, and accordingly Bä., Dr., al., think of Egypt here ; but there is no reference to nations in the context. The *enemies* should be referred to other destructive sea monsters, and not to men. — *as one deadly wounded*], pierced through by sword, arrow, or spear, and so wounded unto death ; cf. 69²⁷ Je. 51⁵² Ez. 26¹⁵ 30²⁴ La. 2¹², and so slain Ps. 88⁶ Nu. 19¹⁸ 31⁸. ¹⁹ (P) etc. ; cf. God's destruction of Leviathan 74¹³ᵇ⁻¹⁴ᵃ in similar terms. — *With Thy strong arm Thou didst scatter*], drive away, disperse all enemies in the sea ; cf. Is. 51⁹ 62⁸.

Str. V. sets forth the beneficent power of Yahweh in creation, in two couplets, the first synth., the second syn. — **12.** *Thine are the heavens*]. They belong to Thee as their owner ; Thou hast them in Thy possession and under Thy government. The heavens are chiefly thought of here as in v.³· ⁶· ⁷. — The Ps. for completeness of ownership adds, *yea, Thine is the earth*], cf. 74¹⁶, both summed up in *The world in its fulness*, cf. 50¹², that which fills it full, all its contents. — The reason for ownership is, *Thou didst* *found them*], in the sense of creation, cf. 24^2 78^{69} 102^{26} 104^5, involving the image of the founding of a building. — **13**. *North and South*], for the northern and southern sections of the world. — *Thou didst create them*], cf. v.[48] for creation of mankind, 104^{30} of creatures, 148^5 of heavens, Gn. 1^1 of heavens and earth. — *Tabor and Hermon*], the chief mountain peaks of the Holy Land, Tabor, commanding the great plain of Esdraelon, and Hermon, the giant of Lebanon, commanding the greater part of the entire land, representatives therefore of the mountains. — *In Thy name ring out joy*], returning to the conception of Str. I. where the psalmist sings at the head of the people. In Str. II. the heavens celebrate, in Str. III. the angels revere, so now the mountains join the choir; cf. Ps. 29^6 65^{13} 96^{11-12} 98^{7-8} Jb. 38^7 for similar jubilations of nature.

Str. VI. has two syn. couplets, returning from the deeds of power and kindness to the attributes themselves. — **14**. *Thine is an arm*], followed by relative clause, with relative omitted as usual, the vb. to be supplied, *that is endued with might ‖ Thou strengthenest Thy hand ‖ exaltest Thy right hand*, cf. v.[11b], thus emphasizing the exceeding great strength and might of God. But this might is always in the interest of justice and kindness. He is King of angels, of the world and mankind, and He rules from a divine throne. — **15**. *Righteousness and justice are the foundation of Thy throne*]. On these two syn. attributes as on a base or platform the throne of Yahweh is built. This is cited in Ps. 97^2. — *Kindness and faithfulness come to meet Thy face*]. They are personified, cf. v.[9], there as attendant upon Him, here as messengers coming to meet Him, having done His bidding, or coming to receive His commission to do it; cf. 85^{11-14}.

16–17. A late editor inserts a liturgical conclusion to the Ps. It did not belong to the original Ps., for there is no reference in it to the theme of the Ps., "kindness" and "faithfulness," but the more general terms, "name" and "righteousness" take their place. It is a syn. triplet. —

> Happy the people knowers of the sacred shout!
> Yahweh, in the light of Thy face they walk,
> In Thy name they exult, all day long in Thy righteousness.

Happy the people], exclamation, pl. abst. emphatic, cf. 1^1. — *knowers of the sacred shout*], accustomed to the sacred service

s

of the temple and especially to the *Teruah*, the sacred shout which accompanies the musical service at the sacrifices in the temple, cf. 33^3 $47^{2.6}$ 66^1 81^2 95^{1-2} $98^{4.6}$ 100^1. — *in the light of Thy face*]. The face of Yahweh, looking forth from the throne room of the temple, is illuminating ; cf. 4^7 44^4. — *they walk*], in sacred procession, cf. 42^5. — *In Thy name they exult*], so 9^{15} 13^6 21^2 in Thy salvation, 35^9 in Yahweh, — *in Thy righteousness*]. MT. attaches *all day long* to the first part of the verse, and adds the vb. "are exalted," but this makes a pentameter and the vb. "exalt" is not suited to the previous context. It probably came in from the line below.

PSALM LXXXIX. *B.*

Part I. has three advancing trimeter tetrastichs, and a tetra-stich Rf. — **18-19.** This tetrastich is syn. throughout, and with assonance : *our* strength, *our* horn, *our* shield, *our* king, all refer-ring to the Davidic dynasty. — *Thou art the glory of our strength*]. Yahweh is the One in whom the king, the strength, the strong hero of his people, glories, or the One who makes the strength of Israel beautiful and glorious. — *By Thy favour Thou exaltest our horn*], the horn of the nation, its honour and dignity, in their king. The exaltation of his horn is the exaltation of their horn, cf. v.^{25} 112^9 148^{14} and similar phr. 132^{17}. — *For Yahweh's is our shield*], to Yahweh he belongs, according to the covenant to be mentioned below. The king is the shield of his people as their heroic chieftain and defender, just as Yahweh is their shield and his shield Pss. 3^4 7^{11} $18^{3.31.36}$. — *the Holy One of Israel*], the divine name based on the Trisagion Is. 6^3. — **20.** This tetrastich has two couplets, the second synth. to the first. — *Then Thou didst speak*], referring to the time of the giving of the covenant to David through the prophet Nathan 2 S. $7 = 1$ Ch. 17, — *in a vision*], so 2 S. $7^{17} = 1$ Ch. 17^{15}, to the prophet, when in the ecstatic state. — *To Thy son*]. Codd. of 𝕳 differ ; the most authoritative have pl., " to Thy pious ones," referring to Nathan the prophet, Samuel, the book in which it is recorded, and the prophets depending on them ; cf. Acts 3^{24}. But many codd. and editions have sg., " Thy pious one," referring to Nathan. 𝕲 "Thy sons " suggests the true reading, which is "Thy son," the title given to the Davidic dynasty in the covenant, cf. v.[27]. — *Thou gavest a word*], so by an easy change of text, cf. 68[12] 77[9] ‖ speak in vision, instead of the prosaic and incomplete line of 𝕳, "and saidst," which requires that all up to this point be taken as one clause, and so as a pentameter, destroying the measure of the poem and losing a line from the Str. — *I have laid help on a hero*], made the hero a bearer of help for the people. — *I have exalted one chosen from the people*], cf. v.[4] 2 S. 7[8], where David was taken by Yahweh from a shepherd's life to be leader of His people. — **21–22** has two couplets, the first synth., the second syn. — *I found David My servant*], (cf. 18[1]) referring to the finding of David by Samuel. — *With My holy oil I anointed him*], his anointing at Bethlehem 1 S. 16[1-13]. — *My hand is established with him*]. Yahweh's hand was continually with David to sustain him in his arduous career, cf. Ps. 18[35-36]. — *Yea, Mine arm doth strengthen him*]. The tetrastich v.[4-5] comes in appropriately here, as indicated by the syn. tetrastichs at the close of Pt. II. v.[29-30] and Pt. III. v.[37-38]. It is composed of two syn. couplets. — **4**. *I made a covenant with My chosen*], cf. v.[29. 35. 40]. The covenant with David is also mentioned 132[12] Je. 33[21]. — *I sware to David My servant*]. The oath is not mentioned in 2 S. 7 any more than the "covenant." Both are interpretations by later writers of the divine promise. It is interpreted as oath also v.[36. 50] 110[4] 132[11]. — **5**. *Forever will I establish thy seed* ‖ *And build thy throne for all generations*], paraphrase of 2 S. 7[12-15] = 1 Ch. 17[11-14], where "seed" and "throne" are in syn. parall. as here.

Part II. has three advancing tetrastichs with a concluding Rf. going back upon the terms of the original covenant. — **23–24.** Two syn. couplets. — *The enemy shall not come treacherously upon him*], so 𝕵, 𝚺, cf. 55[16]; but 𝕲 "make exactions of." Usage is insufficient to determine with certainty. — *And the son of wrong*]. Hebraism for wrong-doers, persons who belong to the class or condition of men characterised by wrong. — *Shall not any more afflict him*], so 𝕲 and also the original passage from which it is cited 2 S. 7[10] (cf. 1 Ch. 17[9]). 𝕳 omits the aux. vb. and impairs the measure. — *But I will beat his adversaries to pieces before him*], cf. Nu. 14[45] (J, E) Dt. 1[44], illustrated by other terms Ps. 18[43]. — *And them that hate him will I smite*], so 𝕳, but the line is too

short; add therefore *before him*, as usual with this vb, Ju. 20³¹
1 S. 4³ 2 Ch. 13¹⁵ 14¹¹. It seems tautological in English, but not
to a Hebrew poet, who delights in assonance and the same or
similar endings to lines. — **25-26**. The first couplet is synth., the
second syn. — *But My faithfulness and My kindness shall be
with him*], in accordance with the promise 2 S. 7¹⁵; cf. also v.³⁴.
" Faithfulness " is added because of the line 2 S. 7¹⁶ " thy house
and thy kingdom shall be made sure forever," " faithfulness " being from the same stem in Heb. as the vb. " made sure." — *And
through My name shall his horn be exalted*], cf. v.¹⁸ᵇ. — *And I
will set his hand also on the sea*], the Mediterranean Sea, the
limit of the Davidic monarchy, the West according to the primitive idea. The " setting of the hand on " is the taking possession
of, cf. Is. 11¹⁴. — *And his right hand will I put on the river*], that
is, the Euphrates, the eastern limit of the Davidic monarchy.
𝔋 omits vb., leaving the line too short, and reads " rivers." This
might be interpreted of streams, canals, or channels of the
Euphrates, cf. 137¹; but elsewhere in the limits of the Davidic
dominion it is always sg., cf. 72⁸ 80¹², and probably it was so here.
The pl. ending is the mistake of a copyist for the original vb. The
actual limits of the Davidic monarchy were the sea and the river
in the time of David and of Jeroboam II.; but late poets gave
a world-wide dominion to the Davidic monarchy, such as that
of the great world powers; cf. Ps. 72⁸ after Zec. 9¹⁰. — **27-
28**. A syn. tetrastich. — *He will call Me : My Father*], to which
𝔋 adds " art Thou," making the line one word too long. It is
doubtless a prosaic enlargement of the original; cf. 2 S. 7¹⁴ =
1 Ch. 17¹³, " I will become a father to him, and he shall become
a son to me." " Son " is here used, not in the natural sense, but
of official adoption, as a king reigning in the place of God over
His kingdom of Israel, cf. Ps. 2⁷. He calls God " Father " and
also *My God and the Rock of my salvation*], cf. 18³. The exact phr.
" Rock of my salvation " is elsw. only Dt. 32¹⁵, cf. Ps. 95¹. — *Yea,
I will make him My first-born*]. The term is not used in the
Davidic covenant, though implicitly involved, if other kings are
also to be considered sons of God ; but it was used in the more
fundamental covenant with Israel, " Israel is my son, my first-
born " Ex. 4²² (J), cf. the paraphrase Dt. 32⁶ ˢ𝑞. — *Most high above*

the kings of earth], so adapted from the promise to Israel Dt. 26[19] 28[1]. — **29–30** returns as Rf. to the exact terms of the covenant: a tetrastich of two syn. couplets. — *Forever will I keep My kindness for him*], 2 S. 7[15], cf. v.[25]. — *And My covenant shall be firm for him*], cf. 2 S. 7[15], where his house is made firm or sure. — *And I will set his seed ‖ his throne*], v.[5] cf. 2 S. 7[12-13]. — *forever ‖ the days of heaven*], cf. "as the sun" v.[37], "moon" v.[38], "with the sun and before the moon" Ps. 72[5].

Part III. has the same structure as the other parts. — **31–32** is a syn. tetrastich, a paraphrase of 2 S. 7[14] "when he commits iniquity" or "acts perversely," omitted 1 Ch. 17. — *If his sons forsake My Law*]. The original was general and indefinite, and entirely apart from any conception of a code of Law ; but this paraphrase interprets the perverse action as a violation of the code of Law. There are four syn. terms : (1) *forsake My Law*], cf. Je. 9[12] Dt. 29[24] Je. 22[9] ; (2) *walk not in My judgments*], cf. Ez. 37[24] ; (3) *profane My statutes*], a.λ., but cf. v.[35], profane the covenant Mal. 2[10] Ps. 55[21], and profaning sacred places and things characteristic of H and Ez. ; (4) *keep not My commands*], a phr. of Dt. 4[2] 5[26] 7[9] + Lv. 22[31] 26[3] (H) and Ex. 20[6] = Dt. 5[10]. These phrases shew the influence not only of D, but also of H, and imply a contemporary of Ez. and one nearer to him than to Je. — **33–34**. This tetrastich has two syn. couplets in antith., the second to the first. — *Then will I visit their transgressions with a rod ‖ And their iniquity with stripes*], a paraphrase of 2 S. 7[14], "I will chastise him with a rod of men and with the stripes of the children of men," which is probably an expansion of an original "I will chastise him with stripes of the children of men." We should probably supply the vb. *chastise* to make a complete line, cf. 2 S. 7[14]. It has been omitted by txt. err. — *But My kindness I will not remove from him*], cf. 2 S. 7[15], which has the Qal, where the later 1 Ch. 17[13] has the Hiph. as here. Doubtless Hiph. was original even in 2 S., as ⅖, the pointing of 꽖 being an error. It is improbable that the psalmist would change the easy technical word "remove" of the original for the new vb. of 꽖 "break off," and use it in a sense which cannot be sustained elsewhere. — *And I will not belie My faithfulness*], cf. Ps. 44[18] with covenant, Lv. 19[11] with a person. — **35–36**. This tetrastich is syn. throughout.

— *I will not profane My covenant*], antith. to v.[32], profaning the divine statutes, — *And that which has issued from My lips*], cf. Je. 17[16] Dt. 23[24] Nu. 30[13] (P) ; syn. "covenant," its verbal contents. — *I will not change*], cf. 34[1]. — *Once*], for all, 𝔊, 𝔍 ; cf. Heb. 7[27]. — *have I sworn*], cf. v.[4]. — *by My holiness*], cf. Am. 4[2], by the majestic separateness, aloofness, of Yahweh above all creatures. — *I will not lie unto David.* — Rf. is a tetrastich, syn. throughout and syn. v.[4-5. 29-30]. — *His seed shall be forever*], cf. v.[5a. 30a]. — *And his throne as the sun before Me*], cf. v.[5b], built for all generations ; v.[30b] "as the days of heaven." — *As the moon shall it be established forever*, cf. 72[5], *And forever as the sky be firm*], by easy change of pointing "forever" for "witness," and of preposition "as" for "in the sky," which introduces a new conception in the climax not easy to explain. Some think of the moon as a witness in the sky, others of God Himself as in Jb. 16[19]. But the term "firm," "sure," in the original 2 S. 7[16] is attached to the "house" or dynasty, and in v.[29] to the covenant, and it seems best to attach it to the throne here, to make the "sky" ‖ "moon," and to find a syn. word for "forever."

Part IV. laments that God has acted contrary to His covenant, in His present dealings with the king. It has the same structure as the previous parts, four tetrastichs, the last a sort of Rf. — **39–40** is a syn. tetrastich. — *But Thou hast cast off and rejected*] David and his present representative on the throne. — *Thou art become enraged with Thine anointed*], cf. 78[21. 59. 62] Dt. 3[26]. These three terms are strong expressions to indicate Yahweh's attitude towards the present king. They imply, in accordance with v.[31-33], that this king had forsaken the Law, and consequently was undergoing the chastisement predicted v.[33]. — *Thou hast spurned the covenant of Thy servant*]. This seems inconsistent with the perpetuity of the covenant v.[4-5], its firmness v.[29], and the promise that Yahweh would not profane it v.[35]. But the Ps. certainly had in mind that the chastisement would be temporary, and that the covenant kindness and faithfulness would not be removed v.[34]. That has been so strongly expressed in the previous context that it is implied here. — *Thou hast profaned to the ground his crown*]. The crown, in the term used here, implies consecration to the royal office, or anointing, cf. 132[18]. The profanation of the crown of the present king is because of his profanation of Yahweh's statutes v.[32a]. — **41-42** has two syn. couplets, setting forth the devastation of the land of the king. — *Thou hast broken down all his fences*], cf. Ps. 80[13]. The boundaries of the land no longer keep out the enemies, it is all open to them. — *Thou hast made his fortresses a ruin*]. The strongholds constructed for the defence of the land had been captured by enemies, and have been reduced to a mass of ruins. — *All the passers-by spoil him*], cf. Ps. 80[13] La. 1[12] 2[15]. The land is open and defenceless to all the neighbours who would despoil it. Just such a spoiling by neighbours is related 2 K. 24[2]. — *He is become a reproach to his neighbours*], defenceless, plundered by all who take advantage of his misfortunes. The land is become the reproach and contempt of all the nations round about. The phr. is used also 44[14] 79[4], cf. 80[7] all Pss. dependent on this one. — **43-44** is a syn. tetrastich describing the defeat of the king in battle. — *Thou hast exalted the right hand of his adversaries*], in battle, giving them the victory over the king of Israel, cf. v.[20]. — *Thou hast gladdened all his enemies*], cf. 30[2], giving them the joy and gladness of triumph and its spoils. — *Yea, Thou turnest back his sword*], so that it is ineffective, does not pierce or cut down the enemies. — *And hast not made him stand in the battle*], that is, he has not stood firm, he has fallen back, retired, fled before his enemies. — **45-46** has a syn. couplet and a synth. one. — *Thou hast taken away the sceptre of his majesty*], so by an easy change of text, which gives a good meaning, syn. with following line. — *And his throne flung down to the ground*], cf. Ez. 21[17] for other use of vb. The humiliation to the ground of the throne here is parall. with that of the crown v.[40]. Such an overthrow of the throne is in strong antithesis to the building of the throne " to all generations " of v.[5], " as the days of heaven " v.[30], " as the sun before me " v.[37], and implies that this overthrow is a temporary one. — *Thou hast shortened the days of his youth*]. This seems to imply that the king who suffered this humiliation was a young man. We might think of the shortening of his youth by death, were it not for the following line, which implies that he continued to live in shame. — *Thou hast wrapped him up in shame*]. It is evident, therefore, that the joyous days of his youth have given place to an experience of the greatest shame and humiliation. These envelop him and wrap him up as in a robe. The descriptions of this part of the Ps. are so graphic and realistic that they may most naturally be referred to a real historic experience ; and if so, the only one who exactly fits the description is Jehoiachin, who began to reign at eighteen, but reigned only three months before he was taken captive to Babylon by Nebuchadnezzar 2 K. 24[8-16]. The Ps. closes here, and it was probably written by one of the exiles with Jehoia-chin before the more terrible calamities which fell upon the nation in the reign of Zedekiah, his successor.

PSALM LXXXIX. *C.*

This Ps. returns to the tetrameter movement, but the Strs. are not tetrastichs, but hexastichs. It presupposes both of the pre-vious Pss., and is not of the style of either of them. It is an addition, reflecting a much later and more impatient attitude. — **47-49.** This hexastich has a syn. couplet and a syn. tetrastich. — *How long, Yahweh*], cf. 4[3] 79[5], will this sad state of things continue? the humiliation of the Davidic monarchy, the postpone-ment of the covenant? — *Wilt Thou hide Thyself forever ?*], im-plying a long-continued hiding from the people, and justifying the expostulation lest it should endure forever. — *Shall Thy hot wrath burn like fire ?*], cf. 79[5] for similar phr. and the same situation. — *Remember, Adonay*], so by the insertion of a single letter to cor-respond with v.[51a], omitted by copyist's mistake, so that 𝔐 has "Remember I," or "as for me." — *what duration is*], duration of life, what it is : how short and worthless it is, as explained in the next line. — *For what nothingness*], empty, vain, worthless thing, of no value or importance. — *Thou hast created all the sons of men*]. The author is here thinking of mankind in general, and not of the fortunes of the king or the nation. He is moralis-ing over the frailty of human life, as the author of the book of Job. He conceives of it in a pessimistic spirit, as even in the pur-pose of God in the creation of man. The same term for creation is used in v.[13]. This is more fully explained in v.[49]. — *What is man, that he should live and not see death*], α.λ. phr., death, the inevitable destroyer of mankind. — *Can he deliver his life*], com-mon phr. 1 S. 19[11] 2 S. 19[6] Je. 48[6] Ez. 33[5] Am. 2[14] Ps. 116[4] +. —

from the hand of Sheol]. Sheol is syn. of Death, and both are conceived as having power over the life of men; cf. 49[15-20] for the dominion of Sheol, 30[4] 86[13] for deliverance from it. Thus the shortness of time and the nearness of death are the basis for the plea that Yahweh would restrain His wrath and grant His presence and favour. — **50-52** is a hexastich having a synth. couplet and a syn. tetrastich. — *Where are Thy former deeds of kindness, Adonay ?*], cf. v.[2], but in an entirely different spirit. There, the poet resolves to sing of them forever; here, he complains bitterly of their absence and refers to them as ancient. — *Which Thou didst swear to David in Thy faithfulness*]. This is more specific, for the special kindness in the covenant of David, v.[4 25. 34]. The combination of the general " deeds of kindness " and the specific kindness to David here resembles the editorial combination of v.[4-5] with v.[2-3]. The editor who made the combination may be the author of these words. — *Remember, Adonay, the reproach of Thy servants*], cf. v.[42]; but that was the reproach of the king, this is more general, one of the nation of Israel, implying a later point of view. — *My bearing in my bosom the shame of the peoples*], by an easy emendation of the text suggested by Bä., because 𝕳 gives an ungrammatical construction which is only paraphrased in " the whole of many peoples," and 𝕲 and 𝔍 had a different text, or conjectured ways out of the difficulty. — *With which Thine enemies reproached, Yahweh*]. The line pauses, not giving the object, in order that by stairlike parall. the next line may begin with a part of the previous line and give its conclusion with emphasis. — *With which they reproached the footsteps of Thine anointed*], the humiliation of the Davidic monarchy, as in the closing part of the trimeter poem.

LXXXIX. A.

2. חֲסְדֵי] pl. *deeds of kindness* v.[50] 4[1] 17[7] 25[6] 107[43] Is. 63[7]. — אוֹדִיעַ] should be cohortative, as אָשִׁירָה. ה‑ has fallen out before א. — **3.** אָמַרְתִּי] but 𝕲, 𝕾, 𝔍, אָמָרְתָּ. The author cites words of God and not his own words. But אמרת suits better v.[4] than v.[3]; so Bi., Du. It is therefore prob. a later insertion to distinguish words quoted. בפי then belongs with l.[3] and should be בפיו *By His* (God's) *command;* cf. use of פי for command Dt. 1[26] 1 S. 12[14] 1 K. 13[26] +. — שָׁמַיִם] emph. in position, followed by rel. clause defined by בָּהֶם. — These four ll. are tetrameters. **4-5** are a trimeter insertion, belonging originally with trimeter poem v.$^{19\,sq.}$ So Horsley would put them between v.^{36} and v.^{37}. — **4.** כרתי ברית]. This cites the Davidic covenant 2 S. 7 = 1 Ch. 17; cf. v.$^{29.\,35.\,40}$ 132^{12}. כרת ברית is phr. of J, E, D, c. ל Ex. 23^{32} $34^{12.\,15}$ Jos. $9^{6.\,7.\,11.\,15.\,16}$ 24^{25} (J, E) Dt. 7^{2} Je. 32^{40}; P uses הקים ברית. — בְחִירִי] so 𝔖, but 𝔊, 𝔙, pl. † בָּחִיר n. *chosen, elect*, always of Yahweh, refer. to Saul 2 S. 21^{6}, Moses Ps. 106^{23}, Servant of Yahweh Is. 42^{1}, children of Jacob 1 Ch. 16^{13} = Ps. 105^{6}, Israel Is. 45^{4}; so His people Ps. 105^{43} 106^{5} Is. 43^{20} $65^{9.\,15.\,22}$; David only here, but vb. is used for David 1 S. 10^{24} $16^{8.\,9.\,10}$ 2 S. 6^{21} 1 K. 8^{16} (= 2 Ch. 6^{5}) 1 Ch. $28^{4.\,5}$ 29^{1} 2 Ch. 6^{5} Ps. 78^{70}. — נִשְׁבַּעְתִּי] the oath to David is not mentioned in 2 S. 7, but the covenant is interpreted as an oath Ps. 110^{4} also. — דוד עבדי] David as the servant of Yahweh elsw. v.^{21} 78^{70} 132^{10} 144^{10}; elsw. titles 18^{1} 36^{1}, David's seed v.^{40}, so in 2 S. 3^{18} $7^{5.\,8.\,26}$, altogether 31 t. in OT. — אכין זרע] ‖ בניתי כסא. Cf. phrs. 2 S. 7^{12-15} = 1 Ch. 17^{11-14}: הקים זרע, הכין ממלכת, כסא יהיה נכון עד עולם, בננתי כסא עד עולם. The couplet is therefore a paraphrastic summary of the promise. — **6.** וְיוֹדוּ] ו does not connect as conj. with the previous tetrastich of covenant. It connects with the first tetrastich v.$^{2-3}$ and the impfs. יִבָּנֶה and תָּכִן. It is ו coörd. of late style. 𝔊 interprets as future. It is, as in v.^{3}, present. — פִּלְאֲךָ] as 77^{12} 88^{13}. — קהל קדשים] phr. α.λ. *congregation of angels*, cf. סוד קדשים v.^{8}, קהל (*22*^{23}), קדשים (*16*^{3}) for angels elsw. Jb. 5^{1} 15^{15} Dn. $8^{13.\,13}$ Zc. 14^{5}, late usage. — **7.** מי יערך ל] cf. 40^{6}. — יִדְמֶה] dependent on מי also (*17*^{4}). — בְּנֵי אֵלִים] angels, as 29^{1} = בני (ה)אלהים Jb. 1^{6} 2^{1} 38^{7} Gn. $6^{2.\,4}$ (J). — **8.** אֵל נַעֲרָץ] phr. α.λ. (*10*^{18}). — רַבָּה] is attached by MT. to first l., but that makes it too long and second l. too short. 𝔊 attaches it rightly to the second; rd. μέγας, רָב; therefore the fem. form is interpretative. — **9.** יהוה אלהי צבאות] (*24*^{10}). — מִי־כָמוֹךָ] takes place of 3 pers. v.^{7} and goes back on 2 pers. v.^{6}. — חֲסִין יָהּ] attached to first part of v. by MT.; but that makes first l. too long and second too short. 𝔊 rightly attaches it to second part: δυνατὸς εἶ Κύριε, καὶ ἡ ἀλήθειά σου; so 𝔍 *fortissime domine.* חֲסִין α.λ. adj. *strong, mighty*, an Aramaism; but † חָסֹן adj. *strong* Am. 2^{9} Is. 1^{31}; txt. err. for חסדך, which is theme of Ps., and ‖ אמונתך v.$^{2.\,3}$. — **10.** בְּשׂוֹא גַלָּיו] inf. cstr. שׂוא for נְשׂוֹא Je. 10^{5}, נשׂא Is. 1^{14} Jb. 20^{6}; "perhaps only a scribal error," Ges.$^{76.\,b}$. 𝔊 σάλον, 𝔍 *elationes.* — **11.** דִּכִּאתָ] (*72*^{4}) vowel of ל״ה (Ges.$^{75.\,oo}$). — רַהַב] is the mythical sea monster "Tiâmat" of Ass.-Bab. mythology Jb. 9^{13} 26^{12}; emblematic name for Egypt Ps. 87^{4} Is. 30^{7}, so here Bä. It is ‖ תנין and prob. refers to the sea monster in Is. 51^{9}, so here; and the stilling of the sea has nothing to do with the Exodus, but is parall. with the reference to other great objects in nature in context. — בִּזְרוֹעַ עֻזְּךָ] phr. Is. 62^{8}, cf. Is. 51^{9}. — פִּזַּרְתָּ] *v. 53*^{6}. — **12.** תבל ומלאה] phr. elsw. 50^{12}, with ארץ 24^{1}, ים 96^{11} 98^{7}, cf. 74^{16}. — **13.** צָפוֹן וְיָמִין] phr. α.λ. *north and south*, for the countries in these regions; cf. 74^{17}. — תבור וחרמון] the two great mountains of Palestine: † תבור commanding the plain of Esdraelon, elsw. Jos. $19^{22.\,34}$ Ju. $4^{6.\,12.\,14}$ Je. 46^{18} Ho. 5^{1}, and חרמון North Galilee and Syria. — **15.** צֶדֶק וּמִשְׁפָּט מְכוֹן כִּסְאֶךָ] = 97^{2}. It is doubtless original here, for it has the parallel חֶסֶד וֶאֱמֶת יְקַדְּמוּ פָנֶיךָ, the four attributes grouped as elsw. in pairs. In 97^{2} it is not necessary to context and might be removed without being missed;

cf. 85¹¹⁻¹⁴ for grouping of attributes personified in a similar way. — †[מָכוֹן] n.m. √כון, *fixed, established place*, (1) usually of God's abode on earth Ex. 15¹⁷ 1 K. 8¹³ = 2 Ch. 6², of temple Ezr. 2⁶⁸ Is. 4⁵ Dn. 8¹¹, elsw. heaven 1 K. 8³⁹· ⁴³· ⁴⁹ = 2 Ch. 6³⁰· ³³· ³⁹ Ps. 33¹⁴ Is. 18⁴; (2) *foundation* Pss. 97² 104⁵, so here. — **16.** [וְיֹדְעֵי תְרוּעָה] those experienced in and accustomed to the musical service at the sacrifice in the temple ; cf. 'זִבְחֵי ת 27⁶, 'צִרְצְלֵי ת 150⁵, and more generally of the shouting at musical service 33³ 47⁶; also vb. 47² 66¹ 81² 95¹· ² 98⁴· ⁶ 100¹. — [בְּאוֹר־פָּנֶיךָ] phr. elsw. 4⁷ 44⁴, always of the illuminating face of Yahweh as looking forth from the most holy place of the temple. — [יְהַלֵּכוּן] fuller form impf. Pi. הלך, frequentative; Pi. intensive chiefly poetic and late, of frequenting the temple ‖ familiarity with the sacred shout ; cf. 55¹⁵ walking with the throng in procession to the house of God, also 42⁵. — **17.** [בְשִׁמְךָ יְגִילוּן כל היום ובצדקתך ירומו]. This is too long for one l., and for two makes two trimeters. We might reduce it to a tetrameter by throwing out either the last word as assimilation to v.¹⁸, or כל היום as an insertion. Gr. suggested the reading יָרִונוּ. If we read יְרַנֵּנוּ with Bä., we shall have to complete l. by adding יהוה to make a tetrameter. This is possible. V.¹⁶⁻¹⁷ are liturgical in character It seems better to regard them as a seam.

LXXXIX. *B.*

18. This v. changes to trimeter which then continues till v.⁴⁷. — [עֻזָּמוֹ] c. archaic sf. for עֻז referring to previous context. But 𝔖, so Gr., rd. עֻזֵּנוּ ‖ קרנינו, מלכנו, מגננו. This is more prob. We then have assonance in these four words, all referring to the Davidic king, and we should rd. קַרְנֵנוּ after 𝔊 τὸ κέρας ἡμῶν, 𝔍 *cornu nostrum*, so 𝔖, 𝔗, many codd., and not MT. קרנינו, which is difficult to understand. This gives us a quartette of trimeters referring to the king, to be compared with the quartette v.⁴⁻⁵. Transpose אתה with יָזֵנוּ תפארת. The כי is prob. a seam to connect this tetrastich with the previous context. It was not in the original trimeter poem, which begins here. — [תרים] of Kt. is more prob. than תרום of Qr. — **19.** [קְדוֹשׁ יִשְׂרָאֵל] divine name of the trisagion Is. 6³ (*v.* 71²² 78⁴¹). These four ll., referring to king under the syn. terms עֻז, קרן, מגן, מלך, constitute the first tetrastich of the poem. — **20.** [אָז דִּבַּרְתָּ בְחָזוֹן]. The אז refers to the time of the covenant 2 S. 7 = 1 Ch. 17. The חזון *vision* is that of Nathan 2 S. 7¹⁷ כְּכֹל הַחִזָּיוֹן הַזֶּה = 1 Ch. 17¹⁵. — [לַחֲסִידֶיךָ] pl. text of Baer and Ginsb. refers not only to Nathan but to Samuel also, and possibly to a number of prophets. But many codd. and texts give sg. חֲסִידְךָ, which then must refer to Nathan. The conception of the prophet as a חסיד is very late. The text is dub., for 𝔊 τοῖς υἱοῖς σου, בָּנֶיךָ. This is also a late conception; but if pointed in sg. *thy son*, it is in accord with the conception of the prophecy that the king was son of God. — [וַתֹּאמֶר] added, is unpoetical, cf. v.³ᵃ; the first half of v. as it stands is pentameter. To make two trimeters another word must be conjectured. We may find it in אמר חזון, as 68¹² אֲדֹנָי יִתֶּן אֹמֶר and 77⁹ אֹמֶר שׁו, and so rd. לְדַבֵּר חזון אמר. A copyist gives prosaic וְתֹאמֶר for תתן אמר. The v. then is the second tetrastich of the original trimeter poem.

—שֻׁוִּיתִי] pf., as v.⁴ כָרַתִי *16⁸* 21⁶. — **21–22.** מְשַׁחְתִּיו] historical reference to the anointing of David by Samuel 1 S. 16¹⋅¹². — אשר] prosaic insertion. This is a third tetrastich. Here is the proper place to bring in the tetrastich v.⁴⁻⁵, as a sort of refrain to the three previous tetrastichs, making a group of four. The ground for this is the fact that v.⁴⁻⁵ are parall. with v.³⁷⁻³⁸, closing a group of four tetrastichs and also with v.²⁹⁻³⁰, closing another group. — **23.** לֹא־יַשִּׁיא]. ⅏ ὠφελήσει, 𝔙 *proficiet*, so 𝔖, but Σ ἐξαπατήσει, 𝔍 *decipiet*. *B*DB. follows ⅏, *act the creditor against, make exactions of;* but Bä., Du., 𝔍, Σ, so 55¹⁶, *come deceitfully upon;* the latter more prob. — וּבֶן עַוְלָה לֹא יְעַנֶּנּוּ] is cited from 2 S. 7¹⁰ וְלֹא־יֹסִיפוּ בְנֵי עַוְלָה לְעַנּוֹתוֹ; cf. 1 Ch. 17⁹ ולא יוסיפו בני עולה לְבַלֹּתוֹ, referring to the people; here applied to the monarch. ⅏ of Ps. has καὶ υἱὸς ἀνομίας οὐ προσθήσει τοῦ κακῶσαι αὐτόν; but 𝔍 is same as 𝔐. ⅏ of 2 S. 7¹⁰ has προσθήσει τοῦ ταπεινῶσαι. It is evident that ⅏ of Ps. did not quote from ⅏ of 2 S. or 1 Ch. It must have found לא יסיף in its text, and indeed וּבֶן־עַוְלָה לֹא־יֹסִיף לְעַנּוֹתוֹ. This makes better measure and gives assonance with כו, and is prob. original. It is then more decidedly still a citation from Heb. text of S., and not from text of Ch. This v. interrupts 1 pers. of divine action by a distich making enemies the subj. It is not closely connected with previous context. It begins the *second part of the poem.* — **24.** וְכַתּוֹתִי] is pointed as ו consec.; if so, it must depend on impfs of v.²². Qal ‡ כתת *beat* or *crush fine*, of potter's vessel Is. 30¹⁴, golden calf Dt. 9²¹, sacrificial victim Lv. 22²⁴ (P); only here of enemies. Hiph. *beat in pieces*, an enemy Dt. 1⁴⁴ Nu. 14⁴⁵ (J, E). It is an early word therefore, but not elsw. in ψ; cf. 18⁴³. — **26.** וְנַהֲרוֹת] *streams* for נהר river Euphrates of other passages 72⁸ 80¹², where limits of Davidic kingdom are given. We might think of the canals of Euphrates as נהרות בבל 137¹. — **27.** הוּא יִקְרָאֵנִי אָבִי אָתָּה]. The l. is one word too long; either הוא or אתה should be elided. Neither is necessary to the sense; both are emph. אתה is the least likely. Cf. 2 S. 7¹⁴ = 1 Ch. 17¹³ קָרֶן יִשְׁעִי, אֵלִי צוּרִי [אֵלִי וְצוּר יִשׁוּעָתִי cf. *18⁸*. — אָנִי אֲהֶיה־לּוֹ לְאָב. The exact phrase צוּר יְשׁוּעָה elsw. Dt. 32¹⁵, but צור ישע Ps. 95¹. — **28.** אַף־אָנִי בְכוֹר אֶתְּנֵהוּ]. In Ex. 4²² Israel as son is compared with other nations as בכור; so Dt. 26¹⁹ 28¹:

26¹⁹ לְתִתְּךָ עֶלְיוֹן עַל כָּל הַגּוֹיִם
28¹; נְהָנֶךָ עֶלְיוֹן עַל כָּל גּוֹיֵי הָאָרֶץ

here, as in Ps. 72, passages originally referring to Israel are applied to the king. — **29.** וּבְרִיתִי נֶאֱמֶנֶת לוֹ]. — הַסְרִי לֹא־יָסוּר מִמֶּנּוּ cf. 2 S. 7¹⁵ לְעוֹלָם אַשְׁמוּר־לוֹ חַסְדִּי cf. 2 S. 7¹² וְשַׂמְתִּי לָעַד זַרְעוֹ]. — נֶאֱמָן בֵּיתְךָ וּמַמְלַכְתְּךָ עַד עוֹלָם לְפָנֶיךָ 30. cf. 2 S. 7¹⁶ הֲקִימֹתִי אֶת־זַרְעֲךָ אַחֲרֶיךָ — וְכִסְאוֹ כִּימֵי שָׁמָיִם] cf. 2 S. 7¹³; cf. 1 Ch. 17¹² כֹּנַנְתִּי אֶת־כִּסְאוֹ עַד עוֹלָם. The phr. יְמֵי שָׁמַיִם is α.λ., but cf. כִּשִׁשִׁישׁ v.³⁷, כְּיָרֵחַ v.³⁸, and עַם יֶרַח לִפְנֵי שֶׁמֶשׁ 72⁵. This completes the second part of poem. — **31–32.** אִב־יַעַזְבוּ בָנָיו תּוֹרָתִי]. This tetrastich is paraphrase of 2 S. 7¹⁴ אֲשֶׁר בְּהַעֲוֹתוֹ, which clause is not in 1 Ch. 17. There are four syn. clauses here: עֻזְב תּוֹרָה, שְׁמֹר דְּרָכִים, הֲלֹל חֻקּוֹת, לֹא שָׁמַר מִצְוֹת; cf. the gl. Ps. 18²²⁻²³ לֹא הֵלֵךְ בְּמִשְׁפָּטִים, הֵסִיר מֵחֻקּוֹת, מִשְׁפָּטִים לְנֶגְדִּי. Here תּוֹרָה and מִצְוֹת are added. These phrs. are used frequently elsw.: (1) עָזַב תּוֹרָה 119⁵³ Je. 9¹² Pr. 28⁴ (of law of father

Pr. 4²); cf. עֹזֵב בְּרִית Dt. 29²⁴ Je. 22⁹ Dn. 11³⁰, פֵּרוּב Ps. 119⁸⁷. (2) הִלֵּל בְּמִשְׁכָּנֹת
Ez. 37²⁴, elsw. vb. c. בְּמָצוֹת 2 Ch. 17⁴, בַּחֲקִים Ez. 11¹² 36²⁷ 1 K. 8⁶¹, **Lv.**
26³ (H) 1 K. 6¹² Ez. 5⁶. ⁷ 11²⁹ 18⁹. ¹⁷ 20¹⁸. ¹⁶. ¹⁹. ²¹ 33¹⁵, cf. Lv. 18⁴, בַּתּוֹרָה **Ex.**
16⁴ (J?) 2 K. 10³¹ 2 Ch. 6¹⁶ Ne. 10³⁹ Je. 26⁴ Pss. 78¹⁰ 119¹, בַּתּוֹרוֹת Dn. 9¹⁰,
בַּתּוֹרֹתַי וּבְחֻקֹּתַי Je. 44¹⁰, בְּתֹרָתִי וּבְחֻקֹּתַי וּבְעֵדְוֺתָיו Je. 44²³. (3) חִלֵּל חֻקּוֹת phr. a.λ.,
but הִלֵּל בְּרִית Mal. 2¹⁰ v.³⁵, cf. Ps. 55²¹. The defiling of sacred places and
things is especially characteristic of H and Ez., cf. Ps. 74⁷ חִלֵּל מִשְׁכַּן שֵׁם.
חִלֵּל is also used in v.⁴⁰ of violating the honour of the Davidic kingdom.
(4) שָׁמַר מִצְוֹת Ex. 20⁶ = Dt. 5¹⁰ Lv. 22³¹ 26³ (H) Dt. 4² 5²³ 7⁹ 8². ⁶ 13⁵. ⁹ 26¹⁸
28⁹ 1 K. 8⁶¹ 9⁶ 14⁸ 2 K. 17¹⁹ 18⁶ Ne. 1⁵. ⁹ Dn. 9⁴ Ps. 119⁶⁰ Ec. 12¹³. —
33. וּפָקַדְתִּי בְשֵׁבֶט פִּשְׁעָם וּבִנְגָעִים עֲוֺנָם]. This v., as it stands, is pentameter paraphrase of 2 S. 7¹⁴, not in ‖ 1 Ch. 17; וְהוֹכַחְתִּיו בְּשֵׁבֶט אֲנָשִׁים וּבְנִגְעֵי בְּנֵי אָדָם 2 S. 7¹⁴
has been expanded from an original וְהֹכַחְתִּי בְּנִגְעֵי בְּנֵי אָדָם. A vb. is missing
in Ps. We cannot do better than supply the original הוֹכַחְתִּי. — **34.** וְחַסְדִּי
וְחַסְדִּי לֹא־אָפִיר מֵעִמּוֹ] cf. 2 S. 7¹⁵ וְחַסְדִּי לֹא־יָסוּר מִמֶּנּוּ, 1 Ch. 17¹³ [לֹא־אָפִיר מֵעִמּוֹ.
The text of Chr. is more correct. 𝕲 of S. has Hiph. The vb. אָפִיר is prob.
txt. err. for אָסִיר, Ols., Gr., Bi., Bä., Che. There was no reason to change this
technical word, and אָפִיר for אָרֵר √כרר is not congruous with the noun. —
[מוֹצָא־שְׂפָתַי] cf. 44¹⁸ [לֹא אֲשַׁקֵּר בַּאֲמוּנָתִי (בַּבְּרִית), with בְּ pers. Lv. 19¹¹. — **35.**
elsw. Je. 17¹⁶ Dt. 23²⁴ Nu. 30¹³ (P); מוֹצָא פִי Dt. 8³. — [אֲשַׁנֶּה] cf. v.⁴ᵃ. ²⁹ᵇ, Pi.
impf. שָׁנָה change, elsw. in ψ only 34¹ (title). — **36.** [אַחַת] once for all, Bä.,
Kau., cf. Heb. 7²⁷; Du. one thing, or once, one time, 𝕲 ἅπαξ, 𝕵 semel. —
[בְקָדְשִׁי] in my apartness, sacredness, with נִשְׁבַּע elsw. Am. 4²; cf. for the
oath v.⁴ᵇ נִשְׁבַּעְתִּי לְדָוִד. — [אִם] after oath strong negation, so 95¹¹ 132³. ³. ⁴. —
— **37.** זַרְעוֹ לְעוֹלָם יִהְיֶה = v.³⁰ שַׂמְתִּי לָעַד זַרְעוֹ = v.⁵ עַד־עוֹלָם אָכִין זַרְעֶךָ
וּבָנִיתִי לְדֹר־וָדוֹר כִּסְאֶךָ = וְכִסְאוֹ כִּימֵי שָׁמָיִם וְכִסְאוֹ כְשֶׁמֶשׁ נֶגְדִּי.
Thus v.³⁷⁻³⁸ ‖ v.⁴⁻⁵ ‖ v.²⁹⁻³⁰. — **38.** [הֵכִין יִכּוֹן עוֹלָם ‖ וְיֵרַח בְּשַׂחַק נֶאֱמָן] cf. v.⁸. The first
l. refers to throne or seed, as v.⁵, and 2 S. 7¹⁶ כִּסְאֲךָ יִהְיֶה נָכוֹן עַד עוֹלָם. Then
we would expect the ‖ נֶאֱמָן בֵּיתְךָ עַד עוֹלָם, and this would be the most appropriate climax for the paraphrase v.³⁸. The vb. is the same. The subj. may be
understood as in previous l. וְעֵד may be for לְעֵד, the ל having been omitted
by copyist, who interpreted it as the familiar phrase עֹולָם וָעֵד, not observing
the measure; later, when parall. was observed, it was pointed as עֵד. Du.
reads בְּעוּר ה', but this is not so easy. בְּ before שַׂחַק should be כְּ, as in ‖ כַיָּרֵחַ.
If we regard עֵד as correct, it is better to think of the moon as witness to the
oath during its perpetual existence. But many think of God, as in Jb. 16¹⁹.
— **39.** [זָנַחְתָּ] pf. hist.; people 43² 60³ 77⁸ 88¹⁵, king only here. — [הִתְעַבַּרְתָּ] pf.
Hithp. denom. עֶבְרָה, v. 78²¹. — **40.** [וְאֵרְתָה] fuller form Pi. pf. 2 m. † [נאר]
abhor, spurn, elsw. La. 2⁷: dub., Hu. נאץ, Du. נֵעַר shake off, 𝕲 κατέστρεψας,
Σ εἰς καταρἁν ἔδωκας, 𝕵 attenuasti, 𝕿 אַשְׁנִיתָא, 𝕾 אֶסְלִית. — ‡ [נֵזֶר] n.m. crown
(sign of consecration) of king, as 132¹⁸ 2 S. 1¹⁰ 2 K. 11¹² = 2 Ch. 23¹¹. —
41. [מִבְצָר] fortification, fortress; v. 60¹¹. — ‡ [מְחִתָּה] ruin of fortress, only here
in this sense; but ruin of a prince without people Pr. 14²⁸, ruin of the poor
in their poverty Pr. 10¹⁵. — **42.** [שַׁסֻּהוּ כָּל־עֹבְרֵי דָרֶךְ] cf. יָאֹרִיךְ כָל־עֹבְרֵי דֶרֶךְ
80¹³. — † [שׁסס] Qal plunder, only here ψ, elsw. 1 S. 17⁵³ Ju. 2¹⁴ Je. 30¹⁶; Niph.

Is. 13[16] Zc. 14[2]; cognate c. שׁסה‎, c. ל‎ Ps. 44[11]. — [עֹבְרֵי דָרֶךְ‎] † phr. elsw. 80[13]
La. 1[12] 2[15]; in all cases of those who gloat over misfortune of Jerusalem or
Israel, or the king; and in Jb. 21[29] of travellers, in Pr. 9[15] of those who go
straight on their way. — [הָיָה חֶרְפָּה לִשְׁכֵנָיו‎] cf. 44[11] 79[4] 80[7], all related Pss.
and all prob. dependent upon our Ps. This completes two quartettes. —
43. [הֲרִימֹתָ יְמִין‎] Hiph. pf. רים‎; elsw. v.[20], of the בחור‎; of קרן‎ 75[5] 148[14], in
victory 75[7], ראשׁ‎ 3[4] 110[7], למרום‎ 75[6]. — [הִשְׂמַחְתָּ כָּל־אוֹיְבָיו‎] Hiph. pf. שׂמח‎ rejoice.
Hiph. α.λ. It is a scribal assimilation to הרימוֹתָ‎; originally Pi. gladden enemies, as 30[2]. — **44.** [אַף תָּשִׁיב צוּר חַרְבּוֹ‎] צוּר‎ is difficult; for stone knife Jos. 5[2]
does not justify the mng. edge or knife here. 𝕲 τὴν βοήθειαν, 𝕵 robur, show
their perplexity. Ols. thinks it vocative of God. Du. would rd. כְצֵר‎ after
44[11], Gr. אחור‎ after 𝕿. צוּר‎ is really not needed for measure. We might take
it as צר‎ adversary of v.[43], and transpose to צריו‎ חרב‎, or regard it as a gl. defining חרב‎. — **45.** [הִשְׁבַּתָּ מִטְּהָרוֹ‎] is a defective l. 𝕲 κατέλυσας ἀπὸ καθαρισμοῦ
αὐτόν, 𝕵 quiescere fecisti munditiam eius. Aq., Σ, 𝕾, AE., Ki., take מטהר‎ as
noun. The separable preposition is necessary for measure unless we supply
a word. But then there is no other example of such a noun as מְטָהֵר‎ Ges.[L. 10. 2. b],
or מְטַהֵר‎ Ols.[§ 173. b] Bö.[286], or מְטֹהַר‎ Ges.[L. 20. 2. (2) b], v. Kö.[II. 1. 35]. Bä. suggests
מַטֵּה מִיָּדוֹ‎ sceptre from his hand, which is good parall. But still better הוֹדוֹ מַטֵּה‎
sceptre of his majesty, v. 8[2] 21[6]; cf. מַטֵּה עֻזְּךָ‎ 110[2]. הִשְׁבִּית‎ cause to cease from, do
away with, c. מִן‎ Ex. 12[15] Lv. 26[6] Ez. 23[27. 48] 30[13] 34[25] Is. 30[11] Je. 7[34], c. acc.
Pss. 8[3] 119[119] 46[10] (wars). — [מִגַּרְתָּ‎] fully written Pi. 2 m. † מוֹר‎ throw, toss,
elsw. only Qal Ez. 21[17]. — **46.** † [עֲלוּמָיו‎] his youth, only found with sf.; elsw. Jb.
20[11] (Kt.) 33[25] Is. 54[4]. — [הֶעֱטִיתָ‎] Hiph. עטה‎ wrap, envelop oneself (71[13]). —
† [בּוּשָׁה‎] n.f. shame, elsw. only Mi. 7[10] Ob.[10] Ez. 7[18]; usually בֹּשֶׁת‎ Pss. 40[16] 69[20]
70[4], לבשׁ ב׳‎ 35[26] 132[18], עטה ב׳‎ 109[29]; cf. 44[16]. V.[39-46] constitute four tetrastichs
of expostulation, the fourth part of the trimeter Ps. which concludes here.

LXXXIX. C.

47. [עַד־מָה יהוה תִּסָּתֵר לָנֶצַח‎] here begin tetrameters which continue to the
end of Ps. — [עַד־מָה‎] how long? cf. 4[3] 79[5]. — **48.** [זְכָר אֲנִי מֶה חָלֶד‎]. The l. is
difficult and too short. אני‎ error for אדני‎, Houb. זכר אדני‎ as v.[51], so Ew., Hi.,
Ols., Bä., Ehr. — [חָלֶד‎] duration, of life 39[6] Jb. 11[17], so here; of world Pss.
17[14] 49[2]. — [עַל מַה שָׁוא‎] for what worthlessness, worthless thing (merely to die)
(v. 12[3]). — **49.** [יִרְאֶה מָּוֶת‎] phr. α.λ. — **50.** [רַאֲשֹׁנִים‎] has two accents, cf. v.[2].
— **51.** [כָּל־רַבִּים‎] defective text; 𝕵 quia portavi in sinu meo omnes iniquitates
populorum, 𝕲 οὗ ὑπέσχον ἐν τῷ κόλπῳ μου πολλῶν ἐθνῶν; the rel. refers to
חרפת‎, 𝕵 conjectures iniquitates; Du. suggests כל ריב‎. Bä. כְּלִמַּת‎ is probable.
— **52.** [עִקְּבוֹת מ׳‎] footprints of Messiah, cf. 56[7] 77[20].

PSALM XC., 6 STR. 5³.

Ps. 90 is a prayer of Israel. It bases itself on the fact that the everlasting God has been the habitation of Israel in all generations (v.$^{1-2}$), prays that the nation may not incur the primitive sentence for sin from Him with whom a thousand years are of so short duration (v.$^{3-4}$). Israel's iniquities from his youth are in the sunshine of God's face, and he is consumed by the divine anger as the grass by the sun (v.$^{5, 6b-8}$). His days rapidly decline, are but a sigh, and are about to fly swiftly away (v.$^{9-10ade}$) ; therefore he prays for instruction as to the meaning of the divine anger and for true wisdom, and importunately complains of delay (v.$^{11-13a}$). The Ps. concludes with a petition for divine kindness, and gladness in proportion to the years of affliction (v.$^{13b-15}$). There are several glosses of interpretation (v.$^{6a, 10b-c}$), and of intensification (v.$^{16-17}$).

(YAHWEH), Thou art our dwelling place:
    Thou art ours in all generations.
    Before the mountains were born,
    And the earth and the world were brought forth,
    From everlasting to everlasting art Thou.
(DO not) turn man back to dust;
    And say : " Return, ye sons of mankind."
    For a thousand years in Thine eyes
    Are as a day, yesterday when it passeth away.
    As a watch in the night Thou dost flood them away.
AS in the morning grass shooteth up,
    In the evening is mown down and withereth ;
    So we are consumed in Thine anger.
    Thou hast set our iniquities before Thee,
    Our youth in the sunlight of Thy face.
FOR all our days do decline ;
    In Thy wrath we bring our years to an end.
    As a sigh are the days of our years,
    And their breadth is travail and trouble :
    For it is quickly gone, and we fly away.
WHO knoweth the strength of Thine anger,
    Or can number (the awful deeds) of Thy wrath?
    Thine hand so make us to know,
    That we may get a mind of wisdom.
    O return, Yahweh ! How long?
BE sorry for Thy servants.
    Satisfy us in the morning with Thy kindness,
    That we may jubilate and be glad in our days.
    Make us glad according to the days Thou hast afflicted us,
    The years when we saw adversity.

Ps. 90 is properly designated in the title as a תפלה, and is ascribed to "Moses the man of God," cf. Dt. 33¹, not with the meaning that it was composed by him, as was usually supposed in former times, but that it was put in his mouth as a pseudograph, just as its neighbours, 88 (ascribed to Heman), and 89 (to Ethan) (*v.* Intr. 1, 30). The Ps. resembles in many respects Dt. 32 ; cf. v.¹ᵇ with Dt. 32⁷, v.¹⁰ שנות and v.¹⁵ ימות with Dt. 32⁷; v.¹³ with Dt. 32³⁶. Its use of מעון v.¹ depends upon Dt. 33²⁷. Moreover the Ps. shows familiarity, v.³ with Gn. 3¹⁹ (J), v.² with Gn. 2⁴ (P). The neglect of other Lit. and this dependence on the historic songs of the Pentateuch were doubtless intentional to make the language appropriate to the pseudograph. The measure and rhythm are also those of these older poems. The Ps. looks back to the youth of the nation through a long history. It expresses an experience of affliction due to the anger of God with the nation for its sins, which has long continued. The prayer is for a restoration of divine favour. The use of לבב v.¹² is in accordance with the usage of the Exile and early Restoration, and the use of חכמה is the earlier one of Je., before the development of WL. The thought of God as the dwelling place of His people resembles Ez. 11¹⁶⁻²⁰, where He is their sanctuary during the Exile. The estimate of proportion between the affliction and the gladness is in accordance with Is. 40². The late Exile is the most probable period of composition.

Str. I. Two syn. couplets and a synth. line. — **1.** *Yahweh*] was doubtless the divine name of the original, subsequently displaced by "Adonay" to correspond with the gloss v.¹⁷. — *Thou art our dwelling place*], based on Dt. 33²⁷, cf. Ps. 91⁹, a richer expression than "refuge" of 𝔊; for it adds to this more frequent conception (cf. 27¹ 31⁵ 37³⁹ 52⁹) the comforting thought that God was the everlasting home of His people. This is an unfolding of the idea of the temple as not only the dwelling place of God, but the place whither His people resort as guests, cf. Ps. 15¹ ˢ𝐪· 84²⁻⁵. During the Exile, when they could not resort to the temple, God Himself became their living temple, cf. Ez. 11¹⁶⁻²⁰ (*v.* Br.ᴹᴾ· ²⁶⁸). — *Thou art ours in all generations*], our own God, belonging to Israel in all the generations of the past. By attaching this to the previous sentence, 𝕳, followed by EVˢ., destroys the measure and the parallelism, and fails to get the additional thought. — **2.** *Before the mountains were born ‖ And the earth and the world were brought forth*], both passive, as 𝔊, Aq., 𝚺, 𝕿, 𝓥, followed by PBV., which suits the parallelism better than with 𝕳, 𝕵, AV., RV., JPSV., to interpret the second vb. as active. The conception is practically the same : that God was not only the Father

of Israel as Dt. 32⁶, but also of the physical universe, the author
probably giving that interpretation to Gn. 2⁴. — *From everlasting
to everlasting art Thou*], asserting the divine existence and activity
during all this interval, from an everlasting time prior to the creation of the world on until an everlasting time in antithesis thereto.
𝔐, followed by EVˢ., attaches the divine name to this sentence ;
but 𝔊, 𝔙, are more correct in interpreting the form as a negative
belonging to the next sentence.

Str. II. Two syn. couplets enclosing a line mediating between
the two. — **3**. *Do not turn man back to dust*], as 𝔊 ; a petition
that the sentence pronounced upon the first parents for their sin
Gn. 3¹⁹ may not be carried out in the case of Israel ‖ *And say*],
in command, *Return, ye sons of mankind*], to the dust from which
ye were made. This is the most natural interp., cf. 146⁴, taking
"man" in its usual collective sense ‖ with "sons of mankind,"
and considering both as emphasizing the humanity of Israel, notwithstanding their privilege of having their home in God. The
usual interpretation, as given in EVˢ., that the couplet states God's
usual dealings with mankind, has grammatical difficulties in the
way, and is hard to reconcile with the course of thought of the Ps.
The PBV. "come again, ye children of men" makes the two lines
antithetical, the turning to death of one generation, the coming
up out of the dust of another generation in constant succession.
This, though favoured by Luther and attractive as a conception, is
not suited to the context. — **4**. *For a thousand years in Thine
eyes*], as compared with the divine existence from everlasting to
everlasting. A thousand years of existence of Israel as a nation
in the eyes of man is a long time from generation to generation ;
but in the eyes of God it amounts to very little. This is urged as
a reason why Israel should not be condemned to death. — *Are as
a day*], a single day, cited 2 Pet. 3⁸ to warn Christians against
thinking God slack concerning His promises. — *Yesterday when it
passeth away*]. The day whose hours are counted as they pass is
not so short to man's mind as yesterday as one sees it passing
away forever. — *As a watch in the night*], one of the three
divisions of the ancient Hebrew night, cf. La. 2¹⁹ Ju. 7¹⁹ 1 S. 11¹¹.
This is not a complement of the previous yesterday, which would
be against the measure. It begins a syn. line whose vb. is :

T

5 a. *Thou dost flood them away*]. Thus we get a fine parallelisᵣ between the passing away of the thousand years, as if they were yesterday, and their being swept away in a flood of rain as if they were no more than a watch in the night. The usual interpretation, that it is man who is swept away in the flood, is favoured by the attachment of this word to the next line against the measure, and also because of the gloss which in 𝕳 is : *they become sleep*], they pass over into the sleep of death.

Str. III. has two syn. couplets with an intermediate line. — **5 b–6.** *As in the morning* ‖ *in the evening*], the beginning and end of the day ; used in the more general figurative sense of the beginning and end of a time, here of the duration of grass, cf. 30⁶ 46⁶ Jb. 11¹⁷ of the duration of trouble, and Gn. 1⁵·⁸·¹³+ of the beginning and end of a divine day's work. — *grass shooteth up* — *is mown down and withereth*], a figure of frailty and transitoriness, cf. Is. 40⁶⁻⁸ Ps. 103¹⁵⁻¹⁶. A glossator inserts an explanatory doublet to the first clause : *in the morning it blossometh and shooteth up*, probably in order to avoid the interpretation of the previous vb. in the sense of " pass away," " fade away " ; but it has not in fact prevented that interpretation by 𝕲, 𝕵, PBV. — **7.** *So we are consumed in Thine anger*]. By ancient copyist's mistake a particle usually rendered " for " took the place of " so " ; but it is difficult to find a reason in this clause. A glossator intensifies this by the ‖ *and in Thy heat are we dismayed*, which cannot be brought into the measures of the Str. The point of the comparison is not stated in this line, but suggested. That which so speedily consumes the grass is the heat of the sun. That which is implicit here is explicit in the next couplet. — **8.** *Thou hast set our iniquities before Thee* ‖ *Our youth in the sunlight of Thy face*]. The face of God is compared to the sun, which consumes the nation because of the iniquities Israel has committed from his youth, just as the sun consumes the grass of the field. The face of God is elsewhere compared to the sun in its enlightening power, cf. 27¹ 84¹² Is. 60¹⁹·²⁰. The word translated above " our youth," in accordance with good usage, after 𝕿, Quinta, is given by 𝕲, 𝕵, as " our age," and by 𝕳, followed by EV⁸., as " our secret sins," all interpretations of the same Heb. consonants in the unpointed text.

Str. IV. A syn. tristich with a syn. couplet between its second and third line. — **9-10.** *For all our days ∥ our years*, summed up in *days of our years ∥ their breadth*]. The days of the years of Israel's life are conceived as extending in breadth over a wide space of time. This, the most natural interpretation, is that of 𝔊, 𝔙, 𝔍. 𝔥, followed by EVˢ., gives a slightly different form supposed to mean " pride " ; but this is α.λ. and not so well suited to the context, for the vbs. all imply extent, measurement. — *decline*], of the swiftly falling day ∥ *bring to an end ∥ quickly gone*, and in the climax *fly away*], in the swiftest movement, as time flies, cf. Jb. 20⁸. The whole duration of the nation's life is compared to a *sigh ∥ travail and trouble*], cf. Gn. 47⁸⁻⁹. All this is because of the divine *wrath*, as v.⁷. A glossator inserted a prosaic statement as to the usual duration of human life : *In them are seventy years, or if, by reason of extraordinary might, eighty years.* But it interrupts the thought and destroys the measure of the original.

Str. V. Syn. couplet, synth. couplet, and a line synth. thereto. — **11.** *Who knoweth ? ∥ can number ?*], implying the negative answer : no one, — *the strength of Thine anger ∥ the awful deeds of Thy wrath*]. As the previous context shows, Israel did know by generations of experience somewhat of the strength of the divine anger against himself as well as other nations, and he could enumerate many awful deeds of wrath in the past history. But he is yet conscious that the divine wrath is much stronger than he has experienced it, and that the full number of awful deeds that God might do has not yet been estimated. He dreads the full measure of the divine wrath, which he knows has been held back. The simple and powerful parallels of this couplet and its measures, essentially preserved by 𝔊, 𝔙, have been destroyed by 𝔥, 𝔍, followed by EVˢ., both by misreading the noun so as to compel the translation : " and according to the fear that is due unto Thee," and by attaching the vb. " number " to the next line. — **12.** *Thine hand so make us to know*], so 𝔊, 𝔙 ; the hand as stretched out in anger and in doing awful deeds. The petition of Israel is that he may so know the divine hand in discipline that he *may get a mind of wisdom*], and so in the future be able to think and act wisely in accordance with the divine will and guidance. 𝔥, 𝔍, followed by EVˢ., read : " to number our days so make us know," implying that the lesson is to be learned from the brevity and affliction of life. — **13**. *O return, Yahweh*], the importunate petition for restoration of favour, cf. Dt. 32³⁶ Ps. 6⁴; with the complaint: *How long?*], cf. 74¹⁰ 80⁵ 82² 94³.

Str. VI. A synth. triplet and a syn. couplet. — **13 b.** *Be sorry for Thy servants*], as Dt. 32³⁶ Ps. 135¹⁴. — **14**. *Satisfy us in the morning with Thy kindness*], after the long night of affliction, cf. v.⁵⁻⁶, — *that we may jubilate and be glad in our days*], rejoice in the renewed favour of their God in their resort to Him as their everlasting home. A glossator intensifies by inserting "all" before "days," without need and against the measure — **15**. *Make us glad according to the days ‖ the years*], those mentioned in the previous Strophes. — *Thou hast afflicted us ‖ we saw adversity*]. Israel desires that his joy in salvation may at least be equal in extent of duration, and probably also in intensity, with the afflictions he has so long experienced, cf. Is. 40².

The Ps. has reached a most appropriate conclusion; but a later editor, doubtless for liturgical reasons, wished to emphasize the situation, and so he added v.¹⁶⁻¹⁷. — **16**. *Let Thy work appear unto Thy servants*], that is, work of salvation, cf. Dt. 32⁴ Ps. 92⁵. — *and Thy majesty upon their children*], so 𝔐, but 𝔊, 𝔙, "lead their children," by a different pointing of the same Hebrew consonants, making it more in accord with v.¹². — **17**. *And let the sweetness of Adonay our God be upon us*], cf. 27⁴; the graciousness, kindliness of God; syn. with "kindness," v.¹⁴ᵃ, rather than with majesty. — *the work of our hands O establish upon us*], give us success and prosperity in our labours. This is repeated, in part, for emphasis: *and the work of our hands establish it.*

1. ארני] dub. rd. יהוה as v.¹³. — מָעֹון] *v. 26⁸ dwelling*, as 91⁹, cf. 71³, מְעֹונָה Dt. 33²⁷ Ps. 76³; so 𝔍, Dr., Kirk., *BDB.*; but 𝔊 καταφυγή מעוז, so Street, Ols., Gr. — **2.** בְּטֶרֶם] usually sq. impf.; but older usage abandoned here, Dr.²⁷ ᴮ·ⁿ. — וַתְּהֹולֵל] ו consec. impf. Polel חול (29⁸), so 𝔍, Bä., as Dt. 32¹⁸; but 𝔊, Aq., Σ, 𝔗, 𝔙, PBV., Polal, as Pr. 8²⁴·²⁵ Ps. 51⁷; so Street, Bö., Hi., Moll., Hu.³. — **3.** אֵל] divine name, so 𝔖, 𝔍, and most; but 𝔊 neg. אַל attached to the juss. תָּשֵׁב, which indeed is difficult to explain otherwise, so Gr., Bruston. 𝔙 has both אֵל and אַל by dittog. הָשֵׁב is explained by some as equivalent to ו consec. impf. with ו omitted, Dr.⁸⁵ ᴮ. It might be explained as prot. of conditional clause with ותאמר in apod.; but neither of these is suited to the context. — † דַּכָּא] n.m. α.λ.; but adj. Ps. 34¹⁹ Is. 57¹⁵; 𝔊 ταπείνωσιν, 𝔙 *in*

ו [וַהֹּאמֶר] — עפר. Gn. 3¹⁹. *humilitatem* improb. It is doubtless a variation of consec. impf. emph. present: but Aq., 𝔍, Gr. ו conj., which is to be preferred. —
4. †[אֶתְמוֹל] adv. *yesterday*, 1 S. 4⁷ 10¹¹ 14²¹ 19⁷ 2 S. 5², cf. Is. 30³³; prob. apposition with יוֹם. — [כִּי יַעֲבֹר] impf. of graphic description of the movement in process. — **5.** [זְרַמְתָּם] pf. זרם vb. denom. יֶרֶם, *flood away*, Qal a.λ., but Pol. 77¹⁸. 𝔊 τὰ ἐξουδενώματα αὐτῶν, 𝔙 *quae pro nihilo habentur eorum;* 𝔖 זרעתם *their seed*, cf. Ez. 23²⁰ זרמה *issue*, so Ehr. — [שֵׁנָה יִהְיוּ] so 𝔍, Σ; but 𝔊 ἔτη, 𝔙 *anni* שָׁנִים more prob. In any case it is explan. gl., against the measure. — [יַחֲלֹף׀] Qal impf. ‡ חלף as v.⁶ 102²⁷, 𝔊, 𝔙, *pass away*, so Ew.; but *come anew, sprout again*, De., Hi., Bä., *BDB*. Hiph. *change* garments 102²⁷ Gn. 35² (E). — **6.** [בבקר יציץ וחלף] is explan. doublet and a gl. — **7.** [כִּי כָלִינוּ] though sustained by Vrss. is improb. as causal clause; rd. כֵּן as Street. — [ובחמתך נבהלנו] is gl. of intensification, against the measure. — **8.** [שַׁתָּ] Kt., defectively written שַׁתָּה as Qr. — [עֲלֻמֵנוּ] defectively written pl. pass. ptc. עָלֻם, *our secrets;* so 𝔍, Σ, cf. העלמה Ps. 44²² Jb. 28¹¹; but Qal of vb. a.λ. and improb. 𝔊 ὁ αἰὼν ἡμῶν, 𝔙 *saeculum nostrum* עוֹלָמֵנוּ; but this late usage of עוֹלָם. 𝔗, Quinta, עֲלוּמֵנוּ *our youth*, cf. 89⁴⁶ Is. 54⁴ Jb. 20¹¹ 33²⁵ most prob. — [מְאוֹר פָּנֶיךָ] phr. a.λ. in this sense, but cf. Pr. 15³⁰; well suited to context in the sense of *luminary*, the face of God being cf. to the sun with its scorching heat; cf. Ps. 74¹⁶. — **9.** [כְּמוֹ הֶגֶה] should go to next l. for good measure. †הֶגֶה n.m. (1) *sound of God's voice, thunder* Jb. 37²; (2) here *sigh*, BDB, *murmur*, Dr., cf. Ez. 2¹⁰, 𝔊 ἀράχνην ἐμελέτων, 𝔊ᴺ·ᶜ·ᵃ·ᴬ·ᴿ·ᵀ, ἀράχνη. —
10. [יְמֵי שְׁנוֹתֵינוּ] phr. cf. Gn. 25⁷ 47⁸·⁹ (P) 2 S. 19³⁵ Ec. 6⁸; pl. f. שנות elsw. v.¹⁵ Dt. 32⁷ + 18 t. — [בָּהֶם] emph. in position, introducing gl. extending through שבעים שנה. — [גְּבוּרֹת] if correctly pointed, abstr. intensive pl. *great might* or *extraordinary might* (20⁷). — [רָהְבָּם] 3 pl. sf. with † רהב a.λ. *pride;* but 𝔊, 𝔙, 𝔍, רחבם *their breadth* most prob. — [יָמֵל וָאֹון] phr. elsw. 10⁷ Jb. 4⁸ 5⁶ Is. 10¹. — [גָּז] Qal pf. † גוז Qal *pass away*, elsw. Nu. 11³¹ of quails. — [חִישׁ] adv. a.λ. *quickly*, cf. חוּשׁ vb. 22²⁰; but 𝔊 ἐπῆλθεν πραΰτης ἐφ᾽ ἡμᾶς, 𝔙 *supervenit mansuetudo*, cf. השׁה 28¹, also Is. 57¹¹ 65⁶. — **11.** [וּכְיִרְאָתְךָ] so 𝔍, with obj. sf. *according to the fear that is due Thee.* But 𝔊 ἀπὸ τοῦ φόβου τοῦ θυμοῦ σου has no sf. nor prep. כ; both are prob. interp., as indeed the ἀπὸ of 𝔊, leaving יראת as the common original, which was then prob. pl. referring to the awful deeds; and נוראת as usual. — **12.** [לִמְנוֹת] as in 𝔊 belongs with previous l. to complete its measure. — [יָמֵינוּ] so 𝔍; but 𝔊 τὴν δεξιάν σου, 𝔙 *dexteram tuam*, is more prob., ימין, the sf. in both cases, being interp. — [כֵּן הוֹרַע] so 𝔍, 𝔊ᴺ·ᶜ·ᵃ·ᴬ·ᴿ·ᵀ, but 𝔊ᴮ·ᴺ omits כֵּן, needed for measure. — ו [וְנָבִא] subord. Hiph. impf. 1 pl., cf. La. 5⁹. — [לְבַב חָכְמָה] phr. a.λ., but cf. חכם לבב Jb. 9⁴, לב חכם 1 K. 3¹² Pr. 16²³ Ec. 8⁵, לב הבמיה Ec. ⁷⁴ 10². — **13.** [הִנָּחֵם] Niph. imv. נחם c.; with אל Ju. 21⁶; prob. originally הִנְחֵם, which is used in the same phr. Ps. 135¹⁴, both based on Dt. 32³⁶. — **14.** [וּכְבַל־יָמֵינוּ] so 𝔊; but בל is unnecessary and makes l. too long. — **15.** [ימות] pl. f. elsw. Dt. 32⁷. — **16.** [יֵרָאֶה] Niph. juss.; so all Vrss., but 𝔊 καὶ ἴδε, 𝔙 *respice* וּרְאֵה Qal imv. — [פָּעֳלֶךָ] as 44² 77¹³; all Vrss. except 𝔍 have pl.; 𝔐 codd. differ: 65 Kenn., 117 De R., sg.; v. Baer. — [וַהֲדָרְךָ] (8⁶); but 𝔊 ὁδήγησον הַדְרֵךְ Hiph. imv. דרך *lead* as 25⁵ 107⁷ 119³⁵,

𝔙 *dirige filios eorum;* עַל of 𝔐 interp. — **17.** [וַיְהִי ו conj. juss. — [נֹעַם *v.*
27⁴. — [אֲדֹנָי אֱלֹהֵינוּ] cf. Dn. 9⁹·¹⁵, late phr. — [מַעֲשֵׂה יָדֵינוּ כּוֹנְנָה] repeated for
emphasis with the variation of sf. הוּ־ to vb. The repetition is not in 𝔊ᴮ, but
in 𝔊ᴺ·ᴬ·ᴿ·ᵀ· without sf., which is prob. interp. in 𝔐.

PSALM XCI., 4 STR. 7³.

Ps. 91 is didactic in character : (1) assures Israel of the safety
from peril of those who make the temple of God their habitual
resort (v.¹⁻³, ⁴ᶜ) ; (2) then, in a direct address, exhorts not to fear
the pestilence which is destroying multitudes on every side (v.⁵⁻⁷) ;
asserts that God will keep them safely in the hands of guardian
angels (v.⁹· ¹¹⁻¹³) ; and finally (3) speaks in the name of God,
assuring those who know and love God that He will deliver them
from all trouble and honour them in a long life (v.¹⁴⁻¹⁶). Glosses
emphasize the promise (v.⁴ᵃᵇ· ¹⁰), and assert that they will see the
recompense of the wicked (v.⁸).

> AS for him who dwells in the secret place of 'Elyon,
>   In the shadow of Shadday abides,
>   Saith of Yahweh : " My refuge !
>   My fortress ! my God in whom I trust ! "
>   Surely He will deliver from the snare,
>   The one ensnared from the engulfing pestilence ;
>   With a shield His faithfulness will surround him.
> THOU shalt not be afraid of the terror by night,
>   Of the arrow that flieth by day,
>   Of the pestilence that goeth in darkness,
>   Of the destruction that wasteth at noonday.
>   Though a thousand fall at thy side,
>   And a myriad at thy right hand,
>   Unto thee it will not come nigh.
> SINCE 'Elyon thou hast made thy dwelling,
>   He will give His angels charge over thee
>   To keep thee in all thy ways.
>   Upon their palms they will bear thee up,
>   Lest thou dash thy foot against a stone.
>   Upon reptile and cobra thou wilt tread ;
>   Thou wilt trample the young lion and dragon.
> SINCE he hath set his love on Me, I will deliver him.
>   I will set him on high, because he doth know My name.
>   He will call upon Me, and I will answer him.
>   With him I will be in trouble.
>   I will deliver him, and I will honour him.
>   With length of days will I satisfy him,
>   And make him gaze on my salvation."

Ps. 91 in ￥, ﬡ, is without title. But 𝕲 has αἶνος ᾠδῆς τῷ Δαυείδ. This was the conjecture of a late editor, due to the large number of terms in this Ps. familiar in 𝕯: סתר and צל v.[1] for the refuge in the temple, as 17[8] 27[5] 31[21] 36[8] 61[5] + ; מצודה v.[2], cf. 18[3] 31[4]; צנה v.[4], cf. 5[13]; the guardian angel v.[11], cf. 34[8] 35[5, 6]. The author also used אנכי v.[15] and חשק v.[14], both characteristic of D, and was especially familiar with Dt. 32, using the terms חץ, קטב, v.[5, 6], cf. Dt. 32[23, 24]; רבבה, אלף, v.[7], cf. Dt. 32[30]; זהל, פחן, and תנין v.[13], cf. Dt. 32[24, 33]. V.[4a] is similar to Dt. 32[11], and v.[4b] uses the familiar image of Pss. 17[8] 36[8] 57[2] 61[5] 63[8] (all 𝕯), though in a form found elsw. only Ru. 2[12]; but both phrs. are gl. The characteristic divine names are : עליון v.[1, 9], cf. Dt. 32[8] Ps. 18[14]; שרי v.[1], cf. Gn. 49[25] Nu. 24[4, 16], a poetic rather than an early usage. The use of מעון v.[9] is similar to that of 90[1], only here it is of the temple, there of God Himself. The phr. ידע שם v.[14] is elsw. 9[11] Is. 52[6] Je. 48[17]. The Ps. was evidently written in peaceful times, when there was constant access to the temple, and when the chief evils to be feared were pestilence and such like. The Ps. belongs to the late Persian or more probably to the early Greek period. It is dramatic in character. The change of persons does not imply responsive voices ; but the poet now speaks for himself of the general principles of the divine government, then addresses the people with personal application of these principles, and finally utters the words of God Himself. The use of v.[11-12] with reference to Jesus Mt. 4[6] = Lk. 4[10-11], and the dominion over the lion and the serpent v.[13], similar in some respects to Is. 11[6-9], give the Ps. a Messianic character.

Str. I. a syn. tetrastich and a syn. tristich. — **1.** *As for him who dwells*], emphatic in position, introducing the protasis whose apodosis begins in v.[3]. — *abides*]. The ptc. expresses the continual dwelling, the impf. the habitual resort. The place was the temple, — *the secret place of 'Elyon ‖ the shadow of Shadday*], as 17[8] 27[5] 31[21] 32[7] 36[8] 57[2] 61[5] 63[8] (all 𝕯). The divine names are the poetic ones based on Gn. 49[25] Dt. 32[8] Ps. 18[14]. — **2.** *Saith*], taking the form as ptc. after 𝕲, 𝔘, 𝔖, syn. with previous ptc. ￥, ﬡ, followed by EV[s]., interpret the form as 1 sg., " I will say," which makes an abrupt change, introducing another voice. — *of Yahweh*], of AV., RV., JPSV., seems better than " unto Yahweh " of PBV., although either is a proper translation. — *My refuge*], cf. v.[9] 14[6] 46[2] 61[4] 62[8, 9] + ‖ *my fortress*], cf. 18[3] 31[4] 71[3] + ‖ *my God in whom I trust*] : all this emphasizing the general principle that Yahweh in His temple was the habitual resort and refuge of His people. — **3.** *Surely*], introducing the apodosis with an asseveration, as AV., and not with the causal particle " for," as PBV., RV. — *He will deliver*], namely, the one indicated in the protasis ;

but 𝔥, 𝔍, followed by EVˢ., interpret obj. as sf. 2 pers. "thee," another abrupt change of person, due doubtless to assimilation to the gloss v.⁴ᵃᵇ. — *from the snare*], defined in the ‖ as *engulfing pestilence*, ensnaring multitudes in engulfing ruin, cf. v.⁵⁻⁷. Israel is in great peril from this pestilence. He is *one ensnared* in it already, and therefore needs deliverance : for so we should translate this first word of the line, and not make it dependent upon the previous word, as EVˢ., and translate "of the fowler," which destroys the measure. — **4.** *With a shield His faithfulness will surround him*], so 𝔊, 𝔍, 𝔖, which is better suited to the parall. than 𝔥, followed by EVˢ., interpreting the Heb. word as a noun α.λ. "buckler " ‖ *shield.* On the one side God will deliver His faithful people from the pestilence in which they are already ensnared, and on the other side will shield them from it in the future. — A glossator makes a personal application of this prematurely in v.⁴ᵃᵇ, using the terms of earlier Pss. of 𝔅 17⁸ 36⁸ 57² 61⁵ 63⁸, cf. Dt. 32¹¹ : *With His pinion He will cover thee, and under His wings thou wilt take refuge.*

Str. II. A syn. tetrastich, a syn. distich, and an emphatic conclusion. — **5–6.** *Thou shalt not be afraid*], a direct address based on the doctrine of the previous Str. The pestilence is now described in several terms : *the terror by night* ‖ *the arrow that flieth by day* ‖ *the destruction that wasteth at noonday*]. At all hours of day and night *the pestilence* is at work, causing terror in the *darkness* of the night, swift and sudden as an arrow in its flight, piercing the very soul in the daylight, and making havoc and devastation at noon. 𝔊 thinks of the pestilence as a demon, and it is possible that 𝔥 had the same idea. Both vary on this account from the vb. that was probably original to the text. So terrible was the pestilence that it is stated as a possibility : **7.** *Though a thousand fall at thy side* ‖ *And a myriad at thy right hand*], and so the people of God were exposed to the utmost possible degree, — yet *Unto thee it will not come nigh*], resuming v.³·⁴ᶜ; safe in the protection of their God, the plague cannot approach them. — A glossator appends **8**, probably in order to show that God distinguishes between the righteous and the wicked ; and that while He delivers those who have made Him their refuge, He does not spare the wicked. The pestilence will spend itself on them, and the righteous will see them suffer the recompense of their wickedness. — *Only with thine eyes wilt thou behold and see the recompense of the wicked*]. This glossator seems to have held the older opinion, contested in the book of Job, that the wicked and the righteous are carefully discriminated in plagues and other evils.

Str. III. An introductory line, a synth. tetrastich, and a syn. couplet. — **9**. *Since 'Elyon thou hast made thy dwelling*], resuming the thought of v.¹⁻² : hast made the presence of God in the temple, the place of habitual resort, a real home. — A marginal gloss claims that this very thing has been done : *For Thou, Yahweh, art my refuge*]. This subsequently crept into the text prior to the first line of this Str., making another of those abrupt transitions characteristic of the present text of the Ps. — A glossator before the specific promises of v.¹¹⁻¹² introduces a general one : **10**. *Evil will not befall thee, nor plague approach thy tent*]. This breaks the force of the antithesis with the previous Str. — **11**. *He will give His angels charge over thee*]. The guardian angels, cf. 34⁸ 35⁵·⁶ Gn. 24⁷, now take the place of the shield of v.⁴ as more active agents of the divine protection. — *To keep thee in all thy ways*]. Wherever the pious went, they would be kept in safety by their guardians. — **12**. *Upon their palms they will bear thee up*], when there was any danger of falling, — and that with so much attention to detail, *Lest thou dash thy foot against a stone*]. This passage was used by Satan in the temptation of Jesus, Mt. 4⁶ = Lk. 4¹⁰⁻¹¹, with a logical interpretation to a situation not contemplated in the Ps. The Ps. has in view a real peril, which meets the pious in his normal course of life. Satan applies the promise to a peril into which he urges Jesus to cast himself. This interpretation of the promise is rejected by Jesus as tempting God. — **13**. *Upon reptile and cobra thou wilt tread*], so 𝕲, as Dt. 32²⁴; but 𝕳, by copyist's error of a single letter, introduces prematurely the lion. The context suggests that this treading on venomous snakes, which might in an ordinary case be deadly, in the case of the pious would be harmless. — *Thou wilt trample the young lion and dragon*]. The pious would have dominion over them. This gives the promise a Messianic significance, cf. Is. 11⁶⁻⁹.

Str. IV. Two syn. couplets and a syn. tristich. — **14–16.** *Since he hath set his love on Me*], a Deuteronomic expression, love to God being really implied in the dwelling in the temple v.[1. 9]: ‖ *he doth know My name*], personal acquaintance with the name of God as manifested in the sanctuary, cf. 9[11] Is. 52[6] Je. 48[17]. — *I will deliver him ‖ I will set him on high*], resumed in v.[15b], — *I will deliver him and I will honour him*], and in the climax v.[16], — *And make him gaze on my salvation*], cf. 50[23]. The deliverance is to be not a simple one, but an exalted, a glorious one, which he will be permitted not only to experience but to contemplate with joy. It will indeed be in answer to prayer: *He will call upon me and I will answer him*], and connected with the constant presence of God with the one who constantly resorts to Him: *With him I will be in trouble*], cf. 23[4] 46[8. 12]; and as the final result, instead of his days being cut short by the pestilence, as was the case with multitudes of others, *With length of days*, a long life, *will I satisfy him.*

1. [שֹׁדַי] 𝔊. — 61[5] ס׳ כנפיך 31[21], ס׳ פניך 27[5], ס׳ אהלו cf. phr. a.λ. [סֵתֶר עֶלְיוֹן] τοῦ Θεοῦ τοῦ οὐρανοῦ, 𝔍 *domini*. — [יִתְלוֹנָן] Hithp. לין, elsw. Jb. 39[28]; but Qal Ps. 25[13] +. — **2.** [אֹמַר] Qal impf. 1 sg., so 𝔍; but 𝔊 ἐρεῖ, so 𝔙, 𝔖, either אמר ptc. or יאמר 3 sg., so Hu., Pe., Gr., Du., al. — [יהוה] 𝔊[B. א] τῷ Θεῷ, but 𝔊[B. a. b. א. c. a. A. T.] κυρίῳ, 𝔍 *domino*. — **3.** [יַצִּילְךָ] so 𝔍, 𝔊[א. A. R. T] με; but 𝔊[B] יציל sf. interp. — † [יָקוּשׁ] usually n.[m.] *fowler*, as Ho. 9[8]; but ‖ requires independent word, prob. ptc. pass. vb. יקשׁ *one snared*. — [דֶּבֶר] *pestilence*, as Ex. 5[3] 9[15] Nu. 14[12] (J) Dt. 28[21]; but 𝔊 λόγου = דבר. — **4.** [אֶבְרָתוֹ] sf. אֶבְרָה *pinion*, as Dt. 32[11]. — [יֶסֶךְ] impf. סכך (5[12]), not juss. but late, when distinction had disappeared. — [סֹחֵרָה] n.f. *buckler*, a.λ., as Aq., Σ, 𝔗; but 𝔊 κυκλώσει, so 𝔙, 𝔖, סֹחֵרָה ptc. vb. סחר *go round about.* — **5.** [יָעוּף] rel. clause; of arrow only here, *v. 18[11]*. — **6.** [יַהֲלֹךְ] for usual יֵלֵךְ. — † [קֶטֶב] n.m. *destruction*, as Dt. 32[24] of Sheol, Ho. 13[14] Is. 28[2]. — [וְיָשׁוּד] denom. שֵׁד, originally *lord*, subsequently *demon, god*, Dt. 32[17] Ps. 106[37] (𝔊); 𝔊 δαιμονίου, 𝔙 *daemonio*, שֵׁד here; but more prob. impf. שדד *lay waste.* — **8.** [בְּעֵינֶיךָ תַבִּיט] phr. a.λ., the line a gl. — [וְשִׁלֻּמַת רְשָׁעִים תִּרְאֶה] gl. from 73[8]. — **9.** [כִּי אַתָּה יהוה מַחְסִי] gl. originally marginal note, referring to v.[2]. — [מְעוֹנֶךָ] as 90[1], but 𝔊 here as there καταφυγήν σου, מַעוֹן. — **10.** [תְאֻנֶּה] Pu. impf. † אנה vb. not used in Qal. Pi. *cause to meet* Ex. 21[13] (E). Pu. *be allowed to meet*, elsw. Pr. 12[21]. Hithp. 2 K. 5[7]. — **13.** † [שַׁחַל] n.m. poetic, *lion* as Ho. 5[14] 13[7] Jb. 4[10] 10[16] 28[8] Pr. 26[13]; but 𝔊 ἀσπίδα = חל׳, so 𝔖, 𝔍, as Dt. 32[24] Mi. 7[17], more prob. with פרן *venomous serpent*, prob. cobra Ps. 58[5] Dt. 32[33]. — **14.** ‡ [חָשַׁק] vb. Qal *be attached in love*, c כ. Dt. 7[7] 10[15] 21[11] +. — [יָדַע שְׁמִי] phr. elsw. Ps. 9[11] Is. 52[6] Je. 48[17]. — **15.** [אָנֹכִי] *long form* as in D. It is also needed for measure.

PSALM XCII., 4 STR. 6³.

Ps 92 is a song in praise of Yahweh : (1) rejoicing in the act of praising day and night with instrumental music (v.²⁻⁴) ; (2) wondering at the greatness of the divine works and thoughts, especially in permitting the wicked to flourish only to their eventual destruction (v.⁶·⁸⁻⁹) ; (3) the wicked will surely perish in full view of the righteous, who will be exalted in their stead (v.¹⁰⁻¹²) ; (4) the righteous will flourish in the temple, as the palm and cedar, even to old age (v.¹³⁻¹⁵). Glosses emphasize the gladness (v.⁵), the ignorance of man (v.⁷), and the uprightness of God (v.¹⁶).

IT is good to give thanks to Yahweh,
 To make melody to Thy name, 'Elyon ;
 To declare Thy kindness in the morning,
 And Thy faithfulness in the dark night,
 With a ten-stringed harp,
 With melody on the lyre.
O HOW great are Thy works !
 How very deep Thy thoughts !
 When the wicked sprout forth as herbage,
 And all the workers of iniquity blossom,
 It is in order that they may be destroyed forever,
 Since Thou art on high everlastingly.
FOR lo ! Thine enemies shall perish ;
 All the workers of iniquity shall be scattered.
 But Thou wilt exalt my horn as a yore ox ;
 (Thou hast enriched me) with fresh oil ;
 And mine eye shall look on my lurking foes ;
 Evil doers mine ears shall hear.
THE righteous will sprout forth as the palm tree,
 Wax tall as the cedar in Lebanon.
 Transplanted into the house of Yahweh,
 They will sprout forth in the courts of our God.
 Still in old age they will bear fruit :
 They will be full of sap and freshly green.

Ps. 92 was originally a שיר, a term appropriate to its contents. מזמור was added at a later date. It was eventually assigned for use in the liturgy: ליום השבת (*v.* Intr. §§ 24, 31, 39). It is a Ps. eminently suited for worship, whether in the temple or the synagogue. It was composed in the time when Israel was exposed to peril from enemies, and when the musical service of the temple was in full operation ; therefore probably in the late Greek period. The language is not late : הגיון v.⁴ **as** 9¹⁷ ; **v.⁶** depends possibly on Is. 55⁸·⁹ ; v.⁷ is related to 49¹¹ 73²², but is a gl.

Str. I. A syn. tetrastich and a syn. couplet. — **2–4.** *It is good*] pleasant, delightful, — *to give thanks ‖ to make melody*], terms usual in public worship in the temple, cf. 33^2 105^{1-2} 106^1 $107^{1.\ 8.\ 15.\ 21.\ 31}$ $118^{1.\ 29}$ 136^1. The theme is *Yahweh ‖ Thy name Elyon*], cf 18^{50} 135^3; *Thy kindness ‖ Thy faithfulness*], the pair of divine attributes usually associated in such songs, — *in the morning ‖ in the dark night*] implying public worship in the temple at night, cf. 134^1, as well as in the morning, and indeed not only with vocal music, but with instruments as well, — *with a ten-stringed harp*], as 𝕲, cf. 33^2 144^9, *and with melody on the lyre*, cf. 81^3. 𝕳, followed by EV⁸., interprets the word meaning " ten-stringed " as another instrument than the harp. 𝕵 also interprets " melody " as song accompanying the lyre, and so PBV. as a separate " loud instrument," but all this is improbable. — **5.** A glossator inserts a reason here, which the original reserves for the subsequent Strs., — *For Thou hast made me glad ‖ I shall ring out praise*], the theme of which was some deliverance just wrought, probably in the Maccabean times. — *Thy deed ‖ the works of Thy hands*], cf. 28^5 77^{13} 90^{16}.

Str. II. Two syn. couplets and a synth. one. — **6.** *How great*], exclamation of wonder and praise ‖ *How very deep*], for the exclamation is continued in the syn. line, which is not a mere statement of fact, as EV⁵. The *works* of Yahweh are wonderfully great, in intensity rather than in number, as implied in the syn. " deep," which is appropriate to the divine *thoughts* as unsearchable and profound, cf. 40^6, but especially Is. $55^{8.\ 9}$. These divine works and thoughts are with reference to the wicked, in the antithesis between their prosperity and their ultimate destruction v.$^{8-9}$. But a glossator interposed a couplet emphasizing the profundity of the divine thoughts. — **7.** *A brutish man ‖ a dullard*], cf. 49^{11}, as distinguished from a wise and understanding man, living in the fear of God ; characteristic of WL. — *knoweth not ‖ understandeth this not*], that which the psalmist knows in his experience and what the people understand in the use of the song of praise. — **8.** *When the wicked ‖ all the workers of iniquity*], doubtless the same as those of v.$^{10.\ 12}$, and therefore not wicked men in Israel, but foreign enemies and treacherous foes. — *sprout forth as herbage ‖ blossom*], in sudden luxuriant success and prosperity. The simile implies also frailty and transitoriness, cf. 90[5-6], which is then expressed in the apodosis in the strongest terms. — *It is in order that they may be destroyed forever*], and the reason for it is — **9**. *Since Thou art on high everlastingly*]. Yahweh reigns in the height of heaven, everlastingly His dominion continues. This makes it certain that the prosperity of the wicked will only be temporary, and their doom sudden and irrevocable. The antithesis between the everlasting reign of God and the everlasting destruction of the wicked brings the Str. to its climax.

Str. III. Three syn. couplets. — **10**. *For lo ! Thine enemies*], repeated for emphasis with the divine name in 𝔊, 𝔍, EVᵉ., but not in the original. The wicked are the divine enemies, as usual in the ψ. — *shall perish ‖ shall be scattered*], in defeat on the battle-field and in the panic of a disastrous rout. — **11**. *But Thou wilt exalt my horn*], in victory, cf. 75[5.6] 89[18] 148[14] : *as a yore ox*], the gigantic wild bull of the ancients, cf. Nu. 23[22] Dt. 33[17] Ps. 22[22] Jb. 39[9 sq.], whose furious onset was greatly to be feared by the hunter. — *Thou dost enrich me with fresh oil*], that is, at the festival celebrating the victory he is anointed so richly with oil by Yahweh that he will be saturated with it as are cakes when prepared for the sacrifice. This is a parallel simile. As Horsley, " a penetration of the whole substance of the man's person by the oil," cf. 23[5]. — **12**. *Mine eye shall look on*], with the gaze of the victor, seeing his enemies slain on the battle-field and rushing panic-stricken away from his pursuit ‖ *Mine ears shall hear*], doubtless the outcries of terror and anguish of the vanquished.

Str. IV. Three syn. couplets. — **13**. *The righteous*], Israel, and not the righteous in Israel, — *will sprout forth as the palm tree*], an appropriate simile of rapid, vigorous growth and luxuriance of life, — *wax tall as the cedar of Lebanon*], a simile of strength and durability, cf. Ho. 14[5.6] ; both in antithesis with the luxuriant but perishable herbage to which the wicked had been compared v.[8]. — **14**. *transplanted into the house of Yahweh ‖ courts of our God*]. The temple in its larger sense, as explained by courts, is conceived as exceedingly fertile soil. The trees that are removed from other places and planted there will have a luxuriant growth, cf. 1[3] 84[5]. — *They will sprout forth*, as young plants, and, — **15**. *still in old age they will bear fruit*], doubtless combining in the figure the fruitfulness of the palm and the longevity of the cedar. — *They will be full of sap and freshly green*], everlastingly animate with the fulness of life and ever green with the richest of foliage.

The Ps. comes to its most appropriate end here; but a glossator, wishing to give it a dogmatic ending, adds: **16.** *That they may declare that Yahweh is upright, my Rock in whom is no iniquity*]. This seems to be based on Dt. 32⁴, where the uprightness of God was properly emphasized; but here it is inappropriate, for the Ps. praises rather the divine kindness and faithfulness.

3. וַאֱמוּנָתְךָ] has two tones. — לֵילוֹת] abstr. intensive pl. *dark night*, as 134¹ Ct. 3¹·⁸. — **4.** עֲלֵי עָשׂוֹר וַעֲלֵי נָבֶל] 𝔐, 𝔍. עֲלֵי archaic for עַל. The repetition makes l. tetrameter and interp. עָשׂוֹר as a different instrument from נבל. But 𝔊 had only נבל עָשׂוֹר or נבל עשור as 33² 144⁹, *a ten-stringed harp.* — הגיון] as 9¹⁷, *melody, resounding music,* 𝔊 μετ᾽ ᾠδῆς, Σ μελῳδίας. 𝔍 *cantico et* interprets it as apart from בְּכִנּוֹר just as in previous line. — **5.** יהוה, though in Vrss., makes the l. tetrameter. The v. is doubtless a gl., giving a premature reason. — **7.** אִישׁ בַּעַר] cf. אני בער 73²² with the same vb. כסיל implies WL. and indicates a gl. — **8.** לְהִשָּׁמְדָם] Niph. inf. c. sf., with לְ. This is prob. for an earlier למען needed for the measure. — **9.** יהוה] is gl.; unnecessary and makes l. too long. — **10.** כִּי הִנֵּה אֹיְבֶיךָ יהוה] 𝔐, 𝔍, is not in 𝔊ᴮ, but in 𝔊ᴬ·ᴿ·ᵀ, and is dittog. or emph. repetition; in either case a gl. — יִתְפָּרְדוּ] Hithp. impf. in the sense of *dispersed*, as Jb. 4¹¹; *separated*, Ps. 22¹⁵. — **11.** וַתָּרֶם] ו consec. of 𝔐 is wrong interp. 𝔊, 𝔍, 𝔙, all have simple ו and make the vb. future as the context demands. — בַּלֹּתִי] Qal pf. 1 sg. בלל usually after Ki. intrans. *anointed*, but without justification in usage. 𝔖, 𝔗, Ols., Du., בַּלֹּתִי most prob. 𝔊 τὸ γῆράς μου, 𝔙 *senectus mea*, 𝔍 *senecta mea*, Σ ἡ παλαίωσίς μου. Hu., Bä., בְּלוֹתִי inf. cstr. sf. 1 sg. בלה *my wasting* in old age, cf. 32³ 49¹⁵. The man by the anointing of his head with oil is enriched as the cakes of the מנחה. — **12.** וַתַּבֵּט] ו consec. is interp.; the context demands simple ו. — בְּשׁוּרָי] error for שׁררי, *v.* 5⁹, 𝔊 ἐν τοῖς ἐχθροῖς μου. — בַּקָּמִים עָלַי] makes l. too long, destroys the simplicity of the parall., and is gl. — **13.** יִשְׂגֶּה] Qal. impf., *v.* 73¹². — **14.** שְׁתוּלִים] Qal ptc., cf. 1³, *transplanted*, not *planted*. — חַצְרוֹת אלהינו] phr. a.λ., but י יהוה 84³, חַצְרֶיךָ 65⁵ 84¹¹, חַצְרוֹתָיו 96⁸ 100⁴, ה׳ בֵּית 116¹⁹ 135², all referring to second temple. — **15.** יְנוּבוּן] full form Qal impf. נוב (62¹¹) *bear fruit.* — **16** depends on Dt. 32⁴; introduces a legalistic conclusion, and is a gl. — עֲלָתָה] Kt. defective for עַוְלָתָה Qr., fuller fem. form because of following monosyl. בֹּ, rel. clause.

PSALM XCIV., 6 STR. 4^3.

Ps. 94 is an importunate prayer of Israel for a theophany of the God of dire vengeance (v.$^{1-2}$), expostulating at the long impunity of the wicked (v.$^{3-4}$), meekly congratulating himself upon divine discipline and instruction out of the Law, while awaiting the doom of the wicked (v.$^{12-13}$), assured that Yahweh will not abandon His people and that righteousness will ere long return (v.$^{14-15}$). The question whether the throne of the oppressor can be allied to Yahweh is raised (v.$^{20-21}$), only to be denied by the assertion that God is the refuge of His people, and that He will surely exterminate their enemies (v.$^{22-23}$). Glosses emphasize the wickedness of the enemies, and their ignoring of divine interposition (v.$^{5-7}$), rebuke the dullards for not understanding (v.^{8}), assert that God is the creator and teacher of the nations (v.$^{9-10}$), though man's thoughts are but breath (v.^{11}), resume the plea for interposition, lest the people go down to Sheol (v.$^{16-17}$), and affirm the sustaining kindness and delightful comfort that Yahweh bestows (v.$^{18-19}$).

O GOD of dire vengeance, Yahweh!
  O God of dire vengeance, shine forth!
  Lift up Thyself, O Judge of the earth;
  Render the proud a recompense.
HOW long shall the wicked, Yahweh,
  How long shall the wicked exult?
  Pour forth, speak arrogantly,
  Speak boastfully, all the workers of trouble?
HAPPY is he whom Thou disciplinest, Yah!
  And whom Thou teachest out of Thy Law,
  To give him rest from days of evil,
  Until a pit be dug for the wicked.
YAHWEH abandons not His people,
  And forsakes not His inheritance,
  Until righteousness return to judgment,
  And following after it all the upright of mind.
CAN the throne of engulfing ruin be allied to Thee,
  Which frameth trouble by statute;
  Those who make attacks upon the life of the righteous,
  And innocent blood condemn?
NAY! Yahweh is become to me a high tower,
  And my God, my rock, my refuge.
  And He hath recompensed their troubling upon them,
  And in their own evil Yahweh will exterminate them.

Ps. 94 has no title in 𝔐, but in 𝔊 ψαλμὸς τῷ Δαυείδ τετράδι σαββάτου. It
was assigned to the fourth day of the week in the Alexandrian liturgy. The
same assignment is known in 𝔗 (v. Intr. § 39). The Ps. was supposed to be
Davidic because of resemblances to 𝔇, especially in v.²⁾⁻²³. The original Ps.
had six trimeter tetrastichs, v.¹⁻⁴· ¹²⁻¹⁵· ²⁰⁻²³; the intervening vss. are gls. of
various dates. The original Ps. in v.¹ implores a theophany in the style of 50²
Dt. 33². Its conception of God as judge v.² is that of 50⁶ 75⁸, עהק רבר v.⁴, cf.
75⁶, all 𝔄 ; רע ימי v.¹³ elsw. 49⁶, personification of צרק v.¹⁵ as 85¹¹· ¹²· ¹⁴, use
of אחריו v.¹⁵ as 45¹⁵, all 𝔙. The use of גאים v.² is as 140⁶; יהברך v.²⁰, cf. 122³.
There are besides α.λ. נקמות אל v.¹, הוות כסא v.²⁰, עמל יצר v.²⁰. The use of
הורה v.¹² implies a legal attitude of mind. Israel is in grave peril from foreign
enemies. It was probably the peril of the late Greek period. הוות כסא well
expresses the situation of the hostile monarchs. The glosses show evidence
of later date: v.⁵⁻⁷ has been influenced by 10⁴· ¹⁰⁻¹³· ¹⁸; v.⁸ is based on 49¹¹, cf.
92⁷, and implies WL.; v.⁹⁻¹¹ is universalistic in its conception of the divine instruction of the nations, and implies a time of peace and hopefulness ; v.¹⁶⁻¹⁷
implies extreme peril, probably Maccabean, to which the use of דומה v.¹⁷
points, elsw. 115¹⁷ as a syn. of Sheol ; v.¹⁸⁻¹⁹ abounds in rare words of Aramaic
type, שרעפי, הנחומיך, ישעשעו.

Str. I. Two syn. couplets. — **1.** *O God of dire vengeance*],
repeated for emphasis, the first line having the divine name *Yahweh*, the second the verb *shine forth*. The divine name 'El is
used with various predicates on account of its brevity. The plural
is an abstract plural of intensity, which should not be ignored, as
in EV⁵., by the use of the sg. " to whom vengeance belongeth " ;
but might possibly refer, as such pls. often do, to *acts* of vengeance.
Yahweh is importunately called upon to shine forth in theophany
as 50² Dt. 33². — **2.** *Lift up Thyself*], rise from a recumbent
posture in order to interpose, cf. Is. 33¹⁰ Ps. 9²⁰. — *O Judge of the
earth*]. Yahweh was the governor and judge of all the earth as
well as of Israel, and it was His prerogative to enter into judgment and right all wrongs, cf. Gn. 18²⁵ Pss. 50⁶ 75⁸. — *render a
recompense*], retributive justice, cf. 28⁴ Is. 35⁴. — *the proud*], cf.
123⁴ 140⁶, the first of a number of terms to characterise the enemies of Israel, more completely described in the subsequent Strs.

Str. II. Two syn couplets. — **3.** *How long shall the wicked*],
repeated for emphasis, as v.¹, with *Yahweh* in the first line and
the verb *exult* in the second, in fine antithesis therefore with v.¹.
The wicked are conceived as exulting in the gratification of their
wicked desires, while Yahweh remains passive. This exultation

is then described as chiefly in speech : **4**. *Pour forth*], that is, words as a torrrent, cf. 19³ 59⁸ 78². — *speak arrogantly*], cf. 31¹⁹ 75⁶ 1 S. 2³. — *speak boastfully*], the most probable meaning of a form α.λ. ; all enlarging upon " the proud " of v.², who are now in the climax described as *workers of trouble*. — Several glosses were inserted between this Str. and the next v.¹² : **5**. *Thy people, Yahweh, they crush, and Thine inheritance afflict*], a pentameter line, cf. 10¹⁰ 28⁹ 143³. — **6**. *The widow and sojourner they slay and orphans murder*], another pentameter line to indicate the heinous nature of their crimes in murdering the helpless, those under the especial protection of Yahweh according to the Law, Dt. 10¹⁸ 14²⁹ 16¹¹·¹⁴ 24¹⁷·¹⁹·²⁰·²¹ 27¹⁹, cf. Pss. 10¹⁴·¹⁸ 68⁶. — **7**. *And they say : "Yah seeth not" ‖ " and the God of Jacob perceiveth not"*], cf. 10⁴·¹¹ 14¹. This is not the denial of the ability of God to see and to interpose, but the assertion of His indifference to the oppression of His people. — **8**. *Consider, ye brutish among the people*, the exhortation in the imv. and the ‖ rebuke in the form of a question : *Ye dumb, how long ere ye will understand ?*], a syn. trimeter couplet. The brutish and the dullards here as in 49¹¹ 92⁷ were those among the Jewish people who were insensible to the principles of Hebrew Wisdom, and took no part in the teachings of the wise. — **9**. *He that planted the ear ‖ or He that formed the eye*], fig. terms for creating, used only here of ear and eye, cf. Ex. 4¹¹ Ps. 33¹⁵ 74¹⁷ 95⁵ 104²⁶, — *shall He not hear ? ‖ shall He not see ?*]. The question can have but one answer ; that He sees the affliction of His people by their enemies, and hears their cries and their prayers. This and the following couplet are tetrameters. — **10**. *He that disciplineth the nations ‖ He that teacheth mankind*]. Both clauses indicate that Yahweh carries on a discipline of instruction with other nations as well as with Israel, cf. v.¹². — *Shall He not correct ?* This requires in ‖ *Shall He not make them know ?*], cf. Jos. 4²² Is. 40¹³ ; that is, give the nations a knowledge of His will and ways, as He has given it to Israel. But the latter clause has been by error reduced to a single word, " knowledge," as if it belonged to the protasis and there were no apodosis. — **11**. *Yahweh knoweth the thoughts of mankind that they are breath*]. This is still later, and indeed a prose sentence, asserting on the one hand, over against v.⁷, that God not only knows the deeds of

U

mankind but also their inward thoughts, and on the other hand that He knows how unsubstantial they are.

Str. III. A syn. and a synth. couplet. — **12**. *Happy*], exclamation of congratulation as 1^1. A glossator inserted *the man who*, as 34^9 40^5 127^5, but here at the expense of the measure. The reference is not to the individual man ; but, as the context shows, to Israel, — *Whom Thou disciplinest, Yah* ‖ *And whom Thou teachest out of Thy Law*]. Israel congratulates himself that he has the special privilege of the Law of God for his teaching and divine discipline. — **13**. *To give him rest from days of evil*]. The days of evil are days of discipline. When they have accomplished their purpose they will pass away, and Israel will be given rest and quietness. — *Until a pit be dug for the wicked*]. While God is engaged in the discipline of His people, He is also engaged in preparing a just retribution for their enemies. He is, as it were, digging the pit into which they will eventually fall ; although elsewhere the wicked are conceived as digging the pit themselves 7^{16} 35^7 57^7.

Str. IV. Syn. and synth. couplets. — **14**. *Yahweh abandons not His people* ‖ *And forsakes not His inheritance*]. His people are His inheritance, and as belonging to Him He will not relinquish them to others, or permit them to be seriously injured, cf. Ex. 19^5. He may do it for a time Je. 12^7, but not permanently. — **15**. *Until righteousness return to judgment*]. Righteousness is personified here, as in 85^{11-14}. It is conceived as having departed from the place of judgment. There is a limit to its absence. It will eventually return, when God shines forth in theophany v.^{1}; and justice will be done in vindicating the people of God and bestowing upon the enemies just retribution. — *And following after it*], that is, in its train, cf. 45^{15}. Seeing justice again about to ascend on the throne, *all the upright of mind* follow in the procession to the throne. Glossators make additions here also ; and first an importunate appeal to God, a tetrameter tetrastich : **16**. *O that one would rise up for me !* ‖ *O that one would stand up for me !*], expressing a wish, more probable in this context than the interrogative clause of EV^s. It is a plea for divine interposition, as v.$^{1-2}$. — *against evil doers* ‖ *against workers of trouble*], the same as those of previous Strs. — **17**. *If it had not been that Yahweh* *had been a help to me*], that is, in the past history of the nation, — *I had almost dwelt in the land of silence*], cf. 115[17]. The nation had ceased to exist and had passed with the dead into Sheol, the abode of dead nations as well as individuals, cf. 9[18] Is. 14[9 sq.]. — **18.** *When I said: My foot doth slip*]. When hard pressed by the enemies and deliverance seemed improbable ; when he felt his foot slipping, and that he was about to fall. Then, when he could not sustain himself, God's *kindness held him up*], cf. 3[6] 18[36] 38[17]. — **19.** *When my anxious thoughts were multiplied within me*]. In his intense anxiety thoughts alternately of hope and despair rushed through his mind in multitudes. — *Thy comforts were delighting my soul*]. God gave him oft-repeated comfort and delight in the midst of his trials.

Str. V. A synth. and a syn. couplet. — **20.** *Can the throne of engulfing ruin*], a government whose administration was like a yawning gulf, swallowing up its subjects in irretrievable ruin. — ‖ *Which frameth trouble by statute ?*], whose very laws are iniquitous and ruinous. Can such a government *be allied to Thee ?*], have the divine sanction and support. — **21.** The wicked administration is further described as *Those who make attacks upon the life of the righteous* ‖ *And innocent blood condemn ?*]. Government and law should protect the righteous and justify the innocent. This government had become so corrupt that it did the very reverse of what it ought to have done. The question is raised only to give an emphatic negation.

Str. VI. Syn. couplets. — **22.** *Nay! Yahweh is become to me*], the answer to the question with an emphatic change of tense to emphasize the fact as an established experience. The EV[s]. " but " fails to express the emphasis of the original. — *a high tower*], as frequently in 𝕯 9[10. 10] 18[3] 59[10. 17. 18] 62[3. 7] 144[2] ; also in 𝕶 46[8. 12] 48[4]. ‖ *my God, my rock, my refuge*], terms heaped up as in 18[3] ; the original " rock of my refuge " is α.λ. and prob. error. — **23.** *And He hath recompensed their troubling upon them*], resuming v.[1-2]. — *And in their own evil*], that described v.[20-21], — *will exterminate them*], cf. 18[41] 54[7] 69[5].

1. אֵל נְקָמוֹת] bis α.λ., pl. abstr. intensive, or possibly *acts of vengeance.* — הוֹפִיעַ] Hiph. imv. prob. in original הוֹפִיעָה as 80[2]; final ה overlooked before ה of הִנָּשֵׂא as Hu.[3], Ehr. But 𝕲 has pf., as Dt. 33[2] Ps. 50[2]. — **2.** נֵּאִים ‡ גֵּאֶה

adj. pl. elsw. 123⁴ (?), *proud*, 140⁶ Pr. 15²⁵ 16¹⁹ +. — **4.** [יִרְאֲבְּרוּ] Hithp. a.λ. *act proudly*, BDB., cf. יִתְעַלָּ֑ו Is. 61⁶; context requires *boast, speak proudly*, 𝔊 λαλήσουσιν, 𝔙 *loquentur* = יאמרו. — **5.** A pentameter gl. — **6.** [אלמנה וגר]. 𝔊 χήραν καὶ ὀρφανὸν . . . καὶ προσήλυτον, so Θ, more natural order; a pentameter gl. — **7.** [וַיֹּאמְרוּ] ו consec. result: a trimeter gl. — **8.** A trimeter gl. based on 49¹¹. — **9–10.** A tetrameter gl. — [רָעָה] improb.; the measure requires הלא ידע or הלא יירע. — **11.** A prose sentence, late gl. — **12.** [אַשְׁרֵי הַגֶּבֶר אֲשֶׁר] makes too long a l. — אשר is prosaic and improb. — הגבר has been inserted from 34⁹ 40⁶. אַשְׁרֵי תְיַסְּרֶנּוּ was doubtless original; the exclamation of happiness before a relative clause, *v.* 1¹. — **13.** [יִרְרֶה] Niph. a.λ., but Qal 7¹⁶ +. — **14.** [יִטֹּשׁ] Qal impf. נטשׁ vb. *leave, let alone*, cf. 27⁹. — כי is interp. gl., makes l. too long. — **15.** [כי] is interp. gl., and indeed erroneous; it is not in 𝔊. — [צֶרֶק] personified, so 𝔊, 𝔍, 𝔗, but 𝔖, Σ, צדיק improb. — [וְאַחֲרָיו] *following after it*, as 45¹⁵ 68²⁶. — **16–17.** A tetrameter gl. — [מִי־יָקוּם לִי] fuller form of fem. with retracted accent because of monosyllable that follows, cf. 63⁸. — † [דוּמָה] n.f. *stillness*, for Sheol as 115¹⁷. — **18.** [אִם אָמַרְתִּי] prot. temp. clause with impf. of habitual action, יִסְעָדֵנִי, in apod. — **19.** [בְּרֹב] inf. cstr. with ב temp. prot. with יִשַׁעְשְׁעוּ apod.; but 𝔊 κατὰ τὸ πλῆθος. — [שַׂרְעַפַּי] pl. sf. † [שַׂרְעַף] only pl. n.[m.] *disquieting thoughts*, elsw. 139²³, cf. שְׂעִפִּים Jb. 4¹³ 20². — [תַּנְחוּמֶיךָ] † [תַּנְחוּם] only pl. *consolations*, elsw. Is. 66¹¹ Je. 16⁷ Jb. 15¹¹ 21². — [וִישַׁעַשְׁעוּ] Pilp. impf. † שׁעע Pilp. *delight in*, elsw. Is. 11⁸ Ps. 119⁷⁰, Palp. Is. 66¹², Hithp. Ps. 119¹⁶·⁴⁷. This accumulation of late words indicates a gl. — **20.** [הַיְחָבְרְךָ] dub. form, Ges.⁶⁰ᵇ, and especially Kö.ᴵ·²⁵⁷·⁸, Pu. impf. חבר *be allied with, v.* 58⁶; introducing an interrog. clause whose apod. is v.²². — [כְּמֵא הַוָּה] phr. a.λ., but הוות term of 𝔅 5¹⁰ +. — **21.** [עֲלֵי־חֹק] more euphonic than עַל־חֹק. — [יגודו] Kt. Qal impf. גוד; but Qr. from גדד, cf. 56⁷. — **22.** [וַיְהִי] ו consec. of apod. to emphasize the established fact. — [צוּר מַחְסִי] phr. a.λ.; improb.; rd. צוּרִי מַחְסִי, cf. 18³. — **23.** [וַיָּשֶׁב] ו consec. carries on apod. — [יַצְמִיתֵם] bis, but 𝔊 only once, as measure requires. — [אלהינו] is gl. of intensification; against measure.

PSALM XCV.

Ps. 95 is composite: (*A*) A summons to worship Yahweh, the king above all gods, in the temple, with psalms (v.¹⁻³). He is to be worshipped as the creator and owner of all nature (v.⁴⁻⁶). (*B*) A warning to Israel not to harden their hearts against Yahweh, as their fathers did in the wilderness, when they sorely tempted Yahweh (v.⁷ᶜ⁻⁹), and He loathed them and in His anger excluded a whole generation from the Holy Land (v.¹⁰⁻¹¹). A seam connects the two, asserting that Yahweh was yet the God and Shepherd of His people (v.⁷ᵃ⁻ᵇ).

A. v.[1-6], 2 STR. 6^3.

O COME! let us ring out to Yahweh:
  O let us shout to the Rock of our salvation;
  O let us come to meet His face with thanksgiving;
  With psalms let us shout to Him.
  For Yahweh is a great God,
  And a king above all gods.
IN His hand are the recesses of the earth,
  And the eminences of the mountains belong to Him.
  The sea belongs to Him, since He made it;
  And the dry land His hands formed.
  O come! O let us worship and bow down.
  O let us kneel before Yahweh.

B. v.[7c-11], 2 STR. 5^3.

TO-DAY, if ye will hearken to (My) voice,
  Harden not your heart as at Meribah,
  As in the day of Massah in the wilderness,
  When your fathers tempted Me;
  Tried Me; yea, saw My work.
I WAS loathing a generation, and so said:
  "A people erring in heart are they,
  And they do not know My ways."
  So I swear in Mine anger:
  "They shall not enter into My Resting place."

Ps. 95 has no title in 𝔐; but in 𝔊 αἶνος ᾠδῆς τῷ Δαυείδ, which is evidently
a late editor's opinion. This Ps. has several terms of temple worship at
religious festivals, v.[1. 6] and זמרות v.[2], implying the use of psalmody (see Intr.
§ 1). It could not have been composed before there was a regularly organised
temple choir and a collection of Pss. for their use; not earlier than the late
Persian period, and probably early in the Greek period. The original Ps. had
only two hexastichs v.[1-6]. To it was added by a seam v.[7] from 100[3], another
originally independent Ps., probably a fragment of a historical Ps., giving a
warning based on the experience of Israel in the wilderness, especially at
Meribah v.[7c-11]. The phr. הקשה לב v.[8] is that of P, Ex. 7[3] Pr. 28[14]; but the
use of לכב instead of לב of P implies a subsequent usage of the time of Chr.
מסה (יור) v.[8] as Ex. 17[7] (JE) Dt. 6[16] 9[22], cf. 33[8], כמריבה v.[8] elsw. מי כ׳ Dt. 33[8]
Nu. 20[13] (P) Pss. 81[8] 106[32]+; נסוני v.[9] as Ps. 78[18. 41. 56] 106[14] after Ex. 17[2. 7]
Nu. 14[22] (J) Dt. 6[16]. Phr. תעי לבב v.[10] a.λ., but cf. תעי רוח Is. 29[24]. ידע דרכים
v.[10] is a Deuteronomic term, cf. Ps. 18[22] 25[4. 9] 67[3]+. מנוחתי v.[11], cf. 132[8. 14]
Is. 66[1], based on Nu. 10[33]. This little Ps. seems to depend on a completed
Hexateuch, and to be of the time of the Chronicler.

PSALM XCV. *A.*

Str. I. A syn. tetrastich and a syn distich. — **1–3.** *O come*], exhortation to worship. — *let us ring out* ‖ *let us shout* ‖ *let us come to meet with thanksgiving* ‖ *with psalms let us shout*], all expressions for public worship, especially at festivals in the temple. The use of Pss. implies a fully developed service, with temple choirs and collections of Pss. The object of this worship is *Yahweh*, meeting Him, their faces to *His face*, in the place where He let the light of His face shine upon His people. — *the Rock of our salvation*], the favourite term for God in His relation to His own people from ancient times Dt. 32^{15} Ps. $62^{3.7}$ 89^{27}. But the chief reason for worship on this occasion is given in the causal clause, — *For Yahweh is a great God*], an expression of Dt. 7^{21} 10^{17} Je. 32^{18}, cf. Ps. 77^{14}, as the context suggests, in His dominion, explained in the ‖ *And a King above all gods*], cf. 47^3. The nations all had their own gods; but the God of Israel was king over them all.

Str. II. Three syn. couplets. — **4–5.** *In His hand* ‖ *belong to Him*], bis. They are entirely at His disposal, and the reason is given in the circumstantial clause, — *since He made it* ‖ *His hands formed*]. His ownership is based on creation. The various great objects of nature are mentioned, — *the recesses of the earth*], phr. α.λ. for the secret depths of the earth which cannot be searched by man, cf. Jb. 38^{16} Je. 31^{37}; in antithesis with *the eminences of the mountains*], the highest peaks. Thus from the depths to the heights the earth all belongs to Yahweh as owner. — *The sea* and *the dry land* are also put in antithesis for the same reason. — **6.** The sovereignty of Yahweh over nature is another phase of His reign, which gives the reason for the final couplet of praise, expressed by humble prostration in the service of the temple, cf. 22^{30} 72^9 2 Ch. 7^3 29^{29}. A glossator adds to the divine name, which alone was original, at the expense of the measure, " our Maker "; in order that the creative activity of God may include His worshippers as well as inanimate nature.

A later editor connects this Ps. with another by a seam taken from 100^3 and enlarged: **7 ab.** *For He is our God, and we are the people of His pasture and the sheep of His hand*], implying the strong personal attachment of Yahweh to His people especially needed in view of the sovereignty over the gods and nature of the previous Ps. and the solemn warning of the next Ps.

PSALM XCV. *B.*

Str. I. An introductory line, followed by a syn. and a stairlike couplet. — **7 c–9.** *To-day*], emphatic, referring to some particular time of solemn warning, which we know not how to determine. — *if ye will hearken to My voice*], most prob. in the independent Ps., which throughout is in the personal address. But 𝕳, followed by EVˢ., has "his voice," which was originally a scribe's assimilation to the previous seam. The voice of God is His voice of command, especially as embodied in the Law, requiring hearing in the pregnant sense of *obedience* — *Harden not your heart*], the apodosis: phrase of Ex. 7^3 (P) for stubborn inattention or refusal of obedience. Specimens of such stubbornness are now given. — *as at Meribah*] Nu. 20^{13} (P) Dt. 33^8 Ez. 47^{19} Ps. 81^8 106^{32}, when the offence of Israel was intensified, because it was shared in a measure by their leaders, Moses and Aaron. ‖ *As in the day of Massah*], cf. Ex. 17^7 (JE) Dt. 6^{16} 9^{22}, when Israel murmured for lack of water. These are given in the narrative of the Hexateuch as two different places and two different events; but they were doubtless only variant traditions of the same event (*v.* Br.^{Hex. 79}). The two are closely connected here; and it is not clear whether they are in syn. parallelism, as different terms for the same event, or as two events. — *When your fathers tempted Me* ‖ *tried Me*], by their murmuring unbelief and unreasonable demands. — *Yea, saw My work*], probably the work of giving the water from the rock notwithstanding their lack of confidence. This is better than to refer it to past acts of deliverance, or to the work of judgment upon them.

Str. II. A tetrastich of introverted parallelism and a synthetic line. — **10–11.** *I was loathing a generation*], an entire generation, made more definite in 𝕲, 𝕵, by prefixing a demonstrative "that"; but it then is really not so forcible as the original. The impf. expresses action which was habitual for a long time. A glossator gives that time from the ancient narrative of the Hexateuch, Nu. 14^{26-34}, as forty years — *and so said*], as the definite result of the long-continued and oft-repeated loathing. — *So I swear in Mine*

anger]. What was said was the couplet describing the character
of that generation: *A people erring in heart are they* ‖ *And they
do not know My ways*]. Their heart was disposed to wander from
the divine ways, cf. Is. 29²⁴; and they had no practical, experimental
knowledge of them, cf. Pss. 25⁴·⁹ 27¹¹ 37¹⁴ +. What was silently
sworn was a just retribution: *They shall not enter into My Resting
place*], the Holy Land as the place of the resting of Yahweh as
well as of His people after their long wandering in the wilderness,
cf. Nu. 10³³ Dt. 12⁹ Ps. 132⁸·¹⁴ Is. 66¹.

XCV. *A.*

1–2. [נְרַנְּנָה] cohort. impf. רנן ‖ נָרִיעָה] urgent exhortation ‖ [נְקַדְּמָה] used of
meeting in worship elsw. 88¹⁴ 89¹⁵. The second נריע should be cohort. also.
— [זְמִרוֹת] pl. זְמִירָה] *psalm*, as 119⁵⁴ 2 S. 23¹ Is. 24¹⁶ Jb. 35¹⁰ (*v.* Intr. § 1).—
[אֵל גָּדוֹל] assimilated to 47³. גדול makes l. too long and is gl. — **4.** [אשר בידו].
The rel. makes the l. too long and is prosaic gl. — [מֶחְקְרֵי] *a.λ. range*, *B*DB.;
but more prob. *recesses, depths* (cf. חֵקֶר Jb. 38¹⁶). 𝕲 has πέρατα = מרחקי as
Is. 8⁹, but antith. favours 𝔚. [תּוֹעֲפוֹת הרים] phr. *a.λ.* † [תּוֹעֲפָה] n.f. *eminence*,
of horns Nu. 23²² 24⁸, of silver Jb. 22²⁵ (?); here horns of mountains. 𝕲
τὰ ὕψη.— **5.** [אשר־לו] rel., prosaic gl.; connect לו־הים, with one accent. —
[והוא עשהו] circumstantial clause.— † [יַבֶּשֶׁת] n.f. elsw. Ex. 4⁹ (J); for usual
יַבָּשָׁה Ps. 66⁶ Is. 44³+.— **6.** [נשהחוה] cohort. again as v.¹ נברכה ‖ נכריעה
(5¹³) the latter of kneeling in worship only here. 𝕲 has κλαύσωμεν, 𝔙
ploremus = נבכה txt. err.— **7 ab.** [עם מרעיתו] phr. *a.λ.*; so צאן ידו, amplification
of 100³ with no measure. This is a seam, connecting two independent Pss.

XCV. *B.*

7 c. [אם בקלו] conditional clause with obj. emph.: prot. impf, and apod.
juss.— **8.** [אל תקשו לבבכם] phr. הקשו לב Ex. 7⁸ (P) Pr. 28¹⁴; the fuller form לבב
possibly due to heavy sf. or to later usage of Chr.— **9.** [פְּעָלִי] prob.; but 𝕲 pl.
τὰ ἔργα μου.— **10.** [ארבעים שנה] gl. of historic expl., against measure.— [אָקוּט]
Qal impf. ‡ קוּט] *a.λ. feel a loathing*, habitual action, but Niph. Ez. 6⁹ 20⁴³ 36³¹,
Hithp. Pss. 119¹⁵⁸ 139²¹.— [בדור] 𝕲 τῇ γενεᾷ ἐκείνῃ, so Du., Kirk., Bä., but
against the measure. — [וָאֹמַר] ו consec., emph. change of tense to indicate the
final result of long-continued loathing. — [תֹעֵי לבב] phr. *a.λ.*, but cf. תֹעֵי רוח Is.
29²⁴, cf. 58⁴. — **11.** [אֲשֶׁר] particle of result, so Gn. 13¹⁶.— [אם יבאון] formula
of oath, as 89³⁶ 132³·³·⁴; Ges.¹⁴⁹, with full form of 3 pl. impf.

PSALMS XCIII., XCVI.–C., 3 PTS., 5 STR. 6³.

Pss. 93, 96–100 were originally a song of praise, celebrating
the advent of Yahweh, the universal King, for judgment. It had
three parts, each of two sections, the first describing the advent,

the second a universal summons to celebrate it. I. (*A*) **Yahweh** has put on His royal robes, is seated on His everlasting throne, more magnificent than the stormy sea (93^{1-4}) ; (*B*) He is come in theophany, all nature is in commotion, heaven and earth see and declare His glory $(97^{1-2a.\ 3-6})$; (*C*) He is greatly exalted, awful in holiness ; He loveth justice and hath established righteousness in Jacob (99^{1-5}). II. (*A*) All nations are summoned to sing a new song in praise of His wondrous deeds of victory $(96^{1-3} = 98^{1-2})$; to revere Him above all gods, and join in the sacred dance in which all nature participates $(96^{4-6\ 9b\ 10a.\ 11-12})$; (*B*) to take part in a musical festival in the temple, in which all nature shares (98^{4-9b}) ; (*C*) to worship their Creator and Shepherd with thank offerings, songs, and music in the temple courts (100). The breaking up of the Ps. into six little Pss. for liturgical purposes, involved the addition of many glosses of various kinds $(93^5\ 96^{7-9a.\ 10bc.\ 13}\ 97^{2b.\ 7-12}\ 98^{3.\ 9cd}\ 99^{6-9})$.

I.

YAHWEH *doth reign* in majesty,
  (Yahweh) hath put on His apparel,
  Yahweh hath girded Himself with strength,
  He hath adjusted the world that it cannot be moved.
  Thy throne is established from of old,
  From everlasting art Thou (Yahweh).
THE streams have lifted up, Yahweh,
  The streams have lifted up their voice,
  The streams lift up their (commemoration),
  More than the voices of many waters,
  Magnificent more than the breakers of the sea,
  Magnificent on high, Yahweh.
O *SING to Yahweh a new song :*
  Sing to Yahweh all the earth ;
  Sing (to Him), bless His name :
  Proclaim the glad tidings of His victory from day to day :
  Tell among the nations His glory,
  Among all peoples, His wondrous deeds,
FOR great is Yahweh ;
  He is to be revered above all gods.
  The gods of the peoples are nothings :
  But Yahweh made the heavens ;
  Majesty and glory are in His presence,
  Strength and beauty are in His sanctuary.
$(W$HIRL) before Him all the earth ;
  Say among the nations, " He *doth reign*."

Let the heavens and the earth be glad,
Let the sea thunder and the fulness thereof,
Let the field exult and all that therein is,
Let all the trees of the forest jubilate.

II.

HE *doth reign :* let the earth rejoice,
Let the many coasts be glad.
Clouds and darkness are round about Him,
A fire goeth before Him,
And setteth ablaze His adversaries round about,
His lightnings illumine the world.

THE earth doth see and writhe,
The mountains melt like wax,
At the presence of Yahweh (the King),
At the presence of the Lord of all the earth;
The heavens declare His righteousness,
And all the peoples see His glory.

O *SING to Yahweh a new song,*
(*Sing to Yahweh all the earth*),
For wondrous deeds He hath done.
His right hand hath gotten Him the victory;
Yahweh hath made known His victory,
In the eyes of the nations His righteousness.

SHOUT to Yahweh all the earth,
Break forth and jubilate and make melody;
Make melody to Yahweh with the lyre,
With the lyre, with the sound of psalmody,
With trumpets and the sound of the horn,
Shout before the King.

LET the sea roar and the fulness thereof,
The world and what dwells therein;
Let the rivers clap their hands,
Together let the mountains jubilate,
Before Yahweh, for He is come.
(He is come) to judge the earth.

III.

HE doth reign : the peoples tremble;
He is seated on His throne, the earth quakes
Yahweh is great in Zion,
And high above all the peoples:
Let them praise the great and awful name;
Holy is He and strong.

HE doth reign, He doth love justice,
(He hath) established justice in equity,
And righteousness in Jacob hath wrought.
Exalt ye Yahweh, our God,
And worship at His footstool,
Holy is He (and strong).

O *SING to Yahweh a new song,*
   (*Sing to Yahweh all the earth*).

   .   .   .   .
   .   .   .   .
   .   .   .   .
   .   .   .   .

*S*HOUT to Yahweh all the earth;
   Serve Yahweh with gladness;
   Come before Him with jubilation;
   Know that He is God;
   He made us and we are His,
   His people and the sheep of His pasture.
*C*OME to His gates with a thank offering;
   (Come) to His courts with a song of praise;
   Give thanks to Him; bless His name;
   (Give thanks), for Yahweh is good,
   For His kindness endureth forever,
   And unto all generations His faithfulness.

Ps. 93 is one of the group of royal Pss., 96–100, separated from them for liturgical reasons. In 𝕳 it has no title; but in 𝕲 εἰς τὴν ἡμέραν τοῦ προσαββάτου, ὅτε κατῴκισται ἡ γῆ αἶνος ᾠδῆς τῷ Δαυείδ. It was in Alexandrian usage assigned to the sixth day of the week, and thus was placed between 92, for the seventh, and 94, for the fourth day. The Talmud (*Rosch. has Shana* 31[a]) shows that the Palestinian usage was the same, even if it found no expression in the text of 𝕳 (*v.* Intr. § 39). The second clause of 𝕲 may be interpreted with reference to the peopling of the earth on the fifth day of the creation, as the Talmud, or of the peopling of the Holy Land at the Restoration. The assignment of the Ps. to David as מזמור שיר was doubtless because of resemblances to Pss. of 𝔻. It cannot be recognized as valid. The Ps., as indeed the entire group, was a שיר. The מזמור is, as in all such cases, a later attachment. This Ps., as others of the group, depends on Is.[2], and is in especial accord with the little songs which close the earlier section of trimeters whose theme is the deliverance of the Servant of Yahweh (*v.* Br.[MP. 449 sq.]). In this Ps., cf. v.[1] with Is. 51[9] 52[7], and the use of שאו v.[2] with Is. 44[8] 45[21] 48[3. 5. 7. 8]. The Ps. has two trimeter hexastichs, arranged as strophe and antistrophe, with a liturgical addition v.[5].

Ps. 96 has no title in 𝕳, but in 𝕲 ὅτε ὁ οἶκος οἰκοδομεῖται μετὰ τὴν αἰχμαλωσίαν, ᾠδὴ τῷ Δαυδείδ. The union of these two statements shows that the editor did not think of Davidic authorship, but thought of the Ps. rather as belonging to the Davidic type of Pss. The historical reference to the erection of the second temple probably came from a later hand than the reference to David. It is bracketed in the Psalterium Gallicanum, and the order of the statements varies; 𝕲[N. A] reverse the order of 𝕲[B]. The Ps. is used in 1 Ch. 16[23–33] in connection with the removal of the ark by David to Zion, as sung by the temple choirs. It might therefore have been somewhat older than Chr., and have been used for a considerable time in the temple liturgy as

Davidic, and indeed in its present form, apart from variations due chiefly to scribal mistakes. Attention is called to these in the notes. It is, however, probable that this Ps. with the others cited were later insertions in the text of Chr. The Ps. was originally a section of the great royal Ps. This section had three hexastichs v.[1-6. 9b-10a. 11-12]. The other verses are glosses from various sources and by more than one hand: v.[7-9a] especially is an adaptation of 29[1-2]; v.[10b] is from 93[1d]; v.[10c] is from 9[9b], and was inserted later than the text used by Chr.; v.[13] was from 98[9]. The terms of the ritual service in the temple are used v.[1. 2]; שיר חדש v.[1] = 98[1] is based on the usage of Is. 42[10], cf. Pss. 33[3] 40[4] 144[9] 149[1], and implies a song sung to commemorate a great event which has just transpired. בשר ישועתו v.[2] is also after Is. 40[9] 41[27] 52[7], cf. Ps. 40[10]; v.[4a] is based on 48[2a]; v.[4b] on 47[3]; v.[6] seems to imply that the temple not only was in existence, but that it had not been recently erected, as the title of 𝕲 implies; v.[11-12], the participation of nature in the joy of the people, is in accordance with Is.[2] and also with other sections of the original Ps., cf. 93[3-4] 98[7-8]. This Ps. lends its internal evidence to the time of the overthrow of Persia, rather than Babylon.

Ps. 97 has no title in 𝕳, but in 𝕲 τῷ Δαυείδ ὅτε ἡ γῆ αὐτοῦ καθίσταται, 𝖁 *quando terra ejus restituta est*, which doubtless refers to the restoration of the land by the returned exiles from Babylon. This shows the same inconsistency with the first clause, in referring to David, that appears in the previous Ps.; unless we suppose that by "David" the editor meant no more than the Davidic type of Pss. The greater part of the present Ps. is a mosaic made up of extracts by glossators from other Pss. The only part that is original is two hexastichs v.[1-2a. 3-6]. The Ps. has the same reference to the royal advent of Yahweh v.[1], and the universal call to worship v.[1b. 6b], and the same participation of nature v.[4b-6a], as the other Pss. of the group. The original Ps. uses freely older writings: v.[1b] Ez. 27[3. 15], v.[2a] Dt. 4[11] 5[19], v.[3a] Ps. 50[3], v.[4a] 77[19b], v.[6] 50[6], and v.[6b] Is. 66[18. 19]. The glosses are: v.[2b] from 89[15a], v.[8] from 48[12], v.[9] from 47[3. 10] 95[3], v.[12] from 32[11] and 30[5], v.[7] a prosaic gloss against idolaters, v.[10-11] a fragment of another Ps. which is not without literary merit.

Ps. 98 in 𝕳 has מזמור. It is difficult to see why it should be prefixed to this Ps. rather than to others of the group, all of which have the same character. 𝕲 has ψαλμὸς τῷ Δαυείδ. The ascription to David means no more than in the case of the other Pss. of the group. The Ps. also depends on Is.[2] in the original v.[1a. 4b. 8a], and still more in the glosses v.[1d. 3b]. It is yet original in the phrases v.[2. 6a]. It is identified with other Pss. of the group: v.[1a] with 96[1], v.[7a] with 96[11b]; v.[9ab] is original, v.[9cd] is a gl. in 96[13] as we have seen. The Ps. has thus the same characteristics as others of the group, and was part of the same original.

Ps. 99 has no title in 𝕳, but in 𝕲 ψαλμὸς τῷ Δαυείδ, which has the same significance as in other Pss. of this group. The Ps. differs from the others in that it emphasizes the historical relation of Yahweh to Israel, and is universalistic only in the exaltation of Yahweh over the nations. The participation of nature in the worship is also absent. Therefore the Ps. is not so clearly a part of the same original hymn as the others that precede it or as Ps. 100, which follows. This reference to Israel's peculiar claim on Yahweh, with the related material v.⁶⁻⁹, is, however, a later particularistic addition; when this is removed this Ps. is evidently the first section of the third part of the original. It agrees with the others, in emphasizing the advent of Yahweh as king v.¹, in the justice of His administration v.⁴, and in the summons to worship v.³· ⁵.

Ps. 100 has in 𝔐 the title מזמור לתודה, probably a psalm to accompany the thank offering; Aq. εἰς εὐχαριστίαν, 𝔗 קרבן תודתא על יבהא, 𝔊 ψαλμὸς εἰς ἐξομολόγησιν (v. Intr. § 39). This was, however, a later liturgical assignment, for the Ps. is part of the previous group and with them originally constituted a single Ps. The Ps. remains in its original condition as two of the Strs. of the larger Ps.

A review of these six little Pss. shows that they constituted one original advent hymn of three parts, each of two sections. In the first sections the advent of the King to judgment and the effective administration of the justice of His reign is vividly described in two trimeter hexastichs. In the second sections all peoples and all nature are summoned to a festival in the temple courts in celebration of the advent, in three trimeter hexastichs. As thus reconstructed the original is an advent hymn of wonderful grandeur.

PSALM XCIII.

Pt. I., Str. I. Two syn. tristichs. — **1.** *Yahweh doth reign*], as 96¹⁰ 97¹ 99¹ Is. 52⁷, cf. Ps. 47⁹ 146¹⁰; not the assertion of His everlasting royal prerogative, but the joyous celebration of the fact that He has now shown Himself to be king by a royal advent, taking His place on His throne to govern the world Himself, and no longer through inefficient or wicked servants. — *in majesty*]. This qualifies the coming to reign as king, and so best prepares for the antithesis of the second Str. If the Ps. is a trimeter, it must be so attached. 𝔐, Vrss., all ignore the measure and attach it to the following verb " put on," which they regard as repeated without an object. This has been occasioned by the mistaken omission of the divine name in the second line of the tristich. The lines are real trimeters, " Yahweh " being repeated in each line, and each vb. having its object. — *hath put on His apparel ‖ hath girded Himself with strength*], the apparel suited to His royal state, the strength needed to execute His sovereign will. — **2.** *He hath adjusted the world*], so 𝔊, 𝔍, PBV., better suited to the context than the passive of 𝔐, AV., RV., especially as the context favours a pf. rather than an impf. — *that it cannot be* *moved*], cf. 10⁶ 104⁵. This refers, not to the moral order of the world, but to the whole order of the habitable world, in which inanimate as well as animate nature shares, according to the conceptions characteristic of this Ps. Only thus do we get a proper preparation for the parall. : *Thy throne is established*], the habitable world over which He reigns and the throne from which He reigns alike have been so firmly established that they cannot be unsettled. —*from of old*], a characteristic phrase of Is. 44⁸ 45²¹ 48³·⁵·⁷·⁸ ‖ *From everlasting art Thou, Yahweh*], the same assertion of the everlasting divine activity as in 90².

Str. II. is an antistrophe, two tristichs with stairlike parallelism. —**3-4.** *The streams*], thrice repeated : not rivers or brooks, but, as the context shows, the streams of the Mediterranean, ‖ "many waters" ‖ "breakers of the sea." —*have lifted up*], bis, once without obj.; then with the obj. *their voice*, the sound of the rushing and dashing waters in a storm, ‖ "voices of many waters," the roaring of the breakers as they throw themselves upon the shore. The third line changes the tense to the impf., *lift up*, to emphasize the action, not as completed, but in movement, and gives the vb. an obj. which in 独 is a.λ., translated conjecturally in EVˢ. "their waves," RV.ᵐ "their roaring," Dr., Kirk., "their din," BDB. "their crashing." The most probable reading, as suggested by 𝔖, 𝔗, is *commemoration*, their voices commemorating the wonders of Yahweh. This is a graphic description of the majesty of the sea in a great storm. It is to be interpreted as real and not as symbolical of armies of mighty foes, although this symbol is appropriate and used elsewhere, cf. Is. 17¹²⁻¹³ Pss. 46⁴ 89¹⁰. —*More than*]. The comparison is repeated, the first time with the object with which the comparison is made, *the voices of many waters*, the second time with the predicate, *the breakers of the sea.* — *magnificent*], in order to the climax, where the subject is expressed with the predicate and an additional antithetical statement : *magnificent on high Yahweh*]. The force of this stairlike parallelism is lost by 独 and Vrss., which, by wrong attachment of a letter, change into the pl. form and compel the reading "majestic breakers," making difficult syntax. The poet's conception is, that however magnificent the sea may be in a storm, Yahweh is much more magnificent as He reigns on high, above its tumult and raging, with the implication that He will eventually still it and reduce it to order.

A later editor appended **5**, in order to introduce corresponding thoughts of the Law and the temple. — *Thy testimonies are exceedingly steadfast*]. The Law, conceived from the priestly point of view, as composed of testimonies, is steadfast, like the throne of Yahweh and the habitable world. — *To Thy house sanctity is becoming, Yahweh, for length of days*]. The temple as the house of Yahweh, the place of His presence and of His throne, shares in His majesty; only that majesty partakes of the character of a majestic sanctity, separate and apart from all that is unconsecrated and profane.

PSALM XCVI.

Str. III. is a stairlike hexastich. — **1-3**. *Sing*], thrice repeated, twice with *to Yahweh*]; but the third time in an assimilation of *to Him*] against the measure. In the first line the obj. is given, — *a new song*], based on Is. 42^{10}; not in the sense of a new composition, but of a new outburst of song because of a new event that invokes it; cf. 33^3. — The second line gives the subject: *all the earth*]. The summons to sing is universal; the event to be celebrated had universal significance. The third line defines the song: *bless His name*], cf. 100^4, ‖ *Proclaim the glad tidings*], cf. Is. 40^9, ‖ *tell*]; and indeed not to Israel alone, but *among the nations* ‖ *among all peoples*], a story of world-wide significance. — *His glory* ‖ *His wondrous deeds*]. This can only be explained of some great event, some world-wide transformation, some change that gave joy to the world, which was so extraordinary that it could only be ascribed to the divine intervention. It was probably the overthrow of the Persian empire by Alexander the Great.

Str. IV. Synth., antith., and syn. couplets. — **4**. *For great is Yahweh*], in the great deeds He had done, and in the great glory He had won; and therefore — *He is to be revered above all gods*], who have signally failed the nations that worshipped them, cf. 95^3. A glossator assimilated v.^{4a} to 48^{2a} by adding " and highly to be praised," which suits the previous context rather than its parallels in this Str. — **5**. *The gods of the peoples are nothings*], cf. Lv. 19^4 26^1 Ps. 97^7 Is. $2^{8.\ 18.\ 20}$ 10^{10}; they have done nothing for the people that worship them, they can do nothing, they are in reality nothings, they have no real existence and are not gods at all, cf. Is. 40$^{18\ sq.}$ 44$^{9\ sq.}$ Ps. 115$^{4-8}$. — In contrast with them *Yahweh made the heavens*], created the very place in which these gods were supposed to reside, and which therefore belonged to Him and to Him alone, cf. 95$^{4-5}$. — **6.** *Majesty and glory* ‖ *Strength and beauty*], a heaping up of terms to set forth the admirable attributes of Yahweh; the former of Him as king 21^6 and creator 104^1, the latter in their antithesis possibly suggested by the ancient pillars, Jachin and Boaz in the porch of the temple 1 K. 7$^{13-22}$; especially appropriate to the divine *presence* in *His sanctuary*, cf. Is. 60^7 64^{10}.

7–9 a. A later editor inserts here another universal summons to praise, based on 29$^{1-2}$, in a tetrameter pentastich.

> Ascribe to Yahweh, ye families of the peoples,
> Ascribe to Yahweh glory and strength;
> Ascribe to Yahweh the glory of His name.
> Bring a minchah and come to His courts.
> Worship Yahweh in holy ornaments.

The only variations are the substitution of *families of the peoples* for "sons of gods," angels, of the original; and the insertion of the line exhorting to bring a grain offering (cf. 20^4) to the courts of the temple (cf. 65^5 84^{11} 92^{14} 100^4); both of which changes made it more suited to its context.

Str. V. A synth. couplet and a syn. tetrastich. — **9 b.** *Whirl before Him all the earth*] a universal summons to take part in the sacred pilgrim dance in the temple, cf. 87^7 Ju. 21$^{21-23}$ 1 S. 18^6. The translations, "stand in awe of Him," PBV., "fear before Him," AV., "tremble before Him," RV., JPSV., although based on ancient Vrss., are not suited to the context, which implies worship, while the Heb. word never expresses fear and trembling in connection with worship. — **10.** *Say among the nations*], resumption of the proclamation of v.$^{2-3}$. — *He doth reign*], the theme of the entire group of Pss., cf. 93^1 97^1 99^1. A glossator added here from 93^{1d}: *Yea, the world He established that it cannot be moved*. A later glossator subsequent to the text of 𝔊 added from 9^{9b}: *He will judge the peoples with equity*. A still later glossator added to the ancient Greek and Latin Versions: "the Lord hath reigned from the tree," which is cited in many Latin fathers as a prophecy of Christ, and which Justin Martyr (*Apol.* I. 41) charges the Jews with erasing from their text. There is no evidence from Mss. that it was ever in an ancient Hebrew text. This false reading also gained currency among Christians through its use in the hymn of Fortunatus († 609) *Vexilla regis prodeunt,* used in the Latin church and translated by Neale for English use.—**11–12.** The Ps. now calls upon universal nature to share in the joyous worship, as usual in this group of Pss. and the exilic Isaiah. — *The heavens and the earth* ‖ *the sea and the fulness thereof*], all its animal life, ‖ *the field and all that therein is*], all its animal and vegetable life, ‖ *all the trees of the forest*]. These are all personified and express their joyous worship. — *be glad*], to which ﬡﬡ and Vrss. add another vb., " rejoice," against the ‖ which gives only one vb. to a line, and at the cost of good measure. The more general vb. has in ‖ the more specific *thunder,* the voice of the sea, ‖ *exult* ‖ *jubilate.* The Ps. thus comes to an appropriate conclusion. But a glossator appends from 98[9], — *before Yahweh; for He cometh, for He cometh to judge the earth. He will judge the world in righteousness and the peoples in faithfulness.*

PSALM XCVII.

Pt. II., Str. I. A syn couplet and a synth. tetrastich. —**1.** *He doth reign*], as 93[1] 96[10] 99[1]. — *let the earth rejoice*], as Is. 49[13] ‖ *Let the many coasts be glad*], the coast lands of the Mediterranean Sea, the limits of the west to the Hebrews, cf. Is. 41[1, 5] 42[4, 10] Je. 31[10] Ez. 27[3, 15] Zp. 2[11] Ps. 72[10]. — **2–4 a.** *Clouds and darkness are round about Him*], cited from Dt. 4[11] 5[19] to represent that the advent of the King was in a heavy storm with dark clouds, cf. Ps. 18[10–12]. — *fire goeth before Him*], cited from 50[3] to indicate that the darkness sent forth the fire of lightning, so also 18[9, 13, 14]. — *And setteth ablaze His adversaries round about*]. His thunderbolts strike His enemies dead, cf. 18[15] 77[18], where they are compared to arrows piercing His enemies, and 106[18], where they simply set them on fire and consume them. — *His lightnings illumine the world*], cf. 77[19b]. A glossator wishes to alleviate this awful picture, and so he inserts from 89[15] : *righteousness and justice are the basis of His throne.*

x

Str. II. Three syn. couplets. — **4 b.** *The earth doth see and writhe*], cf. 77^{17} Hb. 3^{10}. The earth is here personified, as usual, and is terrified by the terrible storm, and writhes in the pangs of an earthquake. — *The mountains melt like wax*], cf. Mi. 1^4 Is. 34^3, probably conceived as volcanoes pouring forth molten fiery lava. Thus the earth testifies to the divine presence and participates in its terrors. — *At the presence of Yahweh*], repeated with the predicate. — *the Lord of all the earth*], as its sovereign owner. This suggests that in the previous line the syn. word *king*, characteristic of this group of Pss., has been omitted, the line being just one word too short. — *The heavens declare His righteousness*], notwithstanding the theophanic storm. The object of the theophany is to make known the righteous judgment of Yahweh, — and therefore *all the peoples see His glory*.

Many glosses now appear. — **7 a.** *Shamed be all they that serve graven images, boast themselves of nothings*], a Maccabean imprecation upon idolaters, whose gods are mere images graven by man, cf. 115^{4-8}, and mere nothings, cf. 96^5. — **7 b.** *Worship Him, all ye gods*], probably not from the same glossator ; for he would not in one breath call them "nothings," and in the next call upon them as exalted persons to worship the supreme God. This latter is in accord with 95^3 96^4, and from an earlier editor than the previous line, and is, indeed, of a different measure. — **8** is a gloss from 48^{12} : *Zion heard and was glad, and the daughters of Judah rejoiced, because of Thy judgments, Yahweh.* — **9** is a combination and condensation of $47^{3,\,10}$, adapted to the thought of 95^3 : *For Thou, Yahweh 'Elyon, art above all the earth, Thou art exalted exceedingly above all gods.* — **10 a** is a gloss of exhortation to the pious in Israel by the same hand as the gloss of v.^{12} : *Ye that love Yahweh*], in accordance with the Deuteronomic law, as distinguished from those in Israel who do not, — *hate evil*]. This seems to be a general exhortation, not referring to the evil wrought by the wicked nations, but to evil as in violation of the divine Law. This line was probably an introduction to, and a seam of union for, the little fragment **10 b–11**.

> Preserver of the lives of His pious,
> From the hand of the wicked He delivereth them.
> Light (shineth) forth for the righteous,
> And gladness for the upright-minded.

This fragment was probably from the Maccabean period. — *His pious ‖ the righteous ‖ the upright-minded*], are like those that *love Yahweh*, the faithful adherents to the divine Law. Yahweh is the *preserver of* their *lives ‖ from the hands of the wicked He delivereth them*]. This is on the negative side. On the positive side they enjoy the *light* of prosperity ‖ *gladness*. It *shineth forth*] for them; as 𝕲, 𝕵, 𝕾, 𝕿, 𝖁, which is more probable than "is sown" of 𝕳, followed by EV.ˢ., which introduces a figure difficult to understand in this connection. — **12.** A gloss from 30⁵ combined with 32¹¹: *Be glad, ye righteous, in Yahweh, and give thanks in commemoration of His holiness.*

PSALM XCVIII.

Pt. II., Str. III. Three syn. couplets; the first a repetition of 96¹, the second line of which has been omitted by a copyist. — **1.** *For wondrous deeds He hath done ‖ His right hand hath gotten Him the victory*]. Yahweh has interposed against the oppressor of the nations, and in a marvellous way has won the victory over him, probably the Persian empire through Alexander the Great. A glossator adds from Is. 52¹⁰ the syn. term: *His sacred arm;* but it destroys the measure. — **2.** *Hath made known*], to which a glossator adds in the ‖ *hath declared*, against the measure, — *His victory ‖ His righteousness*], the vindicatory, practical exhibition of His righteousness on behalf of the oppressed, as usual in Hebrew literature, *in the eyes of the nations*]. All the world has beheld these wonderful deeds, and shares in the deliverance from the great oppressor. — **3.** A glossator adds a pentameter line, which in 𝕲, however, appears as a trimeter couplet, representing that Israel is the chief beneficiary of this salvation, in accordance with the ancient covenant. — *He hath remembered His kindness (to Jacob), and His faithfulness to the house of Israel*], cf. 89² ˢᑫ 92³. — The same glossator also adds from Is. 52¹⁰: *all the ends of the earth have seen the salvation of our God*], which emphasizes the statement of the previous verse.

Str. IV. A syn. hexastich. — **4-6.** *Shout to Yahweh all the earth*], the universal call is renewed ‖ *shout before the King* v.⁶ᵇ. These lines enclose first a series of verbs enlarging upon this sacred shout: *Break forth ‖ jubilate ‖ make melody;* and then enumerates the several musical instruments used in the festivals of the temple, *the lyre*, with the *sound of psalmody*, the *trumpets, with the sound of the horn*, cf. 47⁶.

Str. V. A syn. tetrastich and a stairlike couplet. — **7.** *Let the sea roar and the fulness thereof*] as in 96¹¹ᵇ. ‖ *The world and what dwells therein*], probably the animal and vegetable world, and not mankind, cf. 24¹ᵇ, 96¹²ᵃ. — **8.** *Let the rivers clap their hands*]. They are personified, and thus express their joy, and accompany the music and shouting with measured strokes, cf. Is. 55¹². — *Together let the mountains jubilate*]. This participation of nature in the rejoicing is characteristic of this group of Pss. and of the exilic Isaiah. — **9.** *Before Yahweh*], as v.⁶: *for He is come*]. The context requires the pf., referring to the advent celebrated, and not the ptc., referring to an impending advent, as EVˢ. The verb was repeated in the original, as attested by ancient Vrss.; though omitted by 𝕳 and EVˢ., in order to state the purpose, — *to judge the earth*], which sums up in a general term the theme of praise of the first Str. — A glossator adds a pentameter line to emphasize the character of this judgment, and doubtless thought of a future advent : *He will judge the world in righteousness and the peoples in equity.*

PSALM XCIX.

Pt. III., Str. I. Syn. couplet and syn. tetrastich. — **1-3.** *He doth reign*], as 93¹ 96¹⁰ 97¹ ; ‖ *is seated on His throne*]. But a glossator gave it a more specific reference to Jerusalem by adding " on the cherubim," cf. 80²ᵉ, in the throne room of the temple, — *great in Zion*] ; and yet *high above all the peoples*. Before this great and victorious king and God *the peoples ‖ the earth — tremble ‖ quakes*], and yet not in the fear, terror, and anguish that accompany their destruction, but in awe at His august presence, and therefore harmonious with and resulting in : — *Let them praise the great and awful name*]. 𝕳, Vrss., followed by EVˢ., append the sf. *Thy* to " name," but it spoils the measure and is against the context, which speaks of Yahweh always in the third person. — *Holy is He*], that is, majestically holy ; invoking the hallowing of His name, as usual in the OT. and even in the NT. — *and strong*] v.⁴ᵃ. This clause belongs with the previous line to complete its measure. It only makes difficulty in v.⁴, when it has been transposed by txt. err.

Str. II. A syn. triplet, a syn. couplet, and a concluding synth. line. — **4.** *He doth reign*]. The most probable rendering in accordance with the context and usage of the Ps., justified by the unpointed text, although 𝔥, 𝔍, 𝔊, and other Vrss., followed by EVˢ., render by a different pointing, making this an attribute and the subj. of the verb, and giving conceptions which are difficult to understand and which have no analogy in usage. — *He doth love justice*], cf. 11⁷ 33⁵ 37²⁸, —*He hath established justice in equity ‖ righteousness hath wrought.* It is especially *in Jacob* in connection with Zion v.¹⁻². — **5.** *Exalt ye Yahweh, our God ‖ worship at His footstool*], cf. 110¹ 132¹⁷ Is. 66¹. All nations are summoned to Zion, the capital city of the King Yahweh, where He is to be worshipped by all.

6–9. A later editor adds material of a more particularistic character.

> Moses and Aaron among His priests,
> And Samuel among them that call on His name,
> They called unto Yahweh and He answered them;
> In the pillar of cloud He used to speak unto them;
> They kept His testimonies and the ordinance He gave them.
> Yahweh, our God, Thou didst answer them;
> A forgiving God wert Thou to them,
> And a taker of vengeance on evil deeds.
> Exalt ye Yahweh, our God,
> And worship at His holy mountain;
> For holy is Yahweh our God.

6. *Moses and Aaron among His priests*]. The editor now looks back to the ancient history for illustration of the divine government; and first he thinks of Moses and Aaron, whom he regards as priests, in accordance with the conception of his own time, rather than as prophets or rulers, as in the earlier conceptions. With true historic instinct he next mentions, — *Samuel among them that call on His name*], because of this characteristic of Samuel, making him the father of all such, cf. 1 S. 7⁸˙ ⁹ 12¹⁶ˢq· BS. 46¹⁶. It is evident, however, that this calling on the name of Yahweh is conceived as that of priestly mediation, for the terms are in syn. lines, and the three heroes are all combined in the clause: *They called unto Yahweh, and He answered them*]. The author, however, thinks not merely of the ordinary invocation of God in temple worship, or of priestly intercession, with answers in accordance with ordinary providential working. He is thinking of extraordinary answers, which alone he can bring into comparison with the wonderful advent. He is summoning all mankind to celebrate ; and so naturally he thinks of the most characteristic theophany of the period of the Exodus. — **7.** *In the pillar of cloud He used to speak unto them*], cf. Ex. 13$^{21-22}$ (J) Ne. 9$^{12. 19}$. — *They kept His testimonies and the ordinance He gave them*], the ancient poetic term for the Law, " ordinance " (cf. 94^{20}), is combined with the priestly term, " testimonies." — **8-9.** *Yahweh, our God, Thou didst answer them*]. This doubtless refers to the intercession of Moses, Aaron, and Samuel in behalf of the people of Israel in times of sin and divine punishment. — *A forgiving God wast Thou to them*], and on the other side, *a taker of vengeance on evil deeds*]. This doubtless refers to the discriminating justice of the divine judgments in the early history of Israel, when the ringleaders were punished for their evil deeds, but Israel as a whole was forgiven because of the intercession of these heroes of faith and their priestly mediation. — *For holy is Yahweh our God*], the holiness of august sanctity, as in Ez., H.

PSALM C.

Str. IV. A syn. tristich and a stairlike tristich. — **1.** *Shout to Yahweh, all the earth*, as 98^4, ‖ **2.** *Serve Yahweh with gladness*], the glad services of worship with song and music, and not the service of obedience ; and accordingly, — *Come before Him*], into His presence in the temple, — *with a jubilation*], 63^6, cf. 17^1. — **3.** *Know*], not in the sense of coming to a knowledge of the fact ; but know by practical, experimental knowledge, in the recognition of worship, — *that He is God*], the true, the only God, and your own God ; advanced to, — *He made us*], we are His own creatures, — *and we are His*], belong to Him as His rightful creation. This reading of the Qr., 𝔍, 𝕿, and Aq., RV., is to be preferred to the Kt., 𝕲, 𝕾, 𝚺, followed by AV., " and not we ourselves " ; especially as in the stairlike advance it is still further defined as : *His people and the sheep of His pasture*]. The conception of Yahweh as shepherd of Israel is common enough ; cf. 23, 80^2, and in this special phrase also Ez. 34³¹ Pss. 74¹ 79¹³. But here He seems to be the shepherd of all the earth, in accord with the universalism of this entire group of Pss.

Str. II. Two syn. tristichs. — **4–5.** *Come to His gates*], resumes the call of v.²⁵, and has as its ‖ *Come to His courts;* for the measure requires the repetition of the verb, which has been omitted by an early copyist. — *with a thank offering*], the most probable meaning ‖ *a song of praise*, accompanying it; more probable than the more general " thanksgiving " of EVˢ. — *Give thanks to Him, bless His name*], cf. 96² 145¹· ². The first verb is repeated, with the reason, *Yahweh is good*], that is, to His people and flock ‖ *His kindness* ‖ *His faithfulness*, which *endureth forever* ‖ *unto all generations*]. The liturgical formula 1 Ch. 16³⁴ 2 Ch. 5¹³ 7³ Ezr. 3¹¹ Pss. 106¹ 107¹ 118¹· ²⁹ 136¹+ is used with an additional line, containing the attribute of faithfulness, which is usually associated with the divine kindness.

XCIII.

1. [מָלָךְ] Qal pf. ‡ vb. denom. מֶלֶךְ, so 96¹⁰ 97¹ 99¹, cf. 47⁹ 146¹⁰ Ex. 15¹⁸ Is. 24²³ 52⁷; cf. (ה)מֶלֶךְ] Pss. 98⁶ 99⁴. — [גֵּאוּת] *17¹⁰*, qualifies כלך and is not obj. of לבש. — [לָבֵשׁ] bis. Qal pf., cf. Is. 51⁹ 59¹⁷ Ps. 104¹; the second, however, should be לבוש, cog. acc. to vb. לבש requires יהוה for subj. in ‖ with previous and following vbs. for good measure. — [אַף־תִּכּוֹן]. The אף is prob. a gl. of intensification, although used in the duplicate citation 96¹⁰. 𝔊 and all ancient Vrss. have תֵּבֵל, as 75⁴, which is better suited to context. — **2.** [מֵאָז] as Is. 44⁸ 45²¹ 48³· ⁵· ⁷· ⁸. — [מֵעוֹלָם אתה] is dimeter, requires יהוה for good measure. — **3.** [דָּכְיָם] dub. pl. sf. [דָּכְיָ] *a.λ.*, 𝐵DB. *crashing, dashing;* Dr., Kirk., *din.* The l. not in 𝔊ᴮ· ℵ; but in 𝔊ᴺ· ᶜ· ᵃ· ᴬ, Aq., ἐπιτρίψεις, 𝒱 *fluctus*, and needed for completion of Str. 𝔍 *gurgites*, Syr. Hex. עובקתא = עמקיב, 𝔖 ברכוותא *in purity* from זכא = דכא. The context demands, as 𝔗, in the climax: the praise of Yahweh that the voice utters. Rd. זכרם *their commemoration*, as 97¹². — **4.** [אַדִּירִים] 𝔐, Vrss., cf. Ex. 15¹⁰ of waters, which has prob. occasioned the change from an original מ׳ אדיר, which is better suited to the context, as Dy., Hu.³, al. — **5.** [עֵדְתֶיךָ] legal term of P, cf. 25¹⁰ 78⁵⁶ 99⁷ 119²· ²² +. This v. is a prosaic gl. — [נָאֲוָה] Pil. †נאה as Is. 52⁷ Ct. 1¹⁰, but adj. נָאוֶה more freq. Pss. 33¹ 147¹ +, and so possibly here.

XCVI.

1–2. [שִׁירוּ] tris, abbreviated in 1 Ch. 16²³ by omission of v.¹ᵃ· ²ᵃ. — [יהוה] tris also in 𝔐, Vrss., but in l.¹· ³ against the measure. Rd. לֹ, as 100⁴. — [מִיּוֹם לְיוֹם] Chr. אל־יום; both enlargements against measure of an original יֹ׳ יֹ׳, which has the same mng. — **4.** [וּמְהֻלָּל מְאֹד] added from 48² against the

measure. — נוֹרָא הוּא]. The הוּא is gl. of intensification, makes l. too long. —
5. יְיָ] dittog.; makes l. too long. — ‡ אֱלִילִים] pl. *idols* as *worthless things,
nothings*, so 97⁷ Lv. 19⁴ 26¹ (H) Is. 2⁸·¹⁸·²⁰ 10¹⁰ +. ⅌ δαιμόνια, 𝔙 *daemonia.*
— **6.** עֹז] ⅌ ἁγιωσύνη. 1 Ch. 16²⁷ has חֶדְוָה for תפארת, and מקמו for קדשו, the
former prob. an intentional adaptation, the latter an unconscious error. —
7–9 *a.* Gl. from 29¹⁻², except משפחות עמים for בני אלים and insertion of v.⁸ᵇ,
both changes made in the interests of worship in the temple. 1 Ch. 16²⁹ has
לפניו for לחצרותיו, which is an unintentional error. — **9** *b.* חילו] although rendered by Vrss. *be in pain* or *anguish of fear* or *trembling*, cf. 55⁵ Dt. 2²⁵ Je. 5²²
Ez. 30¹⁶, yet never has this mng. in connection with worship; but rather
dance the sacred dance, as Ps. 87⁷ Ju. 21²¹⁻²³ 1 S. 18⁶. — מפניו] 1 Ch. 16³⁰
מלפניו, stylistic change. — **10** *a* in Chr. is transferred to a place after v.¹¹ᵃ. —
10 *b* is a gl. from 93¹ᵈ. — **10** *c* is a gl. from 9⁹ᵇ, not in Chr. — **11** *a.* וְתָגֵל הָאָרֶץ]
assimilated to 97¹ Is. 49¹³; but the vb. makes l. too long and the other ll.
all have but one vb. for a principal and a subord. subj. — **11** *b* = 98⁷ᵃ. —
12. שדי] in 1 Ch. 16³² שדה, variation of writing same word; also in Chr. for
עלו the variant עלי. — וכל־אשר־בו] prosaic for an original וכל־בו. — אָז] as 2⁵,
emphasizes a special feature of the description, B*D*B. But the text is dub. The
measure is better without it. — **13** is a gl. from 98⁹, although כי בא is here given
twice, and באמונה for במישרים. Chr. has only מלפני יהוה כי בא לשפט את־הארץ,
probably representing an earlier couplet:

לפני יהוה כי־בא
כי־בא לשפט הארץ,

which is all that the measure allows in 98⁹.

XCVII.

2 *b.* Gl. = 89¹⁵ᵃ. — **5.** מלפני יהוה] needs a word to complete the l., prob.
אדון ‖ המלך. — **7** *a.* Pentameter l.; whole v. a gl. — עבדי פסל] cf. 2 K. 17⁴¹
2 Ch. 33²². ‡ פֶּסֶל n.m., as Ex. 20⁴ Is. 42¹⁷ +. — מתהללים ב־] as 52³, usually,
however, in good sense 34³ 63¹² +. — **8.** Gl. from 48¹². Variations: שמעה
for ישמח הר ציון and ותשמח ציון; and יהוה added. בנות יהודה ψ. — **9** *a.* Gl.
from 47³ by condensation, כי יהוה נורא מלך גדול על כל הארץ. — **9** *b.* From
47¹⁰ᵈ מאד נעלה, combined with 95³ᵇ על כל אלהים. — **11.** זָרֻעַ] α.λ. in this form.
⅌, 𝔍, 𝔖, 𝔗, 𝔙, זרח, so Hu., Bä., B*D*B., cf. 104²² Dt. 33² Is. 60² +. — **12.** Gl.
from 32¹¹ והורו לזכר קדשו and 30⁵ᵇ שמחו ביהוה וגילו צדיקים.

XCVIII.

1 = 96¹; only the first l. is given in 𝔐 and Vrss., but the other l. of the
couplet is needed and should be inserted. It was omitted by ancient copyist.
— וּזְרֹעַ קָרְשׁוֹ] makes the l. a pentameter. It was added from Is. 52¹⁰ᵃ. —
2. גִּלָּה] makes l. too long and is a gl. — **3.** The first l. is a pentameter in 𝔐,
but ⅌, by giving ליעקב after חסדו, makes it a trimeter couplet. The second
half of v. was added from Is. 52¹⁰ᵇ. — **4.** פִּצְחוּ] imv. † פצח vb. *break forth,
burst forth with joy*, elsw. Is. 14⁷ 44²³ 49¹³ 52⁹ 54¹ 55¹². Pi. *break in pieces*
Mi. 3³. — **5.** וְקוֹל זִמְרָה] phr. α.λ. but noun, *melody* of psalm, as 81³. — **6.** הֲצֹצְרֹות]

the straight metal trumpets ; in religious use elsw. only P, Chr. (*v.* Intr. § 34).
— יהוה] makes l. too long, and is a later insertion.— **7.** The first l. = 96[11b],
the second 24[1c].— **8.** יִמְחָאוּ] juss. † מחא vb. *clap hands*, elsw. with כַּף Is. 55[12]
of trees ; cf. הכה כף 2 K. 11[12], תקע כף Ps. 47[2]. Pi. with יד Ez. 25[6].— **9.** כִּי בָא]
pf. and not ptc. as EV[s]., influenced by impf. ישפט ; for the Ps. is in praise
of an advent that has taken place already. It is repeated in Syr.-Hex. 𝕲[A] as
in 96[13], but not in 𝔖, 𝔍, or 𝕲[B]. The measure requires it. — The last clause
with ישפט = 96[13] is a pent. gl., thinking of a future advent. בְּמֵישָׁרִים for
באמונתו 96[13].

XCIX.

1. הֲנוֹט] *a.λ.*, 𝕲 σαλευθήτω, as 93[2] תמוט ; but this would then be in direct
contradiction with that passage and inconsistent with the context. Ols., We.,
*B*DB., נוע, Gr. נוע.—כְּרוּבִים] makes l. too long and is a gl., particularistic
in character as v.[6 sq.]—**3.** יִירוּ שְׁמְךָ]. The sf. is improb. ; without it we might
retain all the words and have a trimeter l.; with it the l. is tetrameter. Rd.
יודו־שם.—**4.** וְעֹז] although sustained by Vrss. is improb. ; awkward and difficult. Rd. וְעַז adj. as predicate and attach to previous l. to complete the measure ; so Street, Houb., Horsley.—אַתָּה] bis, make ll. too long and are gls.
The change to 2d pers. is also improb. ; rd. כונן and עשה.—**5.** קרוש הוא]. A
word is needed for measure, prob. יְיָ, as v.[3b].—**6.** This v. begins a particularistic gl. which continues to the end of the Ps.—**8.** עֲנִיתָם]. The sf. here might
be referred to the heroes of previous Str. and possibly לְהֶם, but not the sf. in
עֲלִילוֹ־ם. Doubtless they all were meant to have a general reference. But
the sfs. are prob. in all these cases prosaic interpretations.

C.

1 = 98[4].—**2.** בְּרָווֹה] lengthened form for measure, as 63[6], for usual רְנָה.—
3. יהוה] makes the l. too long and is an unnecessary gl.—הוא עשנו]. The
הוּא, emphasizing the subj., is without sufficient reason and makes l. too long.
It prob. was inserted in antithesis to ולא אנהנו Kt., 𝕲, 𝔖, Σ, which is erroneous. The לו of Qr., 𝔍, 𝕿, is to be preferred, and makes the הוא surprising.
— צאן מרעיתו] as Ez. 34[31] Pss. 74[1] 79[13]. The enlargement of 95[7] is the work
of a glossator. — **4-5.** באו] should be repeated for measure in the second l.
—הידו] of v.[4c] should be repeated v.[5a] before כי טוב for measure, and כי is
needed before לעולם in accordance with the usual phr. 1 Ch. 16[34] 2 Ch. 5[13] 7[3]
Ezr. 3[11] Pss. 106[1] 107[1] +.

PSALM CI., 2 STR. 4[5].

**Psalm 101 is a profession of integrity in personal character and
conduct (v.[2c-4]), and in companionship (v.[6-7]). To this was added a
gloss of worship and prayer for the divine presence (v.[1-2b]), and
vows to exterminate the wicked (v.[5, 8]).**

I WALK in integrity of mind in the midst of *my* house.
  I set not any base thing before *mine* eye.
  The making of apostasy I hate. It cleaves not unto *me*.
  Evil I know not: crookedness departs from *me*.
MINE eye is upon the faithful of the land, that they may dwell with *me*.
  The one walking in the way of integrity ministers to *me*.
  The worker of deception dwells not in *my* house.
  The speaker of lies is not established before *mine* eye.

Ps. 101 in 𝕳 has the title לדוד מזמור; so also in 𝕲. This was probably original, and the Ps. belonged to 𝕯 and 𝕸 (*v.* Intr. §§ 27, 31). It had two pentameter tetrastichs, v.²ᶜ⁻⁴· ⁶⁻⁷, each line ending in ־י; to which several glosses have been added, v.¹⁻²ᵇ· ⁵· ⁸, without the ending. The original was a profession of integrity, suited to the congregation of Israel before the legal attitude of mind had become established. The language is early: תם לבב v.²ᶜ = Gn. 20⁵· ⁶ (E) I K. 9⁴ Ps. 78⁷²; דבר בליעל v.³ᵃ = Ps. 41⁹; סטים v.³ *a.λ.* for שטים, cf. 40⁵ Ho. 5²; לבב עקש v.⁴ *a.λ.* error for עקש as Ps. 18²⁷; נאמני ארץ v.⁶ *a.λ.*, but cf. Is. 1²¹; עשה רמיה v.⁷ as 52⁴, cf. 32²; דבר שקרים v.⁷, cf. 63¹². The Ps. was probably composed for the community of the Restoration before Nehemiah. The glosses are of a different character and later. V.⁵· ⁸ express the determination to exterminate the wicked from the land, and give the only reason for thinking of the author as a ruler. They are Maccabean in tone, and the language is late. V.¹⁻²ᵃ is a trimeter tetrastich of introduction: a vow to Yahweh of worship and a petition for the divine presence. It was designed to make the Ps. more appropriate for public worship.

The Ps. begins with a trimeter tetrastich, making it more appropriate for public worship than the original could have been. — **1-2 b.** *Of kindness and justice*], cf. Je. 9²³, divine attributes; especially characteristic of God's administration of government, and of His requirements of mankind, cf. Ho. 12⁷. — *I will sing ‖ I will make melody to Thee, Yahweh*], usual phrases of public worship in the temple. — *In a way of integrity*], cf. v.⁶ᵇ; a course of life which is in complete and entire accord with the divine will. — *I will behave myself wisely*], cohortative form expressing a vow of such conduct. It is possible, with JPSV. and Kirk., to render " consider," " give heed unto "; but this is not so probable. — *When wilt Thou come unto me*], a petition for the divine presence as prepared for by entire conformity to His will.

Str. I. A syn. tetrastich. — **2 c.** *I walk*]. This and the following vbs. are not in the cohort. form as the previous vb. Therefore they do not express a vow; but state what is the habitual conduct of the righteous. — *in integrity of mind*]. The internal mental state is in entire accord with God, and therefore the walk is such, in a way of integrity v.[6b], cf. v.[2a]. — *In the midst of my house*], in the life of the family and of society. — **3.** *I set not before mine eye*], to consider as a possibility for action, or as something to be desired. — *any base thing*], cf. 41[9], such as base men, sons of Belial, do, cf. Dt. 15[9]. — *The making of apostasy I hate*], the swerving or falling away from Yahweh into such evil conduct. — *It cleaves not unto me*], as a power of temptation, or something desirable and attractive. — **4.** *Evil I know not*], by experimental knowledge, resulting from its commission. — *crookedness*], as 18[27], qualified by a glossator, against the measure, as "of the mind," against the context, which regards it no longer as internal, but as external; and which *departs from me*], as an unwelcome guest, or banished from the presence as an enemy. A glossator now inserts a pentameter couplet of a different character. — **5.** *The slanderer in secret of his neighbour*], cf. Pr. 30[10], still further described as *one lofty of eyes*], cf. Ps. 18[28], and *proud of mind*, cf. Pr. 21[4]. These terms do not refer to ordinary men of this class; but to men of position and power who had become oppressors of the people, for otherwise they could hardly be dealt with so severely and summarily. — *will I exterminate* ‖ *I will not suffer*].

Str. II. Two syn. couplets. — **6–7.** *Mine eye is upon*], considering, contemplating with recognition and acceptance, in antith. to v.[3a] and also to v.[7b], — *The faithful of the land*], those faithful to Yahweh, in antith. to the apostasy of v.[3b]. ‖ *The one walking in the way of integrity*], cf. v.[2a. c], and in antith. with *the worker of deception* ‖ *speaker of lies*. The former *dwell with me* ‖ *minister to me*], as household servants; the latter *dwells not in my house* ‖ *is not established*], or settled, as one of my household. The glossator of v.[5] also appends v.[8]. — *Morning by morning*], one after the other, searching for them. — *will I exterminate*], as v.[5a] ‖ *cut off from the city of Yahweh*], cf. 12[4] 34[17] 109[13. 15], where God does this cutting off. — *ull the wicked of the land* ‖ *all the workers of trouble*.

1-2. אָשִׁירָה ‖ אֲזַמֵּרָה ‖ אַשְׂכִּילָה] cohort. impfs. expressing a vow. — לְךָ יהוה] is attached by MT. to אזמרה, by 𝔊 to אשירה; the latter favours a pentameter, the former two trimeters. But the remaining l. is a hexameter or two trimeters. These constitute a trimeter tetrastich, a gl. — אֶתְהַלֵּךְ] Hithp. impf. indic. The change from cohort. is significant. It states a fact instead of a vow. — **3.** [דְּבַר בְּלִיַּעַל] = 41⁹; transpose to beginning of l. for assonance in עֵינִי, which should be read here and v.⁷ᵇ for assonance instead of the usual pl., and so also prob. v.⁶ᵃ at the beginning of v. — [קָטֵיב] α.λ. for שטים ‏†‎ שׁוֹט vb. *swerve, fall away*, 40⁵. ‏†‎ שטים n.[m]. *swerver*, Ho. 5²; here prob. abstr. pl., as Bä., Hu.³, *apostasy*.— **4.** [רֶכֶב עֶקֶשׁ] phr. α.λ. The l. has one word too many; prob. רכב, which does not indeed suit the context. — [רַע לֹא אָדֵעַ] should go to the beginning of the line in order to assonance in יְמֵנִי. — **5.** [מְלָשְׁנִי] Poel ptc. of ‏†‎ לשן denom. vb. elsw. Hiph. Pr. 30¹⁰, both in bad sense, use the tongue for slander, Ges.⁹⁰·ᵐ, Qr. מְלָשְׁנִי. We should rd. Hiph. ptc. מַלְשִׁינִי with Che. — [וּבַהּ עֵינַיִם] phr. α.λ. ‡ גבה *high* of mountain 104¹⁸, *lofty* of לב Pr. 16⁵, of רוח Ec. 7⁸, alone Ps. 138⁶ Is. 5¹⁵ 10³³ 1 S. 2³. — [רְחַב לֵבָב] phr. elsw. Is. 60⁵, cf. רחב לב Pr. 21⁴ ר' נפש 28²⁵, ‏†‎ רָחָב adj. elsw. Ps. 104²⁵ *broad* of sea, 119⁹⁶ of divine command, 119⁴⁵ of divine way. These two pent. without assonance and in a more vindictive tone are a Maccabean gl. — **6.** [וַאֲמֵנֵי־אֶרֶץ] phr. α.λ., but cf. Is. 8² Pr. 25¹³. — [יְשָׁרְתֻנִי] Pi. impf. ‡ שרת vb. of ministerial service ; here of men, but 103²¹ 104⁴ of angels. — **7.** [עֹשֵׂה רְמִיָּה] = 52⁴; transpose to the beginning of the l. for assonance in בֵּיתִי. — **8.** Two pent. ll. without assonance and in the tone of v.⁵; a gloss.

PSALM CII.

Ps. 102 is composite : (*A*) **A prayer of afflicted Israel, beseeching Yahweh to answer in a day of distress** (v.²⁻³) ; **the peril is so great that he is about to perish** (v.⁴⁻⁶) ; **he is desolate and reproached by enemies** (v.⁷⁻⁹). **It is his greatest grief that he has been cast off by his God** (v.¹⁰⁻¹²). (*B*) **expresses confidence that the time has come when the everlasting King will have compassion on Zion and build her up from her ruins, and that all nations will see His glory and revere Him** (v.¹³⁻¹⁸). **The story will be told to all generations of His interposition for the salvation of His people, that His praise may be forever celebrated in Jerusalem, where all nations will eventually gather to serve Him** (v.¹⁹⁻²³·²⁹). **Glosses reassert the seriousness of the situation** (v.²⁴⁻²⁵ᵃ), **and contrast the everlasting creator with the perishable creature** (²⁵ᵇ⁻²⁸).

A. v.²⁻¹², 4 STR. 6³.

YAHWEH, O hear *my* prayer ;
　　And let for help come unto Thee *my* cry.
　　Hide not Thy face from *me*.
　　In the day when I have distress, answer *me*.
　　Incline Thine ear unto *me ;*
　　In the day when I call, O make haste (to *me*).

FOR vanish away like smoke *my* days;
And burned like fuel are *my* bones.
Smitten like herbage is *my* heart.
Yea, I forget to eat *my* bread.
Because of the sound of *my* groaning
My bone doth cleave to *my* flesh.

I AM like a pelican of the wilderness;
I am become as an owl of the wastes;
I watch and am become (a falcon),
A bird solitary upon a house-top.
All the day mine enemies reproach me;
They that (wound) me, do curse by me.

YEA, ashes do I eat as bread,
And I mix my drink with weeping,
Because of Thine indignation and Thy wrath;
For Thou hast taken me up, and thrown me away.
My days are like a shadow stretched out,
And I like the herbage wither.

$$B. \ v.^{13-23.\ 29}, \ 2 \ \text{STR.} \ 6^6.$$

THOU, Yahweh, sittest enthroned forever; and Thy commemoration is in all
generations.
Thou wilt arise, Thou wilt have compassion on Zion; for it is time to be
gracious to her.
For Thy servants take pleasure in her stones, and are looking graciously upon
her dust.
And the nations will revere Thy name, and kings of earth Thy glory,
When Yahweh hath built up Zion, hath appeared in His glory (in her midst);
Hath turned unto the destitute and hath not despised their prayer.

THIS will be written for a generation to come, and a people to be created;
When Yahweh hath looked forth from His holy height, unto the earth hath
looked,
To hear the groaning of the prisoner, to loose those condemned to die;
That they may tell the name of Yahweh in Zion and His praise in Jerusalem.
When the peoples are gathered together and the kingdoms to serve Yahweh,
The children of Thy servants will abide, and their seed will be established
before Thee.

Ps. 102 has in the title of 𝔐, 𝔊, תְּפִלָּה לְעָנִי, *a prayer of the afflicted;* and to
this was added, whether at the same time or later we cannot say, " when he
was fainting," cf. 61³, " and before Yahweh pouring out his complaint," cf. 142³
Jb. 7¹⁸. In other words, the Ps. expressed humiliation for national disaster
and prayer for deliverance. עָנִי is a pseudonym. The author wrote in the
person of afflicted Israel, *v.* Intr. § 30. But this title applies only to v.²⁻¹²,
composed of four trimeter hexastichs. The remainder of the Ps. is of an
entirely different character, and of a much later date. The original Ps. uses
many familiar terms of 𝔅. The author must have been familiar with many of
its Pss., if not with the collection as a whole; cf. v.²ᵃ with 39¹³, v.²ᵇ with 18⁷,

v.³ᵃ with 27⁹, v.³ᵇ with 59¹⁷, v.³ᶜ with 31³ 69¹⁸, also 56¹¹, v.⁴ with 31¹¹ 37²⁰, v.⁹ with 55¹³. But the Ps. is not a mere mosaic. In the remaining Strs. there is great originality, and several simple but beautiful similes v.⁴·⁵·⁷·⁸·¹⁰·¹². The Ps. can hardly be earlier than the closing days of the Persian period. Later, doubtless in the early Maccabean period, another original Ps. was appended, v.¹³⁻²³·²⁹, of two hexameter hexastichs. Zion is here in ruins v.¹⁶, and her people are prisoners and many of them condemned to death v.²¹; and yet the psalmist bases his confidence in the divine advent for their redemption upon the eternal reign of God. Two glosses were inserted: the one based on Is. 38¹⁰ v.²⁴⁻²⁵ᵃ; the other, v.²⁵ᵇ⁻²⁸, with real poetic power, was probably a section of a longer poem which has been lost.

PSALM CII. *A.*

Str. I. A syn. and two synth. couplets ; a mosaic of terms of supplication from 39¹³ 18⁷ 27⁹ 59¹⁷ 31³ 69¹⁸ 56¹⁰ ; not because of a lack of originality in the poet, but because he desired to use the familiar terms of the Davidic prayer book for this day of humiliation and prayer for national deliverance.

Str. II. A syn. tetrastich, enclosing before its last line an embl. couplet. — **4.** *For vanish away like smoke my days*], a common simile of transitoriness, cf. 37²⁰ 68³ Is. 51⁶ Ho. 13³ Ja. 4¹⁴. — *And burned like fuel are my bones*]. In feverish anxiety his bones seem to be on fire, cf. 22¹⁵ 31¹¹ La. 1¹³ Jb. 30¹⁷·³⁰. The unusual Heb. word is rendered by PBV., RV., "firebrand," so Kirk.; by AV. "hearth," so Dr., "fireplace," JPSV. It is most probably, as *B*DB., a burning mass, which may be sufficiently expressed by "fuel" for the fire. — **5.** *Smitten like herbage is my heart*]. As the green herbage is smitten by the heat of the sun and withers away ; so the heart, as the seat of mental and moral states, has been so smitten that it has no more freshness and vigour. The withering is sufficiently suggested by the simile, and the line is complete in its measure without "and withered," which has been added by a glossator. — *Yea, I forget to eat my bread*], appetite has departed ; he can think of nothing else but his trouble, and has no other desire than relief from that. — **6.** *Because of the sound of my groaning*]. This is usually attached to the next line, but it really belongs to the previous one ; for it gives a good reason for the absence of appetite ; the mouth is engaged in the constant utterance of groans. — *My bone doth cleave to my flesh*].

As above the bones were burning with fever, so here from the lack of moisture the bone cleaves fast to the flesh, cf. Jb. 19²⁰ Ps. 32⁴.

Str. III. A syn. tetrastich and a syn. couplet. — **7–8.** *I am like a pelican of the wilderness* ‖ *an owl of the wastes* ‖ *a bird solitary upon a house-top*]. These various birds in their solitariness are similes of his desolate condition in the midst of enemies and rejected by his God. The line before the last is difficult, because it is defective, due probably to the omission of a word. It probably should be, — *I watch and am become a falcon*]. The falcon is famed for its keen vision, and so is appropriate to the verb. He is watching keenly for the help he is imploring from God. — **9.** *All the day mine enemies reproach me*], cf. 55¹³, also 42¹¹ 44¹⁷ 74¹⁰·¹⁸ 79¹² 89⁵²·⁵² ‖ *they that wound me*], more probable than those "mad against me," of EVˢ. — *do curse by me*], use the name of Israel in imprecations and oaths, cf. 132² Is. 65¹⁵ Je. 29²².

Str. IV. A syn. and two synth. couplets. — **10.** *Yea*], intensive assertion ; the usual " For " is improbable. It is difficult to find a reason in this Str. for the statements of the previous Str. — *ashes do I eat as bread*], ashes are the symbol of mourning, and appear in Is. 61³ as a turban, and in La. 3¹⁶ as clothing, cf. Ez. 27³⁰ ; but only here as bread. ‖ *And I mix my drink with weeping*], phr. α.λ., but the idea is expressed in other phrases Pss. 42⁴ 80⁶. — **11.** *Because of Thine indignation and Thy wrath*]. Thus far the lamentation has been because of the distress and the reproaches of enemies ; now it is all carried back to the original cause, the wrath of their God. — *For Thou hast taken me up and thrown me away*], deliberate and violent rejection, cf. Je. 7¹⁵. — **12.** *My days are like a shadow stretched out*], resuming the thought of v.⁴ᵃ. The prolongation of the shadow is an evidence of the approach of sunset, an appropriate simile of the close of life, cf. Je. 6⁴ Ps. 144⁴. — *And I like the herbage wither*], a resumption of v.⁵ᵃ, cf. Is. 40⁷ Ps. 90⁵⁻⁶ Ja. 1¹¹ ; the morning of life, when the herbage sprang up and bloomed, and the noontide, when it was smitten by the sun, have passed ; the evening has come, when it withereth.

PSALM CII. *B.*

Str. I. Synth. hexastich. — **13.** *Thou, Yahweh, sittest enthroned forever*], as everlasting king ; phr. of La. 5¹⁹, cf. Pss. 2⁴ 9⁸ 93² 99¹,

— *and Thy commemoration*], the celebration of the name, cf. 6[6]
30[5] 97[12] 111[4]. The fact that Yahweh reigns forever, and is to be
commemorated forever, is the basis of the confidence in the
restoration of Zion expressed in the Ps. — **14**. *Thou wilt arise*],
the usual term for divine interposition, cf. 9[20] 10[12]. — *Thou wilt
have compassion on Zion*], emphatic coördination without conjunction. Zion, the holy city, was in great need of divine help,
and had been for a long time in this sad condition ; therefore it is
added, — *for it is time to be gracious to her*], it is high time : the
distress is so great, it is now or never with her. A glossator
repeats at the expense of the measure : *for the appointed time is
come*], the time appointed for the fulfilment of the divine promises of her restoration. This is not the restoration from the Exile,
cf. Je. 29[10] Is. 40[2] Hb. 2[3] ; but from the devastations of Antiochus
before the Maccabean victories. — **15**. *For Thy servants*], the
faithful people of God who serve Him in spite of persecutions, —
take pleasure in ‖ *are looking graciously upon*], expressing their
interest in, love for, and attachment to her, — *stones* ‖ *dust*].
Zion has been destroyed by the enemy ; her buildings are in ruins,
mere stones and dust ; and yet these are precious to the servants
of Yahweh, because they are the remains of the holy city of the
divine presence and worship. — **16**. *the nations* ‖ *the kings of earth*].
The restoration of Zion will have universal significance to the
nations and especially to their kings ; and the result of it will be
that they *will revere Thy name* ‖ *Thy glory*], take part in the
worship of the God of Israel. — **17**. *When Yahweh hath built up
Zion*], rebuilt the ruined city, cf. 51[20]. — *hath appeared in His
glory*], manifested it in His advent to interpose for her deliverance.
The line is defective, and therefore we must supply either *in her
midst*, or " in Jerusalem," as v.[22]. — **18**. *Hath turned unto the destitute*]. The city has been stripped and left destitute in her ruin.
A glossator inserted from 1 K. 8[28] " prayer " after the preposition
and before the noun, thereby making an improbable tautology with
the complementary part of the line, — *and hath not despised their
prayer*], cf. 22[25] 51[19] 69[34].

Str. II. Synth. hexastich. — **19**. *This will be written*], recorded
for a memorial and especially for commemoration, cf. v[18b], — *for
a generation to come* ‖ *a people to be created*], the succeeding

generations of redeemed Zion, cf. 22[32] 48[14] 78[4. 6]. The purpose is given after a temporal clause in v.[22], *that they may tell the name of Yahweh in Zion and His praise in Jerusalem*], cf. 9[15] 96[3]. But a glossator could not wait for this, and so he appended to v.[19] at the cost of the measure, " shall praise Yah." — **20.** *When*], as in v.[17. 23], and not causal " for," as EV[s]. — *Yahweh hath looked forth from His holy height*], explained by the glossator as " from heaven," without need and against the measure. This v. resumes the thought of the divine advent of v.[14. 17], especially in the form of divine inspection or investigation of what transpires on earth, — *unto the earth hath looked*], cf. 14[2] 33[13] Dt. 26[15]. — **21.** *To hear the groaning of the prisoner*], the Israelites taken captive by the enemy and imprisoned. — *to loose those condemned to die*]. Some of the captives had been condemned to death, probably because of supposed treason against the dominant power of Syria. The compassion upon destitute Zion of the previous Str. has as its parallel, compassion on her captives in this Str. — **23.** *When the peoples are gathered together and the nations to serve Yahweh*]. A resumption of the universalism of v.[16]. The apodosis of this temporal clause is in **29** : *The children of Thy servants will abide, and their seed will be established before Thee*]. This resumes the thought of v.[19], and with it encloses the other lines of the Str. in an organic whole.

Two different glossators made insertions ; the former v.[24-25a] from Is. 38[10], the so-called song of Hezekiah : *He hath brought down my strength in the way; He hath shortened my days. I say : O my God, take me not away in the midst of my days*]. These two pentameter lines are more in accord with the plaintive tone of the original Ps. than with the calm assurance of the later Maccabean Ps. in which it inserted. It was probably designed to assimilate them. The later glossator inserted the octastich v.[25b-28], doubtless a fragment of a choice Ps. which has been lost.

> I N generation of generations are Thy years.
>   Of old Thou didst lay the foundation of the earth ;
>   And the heavens are the work of Thy hands.
>   They will perish, but Thou wilt endure ;
>   Yea, all of them will wear out as a garment,
>   As a vesture wilt Thou change them, and they will be changed.
>   But Thou (Yahweh) art the same ;
>   And Thy years have no end.
>   Y

The first and last lines of this octastich are syn. and enclose the other six ; the first two of which are syn. The antithesis which appears within the fourth line is enlarged upon in the triplet that follows, whose last line is antithetical to the two syn. lines which precede it. — **25 b.** *In generation of generations are Thy years*], extending in one generation after another are the years of the life of God, and not limited to a single generation, as are the years of men. ‖ **28 b.** *Thy years have no end*]. They come to no completion, as do the years of man. — **26.** *Of old*], cf. Dt. $2^{12. 20}$ for the term ; in remote antiquity ; cf. Ps. 90^2 for the idea. — *Thou didst lay the foundation of the earth*], the conception of creation as an erecting or building, cf. 24^2 89^{12} 104^5 Jb. 38^4, and especially Is. 48^{13}. — *The heavens are the work of Thy hands*]. The same conception being continued ; the heavens being considered as the roof or dome of the earth, cf. Pss. 8^4 19^2 Am. 9^6. — **27.** *They will perish*]. Even the heavens and the earth, the most stable of all created things, upon whose stability all they contain of life and existence depends, however long their duration, will eventually perish. ‖ *All of them will wear out like a garment*], based on Is. 51^6. They have a temporary use as clothing ; when they have been worn out another garment will take their place. ‖ *As a vesture wilt Thou change them and they will be changed*], new heavens and a new earth will take their place, according to Is. 65^{17} 66^{22}. In antithesis with creations *Thou wilt endure*], continue to stand firm after these creations perish. ‖ **28 c.** *Thou, Yahweh, art the same*]. The divine name has been omitted in the transmitted text, but is necessary to the measure. As in Is. 48^{12}, Yahweh is the same identical, unchangeable, ever-enduring being from first to last, so here He is the same during all the transitions from the creation of the heavens and the earth, while He is transforming them into a new heaven and a new earth, and so on forever.

CII. *A.*

3. מַהֵר עֲנֵנִי] assimilated to 69^{18} 143^7 ; but the two words make l. too long ; transfer עֲנֵנִי to l.² for measure. — **4.** † מוֹקֵד] a.λ., *BDB. burning mass*, as Is. 33^{14}; but SS., Dr., *hearth*, as מוֹקְדָה Lv. 6^2. 𝕲 φρύγιον, 𝔍 *frixa*. — **5.** רוּכָה] Hoph. pf. נכה, cf. Ho. 9^{16}. 𝕲 ἐπλήγην, 𝔍 *percussum est*, prob. both interp. infin. abs. — וַיִּבַשׁ] makes l. too long ; gl. from Ho. 9^{16}. — **6.** קוֹל אַנְחָתִי] phr.

a.λ., but אנחה 6⁷ +. — רבקה עצמי לבשרי] phr. a.λ., but cf. Jb. 19²⁰ La. 4⁸. —
7. † קאח] n.f. *pelican*, elsw. Is. 34¹¹ Zp. 2¹⁴; so 𝔊, 𝔍. 𝔖 has קקא, Bar Heb.
קוקנוס, *cygnus*. Bä. objects that the pelican is a water bird, and not a bird
of the wilderness. — † כ ס] n.m , elsw. Lv. 11¹⁷ = Dt. 14¹⁶, an unclean bird,
a species of owl. — 8. אֶהְיֶה] Qal impf. היה with ו consec., instead of jussive
אֱהִי. The text gives no predicate. Ols., Gr., Bä., Du., Kirk., Ehr., rd. וְאֶהֱמָיָה
as 77⁴, but *moaning* leads away from the real point of comparison, solitariness.
A word has been omitted by error, for the measure is defective ; rd. אַיָּה *falcon*, a bird especially appropriate to the vb. — † גַּו] n.m. *roof* of house, as
129⁶. — 9. מְהֹולָלַי] Poal ptc., elsw. Ec. 2², of *madness* of folly ; not suitable
here. 𝔊 oí ἐπαινοῦντές με, 𝔙 *qui laudabant me*, 𝔖 = מְהַלְלֵי, so Ehr. ; but this
does not suit the context. 𝔍 *exultantes* neglects the sf., which may be interp.
It is better to read מַחֲלַי = *those wounding me*.— בִּי נשבעו] = *swear by*, in
imprecation, cf. 132². — 10. שִׁקּוּי] a.λ. *my drink*, for vb. שקה (36⁹).

CII. B.

14. רָקוֹם תְּרַחֵם] impfs. future, emph. coördination, most prob., although
the second vb. might be subordinate. — לְרֶחֱנָה] Qal inf., unusual form,
Ges.⁶⁷·ᶜᶜ; cf. הֲוֶרֶם Is. 30¹⁸, חֲיוֹת Ps. 77¹⁰. For חנן *v.* 4². — כִּי בָא מִיֵּחֵר] duplicate of previous clause ; the two make l. too long. This, although phr. a.λ.,
is prob. the gl. rather than the other, as it emphasizes a promise ; cf. 75³. —
15. יחֹנֵנוּ] Poel, elsw. Pr. 14²¹ *direct favour to.*— 16. יֵם יהוה] so 𝔍, but
𝔊 ישׁבך יהוה. The divine name makes l. too long ; rd. שׁמך ‖ כבורך. —
כָּל־מַלְכֵי הָאָרֶץ]. 𝔊ᴮ has only וכל מלכיב, but 𝔊ᴺ·ᴬ·ᴿ·ᵀ agree with 𝕳, 𝔍.
𝕳 is assimilated to Is. 59¹⁹. The clause is too long for measure. כל is the
most prob. gl. — 17. נראה בכבורו] is defective. We should supply prob.
בהוכך with Du.— 18. הֶפֵּל] is improb. with הִרְבְּ־ב in the same l. It is a gl.;
rd. אל העריר.— † עֲרִיר] adj. *stripped, destitute*; cf. עֲרוּעֵר Je. 17⁶. Aq., Σ, 𝔍,
vacui. Bä. thinks of יְרִירִי adj. as Gn. 15² (JE) Je. 22³⁰ Lv. 20²⁰·²¹ (H).—
19. יְהַלְ־יָה] gl. anticipating v.²², phr. a.λ., but cf. ההלל יה 150⁶, יהללו יה
115¹⁷, elsw. always הרלו יה.— 20. וֹשׁמים] expl. gl. to מִמְרוֹם, making l. too
long. — 21. כְּנֵי רְמוּרָה] phr. elsw. 79¹¹.— 24. Derived from Is. 38¹⁰.— בֹּחִו]
Kt., sustained by 𝔊, 𝔙 ; Qr. כֹּחִי, by Σ, 𝔖, 𝔍, 𝔗, and most critics ; both sfs.
explanatory. — 26. † לְפָנֶה] adv. *formerly* Dt. 2¹²·²⁰ Jos. 11¹⁰ +.— 27. הֵמָּה]
gl. ; makes l. too long. — 28. ואתה הוא] is defective ; add יהוה. הוא emph.
denom. *the same*, based on Is. 48¹².— 29. לְפָנֶיך] but 𝔊 εἰς τὸν αἰῶνα = לְפנים,
as v.²⁶, cf. 𝔍 *ante faciem eorum*.

PSALM CIII., 7 STR. 4³.

Ps. 103 is a summons to Israel to bless Yahweh for all that He
had done for them (v.¹⁻²), His pardon and redemption (v.⁵⁻⁴ᵃ·⁹ᵃ),
His deeds of righteousness and justice (v.⁶⁻⁷), His long suffering

(v.$^{9-10}$), His kindness in removing sin (v.$^{11-12}$), His fatherly compassion (v.$^{13-14}$), His everlasting kindness and righteousness to frail man (v.$^{15.\ 17}$). Glosses emphasize these several things (v.$^{4b.\ 5b.\ 8.\ 16.\ 18}$). A liturgical gloss summons the angels and all creatures to unite in blessing Yahweh, the universal king (v.$^{19-22}$).

BLESS Yahweh, O my soul!
   And all that is within me, His holy name.
   Bless Yahweh, O my soul!
   And forget not His benefits.
WHO pardoneth all thine iniquity;
   Who healeth all thy diseases;
   Who redeemeth from the Pit thy life;
   Who satisfieth (thee) with good things (so long as thou livest).
A DOER of acts of righteousness is Yahweh,
   And of acts of judgment for all the oppressed.
   He used to make known His ways to Moses,
   To the sons of Israel His deeds.
WHILE He strives not alway,
   And restrains not His anger forever;
   Not according to our sins doth He do to us,
   Not according to our iniquities doth He deal to us.
AS high as heaven is above the earth,
   His kindness is mighty upon (us).
   As far as the East is removed from the West,
   He doth remove our transgressions from us.
AS a father hath compassion upon sons,
   Yahweh hath compassion upon (us) ;
   For He knoweth our frame;
   Remembereth that we are dust.
MAN, as grass are his days;
   As a blossom of the field, so he blossometh;
   But the kindness of Yahweh is from everlasting,
   And unto everlasting is His righteousness.

Ps. 103 has in the title לדוד, so 𝔊 ; but probably because of resemblance to Pss. of 𝔐. It is impossible that it could ever have been in 𝔐 ; for it cannot be earlier than the late Greek period. It uses familiarly earlier literature : v.^{9a} Is. 57^{16}, v.^{9b} Je. 3^{12}, v.^{11a} Is. 55^{9}, v.^{14b} Gn. 3^{19} (J), v.^{15} Is. 40^{6} Ps. 90$^{5-6}$. It uses the Aramaic sf. יכי_ v.$^{3-4}$; and several words in late meanings : החלואים v.^{2}, גמול v.^{2}, v.^{3}. It is composed of seven trimeter tetrastichs : v.$^{1-4a.\ 5a.\ 6-7.\ 9-15.\ 17}$. It has a late liturgical addition of two trimeter tetrastichs v.$^{19-22}$. There are also several glosses : v.^{5b} based on Is. 40^{31}, v.^{8} on Ex. 34^{6}, v.^{16} on Is. 40^{7} Jb. 7^{10}, v.^{18} on Ex. 20^{6}.

Str. I. Three syn. lines with a synth. conclusion. — **1-2.** *Bless Yahweh, O my soul*], also v.$^{2a.\ 22}$; adore in gratitude and praise.

The soul stands for the entire personality, ‖ *all that is within me*], the entire being, " with all thine heart, and with all thy soul, and with all thy might," Dt. 6⁵. The object of blessing is Yahweh Himself, especially as manifested in *His holy name*], majestically sacred and so to be hallowed, cf. 33²¹ 105³ 106⁴⁷ 145²¹. — *forget not*] a Deuteronomic warning, Dt. 6¹² 8¹¹, taken by Israel to himself, lest he should neglect grateful recognition of *His benefits*], literally *dealings*, which in their enumeration as the theme of the Ps. are all benefits.

Str. II. Synth. tetrastich. — **3-5.** The ptcs. express the continuous characteristic activities of Yahweh in dealing with His people. All through their past history He has been pardoning all their iniquity, cf. Ex. 34⁷, healing all their diseases, cf. Ex. 15²⁶, redeeming the life of the nation from the Pit of Sheol into which they had gone, in exile, and to which they had been so often exposed through their cruel and all·powerful enemies, cf. Ho. 13¹⁴ Ps. 9¹⁴. The whole is summed up in : *Who satisfieth thee with good things so long as thou livest*], for thus this difficult sentence may be translated. Yahweh had not only preserved His people alive, but had bestowed upon them good things continuously during the entire life of the nation. The translation of EVˢ., " who satisfieth thy mouth with good things," is based on the interpretation of some ancient Jewish scholars ; and, though followed by many, is now generally abandoned. " Thy desire " of 𝔊, 𝔙, whether based on a different Heb. word or a different interpretation of the same word, has its advocates. 𝔗, " days of thine old age," followed by JPSV., is nearer to the true interpretation. The previous line, *who crowneth thee with kindness and compassion*] is a gloss of interpretation, cf. 8⁶, for the figure of speech. Kindness and compassion are the characteristic attributes of the Ps. An additional gloss is taken from Is. 40³¹ : *so that thy youth reneweth itself like an eagle*]. It is doubtful whether there is an allusion to the fable of the eagle's renewing its youth in old age ; but at all events it is the fulness of life and vigour of the eagle that is thought of.

Str. III. Two syn. couplets. — **6-7.** *A doer of acts of righteousness ‖ acts of judgment for all the oppressed*]. These were *His ways ‖ His deeds*, which *He used to make known to Moses ‖ to the* *sons of Israel*, when He delivered His oppressed people from Egypt, and subsequently from all their enemies.

Str. IV. Two syn. couplets. — **8–9.** *He strives not alway ǁ He maintains not forever*] not always expressing His anger, as Is. 57[16]; not forever maintaining it, as Je. 3[12]. This double statement of the divine long-suffering suggests the fundamental revelation of it to Moses Ex. 34[6], which was then prefixed by a glossator : *compassionate and gracious is Yahweh, slow to anger and abundant in mercy.* — **10.** *Not according to our sins ǁ our iniquities*], those of the nation in its history, past as well as present, — *doth He do to us ǁ deal to us*], taking up the theme stated in v.[2], the divine dealings or benefits. He doth not give us our deserts, in letting loose His anger against us for sins.

Str. V. Two similes. — **11.** *As high as heaven is above the earth*], cf. Is. 55[8-9], the greatest height conceivable. — *mighty*], in reach from the height of heaven, is *His kindness*], in the pardon of sin, *upon us*], descending and resting upon us. A glossator, thinking that the statement was too sweeping, substitutes for "upon us" of the original, the more limited statement, "upon those that fear Him"; so also in v.[13b. 17b], against the measure. — **12.** *As far as the East is removed from the West*], the utmost conceivable distance in breadth, — *He doth remove our transgressions from us*]. The removal of sin to the utmost possible distance away from the sinner and away from the divine presence is a syn. idea to pardon and forgiveness, which in Hebrew is properly the taking it up and bearing it away as a burden from the sacred places where God and His people meet in communion, cf. Is. 38[17] Mi. 7[19].

Str. VI. A couplet of simile, and a syn. couplet, giving its reason. — **13.** *As a father hath compassion upon sons*]. Compassion is the paternal form of mercy, implying a sympathetic fellow feeling with the sufferer. Yahweh is here compared to a father in His attitude toward Israel, cf. Ex. 4[22-23] Ho. 11[1-4]. — **14.** *For He knoweth our frame*]. He knoweth it because He framed it, referring to Gn. 2[7], the forming of the frame of Adam out of the dust of the ground, as is evident from the ǁ *Remembereth that we are dust*, made of dust and doomed to return to dust, Gn. 3[19].

Str. VII. A syn. couplet of simile, with an antithetical syn. couplet. — **15.** *Man*], emphatic in position, because a characteristic of humanity is to be mentioned, — *as grass are his days*], so brief, so transient, cf. 90$^{5-6}$ ‖ *as a blossom of the field, so he blossometh*], cf. Jb. 14^2. This statement is enlarged upon by a glossator, who introduces from Is. 40$^{6, 7}$: — **16.** *When the wind passeth over it, then it is no more*], the scorching, withering south wind ; and from Jb. 7^{10} : *and the place thereof knoweth it no more.* — **17.** In antithesis, *from everlasting* and *unto everlasting*, and so through the entire interval are existing and acting *the kindness of Yahweh ‖ His righteousness*, which latter, here, as usual, must be His vindicatory, redemptive righteousness. The glossator who limited v.$^{11b-13b}$ by adding, "them that fear Him," did the same here ; and to this a still further limitation in a legalistic direction based on Ex. 20^6, and using the late legal term of Pss. 19^9 111^7 119$^{4 + 21\,t.}$: **18.** *To them that keep His covenant, and to them that remember His precepts to do them*]. The Maccabean editor made the following addition to the Ps. to make it more suitable for public worship :

> IN heaven He hath established His throne;
> And His kingdom ruleth over all.
> Bless ye Yahweh, His angels,
> His mighty ones that do His word.
> BLESS Yahweh, all ye His host,
> His ministers that do His pleasure.
> Bless Yahweh, all ye His works,
> In all places of His dominion.

This liturgical addition has two Strs. of the same measure and formation as the Ps. itself, all synth. couplets, but the last three syn. with each other. — **19-22.** *In heaven*], emphatic in position, — *He hath established His throne*], set it up, and made it firm and permanent, and therefore, — *His kingdom ruleth over all*], beneath the heavens and within the heavens. Accordingly the summons goes forth to all to unite in adoration, — *His angels ‖ His mighty ones that do His word*], enlarged by a glossator who inserted, "in power," and by an additional line, "hearkening to the voice of His word," the one at the expense of the measure, the other a duplicate making the Str. too long, — ‖ *His host*], the angels, conceived as an organised army, cf. 148^2 Is. 24^{21}, — ‖ *His ministers that do His pleasure*], the angels, conceived as faithful ministerial servants, prompt to do the sovereign will. To these are added :

All His works], the entire creation here personified, ‖ *in all places of His dominion*], throughout the entire heavens and earth, everywhere. The whole Ps. concludes with a liturgical addition most suitable for public worship, however much it disturbs the poetical construction: *Bless Yahweh, O my soul.*

1. את יהוה [אֶת] prosaic addition; so v.[1b. 2a. 12b]. — **2.** [כָּל־גְּמוּלָיו] 𝔊 πάσας τὰς αἰνέσεις αὐτοῦ interp. as praise *rendered* to God; as *benefits*, the usual translation, is an interp. of what God renders to His creatures. The more general mng. is *dealings* (28⁴). כו is an intensive gl. — **3.** [(י)כִי] Aramaic sf. in assonance at the close of each l. of Str., also with vbs. — † [תחלואים [*diseases*, elsw. Dt. 29²¹ 2 Ch. 21¹⁹ Je. 14¹⁸ 16⁴. Aramaism for חֱלִי. — **4** *b* without the assonance is a gl., interpreting **5** *a*. — **5.** [בַּטּוֹב עֶדְיֵךְ] is dub. 𝔊 τὴν ἐπιθυμίαν σου, 𝔙 *desiderium tuum* = אֲוָיֵכִי, 𝔗 יומי סבותיכי *days of thine old age*, so JPSV. 𝔍 *bonis ornamentum tuum*, 𝔖 גושמכי. It is usual to interpret עֱדִי *ornament* as syn. כבוד and referring to the נפש; but as there is no other such usage, it is improbable. The parall. suggests עוֹדֵכִי *so long as thou livest*, as 104³³ 146². The ב of these passages may have been omitted by haplog. — [תִּתְחַדֵּשׁ] Hithp. *a.λ.* 𝔊 ἀνακαινισθήσεται; the change of form from ptc. indicates that the l. is gl. from Is. 40³¹. — ‡ [נֶשֶׁר] n.m. *eagle* or *griffon*, *vulture*, as Dt. 32¹¹+. — **7.** עֲלִילוֹתיו [cf. 9¹², 𝔊 τὰ θελήματα αὐτοῦ prob. paraphrase. — **8** is gl. from Ex. 34⁶. — **9.** [יָשׁוּר] Qal impf. † [נטר] vb. (1) *maintain* anger, Lv. 19¹⁸ Na. 1² Am. 1¹¹ Je. 3⁵. ¹²; (2) *keep safely*, vineyard Ct. 1⁶. ⁶ 8¹¹. ¹². — **10.** [נָּמַל עָלֵינוּ] makes l. too long; late style for sf. גמלנו, cf. 7⁵ 18²¹, which latter was doubtless original. — **11.** [כִּי] is dittog of כְ prep. The l. is better in all respects without it, as v.[12a]. — [וְגָבַר] so 𝔊 and all Vrss. It is tempting to substitute וגבה with Hu., Gr., Du., Che., al.; but improb. as unnecessary. — [עַל־יְרֵאָיו] is a gl. of limitation; so v.[13b. 17b]; here and v.[13b] for עלינו. — **14.** [יִצְרֵנוּ] ‡ יֵצֶר n.m. *thought*, *purpose* framed in mind, Gn. 6⁵ (J), *form* of image made by potter Hb. 2¹⁸, cf. Is. 29¹⁶; only here of the *form* of man, based on the use of יצר Gn. 2⁷⁻⁸, as suggested also by the עָפָר of Gn. 3¹⁹. — [זָכוּר] ptc. pass. 𝔍 *recordatus est.* 𝔊 μνήσθητι = זְכֹר; prob. *is reminded;* but the ‖ suggests pf., which is more prob. — **16** is gl. from Is. 40⁷ and Jb. 7¹⁰. — [וַיְּירֶנּוּ] Hiph. impf. with strong sf. ‡ נכר vb. in ψ only Hiph. (1) *recognise* 142⁵, as Dt. 21¹⁷ 33⁹ Is. 63¹⁶, cf. 61⁹; (2) *be acquainted with*, here as Jb. 7¹⁰ 24¹⁷.—**17.** [עַל־יְרֵאָיו] is gl. as above, and also ו before צדקתו, which is ‖ חסד and belongs to עולם [וְעַד עוֹלָם. — [לִבְנֵי בנים] gl. from Ex. 34⁷. — **18** is a gl. of limitation from a legalistic point of view. — פקדיו [elsw. *19*⁹ 111⁷ 119⁴⁺¹⁹ ᵗ. — **19.** [יהוה] is gl., making l. too long. — **20.** גִּבֹּרֵי כֹחַ [phr. *a.λ.* has two beats and makes the l. too long. כֹח is a gl. of intensification; rd. גבריו.—[לִשְׁמֹעַ בְּקוֹל דברו] is a doublet; makes the Str. too long. — **22** *b.* [ממשלה] n.f. *dominion*, elsw. of God 114² 145¹³, of luminaries 136⁸. ⁹, as Gn. 1¹⁶. — **22** *c* is doubtless a final liturgical gl.

PSALM CIV., 7 STR. 8³.

**Ps. 104 is a praise of Yahweh, who created the light by wrap-
ping Himself in it** (v.¹ᵇ⁻²) ; **who built up stories in the upper
waters, making the clouds His chariot, and His angels into winds
and lightnings** (v.³ᵃᵇ·⁴) ; **who set the earth on immutable foundations, and with His thunder frightened the sea to the boundaries
He had assigned it** (v.⁵⁻⁷·⁹) ; **who made streams to flow to give
water to animals, birds, and the vegetation of earth** (v.¹⁰⁻¹³) ; **who
made the vegetation to give food to man and beast** (v.¹⁴⁻¹⁵ᵇ), **the
trees for the birds** (v.¹⁶ᵃ·¹⁷ᵇ), **and mountains and crags for animals**
(v.¹⁸) ; **who made sun and moon to mark the seasons** (v.¹⁹) ; **and
especially to distinguish night from day, the night for the wild animals seeking their prey, the day for man's labour** (v.²¹⁻²³) ; **who
made the water animals in all their variety** (v.²⁵·²⁶ᵇ), **and the land
animals, all dependent upon His bounty** (v.²⁴ᶜ·²⁷ᵃ·²⁸). **Upon the presence of His Spirit and favour depend the life and death of the creatures** (v.²⁹ᵃᵇ·³⁰). **His glory endures forever, and He rejoices in His
works** (v.³¹). **His people also praise Him with song and music
perpetually** (v.³⁴). **Numerous glosses emphasize various features
of the Ps.** (v.³ᶜ·⁸·¹⁵ᵃᶜ·¹⁶ᵇ·¹⁷ᵃ·²⁰·²⁶ᵃ·²⁷ᵇ·²⁹ᶜ·³²·³³). **Moreover v.²⁴ᵃᵇ is an exclamation of wonder at the number of the works of Yahweh.
V.³⁵ᵃᵇ is an imprecation in the Maccabean tone. V.¹ᵃ·³⁵ᶜ are liturgical glosses.**

> M Y God, Thou art very great;
>   With majesty and splendor Thou art clothed!
>   Who put on light as a garment;
>   Who stretched out the heavens as a tent curtain;
>   Who laid in the waters the beams of His upper chambers;
>   Who made the clouds His chariot;
>   Who made His angels winds,
>   His ministers fire and flame.
> W HO founded the earth upon its bases,
>   That it should not be moved forever and ever.
>   The deep like a garment was (its covering).
>   Above the mountains the waters stood.
>   At Thy rebuke they flee:
>   At the sound of Thy thunder they haste away;
>   That they may not pass the boundary Thou didst set,
>   May not return to cover the earth.

WHO sent forth springs into the valleys,
   That they might flow between the mountains,
   That they might give drink to all the wild animals of the field,
   That the onagers might break their thirst,
   That the birds of heaven might settle down,
   From among the branches give forth song;
   Who watered the mountains from His upper chambers,
   That by His outbursts of water the earth might be satisfied.
WHO caused grass to spring up for cattle,
   And herbage to the labour of mankind,
   In order that they might bring forth bread from the earth,
   In order that they might make their face to shine with oil.
   The trees of Shadday have their fill.
   The stork has her home in the cypresses.
   The high mountains are for the wild goats.
   The crags are a refuge for marmots.
WHO made the moon for seasons,
   The sun to know his time of going down.
   The young lions roar for prey,
   And to seek their food from 'El.
   When the sun rises, they gather themselves in,
   And in their dens they lie down.
   Man goeth forth to his work,
   And to his labour until evening.
YONDER sea great and broad —
   There are gliding things innumerable;
   Living things, small together with great;
   Leviathan which Thou didst form to play with.
   The earth is full of Thy creatures.
   All of them on Thee wait.
   Thou givest to them: they gather it.
   Thou openest Thy hand: they are satisfied.
THOU hidest Thy face: they are troubled.
   Thou withdrawest their spirit: they expire.
   Thou sendest forth Thy Spirit: they are created;
   And Thou renewest the face of the ground.
   The glory of Yahweh endureth forever.
   Yahweh is glad in His works.
   My musing is sweet unto Him:
   I am glad in Yahweh.

Ps. 104 has no title in 𝕳, but in 𝕲 τῷ Δαυείδ as 103, which is improbable. It is first of the group of Hallels 104–107. It is a Ps. in praise of Yahweh as creator. The order of creation is the same as Gn. 1–2³, on which the Ps. is based. And yet it knows of the activity of the divine Spirit in creation of animals, and of death as due to the withdrawal of the Spirit, as Gn. 2⁴-3. The author was thus familiar with both stories of the creation and probably in their combination in the Pentateuch in its present form. The author also knew of various other conceptions of the creation, as Am. 9⁶ v.³; Is. 40²² v.²ᵇ;

Jb. 38⁶⁻¹¹, cf. Pr. 8²⁹, v.⁵⁻⁹, which he interweaves with that of Gn. 1. The Ps. therefore could not have been composed earlier than the Greek period.

Str. I. Two tetrastichs, both beginning with a single line followed by a syn. tristich synthetic thereto. — **1–2.** The Ps. begins and concludes (v.³⁵), as several of the Hallels, with the liturgical phrase : *Bless Yahweh, O my soul*], cf. 103¹·²². — *My God*], emphatic in position : personal address, intensified in 搀 by prefixing "Yahweh," still more in 㿌 by using it twice ; but the measure allows neither. — *Thou art very great*], pf. of state ; as the context indicates, in power and glory. — *With majesty and splendour Thou art clothed*]. Royal attributes are here as elsewhere conceived as royal apparel, cf. 93¹ 96⁶. — *Who put on*]. The ptcs. characteristic of the Ps. must be given a uniform and harmonious explanation throughout. They might in some cases be explained as in present time ; the creative and providential divine activities mingling in the mind of the poet, so that what God once did at the creation, He continues to do throughout all time. But many of the ptcs. cannot be thus explained, even with the exceptions made by MT. of changing original ptcs. into pfs. The Ps. is throughout a poetic description of the creation of the world, based on Gn. 1, and retaining its order of six days' work with a supplementary seventh of rejoicing in a finished creation. We are compelled therefore to translate the ptcs. as referring to the past of the original creation. They serve to emphasize the divine activity in creation, rather than the result. We see it graphically in the process of creation, and not as in Gn. 1 in the result as an obedient servant of the divine command. — *light as a garment*]. Light, the first of the divine creations, appears as the garment which the Creator puts on, or wraps about Him, the expression of His attributes of majesty and glory. How different from Gn. 1³ : " God said, ' Let light be !' and light was." — *Who stretched out the heavens as a tent-curtain*]. This is supplementary to the creation of light. As light is the divine garment, heaven is the tent which God stretches out as His dwelling-place, cf. Is. 40²² Ps. 19⁶. — **3.** *Who laid in the waters the beams of His upper chambers*]. This, as the subsequent v., evidently refers to the second day's work of creation. The waters originally covered the earth when "God said, 'Let there be an expanse in the midst of the waters, and let it divide the waters from the waters.' . . . And God called the expanse, Heaven" Gn. 1⁶⁻⁸. The metaphor of a building is used in the Ps. as in Am. 9⁶. A series of stories are built up in the waters, the beams of one being laid upon the beams of the other in an ascending series; and so the upper waters were divided from the lower waters. — *Who made the clouds His chariot*]. The clouds, so characteristic of the heavens and bearing in them the heavenly waters, constituted the divine chariot in which He moved about swiftly from place to place. — This reminds a glossator of the cherubic chariot of Ps. 18¹¹, and so he adds: *Who goeth about on the wings of the wind.* — **4.** *Who made His angels winds, His ministers fire and flame*]. An ancient copyist, by omitting the conjunction, made grave difficulties of grammar. This rendering is essentially that of 𝔊, 𝔍, Heb. 1⁷, PBV., AV., and is most natural in itself. It is also in accord with the poet's previous thought. As God Himself is conceived as really present in nature, wrapping Himself in light, setting up His tent in the heavens, using the clouds as His chariot; so His angels, the ministrant spirits about Him, are made to assume the form of winds and lightnings. Doubtless the author had in mind a conception similar to that of the cherubic chariot of Ez. 1. But RV., JPSV., follow most moderns in their rendering: "Who maketh winds His messengers, His ministers a flaming fire"; thinking that the winds and the lightnings were constituted the ministering servants of Yahweh.

Str. II. A synth. and three syn. couplets. — **5.** *Who founded the earth upon its bases*]. This Str. begins the story of the third day's work of creation Gn. 1⁹⁻¹². The poet turns from the upper stories of the building to the foundations. The earth is conceived as created by building upon well-settled foundations, as in Jb. 38⁴⁻⁶ Pr. 8²⁵. ²⁹. — *That it should not be moved forever and ever*]. The earth was firmly established once for all, to be immutable forever. — **6.** *The deep like a garment was its covering*], so 𝔊, which is more probable than the vb. of 𝔍, followed by EVˢ., "Thou coveredst it," which involves an awkward change of construction. The primitive *Tehom*, "Deep," Gn. 1², covered the earth, which was buried in its depths even after the separation of the upper waters from the lower by the expanse of heaven. — *Above the mountains the waters stood*]; even the highest mountain peaks were beneath the surface of these primeval waters. — **7**. *At Thy rebuke ‖ At the sound of Thy thunder*]. The voice of God speaking in the thunder of the storm, as He rides in His chariot with His angelic winds and lightnings, frightens the Deep and fills it with terror — and the waters *flee ‖ haste away*]. This graphic poetic description takes the place of the calm command, Gn. 1⁹: "God said, 'Let the waters under the heaven be gathered together unto one place, and let the dry land appear'; and it was so." — A glossator inserts a tetrameter couplet to intensify the description, thinking of the agitation of the sea in a storm: **8**. *They went up the mountains; they went down the valleys, Unto the place that Thou didst found for them*], cf. 107²⁵⁻²⁶. — **9**. *That they might not pass the boundary Thou didst set*]. This v. is directly dependent as a final clause on v.⁷. The waters fled hastily in terror to the boundary fixed for them by Yahweh, beyond which thereafter they dared not pass. The poet evidently had in mind Jb. 38⁸⁻¹¹ Pr. 8²⁹. — *Might not return to cover the earth*]. The separation of earth and sea was to be perpetual.

Str. III. Four synth. couplets. — **10**. *Who sent forth springs into the valleys, That they might flow between the mountains*]. The third day's work of Gn. 1 is really a double work: first, the separation of land and sea v.⁹⁻¹⁰; second, the creation of vegetation v.¹¹⁻¹². The latter is the theme of this and the subsequent Str. The author of Gn. 1 does not think of the streams, so essential to vegetable life. The poet supplies that defect, and emphasizes the refreshing streams. — **11**. *That they might give drink to all the wild animals of the field*]. The animals come in here prior to their creation, in order to emphasize the importance of these streams, which the poet conceives as belonging to this order of creation. — *That the onagers might break their thirst*]. The specification of the beautiful wild ass may have been influenced by Jb. 39⁵⁻⁸. — **12**. *That the birds of heaven might settle down*], also final clause, dependent on v.¹⁰, to introduce the birds as dependent on water, as in the previous couplet the animals. The birds settle down, cf. 55⁷, after their flight, on the banks of these streams. The introduction of "by them" by a glossator was unnecessary, and it impairs the measure. — *From among the branches give forth song*] ; having settled down in the branches of the trees by the streams, they utter their satisfaction in notes of song. — **13**. *Who watered the mountains from His upper chambers*]. The upper chambers are those framed in the upper waters v.[3], where are the storm clouds and the lightnings. This must refer therefore to the rains descending upon the mountains. — *That by His outbursts of water the earth might be satisfied*]. This is the most probable original in accordance with the context. The earth is satisfied with the rains, as the mountains are watered by them. The waters come from the upper chambers and from outbursts of these waters in storms. An ancient copyist mistook the form for " fruit," and then was obliged to explain it by the addition of " Thy works " ; but it is difficult to see how these words can refer to the rain.

Str. IV. Four syn. couplets. — **14–15**. *Who caused grass to spring up for cattle*]. The poet, after giving the previous Str. to the fructifying streams, now takes up the vegetation of the third day's work ; and first of all the grass for the cattle, then — *herbage to the labour of mankind*]. The poet here combines with the narrative of the creation, Gn. 1[11-12], the thought of Gn. 3[17-19], the necessity of human labour in the ground, in order to win the products necessary for subsistence. — *In order that they might bring forth bread from the earth*], dependent upon the previous clause, and defining the herbage as the grain out of which bread is made. — To this is added the cultivation of the olive tree for its precious oil : *In order that they might make their faces to shine with oil*]. While the oil is used for anointing the head, especially at feasts 23[5], it is also used to soften and smooth the skin of other parts of the body as well as the face. The oil is mentioned probably because it is the product of a tree that needs cultivation. — The original limited itself to these ; but a glossator thought that wine could not be omitted, and so he inserted : *and wine that gladdeneth the heart of man*, cf. Ec. 10[19]. — It is difficult to see why any one should have added the variant of v.[14c], *and bread which strengtheneth man's heart*, which is evidently from the same hand as v.[15a]. — **16**. *The trees of Shadday*], gigantic trees, cf. 36[7]. This reading alone explains the variation of 𝕲 " trees of the field," and 𝔐 "trees of Yahweh," followed by EV[s]. — A glossator explains them very properly as *cedars of Lebanon that He planted.* — These trees *have their fill*] of the nourishing rain, as in the previous Str. the animals, mountains, and the earth. AV. "full of sap " has nothing to justify it. — **17.** *Where the birds build their nests*]. This is a glossator's general statement, introductory to the specific statement, which only was original : *The stork has her home in the cypresses*]. Tristram says that where the stork has neither houses nor ruins for its nest, " it selects any tree tall and strong enough to provide a platform for its huge nest, and for this purpose none are more convenient than the fir tree " (*Nat. Hist. Bible*, p. 248). — **18.** *The high mountains are for the wild goats*]. The poet, as the context indicates, is thinking of these lofty mountains as having been well watered, cf. v.[13], and so providing vegetation for these wild goats in regions where no other animals can go. Associated with them in these lofty inaccessible regions are the Syrian marmots. — *The crags are a refuge for marmots*]. This animal "lives in holes in the rocks, where it makes its nest and conceals its young, and to which it retires at the least alarm " (Tristram, *Nat. Hist. Bible*, p. 75).

Str. V. Four syn. couplets. — **19.** *Who made the moon* ‖ *The sun*], the fourth day's work of Gn. 1[14-18]. The stars are omitted by our poet. — *for seasons*], to distinguish the seasons of the month and the year, as Gn. 1[14]. Both authors doubtless had in view the new moons and other religious feasts which are determined by the moons. — *to know his time of going down*], to distinguish between day and night by sunset. — A glossator adds to this simple statement : **20.** *If Thou makest darkness, then it is night, wherein all the wild beasts of the forest creep forth*]. The former is a prosaic repetition of v.[19b], the latter a general introduction to v.[21]. — **21.** *The young lions roar for prey*]. After sunset the young lions first become active. The night is their time to satisfy their hunger. — *And to seek their food from 'El* |, cf. Jb. 38[41] ; while eagerly seeking prey, they really depend upon God for it. — **22.** *When the sun rises, they gather themselves in, And in their dens lie down*], for repose after the hunt of the night. As the night is the lion's time for labour, the day is his time for repose. The reverse is true of man. — **23.** *Man goeth forth to* *his work, And to his labour until evening*]. Man toils during the day, and reposes at night. The sun gives the signal for lion and for man alike.

Str. **VI**. A synth. tetrastich, and synth. and syn. couplets. — A glossator inserts before the creation of the animals an exclamation of wonder : **24**. *O how manifold are Thy works, Yahweh !*]. To this he adds, from the conception of WL. : *in wisdom hast Thou made them all*], cf. Pr. 3^{19} $8^{22\,sq.}$. He then, to make the exclamation apply to all the animals, transposes v.^{24c} from its original place at the beginning of the description of the creation of the land animals. — **25**. *Yonder sea great and broad*]. The fifth day's work of creation, Gn. 1^{20-22}, now begins. — *There are gliding things innumerable; Living things, small together with great*], the innumerable and various-sized creatures that swarm in the sea. — **26**. *Leviathan which Thou didst form to play with*]. Leviathan is the great sea monster Gn. 1^{21}, probably the whale. This monster, too huge for man, is to God a dear little animal to sport with. — A late glossator, moved by what influence it is difficult to determine, thought the reference to the sea would be defective without ships, and so he inserted : *there ships sail.* — **27**. The introductory line, referring to the creation of the land animals, was removed to v.^{24c}. It evidently belongs here : *The earth is full of Thy creatures*], so JPSV., RV.^{m} after $\mathfrak{G}$, which alone suits the context. " Thy riches," EV^s., or " possessions," after Aq., Σ, Θ, $\mathfrak{I}$, while a proper meaning of the Heb. word, is not appropriate here. — *All of them on Thee wait*], looking to God for their sustenance. A glossator adds the purpose : *That Thou mayest give their food in its season.* — But this is more appropriately stated in the following couplet : **28**. *Thou givest to them :* ‖ *Thou openest Thy hand — they gather it* ‖ *they are satisfied.* — A glossator adds, without need and against the measure, the object : *with good.*

Str. **VII**. Four syn. couplets. — **29**. *Thou hidest Thy face*] in displeasure, ‖ *withdrawest their spirit*]. The spirit of life of man and animals was imparted by the divine inbreathing Gn. 2^7 ; when that spirit was withdrawn, man and animals expired Gn. 6^3. — To this was appended by a glossator a corresponding word, the primitive curse Gn. 3^{19} : *and unto dust they return.* — **30**. *Thou* *sendest forth Thy Spirit*], the divine Spirit which invokes in the creature the spirit of life. — *they are created*], creatures live again ‖ *and Thou renewest the face of the ground*], with new living creatures in place of the old that have expired. The poet evidently appends to the six days' work what he conceives as happening on a seventh day; probably thinking of these days as extended periods of time. — **31.** *The glory of Yahweh endureth forever*]. This in the original must have been a statement of fact ‖ *Yahweh is glad in His works*], which is the poet's mode of stating the thought of Gn. 1^{31}–2^3, that everything God had made was very excellent, and that after the completion of the works He rested from them. But a later editor, losing sight of this connection, inserted a jussive substantive vb., making the line too long and putting the entire couplet in the form of a wish. This mistake is perpetuated in RV. — The same glossator, wishing to enhance the glory of Yahweh in this connection, brings in the theophanic manifestation : **32.** *He who looked on the earth and it trembled* ‖ *He toucheth the mountains, and they smoke*], cf. Am. 9^5 Ps. 144^5. — **33-34.** The congregation unite in the gladness of Yahweh over His completed work : *My musing*], contemplation of and meditation upon the works of creation above described. — *is sweet unto Him*] is agreeable and acceptable unto Yahweh ‖ *I am glad in Yahweh.* — A glossator emphasized this couplet by prefixing another from 146^2: *I will sing to Yahweh while I live ; I will make melody to my God while I have my being.* — The Ps. has reached its appropriate end ; but a Maccabean editor is not satisfied until he can add an imprecation : **35.** *Let sinners be exterminated from the earth, and let the wicked not be any more.*

---

1. [ברכי נפשי את־יהוה] is a liturgical addition. — [יהוה] in l.² has arisen from dittog. ⅏ has it a second time. — **2.** [עֹטֶה] (*71¹³*) ptc. here and throughout the Ps. as characteristic. — [שַׂלְמָה] err. for שִׂמְלָה n.f. *mantle* Ex. $22^{8. 25}$ (E). — ‡ [יְרִיעָה] n.f. *curtain* Je. 4^{20} 10^{20} 49^{29} Hb. 3^7 Is. 54^2. — **3.** [הַמְקָרֶה] article with demon. force ; dub. Why here and not v.²? Pi. ptc. † קרה denom. n.f. קֹרָה n.f. *beam,* and so *frame, lay beams,* elsw. Ne. 2^8 $3^{3. 6}$ 2 Ch. 34^{11}; figure of building, as in Am. 9^6. — [עֲלִיוֹת] pl. ‡ עֲלִיָּה n.f. *upper chamber* in roof Ju. $3^{23. 24. 25}$ +; pl. *upper stories,* so v.¹³ Je. $22^{13. 14}$, the successive heights or layers of heaven, here on the upper waters, as in Am. 9^6. Amos uses מַעֲלוֹת. Hence ‖ עבים *dense clouds.* — [רכוב] *chariot;* some think of the כְּרוּב of 18^{11}, especially on account of the כנפי רוח עַל which appears in the parall. l. in

z

both passages, and also on account of the reference to מלאכים in v.⁴; but v.³ᶜ is a gl. from 18¹¹, and without it רכוב is better. — **4.** עָשֶׂה מלאכיו רוחות] is capable of three explanations (Dr.¹⁹⁵ ᴼᵇˢ·) : (1) that of 𝕲, 𝔙, Heb. 1⁷, regarding מלאכיו as primary obj. and רוחות as secondary ; (2) regarding רוחות as acc. of material, " out of winds," Dr., De. ; (3) regarding רוחות as primary obj. and מלאכיו as secondary, AE., Ki., Ew., Hi., Hu., Now., Pe., Bä. — מְשָׁרְתָיו אֵשׁ לֹהֵט] must be interp. ‖ with previous l. The neglect of agreement is striking. 𝕲 has πῦρ φλέγον. Rd. with Ols., Bi., Du., Che., יְלַהֵט. — **5.** יָסַד] pf. 3 m., but this is interp. ; change from ptc. improb. — בַּל־הִמּוֹט] final clause. — **6.** כִּסִּיתוֹ] Pi. 2 m. with sf. 3 sg. 𝕲 τὸ περιβόλαιον αὐτοῦ, יְסַ כְּ ; so Aq., Θ, 𝔙, Street, Bä. The sf. refers to תהום, not to ארץ; cf. Jb. 38⁹. It is prob. interp. — **7.** יְנוּסוּן] fuller form impf. 3 pl., usual in this Ps. — **8.** This l. is parenthetical according to most interpreters. The change of form of pl. from וּן to ו is noteworthy. It is a tetrameter gl., as Bä. — **9.** וּגְבוּל שַׂמְתָּ] not emph. in position, but acc. of place after vbs. of v.⁷; cf. Jb. 38⁸⁻¹¹ Pr. 8²⁹. — בַּל יְעַבְרוּן] final clause. — **10.** הַמְשַׁלֵּחַ] article with ptc. improb. in original, cf. v.³. — **11.** מַעְיָנִים] pl. מַעְיָן spring (74¹⁵). — יְרַכְּבוּן] final clause ; so יִשְׁקוּ Hiph. impf. v.¹¹. — חַיְתוֹ] as in Gn. 1²⁴. — ‡ פֶרֶא] n.m. wild ass, as Gn. 16¹² (J) Ho. 8⁹ Je. 14⁶. + — **12.** עֲלֵיהֶם] makes l. too long ; is interp. gl. — † עֳפָאיִם Kt. a.λ., עֳפָאיִם Qr. pl. foliage BDB., 𝕲 τῶν πετρῶν; so 𝔙, 𝔖, ירא, prob. Aram. כפאים. — **13.** מַשְׁקֶה] Hiph. ptc. resuming the principal clause. — מִפְּרִי מַעֲשֶׂיךָ] makes l. too long. מַעֲשֶׂיךָ is an explan. addition to מִפְּרִי, but that has no mng. here. Rd. פְרָצִים outbreak of waters, as 2 S. 5²⁰. — **14.** צֹמֵחַ] cf. הוֹצִיא, הִרְבִּיא of Gn. 1¹¹⁻¹². — ‡ עֲבֹרָה] n.f. labour of work v.²³, as Ex. 1¹⁴ +. Other kinds of labour not in ψ. — לְהוֹצִיא] takes the place of final clauses of previous Strs. for variation of style. — **15.** וְיַיִן יְשַׂמַּח לְבַב אֱנוֹשׁ is a gl. of different construction from context, by a scribe who thought that so important a product as wine should not be omitted. — וּלְהַצְהִיל ‖ לְהוֹצִיא. † צהל vb. a.λ. Hiph. make shining, NH. ; cf. צהר. — לֶחֶם לְבַב אֱנוֹשׁ יִסְעָד is a repetitious gl. — **16.** יִשְׂבְּעוּ] final clause, as impfs. above. — עֲצֵי יהוה] so 𝔖, 𝕿, but 𝕲 τοῦ πεδίου. The original was doubtless שָׂדַי, which might be either שָׂדַי or יְיָ. — אַרְזֵי לְבָנוֹן אֲשֶׁר נָטָע] explan. gl. — **17.** אֲשֶׁר־שָׁם] improb. ; the whole l. is a gl. — יְקַנֵּנוּ] Pi. impf. ‡ קָנַן denom. קֵן nest (84ᵇ). — † חֲסִידָה] n.f. stork, as Lv. 11¹⁹ Dt. 14¹⁸ Je. 8⁷ Zc. 5⁹, cf. Jb. 39¹³. — ‡ בְּרוֹשׁ] n.m. cypress or fir, as Is. 14⁸ 37²⁴ Ez. 31⁸ + ; acc. of place. 𝕲 ἡγεῖται αὐτῶν = רֹאשָׁם improb. — **18.** † יָעֵל] n.[m.] wild mountain goat, as 1 S. 24² Jb. 39¹. — † שְׁפַנִּים] small animals resembling marmots, Pr. 30²⁴· ²⁶ Lv. 11⁵ = Dt. 14⁷. 𝕲 χοιρογρυλλίοις, 𝕲ᴺ· ᶜ· ᵃ· ᴬ· ᵀ λαγωόις. — **19.** עָשָׂה] pf. of vb. as in Str. II. עָ, but MT. pointing is interp. ; ptc. is more prob. — לְמוֹעֲדִים] sacred seasons, as Gn. 1¹⁴ (P) ; not merely time, as Pss. 75³ 102¹⁴. — יָדַע] pf. Qal seems out of place ; rd. inf. — **20.** תָּשֶׁת] juss., followed by וִיהִי, simple ו and juss. ; prot. and apod. conditional clause. But l. is tetrameter and is a gl. ; so also is the next l. — **21.** לִטְרֹף] inf. carries on the previous ptc., cf. Dr.²⁰⁶. — **22.** תִּזְרַח] juss., temporal or conditional clause as v.²⁰, with יֵאָסֵפוּן in apod. — **23.** יֵצֵא] has two accents. — **24.** מָה־רַבּוּ] exclamation of wonder, interjected gl. ; so also

כְּלָם בחכמה עשיתה, which is premature before the completion of creation. —
‡ קִנְיָן] n.m., a late word from קנה = *get, beget :* "creatures" RV.[m], alone suited
to the context as to the usage of vb.; but noun not elsw. in this sense, but
of thing acquired by purchase 105[21], as Gn. 31[18] 34[23] 36[6] Lv. 22[11] Jos. 14[4]
(all P) Ez. 38[12. 13] Pr. 4[7]. The creatures of earth are out of place here. They
belong after the water animals in v.[27]. The editor who inserted previous
clause transposed the line here as most suitable to this exclamation. —
25. זֶה הַיָּם] *yonder sea,* cf. זה סיני Ju. 5[5], as Che., Ew., De.; not "yonder is
the sea," of Pe., Hu. — וּרְחַב יָדָיִם] makes l. too long; last word needless, gl. —
‡ רֶמֶשׂ] n.m. coll. for the שרץ of Gn. 1[20]; only here of water animals, usually
as 148[10] creeping things of land, but Gn. 9[3] (P) all moving things. — **26.** אֳנִיּוֹת]
ships, improb. in original; the l. is a late gl. — לִוְיָתָן] cf. Jb. 40[25]–41[34], *whale.*
— זֶה] for relative. — לְשַׂחֶק בּוֹ]. The sf. does not refer to the sea; but, as Ew.,
Che., to Leviathan. The vb. takes בְ idiomatically in this sense, as in
Jb. 40[29]. — **27.** יְכֹל] in the context refers to previous water animals of fifth
day of creation; but the subsequent context requires land animals of sixth
day. V.[26c] belongs at the beginning of this Str. — יְשַׂבֵּרוּן] Pi. impf., Aramaism, as 119[166] 145[15] Is. 38[18] Est. 9[1]; *v.* Ps. 69[21]. — לָתֵת אָכְלָם בְּעִתּוֹ] a general
statement, variant of v.[28a] and a gl. — **28.** תִּתֵּן] prot. of temp. clause. —
יִלְקֹטוּן] apod. ‡ לקט vb. Qal *gather* Gn. 31[46] Ex. 16[4. 5. 26] (J) +. — **29.** פֶּן]
Hiph. impf. אסף for הֵאָסֵף. — וְאֶל עֲפָרָם יְשׁוּבוּן] is a gl. from Gn. 3[19]. — **31.** יְהִי כבוד]
יְהִי juss. is improb.; it is an interp. gl., making l. too long. — **32.** הַמַּבִּיט] ptc.
rel. clause. — וַתִּרְעַד ו consec. result. This v. seems out of harmony with Ps.
and is a gl. — יִגַּע] prot. of temp. clause with וְיֶעֱשָׁנוּ in apod., as v.[28-30]. —
33. אָשִׁירָה] cohort. impf. ‖ אֲזַמְּרָה. — בְּחַיָּי] *during my life,* cf. 63[5]. — בְּעוֹדִי]
implies עוֹד. — This v. is a gl., amplification of v.[34]. — **35.** יִתַּמּוּ] impf. תמם, cf.
Nu. 14[35]. The imprecation of this v. is a late gl., altogether unsuited to Ps.
— ברכי נפשי את־יהוה] is a liturgical gl., as at beginning.

PSALMS CV.–CVI., 24 STR. 4[3].

Ps. 105 reminds the seed of Abraham and Jacob that Yahweh
their God remembers forever His covenant with the fathers (v.[6-10]).
The story of the patriarchs is then told till the descent into Egypt
(v.[12. 14. 16-21. 23-25]). The sending of Moses and the plagues of Egypt
are then described, closing with the leading forth of the people
(v.[26-27. 29-37]). An introductory gloss makes the Ps. into a Hallel by
its emphasis upon public worship in its varied phases (v.[1-5]). A
concluding gloss carries on the history in outline until the entrance
into Palestine (v.[38-45]). Sundry glosses illustrate and expand the
history (v.[11. 13. 15. 22]), and at times introduce new elements (v.[28]).
Ps. 106 begins with the history of Israel where Ps. 105 ends,

at the crossing of the Red Sea (v.$^{9.\ 11}$) ; and carries it on through the wilderness (v.$^{14.\ 17.\ 19.\ 21.\ 23-26.\ 28-33}$) ; then briefly sums up the story of the miseries of the time of the judges (v.$^{34.\ 36-37.\ 40-41.\ 44-45}$). It was made into a Hallel by an introductory gloss (v.$^{1-5}$), and an insertion (v.^{12}), to which a penitential character is given by (v.$^{6-8.\ 13}$). Expansive glosses were also inserted (v.$^{10.\ 18.\ 20.\ 22.\ 27.\ 33}$). The Ps. was given greater completeness by glosses referring to the later history of the nation, even till subsequent to the Exile (v.$^{38-39.\ 42-43.\ 46-47}$).

CV.

YE seed of Abraham His servant,
    Sons of Jacob (His) chosen,
    He, Yahweh, is our God :
    In all the earth are His deeds of judgment.
HE doth remember forever His covenant,
    The word He commanded to a thousand generations;
    Which He made with Abraham,
    And appointed to Jacob as a statute.
WHEN they were men that could be numbered,
    As it were few and sojourners in (the land),
    He suffered no one to oppress them,
    And reproved kings for their sake.
AND He called a famine on the land :
    The whole staff of bread He brake
    He sent before them a man ;
    For a slave Joseph was sold.
THEY afflicted his feet with fetters :
    Into irons he entered,
    Until the time His word came to pass,
    The saying of Yahweh that tested him.
HE sent a king and released him,
    A ruler of peoples and set him free.
    He made him lord of his household,
    And ruler over all his possessions.
THEN Israel came to Egypt,
    And Jacob sojourned in the land of Ham.
    When He made His people very fruitful,
    Their heart turned to hatred.
HE sent Moses His servant,
    Aaron whom He had chosen.
    He put miraculous deeds,
    And wonders in the land of Ham.
HE changed their waters into blood.
    Their land swarmed with frogs.
    He commanded and the swarm came,
    Gnats in all their borders.

HE gave them hail for rain,
    Flaming fire in their land;
    And smote their vines and fig trees,
    And brake in pieces the trees of their **border.**
HE commanded and the locusts came,
    And the young locusts without number;
    And ate all the herbage in their land,
    And ate all the fruit of their ground.
AND He smote all the first born in their land,
    The first fruits of all their strength;
    And led forth (His people) with silver and gold;
    And there was none that stumbled among His tribes.

CVI.

AND He rebuked the Sea of Reeds, and it dried up;
    And He led them in the depths as in a wilderness:
    And the waters covered over their adversaries.
    Not one of them was left over.
THEN they desired a desire in the wilderness,
    And tested 'El in the desert.
    And He gave to them their request,
    And sent food according to their desire.
THEN they were jealous of Moses in the camp,
    And of Aaron, the consecrated to Yahweh;
    The earth opened and swallowed up Dathan,
    And covered over the company of Abiram.
(THEN) they made a calf in Horeb,
    And worshipped a molten image;
    They forgat 'El their Saviour,
    Who did great deeds in Egypt.
THEN (Yahweh) had commanded to destroy them,
    Were it not that Moses, His chosen,
    Stood in the breach before Him,
    To turn away His wrath from destroying.
THEN they refused the desirable land,
    And did not hearken to the voice of Yahweh.
    And He lifted up His hand to them,
    To make them fall in the wilderness.
THEN they joined themselves to Baal Peor,
    And ate the sacrificial meals of the dead;
    And provoked (Yahweh) by their doings:
    And a plague broke out against them.
THEN Phinehas stood up and interposed,
    And the plague was stayed (from them);
    And it was counted to him for righteousness
    To generation after generation forever.
THEN they enraged Him at the waters of Meribah,
    And it went ill with Moses for their sake;
    For they rebelled against His Spirit,
    And he spake rashly with his lips.

THEY did not destroy the peoples;
   And served their idols,
   And these became a snare to them,
   And they sacrificed their sons to Shedim.
THEN the anger of Yahweh was kindled against His people,
   And He abhorred His inheritance,
   And gave them into the hand of the nations;
   And they that hated them ruled over them.
THEN He looked upon their distress,
   When He heard their yell;
   And remembered His covenant with them.
   And was sorry according to the abundance of His kindness.

Pss. 105–106 were originally one Ps. The former carries on the history of Israel to the going forth from Egypt. The latter begins with the crossing of the Red Sea, and carries the history through the period of the שׁפטים. It is altogether improbable that a poet would close his poem with the former, or begin his poem with the latter event. The Ps. was divided into two for liturgical reasons; and the first part was put in the form of a Hallel by a long introduction v[1-5]; the latter was given a penitential character by an introduction v.[1-8] and by various glosses. After the separation an editor, seeing the inappropriateness of letting a Ps. conclude with the going forth from Egypt, adds v.[38-45] to carry on the history until the entrance into Palestine. Similar reasons led the editor to append to the second part 106[46-47], and to insert v.[35. 38. 39. 42. 43], in order to mingle with the afflictions and deliverances of the time of the "Shophets" reference to the afflictions and deliverances of the later history even to post-exilic times. Under these circumstances we would expect many interpretative, expansive, and liturgical glosses. 105[9b. 10b. 11. 13. 15. 22. 24b. 25b. 28. 29b. 30b] 106[10. 12. 13. 18. 20. 22. 24b. 25a. 27. 34b]. Throwing off these glosses, the original Ps. had twenty-four trimeter tetrastichs, half of which are now in each of the Pss. into which the original was divided. The original Ps. is based on 78 of 𝔄. The ancient history has been derived from the Hexateuch and Judges in their present form; so that the Ps. cannot be earlier than the latter part of the Persian period. Its dependence on 𝔄 brings it down into the Greek period. The poem also used Is. 63[13] in 106[9b], and Is. 63[10] in 106[33a]. There is a reference in 106[37b] to Dt. 32[17], in 106[26] to Ez. 20[23], in 106[23] to Ez. 22[30], and in 106[24] to Je. 3[19] or Zc. 7[14]. The Pss. indicate a varied use of earlier Lit.: 105[1], cf. Is. 12[4]; 105[36], cf. 78[51]; 105[5], cf. Ps. 119[13]; 105[37b], cf. Is. 5[27]; 105[40. 41], cf. Ps. 78[20. 24]; 106[6], cf. 1 K. 8[47]; 106[9a], cf. Na. 1[4]; 106[20a], cf. Je. 2[11]; 106[27], cf. Ez. 20[23]; 106[5], cf. Ezr. 9[2]; 106[46], cf. 1 K. 8[50]. The Chronicler (1 Ch. 16) combines 105[1-15] 96, 106[1. 47] in a Hallel, which is given as a specimen of Davidic Psalmody. There can be no doubt that the Ps. is older than its use in Chr. But the use that is made of it implies that the Ps. was much older. Besides, it is used in its present form with all the glosses. These could not have originated prior to the Chronicler. There can be little doubt, therefore, that these specimens were later additions

to the Chronicles, and not used by the Chronicler himself. Ps. 105 has no title,
but דרו is given at the end, as also at the end of 104. ⅏ has ἀλληλουιά at
the beginning of 105 and 106, and not at the end of 104 or 105; and this is
doubtless correct. These Pss. are evidently Hallels, and so indicated by הללויה
(*v.* Intr. § 35). For the Doxology 106[48], *v.* Intr. § 40.

PSALM CV.

The Ps. has an introductory gloss, making it into a Hallel.
1. A tetrameter couplet from Is. 12[4]: *Give thanks to Yahweh*],
so 106[1] 107[1] 118[1] 136[1] in the special form of the *Hodu* (*v.* Intr.
§ 35). — *proclaim His name*], as Ex. 33[19] 34[5. 6]. This meaning
alone suited to context. " Call upon His name " of EV[s]., though
a possible meaning of the phr., is not appropriate here. — *make
known among the peoples His doings*], cf. 9[12]. Israel celebrates
the wondrous deeds of deliverance and judgment wrought by
Yahweh by publishing them to the world. — **2.** *Sing to Him* ‖
make melody to Him], with vocal and instrumental music. — *hum
of all His wondrous deeds*], the indistinct humming sound of one
who makes music for himself alone, cf. Ju. 5[10. 11]. — **3.** *Glory in His
holy name*], make boast of the majestic sacredness of the renown
won by Yahweh, cf. 34[3] Is. 41[16]. — *Let the heart be glad*]. Such
praise gives joy to the heart, — *of them that seek Him*]; so
assonance requires; but a glossator enlarged the line by substituting for the sf. the divine name " Yahweh." — **4.** *Seek after
Yahweh* ‖ *seek continually*], two syn. wor.'s used of resorting to
the temple, the place of His abode, — *and His strength*], intermediate between Yahweh and ‖ *His face*, can only refer to the
strength of His lifted hands and outstretched arms. — **5.** *Commemorate*], celebrate by bringing to mind; and not " remember "
of EV ., — *the wonders of His doing*], cf. v[2]; enlarged by glossator
into : " His wondrous deeds that He hath done," — *His marvels*],
used especially of the miracles of the Exodus, cf. v.[27]. — *the acts
of judgment of His presence*]. A copyist, by the omission of a
single letter, has destroyed the assonance and compelled the rendering " judgments of His mouth." But the context requires
deeds of judgment and not proclamations. Thus far the introductory Hallel; the original Ps. begins with v.[6].

Str. I. Syn. and synth. couplets. — **6.** *Ye seed of Abraham* ‖
Sons of Jacob]. The people are summoned in the name of their

original ancestors. — *His servant*], doubtless conceiving Abraham as a prophetic servant, Gn. 15. — ‖ *His chosen*], doubtless in the original referring to Jacob as chosen rather than Esau; but a copyist's error or misinterpretation made it pl. "His chosen ones," referring to all the sons. — **7.** *He, Yahweh, is our God*]. Yahweh is in a special sense the God of all the descendants of Abraham and Jacob, their national God. — *In all the earth are His deeds of judgment*]. Yahweh does not limit His wondrous deeds to the land of Israel, but in all the earth they have been wrought.

Str. II. Two syn. couplets. — **8.** *He doth remember His covenant* ‖ *The word He commanded*]. Yahweh was in covenant relations with Israel from the time of their forefathers, and that covenant was essentially a word of promise. This Yahweh remembers and never forgets. He is faithful to it, — *for ever* ‖ *to a thousand generations*], as Ex. 20⁶. — **9–10.** *Which He made with Abraham*], as Gn. 15, 17; ‖ *And appointed to Jacob as a statute*], Gn. 28, 35. The covenant was not only promise, but a law. A glossator enlarges by inserting a reference to Isaac: *and His oath unto Isaac*, and adds the more general statement: *to Israel an everlasting covenant;* and also the essential promise of that covenant: **11.** *Saying: To thee will I give the land of Canaan, the lot of your inheritance*], cf. 78⁵⁵.

Str. III. Two syn. couplets. — **12.** *When they were men that could be numbered* ‖ *As it were few*], in antithesis with the promise that their seed would be innumerable, and also with the reality in the history of the nation reviewed by the psalmist in his own mind, — *and sojourners in the land*]. The land of Canaan was not yet theirs. It was still in the possession of the Canaanites, and they were sojourners in it, going about from place to place as nomads. A glossator enlarged upon this in **13.** *And went about from nation to nation, from people went to people*]. The last clause was changed by error to " from a kingdom to another people." In any case the gloss indicates a conception of the patriarchal history in terms of the later history of the Exile. — **14.** *He suffered no one to oppress them*], thinking of the relation of Abraham to the Canaanites and of Jacob to Laban, — *And reproved kings for their sake*], Pharaoh Gn. 12¹⁰ ˢ۹·, and Abimelech Gn. 20, 26. To this also the glossator adds words of Yahweh : **15**. *Saying, Touch not Mine anointed*], conceiving of the patriarchs as anointed kings, cf. Gn. 14, — *and to My prophets do no harm*], conceiving of the patriarchs as prophets, cf. Gn. 20⁷. Both of these conceptions of the patriarchs were late ones.

Str. IV. Two syn. couplets. — **16**. *And He called a famine on the land*], Gn. 41⁵⁶⁻⁵⁷ 42. — *The whole staff of bread He brake*], bread as the staff of life, cf. Lv. 26²⁶ Ps. 104¹⁵. — **17**. *He sent before them a man*], a single man to be the means of saving his brethren, Gn. 45⁵·⁷ 50²⁰. — *For a slave Joseph was sold*], Gn. 37. All these events were connected in the purpose of God for the fulfilment of His covenant with the fathers.

Str. V. Two syn. couplets. — **18**. *They afflicted his feet with fetters, Into irons he entered*], so essentially RV., JPSV. He was thrown into a dungeon and put in irons Gn. 39²⁰. The rendering of PBV., "the iron entered into his soul," is sentimental, against the ‖, and altogether improbable. — **19**. *Until the time His word came to pass*], the word of divine promise was fulfilled ; ‖ *The saying of Yahweh that tested him*]. This doubtless refers to the prediction contained in the dreams Gn. 37⁶⁻¹⁰.

Str. VI. Two syn. couplets. — **20**. *He sent a king* ‖ *A ruler of peoples*], Pharaoh, king of Egypt, Gn. 41, — *and released him* ‖ *set him free*], from prison. — **21**. *He made him lord of his household* ‖ *ruler over all his possessions*]. Pharaoh exalted him to the highest dignity in reward for his right interpretation of dreams and his wise counsel Gn. 41³³ ˢᵠ·. A glossator added : **22**. *to bind his princes at his will, and that he might teach his elders wisdom*], arbitrary power and wisdom beyond that of the Egyptian wise men ; an exaggeration of Gn. 41⁴²⁻⁴⁴ in the Maccabean temper.

Str. VII. Syn. and synth. couplets. — **23**. *Then Israel* ‖ *Jacob*], doubtless here referring to the journey of the patriarch himself Gn. 46–47, — *came to Egypt* ‖ *sojourned in the land of Ham*], cf. v.²⁷ 78⁵¹. — **24**. *When He made His people very fruitful*], as Ex. 1⁷. This is enlarged by a glossator on the basis of Ex. 1⁹ into, — *and made them stronger than their adversaries*], certainly an inappropriate exaggeration, which if true made the divine interposition unnecessary. — **25**. *Their heart turned to hatred*], so JPSV., which is more probable than EVˢ., "He turned their heart." A glossator strengthened, as he thought, the statement by adding : *to deal craftily with His servants,* referring to the afflictions of Ex. 1⁸⁻²²; which required him to change the noun " hatred " into an inf. " to hate," and then give the vb. its object, " His people," all at the expense of the measure.

Str. VIII. Two syn. couplets. — **26.** *He sent Moses ‖ Aaron*], cf. Ex. 3–4, — *His servant ‖ whom He had chosen*]. Moses and Aaron now take the same relative positions, as prophet and chosen of Yahweh, as Abraham and Jacob v.⁶. — **27.** *He put miraculous deeds ‖ And wonders in the land of Ham*]. The ancient Vrss. are doubtless correct in making God the subject of the vb., and 𝕲, followed by EVˢ., is in error in making Moses and Aaron the subject. The miracles are the plagues of Egypt, the most of which are now mentioned, based on the narratives of Exodus in their present form. A glossator inserts one which had been omitted in the original, here at the beginning, out of its proper order in the narrative. — **28.** *He sent darkness and it became dark*]. This is a plague peculiar to E, Ex. 10²¹ ˢ⁹· The following line is altogether inappropriate in the context. It cannot be other than a marginal gloss : *And they rebelled not against His word*]. This can hardly refer to the Egyptians, who in no sense could be regarded as in rebellion against Yahweh. It is elsw. used only of the people of God. It was probably a glossator's assertion that at this period, in distinction from that covered by 106, the people did not rebel against Yahweh, but were faithful to Him.

Str. IX. Synth. tetrastich, heaping up four plagues. — **29.** *He changed their waters into blood*], the first plague, Ex. 7¹⁴ ˢ⁹·. A glossator adds : *and slew their fish,* making the line into a pentameter. — **30.** *Their land swarmed with frogs*]. This is the second plague of Ex. 8¹ ˢ⁹·. A glossator makes the line into a pentameter by adding : *in the chambers of their king.* — **31.** *He commanded, and the swarm came*], the plague of Ex. 8²⁰ ˢ⁹· Ps. 78⁴⁵ ; a variation of which by another narrator Ex. 8¹⁶ ˢ⁹· : *Gnats in all their borders.* These four plagues were all connected with the fouling of the Nile in the several narratives of Exodus. It is appropriate that they should be combined together.

Str. X. Two syn. couplets, enlarging upon the plague of Ex. 9¹³ ˢ⁹· Ps. 78⁴⁷⁻⁴⁸. — **32.** *He gave them hail ‖ Flaming fire*], a storm

of thunder and lightning, —*for rain*], instead of rain, in its place.
— **33**. *And smote ‖ brake in pieces*], by the violence of the hail,
— *their vines and fig trees ‖ the trees of their border*].

Str. XI. Also two syn. couplets, enlarging upon the plague **Ex.**
10¹ˢᑫ· Ps. 78⁴⁶. — **34**. *He commanded and the locusts came ‖ young
locusts without number*]. Innumerable locusts came up in obedience to the divine command and devoured the land. — **35**. *Ate*],
repeated for emphasis, — *all the herbage in their land ‖ the fruit
of their ground*.

Str. XII. A syn. and a synth. couplet. — **36**. *And He smote all
the first born in their land ‖ The first fruits of all their strength*].
This is the final plague, Ex. 11¹ˢᑫ· Ps. 78⁵¹, the seventh of those mentioned in this Ps. — **37**. *And led forth His people*]. The original
doubtless was so ; but a copyist, by the omission of a single letter,
reduced the object to the sf. " them." This sf. in all the previous
context was used of Egypt, and it was necessary to distinguish in
some way that Israel was the object of this vb. — *with silver and
gold*], jewels and ornaments, as Ex. 12³⁵ ³⁶. — *And there was none
that stumbled among His tribes*]. All the people were protected
by Yahweh and made vigorous and strong. Thus far the original
Ps., which was continued in 106⁹ˢᑫ·. But when the separation was
made, it was evident that v.³⁷ was no proper ending for a Ps., and
accordingly there was the gradual accretion of the glosses v.³⁸⁻⁴⁵.
— **38** is a glossator's exultation over the terror of the Egyptians. —
*Egypt was glad when they went forth ; for the fear of them had
fallen upon them*], cf. Ex. 12⁻³ 15¹⁶. — **39** is a reference to the
theophanic pillar of Ex. 13²¹· ²² 14¹⁹⁻²⁰, but in terms quite different
from those of the ancient history or even of Ps. 78¹⁴ : *He spread a
cloud for a screen, and fire to give light by night*]. This was probably influenced by Is. 4⁵⁻⁶. In the history the cloud was a theophanic leader and guide, and not a screen from the rays of the
sun. — **40–41**. Three of the miracles in the wilderness are mentioned : *They asked, and He brought quails*], Ex. 16¹¹ ˢᑫ· Ps. 78¹⁸.
The pl. of ancient Vrss. is to be preferred to the sg. of 𝕸. — *and
with bread of heaven He used to satisfy them*], the giving of the
manna, Ex. 16⁴ ˢᑫ· Ps. 78²⁴⁻²⁵. This v. goes over into the narrative
of 106¹⁴⁻¹⁵. — *He opened the rock, and waters gushed out*], Ex.
17¹ˢᑫ· Nu. 20¹ˢᑫ· Ps. 78¹⁵· ¹⁶ ²⁰, — *and they flowed in thirsty lands*

as a river. — **42–44** give a general statement of the Exodus and entrance into the holy land. — *For He remembered*], as v.[8], *His holy word with Abraham His servant*], as v.[9], — *and He brought forth His people ‖ His chosen*], resumption of v.[37], — *with joy ‖ with jubilation*], hardly consistent with the historic narrative, but an ideal situation. — *and gave them the lands of the nations*], the nations of Palestine, which were dispossessed at the entrance and in the subsequent history, — *and the toil of the peoples*], the fruit of their labours, especially in the cultivated fields, — *they inherited*], took possession of as their inheritance, given to them by their God, which they would transmit to their children. — **45** is a legalistic conclusion: *in order that they might keep ‖ observe*]. According to the legalistic mind the final aim and purpose of the entire history of Israel was, — *His statutes ‖ His laws*]. The divine Pentateuchal Law was the supreme purpose of God, as well as the highest ideal of His people.

PSALM CVI.

Ps. 106, after its separation from 105, was made into a Hallel by prefixing v.[1-5]. — **1.** *Give thanks to Yahweh, for He is good; for His kindness endureth forever*], the liturgical phr. 107[1] 118[1] 136[1] Je. 33[11] Ezr. 3[11] 1 Mac. 4[24]. Yahweh is "good" in the sense of kind, benignant, beneficent, being good to His people. — **2.** *Who can utter ‖ make to be heard*], in public praise, — *the mighty acts of Yahweh ‖ His praise*], for the doing of them. — **3.** *Happy they that keep ‖ that do*], in the practice of right conduct, — *justice*, as the ‖ *righteousness* requires; and not "judgment" as EV[s]., whether interpreted in the sense of the Law or more generally. Another hand appends v.[4-5], apparently the petition of an individual, possibly originally a marginal gloss. — **4.** *Remember me, Yahweh ‖ visit me*], the divine interposition is invoked, — *according to Thy favour toward Thy people*], the habitual goodwill shown by Yahweh toward His people, in which the petitioner longs to share. ‖ *Thy salvation*], in the general sense, not only in deliverance from enemies and troubles, but in the enjoyment of prosperity. — **5.** *That I may look upon*], pregnant; with gratification ‖ *that I may be glad with the gladness ‖ that I may glory*] in exultant boasting. That which is so ardently

longed for is — *prosperity*, good things which were enjoyed by —
Thy chosen one ‖ *Thy nation* ‖ *Thine inheritance*], emphasizing
the close personal relation of Israel to Yahweh. — **6-8** is a penitential gloss. — **6**. *We have sinned, we have done iniquity, we have
done wickedly*]; the three vbs., in emphatic coördination without
conjunction, are an explicit and solemn confession of sin, — *with
our fathers*], participating with and sharing in their guilt. — **7**. The
specific guilt of the fathers especially in mind was *in Egypt*. There
they considered not ‖ *they did not remember* — *Thy wondrous deeds*,
of deliverance from the Egyptians ‖ *the abundance of Thy kindness*], in caring for them and providing for their needs. 𝕲, Aq.,
𝕵, 𝕿, have the sg., in accordance with the usage of the phr., but
𝕳, 𝕾, followed by AV., have pl. "deeds of kindness," which was
assimilated to the previous pl. ′On the positive side, — *they rebelled*]. We would expect the name of God against whom they
rebelled ; and so doubtless the original reading was ʿ*Elyon*, followed
by the locality, — *at the Sea of Reeds*] Ex. 14$^{11-12}$. But 𝕳, by an
error, instead of the former, gives "at the sea," followed by 𝕾, 𝕵,
𝕿, and EVˢ., an intolerable repetition. 𝕲 interprets the form
as a ptc., " going up " ; but this does not suit the context. —
8. A general statement prior to the beginning of the original Ps. ;
And He saved them for His name's sake], for His own honour
and reputation, cf. Ez. 20$^{9.14}$; the last clause explained by, — *in
order to make known His might*] ; the putting forth of His might
in the deliverance of His people was a making it evidently known
to all nations.

Str. I. Two synth. couplets. — **9**. *And He rebuked the Sea of
Reeds*]. The sea is conceived as a servant, who had exceeded
his authority and done what he ought not to have done, or rather
neglected something he ought to have done. The sea should
have been prompt to serve Yahweh and His people. — *and it
dried up*]. Its bottom was laid bare by the flight of the waters in
terror of the divine rebuke, cf. 104^7 Ex. 14$^{21-22}$. — *and He led them
in the depths as in a wilderness*]. A mode of statement derived
from Is. 63^{13}. The depths of the sea had become as dry as the
wilderness on its borders. — **10** is an expansive gloss, intervening
between the antithetic couplets. — *And saved them* ‖ *redeemed
them — from the hand of*], repeated in prosaic style, — *him that*

hated him ‖ *the enemy*], the Egyptians. — **11**. *And the waters covered over their adversaries*], having returned to their depths; and so completely were these destroyed by drowning that, — *Not one of them was left over*], cf. Ex. 14²⁸. A glossator inserts a reference to the song Ex. 15: **12–13**. *And they believed in His word* and *sang His praise*. This was followed by a censure in the spirit of v.⁶⁻⁷. — *They hurriedly forgat His works and tarried not for His counsel*], cf. Ex. 15²² ˢᑫ· 16² ˢᑫ· 17² ˢᑫ·.

Str. II. Two syn. couplets. — **14**. *Then they desired a desire*], cf. Nu. 11⁴⁻⁶ Ps. 78²⁹⁻³¹ : had an overpowering desire for fleshly food. This under the circumstances *tested 'El*], tried Him by questioning His ability to provide for them. — **15**. *And He gave to them* ‖ *And sent food*] ; the most probable reading in a difficult passage. An ancient copyist, by the mistake of a single letter, used a word which means "wasting, leanness, disease" according to 𝕳, "satiety" according to 𝕲, 𝕵 ; both implying the punishment for the testing God, and making the line antithetical with the previous one instead of synonymous ; which is altogether improbable, especially in view of the parallelism of the vbs. and also of the nouns : *their request* ‖ *their desire*, cf. 78¹⁸.

Str. III. Two syn. couplets. — **16**. *When they were jealous*], cf. Nu. 16, — *of Moses* ‖ *of Aaron*], the two leaders of Israel; this was partly tribal and partly personal. Aaron is further described as *the consecrated to Yahweh*], doubtless referring to the inscription upon the high priest's mitre Ex. 28³⁶⁻³⁸. — **17**. *The earth opened*], in earthquake, — *and swallowed up Dathan* ‖ *covered over the company of Abiram*]. The author leaves out of consideration altogether the Levitical Korah of the later narrative, and limits his attention to the Reubenite of the earlier narrative Nu. 16²⁵ ˢᑫ·. A glossator, noting the incompleteness of the statement, supplies the defect by introducing a reference to the Korahites in **18**. *And fire consumed their congregation, flame licked up the wicked*], cf. Nu. 16³⁵.

Str. IV. A syn. and a synth. couplet. — **19**. *Then they made a calf in Horeb* ‖ *and worshipped a molten image*], the story of Ex. 32¹⁻⁶. This is enlarged by a prosaic gloss. — **20**. *and changed their glory*], the theophanic glory in which their God manifested Himself to them, — *into the likeness of an ox that eateth herbage*], using the terminology of Dt. $4^{16.\ 17.\ 18}$. — **21.** *They forgat 'El their Saviour, Who did great deeds in Egypt*]. He was their Saviour through the great deeds of salvation He had wrought in delivering them from the Egyptians. This is expanded by a glossator into **22.** *wondrous deeds* ‖ *awe-inspiring deeds, in the land of Ham* ‖ *by the Sea of Reeds.*

Str. V. A synth. tetrastich. — **23.** *Then Yahweh had commanded to destroy them*]. This is the apodosis of a conditional clause, which the protasis shows to have been something about to take place, and not as having actually occurred. "Yahweh" was omitted in text by copyist's error, but it is necessary to complete the measure. — *Were it not that Moses, His chosen*]. Moses was the chosen of Yahweh here, as Jacob 105^6 and Aaron 105^{26}. — *Stood in the breach before Him*], a warrior's interposition, cf. for the phr. Ez. 22^{30} BS. 45^{23}, and for the event Ex. 32^{31-34}. — *To turn away His wrath from destroying*], cf. Ps. 78^{38}.

Str. VI. Two synth. couplets. — **24–25.** *Then they refused the desirable land*], cf. Nu. 14^{31} for the event, and Je. 3^{19} Zc. 7^{14} for the phr. — *And did not hearken to the voice of Yahweh*], to obey Him by going up to take possession of the land. The glossator enlarged this by inserting two lines : *and did not believe His word*], of promised help in battle against their enemies, — *and they murmured in their tents*], from Dt. 1^{27}. — **26.** *And He lifted up His hand to them*], the gesture of the divine oath Ex. 6^8 Dt. 32^{40} Ez. 20^{23} ; and cf. for the event Nu. 14^{28-35}. — *To make them fall in the wilderness*], that is, fall in death until the entire generation except Joshua and Caleb had perished. A glossator, with great historical impropriety, adds a clause which can only refer to the great Exile many centuries later : **27.** *to make their seed fall away among the nations, and to disperse them among the lands.*

Str. VII. A synth. tetrastich. — **28.** *Then they joined themselves to Baal-Peor*], attached themselves to the worship of Baal as celebrated at Peor ; an apostasy from Yahweh Nu. 25. — *And ate the sacrificial meals of the dead*], the feasts attached to the offering of the peace offerings to Baal, whose real existence is denied by this poet, who lives at a time when other deities than Yahweh were considered as not real beings, but lifeless as their images themselves, cf. 135^{15-17}. — **29.** *And provoked Yahweh by their doings*], their apostasy from Him and worship of Baal in fellowship with the Moabites. — *And a plague brake out against them*], sent by Yahweh as a punishment.

Str. VIII. Two synth. couplets. — **30.** *Then Phinehas stood up and interposed*] Nu. 25⁷⁻¹⁵. This interposition of Phinehas was the act of a soldier rather than of a priest, executing vengeance upon the ringleader of the apostasy. AV. "execute judgment" substitutes the result for the act expressed by the vb., and overlooks the mediatorial significance of his act. — *And the plague was stayed*], by Yahweh in response to this interposition. — **31.** *And it was counted to him for righteousness*]. Yahweh estimated it as an act of meritorious righteousness, and rewarded him with a covenant giving him an everlasting priesthood ; which was doubtless in the mind of the psalmist in his phrase — *To generation after generation forever*.

Str. IX. A synth. tetrastich, in which the third line depends on the first, the fourth on the second. — **32-33.** *Then they enraged Him at the waters of Meribah*] Nu. 20⁸⁻¹³. This is explained by — *For they rebelled against His Spirit*], an interpretation of the history based on Is. 63¹⁰, which identifies the divine Spirit with the angel of the presence of the Pentateuchal history. The narrative involves Moses and Aaron in this transgression, although it does not make it clear in what exactly their guilt consisted. So here : *And it went ill with Moses for their sake*]. The author thinks that Moses had to suffer not so much on account of what he had done as for his association with guilty Israel, and yet he tries to explain by : *he spake rashly with his lips*], the most probable mng. of a rare word, which gives practically no better explanation of the sin of Moses than the original passage.

Str. X. A syn. tetrastich. — **34.** *They did not destroy the peoples*]. They were commanded to exterminate the Canaanites, but did not do it, cf. Ex. 23³²⁻³³ 34¹² sq. Dt. 7² sq Ju. 1²¹. ²⁷. ²⁹ sq. 2¹ sq.. A glossator adds : *which Yahweh commanded them ;* and also, **35,** the antithetical positive offence : *and mingled themselves with the nations, and learned their works*, which seems to reflect a post-exilic situation rather than the time of the judges. — **36.** *And served their idols*]. This is the second line of the original tetrastich. The Israelites participated in the idolatry of the Canaanites,

— *and they became a snare to them*], cf. Ex. 23[36]. — **37**. *And they sacrificed their sons to Shedim*]. The Shedim were the ancient gods of Canaan, called "Shedim," originally meaning "lords," and no more objectionable as a divine title than "Baalim" or "Adonay"; but it became so associated with the worship of Baal at a very early date that it won a bad repute, and so in the mind of later Israel it amounted to about the same as demons. Human sacrifice was common in ancient times among all the inhabitants of Palestine, and probably among the Hebrews also before it was prohibited by law. But for a long time it prevailed notwithstanding the prohibition, even down to the Exile. It was not common, however, to sacrifice *daughters*. This word makes the line too long, and was doubtless an insertion, due to the gloss v.[38]. A late glossator, long distant in time from the period when such sacrifices were made, filled with horror at the thought and not knowing much about them, adds : **38–39**. *And shed innocent blood, the blood of their sons and their daughters, which they sacrificed to the idols of Canaan; and the land was polluted with their blood. And they became unclean by their works, and went a-whoring by their doings*]. This glossator is evidently more disturbed by ceremonial desecration of the land and people than by moral or religious considerations.

Str. XI. A syn. and a synth. couplet. — **40**. *Then the anger of Yahweh was kindled against* ‖ *And He abhorred*], both Deuteronomic expressions. The object of the divine wrath was : *His people* ‖ *His inheritance*. As a consequence of this anger and abhorrence — **41**. *And gave them into the hand of the nations*], permitted them to be defeated in battle by the several nations, which subdued them in the times of the judges. — *And they that hated them ruled over them*]. Many times they became a subject people in bondage to their oppressors. A glossator enlarged upon this by adding : **42**. *and their enemies oppressed them, and they were subdued under their hand.* This glossator also called attention to the fact that this was due to oft-repeated rebellions. — **43**. *Many times He used to deliver them, but they rebelled in their counsel and sank low in their iniquity.*

Str. XII. A syn. and a synth. couplet. — **44**. *Then He looked upon their distress* ‖ *When He heard their yell*]. When His people

cried unto Him, He did not neglect them; but looked upon
their distress with His eyes and heard their cries for help with His
ears. — **45**. *And remembered His covenant*], that made with the
patriarchal ancestors 105⁸⁻¹⁰. — *And was sorry*], cf. 90¹³. — *according to the abundance of His kindness*], so Kt.; more suited to the
context and the usage of the phr. than the pl. of EVˢ. after Qr.,
whether we think of "kindnesses," or the more usual "deeds of
kindness." The Ps. here reaches its conclusion with the times
of the judges. But the glossator was not satisfied. From the
point of view of his own times he appended a reference to the
Exile: **46**. *And He gave them for compassion*], a phr. derived
from I K. 8⁵⁰. — *before all who carried them captive*. A liturgical
gloss is appended at the end; a prayer of Israel in the Maccabean
period, for deliverance from among the nations. — **47**. *Save us,
Yahweh, our God; and gather us from the nations, that we may
give thanks to Thy holy name, that we may laud Thy praise.*

CV.

1. From Is. 12⁴. — **3**. בְּשֵׁם קָדְשׁוֹ] cf. 103¹. — **4**. עֻזּוֹ] so 𝔍, 𝔗; but 𝔊
κραταιώθητε, so 𝔖, 𝔙 = עֹזּוֹ, so Houb., Street. — מְבַקְשֵׁי יהוה] prob. for an
original מבקשׁיו. — פְּנָיו תָמִיד] prob. transposed, for thus far we have had
assonance in וֹ_ and יו_. — **5**. נִפְלְאוֹתָיו אֲשֶׁר עָשָׂה] rd. עָשָׂ inf. cstr. with sf. 3 sg.
preceded by נפלאות as Gn. 31²⁸, cf. Ps. 101³. — מִשְׁפְּטֵי פִיו] cf. I Ch. 16¹²; rd. prob.
פָּנָיו. If פיו is retained, we must let l. close with מִפְּתִיו. — **6**. בְּחִירָיו] has been
assimilated to the previous ll.; but בחירו refers to Jacob as עבדו to Abraham.
This couplet begins the original poem. — **8**. זָכַר בְּרִיתוֹ] phr. 106⁴⁵ 111⁵, characteristic of P, Gn. 9¹⁵·¹⁶ Ex. 2²⁴ 6⁵ Ez. 16⁶⁰ I Ch. 16¹⁵ +. — לְאֶלֶף דּוֹר] doubtless
is based on Ex. 20⁶. — **9**. שְׁבוּעָתִי לְיִשְׂחָק] a gl. to bring in this patriarch also.
‡ שְׁבוּעָה n.f. *oath*, as Gn. 26³ Dt. 7⁸ Je. 11⁵ I Ch. 16¹⁶. † יִשְׂחָק n. pr. m. elsw.
Je. 33²⁶ Am. 7⁹·¹⁶ for usual יצחק. — **10**. לְיִשְׂרָאֵל בְּרִית עוֹלָם] is repetition and a
gl. בְּרִית עוֹלָם phr. of P, Gn. 9¹⁶ + 8 t.; also Is. 24⁵ 55³ 61⁸ Je. 32⁴⁰ 50⁵ Ez.
16⁶⁰ 37²⁶. — **11** is an expansive gl. ארץ כנען not elsw. ψ, but only כנען 106³⁸
135¹¹. — חֶבֶל נַחֲלַתְכֶם] cf. Dt. 32⁹ I Ch. 16¹⁸. — **12**. בִּהְיוֹתָם] inf. cstr. sf. 3 pl.,
temporal clause. — בָּהּ] for an original בארץ; change due to use of ארץ in the
gl. — **13** is an expansive gl. — מִמַּמְלָכָה] is strange before אֶל עַם אַחֵר. It is
doubtless txt. err. for מֵעַם הלך. — **15** is an expansive gl. — מְשִׁיחָי] i.p. only here
of patriarchs, from very late point of view, regarding them as kings, cf. Gn.
14. Abraham is conceived as a נביא, however, Gn. 20⁷. — **16**. מַטֵּה לֶחֶם] phr.
Lv. 26²⁶ Ez. 4¹⁶ 5¹⁶ 14¹³. — **18**. רַגְלוֹ] Kt. רגליו Qr. ‖ נפשׁו. — בַּרְזֶל ‖ בַּרְזֶל, so
בכרזל, 𝔖, Ols., Bi., Che., al. — **20**. וַיַּתִּירֵהוּ] Hiph. impf. ו consec. † נתר vb.
only Hiph. *loosen, set free*, as 146⁷ Is. 58⁶ Jb. 6⁹ 2 S. 22³³ (?). — **21**. הִגִּיעֻנִי]

context indicates the usual sense of *possessions*, not creatures as 104²⁴. —
22. לֶאְסֹר] 𝕲 τοῦ παιδεῦσαι, לְיַסֵּר, so 𝔖, Street, Du., Ehr.; expansive gl.;
pentameter l. — בנפשו] *in his pleasure; v.* 𝕲, Aq., 𝔖, כנפשו *like himself.* —
24. וַיֶּפֶר] Hiph. impf. ו consec. ‡ פרה Qal *be fruitful* 128³, Hiph. *make fruitful* Gn. 28³ 48⁴ Lv. 26⁹. — וַיַּעֲצִמֵהוּ מִצָּרָיו] is an intensive gl. not suited to context. — **25.** הָפַךְ לִבָּם] vb. intrans. with לבם subj., and not trans. with God as
subj. — לִשְׂנֹא עַמּוֹ makes l. too long. It has been assimilated to the gl.
לְהִתְנַכֵּל בַּעֲבָדָיו. It was originally noun שִׂנְאָה n.f. *hatred* 25¹⁹ 109³·⁵ 139²².
† נכל] vb. Qal *to be a knave* Mal. 1¹⁴; Pi. *beguile* Nu. 25¹⁸, Hithp. *deal
knavishly*, as Gn. 37¹⁸, c. את, here with ב. — **27.** שָׂמוּ] pl., referring to Moses
and Aaron; but 𝕲, 𝔖, 𝔙, Aq., Σ, 𝔍, Hu., De., Bä., al., שָׂם more prob., as 78⁴³
with God subj. — בָּם] is expansive gl. — דִּבְרֵי אֹתוֹתָיו] cf. דברי נפלאתיך 145⁵, acts
of God which were miraculous signs. — **28.** שָׁלַח חֹשֶׁךְ וַיַּחְשִׁךְ]. This is out of
place in the order of plagues, and doubtless was a later misplaced insertion.
— ולא מרו את דבריו]. 𝕲, 𝔖, have no negative, but all other Vrss. have it.
𝕲ᴺ·ᶜ·ᵃ·ᴬ·ᵀ· have ὅτι for καί. In any case it is not suited to the context, even
if with Hi., Bä., Du., Ehr., we rd. שמרו. It was doubtless a marginal gl.; cf.
מרה פי Nu. 20²⁴ 27¹⁴ (P). — **29.** וַיָּמֶת אֶת־דְּגָתָם] is an expansive gl. against the
measure, making l. pentameter. — **30.** וְחֲדָרֵי מַלְכֵיהֶם] is also an expansive gl.,
making l. pentameter. For מלכיהם rd. מלכם. — **31.** כִּנִּים ‡] prob. *gnats*, as
Ex. 8¹²·¹³·¹⁴ (J). — **37.** וַיּוֹצִיאֵם]. The sfs. in v.²⁹⁻³⁶ have all referred to
Egyptians. It is improb. that a changed reference to Israel would be left
to context only with same sf. Rd. עַם for ם_, which makes no difference in
the measure. — **38–45** are a later addition; they go over into the period
covered by Ps. 106. — **39.** פרש ענן לְבָלָ] phr. α.λ., cf. 78¹⁴. ‡ מָסָךְ n.[m.]
(1) *covering, screen*, elsw. 2 S. 17¹⁹ (of well), Is. 22⁸ (of eye); (2) the veil
of the Tabernacle in P Ex. 26³⁶ +. Here is a novel conception of the עָנָן.

CVI.

2. יְמַלֵּל] Pi. impf. † מלל Aram.; elsw. Gn. 21⁷ (E) Jb. 8² 33³. — **3.** עֹשֵׂה]
pl. as 𝕲 = שֹׁמְרֵי. — **4.** זָכְרֵנִי] so 𝔍, 𝔖, 𝕮, ‖ פָּקְדֵנִי; but 𝕲, Aq., Σ, Θ, Quinta,
Sexta, Bä., Che., pl. נו; better suited to context, though prob. an assimilation.
— יהוה] gl.; makes l. too long. — רְצוֹן עַמֶּךָ] phr. α.λ.; constr. of object. —
5. בְּחִירֶיךָ] should be sg. in assonance with גּוֹיֶךָ and נַחֲלָתֶךָ. V.⁴⁻⁵ a trimeter
pentastich with assonance in ךָ_; a gl. by another hand than v.¹⁻³·⁶⁻⁸. — **6** is gl.
from 1 K. 8⁴⁷. — עם אבותינו is, however, an insertion due to v.⁷ᵃ. — **7.** במצרים]
late explanatory gl. against measure. — רֹב חֲסָדֶיךָ] improb.; 𝕲, Aq., 𝔍, 𝕮, רב הַסֵּר in
accordance with usage of phr. — יָם] is tautological and improb., though
sustained by 𝔖, 𝔍, 𝕮. 𝕲 ἀναβαίνοντες, 𝔙 *ascendentes*, עֹלִים. Venema, Bä.,
Dr., Kau., Du., Che., עֶליון as 78¹⁷. — ‡ יַם סוּף] elsw. ψ v.⁹·²² 136¹³·¹⁵. — **9.** וַיּוֹצֵר].
The original Ps. begins here. The l. is dependent on Na. 1⁴. — וַיּוֹלִיכֵם]. This
l. is based on Is. 63¹³. — **10** is expansive and repetitious gl. — **11.** וַיְכַסּוּ מַיִם]
= Ex. 14²⁸. — אֶחָד מֵהֶם] based on Ex. 14²⁸. — **12.** A tetrameter gl., cf. v.²⁴ᵇ
Ex. 14³¹ 15¹. — **13.** A pentameter gl. — **14.** וַיִּתְאַוּוּ תַאֲוָה v. Nu. 11³⁴ (E), cf.
Ps. 73³⁰. — וַיְנַסּוּ אֵל] = 78¹⁸·⁴¹, cf. Ex. 17²·⁷ Nu. 14²² (𝔍) Dt. 6¹⁶. — **15.** שְׁאֵלָתָם] sf.

‡ שְׁאֵלָה n.f. *asking, request,* with נתן elsw. 1 S. 1[17. 27] Est. 5[6. 8] 7[2] 9[12]. — ‡ רָזוֹן] n. *wasting disease,* acc. *B*DB., elsw. Is. 10[16] *leanness,* Mi. 6[10] *scantiness.* 𝔊 πλησμονήν, so 𝔙 *saturitatem,* 𝔖 סבעא, Houb., Street, Che., Dy., Du., al., זרא Nu. 11[20]. But it is not suited to context. We should have, ‖ לחם, מזון *food,* as Gn. 45[23] 2 Ch. 11[21]. — בנפשׂב =] לנפשׂב 78[18]. — 16. קרוש יהוה] *one conse-crated to Yahweh,* a conception of P. — 17. תפתח ארץ] = Nu. 16[32]. — † זֵרֶד] n. pr. m. *Dathan,* son of Ehab, Reubenite Nu. 16[1. 12. 24. 25. 27] 26[9] Dt. 11[6]. אֲבִירָם n. pr. m. his brother; only in same passages. — 18 is an expansive generalizing gl. — 19. ‡ חֹרֵב] n. pr. loc., term of E, D; elsw. Mal. 3[22] 1 K. 8[9] 19[8] 2 Ch. 5[10]. — 20. וַיָּמִירוּ אֶת כְּבוֹדָם] gl. from Je. 2[11], only sf. ם for י, which latter is, however, given here by 𝔊[S. c. a. A. R. T], cf. Rom. 1[23]. — ‡ תבנית] n.f. *construction* 144[12] Jos. 22[28] (P), *pattern* Ex. 25[9], *image* elsw. Dt. 4[16. 17. 18] Is. 44[13] Ez. 8[3. 10] 10[8]. — 22. Expansive gl. בארץ הם] = 105[23. 27], cf. 78[51]. — 23. ויאמר להשמידם] = Dt. 9[25] להשמיד אהכ כי אמר יהוה: יהוה should be inserted here for good measure. — יְעֵר בְּאֶרֶץ] as Ez. 22[30] BS. 45[23]. — השיב חמתו] as Ps. 78[38]. — 24. אֶרֶץ חֶמְדָּה] phr. elsw. Je. 3[19] Zc. 7[14]. — לא האמינו לדברו] is a gl. of interp. — 25. וירגנו באהליהם] dimeter gl. = Dt. 1[27]. † רגן vb. Qal *murmur* Is. 29[24], Niph. (1) same, elsw. Dt. 1[27]; (2) *backbite* Pr. 16[28] 18[8] 26[20. 22]. — 26. וַיִּשָּׂא יָדוֹ לָהֶם] = Ez. 20[23]. — רהפיל אורם] cf. 37[14] 73[18]. — 27. A gl. from Ez. 20[23], introducing reference to Exile; inappropriate here. — 28. וַיִּצָּמְדוּ] Niph. elsw. Nu. 25[3. 5], Hiph. Ps. 50[19]. — בעל פעור] n. pr. dei., elsw. Nu. 25[3. 5] Dt. 4[3] Ho. 9[10]. — זִבְחֵי מֵתִים] phr. α.λ. — 29. יהוה has been omitted by txt. err. — ‡ מַגֵּפָה] n.f. *plague,* v.[3] Nu. 14[37] 1 S. 6[4]. — 30. וַיַּרִצֵּר] Niph. impf. עצר Qal *restrain* not used ψ; but Niph. *be restrained, stayed,* here as Nu. 17[13] 25[8] (P) 2 S. 24[25]. A word is missing for measure; insert מעליהם. — 32. וַיַּקְצִיפוּ] Hiph. † קצף vb. Qal not in ψ; but Hiph. *provoke to wrath* as Dt. 9[7. 8. 22] Zc. 8[14]. — 33. וַיְבַטֵּא] Pi. † בטא vb. Qal בוטֶה Pr. 12[18] *babbler,* Pi. elsw. Lv. 5[4]. A word is missing for measure. Insert either הוא or משה. — 34. אשר אמר יהוה להם] is gl. — 35 is tetrameter gl. — וַיִּתְעָרְבוּ] Hithp. ‡ ערב vb. Qal *go surety for* 119[122] Jb. 17[3] Gn. 43[9] 44[32] (J). Hithp. *have fellowship with,* elsw. Ezr. 9[2] Pr. 20[19] 24[21]. — 36. עֲצַבֵּיהֶם] ‡ עצבים always pl. *idols* v.[38] Ho. 4[17] 8[4] 13[2] 14[9] Is. 46[1] Ps. 115[4] = 135[15]. — 37. וְאֶת בְּנוֹתֵיהֶם] expansive gl. from v.[38]. Daughters were not usually so sacrificed. — † שֵׁדִים] n. pl. *lords,* old name of divinity as Dt. 32[17]. — 38–39. Expansive gl. — וַיֶּחֱנַף] ‡ [חנף] vb. Qal *be polluted* Is. 24[5] Je. 3[1. 1] of land, Mi. 4[11] of Zion, cf. Ps. 35[16]. — וַיִּטְמְאוּ] *become unclean* religiously, as Ez. 22[4] Lv. 19[31] (H). — וַיִּזְנוּ] as Ho. 2[7] 4[15] Is. 57[3]. — 40–41. Original Ps. is resumed. — 42. Expansive gl. — וַיִּכְנְעוּ תַּחַת] = Ju. 3[30]. — 43. Generalizing gl. — וַיָּמֹכּוּ] מכך vb. Qal α.λ. *be low, humiliated,* BDB. Niph. *sink in decay* Ec. 10[18]. Hoph. *be brought low* Jb. 24[24]. — 45. חסדו] Kt. more in accord with usage. חֲסָדָיו Qr. *deeds of kindness* not suited to context. — 46. וַיִּתֵּן לְרַחֲמִים] gl. from 1 K. 8[50]. — 47. Gl. of final petition with Exile in view. — לְהִשְׁתַּבֵּחַ] form α.λ., Aramaism. — 48. Benediction of the book. — וְאָמַר] 1 Ch. 16[36] וִיאמרו.

PSALM CVII., 4 STR. 12³.

Ps. 107 is a summons to praise Yahweh for His redemption of His people from straits. Four are mentioned : (1) perils of caravans lost in the wilderness (v.⁴⁻⁹), (2) of prisoners (v.¹⁰· ¹²· ¹³⁻¹⁶), (3) of sickness (v.¹⁷⁻²²), (4) the perils of the sea (v.²³ᵃ· ²⁵· ²⁶ᵇ· ²⁸⁻²⁹· ³¹· ³²). An introductory gloss makes the Ps. into a Hallel (v.¹). Other glosses interpret the redemption as from exile (v.²⁻³), give a reason for the imprisonment in exile (v.¹¹), enlarge upon the perils of the sea (v.²³ᵇ· ²⁴· ²⁶ᵃ· ²⁷), upon the gladness of a calm (v.³⁰), heap up deliverances of various kinds mingled with discipline (v.³³⁻⁴³).

STRAYING in the wilderness, in the desert,
  The way to an inhabited city they found not.
  Hungry, yea thirsty,
  Their soul fainted within them.
      Then they cried unto Yahweh in their strait,
      That out of their distresses He might deliver them :
  Then He made them tread in a straight way,
  To go unto an inhabited city.
      Let them give thanks to Yahweh for His kindness,
      And His wondrous deeds to the sons of mankind.
  For He doth satisfy the longing soul,
  And the hungry soul He doth fill with good things.
DWELLING in darkness and dense darkness,
  Prisoners in affliction and iron,
  Their heart was humbled with travail :
  They stumbled and there was no helper.
      Then they cried unto Yahweh in their strait,
      That out of their distresses He might save them :
  And He leads them forth from darkness and dense darkness,
  And their bands He bursts asunder.
      Let them give thanks to Yahweh for His kindness,
      And His wondrous deeds to the sons of mankind.
  For He brake in pieces the doors of bronze,
  And the bars of iron He hewed asunder.
WEAK because of the way of their transgression,
  And because of their iniquities they were suffering affliction,
  All food their appetite was abhorring ;
  And they had drawn nigh the gates of death.
      Then they cried unto Yahweh in their strait,
      That out of their distresses He might save them :
  He sendeth His word and healeth them,
  And delivereth (their life from the Pit).
      Let them give thanks to Yahweh for His kindness,
      And His wondrous deeds to the sons of mankind.

Let them sacrifice sacrifices of thank offering,
And tell of His works in jubilation.
GOING down to the sea in ships,
The stormy wind arose,
And lifted up the waves of the (deep).
Their soul was melting because of trouble.
Then they cried unto Yahweh in their strait,
That out of their distresses He might bring them.
He setteth the storm into a whisper,
And the waves (of the deep) are still.
Let them give thanks to Yahweh for His kindness,
And His wondrous deeds to the sons of mankind.
Let them exult in the assembly of the people,
And in the session of the elders praise Him.

Ps. 107 has no title in 𝔐 ; but in 𝕲 ἀλληλουιά, which is doubtless correct, though in 𝔐 it is attached to previous Ps. and so omitted here. The Ps. is composed in its original form of four parts of three tetrastichs each, and so resembles in length and measure 105, 106. These three Pss. are thus closely united, and may have been from the same poet. This Ps. is, however, more ornate, as it has a double Rf. It depends on Is.[2]: v.[10], cf. Is. 42[7], v.[16] = Is. 45[2]. In other respects the Ps. is original. There are several glosses: v.[1], the הודו phrase of introduction, as 106[1], cf. 105[1]; v.[38-43], a series of additions without strophical organisation, to increase the number of exhibitions of the kindness of Yahweh. These show dependence on Is.[2] and Job: v.[33], cf. Is. 50[2]; v.[35], cf. Is. 41[18]; v.[40a] = Jb. 12[21a]; v.[40b] = Jb. 12[24b]; v.[42] = Jb. 22[19] 5[16]; v.[43a], cf. Ho. 14[10]; v.[43b], cf. Is. 63[7]. The Ps. is interpreted by glosses as referring to the Exile; but in fact it mentions four kinds of deliverance from straits which have nothing to do with Exile. The Ps. is not earlier than the Greek period.

Ps. 107 begins with an introductory tetrastich, the first distich of which is the ordinary formula of the Hallel: **1.** *Give thanks to Yahweh, for He is good; for His kindness endureth forever*], cf. 106[1]. — **2.** *Let the redeemed of Yahweh*], a phr. of Is. 35[9] 51[10] 62[12]. — *say it*], that is, the thanks. — *whom He hath redeemed from the hand of the adversary*]. The nations among which Israel was living in perils of various kinds. — **3.** *and from the lands gathered them; from the east and from the west, from the north and from the sea*]. This is against the entire tenor of the Ps., which has to do not with deliverance from enemies, but from straits of a more general character, which might come upon the people of God not merely during the Exile, but at any time in their experience of life. This is a prosaic gloss.

There are four equal Strs. of exactly the same structure : (1) a synth. tetrastich describing the distress ; (2) a synth. tetrastich describing the cry to Yahweh and the redemption that follows ; and (3) a synth. couplet of thanksgiving, with a syn. couplet of praise or its reason. **Str. I.—4.** *Straying*]. In the other instances nominal or participial forms are used, v.¹⁰·¹⁷·²³. The use of the Pf. here, though sustained by 𝔐 and Vrss., is improbable. — *in the wilderness*], defined more strictly as in *the desert.* — *The way to an inhabited city they found not*]. They were lost in the pathless desert ; they had strayed from the right way, and could not find it again. — **5.** *Hungry, yea, thirsty*]. Having consumed their food and water, they had nothing to eat or drink, and were already suffering from hunger and thirst. — *Their soul fainted within them*]. They had become faint, and were ready to perish. — **6.** *Then they cried unto Yahweh in their strait, That out of their distresses He might deliver them*]. This is the first Rf., which appears regularly in the same place in each of the four parts of the Ps., the only variation being in the vb., which in v.¹³·¹⁹ is *save* and in v.²⁸ *bring out.* In the extreme distress in which they are perishing, they cry aloud to Yahweh their God for salvation. — **7.** *Then He made them tread in a straight way, To go unto an inhabited city*]. Yahweh showed them the right way, and led them straight forward in it until they came to the city of their destination. — **8.** *Let them give thanks to Yahweh for His kindness, and His wondrous deeds to the sons of mankind*]. This is the second Rf., which appears in each Part in the same place, v.¹⁵·²¹·³¹, in identical terms. It is a summons to all who have had such a deliverance to render thanks to Yahweh for it. It is the kindness of Yahweh which induces Him to make such deliverances. They are indeed wondrous works ; not miracles in the technical historical sense, but yet special interpositions of Yahweh in answer to prayer. — **9.** *For He doth satisfy the longing soul, and the hungry soul He doth fill with good things*]. The first clause doubtless refers to the satisfaction of the thirst, the latter to the hunger of v.⁵.

Str. II.—10. *Dwelling in darkness*], emphasized by *and dense darkness*], not "shadow of death" of EVˢ. The darkness is here that of the dungeon, which was usually a pit or vault, deep

down and away from the light of day. — *Prisoners in affliction
and iron*]. They were indeed prisoners, not only in dungeons,
but in fetters there ; and in addition suffering cruel affliction,
probably with stripes also, as usual in such cases. — A glossator
gives this a reference to the Exile by adding : **11.** *because they
rebelled against the words of 'El and the counsel of 'Elyon con-
temned*]. They were punished by exile and imprisonment for
disobedience to the Law. But the context shows that the imprisonment and suffering were not due to any such cause, but were
of a more general character. — **12.** *Their heart was humbled
with travail*]. The forced labour of prisoners was a great humiliation to them. — *They stumbled*], from weakness due to over-
work. — *and there was no helper*]. They were friendless, and in
an entirely helpless condition. — **14.** *He leads them forth from
darkness and dense darkness*], the gloomy dungeon of v.[10a]. —
And their bands He bursts asunder]. The prisoners wear iron
fetters, cf. v.[10b]. They regain their liberty through the help of
Yahweh, and through Him alone. — **16.** *For He brake in pieces
the doors of bronze*], the strong gates of the dungeon. — *And the
bars of iron He hewed asunder*], the iron bars that strengthen
the gates of the prison.

Str. III. — **17.** *Weak*], so many moderns conjecture, ‖ *were
suffering affliction*], 獻, Aq., ℨ, " the foolish," followed by EVˢ.,
does not suit the context any more than the reading of 𝔊, 𝔍.
The strait of this part is evidently mortal sickness. — This sickness the poet ascribes to guilt : *because of the way of their transgression ‖ because of their iniquities*], in accordance with the older
theory combated in the Book of Job and still prevalent in the
time of Jesus, Jo. 9[2], that disease was due to sin. — **18.** *All food
their appetite was abhorring*]. They were so reduced in strength
that they could not eat. — *And they had drawn nigh the gates of
death*]. They were about to die and enter into the city of the
dead, who are here, as Is. 38[10], conceived as dwelling in a city,
which has its gates just as any earthly city ; cf. Mt. 16[18]. —
20. *He sendeth His word and healeth them*]. The healing of the
sick is accomplished by the sending of the divine word, which
is doubtless conceived as a commandment bidding the disease to
depart. It is here personified as a messenger, just as in other

passages divine attributes are personified and sent on missions of kindness or of judgment. — *And delivereth their life from the Pit*], the original reading, which an early copyist, by the omission of a single letter, reduced to the unusual form " their Pits." The first line of the v. corresponds with v.[17], the second with v.[18]. — **22**. *Let them sacrifice sacrifices of thank offering*], offer the thank offerings with their festal meals usual on such occasions. — *And tell of His works in jubilation*], the religious shouts that were usual on festal occasions, of the nature of public applause of the celebration of the divine works of deliverance.

Str. IV. — 23. *Going down to the sea in ships*], mariners, — intensified by the gloss : *doing business in the great waters*, continued in **24**. *They see the works of Yahweh — and His wondrous deeds in the gulf.* — **25**. *The stormy wind arose*], so 𝕲, 𝕵. This is explained by glossator as the great work of Yahweh by the insertion of " He commanded " and the interpretation of vb. as Hiph. " cause to arise." — *And lifted up the waves of the deep*]. The original form required by the measure, reduced by a copyist to " his waves," going back upon " the gulf " of v.[24], which was appropriate enough, if that were original, but impossible if it is a gloss. — A glossator enlarges upon the storm, and with a graphic touch which indicates real experience : **26-27**. *They go up to heaven ; they go down to the depths*], the seamen ascending and descending with the waves. — *Their soul was melting because of trouble*]. This is the only line of these verses which was original in the Ps. The storm is of exceptional violence, and they are in real peril, which they realise in terror. — **27**. *They reel to and fro, and stagger like a drunkard*]. The irregular movement of the sea, in pitching and rolling, makes it impossible for them to keep their feet. — *and all their skill is swallowed up*]. The sailors' technical skill has become useless ; they are at the mercy of the sea, and they can only await in dreadful anxiety the result. — **29**. *He setteth the storm into a whisper*]. The roar of the storm dies away, until nothing but a gentle, whispering wind remains. This corresponds with v.[25a]. — *And the waves of the deep are still*]. They have subsided into a gentle, quiet movement, in correspondence with v.[25b]. — A glossator adds : **30**. *And they are glad, because they are calm ; and He leadeth them unto* *the city of their desire.* — **32**. *Let them exult in the assembly of the people*], give public praise. — *in the session of the elders praise Him*], the gathering together of the elders in council. The Ps. has here its appropriate conclusion, although there seems to be no special reason why the examples of the divine deliverance should be limited to these four. Later editors made the Ps. more suitable for a Hallel by adding a considerable number of other examples of divine redemption of the people, but without the strophical organisation and Refrain of the original Ps. — **33-34**. A tetrastich of three syn. lines and one synth. : *He turneth*], habitual action, and not vivid action in the past. — *streams ‖ water springs ‖ a fruitful land*], three syn. terms referring to an oasis, or fertile, well-watered valley. — *into a wilderness ‖ a thirsty land*, without water, ‖ *a salt waste*]. Such a transformation was due to the withholding of rain, not uncommon in Palestine and neighbouring lands. This tetrastich is not in harmony with the Ps., which set forth straits of people, and not condition of the land. — *Because of the evil of them that dwell therein*], is not in accord with the conception of the original Ps., but of the glossator of v.[11]. — **35-36** is in antithesis with the previous tetrastich. — *He turneth the wilderness ‖ a thirsty land — into a pool of water ‖ into water springs*], by bestowing an unusual provision of rain. — *and He maketh the hungry dwell therein, and establisheth an inhabited city*]. Men in great numbers assemble in this fertile oasis, satisfying their hunger, and dwell therein in such numbers as to constitute a city. — **37-38**. *And they sow fields, and plant vineyards, which yield fruits of increase. He blesseth them, and they multiply greatly; and He suffereth not their cattle to decrease*]. To the blessings of an agricultural life are added those of the nomad life.

Another glossator seems to have added **39, 41**, into which a still later one inserted **40**, and to which he appended **42**. — **39**. *But when they are minished and brought low*]. This glossator is evidently thinking of a time of adversity, the reverse of the prosperity of the previous context. — *through oppression, adversity, and sorrow*], such as that the people had to endure in the Antiochean persecution. — The apodosis is in **41**. *He setteth the needy on high from affliction*], gives them a safe refuge from their oppressors. — *and maketh families like a flock*], gives His people, who have sought and found refuge in Him, wonderful fertility, so that their families increase as rapidly as a flock of sheep. — A later glossator inserts from Jb. 12²¹ : *He poureth contempt upon princes*], doubtless referring to the defeat of the Syrian armies by the Maccabees; — and from Jb. 12²⁴ᵇ : *and causeth them to stray in a pathless waste.* — The same glossator also adds from Jb. 22¹⁹ : *the upright see it and are glad,* — and from Jb. 5¹⁶ : *and all perversity doth stop her mouth.* — He also probably appended the concluding lines from Ho. 14¹⁰ : *Whoso is wise, let him observe these things,* — and from Is. 63⁷ : *and let them understand the kind deeds of Yahweh.*

1 is the ordinary formula of the Hallel, cf. 106¹. It is a gl. in order to make the Ps. into a Hallel. Indeed, v.²⁻³ are also glosses to give the Ps. a reference to the Diaspora. — **2.** [גְּאוּלֵי] Qal ptc. pass. as Is. 35⁹ 51¹⁰ 62¹² 63⁴ (?). V. Ps. 19¹⁵. — צַר [מִיַּד־צָר] *adversary* if part of the gl., but צר *distress* if original to the Ps., as in Rfs., so Bä., Che. — **3.** [מִמִּזְרָח וּמִמַּעֲרָב] as 103¹². — ‡ צָפוֹן [48³ 89¹³. — מִיָּם] for West, cf. 80¹² 89²⁶. — **4.** [בִּישִׁימוֹן] as 68⁸ +. — דָּרֶךְ] i.p. incorrect ; it belongs to next l., as 𝔊, 𝔖. — עִיר מוֹשָׁב] v.⁷·³⁶, cf. Zion as dwelling place 132¹³. — **5.** [הִתְעַטָּף] Hithp. with נפשׁ as Jon. 2⁸, cf. Pss. 77⁴ 142⁴ 143⁴ with רוח. — **6.** † [מְצוּקָה] n.f. v.¹³·¹⁹·²⁸, as 25¹⁷ Jb. 15²⁴ Zp. 1¹⁵. — **7.** [וַיַּדְרִיכֵם] Hiph. דרך, so 25⁵·⁹ — דֶּרֶךְ יְשָׁרָה as Je. 31⁹. — **9.** [שֹׁקֵקָה] Qal ptc. † שׁקק (1) usually c. ב *rush upon* Is. 33⁴ Jo. 2⁹ Pr. 28¹⁵; (2) here *longing*, as Is. 29⁸. Hithp. Na. 2⁵. — **10.** [אֲסִירֵי] as 68⁷ La. 3³⁴ +. — **11** is a gl. giving the reason of the suffering ; interrupts the thought and makes Str. too long. — **12.** [כָּשָׁלוּ] in anxiety, distress, as 27² Is. 59¹⁰. — **14.** [מוֹסְרוֹתֵיהֶם יְנַתֵּק] as 2³. — **16.** ‡ [וְחֹשֶׁת] n.m. *bronze*, here of gates, Ju. 16²¹ Je. 39⁷ + of fetters, also ore Dt. 8⁹, armour 1 S. 17⁵ etc. — [בְּרִיחֵי בַרְזֶל] *bars of iron* ‡ בְּרִיחַ n.m. elsw. ψ 147¹³. — **17.** ‡ [אֱוִילִים] adj. *foolish*, always ethically bad Je. 4²² Is. 19¹¹ +, Aq. ἄφρονες, 𝔍 *stultos*, improb. here, 𝔊ˣ·ᴬ·ᵀ ἀντελάβετο αὐτῶν, 𝔘 *suscepit eos*, 𝔖 עֲדַר. Rd. with Ols., Gr., Dr., Kau., Du., חִילִים. — [יִתְעַנּוּ] Hithp. *afflicted* in discipline ; cf. Pi. *afflict* as divine discipline 88⁸ 90¹⁵ 119⁷⁵ Dt. 8²·³ La. 3³³ Is. 64¹¹. — **20.** [שְׁחִיתוֹתָם] pl. sf. שְׁחִית, elsw. La. 4²⁰ for שַׁחַת *pit.* Rd., however, with Du. מִשַּׁחַת חַיָּתָם. — **23.** The inverted נ here and v.²⁴·²⁵·²⁶·²⁷·⁴⁰ are of the nature of parentheses. They indicate that in the opinion of the early Massoretes the verses were misplaced. They are indeed for the most part glosses. — [עֹשֵׂי מְלָאכָה רַחֵים רַבִּים] begins the gl., though the נ was for practical reasons placed at the beginning of the v. — **24** is a gl. throughout. — **25.** [וַיֹּאמֶר] is a gl. to indicate that the storm originated by divine command, and accordingly וַיַּעֲמֵד Hiph. ו consec.; but 𝔊, 𝔍 rightly have יַּעֲמֹד Qal, 𝔘 *stetit*, so Bä., Kau., Du., Che. — **25.** ‡ [סְעָרָה] v.²⁹ 148⁸ Je. 23¹⁹ 30²³ +, cf. סַעַר Ps. 55⁹. — [וַיְרוֹמְמֵם] a word is needed ; rd. תְהוֹם. — **26.** [תִּתְמוֹגָג] מוג, cf. 75⁴, Hithp. *melt in terror*, cf. Na. 1⁵. This v., except this word with נפשׁ בְּרָעָה, is a gl.; so v.²⁷·²⁹. —

27. יָהֹ֣גוּ] fully written, from חגג *reel* as from festival dancing; *v. 42⁵.* — יָנוּעוּ] *stagger*, as Is. 29⁹. — ‡שִׁכּוֹר] adj. *drunken*, as Is. 19¹⁴ Je. 23⁹ +. — **29.** †דְּמָמָה] n.f. *whisper*, as 1 K. 19¹² Jb. 4¹⁶. — ויחשו] Qal impf. חשה *be silent, still;* here only of waves, 28¹ of Yahweh. — **30.** This v. is a gl. — ‡שתק ישתקו] Qal *rest, be quiet*, of waves, as Jon. 1¹¹. ¹², of conflict Pr. 26²⁰. — †[מָחוֹז] n.m. *city*, loan word *BDB.* V.³³⁻⁴³ are later addition to Ps. — **33.** †צִמָּאוֹן] n.[m.] *thirsty ground*, as Dt. 8¹⁵ Is. 35⁷. — מֹצָאֵי מַיִם] v.³⁵ Is. 41¹⁸, *v.* Pss. 19⁷ 75⁷. — **34.** †מְלֵחָה] n.f. *saltness, barrenness*, elsw. Je. 17⁶ Jb. 39⁶. — **35.** ‡אֲגַם] n.[m.] *pool of water*, as Is. 41¹⁸ Ps. 114⁸. — ארץ ציה] as 63² Ho. 2⁶ Je. 50¹² +. — **37.** ‡הַבוּאָה] n.f. *produce*, as Dt. 22⁹ Nu. 18³⁰ Is. 30²³ +. — **38.** וַיִּמְעִיטוּ] Hiph. impf. ‡מעט Qal *be* or *become small* v.³⁹, as Is. 21¹⁷ Pr. 13¹¹. Hiph. *make small* here, as Je. 10²⁴. — **39.** וַיָּשֹׁחוּ] Qal impf. שחח 42⁶ *be brought low.* — †עֹצֶר] n.[m.] *restraint*, as Is. 53⁸ Pr. 30¹⁶. — **42** is a compound of Jb. 22¹⁹ and 5¹⁶. — קפץ] cf. 77¹⁰.

PSALM CVIII.

Ps. 108 is a mosaic of 57⁸⁻¹² and 60⁷⁻¹⁴, with slight modifications discussed in notes upon these Pss.

PSALM CIX.

Ps. 109 is composite. *A.* The congregation prays that God may no longer remain silent; for their enemies are slandering them (v.¹ᵇ. ²ᵇ. ³ᵃ. ⁵ᵇ), pursuing them to death (v.¹⁶. ¹⁷ᵇ), with nothing but curses (v.¹⁷ᵃ. ¹⁸); they pray Yahweh for deliverance from extreme affliction (v.²¹⁻²²), complain that they are ready to perish (v.²³⁻²⁴), and plead His kindness and the credit He will receive from the enemies (v.²⁶⁻²⁷). *B.* An imprecation is upon a wicked ruler: that he may be condemned by a higher power more wicked than himself (v.⁶⁻⁷), that he may lose his position and leave his family destitute (v.⁸⁻⁹), may be exiled from home and oppressed by creditors (v.¹⁰⁻¹¹), that his posterity may perish in a single generation (v.¹²⁻¹³), and his memory be blotted out (v.¹⁴⁻¹⁵). Glosses harmonize to some extent the two Pss. (v.²ᵃ. ³ᵇ⁻⁵ᵃ. ¹⁹⁻²⁰. ²⁵. ²⁸⁻²⁹), and give a liturgical conclusion (v.³⁰⁻³¹).

A. v.¹ᵇ. ²ᵇ. ³ᵃ. ⁵ᵇ. ¹⁶⁻¹⁸. ²¹⁻²⁷, 6 STR. 4³.

O GOD of my praise, keep not silent;
    For they speak with me with a lying tongue,
    And with words of hatred they compass me about,
    With hatred for my love.

HE remembered not to do kindness;
    And pursued the afflicted and poor,
    The one smitten in heart to kill him;
    And he took no pleasure in blessing.
AND he loved cursing, and it came to him;
    And he clothed himself with it as his raiment;
    And it came like water into his inwards,
    And like oil into his bones.
O YAHWEH, work Thou with me;
    According to the goodness of Thy kindness deliver me;
    For I am afflicted and poor,
    And my heart writhes within me.
AS a shadow, when it is stretched out, I depart.
    I am shaken out (when the light grows stronger).
    My knees totter from fasting,
    And my flesh without oil is (as one hasting away).
HELP me, Yahweh my God!
    Save me according to (the goodness of) Thy kindness;
    And they will know that this is Thy hand;
    Thou, Yahweh, hast done it.

$$B. \text{ v.}^{6-15}, \text{ 5 STR. } 4^3.$$

APPOINT a wicked one over him,
    And let an adversary stand at his right hand.
    When he is judged, let him come forth condemned;
    And let the decision of his case be his guilt.
LET his days be few,
    His office let another take;
    Let his children become fatherless,
    And his wife become a widow.
LET his children wander about and beg;
    Let them be banished from their desolate homes.
    Let a creditor strike him for what he hath;
    And let strangers take his labour as spoil.
LET him have none that extendeth kindness,
    And let there be no favour to his orphans.
    Let his posterity be for cutting off.
    In a generation let his name be blotted out.
LET the iniquity of his fathers be remembered,
    And let not the sin of his mother be blotted out.
    Let them be in the sight of Yahweh continually,
    That He may cut off (his) memory from the earth.

Ps. 109 was in 𝔇, then in 𝔐, and was also in 𝔇𝔎 before it received its present position (v. Intr. §§ 27, 31, 33). The original Ps. of 𝔇 had six trimeter tetrastichs, and is a strong and beautiful prayer, pleading with Yahweh for help against unjust enemies, v.$^{1b.\ 2b.\ 3a.\ 5b.\ 16-18.\ 21-24.\ 26-27}$. An imprecatory Ps. of five trimeter tetrastichs, v.$^{6-15}$, was inserted after the first Strophe of the original Ps. This is smooth and artificial, and of an entirely different temper from the original Ps. The editor who united them introduced v.[2a. 3b-5a], in order to assimilate them, and also additional imprecations, v.[19-20. 28-29], more suited to the composite Ps., and a description of a later situation, v.[25]. The Ps. has an appropriate liturgical conclusion, v.[30-31]. The inserted Ps. is Maccabean, but the original Ps. is Davidic of the early Persian period. In the original Ps. there are many fine poetic conceptions, v.[17. 18. 23. 24]. In the inserted Ps. the use of שׁמע v.[6b] is late; מעטים v.[8] pl. elsw. only Ec. 5[1]. There is little real poetry in this piece.

PSALM CIX. *A.*

Str. I. A syn. couplet, enclosed between an introductory and a concluding line. — **1**. *O God of my praise*], phr. α.λ., the object of the praise of His people, cf. Dt. 10[21] Je. 17[14], — *keep not silent*], cf. 35[22] 39[13] 83[2], implying the positive answer to the prayer for help. — **2-5**. *For they speak with me*], in familiar conversation, and not in hostility as PBV., AV., JPSV., pretending to friendship, and so *with a lying tongue*. At the same time in their association with all others they show their hostility : *with words of hatred they compass me about, With hatred for my love*], cf. 35[12] 38[21]. Israel had responded to the pretended friendship with real love, which only called forth hatred in return. The editor who combined the two Pss. endeavoured to adapt this one to the other by prefixing v.[2a] : *the mouth of the wicked one*], the same as the one of v.[6 sq.] ; emphasized by : *even the mouth of deceit — is open against me*]. The text of 𝔊, 𝔙, 𝔍, followed by PBV., is to be preferred to that of 𝔐, followed by RV., "they opened," assimilated to the following vbs. This line is a prose sentence, and can be made into poetry only by serious changes. The same editor introduced v.[3b-5a] ; in part to still further show the connection of these slanderers with the wicked ruler of v.[6 sq.], and in part to emphasize the gratuitous character of the hostility : *and fight me without cause. For my love they are mine adversaries while I am in prayer, and they lay upon me evil for good*]. This is prosaic, and cannot be made into poetry without entire reconstruction of the sentences. The congregation were so friendly to their secret foes that they were in fact supplicating Yahweh on their account, while the foes were endeavouring to rally a host of enemies against them. At this point the editor introduces the imprecatory Ps. which will be considered later.

Str. II. Introverted parallelism. —**16-17 b.** *He remembered not to do kindness* ‖ *And he took no pleasure in blessing*]. In the friendly relation in which they were placed, he should have responded to the love of Israel and the good which Israel did him, with kindness ; and to Israel's prayer on his behalf with blessing. But his enmity was so great that he forgot benefits received, and took no pleasure at all in Israel's happiness. The editor connects this Str. of the original Ps. with the last Str. of the inserted imprecation by prefixing against the measure *Because that ;* and he also transposed v.[17a and b], and because of the antithesis added the sentence, *and it remained afar off from him,* making the line just these two words too long. The enclosed couplet states emphatically conduct justifying these words : *pursued*], with deliberate, persistent effort, with the purpose *to kill*], and, indeed, not only a friendly people as above, but one *afflicted and poor*], usual terms indicating national affliction ‖ *smitten in heart*], suffering in their inmost souls from the crushing blows they had received.

Str. III. A synth. tetrastich. — **17 a.** *And he loved cursing*], antith. the blessing he should have taken pleasure in, of the previous Str. ; and in ignoring of the love toward him of v.[5b]. — *and it came to him*], as a welcome guest, not in retribution as in the inserted imprecation, and further it took possession of him : **18.** *he clothed himself with it as his raiment*], his habitual and favourite clothing. — *And it came like water into his inwards*], with the refreshment of water to his thirst for doing harm to Israel. — *And like oil into his bones*], healing and soothing his frame, agitated with hatred and malice. The fact that this Str. is placed between two imprecations induces many to think of imprecations here also ; but it is difficult to change the text so as to make the vbs. all jussives ; especially in view of the fact that the jussive forms of the vbs. of the imprecatory Strs. are so well defined. The imprecation which follows, v.[19-20], seems to be editorial, and not a part of the imprecatory Ps. v.[6-15]. — **19.** *Let it be to him as the garment he putteth on* ‖ *and for the girdle with which he is always girded*]. This is the transformation of the statement of fact of v.[18] into a couplet of imprecation with the same simile. — **20.** *Let this be the wage of my adversaries from Yahweh, and of those who speak evil against me*]. This is an imprecation of exact retribution, cf. Is. 40[10] 61[8] 62[11].

Str. IV. Two syn. couplets. — **21**. *Yahweh, work Thou with me ‖ deliver me*]. The deliverance implied is a work which Yahweh alone can work in dealing with His people and on their behalf. A glossator emphasizes the divine name by adding " Adonay " and a plea " for Thy name's sake," and a seam to make it antithetical to the inserted imprecation, " But Thou " ; each and all of which additions impair the measure and the simple poetic conception, — *According to the goodness of Thy kindness*], so 𝕲, which is greatly to be preferred to 𝔥, followed by EV⁸, " for Thy kindness is good," conceived as an additional plea, assimilated to the previous gloss. — **22**. *For I am afflicted and poor*], resuming v.¹⁶ᵇ. — *And my heart writhes within me*], in throes of anguish, as 𝕲, 𝖄, 𝕾, to be preferred to 𝔥, Aq., 𝔍, " is wounded," followed by EV⁸.

Str. V. Two syn. couplets. — **23**. *As a shadow when it is stretched out*], cf. 102¹², as the day declines toward sunset, — *when the light grows stronger*], the advancing light of dawn. By this easy emendation the line harmonizes with the previous one, and we avoid the abrupt introduction of the " locust," which does not seem appropriate in this connection. The locust is indeed shaken up and down by a strong wind, and so might be an appropriate simile of helplessness. But there is no suggestion of a storm in the context, and the vb. properly means *I am shaken out*, that is of life, ‖ *I depart* from life. The conception is, that as the day declines his life departs, and that at the dawn of another day he is shaken out of life as by a spasm. — **24**. *My knees totter from fasting*]. He has fasted so long and so strictly in his humiliation before God and in the anxiety of long-continued pleading that he no longer has strength to walk, ‖ *and my flesh without oil is as one hasting away*]. He has abstained from oil so long that his flesh has become hard, coarse, and shrunken, and resembles that of a man hasting away out of life. A glossator adds **25**. *And I am become a reproach to them : when they see me, they shake their head*], the first line based on 31¹², cf. 79⁴ 89⁴², the second on 22⁸.

Str. VI. Two syn. couplets. — **26**. *Help me ‖ Save me*], renewal of the plea v.¹·²¹. — **27**. *And they*, the adversaries, *will know that this is Thy hand ‖ Thou hast done it*], namely, the work of deliverance of v.²¹.

The glossator appends to the original Ps. **28-29**. *Let them curse, but mayest Thou bless*], taking up the term of v.[17]; it matters little whether they bless as they ought, or curse as they ought not, so long as the people have the blessing of their God. These vbs. are jussives, as EV*., because they come from the same hand as v.[19-20]. — *Let them that rise up against me be shamed*], so 𝔊, 𝔍, PBV., to be preferred to 𝔐, followed by AV., which gives a rendering impossible to either text, and RV. which has protasis and apodosis of a temporal clause, possible but awkward. — *but let Thy servant be glad*], in antithesis with their shame, — *Let mine adversaries be clothed with confusion, and let them put on their shame as a robe*], using the same simile as v.[19] in slightly varying terms.

PSALM CIX. *B.*

Str. I. Syn. couplets. — **6**. *Appoint a wicked one over him*]. Yahweh is invoked to put on trial the wicked ruler, and in exact retribution to make his judge as wicked as himself, ‖ *And let an adversary stand at his right hand*]. The adversary stands in order to make a charge against him and press it home before the wicked judge. While the word for adversary is the same as that for Satan, the context does not suggest a trial in the court of heaven, as Zc. 3[1], where a wicked judge would be impossible, but on earth, where supreme judges are not unfrequently supreme in wickedness. — **7**. *When he is judged, let him come forth* ‖ *And let the decision of his case be*]. The syn. term suggested by Is. 28[7] instead of the " prayer " of 𝔐 and ancient Vrss., followed by EV*.; which does not suit the context, whether we think of a prayer to God, the only usage of the word, or a prayer to the wicked judge, which has no support in Hebrew usage.—*condemned*], as wicked, ‖ *guilt*, of sin. Even a righteous judge would make such a decision in this case ; but that a wicked judge should so decide greatly aggravates the situation to the wicked man, who is in the habit of depending on bribery and wickedness rather than on righteousness.

Str. II. Syn. couplets.—**8**. *Let his days be few*], not of life but of position, as ‖ *His office let another take*]. The whole context shows that a wicked ruler is in mind.—**9**. *Let his children*

2B

become fatherless, And his wife become a widow], by his speedy
death, the implication being that he has been condemned to capital
punishment for the wicked administration of his office.

Str. III. Syn. couplets. — **10.** *Let his children wander about
and beg* ∥ *Let them be banished from their desolate homes*].
The last line is after ⅏, 𝔙, which is more suited to the context
than 𝔐, followed by EV., "seek (their bread) out of their desolate places"; for the former represents that they have been driven
forth from their desolate homes by creditors in accordance with
the subsequent context, and gives the reason why they are home-
less wanderers and altogether destitute. The latter simply represents them as seeking a home and food in desolate parts; strange
places in which to beg for food. Several moderns seek a better
sense from 𝔐 by rendering "far from their ruined home," which
is quite possible, and certainly an improvement on EVˢ. — **11.** *Let
a creditor* ∥ *strangers*]. The creditors, especially as foreigners,
not subject to the restrictions of Hebrew law, take advantage of
his condemnation to death and appear upon the scene; whether
with just claims or not, it matters little, for they will be sustained
by the wicked judge, to whom they will give a share in their spoil;
and their victim is helpless in their hands. — *strike him for what
he hath* ∥ *take his labour as spoil*]. They seize upon his possessions, and take to themselves all that he has laid up by his labour,
by his wicked and unscrupulous dealings with others.

Str. IV. Syn. couplets. — **12.** *Let him have none that extendeth
kindness*]. Ordinarily in such a case a man has some friends or
neighbours who sympathize with him and are kind to him; especially if he has been a man of rank and position, his sudden fall
from so great a height of wealth and power excites the pity even
of strangers. But this man was so wicked that even this would
be withheld from him; and still further his children would share
in his reprobation; *And let there be no favour to his orphans*],
after he had suffered capital punishment for his crimes. — **13.** *Let
his posterity be for cutting off*]. His orphaned children are not
only to be reprobates, banished from home; but their doom is also
a speedy death, as the context indicates, because of destitution
from exposure and hunger. ∥ *In a generation let his name be
blotted out*]. His posterity are not to extend beyond the genera-

tion then living; with their death the name of their father would no longer be on the earth. 𝕲, 𝖁, have " one " before generation, 𝕳, Aq., Σ, 𝕵, "another " or "next," both of which are probably interpretations; although they may have been variant readings, for in Heb. the words differ only by a single letter, which is easily mistaken. There can be little doubt that the text of 𝕲, 𝕵, " his name," the name of the guilty father, is to be preferred to " their name " of 𝕳, that of the children who had not yet made themselves a name.

Str. V. A syn. and a synth. couplet. — **14.** *The iniquity of his fathers ‖ the sin of his mother*]. It is here assumed that the wicked ruler had wicked parents, both on the male and on the female side. The guilt of these parents, not yet adequately atoned for, is imprecated upon him. — *Let (it) be remembered ‖ not be blotted out*], from memory, and so estimated in the amount of retribution. — **15.** *Let them*, these sins, *be in the sight of Yahweh continually*], so that He will never lose sight of them or overlook them, with the purpose *That He may cut off his memory from the earth*], exterminate him, the wicked man and his name, as v.[13b], and not " their memory," that of his ancestors, as 𝕳 and Vrss. by an easy copyist's mistake.

A liturgical addition was ultimately made to the Ps. to make it more suitable for public worship. — **30-31.** *I will give thanks to Yahweh, exceedingly with my mouth. In the midst of the multitude will I praise Him. For He standeth at the right hand of the poor, To save from the adversaries of his life*]. Public praise in the congregation of Israel will be given to Yahweh for His salvation of His people from the wicked oppressor. He stands at their right hand as advocate, in antithesis with the adversary at the right hand of the wicked. The wicked judge would in his unrighteousness condemn Israel, were it not for their divine advocate, because the adversaries of his life are also there. The term " adversaries " of the Ps. is more probable than " judges " of 𝕳 and Vrss.

CIX. A.

1. אֱלֹהֵי תְהִלָּתִי] so 𝕵, Aq., Σ, 𝕸; phr. α.λ., but 𝕲[N. A. R. T] ὁ θεὸς τὴν αἴνεσίν μου, 𝖁 *Deus, laudem meam*, 𝕿 אלהים שבחיי.—2. פִּי רָשָׁע] interp. by פִּי מָרְמָה suggests that we should rd. רָעָיו; so Hare, Houb., De W., Hi., Now., Bä., Valeton. But רָשָׁע prob. refers to an individual, whether Antiochus as Bar. Heb., or some

other tyrant. At all events, l. is a prosaic gl. — פתחו] but 𝔊ᴬ·ᴬ·ᴿ·ᵀ, 𝔍, Du., פְּתוּחַ more prob.; both interp. of an original פרח. — דִּבְּרוּ אִתִּי] phr. of E, P, Je., Ez.; *with*, not *against*. — **3.** וַיִּקְחֲבוּנִי חִנָּם] is a gl. continuing through v.⁵ᵃ, entirely prosaic in character. as חִנָּם as 35⁷. — **4.** יִשְׂטְנוּנִי as 38²¹, due to ישׂטן v.⁶. — וַאֲנִי תְפִלָּה] phr. α.λ., but cf. 120⁷. — **5.** וַיָּשִׂימוּ עָלַי] Bä., Valeton, after 𝔖 וישלמוני improb. — וַיָּשִׂיבוּ, פרעוני; Bi., Che., וישלמוני improb. — רעה תחת טובה] from 35¹² 38²¹.

CIX. B.

6. הַפְקֵד] Hiph. imv. פקד Hiph. *appoint, make overseer, 85* c. עַל as Gn. 39⁴ Je. 1¹⁰ Nu. 1⁵⁰ + 9 t. — ‡ שָׂטָן] n.m. *adversary ; not* Satan as Zc. 3¹·²·² Jb. 1⁶ + 13 t.; cf. v.⁴. — **7.** רָשָׁע] as 𝔊ᴺ·ᴬ·ᴿ·ᵀ, 𝔖, 𝔗, 𝔍, *one condemned as wicked.* — תְּפִלָּתוֹ] although sustained by Vrss., improb. Che. suggests פְלוּטָתוּ; but פליליתו as Is. 28⁷ is better suited to context. — חֲטָאָה] *guilt of sin*, cf. 32¹ 40⁷. — **8.** מְעַטִּים] pl. elsw. Ec. 5¹. — פְּקֻדָּה] ‡ כְּהֻנָּה n.f. *office, charge*, as Nu. 4¹⁶ (P) 1 Ch. 26³⁰ 2 Ch. 23¹⁸. 𝔊 τὴν ἐπισκοπὴν, so Acts 1²); 𝔍 *episcopatum ;* but BDB., Du., *store* as Is. 15⁷. — **9.** אַלְמָנָה] needs vb. to complete l.; prob. תהיה as Che. — **10.** וְנֹעַ יְנוּעוּ] inf. abs. is a gl. of intensification, making l. too long. — וְדֹרְשׁוּ 𝔊ᴺ·ᴬ·ᴿ·ᵀ ἐκβληθήτωσαν, יְגֹרְשׁוּ is more suited to context, as Kenn., Street, Horsley, Houb., Bä., Ecker, Valeton. — מֵחָרְבוֹתֵיהֶם] has two tones: prep. *from* with vb. גרשׁ; if with דרשׁ not *out of* but *away from*. חָרְבָּה n.f. *waste, ruin*, of cities 9⁷, here from context of dwellings, home. — **11.** יְנַקֵּשׁ נוֹשֶׁה] vb. as 38¹³ *strike at*, 𝔊ᴺ·ᴬ·ᴿ·ᵀ, 𝔍, יְבַקֵּשׁ נוֹשֶׁה] Qal ptc. *creditor, usurer*, elsw. Ex. 22²⁴ (E) 2 K. 4¹ Is. 24² 50¹. — יָבֹזּוּ וְ] coörd. with juss. ‡ בזז vb. *spoil* α.λ. ψ, but common elsw. — **13.** אַחֲרִיתוֹ] *his posterity* 𝔊 as 37³⁷, but 𝔖, 𝔍, 𝔗, *his end.* — בְּדוֹר אַחֵר] so Aq., Σ, 𝔖, 𝔍 ; but אחד 𝔊ᴺ·ᴬ·ᴿ·ᵀ, 𝔜, Houb., Horsley, Du., Che ; prob. both interpretations. — שְׁמָכ] but שְׁמוֹ 𝔊, 𝔍, Horsley, Che., more prob. — **14.** אֶל יהוה] makes l. too long and is a gl. — **15.** זִכְרָם] pl. sf. improb.; rd. זִכְרִי, cf. v.¹³ᵇ.

CIX. A.

16. יַעַן אֲשֶׁר] a gl. as a seam, connecting the two Pss. — וְנִרְאָה] Niph. † כאה vb. *be disheartened*, BDB., as Dn. 11³⁾. Hiph. Ez. 13²² (?); but cf. וְנִרְאָה רוּחַ Pr. 15¹³ 17²² 18¹⁴, נְכֵה רוּחַ Is. 66². 𝔊ᴺ·ᴬ·ᴿ·ᵀ κατανενυγμένον τῇ καρδίᾳ, 𝔍 *conpunctum corde*, Aq., Σ, πεπληγμένον τῇ καρδίᾳ, Hi., Bä., rd. וְיִרָא לֵבָב. — **17.** וְלֹא חָפֵץ בברכה]. This makes a complete l. ‖ v.16ᵃ, with which it originally formed introverted parall. It was transposed, and assimilated to its antith. by adding two words, יְרַחֵק רִמֶּנּוּ, at the expense of the measure. — ‡ קְלָלָה] n.f. *curse*, as Dt. 11²⁶ + 10 t. D. It is repeated in v.¹⁸ because of its separation from v.¹⁷ᵃ. The original was prob. אָ.רָה. — **18.** ‡ [יֵ] n.m. *garment*, as Ju. 3¹⁶ +. — **19.** † מֵזַח] n.m. *girdle* BDB., Egyptian loan word, elsw. Is. 23¹⁰, but dub., cf. † מְזִיחַ Jb. 12²¹. — **20.** אֵת יהוה] is prob. a gl., although v.¹⁹⁻²⁰ are a late addition to Ps. — **21.** יהוה אדני] conflation, prob. of Kt. and Qr.; but with the omission of אדני the l. is still too long. Doubtless ואתה is a seam, and לְמַעַן שְׁמֶךָ a gl. of pleading. — כִּי טוֹב] 𝔗, Bä., כטוב is more prob. — **22.** חָלָל] so Aq., 𝔍, *vulnera-*
עָנִי ואביון אנכי] phr. 35¹⁰ 37¹⁴ 40¹⁸ 70⁶ 74²¹ 86¹. —

ium ; but 𝕲ᴺ·ᴬ·ᵀ τετάρακται, 𝖄 *conturbatum est,* so 𝔖 = יחיר Qal impf. חִוּר *writhe in anguish,* as 55⁵, Gr., Kau., Che., Valeton, is more prob. — **23.** וְהִרְלַחְתִּי] Niph. *a.λ.,* i.p. prob. assimilated to נגערתי. Qal is used in the sense required here. — ננערתי] Niph. ‡ נער as Jb. 38¹³ Ju. 16²⁾ *be shaken out.* Pi. *shake off,* Ps. 136¹⁵ as Ex. 14²⁷ (J) Ne. 5¹³. — וְאַרְבֶה] is improb., though sustained by Vrss.; for *locust* may be shaken up and down, to and fro, by the wind, and so rendered helpless ; but the vb. has not this mng., and the context does not suggest a storm. Rd. כאור רבה as *the light* of day *grows stronger.* — **24.** יָחֵש] vb. Qal *a.λ.*; Pi. *cringe 18⁴⁵,* a sense inappropriate here. 𝕲ᴺ·ᴬ·ᴿ·ᵀ ἠλλοιώθη δι' ἔλαιον, 𝖄 *immutata est propter oleum,* 𝔍 *mutata est,* so 𝔖 ; 𝕮 פהרן, Σ ὑπὸ ἀνηλειψίας. The context suggests the prep. כ and the Qal ptc. חָש of חוּש *as one hasting away.* — **25** is a gl.; the first l. from 31¹², cf. 79⁴ 89⁴², the second from 22³. — **26.** וְחִסְרֶךָ]. As this l. is too short, rd. כטוב הס־ך as v.²¹ᵇ, with which it is ∥. — **28.** וְיַחְלְלוּ]. This and the following vb. are prob. juss. of imprecation, as they are gls. of the final editor ; although it is possible to take them as indicatives. — רָבָה and אַתָּה in antith. make l. tetrameter, as the mate is ; not surprising if a gl., although it is against the measure of both original Pss. — קָמוּ וַיֵּבשׁוּ] so 𝔍, followed by ו consec. of pf. may be interpreted as prot. and apod. of temporal or conditional clause ; but 𝕲 οἱ ἐπανιστανόμενοί μοι αἰσχυνθήτωσαν = קָמַי יֵבשׁוּ is better suited to the context and more prob.; so Du., Gr., Bä., Kau., Ehr., Valeton. — **29.** ‡ מְעִיל] n.m. *robe, a.λ. ψ,* but common elsw.; fig. of attribute Is. 59¹⁷ 61¹⁰ Jb. 29¹⁴. — **31.** מִשֹּׁפְטֵי] but 𝕲ᴺ·ᴬ·ᴿ·ᵀ, 𝔖, 𝖄, 𝔍 שעפטיכ, which makes נפשו more suitably obj. of vb. It seems best to rd. משטני, the common term of these gls., v.⁴·²⁰·²⁹.

PSALM CX., 2 STR. 5⁵.

Ps. 110 is a didactic Messianic Ps. (1) The Psalmist lets David cite an utterance enthroning his lord at the right hand of Yahweh, with a strong sceptre to overcome his enemies. People volunteer for the war in multitudes like dewdrops at dawn (v.¹⁻³). (2) He cites an oath of Yahweh, making him priest forever (v.⁴). He goes forth to war, overcomes kings and nations, and is exalted in victory (v.⁵⁻⁷).

UTTERANCE of Yahweh to *my* lord : " Sit enthroned at *My* right hand, Till I make *thine* enemies a stool for *thy* feet.
With the rod of *thy* strength rule in the midst of *thine* enemies."
Volunteers on the sacred (mountains) are *thy* people, in the day of *thy* host:
From the womb of the morn come forth to *thee* the dew of *thy* youth.
YAHWEH hath sworn, He is not sorry : " Thou art a priest forever."
My (lord) at (*His*) right hand doth smite in the day of *His* anger.
He executeth judgment on kings. He doth fill the valleys with nations.
He doth smite chiefs, (going over) a wide land,
(An inheritance) on the way he maketh it, therefore he is exalted.

Ps. 110 was in 𝔅, then in 𝔐 (*v.* Intr. §§ 27, 31). It was not used in 𝔅ℜ. The Ps. in its present form is very late: (*a*) The words הדרי for הררת v.³ᵃ, עַל דברתי for עַל דבר v.⁴ᵇ are late formations, but the latter is a gloss and the former an error for הררי. (*b*) The sentence עַל דברתי מלכי־צדק v.⁴ᵇ is based on the story of Melchizedek Gn. 14, which many critics regard as a post-exilic *midrash*, and also gives an explanation involving an anxiety to distinguish this priesthood from the Aaronic, and so the period of the supremacy of the priestly Law. But this being a gloss, it does not give evidence as to the original Ps. (*c*) There is a reference v.⁷ to the story of Gideon's men lapping water Ju. 7⁴⁻⁸; but it is doubtful whether such a reference was in the original text. On the basis of these, many scholars refer the Ps. to the Maccabean times and to Jonathan, Hi., Ols., Bä., cf. 1 Mac. 10²⁰, or to Simon. The suggestion of G. Margoliouth that Simon's name is in the letters beginning certain lines of the Ps. שמעון, though suggested independently by Bi. and sustained by Du., Charles, al., is based on arbitrary arrangement, and is against the usage of acrostics (*v.* Kö. *Einleitung*, S. 404). There are insuperable objections to any of the Maccabean princes. (*a*) They were not of the posterity of David, and the hopes of the nation as to the Davidic dynasty could not in fact gather about them. The Psalter of Solomon 17²³ ˢᑫ, in the first century B.C., looks for a son of David, and not for a Maccabean. The utterance and oath of Yahweh v.¹· ⁴ refer to the covenant of David 2 S. 7 Ps. 2⁷ and the oath of Yahweh 89⁴· ³⁶· ⁵⁰ 132¹¹. None but a son of David could enter into the mind of a Jewish poet. The reference to the Davidic covenant also favours the view that it is the Davidic dynasty that the poet has in mind, the seed of David of Nathan's prediction. The glorification of the dynasty at its covenant institution was the greatest glorification that could be given to any of the line of succession in that dynasty. We are obliged, therefore, to go back to the time of the Davidic dynasty, unless we regard the Ps. as altogether ideal. (*b*) The priest here is a king, or at least a sovereign lord. The Maccabeans were born priests of the line of Aaron before they attained sovereignty. They were not instituted as priests by divine oath. It was least of all appropriate to speak of any of them as a priest after the order of Melchizedek, implying not after the order of Aaron. In fact, it is just this that is emphasized, that the priest is not a priest as such, of an order of priests; but a priest in the more primitive sense, when a king like Melchizedek could be priest although he was king. The conception of the monarch as priest is a primitive conception, earlier than the establishment of the Aaronic priesthood of P, earlier even than the Deuteronomic conception of the Levitical priesthood, just such a conception as that in the earliest historical documents, of Jethro Ex. 2¹⁶ 3¹ 18¹ (JE) and of princes 2 S. 8¹⁸ 20²⁶ 1 K. 4⁵ (Judaic sources). The Ps. must therefore be pre-Deuteronomic. The words "after the order of Melchizedek" destroy the measure of the Ps. and are a gloss, giving an explanatory distinction, made necessary when the Aaronic priesthood filled the minds of the people and a Ps. using this ancient terminology needed to be explained.

Gr. refers the Ps. to Jeshua, the great high-priest of the Restoration, in accordance with Zc. 6¹²⁻¹⁷, where he interprets the two crowns as for Jeshua and the צמח 3⁸ as referring to Jeshua. But the צמח has already become a title of a Davidic monarch Je. 23⁵⁻⁸ 33¹⁴⁻²² (v. Br.ᴹᴾ·⁴⁹⁶), and Zerubbabel of the Davidic line is in the mind of the prophet rather than Jeshua the high-priest, and the predicted צמח is to be a priest-king, the crowning of Jeshua being symbolical of his crowning and enthronement. The reference to the crowning of Jeshua Zc. 6¹¹ᵇ is denied by We., Now., as a gloss; and Ew., Hi., al., think of two crowns, the royal one and the priestly one, for two different persons. Whatever interpretation we may make of this passage, there is yet an antithesis between king and priest which we do not find in Ps. 110. The same utterance which enthrones him is an oath making him priest, and this was in the covenant of David at the institution of the dynasty and is a very different conception from the reëstablishment of the kingdom. The author of the Ps. knows nothing of a dominion in the future and so postponed, or of a period of humiliation of the king and people such as is seen in Pss. 89, 132. The dynasty installed knows no defeat and is everywhere victorious, therefore the Ps. must be preëxilic, and not only pre-Deuteronomic, but earlier than the Assyrian invasions and not later than Jehoshaphat, who was in some respects appropriate as a representative of the conquering king of David's line. This Ps. is earlier than Ps. 2, because it does not contemplate a universal kingdom and rebellious nations. It resembles Ps. 18 in its victory over an indefinite number of kings and nations. The Ps. probably has the song of Deborah in mind, Ju. 5², in its emphasis upon the volunteering of the people in the army of the king, and possibly the victory of Jehoshaphat over the Ammonites, Moabites, and Edomites 2 Ch. 20 The question now remains, whether a poet here speaks his own mind as a court poet, or the mind of the people and their hopes in the dynasty, or whether he makes David, the father of the dynasty, speak his hopes respecting his own dynasty. The former reference does not seem so appropriate when the people are represented as עמך and ילדתך v.³, unless we suppose that the people who utter the Ps. are thinking of another and a later people and body of young men than themselves. It is improbable that the poet speaks merely for himself. It is most probable that he lets David speak his hopes as those in which the people of the seed may join. The Ps. has two syn. Strs., each of five pentameter lines. In the first Str. the first line before caesura and at end has assonance in i, the remaining four lines before caesura and at the end all in ka. In the second Str. the first line has assonance in am. In the other lines there is no assonance in 𝔐, but the text as restored shows assonance of second line in ō, of third and fifth lines in im, of fourth line in ah.

Jesus cites and interprets v.¹ thus: " David himself said in the Holy Spirit, 'The Lord said unto my Lord, Sit thou on my right hand, till I make thine enemies the footstool of thy feet.' David himself calleth him Lord: and whence is he his son?" Mk. 12³⁶⁻³⁷. Mt. in citing from Mk. changes the first clause into an interrogative, " How then doth David in the Spirit call him Lord, saying"; and makes the quotation, "Till I put thine enemies underneath thy feet," and the final clause, "If David then calleth him Lord, how is he his son?" Mt. 22[43-45]. Lk. also citing from Mk. changes the first clause, "For David himself saith in the Book of Psalms," gives the quotation as in Mk. and slightly varies the third clause: "David therefore calleth him Lord, and how is he his son?" Lk. 20[42-44]. The argument rests upon David's having said these words in the Ps., and it is justified if the author of the Ps. lets David appear as spokesman (*v.* Br.[SHS. p. 265]). It does not require Davidic authorship of the Ps. We might say, furthermore, that Jesus is arguing on the basis of the common opinion as to the author of the Ps., and that either he did not in his Kenosis know otherwise, or else, if he knew, did not care to correct the opinion (*v.* Plummer[Luke. pp. 472-473]); but the latter view can be maintained only on the theory that he is arguing from the premises of his opponents to confute and to silence them, which he actually does without endorsing the premise himself. These words, by whomsoever uttered, have a Messianic reference to the seed of David in accordance with the covenant with David, and they do not lose their Messianic reference even though in the mouth of another. This Ps. is assigned in the Roman and Sarum use for Christmas and the Circumcision of Christ.

Str. I. is composed of a synth. tristich and a syn. distich. — **1.** The psalmist speaks, not for himself as an individual, but for David in his seed, in accordance with 2 S. 7[18-29], where he praises God that He has promised so much greater things for his seed than He has granted to himself. In view of the fact that the seed was to build the temple and as the son of God have an eternal throne, it was not too much for a poet to let David speak of his son as his lord. The view that the people of Israel, over whom the Davidic dynasty reigned by divine appointment, spoke these words, is not sustained by the context. — David cites the covenant with him as an *Utterance of Yahweh*], an utterance to a prophet in the ecstatic state (cf. Nu. 24[3 sq.] 2 S. 23[1 sq.]), a synonym of the "vision" 2 S. 7[17] in which Yahweh spake to Nathan the words of the covenant (cf. Ps. 89[20]), interpreted as an חק Ps. 2[7]. This utterance was mediately through Nathan, but addressed *to my lord*], the sovereign of Israel, the seed of David, the Davidic dynasty. Its contents were: *Sit enthroned at My right hand*], the right hand, the seat of the highest honor (cf. Ps. 45[10]), occupy a throne nearest to Yahweh, implying therefore the sonship relation; cf. Ps. 2[6. 7]. — *Till I make thine enemies a stool for thy feet*]. Yahweh is the one who subdues the enemies here as in 2⁵. The line is synth.; but the second part of it is suggested by the sitting enthroned, the feet resting upon a footstool composed of subdued enemies. — **2**. The enthroned lord now himself becomes active. — *With the rod of thy strength*], the strong, powerful, massive sceptre or mace, suggested as held in the hand, in antithesis to the stool for his feet; cf. 2⁹, where the Messiah rules with a rod of iron. — *In the midst of thine enemies*]. He goes forth into the battle and uses his strong rod; as in 2⁹ he dashes them in pieces like a potter's vessel. — A later editor inserts here a gloss of petition, *May Yahweh send it out of Zion*], implying impatience for the realisation of the promise, such as characterises Pss. 89, 123, but is foreign to the tone of this Psalm. — **3**. The Str. concludes with a syn. distich, which is, however, synth. to the previous tristich. That tells of the activity of Yahweh and the king, this of the people of the king. As in ancient times the people volunteered to follow Deborah and Barak Ju. 5², so here, *Volunteers are thy people*]. They are ready and eager to follow their king, *in the day of thy host*], on the day when the host is mustered for war. They assemble *on the sacred mountains*], as 𝔍, 𝚺, especially appropriate to the syn. simile of the dew. The sacred mountains are sacred because they are God's foundation, the place of His temple 87¹, and as the place of the king's installation 2⁶; but 𝔥, 𝔊, have "in sacred ornaments," cf. 29² 96⁹, implying an army of priests, in accordance with the conception of the nation as a kingdom of priests in the covenant of Horeb Ex. 19⁶. This is the interpretation of Rev. 19¹⁴, and is appropriate in itself and ancient. But it seems premature to mention priestly warriors before the priesthood of the king, which does not appear till the next Str. — The volunteers are compared to *dew*], drops of dew, abundant and fresh in vigor. They are *thy youth*], thy young men, with youthful enthusiasm and strength. They appear on the sacred mountains, as it were covering them in their battle array as dewdrops cover the mountains in the early morning, seeming to be born *From the womb of the morn*], cf. 133³.

Str. **II**. is syn. with the first, composed of three syn. ll. preceded by a single line to which they are synth., and followed by a single line of climax. There is only a general correspondence

with the first Str. — **4.** *Yahweh hath sworn*] ∥ to "utterance of
Yahweh" v.¹, another interpretation of the covenant of David,
sustained by the usage of 89⁴·³⁶·⁵⁰ 132¹¹. — *He is not sorry*]. It
is an unchangeable oath, just as in 2 S. 7¹⁶ the kingdom is made
sure, cf. Ps. 89²⁹. — *Thou art a priest forever*], that is, a priest-
king, as Jethro Ex. 2¹⁶ 3¹ 18¹ (JE), and princes of David 2 S. 8¹⁸
20²⁶ 1 K. 4⁵, all in sources of early history, not involving priestly
office, but priestly functions of king. This is explained by a
gloss : *after the order of Melchizedek*, that is, he was not a Levitical priest of Deuteronomic law, or an Aaronic priest of the priest-
code, but one after the order of Melchizedek, the friend of Abraham, Gn. 14. — **5.** *My lord*], just as in v.¹, and not *Lord* of
MT., which makes God the subject of subsequent vbs., which is
appropriate v.⁵, improbable v.⁶, and impossible v.⁷, there being
nothing to suggest change of subject. The parall. suggests the
same reference as v.¹, and this makes the king the subject of all
following verbs and removes all difficulties. So we must read
at His right hand, which is also favoured by assonance with "His
anger," and not "thy right hand," which was due to the interpretation of אדני as Lord, and which also involves the transposing of the position of Yahweh and the king from that of v.¹. —
doth smite] ∥ rule with strong rod v.². 𝔅 makes "kings" the
obj. of "smite," but this destroys the measure, making this line
too long, the next too short. — *in the day of His anger*], the day
of battle, ∥ with "the day of his host" v.³. — **6.** *He executeth
judgment*], that is, in battle, by overthrow. — *On kings*], obj. here
instead of above, as 𝔅. Kings lead the army of enemies, as in
2²·¹⁰ they plot, and are warned. — *He doth fill the valleys with
nations*], after 𝔊, 𝔍, "valleys," instead of 𝔅 "dead bodies," and
attaching "nations" to the vb. "fill," instead ˜ 𝔅 "fill (it) with
dead bodies." The nations in the valle͜   ⹁ Jo. 4¹²⁻¹⁴, where
they are assembled for judgment in the valley of Jehoshaphat,
based on the narrative of the victory of Jehoshaphat over the
Moabites and Ammonites in the valley 2 Ch. 20¹⁶⁻²⁶, to which
possibly also the Ps. refers. — *He doth smite chiefs*], that is, with
his mace, rod of strength. He smites the leaders of his enemies,
going over a wide land]. The battle-field is extended, and the
land of the enemies over which he pursues them is far away. —

7. A change in text, chiefly in pointing, enables us to read : *An inheritance on the way he maketh it*]. He takes possession of the wide land, the battle-field, and the land of the enemy, as his inheritance ; cf. 2⁸, where Yahweh gives the Messiah the nations as his inheritance. This gives us the climax to the previous lines, and sustains *therefore he is exalted;* that is, in the joy of victory and sovereignty. 𝕳 gives, " of the brook in the way he drinketh," as the men of Gideon lapped at the spring of Harod Ju. 7, in a rough and ready way of drinking, not waiting for drinking vessels, but in a hurry for battle. This suits the context, but does not give a good climax. 𝕳 also has " lifteth up his head." This suits the drinking of the brook, but the line is too long and the conclusion is weak. The word for " head " has crept into the text from the previous line.

1. נְאֻם] *utterance, declaration, revelation; v. 36².* — שֵׁב] Qal imv. ישב pregn. *sit* enthroned 2⁴. — עַד־אָשִׁית] final clause; properly takes cohort. form אָשִׁיתָה, but this rule is not carried out even in earliest and most classic literature. שׁית with double accusative, *make* a person or thing into another thing; so 18¹² 21¹³ 84⁷ 88⁹. — הֲדֹם לְרַגְלֶיךָ] *stool for thy feet;* † הֲדֹם n.m. never apart, never literal: † phr. used of Yahweh ; earth as His footstool Is. 66¹, the sanctuary La. 2¹ (cf. מקום ר׳ Is. 60¹³), place of His enthronement in Israel, the cherubic platform Ps. 99⁵ 132⁷ 1 Ch. 28²; here only of the enemies of the Messianic king. This v. has two pentameters with assonance at the caesura and end of l. : לרגליך, איביך ; לימיני, לאדני. — **2.** מַטֵּה עֻזְּךָ] *thy strong staff,* so Je. 48¹⁷ מַטֵּה עֹז of Moab, cf. שבט ברזל Ps. 2⁹. — יִשְׁלַח יהוה מצּיון] is an abrupt change of subj. in midst of Str., incongruous with 2d pers. which precedes and follows. It is a gl. of petition, destroying the measure and the assonance, for עֻזְּךָ and איביך mark the two parts of the pentameter. — **3.** יֹמְךָ] so 𝕵. μετὰ σοῦ 𝕲ᴺ·ᴬ·ᴿ·ᵀ; Aq., 𝕾, *tecum,* עִמְּךָ. — נְדָבֹת] pl. abstr. *voluntariness,* readiness to volunteer for the war, *v. 54⁸;* Aq. ἐκουσιασμοί, 𝕵 *spontanei.* Some think of *free-will offerings,* but there is nothing to suggest it in context ; cf. התנדב for volunteering for war Ju. 5². ⁹. But 𝕲ᴺ ἀρχή, 𝕲ᴺ·ᶜ·ᵃ·ᴬ·ᴿ·ᵀ ἡ ἀρχή, 𝕾 *principium* נְדִיבָה n.f. as Jb. 30¹⁵; cf. נָדִיב adj. *princely in rank* Ps. 47¹⁰ +. — בְּיוֹם חֵילֶךָ] *in the day of thy host,* the day of the military array for war, of mustering of forces; cf. 33¹⁶· ¹⁷ 136¹⁵. — בְּהַדְרֵי קֹדֶשׁ] *in sacred ornaments,* cf. הֲדְרַת ק׳ Pss. 29² 96⁹ 1 Ch. 16²⁹ 2 Ch. 20²¹, always used in connection with public worship of Yahweh and implying priestly ornaments. This conception is in accord with that of the king as כהן: his army would be a priestly army ; cf. Rev. 19¹⁴, where the cavalry of the Messiah is " clothed in fine linen, white and pure " (probably an interpretation of our passage); cf. Ex. 19⁶, where the nation is " a kingdom of priests." But why הררי for הררת ? 𝕵 has *in montibus sanctis,* cf. 87¹ הַרְרֵי קֹדֶשׁ ; so Σ and many Heb.

codd., Hare, Houb., Ol^{s.}, Hu., We., Bä., Davies, al. This suits the figure of the *dew*, and is also appropriate to the place of mustering and in accord with the installation 2⁶. There has been a transposition of words by copyist, and so the assonance has been destroyed. The original order was prob.: [מֵרֶחֶם מִשְׁחָר] phr. α.λ. — נדבת עמך בהררי־קדש ביום־חילך † מִשְׁחָר n.m. α.λ. for usual שַׁחַר *dawn*, is suspicious; prob. dittog. of מ. ᵍ takes this ם as prep. πρὸ ἑωσφόρου, Θ ἀπὸ πρωΐ, 𝔙 *ante luciferum;* 𝔖 מֵן קריב, also prep., thinking of the dawn of time ; Σ ὡς καθ᾽ ὄρθρον ; Aq. ἐξωρθρισμένης, ptc. שחר. — [יַלְדֻהֶךָ] † ילדתך n.f. *youth*, elsw. Ec. 11⁹. ¹⁰ abstr. for concrete *young men*, those assembled on the sacred mountains at the mustering of the volunteers. But ᵍ ᔆ. ᵉ· ᵃ· ᴬ· ᵀ has ἐκ γαστρὸς πρὸ ἑωσφόρου ἐγέννησά σε ; ᵍ ᔆ ἐξεγέννησά ; 𝔙 *ex utero ante luciferum genui te, from the womb before the morning star I begat thee*, pointing יְלִדְתִּךָ just as Ps. 2⁷. This ignores טַל, prob. because it was simply figurative. ᵍ is followed by Herder, Houb., Kenn., Minocchi, al. Other Vrss. agree with 𝔐. The assonance of this l. is in דך and ילדתך.—**4.** [נִשְׁבַּע יהוה‎ ‖ נאם יהוה v.¹; cf. 89⁴· ³⁶· ⁵⁰ 132¹¹.—[אַתָּה כֹהֵן לְעוֹלָם‎ כהן is usually employed for the priest of one of the historic orders. But there is also a usage in which it is applied to kings Gn. 14¹⁸ (Mid.), chiefs of tribes Ex. 2¹⁶ 3¹ 18¹ כהן מדין (JE), and princes 2 S. 8¹⁸ 20²⁶ 1 K. 4⁵, so prob. Ex. 19²²· ²⁴ (J) ; so Israel as a nation is a kingdom of priests Ex. 19⁶ (E), cf. Is. 61⁶ of Israel's ministry. In none of these instances is a specific priestly office involved. — [עַל־דִּבְרָתִי כַּלְכִּי־צֶדֶק] *after the order of Melchizedek*, that is, of the same kind as that of the ancient king of Jerusalem, to distinguish it from the Aaronic or Levitical priesthood. † [דִּבְרָה] n.f. late word ; without prep. only Jb. 5⁸ *suit, cause;* elsw. with עַל as prep. *because of* Ec. 3¹⁸ 7¹⁴ 8². The reference to the covenant of David and the attachment of the word to the king make it necessary to think of כהן in the earlier sense, in which it does not imply an order of priesthood distinct from royalty. There is no reference to priestly function in this Ps. This explanation involves a time when the Aaronic priesthood was so much in mind that the use of כהן in connection with the king needed explanation ; and it prob. also implies the story of Melchizedek, Gn. 14, as so well known that a reference to it would be readily understood in a congregational poem. Such an explanation would not have been thought necessary in a preëxilic Ps. This v. cannot, as it stands, be arranged in any good measure. It has four beats in the first part and four in the second part, acc. to 𝔐; but the second part has really five words. The Ps. is a pentameter in the first Str., and only one l. is needed in this v. We must therefore throw out the glosses for good measure. This explanation is a gl. of a later age. No poet would have constructed such a line. וְלֹא יִנָּחֵם has been changed from an original לֹא־נִחַם by adding conj. ו and changing pf. to impf. Assonance requires ם‏ָ not ם‏ֵ. The l. in its original form would then be : נִשְׁבַּע יהוה לֹא־נִחַם אַתָּה־כֹהֵן לְעוֹלָם. This is then essentially the same as 2 S. 7¹³, cf. Pss. 89⁴· ³⁶· ⁵⁰ 132¹¹.—**5–6.** [אֲדֹנָי]. The word is pointed as a divine name ; but point אֲדֹנִי, as v.¹. — [מָחַץ] vb. cf. 18³⁹, *smite through*, has מלכים as obj. acc. to verse division ; then ‖ מחץ ראש v.⁶. But this l. has too many words, and the next too few, for good measure. Therefore remove מלכים to next l., and make כהיק abs. — [ביום אפי || ביום חֵירֶך v.³; the day of Yahweh's wrath follows the day of muster of the army of His king. The king shatters the enemy here, as Yahweh makes the enemy His footstool in v.¹. — [וְיָדין Qal impf. דין; *execute judgment* in war, here, c. acc. Is אדני subj. ? This is most natural, carrying on subj. from previous v. This leaves only v.⁷, which it is impossible to attribute to Yahweh; and yet there is no hint of a change of subj., and why should the king drink of the brook unless he had done something to weary him? Most interpreters therefore think of the king as subj. of v.⁶. But the difficulty remains, that in the previous v. he has been referred to in the 2d pers. The difficulty could be easily removed by reading, instead of עַל ימינך, עַל ימיני, and interpreting אדני as אֵדֶ־נִי, referring to the king. This change is desirable (1) as securing the assonance found in previous ll., אפי, ימיני; (2) as making אדני in both Strs. refer to the king, and so avoiding a change of attitude from the right hand of Yahweh to the right hand of the king; (3) as enabling us to regard the king as the subj. throughout the Str. The sf. of 2d pers. originated from interp. אדני as divine name. Read, therefore: אדני עַל־ימיני מהץ ביום אפו. — [בגוים must then be connected with מלא, and constitute that with which the valleys are filled up. We may think of the nations gathered in the valley of Jehoshaphat for judgment, according to Jo. 4², cf. 2 Ch. 20¹⁶⁻²⁶. A good pentameter and assonance are given in the order: יָדין מלכים מלא גאיות בגוים.— [יְמַלֵא וְיָדין. 𝕲ˣ πληρώσει πτῶμα; 𝕲ᴬ·ᴿ·ᵀ πτώματα; 𝔙 *implebit ruinas;* 𝔍 *implebit valles* = מִלֵא Pi., which is certainly more probable. גְוִיָה n.f. (1) *body;* of living body † pl. גְוִיוֹת Gn. 47¹⁸ (J) Ne. 9³⁷ Dn. 10⁶ Ez. 1¹¹·²³; (2) *dead body, corpse, (a)* of man 1 S. 31¹⁰ (so orig. in || 1 Ch. 10¹⁰) v.¹².¹² Na. 3³·³ (coll.); so here 𝕳, 𝕲; (b) of lion Ju. 14⁸·⁹. But Aq., Σ, 𝔍, rd. גאיות *valleys, v. 23⁴;* so Kenn., Horsley. Vb. מלא suits *valleys,* but not *corpses;* for there is no receptacle or place suggested in context. We may point מלא, and make the king the subj. as with other vbs. — [ראש not *heads* of the bodies, corpses; but *heads* of the army, *chiefs,* || מלכים.—[עַל־אֶרֶץ רַבָה] might be regarded as pregnant, and a vb. inserted in thought; but the l. is defective and requires just this vb. for completion. עָלָה has been omitted by error before עַל, *went up* in war, in a campaign against; 𝕲ˣ ἐπὶ γῆν πολλήν; 𝔍 *in terra multa;* 𝕲ᴬ·ᴿ·ᵀ ἐπὶ γῆς πολλῶν, so 𝔙 *in terra multorum.* Assonance is given by the order: מהץ ראש עָלָה עַל־ארץ רַבָה.— 7. [מִנַחַל בַּדֶרֶך יִשְׁהֶה] though sustained by all Vrss. and based upon the story of Gideon Ju. 7, does not give a proper climax to the victory of the king. נחל without the prep., which may be interp., would suggest rather the vb. *divide as a possession,* the broad earth which he has conquered. ישיהה might be ישיהה (cf. v.¹) *he maketh it,* the land. What he makes it, is to be found in בדרך, where again ב is an interp. prep. דֶרֶך would then be *highway,* in accord. with the dividing of the earth as a possession. The pl. דרכים would then be needed, not only on account of the number of such highways required, but also for assonance with ירים. ראש is indeed a gl. from the previous l. The original would then be with assonance: נחל ישיתה דרכים על־כן ירם.

PSALM CXI., 11 STR. 2³.

Ps. 111 is a resolution to praise Yahweh in the congregation o'
Israel (v.¹⁻ ¹⁰ᵇᶜ), for the greatness of His works (v.²), His wondrous
deeds of righteousness and compassion (v.³⁻⁴), His fidelity to His
covenant (v.⁵⁻⁶), His trustworthy precepts (v.⁷⁻⁸), the ransom of
His people (v.⁹ᵃᵇ), and His awe-inspiring sanctity (v.⁹ᶜ⁻¹⁰ᵃ).

> I WILL thank Yahweh with all my heart,
>   In the intimate fellowship of the upright and the congregation.
> GREAT are the works of Yahweh,
>   Sought out of all that delight therein.
> MAJESTY and splendour is His doing,
>   And His righteousness standeth firm forever.
> A COMMEMORATION hath He made for His wondrous deeds;
>   Gracious and compassionate is Yahweh.
> PREY hath He given to them that fear Him:
>   He remembereth forever His covenant.
> HIS power hath He declared to His people,
>   To give (them) the inheritance of the nations.
> HIS works are faithfulness and justice;
>   Trustworthy are all His precepts.
> THEY are established forever and ever;
>   They are done in faithfulness and uprightness.
> RANSOM He hath sent to His people;
>   He hath commanded forever His covenant.
> SACRED and awe-inspiring is His name;
>   The beginning of wisdom is the fear of Him.
> A SOUND understanding have all who do so:
>   His praise endureth forever.

Ps. 111 is one of the Hallels, the first of the group 111–118, each having
the title הַלְלוּיָהּ (v. Intr. § 35). It is composed of twenty-two alphabetical
trimeters in groups of two each. It presupposes both the gnomic and the
legal attitudes, when they were in harmony, before they came into conflict;
and therefore the Greek period.

The couplets of the Ps. are all synth. Their connection is loose,
in the gnomic style. — **1**. *I will thank Yahweh*], resolution of
public thanksgiving, — *with all my heart*], phr. of D; with the
entire inner being. — *In the intimate fellowship of the upright*].
The upright are distinguished from the wicked in Israel, and are
conceived as closely united in an intimate fellowship from which

the wicked are excluded.—*and the congregation*]. This fellowship was that of the congregation of Israel, from which the ungodly usually abstained.—**2**. *Great are the works of Yahweh*]
His doings on behalf of His people,—*Sought out*], by diligent
investigation and study,—*of all that delight therein*], cf. I² the
true attitude of the people of Yahweh.—**3**. *Majesty and splendour
is His doing*], manifesting His glorious majesty,—*And His righteousness*], vindicatory, redemptive, as usual,—*standeth firm forever*], is permanent, steadfast, and reliable.—**4**. *A commemoration
hath He made*], arranged for a celebration of them by the re-
hearsal of them in the congregation, —*for His wondrous deeds*],
in the salvation of His people, as implied in, — *Gracious and
compassionate is Yahweh*], based on Ex. 34⁶. — **5**. *Prey*], taken
from their enemies for their benefit, — *hath He given to them that
fear Him*], to His true worshippers; the provision for them in the
Holy Land as implied by : *He remembereth forever His covenant*],
the covenant of Horeb Ex. 19, 24. — **6**. *His power*] enlarged by
a glossator into " power of His works," cf. v.²ᵃ· ⁴ᵃ, — *hath He declared to His people*], power over their enemies in dispossessing
them of their lands, as implied by, — *To give them*], His people,
the inheritance of the nations], the possession of their land. —
7–8. *His works*], cf. v.²· ⁴; enlarged by glossator to "works of His
hands," at the expense of the measure, — *are faithfulness and
justice*], attributes not usually paired, cf. Je. 4²; the one in the
carrying out of the promises of the covenant, the other in the administration of His government; cf. v.⁸ᵇ, — *done in faithfulness
and uprightness*], the former the same word, the latter a syn. of
justice. — *Trustworthy*], to be depended on as a firm, stable
support, ‖ *established* v.⁸ᵃ, upheld, sustained, maintained, — *are all
His precepts*], a late term for the laws of the Pentateuchal Codes,
cf. 19⁹ 103¹⁸ 119⁴⁺²¹ ᵗ· ⁽ᵉᵐ· ᵗˣᵗ·⁾. — **9**. *Ransom He hath sent to His
people*], originally of deliverance from Egypt, then from Babylon,
Is. 50²: probably here in a comprehensive sense, thereby confirm-
ing His promises. — *He hath commanded forever His covenant*],
cf. v.⁵. — *Sacred and awe-inspiring is His name*]. His name, as
the sum of His manifestation of Himself to His people, is to be
hallowed and revered in worship and in life, in accord with the
Word Ex. 20⁷. — **10**. *The beginning of Wisdom is the fear of*

Him], a fundamental principle of WL., Pr. 1⁷ 9¹⁰ Jb. 28²⁸ BS. 1ᵏ ; the reverential fear of Yahweh is the very first step in the acquisition of ethical wisdom. — *A sound understanding*], another term of WL., syn. of "wisdom," — *have all who do so*], all who have this fear and act accordingly, especially in giving thanks and praise. 𝕳 and 𝕲 both supply objects to the vb. at the expense of the measure : the one pl., doubtless thinking of the precepts of v.⁷, too distant in such a gnomic poem ; the other sg., referring to the "fear," and thus interpreting it against the usage of the phr. as a syn. of the Law ; both doubtless wrong. — *His praise*], concluding with the thought with which the Ps. began, v.¹ᵃ, — *endureth forever*], standeth fast, firm, and sure. Public worship is certain to be rendered in all generations.

1. 𝕲 σοι, 𝖁 *tibi*, explanatory gl. — לְבָב] for לֵב, due to dittog. before בַג ; as Ehr. — ס ד וְישָׁרִיב] phr. α.λ.; cf. Pr. 3³², *v.* Ps. 25¹⁴ for use of חיר — **2.** הֶפְצֵיהֶם] so 𝕾, 𝕿, but 𝕲 τὰ θελήματα αὐτοῦ, 𝖁 *voluntates eius ;* both sfs. interp. an original חבציב. — **5.** טֶרֶף] *prey, v.* 76⁵ ; here in fig. sense of food. — **6.** כֹּח מַעֲשָׂיו] makes l. too long; interp. of נָה; so יְרֵם is interp. of לתה. — **7.** מֶעֱשֵׂי יָדָיו] makes l. too long; rd. יֶיֱעֱ. — **8.** ס וּבְים] Qal pass. ptc., as 112⁸, *v.* 3⁶. — וְישֵׁר] 𝕲, 𝕵, 𝕾, 𝕿; יֹשֶׁר more prob.; Gr., Che., Bä., Valeton, Ehr. — **9.** † פְרוּה] n.f. *ransom*, from exile Is. 50², from iniquities Ps. 130⁷; here more general ; Ex. 8¹⁹ is dub. — **10.** רֵאשִׁית הָכְמָה] α.λ., cf. Pr. 4⁷ 9¹⁰ WL. — יִרְאַת יהוה] makes l. too long; rd. יִרְאָתִי. — ‡ שֶׂכֶל] n.m. (1) *prudence*, 1 S. 25³; (2) *insight, understanding*, here, as also in WL. and Chr.; (3) bad sense, *craft*, Dn. 8²⁵. — דְּרִ־עֹשֵׂיהֶב] 𝕲 τοῖς ποιοῦσιν αὐτήν, 𝖁 *facientibus eum*, 𝕵 *qui faciunt eam*, sfs. all gl.; rd. כָּל־עֹשֵׂה.

PSALM CXII., 11 STR. 2³.

Psalm 112 pronounces happy the one that fears Yahweh and delights in His Law (v.¹) ; his posterity will be blessed (v.²), he will have wealth and prosperity with which he will be benevolent (v.³⁻⁴) ; he maintains justice in all his affairs, and will be held in everlasting remembrance (v.⁵⁻⁶) ; he will be firm and confident, without fear, and sure of victory over his adversaries (v.⁷⁻⁸) ; he is generous to the poor, and will be exalted to the chagrin of the wicked (v.⁹⁻¹⁰ᵃ). The Ps. concludes with the ruin of the wicked (v.¹⁰ᵇᶜ).

HAPPY is he that feareth Yahweh,
    That in His commands delighteth greatly.
HIS seed shall be mighty in the land :
    The generation of the upright shall be blessed.
WEALTH and riches are in his house ;
    And his righteousness endureth forever.
LIGHT doth shine for the upright.
    Gracious and compassionate is the righteous.
IT is well with the gracious and benevolent,
    Who maintaineth his affairs with justice.
FOR he shall never be moved :
    The righteous shall be in everlasting remembrance.
OF evil tidings he is not afraid :
    His mind is fixed ; he hath confidence.
HIS mind is established ; he is not afraid,
    Until he look on his adversaries.
HE doth disperse ; give to the poor :
    His righteousness standeth firm forever.
HIS horn shall be exalted in honour.
    The wicked will see and be vexed.
HE will gnash his teeth and melt away :
    The desire of the wicked will perish.

Ps. 112 is the second Hallel of this group (*v.* Intr. § 35), and the mate of 111 in alphabetical structure, measure, and in the use of words and phrases ; doubtless from the same author and the same time. In 𝕾R it has in the title τῆς ἐπιστροφῆς Ἀγγαίου καὶ Ζαχαρίου, which is a late conjecture without sound basis. It passed over into 𝕍 *reversionis Aggaei et Zachariae*. It is found in the Syro-hexapla of 111 also, but is not in 𝕴. This Ps. has the same attitude as Ps. 1, which it copies in v.[1, 10c]. It has many resemblances with WL.: v.[3a] with Pr. 8[18], v.[5a] with Pr. 14[21] 19[17], v.[6b] with Pr. 10[7], v.[9a] with Pr. 11[24].

1. *Happy is he that feareth Yahweh*], cf. 1[1] ; congratulation of the god-fearing man on his piety and his fidelity to the Law : *in His commands delighteth greatly*], cf. 1[2]. A number of statements now follow, with regard to which it is difficult to determine whether they refer to the present or the future of the man ; the most of them are probably timeless and general in their character. — **2.** *His seed* ‖ *the generation of the upright*], his descendants. — *shall be mighty in the land*], men of power, position, and influence ; ‖ *shall be blessed*], share in their father's congratulations of happiness. — **3.** *Wealth and riches are in his house*]. He enjoys prosperity in accordance with the blessings of the Deuteronomic Law, Dt. 28. — *His righteousness*], doubtless in the

2 C

sense of prosperity, as Pr. 8[18] Jo. 2[23]. — *endureth forever*], will have no end. — **4.** *Light doth shine for the upright*], the light of prosperity in the divine favour, as 97[11] La. 3[2] Jb. 22[28] 30[26]. The original object was probably sg., but by copyist's mistake it became generalized into a pl., and so gave a basis for interpreting "the upright" either as his posterity, or as those under his influence, in the various interpretations represented by EV[s]. The gloss "in darkness" was introduced through a similar mistake, at the expense of the measure; for the context would make it altogether inappropriate to the man who is the theme of the Ps. This ancient error also influenced the interp. of the ‖ line, which originally was: *Gracious and compassionate is the righteous*], by the introduction of a conjunction before the last word, making it into an additional attribute "and righteous," which then makes it difficult to construct the line grammatically. — **5.** *It is well with the gracious and benevolent*], a resumption of the congratulation of v.[1]; so RV., JPSV.; but the PBV., AV., are ungrammatical and against the context in their renderings. — *Who maintaineth his affairs*], so essentially AV., JPSV., after Σ, 𝔗, which suits the context much better than RV., "he shall maintain his cause in judgment," although sustained by 𝔊, 𝔍. — *with justice*], in accordance with his character as a righteous man. — **6.** *For he shall never be moved*], usual phr. for stability of the righteous, cf. 15[5] 55[23] ‖ *shall be in everlasting remembrance*], in the successive generations of his seed, that will inherit his blessedness and congratulations. — **7-8.** *Of evil tidings*], emphatic in position; those which threaten most men as liable to come some time unexpectedly upon them; as the parall. suggests, v.[8b], of *adversaries* coming up against him. — *he is not afraid*], repeated for emphasis v.[8a], ‖ *he hath confidence*], changed by a glossator, at the expense of the measure, into "trusting in Yahweh": true enough, but not exactly the thought of the poet. The reason for his confidence in the future is, that he is prepared to meet adversaries; *His mind is fixed* ‖ *is established*], taking up again the thought of v.[6a]; he is sure of the final result. — *Until he look on*], gaze in triumph, as 22[18] 118[7]. — **9-10** a. *He doth disperse*], free and full distribution of his wealth in alms, cf. Pr. 11[24]. ‖ *give to the poor — His righteousness*], prosperity as v.[3], cf. 2 Cor. 9[9], where it is cited as an encouragement to Christian benevolence. This passage prepares the way for the later usage, where "righteousness" is a syn. of almsgiving, cf. Mt. 6$^{1\,sq.}$. — *His horn shall be exalted in honour*], cf. 75^5 89$^{18.\,25}$ 1 S. 2^1; doubtless here also in triumph over the adversaries of v.^{8b}, who are now represented in the ‖ as *The wicked* — They *will see* his triumph *and be vexed*, while he looks upon them in triumphant gratification, v.^{8b}. — **10 bc**. The final couplet is antithetical to the first one. The wicked *will gnash his teeth*], in the rage of disappointment and contemplation of the triumph of his adversary, and will *melt away* in impotent rage, melting as it were from his own heat. — *The desire of the wicked*], in antithesis with the delight of the righteous v.^{1b}. — *will perish*], go away into utter ruin, as Ps. 1^6.

1. אַשְׁרֵי אִישׁ] as *1*; but אִישׁ is prob. gl. here as well as אֶת; both impair the measure and are needless. — **2.** יְהִי] is prosaic, makes l. too long. — **4.** זָרַח] vb. as 104^{22}, of sun. בַּחֹשֶׁךְ is an interp. gl., making l. too long. — יְשָׁרִים] is also a generalisation of an original יָשָׁר. — וְצַדִּיק] not an additional attribute, but "the righteous man," as Hare, Du., Gr., after $\mathfrak{S}$; ו is gl. — **5.** אִישׁ] as v.^{1}; interp. gl. before ptc. — כַּלְוֶה] ptc. Hiph. לוה; *lend*, as 37^{26}. — וְיְכַלְכֵּל] Pilp. כּוּל *support*, as 55^{23}; Σ οἰκονομῶν τὰ πράγματα αὐτοῦ μετὰ κρίσεως, cf. $\mathfrak{C}$; to be preferred to $\mathfrak{G}$ οἰκονομήσει τοὺς λόγους αὐτοῦ ἐν κρίσει, $\mathfrak{J}$ *dispensabit verba sua in judicio*. — **6.** יִהְיֶה] as v.^{2} a gl., making l. too long. — **7.** ‡ שְׁמוּעָה] n.f. *tidings*, as Je 49^{23} (רָעָה), Pr. 15^{30} 25^{25} (טוֹבָה). — בֶּטַח בַּיהוה] makes l. too long; בַּיהוה is interp. gl.; with Dy. rd. בָּטַח ‖ יִירָא; $\mathfrak{G}$ ἐλπίζειν, בְּטֹחַ inf. — **9.** פַּזֵּר Pi. *scatter;* of alms, cf. Pr. 11^{24}; for other uses *v. 14$^{5-6}$*. — **10.** שִׁנָּיו יַחֲרֹק] phr. 35^{16} 37^{12} La. 2^{16} Jb. 16^9.

PSALM CXIII., 4 STR. 4^3.

Ps. 113 is a summons to Israel to praise Yahweh forever (v.$^{1-2}$) who, exalted above the nations in heavenly glory, is worthy of universal praise (v.$^{3-4}$) ; He is incomparable, from His heavenly throne condescending to see what transpires in heaven and on earth (v.$^{5-6}$) ; He enthrones Zion, taking her from her desolation and barrenness, and making her the glad mother of children (v.$^{7a.\,8ae.\,9}$) ; which last is emphasized by glosses (v.$^{7b.\,8b}$).

> PRAISE Yahweh, ye servants:
> Praise the name of Yahweh.
> The name of Yahweh be blessed
> From now on even forever.

*F*ROM the rising of the sun unto its setting
   The name of Yahweh is worthy to be praised.
   He is high above all nations,
   Above the heavens His glory.
*W*HO is like Yahweh our God ?
   He who exalteth Himself to sit enthroned:
   He who stoopeth to look
   In the heavens and in (all) the earth.
*H*E who raiseth out of the dust:
   He who enthroneth His people:
   He who enthroneth the barren
   To be the glad mother of children.

Ps. 113 is the third Hallel of this group (*v.* Intr. § 35). It begins the Jewish liturgical Hallel, 113–118, sung at the three great pilgrim feasts, at the Feast of Dedication, and at the ordinary new moons. At the Passover 113–114 were sung before the meal, 115–118 after it, in connection with the fourth cup. The group is also called "the Egyptian Hallel." The Roman Catholic Church uses these as the basis of the Sunday vesper service. This Ps. depends upon Mal. 1¹¹ in v.³ᵃ, 1 S. 2⁸ in v.⁷, Is. 54¹ in v.⁹. V.¹ except for a transposition of lines is essentially the same as 135¹. The Ps. doubtless belongs to the Greek period. It has four trimeter tetrastichs, with gls. from 1 S. 2⁸ in v.⁷ᵇ·⁸.

Str. I. Three lines syn., the last synth. — **1-2.** *Praise*], repeated for emphasis ‖ *be blessed.* — The subj. *Ye servants*], as 𝕲, 𝖁, 𝕴, Aq., 𝚺, PBV. : faithful worshippers, the true Israel, to be preferred to " servants of Yahweh " of 𝕳, 𝖘, 𝕿, AV., RV. The first line then gives both those called upon to praise and the object to be praised : *Yahweh*] ; which latter has then as its ‖ *the name of Yahweh*, repeated to emphasize the worship as comprehending the entire divine manifestation. The climax is : *From now on even forever*], everlastingly, without cessation.

Str. II. The first line is followed by three syn. lines synthetic thereto, reversing the order of the previous Str. — **3-4.** *From the rising of the sun unto its setting*] from the remote East to the farthest West ; universal worship in place is thus added to universality of time of the previous Str. — *is worthy to be praised*], as 18⁴ 48² 96⁴ 145³ ; and not " be praised " of EV⁸ as if ‖ with previous Str., when it is really ‖ with *He is high above all nations* ‖ *above the heavens His glory*] : cf. 8¹ 57⁶·¹². The praise is to be universal : among all nations, for He reigns over them all ; and over all the earth, as His glory above the heavens is also above all the earth.

Str. III. An antith. couplet enclosed in an introductory and a concluding line. — **5–6.** *Who is like Yahweh our God?*] a challenge insisting that He is incomparably superior to all others, cf. Ex. 15¹¹ Dt. 3²⁴. — The superiority of Yahweh is now set forth in participial relative clauses : *He who exalteth Himself to sit enthroned*], resuming the "high" of v.⁴. He riseth to supreme heights, when He sits on His heavenly throne. He is incomparable in His divine sovereign majesty. — *He who stoopeth to look*]. From the supreme heights He stoopeth, in order to look through all the regions below — namely, *In the heavens*], for He is conceived as above the heavens ; *and in all the earth*], beneath the heavens. Yahweh is incomparable in His condescension also, cf. Is. 57¹⁵.

Str. IV. Three syn. lines with a synth. conclusion. — **7–8.** *He who raiseth out of the dust*] ; as Yahweh was incomparable in His universal inspection of earth and heaven, so now He is incomparable in His special dealings with *His people*. Israel had been maltreated by the nations and humiliated to the dust. Zion, the wife of Yahweh and mother of her population, had been deprived of her children, who had been slain before her eyes or been taken into captivity ; and so she had become *barren*, cf. Is. 54¹ˢq. — Yahweh is incomparable in that He is the one *who enthroneth*], repeated for emphasis, both in connection with His desolate people and barren Zion, and especially with the latter in order to the climax — making her *the glad mother of children*] ; giving a numerous and happy population. A glossator enlarges this Str. by inserting from 1 S. 2⁸ several clauses : the object *poor* of the first line, an entire syn. line, *from the dunghill lifteth up the needy*, and in the second line *with princes ;* repeated, probably in the original gloss, but changed by an early scribe in the latter case to "with nobles of His people," which gives the clause a reference to individuals against the context, which evidently refers to Israel.

---

1. עֲבְדֵי יי] so אֱ, ℭ, as 135¹ᵇ; but ⅏, 𝔈, 𝔍, Aq., Σ. עבדים more prob. — שֵׁם יי] as 135¹ᵃ; ⅏ שמי, but against measure. — **2.** מְבֹרָךְ] Pu. ptc. ברך; cf. 37²² 112² 128⁴; constructed with יְהִי juss., which is, however, needless and dubious. — **3.** מִמִּזְרַח שֶׁמֶשׁ עַד־מְבֹאוֹ] phr. 50¹ Mal. 1¹¹. — מְהֻלָּל שֵׁם יהוה] Pu. ptc. הלל: elsw. 18⁴ 48² 96⁴ 145³. — **4.** רָם עַל־כָּל־גּוֹיִם] cf. כגוים 46¹¹, על (ה)שׁמים 57⁶·¹² = 108⁶; עַל here assimilated to על השׁמים in syn. clause. — וּכְבוֹדוֹ] is a needless gl. — **5.** הַמַּנְבִּיהִי] Hiph. ptc. גבה; cf. Qal 103[11].— **6.** הַמַּשְׁפִּילִי] elsw. ψ humiliate 18[28](?) 75[8] 147[6]. The ‑ִי is ancient case ending, Ges.[90. 8], for euphony, to get two accents. — **7.** מְקִימִי] should have article as ptcs. above v.[5b. 6a], and then two accents as those. לְ then makes l. too long and is a gl., as also v.[7b] from I S. 2[8]. — ‡ אַשְׁפֹּת n.[m.] (√שפת) dunghill, as I S. 2[8]. — **8.** לְהוֹשִׁיבִי] Hiph. inf. with ‑ִי, prob. assimilated to I S. 2[8]. We should rd. as in other cases הַכִּישִׁיבִי, as v.[9a], and regard עֲמִי as its object. A glossator has enlarged the l. 𝔊[N. A. R. T] καθίσαι αὐτὸν 𝔍 ut eum sedere faciat; so Gr., Now., Du., Che., but doubtless this is an interp. as usual, and does not imply an original להושיבו. — **9.** עֲקֶרֶת הַבַּיִת] cstr. ‡ עָקָר adj. barren, as I S. 2[5] Gn. 11[30] Is. 54[1]. הבית is doubtless interp. gl.

PSALM CXIV., 2 STR. 6[3].

Ps. 114 is a historical poem, describing the transformation of nature at the Exodus (v.[1. 3. 4]), and affirming that it was due to the presence of the God of Jacob, who is at the same time Lord of the earth (v.[5-7]). Glosses add the selection of the holy place in Judah (v.[2]), and the bringing of water from the rock (v.[8]).

> W̲HEN Israel went forth out of Egypt,
> 　　The house of Jacob from a people of unintelligible speech,
> 　　The sea saw and fled;
> 　　Jordan turned backward;
> 　　The mountains skipped like rams;
> 　　The hills (danced) like lambs of the flock.
> W̲HAT ailed thee, O Sea, that thou shouldst flee;
> 　　O Jordan, that thou shouldst turn backward;
> 　　Ye mountains, that ye skipped like rams;
> 　　Ye hills, that ye (danced) like lambs of the flock?
> 　　It was at the presence of the Lord of the earth:
> 　　At the presence of the God of Jacob.

Ps. 114 is also a Hallel, having הללויה in 𝔊, although in 𝔐, 𝔍, this word is attached to the end of previous Ps., doubtless by error (v. Intr. § 35). Originally, however, it was not a Hallel. The title is appropriate only so far as it was used with the previous or the subsequent Ps. Probably in liturgical use it was always used with the latter, and accordingly it is combined with it in 𝔊, 𝔙. The reference to the crossing of the Red Sea and the Jordan is of such a general character that it does not indicate the use of any particular document of the Hexateuch. The use of לְעֹז v.[1] is the only evidence of late Hebrew. The Ps. doubtless belongs to the Greek period. It has two trimeter hexastichs arranged as Str. and anti-Str. V.[2. 8] are late glosses.

Str. I. A syn. couplet and a syn. tetrastich. — **1**. *From a people of unintelligible speech*], speaking a language that Israel did not understand, cf. Gn. 42²³ Is. 28¹¹. The proper apodosis is in v.³⁻⁴; but a glossator, wishing to give a more suitable basis for the use of the Ps. in public worship, and thinking of the final purpose of the Exodus, adds **2**. *Judah became His sanctuary*], the land of Judah, for the usual Jerusalem, the capital city, cf. Ex. 15¹⁷ Ps. 78⁶⁸⁻⁶⁹. — *Israel His dominion*], the entire land of Israel, the land over which He reigned as King of Israel. — **3**. *The sea saw and fled*], the Red Sea, or sea of reeds, which at the Exodus was laid bare, so that Israel might cross. It is personified and represented as fleeing in terror before something that it saw. What this was is reserved for the antistrophe, cf. Ex. 15⁸ Ps. 77¹⁷. — ‖ *Jordan turned backward*]. Its waters became dammed up above, so that Israel might cross in its bed, cf. Jos. 3¹³⁻¹⁷. — **4**. *The mountains skipped like rams* ‖ *The hills danced like lambs of the flock*], personification of the mountains of Horeb, which, in the earthquake at the theophany of the lawgiving (Ex. 19¹⁶⁻¹⁹), resembled young rams and lambs, skipping and dancing about in their terror, cf. Hb. 3¹⁰.

Str. II is the antistrophe, with a syn. tetrastich of inquiry, and a syn. couplet of reply. — **5-6**. *What ailed thee ?*]. What is the reason of your terror? What was it that you saw, that frightened you so much? The question is asked of the *sea*, the *Jordan*, the *mountains*, and the *hills*, repeating exactly v.³⁻⁴ in the form of the question, in order to the emphatic reply. — **7**. *It was at the presence of*], repeated for emphasis. — *the Lord of the earth*], the sovereign owner and possessor of the sea, the Jordan, the mountains, and the hills, and of all other things; who had come in theophany, summoning them to take their part in the deliverance of His people; for He was also, and in a special sense, *the God of Jacob*. This answer has been disturbed by an early copyist's mistake; who, to the great injury of the measure, wrote the vb. in v.⁷ᵃ instead of in v.⁶ᵇ. Thus the vb. " danced," which is syn. with " skipped," had to be given a meaning appropriate to all the objects of nature and interpreted as an imv. " writhe," or " tremble " ; and so instead of answering the question, these great objects of nature are exhorted to do what they have already been represented as doing. A glossator tacks on, with great impropriety, a couplet relating the miracle of bringing water from the rock: **8**. *He who turned the rock into a pool of water, the flinty rock into a fountain of waters*, cf. Ex. 17⁶ Nu. 20⁸ ˢᑫ· Pss. 78¹⁵· ¹⁶· ²⁰ 107³⁵ Is. 41¹⁸.

1. עַם לֹעֵז] a.λ. a people speaking an unintelligible or foreign language, NH. for לְעֵז, cf. Is. 28¹¹. — מֶמְשְׁלוֹתָיו] pl., elsw. only 136⁹ ‡ מֶמְשָׁלָה n.f. *dominion* of God as 103²² 145¹³, elsw. ψ of heavenly bodies 136⁸· ⁹; pl. prob. error of pointing. 𝔊 ἐξουσία αὐτοῦ, 𝔍 *potestas eius*. This whole v. is gl. — **3.** יָשֹׁב] Qal impf. סבב, *v. 17¹¹;* c. אחור *turn about backward*, so v.⁵, not elsw. — **4.** רָקְדוּ] Qal רקד *skip about;* so also v.⁶. Hiph. 29⁶. A parallel vb. needed in next l.; prob. חָלוּ; so also v.⁶ᵇ, cf. 96⁹. — **7.** הוּלִי] displaced from previous l. — אֱלֹהֵי יַעֲקֹב] phr. a.λ.; improb.; error for אֱלֹהֵי יַעֲקֹב. אֱלֹהֵי elsw. in ψ 18³² (for אֵל 2 S. 22³²), 50²² (gl.) 139¹⁹ (gl.). — **8.** הַהֹפְכִי] article relative, ptc. הֹפֵךְ, *v. 30¹²*, archaic ending for euphony. — † חַלָּמִישׁ] n.m. *flint*, as Dt. 8¹⁵ 32¹³ Jb. 28⁹ Is. 50⁷. — מַעְיְנוֹ] archaic, euphonic ending, for cstr. מעין with מים as Jos. 15⁹ 18¹⁵ (P) 1 K. 18⁵ 2 K. 3¹⁹· ²⁵. This v. is gl.

PSALM CXV.

Ps. 115 is composite: (*A*) a prayer to Yahweh to manifest His glory over against the idols of the nations, with an imprecation upon idolaters (v.¹ᵃᵇ· ²⁻⁷ᵇ· ⁸), to which supplementary glosses were added (v.¹ᶜ· ⁷ᶜ); (*B*) a litany of priest and people, the former exhorting to trust in Yahweh, the latter responding that He is their help and shield (v.⁹⁻¹¹); the latter then imploring a blessing upon all classes of the community (v.¹²⁻¹³), the former pronouncing the blessing in the name of the Creator (v.¹⁴⁻¹⁶). To this was added a gloss in the nature of a vow to bless Yahweh forever (v.¹⁷⁻¹⁸).

A. v.¹ᵃᵇ· ²⁻⁷ᵇ· ⁸, 4 STR. 4³·

NOT to us, Yahweh, not to us,
But to Thine own name give glory.
Wherefore should the nations say:
" Where now is their God ? "
OUR God is in heaven (above).
All that He pleaseth, He doeth.
Their idols are silver and gold,
The work of the hands of men.

A MOUTH have they; but they cannot speak.
Eyes have they; but they cannot see.
Ears have they; but they cannot hear.
A nose have they; but they cannot smell.
HANDS have they; but they cannot feel.
Feet have they; but they cannot walk.
Like them be they that made them,
Every one that trusteth in them.

B. v.⁹⁻¹⁶, 3 STR. 6³.

O (HOUSE of) Israel, trust in Yahweh.
He is their help and their shield.
O house of Aaron, trust in Yahweh.
He is their help and their shield.
O ye that fear Yahweh, trust in Yahweh.
He is their help and their shield.
(HE is their help and their shield.)
May Yahweh remember and bless:
Bless the house of Israel;
Bless the house of Aaron;
Bless them that fear Yahweh,
Small together with great.
MAY Yahweh add unto you,
Unto you and unto your children.
Blessed be ye of Yahweh,
Maker of heavens and earth,
The heavens (which are assigned) to Yahweh,
The earth which is given to the sons of mankind.

Ps. 115 is a Hallel, incorporated by 𝔊, 𝔙, 𝔖, Θ, 𝔍, and some codd. 𝔚, 52 de Rossi, with previous Ps. for liturgical reasons; without הללויה in 𝔚, but the space with ο in codices indicates its omission, due probably to the liturgical use of this with the previous Ps. Ps. 115 is composite: *A,* four trimeter tetrastichs, v.¹ᵃᵇ· ²⁻⁷ᵇ· ⁸, contrasting the God of Israel with idols, cited in 135⁶ᵃ· ¹⁵⁻¹⁸; with glosses v.¹ᶜ from 138², and an additional characteristic of idols v.⁷ᶜ; *B,* three trimeter hexastichs, a litany of priest and people v.⁹⁻¹⁶, with a later gloss v.¹⁷⁻¹⁸. *A* is earlier, indicating a period of conflict with idolatry, cf. Is. 44⁹⁻²⁰ Je. 10¹⁻¹⁶, probably from the Babylonian period. *B* implies established worship in the temple. The prominence of the Aaronic priesthood in v.¹⁰⁻¹², and the distinction of proselytes v.¹¹· ¹³ from the house of Israel, with the absence of any mention of a king, imply the Greek period. The glosses are of later date.

PSALM CXV. *A.*

Str. I. Two synth. couplets. — **1.** *Not to us*], repeated for emphasis, appealing to *Yahweh,* in order to the antithesis: *But to Thine own name give glory.* — A glossator adds from 138²: *for*

the sake of Thy kindness, (and) *for the sake of Thy faithfulness*],
to do honour to those divine attributes, cf. Ex. 34⁶. — **2.** *Wherefore should the nations say: "Where now is their God?"*],
because He had not displayed the glory of His name in the
redemption of His people, cf. Ps. 42⁴·¹¹ 79¹⁰.

Str. II. Synth. couplets in antithesis. — **3.** *Our God is in
heaven*], to which 𝔊 very properly adds *above,* as the measure
requires; implying, on the one hand, that His throne was there,
and on the other hand, that the gods of the nations were not
there. — *All that He pleaseth, He doeth*]. His divine sovereign
will knows no restrictions or restraints. — **4.** *Their idols*]. The
gods of the nations are thus identified with their images. — *are
silver and gold*], of the most precious metals — and yet *The work
of the hands of men*], not creators, but creations.

Str. III. A syn. tetrastich. — **5–6.** *Mouth — eyes — ears —
nose*], these features of the face, common to men and to heavenly
intelligences when they manifest themselves, — *have they*], these
idols; but they have no life in them. — *they cannot speak — see
— hear — smell*]. They cannot use these features as living
beings do.

Str. IV. A syn. couplet and a synth. one. — **7.** *Hands — feet
— have they*], chief instruments of the activity of the body; but
they cannot use them. — *they cannot feel — they cannot walk*].
A glossator adds — *they utter not with their throat*], which makes
the Str. just this line too long, is in a different style from the
other lines, and really is a repetition of v.⁵ᵃ and not homogeneous
with its immediate context. — **8.** *Like them be they that made
them*], an imprecation not only upon the craftsmen that made
the images, but also upon those who employed them; that they
may become as impotent and probably also as dead as these
images. — The imprecation is extended in the climax to all idolaters, *Every one that trusteth in them.*

PSALM CXV. *B.*

Str. I. Litany of three syn. lines by the priest, with three identical lines of response by the people. — **9–11.** *O house of Israel*],
so 𝔊, 𝔖, 𝔙, PBV., as v.¹² 135¹⁹; to be preferred to "Israel" of
𝕳, AV., RV., although the mng. is the same — the organisation

of Israel as a household or nation. ‖ *house of Aaron*], the Aaronic priesthood, the rulers of Israel at the time of the composition of the Ps., in the Greek period. ‖ *ye that fear Yahweh*], the proselytes from other nations than Israel, for thus we must interpret it here as additional to the " house of Israel " v.[12-13], and not in the usual sense of the " pious " in Israel as distinguished from the ungodly. — The priest exhorts each and all to *trust in Yahweh*]. ⅏, ⅀, 𝔘, 𝔍, all have the pf. here, stating as a fact that they do trust in Yahweh, which makes a better antithesis with the idolaters of the last line of the previous Ps., who trust in their idols, and also harmonises better with the sfs. of the thrice repeated line : *He is their help and their shield*]. But, on the other hand, the change of person best suits the nature of the litany with the people responding to the priest, which in any case appears in the subsequent Strs., in the last of which the priest responds to the people. Furthermore, the threefold repetition of identical lines is appropriate to such a litany, and not to statements of fact. God is conceived as help and shield of His people, as 3^4 28^7 33^{20}.

Str. II. A synth. couplet, a syn. triplet, and a synth. line in conclusion. — **12–13.** *May Yahweh remember and bless*]. The subsequent context makes this rendering most probable. ⅏ interprets both vbs. as in the same construction and with the same sf. 𝔥 takes the former as pf., which then must be in a relative clause, as JPSV. " who was mindful of us," or a statement of past experience, as PBV., AV., RV., " hath been mindful of us." EV[s]. all take the impfs. here and in subsequent clauses as futures, " He will bless " ; but JPSV. more correctly as jussives. — A line is missing in 𝔥 and Vrss. of this Str. It seems most probable that the people here begin their petition with the same words they have used in the previous Str. : *He is their help and their shield.* — The people then pray : May He *bless*] each of the classes mentioned above, *the house of Israel, the house of Aaron,* and *them that fear Yahweh ;* comprehending all in the climax, *Small together with great*], all portions of the community, whether exalted in position or of humble condition ; cf. Je. 6^{13} 16^6 31^{34}.

Str. III. Two synth. couplets and an antith. couplet. The priest responds to the petition of the people in this Str. — **14.** *May Yahweh add unto you*], increase your numbers, ever an important divine favour to ancient Israel;— and not only *Unto you*, but also *unto your children*], giving increase to all subsequent generations. — **15**. *Blessed be ye of Yahweh*], as approved and favoured by their God, receiving all manner of blessings from His hands. — *Maker of heavens and earth*]. The creator is the sovereign owner of all things, and therefore able and competent to bestow them in blessings on His people. — **16**. *The heavens*], not only created by Him, but *assigned to Yahweh*], reserved to Him for His divine throne and royal residence. The unpointed text suggests this rendering, as does the antithetical line ; but 𝔐, 𝔊, and all Vrss. read " heavens," the former making it predicate, as RV., JPSV., " the heavens are the heavens of Yahweh," or in apposition, as AV. " the heaven, even the heavens are Yahweh's." But PBV., " all the whole heavens are Yahweh's," follows the Vrss. in taking the two as in the construct relation. — *The earth which is given to the sons of mankind*], for a residence and for the use of its products. It is given by Yahweh, whether we regard Him as the subj. of the vb., as most, or take the vb. with an indef. subj. to be rendered in Eng. by the passive, which best accords with the previous line, if our interpretation is correct.

A glossator adds **17–18**, a trimeter tetrastich of the nature of a vow, implying the deliverance of the nation from a deadly peril, probably therefore in the early Maccabean times. — **17**. *The dead cannot praise Yah*], that is, in the temple worship, as 6⁶ 30¹⁰ 88¹¹ Is. 38¹¹. ¹⁸⁻¹⁹. ‖ *Nor any that go down to Silence*], a syn. of Sheol, as 94¹⁷. — **18**. *But we*], " the living," as 𝔊 interprets by a gloss, who have been preserved from death and Sheol. — *will bless Yah*], in the temple worship. — *From now on even forever*], in all subsequent generations and ages.

CXV. A.

1. לא] 𝔊ⁿ·ᴬ·ᴿ·ᵀ μή = אַל more proper in ‖ with imv. תֵן. If לא is retained, כי must be not adversative, but intensive. — עַל־חַסְדֶ־ךָ עַל־אֲמִתֶ־ךָ] gl. from 138², without intermediate ו, which, however, is given by 𝔊ⁿ·ᴬ·ᴿ·ᵀ. — **3**. בשמים]. 𝔊ⁿ·ᴿ adds ἄνω = לְעַל, which is needed for good measure, but it is omitted in 𝔊ⁿ·ᶜ·ᵃ·ᴬ·ᵀ. 𝔊ⁿ also has ἐν τοῖς οὐρανοῖς καὶ ἐπὶ τῆς γῆς, 𝔊ⁿ·ᶜ·ᵃ·ᴿ·ᵀ ἐν τῇ γῇ, which is an expansive gl. — **4**. עצביהם] *their idols*, as 106³⁶·³⁸ 135¹⁵. 𝔊, 𝔖, τῶν ἐθνῶν instead of sf., as 135¹⁵. — **6**. יריחון] Hiph. impf. full form 3 pl. ‡ ריח denom. רֵיחַ *scent, odour*, and so *to scent, smell*, as

Dt. 4²⁰ Gn. 8²¹ 27²⁷ (JE) Jb. 39²⁵. — **7.** רגליהם] so רגליהם, but awkward. ⅁
להם ידים ,רגלים להם. — ‏יְמִישׁוּן] Hiph. impf. full form 3 pl. † [מוּשׁ]
vb. *feel*, Qal only Gn. 27²¹. Hiph. elsw. Ju. 16²⁶ (?) *idem*. ⅁ has the same
construction here as in v.⁵⁻⁶, and that is intrinsically more prob. But the last
l., of different constr., לא־יהגו בגרונם, is a gl.

CXV. B.

9. ישראל] but ⅁ᴺ·ᴬ·ᴿ·ᵀ, 𝕾, 𝔍, בית ישראל, as v.¹² 135¹⁹. — בְּמַח] imv.; but
⅁ᴺ·ᴬ·ᴿ·ᵀ, 𝕾, 𝔍, pf. as v.¹⁰· ¹¹. — **10.** בֵּית אַהֲרֹן] as v.¹² 118⁸ 135¹⁹. — **12.** זְכָרָנוּ
יְבָרֵךְ [‏ ⅁ᴺ·ᴿ ἐμνήσθη ἡμῶν καὶ εὐλόγησεν ἡμᾶς, ⅁ᴺ·ᶜ·ᵃ·ᴬ·ᵀ μνησθείς; prob.
sfs. all interpretative. — **16.** השמים שמים] ⅁ᴺ·ᵀ ὁ οὐρανὸς τοῦ οὐρανοῦ, ⅁ᴬ·ᴿ
τῷ οὐρανῷ = שמי השמים, so 𝔼, 𝕾, 𝕿, 𝔍; but ‖ suggests שָׂמִים = ptc. שִׂים *are
assigned to*. — **17.** יֹרְדֵי דוּמָה] phr. a.λ., cf. ירדי בור Pss. 28¹ 143⁷. דוּמָה elsw.
= שְׁאוּל 94¹⁷. — **18.** אנחנו] ⅁ᴺ·ᴬ·ᴿ·ᵀ interprets by the gl. οἱ ζῶντες.

PSALM CXVI., 8 STR. 3³, RF. 1³.

Ps. 116 pledges Yahweh the love of His people and continual
prayer, because He had proved Himself the hearer of prayer (v.¹⁻²),
had delivered them from death (v.³⁻⁴ᵃ), was the gracious keeper of
the simple-minded (v.⁴ᵇ· ⁵ᵃ· ⁶ᵃ), and had dealt bountifully with them
(v.⁷· ⁸ᵃᶜ) ; assures Yahweh of their faith in Him and their continual
prayer, though greatly afflicted by false men (v.¹⁰⁻¹¹), and vows a
libation of gratitude for benefits (v.¹²⁻¹³), thank offerings (v.¹⁶ᵃᵇ· ¹⁷),
and votive offerings in the courts of the temple (v.¹⁸⁻¹⁹ᵃ).
Glosses emphasize still further various statements of the Ps.
(v.⁵ᵇ· ⁶ᵇ· ⁸ᵇᵈ· ⁹· ¹⁴· ¹⁵· ¹⁶ᶜ· ¹⁹ᵇ).

I LOVE (Yahweh, my strength).
  Verily He heareth the voice of my supplications;
  Verily He doth incline His ear to me:
    Therefore on the (name of Yahweh) will I call.
THE snares of Death encompassed me,
  And the straits of Sheol found me.
  Trouble and sorrow I find:
    Therefore on the name of Yahweh will I call.
AH now, deliver my life,
  Yahweh, gracious and righteous!
  Yahweh, keeper of the simple-minded!
    (*Therefore on the name of Yahweh will I call.*)
RETURN, my soul, to thy resting place;
  For Yahweh hath dealt bountifully with thee;
  For He hath rescued mine eyes from tears:
    (*Therefore on the name of Yahweh will I call.*)

I BELIEVE, though I speak ך.
  I was greatly afflicted.
  I said: Every man is a liar.
      (*Therefore on the name of Yahweh will I call*.)
WHAT shall I render to Yahweh,
  For all His benefits unto me?
  The cup of salvation will I lift:
      Therefore on the name of Yahweh will I call.
AH now, I am Thy servant:
  I am Thy servant, the son of Thine handmaid.
  To Thee will I sacrifice a thank offering:
      Therefore on the name of Yahweh will I call.
MY votive offerings to Yahweh will I pay,
  I will declare it to all His people,
  In the courts of the house of Yahweh:
      (*Therefore on the name of Yahweh will I call*).

Ps. 116 is a Hallel in $\mathfrak{G}$, preceded by ἀλληλουιά; but in $\mathfrak{H}$ הללויה is at the close of the previous Ps., and also at the close of v.[19], in both cases txt. err. $\mathfrak{G}$ also divides the Ps. into two Pss., making the second begin with v.[10] preceded by ἀλληλουιά; which, however, is not in $\mathfrak{H}$. The separation was doubtless for liturgical reasons, for though there is a natural break at this place in the Ps., yet the two parts have so many features in common that they must be regarded as parts of the same original; cf. אנה v.[4. 16]. The Rf. יבשם יהוה אקרא, given v.[4a. 13b. 17b] and in a corrupt form v.[2b], has been omitted v.[6b. 9b. 11b. 19b]. $\mathfrak{G}^{\text{א}}$ also omits it in v.[17b], but it is given by $\mathfrak{G}^{\text{א. c. a. A. T.}}$ The Ps. is an artistic trimeter of eight tetrastichs arranged as $2 \times 2 \times 2 \times 2$. There are several glosses: v.[8bd. 9] from 56[14], v.[11a] from 31[23]; also v.[5b. 6b. 15. 16c. 19b] for various reasons, as explanation or expansion. v.[14] is v.[18] displaced, and is omitted in $\mathfrak{G}$. The original Ps. uses: v.[1a] 18[2], v.[3] 18[5. 6]. V.[19a] = 135[2], but the latter is probably later. The original has two rare forms: מצר v.[3b], תגמולוהי v.[12b]. נגרה v.[18b] may be otherwise explained. There is no evidence of the use of any literature except $\mathfrak{D}$. This favours an early date. But the stress laid upon sacrificial worship in the temple v.[17-19] favours the early Greek period.

Str. I. A syn. couplet enclosed by introductory l. and Rf. — **1-2.** *I love*], absolute in $\mathfrak{H}$ and Vrss.; but as it is based on 18[2] the original object was probably *Yahweh, my strength*], which has been omitted by copyist's error at the expense of the measure and the parallelism, and of the interpretation. The people here affirm and pledge their love to Yahweh, who has been their strength in all their past experience. The specific ground of love in this Str. is, that He has been the answerer of prayer: *Verily*] asseverative rather than causal particle as EV[8].—*He heareth || doth incline His ear to me—the voice of my supplications*], familiar terms, cf.

$28^{2.6}$ 31^{23} $86^{1.6}$ +. — *Therefore on the name of Yahweh will I call*], a vow of prayer, which was repeated at the end of every Str. in the original Ps., but which has been retained only in part by copyists; cf. v.$^{4a.\ 13b.\ 17b}$. Here it has been changed by an early copyist's error of a single letter into "in" or "during my days," which is rendered "as long as I live" by EV^s.

Str. II. A syn. triplet and Rf. **3.** *The snares of Death encompassed me* ‖ *the straits of Sheol found me*], cf. 18^{5-6}, upon which the thought is based; explained as *Trouble and sorrow;* not individual but national, as throughout the Ps.

Str. III. A syn. couplet enclosed by introductory line and Rf. as Str. I. — **4 b–6.** *Ah now*], exclamation of entreaty as v.^{16}. — *deliver my life*], from the peril of death, of the previous Str. — *Yahweh*], repeated for emphasis, and indeed vocative, as in apposition with the subj. of the imv., and not a statement of fact as EV^s. — *keeper of the simple-minded*], those especially in need of divine favours, because of their liability to be misled into peril owing to lack of experience, cf. 19^8. In WL. it indicates those who are on the one side open to instruction, on the other exposed to temptation and error. A glossator adds to the attributes *gracious* and *righteous: Yea, our God is compassionate*, and to v.^{6a} a statement of the past peril: — *I was brought low, but me He saved*, which is not consistent with the prayer for deliverance characteristic of the Str.

Str. IV. A syn. couplet enclosed as in previous Str. — **7.** *Return, my soul, to thy resting place*]. The resting place is doubtless Yahweh Himself; for just as the temple is the refuge of God's people and in a higher sense God Himself (cf. 90^1 91^1); so the temple is the resting place of God 132^8, and the temple and God Himself are the resting place of His people. — *For Yahweh hath dealt bountifully with thee*], cf. 13^6. There is but a single specification in the original. — **8–9.** *For He hath rescued mine eyes from tears*], resuming the thought of the trouble and sorrow of v.^{3}. But a glossator adds from 56^{14} three other items : *Thou hast rescued my life from death, my feet from stumbling; I will walk before Yahweh in the land of the living.*

Str. V. Synt. lines. — **10.** *I believe*], absolute ; expression of confidence and trust in Yahweh. — *though*], as JPSV., and not

" for " RV., or " therefore " PBV., AV., after ⑥, 𝔙, 𝔍. — *I speak it*], that which follows, which might seem to evidence a lack of confidence. — *I was greatly afflicted*], resuming v.³·⁸.—**11.** *I said*], to which the glossator adds from 31²³: *in my alarm — every man*], as ⑥, required by the sg. ptc. — *is a liar*], emphasized by 𝕳 into " all mankind," against the grammatical construction, which JPSV. tries to avoid by the unjustifiable rendering " the whole of man." The people were exposed on every side to liars and slanderers.

Str. VI. Synth. couplets. — **12.** *What shall I render to Yahweh?*], by way of recompense for His bounties. — **13.** The question is raised in order to the answer in the vow: *The cup of salvation will I lift*], in a drink offering, expressing thanksgiving for the blessings of salvation received and enjoyed. 𝕳 adds here v.¹⁴, a premature repetition of v.¹⁸, not in ⑥ and against the strophical organisation.

Str. VII. Syn. couplet and synth. lines. — **15–16.** *Ah now, I am Thy servant*, emphasized in the ‖ *I am Thy servant and the son of Thine handmaid*], cf. 86¹⁶. The relation of His people to their God as worshipping servants is the basis of the vow. 𝕳 inserts an interpretative particle; which was probably designed as asseveration " truly " as AV., RV., but is interpreted by PBV. as " how," by JPSV. as causal " for." But it is not in ⑥, and it impairs the measure. The glossator prefixes and adds reference to the trials from which the people had been delivered; the former: *Precious in the eyes of Yahweh is the death of His pious*], a pentameter based on 72¹⁴, and in late Maccabean style and temper; the latter: *Thou hast loosed my bonds*], probably referring to deliverance from captivity in the Maccabean wars, cf. Is. 52² Jb. 12¹⁸ 39⁵.— **17.** *To Thee will I sacrifice a thank offering*], accompanying the drink offering of v.¹³.

Str. VIII. Syn. triplet and Rf. — **18.** *My votive offerings to Yahweh will I pay*]. The thank offering is thus specified as one that had been vowed and was now to be paid. The context makes it evident that the kind of vow is that of sacrifice. — *I will declare*], the most probable interpretation of a difficult form, which by an ancient error of a single letter has been changed into an anomalous form, interpreted by PBV. after ⑥, 𝔙, 𝔍, " in the sight of," but by other EVˢ. after 𝕳, which introduces a particle, " now

in the presence of," AV., "yea, in the presence of," RV.,
" I would it were in the presence of," JPSV. The vb. asserts
that the votive offering will be accompanied by an oral declaration of the praise of Yahweh, probably in sacred song : *to all
His people*]. — **19.** *In the courts of the house of Yahweh*], the
place where the sacrifices were made and the sacred songs and
music were rendered. This is enlarged upon by a gloss : *In thy
midst, O Jerusalem.*

1. אָהַבְתִּי] for ארחמך of 18². It is then tempting with Bä. to give the vb.
sf., which might have been absorbed in the following כי. This, in accord with
‖ v.², goes with the second l. There is no sound reason to substitute האמנתי
with Bruston, Gr., Che. 𝕲ᴺ has for יהוה ὁ Θεὸς, but 𝕲ᴺ·ᶜ·ᵃ·ᴬ·ᴿ·ᵀ κύριος. In
such cases of difference both are usually interpretative. If then the second l.
begin with כי־ישמע without the divine name, then the first l. is defective, two
words being missing. These were prob. those of 18²: יהוה חזקי. Then the
omission of sf. is explained, and כי is not causal, but asseverative. — קולי]
archaic ending in order to get two accents. — תחנוני] i.p. as 28²·⁶ 31²³ 86⁶ 130²
140⁷. — **2.** בימי] so 𝔍, 𝕲ᴺ·ᶜ·ᵃ·ᴬ·ᴿ·ᵀ, but 𝕲ᴺ, ἐν ταῖς ἡμέραις αὐτοῦ. The l. is
defective ; it is the Rf. ; rd. ביום יהוה as v.⁴·¹³·¹⁷, so Hu., Du. — **3.** אפפוני]. This
l. is cited from 18⁵. — מצרי שאול] phr. α.λ. = חבלי שאול 18⁶. † מצר n.m. *straits,
distress,* elsw. La. 1³ Ps. 118⁵. — מצאוני] for סבבוני 18⁶. — **4.** מלטה נפשי Pi. imv.
cohort. ; phr. elsw. 89⁴⁹ 1 S. 19¹¹ Je. 48⁶ Am. 2¹⁴·¹⁵. יהוה is gl., making l. too
long. — **5.** ואלהינו מרחם]. 𝕲ᴺ prefixes יהוה, but not 𝕲ᴺ·ᶜ·ᵃ·ᴬ·ᴿ·ᵀ. This phr.
is gl. — **6.** פראים] cf. *19*⁸. For form *v.* Ges.⁹³·ˣ. — דַּי] Qal pf. 1 sg. ‡ דלל
be brought low, as 79⁸ = 142⁷. — יהושיע] Hiph. impf. old form ישע 1 S. 17⁴⁷ for
יושיע ; 𝕲 καὶ ἔσωσέν με ישיע. Gr. thinks that י is dittog. This whole clause is gl.
— **7.** מנוחיכי] כי Aramaising sf. for ך, unless dittog. (*v.* 103³), but cf. עליכי.
‡ מנֹיחַ n.m. *rest ;* other mngs. not in ψ ; cf. מנוחה 23². — **8**ᵇᵈ = marginal gl.
from 56¹⁴. — **9.** ארצות החיים] phr. α.λ. for (ה)חיים ארי 27¹³ 52⁷ 142⁶ + ; prob.
txt. err. The l. is pent. gl. from 56¹⁴ᶜᵈ. — **10.** 𝕲 makes v.¹⁰⁻¹⁹ separate Ps.
It was prob. divided for liturgical use. — כי] 𝕲 διὸ, 𝔍 *propter quod.* — **11**ᵃ =
31²³ᵃ. — **12.** תגמולוהי] † תגמול] n.m. α.λ. *benefit,* Aramaism for גמור with Aramaic sf. — **13.** כוס ישועות] phr. α.λ., כוס in good sense elsw. ψ 16⁵ 23⁵ ; *v. 11*⁶.
ישועות pl. abstr. intensive. — **14 = 18.** V.¹⁴ om. 𝕲 ; due to displacement of
v.¹⁸. — ונדרה־נא] α.λ. נדרה usually interp. as local acc. for נגר. But נא implies
vb. cohort. as elsw. ; rd. אגידה as 40⁶. This suits the ‖. However, 𝕲, 𝔍,
show no traces of נא. — **15.** המותה] α.λ. fem. for מוה. — להסירו] ל of late style.
The v. is a late gl. — **16.** כי] is interp. gl., not in 𝕲ᴺ·ᴬ·ᴿ·ᵀ. יהוה is also gl.
as v.⁴. — בן אמתך] cf. 86¹⁶. — פתח מוסר] a gl. ; phr. elsw. Is. 52² Jb. 12¹⁸ 39⁵,
cf. נתק מ Ps. *2*³. — **17.** וזרה is an unnecessary gl. of interp., and impairs the
measure. — **19.** בתוככי] הוך with כי sf. v. above v.⁷ ; but following י of ירושלם
makes it dubious ; besides, the clause is a dimeter and is doubtless a gl.

2 D

PSALM CXVII., 1 STR. 4[3].

Ps. 117 summons all nations to worship Yahweh for His kindness and faithfulness (v.[1-2]).

> PRAISE ye Yahweh, all nations;
> Laud Him, all peoples :
> For His kindness is mighty over us,
> And the faithfulness of Yahweh endureth forever.

Ps. 117 is a Hallel, preceded by ἀλληλουιά in 𝕲. But in 𝕳 the הללויה is at the close of the previous Ps. and also at the close of this Ps. It has a single Str., a trimeter tetrastich. Originally it was part of a longer Ps.; but neither of the one that precedes, nor of the one that follows, although in many codd. Kenn., de Rossi, it is connected with the following Ps. It is of an entirely different temper toward the nations. It is of late date, as is evident from אֻמִּים v.[1], unless that be error for לְאֻמִּים. It was used for liturgical worship at the feasts.

Two syn. couplets. — **1.** *Praise ‖ laud*], in public worship. — *all nations ‖ all peoples*], universal, as in the royal group 96–100. — **2.** *For His kindness ‖ faithfulness of Yahweh*], attributes most frequently combined in songs of praise. — *is mighty over us*], phr. elsw. 103[11]. The psalmist combines other nations, whom he addresses, with Israel in personal relation to Yahweh, as the recipients of His kindness and faithfulness.

1. הָאֻמִּים] a.λ. Aramaism for אֻמוֹת Nu. 25[15], אֻמָּתָם Gn. 25[16], for usual Heb. לְאֻמִּים. — **2.** גבר עלינו חסדו] phr. elsw. 103[11].

PSALM CXVIII.

Ps. 118 is a composite processional with responsive voices : I. In the streets of Jerusalem the leader calls upon the three classes of worshippers to speak, and the chorus responds with the liturgical phrase, "His kindness endureth forever" (v.[2-4]). The solo proclaims the deliverance of the people by Yah from great straits, and their confidence in Him who has helped them to triumph over their enemies (v.[5-7]). The leader recalls the multitude of enemies, and the chorus responds in a vow to exterminate them (v.[10-12]). The leader bids them hearken to the shouts of victory ; the chorus

responds that it is due to the right hand of Yahweh (v.[15-16]).
II. Entering the temple, the call to open the gates (v.[19]) is
answered by the priest that only the righteous may enter (v.[20]).
The statement that the rejected corner stone has been made the
head of the corner (v.[22]), is answered by the recognition that this
is the work of Yahweh (v.[23]). The call to recognize the day as
Yahweh's feast (v.[24]), is answered by a priestly blessing from the
house of Yahweh (v.[26]). Many glosses emphasize various things
(v.[8-9. 13-14. 17-18. 21. 25. 27-28]). The Ps. in its present form begins and
ends with the liturgical summons to thanksgiving (v.[1. 29]).

A. v.[2-7. 10-12. 15-16], 4 STR. 6³.

O LET (the house of) Israel say:
  For His kindness endureth forever.
  O let the house of Aaron say:
  For His kindness endureth forever.
  O let them that fear Yahweh say:
  For His kindness endureth forever.
OUT of my straits I called upon Yah;
  (Yah) answered me in a broad place.
  Yahweh is for me; I fear not.
  What can man do to me?
  Yahweh is for me, as my great Helper;
  And so I look in triumph upon them that hate me.
ALL nations encompassed me,
  In the name of Yahweh will I circumcise them.
  They encompassed me, yea encompassed me.
  In the name of Yahweh will I circumcise them.
  They encompassed me, as bees (encompass) wax.
  In the name of Yahweh will I circumcise them,
HARK! a shout of joy and victory!
  (*The right hand of Yahweh doeth valiantly.*)
  Victory in the tents of the righteous!
  The right hand of Yahweh doeth valiantly.
  The right hand of Yahweh is exalted.
  The right hand of Yahweh doeth valiantly.

B. v.[19-20. 22-24. 26], 3 STR. 4³.

OPEN to me the gates of Zedek,
  That I may enter therein to give thanks to Yah.
  This is the gate that belongs to Yahweh.
  The righteous may enter therein.
THE stone that the builders rejected
  Has become the head of the corner.
  From Yahweh this has come,
  It is wonderful in our eyes.

T HIS is the day that Yahweh hath made.
　　Let us exult and let us be glad in it.
　　　　Blessed be he that cometh, in the name of Yahweh.
　　　　We bless you from the house of Yahweh.

Ps. 118 is a Hallel; introduced by ἀλληλουιά in 𝕲, but not in 𝔚, which omits it also at the end of the Ps. There can be little doubt that 𝕲 is correct. The Ps. resembles 115 B in its structure of trimeter hexastichs, in its use of responsive voices, in its division of the worshippers into three classes v.[2-4]. But it differs from that Ps. in that it celebrates in a temple festival a victory that has just been won, and looks forward to other and greater victories. Accordingly, as the Ps. cannot belong to the period of the Hebrew monarchy, we are compelled to think of the Maccabean victories: and the temper of the whole Ps. favours this date, as does its language and style. The Ps. uses earlier ones: v.[5] 18[20]; v.[6] 56[12]; v.[7] 54[6, 9]; v.[22] Is. 28[16]. The uses of Ex. 15 are in glosses, v.[14, 21, 28]. The Davidic Psalter was in the mind of the psalmist. But the Ps. is modelled after the earlier 115: v.[2-4]; cf. 115[9-11]; and uses מצר v.[5] as 116[3]. The use of אמילם v.[10-12] is probably in the ironical sense, and as such is peculiarly appropriate to the earlier Maccabean times, when circumcision was forbidden to Israel by the Syrians. The only objection of Bä. to the Maccabean date is the use of v.[25] in the prayer of Nehemiah, Ne. 1[11]: but as this v. is a gl. in the Ps., the objection falls; and his reasons for thinking of the feast of Tabernacles of Ne. 8[14-18] have little force. The Ps. is introduced and concluded with a liturgical couplet, which in neither case was original. There are several other glosses: (1) v.[8-9] is a pentameter couplet; (2) v.[13-14] a pentameter couplet based on Ex. 15[2]; (3) v.[21] a pentameter l. also based on Ex. 15[2]; (4) v.[25] a tetrameter couplet from Ne. 1[11]; (5) v.[28] a pentameter also based on Ex. 15[2]; (6) v.[17-18] a trimeter tetrastich, original to the glossator, but involving a different situation from the victory celebrated in the Ps.; (7) v.[27] an interpretation of the blessing in accordance with Nu. 6[25] (P), and a direction as to the procession in the temple. After these gls. have been stripped off, the first Pt. is composed of trimeter hexastichs. Three of them, v.[2-4, 10-12, 15-16], are responsive, each with thrice repeated solo voices and responses. One of them, v.[5-6], is a solo recital of the victory. The second Pt. of Ps. has three tetrastichs, owing to the fact that the voices use couplets instead of single lines. This part of the Ps. was sung in the temple by priest and people, the other part exterior to the temple by a procession in the streets in which a solo led and a chorus responded.

PSALM CXVIII.　*A.*

The Ps. is introduced and concluded by the liturgical formula : *Give thanks to Yahweh; for He is good; for His kindness endureth forever*], cf. 106[1] 107[1] + ; which was not in the original Ps. because it has no place in the strophical organisation. — **Str. I. 2–4.** The leader of the procession in the streets of Jerusalem calls upon the three classes, *house of Israel, house of Aaron*, and *them that fear Yahweh* (cf. 115[9-13]), to *say*]. What they are to say, is the liturgical phrase so suited to the situation, repeated after each of the three summons.

Str. II. The leader recites, in a hexastich synth. and progressive throughout, the deliverance and the victory. — **5.** *Out of my straits*], the great trials due, as the context suggests, to enemies; out of a deep experience of agony. — *I called upon Yah*], in prayer for relief; using the poetic abbreviation of "Yahweh." — *answered me*] in response to the call and — *in a broad place*], pregnant, implying the vb. "set me," in antithesis with the "straits." — **6.** *Yahweh is for me*], repeated v.[7a]; on my side. — *I fear not*] with the best of reasons; because Yahweh so shields me, that the challenge can be uttered. — *What can man do to me ?*], citation from 56[12], and cited in Heb. 13[6]. — **7.** *As my great Helper*], cf. 54[6] in antithesis with *them that hate me.* — *Upon* these last he *looks*] pregnant; in triumph, as the result of the divine help, cf. 59[11] 92[12]. — **8-9.** A glossator adds a pentameter couplet of gnomic experience :

> It is better to take refuge in Yahweh, than to trust in mankind.
> It is better to take refuge in Yahweh, than to trust in princes.

Str. III. 10-12. The leader describes the serious situation in three syn. lines, in which the vb. *encompassed me*, is repeated four times; at first with the subject *all nations*, then twice for emphasis without subj., and finally with a simile. — *as bees* encompass *wax*], for thus the text should be restored. — It has been confused by the gloss : *They are quenched as the fire of thorns*], which certainly is not suitable as the words of the leader, and impairs the strong statement thrice repeated by the chorus in identical language : — *In the name of Yahweh will I circumcise them*] ; this vb. is used here ironically. The Syrian oppressors had forbidden circumcision to Israel. Israel would take vengeance by circumcising them ; yet not with a religious significance, but as the performance of an operation extremely painful to adults ; cf. Gn. 34. — A glossator appends a pentameter line referring back to the straits. — **13.** *Thou didst thrust hard at me* *that I might fall*]. The change of subj. common in glosses makes a direct complaint against the enemy in antithesis with : *but Yahweh was my helper*, cf. v.⁷ᵃ. The latter clause is then strengthened **14** by a loose citation from Ex. 15² : *Yah is my strength and psalm, and has become my salvation.*

Str. IV. has the same structure as Str. I., III. **15–16.** The leader calls attention to the celebration of the victory. — *Hark*], exclamation, as JPSV., more probable than " voice of " EVˢ. — *a shout of joy and victory*], " salvation " of EVˢ. is too general to suit the situation. — *in the tents of the righteous*], the army of righteous Israel triumphing over the enemy. — *The right hand of Yahweh is exalted*], the lifting up of His hand has given the victory. — The chorus responds in three identical lines : *The right hand of Yahweh*, personified, *doeth valiantly*] in battle. — Again, the glossator returns to the previous straits in a trimeter tetrastich. **17.** *I shall not die*], a national death, *but I shall live*], in the renewal of national existence and independence. — *And I shall declare*], in the temple worship, *the deeds of Yah*], His victorious doings. — **18.** *Yahweh hath sorely chastened me*]. The people recognize that they have been under divine discipline. — *But He hath not given me over unto death*], delivered me into the hands of mine enemies.

PSALM CXVIII. *B.*

A procession has come up to the gates of the temple, and the chorus speaks in couplets, and a priest responds in couplets. **19.** *Open to me the gates of Zedek*]. It is probable that this is an ancient proper name of the Holy City, which is called " the city of Zedek " Is. 1²⁶ ; cf. Je. 31²³ 50⁷, and whose ancient kings were called Adonizedek Jos. 10¹·³ and Melchizedek Gn. 14¹⁸ ; as " Salem " is used 76³. — *That I may enter therein to give thanks to Yah*]. The purpose of the procession is to offer a thank offering and celebrate a festival for the victory given by Yahweh. — **20.** To this the priest replies : *This is the gate that belongs to Yahweh*]. Only those may enter whom He permits access to His presence, and only *The righteous* people of Israel — *may enter therein*]. This is an implicit inquiry whether they were such. — The glossator now adds : **21.** Another statement based on Ex. 15² : *I will* *give Thee thanks that Thou hast answered me, and become mine for victory*], which is a further unfolding of v.[20b].— The true reply of the chorus is, however : **22**. *The stone that the builders rejected, has become the head of the corner*]. Zion is the cornerstone of the kingdom of God in accordance with Is. 28[16]. The nations had done their best to reject and destroy it. The last effort had been made by Antiochus, the king of Syria, but in vain. He had been overcome. Zion had regained her strength and glory through the victorious armies of the Maccabeans, and the omnipotent right hand of Yahweh. The Messianic application of the passage is due to the fact that the person of the Messiah bears the same relation to a kingdom of living persons that Zion, the capital of the kingdom, does to the kingdom. The metaphor stands equally well for both relations : cf. Mt. 21[42] = Mk. 12[10-11] = Lk. 20[17] Acts 4[11] 1 Pt. 2[4-7] Eph. 2[20] (Br.[MP. 208-209]).— **23**. The priest responds : *From Yahweh this has come. It is wonderful in our eyes*]. The elevation of Zion is due to the wonderful victory wrought by Yahweh Himself. — The final word of the chorus is : **24**. *This is the day that Yahweh hath made*]. This festival day, this day of celebration, is due to the victory wrought by Yahweh ; it is therefore His day.— *Let us exult and let us be glad in it*], in the festival celebration in the temple. — The priest replies with the blessing : **26**. *Blessed be he that cometh, in the name of Yahweh. We bless you from the house of Yahweh.*] The blessing is pronounced upon those coming or entering the gates of the temple with the purpose of celebrating this festival. And thus the Ps. reaches its most appropriate conclusion. A glossator, in view of a later situation of trial, interjected before the blessing of the priest an urgent petition, which is not suited to its context. — **25**. *O now, Yahweh, give victory ! O now, Yahweh, give prosperity.* — The same or another glossator adds to the blessing of the priest **27**, which in its original form was a trimeter couplet : *Yahweh it was*] who hath done all these glorious deeds. By error אל came into the text and forced the translation "Yahweh is God," which has no propriety in this context. — *And He hath given us light*], the light of His countenance, in the priestly blessing Nu. 6[25]. — *Even to the horns of the altar*], in accepting the sacrifices offered in the festival they were celebrating. — A

liturgical direction was written on the margin of ancient codices:
Begin the feast with dense boughs], as the feast of Tabernacles
Lv. 23⁴⁰; so essentially all ancient Vrss. But when these words
crept into the text, they made endless difficulty. The easiest
explanation of the combination is that the decoration of the courts
of the temple extended even to the horns of the altar (cf. Succa,
IV. 5). EVˢ. "bind the sacrifice with cords, even unto the
horns of the altar" is not in accord with sacrificial laws or usage.
Or the vb. might be taken in a pregnant sense, as Hu., Now., Dr.,
"and lead it unto," which, while more reasonable, is still against
usage, for the blood of the victim was applied to the altars by the
officiating priest: the animals were never brought thither. De.,
after Ainsworth, thinks of the festival offerings as so numerous
that they filled the entire court, even to the horns of the altar.
But Ainsworth in his alternative, "many sacrifices or boughs," is
uncertain which to choose. Moreover, there is no usage in OT.
to justify taking חג in the sense of festival offering. The view of
Bä. that חג is to be taken in the ancient sense of the sacred
dance, and that "the dance" is to be joined with "dense boughs"
or garlands, however tempting it may be (cf. JPSV. "wreathe
ye the festival march with branches of myrtle") is not sustained by the usage of the word, and is altogether improbable
at the late date of the Ps. — **28.** The glossator adds another
pentameter on the basis of Ex. 15², as he had already done in
v.¹⁴· ²¹ : *My'El art Thou, and I will give Thee thanks ; my God,
and I will exalt Thee.*

CXVIII. *A.*

5. הַמֵּצַר] *the straits*, elsw. 116³ La. 1³. — מֶרְחָבְיָה] composed of יָה and מֶרְחָב
broad, roomy place 18²⁰ 31⁹; as 𝔍 *in latitudine dominus* and Eastern Mas.
𝕲ᴺ· ᴬ· ᴿ· ᵀ, Western Mas., regard it as enlarged fem. form. — **7.** בְּעֹזְרִי] i.p.
among my helpers or emphatic pl. with ב *essentiae, as my Helper*, Dr. better, but 𝔍 *mihi auxiliator*, 𝕲ᴺ· ᴬ· ᴿ· ᵀ ἐμοὶ βοηθός, וְעֹזְרִי Che., בְּעֹזְרִי Gr.—
10. כִּי אֲמִילַם] Hiph. impf. 1 sg., sf. 3 pl. Ges.²⁶ᵈ. 𝕲, 𝔍, do not translate כִּי.
It is prob. a gl. of asseveration. ‡ מול vb. Qal *circumcise*, Niph. *be circumcised*, neither in ψ ; Hiph. *make to be circumcised* BDB. here and v.¹¹· ¹² ;
but De. *cut in pieces*, 𝔗 אהישנון, 𝔖 אסיפה, 𝕲ᴺ· ᴬ· ᴿ· ᵀ, Aq. ἠμυνάμην, Σ διέθρυψα,
𝔍, 𝔙, *ultus sum*. Du., Valeton rd. אֲפִילֵם. — **12.** כדברים] pl. † דְּבוֹרָה n.f. *bee*,
Is. 7¹⁸, pl. דברים elsw. Dt. 1⁴⁴ Ju. 14⁸.--דֹּעֲכוּ] Pu. pf. 3 pl. † דָּעַךְ] vb. Qal *go
out, be extinguished*, of lamp, fig. of wicked, Jb. 18⁵· ⁶ 21¹⁷ Pr. 13⁹ 20²⁰ 24²⁰, of

hostile armies Is. 43¹⁷, Niph. of brooks Jb. 6¹⁷, Pu. of enemies only here.
𝕲 ἐξεκαύθησαν, 𝖁 *exarserunt*, בערו, so Oort, Bä., Che., Gr. As a word is
missing, the text was prob.:

סבוני כדברים דונג

בערו כאש בקוצים

The second l., however, is a gl. — קוֹצִים] pl. ‡ קוֹץ n.m. *thorn bush, thorn*, Ex. 22⁵
(E) Is. 33¹² Je. 4³ 12¹³ +. — **13.** וָחֹה] Qal inf. abs. דהה vb. *thrust, push*, followed by pf.; cf. 35⁵ 62⁴ 140⁵. This v. is a gl. — **14.** עָזִי וזמרת יה], as Ex. 15²
v. Intr. § 1. This v. also is a gl. — **15.** קוֹל] exclam. *hark!*, as JPSV. —
יִשׁוּעָה] should be in both clauses; the second was omitted by haplog. —
עֹשֵׂה היל] as 60¹⁴ = 108¹⁴; of warlike valour. — **18.** יַסֹר] Pi. *v.* 2¹⁰ *discipline
with severity*, as 94¹².

CXVIII. *B.*

19. אָבֹא] final clause; so אוֹרֶה. — **22.** ‡ פִּנָּה] n.f. *corner*, of stone, as
Is. 28¹⁶. — **25.** הַצְלִיחָה] Hiph. Imv. cohort.; cf. *1³* 37⁷. — **27.** אֶל יהוה] conflation of two divine names though in 𝕲. אל came in from below. — וָאֵר] Hiph.
impf. ו consec. copula in previous clause. אור *make shine* the face of Yahweh,
as Nu. 6²⁵ (P) Ps. 31¹⁷ 67² 80⁴·⁸·²⁰ 119¹³⁵; cf. 4⁷ 13⁴. 𝕲^{א. A. R. T} καὶ ἐπέ-
φανεν, 𝖃 *et apparuit*. — אסרו חג בעבתים] 𝕲 συστήσασθε ἑορτὴν ἐν τοῖς πυκά-
ζουσιν, 𝖁 *constituite diem solemnem in condensis*, 𝖃 *frequentate sollemnitatem
in fronduosis*, Σ συνδήσατε ἐν πανηγύρει πυκάσματα. These Vrss. all take
חג in the usual sense of *feast*, and עבתים in the sense of *boughs with dense foliage*. Lag. would rd.: ערבים Lv. 23⁴⁰ for עבתים, but this is unnecessary and
improb. The difficulty in this interp. is with the vb. אסר, which means to
bind, tie; but אסר מלחמה 1 K. 20¹⁴, 2 Ch. 13³ means to *join battle*, cf. German
"den Streit anknüpfen"; so here *begin the feast with dense boughs*, as Lv. 23⁴⁰,
the first day of the feast of Tabernacles. The interp. of חג as *festal victim*, cf.
חֲגִינָה, though sustained by Ew., Ol., De., Hu., Now., Dr., *al.*, has no support
in usage of OT.; and the interp. as *sacred dance* or *procession* of Bä., Davies,
Minocchi, JPSV., is a rare and early usage, not to be thought of in so late a
Ps. or gl.

PSALM CXIX., 22 STR. 8⁵.

Ps. 119 is a prayer of the congregation in twenty-two parts, based
on the observance of the Law. (1) Happy are those who perfectly
obey the Law. (2) They observe it with heart, lip, and way, and
rejoice in it. (3) The Law is their counsellor against plotting
princes. They pray that Yahweh may uncover its wonders;
(4) may quicken and strengthen them according to it, and deliver
them from humiliation. (5) They pray that He may teach them

the Law, that they may turn unto it away from covetousness.
(6) They assert their trust in the Law, and vow to observe it with
delight and love. (7) Proud seducers like a sirocco torment them
for keeping the Law, but cannot deprive them of their comfort and
joy in it. (8) The cords of the wicked enclose them, but they still
are companions to those that observe the Law. (9) Yahweh is
good and the doer of good, even in their affliction by proud enemies.
(10) Yahweh is their maker and His Law is righteous, therefore
they pray that not the perfect but the proud may be shamed.
(11) They pine for salvation, but hope in the Law. The proud
have well-nigh overcome them by treachery. (12) The Law is
fixed eternally in heaven and on earth. It has no end, and is
exceeding broad. (13) They love the Law, which imparts wisdom,
and hate every evil way. (14) The Law is a lamp. Their life is
risked by the snares of the wicked, but they rejoice in their inheritance in the Law. (15) They pray for support against backsliders,
whom they hate, but they reverence and love the Law; (16) they
pray that He will save them from oppressors, and give them understanding in the Law which they love. (17) The Law is wonderful,
giving light. They long to understand it, and pray for redemption
from oppressors who break it. (18) Yahweh is righteous, and His
Law is upright. Jealousy for the Law has destroyed them, but
they have not forgotten it. (19) In great peril they anxiously
pray for salvation from enemies. Their hope is in the everlasting
Law. (20) They plead for redemption from treacherous persecutors.
The Law is the sum of faithfulness. (21) Persecuted by princes
without cause, they yet praise the Law and hope for salvation.
(22) They plead for salvation with a vow of praise with lip and
tongue.

HAPPY are they that are perfect in way, who walk in (*Thy*) Law;
  Happy are they that seek (Thee) with the whole heart, who keep (*Thy*)
    Testimonies.
  Thou (Thyself) hast commanded to observe diligently *Thy* Precepts:
  Then shall I not be ashamed in looking unto all *Thy* Commands.
א Yea, they do no iniquity that walk (according to *Thy* Word);
  Ah: that my ways were established to observe *Thy* (Saying).
  I will thank Thee with uprightness of heart, learning Thy righteous Judgments:
  Do not forsake me utterly; I will observe *Thy* Statutes.
WHEREBY shall one keep his path pure? By observing *Thy* Word;
  Within my heart, that I may not sin against Thee, I have stored up *Thy* Saying.

Blessed be Thou, Yahweh! Teach me *Thy* Statutes:
With my lips I told all the Judgments of *Thy* mouth.

ב In Thy (Law) I delight myself, I forget not (*Thy*) Way.
In Thy Testimonies I rejoice, over above all riches in (*Thy*) Way.
With my whole heart I seek Thee; let me not err from *Thy* Commands;
In Thy Precepts I muse, and I look unto *Thy* paths.

DEAL bountifully with Thy servant, that I may live, and I will observe *Thy* Word:
Yea, princes sit down, talk together against me, while I muse on *Thy* Statutes.
A sojourner am I in the earth; do not hide from me *Thy* (Saying);
My soul is in exile in longing at every time for *Thy* Judgments.

ג Uncover mine eyes that I may behold wonderful things out of *Thy* Law:
Uncover reproach and contempt; I have kept *Thy* (Precepts).
Thou dost rebuke the proud, the accursed that err from *Thy* Commands;
Yea, my delight, the men of my counsel, are *Thy* Testimonies.

MY soul doth cleave to the dust; according to Thy Word quicken *me*:
My ways have I told, and Thou hast answered me; Thy Statutes teach me.
The way of Thy wonders will I sing; Thy (Judgments) make *me* understand;
My soul doth drop away from heaviness; according to Thy (Saying) raise
    me up.

ד The way of falsehood remove from me, and with Thy Law be gracious to *me*;
The way of fidelity have I chosen; with Thy (Precepts) compose *me*.
I cleave unto Thy Testimonies, Yahweh; put *me* not to shame;
The way of Thy Commands will I run; for Thou wilt encourage *my* heart.

MAKE me understand Thy Law, and I will observe it with all (*my*) heart.
Show me the way of Thy (Precepts) and I will keep it as (*my*) reward.
Make me tread in the path of Thy Commands; for in it *I* delight;
Incline unto Thy Testimonies and not unto covetousness *my* heart.

ה Remove mine eyes from worthlessness, (according to Thy Word) quicken *me*.
Behold, I long for Thy (Statutes); in Thy righteousness quicken *me*.
Establish to Thy servant Thy Saying; according to the fear that is due Thee
    (*my* step);
Remove my reproach; Thine excellent Judgments *I* stand in awe of.

VERILY let Thy kindness, Yahweh, bring me Thy salvation according to *Thy*
    Word;
And I will lift up my palms unto what I sing of, even *Thy* Statutes.
Verily do not snatch away the word of faithfulness; I hope in *Thy* Judgments.
And I will return word to him that reproacheth me that I trust in *Thy* (Saying).

ו Verily I will observe continually, forever and ever, *Thy* Law;
And I will walk in a roomy place, because I study *Thy* Precepts;
And I will speak before kings, and I will not be ashamed of *Thy* Testimonies;
And I will delight myself in what I love, even *Thy* Commands.

REMEMBER Thy servant, because Thou hast made me hope in (*Thy*) Word;
This is my comfort in mine affliction, that Thou hast quickened me according
    to *Thy* Saying.
The proud scorn me exceedingly; I have not inclined from *Thy* (Testimonies);
I remember of old, Yahweh, and comfort myself in *Thy* Judgments.

ז A burning wind has seized me from the wicked, the forsakers of Thy Law.
Songs have I in the house of my sojourning, even *Thy* Statutes.
I remember in the night Thy name, and observe *Thy* (Commands);
This have I because I keep *Thy* Precepts.

I ENTREAT Thy favour with my whole heart; be gracious to me according to
    Thy Saying;
    My portion, Yahweh, I have said that I would observe *Thy* Word.
    At midnight I rise up because of *Thy* righteous Judgments;
    I have considered my ways and (turned) unto *Thy* Testimonies.

ח The earth is full of Thy kindness; teach me *Thy* Statutes:
    The cords of the wicked have enclosed me; I do not forget *Thy* Law.
    A companion am I to all that fear Thee, and to them that observe *Thy* Precepts:
    I made haste and delayed not to observe *Thy* Commands.

WELL hast Thou dealt with Thy servant, Yahweh, according to *Thy* Word:
    Well was it for me that I was afflicted that I might learn *Thy* (Testimonies).
    Before I was afflicted I erred; but now I observe *Thy* Saying:
    Better to me than thousands of gold are the (Judgments) of *Thy* Mouth.

ט The proud have smeared lies over me; I keep *Thy* Precepts.
    Their heart is gross with fatness; I delight in *Thy* Law.
    Good taste and knowledge teach me, I believe in *Thy* Commands:
    Good and the doer of good art Thou: teach me *Thy* Statutes.

LET them that fear Thee turn to me that they may know *Thy* Testimonies:
    Let them that fear Thee see me and be glad, that I hope in *Thy* Word.
    I know, Yahweh, that righteous and faithful are *Thy* Judgments:
    Let Thy kindness be to Thy servant, to confirm me according to *Thy* Saying.

י Let Thy compassion come to me, that I may live; my delight is in *Thy* Law.
    Let the proud be shamed; while I muse on *Thy* Precepts.
    Let my heart be perfect, that I may not be ashamed of *Thy* Statutes.
    Thy hands made me and prepared me, that I might learn *Thy* Commands.

MY soul doth pine for Thy salvation: I hope in *Thy* Word:
    Mine eyes fail: how long ere will comfort me *Thy* Saying?
    Though I am become like a wineskin in smoke, I forget not *Thy* Statutes.
    How many are the days of Thy servant? How long ere (*Thy*) Judgments?

כ The proud have dug for me pits: for one who is according to *Thy* Law.
    According to Thy kindness quicken me, that I may keep the Testimonies of
        Thy Mouth.
    All with falsehood pursue me; faithful are *Thy* Commands.
    Almost had they consumed me, and yet I have not forsaken *Thy* Precepts.

FOREVER fixed in heaven, Yahweh, is *Thy* Word.
    To all generations Thou hast established (in) the earth and there standest fast
        Thy (Saying).
    As regards Thy Judgments, they stand fast to-day; for all are *Thy* servants.
    Forever will I not forget; for Thou dost quicken me according to *Thy*
        (Statutes).

ל Though I had perished in mine affliction, my delight had been in *Thy* Law.
    For me the wicked wait to destroy me; I consider diligently *Thy* Testimonies
    Thine am I; save me; for I study *Thy* Precepts.
    To all completeness have I seen an end; broad are *Thy* Commands.

O HOW I love Thy Law! All the day is it *my* musing:
    More wise than mine enemies, Thou makest me with Thy Commands; forever
        they are *mine*.
    More insight than all teachers have I; for Thy Testimonies are *my* musing:
    More understanding than my seniors have I; for Thy Precepts *I* keep.

מ From every evil way, that I may observe Thy Word, do *I* refrain;

From Thy Judgments I do not turn aside; for Thou dost instruct *me.*

From Thy (Statutes) have I understanding; for every word of falsehood *I* hate:

O how sweet is Thy Saying to my palate! sweeter than honey to *my* mouth.

A LAMP to my foot and a light to my path is *Thy* Word:

I have sworn and confirmed it, to observe *Thy* righteous Judgments.

I am sore afflicted, Yahweh: quicken me according to *Thy* (Saying):

The freewill offerings of my mouth, O accept, and teach me *Thy* (Statutes).

ℶ My life is in my palm continually; but I forget not *Thy* Law:

The wicked have laid a snare for me; but I err not from *Thy* (Commands).

I incline with my heart to do as a reward *Thy* (Precepts).

I have an everlasting inheritance; for the joy of my heart are *Thy* Testimonies.

MY hiding place and my shield art Thou: I hope in *Thy* Word:

Uphold me, and shame me not in my hope, that I may live according to *Thy* Saying.

Those that backslide Thou dost cause to cease: therefore I love *Thy* Testimonies.

My flesh bristles up in awe of Thee and I reverence *Thy* Judgments.

ס Those that swerve with their mouth I hate; but I love *Thy* Law:

Support me that I may be saved, and I will (delight) continually in *Thy* Statutes.

Thou dost set at naught the falsehood of their deceit: all that backslide from *Thy* (Precepts).

As for them that turn aside, their portion is adversity; but I keep (*Thy*) Commands.

MINE eyes pine for Thy Salvation and for *Thy* righteous Saying:

Take (Thy Word) in pledge; let not the proud oppress (*Thy* servant).

I have done (Thy) Judgments: do not abandon to the oppressor (*Thy* servant).

Thy servant am I; make me have understanding that I may know *Thy* Testimonies.

ע Do with Thy servant according to Thy kindness, teach me *Thy* Statutes.

It is time for Yahweh to act: they have broken *Thy* Law.

Therefore more than gold or than fine gold I love *Thy* Commands.

Therefore the way of falsehood I hate, I direct my steps according to (*Thy*) Precepts.

THE opening of Thy Word giveth light, giveth understanding to the *simple.*

Wonderful are Thy Testimonies; therefore keepeth them *my* soul.

Turn to the one that loves Thy name, and according to Thy Judgments be gracious to *me.*

My footsteps confirm according to Thy Saying, and let not iniquity have dominion over *me.*

צ Streams of water, because they keep not Thy Law, run down *mine* eye.

Redeem me from the oppression of man: Thy Precepts *I* keep.

Thy face make shine on Thy servant, and Thy Statutes teach *me.*

My mouth I open wide and pant: for Thy Commands *I* long.

IN righteousness and faithfulness exceeding Thou hast commanded *Thy* Testimonies.

My jealousy hath destroyed me, that mine adversaries have forgotten *Thy* Word.

Smelted exceedingly is Thy servant, but he doth love *Thy* Saying:
Righteous art Thou, Yahweh; and upright are *Thy* Judgments.

צ I am small and despised, but I forget not *Thy* Precepts.
Thy righteousness is righteousness forever; and faithfulness is *Thy* Law.
Trouble and distress have overtaken me: my delight are *Thy* Commands.
Thy righteousness is forever; give me understanding that I may live according
to *Thy* (Statutes).

I AM beforehand with the twilight of dawn, and cry for help: I hope in *Thy* Word:
Mine eyes are beforehand with the night watches to muse of *Thy* Saying.
My voice, O hear, according to Thy kindness; quicken me according to *Thy*
Judgments:

I call with my whole heart; answer me; I will keep *Thy* Statutes.

ק They draw near that pursue (me) with evil devices, that are far from *Thy* Law:
I call upon Thee (Yahweh); O save me; and I will observe *Thy* Testimonies.
Be Thou near, Yahweh; faithful are *Thy* Commands:
Of old I know (them); forever Thou hast founded *Thy* (Precepts).

PLEAD my cause and redeem me: quicken me according to *Thy* (Word):
I see the treacherous and loathe them that do not observe *Thy* Saying.
Far off from the wicked is salvation: they study not *Thy* Statutes.
Many are Thy compassions, Yahweh: quicken me according to *Thy* Judg-
ments.

ר O see mine affliction and rescue me: I do not forget *Thy* Law:
Many are my persecutors and mine adversaries: I do not decline from *Thy*
Testimonies.

O see, quicken me, according to Thy kindness; I love *Thy* Precepts.
The sum of faithfulness and forever are *Thy* righteous (Commands).

PRINCES persecute me without cause; I stand in awe of *Thy* Word:
I rejoice, as one that findeth spoil, over *Thy* Saying.
Seven times a day I praise *Thy* righteous Judgments:
Lying I hate and abhor; I love *Thy* (Statutes).

ש Great peace without a cause of stumbling have they that love *Thy* Law:
My soul doth observe and love exceedingly *Thy* Testimonies.
I hope for Thy salvation, Yahweh; I do *Thy* Commands.
I observe Thy Precepts: yea, all my ways are before *Thee*.

LET my yell come near before Thee; make me to have understanding according
to *Thy* Word:

Let my supplication come before Thee; deliver me according to *Thy* Saying.
My lips will pour forth praise, that Thou teachest me *Thy* Statutes:
My tongue will respond in faithfulness of *Thy* righteous (Judgments).

ת I long for Thy salvation, Yahweh, my delight is in *Thy* Law:
Let me live and praise Thee, and make to help me *Thy* (Testimonies).
Let Thine hand be ready for my help; I have chosen *Thy* Precepts.
I stray as a lost sheep: but I do not forget *Thy* Commands.

Ps. 119 (118 𝕲, 𝖅) is the most artificial of the Psalms. It is composed of
twenty-two alphabetical Strs., in the order of the Hebrew alphabet. Each
Str. has eight lines, each line beginning with the letter characteristic of the
Str.; cf. La. 3, which has twenty-two alphabetical Strs. of three lines each,
every line beginning with the letter characteristic of its Str. The Ps. is also

artificial at the close of its lines, rhyming with the characteristic suffix, or some form corresponding with it in utterance. Copyists and glossators have disregarded this feature; but by transpositions and a few modifications of the text justified for other reasons, it is easy to so restore them that they always rhyme either in ךְ_ or יִ_. Dr. Littmann has called my attention to the fact that the same kind of syllabic play is found in Arabic poetry. The Ps. has also its regular, uniform measure throughout. It is not always easy to distinguish pentameters from hexameters, especially when the text has been often corrupted by prosaic copyists; but the measure of this Ps. is really pentameter. The most significant feature of this Ps. is its use of eight terms for the Law. These are: דבר, אמרה, הקיב, משפטים, חורה, מצות, ערות, and פקורים. The only other word used for Law in this Ps. is v.[16] חקוּת. But this single instance is doubtless an error. It has been inserted for another term which is missing from the Str. Since just these eight terms are used, and used uniformly throughout the Ps., the presumption is that each one was used once, and once only, in each Str. This is the case with some exceptions, due to corruption of the text. It is not difficult to restore the original text, so far as these eight terms are concerned, and to show that each term was used once in each of the Strs., and that all were used in every Str. It was not understood by later copyists that these were all legal terms, and hence there arose gradually textual errors due to the giving of other interpretations to these terms. All Christian translations err greatly in this particular.

These eight terms represent in their original meaning several types of Hebrew Law (v. Br. [Hex. 242 sq.]). But in this Ps. they seem to have lost for the most part their original force. (1) The term דבר is the *Word* or *sentence* of Law, originally of the type: *Thou shalt* or *shalt not*, a prophetic word addressed to Israel as a nation conceived as one person. דבר is the earliest term, and the most prominent one in this Ps. (2) The term אִמְרָה, *Saying*, is a poetic syn. of דבר, based on Dt. 33⁹. It is so used in sg. throughout the Ps.; prob. also in 19¹⁰, for which יִרְאַת has been substituted by mistake. (3) The term חקים indicates the brief, terse *Statutes* of the primitive Hebrew administration of Law, usually with penalty attached. This term is used in pl. throughout the Ps. (4) A later type of the חקים are the משפטים, *Judgments*, used also in pl. throughout. The sg. in v.⁴³·⁸⁴·¹²¹·¹³²·¹⁴⁹·¹⁶⁰·¹⁷⁵ is due to txt. err. (5) חורה, *the Law*, as teaching, instruction; originally a term for a body of law, in P for specific laws also; used throughout in sg. (6) מצוה is used in pl. for Deuteronomic or later prophetic *Commands*. (7) עירות, *Testimonies*, term of P, used in pl. (8) פקרים, *Precepts*, a poetic term in late Pss. 𝔊 renders ἐντολαί same as מצוה, for which indeed it is a synonym; 𝔍 renders *praecepta* same as חקים. It is used throughout the Ps. in pl. with sf. These eight terms for Law, so far as 𝔐 and Vrss. are concerned, are used with such variation that there seems to be no more order than in a kaleidoscope. There are variations in the Vrss., but these are not sufficient in number or helpful in character to change this situation. It is improbable that an author, who in all other respects was so artificial and ornate in style, would in this essential matter be so artless and unconventional. This Ps. was composed for recitation as an ABC for the training of the young scribe in the Law. One would expect the author to give aid to the memory by an orderly arrangement. When we examine these terms in their present usage, and emend the text in the cases already mentioned, some trace of order becomes apparent in the midst of the chaos. The question then arises whether the disorder is not the result of the carelessness of scribes, or due to variations of memory in the ancient schools. Bä. tells us that "jeder Vers bildet in der Regel einen für sich abgeschlossenen Gedanken ; nur selten (z. B. 89–91, 97–100) hangen mehrere Verse enger zusammen." This is as much as to say that this Ps. lacks parall., the essential feature of all Heb. poetry, and is in fact no poetry at all. A careful search for parallelism in this Ps. makes it evident that there is no Ps. more marked by parall. in its varied forms, and that no Heb. poetry known to us has a greater variety of these forms than this Ps. By copyists' errors and glossators' neglects, by readjustments due to defective memory or slips of the eye, or supposed improvements of editors, the original parall. is often obscured or destroyed ; but it is not difficult to restore it in most cases, as the subsequent comment shows.

Much time has been spent and no pains have been spared in the effort to discover the principle which determines the variation of terms in the Strs. The following scheme is presented as the best that we can offer at present. If the problem is not fully solved, it is hoped that the solution is not far distant. The principle of arrangement has been determined chiefly through a study of the parallelisms. These seemed to require a transposition of lines in many Strs. The frequent omissions and duplications of terms in 𝕳, and the many and remarkable variants presented by 𝕲, 𝖅, seemed to justify an occasional transposition of terms, as well as the substitution of missing terms for duplicates. The scheme is as follows: (1) The Strs. are grouped in pairs by a similar use of the terms. (2) They are divided into larger groups of four, eight, and ten Strs., by the interchange of all four terms between the tetrastichs (Strs. 1–2, 5–6, 13–14). (3) These groups are subdivided by changes in the terms of the opening couplets of the tetrastichs. Throughout the Ps. the tetrastichs use in their first lines דבר and תורה, excepting in Strs. 7–10, 15–18, where the terms of the first couplet change places, and דבר and תורה take the second place. With דבר is used אמרה in Strs. 1–2, 7–8, 11–12, 15–16, 19–22 (12 Strs.), משפטים in Strs. 13–14 (2 Strs.), חקים in Strs. 3–6 (4 Strs.), עדוה in Strs. 9–10, 17–18 (4 Strs.). With תורה is used: פקורים in Strs. 3–6, 9–10, 17–18 (8 Strs.), מצות in Strs. 13–14 (2 Strs.), עדות in Strs. 1–2, 11–12, 19–22 (8 Strs.), חקים in Strs. 7–8, 15–16 (4 Strs.). This variation of the second term divides Strs. 1–4 into two pairs, Strs. 5–12 into four pairs, Strs. 13–20 into four pairs. The final Strs., 21–22, seem to form a group by themselves, as they repeat the arrangement of the first pair of Strs. and of the closing Strs. of the larger groups, 5–12, 13–20, varying only by using the order of the first Str. in one tetrastich and the order of the second Str. in the other tetrastich, *i.e.* 1^a is combined with 2^b, and 1^b with 2^a. (4) The tetrastichs always retain three of their terms, but occasionally interchange one. The terms thus common to both tetrastichs are הקים and עדות. חקים is used with דבר and its mates אמרה and משפטים in Strs. 1–6, 11–14, 19–22; עדות with הורה and its mates פקודים and מצוה in these same Strs. The two terms are interchanged in Strs. 7–10, 15–18. This variation serves to unite two of the four pairs in Strs. 5–12 and 13–20, making the subdivision of each group 2 + 4 + 2. (5) The order of terms in the first couplet of the tetrastichs is reversed only in Strs. 7–10, 15–18, *i.e.* where the variable terms are interchanged. This variation serves to emphasize the union of these pairs in quartettes. (6) The order of terms in the second couplet is regularly reversed throughout the Ps.; so that no Str. repeats exactly the combination of the preceding Str. (7) There is the same selection of terms, with variation in order only, in the opening and closing groups of the Ps., Strs. 1–4, 21–22, and in the opening and closing pairs of the groups 5–12, 13–20. There is correspondence in order as well between Strs. 1–2, 11–12, 19–20, 21–22; and between Strs. 3–4, 5–6. The same general correspondence appears between Strs. 7–10, 15–18, and the exact correspondence between Strs. 7–8, 15–16 and between Strs. 9–10, 17–18. This resemblance serves to unite the several groups into an organic whole. The scheme may be presented most clearly in the form of a table (see p. 418).

There is undoubtedly a considerable amount of repetition of phrases in this Ps., and this to the superficial reader gives the impression of monotony; but in fact such phrases are comparatively few in number, and their repetition is due to the emphasis the poet desires to put upon them and upon them alone. The great majority of the terms used in connection with the Law are used no more than once or twice in these 176 lines; so that in fact there is a wonderful variety in the Ps., a variety so great that it seems to exhaust the possibilities of usage.

The psalmist writes in the midst of great trouble, affliction, and indeed persecution. He is encompassed by proud, powerful enemies, who scorn him for his fidelity to the Law, and heap reproaches and contempt upon him. At the same time they seek to ensnare him by craft and lies. Notwithstanding all this, the psalmist is entirely loyal to the Law. The Law has become to him the representative of his God. Throughout the Ps. he ascribes to the Law the attributes older writers ascribe to God; looks to the Law for the help and salvation that ordinarily come from God alone. The Law is to him almost hypostatical, almost what the *Memra* became to later Judaism. It was eternal in heaven before it came to the earth: it came to the earth and to man to remain everlastingly. Upon its observance depend life, salvation, knowledge, wisdom, happiness, and every joy. It is not true that this author has the Deuteronomic spirit. The personal allegiance to Yahweh of D has become a legal allegiance. The psalmist is far in advance of the priestly attitude of P. He is a scribe, an early Pharisee of the highest and noblest type. The Ps. originated, therefore, after the rise of the Pharisaic party, at the time of their persecution because of zeal for the Law by the Hellenistic party in

2 E

חקם	משפטים	אמרה	דבר	מצות	פקודים	עדות	תורה	א
פקודים	מצות	עדות	תורה	משפטים	חקים	אמרה	דבר	ב
עדות	מצות	פקודים	תורה	משפטים	אמרה	חקים	דבר	ג
מצות	עדות	פקודים	תורה	אמרה	משפטים	חקים	דבר	ד
משפטום	אמרה	חקים	דבר	עדות	מצות	פקודים	תורה	ה
מצות	עדות	פקודים	תורה	אמרה	משפטים	חקים	דבר	ו
פקודים	מצות	חקים	תורה	משפטים	עדות	אמרה	דבר	ז
מצות	פקודים	תורה	חקים	עדות	משפטים	דבר	אמרה	ח
חקים	מצות	תורה	פקודים	משפטים	אמרה	עדות	דבר	ט
מצות	חקים	פקודים	תורה	אמרה	משפטים	דבר	ערות	י
פקודים	מצות	ערות	תורה	משפטים	חקים	אמרה	דבר	כ
מצות	פקודים	ערות	תורה	חקים	משפטים	אמרה	דבר	ל
אמרה	חקים	משפטים	דבר	פקודים	עדות	מצות	תורה	מ
עדות	פקודים	מצות	תורה	חקים	אמרה	משפטים	דבר	נ
מצות	פקודים	חקים	תורה	משפטים	עדות	אמרה	דבר	ס
פקודים	מצות	תורה	חקים	עדות	משפטים	אמרה	אמרה	ע
מצות	חקים	פקודים	תורה	אמרה	משפטים	עדות	דבר	פ
חקים	מצות	תורה	פקודים	משפטים	אמרה	דבר	עדות	צ
פקודים	מצות	עדות	תורה	חקים	משפטים	אמרה	דבר	ק
מצות	פקודים	עדות	תורה	משפטים	חקים	אמרה	דבר	ר
פקודים	מצות	עדות	תורה	חקים	משפטים	אמרה	דבר	ש
מצות	פקודים	עדות	תורה	משפטים	חקים	אמרה	דבר	ת

Israel, and especially by the haughty leaders and princes who represented the Syrian interest, toward the close of the Greek period.

Str. **א.** The first tetrastich has syn. and synth. couplets; the second, antith. and synth. couplets.—**1–8.** *Happy*], congratulation; repeated for emphasis v.^{2}, cf. 1^1.—*perfect in way*], who have integrity in their walk of life, cf. 15^2 $18^{22\,sq.}$ ‖ *Seek Thee with the whole heart*], so v.^{10}: personal acquaintanceship with Yahweh is the goal of their way. — *Walk in Thy Law*], as assonance and measure require; enlarged by glossator into " Law of Yahweh " to make the reference more definite; cf. *walk according to Thy Word*], v.^{3}, which an early copyist changed by error into the similar Heb. " in His way." — *keep Thy Testimonies*], v^2. This vb. is frequently used in this Ps. : with Testimonies also v.$^{22.\,129}$, with Law v.^{34}, with Precepts v.$^{56.\,69.\,100}$, with Commands v.^{115}, with Statutes v.$^{33.\,145}$. It is ‖ *observe Thy Precepts*], v.^{4}: vb. used with Precepts also v.$^{63.\,134.\,168}$, with Statutes v.$^{5.\,8\,(?)}$, with Word v.$^{9.\,17.\,57.\,101}$, with Law v.$^{34.\,44.\,55\,(?).\,136}$, with Commands v.^{60}, with Saying v.$^{67.\,158}$, with Testimonies v.$^{88.\,146.\,167.\,168\,(?)}$, with Judgments v.^{106}; the only vb. used with all the legal terms. These vbs. imply watchful, careful observance of the Law. It is evidently the chief thing in the mind of the author of the Ps. — *Thou Thyself hast commanded*], v.^{4}. The Law is the personal command of God, involving personal allegiance in seeking Him with the whole heart, and the resultant happiness. — *Ah : that*], v.^{5}, strong expression of longing, with its antithesis in the negative jussive v.^{8}. — *my ways were established*], fixed right, directed aright by God; so that I might walk aright in the way, be " perfect in way " v.^{1}. — Cf. for the negative side v.^{8}. *Do not forsake me utterly*], leaving me to walk alone, without divine direction; one who " seeks Thee with the whole heart " v.^{2}. — *Then shall I not be ashamed*], v.^{6}, put to shame by transgression — but, in antithesis, *thank Thee*], v.^{7}, giving God the praise. — *with uprightness of heart*], the heart being upright because without transgression, and with completeness of devotion. — *in looking unto all Thy Commands*], with a teachable spirit to learn; cf. v.^{15} ‖ *learning Thy righteous Judgments*]. The vb. " learn " is used also with Commands v.^{73}, with Statutes v.^{71}. The phr. " righteous Judgments " is used elsw. v.$^{62.\,106.\,164}$, also with corrected text v.$^{121.\,160.\,172}$, cf. v.^{75}, a favorite term of this author; cf. 19^{10} for the idea.

Str. ב. The first quartette is composed of two synth. couplets; the second of lines essentially syn. — **9–16.** *Whereby shall one keep his path pure?*], a question directed to God; cf. the antith. v.³·⁵. An early copyist under the influence of WL. inserted in the text "young man"; but the context has no more to do with young men than with other persons, and this being the only passage in the Ps. applied specifically to young men, the reference is improbable. The path is a pure path ‖ "perfect" v.¹, and is to be kept pure. The EVˢ. "cleanse" implies a way not already pure but to be made so; which suits admirably the Augustinian doctrine of sin, but does not suit the conception of this poet. — *Within my heart*], v.¹¹, in antithesis with *my lips* v.¹³. Within the heart *that I may not sin against Thee*] as a preventive of sin against God by violating His Law. — *I have stored up Thy Saying*], as a treasure ever to be kept in mind and guarded. In this way, the heart, the mind, the will, the entire inner man is restrained from sin. — The same is accomplished in the outer man by oral recitation: *I told all the Judgments of Thy mouth*], v.¹³. Telling them to others impresses them upon the mind of him who tells them; and is a public recognition of their obligation; and therein an effectual restraint from outward sin. — *Blessed be Thou, Yahweh!*], v.¹². An ascription of blessedness to Yahweh, the great Teacher, Himself the sum of the Law. — *Teach me Thy Statutes*], phr. of D, also v.²⁶· ⁶⁴· ⁶⁸· ¹²⁴· ¹³⁵· ¹⁷¹. The vb. is also used with Judgments (error for Statutes) v.¹⁰⁸. — *In Thy Testimonies I rejoice*], v.¹⁴, cf. Thy Saying v.¹⁶² ‖ *In Thy Law I delight myself*], v.¹⁶; so in Thy Commands v.⁴⁷; cf. also use of noun from same stem: "my delight is Thy" Testimonies v.²⁴, Law v.⁷⁰· ⁷⁷· ⁹²· ¹⁷⁴, and Commands v.¹⁴³. — The intermediate *in Thy Precepts I muse*], v.¹⁵, is not simply the musing of meditation and study, which does not suit the ‖ here or in v.⁷⁸, or in v.²³· ⁴⁸ (with Statutes), where this vb. is in the same parallelism with terms of rejoicing. It is the musing of talking or singing to oneself about a joyous theme. And the other passages v.¹⁴⁸ with Saying, and v.²⁷ with "wonders," and even the cognate noun of v.⁹⁷· ⁹⁹ favour this general mng. for all the passages of this Ps. — *over above all riches*]. The Law is the most valuable of all things, worth all things else; cf. Jesus' Parables of the Kingdom Mt. 13⁴⁴· ⁴⁵. This tristich has also the syn. terms *Way* used twice and *Path*, which is the way of the Law, cf. v.[9] — Unto this the pious *look*], cf. v.[6] and they *forget*] it not ; cf. v.[61. 109. 153] used with Law, v.[83] with Statutes, v.[93. 141] with Precepts, v.[139] with Word, and v.[176] with Commands. — *Let me not err from Thy Commands*], v.[10] ; so v.[21], cf. v.[118], where the same vb. is used with " Statutes " ; cf. also 19[13] and the conception of sin as error in P.

Str. J. The first quartette has synth. and syn. couplets, the second antith. couplets. — **17–24.** *Deal bountifully with Thy servant*], as 13[6] 116[7] 142[8]. — *that I may live*], not physical but religious, as v.[25. 37. 40. 50. 77. 88. 93. 107. 116. 144. 149. 154. 156. 159. 175]. This writer evidently thinks that the only true life is in knowing and obeying the divine Law. — *Yea princes sit down*], v.[23], in council. — *talk together against me*], plotting and conspiring, as v.[61. 69. 85. 95. 110 +]. A glossator inserts at the expense of the measure *Thy servant*, requiring the change of its vb. from the first person to the third. — *A sojourner am I in the earth*], v.[19]. The earth was not his native land. He was an alien, residing in it by sufferance with only the rights of a guest. — The ‖ was probably also *My soul is in exile*], v.[20], for 𝔐 and Vrss. differ in text. 𝔐 has an Aramaic word which is usually rendered after La. 3[16] " is crushed " ; but this is dubious and harsh in the context. The Vrss. seem to have had a vb., syn. with the following infinitive. — *in longing*]. The psalmist is not content with the provisions for his comfort which he finds on the earth. He longs for something which is over and beyond the earth, for heavenly things. — *at every time*]. There is no cessation of this longing ; and it is for the divine Law, which he implores that God may *not hide*], but reveal to him. — *Uncover mine eyes*], v.[18] ; unable to see without the divine help. This is moral indistinctness of vision, not physical ; cf. the words of Jesus Mt 6[22-23] 7[3-5] Jn. 9[30-41]. — *wonderful things*], cf. v.[27. 129], a term used elsewhere for the wonderful acts of Yahweh in judgment and redemption ; here for the wonderful features of the Law itself, and so it is defined : — *out of Thy Law*], manifesting themselves from the Law in the attentive study of it, so soon as the religious eyes are opened to see. — *Uncover reproach and contempt*], v.[22]. Reproach and contempt are conceived as garments clothing the Psalmist. His prayer is that he may be uncovered, that they may be stripped off. A glossator to make this clearer inserts " from upon me." — *Thou* *dost rebuke the proud*], v.[21]. The author was evidently living at a time when there were many of these proud, arrogant men, who are here described as *accursed* of God, and such as *err from Thy Commands*, cf. v.[10]; elsewhere as deriding v.[51], misrepresenting v.[69], subverting v.[85], and oppressing him v.[122], and as put to shame v.[78]. In antithesis with the conspirators already mentioned, the psalmist consults the divine *Precepts* as *the men of my counsel*], v.[24], his advisers and helpers.

Str. ד. In the first tetrastich antith. lines are enclosed by syn. ones. The second tetrastich has antith. and syn. couplets. — **25–32.** *My soul doth cleave to the dust*], prostrate on the ground, the face in the dust, unable to rise ‖ *doth drop away from heaviness*], v.[28], dissolving in tears, in the intensity of affliction, due doubtless to persecution. — *according to Thy Word quicken me*], in accordance with the principle that the divine Law imparts the only true life, cf. v.[17]. This phr. is used also v.[37. 107], with Saying v.[50. 154], with Judgments v.[149. 156], cf. also v.[93. 144] ‖ *according to Thy Saying raise me up*] from the prostrate condition into new life and energy. — *My ways have I told*], v.[26], in confession to God — *and Thou hast answered me*], with forgiveness and favour. — *The way of Thy wonders will I sing*], musing on it in praise. The way is the way of the Law and of its wonders, as v.[18]. A later scribe at the cost of measure and parallelism makes this more evident by transposition. — *make me understand*], give intellectual and moral discernment, ‖ *teach*, cf. v.[7] — *The way of falsehood*], v.[29], leading away from the Law; implying unfaithfulness to legal obligations; and so antithetical to *The way of fidelity*], v.[30], faithful adherence and obedience to the Law. The former he prays that God will *remove;* of the latter he affirms that he has *chosen* it. On the basis of both is the petition: *with Thy Law*], as an instrument ‖ *with Thy Precepts.* — *be gracious to me*], make the Law a means of grace. — ‖ *compose me*], reduce the agitated soul to calmness and an even temper. This term, suggested by the parall., seems to be the most probable explanation of a difficult phr. in which 𝕳 and Vrss. greatly differ. — *I cleave unto Thy Testimonies*], v.[31], the deliberate adherence of affection as distinguished from the forced physical adherence of v.[25]. — *The way of Thy Commands will I run*], v.[32], as eager, and so impatient of the slower "walk" of v.[1]. —

put me not to shame], petition on the negative side ‖ *Thou wilt encourage my heart*], the positive side. There will be no discouragement, but encouragement to run the divine race of the Law.

Str. ‌ה. The first tetrastich has two syn. couplets, the second introverted parallelism. — **33–40.** *Show me the way*], as 27[11] 86[11], cf. v.[102] : give instruction in the way of the divine Law ‖ *Make me to understand — as my reward*], cf. v.[112] ; the most probable explanation of a difficult passage where 𝕳 and Vrss. differ, and suited to the ‖ *with all my heart.* — ‖ *I delight*], v.[35]. The Law itself is the reward of the servant of God ; the very keeping of it is its own reward, as 19[12], and gives delight to the heart whose whole affections are set upon it. " Unto the End " of EV[s]. is not sustained by usage, and does not give an appropriate sense. JPSV. " with every step " is more probable, but not so well suited to ‖. — *Make me tread in the path*], v.[35], as guide and helper ‖ *Incline my heart*], cf. Jos. 24[23] (E) Pr. 2[2] Ps. 141[4]. — *not unto covetousness*]. The antithesis of God and His Law with Mammon and the greed for unjust gain, cf. Is. 33[15] Mt. 6[24] Lk. 16[13]. — *Remove mine eyes from worthlessness*], v.[37]. The glossator inserts, at the expense of the measure, the unnecessary "seeing." The vanity that he would not see is worthlessness of evil conduct as the ‖ *my reproach*, v.[39], suggests. These worthless men, cf. 26[4], heap reproaches upon him for not sharing in their worthless conduct. He desires to avoid them altogether, and to see nothing of them. — *my steps*], the most probable explanation of a word misunderstood and interpreted as a relative by 𝕳 and Vrss., or else omitted. — *Establish to Thy servant Thy Saying*], v.[38], make it firm, sure, certain, cf. v.[5]. — *according to the fear that is due Thee*], the reverential fear that God invokes from His servants. — ‖ *Thine excellent Judgments I stand in awe of*], v.[39], cf. 22[24] 33[8]. As usual in this Ps. there is a constant interchange of God and His Law, which are practically identical to this psalmist. — *In Thy righteousness*], v.[40], by instrumentality of, shewing it, putting it forth as a means of grace. It is as usual in ψ and Is.[2] a saving attribute.

Str. ‌ו. The first tetrastich has synth. couplets ; the second, a syn. couplet enclosed in synth. lines. — **41–48.** *Verily*], so v.[43. 44] ; asseverative ‌ו, usually neglected. — *let Thy kindness bring me*],

the most probable rendering for "come to me," in pl., MT., 𝔖,
𝔗, 𝔍, followed by AV., RV.; in sg. 𝔊, 𝔈, PBV., JPSV. — *And I
will lift up my palms unto*], v.[48]. The gesture of prayer, especially
in the form of invocation and adoration. This attitude of worship
of the Law is a late conception, instead of the earlier conception,
which is always a lifting up of the palms to God Himself 63[5] La. 2[19]
3[41], or to His shrine Pss. 28[2] 134[2]. A copyist's error inserts from
v.[47] (after the transposition of v.[48] to its present place), the clause :
" unto Thy Commands which I love ; " but in both lines the relative is determined by the last clause, here : *what I will sing of,
even Thy Statutes*], cf. v.[15]. — *Do not snatch away the word of
faithfulness*], v.[43]. This is the word that the psalmist would
speak in fidelity to His God. He implores that he may not
be made incapable of speaking it, or that, just as he is about
to speak it, it may not be taken from him by Yahweh's abandonment of him to his enemies. — *I hope in Thy Judgments*],
elsw. Word v.[49, 74, 81, 114, 147]. The poet waits in hope on the divine
Law, as elsw. on God Himself, 31[25] 33[22] 69[4]. — *And I will return
word to him that reproacheth me*], v.[42]; respond to his reproaches,
cf. v.[22]. — *that I trust in Thy Saying*], phr. α.λ.; trust in the Law
secures life and salvation, and this is the sufficient answer to the
proud enemies. Trust in the Law to this poet stands for the
usual trust in God (9[11] + 21 t. ψ). — *In a roomy place*], v.[45], where
there is ample room for liberty of movement, like a public square ;
so v.[96] the Commandment itself is spacious, exceeding broad ; and
v.[32] Yahweh enlarges, encourages the heart. — *because I study Thy
Precepts*], so v.[94], with Statutes v.[155], cf. Ezr. 7[10] 1 Ch. 28[8]: seek
with application, study in order to practise. — *And I will speak
before kings*], v.[46], the word of faithful testimony to the Law. The
kings were doubtless the Egyptian and Syrian monarchs of the
later Greek period. — *And I will not be ashamed of Thy Testimonies*], implying the reverse ; full of hope and courage, joy and
pride in the Law ; as expressed by v.[47]. — *I will delight myself in
what I love, even Thy Commands*], cf. v.[16]. Love to the Law is
characteristic of this poet: in the form of Commands elsw. v.[48]
(gl.), also v.[127] ; of Testimonies v.[119, 167] ; of Precepts v.[159]; elsw. of
Law v.[97, 113, 163, 165]. Love to Law takes the place of the earlier
Deuteronomic love to Yahweh Dt. 5[10] 6[5] + 10 t. (Dt.) Pss. 31[24]

97^{10} 116^1 145^{20}; or to the name of Yahweh 5^{12} 69^{37}, as v.^{132}, His house 26^8, His salvation 40^{17} = 70^5, Jerusalem 122^6.

Str. 7. The first tetrastich has synth. lines enclosed by antith. ; the second, antith. and synth. couplets. — **49–56.** *Remember Thy servant*], v.^{2}, cf. 136^{23} (with ל), 9^{13} 74^2 115^{12} (with acc.). This is the most probable reading, so soon as the term for Law goes to the end of the line as in all other cases in this Str. " Word to Thy servant " of 獨 is most naturally a promise, which is not suited to the usage of terms in this Ps. ; and moreover the Vb. " hope " requires an object as in v.^{43}. — *because Thou hast made me hope*], as RV. The prayer is based on the fact that God Himself has inspired the hope. This is more probable than " wherein " PBV., " upon which " AV., or " when " JPSV. — *This is my comfort, that Thou hast quickened me*], v.^{50}, cf. RV.^{m}, JPSV. The experience of quickening in the past is the ground of comfort for the present and the future. — *in my affliction*]. This is explained, v.^{51}, as from *The proud*, cf. v.^{21}. — Who *scorn me exceedingly*], cf. 1^1. These, in the Greek period when the study of Hebrew Wisdom and devotion to the Law alike prevailed among the pious, treated all who engaged in such studies with scorn, and heaped reproaches upon them ; cf. v.$^{21-22}$. — *I have not inclined from Thy Testimonies*], so v.^{157}. The Law is conceived as a straight line, a rule of conduct from which the psalmist does not deviate to the right or the left. — || *forsakers of Thy Law*], v.^{53}, cf. v.^{87} Dt. 29^{24} + 14 t., for the earlier " forsake God," Ju. 10^{10} Dt. 28^{20} 31^{16} + 39 t. — *A burning wind has seized me from the wicked*]. The scorning coming from the wicked is compared to the Sirocco, a burning, enervating wind which enfeebles and afflicts him. The || and the usage of the noun, v. 11^6, makes this rendering more probable than the various explanations of the Vrss. ancient and modern : " horror " AV., after ℨ, Σ, " hot indignation " RV., JPSV., which have no justification in Hebrew usage, and require the rendering " because of the wicked," which then entirely destroys the parall. — *I remember*], v.^{52}, also v.^{55}, in antithesis with the divine remembrance v.^{49}. That which is remembered in the latter case is the *name* of Yahweh. The || suggests that *Yahweh* Himself should be the object in the first case, and that the divine name should not be vocative. 獨 and Vrss. all make the obj. " Thy judgments " ;

but usage and assonance require that this should be at the close of the line with the final Vb. — *comfort myself*], cf. v.[50]. The first remembrance v.[52] is *of old*, of the historic deliverances of Yahweh from ancient times, cf. v.[49]; the second v.[55] is *in the night*, the time of reflection and consideration, cf. v.[62]. — *Songs have I*], v.[54], joy expressed in songs, whose theme is the *Statutes* of the Law. The ‖ *This have I*], v.[56], suggests that the remembrance in the night is a joyous one, expressed orally, cf. Jb. 35[10]. — *in the house of my sojourning*], the earthly life, cf. v.[19-20] Gn. 47[9].

Str. ‎ח. Both tetrastichs have synth. couplets. — **57–64**. *My portion, Yahweh*]. Yahweh is the portion of His people 16[5] 73[26] 142[6]. — *I have said*], resolved, promised, as 1 Ch. 27[23] 2 Ch. 21[7]. — *I entreat Thy favour*], v.[58], cf. 45[13]. — *At midnight I rise up*], v.[62], as the glossator rightly interprets, though at the expense of the measure, " to give thanks unto Thee," in the songs of praise of v.[54], making the midnight hour a vigil of worship. — *I have considered my ways*], v.[59], attentively examined the course of life and conduct. — *and turned unto Thy Testimonies*], the positive side of repentance. This psalmist is unconscious of violation of Law, and therefore says nothing of the negative side of turning away from sin. A glossator inserted at the expense of the measure " my feet," thinking of walking in the way. — This is enlarged upon in : **60**. *I made haste and delayed not*]. The turning was prompt, without hesitation or procrastination. — *The earth is full of Thy kindness*], v.[64], as 33[5], cf. 145[8-9]. — *The cords of the wicked have enclosed me*], so essentially RV., JPSV., " wrapped me round." These wicked men are doubtless the proud scorners of the previous Strs. They are here regarded as hunters who for the time have succeeded in snaring him and binding him fast with their cords. But they cannot withdraw him from the Law. PBV., AV., " have robbed me," has no justification. — *A companion am I to all that fear Thee*], v.[63]. He voluntarily unites himself with ties of fellowship to the true worshippers of Yahweh, because they are observant of the Law.

Str. ‎ט. The first tetrastich has introverted parallelism, the second syn. couplets. — **65–72**. *Well hast Thou dealt with Thy servant*], doing him good. ‖ *Thou art good and a doer of good*], v.[68]; as benignant, beneficent, and bestowing good things on His servant. —

Well was it for me that I was afflicted], v.[71]. The affliction was not merely a suffering from injustice and wrong through proud and scornful enemies; but was a divine discipline, doing him good; cf. La. 3[27. 32-33]. — ‖ *Before I was afflicted I erred*], v.[67]. Affliction has brought him to repentance of his errors, cf. v.[59]; so that now he errs no more. — *Better to me than thousands of gold*], v.[72], more precious than great wealth is the Law, cf. v.[14]. — *smeared lies over me*], v.[69]. The proud so frequently mentioned v.[21], as talking together against him v.[23], and scorning him v.[51], here smear him over with falsehood. — *Their heart is gross with fatness*], v.[70]. In their pride they have so greatly indulged themselves that they have become incapable of right thoughts, right feelings, or right judgments, cf. 17[10] 73[7]. — *Taste*], v.[66], intellectual discernment, defined as having the quality of *goodness*, excellence, and so associated with *knowledge*. The context sufficiently indicates that the object of this taste and knowledge is the Law. — *I believe in Thy Commands*], phr. a.λ.; for the earlier belief in God Himself Gn. 15[6] (E) Ex. 14[31] Nu. 14[11] (J) Ps. 78[22], His works 78[32], His word of promise 106[12].

Str. י. The first tetrastich has syn. and synth. couplets; the second, antith. and synth. couplets.—**73-80.** *Let them that fear Thee*], v.[74], repeated v.[79]; the true worshippers of God. — *see me and be glad*] ‖ *turn to me that they may know*, v.[79]. As in v.[63], the psalmist was their companion, so here they resort to him to see him and be glad with him, and learn from him to know the Law in which he hopes. The Kt. is to be preferred to the Qr., though the latter is sustained by Vrss.; since it gives in the phrase " them that know Thy Testimonies," an unnecessary addition to " them that fear Thee," and omits altogether the purpose of their resorting to the psalmist. — *I know, Yahweh*], v.[75], not only the Law as such, but also its attributes *righteous and faithful*, which indeed in the same combination are attributes of God Himself, 96[13] 143[1], cf. 85[11-12]. A glossator put upon the margin *Thou hast afflicted me* after v.[67. 71] to indicate that the divine affliction also had these characteristics. When it crept into the text at the cost of the measure and assonance, " faithful " was attached especially to it. — *Let Thy kindness be to Thy servant*], v.[76], ‖ *Let Thy compassion come to me*], v.[77]. The scribe who transposed " Thy servant " to the close of the line, interpreted *Saying* as a divine promise, against the usage of this Ps. — *to comfort me*], as v.[50], ‖ *that I may live*], as v.[17]. — *Let the proud be shamed*], v.[78], the same proud scorners who constantly appear in the Ps. — In antithesis with this he imimplores that : *I may not be ashamed,* — and in order to this : *Let my heart be perfect*], v.[80], entire, complete in conformity to the divine Law, cf. v.[1]. — *Thy hands made me and prepared me*], cf. Dt. 32[6] Jb. 10[8]. The author conceives that he as an individual was made by the hands of God : and that the purpose of his creation was that he might study and learn the divine commands. This is in accord with the doctrine of later Judaism, that the world was created in the interest of the divine Law. An early glossator, not understanding this, inserted the imv. "make me to understand," cf. v.[34].

Str. **ב**. Both tetrastichs are composed of syn. and synth. couplets. — **81-88**. *My soul doth pine*], cf. 84[3], ‖ *Mine eyes fail*], cf. v.[123] 69[4]; with the strain of watching and eager longing with its wasting effects upon the physical organisation. — *for Thy salvation*], as the subsequent context indicates, from the persecution of the proud. — *How long ere*], v.[82], a frequent complaint in ψ at the delay of divine interposition, cf. v.[84]. — *will comfort me Thy Saying*], cf. v.[50. 52. 76]. It is in accord with the constant usage of this Ps. that the Law should do what the older psalmists thought that God Himself would do. An early copyist by transferring "Thy Saying" from its proper place at the close of the line made it the object for which the eyes fail, and made God the subject of comfort. — *Though I am become like a wineskin in smoke*], v.[83]. The skin of wine, the bottle of the ancients, hung up on the beams of the room becomes blackened and shrivelled when the room is filled with smoke. Thus the body of the psalmist becomes emaciated, as his eyes fail, with long-continued pining for the long-postponed deliverance. — *How many are the days*], explained by *How long ere;* the days of waiting for the Law to give the comfort and salvation longed for. An early scribe, not understanding the terse sentence in its parallelism with v.[82], inserted at the expense of the measure an explanatory clause "ere Thou wilt do on those that pursue me," which forced the explanation of "Judgments" as judicial punishment, against the usage of the Ps., where it always means the judgments of the Law. — *The proud have dug for me pits*], v.[85], cf. 7[16] 57[7], a figure for plotting. — *one who is according to Thy Law*], v.[85], whose life and conduct correspond with the Law's requirements, cf. v.[9]. This is the most probable explanation of a difficult passage, where 𝔊 and Vrss. differ and all are alike prosaic. — ‖ *All with falsehood pursue me*], v.[86], cf. v.[61. 69]. The "all" must be at the beginning of the line, in accordance with the alphabetical arrangement, and refer to the proud of v.[85]. An early copyist by mistake attached it to the term for the Law, which assonance requires at the close of the line. — *faithful are Thy Commands*], v.[86]. This divine attribute, 88[12] 89[2. 3. 6. 9] +, is here attached to the Law, cf. v.[75. 142. 151. 160] 19[10]. — *Almost had they consumed me*], v.[87]. He had well nigh perished from the persecution of these proud and slanderous enemies, and yet he was faithful to the Law notwithstanding all.

Str. ל. The first tetrastich is composed of a syn. triplet and a synth. line, the second of two synth. couplets. — **89–96.** *fixed in heaven is Thy Word*]. The divine Law was everlasting, preëxistent in heaven before it came down to earth as the later rabbins understood it. — ‖ *Thou hast established and there standeth fast*], immutable for all future time in generation after generation of mankind. The ‖ indicates that it is the Law as *Saying* which is thus established, and that we should read *in the earth* in antithesis with "in heaven." An early scribe, mistaking "Thy Saying" for "Thy faithfulness," a similar form in Heb., made "earth" the object of the Vb. as that which was established forever. The psalmist, however, was not thinking of the creation of the earth or its permanence, but of the Law. — *As regards Thy Judgments, they stand fast to-day*], v.[91]. The Law not only was preëxistent and so everlasting in the past, and extending to all generations in the future ; it was also in the present alike immutable. The error in the previous v. compelled the Vrss. to think of heaven and earth as immutable in accordance with the laws of God, which is a later conception certainly not in the mind of this poet. — *for all are Thy servants*], heaven and earth in which the Law has been immutably established. — *Though I had perished in mine affliction*], v.[92]. A scribe, transposing this clause with the next, lost the parallelism and the sense. The poet makes the extreme statement that he would have still continued to delight in the Law, even if his affliction had resulted in his death, cf. v.[87]. The EV[s]., finding the clauses transposed, give the rather weak "unless Thy Law had been my delight." — *For me the wicked wait to destroy me*], v.[95]. The proud, scornful, slanderous enemies are waiting for an opportunity for his destruction. — *I consider diligently Thy Testimonies*], make an earnest study of them, cf. v.[100. 104]. — *Thine am I: save me*], v.[94]. The consciousness that he belongs to Yahweh gives him confidence to implore salvation from his enemies. — *To all completeness have I seen an end*], v.[96]. This verse sums up the thought of the Str. All things else, however complete, have their limit; they come to an eventual end; but in antithesis the Law is *broad*, limitless in breadth, without end in time, past, present, or future.

Str. מ. The first tetrastich has three syn. lines synth. to an introductory line; the second has antith. and synth. couplets. — **97–104.** *O how I love Thy Law*], v.[97]. The Deuteronomic love of Yahweh has become to the psalmist a love of the Law. This thought appears also v.[113. 163. 165] of the Law itself, v.[119. 167] of the Testimonies, v.[47. 127] of the Commands, v.[159] of the Precepts. — *More than mine enemies*], the proud, lying scorners of the previous context. — ‖ *all teachers*], as the context shows, not teachers of the Law, but other teachers who would lead him into other paths of instruction. He means to say that God is the great Teacher, and that His Law is far superior to all other teachers. — ‖ *the seniors*], not the official elders of his people, but old men who ought to know and to be able to teach. The Law is a better teacher than they. — *wise Thou makest me with Thy Commands*], givest me their instruction in divine wisdom, so 𝔊, 𝔙, 𝔍, to be preferred to EV[s]. — ‖ *insight have I* ‖ *understanding have I*], cf. v.[104]. — In the supplementary clause the reason is given: *forever they are mine*]. The Law is his everlasting personal possession. — *From every evil way*], v.[101], way leading to evil; taking up the thought of the previous line. — *I refrain*], restraining himself, withholding his *feet* from walking in the way, which word indeed the glossator inserts at the expense of the measure. — In antithesis with the evil way is the right way from which he does not deviate: *From Thy Judgments I do not turn aside*], v.[102], but he goes straight forward in their way. This Deuteronomic term is frequent in OT. even in Pr. — *For Thou dost instruct me*]. Usually the psalmist thinks of the Law as the instructor ; but here of Yahweh Himself, showing that he still ever sees God behind the Law. — *From Thy Statutes have I understanding*], v.[104]. In this, the climax, it appears that from the Law and from no other instructor whatever, all his wisdom and knowledge come. — *every way of falsehood I hate*], the way leading from the Law into falsehood. — *O how sweet is Thy Saying to my palate ! sweeter than honey to my mouth*], v.[103], based on 19[11b]. The Law is the sweetest, the most delicious of all things. It is the most dainty food of the soul.

Str. ן. The first tetrastich is composed of synth., the second of syn. couplets. — **105–112.** *A lamp to my foot ‖ a light to my path*]. The Law is conceived as a lamp giving light upon a path which would otherwise be dark, cf. Pr. 6[23]. — *I have sworn and confirmed it*], v.[106], so RV., after 𝔥, 𝔊, 𝔙, 𝔖, 𝔗. The oath has not only been sworn but ratified by a solemn act as in a court of justice, or by the recording of it with a seal; but AV., JPSV., "and I will perform it," follow 𝔍. — *The freewill offerings of my mouth, O accept*], v.[108], the praises for deliverance, cf. 19[15]. — *I am sore afflicted*], v.[107], cf. v.[22–23. 50–51. 67. 69. 71. 85–87. 92. 95]. — ‖ *My life is in my palm continually*], v.[109], a phrase indicating the great risk and peril that he incurred. This is explained v.[110]. — *The wicked have laid a snare for me*], as v.[69. 85]. — *I have an everlasting inheritance*], v.[111], cf. v.[19. 20. 54]. He is not thinking of the holy land, but of the holy Law and the everlasting holy life with God resulting from it. This, says he, is the *joy of my heart*, that in which he has the greatest delight, cf. v.[72. 103]. — *I incline with my heart to do*], v.[112]. Here he inclines toward the Law, as in v.[51. 157] he does not incline or decline from it. To do the Law is to obey it, act in accordance with it ; here in the form of Precepts (so prob. as Statutes is required for v.[108], cf. v.[12]), v.[121] of Judgments, v.[166] of Commands. — *as a reward*], finding his reward in the Law itself, as it was his inheritance and joy, cf. v.[33].

Str. ם. The Str. has synth. couplets enclosed by syn. couplets which are antith. — **113–120.** *My hiding place and my shield art Thou*], v.[114] ; cf. 28[7] 32[7] ; protecting from the enemies of the previous tetrastichs. — *My flesh bristles up in awe, and I reverence*], v.[120].

The context and the entire thought of the Ps. indicate that the psalmist holds the Law in great reverence and awe. The more ancient reverence of Yahweh has become reverence for His Law. There is no thought of his having terror or being afraid of it, as EV[s]. variously express it. — *Uphold me*], v.[116], ‖ *Support me* v.[117] ; cf. 3^6 $37^{17.\ 24}$ 51^{14}. The personal relation to Yahweh and the divine sustaining grace are here emphasized. — *and shame me not in my hope*], ‖ *that I may be saved* v.[117]. Let me not be put to shame by the failure of the salvation hoped for, cf. v.[6. 31. 80]. — *Those that swerve with their mouth*], v.[113], from truth and the Law, cf. 101^3. The most probable explanation of a difficult and defective sentence, in accordance with the parallelism. "Them that imagine evil things" PBV., "vain thoughts" AV., "them that are of a double mind" RV., JPSV., are all conjectural translations of a word elsewhere unknown and otherwise explained in ancient Vrss. — *I will delight*], v.[117], so 𝔊, 𝔖, 𝔍, PBV., JPSV., as v.[16. 24. 47] + ; to be preferred to 𝔥 followed by AV., RV., "have respect unto." — *Thou dost set at naught*], v.[118], cf. v.[119], the doom of the wicked. — *the falsehood of their deceit*], syn. with v.[113]. The wicked of this Ps. were essentially false and liars, cf. v.[23. 29. 69. 104]. Through the transfer of this clause to the end by an early copyist, at the expense of the assonance, the rendering originated which is given most literally in RV. : "for their deceit is falsehood," a tautological expression giving no real reason for the previous statement. — *all that backslide*], from the Law ; repeated in v.[119] according to 𝔊, 𝕱 ; but 𝔥, Σ, 𝔍, followed by EV[s]. read "as dross," which required the insertion at the expense of the measure of the explanatory "all the wicked of the earth." — *As for them that turn aside, their portion is adversity*], v.[115], cf. 11^6. This is in accordance with the parall., and is gained by slight changes, chiefly in the separation of the letters of the Heb. text. The reading of 𝔥 and Vrss. : "Depart from me, ye evil doers, that I may keep the Commands of my God," is against the context, refers to God in the third person instead of in the second which is the usage of the Ps. throughout, and makes the line overfull.

Str. 𝕍. The first tetrastich has introverted parallelism ; the second synth. and antith. couplets. — **121–128.** *The oppressor* ‖ *let not the proud oppress*]. These same proud oppressors are constantly reappearing in the Ps. — *Do not abandon* ‖ *Take Thy Word in pledge*], interpose on my behalf, and be my pledge and guarantee over against them. — *Thy servant am I* ‖ *Do with Thy servant*], v.[124-5]. The personal relation as a faithful worshipper of God justifies him in making his plea. — The greatest *kindness* is : *make me to have understanding that I may know Thy Testimonies*], cf. v.[152]. — *It is time for Yahweh to act*], v.[126], high time for Him to interpose ; not only because of the peril of the psalmist, but also to vindicate His own Law which these proud oppressors *have broken*, thus far with impunity. — *more than gold or than fine gold*], v.[127], the most precious of all things is the divine Law, cf. v.[14, 72]. — *I direct my steps according to Thy Precepts*], v.[128], so 𝕲, 𝕭, 𝕴, which is much better suited to the context than the other possible meaning : " I esteem right," which is rather prosaic and tame.

Str. ⅃. The first tetrastich has syn. and synth. couplets ; the second, synth. couplets. — **129–136.** *The opening of Thy Word giveth light*], v.[130] : the uncovering, the manifestation of it, lets light break forth from it. ‖ *Thy face make shine*] v.[135] ; cf. 4[7] 31[17]. The Law like Yahweh's face gives light. — *the simple*], are the open-minded, who may be led aright or led astray according as they are taught ; cf. 19[8]. — *Wonderful are Thy Testimonies*], v.[129]. They contain and set forth wonderful things, cf. v.[18]. — *Turn to the one that loves Thy name*], v.[132]. Love for the name of God is another phase of the love of God Himself and of His Law so characteristic of this Ps. It corresponds with the eager longing of v.[131], and the grief of v.[136]. An early scribe, misunderstanding the line, at the expense of the measure and assonance and the term for Law, gave by transposition and readjustment, the text followed by EV[s]. " as Thou usest to do unto those that love Thy name."— *My footsteps confirm*], v.[133], that I may walk in the right way, cf. v.[5, 128]. — *let not iniquity have dominion over me*] ‖ *Redeem me from the oppression of man*], v.[134] : the proud oppressors who wrought mischief and trouble, and broke the Law with impunity, cf. v.[121, 122, 126]. — *Streams of water run down mine eye*], v.[136], from excessive weeping, cf. La. 3[48]. — *My mouth I open wide and I pant*], v.[131]. The eagerness is expressed physically by the wide open mouth and the panting of hasty movement, which correspond with the longing of the soul.

2 F

Str. צ. The first tetrastich has introverted parallelism ; the second, synth. couplets whose corresponding lines are syn. — **137–144.** *Righteous art Thou,* v.[137], ‖ *In righteousness and faithfulness exceeding,* v.[138], ‖ *Thy righteousness is righteousness forever,* v.[142], the last repeated v.[144]. This Str. emphasizes the righteousness of *Yahweh ;* but the context shows that it is a righteousness syn. not with justice, but rather with faithfulness and accordingly a saving attribute. — *upright are Thy Judgments*], v.[137], cf. 19[10]. The Law has the same attribute of uprightness as God Himself : — so *faithfulness is Thy Law,* v.[142], as God Himself has faithfulness. — *My jealousy hath destroyed me*], v.[139]. Jealousy for the Law and its observance has brought upon him persecution from his adversaries who violate it, cf. v.[126. 136] also 69[10]. ‖ *Smelted exceedingly is Thy servant*], v.[140], in the furnace of affliction, cf. Dn. 11[35]. An editor, misled by Ps. 18[31] Pr. 30[5], thinks of the Law as refined and so loses the parallelism. EV[s]. follow this mistake. — *I am small and despised*], v.[141], as compared with the proud enemies who heap upon him scorn and contempt, cf. v.[21–23]. ‖ *Trouble and distress have overtaken me*], v.[143], due to his fidelity to the Law. Notwithstanding all, he asserts his love for the Law, that his *delight* is in it, and that he has not forgotten it. — *that I may live according to Thy Statutes*], v.[144], so the text is best arranged in accordance with v.[25. 40. 50. 88. 93. 107. 116].

Str. ק. The first tetrastich is syn. ; the second has synth. couplets whose first lines are antith. — **145–152.** *I am beforehand*], v.[147], anticipate in my prayer ; repeated in v.[148] : in the former v. with *the twilight of dawn,* before the break of day, in the latter with *the night watches ;* before each of the three watches of the night, cf. v.[62] 63[7] La. 2[19] ; all indicating oft-repeated importunate prayer. — *My voice, O hear*], v.[149], the invocation of prayer. — *I call*], v.[145] ; repeated in v.[146] ‖ *cry for help* v.[147] ; qualified in the former line by the intensity of the invocation *with my whole heart,* in the latter by the personal address *upon Thee, Yahweh ;* having in the former line the additional petition *answer me* ‖ *O save me* in the latter. — *They draw near that pursue me with evil devices*], v.[150] ; so 𝕲, 𝔙, 𝔖, cf. PBV., to be preferred to MT., followed by AV., RV., "pursue evil devices." The proud and wicked enemies of the previous Strs. approach him, yes, pursue him, to execute upon him the evil they have devised, cf. 17^3 26^{10}. — *They are far from Thy Law*], have departed a long distance, are far from observing it. — *Be Thou near*], v.[151], petition, as PBV., is more suited to the context than the statement of fact of AV., RV. When his enemies draw near, he implores that Yahweh will draw near also to oppose them. — *Of old I know them*], v.[152], in past experience, having learned the Law from childhood on. —*forever Thou hast founded*]. The divine Law was founded as a structure which will endure forever, cf. v.[90].

Str. ר. The first tetrastich has introverted parallelism, the second couplets whose first lines are syn. and whose second lines are antith. — **153–160**. *O plead my cause ‖ O see my affliction*], cf. v.[159], an urgent plea for the interposition of God in the vindication of His servant, cf. Ex. 3^7 La. 1^9 Ps. 35^1 43^1. — *redeem me ‖ rescue me*], from the affliction, which, as subsequent context and the thought of the entire Ps. shows, was due to proud, malicious enemies, described as *the treacherous*], v.[158], those who are faithless and deceitful in their conduct toward him, cf. 25^3 59^6. These the psalmist *loathes ;* they are disgusting to him, cf. 139^{21}. — *Far off from the wicked is salvation*], v.[155], because they are far off from the Law, which alone gives it, cf. v.[150]. In antith. are the *Many compassions*], v.[156] of *Yahweh* toward His servant, which are near him to save, cf. v.[151]. — *Many are my persecutors and mine adversaries*, v.[157], cf. v.[150]; the same proud, contemptuous, reproachful enemies that appear throughout the Ps. — *The sum of faithfulness*], v.[160]. The chief, the highest degree of faithfulness is that of the divine Law, as v.[142. 151], cf. v.[86. 138]. A glossator, misunderstanding this, inserted " Thy Word," making the phr. " the sum of Thy Word," and he has been followed by all Vrss., excepting that 𝕲, 𝖁, 𝕵, have the pl. " Thy Words." The sum of the words in this case is their sum total. But the attribute of faithfulness is not only most appropriate to the thought of the Ps., but also to the other term, —*forever*] cf. v.[90. 152].

Str. ש. The first tetrastich has introverted parall. ; the second synth. and syn. couplets. — **161–168**. *Princes persecute me*]. The proud, malicious enemies and oppressors here seem to have princes at their head, probably the officials of the Syrian kings, cf. v.[23. 46]. — *without cause ‖ Lying*], the false charges of the enemies, cf.

v.[69. 86. 128. 158]. — *I stand in awe of Thy Word*], reverence it greatly, cf. v.[120]. — *I rejoice, as one that findeth spoil*], v.[162], cf. Is. 9[3] : the victor who, having conquered his enemy, appropriates to himself the treasures which they have abandoned. — *Seven times a day I praise*], v.[164] ; probably not implying seven fixed times of worship, but used as the holy number of completeness. The object of the praise is the Law ; but a later editor makes God the object by a change of text at the expense of the measure. — *Great peace*], v.[165], inward, of soul, and so explained as *without a cause of stumbling*, with nothing to scandalize them, offend their minds or consciences in their relation to God. Outward peace was excluded by the fact that their persecutors were princes, v.[161]. — *Yea, all my ways are before Thee*], v.[168]. The psalmist is assured that God knows thoroughly all his course of life ; and that is to him a ground not of fear but of hope and courage. — *I hope for Thy salvation*], v.[166], confidently look for it and expect it, cf. v.[116] 104[27] 145[15] 146[5].

Str. נ. The first tetrastich is composed of two syn. couplets, the second has introverted parallelism. — **169–176**. *Let my yell come near before Thee* ‖ *Let my supplication come before Thee*], urgent petition for deliverance. — *My lips will pour forth praise*], v.[171], in a stream of song, cf. 19[3] 78[2] ‖ *My tongue will respond*], v.[172], in responsive song, as an antiphone. — *in faithfulness*], faithfully. The theme is, — *Thy righteous Judgments*], and so most probably ‖ *that Thou teachest me Thy Statutes*], taking the clause as objective rather than as temporal, PBV., AV., or causal, RV., JPSV. — *I long for Thy salvation*], v.[174], eagerly desiring it and greatly needing it, cf. v.[81. 123. 131]. ‖ *I stray as a lost sheep*], v.[176], not in the ethical or religious sense of v.[110] ; but in the physical sense of losing the way, as 107[4], and so becoming lost and needing help and salvation. — *Let me live and praise Thee*], v.[175], resuming v.[171]. — *and make Thy Testimonies to help me*], ascribing to the Law what usually is ascribed to Yahweh Himself, and so ‖ *Let Thine hand be ready for my help*], v.[173].

1. The Ps. throughout, except v.[1-3. 115], has 2 pers. sf. with legal term. It is improb. that these are exceptions, especially as measure and assonance both require the usual sf. A prosaic scribe substituted תורת יהוה for תורתך, because it seemed better to use the divine name at the beginning of the Ps. And then it became necessary to change the sfs. of v.[2-3] from the 2 p. to the

3 p., and the order of words in the sentence was changed accordingly. — **3.** בִּדְרָכָיו] txt. err. for כדבריו, which is absent from Str. and needed to complete its usage of legal terms. The original was certainly כדברך, needed for assonance at close of l. — **4.** This l. should be transposed to follow v.², where such an emphatic statement seems most appropriate. — פקודיך] should stand for assonance at close of l. — **5.** † אַחֲלַי] *ah that;* elsw. אַחֲלֵי 2 K. 5³. אח־לי Aram., *v.* BDB. This should be l.⁶. — חֻקֶּיךָ] used also v.⁸. Probably it has here, through carelessness of a scribe, taken the place of an original אמרתך which is missing from the Str. — **6.** בְּהַבִּיטִי] Hiph. inf. with sf. and ב; not temporal, but circumstantial. This should be l.⁴. — **7.** לֵבָב] makes l. too long; reduce to לֵב. The second ב dittog. of the next letter. — **8.** אֶת־חֻקֶּיךָ]. The order of the sentence has been changed. The v. should begin with אַל and close with חקיך.

9. נער] is a gl., too restrictive for context or Ps., making l. too long. — כדברך] 𝔍 *custodierit verba tua,* 𝔊 φυλάσσεσθαι τοὺς λόγους σου = דבריך. The sg. without prep. is most prob. — **10.** תַּשְׁגֵּנִי] Hiph. juss. שׁגה; Qal used v.²¹· ¹¹⁸ ‖ שׁגג v.⁶⁷, cf. 19¹³. This should be l.⁷. — **11.** צפנתי אמרתך] belongs at the end of l. for assonance, as usual. — לְמַעַן לא] is prosaic for an original ולא. This should be l.². — **14.** בדרך עדותיך] is improb. The ‖ of v.¹⁵· ¹⁶ requires דרכך at the end of l. and the prep. ב with עדותיך at the beginning. — **15.** וְאַבִּיטָה] cohort. Hiph. נבט requires אֶל, the usual prep., for good measure, as v.⁶. This should be the last l. — **16.** בְּחֻקֹּתֶיךָ] חֻקּוֹת term of H is improb.; only here in Ps. for חקים, which has already been used in v.¹². Substitute for it תורה and make l.⁵. — אֶשְׁתַּעֲשָׁע] Hithp. שׁעע as v.⁴⁷, Pilp. v.⁷⁰; *v.* 94¹⁹. — דְּבָרֶךָ] is for דרכך as ‖ requires. דברך has been used already v.⁹, and the term for Law has already been given in this v.

18. גַּל] Pi. imv. גלה for גַּלֵּה *uncover.* Transpose this l. to begin second tetrastich. It is too important a l. to come in middle of a tetrastich, and is ‖ v.²⁴ as well as v.¹⁷. תורה is also needed in l.⁵ of Str. as usual. — **19.** אנכי] the long form improb.; makes l. too long; rd. גֵּר־אֲנִי. — מצותיך] used also v.²¹; this is prob. err. for אמרתך, needed in Str. — **20.** גָּרְסָה] Qal pf. 3 f. † גרס (גרשׂ) Aram. *be crushed,* BDB., cf. Hiph. La. 3¹⁶; but 𝔊 ἐπεπόθησεν, 𝔙 *concupivit,* 𝔍 *desideravit:* prob. error for גרשה *one thrust out, separated, exiled,* ‖ גר v.¹⁹. — לתאבה] תַּאֲבָה n.f. α.λ. *longing,* BDB.; but 𝔊 τοῦ ἐπιθυμῆσαι, 𝔍 *desiderare,* imply inf. vb., so most prob. inf. f. תאב; cf. v.⁴⁰. — בכל־עת] should be transposed, that l. may end for assonance in משפטיך. — **21.** This should be l.⁷. — **22.** גַּל] *uncover,* here shame, conceived as a garment. It is usually regarded as imv. גלל *roll,* and then should be גֹּל. The l. is overfull. Either מעלי or ובוז is a gl., prob. the former. — כי] is an interp. gl. — עדתיך] used also v.²⁴. Substitute here the missing פקדיך; and tr. to end of l. for assonance. This v. is parall. with v.¹⁸. — **23.** שָׂרִים]. 𝔖 rd. רשעים. — עבדך] is gl., making it necessary to change אשיח into ישיח. 𝔖 rd. אשיח. This should be l.². — **24.** עדתיך] must go to end of l. for assonance. 𝔊 adds at close of l. τὰ δικαιώματά σου = חקים; so also 𝔙.

25. חַיֵּנִי] should be at the end for assonance; so למדני v.²⁶. — **27.** פקודיך

הביגני]. Substitute for פקודיך, משפטיך. ⅏ δικαιώματα has חקים, so also 𝔙. The phr. should be at the end, in accordance with the assonance of the v. We should therefore rd. בדרך נפלאותיך אשיחה, which also gives better parall. — **28.** דלפה] Qal pf. † דלף vb. *drop*, elsw. in tears Jb. 16²⁰, *leak* (of house) Ec. 10¹⁸. — † הוגה] n.f. *grief,* elsw. Pr. 10¹ 14¹³ 17²¹, cf. יגון Ps. 13³. — קימני] should go to close of l. for assonance. — כדברך] already used v.²⁵; error for אמרתך, needed in Str. — **30.** שויתי] Pi. pf. 1 sg. שוה *set (16⁸),* so Σ προέταξα, 𝔍 *proponebam ;* but absence of prep. suspicious. ⅏ οὐκ ἐπελαθόμην, 𝔙 *non sum oblitus,* imply שכחתי or synonym. 𝔖 had before it האבתי v.⁴⁰. Zenner, Bä., suggest אויתי, but all other ll. end in ־ֵי. We would therefore expect vb. with sf.; rd. שוֵיני *smooth, compose me,* which suits ‖ הנני, cf. 131² Is. 38¹³. — משפטיך]. Substitute פקודיך, usual term after חורה in this part of Ps., משפטיך being needed in v.²⁷.

33. יהוה] gl., making l. too long. — חקיך]. Substitute פקודיך, needed after חורה, if there is to be order in use of terms. — עקב] so v.¹¹². ⅏ here διὰ παντός, there διὰ παντὸς ἄμειψιν ⅏ᴺ, but δι’ ἀντάμ(ε)ιψ(ε)ιν ⅏ᴺ·ᶜ·ᵃ·ᴬ·ᵀ; 𝔍 here *per vestigium,* there *propter retributionem.* The assonance requires in both vs. עקבי; and then, as Bä., *reward,* rather than JPSV. *step.* This l. should be transposed with v.³⁴, that חורה may begin Str. — **34.** ואצרה] gl. of amplification. — בכל לב] assonance requires לבי. — ואצרה] is gl. disturbing the connection. — **36.** לבי] goes to end of l. for assonance. — **37.** מראות] gl., making l. too long ; rd. משוא. — בדרכך] err. for בדרכך. — **38.** אשר ליראתך]. ⅏ εἰς τὸν φόβον σου, 𝔍 *in timorem tuum,* ignore אשר. It is prob. due to assimilation to v.³⁹, where it is a gl. But a word is needed for measure and assonance ; rd. אשרי *my step* (cf. 4⁵ 17⁵ 37³¹ 40³ 44¹⁹ 73²) and transpose to end of l. — **39.** יגרתי] belongs at end of l. for assonance, and has for obj. not חרפתי, but ייראתך ‖ משפטיך † יגר vb. *be afraid of* Dt. 9¹⁹ 28⁶⁰ Jb. 3²⁵ 9²⁸; here as Pss. 22²⁴ 33⁸ *stand in awe of.* — כי] is gl., not needed, and spoiling measure. This should be last l. of Str. — **40.** ראבתי] † האב vb. *long for, desire,* as v.¹⁷⁴; cf. יאב v.¹³¹ and האבה v.²⁰. — פקודיך]. Substitute חקיך, if פקודיך is supplied v.³⁸, as order seems to require. This v. then should be l.⁶.

41. ו] begins each l. of this Str. Here and v.⁴³·⁴⁴ it is asseverative ; in all other cases it introduces the apodosis of the juss. — ויבאני חסרך] MT. pl., so 𝔖, 𝔗, חסרך defective pl. for חסריך; but ⅏ sg. more prob. Then vb. is also more prob. Hiph. ויביאני. — אמרתך] is for an original כדברך here. This v. has been by err. transposed with v.⁴². — **42.** This v. should be l.⁴. — **43.** מפי] is expansive gl.; so also עד־מאד כי. The measure is complete without them. — למשפטך]. This term should be in pl. as usual. It goes to the end of l. for assonance ; so also הורתך v.⁴⁴, פקריך v.⁴⁵, עדתיך v.⁴⁶, מצותיך v.⁴⁷. — **44.** This should be l.⁵ as usual, followed by v.⁴⁵. — **46.** ולא]. The measure requires that לא should be united with אבוש in one tone ; therefore ו is a gl. — בעדתיך] כ also gl., due to transposition. — **47.** This v. should be l.⁸. — **48.** אל מצותיך אשר אהבתי] makes l. too long. The original was only אל־אשר ; the other words crept into the text from the previous l. To this is due ו before אשיחה. This v. should be l.².

49. דָּבָר] so 𝔍 *sermonis;* 𝔊ᴿ τὸν λόγον σου; 𝔙 *verbi tui,* also 𝔖; 𝔊ᴺ· ᶜ· ᵃ τῶν λόγων ἐμοῦ; Σ λόγων ἐμοῦ. דברך is required in this Str., and as usual at the close of the l. Then transpose ל with it as needed after יחל rather than after זכר, where it is lacking 𝔊ᴺ· ᵀ. — **50.** כִּי אמרתך] err. for the usual נאמרתך, cf. v.²⁵ +; and it should be at the close of l. — **51.** הֱלִיצֻנִי] Hiph. ליץ vb. *scorn,* Qal *1¹.* Hiph. also Jb. 16²⁰. — מהורתך] err. for עֵדְוֹתִךָ and should be at close of l. הורתך is given in v.⁵³. This v. om. by 𝔊ᴺ, but given by 𝔊ᴸ· ᴿ· ᵀ. — **52.** משפטיך] is required at close of l. as usual. יהוה, represented by sf. ה, is then obj. of זכרתי ‖ שְׁבֵך v.⁵⁵. — **53.** זַלְעֵפָה] as *11⁶,* the burning wind of the Sirocco. Vrss. differ: 𝔊 ἀθυμία, 𝔙 *defectio,* Aq. λαῖλαψ, Σ φρίκη, 𝔍 *horror.* — **54.** חֻקֶּיךָ] belongs at close of l. as usual. — **55.** תורתך] not needed, as used v.⁵³; מצותך is required. — יהוה] is gl. — **56.** פקריך] belongs at close of l.

57. דבריך] pl. improb.; rd. sg. as usual. 𝔊ᴺ τὰς ἐντολάς σου = either פקריך or מצותיך, 𝔊ᴺ· ᶜ· ᵃ· ᴬ· ᴿ· ᵀ τὸν νόμον σου = תורתך, shows that after the separation of the texts of 𝔊 and 𝔐, in 𝔊 as in 𝔐 interchange of terms took place. This v. should be transposed with v.⁵⁸. — **59.** רַגְלָי] makes l. too long. Its insertion was due to the interp. of ואשיבה as Hiph. instead of Qal. This should be l.⁴. — **60.** הִתְכַהְמָהְתִּי] Hithpalp. ‡ [מהה] vb. only this form, *linger, tarry, delay* Gn. 19¹⁶ 43¹⁰ (J) Ex. 12³⁹ (E) +. — **61.** יְיִרֻנִי] Pi. pf. sf. עוּר *surround, v. 20⁹.* — הורתך] should be at close of l. This v. should be l.⁶. — **62.** חֲצוֹת לַיְלָה] phr. elsw. Ex. 11⁴ (J) Jb. 34²⁰, cf. Ex. 12²⁹ (J) Ju. 16³· ³ Ru. 3⁸. — להורות לך] is an interp. gl. This v. should be l.³. — **64.** חקיך] should be at close of l. This should be l.⁵.

66. כי] gl. impairing measure. — מצותיך] should be at end of l. as usual. This v. should be l.⁷. — **67.** אמרתך] should be at close of l. for assonance. — **68.** This v. should close the Str. — **69.** טָפְלוּ] Qal pf. † [טפל] Qal *smear, plaster over,* elsw. Jb. 13⁴ 14⁷. — אֲנִי בכל לב] is a gl. of intensification. This should be l.⁵., followed by v.⁷⁰. — **70.** † טָפַשׁ] vb. *be gross, fat,* α.λ. Aram. — אֲנִי] emph. gl. — תורתך] should be at close of l. for assonance. — **71** should be l.². — **72.** תּוֹרַת פִּיךָ] תורה has already been used v.⁷⁰. משפטי is needed in Str. This phr. should go to end of l. for assonance. — וְכֶסֶף] is gl. of amplification. This v. should be l.⁴

73. הֲבִינֵנִי] gl. of interpretation; so כִּי v.⁷⁴· ⁷⁷. V. has been transposed from last l. to the first l. by error. — **75.** עִנִּיתָנִי] a marginal gl. that has crept into the text and occasioned the transposition of ואמונה and משפטיך. The latter belongs to the close of the l. for assonance. — **76.** לְעֶבְדֶּךָ] belongs in the first half of l. It has been removed to this place by misinterpretation of אמרתך as "promise." — **77.** הורתך] belongs to the close of l. as usual. — **78.** כִּי שֶׁקֶר עִוְּתוּנִי] gl. of expansion; on the basis of v.⁶⁹. — אֲנִי] not emphatic, but introducing a circumstantial clause. — **79.** וירעי] Kt. is to be interp. as ו with subjunctive, expressing purpose. Qr. וְדֵעֵי, though sustained by Vrss., is improb. This v. should be l.¹ — **80.** נִדְחֵיךָ] as usual belongs at close of l. — לְמַעַן לֹא] for an original ולא. This v. should be l.⁷

81. לִדְבָרֶךָ] goes to close of l. for assonance; so חקיך v.⁸³. — **82.** אמרתך] has been transposed from close of l. and ל prefixed because of the לֵאמֹר. It was really originally the subj. of הנח׳ר. — לְאֹר] is a prosaic gl. — **83.** † קיטור] n.m. *thick smoke* as 148⁸ Gn. 19²⁸·²⁸ (J). 𝔊 πάχνη, 𝔙, 𝔍, *pruina* improb. — **84.** תְּעֶשֶה בְלִרְפִי] is an explan. gl., making l. much too long, and indeed giving a false explan.; for משבט here as elsw. in Ps. refers to the law itself and not to its execution. The sf. יךָ was dropped from משפט by haplog. — **85.** שִׂיחות] pl. † שִׂיחָה n.f. *pit;* phr. also 57⁷ Je. 18²² (Kt.): so 𝔖, 𝔍, 𝔗; but 𝔊 διηγήσαντό μοι ἀδολεσχίας, 𝔙 *narraverunt mihi fabulationes* = ח׳ ר׳, which, however, is given a mng. unknown elsw., as also the vb. כרה. — אֲשֶׁר לֹא] tame and improb. 𝔊ˣ οὐχ ὡς ὁ νόμος σου depends on לֹא אשׁר, which is an interpretation of an original רָי ‖ ‖ רַאֲשֶׁר. — **86.** כל מצו׳תיך] is impossible, for כל is needed at the beginning of the l. and מצותיך at the close for assonance. כל refers to the זדים of v.⁸⁵, and should be followed by שקר רדפוני. — עֻזרני] is a gl. due to the transposition above mentioned. — **87.** בארץ] is gl., as Bi., Du. — וַאֲנִי] circumstantial clause. This should be the last l. of Str. — **88.** עֵדוּת] impossible; rd. עֵדוּת as usual. This should be l.⁶.

89. דברך] goes to close of l. for assonance. — **90.** אֱמוּנָתֶךָ] is an error for אמרתך, which is needed in Str. and here as ‖ דברך. It goes, however, to close of l. — ארץ] should be בשׁמים > בארץ. — **91.** ל למשפטיך has the force of *as for, as regards,* summing up; and not "according to," as EVˢ., due to error of previous l. — **92.** לוּלֵי] dittog. for לי, due to the transposition of the clauses. It goes with אברתי, and הורתך with its vb. belongs at close of v. as usual. — אָז] is a gl. The v. should be l.⁵. — **93.** זִקְרֵיךָ] is used also v.⁹⁴; it is here error for חקיך needed in Str.; so 𝔊, 𝔙, which, however, give חקיך also v.⁹⁴. The term belongs at close of l., after חייתני. — בָּם] is a gl., due to the transposition. Transpose this l. to close of first tetrastich, ‖ v.⁸⁹. Then v.⁹² will be followed by v.⁹⁴⁻⁹⁵, with which it is ‖, and הורה will begin second tetrastich as usual. — **94.** פקודיך] belongs at close of l.; so עדתיך v.⁹⁵. This v. should be l.⁷. — **96.** † תִּכְלָה n.f. a.λ. *completeness, perfection,* for תכלית 139²². This should be l.⁸. — מְאֹד] is a gl. of intensification. — מִצְוָתֶךָ] sg. here only in Ps.; error of pointing for usual מִצְוֹתֶיךָ

98. תְּחַכְּמֵנִי] Pi., usually 3 f. sg. with pl. noun Ges.¹⁴⁵·⁴, but 𝔊, 𝔍, 𝔙, 2 sg. referring to Yahweh as v.¹⁰²; then מצותך is the second subj., v. 3⁵. This on the whole seems more prob. — היא לי]. The f. sg. came into the text from the previous l.; it does not agree in number with מצותך. — **99.** מְלַמְּדַי] Pi. ptc. as Pr. 5¹³; *teachers.* The sf. is, however, not original, but an assimilation to previous l. It was indefinite, as זקנים of next l. — **101.** כלאתי] goes to close of l. for assonance in יִ which characterizes this Str. — רגלי] is an explan. gl., making l. too long. — למען] is interp. of an original ו, also making l. too long. — **102.** 𝔙 adds הורה at close of this l. — **103.** נָמְלְצוּ] Niph. pf. 3 pl. מלץ; a.λ.; prob. *be smooth, pleasant;* pl. vb. with sg. subj. is improb. אמרתך is pl. in 𝔊, 𝔙, 𝔖, 𝔗, but that is against the usage of this term for Law in 𝔥. The pl. of vb. must therefore be a copyist's error. — **104.** פקודיך]. This term already used in v.¹⁰⁰. Here prob. error for חקיך missing from Str. — עֲל־כֵּן] is interp. of an original כי. — שׂנאתי] should go to end of l. for assonance. This v. should be transposed with previous one.

105. דְּבָרֶךָ]. ⅏ has תורה. Term should be at close of l. for assonance ; so תורתך v.[109], פקודיך v.[110].—**106.** וָאֲהַלְיֶ֫ה] consec. with Pi. cohort. *confirm*, as ⅏, 𝔖, 𝔗 ; but 𝔍 *et perseverabo*, followed by AV., Bä., ו in apod. of juss.—**107.** דְּבָרֶךָ] already used v.[105]; rd. אמרתך, which is needed in Str.—**108.** יהוה] is unnecessary gl., making l. too long.—מִשְׁפָּטֶיךָ] already used v.[106]; rd. חקיך as usual with לכד in this Ps. (7 t.), in Dt. 4[1] + 10 t. Transpose to end of l. for assonance.—**110.** פַּקֻּדֶיךָ]. Substitute מצותיך.—**111.** עֵדְוֹתֶיךָ] should be at close of l. Its use here made הֵמָּה necessary at end, and so brought one word too many into l. This v. should be transposed with the next.—**112.** לְעוֹלָם] explan. gl., due to misinterp. of עֵקֶב, cf. v.[33], resulting in transposition of legal term, which belongs at end of l. as usual.— הֻקֶּיךָ] needed with לכד in v.[108]. Substitute פקודיך.

113. סֵעֲפִים] pl. [סֵעֵף] a.λ. adj. *divided, half hearted* BDB. ; but Vrss. all otherwise. ⅏ παρανόμους, 𝔘 *iniquos*, Aq. διαφόρους, Σ παραβάτας, 𝔍 *tumultuosos*. A word is lacking to Str., prob. two words are contained by compression in the one Heb. word. Gr. suggests סעים as 101[3], which is most prob. ; but פיהב should follow to complete the measure. סעים is favoured by ‖ סרים v.[115] (*v.* below), שגים v.[118], סוגים v.[119].—יְהוּרֹתֶ֫ךָ] goes to close of l. for assonance ; so דברך v.[114]. This v. begins second tetrastich as usual with תורה. —**114.** This v. properly begins Str.—**115.** סוּרוּ מִמֶּנִּי מְרֵעִים] is improb. in the context, though sustained by Vrss. ; all the more that it compelled the substitution of מצות אלהי for מִצְוֺתֶיךָ, which assonance and the uniform usage of the Ps. require. For second pl. imv. of vb. סור rd. ptc. סרים ‖ שׁגים. The final ם has been wrongly connected with מִנִּי, which stands for an original מנית *portion* (11[6]) with sf. כ wrongly attached to רעים, which then instead of Hiph. ptc. is the noun רֵעַ with intensive pl. This should be last l. of Str.—**116.** כְּאִמְרָתְךָ] belongs as usual with חיה, and the two words transposed for assonance at close of l.—שִׂבְרִי] † [שֵׂבֶר] n.m. elsw. 146[5]. This v. should be l.[2].—**117.** וְאֶשְׁעָה], *look at* (39[14]); but ⅏, 𝔖, 𝔍, the usual אשתעשע, which is better suited to the context.—חֻקֶּיךָ] goes to close of l. This v. should be l.[6]. —**118.** סָלִיתָ] Qal pf. 2 S. † [סלה] *make light of, set at naught*, elsw. Piel La. 1[15].—כָּל־שֹׁגִים מֵחֻקֶּיךָ] belongs at close of l. As חקים has been used already in v.[117], substitute here the missing פקודיך.—כִּי] is interp. gl.—תַּרְמִיתָם sf. 3 pl. † תַּרְמִית n.f. *deceitfulness*, as Je. 8[5] 14[14] 23[26] Zp. 3[13]. ⅏, 𝔖, 𝔘, 𝔍, תרמיתם *their thought*, which would suit the context if such a word could be found in Heb., as it avoids the tautology or unnecessary emphasis whichever way the form is explained. While the formation from the stem is possible, there is no sufficient evidence of its reality. This v. should be l.[7].—**119.** סִיגִים] pl. ‡ סיג n.(m.) *dross*, as Is. 1[22. 25] Pr. 25[4]; so Σ, 𝔍 ; but ⅏ παραβαίνοντας, 𝔘 *praevartcantes*, suggests rather שׁגים = סוגים, cf. 53[4] 80[19].—הִשְׁבַּתָּ] Hiph. שׁבת ; ⅏ ἐλογισάμην, חֲשַׁבְנוּ, not so prob.—כָּל רִֽשְׁעֵי ארץ] expl. gl., making l. overfull. This v. should be l.[3].—**120.** † סָמַר vb. *bristle up*, BDB.; elsw. Pi. Jb. 4[15].— מִמִּשְׁפָּחֶיךָ] transpose with יראתי. The first מ is dittog. and changes the original *fear of reverence* into one of *terror*. This v. should be l.[4].

121. שְׁפַטְתָּ צֶדֶק] an evident err. for the usual מִשְׁכְּבֵי צדקך. It has, however, been lengthened from an original מִשְׁפָּטֶיךָ. The assonance then requires עַבְדֶךָ

at the close of 1. This v. should be 1.³. — **122**. ערב ‡ [עֲרֹב עַבְדְּךָ Qal *take in pledge, go surety for*, here as Jb. 17³ +; Hithp. Ps. 106³⁵. עַבְדְּךָ is out of place. It is needed at the close of this 1. and also of the previous 1. for assonance. The term for Law is missing. דברך is needed. לטוב is a gl. due to previous txt. err. — **123**. This v. should begin Str. — **124**. חֻקֶּיךָ] belongs at close of 1. This v. should be transposed with the next. — **127**. אהבתי מצותיך] as usual belongs at close of 1. — **128**. כל פקודי כל]. The last כל is an evident err. for sf. ה, which the noun requires. 𝕲, 𝖁, have לכל which stands for an original לפקודיך. But the legal term belongs as usual with its vb. at close of 1. — יִשָּׁרְתִּי] *make straight, right*, of the steps, 𝕲, 𝖁, 𝔍, suits the context better than AV., RV., "esteem right," Piel in this sense α.λ.: *v. 5⁹*. — כל־ארח]. This כל also is gl., due to its use with פקודים.

129. This v. has been transposed with the following, doubtless because it seemed the most important one in the Str. — פְּלָאוֹת] pl. f. פֶּלֶא (9²) as Dn. 12⁶ for פלאים La. 1⁹. — **130**. † פֵּתַח] n.m. abstr. *opening, unfolding*, as 𝕲; but 𝔍, Σ, so Bä. פֶּתַח *door*, less probable. — דבריך] evident err. for the usual דברך. — פְּתָיִים] for פְּתִי; sg. required for assonance. — **131**. פְּעַרְתִּי pf. † [פָּעַר] vb. *open wide*, mouth, elsw. Is. 5¹⁴ Jb. 16¹⁰ 29²³ so prob. Ps. 69¹⁶. — ו [וָאֶשְׁאָפָה consec. cohort. † שָׁאַף *pant after* as Is. 42¹⁴, cf. Je. 2²⁴ 14⁶ with רוח, c. אֶל Ec. 1⁵, c. acc. Jb. 5⁵ 7² 36²⁰. — כי is gl. of interp. — וָאֶבְתִּי † יאב α.λ. Aramaism, *long, desire* = תאב, cf. v.⁴⁰. This v. should close the Str. — **132**. אֵלַי] gl. after the removal of לְאֹהֵב שְׁמֶךָ, the original reading, to the close of the 1. and its change into לְאֹהֲבֵי שְׁמֶךָ, which was connected with a misinterpretation of כמשפט after a copyist had omitted the usual sf. with pl. of this term for Law. — הָכִינֵנִי] belongs at close of 1. for assonance. — **133**. הַשְׁלֶט] Hiph. Juss. † שלט vb. Qal *have dominion* Ec. 2¹⁹ 8⁹ Ne. 5¹⁵ Est. 9¹·¹. Hiph. elsw. Ec. 5¹⁸ 6². — כָל־אָוֶן] makes 1. too long. כל is gl. of intensification. און goes with אל, בי closing 1. for assonance. — **134**. וְאֶשְׁמְרָה] weak ו with apod. in form of cohort. But assonance requires שמרתי at close of 1. — **135**. בְּעַבְדֶּךָ] improb., rd. ל = ἐπί 𝕲. — לַמְּדֵנִי] belongs at close of 1. — **136**. עֵינַי should be עֵינִי for assonance, and be with its vb. at close of 1. — עַל] is interp. gl. before לֹא־שָׁמְרוּ. This v. should begin the tetrastich.

137. This v. should close the first tetrastich. — **138**. צִוִּיתָ] has been incorrectly placed at the beginning. The 1. should begin with צֶדֶק וֶאֱמוּנָה מְאֹד. The vb. belongs with the noun for Law at the close of v. — **139**. דבריך] manifest error for the usual דברך. It should also be at close of 1. — **140**. צְרוּפָה אִמְרָתֶךָ] assimilated to 18³¹ Pr. 30⁵. The ‖ requires צָרוּף agreeing with עַבְדְּךָ, and that אמרתך should go to close of 1. after אָהֵב, which should be read instead of אַהֲבָה. — **141–144**. פקודיך v. 141 goes to close of 1.; so תורתך v.¹⁴², מצותיך v.¹⁴³, and עֵדוֹתֶיךָ v.¹⁴⁴. The latter should be preceded by כ as usual with term of Law connected with חיה; but as עֵדוּת has been used already, v.¹³⁸, the missing חקיך should here take its place. 𝕲, 𝖁, give חקים for פקדים v.¹⁴¹. 𝕲ᴬ has for תורה, v.¹⁴²; דבר; and for דבר v.¹³⁹, the ambiguous term ἐντολαί used by 𝕲 both for מצות and for פקודים.

145. יהוה] has been transposed from v.¹⁴⁶. Here it makes 1. overfull; there it is needed to complete 1. — חקיך] goes to close of 1. as usual; so תורתך

v.[150]. This v. should close the first tetrastich. — **146.** עֲדֹתֶיךָ] 𝔙 *mandata* = either מצות or פקדים, doubtless the latter. The v. should be l.[6]. — **147.** ‡ נֶשֶׁף] n.m. *twilight*, usually of evening, but here as Jb. 7[4] of the dawn. — דבריך] Kt. though sustained by 𝔊, is manifestly wrong for the usual דברך Qri ; so 𝔖. It also goes to close of l. This v. should begin the Str. followed by 148. — **149.** יהוה] is gl., making l. overfull. — כְּמִשְׁפָּטֶךָ] sg. impossible ; rd. pl. as usual. It should also go to cl. of l. This v. should be l.[3]. — **150.** רֹדְפֵי] 𝔊 οἱ καταδιώκοντές με ; רֹדְפַי ; so 𝔖, 𝔙, more prob. This v. should begin second tetrastich. — **151.** וכל מצותיך אמת] כל is gl. of amplification, and מצותיך goes to cl. of l. 𝔊 gives for מצות ὁδοί, so also 𝔙 *viae*. — **152.** כי מֵעֵדֹתֶיךָ כי is dittog. of ך or gl. of interp. The sf. 3 pl. belongs to ידעתי rather than to יסרתם, and may be found in מ of מעדתיך ; for word for Law goes to close of l. as usual. But since עדות has been used already, v.[146], the missing פקודיך should be substituted.

153. כי] is, as often in Ps., expl. gl. ; so v.[155. 159]. — תורתך] as usual belongs at close of l. ; so הקיד v.[155], עדותיך v.[157], אמרתך v.[158]. Trsp. this l. to beginning of second tetrastich. — **154.** לְאִמְרָתְךָ]. The ל is error for כ, invariably used with חיה. Term for Law goes to close of l. Furthermore as this word is used also v.[158], it here stands for the missing דברך. — **156.** מִשְׁפָּטֶיךָ] goes to close of l. — **157.** This v. should be l.[6]. — **158.** וָאֶתְקוֹטְטָה ו consec. Hithpolal cohort. [קוט], Hithp. elsw. 139[21], cf. 95[10]. — אֲשֶׁר] gl. of expl. This v. should be l.[2]. — **159.** פקודיך אהבתי] belongs in reverse order at close of l. — יהוה] is gl., making l. overfull. — **160.** ראש דברך אמת] l. is overfull. דברך is gl. of misinterp. The term for Law of this l. is the missing מצות, the משפטים having been used already, v.[156].

161. לְבִּי] makes l. overfull ; rd. פַחֲדִי, cf. v.[120]. — דבריך] Kt. as 𝔊, 𝔙, 𝔍 ; manifest error for דברך Qr. 𝔖, 𝔗. It goes to the close of l. — **162.** שָׂשׂ אָנֹכִי] makes two beats. It should be שָׂשׂ־אָנִי. — עַל־אִמְרָתֶךָ] with two beats goes to close of l. — רָב] is gl. of intensification. — **163.** תּוֹרָתְךָ] used also v.[165], is for the missing חקוק. It goes to close of l. This v. should be transposed with the following v. — **164.** הִלַּלְתִּיךָ על משפטי] makes l. overfull. It is an editorial change from an original הללתי משפטי. — **165.** לְאֹהֲבֵי תורתך] as usual goes to close of l. — לָמוֹ] is gl. due to the transposition. — **166.** מצותיך] goes to close of l. — **167.** עֵדֹתֶיךָ] has been transposed from end of l. — וָאֹהֲבֵם] suffix due to the transposition. This v. should be l.[6]. — **168.** וְעֵדֹתֶיךָ] is dittog. of terms for the Law, implying variant readings at an early date.

169. יהוה] gl. making l. overfull. — דברך] goes to close of l. as usual ; so אמרתך v.[170], פקודיך v.[173], תורתך v.[174]. — **171.** תַּבִּעְנָה] Hiph. juss. נבע, apod. — כי תלמדני חקיך] l. is overfull. כי, as often, is gl. of interp. The clause is really an objective one, giving the theme of the praise. — **172.** הַעַן] juss. ענה, of responsive song, as 88[1] 147[7]. — אמרתך] already used v.[170], is error for אמונה used adverbially. — כל כִּי] makes l. overfull ; the former word is gl. of interp., the latter gl. of intensification. — מצותיך צֶרֶק] מצותיך is used v.[176]. צֶרֶק stands for צדקך. The usual phr. is משפטי צדקך ; so prob. here. — **173.** כי] is an interp. gl. as often. — **175.** מִשְׁפָּטֶךָ] sg., err. for pl. ; but if משפטי is correct in v.[172], it must here stand for the missing עֵדְוֺתֶיךָ. — **176**. בקשׁ עברך] makes l. overfull. It was originally a marginal gl. The order of ll. should be, in last tetrastich: 174, 175, 173, 176.

PSALM CXX., 2 STR. 4[6].

Ps. 120 is a prayer to Yahweh for deliverance from treacherous foes, whose tongue is compared to sharp arrows and burning coals (v.[1-4]); complaining of the woe of dwelling with people who hate peace and prefer war (v.[5-7]).

UNTO Yahweh in mine own trouble I call, and Yahweh doth answer me.
O deliver me from the lying lip, from the deceitful tongue.
What shall one requite thee, and what more, O deceitful tongue?
Sharpened arrows of a warrior with glowing broom-coals.
WOE is me, that I sojourn with one that draweth it!
(Woe is me), that I dwell among the tents of Kedah!
Full long have I dwelt with one that hateth peace.
I am for peace; but when I speak, they are for war.

Ps. 120 is the first of the Pilgrim Pss. (*v.* Intr. § 36), without any other title. It is essentially a prayer for deliverance from treacherous foes. These are compared with the Bedouin Kedah. Meshek, referring to the Moschi of the region of the Black Sea, is a later conjecture of MT. and improbable. These treacherous foes seem rather to be Israelites than foreigners, and probably represent the irreligious party of the Greek period.

Str. I. A tetrastich of stairlike parall. — **1**. *Unto Yahweh*], emph.; unto Him and to no other. — *in mine own trouble*], the trouble belonging especially to me. The people are speaking in their unity, and not an individual. — *I call, and Yahweh doth answer me*]. The pf. expresses the general truth of the emphatic present. The call has, as its immediate consequence, the divine answer. This has been and is the experience of His people. — **2**. *O deliver me from the lying lip*]; in the complementary clause, *the deceitful tongue*]. The peril is from crafty, treacherous foes; probably a party in Israel, and not foreign foes. — **3**. *What shall one requite thee?*]. What retribution, or penalty, shall be given for such treachery? — *and what more?*], as usual in this phr., an addition to the usual penalty of exact retribution, in accordance with the *lex talionis*, on account of the enormity of the offence. — **4**. *Shar-*

pened arrows of a warrior]. The treacherous tongue is compared to a bow, shooting forth words like arrows; cf. Je. 9$^{2.7}$ Pr. 26^{18} Ps. 64^4. The words have been sharpened for the purpose of doing deadly injury. — *with glowing broom-coals*]. The broom shrub makes the best charcoal, and therefore the best coal to burn and glow.

Str. II. Three syn. and one synth. line. — **5-6.** *Woe is me*], repeated for emphasis, with the variation *Full long*, in the third line. — *that I sojourn with* ‖ *dwell among*], the last repeated in the third line with the third fem. of the person as subj., as a variation of the first person. — *among the tents of Kedah*], an Arabian tribe descended from Ishmael Gn. 25^{13}, doubtless mentioned here because of their well-known treachery: not that the author was in fact living among them, but that the treacherous foes may be compared to them. — *with one that draweth it*], the tongue as a bow, cf. 1 K. 22^{34}, and so ‖ *with one that hateth peace*]. This is the most probable explanation of a difficult word, which in most ancient Vrss. is interpreted as a vb. with the meaning "prolonged," thinking usually of a prolonged sojourn. MT., 𝕿, EV^s., interpret as a proper name, "Meshech," a tribe dwelling on the southeast of the Black Sea, in the Persian period; cf. Ez. 27^{13} 38^3 Is. 66^{19}. It is probably only a late conceit. — **7.** *I am for peace*]. The faithful have the attribute of peace; they are, as it were, all peace. — *when I speak, they are for war*]. The faithful people of God speak the language of peace, friendly words: their treacherous foes speak not only lying, but warlike words.

1. [בצרתה לי] retracted accent 2^{12}. — **2.** [יהוה] belongs in l.1. — [הַצִּילָה] cohort. imv., urgent petition. — **3.** [יֹסִיף לָךְ יֵּמֶה]. The לך is prob. a late addition, though in 𝕲, where it is inconsistent with πρὸς γλῶσσαν. It makes the clause too long, and is not elsw. found with the phr., cf. 1 S. 3^{17} 14^{44} 20^{13}. — **4.** [וְחַלֵּי רְכָמִים] phr. α.λ., but cf. גהלי אש 18^9. † רֹכֶם n.m. *broom plant*, elsw. 1 K. 19$^{4.5}$ Jb. 30^4. — **5.** [אֲיָּה לִי] α.λ., accent retracted as v.¹. The strengthened form of אוי, cf. Is. 6^5 Je. 4^{13} 6^4 +. The measure requires it in the next l. A careless scribe omitted it. — [יָרֵחִי מֶשֶׁךְ] so 𝕿, but most ancient Vrss. regard משך as vb., and some גרתי as noun. 𝕲 ἡ παροικία μου ἐμακρύνθη גוּרִי מָשׁוּךְ, so 𝕻, 𝕾; *peregrinatio mea prolongata est* 𝕵; cf. Σ παρείλκυσα, Aq. ἐν μακρυσμῷ. It seems better to regard the form as active ptc. מֹשֵׁךְ ‖ שׁוֹנֵא, and think of drawing the bow, as 1 K. 22^{34}, cf. Is. 66^{19}. ‡ מֶשֶׁךְ n. pr. gent. the *Moschi*, Ez. 27^{13} 38^3 39^1, is not prob., and seems to be a late conjecture of Massoretic period. The use of vb. ‎זור‎, measure and ‖, require insertion of ‎עם‎. — ‡ ‎הֲדָר‎] n. pr. gent. an Arabian tribe Is. 21¹⁶ 42¹¹ 60⁷ Je. 2¹⁰ 49²⁸ Ez. 27²¹.— **6.** ‎רַבַּת‎] adv. of quantity, *much*, or time, *too long, full long*, Ps. 123⁴ 129¹⁻². ², for the usual ‎רַבָּה‎ 78¹⁵ 89⁸. — ‎לָּה‎] is the ethical dative. The vb. ‎שכנה‎ suggests ‎נפשי‎ as subj.; but it was not necessary to write it. It is a gl., making l. too long. — **7.** ‎שלום‎] as noun is emph. as predicate of the faithful. It is not for adj., nor does it stand for ‎איש שלום‎, nor can it be obj. of ‎אדבר‎, thrown before for emphasis, Ew.³⁶². ᵇ.

PSALM CXXI., 2 STR. 4⁶.

Ps. 121 is a pious resolution to lift up the eyes to the mountains for help (v.¹); with a petition for Yahweh's sleepless protection (v.³). A response gives assurance that help cometh from Yahweh, who never slumbers (v.². ⁴). Yahweh protects on every side as a shade from sunstroke and moonstroke (v.⁵⁻⁶), from every evil forever (v.⁷⁻⁸).

I LIFT up mine eyes unto the mountains. Whence cometh my help?
　Help is from Yahweh, Maker of heaven and earth.
　May He not suffer (my) foot to be moved, (and) may He that keepeth (me)
　　not slumber!
　Lo! He slumbereth not, and He sleepeth not, the Keeper of Israel.
YAHWEH, thy keeper; Yahweh is thy shade on thy right hand.
　By day the sun will not smite thee, nor the moon by night.
　Yahweh will keep thee from every evil, He will keep thy person.
　Yahweh will keep thy going out and thy coming in from this time forth and
　　forevermore.

Ps. 121 doubtless belongs with this entire group to the Greek period. It has the stairlike parall. in a marked degree; v.¹⁻⁴ also is antiphonal in character.

Str. I. Is antiphonal, the first and third lines having their response in the second and fourth. — **1.** *I lift up mine eyes to the mountains*], the sacred mountains of Jerusalem 87¹, where Yahweh dwells, the source of deliverance 3⁵ 20³ 134³. — *Whence cometh my help?*] so RV., JPSV., and most moderns; implying not perplexity or doubt, but, in accordance with the context, expectation. The indirect question of PBV., AV., although sustained by Jos. 2⁴, is improbable here. — **2.** *Help*], in general; not "my help," assimilated to previous word by early copyist's error. This is a response to the previous question by another voice. — *is from*

Yahweh, Maker of heaven and earth], the source of help is the creator of the universe; whether conceived as resident on earth in Zion, or in heaven, the place of the throne of His majesty. — **3.** *May He not suffer my foot to be moved*], the same voice as v.[1], and therefore " my foot " is necessary. An ancient copyist, not perceiving the antiphonal character of the Ps., assimilated this line to the second Str. with the second person, doubtless at the same time mistaking the difference in the negation of v.[3] and v.[4]. This has been followed by EV[s]. also. But the negative of the juss. certainly implies a petition, as RV.[m]. The help needed in v.[1] is here defined : support from tottering to a fall, cf. 55^{23} 66^9. — *May He that keepeth me not slumber*], sleepless vigilance is needed for protection against foes. — **4.** *Lo! He slumbereth not, and He sleepeth not*], an exact and definite response, giving assurance that the petition was granted in its own terms. — *The Keeper of Israel*]. The promise to Jacob, Gn. 28^{15}, to keep his descendants as a shepherd does his flock, Yahweh has always fulfilled.

Str. II. The second voice speaks throughout this Str. in stair-like parall. — **5.** *Yahweh thy keeper*], so probably in apposition, and not predicate as EV[s]., taking up the great thought in the climax of the previous Str. — *Yahweh is thy shade*], in the more general sense of shelter, protection, cf. 91^1, as is evident from — *on thy right hand*], the place where the advocate and protector stands, cf. 16^8 109^{31}. It is improbable that the author is here thinking of the shade of the wings, as 17^8 36^8 57^2, or of a booth or rock from the heat Is. 4^6 32^2. — **6.** *By day the sun will not smite thee*]. There will be protection from sunstroke, of which there was special danger in Palestine, 2 K. 4^{18-19} Is. 49^{10}, making the use of turbans necessary. — *nor the moon by night*]. The rays of the full moon are also generally regarded as danger-ous, especially in the East. — **7.** *Yahweh will keep thee from every evil*], from every kind of evil, rather than the inexact generaliza-tion of EV[s]. " all evil." — *He will keep thy person*], the whole man, poetic for " me," in accordance with Heb. usage ; and not the specific " soul " as distinguished from the body, of EV[s]., which is against the context. — **8.** *Yahweh will keep thy going out*], from home to labour, *and thy coming in*], return from labour ; including

all the intervening activity, the entire course of life, cf. Dt. 28⁶
1 S. 29⁶ 2 S. 3²⁵ Ps. 139²⁻³. —*from this time forth and forevermore*],
throughout all future time, in the life of the nation.

1. מֵאַיִן] prob. direct question, *whence?* as usual Gn. 29⁴ Nu. 11¹³ Ju.
17⁹ 19¹⁷ +; indirect only Jos. 2⁴. — **2.** עֶזְרִי] assimilated to previous word.
עֵזֶר alone is proper. — **3.** רַכִּיט] prep. with noun, cf. 55²³ 66⁹. — אַל] neg. juss.
The second אַל requires ו for measure. — רַגְלֶךָ] assimilated to subsequent context. The juss. of petition, ‖ v.¹, makes it impossible that the sf. should be
the 2 pers. The sf. is prob. a wrong interp. of the article הֲרָרֶיךָ; rd. הַשֹּׁמֵר for
שֹׁמְרֶךָ. — **4.** הִנֵּה לֹא] the change of negative to emph. positive assertion implies
a response to the petition by another voice. — **6.** יִרְיָה] full and strong sf.
with יָהּ. — **7.** מִכָּל־רַע] without article, *every.* If the poet had thought of two
beats, he would have inserted the article and made it "all."

PSALM CXXII., 2 STR. 4⁶.

Ps. 122 expresses the gladness of pilgrims to Jerusalem (v.¹⁻²);
admiration for the city (v.³⁻⁴); implores peace upon the city (v.⁶⁻⁷)
for the sake of friends, and especially the temple (v.⁸⁻⁹). Glosses
remind that the royal throne of David was once there (v.⁵), and
that the pilgrimage was according to the Law (v.⁴ᶜ).

I AM glad when they say to me: "To the house of Yahweh we go."
  (I am glad) when our feet stand within thy gates, O Jerusalem.
  O Jerusalem! rebuilt as a city which is compacted together;
  Whither the tribes ascend, the tribes of Yah, to give thanks to His name!
PRAY: "Peace be (to thee), Jerusalem, and prosperity to them that love thee."
  "Peace be within thy ramparts; prosperity within thy palaces."
  For the sake of my brethren and my friends I will bespeak thee peace.
  For the sake of the house of Yahweh our God I will seek for thee prosperity.

Ps. 122 has in the title לְדָוִד, so 𝔐 and 𝔊. But it is impossible that the Ps.
could have been in 𝔇. It is a late conjecture, due to the gl. v.⁵. The Ps. is
late in syntax, and abounds in Aramaisms. The Ps. could hardly have been
earlier than the late Greek period. Ptc. for finite vb. v.¹·²; שֶׁ relative v.³·⁴;
עֵדוּת v.⁴, term of P for Law, is, however, in gl.

Str. I. Two synth. couplets. — **1.** *I am glad*], as a present and
habitual state: repeated in the stairlike parallel., but omitted by a
prosaic copyist in second line. — *when they say to me*]. At the
time when the proposition is made by friends and relatives ready

to proceed to Jerusalem to the pilgrim feasts. — *To the house of Yahweh we go*]. "We are about to go up to the temple: will you not go with us?" — **2**. *When our feet stand within thy gates, O Jerusalem*]. The gladness is renewed and intensified at the end of the pilgrimage, as it was begun at the start. — **3**. *O Jerusalem*], vocative expressing admiration. — *rebuilt*], as usual in the Pss.; and not "built" of the EV^s., as if it referred to the original city. — *as a city which is compacted together*], its walls and buildings rising up in a compact and harmonious mass; and so different from the small towns and villages from which the pilgrims generally came. — **4**. *Whither the tribes ascend*], all the tribes of Israel from all parts of the land, ‖ *the tribes of Yah*], indicating that they belong especially to Yahweh, the God of Israel. — *to give thanks to His name*], the purpose of the pilgrim's feast in the public worship of Yahweh by the entire nation assembled together in the temple. — A glossator, probably at first on the margin, inserted: *It is a testimony to Israel*], using the term of P for the Law. It is Israel's law to observe these pilgrim feasts. This insertion in the text occasioned the change "name of Yahweh" for "His name," all this against the measure. Another glossator, careless of the measure, inserts a historical statement, making the line too long: **5**. *For there sat they on thrones of judgment, thrones of the house of David.*

Str. II. Two syn. couplets. — **6-7**. *Pray*]. Exhortation, the theme embracing the first distich. — *Peace be to thee, Jerusalem*], so most probably, in accordance with usage and ‖ *Peace be within thy ramparts*. The omission of "to thee" by an early copyist at the cost of the measure occasioned the MT. "peace of Jerusalem" as the obj. of the vb., followed by all EV^s., against 𝔊, 𝔍. — *and prosperity to them that love thee*], so 𝔊, 𝔍, most naturally, ‖ *prosperity within thy palaces* v.⁷. 𝔐 by mistake of the initial letter, followed by EV^s., interpreting noun as vb. impf., makes it parallel with the juss. that follows in "They shall prosper that love thee!" — **8**. *For the sake of my brethren and my friends*], those who accompanied him to the pilgrim feast from their common abode; — still more, **9**. *For the sake of the house of Yahweh our God*], the temple, the common resort of all the people of Yahweh. It is probable that this couplet is an antiphon to the

2 G

previous one by another voice. — *I will bespeak thee peace* ‖ *I will seek for thee prosperity*], closing with the stress on " peace," the keyword of the Str., and the synonym " good, well-being, prosperity."

1. בְּאֹמְרִים] Qal ptc. with prep. Both may be variously interpreted. In classic style the ptc. would express continuous, uninterrupted saying, which is improb. here. It is therefore doubtless the ptc. for finite vb. of late Heb. as v.², which may refer to past, present, or future, in accordance with the interp. of שׂמחתי; prob. emph. present, rather than aorist referring to a definite past. ב may be temporal as most Vrss. and interp.; or obj. of vb. *be glad at*, or *rejoice over*, as Pe., De., Dr., 𝔊 ἐπί, 𝔍 *eo quod.* — נֵלְכָה] indic. and not cohort. as EVˢ., which would require נֵרְכָה. — **2.** This l. requires an additional word for measure and parall., possibly ב ירילי, but inasmuch as these Pss. use repetition ב שׂמחתי. — בְּעֵינִיריד] so 𝔍, 𝔊 ; e. a. A. R. T; but 𝔊 ˢ without sf. — **3.** הבנויה] Qal ptc. f. with article, doubtless vocative with the mng. *rebuilt.* — שֶׁחֻבְּרָה] shortened relative שׁ with Pu. pf. 3 f. חבר (58⁶) here of walls of city, with ה־ pleonastic Aramaism. — **4.** עֵדוּת לישׂראל] gl. to indicate that such pilgrimage feasts at Jerusalem were according to the Law, using the term of P, cf. Ex. 23¹⁷ 34²³ Dt. 16¹⁶. Other expl., making it part of Ps., are unsatisfactory; and indeed it makes l. much too long. — לְשֵׁם יהוה] makes l. too long; after ה־, שׁבֵּי would be most natural. The insertion of the gl., separating שׁם further from ה־, occasioned the change. — **5.** כי שׁמה ישׁבו כסאות למשׁפט. — כסאות לבית דוד] is a historic gl., making Str. too long. — **6.** שׁאֲלוּ שׁלוֹם] 𝔊 ἐρωτήσατε δὴ τὰ εἰς εἰρήνην τῇ Ἰερουσαλήμ. 𝔊ᴿ omits τῇ, 𝔊ᵀ τὴν. Both readings difficult and improb.; the latter did not interpret שׁלום as construct, but in the usual sense שׁלוֹם with prep., prob. לְ. A word is missing; rd. לָךְ. Indeed the vocative best suits the context. — יִשְׁלָיוּ] Qal impf. *plene* for יִשְׁלוּ. † שָׁלָה vb. elsw. Qal *be quiet, secure, without care*, Jb. 3²⁶ 12⁶ Je. 12¹ La. 1⁵. Niph. 2 Ch. 29¹¹. Hiph. 2 K. 4²⁸. But 𝔊 εὐθηνία rd. שׁלוה as v.⁷, and this is indeed most prob. The transposition of clause in 𝔊 ˢ is doubtless txt. err. — **8.** אֲדַבְּרָה־נָּא]. The נא makes l. too long. — **9.** טוֹב] is not in 𝔊ᴺ, though in 𝔥, 𝔊ᴺ. c. a. A. R. T.

PSALM CXXIII., 4⁶.

Ps. 123 asserts fidelity to Yahweh, waiting for His signal as faithful servants (v.¹⁻²). A gloss implores favour, because of contemptuous treatment (v.³⁻⁴).

UNTO Thee I lift up mine eyes, O Thou who art enthroned in heaven.
   Lo! as the eyes of menservants are (lifted up) to the hand of their lords;
   (Lo!) as the eyes of a maidservant are (lifted up) to the hand of her lady;
   So our eyes are unto Yahweh, our God, until He be gracious to us.

Ps. 123 belongs to the Greek period, when fidelity to Yahweh was emphasized.

The Ps. has introverted parall. — **1–2.** *O Thou who art enthroned in heaven* ‖ *Yahweh, our God*], the supreme sovereign and lord of all, whose majestic throne was in heaven, cf. 2^4. — *I lift up mine eyes*], in attentive, patient waiting, — defined by *until He be gracious to us*], manifest His favour. This attitude is compared to that of *menservants* ‖ *a maidservant*], whose eyes are lifted up to the *hand*, which usually in ancient times gave the signal of the kind of service required, or of the bestowal of favour, both on the part of *lords* and the *lady* of the house. This little Ps., a tetrastich complete in itself, was enlarged in the Maccabean times by a trimeter pentastich, which changes the patient attitude of the servant to the importunate plea of one in great need.

> Be gracious to us, Yahweh ! Be gracious to us !
> For exceedingly we are filled with contempt.
> Exceedingly our soul is filled
> With the scorn of those without care,
> The contempt of the proud oppressors.

3–4. *Be gracious to us, Yahweh !*], repeated in importunity. — *For exceedingly*], the reason for the plea, with the emphasis laid upon the exceeding greatness of the need ; repeated for emphasis. — *we are filled* ‖ *our soul is filled*], so full that we cannot contain or endure any more. — *with contempt*, defined as that of *proud oppressors* ‖ *scorn of those without care*]. The Antiochian party was so prosperous, strong, and proud, that they looked with contempt and scorn upon the few faithful servants of Yahweh, and their attitude was so aggressive that the situation had become intolerable.

1. אֵלַי] emph. — נָשָׂאתִי] emph. present. — הַיֹּשְׁבִי] vocative, with final י to get an additional syll. and two accents ; required if this, as all other Pilgrim Pss., is hexameter. Vb. pregnant, as 2^4. — **2.** אֶל יי] ⅏, 𝔍, pl. improb. ; assimilation. The l. needs vb. for completeness : עֵינֵינוּ ; so next l., which also needs יי. These were deemed unnecessary by prosaic copyist. — ‡ שִׁפְחָה] n.f. *female slave*, as Gn. 16^1 25^{12} Is. 24^2. — גְּבִרְתָּהּ] sf. 3 f. with ‡ גְּבֶרֶת n.f. *lady, queen*, Gn. $16^{4.8.9}$ (J) 2 K. 5^3 Is. $47^{5.7}$ — שֶׁיְּחָנֵּנוּ] rel. שׁ with impf. הנן and sf. 1 pl. — **3.** רַב] emph.; adv. for which רָבַּת v.[4] as 120^6. A gl. begins with this v. in trimeter measure. — **4.** לָהּ] ethical dative as 120^6. — הַלַּעַג]

article with cstr before הַשְׁאֲנַנִּים impossible in Heb. grammar. It should be
followed by בְ as 𝕲, τοῖς εὐθηνοῦσιν, and as in subsequent clause ; so Ehr. —
‡ שַׁאֲנָיב] with בְ prefixed has two accents : intensive adj., generally in bad sense,
careless, easy ones, Am. 6¹ Zc. 1¹⁵, cf. Is. 32⁹· ¹¹. — רֹאיִיב] Kt. as one word
for ואינים a.λ. *proud*, so all ancient Vrss.; but Qr. two words, לְאֵי pl. cstr.
יָאֶה *proud* 94², and יָרִיב ptc. pl. יוה (17¹²) *violent, cruel*. This is most prob.
In any case two accents are needed for the measure.

PSALM CXXIV., 2 STR. 4⁶.

**Ps. 124 is a reminiscence of repeated deliverances of the people
by their own God from enemies of overwhelming power (v.¹⁻⁴);
and an ascription of blessedness to Yahweh for not having given
them up, but having given them escape from snares (v.⁶⁻⁷); concluding with the assurance that help is only in the name of
Yahweh, the creator (v.⁸). V.⁵ is a gloss of repetition.**

" IF it had not been Yahweh who was ours," let Israel say ;
     " If it had not been Yahweh who was ours, when they rose up against us ;
     Then alive they had swallowed us up, when their anger was kindled against us :
     Then the waters had swept us away ; the torrent had passed over us."
" BLESSED be Yahweh ! who hath not given us over as a prey to their teeth.
     (Lo) We are like a bird, that has escaped out of the trap of the fowler.
     (Lo!) the trap was broken, and we escaped (from it).
     Our help is in the name of Yahweh, Maker of heaven and earth."

Ps. 124 has in the title of 𝕳, 𝕲 ᵍ, לדוד. But this must be a late conjecture ;
for the language is of the Greek period : יהיה v.¹· ², אזי v.³· ⁴· ⁵. The זרונים
v.⁵, a word of post Bib. Heb., is, with the entire v., a late gloss. The Ps.
must have been written in troublous times of party strife.

Str. I. two syn. couplets. — **1–2.** *If it had not been Yahweh who
was ours*], our God and therefore on our side against the enemies. This is repeated for emphasis. — *let Israel say*], cohort.
RV., JPSV. ; exhortation to the people to give utterance to their
experience. The PBV., AV., " may say " is incorrect. — *when
they rose up against us*]. The context makes it sufficiently evident
who these enemies were ; but an ancient scribe at the expense of
the measure inserted the unnecessary " man," which indeed is too
general and not well suited to the context. — **3.** *Then*], repeated
for emphasis ; apodosis of the temporal clause. — *alive*], emphatic
in position. — *they had swallowed us up*], implying the figure of
an earthquake, and probably having in mind the story of Korah,

Nu. 16³⁰⁻³⁴ ; although the same terms are used of Sheol Pr. 1¹², and of Babylon, compared to a great monster Je. 51³⁴. — *when their anger was kindled against us*], another figure, of devouring fire. — **4**. *Then the waters*], a common figure of peril from enemies, Pss. 18¹⁷⁻¹⁸ 69²⁻³ Is. 8⁷⁻⁸ La. 3⁵⁴. — *had swept us away*], as in a flood or cataract. — *the torrent had passed over us*], drowning us in its depths. — A glossator added a variant in **5** : *Then the raging waters had passed over us*.

Str. II. Tetrastich with introverted parallel. — **6**. *Blessed be Yahweh*], based on the previous statements, and introductory to those of this Str. — *who hath not given us over as a prey to their teeth*]. The enemies are compared to ravenous beasts of prey, cf. 7³ 10⁹. — *We are like a bird*], cf. 11¹. — *that has escaped out of the trap of the fowler ‖ Lo ! the trap was broken, and we escaped from it*]. The enemies are here, as 91³, Pr. 6⁵, compared to fowlers setting traps for birds. They fail only because their traps are broken, as is suggested, by Yahweh. — **8**. See 121², the only difference being that there *help* is "from Yahweh," here *in the name of Yahweh*.

1. לוּלֵי] hypothetical negative, 27¹³. — לָנוּ] dative of possession, *ours*. — שֶׁהָיָה] accent retracted before קָם. Hu., Pe., *al.* take the rel. as complement of לוּ ל *if that*, and regard it as pleonastic. It is better to take it as simple relative: "Were it not Yahweh *who*," as Ew., Dr., *al.* — ויאמר־נא] juss. — **3**. אֲזַי] Hu., Kö.II. 1. 245 take it as older form of אז. BDB. dialectic form of אז ; *then, in that case*, cf. 119⁹². — **4**. † הַלְהָבָה] n.m. as Aramaic נחלא, cf. Nu. 34⁵ as local acc. ; for נַחַל (18⁵) *stream, brook*. — ויהרגונו] *us*, not *our souls*.— **5**. † הַזֵּידוֹנִים] adj. *a.λ. insolent, raging*, from זוּר *boil, swell, rage ;* and so *proud*. This is a word of late Heb. — This l. is a variant of the previous one and a gl. — **6**. שֶׁלֹּא] rel. שׁ and neg. **7**. The measure requires that הנה should be prefixed to both ll. and ממנו added to l.² all omitted as unnecessary by prosaic scribes.

PSALM CXXV., 4⁶.

Ps. 125 expresses confidence that the faithful will be as immovable as Jerusalem, encompassed by protecting mountains (v.¹⁻²) ; that Yahweh will not permit the wicked to rule in their lot (v.³ᵃ). Glosses state the divine protection restraining His people from iniquity (v.³ᵇ) ; and implore the divine guidance for the upright (v.⁴), and banishment for those who go astray (v.⁵).

THEY that trust in Yahweh are as Mount Zion, which cannot be moved.
   Forever Jerusalem sits enthroned, mountains round about her;
   So Yahweh is round about His people from henceforth and forevermore.
   For He will not suffer the sceptre of the wicked to rest upon the lot of the
      righteous.

Ps. 125 in its original form, v.¹⁻³ᵃ, gives little evidence of date, save that
Jerusalem seems to have been in security, reigning as a king on the hills in
the midst of the surrounding mountains. It doubtless came from the prosperous times of the Greek period. The glosses indicate a later date, when
there was a strife of religious parties, v.³ᵇ⁻⁵.

An emblematic tetrastich. — **1-2.** *They that trust in Yahweh*],
the faithful among the people. — *are as Mount Zion*], the sacred
mountain, the chief hill of Jerusalem. — *which cannot be moved*],
will remain firm and unshaken, cf. Is. 28¹⁶ Ps. 46⁶. — *Forever
Jerusalem sits enthroned*]. This is parall. to the previous line.
The royal city is enthroned as a king, cf. 48²˙⁸³·. 𝔥 and Vrss.
mistake the measures and the connection. 𝔊, 𝔍, attach to the
previous clause and render "the inhabitant of Jerusalem will never
be moved," which altogether destroys the measure. 𝔥 followed
by EVˢ. attaches the vb. "abideth forever" to the previous clause,
but "Jerusalem" to the next line ; making the one too long, the
other too short, and impairing the parall. — *mountains round
about her*], although Jerusalem is enthroned on hills and from the
south is in a commanding position, yet in all other directions are
mountains. "All around Jerusalem are higher hills : on the east,
the Mount of Olives; on the south, the Hill of Evil Counsel, so
called, rising directly from the Vale of Hinnom ; in the west the
ground rises gently . . . while on the north, a bend of the ridge
connected with the Mount of Olives bounds the prospect at the
distance of more than a mile " (Rob.*Bibl. Res.* I. 259). — *So Yahweh*],
like these mountains *is round about His people*], the faithful ones
compared to Zion above, *from henceforth and forevermore*]. They
will be shielded and guarded forever, cf. Zec. 2⁵. — **3.** *For He
will not suffer to rest*], so 𝔊, with Yahweh as subject ; more probable than 𝔥 followed by EVˢ., making the sceptre as subj. — *the
sceptre of the wicked*], in antithesis with *lot of the righteous*].
These are wicked nations whose sceptre of dominion would be
lifted up over the holy city given by lot of Yahweh to righteous

Israel. This must have been written during the mild rule of the Egyptian monarchs some time before the Syrian oppression. — We are not surprised that in the troublous times of the Maccabees glosses were found necessary, and added by different hands. One states the purpose of the divine protection from a legal point of view : *that the righteous put not forth their hands on iniquity.* — **4-5.** Another and probably an earlier glossator adds the antithetical couplet : *O do good, Yahweh, to the good and to the right minded*], distinguishing them, not from wicked enemies as in v.³, but from wicked Israelites, the unfaithful in Israel itself. — *But those that turn aside to their crooked ways, may Yahweh lead forth*], from the holy city and from the people of Yahweh ; *together with the workers of trouble*], probably external enemies. — The Ps. concludes with the additional gloss of congratulation, *Peace unto Israel.*

1. יָמִיט לֹא] Niph. impf., rel. clause ; but 𝔊 makes it an independent clause with שֵׁבֶ subj. — יָרֵכְ] attached by 𝔇 to יֵשֵׁב, by 𝔊 to יָמִיט. — יֵשֵׁב] 𝔊 = ὁ κατοικῶν; attached by both to previous context, really has ירושלם as subj.; and בֵיכ has its pregnant mng. — **3.** יָנוּח] 𝔊 οὐκ ἀφήσει τὴν ῥάβδον more prob. יָניח — יֵרֵשׁ] but 𝔊, 𝔖, 𝔙, יֵרֵשׁ = τῶν ἁμαρτωλῶν more prob., as Gr., Che., Davies, Minocchi. — יֵרֵ] introducing a gl. The Str. has been completed in previous l. — יֵרֵ־ה] fuller form of יֵירֵה. — **4.** הֵיטִיבָה] Hiph. imv. cohort. יטב. — הֵטִילַהְדֵיכֵם] pl. sf. † הֵטִילַהְדֵיכֵם] יֵישֵׁרֵי לֵב. — **5.** יֵישֵׁרֵי לֵב. 𝔊 τοῖς εὐθέσι τῇ καρδίᾳ ליישרים בלנוּים] adj. intensive, *crooked*, elsw. Ju. 5⁶. — פֵעֵלֵי האון] for usual פֵעֵלֵי און. — שלום עֵל ישראל] liturgical addition.

PSALM CXXVI., 2 str. 4⁶.

Ps. 126 is an assertion of the festive joy of the people when Yahweh restores their prosperity (v.¹⁻³) ; preparatory to the prayer that He may grant abundant harvests (v.⁴⁻⁶).

WHEN Yahweh restores the prosperity of Zion, we are like dreamers.
    Then is our mouth filled with laughter, and our tongues with jubilation.
    Then they say among the nations: " He hath done great things with them."
    Yahweh doth great things with us: we are glad men.
O RESTORE, Yahweh, our prosperity, as (do) streams in the south country.
    They that sow (seed) in tears, may they reap with jubilation.
    He may go forth weeping, bearing (a load) of seed;
    Let him come home with jubilation, bearing (a load of) sheaves.

The date of Ps. 126 cannot be determined by שׁוּב שֵׁבִית, because that phr., while it might refer to restoration from captivity, frequently means restoration of prosperity, which alone suits Str. II. The phr. הגדיל לעשות v.^{2. 3}, as Jo. 2²⁰, is postexilic. The Ps. doubtless belongs to the Greek period, when the people long for a return of prosperity, probably more favourable years for crops.

Str. I. Introverted parallelism. — **1.** *When Yahweh restores the prosperity of Zion*], a general statement in the protasis of the temporal clause, whose proper apodosis is the syn. v.³, *Yahweh doth great things with us,* with the complementary *we are like dreamers* v.¹. The realisations of the hope are so great, that they seem to be incredible. ‖ *we are glad men*]. There is no specific reference to a restoration from captivity as EV^s., which does not suit the prayer, or the thought of v.⁴⁻⁶. Between these two syn. lines, in accordance with the principle of introverted parallelism, a synth. couplet was inserted by the author v.². — **2.** *Then is our mouth filled with laughter*], the ecstatic state of joy, which in v.¹ is conceived as like dreaming, is here represented as laughter, — and then in the complementary part of the line : *and our tongues with jubilation*], loud shouting expressive of the gladness. — *Then they say among the nations*]. The neighbouring nations observe the prosperity of Zion, and speak about it among themselves, making the same remark that the people make v.^{3a}.

Str. II. A synth. and an antith. couplet. — **4.** *O restore, Yahweh, our prosperity*], petition taking the place of the conditional clause v.¹. — *as do streams in the south country*]. The Negeb, or "south country," lies between Palestine and Egypt. In the rainy seasons the channels that run down from the mountains are full of water, which refreshes the soil and causes it to burst forth with fresh vegetation and flowers. The greater part of the year except in close proximity to perennial fountains it is dry and barren. — **5.** *They that sow seed in tears*], doing their best to obtain crops, but sad and sorrowful as they contemplate a failure owing to a bad season. — *may they reap with jubilation*], a jussive in continuation of the prayer, and not indicative expressing assurance that it will be so, of EV^s. The prosperity longed for is a change from bad seasons to a good one, cf. Jo. 1. — **6.** *He may go forth weeping* (as he goes)], resuming v.^{5a}. — *Let him come home with jubilation*], resuming v.^{5b}. — But the significant thing is that when he goes forth, it is *bearing a load of seed,* when he comes home, it is *bearing a load of sheaves*], a very successful harvest. The simple meaning of the original has been obscured by a copyist, who mistook the word meaning "load" and used a word to which it is difficult to give an appropriate meaning.

1. הֲשִׁיב] prot. temp. clause with apod. — הֵיִינוּ] pf. of state, not referring to the past. — שׁיבת] a.λ. doubtless err. for יבית = שבות in the phr. שוב שבות v.⁴; not referring here to the restoration from captivity, but to the restoration of prosperity (v. *14⁷*). — הֹלְמִים] Qal ptc. nominal force cf. 73²⁰ ‖ שמחים v.³. — **2.** אז יִפָלֵא] impf. after אז, which in early usage has the force of ו consec., doubtful, however, in this late Ps.; so יאברו אז. In any case the time is present, carrying on the previous apod. as second and third members of it. — ‡ שְׂחֹיק] n. *laughter*, as Jb. 8²¹ and elsw. WL. The earlier mng. was *derision* Je. 20⁷ 48²³·²⁷ La. 3¹⁴. — הנריד לְ,שׂוּת] phr. Jo. 2²⁾; the first vb. has auxiliary or adverbial force. — יהוה] is a gl., though in 𝕳, 𝕲, as it makes l. too long and was unnecessary. — **5.** The l. as it stands is tetrameter; but that is improb. Probably the obj. of the first vb. זרע, and the emph. demonstr. as subj. of the second vb. have been omitted by txt. err. — **6.** הָלוֹךְ יֵלֵךְ] inf. abs. before vb., intensifying its meaning: *goes on*. — וּבָכֹה] inf. abs. after vb. emphasizing its temporal character: *continually weeping;* but 𝕲 ἔκλαιον. — נשֵׂא מֶשֶׁךְ הַזָּרַע] 𝕲 ˢ·ᴬ only αἴροντες τὰ σπέρματα αὐτῶν, 𝕲 ˢ·ᶜ·ᵃ·ᵀ βάλλοντες, 𝕲ᴿ φέροντες. † מֶשֶׁךְ n.m. elsw. Jb. 28¹⁸ *drawing up* (in fishing); here usually explained as the drawing out of the seed as it is scattered, so Ew., Pe., Conant; *trail* Dr.; cf. Am. 9¹³ where the vb. משׁך means to trail or draw out the seed. But in its absence from 𝕲 it is improb. It is prob. txt. err. for מֵיִשָׂא n m. *load, burden* (*38⁵*), which same word is needed in v.⁶ᵇ after נשׂא to complete the l. — בא יבא] inf. abs. intensive with vb. *come in* or *home*. — אלמתיו] sf. 3 sg. † אֲלֻמָּה] n.f. *sheaf*, as Gn. 37⁷ (E).

PSALM CXXVII.

Ps. 127 is composite: I., asserting that all depends on Yahweh, whether the building of a house, the watching of a city, or success in daily toil (v.¹⁻²); II., asserting that children are an inheritance of Yahweh, enabling a man to meet his enemies with confidence at the gate of his city (v.³⁻⁵).

A. v.¹⁻², 4⁶.

EXCEPT Yahweh build the house, in vain the builders labour.
Except Yahweh keep the city, in vain the keeper waketh.
It is vain for you, who rise up early, sit down late,
Eat the bread of toil. He giveth to His beloved in sleep.

B. v.$^{3-5}$, 4^6.

L O! an inheritance of Yahweh is the reward of the fruit of the womb.
   As arrows in the hand of a warrior, so are sons of youth.
   Happy he who hath filled his quiver with them!
   They shall not be put to shame, when they speak with enemies in the gate.

Ps. 127 is composed of two independent Pss.: v.$^{1-2}$, v.$^{3-5}$; which have no manner of connection in thought; so Bi., Peters, Bä., Du., Che., Davies. The לשלמה of 𝔐, Aq., Σ, 𝔍, 𝔗, is later than 𝔊, which had it only in 𝔊^R; and is a conjecture due to the בית of v.^{1}, the ידידו and ישנא v.^{2}. There is no good reason to doubt that both Pss. belong to the more prosperous days of the Greek period.

PSALM CXXVII. *A.*

Syn. and synth. couplets. — **1.** *Except*], conditional clause, repeated in ‖. — *Yahweh build the house*], not the temple, but any house whatever, ‖ *keep the city*], from falling into the hands of the enemy. — *in vain*], repeated for emphasis. — *the builders labour* ‖ *the keeper waketh*]. The essential thing, the coöperation of Yahweh, remains lacking, which alone gives success and security. — **2.** *It is vain for you*], change of the order of the sentence, with the personal address for the previous, more objective third person. — *who rise up early*], to go forth to labour earlier than usual. — *sit down late*], after an unusually prolonged day of work. — and so : *Eat the bread of toil*], emphasizing the intensity of the hard labour during the lengthened time. All this extra hard toil is vain, unless Yahweh shares in it. — Indeed *He* (Yahweh) *giveth*], without any kind of toil; *to His beloved*], the one who is dear to Him ; *in sleep*], even when he sleeps quietly in his bed, without thinking of anything needed, or making any effort to gain it.

PSALM CXXVII. *B.*

3–5. Synth. tetrastich. — *Lo*], calling attention to the fact as often in Pilgrim Pss. — *an inheritance of Yahweh*], given by Yahweh. — A glossator inserts "sons" at the expense of the measure and the unity of the line. In fact the subj. is, — *the reward of the fruit of the womb*]. The fruit of the womb, children, are a reward or recompense given by Yahweh as a token of His favour, as an inheritance to His favoured ones. — *As arrows in the* *hand of a warrior*], potent weapons of war. — *so are sons of youth*], born during the youthful vigour of the father, and so well grown and strong while he himself is still able to do battle. — *Happy he*], as 𝕲; not needing the inserted " man " of 𝔎 followed by EV⁸. — *who hath filled his quiver with them*], hath very many sons, a house full of them. — *They shall not be put to shame*], these sons by defeat. — *when they speak with enemies*], meet them face to face and indulge in sharp words preliminary to battle. — *in the gate*], the entrance to the city, where battle is usually waged with enemies who strive to capture a city. The whole conception is warlike. It is altogether against the context to think, as some do, of maintaining a cause against powerful enemies, who would do a man injustice were it not for the support of numerous and stalwart sons.

CXXVII. *A.*

1. אם יהוה] conditional clause : יהיה emph. — בוניו בו] but 𝕲ᴺ·ᴬ·ᴿ οἰκοδο-μοῦντες αὐτόν ; 𝕲ˣ·ᶜ ᵃ ᵀ omit αὐτόν ; 𝔍 *aedificant eam*, only בוניו or בנים. בו dittog. — ימלו] Qal 3 pl. † ימר denom. ימר n.m. (7¹⁵). Qal elsw. Jon. 4¹⁰ Pr. 16²⁶ Ec. 1³ 2²¹ 5¹⁵·¹⁷ 8¹⁷, cf. 2¹¹·¹⁹·²⁰. — 2. משכימי] Hiph. ptc. cstr. before inf. : שכב vb. denom *do a thing early in the morning*, with adverbial force before קום. Its antithesis is מאחרי Pi. ptc. אחר *delay*, adverbial *late* (4c¹⁸). 𝕲ˣ·ᴬ ἐγείρεσθαι μετὰ τὸ καθῆσθαι, 𝕲ᵀ ἐγείρεσθε, 𝖁 *surgite postquam sederitis*, mistake the ptc. for prep. and fail to see the antith. — ירי] third ptc. clause. — כן] so 𝔍, but 𝕲 ὅταν; both interp. of a clause which is better without either. — שנא] Aramaism שנה (7⁶⁶) is acc. of time or condition, not obj. acc. as Vrss.

CXXVII. *B.*

3. בנים] interp. gl.; makes l. too long. — 5. הגבר איר] 𝕲 only δs. — † אשפה] n.f. *quiver*, as Is. 22⁶ 49² Je. 5¹⁶ La. 3¹³ Jb. 39²³; but 𝕲 τὴν ἐπιθυμίαν.

PSALM CXXVIII., 4⁶.

Ps. 128 is a wish for happiness to the godfearing (v.¹), especially when such eat their daily bread (v.²), that the wife may be a fruitful vine, the children numerous olive plants (v.³). Glosses assert the divine blessing upon the godfearing (v.⁴) ; invoke the divine blessing from Zion (v.⁵ᵃ) ; wish that he may look on the welfare of Jerusalem (v.⁵ᵇ· ⁶ᵃ) ; concluding with a later gloss, wishing peace for Jerusalem (v.⁶ᵇ).

HAPPY be every one fearing Yahweh, walking in the way of Yahweh!
  The toil of thy hands when thou eatest, happy be thou, and may it be well
    with thee!
  May thy wife be as a fruitful vine in the inner room of thy house!
  May thy sons be as olive plants round about thy table.

Ps. 128 was originally only v.[1-3]; but several later glosses were added, v.[4-6]. It resembles 127, and doubtless belongs to the same period and possibly the same author.

1–3. Synth. tetrastich. — *Happy be every one*], a wish, not a congratulation or statement of fact as EV[s]. — resumed in v.[2] in the more personal second person : *Happy be thou*], intensified in *and may it be well with thee — fearing Yahweh*], having the reverential fear of true religion, — the complement : *walking in the way of Yahweh*], the way of the divine Law ; shortened in ancient texts at the expense of the measure into " His ways." — *The toil of thine hands*], the product of toil, the food thereby gained, thrown before for emphasis. — *when thou eatest*], after the toil is over and the man sits down at his table to enjoy his evening meal — in accordance with which numerous sons are conceived as gathered *round about thy table* v.[3b], — and so the wife *in the inner room of thy house*], where the table was placed, and not the woman's apartments. — *May thy wife be*], wish as above, and not a promise as EV[s]., or statement of fact as JPSV. — *as a fruitful vine*], bearing many children, as a vine does grapes. — *May thy sons be olive plants*], full of vigour and vitality, cf. 52^{10} Je. 11^{16}. The Ps. thus reaches its appropriate conclusion.

Later editors and glossators enlarged it, and, as they thought, improved it and made it more appropriate for public use. — **4.** *Lo! verily thus*], emphatic, calling attention to the fact based on previous wish, so JPSV., PBV. AV., RV., render : " Behold that thus," which is not so well sustained. — *shall the man that feareth Yahweh be blessed*], the divine blessing taking the place of the wish for happiness v.[1]. — **5–6.** It is difficult to determine whether the glossator wished to state a fact as EV[s]. : *Yahweh will bless thee out of Zion*], or to express a wish as JPSV. ; doubtless the former, if it be by the same hand. — *And look thou on the welfare of Jerusalem all the days of thy life, and look thou on thy children's children*]. This is doubtless a wish, and by a different and indeed an earlier hand than the previous gloss. It is prosaic and does not make any good measure. The wish is, that all his life the pious man may share in the prosperity of Jerusalem, and may live long enough to look in the faces of numerous grandchildren. — The whole concludes with a still later gloss, as 125⁵ : *Peace be upon Israel.*

1. [אַשְׁרֵי] (*1¹*) prob. with juss. not indicative understood. — [יִרְאֵ] sg. cstr. ; 𝕲 takes it as collective, and so renders pl. ; also for [וּרְאֵה] — [וְרָאֵיתָ] for an original ברוך יהוה which the measure requires. — **2.** [יְגִיעַ] (*78¹⁶*) emph. — [כִּי הֵיטִיב] though כִּי not in 𝕲, it is required for measure. It is temporal as Ew., not asseverative as De., or causal as Hu. — [אֶשְׁרֶיךָ] a wish and not an asser-tion of fact. — **3.** [אֶשְׁתְּךָ] variant for אִשְׁתְּךָ. — [פֹּרִיָּה] fuller fem. for פֹּרֶה, more euphonic ; cf. בֹּנִיָה La. 1¹⁶. — [שְׁתִלֵי] pl. cstr. שְׁתִיל *a.λ.* transplanted shoot, cf. שתל vb. (*1³*). — **4.** [כִּי־כֵן] late prosaic expression ; so גֶּבֶר יְרֵא for יְרֵא v.¹, and the variant and later יברך for אשרי. A late prosaic gl. — **5.** [רְאֵה] Imv. not harmonious with יברכך, doubtless begins a new l. — **6.** [שָׁלוֹם עַל יִשְׂרָאֵל] as 125⁵.

PSALM CXXIX., 2 STR. 4⁶.

Ps. 129 is an exhortation to Israel to acknowledge that they have not been overcome by the frequent affliction of enemies from the youth of the nation because of the interposition of Yahweh (v.¹⁻⁴) ; followed by an imprecation upon present enemies (v.⁵⁻⁸).

" GREATLY have they afflicted me from my youth," let Israel now say,
    "Greatly have they afflicted me from my youth; verily they have not pre-
      vailed over me.
    Upon my back (the wicked) ploughed, prolonged their (iniquities)."
    Yahweh (vindicated) the righteous, cut off the (backs) of the wicked.
LET them be put to shame, and let them be turned backward, all the haters of
    Zion.
    Let them become as grass of the housetops, which before (one can draw the
      scythe) withereth :
    Wherewith the reaper does not fill his hand, or he that bindeth sheaves his
      bosom.
    And they who pass by, say not : " The blessing of Yahweh unto you."

Ps. 129 has historical reminiscences of enemies from the youth of the nation, and an imprecation upon present enemies. It is probably Maccabean, at least in the second half, which may possibly be a later addition, although of the same structure as the first half.

Str. I. Stairlike and antith. couplets. — **1–2.** *Greatly have they afflicted me*], repeated in v.². The adv., emphatic in position, emphasizes the magnitude of the afflicting, which has been that of wicked enemies, especially in wars. — *from my youth*], the youth of the nation, when Israel was led up out of Egypt and was disciplined to war by a long series of conflicts. — *let Israel now say*], as 124¹, in an oral recognition of the historical experience of the nation. — *Verily*], asseverative. — *they have not prevailed over me*], Israel still remains notwithstanding it all. — **3**. *Upon my back the wicked ploughed*], so 𝕲, 𝖁. The back is compared to a field, which has been ploughed up and down. It is lacerated with deep wounds like furrows in a field. The wicked are as usual the enemies of the people of Yahweh. — *prolonged their iniquities*], so 𝕲, 𝖁, "their iniquitous affliction." 𝕳 by error has a word α.λ., which is rendered by EVˢ. "furrows," but by most moderns more correctly "field for working," which is, however, a conjectural meaning, derived from the meaning of a late Heb. word and improbable in itself. — **4**. *Yahweh vindicated the righteous*], in accordance with the context, and in antithesis with the next clause. An early copyist, omitting the vb. needed for measure because of similarity of form with the adj., made it necessary to connect the latter with "Yahweh," either as adjective as PBV., or predicate as AV., RV., JPSV. — *cut off the backs of the wicked*], so essentially 𝕲, 𝖁: the cutting off of the enemies' backs being in retribution for their abuse of Israel's back. But 𝕳 by error of a single letter has a word meaning "cords." This is variously explained : by some as referring to the straps of the yoke of the oxen at the plough, the cutting of which made further ploughing impossible. But the words in themselves do not readily suggest this idea. Others think that the figure is changed, and that the cutting of the cords is the release of Israel from bondage, cf. 2³. But such a reference to bondage is not consistent with v.², and is an abrupt transition of the thought, for which there is no suggestion in the context.

Str. II. A synth. imprecation. — **5**. *Let them be put to shame*], the enemies, by defeat. — *and let them be turned backward*], in retreat, cf. 40¹⁵. — *all the haters of Zion*]. The enemies are not only hostile ; but have a deadly hatred of Zion. This suits best the time of the Antiochian persecution. — **6**. *Let them become as grass of the housetops*], grass springs up easily and quickly on the

flat roofs of houses in Palestine, which are much used by the
people. — *which before one can draw the scythe*], to cut it down
for use ; that is, before it has grown sufficiently for the purpose.
This is the most probable meaning of a vb. variously paraphrased
in the Vrss., ancient and modern. — *withereth*]. The depth of
soil (Mt. 13^{3 89.}) is so slight, that it cannot grow to maturity ; and,
exposed to the full blaze of the sun, it is speedily scorched and
withered. — **7.** *Wherewith the reaper does not fill his hand*],
when he gathers the grass in his hand to cut it with his scythe.
— *or he that bindeth sheaves (fill) his bosom*]. The new-mown
hay is bound in sheaves and placed in the loose fold of the garment, in order to take it to the barn. — **8.** *And they who pass by*],
wayfarers, travellers, beholding the haymakers. — *say not*], as they
would if it were a good harvest. — *The blessing of Yahweh unto
you*], cf. Ru. 2^4 : in congratulation of them as having received
this blessing from Yahweh. — A glossator repeats this congratulation : *We bless you in the name of Yahweh.*

1. רַבַּת] adv. ; also v.^2, as 120^6 123^4 ; emph. — יאמֵר נָא] juss., as 124^1. —
צְרָרוּנִי] also v.^2; Qal pf. a.λ. ψ, elsw. ptc. 6^8. — **2.** גם לא] intensive, not advers.
— **3.** עַל־גַּבִּי] emph. ‡ גב n.m. *back*, only here of men ; in Ez. 10^12 of cherubim ; elsw. in other senses. — חָרְשׁוּ] Qal pf. 3 m. ‡ [חרשׁ] vb. *plough* Dt. 22^10
1 S. 8^12 Am. 6^12 9^13. Ptc. הֹרְשִׁים not in 𝔊 here, but οἱ ἁμαρτωλοί, 𝔙 *peccatores* =
רשׁעים more prob., as in v.^4. — [למענותם Kt. ; but Qr. לְמַעֲנִיתָם; both forms dub.
† מַעֲנָה n.f. acc. to *BDB*. *place for task (?)*, spec. *field for ploughing ;* מענה elsw.
1 S. 14^14 " where text corrupt and meaning dub." 𝔊 τὴν ἀνομίαν αὐτῶν,
𝔙 *iniquitatem suam* = עונותם seems more prob. — **4.** צַדִּיק] is difficult to connect with יהוה, whether apposition or predicate. It seems to be in antith.
with רשׁעים. In that case a vb. is needed ; prob. הצדיק, omitted by mistake
because of similarity of form. — [עֲבוֹת] *cords, bonds* (2^3); but of what ? No
suitable mngs. can be found for the word in this context. 𝔊 αὐχένα, 𝔙 *cer-
vices*, prob. גַבּוֹת: most prob. in exact retribution, same as v.^3. This suits the
vb., used of cutting of thumbs, toes, Ju. 1^6, hands and feet 2 S. 4^12 ; here
similarly of back. — **5.** יבשׁו ויסגו אחור] frequent in imprecations v. 40^15. —
6. הַצִיר גַּגּוֹת] phr. elsw. Is. 37^27 = 2 K. 19^26. — [שֶׁקַּדְמַת־ rel. 'ש with † הַרְמָה
n.f. *antiquity* Is. 23^7, *former state* Ez. 16^55 36^11, mngs. unsuitable here. The
Aramaic mng. *before* Ezr. 5^11 Dn. 6^11 is alone appropriate. — ‡ [יָרַף] vb. *draw
out*, weapon Ju. 3^22 1 S. 17^51. 𝔊 τοῦ ἐκσπασθῆναι, 𝔙 *evellatur*, Aq. ἀνέθαλεν,
𝔍 *statim ut viruerit*, Σ ἐκκαυλῆσαι, Sexta τοῦ ἐκστερεῶσαι. Ortenberg, We.,
Du., rd. חלף, Hu. שלף. The Vrss. all seem to paraphrase. It is better to
think of drawing out the scythe to cut the grass, than of drawing or pulling
up the grass. — **7.** [שֶׁרָא] rel. with לא. — [חַצְנוֹ] sf. with † חֵצֶן n.m. *bosom* a.λ.,

but חֵצֶן Is. 49²² bosom of parent; doubtless the same word variously pointed.
— [מְעַמֵּר Pi. ptc. † עמר vb. denom. עֹמֶר, *bind sheaves.* — **8.** ברכנו אתכם בשם יהוה
is a gl., a variant of previous l.

PSALM CXXX., 2 STR. 4⁶.

Ps. 130 is a cry of Israel to Yahweh for help in deepest distress, with a confession of iniquity and ill-desert, but reliance upon Yahweh for pardon (v.¹⁻⁴). Israel waits on Yahweh, hoping in His word and watching from day to day, with confidence that with Him is kindness and ransom from all iniquities (v.⁵⁻⁸).

OUT of the depths I cry unto Thee, Yahweh. O hearken to my voice.
   Adonay, let Thine ears be attentive to the voice of my supplications.
   If iniquities Thou shouldst mark, Yah, who could stand?
   For with Thee, Adonay, is pardon; that (Thy Law) may be revered.
I WAIT on Yahweh; my soul doth wait; for His word I hope;
   My soul for Adonay, from morning watch to morning watch.
   For with Yahweh is kindness, and plenteous with Him is ransom:
   Inasmuch as He ransometh Israel out of all his iniquities.

Ps. 130 v.² is cited in 2 Ch. 6³⁹⁻⁴⁰. It must therefore be earlier. סליחה v.⁴
elsw. Ne. 9¹⁷ Dn. 9⁹, רַשָּׁבֻיֹת v.² elsw. 2 Ch. 6⁴⁰ 7¹⁵. The divine names are
יהוה, אדני, and יה, which, however, are several times misplaced in 𝕲. These
resemblances to Chr. make it probable that the Ps. was written early in the
Greek period.

Str. I. Syn. and synth. couplets. — **1–2.** *Out of the depths*], emphatic in position. Trouble is compared to deep waters 69³. ¹⁵
Ez. 27³⁴. — *I cry unto Thee*], emphatic present, as JPSV., and not
proper pf. " have I cried " of EVˢ. — *O hearken to my voice* ‖ *let
Thine ears be attentive to the voice of my supplications*], urgent entreaty expressed by loud crying and pleading. — The divine names
Yahweh, Adonay, and *Yah,* are used in the several lines of the Ps.
without apparent consciousness of any difference in their meaning.
— **3.** *If iniquities*], emphatic in position, cf. v.⁷ᵇ. Probably another voice responds with the consolation. — *Thou shouldst mark*],
observe them closely, and strictly record them with their ill-desert
and well-deserved punishment. — *who could stand?*], implying a
negative answer: no one; as the condition itself implies the negative that *Yah* does not so deal with the iniquities of His people.

cf. 103¹⁰. — **4.** *For with Thee*], emph.; Thee especially. — יֵשׁ
pardon], of sins, cf. Ne. 9¹⁷ Dn. 9⁹ Ps. 86⁵, which, according to
the Heb. conception is the removal of them from the divine
presence and observation. — *that Thy Law may be revered*]. This
alone explains the use of the vb. in 𝔊 and the noun in most ancient Vrss.; and at the same time makes the measure of the line
complete. Reverence for the divine Law is not only promoted
by the visitation of its penalties, but by the removal of the iniquities and their penalties after the iniquities have been confessed
and put away by sincere repentance.

Str. II. Stairlike couplets. — **5–6.** *I wait*], emphatic present as
v.¹, with the same speaker. ‖ *my soul doth wait* ‖ *I hope*], heaping
up of vbs. to emphasize the anxious yet confident looking for help.
— *to Yahweh* ‖ *His word*], of promise. — *from morning watch to
morning watch*], as 𝔍, 𝔖; "fro the one morning to the other,"
Coverdale. This is much more suited to the context and more
probable in itself than 𝔊 followed by AV.: "more than they that
watch for the morning"; RV., JPSV.: "more than watchmen for
the morning"; with the same words repeated. A glossator appends an exhortation *Israel hope in Yahweh*, which has no place
in the measure of the Ps. — **7.** *For with Yahweh*], cf. v.⁴, and
doubtless by the same responsive voice. — *is kindness*], that divine
attribute which is the source of forgiveness, cf. Ex. 34⁶⁻⁷. — *and
plenteous*], emph., full and abundant. — *with Him is ransom*], a
term ordinarily used for ransom from enemies and troubles; but
here, as the vb. implies in the climax, in the late and unusual
sense: from iniquities. — **8.** *Inasmuch as*], a circumstantial clause.
— *He ransometh Israel out of all his iniquities*]. The ransom is
doubtless syn. with the pardon of v.⁴.

1. [מִמַּעֲמַקִּים] *depths, deep waters*, elsw. with מַיִם as 69³ ¹⁵ Ez. 27³⁴. It has
two accents. — **2.** [יְדֹנָי] belongs with next l., but שִׁמְעָה בְקוֹלִי is the necessary
complement of the first l. — † [הַקְשִׁיבֵ־] elsw. 2 Ch. 6⁴⁾ 7¹⁵. † [קֶ֫שֶׁב] adj. of vb.
קשׁב *hearken, attend to*. — **3.** [יָ־] shortened יהוה. אֲדֹנָי goes with next l.··
4. [שֶׁ֫וָּרֵא] n.t. elsw. Dn. 9⁹ Ne. 9¹⁷; סלח vb. (25¹¹). — [לְ־עַן וְיֵרָא] so Aq.
ἕνεκεν φόβου, 𝔍 *cum terribilis* 𝔊ˣ·ᴬ·ᵀ ἕνεκεν τοῦ ὀνόματός σου; Sexta ἕνεκεν
τοῦ γνωσθῆναι λόγον σου suggests the solution, especially as the line needs an
additional word, תורה הורא; prob. originally τοῦ νόμου, as 𝔙 *propter legem
tuam*, Σ ἕνεκεν νόμου, so Θ and 𝔊ᴿ, all reading תורה (*v.* Jerome, *Epistola
ad San.* 78). — **5.** [וְלִדְברוֹ] but 𝔊 had not י, and connecting this noun with

previous vb., rd. נפשי הוהלת. The measure favours 頒. — **6.** שמרים לבקר]
bis; ᵍ⁵ ἀπὸ φυλακῆς πρωίας μέχρι νυκτός, but ᵍᴬ·ᴿ·ᵀ ἀπὸ φυλακῆς
πρωίας bis, 𝔍 *a vigilia matutina usque ad vigiliam matutinam*, so 𝔖,
giving the true reading לבקר יבׄהר יׄבׄר. — **7.** מישׄׄׄר לׄבהר אל יהוה] gl , not
in ᵍ⁵, but ᵍˢ·ᶜ·ᵃ·ᴬ·ᴿ·ᵀ.— יכׄי רׄרבה] adv. as Ez. 21²⁾.— פׄדוׄת †] as 111⁹ Is.
50² Ex. 8¹⁹ (?). — **8.** והוא] emph.

PSALM CXXXI., 4⁶.

**Ps. 131 is an assertion of the humility of the people, in heart,
look, and walk (v.¹), and of the quieting the soul as a weaneᴅ child
upon the mother's breast (v.²). A gloss urges Israel tu hope
always in Yahweh (v.³).**

> YAHWEH, my heart is not haughty, and mine eyes are not lofty;
>   And I do not walk about in great things, or in things too wonderful for me.
>   Surely I have composed (my soul); surely I have quieted my soul.
>   As a weaned child upon his mother, so is bountiful dealing unto my soul.

Ps. 131 has, according to ᵍˢ·ᴬ·ᴿ, 頒, Aq., Σ, לדׄוׄ; but that was a later
addition; it is not in ᵍᵀ, and the omission in 𝔍, 𝔗, makes it still more
doubtful. The Ps. is doubtless one of the late Greek period.

A syn. and an emblematic couplet. — **1.** *Yahweh, my heart is
not haughty*], I am not high-minded. — *and mine eyes are not
lofty*], looking only at lofty things. — *And I do not walk about in
great things*], neglecting little things. — *or in things too wonderful
for me*], beyond my ability to understand. The people have in
fact renounced all ambition and are content with their lot. —
2. *Surely*], strong affirmation, repeated in complementary half of
the line, though omitted by the condensation of a prosaic scribe
at the expense of the measure. — *I have composed my soul ‖ I
have quieted my soul*], the obj. was needed in both cases for meaning and measure. In the former it was omitted by a prosaic
scribe. The soul, which might well have been agitated by ambition, or the failures of life, was by deliberate action reduced to
a calm, gentle, submissive, patient, and contented state. — *As a
weaned child upon his mother*], resting quietly on the breast of the
mother, already satisfied with nourishment and no longer fretting
for the breast. — *so is bountiful dealing unto my soul*]. This is

essentially the interpretation of 𝔊, 𝔍, Σ, representing the soul of the people as having received from Yahweh all needed benefaction and as being in a calm, peaceful condition, without agitation, just as is the child already amply nourished upon the mother's breast. 𝕳, 𝕵, followed by EVˢ., " my soul is even as a weaned child," is essentially repetition without good reason for emphasis upon the simile, and leaves it unexplained. — **3.** A glossator adds the exhortation, as 130⁷ᵃ : *O Israel hope in Yahweh*, with the temporal addition : *from this time forth and forever.*

1. הִלַּכְתִּי] Pi. intensive *walk about*, emphatic present. — **2.** [אִב־לֹא שִׁוִּיתִי strong asseveration, *surely*, should be repeated before vb. ‡ שׁוה Qal *be like* Is. 40²⁵ Pr. 26⁴+, Pi. *make like, level* Is. 28²⁵, *compose*, as a stormy sea, Hu.; cf. Is. 38¹³. נפשׁי is needed by the vb. and the measure. — [דוממתי Polal *to quiet*, דמם Qal *be silent* (4⁵). — [גָּמַר] Qal ptc. גֹּמֵל : (1) *deal bountifully* c. עָל 13⁶, (2) *requite* 7⁵, (3) *wean* here and Is. 11¹⁸. All Vrss. rd. גמל *weaned* in first clause, but 𝔊, 𝔍, Σ, גְּמֻל inf. cstr. vb. as (2); prob. we should think of (1).

PSALM CXXXII., 4 STR. 4⁶.

Ps. 132 is a prayer in two parts. (1) Yahweh is implored to remember the affliction of David, in his first failure to remove the ark to Jerusalem, and the solemn oath he then made to resort to the holy place (v.¹⁻³⁽ ⁵⁾). The people find the ark in Jearim and urge Yahweh to rise up, for the sake of His priests and His pious ones (v.⁶⁻¹⁰). (2) A paraphrase of the Davidic covenant is given (v.¹¹⁻¹²). Yahweh hath chosen Zion for His everlasting throne, and provides there for His priests and His pious ones (v.¹³⁻¹⁶). Glosses predict the sprouting forth of the Messianic king and the shame of the enemies (v.¹⁷⁻¹⁸), and urge Yahweh not to reject the reigning king (v.¹⁰). V.⁴ is a gloss of intensification.

Yʜ AHWEH, remember unto David (for good) all his affliction :
  How he sware to Yahweh, vowed to the Mighty One of Jacob,
    (Saying) : " I will not enter the tent of my house, I will not go up on the couch of my bed,
    Till I find the place of Yahweh, the great tabernacle of the Mighty One of Jacob."
Lᴏ O! We heard of it in Ephrathah, we found it in the fields of Jear(im).
    (We said) : " Let us come to His great tabernacle, let us worship at His footstool."

Arise, Yahweh, to Thy resting-place; Thou and the ark of Thy strength.
Let Thy priests be clothed with righteousness, and let Thy pious ones shout
    shouts of joy.

YAHWEH sware to David in truth; He will not depart from it.

"Of the fruit of thy body will I set (thy seed) upon a throne for thee.

If thy sons keep My covenant and My testimonies, which I teach them,

Also their sons shall be forever; they shall sit enthroned on a throne for thee."

FOR Yahweh hath chosen Zion, desired it for a habitation for Himself,

(Saying): "This is my resting place for ever; here will I sit enthroned, for I
    desired it.

Her provision will I greatly bless; her poor will I satisfy with bread;

And her priests will I clothe with salvation, and her pious ones will shout shouts
    of joy."

Ps. 132 agrees with 89¹⁸⁻⁴⁵ in citing and paraphrasing the Davidic covenant
2 S. 7¹¹ ˢᑫ·. It represents, however, a much later date. (1) The condition
appended to the Davidic covenant is interpreted v.¹² in a term of Ps. 119,
עֵדוֹת, and implies the legislation of P. (2) The Ps. uses the narrative of
the removal of the ark to Mt. Zion in the spirit of 1 Ch. 15¹²· ¹¹, emphasizing
the share of the priests in it; rather than in the spirit of the Judaic narrative
of 2 S. 6¹⁻¹⁹, or its Deuteronomic redactor. (3) The reference to the sprouting of the horn v.¹⁷ is based on Ez. 29²¹, but that is combined with the צֶמַח of
Jer. 23⁵ in the form of Zec. 3⁸, 6¹², looking forward to a future Messianic
king from the point of view of one who knew nothing of the monarchy in his
own time. (4) The relation between v.⁸⁻¹⁰ and 2 Ch. 6¹¹⁻¹² is more difficult.
This passage of Chr. was not in the source 1 K. 8, which gives a Deuteronomic
redaction of the prayer of Solomon at the dedication of the temple. It was
appended by Chr. from some other source, probably, therefore, our Ps. They
both cite from the song of the ark Nu. 10³⁵. The variations, adding אֱלֹהִים,
probably Qr. of יהוה, and using נוחך for מְנוּחָתֶךָ v.⁸ᵃ, adding יהוה ארהיב and substituting הַיְשׁוּעָה for צדק and יֹשְׁבוּ נְטוֹב for יֹשְׁבוּ יָרַנֵּנוּ v.⁹, cf. v.¹⁶, and the addition
of יהוה אהים v.¹⁰ before אֵל הַיֵּיב, all seem like adaptations of an original Ps.
The one serious difference, זִכְרָה לְחַסְדֵי דָוִד עַבְדֶּךָ at the end for בַּעֲבוּר דָּוִד עַבְדֶּךָ
at the beginning of v.¹⁰, seems to be in the latter a glossator's variation of זכר
and substitution of הֶסֶד deeds of kindness for the חֶסֶד of the covenant and
the יָנוּחַ of v.¹. It is altogether probable, therefore, that Chr. uses the Ps.
(5) The emphasis upon priests and the *Chasidim* v.⁹· ¹⁶ as the real con-
stituents of the Jewish community, not only points to a time of the predomi-
nance of the priesthood, but also to the harmony of the priesthood with the
Chasidim, probably therefore in the early Greek period. (6) V.¹⁵ recognises
a time when provision was made for the poor in the temple, probably from
the numerous thank offerings and festival offerings. We are reminded of the
praise of good works by Simon the Just. (7) The author of the Ps. lived in
peaceful, prosperous times. There is no impatience at the delay of the establishment of the Davidic king, no trace of shame and suffering among the
people, such as we see at the close of Ps. 89. (8) V.⁴ is in such close agree-

ment with Pr. 6⁴ that there must be a definite relation. It is not probable that the Ps. is sufficiently late to borrow from the *Praise of Wisdom*, one of the latest parts of Pr. The Ps. might be a trimeter poem, were it not for several lines where the break comes most naturally after the fourth tone. This looks like a caesura rather than the close of the line, so v.¹· ¹¹ᵃᵇ, and favours a hexameter. Moreover, all the Pilgrim Songs have the long measure. There is no trimeter among them. Both the Ps. and the Pr. probably cite an earlier familiar proverbial expression. It might be taken as a gl. to the Ps., but this would force us to see with Du. a gl. also in v.¹⁰, which is indeed quite possible. The difficulty would then be that the second half of the Ps. would be two lines longer than the first half. It would be easy to find in it two tetrastichs, and to regard v.¹⁷⁻¹⁸ as a closing couplet, referring to the Davidic covenant. In this case it might be regarded as a later Messianic addition. The uniform strophical organisation of the Pilgrim Pss. as hexameter tetrastichs forces us to regard all these as glosses.

Str. I. is a synth. tetrastich. — **1.** *Yahweh remember unto David*], cf. 89⁴⁸· ⁵¹, a plea of intercession, composed for congregational worship. — *for good*], is not in the text, but is required by measure, as in Ne. 13³¹. — *all his affliction*], the context implies that which David suffered on account of the failure of the first attempt to remove the ark to Jerusalem, and during its abode in the house of Obed-Edom 2 S. 6¹⁻¹¹. — **2.** *How he sware to Yahweh*]. This oath is not recorded in the historical narrative, but either rests on tradition or conjecture, based on the resolve to make a second attempt to remove the ark, when the prosperity of the house of Obed-Edom was reported to him 2 S. 6¹². — *vowed to the Mighty One of Jacob*], possibly referring to the humiliation of David before the ark, rebuked by his wife 2 S. 6¹⁶· ²¹⁻²². This divine name is based on Gn. 49²⁴, used elsewhere Is. 49²⁶ 60¹⁶, cf. Is. 1²⁴. — **3-4.** *I will not enter the tent of my house*], tent, which is my house, tent used poetically, cf. La. 2⁴, Zc. 12⁷, Is. 16⁵. — *I will not go up on the couch of my bed*], as above, couch, which is spread for my bed. — A glossator adds as an intensification: *I will not give sleep to mine eyes, to mine eyelids slumber*], so Pr. 6⁴, both using a proverbial expression. All this is a strong oath, not to sleep, not to go to bed, not to enter his tent, until he does that which he proposes. — **5.** *Till I find the place of Yahweh*], interpreting the preposition as the genitive of late style, and not dative *for* Yahweh, though that is sustained by 𝕲, 𝔍,

and other Vrss. David had already provided a place for Yahweh in the tent which he had pitched in Jerusalem 2 S. 6¹⁷:
he vows to go to the place of Yahweh and find it in the usual
sense of arriving at a place of destination. The place of the ark,
he knew well, was in the house of Obed-Edom. — *the great tabernacle of the Mighty One of Jacob*], the pl. is the plural of intensity ;
great, not on account of its size or grandeur, because it was altogether unworthy, a mere temporary structure, but because of the
majesty and sanctity of Yahweh who inhabited it, evinced by the
terrible punishment of Uzzah 2 S. 6⁶⁻⁷.

Str. II. is also a synth. tetrastich. — **6**. *Lo ! we heard of it*],
the ark of subsequent context v.⁸ᵇ. — *in Ephrathah*], probably the
name of the district of Bethlehem, Mi. 5¹ Ru. 4¹¹. The Ps. is
here referring to the people of Judah in general as distinguished
from the people of the North. — *we found it in the fields of
Jearim*], Kirjath Jearim, where the ark abode twenty years 1 S. 7².
" Fields of the wood " probably originated from abbreviation and
was a misunderstanding of the original. It is true, it was removed
from its abode there, on the first attempt of David, and taken
part of the way to Jerusalem ; but how far we are not told in the
narrative of Samuel, or the later story of the Chronicler. The
poet is to be excused for thinking of Kirjath Jearim here. But 𝕿
thinks of Lebanon as " fields of the wood," so Ew., and thus the
North in antithesis with Bethlehem in the South, and so North
and South were summoned to take part in the removal of the ark
to Jerusalem. This is tempting but improbable. In any case the
following lines constitute the words of the people as they journey
to the place of the ark. — **7**. *Let us come to His great tabernacle*],
the same as v.⁵. — *let us worship at His footstool*], namely, the
place of the presence of Yahweh, enthroned, and standing with
His feet on the cherubic platform, according to the conception of
the cherubic throne above the ark. — **8**. *Arise, Yahweh*], the first
words of the ancient song of the ark, when it set forward on the
journeys, during the wanderings in the wilderness Nu. 10³⁵. —
Thou and the ark of Thy strength], a phrase only here and in the
prayer of Solomon at the dedication of the temple, according to
2 Ch. 6⁴¹. — **9**. *Let Thy priests be clothed with righteousness*], so
2 Ch. 6⁴¹ and v.¹⁶, except that these passages use " salvation " of

which indeed righteousness is a common syn.   Attributes are often
represented as clothing put on, so of Yahweh 93¹ 104¹, also cursing
and shame by men 35⁻⁵ 109¹⁸ ⁻¹⁹.   Righteousness or salvation, as the
special clothing of priests here, may be compared with the narrative of the Chronicler, which represents the priests and Levites
sanctifying themselves to bring up the ark 1 Ch. 15¹². ¹⁴ ; which is
doubtless a conjectural modification of the original narrative 2 S. 6,
in accord with the priestly legislation the emphasis upon priests
here, in connection with the ark, implies a period when the priests
were to the people the chief representatives of Yahweh, as bearers
of His righteousness and salvation. — *let Thy pious ones shout
shouts of joy*], so by insertion of infin. abs. to emphasize the
idea of the vb. here, as in v.¹⁶, as indeed the measure requires.
2 Ch. 6⁴¹ varies by "let Thy pious ones rejoice in good (prosperity)."   The reference to the pious ones, the *chasidim*, over
against the priests, also implies a period when they were the
dominant religious force in Israel.   The Ps., without historic
sense, puts them and the priests of the time back, in imagination,
into the time of David, and lets them speak in the bringing up of
the ark to Jerusalem. — **10.** *For the sake of David Thy servant
turn not away the face of Thine anointed*].   This is a gloss from
2 Ch. 6⁴²: Do not reject the anointed king for David's sake.
This implies a much later situation than that of the previous context.   It probably refers to the Maccabean kings.

Str. III. is also a synth. tetrastich. — **11.** *Yahweh sware to
David*], cf. 89⁴ᵇ· ³⁶ both paraphrase of 2 S. 7¹¹ ˢᵠ·.   The oath of
Yahweh is antith. to the oath of David v.². —*in truth*], truly,
cf. Je. 10¹⁰ Ps. 145¹⁸.   𝔊, 𝔍, make truth acc., cf. vb. Hu., Pe., Hi.,
an independent clause : "It is truth we will not depart from it,"
cf. 89³⁴⁻³⁵. — *Of the fruit of thy body*], cf. 2 S. 7¹², "thy seed who
goeth forth from thy bowels." — *will I set*], the obj. *thy seed* must
be supplied to complete the measure. — *upon a throne for thee*],
as his successors in a dynasty.   This covenant had a condition
attached 2 S. 7¹⁴, so Ps. 89³¹⁻³³, cf. 18²²⁻²⁴. — *If thy sons keep My
covenant*], cf. 89³¹. — *and My testimonies which I teach them*], a
late phrase, both in the use of the term for Law of P, and of
God's teaching, cf. 18³⁵ 25⁵· ⁵· ⁹ 71¹⁷ 94¹⁰ 119¹²⁺⁸ᵗ·, implying the
period of the supremacy of the priestly legislation.   The Ps. thus

represents Yahweh as requiring of the seed of David observance of the priestly Law, just as Ps. 89 requires the Code of Holiness. The original covenant knows nothing of a prescribed Law. — *Also their sons shall be forever*], a continuous line of sons in succession. — *they shall sit enthroned on a throne for thee*], reign as kings over Israel.

Str. IV. is also a synth. tetrastich. — **13**. *For Yahweh hath chosen Zion*]. The connection of the choice of Zion with the covenant with David is due to the covenant itself, which was based on the desire of David to build a temple to Yahweh in Jerusalem 2 S. $7^{1\,sq.}$; and the promise in the covenant that David's seed should build it. The selection of Zion in the subsequent narrative, and of the exact place for the temple, is thus wrapped up in the covenant itself. — *desired it for a habitation*] or place of enthronement, the former favoured by v.$^{5,\,7}$, the latter by v.^{14}. — **14–16**. The words of Yahweh, antith. the words of the people v.$^{7-9}$. — *This is My resting place forever*], cf. 5^8, the technical term for the place where the ark rests from journeyings, cf. Nu. 10^{36}. — *here will I sit enthroned*], usually pregnant meaning of the vb. in connection with God and kings, cf. 9^8 29^{10} 33^{14} 55^{20} 68^{17} 102^{13}. — *Her provision will I greatly bless*], all the supply of food of Zion. — *her poor will I satisfy with bread*]. The Ps. here conceives of a provision of bread in the temple for the poor, probably thinking of the abundant thank offerings and festival offerings in the temple in which the poor shared. — *And her priests will I clothe with salvation*], in response to the prayer of the people v.^{9}, so also *and her pious ones will shout shouts of joy*.

A Maccabean editor adds v.$^{17-18}$. — **17**. *I will cause a horn to sprout for David*]. The writer had in mind, in the use of horn, Ez. 29^{21}, the Branch of Je. 23^5, Zc. 3^8 6^{12}, looking forward to a future king to fulfil the Davidic covenant, and so the passage is Messianic, implying the absence of the Davidic king in the time of the writer. — *I have arranged a lamp for Mine anointed*], cf. 18^{29}, and especially 1 K. 11^{36}, where the prophet Ahijah represents that Yahweh gives one tribe to the son of David, " that David My servant may have a lamp alway before Me in Jerusalem." — **18**. *His enemies will I clothe with shame*], antith. v.^{16a}. — *and upon him* *his crown will bloom*]. The blooming of the crown parall. with sprouting of the horn, involves a metaphor of the Branch, cf. also the swan song of David 2 S. 23[4-5].

1. זְכוֹר יהוה לְ] cf. 89[48. 51], זכר אדני with acc.; לְ is sign not of acc. and so Aramaism, but of dative *for*, cf. Ne. 13[14. 22] זָכְרָה לְ, Ne. 13[31] זְכרה לי לטובה. Bi. adds לטובה here also. The measure requires such an addition, and it is probable. — עֻנּוֹתוֹ] Pu. inf. *his being afflicted* as Ps. 119[71], cf. Is. 53[4]. 𝕲 τῆς πρᾳύτητος αὐτοῦ, so 𝕾, Perles, implies עֲנָוֹתוֹ *humility*, Ehr. in sense of " Entbehrung," Aq. κακουχίας, Σ κακώσεως, 𝕵 *afflictiones.* — **2.** אֲשׁר נשׁבע ליהוה]. The oath of David, || נדר *vow*, is not mentioned in the history. This is poetic enhancement of the story, 2 S. 7, that David had in mind to build a temple to Yahweh. אשׁר = *that* or *how*, obj. clause. — אֲבִיר יעקב] also v.[5]; ancient divine name, based here on Gn. 49[24], and then Is. 49[26] 60[16], אביר ישׂראל Is. 1[24]. The pointing is prob. a Massoretic expedient to distinguish it from the ordinary אַבִּיר *mighty*, as applied to men. — **3.** אם] with oath, strong negative; cf. v.[4] 89[36b]. — בֹּא;]. We would expect in classic style אבאה. — אֹהל בֵּיתִי] cstr. apposition. אֹהל used prob. because of 2 S. 7[6], cf. Is. 16[5] La. 2[4] Zc. 12[7]; poetic for house. — יְצוּעֵי עֶרֶשׂ] also cstr. apposition (6[7] 63[7]). — **4.** אם אתן שׁנת] = Pr. 6[4] אל תתן שׁנה לעיניך ותנומה לעפעפיך. The variation is only sufficient to adapt the passages to their context. 𝕲 has conflation in three clauses : —

> εἰ δώσω ὕπνον τοῖς ὀφθαλμοῖς μου
> καὶ τοῖς βλεφάροις μου νοσταγμὸν
> καὶ ἀνάπαυσιν τοῖς κροτάφοις μου;

The last l. a gl. from Θ, as Agellius, Ecker, Bä. עפעפים elsw. ψ 11[4]. ‡ תְּנוּמָה n.f. *slumber*, elsw. Pr. 6[4. 10] 24[33] Jb. 33[15]. שְׁנָת is explained by Ew.[§173d], De., as Aramaism ; better Hu., Kö.[II. 1. 425], as apocopated שְׁנָתִי, cf. 76[6] Bö. for fuller fem. שֵׁנָתָה, Ges.[2b] poetic older fem. form. The phr. is unnecessary here, and is possibly a gl., as the l. v.[5] seems better prepared for by the l. v.[3] than by a couplet including v.[3-4]. The uniform strophical organisation of the Pilgrim Pss. requires us to find a gl. of one l. in this Str. V.[4] was cited from Pr. 6[4] for intensification. — **5.** עד אמצא] final clause ; not *discover*, but *arrive at* the place sought. — מִשְׁכָּנוֹת] pl. is used of the tabernacles of Israel 78[28] 87[2], of the tomb 49[12] (cf. sg. for tomb Is. 22[16]), and of the holy mount 43[3], the courts of the temple 84[2]. — לְ is לְ of genitive of late style, and not לְ of dative, 𝕲, 𝕵, AV., RV. — **6.** ‡ אֶפְרָת is prob the region or district ; not elsw. in ψ ; but (1) near Bethel where Rachel died Gn. 35[16. 19], (2) name of Bethlehem Mi. 5[1]. — וּמְצָאנוּהָ]. The measure requires יְעָרִים ; otherwise the two accented syllables come together. It is improb. that a poet would do this, when he could have so easily avoided it. The sf. in שְׁמַעֲנוּהָ may refer to the resolution of David, and אפרתה may then have its usual mng., referring to Bethlehem : *we heard of it in Ephrathah*, that is, in

Bethlehem; so Bar Heb. The difficulty then would be with the ‖ מצאנוה.
We might render "found it," "came unexpectedly upon the news of it";
that is, the report. שדי יער is understood by 𝔗 of Lebanon, so Ew.; and
thus Bethlehem on the south and Lebanon on the north hear of David's resolution. This suits the subsequent context, but is not a natural interp. of the
text. — **7.** [וְנָ אֶה] cohort. implying vb. אמרנו, usually omitted in poetry. The
sf. 3 m. refers to Yahweh as the 3 f. to the ark; although neither Yahweh
nor the ark is in the immediate context. — **8.** [קומה יהוה למנוח־ך אה־ה וארון עזך].
The first two words are a reminiscence of the ancient song of the ark Nu.
10³⁵. The third word is a reference to the term מנוחה Nu. 35³⁶, introducing
the second couplet. מְנוּחָה, cf. v.¹⁴ 95¹¹, *resting place* of Yahweh; that is, the
sacred place where He granted His presence to His people. אֲרוֹן עֻזֶּךְ phr.
elsw. in citation 2 Chr. 6⁴¹ at close of prayer of Solomon at dedication of temple;
the only change being addition of אלהים for יהוה, and use of נוחך for מנוחך. —
9. [כהניך ילבשו צדק] corresponds with citation in Chr., save that for צדק is substituted הַתְּשׁוּעָה, and that the divine names אלהים, יהוה, are inserted. — וחסידיך
יְרַנֵּנוּ] is certainly defective. A word is missing. ישמחו בטוב of Chr. is much
weaker and much less poetical. It is prob. that inf. abs. has been omitted by
txt. err., cf. v.¹⁶ רַ נֵּן יְרַנֵּנוּ. — **10.** [בעבור דוד עבדך] is a late gl. — [אל־תשב פני משיחך]
is identical in Chr. אל תשב פני כנים I K. 2¹⁶·¹⁷·²⁾ *refuse not*, as Bä., cf. הבט פני
Ps. 84¹⁰. This v. is incongruous with the context. It is a gl. from Chr. The
other vs. were not derived from Chr., as Du. supposes; rather Chr. derives
them from ψ, as Bä. — **11.** [נשבע יהוה לדוד] cf. 89⁴ᵇ·³⁶ paraphrase of 2 S. 7¹¹ ˢᵍ·
without the oath. — [אמת] adv. *truly, in truth*, cf. Je. 10¹⁾, for באמת Ps. 145¹⁸
Je. 26¹⁵ 28⁹ 32⁴¹. If it qualifies the vb., the first part of the v. has four beats
and the second part two. Bä., after 𝔊, 𝔍, ἀλήθειαν, *veritatem*, makes it acc.
of vb., and then against 𝔊, 𝔍 makes it begin a second l., which is improbable.
Ew., Bu., attach it to first part of l., De. to the second. Hu., Pe., Hi., make
it an independent statement: "It is truth." — [אֱמֶת] either refers to אֱמֶת, as
Bä.; or to the oath as such, so most. — [מפרי בטנך אשית לכסא לך] is pentameter
as it stands. This is a paraphrase of 2 S. 7¹²⁻¹³. זרעך is the word we
would most naturally expect to complete the l. — **12.** [אם ישמרו בניך בריתי].
This is a condition to the promise of the covenant involved in the discipline
2 S. 7¹⁴. — [עֵדֹ־יִי] is much more concise than 89³¹·³², where the four terms,
תורה, משפטים, צוה, of D, and חקות of D² and H are used; but it is later,
because here דות, the characteristic term of P, is used, cf. Ps. 18²²⁻²³. — [זו
rel., cf. Ho. 7¹⁶; txt. err. for זי Ex. 15¹³ Is. 42²⁴ 43²¹ Pss. 9¹³ 10² 17⁹ 31⁵ 32⁸ 68²⁹
142¹ 143⁸, so 𝔍, BDB., Bä., Du.; but 𝔊 makes it demonstrative, with rel.
omitted, τὰ μαρτύριά μου ταῦτα ἅ. — [עֵדֹ־יִר] cf. v.¹⁴; so 83¹⁸ 92⁸. — [לך] ethical
dative as v.¹¹ᵇ. — **13.** [כי־בחר יהוה בציון] כי of reason, בחר of divine choice c. בְּ
Aaron 105²⁶, tribe of Ephraim 78⁶⁷ (neg.), espec. David 78⁷⁰; Zion here. —
אִוָּהּ] Pi. pf. ‡ אוה; sf. refer. to Zion; only here and v.¹⁴. Vb. ψ usually Hithp.
45¹² 106¹⁴. — **14.** [פה] *here*, in this place; α.λ. in ψ, BDB. — [צידה] *her
provision*, in this sense elsw. Ne. 13¹⁵ Jb. 38⁴¹, cf. צֵידָה Ps. 78²⁵. — **16.** Cf. v.⁹.
— **17-18.** Late gl. — [אצמיח קרן לדוד]. This seems to be derived from Ez. 29²¹,

where only elsw. the phr. occurs. But the glossator doubtless had in mind Je. 23⁵ הקימותי לדוד צמח צדיק, and especially in the later form, אצמיח לדוד צמח צדקה, of Je. 33⁵, cf. Zc. 3⁸ 6¹². The l. is later than all these passages, and doubtless the glossator knew of them all. — נרי] cf. 1 K. 11³⁶, doubtless in the mind of the glossator. — יָצִיץ נִזְרִי] phr. α.λ. נז blooming of flowers 72¹⁶ 90⁶ 103¹⁵, metaphorically of the wicked 92⁸, Israel Is. 27⁶. ⅏ ἁγίασμά μου, 𝔙 sanctificatio mea, take נזר in the sense of consecration, Lv. 21¹² Nu. 6⁷·¹¹ +, and make the sf. 1 per.; and Aq., Σ, have αὐτοῦ. The reference to crown is justified by Ps. 89⁴⁰. The crown, like the קרן, is compared to vegetation or flowers.

PSALM CXXXIII., 4⁶.

Ps. 133 is a congratulation of Israel because of the fraternal dwelling together of the people under the blessing of Yahweh (v.¹·³ᵇ). This is compared to choice oil upon the head (v.²) and to the most abundant dew upon the mountain of Zion (v.³ᵃ).

BEHOLD how good and how lovely is the dwelling also of brethren together;
    As goodly oil upon the head, which goes down to the collar of the garment;
    As dew (upon) Hermon, which goes down upon the mountains of Zion:
    For there Yahweh hath commanded His blessing, life forevermore.

Ps. 133 has לדוד in the title of 𝔅, but not in 𝔍, 𝔗. The texts of ⅏ vary. The term cannot be original. The Ps. belongs in the Greek period with all the Pilgrim Pss.

Introverted parallelism. — **1.** *Behold*], calling attention to the fact with mutual congratulation. — *how good*], intensified in *how lovely — is the dwelling also of brethren together*], probably referring not to a reconciliation of the alienated tribes, or to peaceful communion in the holy land or holy city; but to their gathering together in Jerusalem at the pilgrim feasts; for this dwelling together is evidently in Zion, where, as the syn. line indicates : *Yahweh hath commanded His blessing, life forevermore*], v.³ᵇ a blessing not only to the permanent inhabitants of the city, but to all those who come up to the pilgrim feasts to share with the inhabitants in the common national worship, which brings upon them the divine blessing and fresh life and vigour with which to return to their homes. The intervening lines gives two simple and beautiful similes. — **2.** *As goodly oil*], choice, select, the best olive oil. — *upon the head*], used to anoint the heads of guests at feasts,

cf. 23⁵. — *which goes down to the collar of the garment*], copious
in quantity as well as choice in quality, it goes over all the head
and beard even to the upper border or collar of the garment. —
A glossator wishing to give it a reference to the most sacred cere-
mony of the consecration of the priesthood, Lv. 8³⁰ ˢᑫᵛ, inserted at
the expense of the measure : *going down upon the beard, the beard
of Aaron*]. But such a specific reference to the consecration of
Aaron, while it might illustrate the copiousness and richness of the
anointing, would not illustrate the dwelling together of brethren
so well as the festal anointing of brethren when assembled at a
common meal. — **3.** *As dew upon Hermon*]. The measure and
the parallel. require the preposition which has been omitted as
unnecessary by a prosaic copyist. — *which goes down upon the
mountains of Zion*]. It is not necessary to think that the author
supposed that the same dew which descended so copiously on
Hermon, subsequently descended upon the mountains of Zion in
the South ; although it is quite possible that the author, knowing
nothing of the real origin of dew, might have had that notion.
But the parall. suggests that the dew upon Hermon is mentioned
because of its extraordinary richness and copiousness. It imparts
life and fertility, and that is the point of the comparison.

1. נָעִים] adj. *sweet*, *pleasant* (16⁵). — כ־יַ] intensifies the יחד. — **2.** הַטּוֹב]
the precious oil of anointing preserved in the tabernacle. It is not in 𝔊 but
in 𝔍, and is needed for measure ; cf. Ex. 30²²⁻³³. — ירד על־הזקן זקן אהרן].
This is a gl. of intensification, making l. overfull. — שֶׁיֹּרֵד] late rel. with ptc.,
which must therefore have its verbal force. — עַל־פִּי] *upon the edge* or *border*,
the upper border of the robe above the bosom.— ‡ מִדָּה] n.f. usually *measure*,
39⁵; in the sense of garment only here ; cf. מַד 109¹⁸. The sf. is due to the
gl., and is not original. — **3.** טַל הֶרמוּן] Hermonlike dew, because of its copiousness. — הַרְרֵי] poetic form for prose הָרֵי.

PSALM CXXXIV., 4⁶.

**Ps. 134 is a call upon all the servants of Yahweh to bless Him,
especially in the courts of the temple (v.¹⁻³).**

BEHOLD! Bless ye Yahweh, all ye servants of Yahweh.
    (Bless ye Yahweh), ye who stand in (the courts of) the house of (our God).
    In the dark night lift up your hands to the sanctuary and bless Yahweh.
    Bless in Zion Yahweh, maker of heaven and earth.

Ps. 134 is the last of the Pilgrim Pss., composed at a time when regular worship, even at night, was carried on in the temple by Levitical singers. It doubtless belongs to the Greek period.

Stairlike parallelism. — **1.** *Behold*], emphatic call to attention. — *Bless ye Yahweh*], repeated in each line ; omitted by early copyist in the second at the cost of the measure, and changed to "May Yahweh bless thee" in the last line by error. An emphatic call to worship. — *All ye servants of Yahweh*], all His worshippers, the entire congregation ; not to be limited to Levitical singers, who are especially mentioned in : *ye who stand in the courts of the house of our God*], so ⅏, 𝔙, best suited to measure, cf. 135². The Levitical choir stood in the courts of the temple, when engaged in worship. 𝔐, followed by AV., RV., condenses and assimilates it to the context in "in the house of Yahweh," at the expense of the measure and the graphic style. It was only in the more general use of "house" for temple and its courts, that it could be said that these worshippers stood in the house of Yahweh. — **2.** *In the dark night*], attached by ⅏, 𝔙, 𝔍, in accordance with the measure and with the introduction of a new idea, emphatically to this v. — *lift up your hands*], a gesture of prayer and also of blessing 28². — *to the sanctuary*], the temple itself, fronting the singers standing in the court. — **3.** *in Zion*], the abode of Yahweh, King of Israel. The mistake in the vb. occasioned the interpretation "from Zion" of 𝔐 and all Vrss., making the v. out of harmony with its context. — *maker of heaven and earth*], Yahweh, the King reigning in Zion, was also the creator of the universe.

1. ברכו את־יהוה] should be repeated in each l. But it has been omitted in v.¹ᵇ at the expense of the measure ; and in v.³ it has been changed by earlier copyist to יברכך, prob. by dittog. — בבית יהוה] but ⅏ˣ ἐν αὐλαῖς οἴκου θεοῦ ἡμῶν = 𝔙 *in atriis domus Dei nostri*, בחצרות בית אלהינו as 135² is more prob., as it makes good measure. ⅏ · ᴬ· ᴮ· ᵀ prefix ἐν οἴκῳ κυρίου, 𝔙 *in domo domini*. — בלילות] pl. either of number, *nights;* or of emphasis, *dark night;* prob. latter. It is attached by ⅏, 𝔙, 𝔍 to v.², and is needed there for measure. 𝔐 attaches it to previous l. — **2.** קֹדֶשׁ] ⅏ εἰς τὰ ἅγια, 𝔍 *ad sanctum*.

PSALM CXXXV., 3 STR. 6³.

Ps. 135 is a Hallel of the Levites in the temple, praising Yahweh for His goodness and loveliness (v.¹⁻³), for His deliverance of Israel and giving them possession of the Holy Land (v.⁸·¹⁰·¹²) ; summoning all classes in Israel to unite in blessing Yahweh, who dwelleth in Jerusalem (v.¹⁹⁻²¹). Glosses specify the goodness of Yahweh in choosing Israel (v.⁴), His supremacy over the gods of the nations (v.⁵), and over nature (v.⁶⁻⁷) ; refer to the miracles in Egypt (v.⁹), to Sihon and Og (v.¹¹) ; mention on the one side Yahweh's commemoration (v.¹³), and on the other His compassion (v.¹⁴) ; and contrast Him with dead idols (v.¹⁵⁻¹⁸).

> PRAISE ye the name of Yahweh :
>   Praise Yahweh, ye servants,
>   Ye that stand in the house of Yahweh,
>   In the courts of the house of our God.
>   Praise ye Yah ; for He is good.
>   Hymn to His name, for He is sweet :
> TO Him who smote the firstborn of Egypt,
>   From man even unto beast ;
>   To Him who smote many nations,
>   And slew numerous kings ;
>   And gave their land for a possession,
>   A possession to Israel His people.
> YE house of Israel bless Yahweh ;
>   Ye house of Aaron bless Yahweh ;
>   Ye house of Levi bless Yahweh ;
>   Ye that fear Yahweh bless Yahweh :
>   Bless Yahweh of Zion ;
>   (Bless) Him that dwelleth in Jerusalem.

Ps. 135 is a Hallel (הללויה, *v.* Intr. § 35). It resembles 113¹ in v.¹, only the lines are transposed : 134¹ in v.²ᵃ, 134³ in v.²¹ᵃ. It has the relative שׁ with ptc. v.²ᵃ and with the pf. v.⁸ᵃ·¹⁰ᵃ. It has many glosses : v.⁴ from Dt. 7⁶ ; v.⁵ from Ex. 18¹¹ ; v.⁶ from Ps. 115³ ; v.⁷ from Je. 10¹³ ; v.⁹ a prosaic statement ; v.¹³ from Ex. 3¹⁵ ; v.¹⁴ from Dt. 32³⁶ ; v.¹⁵⁻¹⁸ from Ps. 115⁴⁻⁸. V.¹¹, as 136¹⁹ᵃ·²⁾, is a gloss of specification. The Ps. cannot be earlier than the late Greek period.

Str. I. Three syn. couplets. — **1–3.** *Praise ye*], thrice repeated, ‖ *Hymn*], public worship with song in the temple. — *the name of Yahweh* ‖ *Yahweh* ‖ *Yah* ‖ *His name*]. Those summoned to praise are *servants*], not Israel in general, but specifically : *Ye* *that stand in the house of Yahweh* ‖ *In the courts of the house of our God*], those accustomed to minister in the courts of the temple, the Levitical singers and musicians as 134¹, the "house of Levi" v.²⁰. — The reason for the praise is : *for He is good*], as usual, benignant, and so ‖ *sweet* in His dealings with His people. Both of these attributes are ascribed to Yahweh as JPSV., and not the latter to the name as EVˢ., cf. 54⁸, or to the action of praise, cf. 147¹. — A glossator adds a number of specifications to these attributes from other Scriptures. — **4.** *For Yah chose Jacob for Himself, Israel for His peculiar treasure*]. This is derived from Dt. 7⁶, with the Deuteronomic idea of the divine selection of Israel, cf. Ps. 33¹², and the terms of the original covenant of Ex. 19⁵, by which Israel was selected out of all nations to be the treasure or property of Yahweh in a special or preëminent sense ; cf. also Mal. 3¹⁷ 1 Peter 2⁹ Eph. 1¹⁴ Tit. 2¹⁴ (Br.^{MP. 102. MA. 52. 191. 235}). — **5.** *Verily I know that Yahweh is great, and that our Lord is above all gods*]. This is an expansion of Ex. 18¹¹, the words of Jethro to Moses in recognition of the deliverance of Israel from Egypt as a divine act of Yahweh, cf. Pss. 95³ 96⁴. — **6.** *All that He pleaseth Yahweh doeth in heaven and on earth, in the seas and all depths*]. This is an expansion of Ps. 115³. — **7.** *Bringing up the vapours from the ends of the earth, the lightnings making for rain, leading forth the wind from his treasure houses*], a citation from Je. 10¹³, to illustrate the power of Yahweh over nature, doubtless with a view to the beneficent effects of the rain upon the land and its vegetation, cf. Pss. 33⁸ 65¹⁰ ˢᵍ·.

Str. II. Synth., syn., and stairlike couplets. — **8.** *To Him who*], relative obj. of the praise. — *smote the firstborn of Egypt, From man even unto beast*]. This, as the most significant and the climax of the plagues of Egypt, is given as a specimen, cf. 78⁵¹ 105³⁶. — A glossator, not satisfied with this, and wishing to recall to mind the numerous plagues of the historical narratives, adds : **9.** *He sent signs and wonders in Thy midst, O Egypt, against Pharaoh and against all his servants.* — **10.** *Him who smote many nations, And slew numerous kings*], a general statement referring to the victories of Moses and Joshua over the kings of the Canaanites. The Vrss. ancient and modern differ very much, some rendering "great and mighty" instead of "many and numerous," and others rendering the one way in one line, the other way in the other line. While etymologically either rendering is possible, the one given above seems to be most probable. — **11.** The glossator again specifies from the ancient history, in this case citing from 136[19-20], *Sihon, king of the Amorites, and Og, king of Bashan,* and making the summary addition to v.[10a], *and all the kingdoms of Canaan,* cf. Nu. 21[21 sq.] Dt. 2[30 sq.] 3[1 sq.] Jos. 12[1 sq.]. — **12.** *And gave their land for a possession — to Israel His people*], all the lands of the many nations and kings that He had smitten for their sakes, the entire land of Canaan, east and west of the Jordan. — A glossator again adds from other Scriptures several passages. — **13.** *Yahweh, Thy name endureth forever. Yahweh, Thy commemoration endureth for all generations*], a couplet from Ex. 3[15], changing the words of Yahweh to Moses, at the revelation of the divine name "Yahweh," into the form of the words of Israel in recognition and praise. — **14.** *For Yahweh will judge His people, and upon His servants have compassion*]. This is an exact citation from the song Dt. 32[36], predicting a divine judgment upon His people for their transgression, and yet one carried on with regretfulness and compassion. The Maccabean editor inserts v.[15-18] : —

> The idols of the nations are silver and gold,
> The work of the hands of man.
> Mouths have they; but they speak not.
> Eyes have they; but they see not.
> Ears have they; but they hear not.
> Like them be they that made them,
> All that trust in them.

This is a citation from 115[4-6a. 8], omitting the gloss to that passage. An additional line is given v.[18b] : — *Yea, there is no breath in their mouth*]. They are breathless, and so not alive.

Str. III. A syn. tetrastich, and a syn. couplet. — **19-21.** The *house of Levi*], resuming the "servants" of v.[1-2]. The three classes of worshippers are summoned : — the *house of Israel,* the *house of Aaron,* and them *that fear Yahweh,* cf. 115[9-13] 118[2-4], to *bless Yahweh*], six times repeated, the last omitted by error of early copyist at the expense of the measure. — In the fifth line Yahweh is described as *of Zion,* which must be interpreted as ‖ with *Him that dwelleth in Jerusalem,* as indicating that He goes forth from

Zion, His royal residence, when He would do His works of interposition and judgment. It is against the parallelism and the attitude of the Ps. to think of blessings resounding from Zion.

1. יְדִי], but 𝔊, 𝔈, 𝔍, עברים, as in 113¹. — **2.** יַעֲמִדים] יְ rel. with Qal ptc.,
cf. 134¹. — **3.** יהוה] gl., though in Vrss.; due to the fact that יְ with הללו had
lost its significance. — יִמִים] adj. *delightful*, cf. *16⁶*. — **4.** † סְגֻלָּה] n.f. (1) *valued
property, peculiar treasure*, of Yahweh, that is, Israel Ex. 19⁵ (E) Mal. 3¹⁷,
עַב ס׳ Dt. 7⁶ 14² 26¹⁸· ³⁰ here; (2) *treasure* of king 1 Ch. 29³ Ec. 2⁸. V. is gl.
from Dt. 7⁶. — **5.** Gl. from Ex. 18¹¹. — **6.** Gl. from Ps. 115³. — **7.** Prosaic gl.
from Je. 10¹³. — יְיִיאִיב] pl. † [וְיִשִיא] n.[m.] *vapour*, elsw. Je. 10¹³ = 51¹⁶ Pr.
25¹⁴. — אֵץ מ] txt. err. for יִשִׂיב; cf., however, Ges.⁵³· ³· Anm. ⁵. Je. 10¹³ = 51¹⁶
has יִשִׂיא, but Vrss. ptc. here. A scribe has been influenced by the original
passage to write the form in this way. — **8.** שֶׁהְיָה] יְ rel. for אִיבר, with pf.
is needed before עֵ for measure. — **9.** בְּיוֹרְגֵי] dittog. בְ. 𝔖 has it not. —
פִרְעֹה] n. pr., title of kings of Egypt; elsw. ψ, 136¹⁵. This v. prosaic gl. —
11. † [פ חִין] n. pr. m. *Sihon* Nu. 21²¹ +; elsw. ψ, 136¹⁹. — † [אֱמִרִי (ה)] מִלֶך]
elsw. ψ, 136¹⁹; *Amorites*, chief of peoples dispossessed by Hebrews; here
those E. Jordan Nu. 21¹³ +. — † עֹגֵ] n. pr. m. *Og*, king of Bashan, 136²⁰
Nu. 21³³ (JE) +. This v. is gl. from 136¹⁹⁻²⁰. — **13.** Gl. from Ex. 3¹⁵. —
14. Gl. from Dt. 32³⁶. — ירדן] 𝔚, 𝔍; but 𝔊 οἰκτείρει, to make better parall.
— **15–18** = gl. from 115⁴⁻⁸. — **17.** יאזינו] Hiph. of אזן, denom. אֹזֶן (5²). —
20. בית הלוי] † לֵוִי adj. gent. *Levite*, cf. בני הלוי 1 Ch. 12²⁶. — **21.** שכן ירושלם]
defective l.; prefix ברוך for measure, in acc. with style of Ps.

PSALM CXXXVI., 2 STR. 6³.

Ps. 136 was originally a song of praise to Yahweh, the supreme
God, for all His wondrous deeds (v.²⁻⁴), for His creation (v.⁵⁻⁷), for
His deliverance of Israel from Egypt (v.¹⁰· ¹³· ¹⁶), for His disposses-
sion of the kings of Canaan, and giving His people their inheritance (v.¹⁷· ²¹· ²⁵). To this additions (v.⁸⁻⁹· ¹¹⁻¹²· ¹⁴⁻¹⁵· ¹⁸⁻²⁰· ²²) were made,
changing it into an alphabetical Ps., with a solo voice giving the
theme and a chorus responding to each line with the common
liturgical phrase. Finally two lines were added (v.²³⁻²⁴), and the
introduction (v.¹) and conclusion (v.²⁶).

GIVE thanks to the God of gods;
Give thanks to the sovereign Lord of lords:
To Him that did great wonders;
To Him that made heaven by His understanding;
To Him that spread out the earth upon the waters;
To Him that made the great lights.

TO Him that smote the Egyptians in their firstborn;
   To Him that divided the Red Sea into parts;
   To Him that led His people in the wilderness;
   To Him that smote great kings;
   (To Him that) gave their land for a possession;
   (To) Him that giveth bread to all flesh.

Ps. 136 is a Hallel, with ἀλληλουιά at the beginning acc. to 𝕲, but הללויה
at close of previous Ps. acc. to 𝕳 ; *v.* Intr. § 35. It has in its present form
26 couplets, each of which begins with a solo voice, the leader of the choir
giving the object or attribute to be praised ; and it concludes with the chorus,
using the identical liturgical phrase: " For His kindness endureth forever."
According to Soph. 18¹² it was sung on the seventh day of Mazzoth. The
original Ps. was much shorter, composed of two hexastichs without the Rf.
The original is easily detected by the use of ל with the ptc. at the beginning
of each l., v.²⁻⁴· ⁵⁻⁷· ¹⁰· ¹³· ¹⁶· ¹⁷. In v.²¹· ²⁵ ל has been omitted because of intervening glosses. The glosses are all of a different construction, showing that
they have been tacked on. V.¹ is the general liturgical phrase frequently
appended to Hallels, cf. 106¹ or 118¹; v.⁸⁻⁹ are specifications from Gn. 1¹⁶· ¹⁸ ;
v.¹¹⁻¹² is a phr. of D. ; v.¹⁴⁻¹⁵ is a specification from Ex. 14²⁷ ; v.¹⁸ is a variant of v.¹⁷ ; v.¹⁹⁻²⁰ are specifications from the history = 135¹¹ ; v.²² is inserted
from 135¹²; v.²³⁻²⁴ is a pentameter of entirely different style from any other
part of the Ps., and by a different hand from the other glosses ; v.²³ is a conclusion, using the term " God of heaven," over against the introduction v.¹.
The original Ps. uses Dt. 10¹⁷ in v.²⁻³, Je. 10¹² in v.⁴⁻⁵, Ps. 24¹⁻² in v.⁶. It is
probable that the Ps. had three stages in its development: (1) the original
composition was of two hexastichs without the Rf. of the chorus ; (2) it was
enlarged to 22 lines with the chorus v.²⁻²²· ²⁵ ; (3) last of all it received the
glosses v.¹· ²³· ²⁴· ²⁶.

Str. I. Syn. couplet with synth. line and syn. triplet. —
1-3. *Give thanks*], once repeated, but implied in every line that
follows. — The third hand prefixed the liturgical formula : *Give
thanks to Yahweh : for He is good ; for His kindness endureth
forever. — to the God of gods ‖ sovereign Lord of lords*], both
cited from Dt. 10¹⁷ ; implying the sovereignty of Yahweh, the God
of Israel, over all the gods of the nations, cf. Ps. 135⁵. — The Rf. :
For His kindness endureth forever], was attached to each line,
probably by the second hand, and sung by a chorus in response
to the leader, who gave in each line the theme. — **4.** *To Him
that did great wonders*], a general term, comprehending all the
divine deeds that follow. A glossator added " alone " to emphasize the uniqueness of the divine activities of Yahweh ; but at the

expense of the measure. — **5-7**. *To Him that made*], at the creation; twice with the intervening ‖ *To Him that spread out*, a specific mode of creation in the style of Is. 42^5 44^{24}, involving the image of the expanse of a tent or curtain spread *upon the waters;* usually applied to *heaven*, but here to *the earth*]. It is possible that there was a transposition of the Ptcs. by copyist's mistake. — *by His understanding*], cf. Je. 10^{12}. The creative activity was an intelligent one, and the creations display the knowledge of their Creator. — *the great lights* only are mentioned in addition to heaven and earth. — **8-9**. A glossator specifies from Gn. $1^{16.18}$, *the sun for ruling over the day, the moon and the stars for ruling over the night*.

Str. II. Enumerates the several divine acts of redemption in six synth. lines. — **10**. *To Him that smote the Egyptians in their firstborn*], here as 135^8, the supreme plague as a specimen. — To this a glossator adds: **11-12**. *And brought forth Israel from their midst by a strong hand and an outstretched arm*], in accordance with the Deuteronomic narrative. — **13**. *To Him that divided the Red Sea into parts*], the supreme act of divine deliverance as a specimen. — To this a glossator adds from the narrative Ex. 14^{27}: **14-15**. *And made Israel pass over in the midst of it; and He shook off Pharaoh and his host into the Red Sea*. — **16**. *To Him that led His people in the wilderness*], a general statement covering the entire journey to the borders of Canaan. — **17**. *To Him that smote great kings*], a general statement, as 135^{10}. The glossator varies the statement slightly by saying: **18**. *And slew noble kings*, cf. 135^{10b}. It is quite possible that one of these originally was "nations" as 135^{10a}, or "kingdoms" as 135^{11}. He also specifies in **19-20**, as 135^{11}, *Sihon, king of the Amorites, and Og, king of Bashan*. — **21**. *To Him that gave their land for a possession*]. This has in 𝕳 been assimilated to 135^{12}, and so the second line has been added: — *A possession for Israel His servant*. — The third hand appends a pentameter in a different tone, and with different and later terminology: **23-24**. *Who in our low estate was mindful of us, and delivered us from our adversaries*, which probably refers to Maccabean afflictions. — **25**. *To Him that giveth bread to all flesh*]. This is a general conclusion. It is probable, however, that the original reference

was to provision for the wants of His people. — The latest glossator adds : **26.** as a conclusion, over against the introduction v.[1] :
Give thanks to the God of heaven], a phr. of Ezr. 1[2] Ne. 1[4] 2[4],
which, however, in 𝔍 is interpreted as a summons to the heavens
to praise their God, as in the Hallel 148[4].

3. אֲדֹנֵי] pl. emphatic, ‖ ֗־לָ֗ as Dt. 10[17]. — **4.** לִבְדוֹ] though in Vrss. makes
l. too long and is gl. — **7.** ־רִים] for בְּאוֹרִב־. — **8–9.** Gl. from Gn. 1[16. 18]; the
l. too long for the measure. — **11–12.** Explanatory gl. from Dt., cf. 4[34]
5[15] + ; prosaic sentence. — **13.** ־־] Qal ptc., *v. 886*. — וְיָ֫רִיב־] pl. † [יֶ֫רֶ]
n.m. only pl. ; here sections of sea ; elsw. halves of animals Gn. 15[17]. —
14–15. Explanatory gl.; last l. too long for measure. — ־־] Pi. pf. *shake
off*, cf. Niph. 109[23]. — ־־ ֗־֗]. ־־ ֗־ n.m , here *host, army*, as 33[6], cf. 59[12] 110[3].
— **16.** מֵילִיך] ptc. Hiph. דרך as Dt. 8[15] Is. 63[12. 13] Je. 2[6. 17] Zc. 5[10] +. —
18. Variant of v.[17] tacked on, cf. 135[10b]. — **19–20.** Gl. of specification, as
135[11a. b]. — **21.** ־ ־] but 𝔊 · A. T καὶ δόντι implies ptc. whose ־ has been
omitted because of intervening gl., and which has been assimilated to 135[12],
but 𝔊R ἔδωκεν. — **22.** Gl. ; cf. 135[12b]. — **23.** יִֽרְשִׁירְלֵנוּ] † [שַׁרְ] n. *lowliness,
low estate*, elsw. Ec. 10[6]. The ־ late form rel. Gl. of diff. structure from
original sentences. — **24.** Sentence of diff. construction from the original l.
and a dimeter. — **25.** וְרֵן] for usual ־רֵן. ־ has been omitted because of
intervening gl. — **26** is a gl. whether אֵל be construct before השמים as 𝔐,
𝔊א. c. a. R. T, or השמים be vocative as 𝔍. 𝔊 · has κυρίῳ, manifestly error.

PSALM CXXXVII., 3 STR. 4[5].

**Ps. 137 narrates the bitter experience of the exiles when their
captors demanded of them songs of Yahweh** (v.[1-3]), **which they
could not sing in a foreign land, in forgetfulness of Jerusalem,
whose remembrance was their chief joy** (v.[4-6]). **With a vivid
recollection of the treacherous cruelty of the Edomites, they look
forward to the time of vengeance upon them** (v.[7-9]).

> BY the streams, there we sat down, yea, we wept;
> By the poplars in the midst we hung up our harps:
> For there our captors asked us words of song;
> (Yea, they asked us), "Sing to us some of the songs of Zion."
> "HOW can we sing the songs of Yahweh in a foreign land?"
> If I forget thee, O Jerusalem, may my right hand be forgotten.
> May my tongue cleave to my palate, if I remember thee not;
> If I exalt not Jerusalem above my chief gladness.
> REMEMBER to the sons of Edom the day of Jerusalem:
> Who said: "Lay it bare! Lay it bare! To the foundation with it."
> Happy be he who repayeth thee what thou didst deal to us.
> Happy be he who taketh and dasheth thy sucklings against the crag.

Ps. 137 has no title in 𝔥. In 𝔊 however it has τῷ Δαυείδ. This certainly did not mean that it was composed by David, but that it was of the Davidic type. It is not probable that this Ps. was in 𝔇, although it intervenes between a series of Hallels and the Davidic group 138–145; *v.* Intr. § 27. The date of the Ps. from internal evidence cannot be long after the destruction of Jerusalem, when the treachery and cruelty of the Edomites was fresh in the minds of the exiles. The Ps. was evidently written early in the Babylonian exile, for it breathes the spirit of the bitter experience of those times. The Ps. is composed of three pentameter tetrastichs. בת בבל השרודה v.⁸ is a late gl. against the context, which makes the Edomites the chief offenders. It was introduced at a time when the share of the Edomites in the destruction of Jerusalem had become effaced. בבל in the first line was also not in the original.

Str. I. Syn. and stairlike couplets. — **1-2.** *By the streams*], the canals uniting the Euphrates and the Tigris, and fertilizing the land of *Babylon*, which in the original was implied, but by a glossator inserted in the text. — ‖ *By the poplars in the midst*], between the canals : changed by the glossator into " her midst," the midst of Babylon, which certainly does not suit the locality of the parallel line. To these places the people had retired for solitary grief and reflection. — *there we sat down*], in the posture of sorrow, with head bowed in humiliation. — *Yea, we wept — we hung up our harps*], having no further use for them. It is not probable however that they were hung "upon" the trees as the EV⁸. have it. — **3.** *For there*], giving a special reason for the sorrow. — *our captors asked us words of song*], the measured lines of psalmody. The vb. *asked* is repeated for stairlike parall. acc. to a probable emendation. 𝔥 has a form α.λ. and there is no agreement among Vrss. or commentators. PBV. takes it as a noun " in our heaviness"; AV., RV., as a vb. " they that wasted us"; JPSV., " our tormentors"; none of which is sustained in form or usage. — *Sing to us some of the songs of Zion*], the songs of Yahweh, songs composed and used in the worship of Yahweh ; not songs of a non-religious character, which might have been sung with propriety.

Str. II. Has an introductory line, and a syn. triplet. — **4.** *How can we sing the songs of Yahweh in a foreign land?*]. These songs were alone appropriate in the land of Yahweh in the temple of Yahweh. — **5-6.** *If I forget thee, O Jerusalem*], in antithesis with the foreign land. — ‖ *if I remember thee not*], intensified in : *If I exalt not Jerusalem above my chief gladness*], finding the chief joy during the exile in the recollection of Jerusalem. — The psalmist imprecates paralysis upon himself, if it should be otherwise : *may my right hand be forgotten*], because paralysed and no longer felt, or within the experience of the mind. — ‖ *May my tongue cleave to my palate*], also paralysed and unable to move.

Str. III. A synth. and a syn. couplet. — **7.** *Remember*], an appeal to Yahweh to join with His people in recalling the bitter experience of the past. — *to the sons of Edom*]. The Edomites were especially zealous against the Jews in their tribulations, cf. La. 4²¹ ˢᑫ· Ob.¹⁰ ˢᑫ· Ez. 25¹² ˢᑫ·. — *the day of Jerusalem*], the day when the city was captured and destroyed by the king of Babylon. — *Who said : " Lay it bare ! "*], repeated for emphasis. — *" To the foundation with it ! "*]. Let it be laid bare and stripped even to the foundation, so that nothing be left standing. — **8.** *Happy be he*], repeated at the beginning of the concluding line. — *who repayeth thee*], referring to Edom, whose cruel zeal against Judah exceeded that of the Babylonians, and who was the instigator of greater severity in dealing with Israel than the Babylonians themselves proposed. — But a later glossator at the expense of the measure prefixed : *O daughter of Babylon, waster*], thinking of Babylon as chiefly responsible for the destruction of the city, at a time when the part that Edom had taken had become obscured, and doubtless because of the mention of Edom in the previous couplet, unwilling that the chief oppressor should be left out. — *what thou didst deal to us*], in exact retribution, intensified by a glossator by the insertion of " thine own dealing " at the expense of the measure. — *who taketh and dasheth thy sucklings against the crag*], the cruel extermination of male offspring, according to the custom of the ancients : due to the principle of blood revenge transmitted as a duty to offspring, making it necessary to exterminate all males in order to prevent future vengeance, cf. Is. 13¹⁶ Ho. 10¹⁴ Na. 3¹⁰.

1. בָּבֶל] is dub. here as in v.⁸. — **2.** † עֲרָבִים] only pl. *poplars*, Is. 15⁷ 44⁴ Lv. 23⁴⁰ (H) Jb. 40²². — בְּתוֹכָה] sf. is improbable if בָּבֶל a gl. — כִּנֹּרוֹתֵינוּ] has two accents. — **3.** שׁוֹבֵינוּ] Qal ptc. שׁבה, *v.* 68¹⁹. — † תוֹלָלֵינוּ] a.λ. 𝔊 οἱ ἀπαγαγόντες ἡμᾶς, 𝔙 *qui abduxerunt nos*, so 𝔖, = מֹילִיכֵינוּ as Jb. 12¹⁷, so Agellius ; 𝔗 בָּזוֹזָא *our plunderers* = שׁׁבֵינוּ, as Ez. 39¹', so Hu., Gr., Bä., Kau., Valeton ; Σ οἱ καταλαζονευόμενοι ἡμῶν ; 𝔍 *qui adfligebant nos.* הֵיר does not exist. עֹלֵל does not explain any of the Vrss. except 𝔗. Ehr. suggests מֵאֵלוֹנוּ, which best suits context. — הֵּׁׁב is not in 𝔊, and is late gl. — ר שֵׁׁ .] 𝔊 ἐκ τῶν ᾠδῶν. — **5.** הֵּׁׁכח יְמִינִי] *obj.* omitted in order to emphasize the idea of forgetfulness itself, an obj. being given in the next l. But 𝔊 ἐπιλησθείη, הֵׁׁרָה, so 𝔍 *in oblivione sit*, 𝔙 *oblivioni detur.* — **6.** אֹזכרי] sf. Aramaism, but prob. due to assimilation to אֹם. — **7.** הֵה] gl. — עָרוּ] Imv. Pi. עָרה : *make naked, lay bare*, demolish, cf. 141⁸. Hithp. *v.* 37³⁵. — **8–9.** בֵּ ת בכל היצורה] is doubtless a gl. ; there is no place for it in measure and it is against the context, which makes Edom the enemy. — הֵׁשִׁי־יֵרָה pass. ptc., *be wasted*, as Rödiger, De., Bä., *vastata* 𝔍, *v.* Kö.ᴵᴵ· ¹· ¹⁹⁴. Bö., Hi., Ew., Hu.³, הֵׁשִׁי־יֵרָה = *oppressor, waster;* Street, Dy., Kau., Gr. הֵׁשׁׁי־דֵרָה. — אֹשֵׁרֵי] as *1¹*, so v.⁹. — שֵׁיׁשֵׁׁׁם] late rel. with impf. ; so with גֹמלח, also with יאהו v.⁹. — אֹת־גֹמוּלך] gl. of intensification, at cost of measure. — וֹנֵפֵּץ] ו consec. after impf.

PSALM CXXXVIII., 3 STR. 6³.

Ps. 138 is a thanksgiving to Yahweh for His kindness and faithfulness (v.¹⁻³). The kings of the earth share in this thanksgiving, for they have heard His words and mused upon His ways, and see and know His glory (v.⁴⁻⁶). Though Israel must undergo trouble, Yahweh's hand saves him from enemies ; therefore he prays Him to continue benefits, and not to discard His handiwork (v.⁷⁻⁸).

WITH my whole heart I give *Thee* thanks :
  In the sight of divine beings I make melody unto *Thee*.
  Thee I give thanks for *Thy* kindness,
  And Thy name for *Thy* faithfulness :
  For Thou hast magnified above all things *Thy* word,
  And strengthened me in my soul with (*Thy*) strength.
ALL earth's kings give *Thee* thanks,
  Because they have heard the words of *Thy* mouth ;
  And they muse, Yahweh, upon *Thy* way,
  For great is *Thy* glory :
  For exalted, Yahweh, they see *Thee*,
  And lofty from afar they know *Thee*.
IN the midst of trouble must I walk,
  Against mine enemies Thou stretchest forth *Thy* hand,
  And Thou savest me with *Thy* right hand.
  Yahweh, on my behalf be *Thy* benefits ;
  Yahweh, forever be *Thy* kindness ;
  Do not discard the works of *Thy* hands.

Ps. 138 was doubtless in 𝔻, as it begins a group of Pss. with לדוד in 𝔅, extending to and including 145; of which 139, 140, were in 𝔻ℜ also, and of which 139, 140, 141, 143, were in 𝔐, 142 was a משכיל and also a הפדה, 145 a תהלה. None were in 𝔈. These were given their present place by the final editor of the ψ (*v.* Intr. §§ 26, 27, 31, 33, 38). 𝔊ᴮ·ᴺ of Ps. 138 had τῷ Δαυείδ, 𝔊ᴬ also Ζαχαρίου, 𝔊ᵀ Ζαχαρίας; 𝔍, Θ, 𝔗, have only "David"; but Aq. and Sexta have not even this. There is no good reason, however, to doubt its originality. The original Ps. had three trimeter hexastichs; but it was considerably modified by the insertion of glosses: v.²ᵃ from 5⁸, v.³ᵃ, and one in 𝔊 between v.¹ᵃ and v.¹ᵇ; also by minor changes throughout the Ps., made at the expense of the measure and to the destruction of the assonance. The Ps. in its original form had every line ending in *ka*. It belonged to the Persian period in its happier times, after Nehemiah.

Str. I. Two syn. and a synth. couplet. — **1.** *With my whole heart I give Thee thanks*], PBV. after Vrss. adds "Yahweh" at the expense of the measure. 𝔊, 𝔙, also add from v.⁴ᵇ, "because Thou hast heard the words of my mouth"; which was not original, though accepted by Gr., Bi., Du.; for there is no place for it in the Str. — *In the sight of divine beings I make melody unto Thee*]. The psalmist conceives that the temple worship is in the presence of heavenly beings, the angels, cf. 8⁶ 89⁶⁻⁹. — **2.** 𝔅 and Vrss. add from 5⁸, *I worship toward Thy holy temple*], which is implied in the Ps and needed no expression. This line has no place in the Str. — *Thee* ‖ *Thy name* — *I give thanks for Thy kindness* ‖ *for Thy faithfulness*]. This syn. couplet has been reduced to a prose sentence by a prosaic scribe. — *For Thou hast magnified above all things Thy word*]. The divine word of promise has been made great and glorious in its fulfilment. By a copyist's error the divine "name" came into the text from the previous line at the expense of the measure, and occasioned great difficulty to the Vrss. "Above every name" was so incongruous to "word" that the latter was easily mistaken by the Greek translators for the similar Greek word "holiness" which appears in the earliest Greek codices. 𝔍, however, retains "word." 𝔅 has "Thy name," and thus gives the rendering of AV., RV., JPSV., "Thy word above all Thy name," which cannot be satisfactorily explained; for how can the fulfilment of the divine promise or of any divine utterance be magnified above the divine name? — **3.** A glossator inserts the general statement, — *In the day I called, Thou didst* *answer me*], which is true enough, but has no relation to the context. — *And strengthened me in my soul with Thy strength*], given me inward strength, by the comfort derived from the fulfilment of the divine promises. 𐤇 and Vrss. differ exceedingly in the form of the vb. But the rendering given above after 𐤂, 𐤉, 𐤔, 𐤕, so essentially PBV., AV., is more probable than 𐤇, followed by RV., JPSV., " didst encourage me," which has little support in OT.

Str. II. Two synth. and a syn. couplet. — **4.** *All earth's kings*], share in this praise of Israel ; cf. 96, 97, 98, 100. — *Because they have heard the words of Thy mouth*], the prophetic words of promise with reference to Israel's deliverance, cf. Is. $41^{26\ sq.}$ 42^9 44^{6-8}. — **5–6.** *And they muse upon*], more probable than " sing " of 𐤇, and Vrss., which is nowhere else used in this construction. — *Thy way*], required for assonance, changed by glossator into " ways of Yahweh." The divine ways are in accordance with the divine promises. — *For great is Thy glory*], required for assonance instead of " glory of Yahweh," of 𐤇 and Vrss. — *For exalted* ‖ *And lofty*]. These were predicates of *Yahweh* in the vocative, ‖ " glory " of previous line and continuing the reason for the thanksgiving of the kings. But an early scribe interpreted the second adj. of proud men against the ‖, for יהוה makes it necessary to interpret the first of God. Accordingly the insertion of an obj. with vb. became necessary, and " the lowly," the antithesis to " the proud," came into the text at the expense of the measure. The vbs. were originally in accordance with the context and the assonance : *they see Thee* ‖ *they know Thee from afar*], the recognition of the exalted majesty of Yahweh by the kings even of the most distant parts. But the interpretation already mentioned compelled the ignoring of the sfs., and so the text became that followed by Vrss. and EVˢ., " though Yahweh be proud, yet hath He respect unto the lowly ; but the proud He knoweth afar off " ; which might be regarded as a good gnomic sentence though in bad measure, but which gives an abrupt change of person and results in a conception heterogeneous to its context and altogether inappropriate to the conclusion of a Str. whose theme is : the praise of Yahweh by all the kings of the earth.

Str. III. Two tristichs : the first, an introductory line followed by a syn. couplet ; the second syn. throughout. — **7.** *In the midst*

of trouble must I walk]. The cohortative form was required for
assonance, but was changed by a copyist into the more usual form.
A glossator at the expense of the measure adds the apodosis here
prematurely in the vb. " Thou revivest me." — *against mine
enemies*]. The trouble had been occasioned by enemies. A
glossator inserted " anger " in the text, after the prep., making it
the anger of the enemies, against the measure. — *Thou stretchest
forth Thy hand* ‖ *with Thy right hand*], the usual divine interposition on behalf of His people, cf. Ex. 15⁶·¹² Ps. 20⁷ 77¹¹ 98¹. —
Thou savest me], from the enemies and troubles ; or possibly
"givest me the victory " over them, for the Heb. word has both
mngs., and we cannot always determine which the author had in
mind. — **8.** *Yahweh, on my behalf be Thy benefits*]. The jussive
of last line makes it necessary to interpret the two previous lines
as jussive also. Moreover, the assonance could hardly have failed
in the original, which prob. had a noun with sf. subsequently
changed by a copyist into the jussive of a late Aramaic vb. of the
same meaning. — *Yahweh, forever be Thy kindness*], resuming
the thought of v.². — *Do not discard the works of Thy hands*],
the works of kindness and faithfulness undertaken in fulfilment of
His promises, which need still to be carried on, in behalf of His
people. To discard them would be to break them off before they
had been completed, and prior to the complete accomplishment
of their purpose.

1. אוֹדְךָ] transpose to end of l. for assonance. 𝕲, 𝔖, 𝔍, 𝕿, insert יהוה, so
Bi., Che., Du. But it is not needed for measure or sense. 𝕲 ·ᶜ·ᵃ· T, 𝔈, insert ὅτι ἤκουσας τὰ ῥήματα τοῦ στόματός μου, which is accepted by Gr., Bi.,
Du. It is not, however, in 𝕲ᴬ. — **2.** אשתחוה אל היכל קדשך] gl. frcm 5⁸. —
ואירה את־שמך] cf. 44⁹ 54⁸ 99³ 142⁸. — על־הסיד ועל־אמ־ך] is prosaic ; one belongs to each l. and the first l. should have sf. with vb., the second את־יאמך.
— הגדלת על־כל] *magnify over all*, cf. 18⁵¹ Is. 42²¹. — שמך אמרתך] so Σ ; 𝕲
ὄνομα τὸ ἅγιόν σου, but ἅγιον error for λόγιον ; 𝔍 *nomen eloquium tuum* ;
שמך gl., as Bä. — **3.** תרהבני] Hiph. ‡ רהב, cf. Ct. 6⁵ ; Bu. denom. רהב *pride*,
and so *fill with pride* ; Aq., 𝔍, *dilatabis animae meae*, interpret as רהב (cf.
18²⁰). 𝕲, 𝔖, 𝕿, rd. prob. תרבני. It is prob. that there has been a confusion
between Heb. רהב and Aram. רהב. — עז] 𝕲ˣ ἐν δυνάμει πολλῇ, but πολλῇ not
in 𝕲ˣ·ᶜ·ᵃ·ᴬ· ʀ· ᵀ·. — **4.** יהוה] excessive gl., cf. v.¹. — כל־מלכי ארק] phr. 102¹⁶
(2². ⁶). — אמרי] (12⁷). — **5.** וישירו ב] not elsw. with ב. Gr. ישיח, cf. 6⁷. Rd.
דרכה for assonance. The ך of sf. fell off by haplog., and so after transposition
of יהוה the noun was taken as cstr. — כבוד] used with רום 113⁴ 57⁶· ¹² = 108⁶.

Rd. כְּבוּדְךָ for assonance, instead of כְּבוֹד יְ.— **6.** ‡שָׁחַל] adj. *lowly* 2 S. 6[22] Ez. 17[14] Mal. 2[9]. It is a gl. here, making l. too long. — ‡מִמֶּרְחָק] *from afar* Pr. 31[14] Is. 10[3] 30[27] Je. 5[15] Ez. 23[40]. The vbs. require sf. for assonance ; rd. יְדָעֶךָ, יִרְאֶךָ. The form יֵרֵעַ arose from dittog. of יְ. It cannot be rectified by pointing יֵרָע Ges.[§ 69. 2. R. 3.] — **7.** אֵם־אֶרֶךְ בְּרֵרֵב צָרָה] cf. 23[4] כִּי אֵלֵךְ בְּגִיא צַלְמוֶת. Assonance requires אֵלְכָה.— [וַתְּחַיֵּנִי] *preserve alive*, as 33[19] 41[3]. — אַף [עַל־אַף expl. gl. — [הַשְׁלָה יַד Gn. 3[22] 8[9] 19[10] +. — [וַתוֹשִׁיעֵנִי יְמִינֶךָ cf. Ex. 15[6. 6. 12] Pss. 20[7] 77[11] 98[1] +. — **8.** וְיִכְלָב] *be complete, come to an end*, 7[10] 12[2] 77[9]; trans. *bring to an end, complete*, 57[3]; but here as well as in 57[3] 𝕲 seems to have had יְמֵר. The form is prob. glossator's change from an original גְּמֹלֵךְ, which gives the assonance needed. — [בַּעֲדִי] *on my behalf.* — [יָרִיד] should close l. for assonance, as also רְסִ״ךְ. — [אַל הֶרֶף Hiph. juss. רפה *abandon, forsake*, c. יְ, יָדִים ; so without יְ c. acc. Ne. 6[3] Dt. 4[31] 31[6. 8] Jos. 1[5].

PSALM CXXXIX.

Ps. 139 is composite. (*A*) A didactic Ps., represents that the divine Spirit, which is identified with the divine Presence, is omnipresent, and that it is impossible to flee or to hide from it (v.[7-12]). (*B*) is also didactic, expressing the conviction that Yahweh searches and knows His people thoroughly and wonderfully in all their actions and in all their relations (v.[1-6]). This knowledge is based upon the creation of man, his protection even in the womb, and the predetermination of his days and fortune in life (v.[13. 15ab. 16]). The Ps. concludes with a prayer that this searching may be for everlasting guidance (v.[23-24]). (*C*) is also didactic, exclaiming at the numerous poor among the friends of God, with the petition that He would slay the wicked (v.[17. 19a. 20a]), and affirming hatred and loathing of them (v.[21-22]). Glosses express wonder at the divine works (v.[14. 18a]), confidence in the resurrection from the underworld (v.[15c. 18b]), and abhorrence of the wicked (v.[19b. 20b]).

A. v.[7-12], 3 STR. 4[3].

WHITHER can I go from Thy Spirit?
 And whither can I flee from Thy presence?
 If to heaven, Thou art there;
 And if to Sheol, behold Thou art there.
WOULD I lift up my wings to the Dawn?
 Would I dwell in the uttermost sea?
 There Thy hand Thou wouldst cause to rest upon me,
 And (there) Thy right hand would lay hold of me.

H AVE I said : " Surely my morning twilight shall be darkness;
    And daylight about me be night";
    Surely darkness maketh not too dark for Thee;
    And the night shineth as the day.

B. v.[1-6. 13. 15ab. 16. 23-24], 6 STR. 4[3].

Y AHWEH, (Thou) dost search me,
    And Thou dost know (me).
    Thou knowest my downsitting and mine uprising;
    Thou perceivest (my friends) from afar.
T O my path and my resting place Thou dost (turn aside),
    And to all my ways Thou art accustomed :
    For there is nothing, Yahweh, on my tongue,
    But lo ! Thou knowest it altogether.
B EHIND and before Thou dost watch me,
    And put Thy palm over me.
    (Thy) knowledge is too wonderful for me:
    It is inaccessible ; I cannot attain to it.
V ERILY Thou didst beget my reins;
    Thou screenedst me in my mother's womb.
    My frame was not hid from Thee,
    Which Thou didst make in the secret place.
M Y (lot) Thine eyes did see,
    And on Thy book was it all.
    Days were inscribed, preordained,
    When there was not one of them.
S EARCH me and *know* my mind,
    Try me and *know* my thoughts;
    And see if there be any wickedness in me,
    And lead me in the way everlasting.

C. v.[17. 19a. 20a. 21-22], 2 STR. 4[3].

O HOW precious are Thy (friends), O God !
    How numerous (the poor) among them !
    O that Thou wouldst kill the wicked, O God !
    Those who speak with wicked intent.
D O not I hate them that hate Thee ?
    And loathe them that rise up against Thee ?
    I hate them with the perfection of hatred ;
    They are enemies to me.

Ps. 139 was in 𝔇 and 𝕸, and subsequently in 𝔇𝕽 according to 𝕳 (*v.* Intr.
§§ 27, 31, 33), to which 𝕾[A. T] adds Σαχαρίου, and 𝕾[A. a. (mg.) T] ἐν τῇ διασπορᾷ
as in other instances, thinking of its composition in the times of the postexilic
prophets. But it is impossible that the Ps. in its present form could have been
in 𝔇 ; and it is improbable that it was in 𝔇𝕽, because of the numerous Aramaisms and late forms and expressions. It is true that many of these are dubi-

ous, the Vrss. having other readings; but a sufficient number remains to make
a very late date for the present Ps. imperative. (1) רֵעַ v.^{2. 17}, usually taken as
a.λ. and Aramaism; but more probably the usual רֵעַ *friend*, as ⅏, ℑ, 𝔘, v.¹⁷.
(2) רבע v.³ for רבץ; elsw. thrice in P in another sense. (3) זרית v.³ in a sense
unknown elsw. Vrss. differ. Probably error for זרה = סרה. (4) מְלָּה v.⁴,
Aram.; דבר; possibly a gl. (5) צרתני v.⁵, interpreted by Vrss. as from יצר;
more probably error for נצרתני. (6) אֶכָל v.⁸, a.λ., Aramaism; prob. gl.
(7) יְנַחֵי שחר v.⁹, a.λ.; error for יְנַחֵי שׁ ⅏, 𝔘. (8) ישופני v.¹¹, elsw. Gn. 3¹⁵ Jb.
9¹⁷, all dub. Vrss. differ; probably error for וְשֻׁפִי as Jb. 7⁴. (9) בַּעֲרֵני v.¹¹,
a.λ. for בעדי; ⅏, 𝔘, otherwise. (10) עַל כִּי v.¹⁴ for אשר. (11) רקמתי v.¹⁵
in a usage a.λ.; probably error for קמתי, as ⅏. (12) גָּלְמִי v.¹⁶, a.λ., Aramaism; probably error for גרלי. (13) יקרו v.¹⁷, in the sense generally given,
a.λ.; but probably the vb. has the usual sense; the difference due to different
interp. of רֵעַ. (14) הקטל v.¹⁹, Aram.; elsw. Jb. 13¹⁵ 24¹⁴. (15) הכלית v.²²,
elsw. in another sense Ne. 3²¹ Jb. 3 t. (16) שרעפי v.²³, elsw. 94¹⁹. (17) עֹצֶב
v.²⁴, elsw. 1 Ch. 4⁹ Is. 14¹³. Of these only (6) (7) (8) (9) are in v.⁷⁻¹², and
these all txt. err. or gl. The doctrine of the divine Spirit in v.⁷⁻¹² is in advance
of anything in the O.T. But it is probable that Is. 63⁹⁻¹⁰ lies back of it.
There is also a similarity with Am. 9²⁻³, which probably was in the mind of
the author. This section of the Ps. is entirely independent of its context;
has simplicity and parallelism; and is more poetic in style and conception.
This was probably the original Ps. of 𝔅, 𝔅𝔈, and 𝔅𝔎, from the Persian
period subsequent to Nehemiah. The other parts of the Ps. were later.
V.¹⁻⁶ and v.¹³⁻¹⁶, apart from glosses, belong together, and probably with them
the conclusion, v.²³⁻²⁴. V.¹⁷⁻²² seem to be later, in the Maccabean temper.
The glosses v.^{14. 15c. 18. 19b. 20a} are later still. Davies does not recognise the
difference between *A* and *B*, but thinks v.¹⁹⁻²⁴ an interpolation.

PSALM CXXXIX. *A.*

Str. I. has two syn. couplets. — **7**. *Whither can I go?*
‖ *whither can I flee?*], cf. Am. 9²⁻³, where, however, escape from
divine retribution was thought of; while here the question is raised
in order to set forth by its negative answer the divine omni-
presence. — *from Thy Spirit* ‖ *from Thy presence*]. In the OT.
the divine Spirit is the divine energy: in the earliest times imparting religious enthusiasm to men; then later imparting other
gifts and endowments, physical, intellectual and moral; also in
Ezekiel the energy of theophanic manifestations. In Is. 63⁹⁻¹⁰, the
Spirit is identified with the angel of the presence of the Exodus;
and in the postexilic prophets with the divine power restoring and
guiding Israel at the Restoration. From this basis the poet rises
to the supreme height of identifying the divine Spirit with the

divine presence, not only in the theophanic, but also in the invisible activities of God throughout the universe. — **8.** *If to heaven*, and its antithesis *if to Sheol*], the underworld, the abode of the dead ; so Am. 9². — *Thou art there ‖ behold Thou art there*]. The original had no vbs., as they were not needed and the measure was better without them. They were later insertions in the text by a prosaic scribe.

Str. II. has syn. couplets. — **9.** *Would I lift up my wings to the Dawn*], so 𝔊, cf. 11¹ 55⁷ ; to be preferred to 𝔥, followed by EVˢ., "wings of the Dawn," a phr. unknown to OT. and improbable, especially as it obscures the antithesis between the East whence the Dawn springs and the West, here as elsewhere indicated by, — *dwell in the uttermost Sea*], cf. Dt. 11²⁴. — **10.** *There*], the place of the Dawn, the extreme East ; and again, the place of the uttermost Sea, the extreme West. — *Thy hand ‖ right hand — would lay hold of me ‖ Thou wouldst cause to rest upon me*], a more natural explanation of the original (requiring no change in the unpointed text), than MT. followed by EVˢ., "lead me," which is of the nature of an anticlimax. The conception of the hand resting upon, laying hold of, is especially appropriate to the rays of both the dawning and the setting sun, cf. Jb. 38¹³.

Str. III. also has syn. couplets. — **11.** *Have I said*], in resolution. — *Surely my morning twilight*], the most probable original reading, cf. Jb. 7⁴ : ‖ *daylight about me*], for which by early copyist's mistake a vb. was substituted which is elsewhere used but twice and is in these cases dubious in form and meaning, and which here gives the Vrss. great difficulty and is variously rendered : PBV., AV., "cover" after 𝚺, 𝔍 ; RV. "overwhelm," or more properly after 𝔊, 𝖌, "crush me " : but none of these give a sense suited to the parallelism. — *shall be darkness ‖ night*]. There shall be no day with its dawning light, but the darkness of night shall continue all day long. — **12.** *Surely darkness ‖ the night — maketh not too dark for Thee*], so that Thou canst not see distinctly in it where I am and what I do. — with the antithesis : *shineth as the day*]. To this a glossator adds the summary statement : "the darkness and the light are alike," which 𝔊ᴮ substitutes for the previous lines ; and so 𝔊ᴮ reduces the Str., making it just one line too short ; while 𝔥 lengthens the Str., making it just one line too long. This singularly beautiful Ps. comes to a proper climax and conclusion here ; and is complete and symmetrical in itself, needing no introduction and no conclusion.

PSALM CXXXIX. *B.*

Str. I. is a syn. tetrastich. — **1.** *Yahweh, Thou dost search me ‖ And Thou dost know me*]. The structure of the Str., the measures, and the parallelism require two lines, which an ancient copyist has reduced to one. The poet is conscious that the people are searched through and through by their God, and are thoroughly known, cf. Je. 17¹⁰ Ps. 14². — **2.** *Thou knowest ‖ perceivest from afar*], both kinds of knowledge, that of conception and that of perception. — *my downsitting and mine uprising*], cf. Dt. 6⁷ : the entire activity of the day, looking backward from the coming home to rest to the rising up to go forth to the day's occupation. — *my friends*], so most probably, in accordance with the usual mng. of the word given by the letters of the unpointed text, rather than " my thoughts " based on a word used possibly v.¹⁷, but nowhere else in OT. The latter emphasizes, it is true, the searching of the mind, as the complement to the searching of the external life ; but it is improbable, as this line is followed by six lines, all of which refer to the external life. If the internal mind were to be referred to, we would expect at least one couplet out of the four to be given to it. Moreover, the previous line of the couplet referring to the external life suggests that its mate should do so also. This we have, if we think of association with friends during the interval between the rising up and the sitting down. Since this is sustained by the usual mng. of the original word, it is surprising that any other mng. should have been thought of.

Str. II. has a syn. and a synth. couplet. — **3.** *my path and my resting place*], the path followed when he rose in the morning and the resting place to which he returned for the night. — ‖ *all my ways*], between the two. The vbs. are unusual and difficult, and variously rendered by ancient and modern Vrss. The most probable vb. in the first line is *turn aside to*], visit, inspect, and so know ; ‖ *Thou art accustomed to*. But 𝔐 gives a rare form, which can only be interpreted in an unnatural sense : PBV. " art

about," AV. " compassest," RV., JPSV., " searchest," RV^m. " win-
nowest."— **4**. *For there is nothing on my tongue*], ready to be
spoken but not yet uttered. — *But lo! Thou knowest it altogether*],
its meaning as well as the expression that will be given to it.

Str. III. has two syn. couplets. — **5**. *Behind and before*], on
all sides round about. — *Thou dost watch me*], the probable mng.
of an original which is dubious.   𝕳 seems to give a vb. meaning
" beset," " besiege," so AV., RV., JPSV., implying the metaphor
of a siege, cf. Jb. 19^12 ; but this would imply hostility, which is
alien to this entire Ps. and improbable in this couplet alone.
𝕲, Σ, 𝔖, 𝔍, had another vb. meaning " fashion," " form," of creation, so PBV. ; but this conception belongs to Strs. IV. and V., and
would be premature here.   It is just as easy to think of the vb.
" watch," " guard," suited to the context and to the ‖ *put Thy
palm over me*].   This phr. has then the usual meaning of protection, which certainly suits the entire course of thought thus far
much better than " lay Thine hand upon " of EV^s., due doubtless
to the influence of v.^10 of the other Ps. — **6**. *Thy knowledge*],
interpreting the article, which, according to the original text, belonged to this noun, as possessive, rather than demonstrative. —
is too wonderful for me], to be wondered at, but not understood.
— ‖ *It is inaccessible*], too high to be reached. — *I cannot attain
to it*].   This completes the first part of the Ps., between which
and the second part an earlier Ps. was inserted by a later editor.

Str. IV. Two syn. couplets. — **13**. *Verily*], asseverative particle,
and not causal as EV^s. — *Thou didst beget my reins*], implying
a paternal conception of creation, as Gn. 14^{19. 22} Dt. 32^6 Pr. 8^{22},
weakened by JPSV. into " formed," and still further by EV^s. into
" possessed " after 𝕲, 𝔙.   The " reins " represent the inward man,
cf. Ps. 7^10 16^7 26^2. — *Thou screenedst me*], protecting me from all
harm, *in my mother's womb*, after I was begotten ; so " covered
me " EV^s.   This is the most natural interpretation, in accordance
with 22^{10-11}, and with the usual meaning of the Heb. word, of which
𝕲, 𝔙, give probably only a paraphrase.   JPSV., " weave me," as
a mode of creation, a common rendering among modern scholars,
gives a meaning to the Heb. word unknown elsewhere ; and while
it gives a good conception of the mode of creation, has really no
proper support in OT. — **14**. A glossator renews the wonder

expressed already in v.[6], *I thank Thee for (all) Thine awe-inspiring works; Thou art wonderful: wonderful are Thy works*] ; a heaping up of terms of admiration of the creation of man and the providential care over him. This is the most probable interpretation of this difficult v., although it is given a more prosaic form in 뀼, followed by EV[s]. : "for I am fearfully and wonderfully made : marvellous are Thy works." The last clause in 뀼, 𝔍, followed by EV[s]. is : "my soul knoweth right well." This is not so probable as "Thou knowest right well my soul"; which is suited to the entire course of thought of the Ps., which emphasizes divine knowledge and not human. — 15. *My frame was not hid from Thee*], the frame as constituted of bone, in its earliest formation in the mother's womb. — *Which Thou didst make in a secret place*]. It was not hidden from God, though in the hidden place of the womb it might well be ; because He indeed had made it. This rendering of 𝔊, and most other Vrss. is more probable than that required by 뀼 followed by AV., RV., JPSV., "when I was made," or "though I be made" PBV. — An original marginal note, which eventually crept into the text, has given untold difficulty to Vrss. and interpreters. It doubtless was an expression of confidence in the resurrection of the body suggested by its original formation : *I certainly shall rise from the underworld*], 𝔊, 𝔙, interpret the Heb. word as a noun, "my substance" ‖ "my frame"; which then involves either the conception of the creation of the substance of the human body in Sheol, the abode of the dead, beneath the earth, with the suggestion of preëxistence, a thought elsewhere unknown to the OT. and improbable in itself; or else the conception that the womb is the underworld, which has no usage to justify it, even if we regard the conception as virtually a metaphor. 뀼 by dittography gives a vb. with the meaning "I embroidered," "wove together of various colors," which gives an interesting conception of the mode of creation, but one which is not exactly represented in AV., RV., "curiously wrought," still less in the more general "fashioned" PBV., "wrought" JPSV.; and which in any case does not escape the difficulties attached to the use of the term "underworld."

Str. V. Two synth. couplets. — 16. *My lot*], the word suggested by 𝔖 and suited to the context. This is more probable

2 K

than the a.λ. " embryo," " unformed substance," though sustained by other Vrss. — *Thine eyes did see*], the entire lot in life assigned to man was foreseen by the eyes of God. — *And on Thy book was it all*]. It was all registered and so predetermined before the birth of man. ⅁, 𝔍, 𝔘, have only "all," which refers to the antecedent "lot" or "fortune" in life. But 𝔚 interprets by a pl. sf. "all of them," interpreting the "embryo" in its constituent elements. — *Days*], of human life, syn. with the fortune or lot in life. — *were inscribed*], in the book, as that was. The pl. of the vb., as well as the measure, requires "days" as the subj. — *pre-ordained*], literally "formed," "constituted," in accordance with the usage of the vb., which is appropriate to all divine originations. — *When there was not one of them*], before a single one of these days of human life took its place in its temporal order.

Str. VI. Syn. and synth. couplets. — **23.** *Search me* ‖ *Try me*], renewing the statement of fact of v.[1], in the form of imv. — *and know*], repeated in each line for emphasis. — *my mind* ‖ *my thoughts*], the inner man, in addition to the outer man of Str. I. — **24.** *And see if there be any wickedness in me*], enlarged by a glossator against the measure by the insertion of "way" from the following line. The thought is, that God might see wickedness of which the poet himself was unconscious, cf. 19[13 sq.]. — *And lead me in the way everlasting*], the way which knows no end, as ⅁, 𝔘, 𝔍, cf. 1[6] 25[4-5]; not "the way leading to everlasting life," which, while true enough as a deduction from the statement, is not in accord with OT. usage of these terms; nor "the way of old," as Ols. after ℭ, cf. Je. 6[16] 18[15], which is not suited to the context.

PSALM CXXXIX. *C.*

Str. I. Two syn. couplets in antithesis. — **17.** *O how precious are Thy friends*], so all Vrss.; but EV. interpret the Heb. word here as in v.[2] in the sense of the divine "thoughts," without justi-fication in OT. — *How numerous the poor among them*], so 𝔍, ⊙, which is more probable and better suited to the context than "their chiefs" of ⅁, 𝔘, or "their sum" of EV[s]. The poor are such as have become poor through the wickedness of the enemies of v.[19]. — **18.** Is in the first line a gloss of expansion: *Would I count them? they are more in number than the sand;* in the second line an expression of faith in the resurrection : *Have I wakened*, from the sleep of death, *I am still with Thee*, cf. v.^{15c} 73²⁴⁻²⁵. — **19-20**. *O that Thou wouldst kill the wicked*], an imprecation on the wicked enemies of the poor friends of God. — *Those who speak with wicked intent*], slanderous enemies, those who seek to injure by falsehood and misrepresentation, as frequently in ψ. — An ancient glossator has, by the insertion of an interpretative sf., against the usage of the word, introduced grave difficulty into the passage, which is then variously rendered by other Vrss. — An earlier glossator added to v.¹⁹ an imprecation in the form of a wish : *Ye men of blood depart from me*, and to v.²⁰ a line : *who take Thy name in vain*, which interprets the speech of the previous line as blasphemy in violation of the Third Word, Ex. 20⁷ ; and concludes with an emphatic restatement of the subject : *even Thine adversaries ;* so Aq. Σ, 𝔍, 𝔗, followed by EV^s. But 𝔊, 𝔘, 𝔖, following the most natural interpretation of the text given in 𝔥, render : " in vain they take Thy cities," which, however, is so difficult in the present context, that modern scholars make various emendations, or else regard the text as hopelessly corrupt.

Str. II. Two syn. couplets. — **21**. *Do not I hate them ? ‖ loathe them ?*], implying a positive answer. The temper of the Maccabean wars is unmistakable in this Str. — *that hate Thee ‖ rise up against Thee*], identifying the enemies of the Jews with the enemies of their God. — **22**. *I hate them with the perfection of hatred*], with such a degree of hatred, with such an intensity, that no higher degree can be thought of. — *They are enemies to me*], my personal enemies.

CXXXIX. B.

1. הֲחָרַבֵנִי] elsw. ψ, 44²²; Je. 17¹⁰ +. — [וַחֲדָעֵ׳] ו consec. result: 𝔊, 𝔍, sf. וַתֵּדָעֵנִי, which has two beats and belongs to l.². — אחד was used at the end of each l., a relic of which is the אחד of v.², which makes l.³ too long. — **2.** [בַּנְתָּה] fully written pf. 2 m. sg. בִּין. — [דְעִי׳] 𝔊^{B. א} πάντας τοὺς διαλογισμούς μου כָל רֵעַ׳, more prob. and better measure than ל of late style for acc., but 𝔊^{א. c. a. A. R. T} have not πάντες. † [דֵעַ] n.[m.] *purpose, aim*, BDB., elsw. v.¹⁷; cf. רֵעִית *longing, striving*, Ec. 1^{14 (+ 6 t. Ec.)}; in Aram. *thoughts, will ;* but this does not suit the context. 𝔍 *malum meum* רָעִי improb. Rd. רֵעִי *my friends*, as 𝔊, 𝔘, 𝔍, in v.¹⁷. — [מרחוק] as 38¹², cf. 138⁶. — **3.** [ארחי] *my path* (of life), cf. 142⁴. — [וְרִבְעִי] Qal inf. † רבע Aram. for רבץ; elsw. Lv. 18²³ 20¹⁶, Hiph. Lv. 19¹⁹, but these in another sense. 𝔊 σχοῖνον, 𝔘 *funiculum* =

‡ רֵבֶץ n.[m.] *resting place*, the *mat* or *spread*, cf. Pr. 24¹⁵. — זֵרִיתָ] Pi. pf.
‡ זרה Piel (1) *scatter, disperse*, 44¹² 106²⁷, not suited to context and so (2) *win-
now, sift*, BDB., Dr., a mng. not elsw. in Pi. and improb. ⅏ ἐξίχνίασας, 𝔙
investigasti, 𝔍 *eventilasti*, Bu., take it as possible Aram. זור = סור *turn aside to
visit*. This best suits context. — הִסְכַּנְתָּה] Hiph. pf. fully written 2 m. ‡ [סכ]
vb. Qal *be of use* or *service* Is. 22¹⁵ 1 K. 1²˙⁴, (2) *benefit* Jb. 15³ (+ 4 t. Jb.).
† Hiph. *be used, wont, accustomed to do* a thing, Nu. 22³⁰˙³⁰ (J) Jb. 22²¹ and
here. ⅏ πρόϊδες, 𝔍 *intellexisti*. — **4.** מִלָּה] ⅏ λόγος ἄδικος, Aram. word, cf.
עַל לְשׁוֹנִי 2 S. 23²; elsw. Ps. *19*⁵ Pr. 23⁹ Jb. (34 t.). Prob. the word is a gl., and
יהוה belongs in this l. It makes the next l. too long.—**5.** אחור וקדם]. ⅏ attaches
to ירעת τὰ ἔσχατα καὶ τὰ ἀρχαῖα. — צַרְתָּנִי] ⅏, Σ, 𝔖, 𝔍, from צור = יצר *fashion;*
but BDB., Dr., ‡ צור *confine, besiege, enclose, shut up*. Neither of these suited
to context : rd. נצרתני *watch.* — יָדֶךָ] sf. 2 sg. full form. — **6.** פְּלִיאָה Qr. פְּלִיאָה;
Kt. פְּלִאָיה ‡ [פלאי] adj. *wonderful, incomprehensible* ; elsw. only Ju. 13¹⁸ (of
name of theophanic angel). The ה belongs to דעה as ⅏.

CXXXIX. *A.*

7. אֶבְרַח] Qal impf. ‡ ברח vb. *flee*, c. מִן; elsw. in ψ only titles 3¹ 57¹. —
8. אֶסַּק] = אֶסְלַק Qal impf. סלק Aram., a.λ. *ascend;* prob. late gl., for the
cohort. form could hardly be missing in the first l. when it appears in the
second. — אַצִּיעָה] Hiph., † יצע only Hiph. *spread out* (as bed), elsw. only Is.
58⁵, Hoph. Is. 14¹¹ Est. 4³. ⅏ καταβῶ, so 𝔖 ; 𝔍 *jacuero*, Σ, Quinta, στρώσω.
These vbs. are interp. The ll. were both without vbs., but with assonance in
שאול.—אם] acc. direction ⅏ εἰς τὸν ᾅδην; acc. vb. Bä., Dr. — **9.** כַּנְפֵי שָׁחַר]
phr. a.λ., cf. wings of wind 18¹¹ 104³, of sun of righteousness Mal. 3²⁰; כנפי
also extremities of the earth and so of dawn ; but ⅏ more prob., τὰς πτέρυγάς
μου κατ᾽ ὀρθόν, כַּנְפֵי.— אֶשָּׂא] Qal impf. נשׂא, cf. נ׳ כנפים lift up *wings* to fly Ez.
10¹⁶˙¹⁹ 11²², נ׳ רגלים *lift up feet* to walk Gn. 29¹. — † בְּאַחֲרִית יב] only here of
place, elsw. of time or persons ; *after part, end ;* cf. הים האחרון *the hinder sea,*
the Western, *e.g.* Mediterranean Dt. 11²⁴ + ; cf. Gn. 49¹ for the phr. באחרית הימים
in the end of days. — **10.** יַנְחֵנִי] ⅏ ὁδηγήσει με, √נהה not suited to ‖ ; rd.
נוח√ ,הנחני *rest*, sq. acc. יד Ex. 17¹¹ (E). — וְתֹאחֲזֵנִי] Qal impf. ı coörd. Line
too short ; prefix יָם, repeated as אנה v.⁷. — **11.** וָאֹמַר] ı consec. impf., protasis
conditional clause, *have I said.* — יְשׁוּפֵנִי] Qal impf. † שׁוף, vb. as Gn. 3¹⁵ Jb.
9¹⁷, all passages dub. Ew., Bä., Dr., Du., יְשֹׁרֵנִי שׁכך√ for סבך *cover* (5¹²), after
Σ, 𝔍. ⅏ καταπατήσει με. Rd. וְנִשְׁפִּי *my morning twilight* as Jb. 7¹, cf. Ps.
119¹⁴⁷.— בַּעֲדֵנִי] a.λ. for בַּעֲדֵי, assimilated to previous vb. ⅏ ἐν τῇ τρυφῇ μου
= בַּעֲדְנִי.— **12.** ⅏B. a. b. mg. inf. א. R. T have v.¹²ab and ⅏A v.¹²a, but ⅏B has only
חשיכה כאורה, which is regarded by Bä., Du., as gl. of interp. It makes the
Str. too long. הַחֲשֵׁיכָה a.λ. variant of הַחֹשֶׁךְ n.f. (*18¹²*). † אוֹרָה n.f. *light*, elsw.
Est. 8¹⁶, light of joy; Is. 26¹⁹ pl. light of life.

CXXXIX. *B.*

13. כִּי אתה]. כי can hardly be causal; it is rather asseverative. It is regarded
by Hi., We., Du., as transposed from after v.¹⁴ᵇ. But it is more likely that

v.¹⁴ is a gl. — [כליתי] *my kidneys, reins,* as seat of emotions 7¹⁰ 16⁷ 26² 73²¹.
𝕲 inserts κύριος, but it makes l. too long. — [וְסֻכְּ‍־] impf. Qal † סכך vb. a.λ.
weave together, BDB., Dr., Bä., cf. Jb. 10¹¹ הסככני; but ס_ך elsw. = *screen,*
cover; so prob. 𝕲 ἀντελάβου μου ; 𝖄 *suscepisti me,* so 𝕾. — 14. [עַל כִּי =] עַל אשר;
Du. כֹּר ‍‍.‍‍ע.ַר — [נוֹראִי] adverbial ptc. Niph. ירא as 65⁶; *v.* 45⁵. — [וְפְלִיתִי] Niph.
pf. פלה Niph. *be separate, distinguished,* as Ex. 33¹⁶ (J). But context urges
פלא (9²) *be extraordinary, wonderful,* cf. for נפלא Ps. 118²³ 119¹⁸. Vrss. 2
pers. *Thou art wonderful,* so Hu., Now., Bä., We. — [וכלאים] Niph. ptc. as adj.
a.λ.; *v.* 9². — [וְנַפְשִׁי יֹדָעַת] so 𝖏. — 15. [איבר]. All Vrss. refer to עצמי; so Bä.; most
moderns interpret as rel. time. — [עֻשֵּׂיתִי] Pu. pf. 1 sg. ; 𝕲 ὃ ἐποίησας עָשִׂיתָ, so 𝕾, Θ,
𝖄. — [בַּחֲחֶר‍] (8¹²) *in a secret place.* — [רֻקַמְתִּי] Pu. pf. a.λ. ‡ רקם ; *woven, embroi-*
dered of various colours. Qal freq. in ptc. *variegator, weaver in colours* Ex. 26³⁶
+ 7 t. (P). Aq, Σ, ἐποικίλθην, 𝖏 *imaginatus sum.* 𝕲 ἡ ὑπόστασίς μου = חָכְיִי.
ר is dittog.; rd. הקיצתי ‖ חמתי *v.*¹⁸. — [בחחתיות ארץ] *underworld* (63¹⁰), as Is. 44²³
Ez. 26²⁾ 32¹⁸·²¹; inappropriate here. The whole l. is a gl. as v.¹⁸ᵇ, expressing
confidence in a resurrection. — 16. [גָּלְמִי] a.λ. *embryo,* BDB. = N.H. גּוֹלֶם. Σ
ἀμόρφωτον, 𝖏 *informem,* 𝕲 ἀκατέργαστόν, 𝖄 *imperfectum.* But 𝕾 suggests גרלי,
which is prob. the correct reading. — [עַל ספרך] *on Thy book of record.* — [יְכְָלֹם]
requires pl. antecedent. 𝕲, 𝖏, have only כֹּר and are doubtless correct. The
measure requires that יכהבו should be construed with יָמִים. — [יְצָּרוּ] Pu. a.λ.
days that were *preordained.* — [ולא אחד] circumstantial clause.

CXXXIX. C.

17. [וליִ] is an interp. gl. — [יקרו] *be precious,* 𝕲, 𝖄, cf. 49⁹; but Ew., Hi.,
Hu., Bä., Du., Aram. יקר *hard, difficult,* or *weighty* (not elsw. Bibl. Heb.). —
[רֵעֶיךָ] 𝕲, 𝖄, 𝖏, οἱ φίλοι σου. — [אֵל] divine name. — [מַה עָצְמוּ] *how numerous,*
strong, mighty in number, as 38²⁰ 40⁶·¹³ 69⁵. — [ראשׁיהם] 𝕲 aἱ ἀρχαὶ αὐτῶν,
𝖄 *principatus eorum;* but 𝖏 *pauperes eorum,* so Θ οἱ πένητες αὐτῶν, רשׁיהם
from רָשׁ. — 18. [הקיצתי] fig. Je. 15⁸ Gn. 22¹⁷ (J) 32¹⁸ (E). — [אֶחוּר ירבוּן] is
usually taken as a waking from the sleep of death, Is. 26¹⁹ Jb. 14¹² so Σ, T.
It is then a gl. — 19. [תּקטֹל] † קטר Aram.; elsw. only Jb. 13¹⁵ 24¹⁴. — [אֵל הַ]
rare in ψ (*v.* Intr. p. lxxi.); gl. — [אנשׁי דמים] 26⁹ 55²⁴ 59³ Pr. 29¹⁰. — [סורו]
imv. incongruous. Either l. is a gl. (cf. 6⁹), or we must rd. יסורו as 𝕾, 𝕿.
In any case בני makes the l. too long. — 20. [יְאמְרוּ] contr. of יאמְרוּךָ; but אמר
is not used with sf. elsw., and it is doubtless a gl. 𝕲 only ἔρεις, 𝖄 *dicitis;*
Aq. ἀντιλέξουσί σοι, 𝖏 *contradicent tibi,* Σ ἀντελάλησάν σοι interpret אמר and do
not imply מרה, Hiph., *shew disobedience,* Dr. *defy* (78¹⁷·⁴⁰·⁵⁶ 106⁷·³³·⁴³ 107¹¹), as
Houb., Hu., Dr. Du., who rd. מריוּך. — [יאמרוּ] *wickedness* in intention (10²) as 𝖏
scelerate; but 𝕲 ¹·ᴺ εἰς διαλογισμόν, 𝕲 ²·ᶜ·ᵃ·ᵀ διαλογισμούς, 𝕲ᴿ ἐν διαλογισμῷ,
𝖄 *in cogitatione.* — [שׁוא ליו] ‍‍‍ refer to Third Word, Ex. 20⁷. Bö., Ol., Kau., rd.
נשׂאו. — [עריך] *cities,* 𝕲 πόλεις, so 𝖄, 𝕾, gives no good sense ; rd. צריך as Aq.
Σ, 𝖏, 𝕿. So De., Eck. Modern scholars suggest various emendations ; Hu.,
Now., שׂ‍‍־ר ‍‍, but admit that there is no usage to justify this construction ; Hi. עֲרֶיךָ;
Bö., Ols., Bruston, Gr., Bi., Du., Minocchi., שַׂמֶךָ. — 21. [יהוה] gl. — [וּבתקוּמְמֶיךָ]

Du. ‫מתקוממיך‬.— ‫אֶרְקִמָט]‬ Hithp. ‫קוט‬ *feel a loathing*, as 119[158], cf. 95[10].—
22. † ‫הִכְלִית]‬ n.f. *completeness*, late word; elsw. *end* Ne. 3[21] Jb. 11[7] 26[10] 28[3].

CXXXIX. *B.*

23. ‫לבבי]‬ full form for euphony. — ‫בחנוי ודע]‬ *test, try*, and *know*. — ‫[שרעפי‬
thoughts, elsw. Ps. 94[19]. — **24.** ‫דרך עצב]‬. 𝔊[B. א] εἰ ἴδες ἀνομίας; εἶδες,
𝔊[B. a. b. א.* A] err. for ὁδός 𝔊[c. c. a. R. T.] ‫דרך‬ is a gl. † ‫עֹצֶב‬ n.[m.] *pain, hurt,*
sorrow, as 1 Ch. 4[9] Is. 14[3].

PSALM CXL., 3 STR. 6[4].

Ps. 140 is a prayer for rescue from violent and crafty enemies
(v.[2-4]) ; **for preservation from the snares they have laid** (v.[5-6]) ;
with expression of confidence in Yahweh and a final plea that the
desires of the wicked may not be accomplished (v.[7-9]). **Subsequent**
additions were: (1) A Maccabean imprecation (v.[10-12]). **(2) A**
liturgical gloss expresses confidence in Yahweh (v.[13-14]).

> R ESCUE me, Yahweh, from evil men,
> From men of violent deeds preserve me;
> Who have devised evil things in their mind,
> All the day stir up wars;
> Who have sharpened their tongue like a serpent,
> Who have the poison of a viper under their lips.
> K EEP me, Yahweh, from the hands of the wicked,
> From men of violent deeds preserve me;
> Who have devised to trip up my feet:
> From the proud who have hid traps for me,
> And cords have spread as a net (for me),
> At the side of the track have set snares.
> I SAY unto Yahweh: " My God art Thou.
> O give ear, Yahweh, to the voice of my supplications.
> Yahweh, my sovereign Lord, my stronghold, my salvation,
> Who hast screened my head in the day of weapons.
> Do not promote, Yahweh, any of the desires of the wicked:
> They have plotted ; grant not that they lift up the head."

Ps. 140 was in 𝔇 ; and 𝔐, and later in 𝔇ℜ (*v.* Intr., §§ 27, 31, 33). There
is no reason to doubt these statements, so far as v.[2-9] is concerned. But they
are untenable for v.[10-14]. Indeed, the former only was the original Ps., of
three tetrameter hexastichs, symmetrical and poetical. Its language and conceptions are those of 𝔇 ; cf. ‫הרצוי‬ v.[2] with 18[2)] 34[8] ; ‫איש חמכים‬ v.[2] with 18[49];
‫הנצרני‬ v.[2. 5] with 12[8] 32[7] 64[2] ; ‫יגורו‬ v.[3] with 56[7] 59[4] ; v.[4] with 58[5] or 64[4] ;
‫יהוה‬ v.[5] with 35[5] 36[13] 56[14] ; ‫כעמי‬ v.[5] with 57[7] 58[11] ; ‫רוש‬ and ‫כעץ‬ v.[6] with 9[16]
31[5] 35[7. 8] 64[6] ; ‫מעגל‬ v.[6] with 17[5] 23[3] 65[12] ; ‫מקשים‬ v.[6] with 18[6] 64[6] 69[23] ;

קול תחנוני v.⁷ with 28². ⁶ 31²³ 86⁶ ; עז ישועה v.⁸ with 28⁸. The only difficulties are these : יהוה אדני v.⁸, but אדני is to be interpreted, not as a divine name, but in the original sense of "my sovereign lord"; ביום נשק v.⁸, phr. a.λ., but cf. Jb. 39²¹ ; נאזרו v.⁹ a.λ. Aramaism, was not in 𝕲 which rd. יזאמרו, which is not uncommon in early Heb. Rd. יעפ. זממו v.⁹ noun with sf. a.λ., not in 𝕲 which rd. יזמו vb. Gn. 11⁶ Dt. 19¹⁹ Je. 4²⁸ + ; אל הפק v.⁹, cf. 144¹³, though in sense of Aramaic נבא is yet in Is. 58¹⁰. The Ps. was composed in the troublous times prior to Nehemiah's reforms. The remainder of the Ps. is composed of glosses : v.¹⁰⁻¹² a Maccabean imprecation. בהמרות v.¹¹, מדחפת v.¹² a.λ., terms for the Pit in Sheol. V.¹³⁻¹⁴ was a still later gloss of confidence in Yahweh, necessary for the liturgical use of the Ps.

Str. I. A syn. couplet and a syn. tetrastich. — **2.** *Rescue me, Yahweh ‖ preserve me*], importunate plea of Israel when in peril, cf. 6⁵ 12⁸ 18²⁰ 32⁷ 34⁸. — *from evil men ‖ men of violent deeds*], cf. 18⁴⁹; bitter enemies who are evil in their character, and, so far as practicable, commit deeds of violence. These are then described in four syn. lines. — **3.** *devised evil things in their mind*], conceived and planned evil. — *All the day stir up wars*], strive to stir up the Persian government to make war upon the feeble community in Jerusalem ; or to rally the neighbouring nations against them. — **4.** *Who have sharpened their tongue like a serpent ‖ Who have the poison of a viper under their lips*]. They strive to accomplish their purpose by craft, with the subtlety and venom of a serpent, making misrepresentations and slanders of every kind against the people of God, cf. 52⁴ 55²² 57⁵ 58⁵ 64⁴ Rom. 3¹³.

Str. II. Syn. to the previous Str. and of the same structure. — **5–6.** V.⁵ a variation only of v.², the second line being identical, the first varying in the use of *Keep me* and *from the hands of the wicked ‖ the proud.* — Their wickedness is also described in four syn. lines : *Who have devised*], v.³ᵃ, only here more specifically. — *to trip up my feet ‖ hid traps for me ‖ cords have spread as a net ‖ At the side of the track have set snares*], using, instead of the image of the venomous, crafty serpent, that of the hunter in his various efforts to ensnare and capture animals, cf. 9¹⁶ 31⁵ 35⁷ ⁸ 64⁶ 141⁹ 142⁴ Mt. 22¹⁵.

Str. III. Two synth. and one syn. couplets. — **7–8.** *I say unto Yahweh*], cf. 16² 31¹⁵, a profession of faith and confidence. — *My God art Thou*], the personal God of Israel His people, belonging to them as they to Him in a unique relation. — ‖ *my sovereign lord*], the sovereign lord of Israel. — *O give ear to the voice of my supplications*], phr. 28². ⁶ 31²³ 86⁶ 130². — *my stronghold, my salvation*], the stronghold or refuge in which salvation is found, cf. 28⁸. — *Who hast screened my head in the day of weapons*]. In the battles in which Israel had been engaged in her national history, Yahweh had been as a helmet, protecting the head from weapons, cf. 60⁹. — **9**. *Do not promote* ‖ *grant not*], the final pleading. — *any of the desires of the wicked*], to be accomplished; those expressed in the devisings of v.³·⁵. — *They have plotted*], so 𝔊, 𝔘, 𝔖; to be preferred to the noun " their plot " or " wicked device " of 𝔐, followed by EVˢ. — *that they lift up the head*], by success, in accordance with their pride, cf. v.⁵ᵈ. The error of an early copyist, attaching ראש to the next line, injures the measure of both and makes the interpretation difficult. The Vrss. vary. The original Ps. ends here; but later glossators enlarge it.

The first of these gls., 10–12, is Maccabean in character, and is an imprecation on the enemies, of an entirely different temper and language from that of the original Ps.

As for those round about me, with the trouble of their own lips may He overwhelm them.
May He rain coals of fire upon them.
May He make them fall into the Pit of deep waters, that they may rise no more.
Let not the men of tongue be established in the land.
Let evil hunt the men of violence to the Pit of utter banishment.

This is a syn. pentastich. — **10**. *As for those round about me*], the enemies of the Ps. — *with the trouble of their own lips*], that which they in their speech would bring upon the people of God. — *may He overwhelm them*], taking God as the subj. of this and the following vbs., and not " the trouble " as EVˢ. — **11**. *May He rain coals of fire upon them*], as most recent scholars in accordance with usage, cf. 11⁶; instead of the expression of 𝔐, though favoured by Vrss., which is peculiar and which is rendered in EVˢ. " fall " with " coals " as subj. : " Let them be cast into the fire," EVˢ., is based on 𝔐, which interprets by the insertion of a preposition. The author is thinking of divine retribution through a theophanic storm coming upon the enemies; possibly such as that upon Sodom, but more probably such as decided the battles of Beth-horon and the Kishon, Jos. 10[11 sq.] Ju.[5], cf. also Ps. 18[7-16]. — *May He make them fall into the Pit of deep waters*]. This is the Pit in Sheol, whither the enemies of Yahweh are cast, cf. Is. 14[15 sq.] Pss. 9[18] 88[11 sq.] Ez. 26[20] 32[17-30]. — *that they may rise no more*], have no resurrection, as Is. 26[14]. — **12.** *Let not the men of tongue*], graphic phr. for the venomous slanderers of v.[4]. — *be established in the land*], gain the supremacy, and so become firmly fixed in the land of Yahweh in place of His people. — *Let evil hunt the men of violence*]. Evil is personified as a hunter, hunting those who hunted the people of God, cf. v.[6]. — *to the Pit of utter banishment*], a syn. term to the Pit of deep waters of v.[11], the Pit of Sheol, as a place whither there is the utter, complete, and final driving, or thrusting forth of the wicked. This is the conception of the Vrss., well paraphrased by 𝔗: "the angel of death shall drive him down to hell." The interpretation of the form as a vb. "to overthrow him," EV[s]., cannot be sustained.

A liturgical gloss was finally added, v.[13-14], to make the Ps. more appropriate for public worship. — **13.** *I know*], affirmation of confidence in God as v.[7]. — *that Thou maintainest the cause of the afflicted, the right of the poor*], thinking of Israel, and not of individuals, as 9[5]. — **14.** *Surely the righteous will give thanks to Thy name*], ritual worship in the temple, cf. 106[47] 122[4]. — *the upright will dwell in Thy presence*], have a permanent right of entrance into the temple as the guests of Yahweh, cf. 11[7] 15[1] 23[6] 84[5].

2. רִגְרֵי] = v.[5]. L. is defective; substitute ובני for sf. — **3.** [כל־יום rd. for measure כר־היום, 𝔊 ὅλην τὴν ἡμέραν, as Kenn., Street, Che.; two beats are necessary. — [יגורו מלחמות] Qal impf. גור (II.) *stir up strife, quarrel,* cf. 56[7] 59[4] 94[21], but all dub. Ols., Hu., Che., Dr. rd. here יגרו √גרה *stir up wars,* 𝔊 παρετάσσοντο πολέμους. — **4.** [שננו לשונם] phr. 64[4]. — † [שוב] a.λ., *asp, viper,* so 𝔊, 𝔙, 𝔍; dub. cf. עכביש *spider.* — **5.** [ירחות] Qal inf. cstr. הה · *push, thrust*; 𝔊 ὑποσκελίσαι, 𝔍 *subplantare,* cf. 35[5] רחה, Pu. 36[13], also [רה] n. 56[14] = 116[8]; Che. *trip up my feet.* — **6.** [ופחים] = 142[1]; but pl. פחים is needed for measure; 𝔊 παγίδα μοι. — [אִיש] not subj., but in apposition with subj. which is in relative clause as other ll. — [חבלי מעגל] 𝔊 τοῖς ποσίν μου ἐχόμενα τρίβου. — שרוגלי. The ל has come down from previous l., where it is needed for measure. It is superfluous here. — **8.** [יהוה ארני] both needed for measure. — [סכותה] phr. a.λ.; so 𝔊, but cf. מעז ישועות 28[8]; rd. prob. עזי. — [עד ישועתי

fully written 2 m. sg. pf. סְכַ Qal *screen, cover*, usually c. עַל of thing covered;
c. לְ elsw. La. 3⁴⁴. — נֶשֶׁק בְּיוֹם] *in the day of equipment, battle;* phr. a.λ., cf.
Jb. 39²¹ ‡ נֶשֶׁק n.(m.) elsw. 1 K. 10²⁵ Ez. 39⁹+. — **9.** אַוֵּי] a.λ., cstr. pl.
[אַוֵּי] BDB.; so Aq., 𝔍 *desideria impiis*, 𝔊 ἀπὸ τῆς ἐπιθυμίας μου ἁμαρτωλῷ;
rd. מַאֲוֵי. — זְמָם] (זְוֹמִ) n.m. a.λ., *plan, device* (in bad sense); but dub.;
𝔊 διελογίσαντο κατ' ἐμοῦ, Σ ἐβουλεύσαντο לִי, זָמְמוּ, cf. 37¹². — אַל־תָּרֵק]. † פוק
vb. only Hiph.: (1) *produce, furnish,* Is. 58¹⁰ Ps. 144¹³; (2) *elicit, obtain,*
Pr. 3¹³ 8³⁵ 12² 18²²; (3) *promote,* so here. Bu., cf. Aram. פנק *grant.* 𝔊 ἐγκα-
ταλίπῃς με, Ki. אַל הוֹצִיא, Ra. אַל הַבְּרִיחַ. — וְיֻרְמוּ] transposed to next l., Du.,
Dr., al.; but needed here for measure and to complete the Str. — **10.** רֹאשׁ]
the obj. of יְרֹמוּ; either *head,* 𝔊, Aq., Θ, 𝔖, 𝔗, or *poison,* Σ, 𝔍. — מְסִבַּי] cf.
מְסִבּוֹת Jb. 37¹² and also 1 K. 6²⁹. 𝔊 τοῦ κυκλώματος αὐτῶν, 𝔍 *convivarum
eorum;* Hiph. ptc. Ginsb., cf. Je. 21⁴. Aq. καταστρεφόντων με, Σ τῶν κυκλούν-
των με, *those encompassing me,* so Dr. — יְכַסֵּימוֹ] Qr. is to be preferred, with
God as subj. 𝔊 καλύψει αὐτούς (3ᵉ¹). — **11.** יִמּוֹטוּ] Kt. Hiph. form elsw. 55⁴
let drop; Qr. Niph. *be shaken, overthrown,* Dr. *dislodged;* but Hu., Dys., Gr.,
Bi., Bä., Du. rd. יָמִיר. 𝔊 πεσοῦνται favours 𝔥. For ordinary usage *v.* 10⁶.
— בְּאֵשׁ] 𝔊^{B. ℵ}, 𝔍 omit ב, but 𝔊^{℃ e. a A. R. T} ἐν πυρί; it is interpretive. —
בְּמַהֲמֹרוֹת] a.λ. (√ המר) BDB. *watery pit,* Dr. *waterfloods;* Gr. מכמרות *nets,*
√ מכר, as Is. 51²⁰, but that is a.λ. and dub. also. 𝔊 has ἐν ταλαιπωρίαις,
𝔍 *in foveas,* so Σ, 𝔗. Du. thinks it is *Hölle.* — **12.** יְרֵדֵמוּ] ‡ צוד vb. *hunt,* as
La. 3⁵² Mi. 7² Je. 16¹⁵. 𝔊 has θηρεύσει without sf., which is interpret. of 𝔥.
— לְמַדְחֵפֹת] a.λ., *v.* [† דחף] vb. Qal *drive, hasten,* Est. 3¹⁵ 8¹⁴; Niph. Est. 6¹²
2 Ch. 26²⁰. Che., Dr., BDB., "*thrust upon thrust,*" so Bä., Du., dub. 𝔊 εἰς
καταφθοράν, 𝔍 *in interitu;* prob. the ב is local, the place of utter thrusting
out. — **13.** יָדַעְתִּי] Qr. 1 sq., 𝔊 ἔγνων; Kt. 2 sg. Du. changes to יָדְעוּ. — דִּין עָנִי]
with עָשָׂה *maintain the cause of, v.* 9⁵. — **14.** יֹדוּ לִשְׁמֶךָ] of ritual worship, as
106⁴⁷ 122⁴.

PSALM CXLI., 4 STR. 4⁴.

Ps. 141 is a prayer at the evening sacrifice (v.¹⁻²), **that Yahweh
would guard the mouth, and prevent evil thoughts and wicked
deeds** (v.³⁻⁴ᵃᵇ), renouncing **social intercourse with evil doers**
(v.⁴ᶜᵈ· ⁵ᵇᶜ), and begging **salvation from their snares** (v.⁶ᵇ· ⁸· ⁹ᵃ).
There are Maccabean glosses of imprecation upon enemies (v.⁶ᵃ· ⁷),
and other glosses, of qualification (v.⁵ᵃ), of expansion (v.⁹ᵇ), and of
harmonistic conclusion (v.¹⁰).

> YAHWEH, on Thee I call: O make haste to me.
>   O give ear to my voice, while I call to Thee.
>   My prayer is prepared at the Incense before Thee,
>   The lifting up of my hands at the evening Minchah.

O SET a guard, Yahweh, to my mouth:
   O keep ('Elyon) the door about my lips.
   Incline not my mind to an evil thing,
   To practise practices of wickedness.
A S for men who are workers of trouble,
   I will not eat of their dainties.
   The oil of the wicked, let it not grease my head.
   While I live, my prayer will be against their wickedness.
H EAR my words; for it will be lovely:
   For mine eyes are unto Thee, Yahweh.
   In Thee I seek refuge; do not pour out my life.
   Keep me from the power of the snare they have laid for me.

Ps. 141 was in 𝔻 and 𝕱𝕳, but not in any other of the major Psalters (v. Intr., §§ 27, 31). There is no reason to doubt this, as to the original Ps.; but like others, especially of this group, it has been greatly changed by glosses and assimilated to them. In its original form it was a simple and beautiful prayer of four tetrameter tetrastichs, v.[1-2. 3-4b. 4cd. 5bc. 6b. 8. 9a]. In the original there are rare terms and expressions: כפי תיצא v.[2] a.λ., but the phr. though original is quite simple and natural; ערב מוחה v.[2] as 2 K. 16[15] Ez. 9[4. 5] Dn. 9[21] implies the fully established sacrifice in the temple at evening prayer; שמרה v.[3] is a.λ. as pointed by MT. as a noun, but it is prob. a ptc. and without difficulty. על דל v. 3 is improbable, rd. עלי דלה as 𝔊, and the strangeness is removed; העולל עללות v.[4] phr. a.λ. but not late; איישים v.[4] elsw. Is. 53[8] Pr. 8[1]; אלחם v.[4] poetic as Dt. 32[24]; מנעמיהם v.[4] a.λ., but rd. במי נעמיהם, cf. Ps. 16[6. 11]; אל הגר v.[8], cf. Is. 53[12]. The Ps. belongs to the peaceful times of temple worship in the Persian period subsequent to Nehemiah. V.[6a. 7] are imprecations of the Maccabean times. V.[5a] came into the text from the margin. V.[9b] is a gloss of expansion. V.[10] is a late harmonistic conclusion.

Str. I. Two syn. couplets. — **1.** *Yahweh, on Thee I call ‖ while I call to Thee*]. The people are engaged in prayer. It is not a general statement " when " as EV[s]. — *O make haste to me*], give a speedy answer, cf. 22[20] 38[23] 40[14] 70[2. 6] 71[12]. ‖ *O give ear to my voice*], enlarged in 𝔊 into "voice of supplication," as 140[7], a true explanation but against the measure. — **2.** *My prayer ‖ The lifting up of my hands*], the gesture of invocation and supplication, cf. 28[2] 63[5] La. 3[41] 1 Tim. 2[8]. — *at the Incense ‖ the evening Minchah*], the time of the offering up of incense at the altar of incense in the temple, and of the grain offering on the altar of burnt offering in the court, at evening prayer according to the ritual of the temple worship Ex. 29[38-42] 2 K. 16[15] Ez. 9[4. 5] Dn. 9[21]. The people are actually engaged in prayer in the temple. It is not a comparison of prayer with incense and sacrifice as EV[s].

Str. II. A syn. and a synth. couplet. — **3**. *O set a guard ‖ O keep the door*], for safety from without, but also and here especially, against that which was within. — *to my mouth ‖ about my lips*], against the peril of evil speech. The congregation feel the need of protection from themselves from the evil that was within them, showing the high ethical sense of the late Persian period. — **4 ab.** *Incline not my mind*], going back of the mouth and lips into the mind, that controls and directs them. The mind needs the divine restraint from evil as well as the lips. Cf. the words of Jesus Mk. 7¹⁵⁻²³. — *to an evil thing ‖ To practise practices of wickedness*]. The wickedness of external practice originates in the mind and issues forth from the mouth and lips. The congregation pray to be restrained from all evil, internal and external.

Str. III. Synth. couplets. — **4 cd.** *As for men who are workers of trouble, I will not eat of their dainties*], partake of their hospitality in social meals, be their guests. These lines do not belong to the previous Str. as EVˢ. after 𝕳, but begin this Str. in an emphatic position. — **5**. *The oil of the wicked, let it not grease my head*], the oil with which honoured guests were anointed before the feast, cf. 23⁵. He will not accept such an honour from the wicked. This seems to be the most natural interpretation of a difficult passage, after 𝕲, 𝕵, 𝕾. But the gloss : *Let the righteous smite me in kindness, and let him reprove me*, made the whole difficult. It asserted that the blows given by a righteous man would be more acceptable than the hospitality however honourable of the wicked. And so EVˢ. interpret the oil after 𝕳 as " oil for the head," and make it a metaphor of the discipline ; but interpret the vb. as " break my head," PBV., AV., which is without justification ; " let not my head refuse it," RV., JPSV., which may be sustained, but is awkward in the context both in grammar and in sense. — *While I live*], as JPSV., cf. 104³³ 146², alone suited to the context. " Yea " PBV., " For yet " AV., " For even " RV., show the difficulty in the minds of the translators, and indicate that they did not see their way. — *my prayer will be against their wickedness*], as it had been in the previous Str. against wickedness of themselves, in mind, lip, or deed.

Str. IV. Two stairlike couplets. — **6**. *Hear my words*], a renewal of the prayer, continued in v.⁸· ⁹ᵇ. — *for it will be lovely*], so to do, as elsewhere other actions are, 133^1 135^3 147^1. — The insertion of an imprecatory gloss, which came into the text from the margin, partly before v.^{6a} and partly after v.^{7}, entirely changed the interpretation of it. The gloss was Maccabean in origin : *O that their governors had been thrown down by the sides of the crag*], cast over a precipice to their destruction, cf. 2 C. 25^{12} Lk. 4^{29}. These were doubtless the Syrian governors and oppressors. The pf. in an optative sense, as Hu., Gr., alone suits the situation ; rather than the statement of the fact as EV^s. — The result of their fall is then given : **7**. *As one splits open and bursts asunder on the ground*]. Falling down to the ground, the body bursts asunder, as did that of Judas Acts 1^{18}. This simple and natural explanation became confused, when this line was separated from its mate by v.^{6b} ; and that line was interpreted as referring to the wicked governors in the rendering : "And they shall hear my words, that they are lovely " ; that is, the people will hear the words predicting the downfall of those governors and only then appreciate their loveliness. But this thought is not at all natural to the context, and is a makeshift of interpretation. It moreover made the subsequent line difficult, and forced its connection with v.^{7b} rather than with v.^{6a}. 𝕾 and Lucian alone of Vrss. give the correct interpretation. — *O that their bones were scattered at the mouth of Sheol*], the bones of those governors, their bodies burst asunder and their bones scattered about at the entrance to the abode of the dead. But 𝕳 and most Vrss. as EV^s. interpret the bones as the bones of Israel, which would seem to imply that Israel was practically dead, as in Ez. 37^{1-14}, needing resurrection to national life. But that is certainly against the context, which implores deliverance from snares, and preservation of life. The limitation of the reference to the slaughtered among the people can hardly be justified in this Ps. But that interpretation forced the interpretation of v.^{7a} to the bones ; and accordingly, after 𝕳, EV^s. render : "like as one breaketh and heweth (wood) upon the earth " PBV., "as when one cutteth and cleaveth (wood) upon the earth " AV., thinking of the chips as a simile of the bones ; or more correctly : "as one plougheth and cleaveth the earth " RV., JPSV., after Aq., 𝚺, 𝔍, 𝕿, but it is then difficult to see a point of comparison with scattered bones. — **8**. *For mine eyes are unto Thee, Yahweh ‖ In thee I* *seek refuge*], cf. 25[15], the attitude of supplicatory prayer. — *do not pour out my life*], as Is. 53[12]. The people are in mortal peril from enemies, and supplicate Yahweh for the salvation of their life. — **9.** *Keep me from the power of the snare they have laid for me*]. These enemies are crafty and treacherous, cf. 140[6]. — The v. is enlarged by the gloss : *the snares of the workers of trouble*], referring back to v.[4c]. — The Ps. received a harmonistic conclusion in **10.** *Let the wicked fall into their own toils*], a usual imprecation of exact retribution, cf. 7[16. 17] 9[16. 17] 140[10]. — In antithesis : *I, on my part, shall rejoice, while I pass by*], so by an easy emendation of a difficult text, which varies in 𝔐 and 𝔊, and is variously interpreted in Vrss. The variation of EV[s]. : " and let me ever escape them " PBV., " whilst I withal escape " AV., " while I pass by safely " JPSV., " whilst I at the same time pass by " Dr. ; show sufficiently their perplexity.

1. *חוּשָׁה לי*] = 70[6](?); elsw. *לעזרתי* 22[20] 38[23] 40[14] 70[2] 71[12] (Qr.), so 𝔍 *festina mihi;* 𝔊 εἰσάκουσόν μου. — **2.** *הקשיבה הבּיט*] phr. α.λ., but cf. 2 Ch. 29[35] 35[10. 16] of temple service, cf. 2 Ch. 8[16] Pr. 19[20]. — *קשׁיֶאֵת כַּפּי*] phr. α.λ., but cf. Ez. 20[40]. — *מִנְחַת עֶרֶב*] phr. elsw. 2 K. 16[15] Ezr. 9[4. 5] Dn. 9[21], cf. Pss. 20[4] 40[7]. — **3.** *שׁיָרָה*] cohort. Imv. *שׁית.* — *שָׁמְרָה*] n.f. *watch,* α.λ. ; dub. rd. *שׁמְּרָה* Qal ptc. 𝔊 has θύραν περιοχῆς περὶ τὰ χείλη μου. — *דָּל*] † [*דַּל עַל שׂפתי*] *door,* α.λ., dub. rd. *דֶלֶה,* fig. for lips Ec. 12[4]. *עַל* not used with vb. ; rd. *עֵלי*; needed for measure. — **4.** *הִתְעוֹלֵל*] Hithpo. *עלל* α. λ. ; BDB. *practise practices,* in wickedness, Dr. *occupied in deeds.* Poel *act severely* toward La. 1[22] 2[20] 3[51]. Hith. *busy, divert one's self with,* Ex. 10[2] (J.), *deal ruthlessly with* c. *ב* 1 S. 6[6] Nu. 22[29] (JE.) Ju. 19[25] +. — *אֶת־אִישִׁים*] *אישים* elsw. Is. 53[3] Pr. 8[4], for *אנשים.* — *אֶלְחַם*] Qal. impf. † *לחם* denom. *לחם* ; *eat as food,* elsw. Dt. 32[24] Pr. 4[17] 9[5] 23[1. 6]. — *מִנְעַמֵּיהֶם*] α.λ. two tones, *delicacies, dainties,* as *נעמים* Ps. 16[6], *נעמות* 16[11]. — **5.** *שׁמן ראשׁ*] *choice oil* 𝔗, Dr. ; but 𝔊 *שׁמן רשׁע* *oil of the wicked,* better suited to context, 𝔍 *oleum amaritudinis.* — *אל יָני*] Hiph. juss. *נוא* *forbid,* cf. 33[10], *frustrate* elsw. vb. only in P. 𝔊 has μὴ λιπανάτω, so 𝔖, 𝔍, after Arab. *be fat.* — *כי עוד*] rd. *כי עורי.* — *בְרָעוֹתֵיהֶב*] two accents. 𝔊 has ἐν ταῖς εὐδοκίαις αὐτῶν. — **6.** *נִשְׁמְטוּ*] Niph. α.λ. ‡ *שׁמט* Qal *throw down* 2 K. 9[33] (rare word), so here *be flung down.* Pf. in the sense of optative as Hu., Gr. — *ירי סלע*] *by the sides of the crag.* This l. is a gl. — *ישְׁמְעוּ*] has no appropriate connection with foregoing. Rd. *שׁמְעוּ* *Hear !* Imv. beginning new Str. — *יְאֵמְרוּ*] not used elsw. of words ; dub. unless we consider them the words of prayer ; vb. elsw. Gn. 49[15] 2 S. 1[26] + ; pl. adapted to previous vb.; rd. *נָעֵים* adj. (cf. Pss. 135[3] 147[1] (of praise)). — **7.** *כמו*] full form prep. — *פֹּלֵחַ*] Qal ptc. † *פלה* *cleave,* elsw. Pi. *cleave open, cut open, split,* Jb. 16[13] Pr. 7[23] 2 K. 4[39], of animals bringing forth young Jb. 39[3]. — *ובְֹּקַע בארץ*] *cleave the earth,* *בקע*

(74^{15}). There is no Biblical usage to justify our thinking of *ploughing* here. Vb. means *burst open*, in Niph., cf. 2 Ch. 25^{12}, of men hurled from a rock. This best suits the context here. — נפזרו] Niph. פזר only here; rd. עצמיו *his bones*. Qal Je. 50^{17}. Pi. Ps. 53^6 +, *v. 14^5.* — **8.** יהוה אדני] conflation of divine names. אדני makes l. too long. — הָנֶּה] prep. with fuller sf. — [אל הָגֵּר Pi. impf. juss. *pour out* my life, as Hiph. Is. 53^{12}, Niph. Is. 32^{15} *lay bare*, Ps. 137^7, cf. 37^{35}. — **9.** [⁝⁝⁝⁝] pl. fem. *a.λ.*; pl. in יס 64^6 140^6, cstr. מוקשׁי 18^6. — **10.** מַכְמֹרָיו] *a.λ.* unless with Gr., Che., for מהמרות 140^{11}, which is expl. of one dub. word by another of the same kind; cf. מִכְבָּר Is. $51^{2)}$. The v. is however a late gl. — יַחַד] BDB. *at the same time;* but dub. ⑯ κατὰ μόνας = יחיד *solitary.* ₰ *simul*, attached to the previous clause. But none of these give good sense. A vb. is required; rd. אחר Qal impf. 1 S. חדה, *I shall rejoice*, cf. 86^{11} (⑯) Jb. 3^6.

PSALM CXLII., 2 STR. 10^3.

Ps. 142 is a prayer of the congregation to Yahweh in great trouble (v.$^{2-4a}$). Yahweh knows that they are friendless and without any way of escape (v.$^{4b. 5}$). Yahweh is their only refuge in their extremity (v.$^{6-7ab}$). Therefore they implore Him to save their life, delivering them from prison, that the righteous may recognize that He does good to His people (v.$^{7c-8a. 8cd}$). There are glosses of explanation (v.^{4c}) and liturgical expression (v.^{8b}).

> UNTO Yahweh I cry with *my* voice;
>   Unto Yahweh I make supplication with *my* voice.
>   I pour out before Him *my* plaint;
>   I declare before Him *my* trouble:
>   Because that within me fainteth *my* spirit.
>   But Thou knowest *my* path;
>   Lookest and seest on *my* right hand,
>   That there is none that recogniseth *me;*
>   Escape fails *me*,
>   There is none that careth for *me*.
> UNTO Thee, Yahweh, do *I* cry,
>   I say: "Thou art *my* refuge;
>   In the land of the living *my* portion."
>   O attend unto *my* yell,
>   For very low am *I* brought.
>   Deliver me from them that pursue (*my* life),
>   For they are too strong for *me*.
>   O bring forth from prison *my* person;
>   That the righteous may recognise with *me*,
>   That Thou doest good to *me*.

Ps. 142 was in 𝔅, of the class ‫משכיל‬ like the group 52–55. But the original title was doubtless ‫תפלה‬ (v. Intr. §§ 1, 26, 27). The Ps. shares with the
group 51–63 in historical references, which in all cases are conjectural of
appropriate situations for the thought of the Ps. ‫בהיותו במערה‬, cf. 57¹;
whether the cave of Adullam (1 S. 22), or of Engedi (1 S. 24), is difficult
to determine. The Ps. is composed of two trimeter decastichs, each line ending in assonance in ‫‬. There is nothing in Ps. to suggest a late date, except
v.⁸ ‫יכתרו‬, a dubious form, which is probably a txt. err. The phr. v.⁴ ‫בהתעטף‬
‫עלי רוחי‬, as 143⁴, is used Jon. 2⁸. ‫ארץ ההיים‬ v.⁶ = Is. 38¹¹ 53⁸ Je. 11¹⁹ Pss. 27¹³
52⁷. ‫דלותי‬ v.⁷, cf. 79⁸ 116⁶. ‫מסגר‬ v.⁸ cf. Is. 24²² 42⁷. V.⁴ᶜ·⁸ᵇ are glosses injuring the measure, the former expansive, the latter liturgical. The Ps. was
composed during the early exile at Babylon, when the life of the nation was
in peril and the people were prisoners v.⁷⁻⁸ᵃ.

Str. I. A pentastich of four syn. lines followed by a synth. one,
and a pentastich of syn. couplet and triplet. — **2-3.** *Unto Yahweh*], repeated for emphasis ; ‖ *before Him*], also repeated for
emphasis. — *I cry* ‖ *I make supplication*], of importunate prayer.
— *with my voice*], repeated to emphasize the fact that it was oral ;
it could not be restrained within the secret breast, but burst forth
in loud cries. — *I pour out*], in a stream of words : ‖ *declare.* —
my plaint], defined by *my trouble.* — **4.** *Because*], the reason,
and not temporal : " when " as EVˢ. — *within me fainteth my
spirit*], discouraged and in the extremity of weakness, cf. 77⁴ 107⁵
143⁴ Jon. 2⁸. — *But Thou*], emphatic : and no other. — *knowest
my path*], the way in which the people have been compelled to
go in their exile. — A glossator in a different situation explains :
in the way that I walk they hid a trap for me], cf. 140⁶, suiting
the situation of the congregation of the Restoration, but not that
of the Exile. Moreover, the measure of the line is different, and
it makes the Str. just this much too long. — **5.** *Lookest and seest*],
so 𝔊, 𝔖, 𝔙, 𝔗, as inf. abs., carrying on previous pf. ; interrupted
by gloss, and thus in MT., followed by EVˢ., rendered as imv. :
" look and see," as a renewal of the petition. — *on my right hand*],
the sf. required for assonance and by the ‖ *my path*, v.⁵ᵇ. The
right hand is the place of the advocate, cf. 16⁸ 109³¹ 110⁵ 121⁵. —
This missing advocate is defined : *That recogniseth me,* ‖ *that
careth for me*], and intermediate *Escape*, which cannot, therefore,
be interpreted as the act of escaping, or the place of escape, but
as the person to whom they would escape as a refuge. — Such an

advocate is emphatically denied in the repeated : *There is none*, and also in the intermediate *fails me*], literally " is perished," utterly lost away from me.

Str. II. A pentastich, composed of a syn. couplet preceded by an introductory line and followed by a synth. couplet ; and also a pentastich, composed of synth. couplet and triplet. — **6.** *Unto Thee, Yahweh, do I cry*], a renewal of the petition of v.$^{2-3}$. — *Thou art my refuge*], Yahweh, and no one else ; in antith. v.^{5c} ; ‖ *my portion*, cf. 16^5, as the share or allotted section *In the land of the living*], cf. 27^{13} 52^7. Even in the holy land, where each one of the congregation had his portion, Yahweh was yet the supreme portion, cf. 73$^{25-26}$. — *O attend unto my yell*], renewing v.^{2}, the loud, importunate pleading. — *For very low am I brought*], cf. 79^8 116^6, reduced to the lowest degree of misery ; cf. v.^{4a}. — *Deliver me from them that pursue my life*], reduced to " me " in text at the expense of the measure, and to the ignoring of the peril to the life of the nation. — *For they are too strong for me*], the Babylonians have overcome them, and they are helpless captives in their hands. — **8.** *O bring forth from prison my person*]. The captives were at first prisoners of war, and many of them at least were kept in prisons. What was immediately needed, next to preservation of life, was deliverance from imprisonment. — *That the righteous may recognise with me*], the most probable rendering of a difficult passage, where 𝕳 and Vrss. greatly vary. The chief Vrss. with 𝕲, after Aramaic, render : " the righteous will wait for me." AV., RV., " compass me about," has no support in Vrss. RV.^{m} " crown themselves because of me," JPSV. " will glory in me," Dr. " shall put out crowns because of me," are based on 𝔖, 𝕿, and ancient Jewish authorities, and is most probable, if the text be correct. But the text is probably corrupt, and the change of a single letter gives the reading followed above. — *That Thou doest good to me*], in giving me the deliverance implored throughout the Ps. — A glossator inserts a liturgical gloss : *that I may give thanks unto Thy name*], in public worship.

2. קוֹלִי] in both instances changed for emph. from the original order at close of l. as assonance required. — **3.** אֵיכֹך יָשִׂיחַ] cf. 102^1. — צָרָתִי] cf. 22^{12} 78^{49} 116^3 ; originally at close of l. — **4.** בְּהִתְעַטֵּף עָלַי רוּחִי] causal and not temporal, cf. 77^4 107^5 143^4 Jon. 2^8. — ‡ נְתִיבָתִי] n.f. sf., as 119^{105} = נָתִיב 78^{50} 119^{35}.

2 L

—וּ] rel. ; 1. is a pentameter gl. —כה מִמֶּנּוּ] = 140⁶. — 5. [הַבֵּיט] fully written Hiph. imv., as ᴶ ; but better as 𝕲, 𝔖, 𝔙, 𝕿, Bä., inf. abs. and so for pf. 1 sg.; so רָאה for רָאֶה. —[יְמִין] should be at the end of 1. with sf. for assonance ; so also לי of next 1. —[מַכִּיר] Hiph. ptc. נכר *recognise, acknowledge*, as Dt. 21¹⁷ 33⁹ Is. 63¹⁶, cf. 61⁹ ; *be acquainted with* Ps. 103¹⁶. —[אבד מנוס מן] phr. elsw. Am. 2¹⁴ Je. 25⁸⁵ Jb. 11²⁰. — 6. [זעקתי] goes to end of 1. for assonance ; so also חֶלְקִי.—[דַלּוֹתִי] 7. pf. דלל *hang down, be brought low*, as 79⁸ 116⁶; should be at the end of 1. —[רְדֹף] for רדף נפשי; assonance requires sg. sf. — 8. †[מַסְגֵּר] *dungeon*, elsw. Is. 24²² 42⁷, cf. מַסְגֵּרֶת Ps. *18⁴⁸.* — [להודות את שמך] is a gl., destroying measure. — [בִּי יַכְתִּרוּ] Hiph. impf. ‡ כתר vb. Pi. *surround*, c. acc. 22¹³ Ju. 20⁴⁸. Hiph. elsw. Pr. 14¹⁸ (dub.), ptc. Hb. 1⁴ *surround* c. acc. The construction with בְּי α.λ. and difficult, and this derivation not sustained by any ancient Vrs. 𝕲 ἐμὲ ὑπομενοῦσιν, ᴶ *me expectant justi ;* so 𝔖, 𝔙, Aq. : all derive from כתר Aram. *wait, hope for*, cf. Jb. 36². But Σ, 𝕿, Ra., AE., and prob. MT., regarded it as denom. of כֶּתֶר *crown ;* so Thes., De., Dr., JPSV., which, however, is only used in Est. 1¹¹ 2¹⁷ 6⁸ and prob. as Persian loan word. There is doubtless a txt. err. בי, as assonance requires, should be at end of 1. ; and so connected with צדיקים rather than with the vb. The original vb. was prob. יַכִּירוּ; see v.⁵ᵇ. — [הגמל על]. 𝕲 ἕως οὗ ἀνταποδῷς μοι, ᴶ *cum retribueris mihi,* so Aq. ; but Σ ὅταν εὐεργετήσῃς με. עָלֶי has been assimilated to 116⁷ 119¹⁷; but assonance requires sg. sf. The original was doubtless לי.

PSALM CXLIII., 2 STR. 5⁵.

Ps. 143 is an importunate prayer of the congregation to Yahweh in great peril for speedy deliverance, pleading His faithfulness, righteousness, and kindness (v.¹· ⁴ᵇ· ⁶⁻⁷ᵃ· ⁸) ; that He would deliver from enemies, teach, lead, and quicken them (v.⁹⁻¹¹). Many glosses, chiefly citations, emphasize the perils (v.³⁻⁴ᵃ· ⁷ᵇ), recall former deliverances (v.⁵), express the dogma that no living being can be righteous in Yahweh's sight (v.²), and imprecate ruin upon enemies (v.¹²).

*M*Y prayer, O hear, in *Thy* faithfulness; O give ear to *my* supplication.
   Answer *me* in *Thy* righteousness; within me is bewildered *my* heart.
   I spread out unto *Thee*, as a weary land, *my* soul.
   Answer *me* speedily (in *Thy* righteousness) : pine doth *my* spirit.
   Make *me* hear in the morning *Thy* kindness; for in Thee do *I* trust.
*M*AKE *me* know *Thy* way; for unto Thee I lift up *my* soul.
   Deliver *me*, Yahweh, from *Thine* enemies; for unto Thee *I* (flee).
   Teach *me* to do *Thy* will; for Thou art *my* God.
   Lead *me* for *Thy* name's sake in uprightness, *my* God.
   Quicken *me* in *Thy* righteousness : bring out of trouble *my* soul.

Ps. 143 was in 𝔅 and 𝕸, *v*. Intr., §§ 27, 31. In 𝔊 it has also ὅτε αὐτὸν ὁ υἱὸς καταδιώκει, which is a late conjecture of an appropriate historical illustration. It is the last of the Penitential Pss. of the Church. It, like all others of this group, has been greatly changed from its original form, in which it was a prayer of two pentameter pentastichs, v.[1. 4b. 6b. 7a. 8-11]. It doubtless belonged to the troublous times before Nehemiah. The language and style are those of 𝔅. The original was ornate, with threefold assonance in every line: in ‫ִי‬, ‫ָה‬, and ‫ִי‬. This has been obscured by transpositions in some cases by late copyists; but it is evident in most lines and easily restored in others. There are many glosses, which lack this assonance and are chiefly citations or adaptations of older Pss. V.[2] reminds of Jb. 9[32] 22[4] in its recognition of universal lack of righteousness before God; is dogmatic in spirit, and tetrameter in form, if not prosaic. V.[3b] is from 7[6b]. V.[3c] was derived from La. 3[6]. V.[4a. 5] are adaptations to 77[6. 12. 13]. V.[7b] is from 28[1], and v.[7a] is a phr. common in 𝔅. V.[12] is a Maccabean imprecation. V.[10b] ‫רוחך טובה‬ is a gloss from Ne. 9[20]. All evidences of late date are in the glosses.

Str. I. Syn. pentastich. — **1.** *My prayer ‖ my supplication*], expressed by the gesture, *I spread out unto Thee*], v.[6a], defined by gloss as " my hands," but really *my soul*, as La. 3[41], the heart into the outspread hands; and so ‖ *lift up my soul*], v.[8b]. This attitude of soul is compared to a *weary land*], thirsting for refreshing rain, cf. 63[2]; and is interpreted as : *pine doth my spirit*], v.[7a], cf. 71[9] 73[26], and qualified by *in Thee do I trust*], v.[8a]. — Notwithstanding the desperate situation, described as : *bewildered my heart*], v.[4b] (stupefied by the extreme peril from which there is no escape unless divinely given), and the importunity of the prayer; their trust in Yahweh is firmly maintained. — *O hear ‖ O give ear ‖ answer me*], repeated in v.[7a] with the adv. *speedily*] and the ‖ *make me hear in the morning*], after the night of trial, cf. 30[6]. — The divine attributes are the sanctions of the pleading : *faithfulness*], to His covenant and people ; *righteousness*], in their vindication against their enemies, repeated v.[7a] ; and *kindness*], v.[8a], which in earlier literature is the nearest syn. to the divine love rather than " mercy," the usual mistaken translation. This Str. has been greatly enlarged by glosses of various kinds. — **2.** *And*], an additional petition, not homogeneous with the original Ps. — *enter not into judgment with Thy servant*]. Israel as the servant of Yahweh is here conscious of sin and guilt, that makes him dread the divine judgment, which the previous context has implored. — *for no living being is righteous before Thee*], a dogmatic statement corresponding with Jb. 9^2 25^4, as regards man, and extended even to the angels Jb. 4^{17-18} 15^{14-15}. This v. is cited by St. Paul, Rom. 3^{20} Gal. 2^{16}. It adds the penitential element to the pleading, and justifies the use of the Ps. as the seventh of the Penitential Pss. of the Church. Doubtless the Ps. thereby became more suited to public worship, notwithstanding inconsistency with the context, which pleads for divine interposition in righteousness and a righteous judgment on enemies. — **3 a.** *For the enemy doth pursue my life*], a gloss from 7^6. The enemies are mentioned in the original for the first in v.^{9}. — *He hath crushed my life to the earth*]. The people are utterly crushed and prostrate on the ground before their enemies. — **3 c.** *In the region of dense darkness he hath made me dwell as those long dead*], a citation from La. 3^6. There is no good reason to think of a different meaning here from there. The people after the destruction of Jerusalem, in exile, are conceived as having died and descended into Sheol, which is a region of dense darkness and gloom, where the shades of the dead dwell, even those dead from ancient times. It is possible to interpret the term as "dead forever," having no hope of resurrection, in accordance with the denial of resurrection to the wicked Is. 26^{14}. But it is not probable that the question of a resurrection was in the mind of this glossator any more than in that of the author of La.; or that he was thinking even of a long-continued, indefinite period for the continuation of the dead in Sheol. It is most natural with EV^s. after most ancient Vrss. to think of those who had been long dead; so that the glossator is complaining here of the long continuance of the death of the nation. — **4.** *And my spirit fainteth upon me*], is a gloss from 77^{4b} adapted to 142^4. — **5.** *I remember the days of old*], adapted from 77^6 ‖ *I meditate on all Thy work*, citation from 77^{13} ‖ *I muse on the work of Thy hands*, variation of 77^{12}. — **7 b.** *Do not hide Thy face from me*], a phr. common in Pss., 13^2 22^{25} 27^9 69^{18} 88^{15} 102^3; in different measure from the context, and a gloss of intensification. — *I become like them that go down to the Pit*], derived from 28^1 by glossator and tacked on without care for grammatical construction. It really implies the protasis "lest if Thou be silent unto me"; but there is no sufficient reason for inserting it with Che., whose reconstruction of this Ps. is of the most arbitrary character.

This glossator conceives of the nation as in extreme peril of death and of descending to the Pit of Sheol; and is accordingly at variance with the glossator of v.[3c], who thought of the nation as already for a long time dead. Such different points of view are not uncommon in such mosaics of religious phrases, and do not really disturb their liturgical use.

Str. II. Syn. pentastich. — **8 b–11.** *Make me know* ‖ *teach me* ‖ *lead me*]. Petition for divine instruction and guidance quite frequently is intermingled with petitions for deliverance, cf. 25[4-5]. — *Thy way*], the course of life prescribed by the divine Law; enlarged by a copyist, by assimilation to 32[8], into "the way wherein I should go." — *Thy will*], the divine will as the norm of human conduct, elsw. 40[9]; even of angels 103[21]. — *in upright-ness*], interpreted and enlarged into "in a land of uprightness"; probably an error for "path of uprightness" as 27[11], which cer-tainly is better suited to the context. These petitions are ‖ with petitions for deliverance, resuming those of the previous Str. — *Deliver me, Yahweh, from Thine enemies*]. The enemies of the people of Yahweh are the enemies of Yahweh Himself, as usual. A later scribe destroyed the assonance by substituting "mine" for "Thine." — In the climax, v.[11], two petitions appear : *quicken me*, revive my life, *in Thy righteousness*, as v.[4b. 7a]; ‖ *bring out of trouble my soul*], my person, me, myself. — Three of the lines in their complementary parts assign reasons for the petition in-troduced by "for": *unto Thee I lift up my soul*], resuming the attitude of soul of v.[6]; ‖ *unto Thee I flee*], so 𝔊. This by an early error of a single letter in 𝔐 and most Vrss. was changed into a vb. meaning to cover, conceal, overwhelm; but having no meaning suited to the preposition used here or to the context. The Vrss. and interpreters dependent on 𝔐, therefore resort to paraphrases; or seek meanings for the vb. unknown else-where, or unsuited to it, such as "flee to hide me," EV[s]. Most modern critics recognise an error in the text and propose various remedies. The simplest is that given above. — *For Thou art my God*], the personal relationship of Israel to Yahweh as their own national God inspires them with confidence and the right to expect guidance and the obligation of obedience. — *for Thy name's sake*], is a syn. thought, though varied in expression.

The name, reputation, and honour of Yahweh is involved in the guidance of His people, and that is a reason for their petition for it. — A glossator inserts in v.[10b], at the expense of the measure, from Ne. 9[20], *Thy good Spirit*], which represents the divine Spirit as having the attribute of goodness, in being good, benignant, and the benefactor of the nation ; and also that the divine Spirit is the teacher and guide, a doctrine which appears also in the "holy Spirit" of Ps. 51[13] Is. 63[10. 11]. — **12.** A Maccabean glossator appended this prosaic v. of imprecation on enemies. — *And in Thy kindness*], that is, to Israel. — *mayest Thou exterminate mine enemies, and destroy all the adversaries of my life*]. It is difficult for a modern to reconcile the divine attribute of kindness with the extermination of the enemies of Israel. But even to the author of the original Ps. the enemies of Israel were the enemies of Yahweh ; and in the Maccabean times it was indeed a kindness of Yahweh to Israel to exterminate their implacable foes. — *for I am Thy servant*]. It is a sufficient reason for this imprecation, as indeed for all the petitions of the Ps., that Israel was in a special relation to Yahweh as His own servant and worshipper, cf. v.[2] 86[16] 116[16] 136[22].

---

1. יהוה] is gl., making l. too long. — שמע תפלתי]. The usual order ; but assonance of Ps. requires transposition. The imv. should be cohor., ‖ האזינה. — אֵל] as 39[13], with this vb.; elsw. acc. 5[2] 17[1] 55[2] 86[6] 140[7] 141[1]. 𝔊 has acc.; prob. prep. txt. err., as it makes l. too long. — באמנתך] attached by 𝔊 to האזינה, but by 𝔐 to עֵנני; the latter destroys parall. Assonance and ‖ require that it should go with שמעה. — **2.** הבוא במשפט] judicial phr. of Jb. 9[32] 22[4], which seems to have been in the mind of the author, as well as the doctrine that no creature can be regarded as righteous in God's sight. This late dogmatic statement is contrary to the tone of the Ps. The v. is a prosaic gl. — **3.** כי רדף אויב נפשי]. This l. is not in 𝔊[B], but in 𝔊[B. ab. (mg).] א. R. T; a gl. from 7[6]. — דכא לארץ חיתי] from 7[6], save that the vb. דכא is substituted for רמס. — הושיבני במחשכים כמתי עולם] a pentameter gl. from La. 3[6]. — **4.** ותהעטף עלי] from 77[4b] adapted to 142[4]. — יְשְׁתוֹמֵם] Hithp. שמם 40[16], with לבי a.λ.; belongs to the original Ps. — **5.** ימים מקדם] from 77[6]. Vb. changed from היבחתי to the more usual זכרתי. — חגיתי בכל פעלך] phr. from 77[13]. 𝔊, 𝔍, 𝔖, 𝔘, Aq., 𝔗, all pl.; but improb. — אשוחח] Polel שיח 6[7]; variation of 77[12]. — **6.** פרשתי ידי] gesture of prayer ; but ידי makes l. too long and is unnecessary ; better think with La. 3[41] of attitude of the לב. — לך] an unnecessary pedantic insertion, making l. too long. — נפשי] belongs to end of l. — **7.** מַהֵר עֲנֵני] transposed from original order. עֵנני came first for assonance. A word is missing with assonance in ךָ_; doubtless צדקתך as v.[1b]. יהוה was a later insertion. —

וחי רוח כלחה] phr. a.λ., but cf. 71[9] 73[26]. — אל הסתר פניך] phr. 51[11]; but gl. — בור ירדי עם ונמשלתי] gl. from 28[1], where it is apodosis of ממני רחשה פן. But here there is no proper grammatical connection. The י does not admit of the translation "lest" of EV[s]. It is possible with Dr. to regard it as י consec. pf. expressing result; but it was tacked on by the glossator without regard to grammatical connection. — **8.** אֶרֶךְ וֹ דְּרֶךְ] makes l. too long; amplification of דַּרְכְּךָ. — **9.** מֵאוֹיְבַי] assonance requires מֵאִיבָךְ. יהוה has been transposed. — אֵלֶיךָ כְּסֵי]. So 𝕲[N. c. a. T], but 𝕲[B. N. A. R] has ὅτι = כִּי, and that is doubtless correct, as it is more euphonic and harmonious with ‖ ll. This vb. is not suited to the prep. and none of its meanings is suited to context. It is doubtless error for נסי, 𝕲 κατέφυγον, as Street, Du., Valeton. Hu., Now., Ols., Dy., after AE., would rd. חסיו, but that would require בְּ. Bach., Bä., חֲבִיתִי, Gr. קויתי. 𝔍 *protectus sum* = כָּסִיתִי Pu. — **10.** אֱלֹהִי] for אֵלַי, required for assonance. — רוּחַהְ טיבָה] gl. from Ne. 9[20] by careless scribe, who omitted the article with adj., which the original had and Heb. grammar requires.— מישׁוֹר בארץ] a.λ., so Σ, 𝔍, 𝕲[A. R. T]; cf. מישׁוֹר בארח 27[11], so here acc. Hu., Bä., במישׁוֹר 26[12]. 𝕲[B. N] ἐν τῇ εὐθείᾳ favours the latter. The others make l. too long; for a word in assonance in ִי_ is needed, which was prob. as above אֱלַי instead of יהוה v.[11a]. — **12.** והאבדת ו consec. pf. after תצמית. This v. is a prosaic Maccabean gloss.

PSALM CXLIV.

Ps. 144 is composite. I. A prayer for deliverance from treacherous foreigners, repeated in Rfs. (v.[7a. 8. 11]), the first introduced by blessing Yahweh for warlike skill (v.[1]), and recognition of Him as Kindness in whom they have taken refuge (v.[2a]). The second is introduced by a vow of public praise for the victory given (v.[9.10]). Glosses emphasize the fact that Yahweh is their refuge (v.[2b]), and petition for theophanic interposition (v.[5-6. 7b]); represent the insignificance of man (v.[3]) and his transitory life (v.[4]). II. A fragment of a Ps. representing the blessedness of the people in their children (v.[12]), their stores (v.[13a]), their cattle (v.[13b-14a]), and freedom from war (v.[14b]), with a Rf. declaring their supreme happiness in having Yahweh for their God (v.[15]).

A. v.[1-2ac. 7b. 8-11], 2 STR. 4[3], RF. 3[3].

BLESSED be Yahweh, my Rock!
　Who traineth my hands for battle,
　My fingers for war.
　My Kindness, and Him in whom I have taken refuge.
　　　　Deliver me from the hand of foreigners,
　　　　Whose mouth doth speak insincerity,
　　　　And whose right hand is a right hand of falsehood.

A NEW song will I sing unto Thee;
    With a lyre of ten strings will I make melody to Thee,
    Who giveth victory to (His) king,
    To His servant from the hurtful sword.
        Deliver me from the hand of foreigners,
        Whose mouth doth speak insincerity,
        And whose right hand is a right hand of falsehood.

B. v.$^{12-15}$, 6^4, RF. 2^4.

THE sons are in youthful vigour, as established towers.
    The daughters are as corner pillars, hewn out as figures.
    The garners are full, affording all kinds of store.
    The sheep are bringing forth thousands, ten thousands in the fields.
    The kine are great with young: there are no miscarriages.
    And there are no goings forth to war, or cries of alarm in the squares.
        Happy the people when they have it so!
        Happy the people, when Yahweh is their God!

Ps. 144 was in 𝔈. The addition of 𝕲 πρὸς τὸν Γολιάθ was suggested by the contents, and is a late conjecture. The Ps. is really composite: of a trimeter poem v.$^{1-11}$, and a tetrameter v.$^{12-15}$, which is a fragment of a lost Ps. The Psalm has many glosses, so that in its present form it is a mosaic. But the Rf., v.$^{7b-8}$ = ^{11}, enables us to find two Strs., v.$^{1.\ 2ac}$, v.$^{9-10}$ +. Even these vs. are dependent, the former on 18$^{47.\ 35}$, the latter on 33$^{2-3}$, and the Rf. on 18$^{45-46}$; so the Ps. must be regarded as essentially an adaptation of earlier material to a later situation, which on account of v.$^{8.\ 11bc}$ may be regarded as the troublous times at the beginning of the work of Nehemiah, when the people were called to arms against their treacherous neighbours. The dependence of the Ps. on Ps. 18 doubtless suggested the many other glosses from that Ps.: v.^{2bd} from 18$^{3.\ 48}$, v.^{5a} from 18^{10}, v.^{6} from 18^{15}, v.^{7} from 18$^{17.\ 18}$. Other glosses were inserted: v.^{3} from 8^5, v.^{4} from 39$^{6.\ 7}$, v.^{5b} from 104^{32}. The fragment v.$^{12-15}$ is a tetrameter octastich in its present form. It is full of Aramaisms and late and unusual words and constructions. It is a remarkable specimen of assonance, in which six lines have four words, in alternate lines, in assonance in ם‎ִ- and ‎ות‎ַ-.

PSALM CXLIV. *A.*

Str. I. A tetrastich with introverted parallelism, and a tristich of Rf. whose second and third lines are syn. — **1.** *Blessed be Yahweh, my Rock*], an adaptation from 18^{47}. — *who traineth my hands for battle, My fingers for war*], enlargement of 18^{35}; the hands probably to wield sword and spear, the fingers to grasp the bow; that is, for warlike skill and vigour against enemies. — **2.** *My Kindness*], as epithet of God elsw. Jon. 2^9, cf. Ps. 59^{18}; as the source and giver of kindness. — *and Him in whom I have taken refuge*], from the enemies. This latter was originally part of the same line as the phrase above ; but a glossator inserted from 18[8] a number of additional terms, emphasizing the fact that Yahweh was the refuge of His people : *my fastness, my high tower and mine own deliverer, my shield;* and also from 18[48] : *who bringeth down peoples under me.* — **3**. A later glossator inserts from 8[5] with slight modification : *Yahweh, what is man, that Thou takest knowledge of him ? The son of man, that Thou considerest him ?* His purpose was to deepen the humility of the congregation and their sense of unworthiness in the sight of God. — **4**. Another gloss from 39[6. 7] states the transitoriness of human life as a reason for immediate deliverance : *Mankind is like unto a breath. His days like a shadow pass away.* — **5–7 a**. The same glossator who inserted v.[2b], adds a petition for theophanic interposition from 18[10. 15. 17. 18] and 104[32], changing descriptive impfs. into imvs.

> Bow Thy heavens and come down.
> Touch the mountains that they may smoke.
> Flash forth lightnings and scatter them.
> Send forth Thine arrows and discomfort them.
> Stretch forth Thine hands from on high :
> Rescue me from mighty waters.

Rf. 7 b–8 = 11. *Deliver me from the hand of foreigners*]. The peril comes from foreign enemies, probably the confederates allied by Sanballat in the time of Nehemiah, when the congregation took up arms to defend themselves, while rebuilding the walls of Jerusalem, Ne. 4. — *Whose mouth doth speak insincerity*]. They were treacherous foes, misrepresenting the congregation to the Persians, and seeking to make a party for themselves in Jerusalem itself. — *And whose right hand is a right hand of falsehood*], probably the right hand lifted in taking oaths : so that they were false witnesses and perjurers.

Str. II. Two syn. couplets, and Rf. **0**. *A new song will I sing unto Thee; With a lyre of ten strings will I make melody to Thee*]. A vow of public worship and praise with song and musical instruments ; an adaptation of 33[2-3]. — **10**. *Who giveth victory to His king ‖ His servant*], doubtless referring to the Davidic monarchy ; but it has been made more definite by a glossator, who inserted at the expense of the measure : *Who snatched away David*]. " His King " was generalised into " kings " in the first line. — *from the hurtful sword*], a phr. α.λ., but poetical and graphic.

PSALM CXLIV. *B.*

Six syn. lines, with syn. couplet of Rf. — **12**. *The sons* ‖ *the daughters*]. 韻 and Vrss. differ in sfs. here, and throughout the Ps.; an evidence here as elsewhere that such sfs. are interpretations. Besides the assonance characteristic of this poem does not allow of them. — *in youthful vigour, as established towers*]. Ehr. suggests that imagery suited to a building is here required with sons as with daughters. The usual interp. after 韻 and Vrss. " are as young plants made to grow up strong in youth," in youthful strength, freshness and vigour, straight, tall, and full of vital energy and beauty, while in some respects appropriate, is rather tame in this context. — *as corner pillars*], JPSV., as ornamental supports used in temples and palaces; not " corner stones " AV., RV., which would hardly be considered from an æsthetic point of view. — *hewn out as figures*], as the caryatides of ancient art. The comparison of a beautiful woman with a building is found already in the story of the creation of Eve, Gn. 2^{22}, obscured in EV[s]. by the generalised " made " for the Heb. " builded " as RV.[m], cf. also Ct. 4^4 6^4 8^{9-10}. By an early misinterpretation of the word rendered " figures," that it had the other and later mng. of " similitude," " model," the word " palace " was supplied against measure and assonance; and accordingly " after the similitude " AV., " fashion " RV., " device " JPSV., " of a palace." — **13–14**. *The garners*], storehouses where the harvests were stored away. — *are full*], because of rich and abundant crops. — *affording all kinds of store*], every kind of harvest has been plentiful. — *The sheep are bringing forth thousands*, amplified to *ten thousands*], wonderful fertility of the flocks. — *in the fields*], RV., or " pastures " JPSV.; not " streets " PBV., AV., where such a thing could not be. — *The kine*], the larger cattle. — *are great with young*], as most moderns in accordance with context, the herds having the same fertility as the flocks; but most Vrss. render " fat " or " strong " and so " strong to labour " PBV., AV., which

seems rather weak in comparison with the other strong lines.
RV., JPSV., render "well laden," thinking of the abundant
harvests laden upon them. But that has been sufficiently mentioned in v.[13a], and a return to it is improbable. — *there are no
miscarriages*]. This phr. is the necessary complement of the
previous sentence, both for measure and assonance. Therefore
we must think that the sing. is an error for an earlier pl., due to
a mistaken view of the connection of the clauses, as if this clause
were in antithesis with the next : "no breaking in and no going
out" AV., RV., JPSV. But the measure requires that these
should be in different lines. — *And there are no goings forth*],
that is, to war, and so suited to the next clause : *or cries of alarm
in the squares*], due to assault upon the city ; and so the climax
is a condition of peace with all their neighbours. — **15.** The Rf. :
Happy the people], repeated for emphasis. — *when they have it so*],
in accordance with the description of peace and prosperity given
above. — *when Yahweh is their God*], all these blessings come
from Yahweh. It is appropriate that the Ps. should conclude
with this recognition.

CXLIV. *A.*

1. ברוך יהוה צורי] cf. 18[47], after which it is modelled. — [הַמְלַמֵּד ידי לקרב] cf.
18[35]; but קְרָב *battle, encounter,* 55[19. 22] 68[31] 78[9]. — [אצבעותי] has two tones, cf. 8[4].
— **2.** [חַסְדִּי] as divine epithet, elsw. Jon. 2[9]; cf. אלהי חסדי 59[18]. It is so unsuited to the following words derived from 18[3] that many think it an error
either for סלעי Du., or הסני Gr., חזקי Dy., Valeton, מחסי Street, Ehr. But these
are really all gls., and the complementary part of l. is ובו הסיתי, well suited to
הסדי. — [הרודד עמי תחתי] from 18[48] ; only עַמִּי 𝕳, 𝕲, but עמים Aq., 𝕵, 𝕾, 𝕿, as
18[48], so Street, Ehr., Valeton. — **3.** Gl. from 8[5], only יהוה is prefixed and כי
subord. changed into ו consec. MT., prob. error of pointing for ו subord. 𝕲,
Σ, ὅτι ; 𝕶, 𝕵, *quia*. The vbs. are also changed from זוכרנו, תפקדנו, to תדעהו
and תחשבהו. — **4.** Gl. from 39[6. 7. 12] with various changes that do not alter the
essential mng., but rather simplify it : דמה as 17[4]; צֵל for צֶלֶם; עוֹבֵר ptc. for
impf. יההלך, but 𝕲, 𝕶, prob. rd. pf. — **5 a.** Change of impf. of 18[10] into imv., and
prefixing of יהוה; so in second half corresponding change of 104[32]. — **6.** Variation of 18[15], also changed to imvs. — **7 a.** Variation of 18[17] with omission of
second vb. יקחני, and insertion of obj. ידיך. — [פְּצֵנִי] imv. with sf. 1 sg. from
† פצה Aramaism, elsw. v.[10. 11] *snatch away,* 𝕲 ἐξελοῦ, so v.[11] in reversed order
of vbs.; but הפוצה v.[10] τῷ λυτρουμένῳ. This variation of order in 𝕲 suggests
insertions in the text, and the variant vb. in v.[10] a variant verbal explanatory
gl. The three uses are all Aramaic gls. — [מים רבים] a late gl. from 18[18];

not in v.[11], and interposing between the vb. הצילני and נכר בני מיד נכר. בני נכר elsw. 18[45. 46] = 2 S. 22[45. 46] +. — **8.** = **11** *bc.* אשר] prosaic gl. — ימין שקר] phr. *a.λ.* — **9.** אלהים] a late insertion, making l. too long. The v. is based on 33[2-3], only ll. are transposed, 1 sg. cohort. of vbs. is used for imv., and sf. of 2 sg. for 3 sg. — **10.** הנותן תשועה] simplification of 18[51]; therefore מלכים is improb.; rd. עבדו ‖ מלכו; but את דוד is an explanatory gl. — מחרב רעה] phr. *a.λ.*

CXLIV. *B.*

12. אשר] rel., inserted as a connective when this fragment was pieced on. 𝕲 ὧν; 𝕵 *ut,* after Aq., Σ. — רָנֵינוּ] sf. 1 pl. interp., not in 𝕲[B. א. R]; αὐτῶν 𝕲[א. c. a. A. T.]. — ונֶטֶים] pl. נֶטַע *a.λ.*; but cf. † ונֶטַע] n.[m.] *plantation* Is. 5[7] 17[10], *planting* Is. 17[11], *plant* Jb. 14[9]. — מְגֻדָּלִים] Pu. ptc. *a.λ. made to grow up strong.* — בִּנְעוּרֵיהֶם] so 𝕲, but sf. improb. here alone; it is interp. The other three words are in assonance in יﬣֵ_; so doubtless this. This v. with this interp. does not harmonise with the next. Ehr. suggests the reading נְטֵּעֵי מִגְדָּלִים "neuen Thurmpfeilern gleichen," giving נטע the mng. of "fixed" Ec. 12[11]. This is an admirable suggestion. We might use the mng. "establish" Is. 51[16] Je. 1[10] 18[9] 31[28], and regard מגדל as Ct. 4[4]. We must transpose the last word of l. and make it second. — בְּנוֹתֵינוּ]. 𝕲 αὐτῶν, sfs. interp. ﬣֵ_ is the assonance of this l. — זָוִיﬨ] pl. † זָוִיﬨ] n.f. elsw. Zc. 9[15] of corners of altar; so here ornamental corners, *anguli ornati,* as 𝕵 after Aq. ἐπιγώνια, Σ γωνίαι; or pillars of a palace. But 𝕲 κεκαλλωπισμέναι, 𝕵 *compositae,* 𝕾 כללﬧﬡ, 𝕿 יﬨﬣﬨ﬩, all thinking of זו Aram. — מְחֻטָּבוֹת] Pu. ptc. *a.λ.* ‡ חטב] Qal *cut or gather* wood Dt. 19[5] Je. 46[22] +, but doubtless = חצב, as Is. 51[1] *hewn out,* cf. Qal *hew pillars* Pr. 9[1]. — תַּבְנִית הֵיכָל] improb., as we should have but a single word ending in ﬨיﬣ_. ‡ תַּבְנִית n.f. (1) *construction* Jos. 22[28] (P); (2) *pattern,* of tabernacle Ex. 25[9], its furniture v.[9. 40], altar 2 K. 16[10], temple 1 Ch. 28[11. 12]; (3) *figure* of animals Dt. 4[16. 17. 17. 18. 18] Ps. 106[20]; איש תבנית Is. 44[13], cf. Ez. 8[3] יד ﬨ. The latter is most prob. in the context, and we are to think of figures of women hewn out of stone, as the caryatides of ancient art. Although the pl. does not occur elsw., there is no reason why it should not have been used here in assonance. Then היכל is an explanatory addition. — **13.** מְזָוֵינוּ] sf., in 𝕲 αὐτῶν; both interp.; rd. מזוים pl. מָזﬣ_] *a.λ. garner, store,* 𝕲 ταμεῖα. — מְפִיקִים] Hiph. ptc. [פוק] *produce,* as Is. 58[10]; cf. Ps. 140[9]. — מִזַּן אֶל זַן] phr. *a.λ.* 𝕲 ἐκ τούτου εἰς τοῦτο, as if Aramaic form זה; but really from † זַן n.[m.], elsw. זֵוִים 2 Ch. 16[14] *kinds, sorts,* so prob. here, as measure and assonance in יﬣﬣ_ require. — צאוננו] Kt.; Qr. without ו. Assonance requires צאנות, which is unknown elsw.; but as referring here to the females, the ewes, there is no sufficient reason against it. — מַאֲלִיפוֹﬨ] Hiph. ptc. אלף denom. אֶלֶף *thousand,* 𝕲 πολύτοκα. — מְרֻבָּבוֹﬨ] Pu. ptc. רבב denom. רבו *myriad,* 𝕲 πληθύνοντα. — בְּחוּצוֹתֵינוּ]. 𝕲 sf. αὐτῶν; both sfs. interp. as usual. חוצות here *fields,* as Jb. 5[10] 18[17] Pr. 8[26]. — **14.** אַלּוּפֵינוּ] 𝕲 οἱ βόες αὐτῶν; sfs. interp.; rd. אלופים pl. אַלּוּף adj. *tame animal* as Je. 11[19], *cattle* as Ps. 8[8]. The mng. *friends* Ps. 55[14] + is improb. here. — מְסֻבָּלִים] Pu. ptc. *a.λ.* ‡ סבל vb.

Qal *bear a heavy load* Gn. 49¹⁵ (J) Is. 46⁷ 53⁴ +. The Pu. is variously interpreted, usually *laden* with young Ges., Hi., Ew., Hu.³; but Bä. after 𝕿 *laden*
with burdens of heavy harvest. 𝕲 παχεῖς, 𝔙 *crassae*, 𝕾 ןיעיט, think of the
animals as large, strong, fat ; so Aq., Σ, 𝔍. The decision remains with the
complementary words. — ץרֶפֶ ןיאֵ]. Assonance requires pl. םיצרפ, which
may refer to bursting forth from womb, as Gn. 38²⁹ (J), or the usual *breach*
in walls Ps. 106²³ Am. 9¹¹ +, as 𝕲 κατάπτωμα φραγμοῦ. — אצֵויֵ] ptc. f. אצֵי
with שׁפֶנ understood. Assonance requires pl. ־ֵיה, goings forth to battle ; cf.
1 S. 17²⁾ Ps. 68⁸. — ןיאֵ] makes l. too long. ו carries on the negative sufficiently. — † החָוָצְ] n.f. *outcry*, as Is. 24¹¹ Je. 14² 46¹². Assonance requires pl.
— וניתֹבֹחְרִבְּ]. 𝕲 αὐτῶν ; sfs. interp.; rd. וחבֹרחב. — **15.** ירֵשְׁאַ] *I.* — הכָּבֶשֶׁ] =
שֶׁ־ rel. and הכֹּ partic. *so, thus.*

PSALM CXLV., 3 STR. 7⁶, RF. 1⁶.

Ps. 145 is an acrostic song of praise to Yahweh the King (v.¹⁻²),
for His greatness, might (v.³), wondrous deeds (v.⁴⁻⁶), and saving
righteousness (v.⁷). His grace and compassion extend to all His
works (v.⁸⁻⁹). He will be praised by all (v.¹⁰), for the glory and
permanence of His kingdom (v.¹¹⁻¹³), His steadfast kindness (v.¹⁴ᵃ).
He raiseth up the fallen (v.¹⁴⁾), supplieth all creatures (v.¹⁵⁻¹⁶), is
kind to all (v.¹⁷), nigh to His worshippers (v.¹⁸), to help and preserve (v.¹⁹⁻²⁰). The whole concludes with a summons to universal
praise (v.²¹).

I WILL exalt Thee, O King! and I will bless Thy name forever and ever.
  Alway will I bless Thee, and I will praise Thy name forever and ever.
  Great is Yahweh and highly to be praised, and His greatness is unsearchable.
  One generation to another will laud Thy works ; Thy mighty deeds declare.
  The splendour of the glory of Thy majesty they will speak ; on Thy wonders
    muse.
  And the strength of Thy awe-inspiring acts they will say ; and Thy deeds of
    greatness tell.
  The commemoration of the abundance of Thy goodness they will pour forth ;
    and Thy saving righteousness ring out.
GRACIOUS and compassionate is Yahweh, slow to anger and of great kindness.
  Yahweh is good to all, and His compassion is over all His works.
  All Thy works will praise Thee, Yahweh; and (all) Thy favoured ones will
    bless Thee.
  The glory of Thy kingdom they will say ; and Thy might they will speak :
  To make known to the sons of men Thy might, and the glory of the splendour
    of (Thy) kingdom.
  Thy kingdom is a kingdom of all ages, and Thy dominion will continue in all
    generations.
  (Yahweh is steadfast in His words, and kind in all His works.)

Y̶AHWEH upholdeth them that fall, and raiseth up all them that are bowed
    down.
  The eyes of all wait upon Thee, and Thou givest to them.
  Thou openest Thy hand and satisfiest all living things with good will.
  Righteous is Yahweh in His ways and kind in all His works,
  Yahweh is nigh to them that call on Him, to all that call on Him truly.
  The good pleasure of them that fear Him He doeth; and their cry for help He
    heareth, and saveth them.
  Yahweh preserveth all them that love Him, but the wicked He destroyeth.
      A song of praise to Yahweh my mouth will speak, and all flesh will bless
      His holy name.

Ps. 145 bears the title תהלה לדוד, but it is probably a later addition. The
Ps. can hardly have been written earlier than the Greek period. It is an
acrostic of 22 hexameters, although in 𝕳 נ is omitted. It has been preserved
in 𝕲. There are several connections with other poems : v.³ גדול יהוה ומהלל מאד
= 48² 96⁴; v.¹⁸ = Dn. 3³³ 4³¹ in Aramaic, quoted from Ps., not the reverse as
Du.; v.¹⁴ זוקף הכפופים Ps. 146⁸; v.¹⁵ a conflation of 104²⁷ with its original. It
is probable that in all these cases our Ps. is earlier; זוקף v.¹⁴ seems to be a late
word. חנון ורחום v.⁸ gives the order of these words, subsequent to Chronicler ;
but in this case the change was necessary on account of acrostic. Therefore it
is doubtful whether this gives evidence of late date. It may be the origin of
the change of order ; and if so, is certainly prior to Ch., Jo., and Jon. There
are no other evidences of late date. The universalism of the Ps. is not the
universalism of Is.², but the larger universalism of the Greek period.

Str. I. Is a syn. heptastich of praise. — **1–2.** *I will exalt Thee*
‖ *bless Thy name*], the latter repeated, in order to the final :
praise Thy name. The name sums up in itself all the renown
that Yahweh has won in the esteem of His people, all that they
know of Him. — *O King*], vocative. The context shows sufficiently that it refers to God as the King of Israel : but a glossator
would make it more definite, and so at the expense of the measure inserts : *my God.* —*forever and ever*], repeated for emphasis.
The praise of the congregation goes on from generation to generation without cessation in the worship of the temple and the synagogue. — **3.** *Great is Yahweh and highly to be praised*], as 48²
96⁴. — *and His greatness is unsearchable*], extends beyond the
bounds of human research in special relations. — **4–7.** *One generation to another*], each generation in its turn transmitting the
praise. — *will laud, declare ; ‖ speak, muse* v.⁵ ; *say, tell* v.⁶] ; all
in sacred song ‖ *the commemoration pour forth*], in a perpetual
stream of celebration ; *ring out*], in jubilant shouts v.⁷. — The

theme of unceasing praise are the wondrous deeds of Yahweh in the deliverance of His people, usually expressed in varied terms referring to the deeds themselves: *works, mighty deeds* v.⁴; || *wonders* v.⁵; *awe-inspiring acts, deeds of greatness*], v.⁶; but intermingled with the divine attributes which urge to those deeds such as — *The splendour of the glory of Thy majesty*], as shewn by the King in His majestic manifestations. — and *the abundance of Thy goodness*], in benefactions to His people || *Thy saving righteousness*], in their vindication against their enemies.

Str. II. has a syn. couplet, a stairlike tetrastich and a synth. line. — **8**. A citation of the primitive revelation of the divine kindness Ex. 34⁶, cf. Ps. 86¹⁵ 103⁸ 111⁴ 112⁴, as a basis for the second Str. of the Ps. — **9**. *Yahweh is good,* as benignant and bestowing benefactions; explained by *His compassion is over*]. He has a tender, fatherly sympathy with and a paternal care over. — *all*], not to be limited as PBV., to "every man," but extending to all His creatures; || *all His works.* — **10–13**. Accordingly, on the basis of these divine attributes: *Thy works,* and especially *Thy favoured ones*], the people of God, the special objects of His kindness: they all take up the praise of Israel of the first part of the Ps. — *will praise Thee,* || *bless* v.¹⁰; *say, speak* v.¹¹; *make known to the sons of men*], to mankind in general. — The theme is the attribute: *Thy might*], v.¹¹, repeated in v.¹²; but especially: *the glory of Thy kingdom* v.¹¹, *the glory of the splendour of Thy kingdom* v.¹²; and above all its perpetuity: *Thy kingdom is a kingdom of all ages, and Thy dominion will continue in all generations* v.¹³. The kingdom is here conceived as universal, not only in time but as extending over all men and all creatures. V.¹³ is cited in Dn. 3³³ 4³¹, in antithesis with the kingdom of Babylon; and probably also was in the mind of the author of 1 Tim. 1¹⁷. — 𝕲 gives the missing line in ℸ, which is needed not only to complete the acrostic, but also to complete the second part of the Ps. It was probably omitted by an early scribe, because he found the climax in v.¹³. But really, while the Ps. sings of the glory of the divine King, His kindness is the main theme to which it ever recurs. We ought not to be surprised therefore that the second part of the Ps. concludes with that thought in the words of 𝕲: *Yahweh is* *steadfast in His words, and kind in all His works*]. The words of such a king are steadfast, and always firm and reliable : the works of such a king are always kind, cf. v.[8-9].

Str. III. now unfolds the divine kindness in a progressive heptastich in : **14.** *Yahweh upholdeth them that fall*], unable to stand upright themselves because of weakness, Yahweh holds them up. — *and raiseth up all them that are bowed down*], when with bowed head and body ready to bend down to the earth. He raiseth them up to an upright posture. This is a graphic description of His goodness to the weak. — **15.** *The eyes of all*], all creatures, as 104[27]. — *wait upon Thee*], for their sustenance. — *and Thou givest to them*], what they have need of; enlarged after 104[27], at the expense of the measure by supplying the object " their food in its season." — **16.** *Thou openest Thy hand*], conceived as full of gifts. — *and satisfiest all living things*], the entire animal world as well as man. — *with good will*], not only the things they need, but the good will to give them all such things, which makes the divine gift so acceptable. — **17.** *Righteous*], in the vindicatory, redemptive sense, as ‖ *kind — in His ways* ‖ *in all His works*], that is, in all His royal government, in all that He does in His administration of the affairs of the world for all creation. — **18.** *is nigh to them that call on Him*], near at hand ready to respond, cf. 34[19]; limited however in the complementary clause. — *that call on Him truly*], sincerely, with confidence in Him ; excluding therefore the insincere, those who are not in a relation of fidelity to Him. — **19.** *The good pleasure of them that fear Him*], what is pleasing to them, acceptable unto them, their desire ; defined by complementary clause as *their cry for help*. — *He doeth*], what pleases them, which is in this case — *He heareth and saveth them.* — **20.** The climax is reached in the antithesis between *them that love Him*]. His faithful and favoured ones, who are in the relation to Him of loving children to a father ; and *the wicked*], who have no such relation to Him. — The former He *preserveth*, the latter *He destroyeth.*

21. The Ps. concludes with a Rf. a universal summons to *all flesh*, all mankind, to *bless His holy name*], as the majestic name of the beneficent King ; introduced by the vow of the congregation itself : *A song of praise to Yahweh my mouth will speak*], the

oral praise with song and music in the temple. — A later scribe
adds : *forever and ever*], preparatory to the Benediction, which,
in the final Psalter at least, always concluded a psalm.

1. אלוהי המלך] a.λ., 𝕵 *deus meus rex ;* but 𝕲 ὁ βασιλεύς μου, so Street,
Che. ; cf. מלכי ואלהי 5³. אלוהי is gl. המלך is vocative and original. — [אברכה
Pi. cohort., cf. 96² 100⁴. — **2.** [אהללה Pi. cohort., cf. 69³¹ 74²¹ 148⁵. — [לעולם ועד
om. in 𝕲ᴮ by err. ; it is in 𝕲ᴺ·ᴬ·ᴿ·ᵀ. — **3.** [גדול יהוה ומהלל מאד = 48² 96⁴. —
† [אין חקר elsw. Is. 40²⁸ Jb. 5⁹ 9¹⁰ Pr. 25³. — **4.** [ישבח Aramaism as 63⁴.
— [גבורתיך pl. *mighty deeds* v.¹² Dt. 3²⁴ Ps. 20⁷ 71¹⁶ 106² 150². But 𝕲 has
sing. here and also v.¹², and is prob. correct. — **5.** [הדר כבוד הודך phr. a.λ.,
but cf. v.¹² 96⁶ 104¹ 111³. — [דברי נפלאתיך phr. a.λ. improb., cf. 105²⁷. 𝕲 λαλήσουσιν ידברו, so 𝔖, 𝔈, Hare, Kenn., Street, Horsley, Che., Bä., Du., Ehr.,
most prob. as it is more suited to ‖. — [אשיחה rd. with 𝕲, 𝔖, 3 pl. ישיחו *sing,
muse,* so Kenn., Street, Horsley. — **6.** [וגדולתיך has two beats and is pl. The
sg. Qr. 𝕲 is not suited to context. — [אספרנה 𝕲 had 3 pl. which is more
prob. יספרון. — **7.** [זכר] = commemoration of ⊙'s character and works 6⁶ 30⁵
97¹² 102¹³ 111⁴. — [רב 𝕲 רב so Bä., Du. — **8.** [חנון ורחום] = 2 Ch. 30⁹ Ne. 9¹⁷·³¹
Ps. 111⁴ 112⁴ Jo. 2¹³ Jon. 4² later order of words ; but 𝕲 has the earlier οἰκτίρ-
μων καὶ ἐλεήμων as Ex. 34⁶ Ps. 86¹⁵ 103⁸. The change of order due to the
acrostic form. — [גדל חסד cf. 1 K. 3⁶ 2 Ch. 1⁸ Ps. 57¹¹ 86¹³ 108⁵. — **9.** [לכל but
𝕲ᴮ·ᴬ·ᴺ substitutes τοῖς ὑπομένουσιν = קוי Bi., Che. ; [למלכבל Bä., σύνπασιν
𝕲ᴺ·ᶜ·ᵃ·ᴿ·ᵀ. — **10.** [יברכוכה Pi. impf. with full form f. sf. — **12.** [לבני האדם
article err. ; the measure requires that the two words should have but one
accent. — [גבורתיו 𝕲 ; גבורתך ; so 𝔐 מלכותו, 𝕲 מלכתך, prob. both sfs. interpretations. — **13.** This v. cited in Dn. 3³³ 4³¹ in Aramaic. 𝔐 omits the l. with נ,
but 𝕲 preserves it : πιστὸς Κύριος ἐν τοῖς λόγοις αὐτοῦ καὶ ὅσιος ἐν πᾶσι τοῖς
ἔργοις αὐτοῦ ; so 𝔈, 𝔖, and prob. 𝕵, although it is omitted in some codd. of
the latter. It fits admirably with the context in measure, style, and thought ;
so Grotius, Cap., Ew., Gr., Bi., Oort, Kirk., Che., al. — **14.** [לכל־הנפלים. The
כל is prob. an assimilation to כל with last word. — [זוקף ptc. † [זקף vb. *raise
up,* elsw. 146⁸ ; no good reason for taking it as late word ; found in As.
zakâpu. — [לכל־הכפופים ptc. pass. כף *bowed down,* cf. 57⁷. — **15.** [ישברו
Pi. impf. *wait,* cf. 104²⁷, to which this l. is assimilated by adding אכלם בעתו,
making it too long. — **16.** [פורח את־ידך measure requires another word : rd.
אתה as 𝕲 for את ; so Bi., Bä., Che., Valeton, cf. 104²⁸. — **17.** [בכל־דרכיו is כל
an assimilation ; it makes l. too long ; so with לכל־קראיו v.¹⁸ and את־כל־הרשעים
v.²⁰ — **18.** [באמת 𝕲 ἐν ἀληθείᾳ, 𝕵 *in veritate ;* so 𝔗 ; but it is adv. *truly,*
as Ju. 9¹⁵ Je. 26¹⁵ 28⁹ 32⁴¹. — **19.** [ואת את prosaic gl. here and v.²⁰. —
21. [לעולם ועד is certainly a late gl., as it makes l. just these words too
long.

PSALM CXLVI., 3 str. 6³.

**Ps. 146 is a resolution of lifelong praise in the temple (v.²),
with a warning to put no trust in princes (v.³⁻⁴) ; pronounces happy
those whose hope is in Yahweh, the creator, who is also faithful
and just (v.⁵⁻⁶ᵃ· ⁶ᶜ· ⁷ᵃ), whose kindness to various classes of need is
specified (v.⁷ᵇ⁻⁹ᵇ). There are expansive glosses (v.⁶ᵇ· ⁹ᶜ), and introductory and concluding liturgical phrases (v.¹· ¹⁰).**

> I WILL praise Yahweh while I live ;
>   I will make melody to my God while I have being.
>   Trust not in princes,
>   In a son of mankind who can have no victory ;
>   (For) he returneth to the ground ;
>   (All) his thoughts perish.
> HAPPY he whose is the God of Jacob,
>   Whose hope rests upon Yahweh his God,
>   Maker of heaven and earth ;
>   Who keepeth faithfulness forever,
>   Worketh justice for the oppressed,
>   Giveth bread to the hungry :
> YAHWEH, who looseth them that are bound ;
>   Yahweh, who openeth the eyes of the blind ;
>   Yahweh, who lifteth up the bowed down ;
>   Yahweh, who loveth the righteous ;
>   Yahweh, who preserveth the sojourners ;
>   The orphan and widow restoreth.

Ps. 146 is a Hallel, with הללויה prefixed in 𝕳 and ἀλληλουιά in 𝕲. It also
in 𝕳 has הללויה at the end, which is dittog., for it is not in 𝕲. *V.* Intr. § 35.
𝕲 adds to the title Ἁγγαίου καὶ Σαχαρίου, which was mere conjecture without
external or internal support. The Ps. has the same structure as the other
Hallels. It depends on Gn. 3¹⁹ in v.⁴ᵃ, on Ps. 103⁶ in v.⁷ᵃ, on 145¹⁵ in v.⁷ᵇ, on
105²⁰ in v.⁷ᶜ. V.⁴ is cited in 1 Mac. 2⁶³ᵇ. The Ps. has three Aramaisms :
(1) the relative ש v.³ᵇ· ⁵ᵃ, (2) the a.λ. עשתנתיו v.⁴, and (3) שברו v.⁵ᵇ, as 119¹¹⁶.
It belongs to the late Greek period. There are several glosses : v.¹ an introductory liturgical phrase, cf. 103¹ 104¹ ; v.⁶ᵇ expansive ; v.⁹ᵇ to get in the fate
of the wicked ; v.¹⁰ conflation of Ex. 15¹⁸ with Ps. 147¹²ᵇ.

Str. I. Three syn. couplets. — **1–2.** *I will praise ‖ I will make
melody*], resolution of public worship in the temple. — *while I live
‖ while I have being*], cf. 104³³ ; lifelong worship. — A later editor
prefixed the liturgical phrase : *Praise Yahweh, O my soul!* —
3. *Trust not in princes ‖ a son of mankind*], the former the

nobles, the latter their sovereign, although the term might as elsewhere be interpreted as collective. These were probably the
Egyptian king and his nobles, who showed themselves not altogether worthy of confidence. — *who can have no victory*], over the
Syrian kings, who pressed upon the Jews from the north. The
specific reference is more probable than the more general " salvation " or " help " of EV⁸. — **4.** *For he returneth to the ground*ᵢ.
as mere man, in accordance with the primitive doom of the human race, Gn. 3¹⁹. This is the citation of 1 Mac. 2⁶³ᵇ, and is more
probable in itself and gives better measure than 頃 and Vrss.ᵢ
which prefix " his breath departeth" to this line and " in that
day " to the next line at the expense of the measure. — *All his
thoughts perish*], so ⑥, in accordance with the measure. The
thoughts to gain a victory on behalf of Judah are transient and
unreliable. They perish as inevitably as one monarch after another
departs from life.

Str. II. A syn. couplet and a synth. tetrastich. — **5.** *Happy
he*], exclamation of congratulation, cf. 1¹. — *whose is the God of
Jacob*], cf. 20² 33¹² 144¹⁵. — A glossator specifies by inserting
" whose help " against the measure ‖ *Whose hope*, which *rests upon
Yahweh his God.* — **6.** *Maker of heaven and earth*], a common
phr. for the creation, cf. 121² 124⁸, which a glossator expands at
the expense of the structure of the Str. by adding from Ex. 20¹¹
" the sea, and all that in them is." The remainder of the Ps.
specifies the constant and varied kindness of Yahweh toward His
people. — *Who keepeth faithfulness forever*], ever faithful to His
covenant and His promises. — **7** *ab. Worketh justice for the oppressed*], as 103⁶. — *Giveth bread to the hungry*], cf. 33¹⁹ 37¹⁹
104²⁷ 107⁹ 136²⁵.

Str. III. Synth. hexastich. — **7** *c. Yahweh*], resuming the subj. ;
repeated five times followed by ptcs., in every line but the last,
where the construction is changed for a climax. — Six acts of
divine kindness are specified : *looseth them that are bound*], prisoners of war as 105²⁰ Is. 42⁷ ; — **8.** *openeth the eyes of the blind*],
cf. Dt. 28²⁹ Is. 59⁹ ˢᵠ· ; probably not in the physical sense by miracle,
but in the intellectual and moral sense, from the darkness, gloom,
and despair of captivity. — *lifteth up the bowed down*], as Ps. 145¹⁴.
— *loveth the righteous*], as the context indicates, by acting in love

toward them. — **9.** *preserveth the sojourners*], cf. 94⁶. These were not limited to proselytes as 𝔊. The term is used in the general sense of D, H, of Hexateuch, which emphasize love and kindness to them on the part of Yahweh and His people. — *The orphan and widow restoreth*]. It is characteristic of D that these are associated with the sojourners as especial objects of divine protection (*v.* Br.ᴴᵉˣ·⁸⁶). — This brings the Ps. to a proper conclusion ; but a glossator wishes to exclude the wicked from the divine benefaction, and so he adds : *but the way of the wicked He maketh crooked*], depending in part upon Ps. 1⁶ and Ec. 7¹³ Jb. 8³ 34¹². — A late editor appends a liturgical conclusion in part based on Ex. 15¹⁸ : **10.** *Yahweh shall reign forever*, and in part on Ps. 147¹² : *Thy God, O Zion, for all generations.*

1 is a gl., a liturgical phrase, cf. 103¹ 104¹· ³⁵. — **2.** [בעורי ‖ בחיי ; cf. 104³³ Je. 15⁹. — **3.** [שֶׁאֵין] late rel. with אין. — **4.** [הֵצֵא רוּחוֹ] gl., not in 1 Mac. 2⁶³ ; so ביום ההוא, both excessive ll. ; prefix כי, as Bi., Du. — [עֶשְׁתֹנֹתָיו] α.λ. [שַׁתֹּנֵה] n.f. Aram. ; *thoughts*, cf. עֶשְׁתּוּת n.f. Jb. 12⁵. כֹּל of 𝔊, 𝔖, 𝔍, required for measure. — **5.** [אֲשָׁרֵי]. *V.* 1¹. — [שֶׁאֵל] late rel., cf. v.³, with אֶל divine name. — [בעזרו interp. gl. — [יֹשְׁבֵרו] † [שֵׂבֶר] n.m. *hope*, elsw. 119¹¹⁶. — **7.** [עֲשׂוּקִים] Qal ptc. as 103⁶ *oppressed.* — [מַתִּיר] Hiph. ptc. נהר *loosen, set free*, as 105²⁰ Is. 58⁶. — **8.** [פֹּתֵחַ] Qal ptc. ‡ פקח vb. *open*, eyes as Is. 42⁷ Gn. 21¹⁹ 2 K. 6¹⁷· ²⁰, cf. Is. 42²⁰. — [יֹחֵף כְּפוּפִים] as 145¹⁴. — **9.** [יְעֹדֵד] Polel עוּר. Qal not used. Pi. *surround*, 119⁶¹. Polel *restore* elsw. 147⁶. Hithp. 20⁹. — [וֹדרך רשעים יְעַוֵּת]. This l. is a gl. of addition. — [וֵיעַוֵּת] Pi. impf. ‡ [עוּת] vb. *make crooked*, elsw. ψ, 119⁷⁸, cf. La. 3³⁶ Jb. 8³. — **10.** This l. is a liturgical addition.

PSALM CXLVII.

Ps. 147 has three parts : I. is a summons of the congregation to praise Yahweh for His goodness and sweetness in rebuilding Jerusalem and restoring her people (v.¹⁻³). Though He numbers and names the stars as their sovereign Lord, He interposes on behalf of His afflicted people against their enemies (v.⁴⁻⁶). **II.** The congregation is summoned to sing and play to Him who sends the rain upon the earth for the service of man (v.⁷⁻⁸), who provideth for the animals, but especially delights in those that fear Him (v.⁹⁻¹¹). **III.** Jerusalem is summoned to laud Yahweh, who hath restored her prosperity (v.¹²⁻¹⁴), whose word governs snow and frost and hail

$(v.^{15-17})$. His word at the same time directs winds and waters, and gives to Israel a Law, thereby distinguishing them from other nations $(v.^{18-20})$.

A. $v.^{1-6}$, 2 STR. 6^3.

PRAISE ye Yah, for He is good.
 Make melody to our God, for He is sweet.
 Yahweh, Rebuilder of Jerusalem,
 The outcasts of Israel gathereth;
 Who healeth the broken hearted,
 And who bindeth up their wounds;
WHO counteth the number of the stars,
 Giving names to all of them.
 Great is our sovereign Lord and abundant in power;
 His understanding has no number;
 Yahweh, restorer of the afflicted,
 Who casteth down the wicked unto the earth.

B. $v.^{7-11}$, 2 STR. 6^3.

SING to Yahweh with a song of thanks;
 Make melody to our God with the lyre.
 Who covereth the heavens with clouds,
 Who prepareth for the earth rain,
 And maketh the mountains to put forth verdure,
 And green herbs for the service of man.
WHO giveth to cattle their bread,
 To young ravens when they cry.
 Not in the strength of a horse,
 Not in the legs of a man,
 But Yahweh delighteth in them that fear Him,
 Them that wait for His kindness.

C. $v.^{12-20}$, 3 STR. 6^3.

LAUD Yahweh, O Jerusalem:
 Praise thy God, O Zion;
 For He hath strengthened the bars of thy gates,
 Hath blessed thy children in thy midst;
 He who maketh thy border, Peace;
 Satisfying thee with the fat of wheat.
WHO sendeth forth His saying to the earth,
 His word very swiftly running;
 Who giveth snow like wool,
 Scattering hoar frost like dust;
 Who casteth down His hail like morsels.
 Before His cold who can stand?

H E sendeth forth His word, and He causeth them to melt away;
    He causeth His wind to blow, and they flow away.
    Who declareth His word to Jacob,
    His statutes and His judgments to Israel.
    Not so hath He done to any nation;
    And His judgments they know not.

Ps. 147 is a Hallel, with the title in 𝔊 ἀλληλουιά · Ἀγγαίου καὶ Ζαχαρίου
(v. Intr., § 35). The same title is at the head of v.¹²⁻²⁰, which in 𝔊 is a
separate Ps. 𝔐 has no title for 147, for the הללויה at the beginning belongs
to the first line of the Ps. As in other cases הללויה is at the close of 146 and
of 147. Du. suggests that v.¹⁻⁶ and v.⁷⁻⁸ were also originally separate. These
parts are all similar in style and resemble 146, all coming from the same
author or at least the same situation. The parts of 147 are so loosely connected that it might be used as one, two, or three Pss. according to liturgical
circumstances, possibly to vary the total number of Pss. from 150 to 153 in
accordance with the three years' readings of the Pentateuch. Ps. 147 is
dependent upon Is.² : v.²ᵇ, cf. Is. 56⁸; v.³, cf. Is. 61¹; v.⁴ᵇ, cf. Is. 40²⁶; v.⁵ᵇ, cf.
Is. 40²⁸; v.¹⁴ᵃ, cf. Is. 60¹⁷; v.¹⁵· ¹⁸, cf. Is. 55¹⁰· ¹¹. Cf. v.¹ with Ps. 135³, v.⁸
with 104¹⁴, v.¹⁰⁻¹¹ with 33¹⁶⁻¹⁸, and v.¹²ᵇ with 146¹⁰. V.² is used in BS. 51² (Heb.
text). Ps. 147¹⁻⁶ has two trimeter hexastichs, v.⁷⁻¹¹ two ; but v.¹²⁻²⁰ three.
There are no glosses except in explanatory words: as v.¹ᶜ from 33¹. The Ps.
belongs to the late Maccabean period.

PSALM CXLVII. A.

Str. I. Three syn. couplets. — **1.** *Praise ye Yahweh ‖ Make
melody to our God*], in public worship. — *for He is good ‖ for He
is sweet*], as 135³, on which this v. is based. This is the most
probable rendering of a difficult passage, where 𝔐 and Vrss.
differ : so JPSV. essentially. The EVˢ. all miss the sense by too
slavish adherence to 𝔐. — *praise is comely*]. This is a gloss from
33¹. Thus the measure and parallelism of the couplet are complete, and they are also harmonious with v.⁷· ¹². — **2.** *Rebuilder of
Jerusalem*], implying at least a partial destruction of the city,
probably in the early Maccabean times. ‖ *The outcasts of Israel
gathereth*], as Is. 56⁸, not, however, from the Babylonian captivity,
but from the Syrian oppression, as 146⁷⁻⁸. — **3.** *Who healeth the
broken hearted*, as Is. 61¹, ‖ *And who bindeth up their wounds*],
those wounded and discouraged by the early Syrian oppression.

Str. II. Two syn. and an antith. couplet. — **4.** *Who counteth
the number of the stars ‖ Giving names to all of them*], taking an
interest in each one of these to men innumerable lights of heaven,

knowing them individually, assigning each a name and a place in the heavens. This conception is based on Is. 40²⁶, and also upon the naming of the created objects, organized as an army under the supreme commander Gn. 1. — **5.** *Great ∥ abundant in power*], having so great and powerful a control over these stars. — *is our sovereign Lord*], pl. abstr. emphatic and not simply " our Lord " of EVˢ. The sovereignty is of His people as well as of the stars. — *His understanding*], as expressed in numbering and naming the stars. — *has no number*], it extends beyond the numbers of the stars, in numbers that cannot be numbered; so that virtually the " infinite " of EVˢ. is practically correct. This is a variation of the " unsearchable " of the original passage Is. 40²⁸. — **6.** *Yahweh, restorer*], as 146⁹. — *the afflicted*], the people who had been oppressed by the Syrians, as v.³. — In antithesis *Who casteth down the wicked unto the earth*], especially the Syrian oppressors, in the humiliation of utter defeat.

PSALM CXLVII. *B.*

Str. I. Three syn. couplets. — **7.** *Sing to Yahweh ∥ Make melody to our God*], resuming the call to public worship of v.¹. — *with a song of thanks ∥ with the lyre*], vocal and instrumental music combine in the temple worship. — **8.** *Who covereth the heavens with clouds*], the clouds are under His sovereign control, and they move to their place in the heavens by His direction. — ∥ *Who prepareth rain,* the clouds are full of rain, *for the earth*], they have a beneficent purpose. — *maketh the mountains to put forth verdure*]. The rain, coming upon the earth, causes it to produce vegetation of all kinds, especially fresh grass and herbage. — A line is missing in 𝕳, and so in AV., RV.; but is given in 𝕲, 𝕴, followed by PBV.: *And green herbs for the service of man*]. Both lines of this couplet are from 104¹⁴.

Str. II. Three syn. couplets. — **9.** *Who giveth to cattle their bread ∥ To young ravens*], providing for the nourishment of the animals, represented by the domestic cattle and the wild ravens. — *when they cry*], in the expression of their need. The relative is temporal and not pronominal as EVˢ. — **10.** *Not in the strength of a horse ∥ not in the legs of a man*], cf. 33¹⁶⁻¹⁷, as the chief means of gaining a victory over enemies. — This couplet is enlarged by glosses inserting at the expense of the measure the vbs. "He delighteth" ‖ "hath pleasure": whereas the original reserves the vb. for the antithetical line : **11.** *But Yahweh delight-eth in them that fear Him* ‖ *Them that wait for His kindness*], depending upon Him alone to give the victory as 33[18].

PSALM CXLVII. *C.*

Str. I. A syn. couplet and a syn. tetrastich. — **12.** *Laud Yah-weh,* ‖ *Praise thy God*], resuming the call of v.[1.7]; but with an especial appeal to — *Jerusalem* ‖ *Zion*], in place of the general summons to the congregation in v.[1.7]. — **13.** *For He hath strength-ened the bars of thy gates*], making the city more defensible against the enemy, cf. Ne. 3. — *Hath blessed thy children in thy midst*]. Zion as in the exilic Isaiah is the mother of her in-habitants. The blessing, as the context suggests, is safety from enemies. — **14.** *He who maketh thy border, Peace*], cf. Is. 60[17]. Peace with neighbours is a boundary of protection. — *Satisfying thee with the fat of wheat*], as Dt. 32[14] Ps. 81[17]: providing richly for the wants of the people.

Str. II. A syn. couplet, a syn. triplet, and a synth. line. — **15.** *Who sendeth forth to the earth*]. Yahweh as sovereign of the earth issues His commands, which are here conceived as the primi-tive prophetic laws, as *His saying* ‖ *His word* (*v.* Br.[Hex. pp. 242 sq.]), cf. Ps. 119, p. 415. — This goes *very swiftly running*], as a faithful, expeditious messenger. — **16–17.** *Who giveth snow* ‖ *scattering hoar frost* ‖ *casteth down His hail*]. These various forms of cold, especially connected with a storm, and compared respectively to *wool* for whiteness, to *dust* for quantity, and to *morsels* for a com-paratively large size, are not given here merely as specimens of the divine sovereignty over nature ; but because they were unusual in Palestine, and only connected with extraordinary storms, which were greatly feared, and which were also associated with theo-phanic manifestations of Yahweh for the deliverance of His people and the destruction of their enemies, cf. Jos. 10[11] Jb. 38[22-23]. — And accordingly the Str. ends with propriety in the challenge : *Before His cold who can stand?*]. No enemy can resist Him when, in accordance with His command, snow, hail, and frost descend in the face of His enemies.

Str. III. Three syn. couplets. — **18.** *He sendeth forth His word*], resuming v.¹⁵, and giving the object to whom it was sent in the ‖ *He causeth His wind to blow*]. The wind of Yahweh is also not unfrequently used in theophanies, cf. 18¹¹. — *and He causeth them to melt away* ‖ *and they flow away*]. 𝔥 and Vrss. connect with the previous lines, and think of the snow, frost, and hail, which are melted by a warm wind and flow away as water. This interpretation indeed was put into the text by the insertion of "waters" before the last vb. But the fact that this couplet begins a new Str. in which Israel is contrasted with other nations, and that the previous Str. refers to the theophanic use of hail, urges that we should here think of a theophanic use of wind to cause the enemies to melt and flow away. — **19.** *Who declareth His word*], the original prophetic type of Law as contained in the Ten Words, and so in the ‖ *His statutes and His judgments*], other primitive types of Law as contained in the Book of the Covenant (Br.^{Hex. pp. 248 sq.}). — These were made known to His people, *Jacob* ‖ *Israel*], in ancient times, and are here in antithesis with the words of command to the forces and powers of nature used in theophanies — and also with the ignorance of such laws by other nations : **20.** *Not so hath He done to any nation* ‖ *And His judgments they know not.*

CXLVII. A.

1. הַלְלוּיָהּ] acc. to 𝔊 and 𝔥 belongs to the text. — זַמְּרָה] Pi. inf. in 𝔥, a.λ. and improb. 𝔊 ψαλμός זַמְרָה also improb. ‖ requires זַמְרוּ as Hare, Street, Ols., Dys., Gr. ; cf. 135³ on which the v. is based. נאוה תהלה is then an expl. gl. from 33¹. — **2.** בֹּנֵה] ptc. without rel., but art. with הרופא; the original was uniform. — יכנס] Pi. (*33*⁷) *gather together* for restoration, as Ez. 39²⁸, for קבץ Is. 56⁸. — **3.** שְׁבוּרֵי לֵב] ptc. עצב from Is. 61¹, cf. Ps. 69²¹. — מְחַבֵּשׁ] Pi. ptc. ‡ חבשׁ vb. (1) *bind, bind on, bind up*, Qal, not in ψ. Pi. here and Jb. 28¹¹. Pu. Ez. 30²¹ Is. 1⁶. — **5.** אין מספר] *There is no number*, cf. Is. 40¹³ Ps. 145³ אין חקר. — **6.** מְעוֹדֵד] ptc. Polel as 146⁹.

CXLVII. B.

7. עֱנוּ] Imv. Qal ‡ עֱנֵה *sing*, as 119¹⁷², cf. 88¹. — **8.** 𝔊^{B. אֲ. R. T} add from 104¹⁴ καὶ χλόην τῇ δουλείᾳ τῶν ἀνθρώπων, which is indeed needed to complete the Str. It is omitted by 𝔊^A. — **9.** אשר] rel. gl. — **10.** ירצה ‖ יחפץ, prosaic gls., making ll. too long.

CXLVII. C.

12 begins a new Ps. with &#5. — **14**. הֵלֶב חטִּים] as Ps. 81¹⁷, cf. Dt. 32¹⁴ Is. 34⁶. — משביעך. &#5, $\mathfrak{S}$, $\mathfrak{S}$, [וישביעך — **15**. עד מְהֵרָה] n.f. as adv., *v. 31³*. — **18**. ביֹשֵּׁב] Hiph. † [נשב] *blow;* Qal Is. 40⁷. Hiph. elsw. Gn. 15¹¹. — [יִזְלוּ] Qal נזל, as 78¹⁶. ⁴⁴ Ex. 15⁸ *flow.* — מים] is a gl. of interp., not needed for measure.

PSALM CXLVIII., 4 STR. 6³.

Ps. 148 is a summons to praise Yahweh : (1) to all in the heavens, especially angels and heavenly lights (v.¹⁻³), also the heavenly waters, to praise the name of their creator and sovereign (v.⁴⁻⁶) ; (2) to all in the earth, especially the great deep, the storm, the trees (v.⁷⁻⁹), also the animals, to praise the glorious name, which is also the praise of all the pious (v.¹⁰· ¹³· ¹⁴ᵇ). A glossator adds men of all classes (v.¹¹⁻¹²), and adds to the ground of praise the exaltation of His people (v.¹⁴ᵃᶜ).

> P̱RAISE ye Yah from the heavens;
> Praise Him in the heights;
> Praise Him all His angels;
> Praise Him all His hosts;
> Praise Him sun and moon;
> Praise Him all ye stars of light.
> P̱RAISE Him heaven of heavens,
> And ye waters above the heavens.
> Let them praise the name of Yahweh,
> For He commanded and they were created;
> And He made them stand firm forever and ever;
> A decree He gave not to be transgressed.
> P̱RAISE ye Yah from the earth,
> Ye dragons, and all ye deeps;
> Fire, hail, snow, vapour,
> Storm, doing His word;
> Ye mountains and all hills,
> Fruit tree and all cedars.
> Y̱E wild animals and all cattle,
> Creeping things and winged bird.
> Let them praise the name of Yahweh;
> For His name alone is exalted,
> His majesty is above earth and heaven,
> The praise of all His favoured ones.

Ps. 148 is a Hallel, having הללויה at the beginning in $\mathfrak{P}$ as well as at the end. &#5 has also as in previous Pss. ἀλληλουιά · Ἀγγαίου καὶ Ζαχαρίου. This Ps. has five trimeter hexastichs ; but inasmuch as there are two parts balanced and the first part has but two Strs., it is probable that v.[11-12. 14ac] are glosses, and that the second part had originally two Strs. also, v.[7-9. 10. 13. 14b], the other verses being liturgical ones. This Ps. is dependent on Gn. 1[7] in v.[4b], Gn. 1[24-25] in v.[10], upon Dt. 10[14] in v.[4a], upon Ps. 33[9b] in v.[5c. 6a], upon 104[4] in v.[8b]. The origin and date of the Ps. were doubtless the same as those of the others of the group.

Str. I. A syn. hexastich. — **13**. *Praise ye Yah*], so probably in the original as the measure demands : resumed in all the subsequent lines as *Praise Him*. — *from the heavens ‖ in the heights*], the praise sounding forth from all the inhabitants of heaven to the earth beneath. — The other four lines give the subjects : *all His angels ‖ all His hosts*], the heavenly intelligences — and then *sun and moon ‖ all ye stars of light*], the heavenly luminaries.

Str. II. A yn. couplet and a synth. tetrastich. — **4**. *Praise Him*], is resumed to connect this Str. with the previous one, and then abandoned. — The subject is given : *heaven of heavens*], the highest heavens, conceived as in an indefinite ascending series ‖ *And ye waters above the heavens*], the source of the rains, above the lower heavens and in the higher heavens, in accordance with the Heb. conception, cf. 104[3] Gn. 1[6. 7]. — **5**. *Let them praise the name of Yahweh*]. The jussive takes the place of the imv. in order to emphasize the name of Yahweh as the object of praise. So in the ‖ v.[13]. — The reason is now given for the praise of the heavenly beings. They were creatures of Yahweh : *For He commanded and they were created*]. The creation is here conceived as by command of the speaking God, as in Gn. 1 Ps. 33[9]. — **6**. *And He made them stand firm forever and ever*]. He established them at their creation in such a firm, abiding position, that they will remain stable and immovable forever. — *A decree He gave*]. He established His law in the heavens, and these heavenly beings, angels and the great luminaries, the ascents of heaven and the rain clouds, all have to submit to it. — *not to be transgressed*]. The decree given to the heaven is immutable. This is the nearest approach to immutable laws of nature that is known to Heb. Literature.

Str. III. Synth. lines. — **7**. *Praise ye Yah from the earth*], in antithesis to v.[1] : the praise from the earth ascending to meet the praise coming down from heaven. The imv. is not repeated, although implied, because the poet needs his space to mention the various creatures who are to share in this praise. — *Ye dragons*], the great sea monsters, cf. Gen. 1^{21}. The mention of dragons here with the elements of nature and apart from the other animals of v.[10] is singular. W. R. Smith's suggestion (*Religion of Semites*, p. 161), that they may be a personification of the water spirit, certainly gives a meaning better suited to the context. It is quite possible that the original was nothing more than the comprehensive " seas." — **8**. The various elements of the thunderstorm are mentioned in heaped-up terms : *Fire*, of lightning, *hail, snow, vapour ;* summed up in the *Storm* — as *doing His word*], obeying the law imposed upon them ; for the " word " here is the word of command, syn. with " decree." — **9**. *Mountains and all hills, Fruit tree and all cedars*] are given as specimens of creatures of the land. All in their way praise Yah.

Str. **IV**. A synth. triplet and a syn. triplet. — **10**. *Ye wild animals and all cattle*], domestic animals, — *Creeping things and winged bird*], including all kinds of animals. These begin this Str. with the imv. praise Him, implied, just as a similar couplet begins Str. II., its counterpart, followed by the same line with the jussive v.[13a] $=$ v.[5a]. But a glossator, noting the omission of any reference to mankind, supplied it by inserting a tetrastich, which is entirely out of proportion in its comprehensiveness to the mention of other creatures in the Ps. **11–12**. Mankind is comprehended in : *kings of earth and all peoples, princes and all governors of the earth, young men and also maidens, old men together with children.* — **13**. A reason is assigned here, as in the counterpart v.[5b] : *For His name alone is exalted ‖ His majesty is above earth and heaven*], cf. 8^2 104^1. The divine glory as manifested is the theme for praise of the earthly beings, as the creator and sovereign was of the heavenly beings. — **14**. *The praise of all His favoured ones*]. This line is syn. with the previous couplet, only in the climax it unites the pious people of God in the praise which sounds through universal nature. A glossator was not satisfied with this modest reference to Israel, and so he prefixes to this line : *And He exalted the horn of His people ;* and appended : *of the sons of Israel, a people near to Him*], which, while appropriate enough in the mouth of the congregation, was not so well suited to the worship of Yah by all nature.

1. הללו את־יהוה] prob. the original here and v.⁷ was הללויה; because מן השמים and מן הארץ have each two beats, and only a single accent should precede. — **2.** כל־צבאיו] as Qr., 𝕲, Aq., Σ, 𝕵, 𝕾, 𝕿, and 103²¹. צבאו Kt. is too short for measure. — **3.** אור]. 𝕲 prefixes καί, but with an interp. of it as an additional object to the "stars." — **4.** אשר] is unnecessary gl. — **5.** כי הוא] cited from 33⁹, to which 𝕲 prefixes from the same passage: ὅτι αὐτὸς εἶπεν καὶ ἐγενήθησαν, making the Str. overfull. — בבראֻו] Niph. pf. ‡ ברא Qal (1) *shape, fashion, create*, Ps. 89¹³·⁴⁸; (2) *transform* 51¹². Niph. (1) *be created*, here as 104³⁰; (2) *be born* 22³² 102¹⁹. — **6.** 𝕲 adds to this v. καὶ εἰς τὸν αἰῶνα τοῦ αἰῶνος, making the Str. overfull. — ולא יעבור] subord. with indef. subj.; cf. Jb. 14⁵. — **7.** תנינים] the *sea monsters, dragons;* strange here at the beginning with תהמות. ימים would be more in accordance with the context. — **8.** קיטיר] is smoke connected with earthquake, cf. 18⁸ 119⁸³ Gn. 19²⁸ (J). The ו is not in 𝕲 and prob. not original. — רוח סערה] prob. רוח is explan. gl. It spoils the measure. — **11–12.** These verses are a late gl. to introduce mankind of all classes. The symmetry of the Ps. is destroyed thereby. — **14.** וירם] ו consec. Hiph. impf. רום. This is a late gl. to bring into the Ps. a glorification of the people; so also the last l. — תהלה לכל הסידיו] is not in 𝕲ᴮ; but in 𝕲ᴺ·ᴬ·ᴿ·ᵀ. It is a proper ‖ to v.¹⁸ᶜ, and gives a suitable conclusion to the Ps.

PSALM CXLIX., 3 STR. 6³.

Ps. 149 is a summons to the congregation of the afflicted but favoured people of God to sing in fresh outburst of song with music and dancing in celebration of a recent victory (v.¹⁻³). Yahweh has adorned them with a glorious victory, which they celebrate with songs in their mouths and swords in their hands (v.⁴⁻⁶). Vengeance is to be taken on the nations; their kings and nobles are to be made prisoners in accordance with a written judgment, a splendid thing to the favoured ones (v.⁷⁻⁹).

SING to Yahweh a new song:
 Let His praise (resound) in the congregation of the favoured:
 Let Israel be glad in his great Maker:
 Let the sons of Zion exult in their King.
 Let them praise His name in the dance,
 With timbrel and lyre make melody to Him.
SINCE Yahweh delighteth in His people,
 Adorns the afflicted with victory;
 Let the favoured exult with glory:
 Let them jubilate at (their great tabernacle):
 Let exaltations of 'El be in their throat,
 And a two-edged sword in their hand.

TO execute vengeance on the nations;
(To execute) chastisements on the peoples;
To bind their kings with chains,
Their nobles with fetters of iron;
To execute the judgment written
Is a splendour for all His favoured ones.

Ps. 149 is a Hallel, with הללויה at the beginning and close in 𝔐, and at the beginning in 𝔊. 𝔖 omits it both at beginning and end. It has the same structure as other Hallels; but is more warlike, and is doubtless expressive of the vengeful military spirit of the Maccabean wars. There are only verbal glosses.

Str. I. A syn. hexastich. — **1–3.** *Sing to Yahweh a new song*], a fresh outburst of praise in celebration of the recent victory, as 33^3 96^1 98^1, based on Is. 42^{10}. — ‖ *Let His praise resound*], as 𝔊, 𝔙, 𝔍, PBV., Bä., is to be preferred to AV., RV., JPSV., which regard " His praise " as the object of the vb. " sing." — ‖ *be glad* ‖ *exult* ‖ *Let them praise His name* ‖ *make melody to Him*. — Those who are to participate in this public celebration of the victory are the *congregation of the favoured*], phr. a.λ., those who are the special objects of the divine kindness, the pious people of Yahweh, cf. v.^{9b}, also $22^{23.26}$ 107^{32}; not with a specific reference to the "Chasedim " of the Maccabean period, who constituted a party in Israel, and who therefore would hardly appear in a national Ps. They were evidently the same as the afflicted people of v.^{4}. They are ‖ with the *sons of Zion* v.^{2b} ‖ *Israel. —in his great Maker*], emphatic pl., cf. Is. 54^5, not sg. " maker " of EV^s. — ‖ *their King*], the usual recognition of the supreme kingship of Yahweh, cf. 146^{10}. — The celebration is not merely with song; it is also *in the dance*, usual in religious festivals, cf. Ex. 15^{20} Ps. 87^7 118^{27} 150^4, and with musical instruments, of which are mentioned *timbrel and lyre*, cf. $150^{3.4}$.

Str. II. Two syn. and an antith. couplet. — **4–6.** *Since*], assigning the reason of the celebration. — *Yahweh delighteth in His people*]. They are the special objects of His good pleasure and His favour, cf. 147^{11}. — He *adorns with victory*]. The victory which Yahweh hath bestowed covers them with splendour and glory, and has become their ornament. — *Let the favoured exult with glory*], with glorification, as 29^9. — ‖ *jubilate* ‖ *Let exaltations of 'El be in their throat*], songs exalting God, as 66^{17}; all resuming the call to celebrate of v.¹⁻³. — Those called to celebrate are *His people ‖ the afflicted ‖ the favoured*, cf. v.¹ᵇ. — The place of celebration can be no other than the temple. The mention of "on their beds," 独 and Vrss., is therefore striking and improbable. It doubtless originated from an ancient textual error of a single letter, and we should read : *at their great tabernacle*], cf. 43³ 84² 132⁷. — *And a two-edged sword in their hand*]. The dance in the temple is a sword dance of the victorious warriors, who shout the praise of Yahweh, their victorious king, and wave their swords above their heads.

Str. III. A syn. pentastich and a synth. conclusion. — **7–9.** *To execute vengeance on the nations*], in victorious battle. — ‖ *chastisements on the peoples*], in retribution for the affliction they had brought upon the people of God. — ‖ *To bind their kings ‖ Their nobles*], in the completeness of an overwhelming victory, taking them all prisoners and putting them to the humiliation and shame of being bound as common criminals — *with chains ‖ with fetters of iron*], all summed up in : *To execute the judgment written*], recorded in the sacred writings against the nations, as in Dt. 32⁴¹ˢᵠ· Is. 41¹⁵ ˢᵠ· Ez. 38, 39 Jo. 3¹² ˢᵠ· Mi. 4¹³ Zc. 14. — To do all such things as have been mentioned *Is a splendour*], resuming the thought of v.⁴ᵇ, the adornment of victory. — *for all His favoured ones*]. It is a glorious work, a splendid thing that their God has given them to do in this victory that they are celebrating. A glossator inserted the demonstrative against the measure to make the reference more distinct ; but it cannot refer to God, as JPSV., "He is the glory of all His pious servants" or be adj. demonstrative agreeing with splendour, as EVˢ. ; but is neuter, summing up the actions previously described.

---

1. ‏[תהלתו‏] not acc. but nom., as 𝕲, 𝔍. — ‏[קְהַל חֲסִידִים‏] phr. a.λ. *v. 22²³.* — **2.** ‏[עֹשָׂיו‏] sf. 2 m. with pl. emph. ‏Jb‏, 35¹⁰ Is. 54⁵. — ‏[רְנוּ ציון‏] ‏La‏. 4² Jo. 2²⁸. — **3.** ‏[מָחוֹל‏] *dance,* as *30¹²,* cf. 150⁴ Ex. 15²⁰ ; 𝕲 *ἐν χορῷ,* 𝔍 *in choro.* — † ‏[הֹף‏] n.m. *timbrel,* as 81⁸ 150⁴. — **4.** ‏[יְפָאֵר‏] Pi. ‡ ‏פאר‏ vb. Pi. *beautify, glorify;* favourite word of Is.², 55⁵ 60⁷· ⁹· ¹³ Ezr. 7²⁷. 𝕲 however *ὑψώσει,* as v.⁶ᵃ, 𝓥, 𝔍, *exaltabit,* interp. of unusual phr. — **5.** ‏[עַל מִשְׁכְּבוֹתָם‏] = *on their bed;* improb. ; rd. ‏עַל מִשְׁכְּנוֹתָם‏ *at their great tabernacle,* the temple, as 43³ 84² 132⁷. — **6.** ‏[רוֹמֲמוֹת‏] pl. f. ‏רוֹמָם‏ ; *exalted words, songs, hymns,* elsw. 66¹⁷. 𝕲 *al ὑψώσεις,* cf. Ne. 4¹¹ II. Macc. 15²⁷. — ‡ ‏[פִּיפִיּוֹת‏] *double edged,* pl. intensive ‏פֶּה,‏

Is. 41¹⁵ cf. Pr. 5⁴. — **7.** הִיּכָחוֹת] pl. as 𝕲 ἐλεγμούς. The l. is defective ; prefix לְעָשׂוֹת. — **8.** ‡ קֶיִם] *fetters*, cf. Jb. 36⁸ Na. 3¹⁰ Is. 45¹⁴. — כַּבְלֵי בַרזֶל] cf. 105¹⁸. — **9.** בהם] interp. gl. — הוּא] dem. neuter 𝔅 as Jb. 31¹¹, is, however, gl.

PSALM CL., 2 STR. 6³.

Ps. 150 is a summons to praise ʼEl for His sanctity and great-ness (v.¹⁻²), with musical instruments (v.³), also with dancing and accompanying musical instruments (v.⁴⁻⁵) ; all that hath breath is to take part (v.⁶).

> ₚRAISE ʼEl for His sanctity :
>> Praise Him for the spreading out of His strength :
>> Praise Him for His great might :
>> Praise Him for the abundance of His greatness :
>> Praise Him with the blast of the horn :
>> Praise Him with harp and lyre.
>
> ₚRAISE Him with timbrel and dance :
>> Praise Him with strings and pipe :
>> Praise Him with sounding cymbals :
>> Praise Him with clashing cymbals :
>> Praise Yah all ye that have breath :
>> Praise Yah ! (Praise Yah ! Praise Yah !)

Ps. 150 is a Hallel, preceded and concluded by הללויה; but the last belongs to the text as 147¹, and should be thrice repeated as the concluding line of the Str. In 𝕲 also ἀλληλουιά is at the beginning and end of the Ps. The Ps. has remained in other respects unchanged.

Str. I. A syn. tetrastich and a syn. couplet. — **1–2.** *Praise ʼEl*], instead of the usual *Praise Yah* v.⁶ ; the two enclosing *Praise Him* of every intervening line. The change of 𝕳 and Vrss. to 3 sg. " let praise Him " v.⁶ᵇ is altogether improbable. — *for His sanctity*], giving the special theme of the praise, ‖ *for the spreading out of His strength* ‖ *for His great might* ‖ *for the abundance of His greatness*]. 𝕳 is usually interpreted as giving the locality of the praise in v.¹ : " in His holy place," which, if ‖ with the usual in-terpretation of v.¹ᵇ " in the firmament of His strength," must refer to heaven. There is no reference in the Ps. to heavenly beings or things, but to *all that have breath* on the earth. This inconsistency makes the reference to place in v.¹ improbable. — **3** mentions instruments of music, which are to accompany the song of praise : *the blast of the horn*, the *harp*, and the *lyre*.

Str. II. A syn. tetrastich and a stairlike couplet. — **4-6**. *With timbrel and dance*]. The timbrel and the other musical instruments of this Str. — *strings and pipe, sounding cymbals*, and *clashing cymbals* — are those that accompany the dance. The Ps. concludes with the thrice-repeated : *Praise Yah*], which the measure requires, though in 𝕳 and Vrss. only a single one remains.

1. בְּקָדְשׁוֹ]. So 𝔍 *in sancto eius* ; but 𝔊 has ἐν τοῖς ἁγίοις αὐτοῦ, less prob. — בִּרְקִיעַ עֻזּוֹ] phr. α.λ.; רְקִיעַ is usually taken after 𝔊 as *19² expanse of heaven ;* but 𝔍 *in fortitudine potentiae eius*, Σ ἐν τῷ στερεώματι τῷ ἀκαθαιρέτῳ αὐτοῦ, so Bä. "*in seiner starken Veste*." But ב precedes all the nouns of v.¹⁻², and it is simpler to give them the same mng. as indicating the object of praise ; then קָדְשׁוֹ is *His sacredness*, as Ex. 15¹¹ Ps. 68¹⁸ 77¹⁴. — **2.** כָּרֹב] improb.; rd. בְרֹב. — גִּדְלוֹ for גָּדְלוֹ. — **3.** † תֵּקַע n.m. *blowing*, α.λ.; from תקע vb. *blow*. — **4.** מִנִּים] pl. † [מֵן] α.λ. n.m. *string*, of harp, cf. 45⁹. — † עֻגָב] = (עוּגָב Gn. 4²¹ Jb. 21¹²) 30³¹. 𝕿 *reed pipe* or *flute*, 𝖁 *Pan's pipe* (organ of several reeds), Now., Benzinger, *bagpipe*. — **5.** צִלְצְלֵי שָׁמַע] α.λ. *clear sounding cymbals*, lit. *cymbals for hearing*, possibly *castanets*, cf. 1 Ch. 15¹⁹ 16⁵. — צִלְצְלֵי תְרוּעָה] *cymbals for giving an alarm*, *clanging*, cf. 2 Ch. 13¹². — †צְלִצְלִים] n.m. pl. *cymbals*, elsw. 2 S. 6⁵, cf. 1 Ch. 13⁸. — **6.** כֹּל הַנְּשָׁמָה] better as vocative than as subj. † נְשָׁמָה n.f. *breath* (1) of God, as destroying wind, Ps. 18¹⁶ = 2 S. 22¹⁶, cf. Jb. 4⁹ Is. 30³³; (2) of man, here as Jos. 10⁴⁰, cf. נְשָׁמָה נפש כל Dt. 20¹⁶ Jos. 11¹¹·¹⁴ 1 K. 15²⁹. — תְּהַלֵּל יָהּ] 3 f. Pi. impf. improb.; rd. הללויה. — הללויה] should be thrice repeated for measure.

INDEXES.

The references are usually in the Hebrew Index, and occasionally in the other Indexes, to the verses of the Psalms where the words are most fully discussed. The prefix † indicates that all uses in the OT. are given, ‡ that all uses in the Psalter are given. In the other Indexes, and occasionally in the Hebrew Index, the Roman numerals refer to the Introduction, the Arabic numerals to the pages of the Commentary in Vol. I., the italicised numerals to the pages of the Commentary in Vol. II.

INDEXES.

I. HEBREW INDEX.

549

II. INDEX OF PERSONS.

III. INDEX OF SUBJECTS.